P9-CLD-534

THE EIGHTEENTH MENTAL MEASUREMENTS YEARBOOK

EARLIER PUBLICATIONS IN THIS SERIES

EDUCATIONAL, PSYCHOLOGICAL, AND PERSONALITY TESTS OF 1933 AND 1934
EDUCATIONAL, PSYCHOLOGICAL, AND PERSONALITY TESTS OF 1933, 1934, AND 1935
EDUCATIONAL, PSYCHOLOGICAL, AND PERSONALITY TESTS OF 1936
THE NINETEEN THIRTY-EIGHT MENTAL MEASUREMENTS YEARBOOK
THE NINETEEN FORTY MENTAL MEASUREMENTS YEARBOOK
THE THIRD MENTAL MEASUREMENTS YEARBOOK
THE FOURTH MENTAL MEASUREMENTS YEARBOOK
THE FIFTH MENTAL MEASUREMENTS YEARBOOK
TESTS IN PRINT
THE SIXTH MENTAL MEASUREMENTS YEARBOOK
READING TESTS AND REVIEWS
PERSONALITY TESTS AND REVIEWS
THE SEVENTH MENTAL MEASUREMENTS YEARBOOK
TESTS IN PRINT II
ENGLISH TESTS AND REVIEWS
FOREIGN LANGUAGE TESTS AND REVIEWS
INTELLIGENCE TESTS AND REVIEWS
MATHEMATICS TESTS AND REVIEWS
PERSONALITY TESTS AND REVIEWS II
READING TESTS AND REVIEWS II
SCIENCE TESTS AND REVIEWS
SOCIAL STUDIES TESTS AND REVIEWS
VOCATIONAL TESTS AND REVIEWS
THE EIGHTH MENTAL MEASUREMENTS YEARBOOK
TESTS IN PRINT III
THE NINTH MENTAL MEASUREMENTS YEARBOOK
THE SUPPLEMENT TO THE NINTH MENTAL MEASUREMENTS YEARBOOK
THE TENTH MENTAL MEASUREMENTS YEARBOOK
THE SUPPLEMENT TO THE TENTH MENTAL MEASUREMENTS YEARBOOK
THE ELEVENTH MENTAL MEASUREMENTS YEARBOOK
TESTS IN PRINT IV
THE SUPPLEMENT TO THE ELEVENTH MENTAL MEASUREMENTS YEARBOOK
BUROS DESK REFERENCE: PSYCHOLOGICAL ASSESSMENT IN THE SCHOOLS
BUROS DESK REFERENCE: ASSESSMENT OF SUBSTANCE ABUSE
THE TWELFTH MENTAL MEASUREMENTS YEARBOOK
THE SUPPLEMENT TO THE TWELFTH MENTAL MEASUREMENTS YEARBOOK
THE THIRTEENTH MENTAL MEASUREMENTS YEARBOOK
TESTS IN PRINT V
THE SUPPLEMENT TO THE THIRTEENTH MENTAL MEASUREMENTS YEARBOOK
THE FOURTEENTH MENTAL MEASUREMENTS YEARBOOK
TESTS IN PRINT VI
THE FIFTEENTH MENTAL MEASUREMENTS YEARBOOK
THE SIXTEENTH MENTAL MEASUREMENTS YEARBOOK
TESTS IN PRINT VII
THE SEVENTEENTH MENTAL MEASUREMENTS YEARBOOK

THE EIGHTEENTH MENTAL MEASUREMENTS YEARBOOK

ROBERT A. SPIES, JANET F. CARLSON,

and KURT F. GEISINGER

Editors

LINDA L. MURPHY
Managing Editor

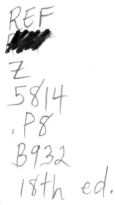

The Buros Institute of Mental Measurements
The University of Nebraska-Lincoln
Lincoln, Nebraska

2010
Distributed by The University of Nebraska Press

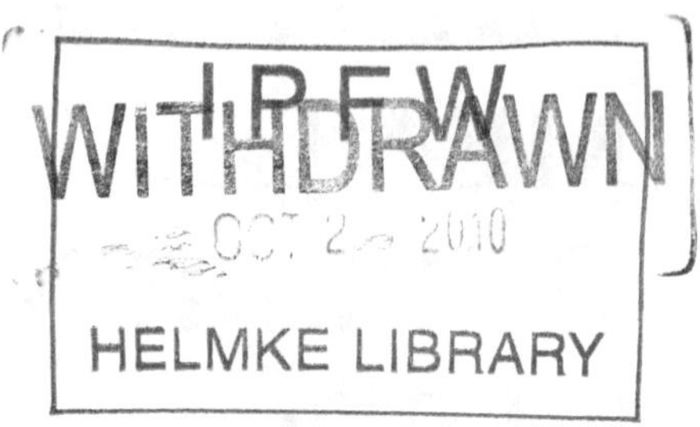

 Published by the Buros Institute of Mental Measurements of The University of Nebraska-Lincoln, 21 Teachers College Hall, Lincoln, Nebraska 68588-0348.

LC 39-3422
ISBN 978-0-910674-61-4

Manufactured in the United States of America.

The paper used in this publication meets the minimum requirements of American National Standard for Information Sciences—Permanence of Paper for Printed Library Materials, ANSI Z39.48-1984.

Note to Users

The staff of the Buros Institute of Mental Measurements has made every effort to ensure the accuracy of the test information included in this work. However, the Buros Institute of Mental Measurements and the Editors of *The Eighteenth Mental Measurements Yearbook* do not assume, and hereby expressly and absolutely disclaim, any liability to any party for any loss or damage caused by errors or omissions or statements of any kind in *The Eighteenth Mental Measurements Yearbook.* This disclaimer also includes judgments or statements of any kind made by test reviewers, who were extended the professional freedom appropriate to their task. The reviews are the sole opinion of the individual reviewers and do not necessarily represent any general consensus of the professional community or any professional organizations. The judgments and opinions of the reviewers are their own, uninfluenced in any way by the Buros Institute or the Editors.

All material included in *The Eighteenth Mental Measurements Yearbook* is intended solely for the use of our readers. None of this material, including reviewer statements, may be used in advertising or for any other commercial purpose.

TABLE OF CONTENTS

DEDICATION

Dedicated to Barbara Sterrett Plake

In 1977, a young, almost newly minted Ph.D. from the well-known quantitative methods program at the University of Iowa drove west with her family along Interstate 80 to Lincoln, Nebraska. She was about to begin her career as an assistant professor at the University of Nebraska-Lincoln after a year's work at the American College Testing Program and work as a graduate assistant in the Iowa Testing Programs.

Dr. Barbara S. Plake was soon promoted to the rank of Associate Professor and, in 1988, to the rank of Professor and Director of the Buros Institute of Mental Measurements. In 1996, she was named the W. C. Meierhenry Distinguished University Professor. During her term as Director, a period of time that lasted from January of 1988 until June of 2006, she transformed a single institute into two institutes and created the Buros Center for Testing. During that same time, she co-edited the journal, *Applied Measurement in Education*, edited and oversaw eight *Mental Measurements Yearbooks* (Volumes 10 through 17) and four *Tests in Print* volumes, as well as other volumes, and served on more than a dozen boards of editors for journals. During her time as an editor, she continued to write for scholarly publications, with more than 130 journal articles and written professional contributions. She served on virtually every major committee in testing and presently co-chairs a committee that is developing new *Standards for Educational and Psychological Testing*. She has been president of the National Council on Measurement in Education and of the Midwestern Educational Research Association. In this limited space we cannot hope to provide a complete list of her many honors. We will enumerate just a few:

National Council on Measurement in Education, Career Award, 2006

Association of Test Publishers' Career Achievement Award, 2005

Commencement speaker, University of Nebraska graduation, 2004

W. E. Coffman Distinguished Lecturer, University of Iowa, 1996

W. C. Meierhenry Distinguished University Professor, 1996-present

Fellow, American Psychological Association, Division 5, 1994-present

University of Nebraska Foundation Trustee's Award for Distinguished Teaching, 1987

We could comprise a volume of this length simply listing Dr. Plake's publications and contributions to our profession. However, instead of doing so, we choose to dedicate this volume to her. She has left an impressive legacy at the Buros Institute of Mental Measurements and, more broadly, to the Buros Center for Testing where she worked with a dedication, spirit, and zeal also attributed to Oscar Buros.

For her broad and valuable service to the profession of educational and psychological testing, for her leadership of the Buros Center for Testing, and for her contributions to the improvement of testing, we proudly dedicate this volume to Barbara Sterrett Plake.

Kurt F. Geisinger
Robert A. Spies
Janet F. Carlson
and
The staff of the Buros Institute of
Mental Measurements

INTRODUCTION

Consistent with all volumes of this long-running series, *The Eighteenth Mental Measurements Yearbook* (*18th MMY*) serves as a guide to the complex task of test evaluation, selection, and use. With its initial publication in 1938, Oscar K. Buros (1905-1978) provided a historic forum that would allow the emerging field of testing to improve in both science and practice.

Criteria for inclusion in this edition of the *MMY* series are that a test be (a) new or substantively revised since last reviewed in the *MMY* series, (b) commercially available, (c) published in the English language, and (d) documented with sufficient test development information and technical data to allow for a comprehensive review process.

THE EIGHTEENTH MENTAL MEASUREMENTS YEARBOOK

The *18th MMY* contains reviews of tests that are new or significantly revised since the publication of the *17th MMY* in 2007. Reviews, descriptions, and references associated with many older tests can be located in other Buros publications: previous *MMYs* and *Tests in Print VII*. Criteria for inclusion in this edition of the *MMY* remain that a test be (a) new or substantively revised since it was last reviewed in the *MMY* series, (b) commercially available from its publishers, (c) available in the English language, and (d) published with adequate developmental and technical documentation.

Content. The contents of the *18th MMY* include: (a) a bibliography of 158 commercially available tests, new or revised, published as separates for use with English-speaking individuals; (b) 301 critical test reviews from specialists selected by the editors on the basis of their expertise in measurement and, often, the content of the test being reviewed; (c) a test title index with appropriate cross references; (d) a classified subject index; (e) a publishers directory and index, including publisher addresses and other contact information with test listings by publisher; (f) a name index including the names of authors of all tests, reviews, or references included in this *MMY*; (g) an index of acronyms for easy reference when only a test acronym is known; (h) a score index to identify for users test scores of potential interest; and (i) a collection of papers presented in April 2010 at a symposium celebrating both the beginning of the Buros Institute of Mental Measurements some 70 years ago and the anniversary of the Institute's arrival at the University of Nebraska-Lincoln during the 1979-1980 academic year.

Appendix. Three separate listings appear in the *18th MMY* for users requiring additional information when a specific test cannot be otherwise located in the *Mental Measurements Yearbook* series. Beginning with the *14th MMY* (2001), a test qualifying for review must provide an adequate developmental history and sufficient evidence describing the instrument's technical properties. Not all tests submitted for evaluation meet these two criteria for review in the *MMY* series. A listing of tests received (but not reviewed) is included to make users aware of the availability of these tests, albeit without supporting documentation or reviews. The Appendix also provides a list of tests that meet review criteria but were received too late for review in this volume. These tests (plus additional tests received in the following months) will be reviewed in *The Nineteenth Mental Measurements Yearbook.* Test reviews that are completed prior to publication of the *19th MMY* are available electronically for a small fee on our web-based service Test Reviews Online (www.unl.edu/buros). A third list in the Appendix includes titles of tests requested from publishers but not yet received as of this volume's publication. This listing includes tests for which publishers refuse to allow their tests to be reviewed as well as those who routinely make their instruments available for review but who have failed at this point to provide a new or revised test for evaluation.

Organization. The current *MMY* series is organized like an encyclopedia, with tests being ordered alphabetically by title. If the title of a test is known, the reader can locate the test immediately without having to consult the Index of Titles.

The page headings reflect the encyclopedic organization. The page heading of the left-hand page cites the number and title of the first test listed on that page, and the page heading of the right-hand page cites the number and title of the last test listed on that page. All numbers presented in the various indexes are test numbers, not page numbers. Page numbers are important only for the Table of Contents and are located at the bottom of each page.

TESTS AND REVIEWS

The *18th MMY* contains descriptive information on 158 tests as well as test reviews by 232 different authors. Statistics on the number and percentage of tests in each of 18 major classifications are contained in Table 1.

The percentage of new and revised or supplemented tests according to major classifications is contained in Table 2. Overall, 102 of the tests included in the *18th MMY* are new and have not been listed in a previous *MMY* although some descriptions may have been included in *Tests in Print VII* (*TIP VII*; 2006). The Index of Titles may be consulted to determine if a test is new or revised.

TABLE 1
TESTS BY MAJOR CLASSIFICATIONS

Classification	Number	Percentage
Personality	28	17.7
Vocations	26	16.5
Behavior Assessment	19	12.0
Intelligence and General Aptitude	14	8.9
Developmental	12	7.6
English and Language	10	6.3
Miscellaneous	9	5.7
Achievement	7	4.4
Speech and Hearing	7	4.4
Neuropsychological	6	3.8
Reading	5	3.2
Sensory Motor	5	3.2
Mathematics	4	2.5
Education	3	1.9
Foreign Languages	1	.6
Science	1	.6
Social Studies	1	.6
Fine Arts	0	0.0
Total	158	100.0

TABLE 2
NEW AND REVISED OR SUPPLEMENTED TESTS BY MAJOR CLASSIFICATION

Classification	Number of Tests	Percentage New	Percentage Revised
Achievement	7	42.9	57.1
Behavior Assessment	19	79.0	21.0
Developmental	12	58.3	41.7
Education	3	66.7	33.3
English and Language	10	40.0	60.0
Fine Arts	0	0.0	0.0
Foreign Languages	1	100.0	0.0
Intelligence and General Aptitude	14	35.7	64.3
Mathematics	4	50.0	50.0
Miscellaneous	9	88.0	11.1
Neuropsychological	6	66.7	33.3
Personality	28	67.9	32.1
Reading	5	60.0	40.0
Science	1	100.0	0.0
Sensory Motor	5	60.0	40.0
Social Studies	1	0.0	100.0
Speech and Hearing	7	42.9	57.1
Vocations	26	84.6	15.4
Total	158	64.6	35.4

Test Selection. A new policy for selecting tests for review became effective with the *14th MMY* (2001). This new policy for selecting tests for review requires at least minimal information be available regarding test development. The requirement that tests have such minimal information does not assure the quality of the test; it simply provides reviewers with a minimum basis for critically evaluating the quality of the test. We select our reviewers carefully and let them and well-informed readers decide for themselves about the essential features needed to assure the appropriate use of a test. Some new or revised tests are not included because they were received too late to undergo the review process and still permit timely publication, or because some reviewers did not meet their commitment to review the test. A list of these tests is included in the Appendix and every effort will be made to have them reviewed for *The Nineteenth Mental Measurements Yearbook*, and included before then through our web-based service, Test Reviews Online (TROL).

There are some new or revised tests for which there will be no reviews although these tests are described in *Tests in Print VII*. The absence of reviews occurred for a variety of reasons including: We could not identify qualified reviewers, the test materials were incomplete so reviews were not possible, the tests were sufficiently obscure that reviews were deemed unnecessary, the publisher advised us the test is now out-of-print before reviews were completed, or the test did not meet our criterion for documentation. Descriptions of all these tests still in print were published in *TIP VII* and are included in the Test Reviews Online database.

Reviewer Selection. The selection of reviewers was done with great care. The objective was to secure measurement and subject specialists who would be independent and represent a variety of different viewpoints. It was also important to find individuals who would write critical reviews competently, judiciously, fairly, and in a timely manner. Reviewers were identified by means of extensive searches of the professional literature, attendance at professional meetings, and recommendations from leaders in various professional fields. Perusal of reviews in this volume also will reveal that reviewers work in and represent a cross-section of the places in which testing is taught and tests are used: universities, public schools, businesses, and community agencies. These reviewers represent an outstanding array of professional talent, and their contributions are obviously of primary importance in making this *Yearbook* a valuable resource. A list of the individuals reviewing in this volume is included at the beginning of the Index section.

Active, evaluative reading is the key to the most effective use of the professional expertise offered in each of the reviews. Just as one would evaluate a test, readers should evaluate critically the reviewer's comments about the test. The reviewers selected are competent professionals in their respective fields, but it is inevitable that their reviews also reflect their individual perspectives. *The Mental Measurements Yearbook* series was developed to stimulate critical thinking and assist in the selection of the best available test for a given purpose, not to promote the passive acceptance of reviewer judgment.

INDEXES

As mentioned above, the *18th MMY* includes six indexes invaluable as aids to effective use: (a) Index of Titles, (b) Index of Acronyms, (c) Classified Subject Index, (d) Publishers Directory and Index, (e) Index of Names, and (f) Score Index. Additional comment on these indexes is presented below.

Index of Titles. Because the organization of the *18th MMY* is encyclopedic in nature, with the tests ordered alphabetically by title throughout the volume, the test title index does not have to be consulted to find a test if the title is known. However, the title index has some features that make it useful beyond its function as a complete title listing. First, it includes cross-reference information useful for tests with superseded or alternative titles or tests commonly (and sometimes inaccurately) known by multiple titles. Second, it identifies tests that are new or revised. Third, it may cue the user to other tests with similar titles that may be useful. Titles for the 40 tests not reviewed because of insufficient technical documentation are included in the Index of Titles. It is important to keep in mind that the numbers in this index, like those for all *MMY* indexes, are test numbers and not page numbers.

Because no *MMY* includes reviews of all tests currently in print, a particular test of interest may not be reviewed in this volume. To learn if a commercially published test has been reviewed in this or an earlier volume of the *MMY*, users may access the Buros page on the World Wide Web (www.unl.edu/buros). A search of Test Reviews Online (TROL) will indicate if a test has been reviewed and also will indicate the yearbook in which the review can be found. TROL also provides electronic access to reviews provided in recent *MMY*s (the most current reviews only) and test reviews that have been finalized since the publication of the most recent *MMY*. Therefore, TROL provides ready access, for a small fee, to the majority of tests that have been reviewed in *The Mental Measurements Yearbook* series. As an alternative, *Tests in Print VII* provides a cross reference to reviews of still-in-print tests in the *MMY* series.

Index of Acronyms. Some tests seem to be better known by their acronyms than by their full titles. The Index of Acronyms can help in these instances; it refers the reader to the full title of the test and to the relevant descriptive information and reviews.

Classified Subject Index. The Classified Subject Index classifies all tests listed in the 18th MMY into 17 of 18 major categories: Achievement, Behavior Assessment, Developmental, Education, English and Language, Fine Arts, Foreign Languages, Intelligence and General Aptitude, Mathematics, Miscellaneous, Neuropsychological, Personality, Reading, Science, Sensory-Motor, Social Studies, Speech and Hearing, and Vocations. (No tests in the Fine Arts category are reviewed in the *18th MMY.*) Each test entry in this index includes test title, population for which the test is intended, and test number. The Classified Subject Index is of great help to readers who seek a listing of tests in given subject areas. This index represents a starting point for readers who know their area of interest but do not know how to further focus that interest in order to identify the best test(s) for their particular purposes.

Publishers Directory and Index. The Publishers Directory and Index includes the names and addresses of the publishers of all tests included in the *18th MMY* plus a listing of test numbers for each individual publisher. Also included are the telephone, FAX numbers, email, and Web addresses for those publishers who responded to our request for this information. This index can be particularly useful in obtaining addresses for specimen sets or catalogs after the test reviews have been read and evaluated. It also can be useful when a reader knows the publisher of a certain test but is uncertain about the test title, or when a reader is interested in the range of tests published by a given publisher.

Index of Names. The Index of Names provides a comprehensive list of names, indicating authorship of a test, test review, or reviewer's reference.

Score Index. The Score Index is a listing of the scored parts of all tests reviewed in the *18th MMY.* Test titles are sometimes misleading or ambiguous, and test content may be difficult to define with precision. In contrast, test scores often represent operational definitions of the variables the test author is trying to measure, and as such they can define test purpose and content more adequately than other descriptive information. A search for a particular test is most often a search for a test that measures some specific variable(s). Test scores and their associated labels can often be the best definitions of the variable(s) of interest. The Score Index is a detailed subject index based on the most critical operational features of any test—the scores and their associated labels.

HOW TO USE THIS YEARBOOK

A reference work like *The Eighteenth Mental Measurements Yearbook* can be of far greater benefit to a reader if some time is taken to become familiar with what it has to offer and how it might be used most effectively to obtain the information wanted.

Step 1: Read the Introduction to the *18th MMY* in its entirety.

Step 2: Become familiar with the six indexes and particularly with the instructions preceding each index listing.

Step 3: Use the book by looking up needed information. This step is simple if one keeps the following procedures in mind:

1. Go directly to the test entry using the alphabetical page headings if you know the title of the test.

2. Consult the Index of Titles for possible variants of the title or consult the appropriate subject area of the Classified Subject Index for other possible leads or for similar or related tests in the same area, if you do not know, cannot find, or are unsure of the title of a test. (Other uses for both of these indexes were described above.)

3. Consult the Index of Names if you know the author of a test but not the title or publisher. Look up the author's titles until you find the test you want.

4. Consult the Publishers Directory and Index if you know the test publisher but not the title or author. Look up the publisher's titles until you find the test you want.

5. Consult the Score Index and locate the test or tests that include the score variable of interest if you are looking for a test that yields a particular kind of test score.

6. If after following the above steps you are not able to find a review of the test you want, consult the Appendix for a list of tests that are not reviewed. Reasons tests are not reviewed include (a) they did not meet our selection criteria, (b) the reviews were not completed in time for publication in this volume, or (c) the publisher failed to respond in a timely manner to our request for testing materials. You also can consult *TIP VII* or visit the Buros web page (www.unl.edu/buros) and use the Test Reviews Online service (TROL) to identify the *MMY* that contains the description and any available reviews for a test of interest.

7. Once you have found the test or tests you are looking for, read the descriptive entries for these tests carefully so that you can take advantage of the information provided. A description of the information in these test entries is presented later in this section.

8. Read the test reviews carefully and analytically, as suggested above. The information and evaluations contained in these reviews are meant to assist test consumers in making well-informed decisions about the choice and applications of tests.

9. Once you have read the descriptive information and test reviews, you may want to contact the publisher to order a specimen set for a particular test so that you can examine it firsthand. The Publishers Directory and Index has the address information needed to obtain specimen sets or catalogs.

Making Effective Use of the Test Entries. The test entries include extensive information. For each test, descriptive information is presented in the following order:

a) TITLES. Test titles are printed in boldface type. Secondary or series titles are set off from main titles by a colon.

b) PURPOSE. For each test there is a brief, clear statement describing the purpose of the test. Often these statements are quotations from the test manual.

c) POPULATION. This describes the groups for which the test is intended. The grade, chronological age, semester range, or employment category is usually given. For example, "Grades 1.5–2.5, 2–3, 4–12, 13–17" means that there are four test booklets: a booklet for the middle of first grade through the middle of the second grade, a booklet for the beginning of the second grade through the end of third grade, a booklet for Grades 4 through 12 inclusive, and a booklet for undergraduate and graduate students in colleges and universities.

d) PUBLICATION DATE. The inclusive range of publication dates for the various forms, accessories, and editions of a test is reported.

e) ACRONYM. When a test is often referred to by an acronym, the acronym is given in the test entry.

f) SCORES. The number of part scores is presented along with their titles or descriptions of what they are intended to represent or measure.

g) ADMINISTRATION. Individual or group administration is indicated. A test is considered a group test unless it may be administered only individually.

h) FORMS, PARTS, AND LEVELS. All available forms, parts, and levels are listed.

i) MANUAL. Notation is made if no manual is available. All other manual information is included under Price Data.

j) RESTRICTED DISTRIBUTION. This is noted only for tests that are made available to a special market by the publisher. Educational and psychological restrictions are not noted (unless a special training course is required for use).

k) PRICE DATA. Price information is reported for test packages (usually 20 to 35 tests), answer sheets, all other accessories, and specimen sets. The statement "$17.50 per 35 tests" means that all accessories are included unless otherwise indicated by the reporting of separate prices for accessories. The statement also means 35 tests of one level, one edition, or one part unless stated otherwise. Because test prices can change very quickly, the year that the listed test prices were obtained is also given. Foreign currency is assigned the appropriate symbol. When prices are given in foreign dollars, a qualifying symbol is added (e.g., A$16.50 refers to 16 dollars and 50 cents in Australian currency). Along with cost, the publication date and number of pages on which print occurs is reported for manuals and technical reports (e.g., 2009, 102 pages). All types of machine-scorable answer sheets available for use with a specific test are reported in the descriptive entry. Scoring and reporting services provided by publishers are reported along with information on costs. In a few cases, special computerized scoring and interpretation services are noted at the end of the price information.

l) FOREIGN LANGUAGE AND OTHER SPECIAL EDITIONS. This section concerns foreign language editions published by the same publisher who sells the English-language edition. It also indicates special editions (e.g., Braille, large type) available from the same or a different publisher.

m) TIME. The number of minutes of actual working time allowed examinees and the approximate length of time needed for administering a test are reported whenever obtainable. The latter figure is always enclosed in parentheses. Thus, "50(60) minutes" indicates that the examinees are allowed 50 minutes of working time and that a total of 60 minutes is needed to administer the test. A time of "40–50 minutes" indicates an untimed test that takes approximately 45 minutes to administer, or—in a few instances—a test so timed that working time and administration time are very difficult to disentangle. When the time necessary to administer a test is not reported or suggested in the test materials but has been obtained from a catalog or through correspondence with the test publisher or author, the time is enclosed in brackets.

n) COMMENTS. Some entries contain special notations, such as: "for research use only"; "revision of the ABC Test"; "tests administered monthly at centers throughout the United States"; "subtests available as separates"; and "verbal creativity." A statement such as "verbal creativity" is intended to further describe what the test claims to measure. Some of the test entries include factual statements that imply criticism of the test, such as "1999 test identical with test copyrighted 1980."

o) AUTHOR. For most tests, all authors are reported. In the case of tests that appear in a new form each year, only authors of the most recent forms are listed. Names are reported exactly as printed on test booklets. Names of editors generally are not reported.

p) PUBLISHER. The name of the publisher or distributor is reported for each test. Foreign publishers are identified by listing the country in brackets immediately following the name of the publisher. The Publishers Directory and Index must be consulted for a publisher's address and other contact information.

q) FOREIGN ADAPTATIONS. Revisions and adaptations of tests for foreign use are listed in a separate paragraph following the original edition.

r) SUBLISTINGS. Levels, editions, subtests, or parts of a test available in separate booklets are sometimes presented as sublistings with titles set in small capitals. Sub-sublistings are indented and titles are set in italic type.

s) CROSS REFERENCES. For tests that have been listed previously in a Buros Institute of Mental Measurements publication, a test entry includes—if relevant—a final item containing cross references to the reviews, excerpts, and references for that test in those volumes. In the cross references, "T7:467" refers to test 467 in *Tests in Print VII*, "14:121" refers to test 121 in *The Fourteenth Mental Measurements Yearbook*, "8:1023" refers to test 1023 in *The Eighth Mental Measurements Yearbook*, "T3:144" refers to test 144 in *Tests in Print III*, "7:637" refers to test 637 in *The Seventh Mental Measurements Yearbook*, "P:262" refers to test 262 in *Personality Tests and Reviews*, "2:1427" refers to test 1427 in *The 1940 Yearbook*, and "1:1110" refers to test 1110 in *The 1938 Yearbook*. In the case of batteries and programs, the paragraph also includes cross references—from the battery to the separately listed subtests and vice versa—to entries in this volume and to entries and reviews in earlier *Yearbooks*. Test numbers not preceded by a colon refer to tests in this *Yearbook*; for example, "see 45" refers to test 45 in this *Yearbook*.

MONITORING ASSESSMENT QUALITY IN THE AGE OF ACCOUNTABILITY

The papers published in the final section of *The Eighteenth Mental Measurements Yearbook* were presented at a symposium entitled "Monitoring Assessment Quality in the Age of Accountability" held in April 2010 on the campus of the University of Nebraska-Lincoln. The symposium commemorated 70 years since the publication of the first *Yearbook* in 1938 and also marked more than 30 years since the Buros Institute of Mental Measurements moved to the University of Nebraska-Lincoln.

We believe that the symposium papers will interest our readers, especially those with long-standing affiliations with the Buros Center. Buros comprises the single most prolific reviewer of tests in the world. Some members of the leadership team here worried that the legacy of the Buros Center for Testing, which presently includes the publisher of this volume (the Buros Institute of Mental Measurements) as well as the Buros Institute of Assessment Consultation and Outreach, could be lost or misremembered without a conscious effort to document its influence on the science and practice of testing. We hope our readers enjoy these special papers.

The scholars whose papers were invited for presentation all have significant connections to the Buros Institute, some as administrators within the Buros Center for Testing, some as editors of previous editions of the *Yearbook*, all with experience in the test reviewer process, and all highly visible for their contributions to the literature in areas related to testing. Collectively, the papers provide both retrospective and prospective views regarding the practice of the profession of testing. We are exceedingly grateful to the symposium presenters whose papers offer a fitting conclusion to the *18th MMY*: Chad W. Buckendahl, Jane Close Conoley,

Kurt F. Geisinger, Terry Gutkin, James C. Impara, Barbara S. Plake, Cecil R. Reynolds, and Robert M. Thorndike.

ACKNOWLEDGMENTS

The publication of *The Eighteenth Mental Measurements Yearbook* could not have been accomplished without the contributions of many individuals. This volume is the first one in some 20 years to be completed without direct guidance from Barbara Plake. We continue to reap the benefits of Barbara's stewardship, which laid a firm foundation for the newest edition of the *MMY*. We miss Barbara personally, but as noted, her presence continues to be felt as a spirit akin to that of Oscar Buros himself.

The editors gratefully acknowledge the talent, expertise, and dedication of our staff at the Buros Center for Testing who have made this most recent version of the *MMY* series possible.

Linda Murphy, Managing Editor, has long been essential to the publication of new editions of the *MMY*. Her historical base of knowledge, attention to detail, good humor, and steadfast commitment is critical to this series and makes our job as editors much more agreeable than it otherwise would be. She sorts out many inaccuracies and omissions as a matter of course, provides fine points on APA style, and alerts us to numerous errors that might occur save for her wise counsel. Publication of this volume also would not be possible without the perseverance of our Assistant Editor, Gary Anderson, who among many other duties continually updates the website, helps to manage voluminous testing materials and databases, provides good-natured communication with all of our reviewers, and carefully proofreads each test review. We would like to acknowledge the efforts of Rasma Strautkalns, Institute Secretary, for key contributions to an efficient office environment and her warm reception for our clients. In addition, we would like to cite other members of the Buros Center for Testing, our parent organization, for their support and encouragement during the publication of this edition of the *MMY*. Brett Foley, Tzu-Yun (Katherine) Chin, and Theresa Glanz have all made generous contributions to discussions of our current and future directions. We appreciate the efforts of all permanent staff, each of whom contributes more than their share to the development and production of products from the Buros Institute of Mental Measurements. We also enjoy the respect and collegiality of others within the University of Nebraska-Lincoln system. In particular, we wish to thank Ralph De Ayala, Chair of the Department of Educational Psychology, and Marjorie Kostelnik, Dean of the College of Education and Human Sciences, for their encouragement and support.

This volume would not exist without the substantial efforts of our test reviewers. We are very grateful to the many reviewers (and especially to those Distinguished Reviewers recognized in this and previous editions of the *MMY* series) who have prepared test reviews for the Buros Institute of Mental Measurements. Their willingness to take time from busy professional schedules and to share their expertise in the form of thoughtful test reviews is very much appreciated. *The Mental Measurements Yearbook* series would not exist without their concerted efforts.

The work of many graduate and undergraduate students helps make possible the quality of this volume. Their efforts include writing test descriptions, fact checking reviews, verifying test references, proofreading, and innumerable other tasks. We thank Graduate Research Students Nancy Anderson, Jeffrey Babl, Allison Champion-Wescott, Rebecca Norman Dvorak, Kristin Jones, Chelsi Klentz-Davis, and Natalie Koziol for their assistance. We also wish to thank Christa Hake and Kaley Smith, who contributed primarily in the area of word processing and proofreading.

Appreciation is also extended to the members of our National Advisory Committee for their willingness to assist in the operation of the Buros Institute of Mental Measurements and for their thought-provoking suggestions for improving the *MMY* series and other publications of the Institute. During the period in which this volume was prepared the National Advisory Council has included Angee Baker, Gregory Cizek, John Fremer, Terry Gutkin, Neal Schmitt, and Jonathan Sandoval.

The Buros Institute of Mental Measurements is part of the Department of Educational Psychology of the University of Nebraska-Lincoln. We have benefited from the many departmental colleagues who have contributed to this work. In addition, we are grateful for the contribution of the University of Nebraska Press, which provides expert consultation and serves as distributor of the *MMY* series.

SUMMARY

The Mental Measurements Yearbook series is an essential resource for both individuals and organizations seeking information critical to the evaluation, selection, and use of specific testing instruments. This current edition contains 301 test reviews of 158 different tests.

Test reviews from recent *MMY* editions are available electronically through Ebsco Publishing or Ovid Technologies at many university, medical, and research libraries. Test reviews also are available over the internet directly from the Buros Institute (www.unl.edu/buros) through our Test Reviews Online ecommerce website.

For over 70 years the *MMY* series has worked to support the interests of knowledgeable professionals and purpose of an informed public. By providing candid reviews of testing products, this publication also serves test publishers who wish to improve their instruments by submitting tests for independent review. Given the critical importance of testing, we hope test authors and publishers will carefully consider the comments made by reviewers and continue to refine and perfect their assessment products.

Robert A. Spies
Janet F. Carlson
Kurt F. Geisinger
July 2010

Tests and Reviews

[1]

A-4 Police Officer Video Test.

Purpose: Designed as an entry-level test to "assess both cognitive and non-cognitive competencies that new police officers need to perform successfully on the job."

Population: Candidates for entry-level police officer positions.

Publication Date: 1999.

Scores: 3 abilities: Ability to Observe/Listen to/ and Remember Information, Ability to Use Situational Judgment and Interpersonal Skills, Ability to Learn and Apply Police Information.

Administration: Individual or group.

Price Data: Available from publisher.

Time: 155 minutes.

Comments: Administered via videotaped scenarios as an alternative to traditional multiple-choice exams; all instructions as well as count down timer are included on the video to facilitate test administration.

Author: International Public Management Association for Human Resources.

Publisher: International Public Management Association for Human Resources (IPMA-HR).

Review of the A-4 Police Officer Video Test by DENIZ S. ONES, Hellervik Professor of Industrial Psychology, University of Minnesota, Minneapolis, MN, and STEPHAN DILCHERT, Assistant Professor of Management, Baruch College, City University of New York, New York, NY:

DESCRIPTION. The A-4 Police Officer Video Test is a 90-item multiple-choice test designed to assess both cognitive and noncognitive competencies relevant for success in police officer jobs. The test is administered using a video tape, which contains all narrated instructions. Administration of the test takes a total time of 155 minutes.

The test consists of three "subtests," designed to assess different domains of job-relevant knowledge, skills, abilities, and traits. The subtests are "Ability to Observe, Listen to, and Remember Information," "Ability to Use Situational Judgment and Interpersonal Skills," and "Ability to Learn and Apply Police Information." Although the technical report provides some information on the subtest scores (e.g., reliability estimates), it appears that only the overall score is recommended for use in personnel decision making.

For the first section, a video vignette (a simulated roll-call meeting) is the stimulus; the 25 items pertaining to the vignette are presented in paper-and-pencil form in the test booklet. For the second section, 40 short vignettes are presented, with each vignette followed by 1 item displayed on the screen as well as narrated. The 25 items of the third section are presented in written format in the test booklet. Test-takers mark their responses to all 90 items on a separate answer sheet. The administration is straightforward, as all instructions (as well as the timing of the subtests) are delivered using the video tape. The technical report does not contain information on administration of the test (a user's manual was neither provided nor reviewed).

Most of the items are multiple-choice (82), with only 8 items using a "matching" format. The test itself consists of a mixture of assessments that can be characterized as memory-recall (Subtest 1), situational judgment (Subtest 2), and reading comprehension (Subtest 3).

The test is intended for the selection of entry-level police officers. The technical manual correctly indicates that "no experience or training in law enforcement" (p. 36) is required to complete the test. Even though the video vignettes and the written items are presented in law enforcement contexts, the items appear to reflect constructs such as memory, reading comprehension, and problem solving, which are largely independent of specific knowledge or law enforcement experience.

DEVELOPMENT.

Job analysis. Test development was guided by a job analysis of police officer jobs. To this end, a previously conducted consortium job analysis was consulted and supplemented with new data that were collected from 45 volunteering agencies across the U.S. A police-specific job-analysis questionnaire (included in the appendix of the technical report) was completed by participating agencies. Ratings of time spent on and importance of job duties, as well as knowledge, skills, abilities, and personal characteristics (KSAPs) necessary to perform job duties were gathered. Results of both the original as well as the supplemental job analysis are presented in the technical report, and are helpful in establishing the link between the original target population of jobs and those of potential test-users.

Over 20 KSAPs were identified as necessary for success in the job of police officer. Because of the test format, a rational decision was made to assess only 11 of these KSAPs. Thus, the test publisher recommends that the test be used as part of a selection *system* in combination with other selection tools (e.g., interviews).

Item development. For Subtest 1 ("Ability to Observe, Listen to, and Remember Information") a simulation was developed to assess test-takers' ability to process and recall information. The script for the video vignette was reviewed by subject-matter experts (SMEs) before production. An initial pool of 37 items relating to this vignette were written. Because test-takers are encouraged to take notes during the presentation of the video, this subtest essentially tests the general ability to process, record, and correctly reproduce relevant information. A few items use pictures to assess memory recall.

The development of Subtest 2 ("Ability to use Situational Judgment and Interpersonal Skills") generally followed accepted principles of situational judgment test (SJT) development. However, the number of items included (40) was determined solely using the average number of items on similar tests developed in prior research studies; no psychometric considerations are mentioned as influencing this decision. An initial item pool of 60 scenarios was developed and eventually resulted in over 80 vignettes after a series of reviews by SMEs. During this process, best and worst answers were also generated. Although the key development yielded SME ratings of each response option on a 4-point scale, a simple scoring key (1 point for choosing the best answer, no points for the remaining options) was chosen. This decision was justified using prior research that—at the time of test development—had not shown any alternative SJT scoring procedures to be superior.

Subtest 3 ("Ability to Learn and Apply Police Information") was developed using written training materials and policy statements from several law enforcement agencies. Forty questions were developed assessing comprehension and reasoning with this type of information. Again, items for this subtest were reviewed by SMEs and their comments were taken into account.

Item selection. A pool of 178 items for the three subtests was completed by 130 police officer job incumbents. Item difficulty was calculated and 53 items were further reviewed because of high (≥98%) or low (≤66%) correct endorsement rates. Thirty-six of these items were eliminated from the final test. An additional 4 items were deleted after an analysis for differential item functioning. "Mantel-Haenszel statistics were run between White/Caucasian and Black/African American incumbents and between White/Caucasian and all minority incumbents. Male (n = 101) and female (n = 22) groups were also analyzed" (manual, p. 44). The final 90 items were chosen based on a combination of test difficulty and item-total as well as item-subtest correlations.

TECHNICAL.

Normative information. The only normative information presented in the technical report is based on 130 completed tests used for finalizing the item pool. Thus, the test was normed on the development sample of job incumbents (job experience ranging from 6 months to more than 8 years). The sample was relatively homogenous with regards to ethnic background (82% Caucasian) and gender (78% male). Means and standard deviations for the total test score as well as the subtests are provided for this sample.

Reliability. Internal consistency reliability estimates (KR-20) for the three subtests and the total score were obtained from the same developmental sample and ranged between .70 and .72. The reliability for the total score was .80. No information on test-retest reliability is provided.

Criterion-related validity. Supervisory ratings of overall performance and 10 job performance dimensions were gathered for the development sample (N = 130). The mean across the 10 dimensions was combined with the overall performance rating to create a criterion measure. The observed correlation of the final 90-item test score with this performance criterion was .35. Interrater reliability for the performance ratings (based on 60 ratings made by two supervisors) was .59. Thus, the appropriate correction for attenuation due to unreliability, which is reported in the technical report, yields an estimate of operational validity of .46. This estimate may be attenuated by restriction in range due to the concurrent design and job incumbent sample. However, due to a lack of job applicant normative data, the exact degree of range restriction in this sample cannot be determined.

Construct validity. The technical report does not contain a section on construct validity. Data that could speak to this issue (convergent or divergent validity) seem to be lacking.

Test fairness. Differential item functioning was investigated during test development. Four items that displayed differential functioning were deleted, and two were retained after their content had been reviewed. An analysis of differential test functioning for the total score is not provided. The technical report does provide an "exam fairness analysis." This portrayal, however, is simply a statement of group mean-score differences (White-Black and male-female comparisons). Results showed no statistically significant difference between White and Black job incumbents, but did reveal a difference between male and female officers (women scoring higher). Unfortunately, this investigation is limited by reliance on statistical significance tests. Due to the small number of minority individuals in this sample (e.g., 12 African Americans), the power for detecting a statistically significant effect was low to begin with. However, standardized group mean-score differences can be computed using the means and standard deviations provided for each group. Cohen's d-values computed by these reviewers indicate that in the development sample, White incumbents on average scored more than half a standard deviation unit higher than African Americans. This finding is a moderate effect which, if found in an applied hiring situation, can result in adverse impact against the minority group if the majority selection ratio is 75% or lower.

COMMENTARY. The A-4 Police Officer Video Test is based on a thorough job analysis for the job of police officer. It tests psychological traits and abilities that are largely independent of prior experience, and is thus appropriate for use with entry-level law enforcement personnel. Job-relatedness is supported by concurrent validity evidence. However, there are some empirical gaps that need to be addressed.

The lack of construct validity evidence (convergent and divergent validity) for the A-4 Police Officer Video Test is disappointing. An inspection of item content suggests that two of the subtests likely assess the intended constructs (memorizing and reproducing information and comprehension of written material). The evidence for the situational judgment part, however (which is purported to measure judgment, logic, interpersonal skills, and common sense), is inconclusive. Recent research has shown that situational judgment tests can measure a variety of psychological traits and abilities (McDaniel & Nguyen, 2001). Yet, what actually is measured by a given test not only depends on its item content but also on the response instructions (Ployhart & Ehrhart, 2003). The instructions for this test ask test-takers to identify the "logical course of action" (technical report, p. 32) in a given situation (i.e., asking them what they *should do*, rather than what they *would do*). Thus, based on the existing literature, we can assume that Subtest 2 mainly measures cognitive ability and problem solving, rather than various "interpersonal skills." The relatively high internal consistency estimate for this subtest (.71), something that is unusual for situational judgment tests that assess a diverse set of traits, would appear to support the conjecture of these reviewers. To evaluate what the A-4 Police Officer Video Test actually measures, data need to be gathered examining the overlap between this test (total score and subtests) and other psychological tests (e.g., cognitive ability, information processing, and personality).

Additional data gathering needs are apparent: Information on job applicants is lacking in the technical report, which constitutes a serious shortcoming for a test intended for personnel selection use. Appropriate normative scores and predictive validity cannot be established without such information. Although the test developers expressed their intent to gather additional information in the original technical report, including information on criterion-related validity, no such information was furnished to the reviewers. Additionally, in future data-gathering efforts, particular attention should be paid to include a sufficient number of minority group members to enable meaningful analyses of group mean-score differences.

Some comments are also in order on the presentation of the test materials. Although the content of the vignettes has probably retained its job-relatedness over time, the test suffers from the inevitable problem that the stimulus material seems somewhat dated. The test publisher should be encouraged to update this material in the near future. For ease of administration as well as quality concerns, the use of alternate media such as DVD or online presentation (compared to the current VHS tape) may be advisable. However, these issues are merely cosmetic in nature.

SUMMARY. Based on a review of the A-4 Police Officer Video Test and accompanying technical report, the test assesses job-relevant KSAPs, mainly cognitive abilities related to memorizing and processing information as well as problem solving. The test appears face valid and easy to administer using the video-based test material. It showed good reliability and criterion-related validity in one sample of 130 job incumbents. Additional data from large samples of job applicants are needed on its predictive validity as well as distributional properties of applicant scores, including data on group-mean score differences. Construct validity evidence shedding light on the meaning of test scores is also desirable.

REVIEWERS' REFERENCES

McDaniel, M. A., & Nguyen, N. T. (2001). Situational judgment tests: A review of practice and constructs assessed. *International Journal of Selection and Assessment, 9,* 103-113.

Ployhart, R. E., & Ehrhart, M. G. (2003). Be careful what you ask for: Effects of response instructions on the construct validity and reliability of situational judgment tests. *International Journal of Selection and Assessment, 11,* 1-16.

[2]

Administrative Series Modules.

Purpose: Designed to assess skills needed in various administrative positions.
Population: Applicants for clerical and administrative positions.
Publication Dates: 1975–1997.
Administration: Individual or group.
Price Data: Available from publisher.
Comments: "Designed in module format so test users can choose the modules that best suit their testing needs"; "hand scoring is available for all individual and combined modules"; "machine scoring is available for all modules except I, K, and L"; previous version listed as SCC Clerical Skills Series.
Author: International Public Management Association for Human Resources.
Publisher: International Public Management Association for Human Resources (IPMA-HR).

a) INDIVIDUAL ADMINISTRATIVE MODULE TESTS.

1) *Grammar (A).*
Score: Total score only.
Time: 15 minutes.
2) *Punctuation (B).*
Score: Total score only.
Time: 11 minutes.
3) *Vocabulary (C).*
Score: Total score only.
Time: 9 minutes.
4) *Spelling (D).*
Score: Total score only.
Time: 6 minutes.
5) *Basic Filing Skills (E).*
Score: Total score only.
Time: 18 minutes.
6) *Reasoning (F).*
Score: Total score only.
Time: 9 minutes.
7) *Following Oral Instructions (G).*
Score: Total score only.
Time: 33 minutes.
8) *Following Written Instructions (H).*
Score: Total score only.
Time: 25 minutes.
9) *Forms, Completion/Listening (I).*
Score: Total score only.
Time: 30 minutes.
10) *Data Proofing (J).*
Score: Total score only.
Time: 13 minutes.
11) *Document Proofing—Part A (K).*
Score: Total score only.
Time: 15 minutes.
12) *Document Proofing—Part B (L).*
Score: Total score only.
Time: 20 minutes.
13) *Mathematical Reasoning (M).*
Score: Total score only.
Time: 35 minutes.
14) *Basic Math Calculations (N).*
Score: Total score only.
Time: 20 minutes.

b) COMBINED ADMINISTRATIVE MODULE TESTS.

1) *Clerical Series 1-A.*
Acronym: CS1-A.
Scores: 5 modules: Grammar, Punctuation, Vocabulary, Spelling, Basic Filing.
Time: 59 minutes.

2) *Clerical Series 1-B.*
Acronym: CS1-B.
Scores: 3 modules: Reasoning, Following Written Instructions, Basic Math Calculations.
Time: 54 minutes.

Cross References: For a review by Lorraine D. Eyde of a previous version, see 9:1074.

Review of the Administrative Series Modules by THOMAS R. O'NEILL, Psychometrician, National Council of State Boards of Nursing, Chicago, IL:

DESCRIPTION. The Administrative Series Modules are a battery of pencil-and-paper tests that are intended to assist employers in selecting the most qualified candidates for clerical positions. There are a total of 14 different modules. All modules are available as stand-alone tests; however, there are also two batteries of modules that come in bundles or "as a series." The Clerical Series 1-A consists of five modules: Grammar, Punctuation, Vocabulary, Spelling, and Basic Filing. The Clerical Series 1-B consists of three modules: Reasoning, Following Written Instructions, and Basic Math Calculations. The remaining six modules are related to more specialized types of clerical work. These modules are: Following Oral Instructions, Forms Completion/Listening, Data Proofing Forms, Document Proofing Part A, Document Proofing Part B, and Mathematical Reasoning. This review is based upon copies of the modules and a 1996 technical report that describes some of the development process.

The modules are typically brief with regard to the number of questions or tasks that are required. Given the time limits for each module, it is apparent that the modules are speeded. The modules are intended to be administered under proctored conditions. Although the modules can be administered by staff in human resources, the scoring can only be performed by the publisher. Also, the manner in which the results are reported back to the test user is unclear.

DEVELOPMENT. The materials provided by the publisher offer a substantial description of the development process. The approach taken by the publisher was to have Subject-Matter Experts (SMEs) develop a list of activities, as well as a list of knowledge, skills, abilities, and other characteristics (KSAOs) and subsequently survey job incumbents with less than 5 years experience and more than 6 months experience. The number of useable surveys returned was unimpressive (n = 108), but it seemed adequate to provide a sufficiently stable mean frequency and importance rating. Of the 147 tasks, 57 were deleted because they were not performed frequently enough or were not regarded as being sufficiently important. Although a typical procedure in job analyses, it seems a little surprising to this reviewer that the publisher bothered with assessing the frequency and importance of the tasks at all because the connection between the tasks and the test specifications described in the documentation is not clearly specified. Clearly the modules are based upon the KSAOs. Only 20 of the 30 KSAOs were retained because 10 were regarded as either "not needed" or "learned on the job" (manual, p. 15). Despite these methodological shortcomings, it does appear that many SMEs have agreed that the resulting constructs have some utility.

TECHNICAL. The publisher does not provide very much technical information about the test. Although the answer key is easy enough to derive for most of the modules, it was not described in the documentation. It would be helpful for a prospective test user (or a reviewer) to be able to evaluate it. It was also unclear if all items are scored right/wrong, with partial credit, or if some items are given more weight than others. The testing theory behind the scoring is also left unspecified. In fact, there is no mention regarding the format of the reported scores at all. It is not known whether they are percentiles, raw scores, or a type of scaled scores. Moreover, score interpretation is not discussed at all. One would hope that this type of information would be included on the score report, but it was not provided by the publisher for this review.

The 1996 technical report does provide some evidence of content validity. A review of the modules themselves also seems to support that modules probably measure the constructs that they are purported to measure (face validity), provided that the scoring is appropriate. However, there is no evidence of any concurrent validity, construct validity, or, most importantly, predictive validity. The 1996 technical report also provides no information on any type of reliability. There is also no information regarding whether the test scores are likely to have an adverse impact on members of protected classes. Similarly, there was no item level information regarding differences across gender or ethnicity in the probability of a correct response after the ability of those two groups was held constant.

COMMENTARY. The tests are clearly speeded, but this feature seems appropriate given that in the workplace the speed with which one can work is quite important. These modules might have received a better review had the publisher documented and submitted information on the scoring procedures, reliability of scores, and predictive validity of the results. Without knowing how the modules are scored and how the scores are to be interpreted, it is difficult to recommend its use. The greatest shortcoming of these modules is the lack of documentation the publisher has provided for review.

Despite this lack, the module approach provides flexibility to the customer and the brevity of the modules makes them attractive as an efficient method of testing. Nevertheless, using the modules in situations in which the employer may have the fairness of the test challenged is unappealing due to the lack of information regarding the predictive power of the module or stability of its scores.

SUMMARY. For the purpose of screening candidates for clerical positions, these modules might prove to be useful. The content seemed relevant to the construct and the ease of administration was impressive; however, the scoring can only be performed by the publisher and the publisher is reticent to specify exactly how it is done. The psychometrics behind the instrument are unknown, as is the interpretation of scores. Therefore, the use of this test for employee selection purposes should be very carefully considered.

[3]

Adolescent and Child Urgent Threat Evaluation.

Purpose: Designed to "assess the risk of near-future violence (both homicidal and suicidal) among children and adolescents."
Population: Ages 8-18.
Publication Date: 2005.
Acronym: ACUTE.
Scores, 8: Threat Cluster, Precipitating Factors Cluster, Early Precipitating Factors Cluster, Late Precipitating Factors Cluster, Predisposing Factors Cluster, Impulsivity Cluster, Overall Threat Classification, Total Score.
Administration: Individual.
Price Data, 2009: $125 per professional manual (64 pages) and 50 rating forms.
Time: (20) minutes.
Comments: Some items may require the examiner to "obtain information from additional sources" to gather the most "accurate information regarding a client."
Authors: Russell Copelan and David Ashley.
Publisher: Psychological Assessment Resources, Inc.

Review of the Adolescent and Child Urgent Threat Evaluation by MARY M. CLARE, Professor of Counseling Psychology, Lewis & Clark College, Portland, OR:

DESCRIPTION. The Adolescent and Child Urgent Threat Evaluation (ACUTE) is a 27-item screening tool designed to identify the likelihood that a child or youth has behaved or is in imminent danger of behaving violently toward self or others. Items are structured in a forced-choice, "yes/no" format. The ACUTE is primarily intended to be used in urgent situations by "school psychologists, counselors, teachers, ... physicians, psychologists, psychiatrists, nurses, and social workers" (professional manual, p. 4). The test authors encourage active solicitation of input from the individual child, her or his family, and others closely involved. However, the instrument's defining application is in quick threat assessments for identification of high risk behavioral and situational indicators.

When completed, the 27 items of the ACUTE produce seven scores for clinical interpretation. These scores include the total, and six cluster scores addressing Threat (8 items), Precipitating Factors (13 items), Early Precipitating Factors (9 items), Late Precipitating Factors (4 items), Predisposing Factors (14 items), and Impulsivity (11 items). Alongside analysis of these scores, the test authors urge consideration of individual items in the context of cluster scores. Their description of cluster score and item interpretation includes emphasis on the fact that no one score or item can have validity as a stand-alone metric. That is, the test authors offer the important reminder that the most useful interpretation of data from the ACUTE will include interpretation across and among clusters and the total score.

Extending this contextual emphasis, the test authors describe the ACUTE as best employed as part of a "guided professional judgment approach" (professional manual, p. 4), one that gives structure and immediate grounding in the current theoretical, empirical, and clinical knowledge bases. In service to this notion, the test authors provide a careful summary of the instrument's conceptual base, emphasizing the importance of considering factors well beyond the presence of depression when gauging potential/imminent violence to self or others.

DEVELOPMENT. The ACUTE is significantly grounded in the test authors' review and synthesis of the empirical bases reflecting current understanding and practice in the identification of urgent threat of violence in children and youth. The approximately 100 reference citations listed by the test authors are drawn primarily from research literature and indicate the rigor of the knowledge base from which the ACUTE has been developed. Based on their analysis of this knowledge base the test authors present their instrument as filling four significant gaps in the assessment of *risk for violence*: (a) providing a unified theory and definition of risk of violence; (b) enhancing validity by assessing historic and social/systemic circumstances beyond evidence of depressive symptomatology or suicidal ideation; (c) using representative sampling for norm development; and (d) reducing false positive and false negative rates to provide strong predictive values.

In the explicit context of their distillation of practical theory, the test authors consulted with two emergency department psychiatrists to develop their pool of items. Item sources included clinical notes, chart entries, and adaptations of existing assessment instruments. The test authors' goal was to isolate factors "other than associated depression and hopelessness" (professional manual, p. 47) predictive of violence and/or suicidality in children and youth. Together with their consultants, the test authors reached agreement on the items and their fit into the three categories of some risk, high risk, or imminent risk.

The 63-item pool was then pilot tested over three data gathering periods: 1980–1984, 1985–1992, and 1992–1994. Based on the data derived from these clinical applications, the ACUTE was distilled into its current form with 27 yes/no questions supporting the score clusters described above. These data also provide the basis for discernment of risk. In addition, interviews (with each child/youth and their parents, teachers, and care providers) and review of clinical records provided data revealing historic, behavioral, and circumstantial predictors defining three clinical groups: suicide threat, homicide threat, and suicide-homicide threat.

TECHNICAL. A 25-year development process led to the 2005 publication of the ACUTE. As mentioned above, the three pilot-testing periods involved children and youth in both inpatient and outpatient settings. Based on the data derived from these pilots, the test authors completed tests of reliability including considerations of internal consistency (item-with-total, .30–.58; cluster-with-total, .70–.85), test-retest stability (correlations from .71–.97), and interrater agreement (Total Score, .94). Each of these outcomes supports the instrument's psychometric reliability.

With regard to validity, the test authors refer to significant differences on every cluster (except Predisposing Factors) from a matched samples t-test between participants from the Non-Threat group and the standardization sample, as evidence of the strong criterion-related validity of the ACUTE for differentiating children/youth with psychiatric histories who are and are not at immediate risk for violence. Additional and explicit report of false positive/negative rates would enhance these data. Convergent and discriminant analyses considered consistency between ACUTE scores and those of related standardized measures to yield sufficient evidence of psychometric validity. Alongside these more conventional analyses, the test authors offer no investigation of logical or treatment validity. Given their emphasis on clinical judgment in the use of the ACUTE, systematic investigation of these forms of validity would enhance the psychometric grounding of this instrument

Related to considerations of logical validity and treatment validity is a potential internal compromise inherent in the test authors' claim that "the ACUTE is the only tool currently available that assigns violence risk levels within minutes of intake (for most cases), thereby capturing high risk situations before the onset of violent behavior and also resulting in more appropriate treatment" (professional manual, p. 4). Even with their parenthetical inclusion of the caveat, *for most cases*, this statement seems at odds with the test authors' earlier emphasis on the importance of consulting multiple informants in order to situate the child/youth's crisis accurately within complex systemic forces of family, environment, and history.

COMMENTARY. Although the test authors emphasize that predictors of violence vary widely across cultures, psychiatric diagnoses, adverse family circumstances, and gender, they provide little depth in their normative samples and no distinction in scoring approaches relative to any of these groups. This feature of the ACUTE limits the logical validity of the instrument to individuals not represented in the sample.

The test authors speak to the considerations of diversity (e.g., ethnic, gender, DSM diagnosis) in their samples and offer interpretations that support their having selected items that generalize across categories; however, these descriptions cannot and do not compensate for sampling limitations. The threats of false positives and false negatives in the assessment of violence are highlighted by the test authors as a rationale for their development of the ACUTE. Given this psychometric and clinical reality, any limitation to the accuracy of the ACUTE must be underscored.

Related to this concern (i.e., limitations in validity relative to individual diagnosis and treatment) is the test authors' own description of the ACUTE as a tool for "guided professional judgment approach" to determining the threat of violent behavior (professional manual, p. 4). The training, experience, and professional network of colleagues supporting the individual employing the ACUTE are significant factors in its ultimate utility. Without immediate access to or thorough familiarity with the manual, completion of this instrument requires extensive subjectivity on the part of the clinician.

SUMMARY. The Adolescent and Child Urgent Threat Evaluation (ACUTE) offers an important advance in the assessment and treatment of children and youth who are at risk of being violent to themselves or others. This instrument can be vital as a tool to seasoned clinicians. Service providers with limited education and experience may carefully study the ACUTE manual and use the instrument well under close supervision. The primary weakness of the instrument resides in its billing as *quick*. The test authors indicate that careful attention, wisdom, and clinical patience are needed for making timely and clinically relevant evaluations under such urgent circumstances. It is only practical to agree that the speed of such an assessment can mean the difference between life and death. However, deference to this or any other metric would risk serious inaccuracies in both diagnosis and treatment. The test authors know and speak to this fact, particularly in their references to *guided professional judgment*. In its current form, the ACUTE falls short in its emphasis on and instruction to address this crucial consideration. In future revisions, it will be helpful for the test authors to field test and provide additional and substantive guidance for how quickly to apply the diverse systemic analyses central to this instrument's clinical purpose.

Review of the Adolescent and Child Urgent Threat Evaluation by THOMAS P. HOGAN, Professor of Psychology, University of Scranton, Scranton, PA:

DESCRIPTION. The Adolescent and Child Urgent Threat Evaluation (ACUTE) purports to "assist in the assessment of risk for violence among children and adolescents" (professional manual, p. 7) by having a trained clinician answer questions about an individual's behaviors. In the ACUTE, risk for violence encompasses threats to others and threats to self, or, in the words of the norm groups for the assessment, homicide threat and suicide threat. Materials consist of the 73-page professional manual and ACUTE rating form. The clinician completes an interview with the individual and, according to the manual, should check extensively with other sources of information before filling out the rating form. The target audience is children and adolescents ages 8–18.

The rating form consists of 27 items answered by the clinician in a Yes-No format. The carbonized four-page form opens so that responses appearing on the inside page may be aggregated into subscores, referred to as clusters. A score summary sheet, including norm conversion tables, appears on the back of the first page. The ACUTE yields a total score and six subscores: a lot of scores for 27 items. The organization of subscores is complex. The Precipitating Factors cluster (13 items) wholly contains three other clusters: Threat, Early Precipitating, and Late Precipitating clusters, and part of the Impulsivity cluster. Furthermore, the Early Precipitating and Late Precipitating clusters partially overlap with the Threat cluster. The Predisposing Factors cluster (14 items) does not overlap with the Precipitating Factors cluster but does partially overlap with the Impulsivity cluster. The total score is based on all 27 items.

Precipitating Factors items deal mainly with specific behaviors such as identifying a victim, involvement with alcohol, and actual plans for violent acts. Ten of the 13 items in Precipitating Factors incorporate the words "violent or suicidal behavior." Predisposing Factors items deal with matters such as previous psychiatric illness, family history, and home environment.

The manual devotes considerable space to describing the rationale, research base, and scoring criteria for each item. The manual also presents three case illustrations, giving the score sheet and commentary for each case.

DEVELOPMENT. The manual refers to using a theoretical model intended to minimize associations with depression and hopelessness. It is not clear why one would want to minimize these associations if, in fact, they are related to the target construct (risk of violence). The manual also refers to classification of items by suicide versus homicide on one dimension and some, high, or imminent risk on the other dimension. However, the final score clusters do not reflect this matrix arrangement.

The manual reports a four-stage process that was used for the ACUTE's development: item development, pilot testing, standardization, and scale development. For item development, the authors refer to adapting items from several extant scales and developing other items from literature reviews and clinical experience, yielding an initial pool of 63 items. Pilot testing is described in terms of three samples: Sample 1 tested from 1980–1984, Sample 2 from 1985–1992, and Sample 3 from 1992–1994. In one place the manual refers to the first sample as consisting of 416 cases but it also refers to analyzing a subset of 100 children; it is not clear which group served as the basis for the analyses. It is also not clear exactly what types of analyses were conducted. In any case, these analyses resulted in reducing the pool of items to 36. Sample 2 consisted of 1,885 cases, including homicide attempters, suicide attempters, and nonviolent youth. Sample 3 consisted of 326 children who were referred to a clinic, in part, for assessment of violence. The final 27 items were obtained using item-with-total correlations and degree to which individual threat groups endorsed the items.

TECHNICAL INFORMATION. The ACUTE standardization sample consisted of 542 cases divided as follows: 298 suicide threat, 103 homicide threat, 71 both homicide and suicide threat, and 70 nonthreat. The manual provides useful demographic information about these cases by gender, ethnicity, and psychiatric diagnosis, but not by geographic origins or urbanicity. In several places, the manual provides age information only in the form of means and standard deviations. Where more detailed information is provided about age, it appears that very few cases represent ages under 13. For example, Table 4.3 shows only 86 cases for the age range 8–12; assuming an even distribution of cases across this age range, we get fewer than 20 cases per year. The earlier description of pilot Sample 1 refers to 3% of the sample being in Grades 4–8, which yields about 2 cases per grade. In effect, the standardization, as well as the pilot testing, appears to apply to ages 13–18, not 8–18.

Raw scores for the ACUTE total and cluster scores are converted into norms represented as four categories corresponding, on the one hand, to percentile ranges 1–33, 34–74, 75–94, and 95+; and, on the other hand, to these qualitative descriptions: low clinical, moderate clinical, high clinical, and extreme clinical. These norm categories appear separately for the nonthreat, suicide, homicide, homicide-suicide, and combined threat groups for total score and for some, but not all, cluster scores. Where norms do appear separately by group for the cluster scores, there are minimal differences between groups (in fact, identical for Late Precipitating Factors). At least for the cluster scores, a single norm group appears preferable, as is done for the Threat cluster.

The manual presents alpha reliability coefficients for the total and cluster scores based on the 542 cases in the standardization sample, with total score at .85 and clusters ranging from .70–.85. Thus, internal consistency is moderate. Test-retest reliabilities, based on 77 cases, with no description of case selection, were exceptionally high, ranging from .91–.97, with the exception of the Predisposing Factors at .71. However, the test-retest interval was only 24–48 hours, an unusually short period of time for a test-retest reliability study. The result for Predisposing Factors is odd because such factors should be exceptionally stable over a short period of time. Interrater reliabilities are given as mostly in the .90s with one cluster at .86 and another at .74. These data are based on only 29 cases, again with no description of case selection, and no description of the raters.

The manual begins its discussion of validity with presentation of correlations among the ACUTE scores based on the entire standardization sample. As might be predicted from the item overlap, correlations tend to be high. The median correlation among the first four clusters is .89, that is, approximately at the level of the internal consistencies for these scales, thus suggesting no useful distinctions among them. The Predisposing Factors cluster has a noticeably low correlation (.24) with the Precipitating Factors cluster (where no item overlap exists). The manual next presents contrasts in scores between the combined threat groups and a nonthreat group. All but one of the differences are significant.

The manual also presents correlations of the ACUTE with the Clinical Assessment of Depression (CAD), the Children's Depression Inventory (CDI), and the Suicidal Ideation Questionnaire (SIQ). All of these correlation studies are based on only 29 cases, with no description of case selection. Oddly, the manual omits correlations between CDI scores and the ACUTE total score. One infers from all of these correlations that (a) relationships are generally going in the desired direction, but (b) the data base is terribly thin.

COMMENTARY. The clinical field contains many instruments for assessing suicidal risk (see Nock, Wedig, Janis, & Deliberto, 2008, for a recent summary). The ACUTE attempts to cover both suicidal and homicidal threats in a single instrument, indeed within single items as noted previously. There appears to be no clinical rationale or empirical basis for conflating homicidal and suicidal populations or behaviors. It may make some sense to ask separate questions about these matters and yield separate scores for them, but the ACUTE does not do so. In fact, the treatment of validity, which includes one (albeit small) study related to suicide, makes no effort to address homicide. An earlier version of the ACUTE, according to the manual, did provide separate scores; reasons for abandoning that scheme were not given but it seems likely that the scheme did not work because of item wording—that is where the conflation occurs.

SUMMARY. The ACUTE aims to provide a clinician's rating for threat of violent (homicidal) or suicidal behavior. The rating form is simple and the manual provides a useful review of background literature on the nature of the problem(s). Two structural problems create difficulties in interpretation: the multiple layers of overlapping items between scales and, more importantly, combining homicidal and suicidal concepts within single items and scales. The ACUTE used a reasonable standardization process, but the extent of information on reliability and validity is inadequate. It is not recommended for clinical use until more complete information becomes available.

REVIEWER'S REFERENCE

Nock, M. K., Wedig, M. M., Janis, I. B., & Deliberto, T. L. (2008). Self-injurious thoughts and behavior. In J. Hunsley & E. J. Mash (Eds.), *A guide to assessments that work* (pp. 158-177). New York: Oxford.

[4]

Ages & Stages Questionnaires®: A Parent-Completed Child Monitoring System, Third Edition.

Purpose: Designed to "screen young children for developmental delays–that is, to identify those children who are in need of further evaluation and those who appear to be developing typically."
Population: Ages 1 to 66 months.
Publication Dates: 1995-2009.
Acronym: ASQ-3™.
Scores, 5: Communication, Gross Motor, Fine Motor, Problem Solving, Personal-Social.
Administration: Individual.
Levels, 21: 2, 4, 6, 8, 9, 10, 12, 14, 16, 18, 20, 22, 24, 27, 30, 33, 36, 42, 48, 54, and 60 months.
Price Data, 2009: $249.95 per starter kit including 21 copies of questionnaires and scoring sheets, CD-ROM, user's guide (2009, 256 pages), and quick start guide; $249.95 per starter kit with Spanish questionnaires; $199.95 per 21 questionnaires, scoring sheets, and CD-ROM in English or Spanish; $50 per user's guide.
Foreign Language Edition: Questionnaires available in Spanish.
Time: (10-15) minutes.
Comments: The questionnaire is to be completed by the child's primary caregiver in the home; the authors state, however, that "professionals will need to establish the screening and monitoring system, develop the necessary community interfaces, train individuals who will score the questionnaires, and provide feedback to parents of children who are completing the questionnaires."
Authors: Jane Squires and Diane Bricker (questionnaires and user's guide); Elizabeth Twombly and LaWanda Potter (user's guide only).
Publisher: Paul H. Brookes Publishing Co., Inc.
Cross-References: For reviews by B. Ann Boyce and G. Michael Poteat of the second edition, see 16:8; for reviews by Dorothy M. Singleton and Rhonda H. Solomon of the original edition, see 14:14.

Review of the Ages & Stages Questionnaires®: A Parent-Completed Child Monitoring System, Third Edition by KENNETH M. HANIG, Adjunct Faculty, Department of Psychology, Indiana University South Bend, South Bend, IN:

DESCRIPTION. The Ages & Stages Questionnaires®: A Parent-Completed Child Monitoring System, Third Edition (ASQ-3™) is an instrument designed to use for the identification of infants and young children who have developmental delays or disorders in order to assess need for the delivery of intervention services. The measure is a first step in screening for services for this population, according to the user's guide authors Jane Squires, Elizabeth Twombly, Diane Bricker, and LaWanda Potter. The measure is composed of 21 questionnaires that are completed by parents or other primary caregivers to children between the ages of 1 month and 5 ½ years of age. The questionnaire age intervals include 2, 4, 6, 8, 9, 10, 12, 14, 16, 18, 20, 22, 24, 27, 30, 33, 36, 42, 48, 54, and 60 months. "Each questionnaire contains 30 developmental items that are written in simple, straightforward language" (user's guide, p. 3). The test authors indicate that the items are organized into five areas: Communication, Gross Motor, Fine Motor, Problem Solving, and Personal-Social. An Overall section addresses general parental concerns. The user's guide authors state that the reading level of each questionnaire ranges from fourth to sixth grade.

The test kit includes the 21 questionnaires, which can be duplicated. The master set of questionnaires is available on a CD-ROM and in an online completion format through a separately purchased subscription to ASQ Family Access. Questionnaires are available in English and Spanish. The test kit includes tabs that allow for easy organization and access by the examiner. Also included among the test materials are the user's guide, Information Summary Sheets for each age level, the ASQ-3 product overview, and an ordering guide. The ASQ-3 starter kit allows the examiner the core materials needed to start screening children. The user's guide includes information regarding planning, organizing, administering, scoring, and evaluating the screening and monitoring system as well as psychometric information on the measure. The test authors indicate that new to the third edition are chapters describing ASQ-3 completion methods and settings and a chapter of case studies illustrating the ASQ-3 in practice. Also, the user's guide has useful appendices which, according to the test authors, are designed to facilitate the screening and monitoring process. A Quick Start Guide is available as "a lightweight, laminated guide to ASQ-3 administration and scoring basics" (user's guide, p. 5). The test authors state that the measure is designed for easy use and little training is needed to use the test. Training DVDs are available as well. Online management and questionnaire completion systems are also available.

DEVELOPMENT. The test authors indicated that they developed the ASQ to monitor the factors in development of designated groups of infants and young children who could benefit from early detection and intervention. These factors included an increase in the population of infants at risk for developmental disabilities, increased emphasis on prevention, and federal and state legal regulations addressing the need for early and effective Child Find programs. The test authors commented that most screening programs conducted with infants focused on populations who are at risk for developmental disabilities as a result of medical, biological, and environmental circumstances (American Academy of Pediatrics, 2006; Batshaw, Pellegrino, & Roizen, 2007; Johnson, Myers, & Council on Children with Disabilities, 2007; Meisels & Atkins-Burnett, 2005). A "multidisciplinary team approach ... began in the 1970s and has been used since then" (user's guide, p. 12). Other tests, such as the Denver II (Frankenburg et al., 1996) and the Pediatric Symptom Checklist (Jellinek et al., 1988) have been used to identify the developmental issues of infants and young children. A parenting monitoring approach has gained acceptance (Bricker & Squires, 1989), relying on measures such as the Denver Prescreening Developmental Questionnaire (Frankenburg & Bresnick, 1998). A community-based evaluation approach, using tools such as the Developmental Indicators for the Assessment of Learning-III (Mardell-Czudnowski & Goldenberg, 1998) is also recommended for early screening efforts.

A challenge for the test authors was to devise a system for the identification of problems in infants and young children that was sensitive to variations in child development. Parent involvement and cost were other issues. The ASQ was initially called the Infant/Child Monitoring Questionnaire. The ASQ-3 addresses the dynamic nature of development by offering multiple assessment intervals. It has three components: questionnaires, procedures for use, and support materials. The involvement of parents in the ASQ system not only makes economic sense, according to the test authors, but also meets the mandates of IDEA 1990 (PL 101-476). As such, it is a good tool to be used by early childhood teachers, kindergarten teachers, school psychologists, school counselors, physicians, speech teachers, occupational therapists, and physical therapists.

Regarding item selection, items were gleaned from standardized developmental tests, nonstandardized tests of early development, textbooks, and other literature concerning developmental milestones. Criteria used to develop items included skills that could be observed by parents, that were likely to occur in a variety of home and child care settings, and were indexed to developmental milestones. Once selected, the items were written in familiar "concrete words that did not exceed a 6th grade reading level" (user's guide, p. 148). A large pool of items was then developed. Then, six items from each of the developmental areas (e.g., Communication) for each age interval were selected. Item selection for each questionnaire interval was restricted by selecting only items that targeted a skill that occurred at the middle to low end of the developmental range for that particular chronological age interval of 75 to 100. The range was chosen, according to the test authors, because one and a half to two standard deviations below the mean is generally regarded as the lower end of the normal range because items above a developmental quotient of 100 would indicate development that fell within normal limits. Developmental quotients for each item were calculated using a variation of the familiar ratio of mental age to chronological age. Revisions include the first revision in 1991, a second revision in 1999, and the current ASQ-3 in 2009.

TECHNICAL. Psychometric data were collected since 2004. The data included completed questionnaires for 15,138 children between 1 and 66 months of age. The entire data set was used to derive new cutoff scores for the questionnaires. Also, Web-based and paper questionnaires were used in comparison studies. The WINSTEPS Rasch Measurement version 3.64.2 computer program was used to analyze the data. Out of the 570 questionnaire items, the findings indicated that only 60 items exhibited significant DIF when comparing the two groups. The gender distribution for the normative sample was 53% male and 47% female. The greatest percentage of mothers (54%) were college educated, whereas 12% had associate degrees, 23% were high school graduates, and 3.5% were nongraduates. Caregivers reported incomes of greater than $40,000 (57%), whereas 36% noted incomes below that.

Reliability studies included test-retest reliability and interobserver reliability. Internal consistency was assessed using correlational analyses and coefficient alphas. Intraclass correlations for test-retest reliability ranged from .75 to .82; for interobserver reliability .43 to .69; and for internal consistency .51 to .87.

Validity evidence was offered through comparisons of questionnaires for risk and nonrisk groups to aid in developing cutoff scores. Three tables are available comparing the standard alphas and correlations between developmental area scores collapsing across questionnaires and overall ASQ-3 scores. These latter correlations ranged from .33 to .79. Concurrent validity was evaluated by comparing children's performance on standardized tests to the ASQ-3. A table highlighting means, standard deviations, and cutoff scores is provided. Two groups were included in this analysis: those tested for eligibility for IDEA services and those presumed to be without problems (known as the typical group). A child's performance on the ASQ was considered identified if the score was at or less than 2 standard deviations below the mean. Comparison to the Battelle Developmental Inventory (BDI) was noted. Overall, the section on validity seemed confusing and somewhat weak, especially compared to the well-ordered and easily understood reliability section.

COMMENTARY. Aside from the validity explanation, the ASQ-3 is a fairly good tool, especially for the school personnel specified above. The test also could be used for autism screenings, students referred for cognitive impairments, and other developmental disabilities. One of the strengths of the measure is the usefulness to parents and other caregivers. The items are easy to read, score, and interpret, and caregivers can get immediate feedback. It is of note, though, that this measure is a screening tool and not a standardized measure such as the Stanford-Binet. It should not be used for placement decisions for special education services, but its value certainly is in identifying potential developmental disabilities that are suspected in infants and young children.

SUMMARY. The ASQ-3 is designed to screen infants and young children in order to assess needs for disabilities services. The test can be used as a monitoring tool as well. Five areas are measured, including Communication, Gross Motor, Fine Motor, Problem Solving, and Personal-Social. Though reliability data are clear, validity evidence is less convincing. Yet, as a screening tool, the ASQ-3 can be recommended.

REVIEWER'S REFERENCES

American Academy of Pediatrics. (2006). Identifying infants and young children with developmental disorders in the medical home: An algorithm for developmental surveillance and screening. *Pediatrics, 118,* 405–420. Available online at http://aappolicy.aappublications.org/cgi/content/full/pediatrics;118/1/405.

Batshaw, M. L., Pellegrino, L., & Roizen, N. J. (Eds.). (2007). *Children with disabilities* (6th ed.). Baltimore: Paul H. Brookes Publishing Co.

Bricker, D., & Squires, J. (1989). Low cost system using parents to monitor the development of at risk infants. *Journal of Early Intervention, 13,* 50–60.

Frankenburg, W., Dodds, J., Archer, P., Bresnick, B., Maschka, P., Edelman, N., et al. (1996). *The Denver II technical manual.* Denver, CO: Denver Developmental Materials.

Frankenburg, W. K., & Bresnick, B. (1998). DENVER II Prescreening Questionnaire (PDQ II). Denver, CO: Denver Developmental Materials.

Jellinek, M. S., Murphy, J. M., Robinson, J., Feins, A., Lamb, S., & Fenton, T. (1998). Pediatric Symptom Checklist: Screening school-age children for psychosocial dysfunction. *The Journal of Pediatrics, 112,* 201–209.

Johnson, C., Myers, S., & Council on Children with Disabilities. (2007). Management of children with autism spectrum disorder. *Pediatrics, 120,* 1162–1182.

Mardell-Czudnowski, C., & Goldenberg, D. (1998). Developmental Indicators for the Assessment of Learning–Third Edition (DIAL-3). Austin, TX: PRO-ED.

Meisels, S. J., & Atkins-Burnett, S. (2005). *Developmental screening in early childhood: A guide* (5th ed.). Washington, DC: National Association for the Education of Young Children.

Review of the Ages & Stages Questionnaires®: A Parent-Completed Child Monitoring System, Third Edition by RACHEL J. VALLELEY, Associate Professor, Munroe-Meyer Institute and Pediatrics, Munroe-Meyer Institute, University of Nebraska Medical Center, Omaha, NE, and BRANDY M. ROANE, Pediatric Psychology Intern, Munroe-Meyer Institute, University of Nebraska Medical Center, Omaha, NE:

DESCRIPTION. The Ages & Stages Questionnaires®: A Parent-Completed Child Monitoring System, Third Edition (ASQ-3™) is a comprehensive developmental screening and monitoring system intended for infants and children between the ages of 1 and 66 months. The ASQ-3 provides a psychometrically sound means to identify infants and children in need of further assessment to determine eligibility for early intervention and early childhood special education services. The ASQ-3 consists of 21 age-specific parent-completed questionnaires that assess five different areas. An Overall section is included to capture common parental concerns. Questions are written in simple, straightforward language requiring a fourth to sixth grade reading level and illustrations are provided to facilitate understanding and enhance accuracy of the report. The ASQ-3 can be used to screen infants and young child and/or track the developmental progress of young children who may be at risk for developmental delays (e.g., low birth weight). A Spanish version of each questionnaire is available.

Questionnaire selection is based on chronological age, but may be adapted based on prematurity status. Questions on the ASQ-3 are categorized according to the five different areas (i.e., Communication, Gross Motor, Fine Motor, Problem Solving, Personal-Social) and progress developmentally within each area (e.g., the question regarding crawling precedes the question regarding walking). Primary caregivers can complete the questionnaire at home while observing their child's behavior with each activity, taking approximately 10–15 minutes to complete. In addition, questionnaires can be completed in a variety of settings (e.g., waiting rooms, clinics, schools). Question response options are *yes, sometimes,* and *not yet* with scores of 10, 5, and 0, respectively, assigned. The Overall section is not scored, but provides a less structured means for parents to express concerns. This section should be reviewed and concerns discussed with the parents to evaluate for potential problems.

Questionnaires are scored by either support staff or the practitioner, and scoring takes approximately 1–5 minutes. Scores are tallied for each of the five areas to yield five total area scores. Area total scores are transferred to the ASQ-3 Information Summary sheet, which includes age-based normative score ranges specific to each of the questionnaires. Based on these normative scores, area total scores are determined to be either above cutoffs, close to cutoffs, or below cutoffs. Above cutoff scores indicate the infant or child's development is progressing typically. Scores falling in the close to cutoff range reflect scores 1 to 2 standard deviations below the mean and suggests the infant or child is at risk and careful monitoring is needed as well as special learning activities. Scores within the below cutoff range indicate the infant or child is functioning 2 or more standard deviations below the mean and further assessment is needed.

DEVELOPMENT. The ASQ-3 is the third revision of the ASQ, which was developed out of the pressing need to establish empirically based screening measures for the early detection of developmental delays in infants and children. The third installment of the ASQ derived from empirical data collected on the second edition of the ASQ from community-based samples since its inception in 1999 and from feedback from professionals and parents. Community based samples were pooled from various state-supported early education programs and other education, health, and social services agencies. To supplement these samples, the test authors established a web-based data collection system in 2004 accessible via a research website for all 50 states. These various data collection methods have established a database of over 18,000 questionnaires for analyses.

The overall goal of the third revision is to enhance generalizability of the measure across the United States as well as in other countries and to promote widespread use of the ASQ-3 as a developmental screener to diverse populations. In order to achieve this goal, five major revisions were made for the ASQ-3. First, the age range expanded and was modified to cover all infants and children between the ages of 1 and 66 months. In order to facilitate this expansion, the ASQ-3 includes two additional questionnaires for 2 and 9 months, which were not part of the second edition of the ASQ. Second, age ranges are now clearly stated on the front of each questionnaire for ease of use. Third, cutoff scores for the 19 previously used questionnaires are empirically derived from the extensive second edition data. Fourth, each questionnaire includes a "monitoring" zone range intended to identify infants and children at risk for developmental delays, but not yet scoring within the below cutoff range. Fifth, feedback from parents and professionals guided changes to wording, illustrations, and examples for several of the questionnaire items. In addition to changes on the questionnaires, revisions were made to the ASQ-3 user's guide to facilitate use of the ASQ-3 with diverse populations. An expansion of case study scenarios was added along with information on using the ASQ-3 in different settings and with different completion methods. The test authors provide extensive references in the ASQ-3 user's guide to support these revisions and additions.

TECHNICAL. The ASQ-3 user's guide provides a detailed description of item selection, questionnaire development, sample selection, and revisions for each ASQ in the Technical Report appendix (pp. 147-175). Between January 2004 and June 2008, over 18,000 questionnaires were completed by primary caregivers (half completed using the paper method and the other half completed on the web). IRT analyses found few differences between the paper- vs. web-completed questionnaires. The standardization sample of children included 53% males and 47% females and was representative of U.S. Census data for ethnicity.

Test-retest reliability data were collected from a group of 145 parents who completed two questionnaires in a 2-week interval, and yielded a 92% agreement rate on classification, with intraclass correlations ranging from .75 to .82. Interobserver data were collected by comparing parents' and trained examiners' classification of 107 children. Results indicated an interobserver agreement rate of 93% on classification, with intraclass correlation ranging from .43 to .69. Finally, internal consistency was calculated on all completed questionnaires with alpha coefficients for developmental area scores ranging from .51 to .87.

The entire sample of completed questionnaires (including children in the nonrisk and risk categories) was utilized to determine normative cutoff scores. Concurrent validity was established by comparing the performance of a typical group (n = 322) and an identified group (n = 257) on the Battelle Developmental Inventory (BDI) and ASQ-3. Overall agreement between the questionnaire and the standardized test on status (e.g., eligible vs. typical) was 85.8% (range 82.6–88.9%) with a sensitivity of 82.5–89.2% and specificity of 77.9–92.1%. Underidentification across the ages ranged from 4.5–7.4%. Limited information was provided on reliability and validity data for the Spanish translation.

COMMENTARY. The ASQ-3 system is an empirically sound screening and monitoring system for the early detection of developmental delays in infants and children. Each questionnaire addresses five key developmental areas in language that is easy to understand for both parents and practitioners. Included in the system are questionnaire-specific Information Summary sheets that make for easy translation of scores to determine possible action via the quick reference cutoff scores provided on each sheet. The comprehensive coverage from 1 to 66 months with 21 different questionnaires is both thorough and efficient. The multiple age-specific questionnaires also allow for monitoring of progress across visits.

The ASQ-3 user's guide provides ample information and guidance regarding administration, scoring, and interpretation of the ASQ-3. The test authors go a step further and provide detailed instructions for the complete implementation of the ASQ-3 system for practitioners via four phases: planning the screening/monitoring program; preparing, organizing, and managing the screening program; administrering and scoring the ASQ-3 and following-up; and evaluating the screening/monitoring program.

In an effort to enhance the accessibility and appeal of the ASQ-3 for practitioners, the test authors provide several user-friendly components to the ASQ-3 including (a) all questionnaires, demographic forms, sample letters, and consent forms that are provided in both paper and .pdf formats and (b) a disclaimer allowing each physical site to maintain one copy of the ASQ-3 system and photocopy necessary questionnaires for use. The test authors also enhanced deliverability for parents and caregivers via numerous completion methods as described in the ASQ-3 user's guide, which provides detailed instructions, considerations, and examples of onsite, home-visit, mail-out, online, and telephone procedures.

SUMMARY. The ASQ-3 is the third installment of the ASQ system and is designed to screen and monitor for developmental delays in infants and children ages 1 to 66 months. The ASQ-3 is an empirically based and comprehensive screening system that uses 21 different age-specific questionnaires to assess five key developmental areas. Questionnaire-specific Information Summary sheets provide quick reference cut-off scores, which allow for easy translation of scores with guidelines suggesting courses of action. The ASQ-3 system allows for continual monitoring of infants and children across visits. In addition, the ASQ-3 user's guide provides a plethora of information on the implementation of the ASQ-3 system and references supporting the validity and reliability of the measure. Data are not yet available for the Spanish translation.

[5]

Assessment, Evaluation, and Programming System for Infants and Children (AEPS®): Second Edition.

Purpose: Designed "to assist interventionists and caregivers in developing functional and coordinated assessment, goal development, intervention and evaluation activities for young children who have or who are at risk for disabilities."

Population: Birth to 3 years, 3 to 6 years.

Publication Dates: 1993-2002.

Acronym: AEPS®.

Scores, 7: 6 developmental areas: Fine Motor, Gross Motor, Adaptive, Cognitive, Social-Communication, Social; 1 Total raw score.

Administration: Individual or group.

Levels, 2: Birth to Three Years, Three to Six Years.

Price Data, 2009: $239 per 4-Volume Set, including Volume 1: Administration Guide (2002, 336 pages), Volume 2: Test: Birth to Three Years and Three to Six Years (2002, 304 pages), Volume 3: Curriculum for Birth to Three Years (2002, 512 pages), Volume 4: Curriculum for Three to Six Years (2002, 352 pages); $179 per Administration Guide, Test, and choice of Birth to Three Years Curriculum or Three to Six Years Curriculum; $65 per each Volume 1: Administration Guide, Volume 3: Curriculum for Birth to Three Years, Volume 4: Curriculum for Three to Six Years; $75 per Volume 2: Test: Birth to Three Years and Three to Six Years; $249.95 per Forms on CD-ROM; annual subscription to web-based management system AEPSinteractive (AEPSi) priced at $19.95–$16.95 per child record, depending on the number of children (1–500) for whom data are being managed (the user is directed to contact the publisher if data will be managed for more than 500 children).

Foreign Language Edition: CD-ROM Forms also available in Spanish; CODRF also available in AEPSi in Spanish.

Time: Administration time varies.

Comments: Administration time depends on several factors; recommended to be administered over a 2-week period to permit observation of the child in a variety of activities. AEPS can also be used for children up to age 9 with significant delays. AEPS is a curriculum-based assessment, not a norm-referenced assessment. As such, the Child Observation Data Recording Form (CODRF) is used by the professional to organize and display assessment information gathered in the six developmental areas that are assessed. Observations for up to four test sessions may be recorded on the CODRF. AEPS is a flexible assessment system designed so that professionals may choose the developmental areas and the number of children who are assessed at each testing session. Each developmental area in each level is composed of strands, or behaviors that are developmentally related. An appendix is included in the Administration Guide that links a child's performance on each developmental area with Individualized Family Service Plan or Individualized Education Program goals. The test elicits family participation through the use of the Family Report, which encourages family assessment of the child. AEPSinteractive (AEPSi) is a "web-based management system (www.aepsi.com) [that] streamlines AEPS administration, provides new reporting features, and includes sets of activities that allow users to assess multiple children at the same time."

Authors: Diane Bricker, Betty Capt, Kristie Pretti-Frontczak, JoAnn Johnson, Kristine Glentz, Elizabeth Straka, and Misti Waddell.

Publisher: Paul H. Brookes Publishing Co., Inc.

Review of the Assessment, Evaluation, and Programming System for Infants and Children (AEPS®): Second Edition by JAMES VAN HANEGHAN, Director, Assessment and Evaluation, College of Education, University of South Alabama, Mobile, AL:

DESCRIPTION. The Assessment, Evaluation, and Programming System for Infants and Children (AEPS) is a curriculum-based assessment system designed for use in the context of early intervention and preschool services for children identified as developmentally delayed. There are four volumes and a CD-ROM with the package: The administration guide, the test items, and curriculum volumes for birth to 3 years and 3 to 6 years. The assessments provide a basis for individualized family services plans and individualized education programs for developmentally delayed infants and young children. Curriculum and ideas for instructional goals are included. It is a comprehensive system for planning, implementing, and assessing the effectiveness of interventions. The current version of the test involves two separate assessments: one for birth to 3 years and one for ages 3 to 6 years. The test items are in one manual so that users can work easily with items that fall into both age ranges. Users should have knowledge of typical and atypical child development and be able to collaborate with specialists who can address communication delays, sensory, and/or motor disabilities. Sometimes it is recommended that specialists administer part of the assessment. There is also a caregiver report form (Family Report) to engage parents and provide further information.

A comprehensive assessment with the AEPS can be time-consuming (several hours). The goal is for most of the items to be observed by the examiner in natural or contrived settings. As noted in the manual, experienced testers may be quicker because they better know contexts where behaviors are most likely to occur. Scorers note whether behaviors were observed, reported, or directly tested. Additionally, indicators and notes about assistance provided, modifications, and other information are part of the recording process. This information can be helpful in planning interventions and providing context for future assessments. After the initial evaluation, the administration guide indicates that subsequent administrations take less time. Further, given that the assessment is associated with curriculum goals that are directly tied to assessment results (the curriculum materials are linked to test items), subsequent assessments can be done to address targets for intervention.

Individual items are scored on a 0 to 2 scale, where 0 means the behavior was not observed, 1 means the skill was inconsistently observed, and 2 means it was consistently observed. The score of "1" is subject to the most interpretation. A "1" could mean that the child needed assistance, could not carry out the task completely, or may only perform in particular contexts. Perhaps "developing" might be a better descriptor than "inconsistently meets," but the criteria for a "1" are clear. A code is recorded indicating whether the assessment was based on a report or observation, whether assistance or modifications were required, whether extraneous behaviors interfered with performance, or whether there were questions about the quality of performance. The score sheet has room for repeated testing of items, raw scores based on summing the items within a domain, and a percent correct score. Finally, there is a place for examiner comments that explain codes and provide curriculum suggestions or other comments. The ability to track several testings has been further improved by the availability of a web-based tool. There are no standard scores, although cutoff scores have been recently developed for each domain to help determine service eligibility in conjunction with other data. The test authors eschew using any kind of normative-based scoring to focus on functional behaviors that can be changed in children.

DEVELOPMENT. The model behind the AEPS involves a functional scaling of basic Social, Cognitive, Social-Communication, Adaptive, Fine Motor, and Gross Motor Skills that emerge with development. Additionally, the system was developed so that the assessment was part of a larger system that focused on cycles of assessment, planning, intervention, and reassessment. Thus, the AEPS is to be used as a comprehensive system.

According to the test authors the assessment system emerged out of the lack of meaningful assessment and curricula for people with disabilities. The administration manual notes that the forerunner to the AEPS was the Adaptive Performance Instrument (API). The birth to 3 version of the system was developed over the course of the 1980s from the API. The AEPS emerged after rewriting and reducing the length of the API. The AEPS for birth to 3 was completed in the 1980s, and in the late 1980s the 3 to 6 AEPS was completed. During this development phase there was extensive revision, rewriting, and feedback collected. Feedback from users and research led to the second edition that was published in 2002. The 2007 printing of the administration guide contains an appendix describing cutoff scores for eligibility determination. The goal in creating these cutoffs was to meet the need expressed by practitioners to help link the determination of eligibility to intervention. The test authors note that the work on eligibility cutoffs is ongoing and they expressed some concerns about reducing false positives. Nevertheless, they report moderate successes in predicting eligibility from AEPS performance.

TECHNICAL. The wide latitude of data gathering and use of multiple sources makes the reliability of the AEPS an important consideration. Interrater and test-retest reliability coefficients are generally good for both the birth to 3 and the 3 to 6 years versions. Some coefficients are not as high, but this is to be expected given the highly variable behavior of infants and preschoolers. Analysis of factors that might influence these reliabilities (e.g., practitioner knowledge and experience) would provide some additional support that the instrument can be reliably used by a variety of practitioners. Additionally, data on caregiver report reliabilities would further strengthen the instrument.

There is evidence of both content and criterion-related validity. The test authors report concurrent validity for the birth to 3 scales with the Gesell Developmental Schedule and the Bayley Scales of Infant Development (statistically significant, but unspecified values). They also report statistically significant but unspecified correlations between scores on the 3 to 6 years measures and the McCarthy Scales of Children's Abilities, and the Uniform Performance Assessment System.

There is a variety of evidence to support the content and construct validity of the AEPS. One kind of evidence the test authors present are data that suggest that the item difficulties correlate with age. Another is evidence from practitioners and experts that confirms the hierarchy of difficulty levels for items. The evidence is stronger with the birth to 3 assessment than for the older age group. The few exceptions the test authors attribute to possible cultural differences, but have not done a formal differential item functioning analysis. As noted above, there is evidence that the AEPS can validly predict eligibility for services. This work used a partial credit Rasch model to generate cutoffs at each age level and is more completely described in Bricker et al. (2008).

The AEPS is part of a larger system of assessment and intervention, thus consequential validity (Messick, 1994) of the AEPS is crucial. Part of the consequential validity evidence surrounds the objectives and interventions generated from the AEPS. Researchers have looked at the quality of objectives generated, treatment suggestions made, and the effectiveness of interventions. In general, these data support the validity of the AEPS. Continued work, especially looking at the effectiveness of interventions based on the AEPS, will strengthen support. An additional element of consequential validity is the ease with which assessment information can be communicated to caregivers and interventionists. The materials provided with the AEPS are easy to follow and easily communicated. Hence, the system is designed to be transparent and authentic. The AEPS appears to have what Frederiksen and Collins (1989) label "systemic validity."

COMMENTARY. The AEPS is an ambitious project based on 30 years of research and development. Perhaps its greatest strength is that it is a complete system that closes the circle between assessment and intervention processes. It provides a transparent assessment and intervention system that can be communicated and implemented by interventionists and caregivers alike. Other reviewers (Bagnato, Neisworth, & Munson, 1997; Horn, 2003) concur. Because of the complexity of the system, there is a need for continued research and improvement. For instance, it would be useful to provide more formal evidence of caregivers' understandings of their part in the assessment and intervention processes. Further, additional treatment studies would be of interest. Likewise, the data on concurrent validity could probably use updating. Finally, analysis of the impact of examiner experience and training on assessment reliability would be of interest. Individuals with a great deal of variability in experience and knowledge purportedly can use the AEPS. Research to confirm the generalizability of the system across different assessors would strengthen its reliability.

SUMMARY. The AEPS is an example of a systematically valid assessment that provides a comprehensive view of infants, toddlers, and preschoolers who are developmentally delayed or disabled. There is evidence that it is a useful tool for the purposes for which it was designed. Because it is a complex system, validating it across the wide ranges of uses is complex and ongoing. It is hoped that work to help improve the system will continue so that the assessments and curriculum can be used to improve the lives of children.

REVIEWER'S REFERENCES
Bagnato, S. J., Neisworth, J. T., & Munson, S. M. (1997). *LINKing assessment and early intervention: An authentic curriculum-based approach*. Baltimore, MD: Paul H. Brookes Publishing Co.
Bricker, D., Clifford, J., Yovanoff, P., Waddell, M., Hoselton, R., Allen, D., & Pretti-Frontczak, K. (2008). Eligibility determination using a curriculum-based assessment: A further examination. *Journal of Early Intervention, 31,* 3-21.
Frederiksen, J., & Collins, A. (1989). A systems approach to educational testing. *Educational Researcher, 18*(9), 27-32.
Horn, E. (2003). Review of "Assessment, Evaluation, and Programming System (AEPS) for Infants and Children, Second Edition." *Topics in Early Childhood Special Education, 23,* 41-42.
Messick, S. (1994). The interplay of evidence and consequences in the validation of performance assessments. *Educational Researcher, 23*(2), 13-23.

[6]

Assessment of Classroom Environments.

Purpose: "Identifies [teachers'] preferences [and approaches] for establishing classroom environments [by comparing] the Leadership Model, the Guidance Model, and the Integrated Model."
Population: Teachers.
Publication Dates: 2000-2008.
Acronym: ACE.
Scores: 3 models (Leadership, Guidance, Integration) for each of 8 scales: Self-Attributions, Self-Reflections, Ideal Teacher, Peers, Students, Supervisors, General Form, Comparative Form.
Administration: Group.
Forms, 8: Self-Attributions (ratings by teacher), Self-Reflections (ratings by teacher [teacher's perception of how students, peers, and supervisors view teacher]), 4 Observation Checklists (General Form [ratings by "community members, parents, visitors, [or] college students in teacher preparation programs"], Peer Form [ratings by teacher's peers], Student Form [ratings by teacher's students], Supervisor Form [ratings by teacher's supervisors]), Ideal Checklist (ratings by teacher [teacher's perception of the ideal classroom environment]), Comparative Form (ratings by teacher [comparison of the teacher's classroom environment, other professional teachers' classroom environment, and the ideal classroom environment]).
Price Data, 2009: $50 per 25 Self-Attributions forms; $50 per 25 Self-Reflections forms; $50 per 25 Observation Checklist-General forms; $50 per 25 Observation Checklist-Peer forms; $50 per 25 Observation Checklist-Student forms; $50 per 25 Observation Checklist-Supervisor forms; $50 per 25 Ideal Checklist forms; $50 per 25 Comparative forms; $40 per test manual (2008, 34 pages); $.40 per scoring/profiling per scale; $40 per analysis report.
Time: Administration time not reported.
Authors: Louise M. Soares and Anthony T. Soares (test).
Publisher: Castle Consultants.

Review of the Assessment of Classroom Environments by AMANDA NOLEN, Assistant Professor, Educational Foundations/Teacher Education, College of Education, University of Arkansas at Little Rock, Little Rock, AR:

DESCRIPTION. The Assessment of Classroom Environments (A.C.E.) is a group-administered battery of rating scales designed to profile an individual's teaching style as reflecting one of three models: Leadership (teacher-centered), Guidance (student-centered), or Integration (information-processing). Although not specified in the test manual or test instruments, the instrument appears to be designed for teachers in the K–12 setting.

The A.C.E. consists of eight scales to be completed by the teacher, peers, students, supervisors, and community members. The Self-Attribution Scale, the Self-Reflection Scale, and the Ideal Teacher scale are all completed by the teacher. Observation checklists are completed by peer teachers, students, supervisors, and a community member such as a parent or other adult. Finally, a Comparative Scale is completed by the teacher that identifies attributes most descriptive of self, others, and the ideal teacher.

All of the scales consist of 25 identical triads of statements that demonstrate a teacher's style preference across six factors: classroom management, learning environment, instructional approach, teacher efficacy, assessment, and instructional practices. Each of the statements in a triad represents one of three teaching models identified by the test authors. The statement that is believed to be most descriptive of the teacher's approach in the classroom is given a rank of +1. The statement that is believed to be least descriptive of the teacher is given a rank of +3. The remaining statement in the triad is given a rank of +2. These rankings are additive and the model with the lowest composite score is then considered to be most indicative of that teacher's style in the classroom.

The technical manual provides instructions for administration as well as instructions for scoring and profiling.

The primary objective for the A.C.E. is to create an accurate profile of an individual teacher's instructional style using an integrated approach of self-report as well as objective observations of others.

DEVELOPMENT. Attempting to establish the theoretical foundation for the A.C.E., the test author provides a brief literature overview of instructional design in the test manual. This description is followed by a general discussion of the emergent literature on brain research in relation to learning. After this discussion, the test author departs from reviewing the literature to conjecture by creating three models of instruction and hypothesizing how each impacts information processing through the process of Organization, Rehearsal, and Elaboration. This entire section, pages 4 through 8, contains no citations to research literature and thus this reviewer assumes that the conclusions reported on these pages are speculation on the part of the test author.

The test author opted to use the triad ranking format without much description as to how she arrived at that decision. Prior to pilot testing, the test author identified five factors: Classroom management, learning environment, instructional approach, teacher efficacy, and assessment. However, the test author does not indicate specifically how she arrived at those factors, whether through an analysis of the research literature or examining other similar assessments. There was additional lack of transparency around how the actual items were developed. The test author simply says that the items were "drawn from the five factors" (manual, p. 13).

The initial pilot study was conducted using 210 teachers, consisting of 70 elementary, 70 middle school, and 70 high school teachers. Each of these teachers completed the Self-Assessment and the Ideal Teacher scales. An additional 105 observers were included, each observing two teachers from two of the three different levels. No description is given about the 105 observers regarding occupations or instructions they were given. These observers completed the Teacher Observation Scale, the Ideal Teacher scale, and most (90) completed the Self-Assessment. This last account by the test author offered a vague indication that most, if not all of these observers may have been teachers as well.

The results of the pilot study were reported without the accompanying description of the statistical analysis used that yielded the results. There were some inconsistencies in the results that caused some confusion when reading the manual. For example, the test authors stated that 70 elementary school teachers participated; however, they reported that at least 155 elementary school teachers "saw themselves as following the Integrated Model" (manual, p. 14). The reviewer can only conclude that the additional 85 elementary school teachers were from the Observer pool of participants.

The test authors used the pilot study data to revise the instruments to include an additional factor (Instructional Practices) composed of 5 clusters or triads with the rationale that the resulting 25 clusters would prove a more reliable instrument than the original 20 clusters. Also, they developed additional scales to include multiple perspectives: Self-Reflection Scale (How I believe others view me); Student Perception Scale (How I believe my own students see me); Supervisor Perception (How I believe my supervisor sees me); and a Comparative Scale (How I believe I compare to other teachers and to an Ideal). There is no discussion by the test author of the value these additional scales would contribute to the overall assessment of a teacher.

A subsequent pilot study of the revised instrument was conducted, using 127 teachers from a metropolitan region. The results indicated that across the three levels (elementary, middle, and high school) the guidance model was the least descriptive of the teachers' teaching style. Although this was described as a significant result, there was no accompanying description of what statistical analysis was completed, or the associated *p*-values.

Based on the information provided in the test manual, there is little assurance that the scales were developed and validated using standard psychometric practices and procedures. Consequently, there exists no basis for confidence that the items included in these scales do, in fact, comprise the six factors as indicated by a factor analytic procedure, or if the six factors are indicative of a teacher's instructional style.

TECHNICAL. Although the technical manual mentioned that there was an in-depth evaluation of the scales by a panel of experts, there was no description of the credentials of these experts or of their results. Test-retest reliability coefficients for an 8-week interval were reported for four of the eight scales with values ranging from .85–.92. These values were based on samples ranging from 75 to 110 participants. The remaining reported validity information was confusing. Content and construct validity were reported for each of the scales with no explanation as to how they were calculated, therefore, making it difficult to interpret. The manual provided no discussion of the validation procedures or of the results.

COMMENTARY. The general description of the A.C.E. provided by the test author in the assessment front matter states that this assessment "was designed to reveal the instructional connections to neural functioning in the students while profiling three major models of teaching style" (general information page). Unfortunately, this assessment does not achieve its goal. None of the assessment activities address how instruction influences neural functioning of the student. The A.C.E. focuses solely on the instructional practices of the teacher as observed by self, other, peer, student, and supervisor.

The A.C.E. is easy to administer, score, and interpret and in that capacity could be a valuable tool for teachers to use to guide reflection upon their own practice. This assessment's strengths stop there. The packaging itself is unprofessional with poor quality graphics, incomplete examples, and spelling errors. In the opinion of this reviewer, the Administration Procedures should include specific instructions for the observers about when to observe and for how long. For example, the first cluster of items asks the respondent to address the teacher's practice of establishing rules of behavior in the classroom during the first week of school. In order to respond to this accurately, the individual would need to observe the teacher during the first week of school as well as several weeks after that. This practice would require a considerable amount of time on the part of the observers. The test author does not address this issue anywhere in the test manual.

The manual does not provide instructions about how to reconcile the various forms into a singular interpretation of teaching style. In other words, the test author does not discuss what to do if the Self-Attribution varies from the Observations or from the Self-Reflections. The test user has no direction about how to use these scores or how to interpret them in tandem.

SUMMARY. The Assessment of Classroom Environments (A.C.E.) consists of multiple instruments designed to identify the instructional style of an individual classroom teacher, consistent with a Leadership Model, a Guidance Model, or an Integrated Model approach. The lack of information regarding the validity of the various scales as well as the questions around the interpretation of the various instruments render this assessment ineffective. It should not be used for teacher evaluation or for the evaluation of classroom environments.

Review of the Assessment of Classroom Environments by STEVEN W. SCHMIDT, Assistant Professor of Adult Education, East Carolina University, Greenville, NC:

DESCRIPTION. The Assessment of Classroom Environments (A.C.E.) examines the characteristics of the classroom environment typically created by teachers, and how those characteristics translate into student learning. The test author notes that a "major task in teacher education is to determine how the latest findings in brain research translate to both the teaching and learning processes" (manual, p. 3). This instrument "was designed to reveal the instructional connections to neural functioning in the students while profiling three major models of teaching style" (information page): (a) Teacher-centered approach (Leadership Model); (b) student-centered approach (Guidance Model); (c) information-processing approach (Integration Model).

All of these models utilize the same sequence for information processing (that process of organization-rehearsal-elaboration). However, in the Leadership Model, these connections are made primarily by the teacher's organizational methods of the content, followed by practice exercises (rehearsal), and more connections to previous and future learning (elaboration). In the Guidance Model, students make such connections in interaction with one another. In the Integration Model, individuals make those connections according to individual style, preferences, abilities, experiences, and the current knowledge base.

The A.C.E. consists of eight scales:

1. Self-Attributions (to be completed by the teacher) examine the teacher's perception of classroom approaches and activities. Respondents are asked to rank a series of 25 clusters of three activities. Ranking is based on which statement is most descriptive of them.

2. Self-Reflections (to be completed by the teacher) examine the teacher's perception of classroom approaches. Respondents are asked to rank a series of 25 clusters of three activities. Ranking is based on which statement is most descriptive of them.

3. Observation Checklists examine perceptions of the observer with regard to various aspects of the classroom environment. Respondents are asked to rank a series of 25 clusters of three activities. Ranking is based on which statement is most descriptive of them. There are separate

observation checklists for the following groups: peers, students, supervisors, and others (e.g., community members, parents, or visitors).

4. Ideal Classroom Environment (to be completed by the teacher) examines the teacher's perception of an ideal classroom environment. Respondents are asked to rank a series of 25 clusters of three activities. Ranking is based on which statement the teacher believes is most descriptive of the ideal classroom.

5. Comparative Forms (to be completed by the teacher) examine attributes that the teacher believes are most descriptive of themselves, of other teachers, and of the ideal teacher. It utilizes a "preference" response of 25 triads of three statements each (75 statements in total). The 3 statements in each triad represent the 3 models (Leadership, Guidance, and Integration). The statement that is believed to be the most descriptive of the teacher's approach in the classroom (the self or the person observed) is given a score of +1. A score of +3 is given to the statement that is least descriptive of the teacher's approach, and a rank of +2 for the remaining statement. The model with the lowest total score is considered to be the one that is most descriptive of the teacher's style.

Completion of each scale, except the Comparative Scale, results in three totals. The lowest total score indicates the teacher's most typical teaching style, and the highest represents the teacher's least typical style (the remaining score is between the high and low scores). For the Comparative Scale, responses are totaled and the highest level indicates the most typical teaching style; the lower totals, the less typical. The end result of completion of the A.C.E. is that the teacher will have a better understanding of his or her teaching style.

DEVELOPMENT. The A.C.E. was developed as a companion set of scales to the Self-Perceptions Inventory/Teacher Forms (SPI/T) and the Teacher Performance Assessment (TPA). "It was designed to reveal the instructional connections to neural functioning in the students while profiling three major models of teaching style" (general information page). The test author's review of existing teaching strategies concluded that three models of instruction appeared in most of the research examined: a teacher-centered approach; a learner centered approach; and an adaptive, individualized approach. These approaches were subsequently named (by the researchers) the Leadership model, Guidance model, and Integration model.

Details on the development of the A.C.E. indicate that scale development began in 1999, with a scale to examine different approaches to teaching. Items, constructs, and instruments that were eventually to become a part of the A.C.E. have been developed and refined since that time, with pilots conducted with pieces of the A.C.E. in a variety of situations. Information garnered in those pilots was used to refine the instrument.

TECHNICAL. Psychometric evidence was based on data collected in an initial study, wherein the three self-report scales were completed by 72 teachers, 56 of whom were rated by 28 peers, 18 supervisors, and 24 students, as well. A panel of 6 experts also evaluated the items. Data were combined with information gleaned from the review panel to generate reliability and validity evidence. Reliability estimates were reported for internal consistency, interrater, and test-retest reliability (8-week interval), ranging from .82 to .89. Concurrent and construct validity were examined, with coefficients reported between .57 and .70.

A pilot study of 75 individuals was conducted on the following scales: Self-Attributions, Self-Reflection, Observations (general or others), and Ideal Classroom Environment. That study yielded test-retest reliability coefficients from .86 to .92 (the interval between test and retest was 8 weeks). Internal consistency coefficients for all four scales ranged from .79 to .89. Content validity ranged from .51 to .61; and construct validity, from .50 to .58. A pilot study of 110 individuals was conducted on the remaining scales: Observations (peers), Observations (students), Observations (supervisors), and Comparative forms. Internal consistency coefficients for these scales ranged from .87 to .92; and construct validity for these scales ranged from .45 to .55.

In summary, reliability coefficients are all at an acceptable range. Validity coefficients are also acceptable, although the student observation and peer observation coefficients were in the low moderate range (.45 and .49, respectively). No demographic information on these pilot studies was reported, and it is important to note that the reliability and validity figures presented were the results of two separate pilot studies.

COMMENTARY. The strengths of the A.C.E. are that it examines the concept of classroom environments from a variety of different perspectives and calls for feedback from many different stakeholders. These strengths may also make the A.C.E. more difficult to properly administer. A weakness of the A.C.E. is that the entire instrument was not piloted all together; the information on reliability and validity presented in the technical manual came from two separate pilot studies. Also, those pilot studies did not include large numbers of participants (n = 75 and n = 110), which may affect reliability and validity findings.

The A.C.E. consists of four scales related to observation: a peer scale, student scale, supervisor scale, and a scale for others. Each scale is basically the same; however, wording was changed based on the audience that is targeted. Based on the wording and on test instructions, it is questionable as to whether students in primary grades could complete the student observation scale accurately. Pilot studies on the student observation scales were conducted only on junior high and high school students (and the number of students participating in pilot studies of this instrument is not noted). Pilot studies on the teacher-related scales seemed broader in scope.

Administration instructions for the A.C.E. are fairly straightforward, and instructions for completion of each scale (with the exception of the Comparative Scale) are basically the same. Instructions for the completion of the Comparative Scale, in which respondents must place checkmarks in three of nine boxes in a matrix-style arrangement, are a bit more confusing. Upon completion of each instrument, respondents will have three numbers that correspond to the degrees to which the teacher in question either demonstrates or subscribes to (depending on who is completing the instrument) each of the three models of teaching style (Leadership, Integration, and Guidance). The technical manual abruptly ends at this juncture. There are no specifics on what these three numbers mean, no instructions for what to do next, and no information on the correlation of these three numbers to the three teaching styles. In the technical manual, there is a graphical representation of a compilation of scores from a pilot study, but it is presented by itself, without any corresponding information. The lack of further instruction, which should deal with the interpretation of scores, is a major weakness of the A.C.E.

SUMMARY. The A.C.E. has the potential to be a very comprehensive tool to measure teaching styles. It considers input from many different stakeholders, both internal and external to the classroom. Reliability and validity, as presented, are fine, although the instrument should be piloted in its entirety to ensure reliability and validity. The technical manual is incomplete, which makes results from the A.C.E. difficult to interpret. Complete instructions and information on the interpretation of scores should be included.

[7]

Assessment of Literacy and Language.

Purpose: Designed to "diagnose children who exhibit language disorders and to identify children who are at risk for later reading disabilities."
Population: Grades PK-1.
Publication Date: 2005.
Acronym: ALL.
Administration: Individual.
Levels, 4: Pre-K (Fall and Spring), K-Fall, K-Spring, 1st Grade (Fall and Spring).
Price Data, 2007: $261 per complete kit including manual (2005, 200 pages), stimulus book, 25 parent questionnaires, 25 record forms, and story cards; $42 per 25 parent questionnaires; $52 per 25 record forms; $78 per stimulus book; $105 per manual.
Time: (60) minutes.
Authors: Linda J. Lombardino, R. Jane Lieberman, and Jaumeiko J. C. Brown.
Publisher: Pearson.

a) PRE-K.
Scores, 16: 6 subtest scores (Letter Knowledge, Rhyme Knowledge, Basic Concepts, Receptive Vocabulary, Parallel Sentence Production, Listening Comprehension); 4 index scores (Emergent Literacy, Language, Phonological, Phonological-Orthographic); 6 criterion-referenced scores (Book Handling, Concept of Word, Matching Symbols, Word Retrieval, Rapid Automatic Naming, Invented Spelling).
b) K-FALL.
Scores, 18: Same as for Pre-K plus Elision and Word Relationships subtest scores.
c) K-SPRING.
Scores, 21: Same as for K-Fall plus Phonics Knowledge, Sound Categorization, and Sight Word Recognition subtest scores.
d) 1st GRADE.
Scores, 21: Same as for K-Spring.

Review of the Assessment of Literacy and Language by ABIGAIL BAXTER, Associate Professor, Department of Leadership and Teacher Education, University of South Alabama, Mobile, AL:

DESCRIPTION. The Assessment of Literacy and Language (ALL) is an individually administered assessment of prekindergarten, kindergarten, and first grade children's language and literacy skills. "The primary purpose of ALL is to diagnose children who exhibit language disorders and to identify children ... at risk for later reading disabilities due to specific risk factors" (manual, p. 1). The kit includes the test manual, stimulus book, listening comprehension cards, record forms, and the Caregiver Questionnaire (demographic information; concerns; medical, family, educational, and developmental histories; attention, oral language, preliteracy, and emergent literacy skills; and reading-related activities). Examiners will need a pencil, stopwatch, piece of paper, and picture book with sentences associated with pictures. The ALL is administered by professionals with experience using standardized tests and expertise in language and emergent literacy and their assessment. The authors estimate ALL administration time to be 1 hour. It has 11 subtests serving initial indicator (Level 1), and/or diagnostic (Level 2) purposes and 6 criterion-referenced subtests (Level 3) providing clinical information. Different aged children take different combinations of indicator, diagnostic, and criterion-referenced subtests. Kindergartners assessed in the spring have more subtests than kindergartners tested in the fall. Prekindergartners' and first graders' subtests do not vary within the school year. Diagnostic subtests follow poor performance on indicator subtests and describe language/emergent literacy problems in terms of four index scores: Emergent Literacy, Language, Phonological, and Phonological-Orthographic. Criteria for poor indicator subtest scores are not specified.

Administration directions for each item are in the easel-format stimulus book. For all but one criterion-referenced subtest the child responds to the examiner's questions by either speaking or pointing. Some items are timed. On the record form, within each subtest, there are starting points for the different age groups and trial or demonstration items (not included in the raw score) to help children understand the task. Basal and discontinuation rules are presented in the manual. Items on all subtests, except for three criterion-referenced subtests, are scored as 0 or 1, for incorrect and correct responses, respectively. It is suggested that scoring be completed after the testing session for some subtests. The scoring rules for the items are relatively straightforward and include dialectal variations. Sample responses are in the record form and further examples for the more complex subtests are available.

For each subtest, raw scores are converted into scaled scores, confidence intervals, and percentile ranks; confidence intervals for the percentile ranks are available. Index standard scores are derived from subtest scaled scores and also have confidence intervals and percentile ranks with confidence intervals. The scaled scores, standard scores, percentile ranks, and confidence intervals are found in tables in the manual for prekindergartners, kindergartners, and first graders assessed in the fall and spring. The index scores are used to "determine the modalities affected by the disorder and to describe the child's language and emergent literacy skills as measured by ALL" (manual, p. 35). Additionally, the Emergent Literacy and Language and the Phonological and Phonological-Orthographic index scores can be compared to determine if the index scores' differences are significant and how rare the differences are in the population.

DEVELOPMENT. In the wake of No Child Left Behind and the National Reading Panel's recommendations, the ALL was developed to address current educational legislation and requirements by identifying students at risk for reading problems so that intervention could begin early. This instrument assesses skills that research has identified as important skills for reading success and is based upon literacy and language models adapted from Seidenberg and McClelland (1989). The literacy model includes the context, phonological, orthographic, semantic, and morpho-syntactic processors involved in both reading and writing. The language model includes the context, phonological, semantic, and morpho-syntactic processors involved in listening and speaking.

Items were developed from the research and clinical practice literatures. Two pilot studies were conducted with 50 children, across the age range, who varied in terms of geographic region, parental education, gender, and race/ethnicity. These studies led to the deletion of some subtests and identification of the most appropriate items. Administration directions were also revised. Next, a tryout version of the ALL was used with 155 typically developing children and 166 children in a clinical sample who varied in age, gender, race/ethnicity, geographic region, and parent education. Ninety eight of the children in the clinical sample were matched to typical children. The tryout study yielded standardized scoring rubrics and the final pool of items, which came from reducing the number of subtests and combining items from different subtests.

TECHNICAL.

Standardization. Fall and spring standardization samples (300 children each) were drawn. The participants were prekindergartners, kindergartners, and first graders who were able to take the ALL without modifications and did not have a moderate or severe behavioral or emotional disorder. English was their primary language although some were bilingual. Some received special education or related services. The samples were stratified on grade, gender, race/ethnicity, geographic region, and parent education level and were very similar to the U.S. population as measured by the 2002 National Census figures. Clinical standardization samples (children diagnosed with Specific Language Impairment (SLI) or at-risk for reading problems due to phonological impairment, environment, or a family history of reading or language disability) were also obtained in the fall (n = 41) and spring (n = 115) using the same stratification. Data from the two samples were used to investigate the clinical utility of the items and to make general comparisons between the responses from children in the standardization sample and children in the clinical sample. However, only data collected from the standardization sample were used for final coding/scoring rules, item placement, and determining starting points and discontinuation rules.

Reliability. The ALL manual presents evidence of test-retest, interrater, internal consistency, and split-half reliability. Test-retest reliability was calculated for 104 children in the spring standardization sample. The average interval between testings, by the same examiner, was 11 days (range 3–21 days). The stability coefficients for the specific indicator tests for each grade level meet reliability standards for screening purposes; however, not all of the index scores at the kindergarten and first grade level meet the .90 criteria for making decisions about individuals (Salvia & Ysseldyke with Bolt, 2007). Split-half and coefficient alpha data are presented as evidence of internal consistency for the subtests and indices for the standardization and clinical samples. Interscorer reliability for subtests involving administrator judgment in scoring is acceptable. Standard errors of measurement for the 11 subtests and the four indices are typically small and acceptable.

Validity. Validity was established in several ways. Content validity was assessed by the test authors, test developers, and an expert panel in terms of appropriateness and potential bias. Evidence for construct validity was established by comparing the test items to the research literature on reading abilities and language, phonological processing, and letter and sound knowledge. Evidence of convergent and divergent validity is presented. Factor-analytic studies verified the emergent literacy and language factor structures for prekindergartners and a language, phonological processing, and phonological-orthographic factor structure for older children. Studies comparing children's scores on the ALL and other measures of similar skills indicate that most correlations among subtests were moderate when the elicitation formats on the two tests were similar. Clinical studies involving SLI and non-SLI children revealed significant score differences for all subtest and index scores. Comparisons of scores of at-risk and typical children revealed significant differences for all but three subtests and for three of the four index scores. Sensitivity analyses indicate acceptable sensitivity at -1 and -1.5 standard deviations and acceptable specificity at -1, -1.5, and -2 standard deviations.

COMMENTARY. The ALL assesses important basic skills for young children who are about to begin or who are beginning to read. The manual describes the test's items and psychometrics adequately. The easel is easy to manipulate and the scoring criteria are clear. However, the manual does not present details about when indicator scores are significant and the examiner should move to Level 2 testing. The Caregiver Questionnaire appears to be a useful tool for understanding a child's risk but it is mentioned in passing in the manual and no guidance is given for interpretation of its results. Likewise, the manual is unclear about the ages of the prekindergartners. There is a great difference between 3- and 4-year-olds, especially in the skills assessed by the ALL. The manual should at least define the ages of the prekindergartners in the standardization sample, if not the minimum age for a prekindergartner.

SUMMARY. The ALL was developed to identify children at risk for language and reading problems to prevent the development of reading difficulties and subsequent school failure. It is unique because it is based on both language and emergent literacy developmental models that include important variables from the reading research literature. Psychometrically, it is adequate and it appears that children will be engaged in the assessment. ALL scores provide information about areas needing remediation as well as areas of emphasis for teachers and clinicians. More detail in the administration manual about using these scores would be helpful for new examiners.

REVIEWER'S REFERENCES

Salvia, J., Ysseldyke, J. E., with Bolt, S. (2007). *Assessment: In special and inclusive education* (10th ed.). Boston: Houghton Mifflin Company.

Seidenberg, M. S., & McClelland, J. L. (1989). A distributed, developmental model of word recognition. *Psychological Review, 96,* 523-568.

Review of the Assessment of Literacy and Language by MILDRED MURRAY-WARD, Professor of Education, California State University, Stanislaus, Turlock, CA:

DESCRIPTION. The Assessment of Literacy and Language (ALL) was developed by Lombardino, Lieberman, and Brown in 2005. Its purpose is to "diagnose children who exhibit language disorders and to identify children who are at risk for later reading disabilities" (manual, p. 1), as mandated by No Child Left Behind (2001). Designed for use with pre-kindergarten, kindergarten, and first grade children, the ALL helps clinicians profile children's "language and emergent literacy strengths and weaknesses and guide" (manual, p. 1) clinicians through instruction and interventions.

The ALL consists of three different types of scores: 11 subtest scores (Letter Knowledge, Rhyme Knowledge, Basic Concepts, Receptive Vocabulary, Parallel Sentence Production, Listening Comprehension, Elision, Word Relationships, Phonics Knowledge, Sound Categorization, and Sight Word Recognition); 4 index scores (Emergent Literacy, Language, Phonological, and Phonological-Orthographic); and 7 criterion-referenced scores (Book Handling, Concept of Word, Matching Symbols, Word Retrieval, Rapid Automatic Naming, Invented Spelling, and Letter Knowledge). The theoretical foundations of the ALL are well documented.

The ALL kit contains a manual with administration, recording, and scoring procedures; score interpretation; clinical uses; theoretical framework; development; and standardization and validity and reliability studies. The ALL uses an administration easel book, two sets of listening cards, recording forms, and a caregiver questionnaire. The examiner provides a book used in the Book Handling subtest.

The ALL requires approximately 60 minutes to complete. Level 1 (Initial Indicator) consists of 2 subtests that help determine if a child is at risk of future reading difficulties and takes 10-15 minutes to administer. Level 2 (Diagnostic) comprises 6 to 11 subtests and requires 45 minutes or less to administer. The use of this level allows the examiner to diagnose and describe the child's language disorder and emerging literacy skill deficits, leading to the identification of children at-risk for later reading problems. Level 3 (Criterion-Referenced) contains 4 to 7 subtests and each subtest requires 1-5 minutes to administer. The amount of administration time and the number of subtests to be administered depends on the purpose of the assessment, grade level of the child, and time of year.

ALL administration is complex and requires practice. Guidelines are provided for establishing starting points, basal levels, and reversal and discontinuation rules, as well as administration guidance that includes creating the test environment, seating, establishing rapport, taking breaks, and taking consideration of cultural and regional language differences in respondents. ALL examiners should be professionals with knowledge and training in language and emergent literacy development, including speech-language pathologists, school psychologists, and reading specialists.

Examiners record raw scores on the record form, which are converted to scaled scores and confidence intervals for the scores. Subtest scaled scores are converted to percentile ranks, with confidence intervals. The scaled scores are also used to determine index scores (mean of 100 and standard deviation of 15) and confidence intervals. Discrepancy comparisons may also be made between the Emergent Literacy/Language and Phonological/Phono-Orthographic Indices. Finally, index and subtest scores are profiled and the criterion-referenced chart is completed. The authors also provide detailed directions on determining if diagnosis is needed (Level 1), diagnosing and describing the disorder (Level 2), and evaluating related clinical behaviors (Level 3). In addition, the authors provide four detailed profiles of children and their typical performances on the ALL.

DEVELOPMENT. As part of constructing the ALL, the authors examined the research and clinical practice literature regarding language and literacy, and merged two models of literacy: the connectionist model (Adams, 1990; Seidenberg & McClelland, 1989) and componential model (Aaron, Joshi, & Williams, 1999; Hoover & Gough, 1990; Wren et al., 2000). The resulting ALL Model involves reading and writing, with a Language Model including speaking and listening.

The ALL pilot items were created after a review of language and literacy literature, and organized into 30 subtests. Pilot studies were conducted with two small groups of children and, on this basis, some subtests were eliminated or changed. The tryout involved 23 revised subtests administered by 85 professionals to the tryout sample consisting of 155 nonclinical children and 166 clinical cases, including 98 matched to the tryout nonclinical children. The tryout resulted in further changes in the subtest components. In addition, an item bias review was conducted on the tryout items. Specialists examined the items and visual stimuli for appropriateness for children from diverse backgrounds.

TECHNICAL.

Standardization. The final standardization subtests were administered to the fall and spring samples containing 300 nonclinical children each. These samples matched 2002 U.S. Census figures in the areas of gender, race/ethnicity, geographic region, and parent education level. In addition, data from 41 (fall sample) and 115 (spring sample) clinical children were used to compare with data from the standardization samples. The items were then arranged hierarchically by difficulty to allow empirical start points and basal and ceiling rules. The start point was selected by noting where 95% of the children passed the items. The discontinuation rule was derived by calculating the probability of a child responding correctly beyond six consecutive incorrect responses.

Reliability. The authors examined test-retest stability, internal consistency, and interscorer reliability. For test-retest reliability, the ALL was administered to 104 children, with intervals ranging from 3 to 21 days. The sample included both genders, and African American, Hispanic, White, and other racial/ethnic groups. Pearson product-moment correlations were calculated on scores from each grade level and all groups combined and corrected for the variability of the standardization sample. The resulting stability coefficients for the subscales at each grade level varied from .71 to .97. Overall, the four indices of combined subscales were more stable, with coefficients from .86 to .96.

Internal consistency was estimated through coefficient alpha and the split-half methods for all groups combined. Alpha coefficients for all groups ranged from .66 to .96 for the normed subtests and from .31 to .85 for the criterion-referenced tests. The split-half reliability indices revealed the same patterns with subtest scores ranging from .68 to .96, and index reliabilities consistently in the .90 range. Similar results were obtained in reliability studies conducted on the scores of clinical groups.

Evidence of interrater agreement was obtained for Parallel Sentence Structure, Word Relationships, Listening Comprehension, and Invented Spelling. The resulting percentages of agreements ranged from .97 to .99 for these subtests. No agreement studies were done on the criterion-referenced subtest scores, which produced several low reliability coefficients.

Standard errors of measurement ranged from .60 for Kindergarten and first grade Sight Word Recognition to 1.70 for Kindergarten Receptive Vocabulary. Indice *SEM*s were larger, ranging from 2.60 for the Phonological-Orthographic index for first graders in the fall and the Emergent Literacy Index for Kindergartners in the spring and first graders in the fall to 4.74 for the Language Index for first graders in the spring.

Differences on scores between the indices were also explored. The authors found that large differences between the Emergent Literacy and Language scores were very rare. Differences in these scores for children at risk for reading difficulties were similar to those of the standardization sample.

Validity. The authors examined validity through content validity, concurrent validity studies with other measures of reading, contrasted group clinical comparisons, and predictive validity to identify children with reading difficulties. Content validity was examined through ALL's foundation areas noted in the literature, and confirmed with factor analysis. In addition, correlations among the subtests and indices were explored, with correlations for the Emergent Literacy and Phonological and Phonological-Orthographic Indices highly positive and correlations for the Language Index and Emergent Literacy, Phonological and Phonological-Orthographic Indices moderate.

Concurrent validity was estimated by examining the relationship of ALL scores to other measures of language, reading, and phonological awareness. Correlations with the subtests of the Clinical Evaluation of Language Fundamentals—Preschool Second Edition (CELF) were moderate, ranging from .46–.79. The Pre-Reading Inventory of Phonological Awareness (PIPA) correlation studies resulted in low correlations with Sound Segmentation (because this subtest addresses skills not addressed in the ALL) and moderate correlations with all other subtests. Correlations with the subtests of the Early Reading Diagnostic Assessment—Second Edition (ERDA) varied greatly, with -.25 for ERDA Letter Recognition and ALL Listening Comprehension, to .82 for ERDA Letter Recognition and ALL Letter Knowledge.

Predictive validity was examined by comparing the ALL scores of typical children from the standardization sample with those children identified with a Specific Language Impairment (SLI). The scores on all 11 subtests for the two groups were statistically significantly different from each other at the .01 level, with the SLI children scoring lower on all subtests. Another such comparison was made of scores of the typical children and those "at risk" of developing a reading disability. "At risk" factors included phonological impairments, "at risk" home environments, or a family history of language and reading disabilities. Statistically significant differences were found in comparison of Letter and Rhyme Knowledge, Sound Categorization, Basic Concepts, Receptive Vocabulary, Parallel Sentence Production, Word Relationships, and Listening Comprehension. Comparison of the typical and "at risk" children's scores resulted in statistically significant differences in the Emergent Literacy, Language, and Phonological indexes. Finally, the ALL's sensitivity in predicting specific language impairments was examined by determining whether the ALL could accurately predict those children with language impairments. The ALL correctly identified 86% of those with SLIs and 96% of those without such impairments.

COMMENTARY. The ALL is a complex clinical instrument used to detect language disorder in young children. The instrument has a strong research base and a well-confirmed set of subtest and index structures. The instrument provides a variety of scores, including indices using scaled scores.

A number of studies explored the technical qualities of the ALL. In the area of reliability, the ALL displays strong reliability for the indices (.86 and above) and acceptable reliabilities for most subtests. Validity studies were extensive and explored test quality and uses. Content validity was confirmed through a literature base and factor analysis. Concurrent validity was estimated by examining correlations of ALL scores with three tests of early literacy and language development. The correlations were in the moderate range. Predictive validity studies were conducted to establish whether the ALL could correctly identify children already identified as SLI or "at risk" for developing a reading difficulty. The children in these groups performed at statistically significantly lower levels than children without impairments. The ALL correctly identified 86% of SLI and 96% of non-SLI children.

SUMMARY. Overall, the ALL is a well-developed, high quality literacy and language test for young children. The instrument provides indices to obtain in-depth descriptions of children's language and literacy levels. Because of its technical complexity, the ALL should be administered only by professionals. The ALL exhibits strong technical qualities with strong reliabilities for the indices at .86 and above. More importantly, the authors validated its use in identifying children with SLI or those "at risk" for developing a reading difficulty. However, several cautions should be noted. First, because the subtests generally displayed reliabilities below .90, their use in diagnoses should be carefully considered. Second, care should be exercised with using the ALL for identifying those "at risk" because no studies have been completed to determine if those "at risk" actually did develop such difficulties. Finally, as with all clinical decisions, determining children's language and literacy levels for interventions should involve use of multiple instruments and data sources.

REVIEWER'S REFERENCES

Aaron, P. G., Joshi, M., & Williams, K. A. (1999). Not all reading disabilities are alike. *Journal of Learning Disabilities, 32,* 120-138.

Adams, M. J. (1990). *Beginning to read: Thinking and learning about print.* Cambridge, MA: MIT Press.

Hoover, W., & Gough, P. (1990). The simple view of reading. *Reading and Writing: An Interdisciplinary Journal, 2,* 127-160.

Seidenberg, M. S., & McClelland, J. L. (1989). A distributed, developmental model of word recognition. *Psychological Review, 96,* 523-568.

Wren, S., Litke, B., Jinkins, D. Paynter, S., Watts, J., & Alanis, I. (2000). *The cognitive foundation of learning to read: A framework.* Austin, TX: Southwest Educational Development Laboratory.

[8]

Attention Test Linking Assessment and Services.

Purpose: "To provide a comprehensive assessment system for diagnosing and remediating ADHD."
Population: Ages 8-18.
Publication Dates: 2001-2007.
Acronym: ATLAS.
Administration: Individual.
Forms, 5: Parent Attention Report, Teacher Attention Report, Attention Performance Assessment, Examiner's Observation Report, Mental Health Interview Screener.
Price Data, 2008: $250 per ATLAS kit including examiner's manual (2007, 129 pages) and 25 each of the Parent/Teacher Attention Report forms, Mental Health Interview Screener, Examiner's Observation Report forms, Attention Performance Summary Report forms, Youth Response booklets, and Client Profile Summary Report forms; $70 per 50 Parent/Teacher Attention Report forms; $40 per 25 Mental Health Interview Screener; $35 per 25 Examiner's Observation Report forms; $35 per 25 Attention Performance Summary Report forms; $40 per 25 Subject Response booklets; $35 per 25 Client Profile Summary Report forms; $65 per examiner's manual.
Time: (50) minutes.
Authors: Gregory R. Anderson and Patricia C. Post.
Publisher: Stoelting Co.

a) PARENT ATTENTION REPORT.
Scores, 6: Inattention, Concentration/Sustained Attention, Organization, Impulsivity, Hyperactivity, Divided Attention.

b) TEACHER ATTENTION REPORT.
Scores, 6: Inattention, Concentration/Sustained Attention, Organization, Impulsivity, Hyperactivity, Divided Attention.

c) ATTENTION PERFORMANCE ASSESSMENT.
Scores, 16: Sustained Attention/Vigilance, Random Letter Response-Vigilance, Trails A(Pathways 1), Complex Figure/Complex Figure for Organization, Memory (Verbal and Spatial), Digit Memory Span Forward, Verbal Memory–Superspan List, Complex Figure/Complex Figure by Memory, Working Memory, Trails B (Pathways 2) Shifting Sets/Attention, Serial Subtraction (7's), Digits Memory Span Reverse, Divided Attention, Divided/Alternating Attention: Cancellation of 4's/Trails A (Pathways 1), Verbal Fluency, Fluency for Names.

d) EXAMINER'S OBSERVATION.
Scores, 8: Inattention, Concentration, Impulse Control, Hyperactivity, Organization for Task Completion, Social Skills, Irritability, Motor Difficulties.

e) MENTAL HEALTH INTERVIEW SCREENER.
Scores, 8: Oppositional Defiant/Conduct Disorderd, Obsessive-Compulsive Disorder, Depression, Bipolar Disorder, Post-Traumatic Stress Disorder (PTSD), Generalized Anxiety Disorder (GAD), Autistic Spectrum Disorder.

Review of the Attention Test Linking Assessment and Services by MARY (RINA) M. CHITTOORAN, Associate Professor, Department of Educational Studies, Saint Louis University, St. Louis, MO:

DESCRIPTION. The Attention Test Linking Assessment and Services (ATLAS) utilizes ratings from home and school, performance assessments, an interview, and behavioral observations during testing "to provide a comprehensive (multifaceted) assessment system for diagnosing and remediating ADHD" (examiner's manual, p. 2) and to rule out other comorbid disorders in children and adolescents between the ages of 8 and 18 years.

The ATLAS includes an examiner's manual, a Youth Response booklet, and several individual assessment components. The Mental Health Interview Screener is administered to the parent/guardian to identify behaviors associated with Oppositional Defiant/Conduct Disorder, Obsessive/Compulsive Disorder, Depression, Bipolar Disorder, Post Traumatic Stress Disorder, Social Phobia, Generalized Anxiety Disorder, and Autism Spectrum Disorder. The Parent/Teacher Attention Report is a rating scale that assesses functioning in the areas of Inattention, Concentration, Organization, Impulsivity, Hyperactivity, and Divided Attention. The Attention Performance Assessment assesses Vigilance, Verbal Memory, Spatial Memory, Working Memory, Divided Attention, and Fluency. The Examiner's Observation Report allows the examiner to rate observed behaviors that are frequently associated with ADHD. Finally, the Client Profile Summary Report allows information gathered from all components to be recorded in one place. The manual also includes the Differential Diagnostic Instrument that helps the examiner make a final diagnostic determination and the Biopsychosocial Treatment Planner that allows the treatment team to develop psychological, social, educational, and other strategies to combat the problem. The ATLAS also offers two levels of intervention: general classroom strategies and advanced strategies for deficit areas noted during performance testing and observation. Finally, the ATLAS manual includes completed sample record forms, descriptions of behaviors associated with comorbid disorders, and case studies.

The ATLAS, which can be administered in approximately 50 minutes, may be used by a variety of professionals including classroom teachers, psychologists, and educational diagnosticians and is designed primarily to be used in the clinical or educational setting in a collaborative, interdisciplinary manner. Training requirements are minimal for most components of the ATLAS; others, like the Mental Health Screener, require a more highly credentialed examiner.

A child's performance on various components of the ATLAS can be measured in the following areas: Inattention, Concentration, Impulse Control, Hyperactivity, Organization for Task Completion, Social Skills, Irritability, Motor Difficulties, and Divided Attention. Raw scores on each component of the ATLAS (except for the Attention Performance Assessment) are converted to Rasch scores rather than the traditional standard scores. The examinee's overall performance on each component of the ATLAS is described as U (Unlike ADHD), NL (Neither Like or Unlike ADHD), or L (Like ADHD).

DEVELOPMENT. The ATLAS was developed over a period of 6 years and was founded on the recognition that ADHD is often misdiagnosed or overdiagnosed and that it typically presents with and is secondary to comorbid disorders such as Depression, Obsessive/Compulsive Disorder, Autism Spectrum Disorders, or Anxiety Disorders. Further, because ADHD is a multifaceted condition, it was felt that a diagnosis of ADHD would be minimally useful if it was not linked to multidisciplinary interventions designed to remediate the condition. Pilot assessments of individuals with and without ADHD were completed in order to develop and refine the ATLAS. These were followed by field trials with subsequent deletion, modification, and refinement of items.

TECHNICAL. The standardization sample included 318 individuals, 274 from the U.S. and 44 from outside the U.S., with approximately 63.5% of the sample being males. Sixty-six percent were White, non-Hispanic; 13.5% were African Americans; 16% were Hispanic; 3% were Asian; and 2% were Native Americans. Forty-two percent of the sample had received special services of some kind, approximately 40% of the sample had been diagnosed with ADHD, and 35% were classified as having learning disabilities. Maternal education, which was used as an indicator of educational level of the home, ranged from less than a high school degree (7%) to some college (45%). Children in the standardization sample ranged in age from 8 to over 16 years; the mean and median age of the sample was 12.73 and 13 years, respectively. Fifty-one percent of the sample resided in the West, 41% in the North Central region, 5% in the Northeast, and 3% in the South.

With regard to reliability, internal consistency data are reported for all but the Attention Performance Assessment using alpha coefficients. Estimates range from .87 to .94 on the subscales of the Parent Attention Report with an overall coefficient of .98 reported across all of the items on the six subscales. Reliability coefficients range from .80 to .96 on the subscales of the Teacher Attention Report with a coefficient of .97 on all items across the six subscales. On the Examiner's Observation Report, reliability coefficients range from a low of .83 to a high of .95 with an overall internal consistency of .98 across all items on all six scales. On the Attention Performance Assessment, test-retest correlations obtained after an interval of 4 weeks ranged from .35 to .85 across the 10 subscales.

Content validity of the ATLAS was established by linking it to research as well as to the Inattention and Hyperactivity/Impulsivity subscales of the DSM-IV. Factor analyses showed that 80% of the variance was accounted for by two factors: Inattention and Hyperactivity/Impulsivity. Efforts also were made to establish racial and ethnic differences in endorsements of behavioral difficulties. Criterion-related validity was established using prior diagnoses of ADHD and mental health conditions as well as parental responses to DSM-like items; coefficients ranged from a low of .13 to a high of .97. With regard to concurrent validity, scores on the Attention-Deficit/Hyperactivity Disorder Test (ADHDT) were correlated with scores from the Parent Attention Report with correlations ranging from a low of .27 on Impulsivity to a high of .96 on the total scale. Construct validity was assessed by measuring the degree to which the ATLAS predicted membership in ADHD, LD, and LD/ADHD groups with evidence that the ATLAS correctly predicted membership in these groups 85% of the time.

COMMENTARY. The ATLAS uses multiple methods to assess behaviors; is relatively easy to administer; makes the assessment-intervention connection that is especially timely, given the national focus on Response to Intervention (RTI); and comes in a neat, portable, relatively inexpensive package. The manual provides detailed guidelines for test administration, a justification for the inclusion of various ATLAS components, and extensive tables of validity coefficients that enhance interpretation of ATLAS scores. The ATLAS is presented as a way to "Map(ping) the way to a better understanding of ADHD and other comorbid disorders" (examiner's manual, front cover) and indeed, it does provide information about these conditions that may prove useful to practitioners. The sample completed Client Profile Summary Report is a useful addition.

Unfortunately, the ATLAS has numerous problematic features that fail to balance its positive ones. The most off-putting aspect of the measure, perhaps, is the fact that the response forms are replete with errors, most of which could have been eliminated by a thorough proofreading. For example, they include grammatical errors, inconsistent and/or incorrect use of words, omissions, wording that is confusing, phrasing or spelling that is unintentionally amusing, redundancies, and sometimes two kinds of errors in the same sentence. There are other errors that are simply too numerous to list within the confines of this brief review; unfortunately, this kind of carelessness immediately–and perhaps unfairly–calls into question the quality of the rest of the measure.

The test authors' approach to ADHD and their use of words and phrases such as "diagnosis" and "diagnostic impressions" reveals an adherence to a medical model, a within-child approach that has been largely discarded within the educational community. Their use of these words is also inconsistent with their emphasis on environmental cues and conditions that influence the child's behavioral functioning.

The standardization sample includes a racially and ethnically diverse group; however, the sample of 318 is a small one and includes minimal representation from the northeastern and southern regions of the U.S. There is not enough information on reliability provided; indeed, the small number of scale items and the brevity of most of the scales are generally linked with low reliability. Further, the omission of interrater reliability is surprising in a measure of this kind. There is very little information on concurrent validity with comparisons drawn only between the ATLAS and the Attention-Deficit/Hyperactivity Disorder Test (ADHDT; 14:30); neither is there adequate information about criterion-related validity. In both cases, there are some extremely low coefficients that are of concern. Further, the test authors' note that doctoral clinical psychology students were used in the validation of the ATLAS raises questions about training, payment, and motivation for participation and how those issues might have affected the quality of obtained results.

Although the manual includes a good deal of information, some of it is placed illogically; for example, a section called General Classroom Interventions is included, mystifyingly, in the chapter on testing considerations when it should have appeared later in the manual. There appear to be two tables labeled 1 with different content and there is no reference in the narrative portion of the text to the numerous tables provided by the test authors. Additionally, there are issues related to the quality of test production that may cause problems, particularly with children who have ADHD and, therefore, experience difficulty with extraneous stimuli. For example, the paper used for the Youth Response Booklet is so thin that the shapes and figures on the other side of the page show through and may serve as a distracter to a child (they certainly did to this reviewer and to a volunteer examinee). Response format on the Mental Health Screener is also problematic, in that the response format is categorical (Yes/No) and limited space is provided for qualification of responses or more detailed descriptions about observed behavior. For example, how often do these behaviors occur? How long have they been occurring?

SUMMARY. The ATLAS is a multidimensional effort at identifying and remediating ADHD in children and young adults. Parts of the ATLAS may be used as a screening device for individuals displaying ADHD-like behaviors and the descriptions of comorbid disorders and interventions may be useful for practitioners. However, numerous errors in the response forms, the quality of test production, and the lack of technical information add up to a measure that cannot, unfortunately, be recommended for use with the population for which it is intended.

Review of the Attention Test Linking Assessment and Services by TAWNYA J. MEADOWS, Assistant Professor of Pediatrics, Munroe Meyer Institute, University of Nebraska Medical Center, Omaha, NE, and ERIC GRADY, Psychology Intern, Munroe Meyer Institute, University of Nebraska Medical Center, Omaha, NE:

DESCRIPTION. The Attention Test Linking Assessment and Services (ATLAS) is designed to measure Attention Deficit/Hyperactivity Disorder (ADHD) in children and adolescents ages 8–18, through a multimodal, multi-informant approach. The ATLAS assists the clinician in the differential diagnosis of other childhood disorders and provides intervention recommendations for children and adolescents with ADHD.

The multimodal, multi-informant battery is conducted through parent and teacher report, clinical observation, and an attention performance assessment task completed by the child. The parent- and teacher-report forms consist of six subscales (Inattention, Concentration/Sustained Attention, Organization, Impulsivity, Hyperactivity, and Divided Attention) and grand total score in which behaviors are rated on a 5-point Likert scale.

The Examiner's Observation Report is a clinician-reported assessment of behaviors observed during the Attention Performance Assessment and comprises seven subscales rated on a 3-point Likert scale (Inattention/Concentration, Impulse Control, Hyperactivity, Organization for Task Completion, Social Skills, Irritability, and Motor Difficulties). An "other Observations/Behaviors" section is present at the end for behaviors that are not included in other categories but may be relevant to assessing ADHD.

The performance measures consist of standard neuropsychological assessments (Trails, Digit Span, Word Memory, Complex Figure Drawing, Serial Subtraction, and Random Letter Response) administered by a trained professional. The test authors included additional behaviors, unrelated to performance, to record during the Random Letter Response and Complex Figure by Memory tasks. These behaviors were observed during the norming process, and were found to be more common in children with ADHD.

The Mental Health Interview Screener is a differential diagnosis aid, completed as part of a clinical interview. The categories included in this screener include Oppositional Defiant Disorder, Conduct Disorder, Obsessive-Compulsive Disorder, Depression and Bipolar Disorder, Post-Traumatic Stress Disorder, Social Phobia, Generalized Anxiety Disorder, and Autism Spectrum Disorders. Parents/guardians are asked to indicate whether or not symptoms are present.

The administration instructions are clearly written for each component, and are easy to follow. Needed materials and a "structure of the response" are described for each subtest. The structure of the response describes how the answer should appear on the response booklet. Instructions for the examiner are provided to assist in accurate scoring. Once scores are determined, criteria are set to determine whether the child is "Like ADHD," "Neither Like or Unlike ADHD," or "Unlike ADHD."

The test authors claim the first level of intervention is appropriate for general classroom management techniques, and the second level is available for students who need more intensive services. The general classroom interventions are bulleted recommendations that may be used based on the areas in which the child has the most difficulty (i.e., Inattention, Concentration, Organization, Divided Attention, Impulsivity, and Hyperactivity).

DEVELOPMENT. The test authors sought to provide a comprehensive ADHD battery that also would assist in differential diagnosis and treatment planning. Dissertation research of the second author of the test led to its development. The impetus for developing the ATLAS grew from the test authors' clinical experience in seeing children with ADHD who also had other mental health and behavioral problems. This, in addition to a lack of "accurate performance measures," led the test authors to conduct additional research and later develop the ATLAS. The test authors approach ADHD from a biopsychosocial perspective, emphasizing deficits in the prefrontal cortex area of the brain.

Items were developed through multiple processes. The Hyperactivity and Impulsivity items of the Parent/Teacher forms were derived from the DSM-IV-TR criteria for ADHD Predominantly Hyperactive/Impulsive type. Items in the Parent/Teacher Form's four Inattentive scales were based on work from Lezak, Howieson, and Loring (2004) and DSM-IV-TR criteria for ADHD Predominantly Inattentive type. The test authors describe internal consistency as "generally very good" and Rasch IRT fit statistics as demonstrating "good fit."

TECHNICAL. The standardization process began with a preliminary pilot study to refine the scales and modify the items as necessary. The test authors reported collecting data on a small number of participants, but did not report a sample size for the pilot portion. The standardization sample was composed of 318 participants, 44 from outside the United States and the remainder from within the U.S. However, the standardization analyses were conducted only on the 274 participants from within the U.S. The test authors stated 40% of the participants had a previous diagnosis of ADHD, and 44% met DSM criteria for ADHD. It was not clear whether this was 44% of the entire sample or 44% of the previously diagnosed portion. The majority of the sample was Caucasian males, with ethnic backgrounds also including Hispanic, African American, Asian American, and Native American. Just fewer than half the sample received some form of special services and 35% received services specific to learning disabilities. Mean child age was 12.73 and ages were grouped by near-age peers due to preliminary analyses revealing age-based group differences. The test authors do not include a breakdown of gender and ethnicity by region or include socioeconomic status data. It is also unclear from where the sample was recruited (i.e., school, clinic, community) or if any other DSM diagnoses were present. The standardization sample was collected though multisite means; however, the majority of the standardization sample was from the Western United States (51%). The test authors also note the Attention Performance Assessment norms are only to be used for younger children, as the performance-based measures were unable to differentiate between older children with and without ADHD.

The test authors report internal consistency (alpha coefficient) values, for all scales, with the exception of the Attention Performance Assessment, in which only test-retest is reported due to the scales containing only one item. The internal consistency estimates for the subscales of the Parent Attention Report (.87–.94) and on the Teacher Attention Report form (.80–.96) were considered "good" using a cutoff of .80 (Field, 2009), with the Concentration/Sustained Memory performing the lowest. Alpha coefficient for the Examiner's Observation Report overall was .98, with individual scales ranging from .89–.95. The Mental Health Screener did not perform as well, with reliability estimates ranging from .69 (Bipolar) to .91 (Autism). The test authors chose to keep the Bipolar scale because of "the importance of assessing the disorder" (examiner's manual, p. 100). The test authors dropped a "psychotic disorders" scale because of infrequency of endorsement and low reliability (.67). The Social Phobia scale was not initially included in the development and norming process and, therefore, was only normed on 137 participants. Despite being normed on a much smaller sample, the reliability estimate still performed well (.80). The Autism scale performed the best; however, the test authors note this scale contains 18 items, which may have contributed to the higher estimate.

The test authors report the length of time between administrations of the Attention Performance Assessment for test-retest was 4 weeks. The test-retest reliability estimates for the Attention Performance Assessment scales ranged from .35 (Random Letter Response) to .85 (Divided Attention). Additionally, the test authors note that a small sample was used in test-retest analyses, although they do not report a number. Furthermore, they note "Trails A" was not included in the test-retest process, resulting in no reliability data for this measure. The test authors acknowledge the low reliability for the Random Letter Response scale and suggest it was due to missing data. However, they did not report any effort to correct this limitation or rerun the analysis at a later time. Additionally, the nature of these types of tests may create difficulty in obtaining accurate test-retest estimates due to practice effects or recall. Any steps that may have been taken to avoid these confounds were not discussed.

The process of initially identifying items to include in the pool may have introduced bias into the selection process and how items were arranged. The initial inclusion/exclusion of items in the content validity process was determined through discussion between the test creators and doctoral students. The test authors note more than one occurrence of doctoral students initially disagreeing with the inclusion of certain items on a particular dimension, but then agreeing "once it had been suggested" (examiner's manual, p. 101). The discussion of the factor analytic process provides limited information, making it difficult to accurately determine how well the data fit the proposed structure. The test authors conducted factor analyses on all components of the battery; however, they do not report the type of factor analysis (i.e., exploratory factor analysis or principal components analysis) that was conducted, and whether or not they chose a rotation method. This information is necessary to determine how the data should be represented. The test authors do report the number of factors that emerge in the analyses, but did not report the criterion used in their decision-making process (e.g., eigenvalues over one; examination of the Scree plot). Concurrent validity was assessed through correlations of the Parent Attention Report raw scores to the Attention-Deficit/Hyperactivity Disorder Test (ADHDT). Impulsivity that correlated low on these two instruments (r = .27).

COMMENTARY. The ATLAS is a comprehensive assessment battery for children and adolescents suspected of having ADHD. The assessment materials appear easy to use and the instructions are clearly written in the manual. A unique aspect of the ATLAS is the connection between the assessment process and the intervention options included in the manual although there are no empirical validations of this claim. There are limitations to the current version that threaten the validity of the instrument and should be addressed to strengthen overall utility. The items on the Parent and Teacher Attention Report forms are all worded such that higher responses indicate greater impairment or symptom frequency. This may establish a response style in which a balance bias is present (i.e., the parent or teacher responds to all items in a high or low manner). The instructions on the Parent/Teacher Attention report are brief, and would benefit from an additional instruction to mark only one "X" per line. Additionally, a response option for "unknown" may prevent some respondents from leaving items blank. The Examiner's Observation Report would benefit from including more specific, operational definitions of the behaviors to be observed. The test authors acknowledge previous work by Barkley (1997) on the risk of false negatives with performance-based assessment. However, the test authors included these types of assessments based on their research showing multiple performance-based assessments can provide good sensitivity and specificity, but then were unable to differentiate between ADHD and non-ADHD children in the older sample. Finally, a larger and more representational normative sample across the United States is warranted.

SUMMARY. The ATLAS is a multimodal multirater assessment battery designed to measure ADHD in children ages 8 through 18 while ruling out other mental health disorders and linking assessment results to intervention. The assessment battery appears reasonably simple to administer and interpret. However, important information regarding the validation and clinical utility of the measure is lacking. It appears that several subscales contained within the battery lack adequate validity and/or reliability and the normative sample is relatively small and not regionally diversified. In addition, this battery is not intended for children younger than 8 years. Based on these considerations, this measure is not recommended for the assessment of ADHD.

REVIEWERS' REFERENCES

Barkley, R. (1997). *ADHD and the nature of self-control* (2nd ed.). New York: The Guilford Press.

Field, A. (2009). *Discovering statistics using SPSS* (3rd ed.). London: Sage Publications Ltd.

Lezak, M. D., Howieson, D. B., & Loring, D. W. (2004). *Neuropsychological assessment* (4th ed.). New York: Oxford University Press.

[9]

Autism Detection in Early Childhood.

Purpose: "Developed to detect Autistic Disorder (AD) in pre-verbal infants ... and very young children."
Population: Ages 12-24 months.
Publication Date: 2007.
Acronym: ADEC.
Scores, 17: Response to Name, Imitation, Stereotypical Behaviour, Gaze Switching, Eye Contact in a Game of Peek-a-Boo, Functional Play, Pretend Play, Reciprocity of a Smile, Response to Everyday Sounds, Gaze Monitoring, Responds to a Verbal Command, Demonstrates Use of Words, Anticipatory Posture, Nestling into Caregiver, Use of Gestures, Ability to Switch from Task to Task, Total.
Administration: Individual.
Price Data, 2008: A$495 per kit including manual (56 pages), Introduction and Training DVD, 10 score sheets, and set of stimulus materials; A$29.95 per 10 score sheets; A$199.95 per manual and Introduction and Training DVD combination; A$269.95 per set of stimulus materials.
Time: (10) minutes or less.
Comments: Parent/guardian should be present during administration.
Authors: Robyn Young.
Publisher: Australian Council for Educational Research Ltd. [Australia].

Review of the Autism Detection in Early Childhood by JOHN J. VACCA, Assistant Professor of Early Childhood Education, St. Joseph's University, Philadelphia, PA:

DESCRIPTION. Educators and pediatric professionals are facing continuing increases in enrollments of very young children with known or suspected Autism Spectrum Disorders (ASD). The prevalence of ASD in the United States ranks as the primary developmental disability over others and may be found in as many as 1 out of 150 children. The push for early intervention is therefore paramount.

Identification of early behaviors of ASD is cumbersome, and some behaviors can be so subtle that they are often seen along the continuum of normal early childhood behavior. Even though professionals are guided by documented milestones in growth and development, the ongoing question addressed concerns determining which of those children who demonstrate delays in or absence of expected behaviors are within normal variance and which of those children are showing early signs of developmental dysfunction. Such questions require the specialized training for all pediatric professionals in order for them to become adept at recognizing early signs of ASD.

Dr. Robyn Young developed the instrument named Autism Detection in Early Childhood (ADEC) to address the needs of pediatric and early education providers to have at their fingertips a tool to identify early signs of autism. The ADEC "is a screening tool that can be used by non-clinicians" (manual, p. 9). The purpose of the ADEC is "to detect Autistic Disorder (AD) in preverbal infants" (manual, p. 1). Young's primary purpose for developing the ADEC is to provide a tool that can be used with other measures to diagnose AD very early as opposed to existing instruments that preclude such early diagnoses given the overemphasis on intact receptive language. Young stipulates that data from the ADEC are to be used to "articulate the specific 'autistic traits' that cause concern rather than suggesting this as a potential and possibly alarming diagnosis" (manual, p. 9). Therefore, it is concluded and recommended that results from the ADEC and other instruments like it, in addition to traditional developmental batteries implemented with young children, be analyzed concurrently to arrive at an informed decision as to the presence or absence of AD.

The ADEC consists of 16 items, including items related to an "Adaptation Period" (manual, p. 5). Each item focuses on core limitations in three domains of behavior: difficulties with social interaction, presence of stereotypical/repetitive behaviors, and bizarre responses to environmental events and stimuli.

Overall, the test manual for administration and scoring is superb. Information is logically organized, and provides not only specifics about test usage but also background information about AD and developmental disabilities in the early childhood population. In terms of administration, the behaviors of focus are observed and then rated (0, 1, 2). Following observation of the child, ratings are tallied to provide an overall score, indicating a risk for underlying autism or a suspicion of a developmental trajectory where such behavior may persist, thereby supporting an AD diagnosis. Test materials accompany the ADEC kit, which includes such things as plastic cups and bowls, blocks, and cause and effect toys (e.g., jack-in-the-box). The materials and their specific measurements and dimensions are clearly identified.

Administration is play-based and child-centered. Provision of the materials is meant to encourage exploration and play on behalf of the child. A suggested sequence for testing is provided, as are suggestions to support children's motivation to play and interact with the toys. A warmup period (Adaptation Period) to allow the child to settle is also recommended (approximately 2 to 5 minutes). Total testing time usually requires less than 10 minutes. The test author is to be commended for providing a comprehensive, clear, and highly organized section on administration. It is obvious that her background and knowledge base of very young children and procedural considerations for evaluating children guided the development of the ADEC.

DEVELOPMENT. Young based the development of the ADEC on the behaviors commonly seen in children with AD and well documented in the literature. An open-ended questionnaire was completed by parents of children with AD (n = 97). The questionnaire centered on the behaviors cited often in the literature. Interrater reliability for 20% of the questionnaires exceeded 90%. The most common reported behavioral concern was delayed language. The behaviors that were rated highly across the sample of parents were then used as the basis for the development of the ADEC items. A follow-up investigation was conducted by Clifford, Young, and Williamson (2007) that involved reviewing videotapes of children with and without AD.

TECHNICAL. Young begins her section about the psychometric properties of the ADEC by stating that "the ADEC has psychometric properties as good as tools that require extensive training and time to administer, and better than some other commonly used tools" (manual, p. 9). The "commonly used tools" to which Young refers are not specifically mentioned at this point.

Psychometric analysis of the ADEC involved collecting data in four samples of young children from Southern Australia. Children were referred to the study mostly by pediatricians or other health care professionals. Additionally, some children were identified to participate based on review of a parent survey that was completed on the Internet. The manner in which these children were recruited was not specified, however. The ADEC was administered in three of the samples "to children with a diagnosis of AD as well as two comparison" (manual, p. 9) groups of children without AD and developing normally or with another disability. The latter was classified as "other developmental disability" (manual, p. 9) but no other information is provided.

The total number of children in the first three samples is not identified, yet Young states that a total of 269 participants were included in the fourth sample. The Early Intervention Research Program at Flinders University in South Australia previously evaluated the children. A total of 131 males and 18 females had a known diagnosis of AD and 60 children were considered typically developing (39 male, 21 female). Finally, children in the Other Developmental Disability category (specified as language disorder or other disorder) included 42 males and 18 females. A chart showing the average ages of the children at their first ADEC assessment in each category of disability (AD, Other, or Typically Developing) indicates the mean age to be about 3 to 3.5 years of age. Data from the Childhood Autism Rating Scale (CARS), Autism Diagnostic Interview–Revised (ADI–R), and the Checklist for Autism in Toddlers (CHAT) were used concurrently in analysis of the observations from the ADEC.

Reported values for validity and reliability are quite remarkable considering the samples of children observed in the study. Users should treat these numbers with caution given the lack of clarity of the exact make-up of the children in all four samples (including sample sizes), the nature of their disabilities, the demographics of children in southern Australia as compared to the U.S., and the limited participation of children under 3 years of age.

Coefficients for reliability (internal consistency, test-retest, and interrater) range from .82 to .97. In terms of validity (convergent), again the reported coefficients are quite impressive with scores ranging from .34 to .84. ANOVAs (with aligned post hoc differences using Tukey's homogenous subtests) were computed in light of the use of the CARS, ADEC, and CHAT. Data from the ANOVAs were primarily used to examine the ADEC's ability to discriminate among three developmental categories (autism diagnosis, typically developing, and other disability diagnosis) when compared against the two measures that are purported to be valid measures of autism. P values for all instruments were $<.001$; for ADEC, $F\ (2{,}265) = 69.15$ using discriminant function analysis, standardized canonical discriminant function coefficients for the CARS, CHAT, and ADEC were also reported across 3 samples. ADEC coefficients ranged from .16 (Function 1) and .84 (Function 2) to .51 (Function 1) and 1.08 (Function 2).

COMMENTARY. Young is to be commended for the development of the ADEC. The play-based/caregiver observation employed in the instrument is consistent with best practice guidelines for developmentally appropriate assessment of very young children. It provides yet another perspective of how young children, namely children with suspected AD, engage in and respond to the play environment. Such data are critical and helpful to have in interpreting the multitude of assessment data that are typical in an evaluation battery for children referred for AD. Although there are concerns about the limited sample size and ambiguity around the formation of the samples themselves, not to mention the fact that the samples were only from southern Australia, the ADEC is a valiant step towards creating more authentic ways of uncovering the world of the child with autism. Young is to be applauded for her development, yet she is strongly encouraged to continue field-testing her instrument with heterogeneous samples.

SUMMARY. The ADEC is a screening tool that can be used by nonclinicians. The purpose of the ADEC is to detect ASD in preverbal infants. It is play-based, and the results can be used easily with other results from both formal and informal measures to document the presence/absence of autistic behaviors in children referred for evaluation. The psychometric properties (though limited to small sample sizes and demographics) "suggest that the ADEC has psychometric properties as good as tools that require extensive training and time to administer, and better than some other commonly used tools" (manual, p. 9). The test manual for administration and scoring is excellent.

REVIEWER'S REFERENCE

Clifford, S., Young, R., & Williamson, P. (2007). Assessing the early characteristics of autistic disorder using video analysis. *Journal of Autism and Developmental Disorders, 37*, 301–313.

[10]

BASC-2 Behavioral and Emotional Screening System.

Purpose: "Designed to determine behavioral and emotional strengths and weaknesses in children and adolescents in preschool through high school."
Population: Ages 3-18.
Publication Date: 2007.
Acronym: BASC-2 BESS.
Score: Total score only.
Administration: Individual.
Forms, 5: Teacher Form–Preschool, Teacher Form–Child/Adolescent, Parent Form–Preschool, Parent Form–Child/Adolescent, Student Form–Child/Adolescent.
Price Data, 2008: $60 per manual (100 pages); $22 per Header Sheets (needed for group scanning); $34 per Test Items on Audio CD; $589 per ASSIST software.
Foreign Language Edition: Spanish edition available for the Parent Form–Preschool, Parent Form–Child/Adolescent, and Student Form–Child/Adolescent.
Time: (5–10) minutes.
Comments: Item development originated with items created for the Behavior Assessment System for Children [Second Edition] (BASC-2; 17:21).
Authors: Randy W. Kamphaus and Cecil R. Reynolds.
Publisher: Pearson.

a) TEACHER FORMS.
Price Data: $26.75 per 25 Teacher Forms–Preschool; $98 per 100 Teacher Forms–Preschool; $26.75 per 25 Teacher Forms–Child/Adolescent; $98 per 100 Teacher Forms–Child/Adolescent.
1) Teacher Form–Preschool.
Population: Ages 3-5.
2) Teacher Form–Child/Adolescent.
Population: Ages 5-18 (Grades K-12).

b) PARENT FORMS.
Price Data: $26.75 per 25 Parent Forms–Preschool; $26.75 per 25 Parent Forms–Child/Adolescent.
Time: (5-10) minutes.
1) Parent Form–Preschool.
Population: Ages 3-5.
2) Parent Form–Child/Adolescent.
Population: Ages 5-18 (Grades K-12).

c) STUDENT FORMS.
Price Data: $26.75 per 25 Student Forms; $98 per 100 Student Forms.
Time: (5-10) minutes.
1) *Student Form–Child/Adolescent.*
Population: Ages 8-18.

Review of the Behavioral and Emotional Screening System by MICHAEL J. FURLONG, Professor, Gevirtz Graduate School of Education, and LINDSEY O'BRENNAN, University of California, Santa Barbara, Santa Barbara, CA:

DESCRIPTION. The BASC-2 Behavioral and Emotional Screening System (BASC-2 BESS) is a mental health screener that assesses for externalizing, internalizing, and school problems, and adaptive skills among youths ages 3–18. This brief assessment can be completed in 5 minutes and uses a cross-informant strategy with teacher (27 items, Grades K–12), parent (30 items, preschool and child/adolescent), and student (30 items, Grades 3–12) forms. There is substantial content overlap, but each version has unique items. A 4-point frequency response scale is used—*never*, *sometimes*, *often*, and *almost always*. Teachers and parents read the administration instructions; however, an audio recording is available for parents with reading difficulties. Students can complete the forms after receiving oral instructions from a teacher or other test administrator, and audio recording is available for students with reading difficulties. Both student and parent forms are available in English and Spanish.

Scoring can be completed manually or using the ASSIST software program. This utility provides the user with individual and group assessment reports (useful for class-wide screening), which includes the total raw score, *T*–scores, percentile rank, classification level, and validity indexes scores (described later in this review). Total *T*–scores are used to indicate if a youth's scores are in one of the following ranges: Normal (*T*–score of 60 or below), Elevated (*T*–score of 61–70), or Extremely Elevated (*T*–score of 71 or above). Forms also can be hand scored using the normative tables provided in the manual, although the test authors do not recommend this practice. An innovative empirical strategy was used to compute three validity indexes (F Index, Consistency Index, and Response Pattern Index) to assess if a respondent provided truthful and accurate information, which is commendable and unique for a mental health screening instrument. Finally, the test authors suggest how to use the BASC-2 BESS during the multiple stages of a comprehensive screening process. They indicate that the BASC-2 BESS can be used during initial screening stages, as part of a comprehensive assessment of at-risk youth, or during intervention to monitor progress.

DEVELOPMENT. The BASC-2 BESS was developed by the test authors to (a) assess an individual's behavioral and emotional strengths and weaknesses; (b) gather information from multiple informants; and (c) provide a quick, reliable screening tool for individuals and groups of children. The items were taken from the widely used Behavior Assessment Scale for Children–2 (BASC–2; Reynolds & Kamphaus, 2004) Teacher Rating Scales (TRS), Parent Rating Scales (PRS), and Self-Report of Personality (SRP). During the BASC-2 BESS item selection process, the test authors began by identifying items with the highest factor loadings on each of the BASC–2 composites (Externalizing Problems, Internalizing Problems, School Problems, Adaptive Skills/ Personal Adjustment, and Inattention/Hyperactivity). These items were then compared across student, teacher, and parent versions to assess whether their properties were maintained across respondents. Items were then tested for reliability and group bias. Most items are the same as those on the corresponding form of the BASC–2; however, there are between one (student) and eight (parent preschool) new items included in the five BASC-2 BESS versions.

The norming sample for the BASC-2 BESS is diverse with regard to race/ethnicity, geographic region, socioeconomic status, and classification in special-education programs. The demographics of the sample closely resemble that of the U.S. population. However, the test authors acknowledge areas where the sample may not match with the population as closely (in a few areas in the preschool samples).

TECHNICAL.

Standardization. The BASC-2 BESS was developed using the original BASC–2 TRS, PRS, and SRP standardization samples. This process was conducted from 2002–2004 using a sample of 3,300 students, 4,450 teachers, and 4,600 parents from 233 cities in 40 states (N = 12,350). The test authors provide ample information on the representation of the sample by age, gender, geographic region, race/ethnicity, and mother's education level. Combined-sex and separate-sex norm groups are provided. They also divided the norms by age due to the developmental differences in average Total scores. There are two groupings for preschoolers (age 3 and ages 4–5) and three groupings for child/ adolescent levels (ages 5–9 [ages 8–9 for the student form], 10–14, and 15–18).

Reliability. Sufficient evidence is provided in the manual related to internal consistency, test-retest reliability, and interrater reliability. Internal consistency on all forms was measured through split-half reliability, with reliability coefficients ranging from .90 to .97. Test–retest reliability was examined using various diverse samples ranging from 78 to 227 participants, and using intervals that ranged from 0 to 88 days. The forms ranged in reliability from .80 to .91, with the student child/adolescent form having the lowest reliability and the teacher child/adolescent form having the highest. Interrater reliability was also examined using diverse, representative samples ranging from 65 to 112 participants. Scores were compared on the same child by different raters (i.e., both mother and father scores; different teachers). Reliability was somewhat higher for parent forms (.83 and .82) than teacher forms (.80 and .71). The test authors ascribed this difference to the fact that students in middle and high school have multiple teachers, which can lead to varying observed behaviors in the school setting.

Validity. Ample evidence is provided that supports the BASC-2 BESS's validity as a screening measure. The global composite score on the BASC-2 BESS shows high correlations with the BASC–2 TRS, PRS, and SRP global composite scores (r = .94, .90, .86, respectively). This was not unexpected because the BASC-2 BESS items are a subset of the BASC–2 items. The manual also indicates that the BASC-2 BESS has relatively strong correlations with global composite scores from the Achenbach System of Empirically Based Assessment measures, including Caregiver-Teacher Report Form (r = .76); Teacher's Report Form (r = .76); Child Behavior Checklist ages 1–5 (r = .71) and ages 6–18 (r = .76); and the Youth Self-Report Form (r = .77).

Relatively strong validity correlations were also shown between the BASC-2 BESS and global composite scores from the Conners' teacher, parent, and student forms (r = .78, .62, .51, respectively). In addition, a positive correlation was found with the global composite score from the Behavior Rating Inventory of Executive Function (BRIEF; r = .78), a measure designed to assess executive functioning. However, only moderate correlations were found between the BASC-2 BESS and adaptive behavior composite scores from the Vineland–II Teacher Rating Form (r = -.39 and -.66 for preschool and child/adolescent levels, respectively) and Survey Interview and Parent/Caregiver Rating Forms (r = -.46 and -.50 for preschool and child/adolescent levels, respectively). Finally, moderate correlations were found when compared to the Children's Depression Inventory (r = .51) and the Revised Children's Manifest Anxiety Scale (r = .55). All samples used for validity testing were relatively large and representative of the population.

Predictive validity was also assessed and the results indicated that the teacher and parent forms could be used to predict future behavioral and emotional functioning (sensitivity values above .50). However, the forms poorly predict preschoolers' internalizing problems. On the other hand, student forms showed good sensitivity for students' future externalizing and internalizing problems. In addition, the manual outlines preliminary findings from longitudinal studies examining the predictive validity of the BASC-2 BESS on academic and behavioral outcomes (see DiStefano & Kamphaus, 2007; Kamphaus et al., 2007). Teacher and parent forms were shown to moderately predict academic achievement in reading and math, whereas the teacher and student forms were able to moderately predict grade-point average.

COMMENTARY. The BASC-2 BESS teacher, parent, and student forms are quick screeners that are easy to use in a variety of settings. Its key strengths are the ample evidence supporting the robust reliability and validity of this measure. In addition, the BASC-2 BESS has high positive correlations with general measures of behavior and emotional problems, ADHD, and executive functioning. The forms also appear to have good sensitivity for predicting future child and adolescent behavioral and emotional functioning.

Although the test authors provide information about how this measure can be used across settings, there is no mention of the theory used in creating the BASC–2 measures. In addition, there was no mention of a pilot study used during the development of the BASC-2 BESS. Finally, it is somewhat less reliable and valid in assessing student internalizing symptoms; however, this is also true of other child and adolescent mental health screening instruments. The BASC-2 BESS shows promise as a youth mental health screener; however, more work is needed to understand how best to measure these problems, especially among the preschool population. Despite these caveats, the BASC-2 BESS is based on a sound record of past and ongoing empirical research. This instrument is arguably the omnibus mental health screener of choice in school settings. Interested users should also examine the Ohio Scales (Ogles & Southern Consortium for Children, 2000).

SUMMARY. The BASC-2 BESS measures a range of behavioral and emotional problems among youth in preschool to high school. It consists of three brief screening measures, including teacher, parent, and student forms that are quick and easy to use. It shows substantial promise as a screening tool based on its good reliability and moderate to high validity with other measures. Moreover, preliminary studies have shown it to have good predictive validity. However, its sensitivity to effectively predict internalizing problems among youth is less clear.

REVIEWERS' REFERENCES

DiStefano, C. A., & Kamphaus, R. W. (2007). Development and validation of a behavioral screener for preschool-age children. *Journal of Emotional and Behavioral Disorders, 15*, 93-102.

Kamphaus, R. W., Thorpe, J. S., Winsor, A. P., Kroncke, A. P., Dowdy, E. T., & VanDeventer, M. C. (2007). Development and predictive validity of a teacher screener for child behavioral and emotional problems at school. *Educational and Psychological Measurement, 67*, 342-356.

Ogles, B. M., & Southern Consortium for Children. (2000). The Ohio Scales–Youth Version. Retrieved May 10, 2008, from www.mh.state.oh.us/oper/outcomes/instruments.english.html

Reynolds, C. R., & Kamphaus, R. W. (2004). Behavior Assessment System for Children (2nd ed.). Circle Pines, MN: AGS Publishing.

Review of the BASC-2 Behavioral and Emotional Screening System by KATHLEEN M. JOHNSON, Psychologist, Lincoln Public Schools, Lincoln, NE:

DESCRIPTION. The BASC-2 Behavioral and Emotional Screening System (BASC-2 BESS) is designed to determine behavioral and emotional strengths and weaknesses in children and adolescents in preschool through high school. The BASC-2 BESS is based on the Behavior Assessment System for Children, Second Edition (BASC-2; 17:21), and includes a set of brief, multi-informant screening instruments. Parent and teacher rating forms are available for two levels (preschool level: ages 3–5 and child/adolescent level: Grades K–12) and a student rating form is available (Grades 3–12). Each of the BASC-2 BESS screening forms yields one total score to be used as a predictor/ screener for a wide range of potential behavioral, emotional, and academic problems. The rating forms include both positively and negatively worded items to minimize rater response sets. Each form is composed of 25 to 30 key items that were selected to tap into commonly identified behavioral and emotional categories: externalizing, internalizing, and school problems, as well as adaptive skills/strengths. The test authors provide detailed guidance regarding the general use of the BASC-2 BESS, such as choosing which children to assess, which forms to use, and how often to do screenings. The BASC-2 BESS is intended for use by schools, mental health clinics, pediatric clinics, communities, and researchers to screen for a variety of behavioral and emotional disorders. The test authors specifically recommend using the BASC-2 BESS as an efficient means of doing systematic, early screening in school settings to help determine which students most need intervention or additional resources. Kamphaus and Reynolds caution users that the BASC-2 BESS is intended to determine risk status and is not a diagnostic tool. Follow-up assessment is needed, after using the BASC-2 BESS, to evaluate specifically the behavioral and emotional needs of some children and adolescents for treatment purposes.

According to the test authors, the BASC-2 BESS measures can be completed in about 5 minutes with no specialized training needed by the person at the point of administration. The directions for completing the forms are straightforward and printed right on the forms. Audio recordings of the directions and the items are also available on a compact disc for both of the parent forms (preschool and school age) and for the student form in English and Spanish, if needed or preferred. Spanish-language versions of the parent and student forms are also available. Each item is briefly stated and the rater marks the frequency rate for each behavior described, using a 4-point scale: *Never, Sometimes, Often, Almost Always* (N, S, O, or A). All forms can be scored by hand or by computer software. Responses can be hand-keyed into the software or scanned in for computer-generated individual scores and other group data reports; the computer-scoring program was not made available for this review. Age-based norm tables are provided in the manual to determine *T*-scores and the percentile ranks based on total raw scores for each form. Classifications are also provided to describe the level of risk that a child or teen may be exhibiting in terms of behavioral or emotional problems. *T*-scores within one standard deviation of the mean indicate normal risk, *T*-scores between one and two standard deviations above the mean indicate elevated risk, and *T*-scores more than two standard deviations above the mean indicate extremely elevated risk. Additionally, score validity indices of consistency, negative response set, and repeated response patterns are available to aid with interpretation of the findings. Although male and female norm groups are available to users, the use of the combined-sex norms is recommended for general use.

DEVELOPMENT. The BASC-2 BESS was developed to provide a brief and efficient method of screening children and adolescents for potential behavioral and emotional problems. All of the BASC-2 BESS items came originally from the BASC-2 item pool. The final items were selected with a primary goal of having a single score from each form (teacher, parent, and student) that would reliably predict the likelihood of behavioral and emotional problems for an individual child or adolescent. Several stages of item selection were utilized. Initially, within each form (teacher, parent, and student) the items that had the strongest correlations with their respective composite scores (e.g., externalizing problems) were selected. These items were then evaluated and the items that had the best overall qualities (e.g., high loadings across forms, unique content) were retained. Based on the selection criteria, a few of the items selected for the BASC-2 BESS were part of the BASC-2 standardization process, but not included in the final published BASC-2 forms. About 30 items were selected for each form and level, and preliminary reliability statistics were used to examine the internal consistency of each form. The final item set was determined for each form, and differential item functioning analyses were conducted to identify bias issues (problem items were replaced with alternate items). The reader may also consult the BASC-2 manual for additional information on the original item development procedures (Reynolds & Kamphaus, 2004).

TECHNICAL. The BASC-2 BESS normative data are part of the standardization data of the Behavior Assessment System for Children—Second Edition (BASC-2; Reynolds & Kamphaus, 2004). The standardization was conducted using a large, nationally representative sample (in terms of sex, socioeconomic status/parental education, race/ethnicity, geographic region, and special education classification), and the demographic targets closely approximated the 2004 U.S. Census. Over 12,000 total forms (parent, teacher, and student forms across the various age groups) from 40 states were collected as part of the standardization process. In the manual, the test authors provide detailed information about the characteristics of the norm group. The BASC-2 BESS reliability data indicate strong internal consistency levels for the parent, teacher, and student forms, with coefficient values above .90. Test-retest correlations were calculated on representative subgroups of the total sample for each form (parent, teacher, and student) and age level (preschool and school-age). The testing interval ranged from 0 to 88 days. The adjusted coefficient values ranged from .80 for the student form to .91 for the teacher child/adolescent form, indicating moderate to strong test-retest reliability. Interrater reliability coefficient values were moderate, ranging from .71 for the teacher child/adolescent form to .83 for the parent preschool form.

The process of item selection using principal components analyses lends support for the construct validity of the BASC-2 BESS total score. Concurrent and predictive studies cited by the test authors also provide validity evidence. For example, the correlations between the BASC-2 BESS total score and the Total Problems score on the Achenbach System of Empirically Based Assessment were strong: .71 to .77 for the parent, teacher, and student forms. Moderately strong negative correlations were also found between the BASC-2 BESS score and the Vineland-II adaptive composite score, as would be expected based on the content of the scales. Correlations between the student form score and self-report measures of internalizing problems (e.g., depression and anxiety) ranged from .51 to .55. Accuracy rates for predicting outcomes (using two classifications: normal range vs. risk range scores) from the BASC-2 BESS to the BASC-2 were also examined by the test authors. The highest predictive relationship was between the BASC-2 BESS score and the Behavioral Symptoms Index (global scores on the parent and teacher forms of the BASC-2) and between the BASC-2 BESS total score and the Emotional Symptoms Index (global score on the student form of the BASC-2). This finding is expected based on the overlap in items, item content, and all of the scores being global measure scores. At more specific composite score levels, there was less predictive value between the BASC-2 BESS score and the BASC-2 score for internalizing problems than for externalizing problems based on the parent and teacher ratings. The student form score was found to have a somewhat stronger predictive correlation with the BASC-2 internalizing problems score as compared to the correlation between the parent and teacher form scores and BASC-2 internalizing problem scores. Data from students identified by parents as having a previous clinical diagnosis indicated slight differences (slightly elevated risk) in group mean scores on the BASC-2 BESS parent and teacher forms (e.g., the group of students reported by parents as having ADHD had a BASC-2 BESS mean scores of 60.8 on the teacher form and 63.8 on the parent form). Reynolds and Kamphaus also present 4-year longitudinal data comparing BASC-2 BESS scores to various school outcome measures. The results indicate at least a mild (inverse) relationship between the BASC-2 BESS score and academic performance in reading and math (e.g., grade-point average, achievement test scores). No clear relationships were found among BASC-2 BESS scores and measures of attendance (e.g., days absent or tardy).

COMMENTARY. The BASC-2 BESS has excellent psychometric properties that are thoroughly documented in the manual. The rating forms are very brief, straightforward in format, and easy to score (by hand or by computer software). Even though the forms are brief, care was taken to include both positively and negatively worded items. Interpretation of the findings is aided by the availability of validity indices (e.g., response consistency). The test authors appropriately caution users that although no specialized training is needed for administration, professional input is needed for making decisions for follow-up on the BASC-2 BESS results. With increased interest in and need for universal screening to better address the needs of children, especially in school settings, the BASC-2 BESS may be a useful option. It can serve as a beginning point in a multistage intervention process for addressing behavioral and mental health problems.

SUMMARY. The Behavioral and Emotional Screening System (BESS) is a Behavior Assessment System for Children, Second Edition (BASC-2) tool, developed since the publication of the BASC-2. It was designed as a means of broadly screening children and adolescents for potential behavioral and emotional problems in school settings, mental health clinics, pediatric practices, and research sites. The BASC-2 BESS includes a set of brief, multi-informant rating forms. Parent and teacher forms are available for two age levels (preschool level: ages 3–5 and child/adolescent level: Grades K–12), and a student self-rating form is available for Grades 3–12. The test authors accurately differentiate screening from assessment and diagnosis efforts. The BASC-2 BESS is not a diagnostic tool and the results indicate only a level of normal, elevated, or extremely elevated risk for students as having or developing behavioral and/or emotional problems. It is a well-developed, valid, and reliable norm-referenced screening tool that may be a useful tool within a multi-stage diagnosis and intervention model.

REVIEWER'S REFERENCE

Reynolds, C. R., & Kamphaus, R. W. (2004). Behavior Assessment System for Children (2nd ed.). Circle Pines, MN: AGS Publishing.

[11]

BECK Youth Inventories for Children and Adolescents: Second Edition.

Purpose: Designed to "assess a child's experience of depression, anxiety, disruptive behavior, and self-concept."
Population: Ages 7-18.
Publication Dates: 2001-2005.
Acronyms: BYI-II, BDI-Y, BSCI-Y, BAI-Y, BANI-Y, BDBI-Y.
Scores, 5: Depression, Anxiety, Anger, Disruptive Behavior, Self-Concept.
Subtests, 5: Beck Depression Inventory for Youth, Beck Anxiety Inventory for Youth, Beck Anger Inventory for Youth, Beck Disruptive Inventory for Youth, Beck Self-Concept.
Administration: Individual or group.
Price Data, 2007: $165 per complete kit including manual (2005, 85 pages) and 25 combination inventory booklets; $95 per 25 combination inventory booklets; $46 per 25 depression inventory booklets; $46 per 25 anxiety inventory booklets; $46 per 25 anger inventory booklets; $46 per 25 disruptive behavior inventory booklets; $46 per self-concept inventory booklets; $85 per manual.
Time: (30-60) minutes for combination form.
Comments: Subtests may be administered separately or via combination form; previous edition was entitled Beck Youth Inventories of Emotional & Social Impairment.
Authors: Judith S. Beck, Aaron T. Beck, John B. Jolly, and Robert A. Steer.
Publisher: Pearson.
Cross-References: For reviews by Mike Bonner and Hugh Stephenson of the earlier edition, see 15:31.

Review of the Beck Youth Inventories for Children and Adolescents: Second Edition by ROSEMARY FLANAGAN, Associate Professor, Graduate School of Education and Psychology, Touro College, New York, NY:

OVERVIEW. The Beck Youth Inventories, Second Edition (BYI-II) is composed of five scales used separately or in combination to obtain self-report data of the experience of Anger (BANI-Y), Anxiety (BAI-Y), Depression (BDI-Y), Disruptive Behavior (BDBI-Y), and Self-Concept (BSCI-Y) for youth aged 7–18 years. The combination of scales can be used as part of a contemporary assessment emphasizing multiple measures and data sources. Youth reports of negative emotional states can be associated with additional matters of great concern, such as suicide ideation and suicide itself. Moreover, the inventories facilitate the assessment of comorbidity, common in youth disorders. The BYI-II may be used in varied settings that include schools, outpatient mental health and medical settings, as well as forensic, residential, and inpatient settings.

ADMINISTRATION, SCORING, AND INTERPRETATION. Administration is straightforward; the inventories are 20 items in length and can be completed in 5–10 minutes. Although the items are written at a second grade reading level, examiners must ascertain that young children as well as those with reading difficulty can read the items. The record form is well-designed; the directions for responding to the questionnaire(s) are clearly printed on each page. Respondents indicate directly on the record form their choice from "never" to "always," scaled from 0–3 points, respectively. The cover sheet provides space to record notes and demographic information about the youngster; the back page provides space to summarize clinical, educational, and assessment information. Scoring is accomplished by tallying item scores and looking up the corresponding *T*-score (*mean* = 50; *SD* = 10) in the appropriate norm table. Although not a complicated task, there is potential for clerical errors. Data can be displayed graphically on the record form.

Interpretation is straightforward. Examiners must first inspect the response sheet for completeness (more than two unanswered items per scale render the data invalid), and are urged to use clinical judgment to decide whether the data are valid when youth seem reluctant to respond in the first place. For the scales that measure depression (BDI-Y), anxiety (BAI-Y), anger (BANI-Y) and disruptive behavior (BDBI-Y), *T*-scores of 55 and below are considered average. *T*-scores of 55–59 and 60–69 represent mild to moderate elevations. The clinical range is reserved for *T*-scores of 70 and above. For the measure of self-concept (BSCI-Y), *T*-scores below 40 represent the clinical range, scores of 40–44 are below average, 45–55 are average, and *T*-scores > 55 indicate greater than average self-concept. As is common with measures of social-emotional functioning, percentile ranks also should be reported because normative data are skewed. Interpretation should extend beyond psychometric cutoffs with consideration given to whether patterns of responding are suggestive of a disorder. Several illustrative case studies of youth with varied problems are provided in the manual to guide practitioners.

DEVELOPMENT AND STANDARDIZATION. Following several pilot studies, a 25-item version of each scale was used to determine the final inventories of 20 items each. Items were removed from each scale based on criteria that included the item not being a pathognomonic indicator, low factor loading, low(er) item-inventory correlation, and an increase in coefficient alpha when the item(s) were removed. The standardization sample of 1,000 individuals was drawn from a larger community sample of youth aged 7-18 from four geographic areas (North, South, Midwest, and West). In addition, clinical samples should be more specific; 107 and 178 were analyzed for the child and adolescent groups, respectively. Stratification variables included age, gender, race/ethnicity, and parental education. A variety of rural, urban, and suburban sites were sampled that included schools, churches, and community centers; individuals also were obtained through advertisements and through professionals who provided services to schools. Other selection criteria for participants included English as the primary language, at least a second grade reading level, attendance at a regular school, and no physical or mental illness that would interfere with the assessment. The standardization sample was composed of 1,000 youngsters (400 at ages 7–10 and 11–14; 200 at ages 15–18). Questionnaires were randomly administered in one of five different orders. Testing was conducted individually or in small groups. In addition, normative data were obtained for a special education sample of 89 youth aged 8–12 who were placed in special education for varying amounts of the school day. This sample included youth with learning and behavior problems. Although the clinical sample is varied, it does not represent census tract data. The adolescent portion of the sample (ages 15–18) is better described in the manual than is the child sample (ages 7–14). Importantly, all individuals in this sample met the criteria for a DSM-IV-TR (American Psychiatric Association, 2000) diagnosis; care was taken to ensure the diagnoses were made by trained clinicians.

PSYCHOMETRIC PROPERTIES. Coefficient alpha is substantial for all scales with values ranging from .86–.96 for a sample of 1,000 youth aged 7–18 (500 males, 500 females); almost 70% of the values are .90 or greater. The Depression scale is the most internally consistent (.90–.95), and the Disruptive Behavior Scale is the least (.86–.91). The average standard error of measurement across scales ranged from 2.12 to 3.37. Test-retest reliability for samples of children (aged 7–14; N = 105) and adolescents (aged 15–18; N = 65) for intervals of 7 and 8 days, respectively, ranged from .74–.93 and .83–.93, respectively. Overall measures of reliability are slightly stronger for adolescents, probably reflecting their higher capabilities in responding to questionnaires as compared to younger children.

Validity was established in several ways. Examination of the internal structure using principal axis factor analysis revealed three factors that underlie the complete BYI-II: negative affect, negative self-concept, and disruptive behavior. Correlations among subscales are substantial and in the expected directions. Relationships with other instruments such as the Children's Depression Inventory (CDI; Kovacs, 1992) and the Piers-Harris Self-Concept Scale, 2nd edition (Piers, 2002) provide further evidence of construct validity. Overall, the relationships are substantial and in the expected directions, with some relationships of particular interest.

The BAI-Y correlates (r = .70/.64) more highly with the Revised Children's Manifest Anxiety Scale (RCMAS; Reynolds & Richmond, 1978) for children (r = .70) than do the other scales. For adolescents, however, the BDI-Y has a slightly stronger relationship with the RCMAS than does the BAI-Y (r = .70 vs. r = .64); most likely reflecting high comorbidity (Brady & Kendall, 1992) between anxiety and depression. Correlations with the Conners-Wells Scales (CASS:S; Conners, 1997) indicate that the Conduct Problems scale correlates most highly with the BDBI-Y, r = .69 and r = .76, for children and adolescents, respectively. Interestingly, the Attention Deficit Hyperactivity (ADHD) index of the CASS:S correlates most highly with the Anger Scale of the Beck (BANI-Y) (r = .73 and .64 for children and adolescents, respectively). These data appear to reflect the overlap that is sometimes observed between some symptoms of ADHD and depression.

Evidence of discriminant validity is provided through group separation. A sample of youth with various disabilities placed in special education scored differently from matched controls on all scales. The effect sizes for these differences are considered medium. Youth from different clinical categories, including depression, mood disorders, anxiety disorders, attention deficit-hyperactivity disorder, adjustment disorders, bipolar disorder, conduct disorder, and disruptive behavior were also studied. Youth with different diagnoses scored differently on the scales, with scale elevations appearing where expected, given the diagnoses. The differences reported are statistically significant and substantial in that the corresponding effect sizes are considered medium to large. Thus, the inventories can distinguish groups.

COMMENT. The revision of the BYI includes an expanded age range and a larger standardization sample. It is important that the scales should assist the practitioner and researcher in the determination of comorbidity, which is common in youth disorders. Although scales of social emotional functioning that can be used in varying combinations in varied settings are needed, practitioners and researchers may prefer to use all scales in order to assess comorbidity in a standard manner. An advantage that the BYI has over other measures of multiple constructs is its relatively briefer length coupled with a focus on the constructs that tend to demonstrate comorbidity. As is good practice, the BYI should not be used in isolation.

REVIEWER'S REFERENCES

American Psychiatric Association. (2000). *Diagnostic and statistical manual of mental disorders* (4th ed., Text Revision). Washington, DC: Author.

Brady, E. U., & Kendall, P. C. (1992). Comorbidity of anxiety and depression in children and adolescents. *Psychological Bulletin, 111*, 244-255.

Conners, C. K. (1997). Conners Rating Scales—Revised. North Tonawanda, NY: Multi-Health Systems.

Kovacs, M. (1992). Children's Depression Inventory. North Tonawanda, NY: Multi-Health Systems.

Reynolds, C., & Richmond, B. (1985). Revised Children's Manifest Anxiety Scale. Los Angeles: Western Psychological Services.

Piers, E. V. (2002). Piers-Harris Self-Concept Scale (2nd ed). Los Angeles: Western Psychological Services.

Review of the Beck Youth Inventories for Children and Adolescents: Second Edition by CARLEN HENINGTON, Associate Professor of School Psychology, Mississippi State University, Mississippi State, MS:

DESCRIPTION. The Beck Youth Inventories for Children and Adolescents (Second Edition; BYI-II) is a brief self-report instrument intended to assess distress in children and adolescents (7–18 years). This latest revision of the Beck Youth Inventories addresses five content areas. The Depression Inventory for Youth (BDI-Y) assesses depression criteria outlined by the *Diagnostic and Statistical Manual of Mental Disorders, Fourth Edition, Text Revision* (DSM-IV-TR; American Psychiatric Association, 2000) with item content appropriate for children and adolescents. The Beck Anxiety Inventory for Youth (BAI-Y) assesses common childhood fears (e.g., school, injury, health), worry, and physiological symptoms often associated with anxiety. The Beck Anger Inventory for Youth (BANI-Y) addresses perceptions of mistreatment, negative thoughts, anger, and physiological arousal. The Beck Disruptive Behavior Inventory for Youth (BDBI-Y) addresses behaviors and attitudes associated with oppositional behavior and Conduct Disorder (see DSM-IV-TR). The Beck Self-Concept Inventory for Youth (BSCI-Y) taps self-perceptions of competence, potency, and positive self-worth. The test authors provide a 4-point rationale for the BYI-II: (a) brevity and ease of use, (b) ability to address comorbidity questions while assessing individual areas of concern, (c) addition of psychometrically sound assessment of anger and disruptive behavior, and (d) norm sampling that reflects United States Census figures.

Although all five inventories of the BYI-II are typically intended to be administered in order (i.e., BSCI-Y, BAI-Y, BDI-Y, BANI-Y, then BDBI-Y), the inventories may be administered individually. Each is a 20-item inventory requiring approximately 5 to 10 minutes to complete for a total administration time of 30 minutes for most respondents, but may require up to 60 minutes dependent upon child characteristics (e.g., age, reading ability, and mental status). Small group and individual administration is possible in school, outpatient mental health, and residential/inpatient settings. However, the authors advise that individuals have privacy (preferably without friends or relatives present) to encourage honest responses.

Responses to each question are rated on a 4-point Likert-type scale (0 = *never*, 1 = *sometimes*, 2 = *often*, 3 = *always*). Scoring is straightforward with raw scores tabulated as the total of the ratings for each inventory and converted to *T*-scores (M = 50, SD = 10) for each sex using one of the age-based conversion tables (i.e., ages 7–10, 11–14, and 15–18). Cumulative percentages are also available. On the BDI-Y, BAI-Y, BANI-Y, and BDBI-Y inventories, higher scores indicate greater severity (i.e., *T*-scores of 60 to 69 or 70+ indicate "moderately elevated" and "extremely elevated" levels, respectively). Lower scores on the BSCI-Y indicate greater severity (i.e., *T*-scores between 40 and 44 and <40 indicate "lower than average" and "much lower than average" levels, respectively). The scores can be plotted on the *T*-Score Profile sheet and qualified individuals can then interpret score profiles, with inclusion of other assessment information, in terms of childhood and adolescent syndromes and disorders.

DEVELOPMENT. The test authors provide theoretical background for consideration (e.g., self-report of children and adolescents; other assessment instruments and research of depression, anxiety, self-concept, disruptive behavior, and anger in youth) in the manual; however, specifics related to test development are lacking. The BYI-II was developed through a pilot study, with item design based on verbal reports of children in therapy with wording altered to reflect a second-grade reading level (see Flesch, 1948). In addition, some items (five for each inventory) were deleted for a variety of reasons. Reviews of the previous Beck Youth Inventories (Bonner, 2003; Stephenson, 2003) report a similar lack of detail in item development.

TECHNICAL. Two phases were used to determine psychometric properties of the BYI-II. Phase 1 involved two children's age groups (7–10 and 11–14 years) in which a community sample (n = 1,100) from urban and rural settings in four U.S. geographic regions (i.e., North, South, Midwest, West) was administered the BYI-II. The sample was stratified to match the 1990 U.S. Census for race/ethnicity (i.e., White, African American, Hispanic, and Other) and parent education level. Phase 2 used 200 adolescents (15–18 years) with similar demographic considerations. Age-by-sex *T*-score norms and descriptive cumulative percentages were developed from these sample data.

The norms groups also were used to determine internal consistency of the BYI-II. The manual provides tables of psychometric characteristics by age group and sex for the five inventories. Coefficient alphas for each of the five inventories were acceptable (.86 to .91 for ages 7–10; .86 to .92 for ages 11–14; and .91 to .96 for ages 15–18) with similar findings for males and females. Test-retest scores across 1 week's time were based on the scores of a subsample of individuals (n = 105 and 65 for children and adolescents, respectively). The authors presented corrected reliabilities (to control for variability of scores on the first of each of the six norm groups), which were also acceptable (.74 to .90 for ages 7 to 10; .84 to .93 for ages 11 to 14; and .83 to .93 for ages 15–18). Slightly lower coefficients were reported for female than male children.

Validity was determined in several ways. First, the BDI-Y, BAI-Y, and BANI-Y inventory scores for norm groups (age and sex) showed high intercorrelations (ranging from .39 to .84 with 29 of the 36 comparisons greater than .60). Only the coefficients for correlations of the BDBI-Y and BAI-Y between female children (7–10 and 11–14 years) and for male children (11–14 years) fell within the moderate range (r < .50). Modest negative correlations existed between these inventories and the BSCI-Y (ranging from -.23 to -.66, with the vast majority of correlations exceeding -.35). In general, the lowest correlations between the BAI-Y and BSCI-Y occurred at the younger ages. Second, an unrotated principal axis factor analysis of items across all inventories showed a first factor of negative affect, accounting for 23% and 34.3% of the variance for children and adolescents, respectively. Third, standardization sample scores on the various inventories were compared to scores on several other instruments (e.g., Children's Depression Inventory, Revised Children's Manifest Anxiety Scale, Conners-Wells Adolescent Self-Report Scale: Short Form, Reynolds Bully Victimization Scales for Schools, Piers-Harris Children's

Self-Concept Scales). These comparisons support appropriate convergent validity for the inventories. Fourth, comparisons were made between a standardization subsample (four groups of approximately 100 children) and matched individuals from two groups: (a) special education (e.g., learning disabled, emotionally disturbed, Attention-Deficit-Hyperactivity Disorder, and behavioral problems; n = 88) and (b) a children's outpatient clinical population (e.g., mood, anxiety, adjustment, attention, disruptive behavior/ODD, and other disorders; n = 107). For adolescents, the comparison group was composed of a clinical adolescent population (n = 178) obtained from a Texas residential facility and a juvenile correctional institution in Colorado that met author-prescribed criteria for anxiety, depression, or Conduct Disorder. A series of comparisons yielded statistically significant t values for all five inventories (BDI-Y, BAI-Y, BDBI-Y, BANI-Y, and BSCI-Y) at all ages, with the exception of depression and anxiety in the child clinical sample for both age groups. Finally, the authors provide profiles of the various clinical groups across the five inventories to facilitate diagnoses differentiation for children and adolescents.

COMMENTARY. The test authors are to be commended for their addition of the self-concept area to the instrument, thereby providing the ability to gather self-reported information from children and adolescents in areas of depression, anxiety, disruptive behavior, anger, and self-concept. The BYI-II is appropriate for school and clinical (inpatient and outpatient) settings. However, the authors make a number of unsupported claims for the instrument: (a) the instrument is purported to be suitable for individual and group administration; (b) administration to lower functioning individuals can be facilitated when the administrator reads items to the individual; and (c) the BYI-II is an appropriate instrument for monitoring change across time. A final shortcoming is the lack of a validity measure or "lie" scale for the instrument. Further, the psychometric properties of the instrument are based on single studies but with groups of children of adequate size to support the claims within the studies (sample sizes ranged from 105 to 192 for convergent studies and 88 to 178 for discrimination studies). Despite these shortcomings, the BYI-II is likely to be a popular assessment tool for clinicians in a variety of settings based on its attributes (e.g., brevity, ease of administration and scoring, assessment of the five areas of concern for a wide age range of children and adolescents). The authors present a number of tables to support the reliability and validity of the BYI-II; however, in the tables the area assessed is interchanged with the name of the inventory of interest (e.g., using "depression" rather than "BDI-Y") making the table entries difficult to match to the instrument. This practice is slightly confusing and interferes with the use of the appropriate name for the inventory, especially within the research context.

SUMMARY. The BYI-II is a useful norm-referenced self-report screener and an efficient tool when paired with other instruments to assess individuals in a variety of settings for five areas of concern (i.e., Depression, Anxiety, Anger, Disruptive Behavior, and Self-Concept). As such, this is likely to be most beneficial in brief assessment of symptom severity in outpatient and inpatient populations. Additionally, the BYI-II may be used in large-scale screening conducted by professionals and supervised nonprofessionals. It yields T-scores and cumulative percentages that may be used in profile analysis across the five areas of concern.

REVIEWER'S REFERENCES

American Psychiatric Association. (2000). *Diagnostic and statistical manual of mental disorders* (4th ed., text revision). Washington, DC: Author.

Bonner, M. (2003). [Review of the Beck Youth Inventories of Emotional and Social Impairment]. In B. S. Plake, J. C. Impara, & R. A. Spies (Eds.), *The fifteenth mental measurements yearbook* (pp. 108-110). Lincoln, NE: Buros Institute of Mental Measurements.

Flesch, R. (1948). A new readability yardstick. *Journal of Applied Psychology, 32,* 221-231.

Stephenson, H. (2003). [Review of the Beck Youth Inventories of Emotional and Social Impairment]. In B. S. Plake, J. C. Impara, & R. A. Spies (Eds.), *The fifteenth mental measurements yearbook* (pp. 110-112). Lincoln, NE: Buros Institute of Mental Measurements.

[12]

Behavioral and Psychological Assessment of Dementia.

Purpose: Designed to "assess changes in behavior and mood associated with the onset of various dementia syndromes."

Population: Ages 30-90.

Publication Date: 2007.

Acronym: BPAD.

Scores, 24: Total Current, Total Past, Total Change, Perceptual/Delusional Current, Perceptual/Delusional Past, Perceptual/Delusional Change, Positive Mood/Anxiety Current, Positive Mood/Anxiety Past, Positive Mood/Anxiety Change, Negative Mood/Anxiety Current, Negative Mood/Anxiety Past, Negative Mood/Anxiety Change, Aggressive Current, Aggressive Past, Aggressive Change, Perseverative/Rigid Current, Perseverative/Rigid Past, Perseverative/Rigid Change, Disinhibited Current, Disinhibited Past, Disinhibited Change, Biological Rhythms Current, Biological Rhythms Past, Biological Rhythms Change.

Administration: Individual.

Price Data, 2010: $260 per software portfolio with on-screen help, quick start guide, professional manual (67 pages), and 25 response booklets; $63 per 25 response booklets; $67 per professional manual.

Time: (15) minutes.

Comments: "Should be completed by family members, paraprofessionals, or other professionals ages 18-90 who have regular contact with individuals who have suspected or diagnosed dementia."

Authors: Kara S. Schmidt and Jennifer L. Gallo.

Publisher: Psychological Assessment Resources, Inc.

Review of the Behavioral and Psychological Assessment of Dementia by SHAWN K. ACHESON, Senior Research Associate, Duke University Medical Center, Raleigh, NC:

DESCRIPTION. The Behavioral and Psychological Assessment of Dementia (BPAD) is a 78-item checklist designed to assess the behavioral and psychological features associated with dementia. It is designed to be completed by someone familiar with the client (e.g., spouse, family member, or other caregiver) in as little as 15 minutes. This instrument is one of few currently available that attempts to capture change in symptomology by asking the informant to rate items based on current status (within the past 4 weeks) and 5 years ago. The intent is to allow clinicians to differentiate the behavioral and psychological features of dementia (which is progressive) from those of a more chronic psychiatric illness. The scores produced are divided into symptom clusters and domains. The Psychopathology symptom cluster consists of the Perceptual/Delusional domain, the Positive Mood/Anxiety domain, and the Negative Mood/Anxiety domain. The Behavioral domain consists of the Aggressive, Perseverative/Rigid and the Disinhibited domains. The last cluster is the Biological symptoms cluster, which contains only the Biological Rhythms domain. Although most of these domains are self-explanatory, a few warrant clarification. The Positive Mood/Anxiety and Negative Mood/Anxiety domains represent an effort to assess affective symptomology that is either inappropriately present (Positive Mood/Anxiety) or inappropriately absent (Negative Mood/Anxiety). The Biological Rhythms domain assesses change in biological functions such as appetite, bowel habits, and sleep. *T* scores and percentiles are provided for each of the domains and the Total BPAD for both present severity and previous severity. These scores are generated using a computer software package included with the price of the instrument.

DEVELOPMENT. The BPAD authors began with 150 items developed from four primary sources: a comprehensive review of the literature, consideration of DSM-IV-TR (APA, 2000) diagnostic criteria of relevant psychopathologies, a review of conceptually similar instruments, and their own clinical wisdom. These items were reduced to 70 by eliminating redundant items and those with little relevance to dementia. These items were then rationally assigned to one of the seven domains. Unfortunately, the rationale for these seven domains (as opposed to other potential domains) is not well articulated. These items were then subjected to rigorous review by relevant professionals including neuropsychologists, geriatricians, and neurologists. During the course of this review process some items were removed, some rewritten and others added based on a rational review of item content, bias, and offensiveness. Confirmation of the domain structure using confirmatory factor analysis would have been useful.

TECHNICAL. The standardization sample is exemplary in terms of number (n = 1,217), demographic make-up (approximates 2003 U.S. Census), and careful inclusion criteria (for both the raters and the individuals being rated). The age range of the sample of rated individuals appears to be 30–90. There appears to be no mean or standard deviation reported for age. Demographic variables such as race/ethnicity, sex, and level of education and age each accounted for little variance (< 5%), except for age, which accounted for almost 8% of the variance in one domain (Disinhibition). Based on these findings, race/ethnicity, sex, and level of education were not used to stratify the norms. Despite the negligible variance accounted for by age, it was used as a stratification variable owing to the importance of age in the onset of dementia. The test authors report that two simple age groups (30–64 and 65–90) best accounted for the age differences observed.

Reliability is described in detail using three different clinical samples as well as the normative sample. Internal consistency reliability is adequate or better in the normative sample for both current symptomology (.80–.97) and past symptomology (.76–.97). It is also adequate in an outpatient dementia sample for all current symptomology domains (.76–.96) and most of the past symptomology domains (.71–.94). However, the Disinhibition and Biological Rhythms domains had internal consistency reliability coefficients of .61 and .67, respectively. Test-retest reliability was assessed in a group of community-dwelling adults over an average interval of approximately 24 days. Correlations varied from .95–.99 for the current symptomology domains and .91–.98 for the past symptomology domains.

The one area of weakness was interrater reliability. Coefficients varied from a low of .49 (Biological Rhythms) to a high of .76 (Positive Mood/Anxiety). Interrater reliability for the Total score was .60 and four of the seven domains had interrater reliability of $\leq$.61. The test authors attempt to dismiss these low values by explaining that the ratings in this pilot sample (which is not described in the manual) were collected over several weeks, making it likely that different raters observed different samples of behavior. The test authors further contend that such interrater values are consistent with other instruments. Although it is true that interrater reliability is often lower than internal consistency values and that this pattern is observed in other instruments, the magnitude of these scores is such that it raises serious questions about the reliability of this instrument. I can say from my own clinical experience with this instrument that this can mean the difference between fully normal domain *T* scores (44–58) provided by one rater to clinically significant scores by another rater (*T* scores: 46–73; 5 of 7 domains clinically elevated). In this clinical example, both raters lived in the home with the patient: one was the primary caregiver and the other worked full-time outside the home. The magnitude of such a difference may reflect problems with specific items or inadequate specificity for rater criterion. In either case, it suggests an absolute need for multiple raters on any given clinical case, and where significant disparities between raters exist, there is a need for additional observations. The interrater reliability coefficients reported in the manual would have been an opportunity to refine items or criteria for appropriate raters. Interestingly, the test authors report an attempt to address this problem by wording items so that "only symptoms that have been observed or witnessed by another individual can be assessed" (professional manual, p. 11). It would have been helpful if raters were given an option to indicate that there was no basis for the observation. There is an important difference between reporting that incontinence was never observed and that there was no basis (no opportunity) to observe incontinence.

Validity scores are also problematic. Although the BPAD total score correlates reasonably well with the Neuropsychiatric Inventory Questionnaire (*r* =.73, NPI-Q; Kaufer et al., 2000) and the Older Adult Behavior Checklist (*r* = .65; Achenbach, Newhouse, & Rescorla, 2004), targeted correlations between subscales on these instruments and the BPAD domains were in many cases inadequate (.43–.75). Four of the seven BPAD scales were not correlated above .6 with relevant NPI-Q or OABC scles. Moreover, there are a few instances where BPAD domains correlate as highly with irrelevant scales as they do with conceptually relevant scales. For example, the Positive Mood/Anxiety domain correlates with the NPI-Q Irritability/Lability scale (.59) and Agitation/Aggression scale (.57) as well as it does with the more relevant NPI-Q Depression/Dysphoria (.51) and the Anxiety scales (.48). Similar problems exist with the BPAD Perceptual/Delusional scale (*r* = .73; NPI-Q Agitation/Aggression) and the Negative Mood/Anxiety scale (*r* = .48; NPI-Q Sleep and Nighttime Behavior Disorder).

Using samples of dementia and psychiatric outpatients and a raw score cutoff of 24 (difference between past and current symptomology), the test authors report modest sensitivity (74.8%) and better specificity (96.2%). That is, the change score was better at detecting psychiatric group membership than dementia group membership. Finally, there are concerns about the absolute validity of retrospective recall, especially when that recall goes back as far as 5 years. This is true for any instrument that makes use of such methods, for example the FrsBE (Grace & Malloy, 2001) not just the BPAD. I am unaware of any studies that have correlated "past" symptomology with current symptomology from an earlier time.

COMMENTARY. On the whole the BPAD fills an important gap in the clinical assessment of dementia. Unfortunately, more work should be done to establish the instrument's validity. This is especially true regarding the assessment of change (current vs. past). I believe the instrument's primary utility lies in the assessment of current behavioral and psychological symptomology that would inform treatment management and caregiver education. There are some other issues that warrant caution in using this instrument in isolation and for the purpose of differential diagnosis. Some of these issues were mentioned above (e.g., the need to use multiple raters, especially where significant discrepancies occur between two raters). Additional concerns relate to the methods used to collect normative data. The normative data were collected through an internet survey, the methods for which are not described in the test manual. Participants were given an incentive in the form of cash prizes. Such methods preclude the opportunity to verify the raters' reports. It is also not clear whether they controlled for multiple entries as can often occur when incentives are provided for completion of anonymous internet surveys. The software used to score the BPAD will be familiar to anyone who has used scoring software developed by PAR. It is generally easy to use but end users would benefit from a number of upgrades. For example, it would be helpful to have Mac versions of scoring software, a common core for all PAR instruments (much like Q-local developed by Pearson Assessments), and an option to administer the instrument on the computer.

SUMMARY. The BPAD is a 78-item, informant-report instrument designed to assess the behavioral and psychological problems associated with dementia, both currently and retrospectively (status of symptoms 5 years ago). It possesses good reliability but only modest validity. Change scores should be used cautiously until further evidence is documented in the literature. Its greatest utility comes from the assessment of current symptomology for the purpose of treatment management and caregiver education. Following additional research, it has the potential to grow into a valuable tool in one's clinical arsenal when assessing older adults with behavioral and psychological complications.

REVIEWER'S REFERENCES

Achenbach, T. M., Newhouse, P. A., & Rescorla, L. A. (2004). *Manual for the ASEBA Older Adult Forms & Profiles.* Burlington: University of Vermont, Research Center for Children, Youth, and Families.

American Psychiatric Association. (2000). *Diagnostic and statistical manual of mental disorders* (4th ed., text rev.). Washington, DC: Author.

Grace, J., & Malloy, P. F. (2001). *Frontal Systems Behavior Scale: Professional manual.* Lutz, FL: Psychological Assessment Resources.

Kaufer, D. I., Cummings, J. L., Ketchel, P., Smith, V., MacMillan, A., Selley, T., et al. (2000). Validation of the NPI-Q, a brief clinical form of the Neuropsychiatric Inventory. *The Journal of Neuropsychiatry and Clinical Neurosciences, 12*, 233–239.

Review of the Behavioral and Psychological Assessment of Dementia by ANITA M. HUBLEY, Professor of Measurement, Evaluation, and Research Methodology, University of British Columbia, Vancouver, British Columbia, Canada:

DESCRIPTION. The Behavioral and Psychological Assessment of Dementia (BPAD) is a paper-and-pencil informant report measure that provides proxy ratings of behavioral and psychological symptoms of dementia (BPSD) in individuals over the age of 30. The BPAD consists of 78 items that cover perceptual disturbances, hallucinations, and delusions (Perceptual/Delusional [PD] domain; 13 items), presence of active symptoms of depression and anxiety (Positive Mood/Anxiety [PMA] domain; 12 items), absence of normal range of affect and activity (Negative Mood/Anxiety [NMA] domain; 11 items), aggressive and/or threatening behavior (Aggressive [AGG] domain; 10 items), inflexibility and perseverative behaviors (Perseverative/Rigid [PR] domain; 9 items), lack of impulse control and inappropriate social behavior (Disinhibited [DIS] domain; 13 items), and changes in eating, bowel movements, and sleep habits (Biological Rhythms [BIO] domain; 10 items). These symptoms are rated using a 5-point frequency scale (0 = *never*, 1 = *once in a while*, 2 = *sometimes*, 3 = *quite often*, 4 = *very frequently*) at two time points ("within the past 4 weeks" and "5 years ago"). Proxy raters may be family members, paraprofessionals, or professionals who have regular contact with the individual being rated.

Administration of the BPAD is straightforward and takes about 15 minutes. The instructions are brief and clear. Scoring may be accomplished by entering the responses to items into the computer scoring program; data entry is fairly quick but the ease with which data entry errors can be made is a concern. The BPAD can be scored by hand, but it is up to the test user to develop a method for doing this easily; tables for converting raw scores to *T*-scores and percentiles are provided in the manual.

DEVELOPMENT. The BPAD was designed to be a comprehensive assessment of changes in behavior and mood associated with the onset and progression of dementia; change over time is meant to distinguish BPSD from longstanding psychiatric illness. The initial pool of 150 items was based on a comprehensive review of BPSD literature since 1980; a review of five published measures assessing neuropsychiatric symptoms of dementia; a review of symptoms associated with depressive and bipolar disorders, anxiety disorders, schizophrenia, and other psychotic disorders in the DSM-IV-TR; and the test authors' clinical experiences and observations of BPSD. Once items with overlapping content and/or less relevance to dementia patients were removed, the remaining 70 items were divided into seven symptom domains as described above. An expert panel ($N = 5$) review resulted in revisions and a 79-item version. Items reflected a sixth grade reading level based on the Flesch-Kincaid Index. A bias panel of five clinicians and nonclinicians from various ethnic groups agreed all items were free from bias. A Delphi panel of eight professionals, asked to rate the suitability of items to their respective domains, rated all items highly. An item tryout was also conducted; some potential item endorsement problems and a few unsatisfactory internal consistencies for a couple of domains were noted. It is unclear how the test authors addressed these problems. Two experts in BPSD conducted a Q-sort and assigned each item to one of the seven domains; overall, their assignments were highly consistent with those of the test authors, except for the Aggressive domain (70% agreement). The final version of the BPAD consisted of 78 items. In reviewing this final version, only two items (#39 – weight loss, #54 – mood change) appear awkward to respond to using the frequency response format. The response booklet is well laid out with an easy-to-read large font used throughout.

TECHNICAL. The final normative sample consisted of 1,217 community adults who completed the BPAD via the Internet. To be eligible, raters had to be 18 years or older, able to read at a Grade 6 level or higher, have regular contact with the rated individual, have no uncorrected hearing or visual impairment, and be able to provide informed consent. The rated individual had to be 30 years or older, living independently in the community, have no history of significant memory problems or neuropsychiatric disease, no evidence of alcohol or drug-related disorders, and no active medical illness that might affect cognition. The normative sample of rated individuals closely approximated the 2003 U.S. Census in terms of gender, race/ethnicity, education, and geographic region. Analyses indicated little or no influence of the rated individuals' age, gender, race/ethnicity, or educational level; the decision to provide separate norms for rated individuals aged 30–64 and 65–90 years was based on the known relationship between age and onset of dementia. It would be useful to know whether raters' age, gender, race/ethnicity, and education impact BPAD total and domain scores.

The computerized Score Report provides raw scores, *T*-scores, and percentile ranks for current, past, and change total and domain scores, a profile of the obtained *T*-scores, and a table showing raw scores for each item. All domain scores and item information is presented by symptom cluster (psychopathological, behavioral, biological). The test authors recommend using a *T*-score of 60 as suggestive of a significant elevation in symptoms. *T*-scores for change are based on absolute raw scores so direction needs to be examined separately, but this is clearly noted in the Score Report. A description of symptom clusters and domains as well as three case studies are provided in the test manual.

Internal consistency estimates were excellent for the BPAD current and past total scores for both the normative sample and a sample of 121 dementia outpatients. Alpha coefficients for the domain scores were satisfactory to excellent (.76 to .92) for the normative sample and unsatisfactory to excellent (.61 to .91) for the dementia outpatients. Test-retest reliability estimates based on ratings of 50 community adults were excellent for both current and past symptoms. The average test-retest interval was 23.92 days. Internal and test-retest reliability estimates for change scores were not provided but would have been useful. Interrater reliabilities of current total and domain scores were examined using raters for 52 residents with dementia from an assisted living facility; estimates were generally unsatisfactory (.49 to .76).

Support for content validity was obtained in the test development phase with the use of a Delphi panel and use of Q-sort analyses. Evidence for convergent validity was obtained by examining correlations between current total and domain BPAD scores and three other measures used to assess BPSD in individuals with dementia who were outpatients or residents at an assisted living facility. These results are generally supportive of the inferences made from BPAD scores, but greater attention needs to be paid to the pattern of correlations presented and similarly high correlations obtained with scores not highlighted by the test authors. Correlations were also examined between BPAD total and domain raw change scores and measures of cognitive functioning, daily activities, and caregiver burden. Although these results also were generally supportive, this evidence would have been stronger if the kind of evidence one would expect to see to support the validity of inferences from the BPAD had been clearly outlined. In examining criterion validity, the BPAD total change score was found to correctly classify 81.4% of cases into the correct diagnostic group (i.e., dementia outpatients vs. outpatients with psychiatric illness). A maximum number of correct classifications were obtained using a raw change score cutoff of 24 but more psychiatric outpatients (96.2%) than dementia outpatients (74.8%) were correctly classified.

COMMENTARY. The BPAD is a brief and easily administered informant report measure of BPSD. Scoring by hand is cumbersome; scoring by computer is easy but subject to data entry errors. The Response Booklet and Score Report are well designed. The development of the BPAD was excellent and unusually thorough. Normative information is well presented. Greater attention needs to be paid to the potential impact of raters' characteristics, including their level of contact with the rated individual, on scores. Internal consistency estimates for current and past total and domain scores were generally very good, but a couple of low alphas in the dementia group suggest some domains need to be examined further. Moreover, the factor structure of the total BPAD and its domains still needs to be examined. Test-retest reliabilities for current and past total and domain scores were excellent. Reliability needs to be examined for the change scores. Interrater reliabilities were unsatisfactory, indicating that the information one obtains can vary significantly across raters. The currently presented validity evidence is limited but promising and would benefit from the presentation of reliability estimates for convergent measures and greater attention to the expected pattern of validity coefficients to support the intended BPAD score inferences. Further validation work is clearly needed.

SUMMARY. The BPAD shows considerable promise as an informant report measure of BPSD. Overall, the test authors are to be commended for the extensive work they have conducted in developing this measure and for the extent of reliability and validity evidence they have presented thus far. As a new measure of BPSD, the BPAD is worth considering but more reliability and validity evidence is needed, especially evidence that supports the use of the BPAD over other available measures of BPSD such as the Neuropsychiatric Inventory Questionnaire (NPI-Q; Kaufer et al., 2000) and the Behavioral Pathology in Alzheimer's Disease Rating Scale (BEHAVE-AD; Reisberg et al., 1987).

REVIEWER'S REFERENCES

Kaufer, D. I., Cummings, J. L., Ketchel, P., Smith, V., MacMillan, A., Shelley, T., Lopez, O. L., & DeKosky, S. T. (2000). Validation of the NPI-Q, a brief clinical form of the Neuropsychiatric Inventory. *The Journal of Neuropsychiatry and Clinical Neurosciences, 12,* 233-239.

Reisberg, B., Borenstein, J., Salob, S. P., Ferris, S. H., Franssen, E., & Georgotas, A. (1987). Behavioral symptoms in Alzheimer's disease: Phenomenology and treatment. *Journal of Clinical Psychiatry, 48* (Suppl. 5), 9-15.

[13]

Bracken Basic Concept Scale: Expressive.

Purpose: Used to measure "a child's ability to verbally label basic concepts."
Population: Ages 3-0 to 6-11.
Publication Date: 2006.
Acronym: BBCS:E.
Scores, 13: 10 subtest scores (Colors, Letters/Sounds, Numbers/Counting, Sizes/Comparisons, Shapes, Direction/Position, Self-/Social Awareness, Texture/Material, Quantity, Time/Sequence); 3 composite scores (School Readiness Composite, Expressive School Readiness Composite, Expressive Total Composite).
Administration: Individual.
Price Data, 2007: $235 per complete kit including manual (2006, 205 pages), stimulus book, and 25 English record forms; $219 per stimulus book; $47 per 25 English record forms; $47 per 25 Spanish record forms; $78 per manual; $149 per Bracken scoring assistant.
Foreign Language Edition: Criterion-referenced Spanish edition included.
Time: 25(30) minutes.
Comments: For use with the Bracken Basic Concept Scale–Third Edition: Receptive (18:14).
Author: Bruce A. Bracken.
Publisher: Pearson.

Review of the Bracken Basic Concept Scale: Expressive by R. ANTHONY DOGGETT, Associate Professor of School Psychology, Mississippi State University, Starkville, MS:

DESCRIPTION. The Bracken Basic Concept Scale: Expressive (BBCS:E) is an individually administered instrument designed for evaluating a child's ability to verbally label basic concepts. The BBCS:E can be administered to children ages 3 years, 0 months through 6 years, 11 months and assesses important educational concepts across 10 categories: Colors, Letters/Sounds, Numbers/Counting, Sizes/Comparisons, Shapes, Direction/Position, Self-/Social Awareness, Texture/Material, Quantity, and Time/Sequence. The first five subtests are combined to yield the School Readiness Composite (SRC), "which is designed to assess educationally relevant concepts children have traditionally needed to know to be prepared for early formal education" (manual, p. 1). In addition, all 10 subtests are combined to yield an Expressive Total Composite score (Expressive TC). Finally, the BBCS:E has been translated into a Spanish version that is similar in format, administration, and scoring to the English version of the instrument.

The BBCS:E may be administered by individuals who have been properly trained to administer, score, and interpret standardized tests and by paraprofessionals receiving appropriate levels of supervision. The BBCS:E requires approximately 20–25 minutes to complete depending on the age and ability of the child being assessed. The English version of the BBCS:E yields scaled subtest scores and composite scores for the Expressive SRC and Expressive TC. Subtest scores have been scaled to a mean of 10 and a standard deviation of 3, whereas composite scores have a mean of 100 and a standard deviation of 15. In addition, percentile ranks, concept age equivalents, and descriptive classifications are provided for all subtests and the Expressive TC score. The Spanish version of the BBCS:E provides percent mastery scores as opposed to norm-referenced scores "and is intended to be used as a criterion-referenced or curriculum-based measure" (manual, p. 4). Basal and ceiling rules have been established to reduce administration time and are clearly outlined in the manual in narrative form and supplemented by several illustrations. Directions for administering and scoring each subtest are provided in the manual and a shortened version of the directions is provided in the Expressive Record Form. Specific instructions also are provided for using the instrument with children who are colorblind, out-of-age range, or have specific special needs.

The BBCS:E is accompanied by a 205-page manual complete with seven chapters providing an overview of the instrument and discussing the administration, scoring, interpretation, development, standardization, reliability, and validity of the English and Spanish versions. In addition, a comprehensive chapter discussing the relationship between the content contained on the BBCS:E and early childhood educational standards influenced by professional organizations, governmental initiatives, and current practices is included in the manual. The easel-backed Expressive Stimulus Book accompanies the manual and contains the full-color picture stimuli necessary to administer all test items. In addition, all 10 subtests are divided by tabs providing a user-friendly method for identifying the beginning of each subtest. A soft black case may be purchased separately to house the manual and stimulus book.

DEVELOPMENT. According to the test author, the *Standards for Educational and Psychological Testing* (American Educational Research Association, American Psychological Association, & National Council on Measurement in Education, 1999) served as the primary resource for providing the criteria necessary for proper test development and use. Based on guidance from the *Standards*, pilot studies were conducted with three separate samples to evaluate the administration directions and scoring rules, subtest and item performance across different ages, success of the visual and verbal stimuli in eliciting the desired response, range of item difficulty, performance of children with typically developing language, performance of children identified with language impairments, and administration time. Modifications were made to the instrument based on the results of the pilot studies and a nationwide tryout including 529 children ages 3 years, 0 months through 6 years, 11 months across the U.S. In addition, a clinical study of 33 children previously diagnosed with receptive and language impairments and receiving services was conducted to select test items with the best clinical utility.

TECHNICAL.

Standardization. The BBCS:E was standardized on a sample of 640 children (drawn from an initial sample of more than 750 children) that included 80 children in each of the 6-month age groups. The sample was representative of the current U.S. population and was stratified on the basis of age, gender, race/ethnicity, geographic region, and parent educational level. Participants were required to take the test in a standardized manner without any procedural modifications, use spoken language to communicate, and could not have been diagnosed with behavioral or emotional disorders. The standardized edition of the BBCS:E was administered by 186 speech-language pathologists, psychologists, and educational diagnosticians in 43 states who met stringent training criteria prior to being allowed to participate in the standardization study. Detailed information regarding the development and standardization of the BBCS:E Spanish version is also included in the manual.

Reliability. The test author reported test-retest stability, internal consistency, and interscorer agreement. Average corrected test-retest stability coefficients for the entire sample ranged from .83 to .90 on the subtests and from .91 to .95 on the two composite scores. Effect sizes ranged from .16 to .23 across the subtests and composites across all ages. Additional test-retest stability data are reported in the manual for the two separate age bands. The typical interval between testing sessions was 7 days. Internal consistency data were reported for participants in the normative sample and two clinical groups (52 children with language impairments, 64 children with intellectual disabilities). Average split-half reliability coefficients ranged from .81 to .96 for the subtests for the normative sample. Overall mean split-half reliability coefficients were .97 for the Expressive TC and .96 for the Expressive SRC. Average split-half reliability coefficients examined by gender and race/ethnicity as well as for the two clinical groups yielded results that were consistent with the coefficients reported for the normative sample. Interscorer agreement was calculated by correlating the subtest total raw scores from two scorers who scored each record form independently. The correlations ranged from .96 to .99 across the subtests.

Validity. Evidence for the validity of the BBCS:E was evaluated based on test content, response processes, internal structure, relationship with other variables, and clinical usage. Content validity was established by reviews conducted by the test author, national and international test developers, and expert panels. In addition, content of the BBCS:E was compared to early childhood educational standards for each of the 50 U.S. states. Additional evidence of validity was established through quantitative and qualitative analyses of the responses provided during instrument development. Evidence for the internal structure of the instrument was established by examining the patterns of intercorrelations between the subtests and composite scores. Intercorrelations across all ages at the subtest level ranged from .53 to .69 and was .77 between the two composite scores. Correlational studies were conducted to examine the relationship between the BBCS:E and the Bracken Basic Concept Scale—Third Edition: Receptive (BBCS-3: R; Bracken, 2006) and the Preschool Language Scale—Fourth Edition (PLS-4; Zimmerman, Steiner, & Pond, 2002). Correlations between the BBCS:E and BBCS-3: R ranged from .54 to .80 for the subtests and .81–.83 for the composite scores. Correlations between corresponding subtests of the BBCS:E and the PLS-4 ranged from .45 to .70 overall. Special group studies were also conducted with 35 children diagnosed with language impairments and 64 children diagnosed with intellectual disability matched to children in the normative sample for age, race/ethnicity, parent education level, and gender. The effect sizes were large for all subtests and composites on both studies with the exception of the SRC in the study comparing the children diagnosed with language impairments to the matched control group. Finally, sensitivity was .83 and specificity was .86 at -1 *SD* providing good evidence for the clinical utility of the instrument.

COMMENTARY. The BBCS:E has several important strengths. These include (a) easy administration and scoring procedures, (b) user-friendly manual that is well-organized and employs graphics to convey technical information and figures to assist with proper scoring of items, (c) colorful and developmentally appropriate visual stimuli designed to capture children's interests, (d) summary and profile components on the record form that aid in the interpretation and explanation of results, (e) thorough and impressive development and standardization procedures, (f) overall good reliability and validity evidence, and (g) development of a Spanish version of the instrument. Despite these strengths, the BBCS:E evaluates only a child's verbal ability to label basic concepts. Therefore, the BBCS:E would be best used as part of a battery that included other measures such as the BBCS-3:R in order to evaluate the child's knowledge of basic concepts using both expressive and receptive measures.

SUMMARY. The BBCS:E was designed to evaluate children's abilities on 10 foundational and functionally relevant educational concepts necessary for formal education. The BBCS:E may be administered to children ranging in age from 3 years, 0 months to 6 years, 11 months in approximately 20–25 minutes. Although efficient for use as an instrument for examining a child's ability to verbally label basic concepts, the instrument will be best utilized as a component of a thorough assessment battery for assessing children's acquired skills and abilities. Finally, further investigation with populations and instruments other than those used by the test author will continue to provide valuable information about the psychometric properties and clinical utility of the instrument.

REVIEWER'S REFERENCES

American Educational Research Association, American Psychological Association, & National Council on Measurement in Education. (1999). *Standards for educational and psychological testing*. Washington, DC: American Educational Research Association.

Bracken, B. A. (2006). Bracken Basic Concept Scale-Third Edition: Receptive (BBCS-3: R). San Antonio, TX: Harcourt Assessment, Inc.

Zimmerman, I. L., Steiner, V. G., & Pond, R. E. (2002). Preschool Language Scale-Fourth Edition (PLS-4). San Antonio, TX: The Psychological Corporation.

Review of the Bracken Basic Concept Scale: Expressive by GREGORY SNYDER, Clinical Child and Adolescent Psychologist, Children's Hospital, Omaha, NE:

DESCRIPTION. The Bracken Basic Concept Scale: Expressive (BBCS:E) is an individually administered test of a child's ability to understand and verbally label pre-academic concepts. Normed along with the Bracken Basic Concept Scale—Third Edition: Receptive, the BBCS:E can be administered to children ages 3 years, 0 months through 6 years, 11 months. The test contains 10 subtests measuring children's comprehension and ability to label colors, directions/positions, letters and sounds, sizes and comparisons, shapes, time and sequencing, numbers and counting, self- and social awareness, textures, and quantities. Authors of the evaluation reported that the above-mentioned conceptual categories and their implicit discriminations are quite useful when determining a child's ability to enter the traditional school setting.

The first five subtests (Colors, Letters/Sounds, Numbers/Counting, Sizes/Comparisons, and Shapes) are summarized as a global School Readiness Composite (SRC) index scale. The remaining subtests (Direction/Position, Self-/Social Awareness, Texture/Material, Quantity, and Time/Sequencing) yield separate scaled scores and are not included in the overall SRC, but are helpful during a more detailed assessment of a child's expressive language abilities and general comprehension of the above mentioned pre-academic skills. Start points for Subtests 1–5 are based on chronological age, whereas start points for the remaining five subtests are staggered based upon the SRC composite score, which aids examiners by reducing administration time.

Scaled scores for all subtests, including the SRC, are separated into 3-month age bands. Corresponding percentile rankings, general descriptors, and age equivalents are also provided.

DEVELOPMENT. The BBCS:E was developed and co-normed with its functional counterpart, the Bracken Basic Concept Scale–Third Edition: Receptive (Bracken, 2006; 18:14). The author of both assessments sought to identify and standardize a collection of basic concepts that children are frequently required to understand upon beginning their formal education. As formal standards were explicated by the National Association for the Education of Young Children (NAEYC) and National Association of Early Childhood Specialists in State Departments of Education (NAECS; 2003), curriculum goals, standards, and definitions became broadly agreed upon for children's initial mastery of basic concepts. Consequently the author of the BBCS-3: R and BBCS:E attempted to include, refine, and measure the latest revisions to curriculum standards set forth by both the NAEYC and NAECS. According to the test author, the recent addition of the BBCS:E arose due to feedback from clinicians and trends in psychoeducational testing of children.

TECHNICAL. The BBCS:E and BBCS-3: R norms were based on a sample of 640 children, stratified on the basis of age, gender, race/ethnicity, geographic region, and parent education level based upon 2003 U.S. Census data. The normative sample included 80 children in each of the 6-month age groups (160 children per year). Of the total sample, 14% of the participant children reportedly received special services or were enrolled in special programs, with less than 1% of these children reportedly receiving gifted and talented services. Reliability of the instrument was reported by the test author in terms of test-retest reliability, internal consistency, and interscorer reliability. Internal consistency estimates of the SRC ranged from .92 to .97 among the 6-month age intervals. Internal consistency estimates of the remaining five subtests were slightly lower and more variable than the SRC, ranging from .64 to .96. Stability coefficients reported by the test author ranged from .87 to .93 for the SRC, and .80 to .91 for the remaining five supplementary subtests. The typical interval between testing sessions was 7 days.

A Spanish translation of the BBCS:E was included in the standardization. Some items on the Spanish version are direct translations from the English counterpart, whereas others are adapted based upon the inexact nature of language equivalence. Because of these challenges, some items are repeated (big and large are both *grande* in Spanish) and some items are skipped entirely due to the inability to identify a direct Spanish equivalent. Therefore, the degree of equivalence between English and Spanish versions is unknown. In the test manual, the test author reports one field research trial that included 61 Spanish-speaking children between 3 years, 0 months and 6 years, 11 months of age residing in the United States. Children were identified by parental report of the primary language spoken in the home. Due to sample size limitations, stratification of the sample based on gender, SES, geographic region, and parent education level could not be performed. Split-half reliability was similar to the standardization sample with the BBCS:E English version with coefficients ranging from .89 for Time/Sequencing to .99 for the SRC index scale. Total Expressive Concept scores yielded good internal consistency (r = .98).

Validity studies conducted by the test author compared the BBCS:E with the Preschool Language Scale—Fourth Edition (PLS-4; Zimmerman, Steiner, & Pond, 2002) and the Bracken Basic Concept Scale—Third Edition: Receptive (Bracken, 2006) assessments. The assumptions of construct, divergent, and convergent validity were largely presupposed based upon prior work with validating earlier versions of the Bracken Basic Concept Scale. The test author cites two studies that were completed as a part of the standardization process of the BBCS:E, one examining the relationship between the Receptive and Expressive versions of the BBCS and one comparing the BBCS:E with a pre-existing, widely used measure of expressive language (PLS-4). As expected, relationships among the Receptive and Expressive versions of the BBCS were significant and most pronounced for the SRC (disparate reports of r = .80 and r = .81). Total composite index scales were also closely related between the two measures (r = .83). The relationship between the PLS-4 and the BBCS:E was moderate to high, with Expressive Total Composite scores on the BBCS:E evincing an r = .77 with the Expressive Composite and .78 with the Total Language Score on the PLS-4.

The author provided some preliminary data about the discriminative power of the BBCS:E when predicting concurrent language impairment. Using the Expressive Total Composite score to predict language impairment among four separate base rates (20%, 70%, 80%, 90%), the BBCS:E yielded Sensitivity and Specificity of .83 and .86, respectively, suggesting adequate discrimination between typically developing and language-impaired children and adolescents.

COMMENTARY. The BBCS:E is a newly developed measure of expressive language and verbal concept formation that was developed out of the original and revised versions of the Bracken Basic Concept Scale. This most recent revision of the Bracken, which is one of the typically used assessments in the preschool age group, attempted to create an equivalent form of its classic receptive basic concept scale. The separation of receptive versus expressive language components is both theoretically and conceptually important; however, the clinical implications and utility of assessing basic concept development with both assessments remains a question to be answered in future research studies. In other words, the test author failed to identify the marginal or incremental utility of adding this assessment to a battery that would likely include either screening for, or formal assessment of, expressive and language functioning. The author provided some evidence, albeit limited, supporting the construct validity and equivalence with the BBCS-3:R. The author supplied very limited information pertaining directly to the BBCS:E with respect to content validity and instead referred to past research with previous versions of the BBCS, none of which had been separated according to expressive/receptive language versions.

In the manual, the author suggests that separating the assessments according to language modality can be an important and clinically useful tool when discriminating between children with potential language impairments that may impact their school readiness and acquisition of fundamental pre-academic skills critical for success in primary school. As the assessment misses some critical aspects of expressive language development, the BBCS:E should not be used solely to distinguish language-impaired from non-language-impaired children. However, poor scores on this evaluation together with age-appropriate scores on the BBCS-3:R would certainly suggest further, formalized language assessment.

Although the construction of a Spanish translation of the BBCS:E is commendable, the validity of the instrument has yet to be established. In the study reported by the test author, the Spanish translation of the BBCS:E was administered to Spanish-speaking children residing in the United States. It remains unclear whether knowledge of the Spanish concepts also predicts school readiness and performance as children enter primary school. It would be critical for future revisions of the BBCS:E to focus on creating a truly parallel Spanish form or simply allowing Spanish responses to the English version. It also remains unclear whether the Spanish form, administered to children residing in the United States, yields similar predictive validity as the English version.

SUMMARY. The Bracken Basic Concept Scale: Expressive version is an extension and expressive equivalent of the classic Bracken Basic Concept Scale (now referred to as the Bracken Basic Concept Scale, Third Edition: Receptive; 18:14). With this latest revision the author has successfully created a parallel version to the BBCS-3: Receptive. Although the author clearly attempts to demonstrate the utility of this assessment when identifying language-impaired children, such an interpretation based solely on this assessment is inappropriate. It is unclear whether this latest revision serves to change the original objective of the BBCS or simply add language as a clinical covariate within the context of a battery of assessment. Specifically, poor scores on this assessment could be attributed to language impairment, limited preschool exposure, or general cognitive delays. Scores from the BBCS:E and its counterpart BBCS-3: R would serve to support the diagnosis of a language disorder, but cannot be made unless more thorough evaluation of a child's language has been completed. The author also attempted to provide a parallel Spanish form; however, caution is suggested when using this assessment because of limited supporting data about the content validity, concurrent validity, and predictive validity of this device with Spanish-speaking children.

REVIEWER'S REFERENCES

Bracken, B. A. (2006). Bracken Basic Concept Scale—Third Edition: Receptive (BBCS-3: R). San Antonio, TX: Harcourt Assessment, Inc.

National Association of Early Childhood Specialists in State Departments of Education (NAECS) & National Association for the Education of Young Children (NAEYC). (2003). *Early childhood curriculum, assessment, and program evaluation: Building an effective, accountable system in programs for children birth through age 8.* Retrieved June 5, 2008, from http://www.naeyc.org/about/positins/pdf/pscape.pdf.

Zimmerman, I. L., Steiner, V. G., & Pond, R. E. (2002). Preschool Language Scale, Fourth Edition. San Antonio, TX: The Psychological Corporation.

[14]

Bracken Basic Concept Scale–Third Edition: Receptive.

Purpose: Designed to measure relevant educational concepts and receptive language skills.
Population: Ages 3-0 to 6-11.
Publication Dates: 1984-2006.
Acronym: BBCS-3:R.
Scores, 8: 5 subtest scores (Direction/Position, Self-/Social Awareness, Texture/Material, Quantity, Time/Sequence); 3 composite scores (School Readiness Composite, Receptive School Readiness Composite, Receptive Total Composite).
Administration: Individual.
Price Data, 2007: $312 per complete kit including manual (2006, 208 pages), stimulus book, and 25 English record forms; $219 per stimulus book; $47 per 25 English record forms; $47 per 25 Spanish record forms; $103 per manual, $149 per Bracken scoring assistant.
Foreign Language Edition: Criterion-referenced Spanish edition included.
Time: (30-40) minutes.
Comments: For use with the Bracken Basic Concept Scale: Expressive (18:13).
Author: Bruce A. Bracken.
Publisher: Pearson.
Cross-References: For reviews of an earlier edition by Leah M. Nellis and Rhonda H. Solomon, see 14:48; see also T5:331 (6 references) and T4:319 (4 references); for reviews by Timothy L. Turco and James E. Ysseldyke of the original edition, see 10:33.

Review of the Bracken Basic Concept Scale–Third Edition: Receptive by GRETCHEN OWENS, Professor of Child Study, St. Joseph's College, Patchogue, NY:

DESCRIPTION. This 2006 revision of the Bracken Basic Concept Scale is designed to determine the extent to which children ages 3 years, 0 months to 6 years, 11 months have developed an understanding of basic terms and concepts needed for success in formal schooling. The test author states that the instrument can be used to assess progress and response to intervention, assist in identifying children with language impairments, and help professionals decide on eligibility for speech-language services. Because the Bracken Basic

Concept Scale—Third Edition: Receptive (BBCS-3:R) was conormed with a new instrument, the Bracken Basic Concept Scale: Expressive (BBCS:E; 18:13), the two measures used in conjunction can indicate whether there is a significant discrepancy between the child's ability to comprehend basic concepts and to verbally label them (i.e., receptive versus expressive language skills). A Spanish version is also available, but the Spanish standardization sample was too small to produce adequate norms. It is solely criterion-referenced.

The manual includes a reproducible Parent/Teacher Conference Form that indicates whether the child has mastered (M) or not mastered (NM) each of the terms. A computerized scoring assistant is available that maintains an ongoing record of M and NM concepts for each child. To complete the curricular link, a separately purchased product, the Bracken Concept Development Program (BCDP), is available. It provides activities and reproducible written materials for individual, small group, and large group instruction in the concepts that appear in the BBCS-3:R. For students with diagnosed special needs, the test author recommends using results from the BBCS-3:R to develop goals for the child's Individualized Education Plan, with the BCDP worksheets used intermittently to assess short-term progress and re-administration of the BBCS-3:R to assess long-term growth.

As in earlier versions, the child points to the picture (out of four presented) that depicts a given concept. The 282 items are grouped into 10 subtests. The first 5 subtests evaluate the child's understanding of 85 concepts that parents and preschool/kindergarten teachers typically teach children to prepare them for formal education (Colors, Letters, Numbers/Counting, Sizes/Comparisons, and Shapes). Instead of providing separate scores for these subtests, raw scores from the 5 subtests are combined and converted to a School Readiness Composite (Receptive SRC). The other 5 subtests (Direction/Position, Self-/Social Awareness, Texture/Material, Quantity, and Time/Sequence) are each scored separately and awarded scaled scores (M = 10, SD = 3). All 10 subtests are then combined for a Receptive Total Composite (Receptive TC) with a mean of 100 and a standard deviation of 15. If the BBCS-Expressive test has also been given, a discrepancy analysis section allows comparison of the child's receptive and expressive skills. The manual states that the School Readiness Composite ordinarily can be completed in 10–15 minutes, the total BBCS-3:R in 30–40 minutes.

DEVELOPMENT. Goals for the current revision included updating test items, artwork, and normative data; adding more low-level items to better identify very young children with concept deficits; providing a way to compare a child's skills in the comprehension and expression of concepts; and organizing content to align with states' standards for early childhood education. After getting user feedback about the previous edition, reviewing recent literature on language development, and having a three-person panel review the tryout items for content and cultural bias, a number of items were added, deleted, or revised to make them more current and culturally universal. Then a nationwide tryout was conducted in 2004–2005 that involved 529 children with no diagnosed language impairments and 33 who currently were receiving speech/language services. Based on feedback from the 214 examiners and inspection of commonly occurring incorrect responses to see whether the directions and/or the pictures required modification, more items were changed or deleted. In 2005–2006, a nationwide standardization and two clinical research studies were conducted in order to develop norms and provide the data needed as evidence of clinical utility and psychometric adequacy.

TECHNICAL.

Standardization. The tryout sample (N = 529) and the nonclinical normative sample (N = 640) closely approximate the 2002 and 2003 U.S. Bureau of the Census statistics, respectively, in terms of sex, race/ethnicity, geographic region, and education level of the child's primary caregiver. Though the original normative sample excluded children with language impairments, the sample was later stratified so that 4.8% of the sample were children with diagnosed language impairments.

Norms were developed using Inferential Norming methods. Conversion tables provide standard scores, percentile ranks, and descriptive classifications for the subtests and composites; age equivalents for the subtests; and confidence intervals for the Receptive Total Composite.

Reliability. Reliability was estimated by means of test-retest stability and internal consistency studies. The stability coefficients were in the upper .70s through the upper .80s for subtests and

.84 for the SRC based on a sample of 87 children who were retested an average of 1 week after the initial administration (range = 2–30 days). The split-half method, applied to the total sample of 640 children, indicated high internal consistency (on average ≥ .90) for both composite scores at all ages and for each subtest when all ages were combined. Coefficients for two clinical groups (52 children with language impairments and 64 with intellectual disabilities) were even higher (.96–.99) than for the normative sample due to the greater range of scores among these groups. Average standard errors of measurement across all age groups ranged from .55–.95 for subtests (which have a mean of 10) and 2–4 points for the composites (mean of 100).

Validity. The test author argues for the test's validity by noting that during the revision process, the content was reviewed by test developers and by "an expert panel of speech language pathologists and psychologists" (manual, p. 112). To determine item appropriateness, he also drew up a matrix showing state educational standards for early childhood education and indicated which standards the test addresses (manual, Appendix G).

Evidence of convergent and construct validity is presented in terms of the moderate intercorrelations (.54–.68) between subtests, which presumably all measure basic language concepts. As further evidence, the test author cites results from published studies of earlier versions, which indicated that the BBCS content is significantly associated with intelligence, academic achievement, and language development. Two new construct validation studies also were conducted. One study showed moderate to high degrees of association between the newer version and the previous one, with subtest correlations ranging from .69 to .84 and correlations between composite scores of .85. (The scores on the newer version were about 7–9 points lower, with practice effects likely accounting for about half of this difference.) In the second study, moderate correlations of .46–.77 were found between BBCS-3:R scores and scores on the Preschool Language Scale—Fourth Edition (PLS-4), indicating that the two tests measure similar but not identical skills.

To investigate discriminant validity, two additional clinical studies were conducted. The first involved 35 children with language impairments (the majority having other conditions as well), each matched with a child from the normative sample. Results showed very highly significant differences between the two groups. In a second study, scores were significantly higher for the normally developing 6-year-olds in the BBCS-3:R standardization sample than for 64 older children with intellectual impairments (ages 7 years, 1 month to 12 years, 8 months).

To evaluate test sensitivity and specificity, the test author used data from the clinical study comparing normally developing children to those with language impairments. Using a cut point of one standard deviation below the mean, the BBCS-3:R accurately identified 71% of the children with language impairments as having language problems that warranted further testing (sensitivity), and it accurately identified 83% of the normally developing children as having no impairment (specificity). The manual provides further sensitivity and specificity data for different prevalence rates (20%, 50%, 70%, 80%, and 90%) that apply to a variety of clinical populations.

COMMENTARY. The test author's provision of information about the test's sensitivity and specificity is appreciated, but these data indicate a rate of false positives and false negatives that warrant caution even for screening purposes. The test's failure to identify a quarter of the children with diagnosed language impairments in the clinical sample is worrisome. With a lower base rate (20%), the rate of false negatives would drop to 8%, but the corresponding 49% false *positive* rate would unnecessarily alarm the parents of half the children identified as possibly needing services. Further studies by the test author or others might reveal a subset of items that have better positive and/or negative predictive power than the Receptive Total Composite score does. In studies of earlier versions, the briefer School Readiness Composite score did a better job of predicting first-grade academic achievement among African American children (Panter, 2000) and of identifying at-risk children (Stebbins & McIntosh, 1996) than the Total Composite score did.

The manual for the BBCS-3:R is comprehensive and frequently instructive, with the test author providing discussions of his rationale for some of the test development decisions and detailed explanations of various psychometric analyses. However, a more careful editing would be beneficial. An unfortunate lack of precision appears in a few portions of the technical chapters. (For example, in the description of the normative sample, does the table showing demographic information include the clinical group or not? How many children were actually in the final norm group?) Clarity is especially crucial when providing procedural directions for examiners. With eight scoring examples provided, it would be helpful if one showed a double basal so users will know whether to use the lower or higher one for calculating a raw score. In addition, the directions for completing the Parent/Teacher Conference Form lack explicit instructions regarding whether to mark items between the basal and discontinue points as Mastered or Not Mastered.

Beyond imprecision, some actual errors need to be corrected in the manual. Some troubling problems appear in the Interpretation chapter, where incorrect scores in a couple sample items lead to erroneous interpretations that leave the reader confused at best and misinformed at worst. In the section on limitations of age equivalents (p. 46), the numbers cited do not coincide with the norms tables, and the conclusions do not make sense. An even more obvious mistake appears in the sample Discrepancy Comparison (p. 50), which—seemingly due to a transposition of numbers—shows a difference score that exceeds the critical value but then has the "Significant Difference?" column marked as "No."

A less easily remedied source of potential confusion has to do with the dual nature of the School Readiness Composite (SRC). Though the sum of the first five subtests is referred to as the SRC and can be converted to a composite score (the "Receptive SRC") with a mean of 100, the SRC also is considered as a subtest that is equivalent to the other five subtests and therefore is converted to a scaled subtest score with a mean of 10. The test author argues that having this option facilitates comparisons with other measures that may be given to the same child, which is a good point, but calling a *subtest* score the School Readiness *Composite* is likely to lead to confusion for readers of the resulting educational reports.

Regarding item content analysis, the omission of early childhood educators from the list of experts who reviewed the test items is regrettable. Having the materials reviewed by early childhood teachers who present these concepts daily and are extremely familiar with the behaviors and thinking of young children might have helped eliminate problems with a number of items that are ambiguous, developmentally inappropriate, or have more than one possible correct response.

One final point is a simple organizational suggestion: Table 3.4 (showing differences between composite scores on the BBCS-3:R and the BBCS:E required for statistical significance) along with Tables 7.7 and 7.8 (showing the prevalence of such receptive-expressive discrepancies) should be placed with the Appendixes so an examiner does not have to search through the manual to find these tables when trying to complete the Discrepancy Analysis section. Along the same line, it would be helpful to readers if the test author would include a column showing current population data in *all* tables that report sample demographics so readers do not have to keep flipping back to Table 5.8 to compare each sample to the U.S. population.

SUMMARY. The BBCS-3:R is designed to measure young children's understanding of 282 educationally relevant terms, many of which are taught by parents before school entrance and all of which should be mastered by the time a child leaves first grade. Because the test is both norm- and criterion-referenced, it can be used to identify children with delays in basic concept acquisition and also as a curriculum-based instrument to help teachers write IEPs and plan instruction. A detailed set of instructional activities and materials, the Bracken Concept Development Program (1986), is available separately. The listen-and-point response format is appropriate for a receptive language measure, and the stimulus book has color drawings that are simple and should be appealing to children. In this new edition, the test author has achieved his main goals of updating the norms, test items, and artwork; improving the floor of the test; revising the (criterion-referenced only) Spanish version; and aligning the subtests with state standards for early childhood education. The data presented on standardization, validity, and reliability generally support its use for most of the stated screening and instructional purposes, and the inclusion of children with language impairments in the normative sample is laudable.

The availability of an expressive measure, the BBCS:E, allows comparisons between a child's receptive and expressive skills. The danger, however, is that as the BBCS comes to look more like a diagnostic language assessment measure—with multiple conversion scores for subtests and composites, discrepancy analyses, and a score profile—users will fail to keep in mind the test author's well-advised warning (manual, p. 127) against using the BBCS-3:R to diagnose language impairments or determine eligibility for special services without performing additional testing.

The test author has made some worthwhile item refinements, and more fine-tuning needs to be done. An expanded group of professionals that includes experienced early childhood educators could be invaluable in critiquing items and identifying those that are problematic so that future editions will be even better. Additional studies of the test's clinical utility (particularly its accuracy in identifying at-risk children) are desirable.

In the meantime, this test can be used with reasonable confidence for screening children's skills in basic concept understanding, providing an indication of a child's relative standing, and helping to identify skills that need further work. Because the BBCS-3:R is considerably longer than other basic concepts tests, it provides more information about concept development, but it is also likely to require two or more testing sessions. The availability of detailed teaching materials (in the Bracken Concept Development Program) is likely to appeal to school personnel who are looking for a curricular link to systematic instructional activities.

REVIEWER'S REFERENCES

Panter, J. E. (2000). Validity of the Bracken Basic Concept Scale—Revised for predicting performance on the Metropolitan Readiness Test—Sixth Edition. *Journal of Psychoeducational Assessment, 18*(2), 104-110.

Stebbins, M. S., & McIntosh, D. E. (1996). Decision-making utility of the Bracken Basic Concept Scale in identifying at-risk preschoolers. *School Psychology International, 17*(3), 293-303.

Review of the Bracken Basic Concept Scale—Third Edition: Receptive by LORAINE J. SPENCINER, Professor of Special Education, University of Maine at Farmington, Farmington, ME:

DESCRIPTION. The Bracken Basic Concept Scale—Third Edition: Receptive (BBCS-3:R) assesses a child's receptive language of basic concepts. Designed for children from 3 years, 0 months through 6 years, 11 months, the materials consist of an examiner's manual, an easel-backed stimulus book with color artwork, and record forms in both English and Spanish. The manual includes a description of examiner qualifications and states that individuals must have experience or training in administering, scoring, and interpreting standardized tests. According to the manual, teachers, speech and language pathologists, psychologists, or educational diagnosticians may use this instrument.

The assessment consists of 10 concept categories: Colors, Letters, Numbers/Counting, Sizes/Comparisons, Shapes, Direction/Position, Self-/Social Awareness, Texture/Material, Quantity, and Time/Sequence. The first five subtests comprise the School Readiness Composite. The Receptive Total Composite comprises all 10 subtests. Administration takes between 10 and 15 minutes for the School Readiness Composite and 30 to 40 minutes for the entire assessment. Scores may be reported as scaled scores with confidence intervals, percentile ranks with confidence intervals, and age equivalents. The test booklet includes a score profile that would be helpful in interpreting the scores to others. A companion instrument, the Bracken Basic Concept Scale: Expressive (BBCS:E; Bracken, 2006; 18:13), allows the examiner to assess the child's ability to use expressive language to label basic concepts and to compare the information with the child's receptive skills on the BBCS-3:R.

DEVELOPMENT. The Bracken Basic Concept Scale—Third Edition: Receptive is the second revision of the original instrument published in 1984. According to the manual, this latest revision was based on feedback from "clinicians and experts in the fields of child language and cognitive development, U.S. and international content reviews, [and] a thorough review of current literature" (p. 75). The latest revision included changes in the artwork of a number of test items. These changes were made to reflect current objects, to improve cultural sensitivity, and to represent objects with universal, rather than regional appeal.

During the development of this revision, there was a national tryout testing involving 529 children, ages 3 years, 0 months to 6 years, 11 months, and a clinical study involving 33 children. This process yielded results that formed the basis for further refinement of items. Experts also reviewed items for content, gender, and cultural/ethnic bias. The manual identifies the individuals who served on the panel of bias and content review.

The BBCS-3:R was standardized on a sample of 750 children from 3 years, 0 months to 6 years, 11 months, with 80 children in each of the 6-month age groups. The sample, representative of the U.S. Census, was stratified on the basis of age, gender, race/ethnicity, geographic region, and parent education level. Examiners who participated in the standardization research are listed in the manual. Based on the standardization research, a few additional changes were made in some test items.

The BBCS-3:R Spanish version was not normed. The manual states that this assessment is intended to be used as a criterion-referenced instrument or a curriculum-based measure. The record form is a translated form with some minor changes to reflect the language. For example, some items required minor adaptations because the concept assessed could not be expressed in a single word.

TECHNICAL. The manual discusses several small studies that present initial evidence of the reliability and validity of this instrument. Additional studies should be completed. Both test-retest stability and internal consistency data suggest that the BBCS-3:R is reliable for assessing basic concept knowledge of young children. The manual presents several sources of evidence that represent different aspects of validity including evidence based on test content, on response processes, on internal structure, on relationships with other variables, and evidence based on special group studies.

COMMENTARY. The Bracken Basic Concept Scale—Third Edition: Receptive provides a contemporary approach to assessing receptive language skills for young children 3 years, 0 months to 6 years, 11 months. The stimulus book includes colorful pictures that would appeal to young children. The manual is clearly written and provides useful information to the examiner who may be new to the field. In Chapter 2, sections such as "Cultural Diversity" and "Special Testing Considerations" are particularly noteworthy. On the other hand, the section on "Establishing Rapport" is not written from an early childhood perspective. Best practice often involves the parent being present while the child is being assessed, depending on the age of the child. General assessment procedures can be discussed with parents to ensure that the quality of the test is not compromised by parent coaching.

Assessing knowledge and skills of preschoolers brings its own special challenges. Unlike assessment tasks used with older children, preschoolers may not wish to comply or follow an examiner's directions. Additional discussions regarding special considerations for working with preschoolers with suggestions for engaging children would be helpful to include in the manual.

Chapter 4 of the manual provides background information on early childhood learning guidelines and standards related to early language. This information would be helpful to examiners who are not familiar with state standards in early childhood education. Furthermore, this chapter provides an important link from assessment to curriculum.

SUMMARY. The Bracken Basic Concept Scale—Third Edition: Receptive assesses a child's receptive language of basic concepts. This instrument, designed for children from 3 years, 0 months through 6 years, 11 months, may be administered by teachers, speech language pathologists, psychologists, or educational diagnosticians. The stimulus book includes colorful pictures that would appeal to young children. Record forms are available in both English and Spanish. The manual presents initial evidence of the reliability and validity of this contemporary instrument.

REVIEWER'S REFERENCE

Bracken, B. A. (2006). Bracken Basic Concept Scale-Third Edition: Expressive. (BBSC-3:E) San Antonio, TX: Harcourt PsychCorp.

[15]

Bruininks-Oseretsky Test of Motor Proficiency, Second Edition.

Purpose: Designed to measure gross and fine motor skills of children.
Population: Ages 4–21.
Publication Dates: 1978–2005.
Acronym: BOT-2.
Scores: 3 scores: Gross Motor Composite, Fine Motor Composite, Battery Composite, for 8 subtests: Fine Motor Precision, Fine Motor Integration, Manual Dexterity, Bilateral Coordination, Balance, Running Speed and Agility, Upper-Limb Coordination, Strength.
Administration: Individual.
Price Data, 2009: $795 per kit including manual (2005, 273 pages), administration easel, 25 record forms, 25 examinee booklets, scoring transparency, balance beam, blocks with string, penny box, penny pad, plastic pennies, knee pad, peg board and pegs, 2 red pencils, scissors, target, tennis ball, shape cards, and shuttle block; $44.50 per 25 record forms for complete battery/short form; $44.50 per 25 examinee booklets.
Time: (45–60) minutes for complete battery; (15–20) minutes for short form.
Comments: Second revised edition of the Oseretsky Tests of Motor Proficiency.
Authors: Robert H. Bruininks and Brett D. Bruininks.

Publisher: Pearson.
Cross References: See T5:353 (22 references) and T4:340 (18 references); for a review by David A. Sabatino of an earlier edition, see 9:174 (7 references); see also T3:324 (3 references) and T2:1898 (15 references); for a review by Anna Espenschade, see 4:650 (10 references); for an excerpted review, see 3:472 (6 references).

Review of the Bruininks-Oseretsky Test of Motor Proficiency, Second Edition, by KATHARINE A. SNYDER, Associate Professor of Psychology, Methodist University, Fayetteville, NC:

DESCRIPTION. The Bruininks-Oseretsky Test of Motor Proficiency (BOTMP), a measure used with children to identify Developmental Coordination Disorder (DCD) and for placement within Adaptive Physical Education Programs, has been updated to the Second Edition (BOT-2). BOTMP assessments have also been undertaken to evaluate motor skill impairments in Mild Traumatic Brain Injury (mTBI; Gagnon, Swaine, Friedman, & Forget, 2004), autism or Asperger's syndrome (Ghaziuddin & Butler, 1998; Ghaziuddin, Butler, Tsai, & Ghaziuddin, 1994; Miller & Ozonoff, 2000), and to cross-validate other measures (Flegel & Kolobe, 2002; Tan, Parker, & Larkin, 2001). Intended for use by physical education teachers, physical therapists, occupational therapists, and researchers, the BOT-2 reportedly assesses fine and gross motor skills in individuals aged 4 through 21 years. Identifying mild to moderate motor control problems is the stated purpose of the BOT-2.

The BOT-2 represents a substantial revision over the BOTMP. Revision goals consisted of the following: Improved functional relevance, expanded coverage, improved measurements of 4- and 5-year-olds, extension of norms through age 21, improved item presentation, and improved kit quality. To enhance functional relevance, BOTMP gross and fine motor skill composites were updated to become the Fine Manual Control (i.e., the hands and fingers grasping, writing, drawing, etc.), Manual Coordination (i.e., using the arms and hands for object manipulation), Body Coordination (i.e., posture and balance), and Strength and Agility Composites of the BOT-2. The BOTMP Visual-Motor Control subtest was divided into the Fine Motor Precision and Fine Motor Integration BOT-2 components. New activities were added and existing ones modified to improve measurement of 4- and 5-year-olds (precise details are lacking).

Administration and scoring of the BOT-2 is fairly straightforward. The full form is recommended (40–60 minutes). Following a brief lateral preference inventory, items are administered by following step-by-step directions in the well-done administration easel. Administration of the BOT-2 is sequenced so that paper-and-pencil activities precede those requiring exertion. Little information on recommended evaluator credentials is provided. In sum, raw scores are converted to standard scores and percentile ranks. Descriptive categories are also provided, but some subscales reach ceilings fairly quickly for older participants.

DEVELOPMENT. In developing the revision, three focus groups, consisting of nine occupational therapists, nine physical therapists, and seven developmental adaptive physical education teachers, revealed the need for more functional items and simplified instructions. A survey was then given to 800 BOTMP users (sample detail is limited). Authors of the instrument assert that "additional information included professional reviews of the BOTMP and analyses of new trends in motor skill assessment, motor development theory, and research on the motor deficits occurring in clinical groups such as autism spectrum disorders, attention deficit/hyperactivity disorder, mental retardation, and developmental coordination disorder" (manual, p. 35). More information about these reviews and trends would be helpful. In sum, nine items were rated as poor or fair by more than 20% of the survey respondents. Eight of these were dropped and the ninth was retained due to balance beam improvements.

A nationwide pilot study was then undertaken with 22 new items, focusing on improving measurement for 4- and 5-year-olds and expanding fine motor skill assessment. With the assistance of 21 occupational therapists, physical therapists, and developmental adaptive physical education teachers, 71 children (3–10 years) were tested in Minnesota. "Based on the results, six of the new items were dropped and the others were modified to function more effectively" (manual, p. 36). Further details are lacking. The BOT-2 balance beam was widened from 1.5 to 1.75 inches to accommodate younger children better.

TECHNICAL.

Standardization. The standardization study included 1,520 examinees from 38 states (4–21 years). Based on 2001 U.S. Census data, sample stratification was across sex, race/ethnicity, SES, geographic region, and disability status. Further information on the disability samples would be useful. Factor analysis revealed seven primary factors (Fine Motor Precision and Fine Motor Integration, Strength, Balance, Upper-Limb Coordination, Manual Dexterity, Bilateral Coordination, and Running Speed and Agility), which were later utilized to construct the subtests and composites of the BOT-2. This analysis is well done; however, it should be noted that some of the factor loadings are small (e.g., .31 for One-Legged Side Hop).

Reliability. Split-half, test-retest, and interrater reliability studies were undertaken. Demographic information is limited. Subscale split-half coefficients were in the .70s and .80s, with only two falling below .70. Composite split-half coefficients are in the .80s and .90s, whereas the Total Motor Composite is in the mid-.90s. A table in the manual is provided for the composite split-half and stratified alpha coefficients. The BOT-2 was administered twice to 134 examinees with an interval of 7 to 42 days, and most subtest and composite test-retest coefficients were in the .80 range. Forty-seven participants (4–21 years) were rated by two examiners during a single administration and interrater coefficients were very high. Prior BOTMP research documented high interrater coefficients between composites and subtests, despite at times low item-to-item agreement and disagreement over the presence of motor problems (Wilson, Kaplan, Crawford, & Dewey, 2000). This reviewer believes that such results (e.g., high interrater reliability, low item-to-item correlations) are likely the case with the BOT-2.

Validity. The authors of the instrument attempted to establish content and construct validity through confirmatory factor analysis, item analysis, and clinical group studies, but findings are at times weak and contradictory. Factor-analytic methods identified the seven factors. However, construct validity findings are difficult to determine because in one place the instrument authors stated that "only the items with a moderately high factor loading on at least one of the seven factors were retained for the final test" (manual, p. 57), and in another place they stated the following: "The Bilateral Coordination Item Touching Nose with Index Fingers–Eyes Closed did not load substantially on any factor; however, because it is commonly used in motor-function evaluation and has a well-established history of providing clinically useful information, it was retained in the final item set" (manual, p. 46). A detailed item analysis was carried out, but findings still at times appear contradictory. For instance, the authors stated the following: "An item with good fit may have been dropped if the skill assessed largely overlapped with another item. On the other hand, some items with marginal fit were retained either because the item covered a range of ability not well-covered by other items or because the item measured an important and unique skill" (manual, p. 38). A convincing argument for construct validity is given by showing that median subscale scores exhibit expected developmental progressions; however, it is unclear why the median as opposed to mean was used. The test authors also report large differences in scores for males and females on the Running Speed and Agility and Strength subtests; however, no significance data are provided. The meaning of many of the tables in the manual are unclear, in the opinion of this reviewer, with the use of categories of sex specific and combined, rather than male, female, and combined. A well-done argument for construct and content validity is that subtest correlations tend to be low, particularly for the 4- through 7-year age range (.3 to .45 range), suggesting that they measure different things.

Clinical group studies were carried out with examinees suffering from Developmental Coordination Disorder (DCD), Mild/Moderate Mental Retardation (MR), and High-Functioning Autism/Asperger's Disorder (AD). Clinical Group membership was verified by diagnoses recorded on school or medical records; no additional supporting documentation was required. Fifty individuals, between 4–15 years old, with DCD exhibited significantly lower scores on all BOT-2 indices. Sixty-six individuals, between 5–21 years old, with mild/moderate MR exhibited significantly lower scores on all BOT-2 indices. Forty-five individuals, between 4–21 years old, with AD exhibited significantly lower scores on all BOT-2 indices.

Convergent validity studies were carried out with the BOTMP, the Peabody Developmental Motor Scales (2nd Edition, PDMS-2), and the Test of Visual Motor Skills–Revised (TVMS-R). Forty-nine participants, ages 6–14, were administered the BOT-2 and BOTMP. Battery composites correlated at .76, whereas the subtests were in the moderate range (.40–.60).

Thirty-eight 4- and 5-year-olds were given the PDMS. The correlation of the BOT-2 Total Motor Composite with the PDMS-2 Total Motor Quotient was .77, whereas the subtests were in the moderate range (.50–.75). Fifty-six individuals, aged 4–13 years, received the TVMS-R. The TVMS-R Visual Motor Skills Composite correlated .55 with BOT-2 Fine Motor Precision, .72 with BOT-2 Fine-Motor Integration, .70 with Fine Manual Control, and .62 with BOT-2 Total Motor Composite.

COMMENTARY/SUMMARY. Overall, the BOT-2 is a useful tool for occupational therapists, special education teachers, and rehabilitation specialists evaluating manual coordination, body coordination, and strength and agility in children. Placement decisions in physical education programs are a good use for the BOT-2. Caution is advised when using the measure to assess academic readiness or clinical syndromes. The BOT-2 represents a substantial revision and improvement of the BOTMP, particularly in terms of the factor structure. Prior research has questioned the validity of the BOTMP short-form (Verderber & Payne, 1987) and the BOT-2 does not substantially improve these issues. Further research with the BOT-2 will help to determine its usefulness with DCD, mild/moderate MR, and AD individuals.

REVIEWER'S REFERENCES

Flegel, J., & Kolobe, T. H. A. (2002). Predictive validity of the Test of Infant Motor Performance as measured by the Bruininks-Oseretsky Test of Motor Proficiency at school age. *Physical Therapy, 82,* 762-771.

Gagnon, I., Swaine, B., Friedman, D., & Forget, R. (2004). Visuomotor response time in children with a mild traumatic brain injury. *Journal of Head Trauma Rehabilitation, 19,* 391-404.

Ghaziuddin, M., & Butler, E. (1998). Clumsiness in autism and Asperger syndrome: A further report. *Journal of Intellectual Disability Research, 42,* 43-48.

Ghaziuddin, M., Butler, E., Tsai, L., & Ghaziuddin, N. (1994). Is clumsiness a marker for Asperger syndrome? *Journal of Intellectual Disability Research, 38,* 519-527.

Miller, J. N., & Ozonoff, S. (2000). The external validity of Asperger disorder: Lack of evidence from the domain of neuropsychology. *Journal of Abnormal Psychology, 109,* 227-238.

Tan, S. K., Parker, H. E., & Larkin, D. (2001). Concurrent validity of motor tests used to identify children with motor impairment. *Adapted Physical Education Quarterly, 18,* 168-182.

Verderber, J., & Payne, V. G. (1987). A comparison of the long and short forms of the Bruininks-Oseretsky Test of Motor Proficiency. *Adapted Physical Activity Quarterly, 4,* 51-59.

Wilson, B. N., Kaplan, B. J., Crawford, S. G., & Dewey, D. (2000). Interrater reliability of the Bruininks-Oseretsky Test of Motor Proficiency–Long form. *Adapted Physical Activity Quarterly, 17,* 95-110.

Review of the Bruininks-Oseretsky Test of Motor Proficiency, Second Edition, by GABRIELLE STUTMAN, Private Practice, Westchester and New York City, NY:

DESCRIPTION. The Bruininks-Oseretsky Test of Motor Proficiency, Second Edition (BOT-2), a revision of the original Bruininks-Oseretsky Test of Motor Proficiency (BOTMP), is a norm-referenced, developmentally based battery of motor skills tests for individuals aged 4 through 21 years. Like its widely used predecessor, it provides information about a broad array of motor skills and identifies motor skill problems in individuals with only mild to moderate motor control problems. In this revision motor functioning is divided into four domains: Fine Manual, Manual Coordination, Body Coordination, and Strength and Agility. As with the BOTMP, these scores can be combined to yield a Total Motor Composite to assess total motor proficiency.

TEST CONTENT AND STRUCTURE. Either the full administration (40–60 minutes) or the Short Form (15–20 minutes) can be administered to all ages, to generate composite scores. The Fine Manual Control Composite consists of the untimed Fine Motor Precision and Fine Motor (visual-motor) Integration Subtests. Fine Motor Precision items include drawing, paper folding, and cutting within a specified boundary. Fine Motor Integration items include reproducing drawings of various shapes. The Manual Coordination Composite consists of the Manual Dexterity and Upper-Limb Coordination Subtests. Manual Dexterity includes timed items: picking up pennies, block stringing, card sorting, and a pegboard. Upper Limb Coordination tasks include catching, dribbling, and throwing a tennis ball. The Body Coordination Composite consists of the Bilateral Coordination and Balance Subtests. Bilateral Coordination requires sequential and simultaneous coordination of the upper and lower limbs; jumping jacks and pivoting thumbs and fingers are included. Balance tasks require (e.g.) walking a line, and utilizing a balance beam for (e.g.) standing on one foot. The Strength and Agility Composite consists of Running Speed and Agility, and Strength subtests. Running Speed and Agility tasks include a shuttle run (100 feet), hopping, and patterned stepping. Strength assessment includes push-ups, sit-ups, and maintaining a seated position against a wall (while standing). Administration and scoring instructions are pictorially presented in a tabbed easel administration booklet. In some cases some optional text may be used in test administration. Test equipment is well constructed. All tasks receive a raw score, which becomes a point score on the record form, is summed with others, and transformed into a standard score.

Standard scores are available for males, females, and both genders combined.

DEVELOPMENT. The BOT-2 is a revision of the Bruininks-Oseretsky Test of Motor Proficiency (BOTMP), originally published in 1978. The revision went through four stages of redevelopment: content development, piloting, national tryouts, and standardization. The goals were to improve the functional relevance of the test content, expand the coverage of fine and gross motor assessment, improve measurement of 4- and 5-year-olds, extend norms upward through age 21, and to improve item presentation and the quality of the kit equipment. Content development was geared toward relevance, and it was initially addressed via a survey of BOTMP practitioners. The BOTMP gross motor and fine motor composites were differentiated into fine manual control, manual coordination, body coordination, and strength and agility. Fine motor assessment was differentiated into fine motor precision and fine motor (visual-motor) integration tasks. Single-item subtests were expanded. The test was standardized on a nationally representative sample of 1,520 examinees, aged 4–21, who were tested at 239 sites in 38 states. Sample selection closely matched the U.S. population and was weighted toward younger, rapidly developing ages, but with balance across sex, race/ethnicity, socioeconomic status, geographic region, and disability status in each age group. Clinical samples include developmental coordination disorder (DCD), high-functioning autism/Aspergers Disorder, and mild to moderate mental retardation (MR). Educational placement was used as a stratification variable in the norm sample. Norms were extended (age 4 to 21) so that the entire age range of the Individuals with Disabilities Education Act (IDEA) is covered. Although behaviors involving large muscles and limb control tend to be highly correlated regardless of limb or muscle group, the BOT-2's final four-factor model of Fine Manual Control, Manual Coordination, Body Coordination, and Strength and Agility resulted in significant improvement of fit over the two-factor model used by the BOTMP. A short form was developed, and subtests were normed separately for males, females, and the combined sample. Point score conversion tables were developed to discriminate levels of performance. Point scores are transformed into normalized Z scores within each of 12 age groups and into a scale score metric with mean of 15 and standard deviation of 5. A conversion table smoothed the scores, with adjustments to remove bias. Composite Score and Total Motor scores were grouped into seven age groups (4, 5, 6–7, 8–9, 10–11, 12–14, and 15–21), then normalized and converted into standard score scales. Expected means are 15 for scale scores, 50 for standard scores, with standard deviations of 5 and 10, respectively. Percentiles and age equivalents are given. Clinical groups (DCD, MR, and Aspergers) are differentiated from each other and the nonclinical population. Reliability studies included internal consistency (split-half), test-retest (7–42 days), and interrater. Correlations are good and increase in value from individual subtests (high .70s to high .90s) to the total composite (high .80s to low .90s). Intercorrelation coefficients among subtest scale scores appear to decrease with age and are generally small to moderate among composite standard scores. Criterion-related validity studies conducted relative to BOTMP (Battery Composite and Total Motor Composite r = .80), Peabody Developmental Motor Scales, Second Edition (PDMS-2; Total Motor Composite and Total Motor Quotient r = .73), and Test of Visual Motor Skills–Revised (TVMS-R; fine motor integration and Visual-Motor Skills Composite r = .74) are acceptable.

COMPUTERIZED SCORING OPTION. The user-friendly computerized scoring has network or single user capacity. Deficiencies include lack of Tab Key data entry and that the data entry sequence does not conform to the sequence of scores on the record form. One may choose gender specific or combined norms and 90% or 95% confidence levels for Short or Full Form. Ample pairwise comparisons, a score profile, a fully informative narrative report, and parent letter are generated.

COMMENTARY. The model of differential development of fine manual control, manual coordination, body coordination, and strength and agility, upon which the BOT-2 is based, is widely accepted and well sampled in this instrument. The test kit contains almost everything one needs, except a 60-foot tape measure. Thankfully, the 50-foot runway is not required for the Short Form, but there is no provision to prorate Speed subtests for the full administration. Test administration requires practice; the examiner must be alert to proper form in task execution. A tabbed, easel-form administration guide, with pictured instructions and scoring aids facilitates administration, but thought is required for Point Score conversions. On Subtest 2: Fine Motor Integration, the Raw Score Column is redundant with the Point Score Column. On Subtest 3: Manual Dexterity, no information is given in the administration easel or record book as to which of the two trials to score; only the manual has that information. Timed norms for Fine Motor Precision Subtest items would add information. Scale Scores have a mean of 15 and a Standard Deviation (*SD*) of 5. Composite Standard Scores have a mean of 50 and a *SD* of 10. The more usual subtest mean of 10 with *SD* = 3, and Index score mean = 100; *SD* = 15 is preferable, but compensated by a conversion table to Percentiles (and Age Equivalents). The four motor composite scores help to target intervention, but there is no table of test-retest coefficients to measure intervention effectiveness.

SUMMARY. The BOT-2 fills an important niche and well serves its stated purpose to provide a battery of normed subtests that differentially assess the full range of motor ability development. Strengths include good quality apparatus, the option of using a short form for screening, reasonable ease of administration: a generally well designed administration easel and record form, and objective scoring. The Short Form is useful to screen for deficits in motor ability. The full administration supports differential diagnoses of motor compromise, placement decisions, development and evaluation of motor training programs, and research purposes. Freedom from bias, generally good subtest reliability, and well-supported validity enhance the examiner's confidence. Weaknesses include occasional scoring ambiguity, the necessity of a 60-foot room for full testing, and the omission of test-retest coefficients to measure intervention effectiveness. The optional computerized scoring CD is strongly recommended.

[16]

Burks Behavior Rating Scales, Second Edition.

Purpose: Designed to measure child and adolescent behaviors that are relevant to school and community activities.
Population: Ages 4–18.
Publication Dates: 1968–2006.
Acronym: BBRS-2.
Scores, 7: Disruptive Behavior, Attention and Impulse Control Problems, Emotional Problems, Social Withdrawal, Ability Deficits, Physical Deficits, Weak Self-Confidence.
Administration: Individual.
Forms, 2: Teacher, Parent.
Price Data, 2007: $105 per complete kit including 25 parent autoscore forms, 25 teacher autoscore forms, and manual (2006, 74 pages); $40 per 25 autoscore forms (specify parent or teacher); $44 per manual.
Time: 15(20) minutes.
Comments: Ratings by teachers or parents; computer scoring options also available, contact publisher for details.
Authors: Harold F. Burks and Christian P. Gruber.
Publisher: Western Psychological Services.
Cross References: See T5:355 (1 reference) and T4:342 (5 references); for reviews by Lisa G. Bischoff and by Leland C. Zlomke and Brenda R. Bush of an earlier edition, see 11:50 (7 references); see also T3:328 (1 reference), T2:1115 (1 reference), and 7:46 (2 references).

Review of Burks Behavior Rating Scales, Second Edition by RONALD A. MADLE, Licensed Psychologist, Mifflinburg, PA, and Adjunct Associate Professor of School Psychology, The Pennsylvania State University, University Park, PA:

DESCRIPTION. The Burks Behavior Rating Scales, Second Edition (BBRS-2) is designed to help diagnose and treat child and adolescent behavior problems through the organized collection of information to supplement interviews and formal intellectual and achievement testing. The scale covers prekindergarten through 12th grade (ages 4 through 18). Parents, teachers, and similar persons (e.g., child care workers, school counselors) who have had experience with the child on a daily basis for at least 2 weeks can complete the ratings in about 15 minutes.

The BBRS-2 includes a manual and 50 AutoScore™ forms (25 each for parents and teachers). Identifying information, directions, and all 100 items are on two sides of a carbonized rating form. Both versions use the same questions that are written at about a fifth grade reading level. A 5-point scale is used to rate the frequency each behavior has been noted, from "not at all" through a "slight," "considerable," "large," and "very large degree." The length of time to consider for the ratings, however, is unspecified.

The AutoScore™ form is opened to work out raw scores for the 19 content and 2 validity scales. Ten or fewer omitted items may be scored using the median item values highlighted in boldface;

more missing items invalidate all ratings. Raw scores are transferred to the detachable, graphical Profile Sheet, with one side for preschool children and the other for school-age children. Only the Profile Sheet differs on the Parent and Teacher forms. The BBRS-2 also can be computer scored using a separately available scoring program and computer answer sheets.

Seven major scales, consisting of Disruptive Behavior, Attention and Impulse Control Problems, Emotional Problems, Social Withdrawal, Ability Deficits (except for preschool), Physical Deficits, and Weak Self-Confidence, as well as the inconsistency and exaggeration validity scales, are converted to *T*-scores (mean = 50; *SD* = 10). No percentile ranks or confidence intervals are included. A moderate to elevated level of clinical concern is indicated by scores of 70*T* or higher, with 60–69*T* scores signifying low to moderate clinical concern.

Nineteen subscales—or components—are organized under the major scales in groups of two to five. For example, the Disruptive Behavior scale includes Poor Anger Control, Distrustfulness, Aggressive Tendencies, Rebelliousness, and Poor Social Conformity. Rather than using *T*-scores, subscales or components have cutoffs labeled as Moderate or Elevated that are applied whenever the parent scale is at or above 60*T*.

DEVELOPMENT. The BBRS-2 revision goals were to maintain the strengths of the original scale while improving weaknesses identified based on published reviews as well as a user survey. At least 20% of users rated three areas as "poor": the lack of *T*-scores based on a representative national sample, outdated and complex language, and certain scale names that tended to be "off-putting" to parents. Published reviews identified the need for improved standardization, as well as better reliability and validity documentation. Ease of scoring and interpretation, coverage of interventions, and face/content validity were consistently noted as strengths.

Dated or confusing items were rewritten and scale names altered. For example, "Excessive Sense of Persecution" became "Distrustfulness." The earlier item clusters became "components" and the validity scales were added. Preliminary analyses with a referred sample (*N* = 860) suggested preservation of scale characteristics, with good component to scale correlations (ranging from .78 to .94) and median item cluster to scale correlations (.54 to .71).

TECHNICAL.

Standardization. The total sample of 2,864 individuals closely approximated the 2005 U.S. Census estimates for gender, age, racial/ethnic background, geographic region, and parental education level. Data were collected from all four major U.S. Census regions, although in only nine states. MANOVA showed that neither gender nor age—except for preschool versus school-age differences on the Ability Deficits scale—showed any meaningful clinical effects. Significant differences in parent versus teacher ratings on several scales, especially Disruptive Behaviors and Emotional Problems, resulted in separate norms for teachers (*N* = 1,481) and parents (*N* = 1,383). In addition, the Ability Deficit scale was not included for preschool norms.

Reliability. Technical characteristics were studied with a referred sample (*N* = 860) with some additional data from the normative sample. Four subsamples, based on rater type and referral status, had median coefficient alpha values from .84 to .89, indicating moderately high internal consistency. Individual scale values ranged from .75 to .96. There were no meaningful differences across groups although *SEM*s are presented for each group only. As is typical, parent reliabilities were lower than for teachers. For teachers (*N* = 81) and parents (*N* = 55), all test-retest correlations used a 1-week interval and all but one yielded values above .80. About half exceeded .90, with a 1 to 2 *T*-score point drop.

Moderate interrater agreement was obtained for 24 parent (.69) and 97 teacher (.62) pairs. The authors note that agreement was higher for longer scales including overt behaviors than for shorter scales with fewer external referents (e.g., internalizing disorders). Interrater concordance analyses, using 102 parent-teacher pairs, found the oft-reported lower level of agreement in both referred (.41) and nonreferred (.46) groups because in these kinds of comparisons, both raters and settings differ. Again, *SEM*s are presented to permit estimation of when scores actually differ across raters.

Validity. Much of the content validation established for the original scale was not redone, given that little test content changed in the revision. In fact, the two versions correlated from .91 to 1.00. Rather than reestablishing the score variations across several special populations, a study was done to determine differences in a mixed referred population versus a nonreferred one. Scales typically differed by about 5 to 10 *T*-score points, although the divergence for Emotional Problems was considerably less (effect size was .15).

Concurrent validity was examined primarily using two broadband scales—the Child Behavior Checklist/Teacher's Report Form (CBCL/TRF; Achenbach, 1991) and the Behavior Evaluation Scale (BES; McCarney, Jackson, & Leigh, 1990). Same type rater (teacher and parent) comparisons with the Achenbach scales showed acceptable validity coefficients (.42 to .78). Parent ratings on the BBRS-2, however, had rather substantial correlations for all scales with both the internalizing and externalizing dimensions on the CBCL. BBRS-2 parent-teacher correlations also were reported for nonreferred and referred samples, whereas the CBCL/TRF used the referred sample alone. The results suggested moderate convergent validity for both scales in the referred group. Discriminant validity was adequate, although the Achenbach scales showed somewhat better discrimination. Parent rating correlations again were nearly as high on dissimilar as similar scales, signifying less discrimination than with teacher-based ratings. The BES study ($N = 79$) showed good concurrent and discriminant validity support for the Ability Deficits and Disruptive Behavior scales, with other scales being weaker. The last validation study, using the Conners' Rating Scales—Revised (CRS-R; Conners, 1997), a narrow band assessment of ADHD symptoms, showed similar results, including the globalizing tendency of the parent ratings.

COMMENTARY AND SUMMARY. The BBRS-2 is a brief, easily used scale designed for assessing disruptive behaviors with a variety of raters. The revision goals, including improved terminology and psychometrics, seem to have been accomplished, and the addition of validity scales is a welcome modification. Technical information indicates moderate to high reliability, with moderate validity for most scales. The validity evidence is most persuasive for externalizing behaviors but less compelling for internalizing problems. Care should be exercised if using the BBRS-2 to detect problems such as depression and anxiety. In spite of the scale improvements, other scales such as the Achenbach system (Achenbach, 1991) and the Behavior Assessment System for Children: Second Edition (Reynolds & Kamphaus, 2004) remain preferred choices for primary broadband information.

The BBRS-2 can be a useful scale when treatment planning is emphasized over clinical diagnosis, making it a useful supplemental rating scale. The manual contains a great deal of practical clinical information concerning factors contributing to scale elevations, related home and school interventions corresponding to elevated scales, and discussion of common scale patterns in various clinically relevant populations.

Some scale characteristics could still be improved, including the use of more objective rating descriptors, specifying a time period to consider for ratings, and adding confidence intervals to facilitate comparison of scale differences. A final practical change would be to consider using separate profile sheets, as the two versions are otherwise identical.

REVIEWER'S REFERENCES

Achenbach, T. M. (1991). *Integrative guide for the 1991 CBCL/4-18, YSR, and TRF profiles.* Burlington, VT: University of Vermont, Department of Psychiatry.

Conners, C. K. (1997). Conners' Rating Scales—Revised. North Tonawanda, NY: Multi-Health Systems.

McCarney, S. B., Jackson, M. T., & Leigh, J. E. (1990). Behavior Evaluation Scale. Columbia, MO: Hawthorne Educational Services.

Reynolds, C. R., & Kamphaus, R. W. (2004). *Behavior Assessment System for Children, Second Edition (BASC-2): Manual.* Circle Pines, MN: American Guidance Services.

Review of the Burks Behavior Rating Scales, Second Edition by HOI K. SUEN, Distinguished Professor of Educational Psychology, Pennsylvania State University, University Park, PA:

DESCRIPTION. The Burks Behavior Rating Scales, Second Edition is a rating scale designed for use with children or adolescents from 4 through 18 years of age who have been referred to school counselors, psychologists, special education, or other mental health specialists for school behavioral adjustment problems. It consists of 100 5-point Likert-type rating items that address seven aspects of child behavior. These include Disruptive Behavior, Attention and Impulse Control Problems, Emotional Problems, Social Withdrawal, Ability Deficits, Physical Deficits, and Weak Self-Confidence. Each of these subscales is further divided into a number of components. For example, Disruptive Behavior is further divided into Poor Anger Control, Distrustfulness, Aggressive Tendencies, Rebelliousness, and Poor Social Conformity. For another example, the subscale of Emotional Problems is further divided into Anxiousness, Self-Blame, and Emotional Distress. Suggestions for intervention or remediation strategies for each of the components are provided.

There is a parent form and a teacher form. The former is to be completed by a parent, foster parent, or other custodial adult; the latter is to be completed by a teacher, a child care worker, or other caretaker. In all cases, the rater used must be well-acquainted with the child and be familiar with the child's current behavior. Separate norms are provided for the parent and the teacher form, respectively.

In addition to the subscale scores and component scores, an *F*-scale score and an I-scale score are provided. The *F*-scale score helps detect possible exaggeration in ratings and the I-scale score helps the user to detect inconsistent responses by a teacher or parent. Finally, common score patterns (i.e., score profiles) for eight types of children are provided along with suggested interventions. These include minority culture or recently immigrated child, the immature child, the shy-withdrawn child, the anxious child, the hyperactive-distractible child, the aggressive-hostile child, the socialized-delinquent child, and the schizophrenic child.

DEVELOPMENT. The original Burks Behavior Rating Scales were published in 1977. The goals of the 2006 revision were to update language and concepts, and to modify items and structure in response to feedback from user surveys as well as suggestions from professional reviewers. The first step taken in the revision was to remove 10 of the 110 original items from the scales due to weak item-whole correlations and, in some cases, outdated language or concepts. Additionally, the original 19 scales were relabeled as "components" and have been grouped into seven new scales representing the seven aspects of behavior.

To verify that the structure of the revised components and new scales is valid, the developer used a somewhat unique method to evaluate convergent and discriminant validity within the conceptual framework of a multitrait-multimethod matrix (MTMM). These analyses indicated that construct validity could be "safely credited to the components and scales created for the BBRS-2 revision" (manual, p. 43).

A large sample of 1,481 teacher reports and another sample of 1,383 parent reports were used as normative data to establish *T*-scores for the two forms, respectively. The two samples are quite representative of the overall U.S. population in terms of race/ethnicity, geographic region, and parents' educational level. Data for the standardization sample also were used to evaluate possible adverse impact due to gender and to evaluate age and rater differences.

TECHNICAL. Reliability and validity analyses were conducted based on data from either the standardization sample, a sample of 860 children who had been clinically referred, or some subsample as appropriate. Reliability was evaluated by estimating alpha coefficients and test-retest correlations. Concurrent validity evidence was gathered through a "broadband assessment" and a "narrow band assessment" approach. These two approaches along with the assessment of reliability coefficients were viewed by the developer as an implementation of an overall generalizability conceptual framework. Additional validity evidence was presented in the form of content validity and comparisons of scores between referred and nonreferred children. Interrater agreements also were evaluated as evidence of convergent validity.

Reliability coefficients reported for scale scores are all high and the standard errors of measurement are relatively small, suggesting that all scale scores are relatively precise. However, no reliability coefficient is reported for any of the component scores. This is in spite of the fact that component scores are to be reported on the score form, interpretations are to be made on the basis of these scores, and intervention strategies are suggested for situations with high scores.

Validity evidence based on content is based on a series of content validation exercises conducted for the original 1977 scales. Because, for the new edition, only 10 items have been removed from the original 110 items, and the fact that the removed items were ones found not to be appropriate, the content-based evidence is sufficiently cogent. Validity is further supported by good correlations with several other related standard behavioral scales. Clinical utility is evidenced by moderate to large scale score differences between referred and nonreferred children. Overall, the preponderance of evidence suggests that the use of scale scores to identify children with the seven specific behavioral problems do lead to valid inferences.

Comparisons between genders and among age groups show negligible score differences, suggesting that there is little adverse impact due to these two variables. No detailed item-level differential item functioning analysis was performed. However, the lack of gender and age difference suggests that the scales are likely to be free from potential gender or age bias.

There does not appear to be any research conducted to gather evidence to support the formulation of the eight score profiles. The developer claims that these profiles were based on "factor analysis studies, clinical observation of scale profiles, and supporting evidence from the literature" (manual, p. 31), yet none of this evidence is provided or referenced in the test manual. There is also no evidence to either evaluate their validity or to support their clinical utility. There is no information on hit rate, sensitivity, specificity, false positive rate, false negative rate, positive predictive power, or negative predictive power.

The developer claims that the reliabilities and several pieces of the validity evidence were gathered and to be understood within the general conceptual framework of generalizability theory. Yet, no G-study or D-study was actually done and some of the known applications of G-theory specifically for convergent validity were not used. Similarly, the framework of MTMM along with its concepts of convergent validity and discriminant validity (which are also related to the generalizability claim) were claimed to be the overarching conceptual framework for many pieces of validity evidence. Yet, the methods used did not actually lead to convergent validity or discriminant validity as were conceptualized in MTMM.

COMMENTARY. Overall, the scale scores are reliable and there is adequate evidence that the use of scale scores to identify possible behavior problems will likely lead to valid inferences and decisions. Therefore, the BBRS-2 has accomplished its overall goal.

There are a number of relatively minor technical issues that need to be addressed for the sake of clarity and to avoid misleading the test user. These technical issues are somewhat esoteric and most do not appreciably diminish the quality of the scale scores or the validity of their interpretation or uses.

One such problem is the repeated claim by the test developer that reliability and validity are analyzed and presented within the framework of the generalizability theory and that of MTMM, when in fact these two approaches were not used at all. The only connection between these two approaches and the actual methods used is a very loose conceptual similarity. For example, according to the manual, the information on reliability and concurrent validity is to be understood within the context of generalizability theory. Yet, all reliability coefficients reported employed classical methods focusing on one single facet at a time (item or occasion). Those reliability coefficients imply two different universes of generalization within the framework of G-theory. Why not a combined two-facet analysis to assess score reliability instead? The absence of an actual generalizability analysis becomes even more pronounced when the publisher provides an illustration of how to use the standard error of measurement to build confidence intervals. The manual provided an illustration using the standard error of measurement value derived from coefficient alpha. What about the standard error obtained from the test-retest reliability? Which should the user use? Of course, a proper generalizability theory would have produced a single standard error of measurement (error variance) corresponding to the proper two-faceted universe.

One can, in fact, derive convergent evidence of validity within the generalizability framework, but not in the manner presented. To do so, one would need a G- and D-study involving a method facet along with other measurement facets. Convergent validity versus reliability are then to be differentiated via the treatment of the method facet as either random or fixed (see, e.g., Kane, 1982). This method was not used in the reported validity evidence and the overall approach actually used can best be described as loosely related to the general idea of having a method facet. Perhaps the developer should consider either removing language about using a generalizability theory from the test manual or actually conducting generalizability analyses and reporting the results in the next printing of the manual.

Another minor technical issue concerns the claim of convergent and discriminant validity via the MTMM approach. The actual analyses were part-whole correlations, which are not actually monotrait-multimethod correlations and are therefore not actually convergent validity coefficients. Discriminant validity (referred to as divergent validity in the manual) needs to be evaluated in light of convergent validity. Again, this mislabel does not diminish the overall reliability and validity of the scale scores; but perhaps the developer should refrain from making these claims.

The use of the part-whole correlation approach also has led to a different relatively minor technical problem that needs to be removed. This is the problem of presenting the same single characteristic of the scales—high part-whole correlations—in different formats (e.g., item-whole correlations, convergent/divergent validity, internal consistency) to make many different claims: (a) That BBRS-2 and its predecessor are parallel, (b) that the 10 items removed were inappropriate, (c) that there is evidence of construct validity, (d) that there is "convergent" and "divergent" evidence of validity, and (e) that there is a high degree of reliability as expressed in the form of alpha coefficients. These are basically the same pieces of part-whole correlation information reorganized into different formats. No new information is gained in each alternative expression as they are essentially redundant information. The claim of convergent and divergent validity is not appropriate as item-whole or component-scale correlations do not meet the definition of convergent validity. Nor is the claim of construct validity on the basis of these part-whole correlations appropriate and these correlations are not meaningful substitutes of factor analyses. Again, this problem has little overall negative impact on the reliability and validity because the overall reliability and validity of the scale scores are already adequate without the redundancy. However, the problem gives the test user an erroneous impression that there is more independent evidence of validity than actually exists.

In addition to these minor technical issues, there are two relatively serious problems and issues that will place limitations on the more fine-grained uses of these scales. One such problem is the high correlations found between components and their corresponding overall scale scores. Although these high correlations do not suggest "convergent validity" as claimed, they actually give rise to the question of whether these components are truly distinct components. This problem is further compounded by the lack of reliability information for these components. In light of the lack of clear evidence of the distinctiveness of these components and the lack of reliability information, users should not be encouraged to interpret and use these component scores as the basis to determine the need for interventions at all—in spite of the fact that the developer did encourage the interpretation of component scores and even suggested intervention strategies for situations in which a child obtains a high component score. There is no evidence that the suggested interpretation and intervention is appropriate or meaningful.

Another relatively serious problem is the lack of literature-based, theory-based, or empirically based support for either the formulation or interpretation of the eight common score patterns. The use of profiles is risky in general because of the inherent problems of reversed conditional probabilities. Without data to evaluate clinical utility, concluding the existence of certain types of children based on the existence of common score patterns and then implementing interventions is inappropriate. Minimally, there is no evidence of correct classification, nor evidence of benefit. Potentially, the classification and intervention can be harmful. The use of the common score patterns should be avoided until there is evidence of classification accuracy and clinical utility, including such information as false positive rates and false negative rates, among others.

In summary, the BBRS-2 is a well-designed and well-constructed scale that is likely to produce reliable scale scores that are useful to determine one of the seven specific behavior problems. However, the use of the component scores and the common score patterns should be avoided until there is evidence of their meaningfulness and utility.

REVIEWER'S REFERENCE

Kane, M. T. (1982). A sampling model for validity. *Applied Psychological Measurement, 6*(2), 125–160.

[17]

The Business Critical Thinking Skills Test.

Purpose: "Developed to assess the critical thinking skills of business professionals and business students."

Population: Adult business professionals and business students.

Publication Dates: 2007-2008.

Acronym: BCTST.

Scores, 6: Analysis, Inference, Evaluation, Deductive, Inductive, Total.

Administration: Group.

Price Data, 2008: $60 per manual (2007, 28 pages) and example test booklet; $250 per one-time client online testing set-up fee; $20 each first 50 online testing uses; $15 each 51-500 online testing uses; $10 each online testing use over 500; $20 each first 50 paper-and-pencil test booklets, answer forms, and scoring sheets; $15 each 51-500 paper-and-pencil test booklets, answer forms, and scoring sheets; $10 each paper-and-pencil test booklets, answer forms, and scoring sheets; discounts available for nonprofit organizations.

Time: (50) minutes.
Comments: This test can be administered online or via paper and pencil.
Authors: Peter A. Facione, Stephen Blohm, and Noreen C. Facione.
Publisher: Insight Assessment–The California Academic Press LLC.

Review of the Business Critical Thinking Skills Test by PATRICIA A. BACHELOR, Professor of Psychology Emeritus, California State University, Long Beach, Long Beach, CA:

DESCRIPTION. The Business Critical Thinking Skills Test (BCTST) was developed to assess the critical thinking skills of business professionals or business students at the graduate and undergraduate levels by human resource professionals, educators, and researchers. The BCTST, a later version of the California Critical Thinking Skills Test (CCTST; 12:58), consists of 35 multiple-choice items that can be administered in groups using an online or paper-and-pencil format. Both formats allow examinees to return to skipped items and all items are scored dichotomously (right answer = 1 point; blank/wrong answers = 0 points). Unless other arrangements are made, examinees have 45 minutes to complete the test. The publisher provides scanning and scoring of the paper-and-pencil version and provides instructions for scoring and downloading of test results to enable establishment of local norms for the online form. A sample item was presented at the beginning of the test to reduce test anxiety and demonstrate how to answer a question correctly.

Instructions to all online examinees included the statement that both men and women do equally well on the BCTST. The authors stated that cultural and ethnic references were avoided and that male and female referents were used equally. Actually, most references to people were gender neutral, which is to be applauded. Unfortunately, although the items were for the most part gender neutral and male and female referents were used sparingly, there were ethnic names and the only two photographs were of women in lower level positions (one a sales clerk and the other a construction worker with a Hispanic name). Both pictures were on the first page of the test. This oversight is particularly disappointing given the proposed avoidance of cultural/ethnic references. No performance data were provided to substantiate the claim of equal performance across genders or to indicate that there were no cultural biases.

DEVELOPMENT. The BCTST is composed of five subscales. The first three subscales were called core critical thinking skills. These were Analysis (identify the relationships among concepts), Evaluation (state the results of one's reasoning), and Inference (draw conclusions based on data). The last two subscales were reasoning skills. Reasoning skills require an examinee to formulate hypotheses and test conclusions drawn from the information provided. The reasoning required to solve the problems is either Inductive or Deductive, so examinees induce, as in statistical inference toward a conclusion or deduce the solution using mathematical principles or proofs. It is reported that 6 items each were used to measure each of the three core critical thinking areas (Analysis, Evaluation, and Inference) and 10 items each were used to assess the Deductive and Inductive reasoning subscales. Hence, some items measure more than one subscale. The authors did not provide item analysis, factor analysis, or any other standard test construction technique to determine scale composition. These analyses could have been extremely helpful in validation studies of the test as well. Despite these glaring omissions, basic guidelines for score interpretation were given. Scores of 0, 1, or 2 are considered as weak performance whereas 5 or 6 are deemed as strong performance for the three 6-item scales (Analysis, Evaluation, and Inference). For the two 10-item scales, weak performances were defined as 3 or less and strong performances were 8 or more. The test items are derived from typical business problems and most answers and distractors are quite well crafted, with some notable exceptions. The test did not have an accompanying key, which would have been extremely helpful. Some items did not seem to have a correct answer whereas other questions were unclear, had extra information, or had presentation errors in the graph/chart. Classical fallacies are used as distractors for pedagogy purposes, and dispositional attributes (impatience, affective responses, and personal bias) were also included in some of the distractors.

TECHNICAL.

Standardization sample. No information was provided in the 2007 test manual that accompanies the BCTST on the 223 persons whose scores were presented as preliminary norms. The manual makes reference to several samples that have taken the BCTST, but no descriptive data were presented about these groups. The manual instructs users to compare their results to three groups (plus the preliminary norms on the validation sample) and use the percentile information of the one that most closely matches their results. For example, a score of 15 could be at the 50th percentile, 25th percentile, or 60th percentile depending on which group of scores one's score most closely resembles (which is at the 35th percentile for the validation sample). It is impossible to compare the performance of any group to another without any normative information and therefore this measure does not meet accepted standardized test construction and use. Unfortunately, at this point the BCTST can only be considered a research tool under development.

Reliability. Internal consistency reliabilities of the BCTST were estimated by calculating KR-20. The coefficients for the five subscales ranged from .86 to .92. KR-20 for the entire 35-item test was .88. Hence these reliability coefficients justify the claim of internal consistency of the BCTST. The authors created five subscales to capture their assumption of five dimensions of critical thinking, but at its heart the BCTST measures essentially one concept: the ability to think critically and possess it as a habit of mind when solving any problem. Items vary in difficulty and critical thinking skills needed to solve problems; hence, the authors should consider performing a factor analysis despite their comments that critical thinking is complex and multifaceted.

Validity. Test items appear to be assessing/measuring the content adequately sampled from the universe of critical thinking items. To determine criterion validity the authors utilized correlations of the CCTST with other standardized measures such as the GRE-Q, GRE-V, ACT, and SAT. Although these values attained statistical significance, these data are for a different test than the one currently under review. Hence, when these data are available for the BCTST the evaluation of criterion validity can be addressed. It was asserted that these data are forthcoming.

The manual states that data to support predictive criterion-related validity is also forthcoming in the next version of the manual. It is expected that correlations between the BCTST and an external criterion measure of successful performance in the field of business would lend support for predictive criterion-related validity. Standardized tests used in admission to graduate and undergraduate programs could also reveal predicted relationships so one could have increased confidence these data are a measure of the attribute under investigation.

COMMENTARY. The BCTST was designed to assess five key skills of critical thinking skills for business professionals and students. Normative comparisons are not possible because no data on the standardization sample were provided. The estimate of the internal consistency reliability of the 35-item test using the KR-20 was .88; the subscale reliabilities ranged from .86 to .92. The high values of KR-20 estimates for the subscales and the total test suggest that the subscales are interrelated; hence, these data suggest that the test is measuring a unidimensional construct. Scale construction was not discussed, nor were the items comprising each subscale. That is unacceptable to test users who need to make decisions about performance on the test. Obviously, scale composition as well as item intercorrelations, item-to-total score correlations, and factor analysis to assist in the evaluation of scale development and an understanding of the factor structure underlying the BCTST is expected to be forthcoming. Content validity was supported by an impressive panel of experts concluding that the items came from the universe of critical thinking items. No acceptable evidence is presented to warrant the construct validity or predictive criterion-related validity of the BCTST to date. However, the manual reports that the BCTST will be correlated with several standardized tests of achievement and/or an appropriate external criterion in the next version. Hence, one should consider this test as experimental and still under development.

SUMMARY. At this time, the BCTST is a research tool only and cannot be used for any statements of normalized performance, admission, or advances. The Business Critical Thinking Skills Test (BCTST) is a standardized test consisting of 35 multiple-choice items and was designed to yield scores on the five subscales (Analysis, Evaluation, Inference, Inductive Reasoning, and Deductive Reasoning) and a total score. No information was provided in the 2007 test manual about the 223 test takers who comprised the standardization sample; hence, no valid normative statements can be made. An estimate of the internal consistency reliability (KR-20) of the total test was .88, whereas the values for the five subscales ranged from .86 to .92. Hence, claims of internal consistency reliability of a unidimensional structure of critical thinking skills are supported. More than 20 years of research conducted by the test authors on the various aspects of critical thinking was convincing evidence that the universe of items had been adequately sampled to establish content validity. Correlations of the BCTST's parent instrument, the CCTST, with other achievement scores were not appropriate for establishing the BCTST's construct validity, however. Unfortunately, we await the next manual for evidence to support predictive criterion-related validity. Hence, currently, claims of the psychometric properties of the BCTST are limited to internal consistency reliability and content validity.

Review of the Business Critical Thinking Skills Test by JEAN P. KIRNAN, Professor of Psychology, The College of New Jersey, Ewing, NJ:

[The reviewer gratefully acknowledges the contributions of Jennifer Kaswin to this critique. Her insights and perspectives contributed significantly to the review.]

DESCRIPTION. The Business Critical Thinking Skills Test (BCTST) is designed to measure critical thinking (CT) skills of business students and business professionals. The BCTST was developed as an offshoot of the California Critical Thinking Skills Test (CCTST; 12:58), to provide a more appropriate measurement of CT. CT is measured through a total score and individual scores on each of five subscales: Analysis, Evaluation, Inference, Inductive Reasoning, and Deductive Reasoning.

The BCTST is composed of 35 multiple-choice questions varying between four and five answer choices. The test can be administered via paper-and-pencil format or online. A major advantage of the online test is that it allows for immediate scoring. Both the paper-and-pencil format and online versions are enhanced by colorful graphs, charts, and pictures. A commendable effort was made to include a mix of male and female characters as well as various ethnic groups in test items. Categories of questions include interpreting graphs, applying logic, calculating percents, and making inferences in a business context. A few items, however, lack face validity and some appear to be measuring verbal skills or English-language familiarity.

The 28-page test manual provides comprehensive instructions for test administrators. Despite these excellent directives, two areas remain unclear. The instructions do not address the use of calculators, which would facilitate responses to five of the test items. This ambiguity serves as a potential source of error if allowed to vary across administrations. Additionally, although a 45-minute time limit is recommended, test publishers note this period can be extended yet fail to offer an explanation of the rationale behind extending the time.

The BCTST can be utilized for three main purposes: group assessment, program evaluations, and at the individual level for admission, placement, or advising. Specifically, the test publishers explain that group assessment can be used in order to establish group statistics and determine baseline, entry, and exit-level CT skills. The BCTST can also aid in evaluating a program's effectiveness in fostering the development of CT skills by measuring if participants' CT ability increased upon completion of the program. For individual decisions, the BCTST can be useful in determining if students or professionals have the basic CT skills to learn and whether they should be exempt from a class or training program that intends to develop CT skills.

The score report includes a total score and a score for each of the subscales in addition to a brief description of the implications of the subscale scores. The paper-and-pencil format must be mailed to the test publisher for scanning and scoring of the test. The test manual and sample test booklet cost $60. There is also a $250 one-time fee to set up online testing. The first 50 online tests or paper-and-pencil tests are $20 each. The next 51 to 500 tests are $15 each, and every test over 500 is $10 each.

DEVELOPMENT. About three pages of the test manual are devoted to the definition of critical thinking and its importance in undergraduate education and ultimately the workplace. The authors refer to "this test instrument, a gold standard in the testing industry" (manual, p. 6). It is unclear how an instrument less than 1 year in use could have already achieved the "gold" standard. There are numerous references in the manual to the CCTST, but the BCTST must provide sufficient documentation to stand on its own. It would be useful if more time was spent documenting the development and validity of this particular instrument, the BCTST.

Although detailed definitions of the subscales are provided, there is no information as to how the scales were derived. There is further confusion on how individual items contribute to the subscales. The manual states that subscales of Analysis, Inference, and Evaluation each use 6 items, whereas Deductive and Inductive Reasoning each use 10 items. However, the score report lists the number of items in each subscale as: Inductive (20), Deductive (15), Analysis (10), Inference (15), and Evaluation (10). These differences require clarification or correction, and they suggest the potential for significant scale overlap in a test of 35 items. Statistical techniques such as factor analysis and interitem correlations should have been conducted to develop or confirm these subscales, or should be described, if they were conducted.

TECHNICAL. It is recommended that users establish local norms, but in the interim, they are encouraged to rely on normative data from a validation sample. Three other sample groups are also provided with the suggestion that the user refer to whichever group more closely resembles their initial BCTST test takers, adopting that group as the normative group. The use of various normative groups is a common practice and indeed is encouraged to ensure the most relevant comparisons for score interpretation. However, the relevance of the normative group should be determined on the basis of demographic information and not score distribution. No information is provided regarding these four samples except for the sample size, which ranges from 153 to 781. One should not use normative samples for interpretation without knowing basic information about these groups such as gender, ethnicity/race, age, educational level, years of work experience, occupation, job type and level, socioeconomic status, and geographical region.

Strong reliability estimates for the BCTST were calculated using internal consistency measures and produced coefficients ranging from .86 to .92. It is unclear if reliability was determined separately for each subscale as well as the total score or if this range results from multiple studies of total score reliability using different samples. Separate reliability measures should be provided for all reported scores. Additionally, consideration should be given to other demonstrations of reliability such as test-retest.

Content validity is claimed but the evidence is insufficient. The publishers state that each of the BCTST items was chosen for its theoretical relationship with the conceptual definition of Critical Thinking expressed in the Delphi Report produced by the American Philosophical Association. Although using the Delphi definition of critical thinking is commendable, what is not explained is the process that was used to determine agreement with that definition. Who determined that these 35 items covered the domains described by the report and what process was used to determine if sufficient coverage and proportional coverage had been achieved?

Although construct validity is discussed, there is insufficient evidence to establish a reasonable level of construct validity for the BCTST. The demonstration of construct validity is often achieved by presenting an accumulation of evidence rather than relying on any individual research study. Although many appropriate studies are discussed, all utilized the CCTST and not the BCTST. Mention was made of a study in progress that would demonstrate score improvement in the BCTST following a course in critical thinking. Demonstration of validity could be expanded to include groups presumed to differ in critical thinking required for jobs or educational programs (Onwuegbuzie, 2001). Anecdotal information from BCTST test takers is also provided. Such statements provide face validity only, which is not recognized as a sufficient demonstration of validity.

Criterion validity is promised in the future and the authors suggest that correlations will be similar to those attained when correlating the CCTST with other measures such as GRE scores, SAT Verbal, ACT score, scores on the Watson-Glaser CTA (another measure of critical thinking of some long standing), and the Nelson-Denny (a measure of reading comprehension). These correlations with existing measures would be welcome; however, they do not constitute criterion-related validity but rather would add to the accumulation of evidence required for construct validity. In fact, criterion-related validity may not be optimal for this instrument. It could only be demonstrated by showing a relationship between BCTST scores and an agreed upon outcome or behavior that demonstrates CT.

COMMENTARY. Data presented for norms, reliability, and validity (of the BCTST) are incomplete in terms of describing the samples used and the methodology for data collection. The

BCTST is a new instrument and the authors cite several studies planned or underway that might address its shortcomings. However, it is troubling that very similar criticisms were cited for other instruments developed by these same authors. For example, the California Critical Thinking Dispositions Inventory (CCTDI; 18:20), a measure of disposition (not ability) to think critically, also had insufficient information on normative samples, development of cutoff scores, and confusion/inadequacy of validity claims (Callahan, 1995). A review of the California Critical Thinking Skills Test (CCTST), although more favorable, still cites inadequacies in reliability, construct validity, and normative information (Michael, 1995).

SUMMARY. The need to develop and measure critical-thinking skills is well documented (Adams, 1999; Braun, 2004; Stein, Hanes, & Unterstein, 2003). The BCTST would appear to have some advantages over the well-established measure of CT, the Watson-Glaser, such as business face validity and better reliability. However, the lack of information on development, insufficient norms, and "in progress" validity studies suggests a "wait and see" approach to recommending this instrument.

REVIEWER'S REFERENCES

Adams, B. L. (1999). Nursing education for critical thinking: An integrative review. *Journal of Nursing Education, 38*(3), 111-119.

Braun, N. M. (2004). Critical thinking in the business curriculum. *Journal of Education for Business, 79*, 232-236.

Callahan, C. M. (1995). [Review of the California Critical Thinking Disposition Inventory.] In J. C. Conoley & J. C. Impara (Eds.), *The twelfth mental measurements yearbook* (p. 142). Lincoln, NE: Buros Institute of Mental Measurements.

Michael, W. B. (1995). [Review of the California Critical Thinking Skills Test.] In J. C. Conoley & J. C. Impara (Eds.), *The twelfth mental measurements yearbook* (pp. 145-146). Lincoln, NE: Buros Institute of Mental Measurements.

Onwuegbuzie, A. J. (2001). Critical thinking skills: A comparison of doctoral and master's level students. *College Student Journal, 35*(3), 477-480.

Stein, B. S., Haynes, A. F., & Unterstein, J. (2003, December). Assessing critical thinking skills. Paper presented at the 2003 SACS/COC Annual Meeting. Abstract retrieved August 26, 2008, from http://209.85.141.104/search?q=cache:LaajIdFYHc0J:iweb.tntech.edu/cti/SACS%2520presentation%2520paper.pdf+Unterstein+%26+%22Assessing+critical+thinking+%22&hl=en&ct=clnk&cd=1&gl=us

[18]

C-BDQ Correctional Officer Background Data Questionnaire.

Purpose: Developed to assess background and personal characteristics.

Population: Candidates for entry-level correctional officer positions.

Publication Date: 1995.

Acronym: C-BDQ.

Scores: 7 biodata subtypes: Unscored Demographic Information, Background, Lifestyle, Interest, Personality, Ability, Opinion-Based.

Administration: Individual or group.

Price Data: Available from publisher.

Time: 60 minutes.

Comments: "It is recommended that this test be given in conjunction with one of IPMA-HR's other entry-level correctional officer tests."

Author: International Public Management Association for Human Resources and Bruce Davey Associates.

Publisher: International Public Management Association for Human Resources (IPMA-HR).

Review of the C-BDQ Correctional Officer Background Data Questionnaire by SUSAN M. BROOKHART, Duquesne University and Brookhart Enterprises LLC, Helena, MT:

DESCRIPTION. The Correctional Officer Background Data Questionnaire (BDQ) is a 68-item multiple-choice questionnaire designed to predict success as a correctional officer. It is intended for use in the hiring process. Item types include unscored demographic information and items about background, lifestyle, interests, personality, ability, and opinions.

DEVELOPMENT AND VALIDATION. The C-BDQ was based on the same job analysis as the C1 and C2 Correctional Officer Examinations by the same publisher. A pilot version of the C-BDQ was developed, with 120 items. A concurrent validation study (correlating items with performance ratings) failed to produce significant results, partly because of restricted range and low interrater agreement on performance ratings.

A predictive validation study was undertaken with a sample of new hires. The criterion employed was a composite performance rating scale based on both supervisor ratings and turnover data. Separate keys were developed that predicted success in Michigan and Louisiana (the two states in the sample), and then cross-validated on the other state. Only items that were significant predictors of success in both states were used in the final key. This key was then subjected to further cross-validation (using five subsamples). The final key included 17 predictor items, with average validity coefficients of .25 for the subsamples and a validity coefficient of .30 for predicting performance for the total sample. Differential prediction (black/white and male/female) was tested; results suggested no adverse impact would result from using the C-BDQ.

No rationale is given for retaining items beyond the 4 demographic items and the 17 keyed items. The identity of the 17 keyed items is not given. Neither examinees nor potential employers could tell from the questionnaire which items are actually scored.

TECHNICAL.

Standardization. Raw scores (total for the 17 items) are converted to standard scores with a mean of 75 and a standard deviation of 10. Sample size for the standardization was 1,101 (the 423 Michigan and 678 Louisiana entry-level correctional officers from the predictive validity study). The actual range for standardized scores was 35 to 100. Expectancy tables were built for standardized scores. No cutoff score is recommended, but the expectancy tables provide information that would allow hiring institutions to decide on a cutoff score for their own use.

Reliability. No reliability data are given except for the low interrater reliability (.39) that was used as a justification for not considering the results of the initial concurrent validity study. An internal consistency reliability for the 17-item final key would be a useful statistic to use to help evaluate the validity coefficients based on it.

COMMENTARY. The self-reflective C-BDQ items are all operational (behavioral)–asking for judgments about how frequently some things happen, for example, or how well one thinks one does certain things. They are not typical of "personality test" items. Some examinees might even enjoy the exercise of answering them and the self-reflection it affords. However, 68 questions seems like a lot of items for examinees in which to embed the 21 (17 keyed and 4 demographic) that are used.

The technical report "Development and Validation of a Background Data Questionnaire for Correctional Officer Selection" seems to be a report submitted to the publisher from the development company. It reads like an unpublished report, and that leads this reviewer to wonder if the lack of reliability information is simply an editorial problem. It does not seem likely that the same people who were able to design such nice validity studies simply "forgot" to check the reliability of the measure.

SUMMARY. The job analysis, item development process, and validation study for the C-BDQ were carefully done. The standardization sample is adequately large. Validity data indicate that the C-BDQ can be used as one of many indicators in the hiring process. Because of the absence of reported reliability information, this reviewer recommends that its main use be as a check on other indicators of fitness for the work (for example, interviewer recommendations, references, and documentation of prior relevant experience). It should not be used as the sole, or even the main, criterion for hiring.

[19]

C-1 and C-2 Correctional Officer Tests.

Purpose: Designed as entry-level examinations for correctional officers.
Population: Candidates for entry-level correctional officer positions.
Publication Dates: 1991–1995.
Scores: 4 knowledge areas: Reading Comprehension, Counting Accuracy, Inductive Reasoning, Deductive Reasoning.
Administration: Group.
Forms, 2: C-1, C-2.
Price Data: Available from publisher.
Time: 120 minutes per test.
Comments: No prior training or experience as a correctional officer is assumed of candidates taking these tests.
Author: International Public Management Association for Human Resources.
Publisher: International Public Management Association for Human Resources (IPMA-HR).

Review of the C1 and C2 Correctional Officer Tests by SUSAN M. BROOKHART, Consultant, Duquesne University and Brookhart Enterprises LLC, Helena, MT:

DESCRIPTION. The C1 (1991) and C2 (1995) Correctional Officer Tests are each 90-item multiple-choice tests designed for entry-level correctional officers. They are intended for use as one of the selection tools for institutions that use written tests to screen applicants for entry-level positions. Four knowledge areas are assessed. Reading Comprehension is assessed with cloze passages; passages are short paragraphs describing scenarios or procedures that would occur in a correctional facility. Counting Accuracy is assessed with two types of items, one requiring visual counts and the other requiring addition and subtraction in word problems. Inductive Reasoning is assessed with items requiring the interpretation of charts and forms and with items requiring applying policy. Deductive Reasoning is assessed with items requiring situational judgment. The context for all items, both scenarios and word problems, is working in a correctional facility.

The test is easy to read, and the directions are clear. The items are clearly written, well edited, and well laid out. The items are written in such a way that the relevance to the job of correctional officer should be clear to examinees.

DEVELOPMENT. The development of the C1 Correctional Officer Examination began with a job analysis conducted in 1990. Twelve correctional facilities in a number of states provided training materials, task lists, and job descriptions. This information was supplemented with on-site observations and interviews at five institutions. Five subject-matter experts (supervisory-level officers) at several institutions were also interviewed. A list of possible knowledge, skills, and attitudes was developed, as was a task list.

The second step in development was a job analysis questionnaire, requesting ratings of frequency and importance of the items on the task list. However, all of the tasks on the list were judged frequent and important. An item pool was developed, reviewed by subject-matter experts, and pilot tested. Items were eliminated if item statistics indicated they were too easy, ambiguous or confusing, or nondiscriminating (low point-biserial correlation). A few items were also eliminated based on differential item functioning for race (Black/White) or gender.

Validity and reliability studies (see below) resulted in the removal or combination of several initial subtests that did not correlate with job performance, leaving the four subtests: Reading Comprehension, Counting Accuracy, Inductive Reasoning, and Deductive Reasoning.

The C2 Correctional Officer Examination used the results of the same job analysis. A different item pool was developed, reviewed by subject-matter experts, and pilot tested. The item pool for the C2 Examination did not include any items for subtests that had not shown validity coefficients of sufficient magnitude in the development of the C1 Examination.

TECHNICAL.

Standardization. There are no normative data except to recommend that 80% or above serves as an effective screening point for the C1. No cutoff score recommendation is made for the C2. For both tests, the publisher recommends use as one of several screening assessments. Test results were based on a sample size of 292 for the C1 and 241 for the C2, with fewer in each group participating in the validity study because of lack of supervisor data.

Reliability. KR-20 for the preliminary C1 with 130 items (the validation study) was .89. No reliability value was given for the 90-item (final) version. KR-20 for the C2 final version (90 items) was .91.

Validity. Several types of validity evidence were presented. The content of the test was based on a job analysis involving correctional officers and their supervisors from around the country, and the content of the resulting test items was also reviewed by correctional officer supervisors. Criterion-related validity evidence was provided by correlating test score performance with supervisors' ratings of job performance (for the C1) and with a composite performance rating combining supervisors' ratings and turnover (for the C2). Subtests that did not correlate significantly ($p < .05$) with performance were dropped. Differential prediction was studied for both race (White/Black) and gender; no evidence of differential prediction was found. Although the criterion-related validity studies used subtest as well as overall scores, an expectancy table built for the C1 used total score, implying that total scores are the ones to be used for screening.

The C1 validity coefficients themselves were somewhat low for subtests and a bit better for total score. Correlation of subtest scores for the C1 with supervisor ratings of performance ranged from .16 to .26; correlation of the total (90-item) score for the C1 with supervisor ratings was .31.

The C2 validity coefficients for subtests (correlations of C2 subtest scores with composite ratings of performance) ranged from .15 to .33. The correlation of the total (90-item) score for the C2 with composite performance was .30.

COMMENTARY. In this reviewer's opinion, presenting multiple sources of validity evidence was the strongest aspect of the C1 and C2. The writing in the manuals "Development and Validation of the C1 Correctional Officer Examination" and "Development and Validation of the C2 Correctional Officer Examination" was uneven in quality, and the tables were not always laid out intuitively. Nevertheless, the implied conceptualization of validity as an argument requiring different kinds of supporting evidence, and the presentation of multiple types of evidence, is a strength of these tests. This is a bit unusual—one usually finds reliabilities or item statistics, the easier things to report, to be the strong points.

SUMMARY. The technical manuals are not without their flaws, but overall this deficiency seems to be more an issue of report-writing quality than the quality of the actual test-development process and data analyses. Reliability is acceptable. Validity coefficients are somewhat low, but are only one part of a several-pronged approach to validity. Differential item functioning and differential prediction were checked; this feature is important for any test and perhaps especially for an occupation like correctional officer that attracts a diverse applicant pool.

Because of the importance of validity evidence and its centrality in the development and documentation of this test, this reviewer can recommend the use of the C1 and C2 Correctional Officer Examinations for the limited purposes their publisher claims for them: as one of several screening measures for entry-level correctional officers for institutions that want one of their screening measures to be a paper-and-pencil test of reading, counting, and reasoning.

[20]

The California Critical Thinking Disposition Inventory [2007 Edition].

Purpose: Designed to measure the dispositional dimension of critical thinking.
Population: Working professionals, high school, and college students.
Publication Dates: 1992-2007.
Acronym: CCTDI.
Scores, 8: Overall score, Truth-Seeking, Open-Mindedness, Analyticity, Systematicity, CT-Confidence, Inquisitiveness, Cognitive Maturity.
Administration: Group.
Price Data, 2008: $180 per 25 test booklets with answer and scoring forms; $45 per manual (2007, 32 pages).
Foreign Language Editions: French, Spanish, Chinese, Hebrew, Japanese, and Thai.
Time: Administration time not reported.
Comments: This test can be administered online or via paper and pencil.
Authors: Peter A. Facione and Noreen C. Facione.
Publisher: Insight Assessment.
Cross References: For reviews by Carolyn M. Callahan and Salvador Hector Ochoa of an earlier edition, see 12:57.

Review of the California Critical Thinking Disposition Inventory by BRAD M. MERKER, Staff Neuropsychologist, Henry Ford Health System, Detroit, MI:

DESCRIPTION. The California Critical Thinking Disposition Inventory (CCTDI) is a measure of an individual's disposition to think critically. This disposition is defined as "a characterological profile, a constellation of attitudes, a set of intellectual virtues, or ... a group of habits of mind" (manual, p. 3). The test is constructed of 75 Likert-style six-choice items designed to profile Critical Thinking (CT) dispositions of individuals and groups. The test also may be used for pre- and posttesting to determine if programs are effective in maintaining or increasing CT dispositions of the class; and in corroboration "with other evidence, for purposes of admissions, placement, or advising" (manual, p. 32). The test can be used by both educators and researchers to assess critical thinking in individuals from high school age up to working professionals. The test may be especially helpful for those in the health sciences professions. It is available in English and numerous other languages.

Specific instructions for administration are provided. The CCTDI can be administered online or via paper and pencil. Online administration results in instant scoring, whereas paper-and-pencil administration requires the return of the score answer sheets to Insight Assessment for scoring.

The CCTDI provides eight scores including an overall score and seven subscale scores. Each scale consists of between 9 and 12 items. The seven subscales assess Truth-Seeking, Open-Mindedness, Analyticity, Systematicity, CT-Confidence, Inquisitiveness, and Cognitive Maturity. Each scaled score ranges from 10 up to 60 yielding a total possible score of 420. Subscale scores at or below 30 reflect a more intensely negative disposition, from 30 to 40 indicate ambivalence, and scores 40 or above reflect an increasingly positive disposition. The test developers recommend using a total score of less than 280 to suggest an overall deficiency in the disposition towards critical thinking and a score at or above 350 as a general indication of strength in the disposition towards critical thinking. A subscale score above 50 on any scale may indicate a strong disposition or aspect.

DEVELOPMENT. The development of the CCTDI began in 1991 and was guided by the conceptualization presented in the 1990 Delphi report. The report defined critical thinking as "the cognitive engine which drives problem-solving and decision-making" (manual, p. 6). Cognitive skills of interpretation, analysis, inference, evaluation, and explanation are at the core of critical thinking. It requires "reasoned, consideration to evidence, context, theories, methods and criteria in order to form this purposeful judgment" (manual, p. 7). Based on the Delphi CT construct "multiple pilot items were written for each phrase of the consensus description of the ideal critical thinker" (manual, p. 13). Subsequently, 250 prompts were reviewed by college-level educators to identify ambiguities. After screening, "150 pilot prompts were retained in a preliminary version of the instrument" (manual, p. 13). The preliminary version was then "administered to 164 students at three different universities, one in Canada, one in California, and one in the Midwestern United States" (manual, p. 13). Seventy-five items were retained "based on both their internal consistency and their ability to discriminate between respondents" (manual, p. 13). The test was published for commercial use in 1992.

TECHNICAL. Limited information on normative data or the development of cut scores is provided in the manual. The test authors discuss a study using 267 undergraduates drawn from the United States and Canada. Of the 267 college students, 22% earned an overall CCTDI score of less than 280. The test authors note that the cutscore tables provided in the manual (p. 28) are not intended to be norms and provide minimal rationale for using cutscores of 40 or 50 as means of evaluating an individual's disposition to critical thinking.

Evidence supporting the reliability of the CCTDI pilot version was provided through estimates of internal consistency. The overall alpha coefficient was .91. The publication version had an overall alpha coefficient of .90 and subscale alpha values ranged from .60 to .78 which suggests the internal consistency of the subscales is generally adequate. Item-to-total correlations also were provided and ranged from .17 to .63.

Face, construct, and convergent validity evidence is detailed in the manual. Face validity evidence was derived from statements of college instructors who noted that the CCTDI prompts "strike them as appropriate to the target dispositions" (manual, p. 16). Factor analysis indicated the test is composed of seven nonorthogonal and nondiscrete factors and that several items load on multiple scales. As such, "when the CCTDI is scored, discrete scales are forced" (manual, p. 14). Item loadings ranged from .03 to .69 and, despite two items having very poor loadings, the developers state the items were retained because of their contribution to overall internal reliability and they were conceptually consistent. Convergent validity was demonstrated by showing the CCTDI was related to the NEO-PI Openness to Experience, the ACT, SAT-Verbal subscale, and a subscale measure of ego resiliency. Finally, research using undergraduate students suggests that there are longitudinal changes in CT dispositions over time and that gender and/or cultural ideology may influence the development of CT.

COMMENTARY. The CCTDI is a well-developed test of critical thinking. It is based on a soundly defined construct and has enough research supporting its use as a research measure of an individuals' disposition to think critically. The test is available in numerous languages and is relatively easy to administer. However, the test is not without its limitations. Unfortunately, there are no normative data available and the developers provide limited rationale on how they determined the recommended cut scores. The lack of normative data is especially concerning given research has shown that age, education, gender, and/or cultural ideology may influence the development of CT. Another limitation of the CCTDI is that several of the items demonstrated low internal consistency and other items overlapped on various subscales. Despite these shortcomings 2 items were retained due to their conceptual consistency with the scales. Finally, another limitation is the need to send paper-and-pencil protocols to Insight Assessments for scoring. This 75-item test could very easily be scored by hand yet no scoring template or directions for scoring are provided in the manual.

In order to improve the test, additional reliability and validity data are needed. For instance, validity studies looking at the CCTDI and measures of executive functioning would be helpful in demonstrating the relationship between the CCTDI and higher order cognitive functioning such as problem solving and complex decision making. Furthermore, normative data would go a long way in supporting the use of the CCTDI for the purposes of candidate selection.

SUMMARY. The CCTDI is a 75-item test designed to assess an individual's disposition to think critically. The test can be completed in a brief period of time and provides an overall score and seven subscale scores measuring Truth-Seeking, Open-Mindedness, Analyticity, Systematicity, CT-Confidence, Inquisitiveness, and Cognitive Maturity. Limited normative data are available and current research suggests that the disposition to think critically may be mediated by age, education, gender, and cultural ideology. Given the lack of normative data and limited evidence of validity the test should not be used by itself for high stakes decision making pertaining to academic entrance or job selection, but in conjunction with other sources of information including ability tests.

Review of the California Critical Thinking Disposition Inventory by JOHN F. WAKEFIELD, Professor of Education, University of North Alabama, Florence, AL:

DESCRIPTION. Since its inception in 1992, the California Critical Thinking Disposition Inventory (CCTDI) has been used to measure an attitudinal construct (and its components) described in the manual as "the disposition to think critically" (p. 1), that is, the willingness to use cognitive skills involved in making purposeful, self-regulatory judgments. The examination packet sent by the publisher included a test manual (2007 edition), a sample item booklet, and a sample answer form. The instrument consists of 75 self-report items in the style of "I hold off making decisions until I've thought through my options." Answer forms allow a person to choose one from among six alternative responses to each item (from "*agree strongly*" to "*disagree strongly*"). Forms are scored by the test publisher. Both individual and group scores are returned for an overall scale ("the disposition to think critically") as well as for seven subscales (described as Truth-Seeking, Open-Mindedness, Analyticity, Systematicity, Critical Thinking Self-Confidence, Inquisitiveness, and Maturity). The constructs of the disposition toward critical thinking and each of its seven components are described in both the test manual and in articles referenced in footnotes (e.g., Facione, Sanchez, Facione, & Gainen, 1995).

DEVELOPMENT. The test manual provides a description of the construct of a disposition to think critically; the seven subscales that correspond to the seven components of the construct; the process of developing the inventory; information for ordering and administering the inventory; and suggestions for interpreting and using the scores. Earlier reviews of the instrument have described how the instrument was developed from a consensual definition of critical thinking that was the product of the Delphi Project sponsored by the American Philosophical Association. Shortcomings in the development of the instrument have less to do with the central construct than with its empirical validation. Items were selected for trial from an initial pool of 250 prompts. College educators screened them, but there is no indication of the reliability of the screening. The resulting 150 items were piloted with 164 college students who are described as attending three regionally diverse comprehensive universities. Factor analysis was used with these results to identify items with common loadings to further select items for the seven subscales, but there is no indication that factor analysis was used to confirm the seven-factor model with the final 75-item instrument. Over the past decade, several independent research efforts (reviewed in Walsh, Seldomridge, & Bedros, 2007) have failed to confirm the seven-factor model from administrations of the inventory to diverse college groups. Collectively, these shortcomings indicate an emerging need for revision of the instrument.

TECHNICAL. The efforts to develop norms for the test appear to be largely post-publication. Consequently, concerns arise about procedures that were followed to standardize scores on the existing instrument. First, there is no description in the manual of any norm group in terms of demographics such as age, gender, ethnicity, and education. Second, there is no description of how raw scores on subscales of various lengths (from 9 to 12 items) are converted into scaled scores (which vary from 10 to 60 on each subscale, and 70 to 420 on the overall scale). Third, users are expected without further evidence to accept score ranges as indicative of weakness (e.g., below 30), ambivalence (e.g., 30 to 40), or strength (e.g., above 40) in specific dispositions represented by the subscales and similarly in the overall disposition to think critically (represented by the sum of the seven subscale scores). One consequence of these shortcomings is that care needs to be taken in the interpretation of data. For example, in one study reported in the manual, 90% of a cohort of 567 freshmen at a selective comprehensive university were reported as strong on "inquisitiveness" because they scored over 40 on the subscale for Inquisitiveness. One might conclude this cohort to be an extraordinarily curious bunch, but with scores this uniformly high, the report raises questions about score scaling and norming that cannot be answered by information provided in the test manual. Other than in one sample score report, there are neither norms nor standard deviations presented in the manual.

The test manual states that the inventory is "based on a conceptual definition, rather than one which presents a cleanly faceted model achieved primarily through empirical methods" (p. 14). As a consequence, empirical methods are inconsistently used to demonstrate reliability and validity. Alpha reliabilities that are reported for the overall score (.91) and subscale scores (.71–.80) are comparable to those of well-known instruments to assess personality, interests, and the like. Correlations between subscale scores, however, are not reported. Evidence of the stability of scores over time is not presented. Correlations between CCTDI subscale scores and the NEO Personality Inventory factor "openness to experience," college entrance exam scores, critical thinking test scores, and some other variables are reported. These correlations surpass criteria of statistical significance (explaining between 4% and 20% of shared variances), but they do not demonstrate the concurrent or predictive validity of CCDTI scores for outcomes assessment. A more robust test of validity for this purpose would be the correlation of CCTDI scores with ratings of a person's disposition to think critically, to seek truth, to be open-minded, and so forth. Indications of concurrent and/or predictive validity are crucial for assessment instruments that are designed to measure outcomes of any kind.

COMMENTARY. The test manual proposes two categories of use for the inventory: research and assessment. Given the absence in the manual of any carefully described norm group, a description of how raw scores are converted into scaled scores, and significant evidence of concurrent or predictive validity, there is no solid psychometric foundation provided through the test manual for using the CCTDI to assess an outcome of education. Nevertheless, the construct of a disposition to think critically is reasonably defined, and scores have sufficient reliability and face validity for research purposes. Some of this research needs to be conducted on the CCTDI to revise the instrument to reflect the results of confirmatory factor analysis and to provide evidence of technical (not just face) validity for outcomes assessment. Other research has provided some insight into relationships between the disposition to think critically and other variables, such as year in college and choice of curriculum (e.g., Giancarlo & Facione, 2001; Lampert, 2007; Walsh & Hardy, 1999). Other good research questions, such as the relationship between a disposition to think critically and the cognitive style known as reflectivity (see the sample item), remain to be explored. Care needs to be taken in the gathering of data and the interpretation of results to account for information that the test manual does not provide with respect to scaling and norming. In the absence of such data, the overall disposition score appears to be the variable from the CCDTI most valid for use in research, unless the structure and interpretation of the subscales are the subjects of investigation.

SUMMARY. Over 15 years ago, the CCTDI was developed as an instrument to assess an important educational outcome, which is the disposition to think critically, but the inventory was not developed primarily through empirical methods. The result is an instrument that reliably measures a construct that may be of interest to educators, but the absence of critical psychometric data in the test manual can only signify to potential users that the CCDTI has yet to be validated for outcomes assessment. More research needs to be conducted on the CCDTI to refine the components of its central construct, to scale and normalize scores so that they are more easily interpretable, and to validate scores for use in outcomes assessment. Researchers who are interested in the measurement of dispositions should themselves be disposed toward critical thinking when they contemplate using the 1992 version of the CCTDI, its scores, or its score interpretations.

REVIEWER'S REFERENCES

Facione, P. A., Sanchez, C. A., Facione, N. C., & Gainen, J. (1995). The disposition toward critical thinking. *Journal of General Education, 44,* 1-25.

Giancarlo, C. A., & Facione, P. A. (2001). A look across four years at the disposition toward critical thinking among undergraduate students. *Journal of General Education, 50,* 29-55.

Lampert, N. (2007). Critical thinking dispositions as an outcome of undergraduate education. *Journal of General Education, 56,* 17-33.

Walsh, C. M., & Hardy, R. C. (1999). Dispositional differences in critical thinking related to gender and academic major. *Journal of Nursing Education, 38,* 149-155.

Walsh, C. M., Seldomridge, L. A., & Bedros, K. K. (2007). California Critical Thinking Disposition Inventory: Further factor analytic examination. *Perceptual and Motor Skills, 104,* 141-151.

[21]

The California Critical Thinking Skills Test [Revised].

Purpose: "Specifically designed to measure the skills dimension of critical thinking."

Population: College students and adults.
Publication Dates: 1990-2007.
Acronym: CCTST.
Administration: Group.
Price Data, 2008: $60 per manual (2007, 23 pages) and example test booklet; $250 per one-time client online testing set-up fee; $20 each first 50 online testing uses; $15 each 51-500 online testing uses; $10 each online testing use over 500; $20 each first 50 paper-and-pencil test booklets, answer forms, and scoring sheets; $15 each 51-500 paper-and-pencil test booklets, answer forms, and scoring sheets; $10 each paper-and-pencil test booklets, answer forms, and scoring sheets; discounts available for nonprofit organizations.
Foreign Language Editions: All forms available in English; Form A is available in Chinese (Beijing and Taiwan), Hebrew, Korean, Spanish (Mexico), and Thai; Form B is available in Portuguese; Form 2000 is available in French (Canadian), Italian, Korean, and Spanish (Spain).
Time: (45) minutes or unlimited.
Comments: This test can be administered online or via paper and pencil.
Authors: Peter A. Facione, Noreen C. Facione, Stephen W. Blohm, and Carol Ann F. Giancarlo.
Publisher: Insight Assessment–The California Academic Press LLC.

a) FORM A.

Scores, 4: Analysis, Inference, Evaluation, Total.

b) FORM B.

Scores, 4: Analysis, Inference, Evaluation, Total.

c) FORM C.

Scores, 6: Analysis, Inference, Evaluation, Deductive Reasoning, Inductive Reasoning, Total.

Cross-References: For reviews by Robert F. McMorris and William B. Michael of an earlier edition, see 12:58.

Review of The California Critical Thinking Skills Test [Revised] by MATTHEW E. LAMBERT, Clinical Assistant Professor of Neuropsychiatry, Texas Tech University Health Sciences Center, Department of Neuropsychiatry, Lubbock, TX:

DESCRIPTION. The California Critical Thinking Skills Test [Revised] (CCTST) is a 34-item multiple-choice test, available in three forms, designed to assess the critical thinking skills deemed essential to college education. It is available in three forms (A, B, and 2000) that can be administered via paper-and-pencil or an internet connection to the publisher's test administration site. The paper-and-pencil format requires a computer-scanned answer form on which test takers "bubble-in" their answers. The individual items address various skills of evaluating information, drawing inferences, and justifying objections to inferences. The updated Form 2000 focuses on evaluating critical thinking skills associated with ideas related to the new century. Item content is nonspecific to any one college discipline with the focus more on underlying skills necessary for a college education.

Standard administration time is 45 minutes, although it can be increased if local norms are to be developed. Regardless of administration procedures, all scoring is completed by the test publisher with results being supplied via electronic media either through the online test site or transmitted to the administrator. In addition, various forms are available in different languages that include English, Chinese, Hebrew, Korean, Spanish, Thai, French, Italian, and Portuguese. CCTST scores include: Analysis, Inference, Evaluation, Deductive Reasoning, Inductive Reasoning, and Total, each of which reflects various aspects of the critical thinking concept.

The 23-page basic manual discusses the development, administration and scoring, and psychometric underpinnings of the instrument. A supplemental manual is also provided, which addresses paper-and-pencil versus online administrations.

DEVELOPMENT. The items that comprise the CCTST Forms A and B were drawn from a pool of about 200 items created as part of a long-term study to assess critical thinking and designed to be discipline neutral. References to sex or social class were avoided with equal numbers of male and female referents in the items. The base item pool had been previously analyzed and determined to adequately discriminate critical thinkers and had high item-total correlations. Item selection for the final forms was designed to reflect five critical thinking skills previously identified by experts as the basis for problem solving and decision making: Interpretation, Analysis, Evaluation, Explanation, and Inference. Unfortunately, no information is provided as to how individual items were selected from the overall item pool.

Form 2000 consists of 22 items from Form A and 12 new items that require application of critical thinking skills to visual information (i.e., diagrams and charts) versus Forms A and B, which present only textual information. No information is presented about how the additional Form 2000 items were constructed or selected.

Regardless of the test form, items are grouped in order of critical thinking complexity although the manual does little to discuss a hierarchical concept of critical thinking skills. Distractors were written to directly address errors associated with the specific critical thinking skill to be assessed. Three or four distractors are associated with each item. The rationale for using the different numbers of distractors is not discussed.

TECHNICAL. Internal consistency estimates for the CCTST were derived from the original validation studies and produced Kuder Richardson-20 values ranging from .68 to .70 for Form A when it was used as a pretest or posttest, respectively, and .71 for Form B for a subgroup of individuals who completed both forms in an equivalency study. For a separate group of graduate nursing students who completed Form B, the Kuder Richardson-20 estimate was .75. Alternate form reliability between Form A and Form B was .78 for students who took both forms. No efforts to address test-retest reliability were presented in the test manuals. Thus, the CCTST has demonstrated adequate internal consistency and alternate form reliability.

Comparison of scores from CCTST items that make up Form A and Form 2000 revealed correlations of .91 and .87, drawn from two divergent samples. Again, Kuder Richardson-20 estimates of internal consistency for Form 2000 were .80 for a sample drawn from a large public university and .78 for a smaller sample of health science school students. As such, the Form 2000 appears to have slightly greater internal consistency than Forms A and B.

Content validity is discussed in terms of the manner in which items were selected from a pool previously analyzed for their ability to discriminate well between individuals in terms of critical thinking skills and by high interitem correlations. The discussion surrounding item selection related to content validity is limited and could benefit from significant expansion.

Construct validity is supported by CCTST pretest to posttest score improvement for students taking a required college level critical thinking course. A .74 score increase was noted across administrations, which was significant at a .008 level. Yet, a matched-pairs analysis demonstrated an average 1.45 point score gain and the average student in the paired sample moved from the 55th to the 70th percentile as compared to pretest scores. Control groups for both cross-sectional and matched-pair groups did not demonstrate significant gains. Other experiments controlling for test experience did not demonstrate differences between test-experienced and test-naïve students following a critical thinking course.

Similarly, criterion validity was assessed by comparing CCTST scores to various measures of academic performance and demographic variables. Dependent upon the measures, significant correlations ranged from .20 for college grade point average to .72 for Graduate Record Examination total score.

At the time of the CCTST manual publication in 2002, Form 2000 normative data were available for 4-year and 2-year college students for the overall score and five subscales. No discussion is presented to describe any aspect of groups upon which these norms are based. The manual also indicates that there is a plan to provide discipline specific or other group norms, but no indication is given when those norms would be available or how they would be developed. That information is reportedly provided when scores are returned by the publisher's scoring service.

Form A and Form B norms are provided for college students who have not taken a critical thinking course, nursing masters' degree students, and law enforcement academy cadets. Details regarding those normative groups are presented in the manual. Nevertheless, users are instructed to develop local population norms if there is a concern that the local population differs significantly from the scoring norms developed for the CCTST.

COMMENTARY. The CCTST appears to be a reasonable measure for assessing the complex concept of critical thinking. The concepts upon which it is based have achieved consensus by experts from multiple disciplines. Administration is rather straightforward via paper-and-pencil or through the test publisher's test administration website. Unfortunately, however, there is no mechanism for obtaining overall and subscale scores other than by submitting completed protocols to the publisher for scoring. The rationale for this process is not discussed in the manual and it would seem reasonable to calculate scores on site and compare them to normative data presented in the manual unless there are complicated calculations required for scoring. Again, such procedures are not represented in the manual.

Internal consistency, reliability, and validity data appear to be reasonable for the CCTST. The descriptions of the populations used in establishing the instrument's psychometric properties also are limited and should be expanded such that there can be a complete understanding of their applicability to populations that may be the focus of prospective test users. Current CCTST norms lack adequate description and only the norms developed for general college students may possess broad utility.

SUMMARY. The CCTST is a 34-item instrument that addresses the concept of critical thinking believed necessary for college achievement. Although there are three forms available, it appears that Form 2000 is the most desirable version as it was developed with items that reflect current issues involved in academic achievement as compared to the other two forms. The CCTST appears to possess adequate psychometric properties, although significant expansion of the manual's technical data is necessary to allow for complete evaluation of the psychometric underpinnings. The utility of generalized CCTST administration for assessing students' critical thinking skills is not justified. As such, the CCTST would be used most appropriately in specialized settings where assessment of critical thinking skills is important to academic planning or progress determination.

Review of the California Critical Thinking Skills Test [Revised] by WILLIAM E. MARTIN, JR., Professor of Educational Psychology, Northern Arizona University, Flagstaff, AZ:

DESCRIPTION. The California Critical Thinking Skills Test (CCTST) [Revised] is a 34-item multiple-choice test to measure core critical thinking skills essential to persons involved in college education programs. The CCTST also has been used with high school students in 10th through 12th grades.

The CCTST generates an overall score of critical thinking skills and five subscale scores identified as Analysis, Evaluation, Inference, Deductive Reasoning, and Inductive Reasoning. No discipline-specific college level content is expected for those taking the CCTST and the items reflect minimal technical vocabulary or jargon. Specific steps for test administration are provided in the manual and test takers are advised that they have 45 minutes to complete the test. The CCTST can be taken online or in a paper-and-pencil administration. Both formats are scored and analyzed by the publisher. The CCTST has three forms: A (1990), B (1992), and 2000. Form B was designed to be statistically equivalent to Form A for use as an alternative form in pretest/posttest designs. Form 2000 has newer item formats combined with those of Forms A and B. According to the test authors, Form 2000 is a "richer and more robust tool for evaluating critical thinking skills" (manual, p. 16).

DEVELOPMENT. The CCTST is based upon a Delphi consensus conceptualization of critical thinking published by the American Philosophical Association in 1990. A panel of 46 theorists, teachers, and critical thinking assessment specialists from several disciplines in the United States and Canada participated in developing the consensus conceptualization. The conceptual architecture was reaffirmed in a national survey and a replication study.

The test authors discuss the core critical thinking cognitive skills as analysis, evaluation, inference, interpretation, and explanation in the context of the consensus study. The five scales of the CCTST reflect Analysis, Evaluation, and Inference but use Deductive Reasoning and Inductive Reasoning in place of interpretation and explanation, respectively. The test authors contend that inductive and deductive reasoning follow a more traditional conceptualization of reasoning. There is no complete explanation given for the derivation of the replaced scales. Parenthetically, metacognitive self-regulation also was identified as a consensus core critical thinking skill but the test authors believed that it could not be assessed apart from the operation of the other skills.

The CCTST items are drawn from a pool of approximately 200 items developed over 20 years of research according to the test authors. They indicate that the items were selected based upon their ability to discriminate well between individuals and their high item-total correlations; however, no supporting empirical evidence is presented. Each multiple-choice item has one correct answer with three or four distractors.

TECHNICAL. The manual does not provide normative information for Form 2000 but does provide information for Forms A and B. Norms are provided for three groups. The first group (n = 781) was undergraduate college students with an average age of 22 years enrolled in a comprehensive, urban, state university. The second group (n = 153) consisted of masters' students in nursing from an urban university. The third group was composed of 224 cadets enrolled in a law enforcement academy. The norms are limited in representativeness and the demographic profiles of the groups lack information including ethnicity and gender of participants.

Information is presented about the equivalence of the CCTST Forms A and B. The test authors reported an $r = .77$ using a sample of 90 undergraduates from both public and private universities studied in 1992. Specific methods and procedures of the study were not discussed. The CCTST Form 2000 has 22 items from Form A and 12 items that are new. The test authors reported correlation coefficients of .91 and .87 for two groups of students from two different institutions comparing scores from Form 2000 to Form A.

Kuder-Richardson 20 coefficients are presented as measures of internal consistency of the CCTST. Three groups produced coefficients of .68, .69, and .70 for Form A. In two groups, Form B showed KR_{20} coefficients of .71 and .75. Form 2000 generated coefficients of .78 and .80 in two additional groups studied.

The primary support for content and construct validity of the CCTST offered by the test authors is the study findings of the panel of experts used in the Delphi conceptualization. The findings of a study of validation by contrasted groups are presented in which undergraduate students who took a course in critical thinking showed significant gains on the CCTST when compared to students who had not completed such a course. A table of correlations with other measures is presented to represent criterion validity. For example, the CCTST total score was reported to be highly correlated to GRE Total, GRE Analytic, and GRE Verbal scores. Also reported was a regression model accounting for 41% of the variance in CCTST scores that was attributed to a combination of SAT-Verbal, SAT-Math, college GPA, and high school GPA.

The test authors found significant gender differences on the CCTST after students completed a college level critical thinking course, but additional information was provided showing that the difference was due to other factors. There is not enough evidence presented to support either finding. Moreover, information is presented to support the position that the CCTST does not favor or disadvantage any particular ethic group. It appears that nonnative English speakers were the primary participants comprising the ethnic group. Again, there is not enough information to substantiate a clear finding.

COMMENTARY. The CCTST is well designed and easy to follow. The items are interesting and stimulate thought. The Delphi consensus conceptualization of critical thinking published by the American Philosophical Association establishes a compelling argument for the foundation of the CCTST. However, more information is needed. A fuller description of the methodology and results of the Delphi study as it directly relates to the development of the CCTST is desirable. Additional specific evidence showing the development and validity of the 200 items in the pool used for the CCTST would be valuable. A more thorough explanation is warranted for creating the two subscales of inductive and deductive reasoning rather than using the core critical thinking cognitive skills of interpretation and explanation. A further explanation for not using the core critical thinking skill of metacognitive self-regulation in the CCTST would be useful.

It is confusing to know which of the three CCTST forms to use. The Form 2000 is said to be a "richer and more robust tool" (manual, p. 16) but there is less supporting technical information presented when compared to Forms A and B. There is no normative information presented in the manual for Form 2000 although comparison norms are provided along with scores as part of the CAPSCORE service. The norm groups used for Forms A and B are composed of undergraduate students from one university, masters' students in nursing, and law enforcement cadets. The representativeness of these three groups is limited, and use of the CCTST would be enhanced if a more complete normative sample were obtained. There is no normative information presented about gender or ethnicity. The information presented about gender and ethnicity differences on the CCTST is incomplete and unconvincing.

SUMMARY. The California Critical Thinking Skills Test (CCTST) was designed to measure core critical thinking skills essential to persons involved in a college education program. The CCTST items are challenging and engaging for the testtaker. More explanation and research is needed to confirm the content and construct validity of the CCTST. Moreover, the normative sample needs to be expanded to be more representative of persons who may use the instrument. The CCTST clearly has potential for useful applications; however, more research is needed before prospective users can be comfortable with the meaning and stability of the CCTST results.

[22]

California Measure of Mental Motivation.

Purpose: Designed to "measure the degree to which an individual is motivated toward thinking."
Population: Grade K through adult.
Publication Dates: 1997-2006.
Acronym: CM3.
Administration: Group.
Levels, 4: IA, IB, II, III.
Price Data, 2008: $60 per manual (2006, 31 pages) and example test booklet; $250 per one-time client online testing set-up fee; $20 each first 50 online testing uses; $15 each 51-500 online testing uses; $10 each online testing use over 500; $20 each first 50 paper-and-pencil test booklets, answer forms, and scoring sheets; $15 each 51-500 paper-and-pencil test booklets, answer forms, and scoring sheets; $10 each paper-and-pencil test booklets, answer forms, and scoring sheets; discounts available for nonprofit organizations.
Time: (15-20) minutes.
Comments: This test can be administered online or via paper and pencil.
Authors: Carol A. F. Giancarlo and P. A. Facione.
Publisher: Insight Assessment–The California Academic Press LLC.

a) LEVEL IA.
Population: Grades K-2.
Scores, 4: Mental Focus/Self-Regulation, Learning Orientation, Creative Problem Solving, Cognitive Integrity.

b) LEVEL IB.
Population: Grades 3-5.
Scores, 4: Mental Focus/Self-Regulation, Learning Orientation, Creative Problem Solving, Cognitive Integrity.

c) LEVEL II.
Population: Grades 6-12.
Scores, 5: Mental Focus/Self-Regulation, Learning Orientation, Creative Problem Solving, Cognitive Integrity, Scholarly Rigor.

d) LEVEL III.
Population: Adults.
Scores, 4: Mental Focus/Self-Regulation, Learning Orientation, Creative Problem Solving, Cognitive Integrity.

Review of the California Measure of Mental Motivation by JOHN J. BRINKMAN, Assistant Professor of Psychology and Counseling, University of Saint Francis, and AMBER CARTER, Graduate Assistant, University of Saint Francis, Fort Wayne, IN:

DESCRIPTION. The California Measure of Mental Motivation (CM3) is a group-administered test that was designed to measure critical thinking skills and dispositional aspects of critical thinking. Four levels of the test are intended for K–12 students and adults in the workplace. Each level or form is available via paper-and-pencil or online administration. Each form is untimed and takes approximately 20 minutes to complete. The paper-and-pencil test includes a test booklet and an answer sheet. Statements are either read aloud by the examiner or read silently by the examinee. The examinee is directed to select the answer that is most representative of how they feel. Levels IA and IB have two choices for each statement. K–2 students filling out Form IA are instructed to circle a smiley face or a frowny face for each answer. Students filling out Form IB are directed to circle either "agree" or "disagree" for each statement. Participants filling out Forms II and III are instructed to choose one of four options on a Likert-type scale ranging from "Agree Strongly" to "Disagree Strongly." Verbal instructions include informing the examinees that the test is an opinion survey and there are no right or wrong answers. Each form of the exam has practice items before the beginning of the exam. Online testing is available for Levels II and III. A fifth scale of critical thinking, called Scholarly Rigor, is included on Level II of the online testing but not available on any other form of the test. Online testing also allows for timed or untimed testing whereas the paper-and-pencil testing instructions explicitly state that the CM3 is an untimed test.

The CM3 is organized into four dispositional domains. The dispositional domains include: Mental Focus, Learning Orientation, Creative Problem Solving, and Cognitive Integrity. Scholarly Rigor, a fifth domain, is included on Level II of the online test. Below is a short description of the five dispositions organized according to their contribution to the CM3's scales.

The Mental Focus scale indicates if an examinee is highly disposed or highly indisposed toward mental focus. Three interrelated factors comprise the Mental Focus scale. These factors include Process, Organization, and Attention. The Process factor assesses an examinee's comfort or frustration level with solving intricate problems. The Organization factor assesses an examinee's capabilities in managing tasks and completing work. The Attention factor measures the abilities to maintain focus when completing tasks. The Learning Orientation scale measures an individual's motivation toward increasing their knowledge and skills. This scale includes two correlated factors: Desire to Learn and Information Gathering. The Desire to Learn factor assesses the examinee's intellectual curiosity whereas the Information Gathering factor assesses the importance an examinee places on gathering complete and adequate information. The Creative Problem Solving scale assesses an examinee's use of creativity in problem solving. The Creative Problem Solving scale is composed of two correlated factors: Innovation and Challenge Seeking. The Innovation factor measures the approach an examinee takes in problem solving, and the Challenge Seeking factor assesses the examinee's preference for completing challenging or complicated tasks. The Cognitive Integrity scale measures the examinee's motivation or resistance to use skills involved in thinking. This scale includes two correlated factors: Intellectual Curiosity and Fair-mindedness. Intellectual Curiosity measures the value an examinee places on seeking out knowledge whereas Fair-mindedness assesses the examinee's desire to equally consider all the alternatives. Finally, Scholarly Rigor assesses the value an examinee places on a deeper understanding of abstract and complicated material.

The administration instructions are detailed in the test booklet and are clear and easy to follow. Scoring of the test is completed by Insight Assessment. Paper-and-pencil answer sheets are mailed to Insight Assessment and the results of the testing are mailed back to the examiner. Online testing is scored after the test is completed and results are available immediately.

The scores are based on a 50-point scale. Scores are provided for each dispositional domain and its corresponding factors. Each score represents an interpretive category (e.g., Strongly Disposed). The score and its interpretive category are as follows: 0–9, Strongly Negative Disposed; 10–19, Somewhat Negative; 20–30, Ambivalent; 31–40, Somewhat Disposed; and 41–50, Strongly Disposed.

DEVELOPMENT. The CM3 was developed to measure both critical thinking skills and dispositions toward critical thinking. The CM3 was written using a theoretical approach from the American Philosophical Association Delphi Project and the California Critical Thinking Disposition Inventory (CCTDI). The Delphi Project researchers described critical thinking in terms of both thinking skills and thinking dispositions. The CCTDI was the first assessment measure available that looked at both thinking skills and thinking dispositions and prompted researchers to examine how these relate to educational success. Building on the CCTDI, the CM3 was designed to investigate critical thinking skills and critical thinking dispositions in school-aged children. Additionally, the test authors developed the test for a broad population including not only K–12 students but also adults in the workplace.

Test item development was conducted by using empirical literature on student motivation and critical thinking dispositions. Items were adapted from the California Critical Thinking Disposition Inventory and modified to encompass secondary-school-aged participants. Other items were created based on research from the Delphi Project and other sources published on the theory of critical thinking. An initial 100 items were created for the test. All test items were written on a 4-point Likert-type scale ranging from "strongly agree" to "strongly disagree." The test booklet provides example statements noting which statements a participant would typically agree or disagree with for each scale. The initial 100 items were categorized into four scales (i.e. Learning Orientation, Creative Problem Solving, Mental Focus, and Cognitive Integrity) using an alpha factor analysis with the delta set to zero. High loading questions were augmented with additional items from the California Critical Thinking Disposition Inventory to increase reliability and validity of the scales. The stability of the four-scale construction of the test was examined through confirmatory factor analysis on samples that were utilized to minimize the time needed for administration by assessing differing grade levels in the secondary school. Chi-square value 2449.40 (1218, N = 246, p < .000) supports the four-scale structure. The four scales were supported additionally by the adjusted goodness-of-fit indices (.73–.89) and comparative fit indices (.77–.90).

TECHNICAL. The standardization sample consisted of classrooms from three separate high schools. The first two samples included students attending public schools in Northern California. These samples consisted of both male and female participants from diverse racial and ethnic backgrounds. The third sample was from a private college preparatory school in the Midwest. This sample consisted of predominantly white females.

Reliability was examined using internal consistency estimate. Alpha coefficients were as follows for each scale: Learning Orientation, r = .79–.83; Creative Problem Solving, r = .70–.77; Mental Focus, r = .79–.83; and Cognitive Integrity, r = .53–.63.

The validity of the CM3 was estimated using external validity, predictive validity, and discriminant validity. External validity was demonstrated by correlations between the four scales of the CM3 and measures of student motivation, classroom behavior, and achievement. The measures of student motivation, classroom behavior, and achievement included the following: Mastery Goal, Self-Efficacy, and Self-Regulation. Correlations ranged from as low as r = .09 (e.g., between Cognitive Integrity and Mastery Goal) to r = .67 (i.e., between Learning and Mastery Goal) with all showing statistical significance at the $p < .05$ level or better.

Predictive validity was measured using scores from the CM3 and students' standardized scores from the Stanford Achievement Test (SAT9) and the Preliminary Scholastic Aptitude Test (PSAT/NMSQT) and students' GPA. Again, correlations ranged from as low as r = .15 (i.e., between PSAT Math and Cognitive Integrity) to r = .46 (e.g., between GPA and Creative Problem Solving) with all demonstrating statistical significance at the $p < .01$ level.

Discriminant validity of the CM3 was demonstrated by analysis of the short version of the Marlowe-Crowne Social Desirability Index. The Marlowe-Crowne Social Desirability Index is a measure of trustworthiness of an examinee's answers. No relationship was found between the Marlowe-Crowne Social Desirability Index and the CM3. The correlations ranged from r = .00 for Cognitive Integrity to r = -.06 for Mental Focus.

COMMENTARY. The CM3 is a well-designed test of critical thinking and dispositional aspects of critical thinking. Strengths of the CM3 lie in its theory, administration, interpretation, target populations, and reliability and validity. Good in-depth theory behind the creation of the test supports the uses of the CM3. The CM3 is quick and easy to administer, taking approximately 20 minutes to complete. The test manual offers clear and complete instructions on administration of the test. Online testing is beneficial allowing for easy testing and timely results. The results of the test are easy to interpret using the information provided in the test manual. The test can be administered to groups which allows for large numbers of examinees at once. The age range, from K–12 students and adults in the workplace, allows for the examination of a broad population of subjects. Additionally, the test offers adequate reliability and validity estimates.

Despite all of the strengths the CM3 offers, there are two areas that could be developed. First, there is one scale that demonstrates only moderate reliability. Reliability estimates for the Cognitive Integrity scale approached only adequate levels (e.g., r = .53–.63).

The second area of the CM3 that could be developed is the amount of information provided in the test manual as the information about studies is limited. For example, in the section about the standardization sample, no information is provided as to the number of students assessed in each sample or the age range of the students in each sample. Additionally, in the reliability section, there is limited information about the population utilized such as sample size. Despite the fact that references for various studies are provided, it would be beneficial to the test administrator, and ultimately to the individual providing an interpretation of the CM3, to have all of the information available to them in the test booklet.

SUMMARY. The CM3 was designed to measure critical thinking skills and dispositional aspects of critical thinking for K–12 students and adults in the workplace. The CM3 is organized into four dispositional domains, with a fifth domain for online testing, all of which were designed to measure the examinee's engagement in critical thinking. The CM3 is easy to administer, taking about 20 minutes to complete. Scoring is facilitated by Insight Assessment and interpretation of scores is easy to understand. Overall psychometric properties of the CM3 have been adequately demonstrated by the test authors. The value of the CM3 goes beyond simple assessment of critical thinking and lies in its potential use for professionals interested in baseline, pretest, or post-test measures, program evaluation, and admissions, placement, and advising for individuals.

Review of the California Measure of Mental Motivation by WILLIAM D. SCHAFER, Affiliated Professor (Emeritus) of Measurement, Statistics, and Evaluation, University of Maryland, College Park, MD:

DESCRIPTION.

Purpose and nature. The California Measure of Mental Motivation (CM3) provides an assessment of dispositional aspects of critical thinking. According to the manual, critical thinking requires not only knowledge about the skill but also motivation to use that knowledge. The latter, so-called dispositional traits have been assessed in postsecondary students since 1992 using the California Critical Thinking Disposition Inventory (CCTDI; 18:20). The CM3 was designed to assess dispositional aspects of critical thinking of elementary and secondary students. It may also be used with adults in the workplace.

The CM3 yields scores on four scales that were derived using factor analysis from items that were adapted for younger examinees from the CCTDI and then augmented. The scales are Mental Focus (comfort with problem solving, organization, diligence), Learning Orientation (curiosity, interest in information gathering), Creative Problem Solving (confidence in problem-solving ability, desire for mental challenge), and Cognitive Integrity (desire to learn, fair-minded toward ideas).

There are four levels, corresponding to grade ranges. Level IA (read aloud during administration) is for Grades K through 2, Level IB is for Grades 3 through 5, and Levels II and III are for Grades 6 and up. The latter may also be computer-administered. The publisher shared Level II Plus and Level III for review (each has 72 items; Levels 1A and 1B have fewer items, according to the manual). The CM3 is not timed but students are expected to be finished within about 20 minutes. Students respond on a separate answer sheet using a 4-point Likert scale. The separate answer sheets need to be sent to the publisher for scoring.

DEVELOPMENT.

Scales. Levels IA and IB report only the four major scale scores. Levels II and III also report subscale scores (see the above scale descriptions). Scores on each scale or subscale range from 0 to 50, but how the scores are calculated is not described in the manual. An interpretive guide suggests that users can apply five category names, Strongly Negative, Somewhat Negative, Ambivalent, Somewhat Disposed, and Strongly Disposed, with approximately 10-point ranges, to describe how the examinee reports himself or herself regarding the scale attribute. There are no norms reported.

TECHNICAL COMMENTARY.

Reliability evidence. Reliability was investigated using three samples, two groups of public school (grades unspecified) students from Northern California and a third predominantly female group from a Midwest college preparatory school. The ranges of alpha coefficients were .79–.83 for Learning Orientation, .70–.77 for Creative Problem Solving, .79–.83 for Mental Focus, and .53–.63 for Cognitive Integrity. No estimates were reported for the subscales.

Validity evidence. The manual reports that scale intercorrelations, some as high as .60, were found in the reliability samples. This finding, coupled with alpha values that were mostly in the .70s, suggests that the scales may not be distinct enough to interpret separately.

Correlations were computed between the four CM3 scales and outside measures of motivation, self-efficacy, and self-regulation; these generally correlated meaningfully (.30 or higher) with all the CM3 scales except Cognitive Integrity. Correlations with the scales of a standardized achievement test were weaker; only the Creative Problem Solving-Math correlation (.33) and the Cognitive Integrity-Reading correlation (.43) were .30 or higher. Two studies evaluated the correlations between the CM3 and GPA. In one, Learning Orientation (.40), Creative Problem Solving (.46), and Mental Focus (.44) were meaningfully correlated, but in the other, only Mental Focus (.35) surpassed .30. Finally, meaningful correlations were found between Creative Problem Solving and PSAT Math (.37), Verbal (.31), and Writing (.33) scores, as well as a PSAT Selection Index used for National Merit Scholars (.40). None of the other CM3 scales yielded a meaningful correlation.

Discriminant validity was evaluated by correlating the CM3 with the Marlowe-Crowne Social Desirability scale. All four CM3 scales were essentially independent of social desirability.

Utility. The CM3 is quite easy to administer. However, it is cumbersome to score because it must be sent to the publisher for scoring.

SUMMARY. The CM3 is a brief assessment of noncognitive aspects of critical thinking that could have value in studies that explore the nature and correlates of this construct. For the present, however, the CM3's reliability and validity evidence and the state of our knowledge about the construct, its determinants, and its effects are not compelling enough to warrant use of the test for individual student counseling or for the design and/or evaluation of educational experiences. Unfortunately, the three examples of use of the CM3 provided in the manual are all examples of these applications. Studies that evaluate these uses are needed before they can be recommended. Moreover, the interpretive guide needs to be augmented by normative results, if for no other reason than to strengthen validity evidence. The CM3 should at present be regarded as an experimental instrument.

[23]

CARE-2 Assessment: Chronic Violent Behavior Risk and Needs Assessment.

Purpose: Designed to identify youth "at risk for violence and aggression and to determine the interventions needed to prevent any future risk of aggression."
Population: Ages 6-19.
Publication Dates: 2003-2007.
Acronym: CARE-2.
Scores, 3: Risk, Resiliency, Total.
Administration: Individual.
Price Data, 2007: $39.95 including manual (2007, 35 pages) and one assessment booklet; $45 per 25 assessment booklets.
Time: (15–30) minutes.
Comments: Clinician obtains information for assessment through interviews with the youth, family, and caregivers; earlier edition entitled Child and Adolescent Risk Evaluation: A Measure of the Risk for Violent Behavior.
Author: Kathryn Seifert.
Publisher: Acanthus Publishing.
Cross References: For reviews by Christopher A. Sink and Beverly J. Wilson and by Jamie G. Wood of the original edition, see 17:40.

Review of the CARE-2 Assessment: Chronic Violent Behavior Risk and Needs Assessment by RANDY G. FLOYD, Associate Professor of Psychology, The University of Memphis, Memphis, TN:

DESCRIPTION. The "CARE" in CARE-2 stands for Child and Adolescent Risk Evaluation, but the manual for its most recent edition does not make this important definition prominent. CARE-2 is a narrow-band rating scale completed by a clinician after reviewing records and interviewing various informants, such as the child or adolescent being assessed, caregivers, and family members. The author stated that information should be collected from as many informants as possible before the rating is completed. The purposes of the CARE-2 are (a) to identify children and adolescents aged 6 to 19 who are at risk for aggressive and violent behaviors and (b) to guide intervention development to prevent further development of these problem behaviors.

The CARE-2 rating form opens with a section devoted to demographic and background information. The next 12 pages consist of the 57 items targeting Risk Factors (Section I) and Resiliency Factors (Section II). The Risk Factors section includes subsections devoted to prior behavior problems, family history, prior substance abuse and neurological problems, and recent psychological and academic functioning. Raters must mark in one of four columns the score associated with the demonstration of the instance described by the item. Each column represents the norm group used for the child or adolescent being rated—preteen males, teen males, preteen females, and teen females. Some items require ratings of severity, but most items are marked using a checklist (i.e., present or absent) format. Each item yields a score ranging from -2 to 10 based on the perceived importance of the item in predicting violent behavior. For example, for males, the item devoted to chronic assaults (i.e., more than three) receives the most weight, and, in addition, raters are also asked to mark an earlier item, with weight of 2 to 6, if this item is marked. What is surprising is that 20 items (35%) do not yield scores for any age group and that some other 29 items (53%) do not yield scores for at least one age group. In particular, no items contribute to the Resiliency score for females, and only 2 to 4 items (contributing a maximum of 6 points) contribute to the Resiliency score for males. The rating form ends with sections devoted to information for interagency communication, listing of the youth's resources and barriers, a detailed description of the author, and a description of other products from the author.

Scoring of the CARE-2 is accomplished by summing all of the Risk Factor item scores, summing all of the Resiliency Factors item scores, and subtracting the latter from the former to obtain the Total score. The Total score reflects whether the youth being rated is not similar, moderately similar, similar, or very highly similar to others with a history of three or more assaults. It is this total score and the resultant classification that is the focal point of interpretation.

DEVELOPMENT. CARE-2 items were developed based on the author's personal observations and perceptions while assessing children and adolescents and through a literature review of risk and resiliency factors and problematic behaviors of youth. There was some apparent pilot testing of items by the author across a variety of raters and a variety of youth across settings, but there appears to have been no external panel of experts evaluating items. Item scores were weighted based on results from bivariate correlations between the item scores and the total score. Items that demonstrated a significant correlation ($p < .01$) with the total score received weighting. It is not apparent that corrected correlations, which remove the item score in question when calculating the total, were employed; how the total score was obtained, such as by summing each item scored as 1 or 0 before weighting; nor how the sizes of the item weights were obtained (e.g., based on the magnitude of the correlation).

TECHNICAL. This reviewer found that the section of the CARE-2 manual devoted to summarizing its technical properties was poorly organized. Headings in this section could be revised to promote better organization, but some text and other content, such as results presented in figures, were largely incomprehensible and should be substantially reworked. For example, it appears that the author attempted to present the results of correlational analyses as well as descriptive statistics in vertical bar graphs. Below is this reviewer's best attempt to make sense of the technical characteristics of the CARE-2.

The CARE-2 score classifications stem from a norming sample totaling 1,026 youth from the Mid-Atlantic and Midwestern United States. It is neither clear what percentages of youth were from each region nor clear who completed the ratings yielding the sample data, but ratings of youth were completed in outpatient treatment programs, residential settings, juvenile detention settings, group home facilities, and school settings. The total sample is diverse in terms of race and ethnicity, and it appears to be primarily a "clinical sample" (versus a normative or community sample). Based on the manual, about 7% of youth in the sample had no history of behavior problems, whereas about 59% had a history of assaults. About 83% had psychiatric problems. It appears that ratings of well more than 100 youths were included in each of the four norm groups. Of some concern is that it appears that ratings of children much younger than the lowest age recommended (i.e., age 6) were included in the preteen samples (i.e., down to age 2).

The author addressed reliability in only two paragraphs—separated by two pages—and in only nine sentences. One must assume that this property refers to the Total score. The author reported the following internal consistency reliability coefficients in the manual: split-half reliability = .73, reliability corrected with the Spearman-Brown formula for equal length tests = .84, and reliability corrected with the Spearman-Brown formula for unequal length tests = .84. However, afterward, another litany of reliability coefficients is reported: coefficient alpha = .82, alpha for first half = .84, alpha for second half = .76; reliability corrected with the Spearman-Brown formula for equal and unequal length tests = .70, and Guttman split-half reliability = .70. Although these values are far from dismal, it is unclear why all of these reliability coefficients were calculated and why they vary without explanation. In addition, it is not clear which items contributed to these coefficients.

The author reported that the test–retest reliability coefficients were .70 and .72, but the length of the retest intervals, descriptive statistics for both measurements, sample descriptions, and details regarding the reason for two coefficients were not presented. Finally, the author reported "correlations between forms" equaling .54, but it is not apparent that the CARE-2 includes alternate forms necessary for such evidence. Although the author noted in the manual that users should consider unreliability in measurement (i.e., error) when determining classifications according to the four specified levels, neither standard errors of measurement nor confidence intervals are reported. Perhaps the CARE-2 Total score has demonstrated acceptable levels of reliability across these analyses, but the veracity of this claim is difficult to determine.

The author reported some validity evidence for the CARE-2 Total score, and this evidence is primarily evidence based on external relations. Some limited evidence based on content is reported above in the Development section and some limited evidence based on internal structure (i.e., internal consistency) is reported in a previous paragraph. No factor-analytic evidence is presented to support the subsections of the Risk Status section, the division between the Risk Status and Resiliency Status sections, or the effect of a single factor on all items.

Validity evidence based on external relations seems to exist, but it is described in such sparse detail and so ineffectively in the manual, it is difficult to evaluate. For example, the author reported that "various analyses were performed on the CARE and CARE-2. The CARE score correlated with the BASC Aggression scale (.92), the PCL-YV (.71) and the SAVRY (.72)" (manual, p. 22), but the comparison scales were not spelled out or cited, the samples were not described, and other convergent and divergent correlations were not presented. It is also unclear if the author was referring to the CARE or the CARE-2. The author also described the results from discriminant function analysis for males 6 to 12, but the groups that were analyzed to produce the discriminant functions are indicated. Bar graphs are presented to compare those youth who completed acts of violence to those who did not (for each of the four norm groups) as well as to compare youth with psychiatric disorders and those without them (for only males), and some statistics, such as basic ANOVA results, effect size estimates, and receiver operation characteristic (ROC) analysis results are presented with no explanation below these charts. Perhaps the most detailed description of a validity study was the one describing the relation between initial CARE-2 scores and the number of assaults reported by therapists 6 months later; however, the author reported only a narrative description of the results and no statistics. No validity evidence was reported for the linking of items to evidence-based intervention.

SUMMARY AND COMMENTARY. Perhaps the most unique and useful feature of the CARE-2 is its listing of interventions that may be useful in responding to a problem described by an item. Several of these intervention descriptions have links to websites and to interventions with well-documented success, such as multisystemic therapy. However, this reviewer cannot recommend adoption of the CARE-2 due to the author's challenges in presenting a coherent collection of reliability and validity evidence for its core measure. Although the instrument may have potential, substantial efforts devoted to scale development, data analysis, and editing are needed.

Review of the CARE-2 Assessment: Chronic Violent Behavior Risk and Needs Assessment by MICHAEL J. FURLONG, Professor, Gevirtz Graduate School of Education, and AMY-JANE GRIFFITHS, Doctoral candidate, Counseling, Clinical, and School Psychology Department, University of California, Santa Barbara, Santa Barbara, CA:

DESCRIPTION. The CARE–2 Assessment: Chronic Violent Behavior Risk and Needs Assessment was developed to facilitate communication among agencies about youth for whom aggressive behavior is a current and possibly future problem and to identify possible interventions. The assessment is used with youths 6 to 19 years of age and has 57 items that describe risk behaviors, experiences, and conditions associated with aggressive behavior, and assets considered to reduce the probability of aggression. Clinicians rate each item after gathering case history data and via interviews with the child, family, and caregivers. The assessor rates as many items as possible but the Total score is computed only if more than two-thirds of the items are known (that is, can be rated with confidence). Previous, repeated, and serious aggressive behavior items contribute the most to the Total score—given their absolute importance to understanding aggression in youth, it is difficult to identify circumstances in which the assessment would be used if knowledge of prior aggression was unknown (even if two-thirds of the items could be rated).

Some items are self-explanatory, whereas others use subjective interpretation; however, item definitions are provided in the manual. These definitions are detailed; hence, it is imperative that raters read and review all of them each time the assessment is completed. An important resource provided with this measure is that for each item general intervention strategies are offered, although there is only very limited empirical evidence provided for the use of these suggested interventions as they relate to the specific item.

A Total CARE–2 score is obtained by summing weighted Risk items and then subtracting the sum of weighted Resilience items. The manual suggests that higher scores are associated with the need for more intensive services; however, no research findings are reported to support this claim. Due to frequent changes in the needs of these youth the author suggests that they be reassessed every 6–12 months.

DEVELOPMENT. The first version of the CARE was developed from a list of common characteristics the author observed in clinical work with youth considered to have aggressive behavior problems. The author added items to the preliminary list by conducting literature reviews of risk and resiliency factors for youth with behavioral concerns. A checklist was created and data were collected using it with youth in a number of settings, such as: public mental health clinics, juvenile detention centers, hospitals for the mentally ill, residential treatment facilities, foster care placements, and typical clinical settings. The CARE–2 uses items drawn from risk and protective factors that research has found to be associated with youth violence; however, no evidentiary support is provided. The manual would be greatly improved if the research supporting the use of each item were systematically presented. Furthermore, fundamental research related to the developmental pathways associated with antisocial and aggressive behaviors in childhood and adolescence (e.g., Rolf Loeber and Delbert Elbert) is not mentioned.

TECHNICAL.

Standardization. The "norms" for the CARE–2 were derived from the ratings of 1,026 youth—369 children (ages 2 to 12) and 636 adolescents (ages 13 to 19). Score comparisons are provided for four groups: males of ages 6–12 and 13–19, and females ages 6-12 and 13-19. The 12 common items included in the Total score across all four groups deal with a history of verbal aggression, physical aggression, weapon use, abuse of animals, delinquency, anger management problems, bullying behavior, lack of remorse, and favorable attitudes toward aggression. In brief, the only items (among all 57) used to ascertain the potential for future aggression are those that assess previous aggression and beliefs that aggression can be justified. Item weighting was used to calculate risk scores. It is stated that correlations were used to weight the items in each group, but is unclear how these analyses were utilized to determine the weights. Items with numerical scores were subject to discriminant analyses; however, the details of these analyses are not provided in the manual. The manual lacked the statistics needed to support the conclusions drawn and information for all groups was not provided—only the results for males ages 6–12 were included, which is the group with the least short-term risk for violence. Furthermore, the first function (aggression) accounted for 97% of the variance, whereas all four functions accounted for 98% of the variance, suggesting that information beyond the aggression category was not crucial in "predicting" violent behavior. Based on the discriminant function analysis, 20 items were listed in the manual, but the assessment included 29 items; the reason for this discrepancy is unclear. Items that significantly contributed to the discriminant functions (differentiating between youths who had three or more assaults from those with two or fewer assaults) were included in the final scale to provide information for intervention planning.

Reliability. The manual presents various internal consistency reliability indices, but it is unclear which sets of items were included in each computation. For example, although 57 items can be rated, only 12 common Risk items and no Resiliency items are used to compute the total score across all four groups. Because a weighted sum of selected items is used to compute the Total score, it is unclear how these weights affected the reliability estimates. In addition, the items are not independent of each other. For example, if a youth assaulted an authority figure (one item) then they would also be rated as having a record of chronic or severe behavior problems (another item). Furthermore, because a Total score is used, the scale is presumed to be unidimensional, but no analysis is presented to support its use in this way. The most critical type of reliability for scales like the CARE–2 is interrater consistency, and this score is not presented.

Validity. Although the stated purpose of the CARE–2 is to assess potential for future violence, there was only one prospective study involving a nonrandom sample of 112 youths. Cooperating therapists submitted case files for a sample of youth who had/had not committed assaults following administration of the assessment. The Total score for these youth was correlated with the number of assaultive behaviors based on case file information. The Total score was found to be positively and significantly related to the possibility of future assaultive behavior and other behavior problems. It is unclear where the evidence for the criterion variable (assaultive and aggressive behavior) was obtained. Although Receiver Operating Characteristic information is provided about the association between the CARE–2 Total score and severity of problem behavior and assaultive behavior, details for these analyses (e.g., the ROC curves, and full sensitivity and specificity information) are not provided.

The authors conducted a retrospective validity analysis by dividing the sample into six groups based on severity of their previous behavior problems, although it is unclear how the youth were categorized. Categories included: (a) no behavior problems, (b) mild behavior problems, (c) moderate behavior problems, (d) severe behavior problems, (e) severe behavior problems with Level 1 assaults (no injury requiring medical attention), and (f) severe behavior problems with Level 2 assaults (severe injury or death). The relationships between the Total score and these six behavior severity groups were examined for each of the four norm groups.

The CARE–2 uses the following wording to describe the Total score ranges: "This youth is (not similar to/moderately similar to/highly similar to/very highly similar to) other youth who have committed chronic (more than 3) assaults against others" (manual, p. 3). These four categories were derived using group means and standard deviations. The manual indicates that the means and standard deviations for the four comparison groups are available in a table, but it was not included in the manual. Furthermore, it is unclear how the cut points were established and from where the category descriptions and intervention suggestions were derived. In addition, the manual is bereft of basic information that is needed for the potential user to assess its utility; for example, the size of each group and the *N*s for all analyses are not given.

COMMENTARY. The CARE–2 includes items with both Risk and Resilience content. In truth, however, the sum of the Risk items can be adjusted by no more than 4 points when adding the Resilience items. And, for preteen females and teen females the Resilience items provide no adjustment whatsoever. As such, the CARE–2 is fundamentally a weighted compilation of internal and external risks associated with aggressive behaviors in a youth's life. Although not stated, the authors apply an additive risk model—the more risk factors present, the more likely the youth has engaged in past aggression, and the supposition, weakly supported in the manual, is that they are at increased risk of future aggressive behavior.

It will be important to consider which professionals complete the assessment and how this information is communicated and stored. For example, it would be very awkward to use this instrument in a school setting because it would then become part of a student's cumulative record. It might be more amenable to use juvenile probation or residential treatment facilities.

As the completion of this assessment requires a great deal of information based on an extensive background review, it may be time-consuming for professionals to complete thoroughly and appropriately. In addition, some of the items are subjective and will depend on the rater's perception of the youth, again reiterating the importance of the professional selected to complete the assessment. As this assessment is relatively new, no published research studies examining this assessment were found.

SUMMARY. Despite the concerns noted about the methods used to develop the CARE–2 and to evaluate its psychometric properties, one is still left with evidence of the link between high CARE–2 ratings and past aggressive behavior. It is important to note that only items used to ascertain the potential for future aggression in this assessment are those that assess previous aggression and youth beliefs that aggression is justifiable. As its name implies, care must be exercised if it is used. A potential problem associated with the use of this assessment would be the misuse of the scores leading to labeling of students as "violent or dangerous." Despite the discussion of the preventative purpose of the assessment in the manual, the cover of the assessment (picture of a child's facial profile with a picture of a gun in the head) implies that this instrument will identify "deadly/violent children" and may be purchased for that purpose. It will be crucial to stress the intended purpose of the assessment as preventative, specifically to be used in the early identification of those at-risk for violent behavior and in providing appropriate interventions.

[24]

Category Test.

Purpose: "Measures an individual's ability to perform in an ambiguous, problem-solving situation" and is intended to be used "in settings that require the assessment of brain damage and/or problem solving ability."

Population: Ages 9-15 (ICat); Ages 16-69 [(HCT, ACat, RCat)].

Publication Dates: 1989-2008.

Acronym: Cat.

Scores: Information available from publisher.

Administration: Individual.

Forms: 4 computer-adapted versions: Halstead Category Test (HCT), Adaptive Category Test (ACat),

Russell Revised Short Form (RCat), Intermediate Category Test (ICat).
Price Data, 2010: $209 per complete kit including Category Test software (version 7.0) and technical guide and software manual (2008, 104 pages); $199 per Category Test software; $30 per technical guide and software manual.
Time: (30-40) minutes; "up to [95] minutes for impaired clients."
Comments: The Cat is composed of four computer-adapted versions administered depending on respondents' ages. The HCT is the full adult version of the Halstead Category Test; the ACat is a shortened version that uses "a subset of responses on items of [each HCT] subtest...to predict the respondent's final score for that subtest;" the RCat is a shortened version that eliminates one of the HCT subtests and reduces "half the number of items from most [other] subtests;" the ICat "is designed for children;" software is Windows compatible; instructions available in visual and auditory form; each score is based on "the ability to discover and apply certain" problem-solving rules.
Authors: James Choca, Linda Laatsch, Dan Garside, Rahul Gupta, and James Fenstermacher.
Publisher: Multi-Health Systems, Inc.
Cross References: For a review by Robert A. Leark of an earlier form, The Computer Category Test, see 15:62.

Review of the Category Test by KAREN T. CAREY, Dean, Division of Graduate Studies, Professor of Psychology, California State University, Fresno, Fresno, CA:

DESCRIPTION. The Category Test (Cat) is composed of four computer-adapted versions and is designed to distinguish between "normal" and brain-injured individuals on their use of problem-solving skills to determine a rule based on positive or negative feedback. The Halstead Category Test (HCT), the full version of the tool, is designed for individuals 16–69 years of age and takes 30 to 40 minutes to administer to "normal" individuals. The Adaptive Category Test (ACat) uses archival data built into the software to compare an individual's responses to a group of previous respondents. The Russell Revised Short Form (RCat) groups the 95 figures on the HCT into six subtests reducing the total number of items. The Intermediate Category Test (ICat) is designed for children ages 9 to 15 and contains 168 items grouped into six different subtests. No information is given regarding administration times for the ACat, the RCat, or the ICat.

The Cat is the computer software version of the original Category Test, with computer-adapted forms for each of the four versions of the test: HCT, ACat, RCat, and ICat. The test requires the respondent to type in a 1, 2, 3, or 4 for each test figure item presented. The respondent is then automatically told whether the item is correct or incorrect and responses are scored automatically, resulting in an output report that includes total number of errors, actual responses, and the response rate for each subtest. For all four tests, the reaction times range from 1.4 to 98.5 seconds per response.

The test authors state that the test can be used in the clinical setting, as a screener, and in research settings. No information relative to the norm sample is provided in the manual and in order to interpret the test, the manual states that "interpretation based solely on criteria presented in this manual would be irresponsible and is strongly discouraged" (p. 25). Thus, there is not enough information contained in the materials to actually make any determinations relative to scores obtained on the computer-based tests. However, the test authors do state scores between 20 and 40 are "excellent" and low scores indicate an "intact brain, reasonable intellectual abilities, and the capacity to think with concentration and efficiency" (manual, p. 25). Scores above 50 could indicate "intellectual impairment" and may include "brain damage, intellectual ability, cognitive development or emotional interference" (manual, p. 26). Interestingly, the test authors state that poor performance on the Cat is "not necessarily indicative of impairment; many fully functioning individuals have trouble with this test" (manual, p. 8). It is unclear if the difficulty stems from the items, the computer administration, or the problem-solving tasks required.

DEVELOPMENT. The Category Test was first described in 1943 in an article by Ward Halstead and Paul Settlage (Halstead & Settlage, 1943) and was developed as a part of the Halstead-Reitan Neuropsychological Test Battery (T7:1137). The test was designed as an object sorting technique to identify normal individuals from those with brain injury. The original version contained 360 items grouped into nine subtests, with the final subtest designed as a memory test of items on previous subtests. A rotating drum apparatus was used for item presentation and switches were used for the examinee to press in order to identify the correct response. Total errors were recorded for the entire test.

In 1947 the test was administered with 360 slides and by 1958 the number of items was reduced to the current number of 208. Different forms have been developed since that time including portable versions, paper-pencil versions, a booklet form, and a card version. The most recent version is computer administered allowing for a "statistical determination of how many items must be administered for any given subtest" (manual, p. 14).

TECHNICAL. Normative data are not included in the technical guide and software manual, and the user is referred to other publications. Scores are obtained based on the number of errors obtained, but again, the user is referred to "norms available in the literature" (manual, p. 30) in order to convert raw scores to *T* scores. Standardizations are also available in the literature for the ACat, non-impaired adults, and for the ICat.

Age, education, gender, and clinical effects are described in general, and the user is directed to a myriad of studies in the literature demonstrating differences (e.g., age and education make a difference in the scores obtained). Unfortunately, the descriptions are based on results from other versions, not the computer version, so the extent to which there are differences between and among groups on the computer version is not known. The test authors provide a critique of different versions of the test, including the short forms. By citing numerous studies they make a case by stating that all adult versions of the test have been found to be equivalent to the standard version (with one exception).

Results of reliability studies performed on an earlier version of the computerized test by Choca and Morris (1992) demonstrated that the two versions correlated at .90. According to the authors, split half reliability of .90 or above "has been reported repeatedly" (manual, p. 36), citing a number of studies from the literature, however, not with the computerized version. Test-retest reliabilities for impaired groups were reported to increase as performance worsens with coefficients of .72 for individuals with schizophrenia, and from .82 to .96 for individuals with brain damage.

Concurrent validity was reported as only modest with the Time task of the Tactual Performance Test, Part B of the Trail Making Test, the Speech and Sounds Perception Tests, and the Halstead Impairment Index, but again these correlations were derived using versions other than the one presented in the manual. Further, correlations of previous versions of the Cat with intelligence tests were reported as between -.30 and -.78, based on a series of studies conducted, and no correlations were found with the Woodcock-Johnson Psycho-educational Battery.

COMMENTARY. Although this test is easy to administer using the computer-based software, the technical properties of this test as described in the manual are not adequate for individual decision making. Rather than reporting numerous studies conducted on other versions by other authors, the developers of the computer version should conduct the necessary studies to address issues of reliability and validity and should opt for a technical guide that thoroughly establishes the technical adequacy of the instrument. Although a case is made for the equivalency of the many versions of the test, without specific studies using the computerized version, equivalency cannot be established.

SUMMARY. The Cat is the computer software version of the original Halstead Category Test and measures an individual's ability to problem solve. The four computer-adapted forms are easy to take and administer and could provide some useful information regarding an individual's problem-solving abilities. However, because the information in the manual relates primarily to other versions of the test and is sparse in some cases, the user of the instrument should be wary about making comparisons between results of other versions and the computer versions.

REVIEWER'S REFERENCES

Choca, J., & Morris, J. (1992). Administering the Category Test by computer: Equivalence of results. *Clinical Neuropsychologist, 6,* 9-15.

Halstead, W. C., & Settlage, P. H. (1943). Grouping behavior of normal persons and of persons with lesions of the brain. *Archives of Neurology and Psychiatry, 49,* 489-506.

Review of the Category Test by CATHERINE P. COOK-COTTONE, Associate Professor of School Psychology, State University of New York at Buffalo, Buffalo, NY:

DESCRIPTION. The Category Test (Cat) is a specialized version of the Halstead Category Test (Halstead & Settlage, 1943) designed for computer use. The Category Test is an integral part of the original Halstead-Reitan Neuropsychological Test Battery (HRNB; Halstead & Settlage, 1943). The Category Test is one of the most frequently administered neuropsychological tests (Sweet & King, 2002). Defined as assessments of executive functioning, both the Cat and the Halstead Category Test (HCT) assess "an individual's ability to perform in an ambiguous, problem solving situation" (manual, p. 4) and capacity to search and discover alternative solutions. The Cat may be especially useful for clinicians and researchers assessing brain damage or problem solving ability. Designed as a self-standing instrument, the Cat also can be used as part of a full neuropsychological battery or as a screener for executive functioning deficits. Those responsible for Cat interpretation should hold an advanced degree in the social, medical, or behavioral sciences and must be very well trained in neuropsychology.

Administration ease is a definitive feature of the Cat. Specifically, the Cat displays a series of test figures on the computer screen and the respondent uses the keyboard to register responses. Following each response, an indication on the computer screen signifies whether the response was right or wrong. If the spoken test instructions are enabled, the computer plays recorded verbal instructions and provides auditory feedback. The output record provides a tally of error, actual responses, and a response rate for each subtest.

The Cat offers alternative administration options that include: (a) the complete Halstead Category Test (HCT), (b) the Adaptive Category Test (ACat), (c) the Russell Revised Short Form (RCat; Russell & Levy, 1987), and (d) the Intermediate Category Test (ICat). The HCT is recommended for clients age 16 years and older and takes about 30 to 40 minutes to administer with impaired responded taking up to 95 minutes. The Cat uses the same standards as the HCT (e.g., the Heaton norms; Heaton, Grant, & Mathews, 1991). The ACat is a shorter version of the Cat that uses archival data (i.e., statistically derived clusters of similar response patterns) to generate a predicted score for each subtest (see Laatsch & Choca, 1994). The RCat is distinct in that it groups the figures of the HCT into six subtests, reduces the number of items in most subtests by half, and discards the memory subtest (i.e., Subtest VII in the traditional version; Russell & Levy, 1987). In addition, Subtests V and VI were reorganized into counting and proportional principles (see Russell & Levy, 1987). Finally, the ICat was designed for children aged 9 to 15 years. Its 168 items are organized into six different subtests. Subtests I and II are identical to those in the adult version (the HCT). Although the principle for subtest III remains the same as the HCT (i.e., differential positioning of the figure), the figures displayed for the ICat are not identical to those in the HCT. In the same way, although Subtests IV and V of the ICat use the proportional principles of the HCT Subtests V and VI, both the figures displayed and the order of presentation differ across the test versions. For the ICat, "subtest VII is a memory subtest that presents figures from the previous subtests" (manual, p. 6). The test authors report that norms for the ICat are available (e.g., Hughes, 1976; Findeis & Weight, 1994, as cited in Strauss, Sherman, & Spreen, 2006). It is important to note that most published research reports on the traditional version of the Category Test.

DEVELOPMENT. In 1940, Halstead "hypothesized that the ability to discover commonalities among objects and/or situations allows individuals to adapt to the environment" (manual, p. 13). Following the development of an object sorting task, Halstead created an assessment of grouping behavior he called the Category Test (Halstead & Settlage, 1943). The initial version of the Halstead Category Test (HCT) contained 360 items that were grouped into nine subtests (Sweet & King, 2002). The original administration involved the presentation of figures through a reading lens and required the respondent to press one of four switches to indicate an answer. Correct responses moved a rotating drum forward to the next item and incorrect responses had no effect. Later versions involved administration via slides, more modern testing equipment, and a reduction of items to the current 208.

The exact nature of what the Category Test measures has been the subject of some debate. The test authors indicate that good performance on the Cat suggests that the respondent is able to adequately solve problems in real-life situations. According to the test authors, effective problem solving requires: (a) "the ability to recognize the problem or nature of the task the individual is asked to perform" (manual, p. 24), (b) "the cognitive capacity to carry out the task including abstractive ability and visuospatial understanding" (manual, p. 24), (c) mental flexibility, (d) mental consistency, (e) patience, (f) the "ability to maintain focus" (manual, p. 24), and (g) "motivation to do well" (manual, p. 24). Shute and Huertas (1990) described the Category Test as a measure of Piaget's formal operations characterized by effective adult reasoning and problem solving. Some purport that this processing capacity is akin to psychometric intelligence, exists on a continuum, and is normally distributed. Others believe that the abilities measured by the Category Test may be more dichotomous in nature being either good/present or poor/not present (Halstead, 1947; Shute & Huertas, 1990). The authors of the technical guide and software manual for the Cat suggest that the best way to interpret the Category Test may be to view the scores along a continuum.

The Category Test was designed to work in total with the sequence of subtests and intersubtest shifts in decision rules serving to inform a total error score and the assessment of problem solving. The main function of Subtest I "is to orient the respondent to the equipment and to the task" (manual, p. 5) and is a simple sequencing task. Subtest II adds abstraction and does not substantially alter the decision rule. Subtests III and IV require a subtle shift in the decision rule, involve the attributes of oddity and spatial position, and are more difficult. Subtests V and VI are also more difficult, shift the decision rule, and involve proportional reasoning. Finally, Subtest VII has no unitary decision principle and can be viewed as a memory task for decision rules learned in previous subtests.

TECHNICAL.

Standardization. The measurement traditionally taken from the Category Test is the number of errors rather than a standard score. Standard scores can be obtained for the HCT and the ICat by referring to the appropriate literature (e.g., Heaton, Grant, & Mathews, 1991; Hughes, 1976, Knights & Norwood, 1980, Strauss et al., 2006). Often the number of errors is converted to a *T* score. For the abbreviated ACat, calculating a norm-referenced score is different only in the calculation of the total raw score (described above).

Reliability. Most information on the psychometric properties of the Cat (composed of four computer-adapted versions) that is reviewed here is derived from research conducted on the Category Test from the Halstead-Reitan Neuropsychological Test Battery (HRNB). The test authors address reliability first in terms of the comparability of the Category Test and the Cat reporting insignificant differences between versions (t = 1.84) and a high correlation between the two versions (r^2 = .90, p = .001; Choca & Morris, 1992). The manual reports a split-half reliability or .90 or above for the full version. Test-retest reliability for normal individuals is low (r = .60) due to practice and learning effects and possibly due to the restricted range of scores (Russell, 1992). Russell (1992) was able to improve test-retest coefficient for normals substantially by redistributing scores (r = .88). For impaired groups, test-retest reliability coefficients tend to increase as performance worsens. To illustrate replicated findings, the manual cites Matarazzo, Matarazzo, Wiens, Gallo, and Klonoff (1976) who reported test-retest for individuals with schizophrenia at r = .72 and from .82 to .96 for respondents with brain damage.

Validity. The validity of the Cat is reflected in studies of the factor structure, concurrent validity, and clinical validity. Various factor analyses of the Category Test have found the test to load on factors such as general intelligence, complex spatial reasoning, symbol recognition/counting, spatial positional reasoning, and proportional reasoning (Sweet & King, 2002). Some research suggests that the subtests may measure unique aspects of executive functioning. Generally, Subtests III, IV, and VII form the spatial positional reasoning factor and Subtests V, VI, and VII form a proportional reasoning factor (Allen, Caron, Duke, & Goldstein, 2007; Donders, 2001). The test authors provide some evidence that the factor structure may vary depending on the population being assessed. For example, for normally functioning individuals the HCT may measure sequential problem solving whereas with severely impaired individuals it may measure visual and memory abilities. Forrest, Allen, and Goldstein (2004) reported that Subtests I and II may be particularly sensitive to malingering. Given the use of neuropsychological assessment in civil litigation involving brain injury or disease, response validity is an important consideration (Sweet & King, 2002).

Concurrent validity is reported as producing only modest correlations with similar instruments (e.g., Time task of the Tactual Performance Test, .53, and Part B of the Trail Making Test, .58; Goldstein & Shelly, 1972; manual, p. 37). The manual cites several studies that report only modest correlations have been found with the Wisconsin Card Sorting Test (.30 to .40). Moderate significant correlations were reported with the Cognitive Deficit subscale of the SCL-90-R (O'Donnell, deSoto, & Reynolds, 1984). The test authors report that there have been no significant correlations found between the Cat and the Minnesota Multiphasic Personality Inventory (MMPI). Similar to factor structure findings, correlations with IQ tests may vary with ability level. That is, although those with low IQs generally perform poorly at problem-solving tasks, those with higher IQ can be both good and bad problem solvers. Accordingly, with IQ tests, the Cat has shown a wide range of relationships (trivial to moderate) depending on the IQ test, the index used, or the specific IQ subtest used. Generally, higher correlations with the Cat have been found between the Wechsler Adult Intelligence Scale-Third Edition (WAIS-III) subtests of Block Design (-.46), Letter Number Sequencing (-.36), Object Assembly (-.36), and Matrix Reasoning (-.34; Titus, Retzlaff, & Dean, 2002).

The Category Test is effective for detecting cognitive impairment and cerebral dysfunction (high sensitivity). However, the number of errors does not necessarily indicate brain damage, and high false positive rates have been reported (low specificity). There is an emerging consensus that a factor-based approach to the assessment of brain damage may improve specificity (Allen et al., 2007). Overall, in those with brain damage the Category Test has been found to measure counting, proportional reasoning, and spatial positioning with decreased performance associated with increased brain injury. No relationship was found between versions of the Category Test with lateralization, acuteness, chronicity, and epilepsy. In regard to other cognitive illnesses and impairments, the test authors report some evidence of the Category Test distinguishing between cortical and subcortical dementias in patients with cortical dementia scoring in the severely impaired range and subcortical patients in the mildly impaired range (see Horton & Siegel, 1990). Notably, the "Category Test score will decrease with acute intoxication, but may return to within the normal range" (manual, p. 43) after a period of sobriety (i.e., 17 days; see Eckardt & Matarazzo, 1981). The test authors report that the cognitive deterioration associated with years of excessive drinking and amount of alcohol consumed per occasion may be uniquely detectable by the Cat. As with other substances (e.g., cocaine and heroin), alcohol may affect the ability to shift from one set to another.

COMMENTARY. There are several advantages to using the Cat computerized version of the Category Test. Given the computer enabled input and data collection, evaluators and researchers can collect data previously difficult to obtain including response latency and perseveration indices. In addition, the computer administration also results in reduced administrator involvement and administration error. A large proportion of the information provided in the manual and available in research journals utilized the traditional version of the Category Test. Additional studies comparing the Computerized Cat and the Halstead Category Test, as well as the alternative forms of the Cat, are needed to confirm the reliability of the computerized format and should be conducted by individuals not affiliated with the test. Clinicians should note that the Category Test appears to be more sensitive than specific and should be used in conjunction with other neuropsychological assessments and within the context of clinical judgment. Interpretation should be completed by individuals well trained in neuropsychology and familiar with the psychometric properties of the Cat and the unique performance of various populations on the assessment tool. The Category Test should be administered and interpreted in total as an assessment of executive function, and subset by subtest or factor-based interpretations should be done as part of a battery.

SUMMARY. The Cat is a computerized version of the Category Test developed by Halstead in 1943. The original Category Test has been used for many years as a component of the Halstead Reitan Neuropsychological Battery. Generally, the Cat form of the Category Test is a useful clinical tool for the assessment of executive functioning in patients with brain damage or cognitive dysfunction, and it may have clinical utility with particular cognitive illnesses and substance abuse. The Cat is easy to administer, may reduce administrator involvement and error, creates score reports, and provides additional data for interpretation (e.g., response latency). More research is needed to confirm the reliability of the Cat and the psychometric properties of the alternative forms.

REVIEWER'S REFERENCES

Allen, D. N., Caron, J. E., Duke, L. A., & Goldstein, G. (2007). Sensitivity of the Halstead Category Test factor scores to brain damage. *Clinical Neuropsychologist, 21,* 638-652.

Choca, J., & Morris, J. (1992). Administering the Category Test by computer: Equivalence of results. *Clinical Neuropsychologist, 6,* 9-15.

Donders, J. (2001). Clinical utility of the Categories Test as a multidimensional instrument. *Psychological Assessment, 13,* 592-294.

Eckardt, M. J., & Matarazzo, J. D. (1981). Test-retest reliability of the Halstead Impairment Index in hospitalized alcoholic and nonalcoholic males with mild to moderate neuropsychological impairment. *Journal of Clinical Neuropsychology, 3,* 257-269.

Findeis, M. K., & Weight, D. G. (1994). *Meta-norms for two forms of neuropsychological test batteries for children.* Unpublished manuscript, Brigham Young University.

Forrest, T. J., Allen, D. N., & Goldstein, G. (2004). Malingering indexes for the Halstead Category Test. *Clinical Neuropsychologist, 18,* 334-347.

Goldstein, G., & Shelly, C. H. (1972). Statistical and normative studies of the Halstead Neuropsychological Test Battery relevant to a neuropsychiatric hospital setting. *Perceptual and Motor Skills, 34,* 603-620.

Halstead, W. C. (1947). *Brain and intelligence: A quantitative study of the frontal lobes.* Chicago: University of Chicago Press.

Halstead, W. C., & Settlage, P. H. (1943). Grouping behavior of normal persons and of persons with lesions of the brain. *Archives of Neurology and Psychiatry, 49,* 489-506.

Heaton, R. K., Grant, I., & Mathews, C. G. (1991). *Comprehensive norms for an Expanded Halstead-Reitan Battery: Demographic corrections, research findings, and clinical applications.* Odessa, FL: Psychological Assessment Resources.

Horton, A. M., & Siegel, E. (1990). Comparison of multiple sclerosis and head trauma patients: A neuropsychological pilot study. *International Journal of Neuroscience, 53,* 213-215.

Hughes, H. E. (1976). Norms developed. *Journal of Pediatric Psychology, 1,* 11-15.

Knights, R. M., & Norwood, J. A. (1980). *Revised smoothed normative data on the Neuropsychological Test Battery for Children.* Ottawa: Carleton University.

Laatsch, L., & Choca, J. (1994). Cluster-branching methodology for adaptive testing and the development of the Adaptive Category Test. *Psychological Assessment, 6,* 345-351.

Matarazzo, J. D., Matarazzo, R. G., Wiens, A. N., Gallo, A. E., & Klonoff, H. (1976). Retest reliability of the Halstead Impairment Index in a normal, a schizophrenic, and two samples of organic patients. *Journal of Clinical Psychology, 32,* 338-349.

O'Donnell, W. E., deSoto, C. B., & Reynolds, D. M. (1984). A Cognitive Deficit subscale of the SCL-90-R. *Journal of Clinical Psychology, 40,* 241-246.

Russell, E. W., & Levy, M. (1987). Revision of the Halstead Category Test. *Journal of Consulting and Clinical Psychology, 55,* 898-901.

Shute, G. E., & Huertas, V. (1990). Developmental variability in frontal lobe function. *Developmental Neuropsychology, 6,* 1-11.

Strauss, E., Sherman, E. M. S., & Spreen, O. (2006). *A compendium of neuropsychological test administration, norms, and commentary* (3rd ed.). New York: Oxford University Press.

Sweet, J. J., & King, J. H. (2002). Category Test validity indicators: Overview and practice recommendations. *Journal of Forensic Neuropsychology: Special Issue: Detection of response bias in forensic neuropsychology: Part II, 3,* 241-274.

Titus, J. B., Retzlaff, P. D., & Dean, R. S. (2002). Predicting scores of the Halstead Category Test with the WAIS-III. *International Journal of Neuroscience, 112,* 1099-1114.

[25]

Children's Aggression Scale.

Purpose: Designed to "evaluate the nature, severity, and frequency of aggressive behaviors in children, distinct from those behaviors better characterized as oppositional/ defiant or hostile."

Population: Ages 5-18.

Publication Dates: 2002-2008.

Acronym: CAS.

Scores, 11: Scale scores (Verbal Aggression, Aggression Against Objects and Animals, Physical Aggression, Use of Weapons, Total Aggression Index), Cluster scores (Provoked Physical Aggression, Initiated Physical Aggression, Aggression Toward Peers, Aggression Toward Adults, Aggression Against Family Members [Parent form only], Aggression Against Non-Family Members [Parent form only]).

Administration: Group.

Forms, 2: Parent (CAS-P), Teacher (CAS-T).

Price Data, 2010: $240 per introductory kit including professional manual (2008, 473 pages), 25 Parent rating forms, 25 Teacher rating forms, 25 Parent score summary forms/profiles, and 25 Teacher score summary forms/profiles; $52 per 25 Parent rating forms; $52 per 25 Teacher rating forms; $37 per 25 Parent score summary forms/profiles; $37 per 25 Teacher score summary forms/profiles; $77 per professional manual.

Time: (10–15) minutes.

Comments: Ratings by parents and teachers (multiple forms may be completed by multiple parents and teachers); Children's Aggression Scale Scoring Program (CAS-SP) offered separately.

Authors: Jeffrey M. Halperin and Kathleen E. McKay.

Publisher: Psychological Assessment Resources, Inc.

Review of the Children's Aggression Scale by JEFFREY A. ATLAS, Clinical and School Psychologist, SCO Family of Services, Queens, NY:

DESCRIPTION. Social welfare agencies are frequently faced with level of care questions, often basing determinations on a combination of referral diagnoses of children and behavioral adjustments in a succession of milieus. In tandem with this process, Committees on Special Education may seek to differentiate attentional and learning deficits from disruptive behavior disorders to determine the least restrictive educational environment for students. Underlying both of these assessments is some evaluation of children's anger expression and targets. The Children's Aggression Scale (CAS) presents itself as an instrument for quantifying and qualifying childhood aggression, potentially aiding in placement decisions.

The CAS consists of Teacher and Parent Rating Forms, the latter containing 33 versus 23 items by virtue of differentiating yelling, cursing, verbal threatening, and physical fighting on the basis of whether such behaviors occur at home or out of the home. Although the test's authors indicate a "group" administration format, the more likely procedure entails distributing the forms to be completed within an evaluation process or in line with the rater's available professional or personal time. A 10-minute estimate for completion of the scales is reasonable, and a carbonless tear-away hand-scorable page provides for rapid assessment. Items are rated on a 5-point Likert-type scale encompassing frequencies of *Never, Once a Month or Less, Once a Week or Less, 2–3 Times a Week,* or *Most Days.* More dangerous behaviors such as fighting or weapon use carry historical incidence anchors of *Never, Once or Twice, 3–5 Times, 6–10 Times,* or *More Than 10 Times.*

The CAS authors suggest that pedagogical personnel know the examinee a minimum of 4 weeks, but elsewhere in the manual 1 year is cited as optimal. The scales themselves have each of seven areas prefaced with "During the past year…" The longer time requisite, presumably used in norming of the scale, is preferable for teachers to bypass "halo" effects as new students may be on their best behavior upon entering classes. The 1-year prerequisite does introduce practical problems in school and agency evaluations in initial assessments. For those entering a new Special Education locale, it is unrealistic to assume an evaluator could locate and enlist the cooperation of raters at some physical and temporal separation. In foster care situations, especially in instances of congregate care, tensions existent from prior placements, often occasioning transfer, lower the likelihood that earlier parenting figures could be located and enlisted to provide the prior year's assessment. In such evaluative contexts the Child Behavior Checklist (Achenbach et al., 2003), canvassing behaviors "now or within the last 6 months," may provide a less detailed but more obtainable measure of aggressive behavior.

The CAS has an age range of 5–18 years, but provides separate preadolescent (5–11 years) and adolescent (12–18 years) norms based on a community sample. The CAS clinical sample did not provide for such bifurcation. The CAS aggregates frequencies of Aggression Against Family Members, Aggression Against Nonfamily Members, Aggression Towards Peers, and Aggression Towards Adults to yield separate *T*-score and percentile values, with suggested qualitative labels.

Verbal Aggression, Aggression Against Objects and Animals, Provoked Physical Aggression, Initiated Physical Aggression, and Use of Weapons are weighted and aggregated to yield summary values. Finally, composite Physical Aggression (Provoked Physical Aggression + Initiated Physical Aggression) and Total Aggression (Verbal Aggression + Aggression Against Objects and Animals + Physical Aggression + Use of Weapons) summary scores and descriptors are provided.

DEVELOPMENT. The test authors reviewed adult aggression scales to narrow down five child aggression domains: verbal, towards objects and animals, provoked, initiated, and use of weapons. Behaviors that upon face validity appeared to represent a continuum of acts were randomized around an anchoring item weighted .50. Subsequently, a group of 30 colleagues of the test authors rated the items to produce mean scores of greater or lesser severity.

TECHNICAL.

Standardization. The CAS Community sample consisted of 438 parents and 516 teachers of children, with overrepresentation of Caucasians (91.3%) for the parent scale. The Clinical sample consisted of 247 parents and 252 teachers, with 84.6% and 84.5% male composition, respectively, a mild overestimate considering a greater proportion of male school/clinic referrals in the U.S. population. In this reviewer's viewpoint the Clinical sample showed overrepresentation of Attention-Deficit/Hyperactivity Disorder participants (64.8% and 58.7%), with underrepresentation of Early Onset Bipolar Disorder (both Parent and Teacher groups at .4%). Regression analyses for the effects of age and gender yielded minimal variance. Nevertheless, separate age and gender tables were developed in line with expected developmental and gender differences for the Community sample. The Clinical sample, about half the size of the Community one and more homogeneous, was not stratified by age or gender. "The raw score distributions were converted to *T*-score distributions with a mean of 50 and a standard deviation of 10 using linear transformations" (professioinal manual, p. 43). Group differences were found in pretesting the Community and Clinical samples (CAS Parent form) utilizing the Community norms. Significant *t*-test differences comparing the groups across all scales and clusters lend support to the instrument's construct validity, and provided a basis for generating the separate Clinical norms.

Reliability. Internal consistency was assessed for the Community samples (CAS Parent and Teacher forms) utilizing alpha coefficients. Although the Total Aggression Index alpha coefficients were high, ranging from .78 to .94, some individual scales or clusters demonstrated moderate values (e.g., Initiated Physical Aggression had alpha coefficients of .53 for the Parent scale and .55 for the Teacher scale). As 98.8% of the Community sample reported no Weapons behaviors, alpha coefficients were not calculated.

The Total Aggression Index provided good internal consistency when samples of externalizing and disruptive behavior disorder children were evaluated. Initiated Physical Aggression produced acceptable alpha coefficients ranging from .60 to .77. Use of Weapons provided alpha coefficients of .63 to .81, comparable to the internal consistency of other scales and clusters.

Stability of the CAS was evaluated using small samples of 31 to 40 participants, utilizing retests after 7 to 52 days. Median correlation coefficients of .91 to .92 reflect the test's reliability.

Interrater reliability was assessed through examining Parent-Parent (N = 84), Teacher-Teacher (N = 169), and Parent-Teacher (N = 181) study samples. Although the median correlation coefficients for the first two studies were high (.87 and .97, respectively), the Parent-Teacher median *r* was a low .39, explaining less than 16% of the variance of scores. As the test authors note, the fact that some items differ between the Parent and Teacher forms and the fact that the child is being rated in different contexts may contribute to lowered comparability. It may also be suggested that the CAS is sampling behavioral states across different contexts rather than less malleable traits.

Validity. The CAS showed low to moderate convergent validity with a number of child rating scales, with higher correlations appearing between the Aggressive Behavior scale of the Child Behavior Checklist and the CAS Parent scale (N = 60; rs ranging from .55 to .82) and the CAS Teacher scale (N = 77; rs ranging from .69 to .78), excluding low correlations with the CAS Use of Weapons scale (.35 and .04, respectively).

Small group comparisons of Conduct-Disordered, Oppositional-Defiant, and ADHD youth reflected sensitivity of the CAS in all scales and clusters except Aggression Against Objects and Animals, Use of Weapons, and Aggression Toward Peers.

COMMENTARY. The present reviewer piloted the CAS on several youth to assess further the scale's strengths and weaknesses. One regular education 5-year-old boy, Ray, had only one item endorsed beyond "Never" on the CAS Teacher form, an Aggression Towards Adults item. Yet his raw score, was referenced at the 90.4th percentile in the norms table. In fact, the descriptor, "Very elevated," is attached to over half the raw scores for this category in the Community norms table (professional manual, p. 269). Visual inspection of the 403 pages of norms reveals many instances in which a surfeit of scores reach the maximal category (e.g., CAS Parent Community norms for females 5–11 indexing 5 of 9 pages for Provoked Physical Aggression and Initiated Physical Aggression at the >99 percentile). This phenomenon indicates a low ceiling level for the scales, lessening discriminant validity.

SUMMARY. The CAS is an easy-to-use, multifaceted scale of aggression in community and clinical populations aged 5-18 living in the U.S. The 1-year recommended observation period for raters may limit its usefulness as part of a psychological assessment intake protocol, whereas the low ceiling for scores may produce too many false positives. Although the Child Behavior Checklist is more restricted in its contours of aggressive behavior, it may be more practical and predictive in placement endeavors. The CAS, given the richness of its data, may find a niche in within-subjects assessments such a tracking the course of anger management treatment.

REVIEWER'S REFERENCE

Achenbach, T. M., Rescorla, L. A., McConaughey, S. H., Pecora, P. J., Wetherbee, K. M., Ruffle, T. M., & Newhouse, P. A. (2003). Achenbach System of Empirically Based Assessment. Burlington: University of Vermont Research Center for Children, Youth, and Families.

Review of the Children's Aggression Scale by DAVID F. CIAMPI, Adjunct Professor, International Homeland Security University Project, Springfield, MA:

DESCRIPTION. The Children's Aggression Scale (CAS) was normed, standardized, and validated to measure the frequency and severity of aggressive behavior among noninstitutionalized, nonhospitalized children and adolescents between the ages of 5 and 18 years. This multiple informant approach, based on the observations of both parents and teachers, necessitates the use of two versions of the CAS: namely, the CAS-P, designed to be completed by parents, and the CAS-T, designed to be completed by the child's principal teacher(s). The administration of the CAS takes approximately 10 minutes.

Both versions of the CAS are administered and scored in the paper-and-pencil form in conjunction with the CAS professional manual, the Teacher Rating Form, the Parent Rating Form, the Parent Score Summary Form, and the Teacher Score Summary Form. Computer-scoring software is also available (referred to as the "Children's Aggression Scale Scoring Program "CAS-SP" as an alternative).

The Parent Rating Form is of the selection type and 5-point Likert scales are provided for responding to the statements and questions on the assessment. Items 1–20 and 23–26 have a rating range from 0 to 4 (0 = *Never*, 1 = *Once a Month or Less*, 2 = *Once a Week or Less*, 3 = *2–3 Times a Week*, 4 = *Most Days*). Items 21–22 and 27 through 32 also have a 5-point scale that ranges from 0 = *Never,* 1 = *Once or Twice*, 2 = *3–5 Times*, 3 = *6–10 Times*, and 4 = *More Than 10 Times*. Additionally, Items 22 and 28 request that the parent describe the nature of any serious physical injury.

The Teacher Rating Form consists of 23 statements and questions. Items 1 to 22 correspond with 5-point scales and Item 23 has a "*Yes, No*, or *Does*

Not Apply" response format. Items 10, 13, 14, and 17 to 22 are equipped with a 5-point rating scale. The range is 0 = *Never*, 1 = *Once or Twice*, 2 = *3–5 Times*, 3 = *6–10 Times*, and 4 = *More than 10 Times*.

Both the CAS-P and the CAS-T have four scales: Verbal Aggression, Aggression Against Objects and Animals, Physical Aggression, and Use of Weapons. The CAS-P has six clusters: Provoked Physical Aggression, Initiated Physical Aggression, Aggression Against Family Members, Aggression Against Non-Family Members, Aggression Toward Peers, and Aggression Toward Adults.

The CAS-T has four clusters: Provoked Physical Aggression, Initiated Physical Aggression, Aggression Toward Peers, and Aggression Toward Adults. Both the CAS-P and CAS-T combine all scores to generate a Total Aggression Index. Each of the scales, clusters, and index scores are easily converted to *T*-scores using conversion tables that are provided in the professional manual. *T*-score ranges and Qualitative Labels are provided in the Parent Score Summary and Teacher Score Summary Forms. The developers mentioned that the CAS has utility in educational, forensic-criminal justice, and research settings.

DEVELOPMENT. The authors of this assessment instrument mentioned that the development of the CAS was initially based on a review of previously constructed scales that measured aggression among adults (Buss & Durkee, 1957; Buss & Perry, 1992; Yudofsky, Silver, Jackson, Endicott, & Wiliams, 1986). The CAS scoring system was piloted by colleagues and associates (N = 30) who were asked to rate all the items within each scale relative to an anchored item. According to the test authors, the raters were not involved in the initial construction of the CAS scales. Those who participated in the pilot study were either mental health professionals, graduate students, or clerical staff.

A one-way analysis of variance (ANOVA) revealed significant differences in ratings across the items in the five domains (e.g., the CAS-P's value was: $F > 12.00$, $p < .001$; the CAS-T had a value of: $F > 11.00$, $p < .001$. The test authors further elaborated that ratings for each item were used to develop a weighting system within the given domains. This process resulted in establishing weighting values for the items so that more severe responses would disproportionately increase the score's value within the respective domain.

TECHNICAL.

Standardization. Community norms were established based on data collected from 438 parents and 516 teachers of children and adolescents between the ages of 5 and 18 years. Clinical norms were established for both the CAS-P and CAS-T based on the sample data (N = 247, parents; N = 252, teachers), as well as (a) direct recruitment of data from sites across the United States and (b) clinical referrals to a research study in New York City on the neurobiology of ADHD and aggression (Halperin, et al., 1997; Schulz et al., 2001). The Clinical sample included four clinical groups: ADHD, ODD, CD, and Social Maladjustment. With respect to the Community norms, two age groups were established: (a) 5 to 11 years of age and (b) 12 to 18 years of age. *T* scores were then calculated for the two age groups by the two gender groups. This procedure was accomplished for both the CAS-P and the CAS-T.

Reliability. A series of tables in the professional manual display the internal consistency, test-retest stability, and inter-rater reliability values. Alpha coefficients were utilized to estimate the internal consistencies of both the CAS-P and the CAS-T scales by gender and age grouping. With respect to the CAS-P, the alpha coefficient ranged from .53 (Initiated Physical Aggression) to .83 (Aggression Toward Peers). Strong alpha coefficients were reported for the Total Aggression Index, .86 to .90. Alpha coefficients for the CAS-T scales were .58 (Aggression Against Objects and Animals) to .86 (Verbal Aggression) in the Community sample. The CAS-T Total Aggression Index alphas across the four normative groups were .78 to .94. It should be noted that internal consistency was not obtained for the Use of Weapons scale, as no alpha values are listed in the tables for either the CAS-P or CAS-T.

The test authors assessed reliability of the Use of Weapons scales based on an examination of the clinical sample, arguing that greater response variability would be expected. Internal consistency of the test scores was then evaluated. Test-retest (interval range of 7–40 days) coefficients for the CAS-P scales and clusters ranged from .69 to .99, and the mean *T* scores and standard deviations from the first to second ratings were from .02 to 2.45. The test authors obtained similar value ranges for the CAS-T, reporting: .84 to .99 for test-retest coefficients (interval range of 13–52 days) along with an absolute mean *T* score change of .01 to .69. Interrater reliability was also calculated and the obtained coefficients were .87 to .97 for the Parent-Parent and Teacher-Teacher samples, respectively.

Validity. The test authors explored validity of the CAS-P and the CAS-T by examining the intercorrelations among the CAS scales and clusters, between the CAS-P and CAS-T scores, and that of other behavioral measures, as well as the ability to identify groups with varying levels of aggression. The CAS-P Community sample's intercorrelations ranged from .05 for the Use of Weapons scale with the Aggression Against Objects and Animals scale and the Physical Aggression scale, and to .88 for the Verbal Aggression Scale with Total Aggression Index. The test authors did report findings using the clinical sample when pairing the Use of Weapons scale with the Aggression Against Objects and Animals scale of .39 and a high Total Aggression Index of .88. Similar results were reported with the CAS-T's Community sample and subsample of the Clinical sample with a range from .18 (Use of Weapons scale with Aggression Against Objects and Animals) to .86 when pairing the Verbal Aggression scale with the Total Aggression Index. Intercorrelations were reported as significant at $p < .01$ with a coefficient range from .27 (Use of Weapons scale with the Verbal Aggression scale) to .91 (Physical Aggression scale with Total Aggression Index).

Convergent validity of domain-specific assessments was also reviewed by the test developers and found to have overall moderate to strong correlations between the CAS-T scales and clusters, and the OAS (i.e., the Overt Aggression Scale; Yudofsky et al., 1986).

COMMENTARY. The CAS purports to measure the frequency and intensity of aggressive behaviors, along with identifying the object of aggression among American children and adolescents. The instructions, attached statements, and question items are parent and teacher friendly. There are, however, some concerns because the Use of Weapons scale's internal consistency was not established for either the CAS-P or the CAS-T. The Use of Weapons scale test-retest values for the Parent Scale and Teacher Scale were quite high, .99 and .99, respectively. The Parent-Parent, Teacher-Teacher, and Parent-Teacher Use of Weapons interrater reliability coefficients were low, -.02, .01, and .25, respectively.

With respect to establishing validity of the scales and clusters, the test authors noted that the Use of Weapons scale did not have a significant correlation with other CAS-P scales for the community sample. The test authors argued that there would be greater utility in pairing the Use of Weapons scale with the Clinical sample as greater variability in item responses would be anticipated. As captioned in the data for the community sample and clinical sample, significant intercorrelations were obtained ($p < .01$) and ranged from a low of .63 (Use of Weapons Scale with Aggression Against objects and Animals) to a high of .88 (Physical Aggression scale paired with the Total Aggression Index).

In general, internal consistency reliability is good among the remainder of the scales, clusters, and Total Aggression Index. There is good test stability for the CAS-P and CAS-T scales and clusters, with moderate to high correlations ranging from .69 to .99, and high test-retest coefficients with the CAS-T from .84 to .99.

Data on the normative sample's race/ethnicity categories are limited to Caucasians, African Americans, Hispanics, and Others. It would be useful to have greater clarity on the ethnic/racial composition of individuals who are labeled as Other.

SUMMARY. The test authors have developed a much needed instrument that puts less pressure on the child by having parents and teachers respond to the survey's questions and statements. Both the CAS-P and CAS-T are easy to administer and score. The ability to quantify aggressive behaviors, and identify the typologies and objects of aggression in both community and clinical contexts based on a relatively rapid administration (approximately 10 minutes) are strong points regarding the utility of this instrument. In general, this instrument has strong psychometric properties. It is recommended that potential test users become familiar with the uses and limitations associated with behavioral rating scales, particularly those that measure aggressive behaviors among children and adolescents, as well as the benefits and limitations associated with such instruments.

REVIEWER'S REFERENCES

Buss, A. H., & Durkee, A. (1957). An inventory for assessing different kinds of hostility. *Journal of Counseling Psychology, 21*, 343–349.

Buss, A. H., & Perry, M. (1992). The Aggression Questionnaire. *Journal of Personality and Social Psychology, 63*, 452-459.

Halperin, J. M., Newcorn, J. H., Kopstein, I., McKay, K. E., Schwartz, S. T., Siever, L. J., et al. (1997). Serotonin, aggression, and parental psychopathology in children with attention-deficit hyperactivity disorder. *Journal of the American Academy of Child and Adolescent Psychiatry, 36*, 1391–1398.

Schulz, K. P., Newcorn, J. H., McKay, K. E., Himelstein, J., Koda, V. H., Siever, L. J., et al. (2001) Relationship between Central Serontonergic function and aggression in prepubertal boys: Effect of age and attention-deficit/hyperactivity disorder. *Psychiatry Research, 101,* 1-10.

Yudofsky, S. C., Silver, J. M., Jackson, W., Endicott, J., & Williams, D. (1986). The Overt Aggression Scale for the objective rating of verbal and physical aggression. *The American Journal of Psychiatry, 143,* 35–39.

[26]

Children's Communication Checklist–2: United States Edition.

Purpose: "Designed to assess children's communication skills in the areas of pragmatics, syntax, morphology, semantics, and speech."
Population: Ages 4-16.
Publication Date: 2006.
Acronym: CCC-2.
Scores, 12: 10 communication domains: Speech, Syntax, Semantics, Coherence, Initiation, Scripted Language, Context, Nonverbal Communication, Social Relations, Interests; plus General Communication Composite, Social Interaction Difference Index.
Administration: Individual.
Price Data, 2008: $165 per complete kit including manual (2006, 112 pages), 25 caregiver response forms, 25 scoring worksheets, and scoring CD; $89 per manual; $39 per 25 caregiver response forms; $22 per 25 scoring worksheets.
Time: (5-10) minutes.
Comments: Scaled scores, general communication composite, social interaction difference index, confidence intervals, and percentile ranks are provided for each scale score.
Author: D. V. M. Bishop.
Publisher: Pearson.

Review of the Children's Communication Checklist-2: United States Edition by REBECCA McCAULEY, Professor of Speech & Hearing Science, The Ohio State University, Columbus, OH:

DESCRIPTION. The Children's Communication Checklist—Second Edition, United States Edition (CCC-2) is intended for use with children between the ages of 4 years and 16 years, 11 months who have normal hearing, speak in sentences, and use English as their primary language. As a caregiver-completed checklist, the CCC-2 provides a source of pre-assessment information for a child scheduled to be evaluated by a speech-language pathologist (SLP), educational diagnostician, or psychologist for speech and language concerns. In particular, the CCC-2 includes content addressing pragmatics—an aspect of language that is infrequently addressed in most language measures, but is critical for the diagnosis of autism spectrum disorders (ASD). The purposes of the CCC-2 are the identification of pragmatic language impairment, screening of receptive and expressive language skills, and assistance in screening for ASD.

In addition to general knowledge of standardized test use, test users should become familiar with the CCC-2 and practice its administration, scoring, and interpretation prior to clinical use. If the child's caregiver is considered unable to provide valid responses, an alternative individual (e.g., a teacher) who has at least 3 months of regular contact with the child is enlisted. Alternatively, the checklist can be given as a guided interview. One potentially confusing feature of checklist completion is that the direction of the 4-point scale used by caregivers is reversed for checklist items reflecting difficulties versus those reflecting strengths. Although this design is clearly stated and intentional on the part of the test publishers, test users will want to insure respondents' compliance with this change in scoring from one section to the next. Specifically, the same scale, 0–3, is used for difficulties and strengths, but a 0 for a difficulty indicates an absence of the difficulty, whereas a 0 for a strength indicates an absence fo the strength. The checklist takes about 10 to 15 minutes to complete. Once completed, the CCC-2 can be scored using a scoring CD in about 5 minutes or a scoring worksheet in about 15 minutes. Both methods result in (a) derived scaled scores and percentile ranks for each scale; (b) a General Communication Composite (GCC) normalized standard score, confidence interval and percentile rank, reflecting the child's performance on the first 8 scales; and (c) the Social Interaction Difference Index (SIDI). The SIDI is intended for descriptive use and is the sum of performances on the scales E, H, I, and J (scales assessing language and nonlanguage features associated with autism) minus the sum of performances on scales A—D (scales associated with knowledge of language structures). Guidelines for administration, scoring, and interpretation are clearly stated in the test manual.

DEVELOPMENT. The United States Edition of the CCC-2 is an adaptation of the CCC-2 (Bishop, 2003), which was developed in the United Kingdom. In addition to making changes in spelling and phrasing, the test developers also made minor additions to rating scale descriptors prior to U.S. standardization. The first predecessors to the British version of the CCC-2 (Bishop, 2003) had been developed to identify patterns of language difficulties (especially pragmatic) in children with diagnosed language impairment. These earlier versions first used respondents who were teachers and speech-languages professionals, later shifting to the use of familiar adults as respondents. The British edition of the CCC-2 was modified so that it could be used in diagnosis and has been the focus of ongoing validity studies by a variety of researchers.

The CCC-2, United States Edition, is composed of 70 items within ten 7-item scales (A. Speech, B. Syntax, C. Semantics, D. Coherence, E. Initiation, F. Scripted Language, G. Context, H. Nonverbal Communication, I. Social Relations, and J. Interests). Within each scale, 5 items relate to communication difficulties and 2 to strengths. The checklist is structured so that all communication difficulties are evaluated first, then strengths are evaluated. The first four scales (A—D) address aspects of language frequently affected in specific language impairments. The second four scales (E—H) address aspects affected in pragmatic impairments (which can occur independently or along with other language impairments). The last two scales (I—J) address nonlanguage behaviors often associated with autism spectrum disorder (ASD). Findings on the last two sets of scales (Scales E through J) are used as a basis for recommending further assessment for ASD.

TECHNICAL.

Standardization. The development of norms and selected technical studies for the current edition were conducted on a sample of 950 U.S. children. Sample sizes by age were 100 children for each year between 4 years and 9 years, 11 months; 100 children for each 2-year period between 10 years and 13 years, 11 months; and 150 children for the period from 14 years to 16 years, 11 months. These samples are well matched to U.S. Census data from 2002 for race/ethnicity, geographic region, and parent education level. Twenty-seven percent of these children were receiving special services (including 7% for gifted and talented/advanced placement). Although the sample as a whole was evenly divided between boys and girls, scaled scores were not reported by gender for each age group. Normative data were presented at 3-month intervals for ages 4 years to 6 years, 11 months; at 6-month intervals for 7 to 7 years, 11 months; and at 12-month intervals for subsequent ages.

Reliability. Reliability studies examined test-retest reliability and internal consistency. Test-retest reliability was examined for 98 children from the standardization sample in three age groups (4 years to 6 years, 11 months; 7 years to 9 years, 11 months; and 10 years to 16 years, 11 months) composed of at least 30 children each and retested over intervals from 1 to 28 days. Results were good for the youngest age group ($r = .86$) and excellent for the older two groups ($r = .96$ and .93, respectively). Coefficient alpha data based on the U.S. standardization data suggest appropriately strong internal consistency for each of the component scales.

Validity. Children with specific-language impairment (SLI) ($n = 54$), autistic/spectrum disorder (ASD) ($n = 62$) and pragmatic language impairment ($n = 46$) were studied to provide validity evidence. As was required for the standardization sample, children in these groups were required to have normal hearing, to have English as their primary language and to speak in sentences. Because many children with ASD do not develop this level of spoken language, the children studied for the CCC-2 seem likely to be more representative of individuals with ASD who are relatively high functioning.

The test manual describes three studies examining the construct validity of the CCC-2 and, in particular, its ability to distinguish among clinical samples. First, the test developer compared each clinical group against a matched sample from the standardization data. Multiple *t*-tests showed significant differences between each clinical group and its matched group on individual scales and on the GCC overall. In a second study, because the SIDI reflects the individual's relative functioning on language structure versus pragmatics, the author predicted differing outcomes across the three groups as well as when each group was compared with a matched control group taken from the standardization sample. Results appeared consistent with predictions. In the third study, the test developer reports the diagnostic accuracy of the GCC in the form of sensitivity and specificity for each group at three criterion levels (1, 1.5, and 2 *SD* below the mean of the matched samples), as well as the Positive Predictive Power (PPP) and Negative Predictive Power (NPP) for these criterion levels at five different base rates. Although not widely reported for children's language tests, such measures of diagnostic accuracy are increasingly called for and represent a level of detail that can help clinicians assess the likely utility of these measures within their own context (Dollaghan, 2007). Except at the lowest base rate, these data generally suggest that the CCC-2 can prove quite helpful in identifying children who have the clinical conditions for which the test was developed.

COMMENTARY. Weaknesses in the current evidence base supporting use of the CCC-2 for its intended purposes include a need for interexaminer reliability evidence and a more thorough description of its content relevance and coverage. Nonetheless, evidence concerning test-retest reliability and diagnostic validity is strong, particularly in comparison to competing measures—few of which attempt to address language use (pragmatics) as well as language structure. The minimal time demands this instrument places on respondents and test users is another very attractive feature.

SUMMARY. The intended purposes of the CCC-2 are screening for ASD and SLI, as well as the identification of pragmatic impairments in children between 4 and 16 years, 11 months. Given evidence supporting it thus far, clinicians who have access to caregivers or other familiar adults to serve as respondents will probably find this a useful addition to their testing protocol. Although it is not suited to children who are lower functioning (i.e., do not speak in sentences), its efficiency, the clarity of its manual, and its focus on both language structure and use (pragmatics) represent considerable strengths. Because the CCC-2 is the product of a long history of research by the test author and other, independent researchers, it seems likely that additional support related to reliability and further validity evidence may be forthcoming.

REVIEWER'S REFERENCES

Bishop, D. V. M. (2003). Children's Communication Checklist—Second Edition. London: The Psychological Corporation.

Dollaghan, C. (2007). *The handbook for evidence-based practice in communication disorders.* Baltimore: Paul H. Brookes Publishing Company, Inc.

Review of the Children's Communication Checklist-2: United States Edition by ROGER L. TOWNE, Associate Professor, Department of Communication Sciences and Disorders, Worcester State College, Worcester, MA:

DESCRIPTION. The Children's Communication Checklist-2 (CCC-2) is a rating checklist whereby a child's language skills are measured by their primary caregiver or other adult familiar with the child. The CCC-2 is designed to assess children's communication skills in the areas of pragmatics, syntax, morphology, semantics, and speech. Further, it is also designed specifically to identify children with pragmatic language impairment, specific language impairment, and those who may require further assessment relative to autistic spectrum disorder. The test can be administered to children between the ages of 4 years to 16 years, 11 months.

The CCC-2 consists of 70 statements about the child's communication behavior that the caregiver rates on a 4-point scale relative to the estimated number of times the behavior is observed during the day or week. For example, a rating of 0 indicates the behavior is observed less than once a week (never), whereas a rating of 3 indicates the behavior is observed several times a day (always). The first 50 statements are written to assess communication skills in which a child may be having difficulty, and the last 20 statements focus on potential strengths in communication skills. The 70 statement items are divided into 10 scales, each representing a different communication skill area (e.g., syntax, initiation, nonverbal communication) with each scale having 7 test items. Four of the scales specifically assess communication areas often impaired in children presenting specific language impairment (SLI), four of the scales assess areas of pragmatic aspects of communication, and two scales assess behaviors often impaired in children with autistic spectrum disorder (ASD).

The CCC-2 consists of a manual, a Caregiver Response Form, a scoring CD, and an optional scoring worksheet. The manual contains information regarding test administration, development, scoring, and interpretation. The Caregiver Response Form contains directions to the caregiver, the rating key, and the 70 test item statements. Scoring can be done using the scoring CD and a computer, or by hand using the scoring worksheet.

The test is administered by giving the Caregiver Response Form to the child's caregiver or other adult (such as a teacher) who knows the child well enough to be able to answer the test items. The caregiver is given instructions to answer all 70 test items and to provide basic demographic information regarding the child and themselves. In addition, the caregiver notes if the child has a permanent hearing loss, if English is not the child's primary language, or if the child does not put words together to form sentences as any of these excludes the valid use of the checklist. The caregiver then assigns a rating score (0 to 3) for each test item indicating how often they observe the child engaging in the described communication behavior. It is estimated that completion of the response form should take 10 to 15 minutes. The response form is then returned to the examiner for scoring. If the caregiver has not answered all the questions, the examiner is to contact the caregiver and encourage them to complete the form.

Scoring can be done on a computer using the scoring CD or by hand using the scoring worksheet. If using the scoring CD, the raw scores given for each of the 70 test items are entered directly from the Caregiver Response Form. The program then calculates total raw scores, scaled scores, and percentile ranks for each of the 10 scales, a General Communication Composite score (GCC), and a Social Interaction Difference Index (SIDI) and presents them in a summary chart that can be printed and saved. The GCC can be used to compare the child's overall communication skills to others of the same age and identify those likely having a significant communication problem. The SIDI is an index that may be helpful in identifying children with language impairment or autistic spectrum disorder.

Alternatively, scoring can be done by hand using the scoring worksheet. Although this method takes a little longer, it is a simple process that is facilitated by the logical and user-friendly organization of the worksheet. The process starts with the professional recording the raw scores for each test item from the Caregiver Response Form to the inside of the worksheet, which is organized into the 10 scales. From these the total raw score for each scale is calculated and then transferred to the front page score summary of the worksheet. From these data, scaled scores and percentiles for each scale, the General Communication Composite, and the Social Interaction Difference Index are derived using tables provided in the manual.

DEVELOPMENT. The present U.S. Edition of the CCC-2 is an adaptation of the first CCC-2 developed and used in the United Kingdom. Both editions are revisions of the author's original Children's Communication Checklist (CCC) published in the United Kingdom in 1998. The CCC was developed by selecting and reorganizing subtests from the author's two previously published language assessment tools: the Checklist for Language Impaired Children (CLIC) and the Checklist for Language Impaired Children-2 (CLIC-2). Items were selected from the CLIC-2, which had "the highest interrater reliability, and were categorized into new scales based on internal consistency" (manual, p. 25). Although the CCC was intended to be used to classify children already known to have a specific language impairment, an adaptation of the CCC as a screening tool for specific language impairments was undertaken. The result of this undertaking was the CCC-2 United Kingdom Edition. With some changes in spelling and wording as well as standardization in the United States, the present United States Edition was generated.

TECHNICAL. The United States Edition of the CCC-2 was standardized in the United States over a 5-month period in 2005. Data were collected on 950 children ranging in age from 4 years to 16 years, 11 months with 100 children in each of the nine yearly age ranges (e.g., 4 years to 4 years, 11 months; 5 years to 5 years, 11 months). The sample was further stratified by caregiver education level, race and ethnicity, and geographic region of the country to similarly reflect the percent of U.S. population as reported in the 2002 U.S. Current Population Survey. In addition to the standardization data, data were also collected on three clinical populations of children that were later used to document and support the validity of the test; specific language impairment (N = 54), pragmatic language impairment (N = 46), and autistic spectrum disorder (N = 62).

Test reliability was established in two ways: test-retest reliability and through internal consistency. Test-retest reliability was established by selecting 98 children from the standardization study who fell relatively evenly into three age groups (4 years through 6 years, 11 months; 7 years through 9 years, 11 months; and 10 years through 16 years, 11 months) and also reflected the demographic stratification of the standardization group. Caregivers of these children were then asked to complete a second CCC-2 within 1 to 28 days of completing the first checklist. Correlations between the General Communication Composite (GCC) obtained on the first and second administrations were calculated using product-moment correlation coefficient. These correlations ranged between .86 and .96, suggesting a high degree of performance similarity between the two administered checklists.

Internal consistency was established by coefficient alpha for each of the 10 scales. This was first done by collapsing across all age groups so the data could also be compared to the United Kingdom edition. Within the United States Edition alone correlations between the two test halves ranged from .69 to .85, suggesting relatively good reliability as well as good homogeneity of content within each scale. Correlation differences between the United States Edition and the United Kingdom Edition ranged between .01 and .09, indicating similarity between the two editions. For the United States Edition, coefficient alpha was also calculated separately for the nine different age groups for each of the 10 scales and the General Communication Composite (GCC). Coefficients (alpha) ranged between .47 and .86 for all scales by ages, and from .65 to .79 across the 10 scales when averaged by age. The GCC coefficients for each age group only ranged between .94 and .96, suggesting a high degree of reliability for that composite.

Evidence of validity was presented based on test content and special group studies, which included performances of children from the clinical samples tested and the ability of the checklist to identify children with clinical conditions. The author noted that "CCC-2 construction and content was developed to reflect developmental communication abilities of children ages 4:0 to 16:11 years" and "to ensure that the items adequately covered established domains of communication with special emphasis on aspects of social communication" (manual, p. 37). That the author is a well-published expert in the area of child language disorders and pragmatic communication strongly suggests that the checklist does reflect content that is current and germane to its intended use.

Evidence of validity based on group studies of the special children was presented in two ways: by examining the scores of children from the clinical samples and the ability of the checklist to identify children accurately within these special groups. Examination of the scores of the children from the three clinical samples (specific language impairment, pragmatic language impairment, and autistic spectrum disorder) began with selecting a child from the standardization group who matched a child from the special groups on age, sex, race/ethnicity, and parent education level. Means and standard deviations for all scales and the GCC were then computed for each of the special groups and matched controls. In each case the special groups had lower mean scores than did their matched control group. *T*-scores between the two samples were all significant at .019 or .001 indicating that the checklist had the ability to differentiate between children with normal ability and children with communication difficulty.

Secondly, the Positive Predictive Power (PPP; i.e., the likelihood that a child with a positive test result actually has the disorder) and Negative Predictive Power (NPP; i.e., the likelihood that a child with a negative test result does not have the disorder) was calculated at -1.00, -1.50, and -2.00 standard deviations for four base rates based on reported screening identification rates and referral identification rates in the public schools (10%, 60%, 70%, and 80%). These were compared to similar calculations for the matched samples at a 50% base rate, or false positive rate. Data were presented for the General Communication Composite (GCC). Although difficult to interpret, the general trend in the three referral base rates and the 50% base rate for the matched sample was that PPPs were considerably higher than NPPs and their differences increased with higher standard deviations below the mean. This is a desired effect. Also, as would be expected, the data at the 10% screening base rate was the opposite in that PPPs were considerably smaller than corresponding NPPs but with differences again increasing at higher standard deviations. Collectively, these data provide broad support for the validity of the checklist by demonstrating its ability to identify children with potential communication problems as well as differentiate between children with specifically identified communication problems.

COMMENTARY. As the author noted, due to the completion of the checklist typically being done by a child's caregiver, responses will be influenced by the subjective bias of the respondent. However, "when combined with other data obtained—such as the administration of other assessments, teacher reports, and clinical observations—you will be able to make clinical decisions regarding the child's communication and language skills" (manual, p. 17). Therefore, the CCC-2 should be viewed as either a screening tool to identify children who are at risk and need additional assessment, or a supplemental tool to other testing and data being collected. Within that context, the CCC-2 has inherent value especially in helping to identify children with pragmatic language disorder in which there are few other assessment tools available. Further, although structured parent reports have been developed for the assessment of communication skills in toddlers and preschoolers (Reed, 2005) few, if any, have been developed that extend into the age ranges incorporated in the CCC-2. In addition, few instruments exist that comprehensively measure pragmatic skills in a natural environment; therefore, those instruments that are generally used to measure language and pragmatic skills may lack the sensitivity to identify pragmatic impairments (Bishop, 1997).

SUMMARY. The CCC-2 appears to be a well-constructed instrument that has both face validity and reliability to accomplish its stated purpose of assisting in identifying children with language and communication problems, especially in the area of pragmatic communication skills. As a caregiver or parent checklist it is unique in the extended age range in which it was standardized and can be used. As a caregiver or parent checklist it is also limited by the observational skills, accuracy in reporting, and potential biases of the respondent. However, when used as intended as a screening tool or in addition to other more comprehensive communication and language assessment tools the CCC-2 should be a welcomed and useful addition for a clinician.

REVIEWER'S REFERENCES

Bishop, D. V. M. (1997). *Uncommon understanding: Development and disorders of language comprehension in children.* Hove, UK: Psychology Press.

Reed, V. A. (2005). *An introduction to children with language disorders.* Boston: Pearson, Allyn and Bacon.

[27]

Children's Organizational Skills Scales.

Purpose: Measures "how children organize their time, materials, and actions to accomplish important tasks at home and school."

Population: Ages 8-13.

Publication Date: 2009.

Acronym: COSS.

Scores, 15: 5 scores per form: Task Planning, Organized Actions, Memory and Materials Management, Total, Inconsistency Index (COSS-Parent & COSS-Teacher only), Positive Impression (COSS-Child only).

Administration: Individual or group.

Forms, 3: COSS-Parent, COSS-Teacher, and COSS-Child.

Price Data, 2010: $209 per complete handscored kit including 25 Parent/Teacher/Child QuikScore forms and technical manual (2009, 153 pages); $262 per complete scoring software kit including 25 Parent/Teacher/Child response forms, technical manual, and scoring software; $93 per online kit including 10 Parent, 10 Teacher, and 10 Child online forms, and technical manual; $42 per 25 COSS-Parent QuikScore forms; $42 per 25 COSS-Teacher forms; $42 per 25 COSS-Child forms; $42 per 25 COSS-Parent response forms; $42 per 25 COSS-Teacher response forms; $42 per 25 COSS-Child response forms; $1.50 per COSS-Parent online form; $1.50 per COSS-Teacher online form; $1.50 per COSS-Child online form; $58 per technical manual; $104 per COSS scoring software; $49 per COSS online subscription; $49 per COSS online subscription renewal.

Time: (20) minutes.

Comments: Global assessment of overall organizational difficulty (COSS-Teacher only) and Impairment Questions (COSS-Teacher & COSS-Parent only) are interpreted qualitatively; ratings by teachers, parents, and child (self-rating); available online and in paper-and-pencil format; forms can be scored by hand, using the COSS scoring software, or using the COSS online program.

Authors: Howard Abikoff and Richard Gallagher.

Publisher: Multi-Health Systems Inc.

Review of the Children's Organizational Skills Scales by MICHAEL S. MATTHEWS, Assistant Professor of Gifted Education, The University of North Carolina at Charlotte, Charlotte, NC:

DESCRIPTION. The Children's Organizational Skills Scales (COSS) was developed to assess how children ages 8–13 manage their time, organize their materials, and plan their actions to accomplish tasks at home and at school. Authors Abikoff and Gallagher conceptualize these three factors, within the broader realm of executive functioning, as adaptive skills that influence children's ability to complete tasks effectively at home and in school. Although developed during clinical work primarily with students with Attention Deficit-Hyperactivity Disorder (ADHD), the COSS also is relevant for typical children who have difficulty with organizational skills but have not presented other symptoms of ADHD.

The COSS consists of three closely related rating scale forms, composed of 42 to 66 items, to be completed by the parent, the child, and the child's teacher. The test authors suggest that COSS results may be useful "in the areas of assessment, intervention, progress-monitoring, and research" (technical manual, p. 1) as well as for "pinpointing the organizational skills that present the greatest difficulty" (technical manual, p. 1) in the child's life. The COSS may be given either in a paper-and-pencil version, which contains a hidden carbon-copy scoring grid in the inner pages of the form, or in an online version. It may be administered either individually or within a group setting. Responses may be hand scored or scored using software (both a local program and an online one are available) to facilitate tracking of multiple scores. Administration time is approximately 20 minutes. Instructions for administration are clear and precise, and they emphasize adherence to relevant professional and ethical standards.

Each of the three self-report forms yields a total score, as well as scale scores in three areas that include Task Planning (the ability to declare steps needed to complete a task on time), Organized Actions (the use of routines and planning aids, such as calendars), and Memory and Materials Management (the ability to recall assignments and their due dates, and to organize and keep track of supplies needed to complete a task). Raw COSS scores are converted to *T*-scores and percentile ranks to allow comparison across raters and contexts. Norm tables are divided by sex and are further divided into 2-year age ranges of 8–9, 10–11, and 12–13 years to address developmental changes in organizational skills as children mature.

DEVELOPMENT. This norm-referenced measure was developed in the course of the test authors' clinical and research work to offer a way to evaluate the outcomes of different interventions for children with ADHD and their families. Items were selected to address salient competencies the test authors encountered in clinical practice with students with symptoms of ADHD, because they found that little normative information and few suitable measures were available to examine children's organization, planning, and time management skills within the real world context. Existing measures of these skills, which the test authors review, were either too broad, too narrow, or lacking appropriate norms.

Abikoff and Gallagher, the test authors, generated an initial pool of items based on themes obtained through interviews, discussion, and as lists of problems reported by parents, teachers, and clinicians in regard to children's ability to complete assigned tasks at home and in school. A pilot version of the Teacher and Child COSS with 49 to 52 initial items was tested on 180 teachers and their 911 students, and the Parent and Child COSS forms were piloted with 135 parents and their children. Exploratory factor analysis was used to create a three-factor model for the Teacher form of the scale. Some items that loaded highly on more than one factor or were judged important for clinical purposes were retained; these items contribute to the total score but are not used in calculating factor scores. The initial scale structure from the pilot studies was verified in subsequent analyses for all three forms based on the norming sample population. It is not completely clear how the initial item counts for the pilot study relate to the final item counts, as the number of items increased for the Child (63 vs. 51) and Parent (58 vs. 52) versions, but decreased (35 vs. 49 items) for the Teacher version of the COSS (final item counts here do not include the global assessment and impairment questions). Further explanation of these changes would strengthen the test authors' description of the development process.

TECHNICAL.

Standardization. An overall sample of 5,047 completed COSS assessments was collected over a 3-year time frame from U.S. and Canadian parents, teachers, and children. Between 23% and 35% of the sample (depending on the comparison) were diagnosed as having either ADHD or a learning disorder. The norming sample consisted of 1,440 representative responses (half male, half female) randomly drawn from this larger sample to be representative of the racial and ethnic makeup of the general population (2000 U.S. Census). The test authors' analyses suggest that race/ethnicity differences had little substantive effect on COSS ratings, but sex and age did show differences.

Reliability. The test authors cite acceptable to strong internal consistency reliability coefficients for the three COSS forms, ranging from .70 to .98, as well as test-retest reliability coefficients ranging from .88 to .99 over periods of 2 to 4 weeks. Standard errors of measurement were relatively small.

Validity. Mean correlations across informants rating the same child ranged from $r = .52$ (teacher to child) to $r = .69$ (parent to teacher). COSS scores differentiated between students diagnosed with ADHD and those with a specific learning disorder, as well as between typical students and those with ADHD. In a study with $n = 186$, the test authors found that similar constructs from the Conners 3 rating scale for ADHD were correlated with COSS results more strongly than were dissimilar Conners constructs. No information is provided regarding students or families from low-SES backgrounds, who should have been examined in the validity comparisons and norming information, but in other respects the evidence presented to support the validity of COSS results is clear and compelling.

Notably, the first step in the COSS interpretation guidelines instructs the assessor to consider a variety of potential threats to validity. Parent and Teacher forms contain a procedure for calculating an Inconsistency Index score as a general check against response inconsistency, and a Positive Impression score may be calculated on the Child form to check for positively biased response patterns.

COMMENTARY. The COSS is a welcome addition to the set of tools that may be used in helping children of all ability levels to become more successful in school and at home. It effectively fills a gap in the area of children's organizational skills that is quite important to parents (Garn, Matthews, & Jolly, in press), but is only rarely quantified. As a measure based in clinical experience, the COSS will be useful to both researchers and practitioners.

Overall, the COSS technical manual is thorough yet accessible. The age range of 8–13 with which the COSS may be used is relatively narrow, and I would encourage the test authors to consider developing a parallel measure for use with children in the upper middle school to high school age range where high ability learners not diagnosed with ADHD often first begin to encounter difficulties in school.

A few minor cautions should be noted. Some COSS items seem likely to reflect mainstream U.S. values, rather than those necessarily of children and parents from other cultures or from low SES households. Some items may unintentionally reflect middle class values and parents' ability to scaffold their child's organization rather than providing a picture of the child's organizational skills on his or her own. In a brief paragraph in the test manual the authors note that "parents from different cultures might have different perceptions of what constitutes desirable behavior" (technical manual, p. 22), but it may not be clear what these differences may look like or what the test administrator should do if such differences are observed. Child scale items are appropriately shorter and less complex, yet with 63 items, the form still may be too long for younger children (especially those prone to inattention) to complete unassisted.

SUMMARY. The Children's Organizational Skills Scales is a strong measure overall that has been developed using a sophisticated understanding of both organizational skills and test development. Some caution appears warranted in using the COSS with low-income and culturally diverse children and families, but overall I expect it will prove quite useful to researchers as well as practitioners. Relevant populations who might be assessed using the COSS include students diagnosed as having ADHD, underachieving academically gifted learners (McCoach & Siegle, 2003), and other children ages 8–13 who may experience difficulty at home or in school due to underdeveloped organizational skills.

REVIEWER'S REFERENCES

Garn, A. C., Matthews, M. S., & Jolly, J. (in press). Parental influences on the academic motivation of gifted students: A self-determination theory perspective. *Gifted Child Quarterly*.

McCoach, D. B., & Siegle, D. (2003). Factors that differentiate underachieving gifted students from high-achieving gifted students. *Gifted Child Quarterly, 47,* 144-154. DOI: 10.1177/001698620304700205

Review of the Children's Organizational Skills Scales by RAYNE A. SPERLING, Associate Professor and Professor-in-Charge of Educational Psychology, The Pennsylvania State University, University Park, PA:

DESCRIPTION. The Children's Organizational Skills Scales (COSS) consists of a multi-informant (parent, teacher, and child) assessment designed to measure how elementary and middle school students "organize their time, materials, and actions to accomplish important tasks at home and school" (technical manual, p. 1). The assessment is specifically designed to measure children's Organization, Time Management, and Planning (OTMP). The COSS has been used in research with children and also may serve as a useful tool in tracking individual children's skills. Data from the COSS may inform the identification of children in need of assistance in OTMP and may aid in the development and progress monitoring of interventions for students with Individual Education Programs. COSS data may also serve to inform the efficacy of treatments and interventions in clinical and research settings. The COSS is independently administered via computer or paper and pencil in approximately 20 minutes. The COSS instrument presents behavioral statements to which a child self-reports and parents and teachers rate agreement on 4-point scales. There are 42 Teacher, 66 Parent, and 63 Child items. Higher COSS scores indicate greater OTMP skills concerns. The COSS can be either hand scored or computer scored. The resulting raw and standard scores provide an overall score and scale scores for Task Planning, Organized Actions, and Memory and Materials Management. The technical manual clearly describes appropriate administration, scoring, and interpretation information and provides extensive data regarding the development and psychometric properties of the COSS.

DEVELOPMENT. The COSS was designed primarily from a clinical and research perspective as an assessment of the OTMP skills and behaviors often reported by those working with children with Attention Deficit Hyperactivity Disorder (ADHD). The COSS was developed in order to define "the construct of organizational skills to reflect children's real-world functioning" (technical manual, p. 45), to detail components of those skills, and to allow evaluators to track changes in children through development or intervention. Initial items were constructed by psychologists based upon observations from practice. Psychiatrists, teachers, social workers, and learning disability experts reviewed and modified initial items. Parallel items were constructed for inclusion across the Child, Parent, and Teacher scales. The pilot scales included a *Does not apply* response that was used to screen items not relevant to the target population of children aged 8–13 years. The pilot administrations were conducted with 180 teachers who rated 911 students as well as administrations to 135 parents and their children.

Results from the pilot administrations indicated sound internal consistency reliability (coefficients ranged from .86 to .94). Test-retest reliability assessed after 2 to 3 weeks by teachers based upon ratings of 144 children yielded coefficients that ranged from .92 to .94. Preliminary factor structures derived from exploratory factor analyses supported three factors and informed the final scales. Items from the pilot administrations that loaded on more than one factor were retained for inclusion in the current instrument to inform overall scores but not scale scores. Of particular importance for clinical practice and application to school settings, items for parents and teachers that address the potential functional impact of OTMP skills deficits are included in the COSS. Items for parents to rate family conflict related to OTMP skills deficits are also included in the COSS scales. Of further importance, an Inconsistency index and a Positive Impression scale are also included in the COSS.

TECHNICAL. The technical manual is well-designed and prepared, and adequately provides all relevant normative information for score and scale interpretations. General population, normative, and clinical samples for the COSS included children, parents, and teachers from the United States and Canada. Participants varied with respect to gender, ethnicity, and parents' education level. The developers clearly made efforts to include an adequate normative sample representative of current United States populations, and the representativeness of the clinical samples are adequate. For example, the general percentages of students by category indicate adequate variance, and as would be expected, more boys than girls were included in the clinical sample. Linear *T*-scores were calculated and empirical percentiles were generated to account for the expected somewhat positively skewed distributions for the COSS overall and scale scores. Overall, boys rated themselves higher and were rated higher by parents and teachers on all forms of the COSS. Parents also generally rated younger children higher than older children. Some race/ethnicity differences were indicated in the normative sample for Parent scores. These differences may warrant additional research. As the COSS is a new measure, future administrations of the COSS scales will serve to inform the existing data regarding the overall and scale scores.

As determined by alpha coefficients, the reported internal consistency reliability of the COSS overall and scale scores range from .70 to .98 across the Child, Parent, and Teacher scales. These reliabilities appear appropriate. When consideration is given to the age of the target population, the lower reliability coefficient observed for the child's task-planning scale (.70) is likely acceptable. The reported high test-retest reliabilities (.88–.99) were determined based upon relatively small samples.

The technical manual reports several forms of validity for the COSS scales. Across-informant correlations were expected to be, and were, moderate. Although statistically significant due in large part to sample size, these ratings ranged from .47 to .73 and were lower than might be expected between ratings by parents, teachers, and children. In order to assess convergent and divergent validity the developers administered the Conners 3, a well-known and often used measure of ADHD (e.g., Conners, 2008), to a sample of children, parents, and teachers. Relative support for the COSS scales is established from the correlations among COSS and Conners 3 scales. For example, some of the strongest correlations, such as those between COSS scale scores and Conners 3 scale scores of Inattention and Executive Functioning indicate convergent support for the COSS. Other correlations, such as those with the Conners 3 Anxiety scale, help to establish divergent validity. Generally, however, the strength of the correlations across these measures is due in large part to sample size, and significance tests reported are inflated due to a lack of adjustments for multiple inferential tests. Nonetheless, taken together, there is some convergent and divergent support provided regarding the validity of the measure. Of critical importance for research and practice, the tests of discriminant validity lend support for the use of the COSS overall and scale scores for the intended purposes of identifying skills deficits.

COMMENTARY. Overall, the COSS appears to assess the OTMP of children as determined by self-report ratings as well as parent and teacher ratings. Although some may argue that there is limited empirical support for OTMP constructs, medical professionals, as well as counseling and school psychologists, learning disability specialists, teachers, parents, researchers, and others working with children who may display deficits in OTMP skills recognize there is a need for sound measures. The COSS can serve to fill an important void in available systematic measures of these critical skills. In my practice administrations of the scale, children were able to complete the scale and the resulting scores illustrated adequate variance across items. The practice administrations with parents did draw attention to questions regarding the degree to which parents were able to rate observed behavior in schools. Parents reported their answers to some of the scale items were speculative. The validity of the ratings provided by parents will likely vary based upon knowledge of their children and their communication with school professionals. This concern is tempered by the multiple-informant approach used with the COSS scales.

SUMMARY. The COSS is a relatively new, easily administered, assessment that can serve an important role in research and practice in clinical and applied settings in an area where sound assessments are currently lacking. The provision for computer administration and scoring likely holds appeal for many prospective users. The cost of the scales is not prohibitive for use in research, clinical, or school settings. The technical manual is an excellent and necessary resource for those who intend to administer, score, or interpret COSS scores. Although the COSS scales may provide information for typical children, those seeking to assess skills related to children's ADHD will find information from administration of the COSS scales helpful in their planning of treatments and interventions.

REVIEWER'S REFERENCE

Conners, C. K. (2008). *Conners 3rd Edition manual.* Toronto, Ontario, Canada: Multi-Health Systems, Inc.

[28]

Chronic Pain Coping Inventory.

Purpose: Designed to "assess the use of coping strategies that are typically targeted for change in multidisciplinary pain treatment programs."
Population: Ages 21-80.
Publication Dates: 1995-2008.
Acronym: CPCI.
Scores, 9: Guarding, Resting, Asking for Assistance, Exercise/Stretch, Relaxation, Task Persistence, Coping Self-Statements, Pacing, Seeking Social Support.
Administration: Individual or group.
Price Data, 2009: $185 per manual (2008, 60 pages), 25 rating forms, 25 score summary/profile sheets, and 25 pain worksheets; price data for computer scoring software available from publisher.
Time: (15) minutes.
Authors: Mark P. Jensen, Judith A. Turner, Joan M. Romano, and Warren R. Nielson.
Publisher: Psychological Assessment Resources, Inc.

Review of the Chronic Pain Coping Inventory by TONY CELLUCCI, Professor and Director of the Psychology Training Clinic, Idaho State University, Pocatello, ID:

DESCRIPTION. The Chronic Pain Coping Inventory (CPCI) is a 70-item self-report measure of positive and negative coping behaviors related to chronic pain. It is recommended as part of a comprehensive evaluation of patients in multidisciplinary pain clinics, and has been used with a variety of types of pain patients (e.g., spinal cord injuries, fibromyalgia, multiple sclerosis). The person responds to each item in terms of the number of days (1–7) in the past week that he or she engaged in that particular coping behavior. The test authors believe this scale provides for meaningful interpretation of scores and comparability across patients. The response booklet uses carbonless paper allowing for easy summation of raw scores. There are nine separate scales (3 Illness-Focused and 6 Wellness–Focused) with varying numbers (4–12) of items. Normalized *T* scores and percentile ranks corresponding to raw scores are provided in the manual and on a separate profile sheet. A score summary sheet also allows examination of a reliable change index with associated probability. A supplemental worksheet for pain intensity ratings (0–10 with 10 representing worst possible) and an accompanying human figure pain drawing are provided to enhance interpretation. The CPCI is based on cognitive-behavioral models of pain that target coping strategies in intervention efforts. The test is said to be appropriate for both men and women, ages 20–80, who suffer from chronic pain, and can be used for both initial evaluation and monitoring treatment progress.

DEVELOPMENT. This is the latest version of an instrument the test authors began investigating over 12 years ago (Jensen, Turner, Romano, & Strom, 1995). The manual describes the procedures used for initial scale development and item selection; a list of pain coping strategies recognized in the literature and by providers was defined and used to construct specific items. Pilot data obtained from volunteers who had been screened for multidisciplinary pain treatment were used to develop the original scales. Items were retained if they were significantly correlated ($r \geq .40$) with their purported scale more so than with other scales. The scales themselves had to have an internal consistency of .70 or greater in order to be retained. This process resulted in eight original scales that generally had expected relationships with other measures (e.g., pain discomfort, activity level). The pacing scale (i.e., what patients do when they moderate activities appropriately) was added separately. Several items related to medication use were dropped due to purported difficulties in coding and scoring. Alcohol and medication misuse to cope with pain must be assessed separately. The remaining items themselves seem well written for the scale constructs and individual interpretation. However, the item content certainly is more behavioral than cognitive, with positive coping self-statements the only real cognitive measure. The manual makes no mention of an earlier abbreviated version of the instrument (CPCI-42) and why this research did not impact the length of the current version (Romano, Jensen, & Turner, 2003).

TECHNICAL.

Standardization. The standardization sample of 527 adults was aggregated from four different samples (i.e., 125 individuals diagnosed with MS, 127 persons with pain due to spinal cord injuries, 163 outpatients in a multidisciplinary chronic pain program, and 112 patients with fibromyalgia). Each of these groups is well described demographically in the manual and in separate articles; the test authors do not provide comparative data on the CPCI. The overall mean age was 47 years (*SD* 10.7) with 59% female. No gender comparisons are provided. Moreover, the sample was 80% Caucasian with less than 2% of African Americans and Hispanics represented. A brief literature search indicated that versions of the CPCI have been used in several European countries, so it would have been appropriate to provide a discussion of ethnicity.

Reliability. The CPCI has demonstrated good to excellent internal consistency. Using the standardization sample, the Resting scale was the least homogeneous (.72), but the Exercise/Stretch, Coping Self-Statements, and Pacing scales all had alpha coefficients above .90. The test authors argue that one might not expect high stability on coping measures, and test-retest stability was lower for many of the scales. In the original 1995 study, 2-week test-retest coefficients ranged from .66 to .90. Additional reliability participants were recruited from the multidisciplinary pain sample and completed the CPCI after treatment and again at 2-week follow-up. Uncorrected reliabilities ranged from .42 (Exercise/Stretch) to .81 (Guarding), with .62 (Resting) being the median coefficient. The Pacing scale had a test-retest reliability of .60 at initial development and .67 following a group of fibromyalgia patients 3 months after treatment. Interestingly, *T*-score differences from posttreatment to follow-up were generally small, indicating at best a modest decline in use of relaxation and exercises.

Validity. The manual provides three types of validity evidence: construct validity (i.e., factor analysis), concurrent validity with other measures, and treatment-related changes. Several confirmatory factor analytic studies have supported an eight factor solution that closely resembles the current scale structure of the CPCI (Tan, Nguyen, Anderson, Jensen, & Thornby, 2005; Truchon, Côté, & Irachabal, 2006). However, the evidence for the higher order grouping of scales as Illness-Focused versus Wellness–Focused is considerably weaker, as many scales (across both Illness and Wellness coping) are moderately correlated. In addition, the Wellness-Focused scales demonstrate intercorrelations that range from -.15 to .54, suggesting that these scales are only nominally related to one another. Regarding concurrent validity, the test authors summarize a number of research studies that involve associations between selected CCI scales and other measures commonly used in pain assessments such as the Coping Strategies Questionnaire (CSQ), Roland Morris Disability Questionnaire, and the West Haven Multidimensional Pain Inventory. The Illness-Focused scales and particularly the Guarding scale have been related to pain, disability, and interference in life activities. Although the CPCI Coping scale has been related to Positive Self-Statements on the Coping Strategies Questionnaire, the CSQ Catastrophizing scale was the most predictive of depression and pain severity in one study of male veterans (Tan, Jensen, Robinson-Whelen, Thornby, & Monga, 2001). In addition, although generally supportive, individual scales (e.g., Coping Self-Statements, Relaxation) in some studies have shown an opposite association than predicted, which the test authors attribute to a possible moderating effect of pain level. According to the manual, the CPCI scales are only weakly associated with pain attitudes and emotions on the Survey of Pain Attitudes (SOPA; 18:134), although again the Illness-Focused scales are related to perceptions of disability. Finally, the CPCI scales have been demonstrated to change as a function of treatment with decreases on the Guarding and Resting scales associated with clinical improvement in depression and disability.

COMMENTARY. The CPCI is a well-designed measure of specific behavioral coping strategies emphasized in pain treatment. The manual is generally well written with the exception of a few typos (e.g., title of Table A.1). Guidelines are provided for appropriate interpretation of the scales along with three illustrative case profiles. One noteworthy feature is the inclusion on the profile sheet of a treatment goal skyline, defined as the mean patient posttreatment score. With only a minority of patients likely to have extreme scores, the major use of the CPCI may be to monitor treatment-guided changes using the reliable change index provided. Otherwise, the Illness—Focused scales appear to have the most validity. Critical review of the CPCI includes questioning the higher order factors, the necessity of all items and unequal items per scale, and need for further normative information regarding possible differences by gender and ethnicity. Perhaps the test's major limitation is that it does not adequately tap negative cognitive coping (e.g., catastrophizing) and affectivity that influence patient perceptions of their disability and quality of life. Pain level and affectivity may affect interpretation of some scores. It would be best to combine the CPCI with other measures tapping cognitive and affective processes as they relate to pain.

SUMMARY. The CPCI provides reliable scores for assessing pain patients' use of various behavioral coping strategies. In particular, the Illness-Focused scales provide a measure of extent of disability. Accurate interpretation of some scales may depend upon considering pain level and affectivity, and cognitive therapists would want further information about patient maladaptive thinking patterns. The CPCI is perhaps most useful in monitoring outcomes of CBT pain treatment against the modal patient and is recommended for that purpose.

REVIEWER'S REFERENCES

Jensen, M. P., Turner, J. A., Romano, J. M., & Strom, S. E. (1995). The Chronic Pain Coping Inventory: Development and preliminary validation. *Pain, 60*, 203-216.

Romano, J. M., Jensen, M. P., & Turner, J. A. (2003). The Chronic Pain Coping Inventory-42: Reliability and validity. *Pain, 104*, 65-73.

Tan, G., Jensen, M. P., Robinson-Whelen, S., Thornby, J. I., & Monga, T. N. (2001). Coping with chronic pain: A comparison of two measures. *Pain, 90*, 127-133.

Tan, G., Nguyen, Q., Anderson, K. O., Jensen, M., & Thornby, J. (2005). Further validation of the chronic pain coping inventory. *The Journal of Pain, 6*, 29-40.

Truchon, M., Côté, D., & Irachabal, S. (2006). The Chronic Pain Coping Inventory: Confirmatory factor analysis of the French version. *BMC Musculoskeletal Disorders, 7*, 13.

Review of the Chronic Pain Coping Inventory by JAMES P. DONNELLY, Clinical Associate Professor, Department of Counseling, School & Educational Psychology, University at Buffalo, Amherst, NY:

DESCRIPTION. The Chronic Pain Coping Inventory (CPCI) is a 70-item self-report measure of pain-related coping strategies. The CPCI was developed to provide a measure suited to cognitive-behavioral approaches to chronic pain assessment and treatment for men and women aged 20 to 80 years of age. In this model, coping behaviors are a primary target of therapeutic activity because of their well-established mediational link to adjustment, functioning, and related outcomes. The CPCI is described as both more comprehensive and more specific than other available measures such as the Coping Strategies Questionnaire (Rosenstiel & Keefe, 1983) and the Vanderbilt Pain Management Inventory (Brown & Nicassio, 1987) in the assessment of patient coping in the treatment cycle from initial assessment to outcome.

The test kit includes the 60-page manual, the patient coping rating form, the pain worksheet, a summary sheet for scores, and a profile plot. The coping measure includes nine scales in two domains, with a focus on rating the frequency of use of each coping strategy in the past week. The Illness-Focused Coping domain includes three scales: Guarding (limiting movement), Resting, and Asking for Assistance. The Wellness-Focused domain includes six scales: Exercise/Stretch, Relaxation, Task Persistence, Coping Self-Statements (purposeful positive thoughts regarding one's resources and abilities), Pacing, and Seeking Social Support. The Pain Worksheet supplements the coping assessment with ratings of pain intensity on four items (current, worst, least, and average pain on a 0–10 scale from "no pain" to "worst possible pain"). The back of the worksheet provides anterior and posterior diagrams of the body so that pain can be localized for each patient.

The CPCI is completed via paper form and is intended for use by psychologists and related health professionals. A professional with psychometric competence sufficient to be able to read and understand the test manual should do the interpretation of results, which include raw scores, normalized *T* scores, percentile ranks, a graphic profile plot, and reliable change scores. The manual does not provide guidance with regard to reading level or expected time to completion. Users are encouraged to check for missing responses immediately upon completion and to attempt to obtain complete data from patients. In the case of missing responses, procedures for prorating scales are provided. The CPCI Rating Form was designed for efficient management of scoring because the form is set up so that patient responses appear on the carbonless scoring sheet hidden below the scale and accessed by removal of a perforated strip on the side of the form. Once the examiner has totaled the raw scale scores, they are manually transferred to a Profile form that provides the norms and graphic aids to interpretation. The reverse side of the Profile page is a Summary Sheet that lists the individual scale scores as well as the Reliable Change Score and associated *p* values (obtained from an appendix in the manual). A complete example is provided in the test manual as are three well-described illustrative clinical cases.

DEVELOPMENT. The CPCI items and scales were developed in a systematic multistep process beginning with generation of a comprehensive list of coping strategies based on the test authors' clinical experience as well as the literature. The strategies were classified in one of three groups: illness, wellness, and neither encouraged/discouraged. The initial set of 103 items representing 14 scales was generated from this source. The manual notes that the response scale chosen (the number of days the strategy was used during the last week) was intended to be more specific than prior scales.

The initial item set was evaluated via examination of interitem correlations, item-total correlations, and internal consistency. The sample utilized in this analysis included 176 respondents from a total of 928 clinic patients seen over the prior 2 years contacted with a request for data. In addition, 111 of the patients who completed the initial item set provided retest data at a 2-week interval. This analysis included an item retention rule specifying an item-scale correlation of at least .40 with the intended scale. In addition, the correlation between an item and its scale had to be at least .15 greater than its correlation with any other scale. The outcome of this analysis was a set of 58 items covering eight scales. Internal scale reliability in this stage was set to a minimum of .70. There was no cutoff reported for test-retest coefficients, but the range was .66–.90. The convergent and discriminant validity of the initial scales were examined in correlational studies of coping, dysfunction, and activity level (citations to prior published work are provided in lieu of details). In addition, a 6-item activity pacing scale was added to the set in what appears to have been a follow-up process intended to create a more comprehensive measure. A medication use scale was dropped because of complications in coding and scoring. The final set of 70 items and nine scales was then included in the standardization study.

TECHNICAL.

Standardization. The standardization sample for the CPCI comprised an aggregate of four separate samples with varying medical conditions. The four groups included patients with multiple sclerosis (*N* = 125), spinal cord injury (*N* = 127), chronic pain treated in an outpatient clinic (*N* = 163), and a group of fibromyalgia patients (*N* = 112) recruited through a treatment study. Demographic summary statistics on age, gender, education, race/ethnicity, employment, and marital status, and at least one condition-specific variable are given for Subsamples 1, 2, and 3. Somewhat less detail is provided on

Subsample 4. Pooled descriptive statistics for age, gender, and race/ethnicity are given for the combined sample of 527. It appears that the patients were primarily residents of the Western United States and Canada. The test authors do not address the representativeness of the aggregated group for the intended sample of chronic pain patients, but it is clear that by including four subsamples with clinically important pain problems, they were attempting to provide normative data that would have some generalizability across diagnostic groups likely to present with significant pain. Surprisingly, there is no comment on whether any analysis of the item or scale characteristics by subsample was conducted.

One of the more notable aspects of this instrument is the inclusion of Reliable Change scores to facilitate interpretation of individual patient change in the context of treatment. The particular method employed incorporates a comparative change index based on the test-retest correlation and the standard deviations obtained at the two measurement points and used to estimate the standard error of the difference (Iverson, 2001). This value is then multiplied by the z score corresponding to p values of .20, .15, .10, and .05 to estimate confidence levels associated with specific changes observed on individual scales. The assessment and follow-up data used in the test-retest correlation were obtained at the end of treatment and 2 weeks later. This procedure may have the benefit of reducing regression artifacts with a tradeoff of data reflecting a posttreatment rather than current-to-post treatment observation period. Enthusiasm for this otherwise excellent addition to the other scores is perhaps further tempered by the fact that only Subsample 3 was used for eight of the scales with Subsample 4 used for the Pacing scale. Given that the computation of Reliable Change is dependent on the size of the test-retest reliability and *SD*, the reliability and validity of the Reliable Change statistics warrants additional study, but it is a welcome contribution to consideration of clinical significance with the scale.

Reliability. The test manual provides internal consistency and test-retest reliability estimates for the CPCI scales. The internal consistency of the scales has been previously reported in published research and is summarized along with estimates derived from the standardization studies, tabled for each of the four subsamples. Across all scales and samples, the CPCI evidences good internal consistency with alpha coefficients ranging from .70 to .94. As with the internal consistency studies, the test-retest reliability of the CPCI has been examined in prior work as well as in one of the standardization subsamples. As the test authors note, coping with chronic pain is a construct that suggests that some change is likely to occur naturally over time thus limiting test-retest correlations. In both reported studies, test-retest correlations were moderate to high (lowest reported was for Exercise/Stretch at .42; highest was Guarding at .81). Both sets of coefficients represent an interval of 2 weeks following completion of treatment. The analysis of the standardization sample is enhanced with a second and more favorable (i.e., higher) set of estimates based on correction for range restriction.

Validity. The validity of the CPCI has been examined in terms of internal structure and relationships to other measures. The structure of the CPCI was addressed in two published studies that are summarized in the test manual. The first was an exploratory factor analysis that provided support for an eight-factor structure that corresponded very well with the original scales. The second was a confirmatory factor analysis that provided further support for the scales with only minor exceptions.

Coping with chronic pain is a construct embedded in a relatively rich nomological network. The related constructs associated with coping with chronic pain include physical and mental health and functioning, other aspects of pain and coping, and responsiveness to treatment. All of these constructs have been studied in relation to the CPCI and the prior work is summarized in the test manual. Overall, the pattern reported is consistent with theoretical and clinical expectations in terms of direction of correlations and to some degree their strength. The manual provides a comprehensive overview of these findings, but in some cases the report is incomplete, as when a result is reported as significant but the level of significance is not specified. Given that many of these studies include clinical samples, nonnormal distributions may underlie at least some of the reported validity coefficients, perhaps attenuating the evidence. It would seem to be in the best interests of the test authors to re-examine the prior validity literature and to report more completely in the next edition of the manual.

COMMENTARY. The CPCI was developed to meet an important measurement need in the context of chronic pain treatment based on cognitive-behavioral principles and practices, the current standard in the field. The instrument appears to have been subject to a generally rigorous development process, and the reliability and validity evidence reflects these efforts. In addition, the fact that this instrument was developed in the context of clinical care has undoubtedly added to the practical value of the CPCI because the test developers are familiar with the trials and tribulations of pain patients and the challenges of helping them to change coping behavior. The standardization sample appears to be adequate, especially given the difficulty of recruiting a nationally representative sample of pain patients, but future work could be done to examine test performance and ultimately provide norms with greater precision based on such patient characteristics as gender, age, and medical condition. In addition, the reliable change score is an important and positive aspect of the test, but future research may, as with norms, provide more precision as well as confidence in interpretation.

SUMMARY. The CPCI can be recommended for its intended use in assessment of pain-specific coping in adult chronic pain patients in the context of cognitive-behavioral treatment. The well-designed kit, test materials, and substantial efforts to develop and refine the measure are likely to contribute to the continued development of evidence-based practice in this challenging field.

REVIEWER'S REFERENCES

American Educational Research Association, American Psychological Association, & National Council on Measurement in Education. (1999). *Standards for educational and psychological testing.* Washington, DC: American Educational Research Association.

Brown, G. K. & Nicassio, P. M. (1987). Development of a questionnaire for the assessment of active and passive coping strategies in chronic pain patients. *Pain, 31,* 53–64.

Iverson, G. L. (2001). Interpreting change on the WAIS-III/WMS-III in clinical samples. *Archives of Clinical Neuropsychology, 16,* 183-191.

Rosenstiel, A. K., & Keefe, F. J. (1983). The use of coping strategies in low back pain patients: Relationship to patient characteristics and current pain adjustment. *Pain, 17,* 33–44.

[29]

Cigarette Use Questionnaire.

Purpose: Designed for "evaluation, referral, and treatment of individuals who smoke cigarettes and wish to quit or must do so for health reasons."
Population: Ages 18-83.
Publication Date: 2006.
Acronym: CUQ.
Scores, 6: Defensiveness, Environmental Cues, Inconsistent Responding, Nicotine Addiction, Negative Emotional Relief, Readiness for Change.
Administration: Group.
Price Data, 2010: $99 per kit including manual (41 pages) and 25 autoscore forms; $45 per 25 autoscore forms; $60 per manual.
Time: (5-10) minutes.
Comments: Self-report.
Author: Ken Winters.
Publisher: Western Psychological Services.

Review of the Cigarette Use Questionnaire by MARK A. ALBANESE, Professor of Population Health Sciences and Educational Leadership and Policy Analysis, University of Wisconsin School of Medicine and Public Health, Madison, WI:

DESCRIPTION. The Cigarette Use Questionnaire (CUQ) is a 44-item (with four options ranging from *strongly disagree* to *strongly agree*) self-report instrument that demands a reading skill at the fifth grade level, designed to help health professionals evaluate, refer, and treat individuals who smoke cigarettes and wish to quit. There are four primary scores derived that pertain to cigarette use: Nicotine Addiction (12 items), Environmental Cues (8 items), Negative Emotional Relief (7 items), and Readiness for Change (7 items), and an additional two scores that pertain to response bias: Inconsistent Responding (differences in 10 pairs of items that are similar) and Defensiveness (5 items). The response bias scores are used to screen the results and, if they are sufficiently large, the user is cautioned that more investigation is needed to determine if the results are valid. The CUQ takes approximately 10 minutes to complete and can be administered and scored by any appropriately trained and supervised technician. Scoring is based upon transfer of responses via carbon paper to an inner form that has both scoring instructions and graphical reporting capability. All scores are reported using *T*-scores, with the mean (50) and standard deviation (10) derived from a standardization sample of 609 individuals recruited from an assortment of venues.

DEVELOPMENT. The CUQ has its roots in the *Diagnostic and Statistical Manual of Mental Disorders–Fourth Edition* (DSM-IV) and various other scales. The Nicotine Addiction (NICADX) scale was derived from the DSM-IV and Fagerstrom's Test for Nicotine Dependence (Heatherton, Kozlowski, Frecker, & Fagerstrom, 1991). The Environmental Cues (ENVCUE) scale is based upon a rational analysis of common environmental features that support the habit of smoking cigarettes as identified by smoking cessation counselors (source unidentified). The Negative Emotional Relief (NEGREL) scale is based upon the Negative Affect Reduction Scale (Copeland, Brandon, & Quinn, 1995) and the Temptation to Try Smoking Inventory (Velicer, DiClemente, Prochaska, & Brandenburg, 1985). The Defensiveness (DEF) scale is based upon the Marlowe/Crowne Social Desirability Scale (Crowne & Marlowe, 1960). The Readiness for Change (READY) scale is based upon the Transtheoretical Stages of Change Model (Prochaska & DiClemente, 1992) and the questions are similar to those asked in drug abuse treatment settings (Cady, Winters, Jordan, Solberg, & Stinchfield, 1996). There are also smoking history items: length of smoking in years, current smoking pattern and frequency, smoking onset, and history of attempts to quit smoking. Much of the scoring and scale development were based upon statistical analyses of the standardization sample.

TECHNICAL.

Scoring. The CUQ reports four primary scores: Nicotine Addiction (12 items), Environmental Cues (8 items), Negative Emotional Relief (7 items), and Readiness for Change (7 items) and an additional two scores that pertain to response bias: Inconsistent Responding (differences in 10 pairs of items that are similar) and Defensiveness (5 items). All scores are reported using *T*-scores, with the mean (50) and standard deviation (10) derived from a standardization sample of 609 individuals recruited from an assortment of venues (see below). The scoring of the CUQ is heavily based upon statistical analyses from the standardization samples.

Standardization. The CUQ has not been standardized in the sense of administering it to a probability sample of some specific population. The manual reports results for 609 individuals who smoke cigarettes aged 18–83 years (mean = 35.4, *SD* = 15) recruited from various nonclinical settings in Minnesota, New York, Maryland, Tennessee, and Florida. "Most of the young adults in the sample were college students. Adult respondents were from a variety of community settings such as college classrooms and faculty, senior centers, work sites, and religious organizations. Some respondents were recruited while shopping at discount tobacco stores" (manual, p. 22). The sample characteristics are described in detail in the manual. The median years smoked was 16.8 and ranged from 1 to 59. Compared to the national population (2000 U.S. Census), the Black/African American population was somewhat overrepresented (18% vs. 13% nationally), and Hispanics and Whites were underrepresented (Hispanics: 3% vs. 13% nationally; Whites: 72% vs. 77% nationally).

Reliability. Internal consistency reliability was estimated for individual scales using coefficient alpha from the standardization sample. The values ranged from .57 for the Defensiveness scale to .93 for the Nicotine Addiction scale. The values for the other three scores were: Environmental Cues = .79, Negative Emotional Relief = .89 and Readiness for Change = .80. To assess test-retest reliability, three subgroups took the CUQ a second time within one week of their first assessment. It is not stated how they were selected, but their ages differed in terms of range. One group of 26 ranged in age from 18–31, a second group of 15 ranged from 32–58, and the third group of 22 ranged from 30–83. The test-retest reliabilities ranged from .63–.99; however, their values were somewhat anomalous. Generally, this reviewer normally expects test-retest reliabilities to be lower than the internal consistency reliability values. For the youngest group (18–31) this pattern was found for all subscales except the Defensiveness scale where the test-retest reliability was .31 higher than the internal consistency value (.88 vs. .57, respectively). For the two older groups, the test-retest reliabilities were about .1 higher than the internal consistency reliabilities for all four scales in the two groups.

Validity. Data are reported on construct and discriminant validity. The evidence for the construct validity was based upon item to scale correlations, interscale correlations, and correlations with other measures intended to assess the same and different things. Although the majority of the data used for construct validity employed the entire standardization sample, the correlations with other measures came from a subset of 21 who also completed the Problem Recognition Questionnaire and another subset of 228 who completed a supplemental questionnaire. The correlations among the Nicotine Addiction, Environmental Cues, and the Negative Emotional Relief scores ranged from .55 to .77 and were at a level considered strongly related, yet enough below the internal consistency reliabilities to appear sufficiently independent to justify separate scoring and interpretation. Correlations with the Problem Recognition Questionnaire and the Supplemental

Questionnaire scores were provided to show that hypothesized relationships to other variables were supported by the data. The Problem Recognition Questionnaire correlations were strongest for the Nicotine Addiction (r = .42) and Readiness for Change (r = .57) scales. Because the Problem Recognition Questionnaire gives higher scores the more a person thinks his or her smoking is a problem, these high positive correlations were considered to support the construct validity of the CUQ. The Supplemental Questionnaire produced two scores: Negative Attributes of Smoking and Behavioral Control. A high Negative Attributes of Smoking score means that a person has a generally negative view of smoking, whereas a high Behavioral Control score indicates that a person believes he or she generally feels in control of his or her own behavior. The Negative Attributes of Smoking score produced moderately high negative correlations (correlations ranged from -.40 to -.54) with the three CUQ subscores: Nicotine Addiction, Environmental Cues, and Negative Emotional Relief. A small positive correlation (.15) was found for the Readiness to Change score. The Behavioral Control score was found to produce relatively small correlations with any of the CUQ scores (-.27 to +.10).

Discriminant validity was assessed by comparing scores of groups known to differ on the characteristics measured by the CUQ. In the standardization sample, they found that individuals who characterized themselves as regular smokers obtained higher scores on Nicotine Addiction, Environmental Cues, and Negative Emotional Relief than did those who characterized themselves as occasional smokers (effect size differences ranged from .8 to 1.4 on the three scores). In another sample of 201 individuals enrolled in a smoking cessation treatment, all scores were statistically significantly higher than for the standardization sample, with effect sizes ranging from .19 for Defensiveness to .41 for Readiness to Change.

COMMENTARY. The CUQ is a relatively simple instrument designed to help health care professionals evaluate, refer, and treat individuals who smoke cigarettes and wish to quit. It is low tech, but provides standardized T-scores to assist in interpreting the various scores obtained as well as having checks on response bias. It takes only about 10 minutes to complete and does not require much training or time to administer and score. The checks on response bias are impressive as they are mostly by-products of answers to the regular questions and do not add greatly to the respondent burden. The estimates of reliability are impressive with the test-retest reliability showing strong stability for scores over a relatively short period of time. The fact that the Defensiveness subscore is composed of only five items and has an internal consistency reliability of only .57 but test-retest reliabilities ranging from .88 to .98 in three different samples indicates that although its construct may be somewhat ambiguous, the responses to it appear extraordinarily stable, at least over a week.

The main problems with the CUQ stem from the lack of attention to establishing the content and predictive validity of the instrument and the representativeness of the standardization sample. In the validity section, there is no reference to content validity. From the description of the item development, it appears that the subscales derive from DSM IV classifications and an array of alternative instruments. The only allusion to the overall basis for the scale design is that "Development of the items was primarily a rational process that consisted of literature review and consultation with content area experts" (manual, p. 21). The type of content area experts and what criteria were used to determine that they are experts was not discussed. The CUQ author's credentials are not even provided, although this may be a case where the author is so well recognized in the field that the publisher believes there is no such need, but even a paragraph with a web-link would be helpful.

There is no predictive validity evidence provided, but with an instrument of this type, that may not be a problem. The instrument is mainly diagnostic to help a therapist determine what to emphasize in helping a person quit smoking. It would be useful to show that making such emphases in treatment plans has helped to improve quit rates, but such evidence may come with time.

The lack of a defined standardization sample may or may not be problematic. In today's environment where smoking is increasingly being banned from public places, it is hard to know what population one is dealing with and where smokers can be found. However, more information on the context and manner in which the standardization sample was obtained would be very helpful. (Were these students and individuals attending presentations that the author was giving? What was the incentive for the individuals to complete the instrument?) The demographics provided for the standardization sample suggest that it is overrepresented by African Americans and that Hispanics and White people are underrepresented.

There are also some other technical issues that are worth consideration. For example, the response options for the items are 4-option Likert-type: *Strongly Agree, Agree, Disagree, Strongly Disagree*. There is no middle point, so someone who genuinely cannot agree or disagree with a particular statement is forced to choose one way or the other or omit the item. The instructions push respondents to answer all questions for the results to be valid. A second issue is that under the construct validity discussion of the instrument, no factor analyses were performed. Factor analysis is a standard tool for determining the integrity of scales and might help to clarify whether or not the different scales are distinct.

SUMMARY. The CUQ is a low-tech, simple tool that takes approximately 10 minutes to administer. It was designed to help health professionals evaluate, refer, and treat individuals who smoke cigarettes and wish to quit. There are four scores derived that pertain to cigarette use: Nicotine Addiction (12 items), Environmental Cues (8 items), Negative Emotional Relief (7 items), and Readiness for Change (7 items) and an additional two scores that pertain to response bias: Inconsistent Responding (differences in 10 pairs of items that are similar) and Defensiveness (5 items). The response bias scores are used to screen the results and if they are sufficiently large, the professional user is cautioned that more investigation is needed to determine if the results are valid. Scoring is based upon transfer of responses via carbon paper to an inner form that has both scoring instructions and graphical reporting capability. All scores are reported using *T*-scores, with the mean (50) and standard deviation (10) derived from a standardization sample of 609 individuals recruited from an assortment of venues.

Internal consistency and test-retest reliabilities (separated by approximately 1 week in three separate samples) ranged from .57–.93 and .63–.99, respectively. For the older two samples (ages 30–83), the stability was substantially higher, ranging from .87–.98, indicating that CUQ results for younger individuals (ages 18–31) may be less stable over a 1-week period (.63–.88). The Nicotine Addiction score is the most reliable of all, having an internal consistency reliability value of .93 and test-retest correlations of .85, .99, and .98 in the three samples. Construct and discriminant validity data are reported that generally support the integrity of the scores reported. The test manual gives no discussion of the content validity of the instrument and no predictive validity data are provided. Further, ambiguities surrounding how the standardization sample was obtained and under- and overrepresentativeness of some ethnic groups raise questions about how representative the standardization sample is of the smoking population. Given that *T*-scores derived from the instrument are based upon the standardization sample, this could be a significant concern.

Although the CUQ has the potential to be useful for helping health care professionals develop treatment plans for individuals who wish to quit smoking cigarettes, there are limited data that support using it for this purpose. The internal structure of the instrument and the scores it produces appear to be promising, but the ambiguities of the standardization sample temper the enthusiasm that this creates. More discussion of the content validity of the instrument would be very helpful to users contemplating its use. At this point, the only guidance that can be given to potential users is that they need to consider whether the four primary scores derived from the CUQ make clinical sense from their own experience and whether having information about the four qualities would be useful in guiding treatment plans for individuals who wish to quit smoking. As more data emerge from its use, a clearer picture of the utility of the CUQ may form.

REVIEWER'S REFERENCES

Cady, M., Winters, K. C., Jordan, D. A., Solberg, K. R., & Stinchfield, R. D. (1996). Measuring treatment readiness for adolescent drug abusers. *Journal of Child and Adolescent Substance Abuse, 5,* 73–91.

Copeland, A. L., Brandon, T. H., & Quinn, E. P. (1995). The Smoking Consequences Questionnaire–Adult: Measurement of smoking outcome expectancies of experienced smokers. *Psychological Assessment, 7,* 484–494.

Crowne, D. P., & Marlowe, D. (1960). A new scale of social desirability independent of psychopathology. *Journal of Consulting Psychology, 24,* 239–354.

Heatherton, T. F., Kozlowski, L. T., Frecker, R. C., & Fagerstrom, K. (1991). The Fagerstrom test for nicotine dependence: A revision of the Fagerstrom tolerance questionnaire. *British Journal of Addiction, 86,* 1119–1127.

Prochaska, J. O., & DiClemente, C. C. (1992). Stages of change in the modification of problem behaviors. In M. Hersen, R. Eisler, & P. Miller (Eds.), *Progress in behavior modification* (pp. 184–214). Sycamore, IL: Sycamore Press.

Velicer, W. F., DiClemente, C. C., Prochaska, J. O., & Brandenburg, N. (1985). Decisional balance measure for assessing and predicting smoking status. *Journal of Personality and Social Psychology, 48,* 1279–1289.

Review of the Cigarette Use Questionnaire by DELORES D. WALCOTT, Professor, Western Michigan University, Counseling and Testing Center, Kalamazoo, MI:

DESCRIPTION. The Cigarette Use Questionnaire (CUQ) is a self-report instrument developed specifically "for assisting health professionals in the evaluation, referral, and treatment of individuals who smoke cigarettes and wish to quit or must do so for health reasons" (manual, p. 3). The manual noted that the CUQ is especially useful in creating an opportunity for a health care provider to initiate a brief discussion with patients about the hazards of smoking; and it might "encourage them to consider making an effort to stop smoking" (manual, p. 3). The CUQ can be used "to provide relevant information to professionals who wish to implement or evaluate smoking cessation" programs (manual, p. 3). It can also serve as a research instrument. The questionnaire also contains two valuable scales that are included to alert clinicians to defensiveness and inconsistent responding on the examinee's part.

The CUQ is a paper-and-pencil questionnaire that is scored by the evaluator using an Autoscore form. It is a questionnaire comprising 44 questions in a multiple-choice format. The convenient Autoscore form and the brevity of the CUQ make it highly useful for screening. This questionnaire asks the examinee about his or her experiences with smoking, about how often certain things happen, and how much the examinee agrees or disagrees with a given statement. The examinee is asked to read each question carefully and to mark the answer that is right for them. Scoring the Autoscore form is reasonably simple. The CUQ scores can be easily transferred to a profile sheet for easy interpretation.

The CUQ protocol is divided into two parts, Part 1 is for general information and Part 2 includes the 44 test statements. The respondent is asked to complete all the CUQ items. The CUQ can be completed in about 10 minutes depending on the respondents' reading level. It can be administered individually or in groups. This 44 item inventory asks about one's smoking habits; and in great detail, it asks about one's attitude toward smoking. The respondent "is asked to designate how much he or she agrees with each item by choosing one of four options: *Strongly Agree*, *Agree*, *Disagree*, or *Strongly Disagree*" (manual, p. 3). The manual indicates that with the exception of the inconsistent Responding Index, all of the CUQ scale scores are converted into *T*-Scores, which make it easy to compare scores directly across scales. It also helps with ease of comparison with the average performance group.

The technical manual outlines the purpose and application for which the test is recommended. The manual also identifies the qualifications required of a user to administer the instrument and interpret its scores and gives limited evidence of validity and reliability studies. The questionnaire was targeted for anyone aged 18–83 years who has at least a fifth grade reading ability. According to the manual "the Flesch Reading Ease Score for the items is 75.5" (manual, p. 5).

DEVELOPMENT. The CUQ is intended to measure factors related to cigarette use for the purpose of discussing, planning, and evaluating effective smoking cessation treatment and how these factors relate to ongoing research about cigarette use. This instrument was "designed to measure four central constructs pertaining to smoking: intensity of nicotine addiction, environment cues for smoking, smoking benefits related to the relief of negative emotions, and willingness to reduce or quit smoking" (manual, p. 21). The questionnaire screens for defensive responses and for biased and inconsistent responses. It solicits a brief history of one's past efforts to quit smoking.

TECHNICAL. The technical manual indicated that the CUQ standardization normative sample was a group of 609, "aged 18–83 from various nonclinical settings in Minnesota, New York, Maryland, Tennessee, and Florida" (manual, p. 22). The majority of the young adults in this group were college students. Adult respondents were from a variety of settings. Individuals from ethnic minority groups were underrepresented. Older adults were also underrepresented. One-third of this group described themselves as occasional smokers. The remaining two-thirds consider themselves as regular smokers, and 70% disclosed that they smoke at least one pack per day.

Although some groups were underrepresented, the CUQ has shown adequate reliability and appears to be a valid instrument for its specific purpose. The manual reports the "alpha estimates of internal consistency on the smoking related scales for the entire sample range from .79 to

.93" (p. 29). The manual also provides a median value of .80, suggesting that the CUQ scales are acceptable for use in clinical practice. The authors also provided several kinds of evidence to support validity, including discriminant validity studies for the CUQ. According to the manual, the CUQ has shown adequate reliability, internal consistency, and median item-to-scale total corrections and test–retest reliability estimates for each scale, based on the normative sample.

The mean age, years smoked, gender, and ethnic background of the samples were used for validation. Validation studies of the CUQ described in the manual found the instrument to be relatively free from age bias.

COMMENTARY. Overall, the technical manual contained enough information for a qualified user or reviewer of a test to evaluate the appropriateness and purpose of the test. An autoscore form is used to administer and interpret this test. This form contains scoring aids that were designed to make scoring rapid, while eliminating the potential for key errors. Responses are easily transferred through to the underlying pages, where the administrator can follow the simple steps for scoring. However, if the client fails to press hard enough and/or erases a response after being told not to do so, the scoring will become smudged and difficult to read. If the client also misses a question and the examiner fails to see this error until after the client has left the testing site, instructions for test users provide no direction to compensate for this error. Likewise, it is important that the scorer proceed with caution when transferring raw scores from the worksheet to the summary sheet, as an error could result in the interpretation.

SUMMARY. The CUQ was designed to determine smoking habits, history, and past efforts to quit. The CUQ is a meaningful questionnaire for clinicians, researchers, administrators, and smokers themselves who are seeking information that may enable them to have a positive impact on a smoking cessation program. However, self-reporting is often vulnerable to underreporting, inaccurate reporting, and denial. It should be noted that underreporting of smoking status is probably less likely when one is focusing on alcohol or other drug usage. Therefore, as with most self-reporting questionnaires, the CUQ should be used in conjunction with other sources to insure a comprehensive assessment.

[30]

Clinical Evaluation of Language Fundamentals—4 Screening Test.

Purpose: "Designed to screen school age children, adolescents, and young adults for language disorders."
Population: Ages 5-0 to 21-11.
Publication Dates: 1995–2004.
Acronym: CELF-4 Screening Test.
Scores: Total score only.
Administration: Individual.
Price Data, 2006: $225 per kit including examiner's manual (2004, 45 pages), stimulus manual, and 25 record forms; $59 per 25 record forms; $220 per 100 record forms.
Time: 15 minutes (untimed).
Comments: A test in the CELF series of language testing instruments; administered orally with visual stimuli; not for diagnostic use; "criterion-referenced."
Authors: Eleanor Semel, Elisabeth H. Wiig, and Wayne A. Secord.
Publisher: Pearson
Cross References: See T5:542 (2 references); for reviews by Billy T. Ogletree and Marcel O. Ponton of an earlier edition, see 13:69 (1 reference); for reviews by Linda M. Crocker and Jon F. Miller of an earlier edition, see 9:234.

Review of the Clinical Evaluation of Language Fundamentals-4 Screening Test by AIMÉE LANGLOIS, Professor Emerita, Department of Child Development, Humboldt State University, Arcata, CA:

DESCRIPTION. The Clinical Evaluation of Language Fundamentals-4 Screening Test (CELF-4 Screening Test) is designed to identify students between 5 years, 0 months and 21 years, 11 months of age who may have language disorders. As a screening instrument, it simply allows users to specify whether a student's language skills are appropriate or not for his or her age and thus provides a basis for further assessment.

The CELF-4 Screening Test kit includes an examiner's manual, a stimulus book, and 25 record forms. The manual provides an overview of the test, instructions for administration and scoring, and information about its design, development, and technical aspects. The easel-type stimulus book contains colored pictures facing the student and information for administering test items facing the examiner. The record form is self-explanatory.

The authors developed the CELF-4 Screening Test in response to feedback from clinicians who had used the CELF-3 Screening Test and out of a need to maintain consistency with its parent test, the CELF-4, a diagnostic test. The screening version includes 47 items divided into seven language tasks. Although the authors fail to identify, both in the examiner's manual and on the score form, what aspect of language each task assesses, they do provide a listing of the CELF-4 subtests from which each task has been taken. These subtest names provide a sense of the language skills involved. Given their claim for maintaining consistency between this test and the CELF-4, this omission is not helpful in the opinion of this reviewer. Buried in the chapter on test development, one can find a list of items by subtest from the CELF-4 that comprise the screening version: "Word Structure, Concepts and Following Directions, Recalling Sentences, Sentence Assembly, Semantic Relationships, and Word Classes" (examiner's manual, p. 17). Absent further discussion, one can assume that the list represents the order of the test items as they appear on the score form.

Professionals in a variety of fields as well as supervised paraprofessionals and teachers' aides are deemed qualified to administer the CELF-4 Screening Test. The authors caution all potential test users to study and practice using the test before administering it. Instructions are provided regarding seating for left- and right-handed examiners and thus ensuring a comfortable test environment. Each test item requires examiners to read the instructions, point to the stimuli, decide when the student has completed his or her response, gauge whether the response is correct or not, and write the student's response out of his or her sight while maintaining rapport with and encouraging him or her.

The examiner selects the items to administer based on a student's age. He or she then presents one stimulus at a time, beginning with a trial item for each task. All correct responses receive a score of 1; all incorrect responses receive a 0. Total raw scores for ages 5–8 (Items 1–28) and for ages 9–21 (Items 14–47) are calculated and entered on the record form. A student's total score is then compared to the criterion score for his or her age, which is found in a table on the first page of the record form. If the student's total score is at or above criterion, the child's language is deemed adequate. Conversely, if the child's total score is below criterion, he or she may have a language disorder and needs additional assessment. The test takes about 15 minutes to administer, a time frame that may preclude its use for routine screenings of large groups of children.

In spite of its ease of administration, using the test raises several issues: For each item, examiners must decide how long to wait for the student's response (e.g., "within about 10 seconds") and when they are "certain" that the student has responded. For some items, they must also gauge what are acceptable dialectal variations and paraphrases of target responses. Even with the admonition of the authors to study and practice administering the test before using it for the first time, given the number of subjective decisions examiners must make, the risk for variations in scoring is high, and thus can affect results.

DEVELOPMENT. The authors offer a sound rationale for the development of the CELF-4 Screening Test and its use, as they wanted (a) to maintain consistency with its parent test the CELF-4 and (b) to make it as easy to use as its predecessor, the CELF-3 Screening Test. After obtaining feedback from clinicians and scholars, they conducted pilot, tryout, and standardization studies. Following the pilot study, the test was revised and the new version was administered to 419 children for the tryout study; the examiners were also questioned about the revisions and additions, as well as several aspects of test administration. Based on the data obtained, the test authors made a final revision of the test for the standardization research. Items and subtests were selected based upon data in the CELF-4 indicating which items and subtests are most discriminating empirically. Because no logical rationale is presented regarding the selection of tasks and test items, users may not understand why the tasks were selected for each age group, why some items were selected, and why the number of items is not consistent for each task.

TECHNICAL. The CELF-4 Screening Test was administered by 281 experienced professionals to "more than 1,200 students" (examiner's manual, p. 19) between the ages of 5 years, 0 months and 21 years, 11 months who were divided in a clinical and nonclinical group (i.e., with and without a diagnosed language disorder or learning disability). These students closely represented U.S. Census demographics in terms of gender, race/ethnicity, geographic region, and education level. Four tables support this information; however, the total number of students in each table equals "725" (examiner's manual, p. 20), not the 1,200 mentioned on the previous page. This discrepancy is not explained, which leads one to wonder whether this is a typographical error or whether data from 475 students were omitted from the final tally, and if so, why. [Editor's note: After considering this review, the test publisher informed the editors that 1,200 students participated in the standardization studies and, of these, 725 is the number used for the development of norms.]

Another table presents the number of students tested at each age, which ranges from 11 to 50. Because age is the factor to consider for selecting test items and comparing students to criterion scores, the number of students at each age level falls short of the mark of 100, which is deemed adequate for test standardization to ensure that norms are stable (American Educational Research Association, American Psychological Association, & National Council on Measurement in Education, 1999; Benner, 2003).

Test-retest reliability was assessed with a representative group of 170 students from the standardization sample, who were retested by the same examiner within about a month of the original administration. Correlations of .89, .90, and .82 for students aged 5 years, 0 months to 8 years, 11 months, 9 years, 0 months to 12 years, 11 months, and 13 years, 0 months to 21 years, 11 months, respectively, reveal that the CELF-4 Screening Test shows adequate stability over time because "for screening instruments a standard of .80 [is] recommended" (Benner, 2003, p. 123). In contrast, split-half reliability coefficients of .70 and .72 for the two younger groups suggest lower internal consistency. Without any explanation, the authors simply dismiss these latter data with a comment that "test-retest stability coefficient is a more appropriate measure of reliability ... for screening tests" (examiner's manual, p. 27).

Given that various professionals, paraprofessionals, and teachers' aides can administer the test, the absence of interexaminer reliability scores is a serious oversight. Because examiners must make subjective decisions during testing, the potential for variability between examiners is high and should have been assessed. Without such information, we do not know if and how examiners affect the scores or the test takers, and in what way, thus weakening the usefulness of the test results (American Educational Research Association et al., 1999).

Criterion-related validity was obtained by comparing 137 students' scores on the CELF-4 Screening Test with their CELF-4 Core Language scores. Correlations ranged from .67 for older students to .75 for the younger ones. As evidence of the clinical utility of the test, a table shows that it identified correctly 80% to 93.3% of students later diagnosed with a language disorder and 84.4% to 93.3% of those not so diagnosed. Data on specificity and sensitivity of the test were also obtained and show that the test has predictive powers of 39% and 99% accuracy for these same groups. The discrepancy between these two sets of data is not discussed and in the opinion of this reviewer begs for an explanation. In addition, the authors do not provide information about the selection of the 137 and 900 students who participated, respectively, in criterion validity and clinical utility testing. Overall, the section on validity is confusing and requires the reader to rely on the authors' assertion that the test has "excellent" (examiner's manual, p. 25) predictive power.

COMMENTARY. The authors offer a sound rationale for the development of the test, which underwent several revisions following pilot and tryout studies. Its standardization with students who represent the U.S. population makes it useful where heterogeneity of culture and ethnicity is the norm. The test's strength resides in its ease of use and appealing presentation and in its potential for identifying children who are at risk for language disorders. Nonetheless, several concerns regarding test administration, item selection, group sizes, interexaminer reliability, validity, and examiner qualifications discussed above weaken the usefulness of the test and leave many unanswered questions. To allay these concerns, additional information about item selection is needed, standardization groups must include at least 100 participants, interexaminer reliability research must be conducted, and the section on validity needs to be clear. Overall, given the amount of time it takes to administer the test, it has limited usefulness as a screening instrument for large groups of children.

SUMMARY. The CELF-4 Screening Test was designed to identify students who are at risk for language disorders. The test meets its goal with five to seven tasks that represent different aspects of spoken language and are administered according to a student's age. Unfortunately, the test has several flaws discussed throughout this review and delineated above that limit its usefulness as a clinical tool.

REVIEWER'S REFERENCES

American Educational Research Association, American Psychological Association & National Council on Measurement in Education. (1999). *Standards for educational and psychological testing.* Washington, DC: American Educational Research Association.

Benner, S. B. (2003). *Assessment of children with special needs: A context based approach.* Clifton Park, NY: Delmar Learning.

Review of the Clinical Evaluation of Language Fundamentals-4 Screening Test by GREGORY SNYDER, Clinical Child and Adolescent Psychologist, Children's Hospital, Omaha, NE:

DESCRIPTION. The Clinical Evaluation of Language Fundamentals-4 Screening Test (CELF-4 Screening) is an individually administered, brief language assessment designed to quickly and efficiently discriminate and identify children who may require additional, more extensive language assessment. The authors of the instrument attempted to revise the screening test with the current revision by extending the age norms, matching that of the complete version of the CELF-4 normative data including children from ages 5 years, 0 months through 21 years, 11 months.

The CELF-4 subtest represented in the CELF-4 Screening include: Word Structure, Concepts and Following Directions, Recalling Sentences, Sentence Assembly, Semantic Relationships, and Word Classes 1 and 2. The entire assessment contains 47 carefully selected items, all of which have been selected from the parent CELF-4 edition. Separate start points are provided for children ages 5 years, 0 months to 8 years, 11 months, and 9 years, 0 months to 21 years, 11 months. Thus, total criterion scores are based on responses to 28 items for younger children and 34 items for the older cohort mentioned above. The above mentioned 47 items are grouped into seven separate, but not freestanding item blocks, two of which are presented only to the 5 years, 0 months to 8 years, 11 months age group, two blocks presented to the entire age range, and the three latter blocks that are only presented to individuals in the oldest age bracket (9 years, 0 months to 21 years, 11 months).

Administration of the CELF-4 Screening is not timed; however, the authors encourage the examiners to allow each student a reasonable amount of time to respond to each test item (but suggest limiting this to about 10 seconds). Total time for administration is quite meager, and would require no more than 15-30 minutes for both administration and scoring. The stimulus book, provided with the assessment, is used for all item blocks with the exception of sentence repetition. Repetitions of individual items are occasionally allowed and the authors clearly demarcate whether or not a single repetition is allowed at the start of each item block. The assessment is rather fast to administer and score for all age groups. Items are scored dichotomously as either correct or incorrect and partial credit is not given for close but not entirely accurate responses. For the oldest age segment (9 years, 0 months to 21 years, 11 months), expressive sentence construction even provides the examiner with all possible correct sentence responses so as to speed the scoring process further.

Youngest children (those aged 5 years, 0 months to 8 years, 11 months) receive criterion scores based on the total number of correct items on the first 28 items. The summed raw score is then compared to the criterion reference, which is located on the cover of the record form. Separate criterion scores are presented for all ages in 6-month blocks for children ages 5 years, 0 months through 8 years, 11 months and 21 years, 11 months in 12-month age blocks for children ages 9 years, 0 months through 21 years, 11 months.

TECHNICAL. The authors of the screening instrument reported having created the instrument by selecting items from the CELF-4 instrument that yielded the most discriminatory power in differentiating children with and without language impairment. The standardization sample for the CELF-4 Screening consisted of 1,200 students ages 5 through 21 years, 11 months. Of this sample, two groups were identified: those students without any previous history of expressive and/or receptive language impairment and those students with some history of having been diagnosed with either a language impairment or learning disability. For all participants in the standardization sample, the authors reported that English was the primary language spoken in the home; however, the authors failed to report the percentage of bilingual or polylingual individuals who were included in the standardization sample. European-American children reflected a majority of the students in the normative sample (60.4%), followed by Hispanic (17.8%), African American (16%), and other nationalities (5.8%). The test authors presented geographic information with percentages of the standardized population roughly equivalent across the north-central, northeast, south, and west regions. They also presented both mean and standard deviation data in the manual provided with the test stimuli.

Because the development of the CELF-4 Screening employed data obtained during standardization of the parent CELF-4 edition, the two instruments were not co-normed. Clearly the goal of the development and standardization of the CELF-4 screening test involves identifying items that have a high discriminative validity between language-disordered and non-language-disordered children. The test authors cited evidence of the convergent validity CELF-4 Screening with their comparison of scores to the CELF-4 Core Language Standard Scores. They reported that a matched sample was used to calculate the classification rates, sensitivity, specificity, positive predictive power, and negative predictive power of the CELF-4 Screening. The test authors cited a study of 450 clinical and 450 nonclinical cases. In the authors' study, the percentage of clinical hits (positive predictive power) ranged on the low end from 82.9% for children ages 13 years, 0 months, to 13 years, 11 months, to 96.8% for children ages 6 years, 0 months, to 6 years, 5 months. The percentage of false-positives using the CELF-4 Screening ranged from 6.7% for children ages 5 years, 5 months, to 15.6% and 16.1% for children ages 9 years, 0 months to 9 years, 11 months and 5 years, 6 months to 5 years, 11 months, respectively. False negatives or failing to identify appropriately abnormal language development ranged widely from a high point of 20% for children ages 15 years, 0 months to 15 years, 11 months and to a minimal 3.2% for children ages 6 years, 0 months to 6 years, 5 months. Taking into account all age brackets, the authors summarized overall sensitivity and specificity of the instrument as being .88 for both. Negative predictive power overall was .99, which suggests that of those children identified as not needing a complete language evaluation, only 1% of the children were misidentified and were false-positives.

Test-retest reliability was demonstrated in a second study conducted by the authors in which they included 170 students who were identified from within the original standardization sample described above. The test authors were careful to select students in a manner reflecting the broader standardization sample in terms of ethnicity and gender. Reliability for children between the ages of 5 years, 0 months to 8 years, 11 months was r = .89, r = .90 for children ages 9 years, 0 months to 12 years, 11 months, and r = .82 for children ages 13 years, 0 months to 21 years, 11 months.

COMMENTARY. The CELF-4 Screening is a rapidly administered assessment designed to identify children in need of further language assessment. Highly discriminative test items from the parent CELF-4 were used to construct this measure. The authors of the assessment aimed to quickly and accurately predict whether children require further expressive and receptive language assessment. The CELF-4 Screening requires very little time to administer and score. Scoring is quite easy for this assessment, and the measure allows the clinician to gauge quickly whether or not further language evaluation needs to occur. This assessment is based on the student's ability to achieve the basic criterion identified on the front of the record form. Normative data are adequate and the test authors clearly appeared to match items to the original CELF-4 and to assess whether or not these items were specific and sensitive enough to identify children at risk who need further evaluation.

A drawback to the CELF-4 Screening is the lack of useful data about children's performance on the four or five subtests that are presented. It remains a challenge to create a screening device that can be rapidly administered/scored and at the same time provide clinically useful trends in performance. With respect to this assessment, the authors clearly focused on creating an extremely brief, objective method or identifying those children in need of more thorough language assessment. With respect to that goal, the authors clearly succeeded as the instrument is quite compact, but does not assume to parse out performance among the subtests. This allows clinicians to postulate hypotheses but not test the veracity of such ideas without further assessment. This is appropriate and consistent with the authors' overall aim in the creation of the assessment. Use of this device alone to diagnose language impairment, then, is quite inappropriate and unethical. Any use beyond the identification of those children in need of more extensive testing is not indicated by the test authors, so users of the CELF-4 Screening should not overinterpret below-criterion scores as definitely language impaired. Moreover, although mean and standard deviation data are available for all item blocks across all age groups in the standardization sample, these should not be used to provide any standardized score to capture variability across item blocks.

Although the degree of nonclinical misclassifications, or false positives, is not as much of a problem, the high variability of false negatives is concerning. Although aggregate sensitivity and specificity indexes, which encompass the entire standardization sample, were quite robust, the authors failed to explain sufficiently the variability and implication of the misclassification rate among the individual age brackets.

SUMMARY. The CELF-4 Screening assessment clearly succeeds as a brief, valid device aimed at identifying children in need of extensive expressive and receptive language assessment. Authors of the assessment selected powerful items and domains that are quite sensitive when predicting possible impairment. Inclusion of sentence repetition and comprehension of instructions are two examples of historically powerful "acid tests" of language impairment. Potential users would clearly find benefit in including this very brief measure in larger batteries of cognitive assessment as a device to lend support for later language assessment or for ruling out the potential of language impairment when explaining/interpreting results.

[31]

Comprehensive Addictions and Psychological Evaluation.

Purpose: Designed to "provide the clinician with a standard set of questions covering specified content of the DSM-IV diagnostic criteria."
Population: Adults.
Publication Dates: 2000-2004.
Acronym: CAAPE.
Scores, 16: Substance Dependence, Substance Abuse, Depression, Mania, Panic, Anxiety and Phobias, Posttraumatic Stress, Obsessions/Compulsions, Psychosis, Conduct Disorder, Antisocial Personality, Paranoid Personality, Schizoid Personality, Borderline Personality, Dependent Personality, Obsessive-Compulsive Personality.
Administration: Individual.
Price Data, 2008: $67.50 per 25 booklets, $20 per manual (2000, 59 pages).
Time: (20) minutes.
Author: Norman G. Hoffmann.
Publisher: The Change Companies.

Review of the Comprehensive Addictions and Psychological Evaluation by TONY CELLUCCI, Professor and Director of the Psychology Training Clinic, Idaho State University, Pocatello, ID:

DESCRIPTION. The Comprehensive Addictions and Psychological Evaluation (CAAPE) is a structured diagnostic interview for psychoactive substance use disorders and related mental health conditions. It is meant to provide qualified professionals, trained in interpreting the DSM-IV diagnostic criteria, with a standardized set of questions for consistent evaluation and documentation. In addition, the information collected may be used in treatment planning and possibly for motivational enhancement. The cover page collects demographic data, which the test author suggests also have prognostic value. The CAAPE includes a generic six-item screen (UNCOPE) for substance use disorders, which may be used to determine the need for completing the substance use section. This section begins with an alcohol and drug use history, allowing the interviewer to later inquire about either all drugs ever used (lifetime) or those drugs used in the last 12 months. Queries about cocaine are separate from amphetamine and other stimulants, and tobacco is not included. There are a few questions related to quantity of alcohol consumed, time typically spent using on weekends and weekdays, "amnesiac episodes" (manual, p. 6), and any intravenous use. Otherwise, the items straightforwardly map onto the DSM-IV criteria for dependence and abuse. Withdrawal effects are not distinguished by substance category. With the exception of tolerance, the patient is asked how often the experience occurred (i.e., once, twice or three or more times in the past 12 months). The CAAPE does not provide a specific algorithm when data pertaining to criteria are mixed, deferring to professional judgment.

The mental health section contains diagnostic screens for both primary Axis I mental health disorders and Axis II personality disorders as well as a final section for psychosis indicators and observations. The Axis I disorders include Depression, Mania, Panic, Anxiety and Phobias, Posttraumatic Stress, and Obsessions/Compulsions. A triage or branching strategy is used in this section such that a patient's response to key questions determines the need for further inquiry regarding that disorder. Not all diagnostic criteria are included so further assessment is required. Affective disorders are covered the most thoroughly, with a probe for whether such periods occurred while not using alcohol or other drugs. The Axis II section covers conduct disorder and ASPD well while screening for a variety of other personality disorder problems (e.g., Schizoid, Dependent). The manual provides detailed guidance as to correct probing and how the items relate to the DSM-IV criteria. There are no scores per se, with a profile sheet summarizing the substance use diagnostic information by drug category as well as the items for mental health and personality disorders. The manual does not estimate an average administration time but both sections can be administered in less than an hour.

DEVELOPMENT. There is limited information on the development of the CAAPE in the revised 2004 manual, although it follows the test author's earlier work on the Substance Use Disorders Diagnostic Schedule-IV (SUDDS-IV; 15:253). The items intentionally address very specific behaviors and experiences, which can be verified by collaterals. The UNCOPE screen questions were reportedly first culled from existing instruments and research reports in 1999, with a few wording changes over the years. The content validity of the CAAPE is based on its close alignment with the DSM-IV substance dependence criteria. Earlier research (alpha coefficients) suggested that these criteria constituted a homogeneous syndrome or construct. The test author cites SUDDS-IV data from the Minnesota correctional system and Schuckit et al.'s (2001) longitudinal research as supporting the differentiation of substance dependence from abuse (Hoffman, in press). More recent work using item response theory has indicated that DSM-IV substance criteria themselves (at least for alcohol) reflect a unidimensional continuum with most abuse and dependence criteria tapping the severe end; the criteria related to amount of time spent, drinking more and longer than intended, and continuing to use despite physical/psychological problems were the most discriminating (Saha, Chou, & Grant, 2006). Although not necessarily in conflict with Hoffman's perspective, such data indicate the DSM-IV criteria themselves might be improved, and the hierarchical arrangement between abuse and dependence is questionable.

It is perhaps more problematic that limited information is provided on how the mental health disorders and related items were selected. Conditions thought to be more prevalent and or posing a greater risk to recovery are said to be covered in more detail. However, there are no questions that directly ask about social anxiety, which is common among alcoholics, whereas OCD would present more rarely. The diagnosis of emotional disorders is difficult without a period of abstinence. CAAPE items reflect the essential features of various disorders with follow-up needed to understand how reported symptoms relate to substance use and associated behavior. It is not clear why questions regarding experiencing depression, manic, and psychotic symptoms apart from alcohol and drug use were specifically included but the respondent is not explicitly asked about panic or anxiety symptoms occurring apart from substance use.

TECHNICAL. The CAAPE manual states that the CAAPE should not be considered a psychometric instrument with norms. Test-retest reliability is discussed as relevant to the diagnostic process with the CAAPE providing standardized questions to reduce information variance. However, no studies of interclinician or test-retest reliability are provided. The DSM-IV substance abuse criteria generally exhibit limited differential criterion functioning by gender or ethnicity, especially at the scale level (Saha et al., 2006), so such bias might not be a large concern. The manual provides the most technical information on the predictive validity of the UNCOPE as a screen for substance abuse. The test author examined the sensitivity and specificity of various cut scores for alcohol, cocaine, and marijuana abuse in large clinical and correction samples. A score of 2 out of the 6 items has high sensitivity (above 97%) and specificity (93%), although specificity for marijuana abuse was somewhat lower (82%). A score of 4 or more indicates a high probability of dependence. Prognostic statements regarding selected demographics (e.g., being young and unmarried) and the need for more extensive treatment appear overly generalized and should be considered cautiously.

Unfortunately, there have been few studies comparing the CAAPE to other substance abuse interviews. Professional staff at an integrated day treatment program compared the CAAPE with the SCID in terms of diagnostic concordance and administration burden (Gallagher, Penn, Brooks, & Feldman, 2006). Twenty patients receiving outpatient treatment were evaluated with both instruments. The CAAPE identified somewhat more substance abuse diagnoses per person but concordance for substance use disorders was very high (95%). Not surprisingly, concordance for mental health diagnoses was much lower (40%) with the Structured Clinical Interview for DSM-IV (SCID) identifying more mental health problems. These authors concluded that the CAAPE was valid for diagnosing substance use disorders, but only provided a quick interview screen for co-occurring disorders. Clearly, further studies are needed to examine the validity of using the CAAPE to identify specific disorders such as depression and antisocial personality disorder.

COMMENTARY. The CAAPE interview provides a cost-effective method for collecting information on DSM-IV substance abuse criteria and screening for mental health problems. It attempts to address a practical need in psychosocial treatment settings for assessing co-occurring disorders and service needs in a population. The UNCOPE provides an effective screening acronym for substance abuse. Like the SUDDS-IV, the CAAPE captures the DSM-IV dependency construct well. Although the DSM-IV substance abuse criteria themselves have been demonstrated to be reasonably reliable, specific evidence for the reliability of the CAAPE is needed. In addition, it may have been preferable to limit the breadth of mental health coverage to selected disorders with greater depth of coverage. This reviewer is particularly concerned about possible overidentification of personality disorders. At best, and following the manual, the mental health section should be conceptualized as a screen indicating what might need further assessment. Also, although summary information can be shared with patients as part of personalized feedback, the use of the CAAPE for motivational enhancement appears limited in that accepting a diagnosis is not typically a part of motivational interviewing. Finally, although the CAAPE makes an attempt to separate the effects of intoxication and withdrawal from mental health symptoms, other instruments such as the AUDADIS and PRISM (see Samet, Waxman, Hatzenbuehler, & Hassin, 2007) are more systematic in their approach to this problem. These measures are more comprehensive but require more training and administration time. Another possible comparative disadvantage is that there is not a computerized version of the CAAPE.

SUMMARY. The CAAPE provides a systematic diagnostic interview for substance use disorders with the items used to identify dependence internally consistent and valid for that purpose. Although it efficiently screens for co-occurring mental health and personality disorders, evidence of validity is needed to support any greater use in such assessments. Nevertheless, the CAAPE has practical utility as an assessment tool in substance abuse evaluations.

REVIEWER'S REFERENCES

Gallagher, S., Penn, P., Brooks, A., & Feldman, J. (2006). Comparing the CAAPE, a new assessment tool for co-occurring disorders, with the SCID. *Psychiatric Rehabilitation Journal, 30,* 63-65.

Hoffman, N. G. (in press). An integrated perspective on the prevalence, diagnoses, and treatment of behavioral disorders in correctional populations. In E. Rhine & D. Evans (Eds.), *What works: Research into practice: Bridging the gap in community corrections.* Washington, DC: ICCA/ACA.

Saha, T. D., Chou, S. P., & Grant, B. F. (2006). Toward an alcohol use disorder continuum using item response theory: Results from the National Epidemiological Survey on Alcohol Related Conditions. *Psychological Medicine, 36,* 931-941.

Samet, S., Waxman, R., Hatzenbuehler, M., & Hassin, D. (2007). Assessing addiction: Concepts and instruments. *Addiction Science & Clinical Practice, 4,* 19-31.

Schuckit, M. A., Smith, T. L., Danko, G. P., Bucholz, K. K., Reich, T., & Bierut, L. (2001). Five-year clinical course associated with DSM-IV alcohol abuse or dependence in a large group of men and women. *American Journal of Psychiatry, 158,* 1084-1090.

Review of the Comprehensive Addictions and Psychological Evaluation by WILLIAM E. MARTIN, JR., Professor of Educational Psychology, Northern Arizona University, Flagstaff, AZ:

DESCRIPTION. The Comprehensive Addictions and Psychological Evaluation (CAAPE) is a structured interview to be administered by individuals qualified to make diagnostic assessments. The structured interview focuses primarily on providing information for diagnosing substance abuse disorders and how these disorders may complicate other mental conditions. As the test author states, "the CAAPE should not be considered a psychometric instrument with scores and norms" (manual, p. 1). The CAAPE consists of 145 questions orally administered by the interviewer who records the client's responses directly on the evaluation form during a 20-minute interview. The first 50 interview questions relate directly to client demographic information and substance abuse and dependency. The next 91 questions focus on DSM-IV and DSM-IV-TR Axis I and Axis II disorders, and the last 4 items generate clinical observation information. The questions have varying structured response formats depending on the nature of the question and the desired information. For example, several questions relate to type of drugs used, for how long, and how often. Other questions target whether a client has experienced certain symptoms related to Axis I (i.e., depression and posttraumatic stress) and Axis II disorders (i.e., conduct disorder and obsessive-compulsive personality). Within the CAAPE are 6 items referred to as the UNCOPE screen that the test author asserts are highly accurate in detecting substance abuse disorders.

The CAAPE manual provides a description of how to score and when to probe client responses to the interview questions. The questions reflect a structured scoring format for the interviewer to record responses. For example, the diagnostician scores a no (0) or yes (1) to the questions related to whether the client has experienced a substance abuse or related mental health condition. In addition, there are scores recorded for the frequency of substance abuse behavior over 12 months. The scores from the structured interview are then transferred to a four-page CAAPE Summary Data form to summarize and document the interview findings from the administration of the CAAPE. A section on interpretation of the CAAPE results is provided in the manual.

DEVELOPMENT. The nine demographic items were chosen to provide both diagnostic and prognostic information for use in treatment planning. For example, according to the test author, marital status is related to the risk for relapse after addictions treatment. Specific content of the DSM-IV was used to develop a set of questions covering substance abuse and Axis I and II disorders. Explanations for some items and how they relate to the DSM-IV criteria are provided in the interpretation section of the manual. However, there is no clear description of how individual CAAPE questions were specifically developed or pilot tested.

TECHNICAL. Standard interviewing procedures are detailed in the manual for each CAAPE item. A brief discussion of validity and reliability of the CAAPE is provided in the interpretation section of the manual; however, much of the discussion is oriented toward defining the concepts of validity and reliability. The test author says that the CAAPE has content validity because the items are based on the diagnostic criteria of the DSM-IV but no empirical evidence is provided. Moreover, there is no evidence provided for the concurrent and predictive validity or reliability of the CAAPE. Accuracy information in screening for addictive disorders and clinical populations is presented for the six screening items of the CAAPE known as the UNCOPE. However, more information about the methods used in the studies to generate these data is needed.

COMMENTARY. The format for administrating and scoring the CAAPE is clear. Useful information is provided about each item of the CAAPE to consider during administration. The direct link to DSM-IV criteria for substance abuse and Axis I and II disorders should be beneficial to diagnosticians of substance abuse disorders.

The CAAPE manual needs to be strengthened by reorganizing and expanding the information presented. Information about specific topics such as administration, scoring, and interpretation are intermingled across several sections of the manual making it difficult to find all information about one topic in one place. The very limited validity and reliability information is presented in the interpretation guide. Concurrent and predictive validity evidence is needed to demonstrate the effectiveness of the CAAPE as a tool to make accurate diagnoses. Temporal consistency and interrater reliability evidence must be studied to determine if there is a stability of ratings over time and among diagnosticians. More information about how the items of the CAAPE were developed and pilot-tested is needed.

SUMMARY. The CAAPE is a structured interview administered by qualified individuals to make diagnostic assessments of substance abuse disorders and how these disorders may complicate other mental conditions using DSM-IV criteria. The CAAPE is user-friendly in administration and scoring. However, supporting information relative to item development, validity, and reliability is too minimal to warrant a recommendation for the clinical use of the CAAPE at this time.

[32]

Computerized Test of Information Processing.

Purpose: Designed to "measure the degree to which various neurological injuries impact the speed at which information is processed" and to detect "whether a traumatic brain injury patient is putting forth maximum effort."

Population: Ages 15-74.

Publication Date: 2008.

Acronym: CTiP.

Administration: Individual.
Scores: 3 subtests: Simple Reaction Time, Choice Reaction Time, Semantic Search Reaction Time.
Price Data: Available from publisher.
Time: (15) minutes.
Comments: Version 5 software package requires Microsoft Windows 98 SE through Windows XP; provides the ability to administer assessments and score and generate reports; scoring is automatic and the test can be administered multiple times to the same individual without high practice effects.
Authors: Tom N. Tombaugh and Laura M. Rees.
Publisher: Multi-Health Systems, Inc.

Review of the Computerized Test of Information Processing by BRAD M. MERKER, Staff Neuropsychologist, Henry Ford Health System, Detroit, MI:

DESCRIPTION. The Computerized Test of Information Processing (CTIP) is an individually administered measure designed to assess the degree to which various neurological injuries such as traumatic brain injury and multiple sclerosis impact the speed of information processing. A secondary purpose of the test is in detecting whether a patient with a suspected traumatic brain injury is putting forth maximum effort. The test is composed of three computerized reaction time subtests–Simple RT, Choice RT, and Semantic Search RT. Each subtest is progressively more challenging than the previous test thus requiring increased cognitive resources and, therefore, progressively longer reaction times. Each of the three subtests begins with 10 practice trials and is followed by 30 test trials.

The first subtest is the Simple RT subtest. It was conceived as a pure speed of information-processing measure and serves as a baseline for the other subtests. During the Simple RT subtest individuals press a key as soon as a single stimulus appears in the center of the screen. The second subtest is the Choice RT subtest, which adds a decision-making component. During this subtest the respondent is provided with one of two choice stimuli and must decide which of the two corresponding keys should be pressed. "The Choice RT subtest measures the time required to process two bits of information and respond differentially" (technical manual, p. 7), thereby significantly increasing response time relative to the Simple RT subtest. The third and final subtest is the Semantic Search RT subtest. This subtest adds a conceptual component to the decision-making process. Specifically, the "respondent must decide if an exemplar word belongs to a specific category" (technical manual, p. 8) by responding appropriately using one of two keys. The processing of the meaning of the stimuli significantly increases response time compared to the two previous subtests. Total testing time is approximately 15 minutes.

After the respondent has completed testing, an automatic scoring program can generate two types of reports: a clinical report and a research report. The clinical report is based on a normative sample of 386 individuals ranging in age from 15 to 74 and contains the median reaction time for each subtest and percentile equivalent. A summary table and graph are provided to facilitate analysis. Additionally, the impact of motor slowing and possible reduced effort or malingering is provided. Several other scores are provided in the research report to facilitate interpretation of the effects of motor dysfunction on performance including median RT, the number of correct responses for the Choice and Semantic Search RTs, the mean and standard deviation of RT, coefficients of variability, and percent chance scores. Supplementary scores include the category and noncategory scores for the Semantic Search RT, anticipatory responses, and median RT for 10 trial blocks.

For psychologists concerned about a respondent's level of effort the CTIP report provides a statement concerning the possibility of reduced effort. The statement is provided if the respondent was identified as having a traumatic brain injury (TBI) and the following condition is met: Simple RT score is significantly slower than expected. If this criterion is met then two additional criteria will be evaluated for indicating possibly reduced effort: Simple RT variability is lower than anticipated, and either the choice RT or semantic search RT tasks produced more than four incorrect responses.

Four case studies are provided highlighting normal and impaired speed of information processing, as well as possible effects of motor abilities and possible malingering. Throughout the manual the developers appropriately caution that the CTIP should not be used as a sole measure of effort or processing speed and instead be used as part of a comprehensive neuropsychological test battery. Further cautionary statements are provided with respect to not using the CTIP with individuals having an IQ lower than 85, documented learning disability or academic history indicative of a learning disability, less than a high school education or GED, significant motor problems such as decreased coordination, and lack of proficiency in English. Finally, the developers note that there is no evidence to date showing the CTIP is capable of detecting malingering in any neuropsychological population other than traumatic brain injury.

DEVELOPMENT. A major factor in the development of the test was the developers' observation that "few, if any, tests measured information processing speed that were not vulnerable to practice effects, were tolerated by participants and did not confound motor effects with cognitive processing" (technical manual, p. 37). The test was also created because numerous experts in the field indicated that RT paradigms could provide a quick and easy clinical tool to assess for cognitive impairment. RT tests "revealed cognitive impairment even when traditional neuropsychological measures failed to do so" (technical manual, p. 37), and RT assessment was helpful in tracking recovery over time.

Initially, several RT paradigms were created using both words and pictures. However, after experimentation only words were used in the final version as most individuals were found to code pictures as words. The three subtests chosen were based on their progressive increase in complexity, their failure to elicit frustration, and their minimal vulnerability to practice effects. Originally 60 trials were used with patients having TBI and MS, though in the end 30 trials was selected as the optimal number of trials that produced the information-processing effect without incurring fatigue or boredom.

Normative data were collected over a 6-year period across community, university, city, and rural sites. In total, data were collected from 386 people ranging in age from 15 to 74 with a mean education of 14.89 years. Normative scores were calculated for each of the four age groups "based on analyses showing that smaller age groups did not yield any differences between them" (technical manual, p. 43). Additionally, analysis showed that with increasing age, individuals' scores tended to slow, and across all age groups increasing task complexity resulted in slower response times. Overall, normative data are available for ages 15–24, 25–44, 45–64 and 65–74. The number of individuals in each group ranges from 54 in the oldest age group to 132 in the second oldest age group.

TECHNICAL. Information describing the normative process is ample. Across the age ranges the sample sizes are generally large enough to provide confidence in using the normative data with respondents of varying gender, education, and community backgrounds. As expected, gender and education variables did not significantly contribute to differences in performance in information processing thereby negating the need for separate gender and education norms.

Reliability evidence is presented in the form of test-retest reliability and investigations of practice effects and fatigue on performance. In the first study, 20 undergraduate students were initially assessed and then re-assessed at 20 minutes and 1 week later. Test-retest reliability ranged from .56 to .80 with greater reliability over the longer interval. In the second study, 20 undergraduates were tested once a week for 4 weeks and then 6 months following the last testing session. Thirteen participants completed all testing, which resulted in test-retest reliabilities ranging from .37 to .85 with the second and third test-retest intervals producing the highest coefficients. In order to determine the effects of practice and fatigue on performance the developers separated the 30 block trials into 3 blocks of 10. Across the 3 blocks, performance was found to be consistent, therefore, not providing any "evidence of either practice or fatigue effects within a single testing session" (technical manual, p. 49). On the whole, the CTIP appears to have good reliability and is not vulnerable to the effects of practice or fatigue.

Validity evidence supporting the CTIP is adequate. In two studies the CTIP was found to have minimal correlations with measures of attention, with the exception of the Trail Making Test where correlations were significant, but low. The CTIP also was shown to have high correlations between the three subtests, which suggest each of the three subtests is measuring a similar construct. A study using functional magnetic resonance imaging (fMRI) supported the notion that the three subtests require progressively greater cognitive complexity. As expected, as task complexity increased greater neuronal involvement was shown, particularly in the prefrontal cortex. Numerous other studies are discussed in the manual supporting the use of the CTIP with TBI,

Multiple Sclerosis (MS) patients, and ADHD/LD populations. In brief and unsurprisingly, as the severity of TBI increased greater deficits in information-processing speed were evident, MS patients demonstrated deficits in information processing speed when compared to controls, and individuals with a history of learning disability performed more poorly than those with a history of ADHD. Appropriately, the developers caution against using the CTIP with individuals having a history of LD as this may confound results.

The use of the CTIP as a measure of effort was investigated in a study looking at performance of controls, individuals instructed to simulate deficits, and mild and severe TBI groups. Overall, simulators obtained longer RT scores, made more incorrect responses, and demonstrated greater variability than did the controls and TBI groups. Sensitivity and specificity are reportedly high though specific values are not reported in the manual. Nonetheless, the developers state the CTIP identified "virtually all members of the control group and mild TBI groups" (technical manual, p. 68). Combination of data from three studies using Simple RT scores and coefficient of variation cutoffs revealed that the Simple RT subtest was the most sensitive (.89) for detecting poor effort. Furthermore, although having lower sensitivity, the coefficient of variation was also suitable for detecting poor effort.

COMMENTARY. The CTIP is easy-to-use computerized measure of information-processing speed. It can also be used confidently for the detection of suboptimal effort in individuals with TBI. The test manual is well written, administration and scoring are simple, and the computerized reports are easy to follow and interpret. Normative data is provided for four separate age groups and the sample size comprising each of the groups is large enough to have confidence in the generalizability to the population at large. Reliability and validity data are sound and the research on the ability of the CTIP to detect poor effort suggests the CTIP has high sensitivity and specificity when used with TBI patients. Overall, the CTIP fills a gap in the neuropsychologist's armamentarium as a more pure measure of information-processing speed and as a unique nonembedded measure of effort. Future research is needed investigating the use of the CTIP with other neurological and psychiatric populations, as well as determining the test's relationship with other measures of effort such as Green's Word Memory Test (Green, 2005) and the Structured Inventory of Malingered Symptomatology (Widows & Smith, 2005).

SUMMARY. The CTIP is a well-developed measure of information-processing speed and effort. It is composed of three subtests of increasing cognitive complexity and can be administered in less than 15 minutes. The test is psychometrically strong and provides unique information on processing speed after accounting for motor deficits. The test has high sensitivity and specificity when used for detecting poor effort in individuals with suspected TBI. This unique test provides an excellent alternative to the more commonly used and well-known tests of malingering.

REVIEWER'S REFERENCES

Green, P. (2005). *Word Memory Test for Windows: User's Manual and program.* Edmonton, Alberta: Green's Publishing.

Widows, M. R., & Smith, G. P. (2005). Structured Inventory of Malingered Symptomatology. Lutz, FL: Psychological Assessment Resources.

Review of the Computerized Test of Information Processing by JEREMY R. SULLIVAN, Assistant Professor of Educational Psychology, University of Texas at San Antonio, San Antonio, TX:

DESCRIPTION. The Computerized Test of Information Processing (CTIP) was designed as a test of information-processing speed, or more specifically as a method of assessing whether processing speed abilities have been compromised by brain injuries or disease (especially Traumatic Brain Injury and Multiple Sclerosis). The test also purports to assess for malingering of cognitive deficits by determining whether examinees are exerting maximum effort as they approach the task. The test authors recommend the CTIP be administered as part of a comprehensive neuropsychological assessment battery that also includes measures of motor ability and potential malingering. The manual clearly states that the CTIP should *not* be used as a stand-alone indicator of malingering potential.

Three subtests are included on the CTIP, administered in the following order using a computer monitor and keyboard: Simple Reaction Time, Choice Reaction Time, and Semantic Search Reaction Time. On the Simple subtest, the examinee is instructed to press the spacebar as quickly as possible when a single stimulus appears in the center of the computer screen. Thus, each trial provides a measure of the number of seconds required to process the stimulus and provide a response. On the Choice subtest, the examinee must choose which of two keyboard keys to press based on which stimulus (of two possible stimuli) appears on the screen. Thus, each trial provides a measure of the number of seconds needed to process two pieces of information and decide on a response. Finally, the Semantic Search subtest requires the examinee to choose which of two keyboard keys to press based on whether or not a stimulus word presented on the computer screen fits into a corresponding semantic category, which also is presented on the screen. Each trial provides a measure of the number of seconds required to recognize and process the meaning of the stimulus word, determine whether the word fits into the stimulus category presented, and press the corresponding keyboard key. Given the increasingly complex demands of each subtest, reaction times tend to increase from the Simple to Choice to Semantic Search subtest. As examinees take more time to process the information contained in these tasks and decide on a response, their reaction time scores increase, indicating decreases in processing speed.

The primary scores for the CTIP are the median reaction times for each subtest, which are converted to norm-based percentile scores. The manual states that most examinees will be able to complete all three subtests in approximately 15 minutes. Further, administration and scoring are completely automated, eliminating the need for paper record forms and written responses. Each subtest starts with 10 practice trials designed to teach the examinee the nature of the task. These practice trials are followed by the actual test trials (30 test trials per subtest). Instructions are provided to the examinee by the computer; the manual also provides specific instructions that should be read by the examiner.

The CTIP manual provides sufficient information on computerized administration, scoring, and report generation. Two types of administration are offered. Clinical administration presents the three CTIP subtests in their standardized order, and therefore provides norm-based percentiles to describe the examinee's performance. Research administration is more customizable, as any or all of the three subtests can be administered in any order. The Research option provides separate reaction times for each trial of each subtest, in addition to other scores that may be useful for research purposes.

DEVELOPMENT. The operational definition of information-processing speed provided in the manual is: "a specific type of attentional processing that represents the speed at which processing operations are carried out" (p. 5). The test authors provide a brief review of the information-processing speed construct, citing its importance to other cognitive functions such as working memory and verbal comprehension. Further, the authors note that deficits in information-processing speed are involved in numerous clinical phenomena, such as normal aging, Traumatic Brain Injury, and neurological diseases such as Multiple Sclerosis.

The test authors developed the CTIP based on research indicating the sensitivity and utility of reaction time tests for detecting cognitive impairment. The authors note that the Simple, Choice, and Semantic Search subtests were selected because they met criteria important in the measurement of information-processing speed, including minimal practice effects after repeated administrations, increasing complexity from one subtest to the next, less frustrating tasks than other measures of reaction time, and minimal reliance on motor abilities for successful task completion.

Overall, this reviewer would like to know more about the process of item and scale development. Specifically, more information is needed on how the items and stimuli were developed, and how important decisions were made, such as how the symbols, words, and categories were selected for use in the subtests (as opposed to numerous other possibilities); why the test authors chose to use a "beep" to provide feedback for premature and incorrect responses; and how the test authors decided on the lengths of between-trial intervals.

TECHNICAL.

Standardization. The normative sample included 386 people (173 males, 213 females) with cognitive functioning within normal limits. Standardization participants ranged from 15 to 74 years of age. For purposes of converting raw median reaction time scores into norm-based percentile scores, the sample was divided into four age groups: 15 to 24 years (n = 109), 25 to 44 years (n = 91), 45 to 64 years (n = 132), and 65 to 74 years (n = 54). The rationale for dividing the sample into these age groups is that reaction times were progressively slower as age increased.

The mean number of years of education among normative participants was either 14.89 or 14.94 (the text presents one value and a table presents another; it is unclear which is correct). Unfortunately, no information is provided about the ethnicity or geographic distribution of the sample, or about the process by which people were selected for participation in the standardization process.

Reliability. Internal consistency analyses are not reported for the CTIP, given the nature of the subtests (i.e., reaction times are the primary index of interest rather than number of correct or incorrect responses). It seems like some sort of internal consistency analysis (e.g., coefficient alpha, item-total correlations) could have been helpful in detecting items that for whatever reason did not function in the same way as other items (see Neuhaus, Carlson, Jeng, Post, & Swank, 2001, for an example of how internal consistency analyses were used with a computerized measure of reaction time). This seems especially important for the Semantic Search subtest, as the content differences among individual items on this subtest are greater compared to the interitem differences on the Simple and Choice subtests.

In the absence of internal consistency analyses, reliability was estimated with two analyses of test-retest stability. In the first study, a sample of 20 undergraduate students took the CTIP on three occasions: The first administration was followed by a second administration with an interval of only 20 minutes, and the third administration occurred 1 week later. Test-retest coefficients for the 20-minute interval ranged from .56 to .66; coefficients for the 1-week interval ranged from .63 to .80.

The second test-retest study followed a group of 20 undergraduates over 4 weeks, with one administration per week. Thirteen of these students participated in an additional administration that occurred 6 months after the fourth administration. Across the first 4 weeks, coefficients ranged as follows: Simple Reaction Time from .37 to .85, Choice Reaction Time from .61 to .85, and Semantic Search Reaction Time from .54 to .84. As was found in the first study, longer time intervals generally were associated with higher coefficients. Coefficients based on the 6-month interval ranged from .49 to .66.

Overall, some of these test-retest coefficients are lower than expected, given the seemingly stable nature of the information-processing speed construct. Additional research using larger samples will be necessary to explore the reasons for these findings, especially with regard to why the short-term stability coefficients are so low.

Validity. Several types of evidence for validity are described in the manual. Evidence for construct validity was evaluated by correlating CTIP scores with scores on other measures of neuropsychological constructs. For example, scores were correlated with scores on the Trail Making Test, Digit Span subtest, and Digit Symbol tests. Using subsamples from the normative group, CTIP scores demonstrated high and statistically significant intercorrelations among the three CTIP subtests and moderate and statistically significant correlations with Trails A and Trails B, but very small and nonsignificant correlations with the Digit Span and Digit Symbol tests. Correlational results also are presented using samples of participants with Traumatic Brain Injury or Multiple Sclerosis, but these correlations were rather inconsistent across groups, with no consistent or predictable pattern of relationships among scores.

Several clinical studies were conducted to establish evidence for criterion-related validity, by demonstrating that different clinical groups performed in distinct and predictable ways on the CTIP. Overall, results of these studies generally support criterion-related validity. For example, one study demonstrated that participants in a Severe Traumatic Brain Injury group performed more poorly (i.e., slower reaction times) than participants in a Mild Traumatic Brain Injury group, who in turn performed more poorly than participants in a Control group on the Semantic Search RT subtest. The sample sizes for some of these clinical groups were relatively small, such as for the ADHD and learning disability analyses. Interestingly, participants instructed to simulate cognitive deficits performed much slower and committed significantly more errors as compared to participants with Traumatic Brain Injury and a Control group, suggesting CTIP performance may be useful in detecting potential malingering or reduced effort in order to feign cognitive impairment associated with Traumatic Brain Injury.

The test authors also conducted a series of studies on the influence of practice and fatigue on CTIP performance. Results of these studies suggest that with the normative sample, practice and fatigue effects were not observed within administrations (i.e., performance did not get significantly better or worse from the earlier to later items in the same subtest) or upon repeated administrations (i.e., performance did not significantly improve after taking the test multiple times). These results provide support for the validity of using the CTIP for the purposes of pre-post testing and progress monitoring.

COMMENTARY. Perhaps the principal strength of the CTIP is the ease of administration and scoring, as the automated procedures eliminate scoring time and the potential for scoring errors. This reviewer installed the CTIP on his laptop computer in order to gain a "hands on" understanding of the instrument. Administration, scoring, and report-generating procedures are simple for the examiner to navigate. It seems that observing the examinee during administration will provide the examiner with clinically useful information such as behaviors or verbalizations indicative of fatigue, motivation, and tolerance for frustration. The Clinical report provides a useful graph that compares the examinee's performance to the normative group for each subtest, which (along with the percentile scores) makes it very easy to see deficits in information-processing speed relative to the normative sample. One caveat related to the computerized administration: Examiners must take care to use a computer monitor without a harsh glare, as this may influence performance.

The chapter on interpretation includes four case studies to illustrate common profiles likely to be observed with the CTIP. These case studies will help users understand the distinction between profiles that are within and outside normal limits. For example, it was interesting to see that individuals with impaired processing speed typically score quite similarly to the norm group on the first subtest (Simple Reaction Time) but show progressively greater deviation from the norm on the second and third subtests, as the tasks become more complex and demanding.

A weakness of the CTIP is the narrow range of potential use, as the test should not be administered with certain groups, such as individuals with learning disabilities, low intelligence scores, limited education, and severe deficits in motor skills or coordination. The CTIP also cannot be used with people who do not speak and read English, due to verbal demands involved in the test (listening to instructions, reading instructions and stimulus words). The Semantic Search task also seems to be influenced to some extent by crystallized intelligence, as the ability to categorize words will depend on an understanding of what the words mean.

From this reviewer's clinical perspective, another weakness is the use of percentiles as the only norm-referenced score. It seems that *T*-scores may be more helpful for users attempting to describe an examinee's performance categorically (e.g., below average, average, above average). Further, most of the percentiles provided in the normative tables are distributed by groups of 5 or 10. *T*-scores typically provide greater precision than percentile ranks, allowing for finer distinctions to be made among examinees.

Psychometrically, more information is needed about the procedures used in developing, standardizing, and validating the use of the CTIP, including more information about the normative group, more complete rationale for choosing particular measures for construct validity analyses, and more explanation of the pattern of results from these analyses. The manual also provides very limited information on score reliability, and the information that is provided is based on inadequate sample sizes. Information about gender or ethnic group differences on CTIP performance also is needed.

SUMMARY. The CTIP shows promise as a measure of information-processing speed. However, within the context of clinical decision making, the CTIP should be used with caution until more data are available to support reliability of subtest scores, and until relationships with scores on other measures are better understood. The CTIP would appear to be most useful as part of a comprehensive neuropsychological battery in order to provide convergent evidence of processing-speed deficits, Traumatic Brain Injury, and potential malingering. It is clear from the manual that using CTIP performance to make inferences of potential malingering should be restricted to examinees with Traumatic Brain Injury, as currently there is no research supporting the use of the CTIP for this purpose with other clinical groups. The manual provides evidence that the CTIP demonstrates no or minimal practice effect, which suggests the test can be used on repeated occasions to monitor deficits or treatment effects over time. It would be interesting for future research to examine how CTIP scores relate to scores on a continuous performance test such as the Conners' Continuous Performance Test–II (Conners, 2000; 15:66), given the similarity in mode of administration.

REVIEWER'S REFERENCES

Conners, C. K. (2000). Conners' Continuous Performance Test–II. North Tonawanda, NY: Multi-Health Systems.

Neuhaus, G. F., Carlson, C. D., Jeng, W. M., Post, Y., & Swank, P. R. (2001). The reliability and validity of Rapid Automatized Naming scoring software ratings for the determination of pause and articulation component durations. *Educational and Psychological Measurement, 61*, 490-504.

[33]

Conners Comprehensive Behavior Rating Scales.

Purpose: Designed to "assess a wide spectrum of behaviors, emotions, and academic problems" in order to diagnose, and develop and monitor treatment plans for children and adolescents.

Publication Date: 2008.

Acronyms: Conners CONNERS CBRS; Conners CI.

Administration: Individual or group.

Forms, 6: Conners CONNERS CBRS–Teacher, Conners CONNERS CBRS–Parent, Conners CONNERS CBRS–Self-Report, Conners Clinical Index–Teacher, Conners Clinical Index–Parent, Conners Clinical Index–Self-Report.

Price Data, 2009: $525 per manual (416 pages), Conners CONNERS CBRS unlimited use software program, and 25 parent/teacher/self-report response booklets.

Foreign Language Edition: Spanish edition available.

Comments: "The Conners Clinical Index (Conners CI) is extracted from the Conners CONNERS CBRS form; the same 24 items used to calculate the Conners Clinical Index score on the Conners CONNERS CBRS form are used on the Conners CI"; The Conners CONNERS CBRS and Conners CI forms can be administered and scored online; paper-and-pencil forms can also be scored online; can be scored using the Conners CONNERS CBRS scoring software program by entering responses from a completed paper-and-pencil administration but cannot be administered through the software.

Author: C. Keith Conners.

Publisher: Multi-Health Systems, Inc.

a) CONNERS COMPREHENSIVE BEHAVIOR RATING SCALE–TEACHER.

Population: Ages 6–18.

Acronym: Conners CONNERS CBRS-T.

Scores, 44: Emotional Distress, Upsetting Thoughts/Physical Symptoms, Social Anxiety, Defiant/Aggressive Behaviors, Academic Difficulties, Academic Difficulties: Language, Academic Difficulties: Math, Hyperactivity, Social Problems, Separation Fears, Perfectionistic and Compulsive Behaviors, Violence Potential Indicator, Physical Symptoms, ADHD Hyperactive/Impulsive, ADHD Inattentive, ADHD Combined, Conduct Disorder, Oppositional Defiant Disorder, Major Depressive Episode, Manic Episode, Mixed Episode, Generalized Anxiety Disorder, Separation Anxiety Disorder, Social Phobia, Obsessive-Compulsive Disorder, Autistic Disorder, Asperger's Disorder, Positive Impression, Negative Impression, Inconsistency Index, Conners Clinical Index, Bullying Perpetration, Bullying Victimization, Enuresis/Encopresis, Panic Attack, Post Traumatic Stress Disorder, Specific Phobia, Substance Use, Tics, Trichotillomania, Impairment in Schoolwork/Grades, Impairment in Friendships/Relationships, Severe Conduct, Self-Harm.

Time: (20) minutes.

b) CONNERS COMPREHENSIVE BEHAVIOR RATING SCALE–PARENT.

Population: Ages 6–18.

Acronym: Conners CONNERS CBRS-P.

Scores, 46: Emotional Distress, Upsetting Thoughts, Worrying, Defiant/Aggressive Behaviors, Academic Difficulties, Academic Difficulties: Language, Academic Difficulties: Math, Hyperactivity/Impulsivity, Social Problems, Separation Fears, Perfectionistic and Compulsive Behaviors, Violence Potential Indicator, Physical Symptoms, ADHD Hyperactive/Impulsive, ADHD Inattentive, ADHD Combined, Conduct Disorder, Oppositional Defiant Disorder, Major Depressive Episode, Manic Episode, Mixed Episode, Generalized Anxiety Disorder, Separation Anxiety Disorder, Social Phobia, Obsessive-Compulsive Disorder, Autistic Disorder, Asperger's Disorder, Positive Impression, Negative Impression, Inconsistency Index, Conners Clinical Index, Bullying Perpetration, Bullying Victimization, Enuresis/Encopresis, Panic Attack, Pica, Post Traumatic Stress Disorder, Specific Phobia, Substance Use, Tics, Trichotillomania, Impairment in Schoolwork/Grades, Impairment in Friendships/Relationships, Impairment in Home Life, Severe Conduct, Self-Harm.

Time: Same as *a* above.

c) CONNERS COMPREHENSIVE BEHAVIOR RATING SCALE–SELF-REPORT.

Population: Ages 8–18.

Acronym: Conners CONNERS CBRS-SR.

Scores, 38: Emotional Distress, Defiant/Aggressive Behaviors, Academic Difficulties, Hyperactivity/Impulsivity, Separation Fears, Violence Potential Indicator, Physical Symptoms, ADHD Hyperactive/Impulsive, ADHD Inattentive, ADHD Combined, Conduct Disorder, Oppositional Defiant Disorder, Major Depressive Episode, Manic Episode, Mixed Episode, Generalized Anxiety Disorder, Separation Anxiety Disorder, Social Phobia, Obsessive-Compulsive Disorder, Positive Impression, Negative Impression, Inconsistency Index, Conners Clinical Index, Bullying Perpetration, Bullying Victimization, Panic Attack, Pervasive Developmental Disorder,

Pica, Post Traumatic Stress Disorder, Specific Phobia, Substance Use, Tics, Trichotillomania, Impairment in Schoolwork/Grades, Impairment in Friendships/Relationships, Impairment in Home Life, Severe Conduct, Self-Harm.
Time: Same as *a* above.
d) CONNERS CLINICAL INDEX–TEACHER.
Population: Ages 6–18.
Acronym: Conners CI-T.
Scores, 6: Overall Conners Clinical Index Score, Disruptive Behavior Indicator, Learning and Language Disorder Indicator, Mood Disorder Indicator, Anxiety Disorder Indicator, ADHD Indicator.
Time: (10) minutes.
e) CONNERS CLINICAL INDEX–PARENT.
Population: Ages 6–18.
Acronym: Conners CI-P.
Scores: Same as *d* above.
Time: Same as *d* above.
f) CONNERS CLINICAL INDEX–SELF-REPORT.
Population: Ages 8-18.
Scores: Same as *d* above.
Time: Same as *d* above.

Review of the Conners Comprehensive Behavior Rating Scales by JEREMY R. SULLIVAN, Assistant Professor of Educational Psychology, University of Texas at San Antonio, San Antonio, TX:

DESCRIPTION. The Conners Comprehensive Behavior Rating Scales (Conners CBRS) was designed as an omnibus measure of emotional, behavioral, academic, and social functioning among children (please note: the term "children" will be used in this review to include both children and adolescents). The Conners CBRS is purported to facilitate decision making with regard to diagnosis, special education classification, intervention planning, progress monitoring, and research. The Conners CBRS includes a parent rating scale (203 items), teacher rating scale (204 items), and self-report scale (179 items), which may be used independently or in conjunction with one another to facilitate multi-informant assessment. The parent and teacher scales can be used with children from 6 to 18 years of age; the self-report scale can be used with children from 8 to 18 years of age.

Given the test author's intent to assess a range of behavioral and psychological problems, the Conners CBRS includes over 40 scales. The Content Scales include broad areas of dysfunction, such as Emotional Distress, Defiant/Aggressive Behaviors, and Academic Difficulties. The Symptom Scales are tied to specific DSM-IV-TR diagnostic criteria, including ADHD (differentiated by subtype), Conduct Disorder, Oppositional Defiant Disorder, Autistic Disorders, Mood Disorders, and Anxiety Disorders. These scales are meant to help the examiner narrow down which diagnoses are likely and unlikely to be appropriate for the child. The Validity scales are designed to detect three possible patterns of responding: Positive Impression (i.e., faking good), Negative Impression (i.e., faking bad), and Inconsistency (i.e., careless or random responding). The Conners Clinical Index attempts to differentiate children with a discernible diagnosis from children without a discernible diagnosis. The Other Clinical Indicators scales assess other potential problems such as Bullying Perpetration and Victimization, Panic Attack, Posttraumatic Stress Disorder, Substance Use, Tics, and Trichotillomania. Two sets of Critical items (Self-Harm and Severe Conduct) may identify immediate safety concerns. Finally, all three forms include Impairment items, which ask the rater whether the problems result in significant impairment in functioning across settings such as home, school, and social settings. The Conners CBRS system also includes a short form of sorts called the Conners Clinical Index (Conners CI). The Conners CI form is meant to be used as a screener, or rough indicator that suggests the child is similar to other children with a diagnosis.

The Conners CBRS and Conners CI can be administered by raters writing directly on the response booklets, or they can be administered online. Items may be read aloud if reading comprehension is a concern, and specific procedures are provided for the examiner to follow in this situation. Across all forms of the Conners CBRS, response options for each item are as follows: 0 = *Not true at all (Never, Seldom)*, 1 = *Just a little true (Occasionally)*, 2 = *Pretty much true (Often, Quite a bit)*, and 3 = *Very much true (Very often, Very frequently)*. Respondents are asked to consider behaviors observed over the past month. Thus, teachers completing the form should have at least 1 month in which to become familiar with the child and his or her behaviors.

Both the Conners CBRS and Conners CI can be scored either with computer software or online. The Conners CI also can be scored by hand using the QuikScore form; the Conners CBRS cannot be scored by hand. If the hard copy version of the Conners CBRS is used, scoring is completed by the clinician typing the rater's responses into the computer scoring program. Raw scores for the Conners CBRS and Conners CI scales are converted to *T*-scores for normative interpretation. Both software and online scoring result in a narrative report inclusive of interpretive guidelines. Overall, the manual provides adequate instruction in administration and scoring procedures.

DEVELOPMENT. Conners CBRS development is described as taking place over three phases: initial planning, the pilot study, and the normative study. The initial planning phase involved developing items based on reviews of the assessment and psychopathology literature. Given the purpose of the Conners CBRS, the DSM classification system served as an important basis of item development, and the Symptom scales were rationally derived from the DSM-IV-TR. The initial Conners CBRS item pool was reviewed and reduced by the development team before the pilot study was conducted; items were revised or eliminated based on their ability to be translated into Spanish, appropriateness across cultural groups, clarity, and clinical importance.

The pilot study phase involved administering the initial item pool to different samples of adults and children, including samples from the general population and various clinical samples. The sample sizes for the pilot study were 232 for the parent form, 271 for the teacher form, and 249 for the self-report. Exploratory factor analysis and other statistical procedures (e.g., coefficient alpha, item-total correlations, item discrimination indices) were used to gain an understanding of item groupings, and to determine which items to retain and which to eliminate. Expert review also was used to evaluate the items for clarity, clinical importance, and cultural sensitivity.

The normative study phase involved administering the revised set of Conners CBRS items to the standardization sample, and then using these responses to develop final versions of scales and subscales, confirm results from the exploratory factor analyses, establish scoring criteria and cutoffs, and evaluate psychometric properties. Several items were removed from each of the Conners CBRS forms before publication of the final version of the Conners CBRS. Reading levels of the Conners CBRS items were found to range from Grade 3.5 (self-report) to 5.9 (teacher report).

TECHNICAL.

Standardization. The norms are based on ratings from 3,400 people, including 1,200 parents, 1,200 teachers, and 1,000 children. The normative sample was taken from a larger sample (4,626) of gathered data, so that at each year of age there would be 50 males and 50 females included who were representative of the United States population in terms of ethnicity. The clinical sample included 704 parents, 672 teachers, and 700 children. The normative and clinical samples are described in great detail in the test manual. The ethnic distributions of participants in the normative sample are generally similar to the United States population for Asian, African American, Hispanic, and Caucasian children. With regard to geographic distribution, the Western states are less represented than the Northeast, Midwest, and Southern states. For the purpose of score conversions, the norms are divided by age and gender due to numerous statistically significant age and gender effects found in the normative data (although most effect sizes were relatively small). Statistically significant effects for ethnicity and parent education level were found for many scales, but again, most effect sizes were small.

Reliability. Score reliability was assessed with internal consistency, test-retest reliability, and interrater reliability analyses. With regard to internal consistency, most alpha coefficients for the Content and Symptom scales were above .70, and many were above .90. An exception is the Asperger's Disorder scale, which fell below .70 for some age and gender subgroups. Alpha coefficients for the Positive Impression and Negative Impression scales were below .70 for many subgroups (even as low as .28), but these lower coefficients are likely due to a lack of variability on the items on these scales. Internal consistency analyses are broken down by gender and age, and coefficients are generally similar across these subgroups. However, this reviewer would like to see evidence in the manual that alpha coefficients are similar across ethnic groups.

Test-retest analyses were conducted with a sample of 84 parents, 136 teachers, and 75 children. The test-retest interval was 2 to 4 weeks. All coefficients were statistically significant at $p < .001$, and adjusted coefficients indicate acceptable stability across administrations with ranges as follows: Parent Content .70 to .96,

Parent Symptom .66 to .95, Teacher Content .80 to .96, Teacher Symptom .76 to .94, Self-Report Content .58 to .82, and Self-Report Symptom .56 to .76.

Interrater reliability was assessed with 199 pairs of parents and 130 pairs of teachers. Within these pairs, the two parents or two teachers provided ratings of the same child, in order to determine level of similarity across two independent raters. Corrected correlation coefficients indicate moderate to high levels of agreement: Parent Content .62 to .89, Parent Symptom .53 to .84, Teacher Content .50 to .89, and Teacher Symptom .53 to .80.

Validity. The test manual provides an abundance of information about validity evidence; only the highlights will be presented here. The development team evaluated validity from several angles, including factorial validity, convergent and divergent validity, and discriminative (or criterion-related) validity. Factorial analyses indicated that the Conners CBRS items grouped into theoretically supported factors. The test manual describes the process of using exploratory factor analyses to establish the factor structure of the parent, teacher, and self-report forms, and then using confirmatory factor analysis to test and confirm the structure. Confirmatory fit indices for the parent form generally suggest good model fit; indices for the teacher and self-report forms were somewhat lower than desired.

Convergent and divergent analyses indicated that scores on the Conners CBRS generally correlated with scores on other measures of psychopathology in theoretically expected ways (i.e., stronger correlations with measures of similar constructs, weaker correlations with measures of dissimilar constructs). The other measures used in these analyses included the Behavior Assessment System for Children–Second Edition (BASC-2; Reynolds & Kamphaus, 2004), Achenbach System of Empirically Based Assessment (ASEBA; Achenbach & Rescorla, 2001), Children's Depression Inventory (CDI; Kovacs, 2003), and several additional measures. As an example, scores on the Major Depressive Episode scale of the Conners CBRS were correlated with scores on other scales as follows: BASC-2 Depression scale .38 to .71, ASEBA Anxious/Depressed scale .43 to .83, and CDI self-report Total Score .55 ($p < .01$ for all). Similarly, Conners CBRS scores were generally correlated with the Adaptive scales of the BASC-2 (e.g., Adaptability, Leadership, Social Skills) in a negative direction, which makes sense given the nature of these scales. The overall pattern of correlations with scores on other measures provides adequate evidence of construct validity.

Finally, discriminative analyses indicated that Conners CBRS scores were able to differentiate children in various clinical groups from those in the general normative sample. For example, children in the Disruptive Behavior Disorders clinical group scored significantly higher on the Defiant/Aggressive Behaviors, Violence Potential Indicator, Conduct Disorder, and Oppositional Defiant Disorder scales than children from both the general population and other clinical groups. Similarly, children in the Pervasive Developmental Disorders clinical group scored significantly higher on the Social Problems, Perfectionistic and Compulsive Behaviors, Autistic Disorder, and Asperger's Disorder scales as compared to children in other groups. Conversely, the ADHD Inattentive scale was not successful at differentiating ADHD subtypes; this was true for the parent, teacher, and self-report forms. Overall, mean correct classification rates based on Conners CBRS scores were as follows: parent = 78.40%, teacher = 81.22%, self-report = 75.25%. The test manual also includes classification statistics for sensitivity, specificity, positive predictive power, negative predictive power, false positive rate, false negative rate, and kappa.

COMMENTARY. It is clear that much care and thought were invested in the development of the Conners CBRS. The test manual is among the best this reviewer has seen in terms of level of detail regarding psychometric issues such as norms, reliability, and validity. The test manual also describes how different scales are tied to DSM and IDEA criteria, thereby facilitating interpretation for clinicians. The chapters on interpretation and intervention discuss these issues in more detail than is often found in test manuals. Tables also are provided for users to determine whether pre-post changes in Conners CBRS scores are statistically significant.

This reviewer took the Conners CBRS self-report as a 16-year-old male, responding with a "2" to all items, and then entered these responses into the computer scoring program. As expected, this response pattern resulted in "Very Elevated" *T*-scores for all Content and Symptom scales (*T*-scores ranging from 79 to 90), yet the Negative Impression Validity scale was in the normal range. Thus, it is possible for raters to give 2-point responses to all items (thereby endorsing multiple symptoms to some degree) without triggering the Validity scales because extreme responses were not given to any of the Negative Impression items. This observation makes sense given the procedures and cutoffs used in developing the Validity scales, but clinicians should be aware of the potential for these scales to "miss" some response patterns.

The tables and handouts provided in the software-based interpretive report make a large amount of data more manageable. *SEM* and percentiles are optional, providing more interpretive information. The computer program makes scoring fast and easy, and the program includes a double-entry option to catch data entry errors.

An additional strength is the similarity of items and scales across parent, teacher, and self-report forms, allowing the clinician to look at consistency across informants and determine possible setting effects. Although not described in detail in this review, the psychometric properties of the Conners CI and Spanish forms were similar to those of the full Conners CBRS, but validity analyses were not reported for the Spanish forms.

Users should also consider some of the weaknesses of the Conners CBRS. For example, on the teacher form, it seems like the Upsetting Thoughts/Physical Symptoms subscale would be more useful if it was split into two scales to facilitate interpretation; in its current form, an elevated score will require consideration of individual responses to determine whether the elevation is due to endorsement of items assessing upsetting thoughts or physical symptoms, or both. Similarly, the Emotional Distress scale combines symptoms of anxiety and depression.

With regard to the validity studies, this reviewer would like to see more explanation for why some of the confirmatory fit indices were lower than expected. Further, not many ethnic minorities were included in the construct validation samples, as compared to Whites. Finally, the Conners CBRS does not include scales specifically designed to detect possible psychosis or thought disturbances; clinicians seeking to assess these issues should consider additional measures.

SUMMARY. Alternative omnibus instruments that include self-, teacher-, and parent-report components include the BASC-2 and ASEBA systems. Although similar, the Conners CBRS is unique in terms of some of the constructs included and in the comprehensiveness of the DSM Symptom scales. One of the goals behind the development of the Conners CBRS was to provide clinicians with a measure that is more diagnostically useful than similar rating scales. More research and clinical use will be necessary to determine whether this goal has been realized, and to determine whether the Conners CBRS contributes to developing appropriate interventions. The Conners CBRS appears to be a high-quality option when comprehensive information is needed about behavioral and psychological functioning from multiple informants. The low to moderate correlations across different informants suggest the importance of gathering ratings from multiple sources, as each will likely provide unique pieces of information about the child.

REVIEWER'S REFERENCES

Achenbach, T. M., & Rescorla, L. A. (2001). *Manual for ASEBA School-Age Forms & Profiles*. Burlington, VT: University of Vermont, Research Center for Children, Youth, & Families.

Kovacs, M. (2003). *Children's Depression Inventory technical manual update*. Toronto, Ontario, Canada: Multi-Health Systems.

Reynolds, C. R., & Kamphaus, R. W. (2004). *Behavior Assessment System for Children–Second Edition manual*. Circle Pines, MN: American Guidance Service.

Review of the Conners Comprehensive Behavior Rating Scales by JOHN J. VACCA, Assistant Professor of Early Childhood Education, St. Joseph's University, Philadelphia, PA:

DESCRIPTION. The early childhood field is confronted now more than ever with a surge in populations of younger children with behavioral and emotional difficulties. Many of these children often go undiagnosed or are misdiagnosed, especially because the presenting behaviors are not completely understood within the context of the environments in which these children are raised. Furthermore, the cultural diversity of families and the ways rituals, routines, and practices are carried out in homes across the United States are factors that researchers continue to see as the primary contributors to how well children cope and manage stress. Therefore, these factors need to be included in any measure of social-emotional functioning.

"The Conners Comprehensive Behavior Rating Scales (Conners CONNERS CBRS) is a comprehensive assessment tool, which assesses a wide range of behavioral, emotional, social, and academic concerns and disorders in children and adolescents" (manual, p. 1). The format of the tool provides a forum for input about a child's behavior from multiple people across multiple settings. Rating forms for teachers and parents are provided for children and adolescents (ages 6 to 18 years). Additionally, self-report forms are available for individuals from 8 to 18. A comprehensive manual, score sheets, record booklets, and a quick reference guide for interpretatioins and interventions are all provided to users. Detailed instructions for administration, scoring, and interpretation (including supporting information for making diagnoses/dual-diagnoses and designing interventions) are provided to the user.

The test author stipulates that the sole use of the scales to make a diagnosis or determine eligibility for specialized support is not only inappropriate but also unethical. His stipulation is upheld not only in federal law but also in research focusing on best practices in the assessment and evaluation of children, adolescents, and adults across developmental levels and concerns. User qualifications allow for administration and scoring by individuals without specialized training; however, only those professionals with advanced levels of training in the mental health/psychiatric fields are considered qualified to interpret and report findings.

DEVELOPMENT. The process for the development of the Conners CBRS was complex and involved three phases: initial planning, pilot study, and normative study. During the initial stage, an in-depth review of research, theories, legislative initiatives, and public policies was done. Focus groups were then formed and information was gathered reflecting public opinion from pediatric, education, and related professionals about issues involving youth and social-emotional functioning.

Overall, the development of the Conners CBRS represented a multifaceted approach that occurred over the course of 4 years and involved more than 7,000 field testing activities across regions and stratified demographics in the United States. Ratings from teachers, parents, and students were gathered over the course of the development of the instrument in multiple settings and contexts. Extensive factor analyses were implemented to render the current scale, and behavioral dimensions that reflected judgments about an individual's behavior were examined. The section on development is exceptional, and provides the user with an in-depth background on not only how the Conners CBRS was established but also on the critical integrity with which the instrument was developed.

The development section for any assessment instrument is one that should be identified and addressed comprehensively for effective appraisals to be completed by experts in the field such as the appraisals published in the *Mental Measurements Yearbook*. This information is also important to address because it demonstrates the integrity of the instrument, the manner in which the factors that it is purported to measure are addressed, and finally, the extent to which the targeted population was included in the inception and field-testing process. Many test authors fall short in discussing with users the process of development for the given instrument and instead stress its purpose and usefulness. The Conners CBRS represents a model for how assessment instruments of any kind should be organized, developed, and implemented.

TECHNICAL. The technical aspects of the Conners CBRS are remarkable and a model for an instrument of this nature. Conners reports that over 6,000 assessments were collected and analyzed. Information from a majority of these assessments came from multiple informants. Specifically, for any given child for whom assessment data were collected, at least two different individuals provided ratings (e.g., teacher and parent). The normative sample was extensive (n = 3,400) and stratified to reflect the heterogeneity of the U.S. population. Within the norming sample, the test author identifies that 50 boys and 50 girls across the age range of 6 to 18 years participated. A smaller subset of the overall normative population (n = 1,616) included individuals who received ratings from other similar measures. This process was used to evaluate the concurrent validity of the Conners CBRS and the ability of the data to support that collected in a typical psychiatric assessment battery.

Extensive measures were undertaken to establish both the reliability and validity of the Conners CBRS. In terms of reliability, multiple measures were completed. Mean alpha coefficients for internal consistency, test-retest, and interrater reliability ranged from .65 (test-retest) to .90 (internal consistency). Generally, alpha coefficients of .70 and above are acceptable. The user should recognize that low numbers of items on any scale can contribute to lower coefficients. The advice in these cases is to compare such results with the rest of the results of the test. All Conners CBRS alpha coefficients that fall below .70 reflect this phenomenon and are therefore not clinically significant.

The measure of internal consistency is an important variable of reliability to examine because it is a reflection of how well all of the items on a given scale not only relate to one another but how they uphold the construct being measured. Other variables that are equally important to evaluate are test-retest and interrater reliability, and the values reported for the Conners CBRS are well within the acceptable range and in some cases above the median level for test construction. This means that any user can expect consistent results across evaluations of individuals. Finally, the fact that Conners recruited the participation of multiple persons for each evaluation of an individual, the values mirror what can be reasonably anticipated when groups evaluate students with the Conners CBRS.

An important issue that needs to be mentioned is the remarkable consistency with which the Conners CBRS aligns with social-emotional disabilities as well as school-related difficulties. Coefficients are well above the acceptable levels. For example, alpha coefficients for the parent form were determined to be at .95 for general Emotional Distress, .94 for Academic Difficulties, .93 for ADHD Inattentive, .90 for Oppositional Defiant Disorder, and .78 for Autistic Disorder.

With measures of validity, the following domains were examined: Factorial, Across-Informant, Convergent/Divergent, and Discriminative. A total of six strongly loaded factors within the instrument were identified and then assessed: Emotional Distress, Aggressive Behavior, Academic Difficulties, Hyperactivity, Perfectionistic and Compulsive, and Social Problems. Factor analyses indicated a stronger model and fit for the parent scale of the Conners CBRS and a slightly lower level of fit for the student and teacher forms. Neither was clinically significant, however, thereby supporting full use of the three scales.

Values for across-informant correlatioins were low to moderate in scale (.29 to .67). Although some coefficients for the Conners CBRS-P and Conners CBRS-T are quite low, the user must remember that it is reasonable for individuals' judgments about behavior for a given student to vary from one individual to another. This supports the critical nature of gathering assessment information from multiple sources.

Coefficients for convergent/divergent validity were moderately strong when compared against the DSM-IV-TR. Finally, scores for discriminative validity (which is the ability to isolate those behaviors/items that truly reflect those that are manifest in individuals with known diagnoses) indicated that the Conners CBRS reflected close to 80% of the diagnostic classifications published in the DSM-IV-TR.

COMMENTARY. The work of Professor Conners on his latest scale represents a significant contribution to the field of education and developmental pediatrics. Given the limited resources available to educators and related professionals, the Conners CBRS provides a forum for multiple persons to collaborate on concerns about a given student. The strongly established psychometric properties of the tool clearly demonstrate the capability to assist professionals in determining diagnoses and etiologies of emotional difficulties, developing appropriate program goals, and identifying teaching and therapeutic interventions to support students in their efforts to cope with the environments in which they participate (including home, school, and beyond).

SUMMARY. The Conners CBRS "is a comprehensive assessment tool, which assesses a wide range of behavioral, emotional, social, and academic concerns and disorders in children and adolescents" (manual, p. 1). The format of the measure provides a forum for input about a child's behavior from multiple people across multiple settings. Given the rise in populations of children and adolescents experiencing emotional distress, teachers, parents, professionals, and students themselves are in need of innovative ways to help support learning and development. The Conners CBRS represents a valuable contribution to the field and provides a critical piece to any team assessment of a student.

[34]

Conners Early Childhood.

Purpose: Designed to "assess a wide range of behavioral, emotional, and social concerns and developmental milestones in preschool-aged children."
Population: Ages 2-6.
Publication Date: 2009.
Acronym: Conners EC.
Administration: Individual or group.
Forms: 5 forms per rater (Parent, Teacher/Childcare Provider).
Price Data, 2010: $329 per Complete Scoring Software kit including 25 each of the Parent and Teacher

response booklets, manual (259 pages), and scoring software; $115 per Online Kit including 20 of each of the Parent and Teacher Online Forms, and Manual; $115 per Global Index Handscored Kit including 25 each of the Parent and Teacher QuikScore forms and manual; $99 per Global Index Online kit including 10 each of the Parent and Teacher Online forms and manual; $45 per 25 Parent or Teacher response booklets; $35 per 25 Parent or Teacher Behavior forms; $35 per 25 Parent or Teacher Developmental Milestones forms; $30 per 25 Parent or Teacher Behavior Short Response forms; $30 per 25 Parent or Teacher Global Index QuikScore forms; $1.50 per each Online form (Parent or Teacher Full-Length, Behavior, Developmental Milestones, Behavior Short, or Global Index form); $80 per manual; $199 per scoring software (USB); prices are identical for the equivalent Spanish forms.
Foreign Language Edition: Spanish version available for all forms.
Comments: Administration available in paper-and-pencil or online format; scoring available online or using the scoring software (Global Index QuikScore form can also be hand-scored).
Author: C. Keith Conners.
Publisher: Multi-Health Systems Inc.

a) CONNERS EARLY CHILDHOOD FULL-LENGTH FORMS.
Acronyms: Conners EC-P; Conners EC-T.
Scores: 22 scores per rater, including 11 Behavior scores (Inattention/Hyperactivity, Defiance/Temper, Aggression, Defiant/Aggressive Behaviors Total, Social Functioning, Atypical Behaviors, Social Functioning/Atypical Behaviors Total, Anxiety, Mood and Affect, Physical Symptoms, Sleep Problems), 5 Developmental Milestone scores (Adaptive Skills, Communication, Motor Skills, Play, Pre-Academic/Cognitive), 3 Validity scores (Positive Impression, Negative Impression, Inconsistency Index), and 3 Global Index scores (Restless-Impulsive, Emotional Lability, Total).
Time: (25) minutes.
Comments: Scoring report also includes item ratings for Other Clinical Indicators and Impairment Items, and rater's responses to two additional open-ended questions.

b) CONNERS EARLY CHILDHOOD BEHAVIOR FORMS.
Acronyms: Conners EC BEH-P; Conners EC BEH-T.
Scores: 17 scores per rater, including 11 Behavior scores (Inattention/Hyperactivity, Defiance/Temper, Aggression, Defiant/Aggressive Behaviors Total, Social Functioning, Atypical Behaviors, Social Functioning/Atypical Behaviors Total, Anxiety, Mood and Affect, Physical Symptoms, Sleep Problems), 3 Validity scores (Positive Impression, Negative Impression, Inconsistency Index), and 3 Global Index scores (Restless-Impulsive, Emotional Lability, Total).
Time: (15) minutes.
Comments: Scoring report also includes item ratings for Other Clinical Indicators and Impairment Items, and rater's responses to two additional open-ended questions.

c) CONNERS EARLY CHILDHOOD DEVELOPMENTAL MILESTONES FORMS.
Acronyms: Conners EC DM-P; Conners EC DM-T.
Scores: 5 Developmental Milestones scores per rater: Adaptive Skills, Communication, Motor Skills, Play, Pre-Academic/Cognitive.
Time: (10) minutes.
Comments: Scoring report also includes item ratings for Impairment Items, and rater's responses to two additional open-ended questions.

d) CONNERS EARLY CHILDHOOD BEHAVIOR SHORT FORMS.
Acronyms: Conners EC BEH-P[S]; Conners EC BEH-T[S].
Scores: 8 scores per rater, including 6 Behavior scores (Inattention/Hyperactivity, Defiant/Aggressive Behaviors Total, Social Functioning/Atypical Behaviors Total, Anxiety, Mood and Affect, Physical Symptoms), and 2 Validity scores (Positive Impression, Negative Impression).
Time: (10) minutes.
Comments: Scoring report also includes rater's responses to two additional open-ended questions.

e) CONNERS EARLY CHILDHOOD GLOBAL INDEX FORMS.
Acronyms: Conners ECGI-P; Conners ECGI-T.
Scores: 3 Global Index scores per rater: Restless-Impulsive, Emotional Lability, Total.
Time: (5) minutes.

Review of the Conners Early Childhood by SHERRY K. BAIN, Associate Professor, and KATHLEEN B. ASPIRANTI, Doctoral Student in School Psychology, Department of Educational Psychology and Counseling, University of Tennessee, Knoxville, TN:

DESCRIPTION. The Conners Early Childhood (Conners EC) was developed to cover the general domains of behavioral and developmental functioning for young children, aged 2 to 6. Besides the full scale format (referred to here as the EC), which contains 190 items on the Parent form (EC-P) and 186 items on the Teacher/Childcare Provider form (EC-T), there are four additional short forms: the Behavior form (BEH), the Developmental Milestone form (DM), the Behavior Short form (BEH(S)), and the Early Childhood

Global Index form (ECGI). The ECGI contains the same global index items available in all of the revisions of the various Conners rating scales (e.g., Conners Third Edition™; Conners, 2008a). Each form is available in both Parent and Teacher/Childcare Provider versions. Spanish versions are also available. Conners recommends that for administration and scoring of the Conners EC, no specialized advanced training is needed; however, to interpret the Conners EC, individuals need to have MHS B-level qualifications.

The Behavior scale on the EC includes Inattention/Hyperactivity, Defiant/Aggressive Behaviors, Social Functioning/Atypical Behaviors, Anxiety, Mood and Affect, and Physical Symptoms. The Developmental Milestone scales include Adaptive Skills, Communication, Motor Skills, Play, and Pre-Academic/Cognitive. Validity scales are available on the EC, BEH, and BEH(S). Additionally, scores on Restless-Impulsive, Emotional Lability, and Total Global Index are available on the EC, BEH, and ECGI forms. Clinical indicators and items indicating degree of impairment across various settings (learning, peer-interactions, and home) are provided on the EC and some short forms. All forms can be administered using a paper-and-pencil or online format and are largely self-explanatory for raters. Questions on the EC, BEH, BEH(S), and ECGI are presented in a 4-point Likert format, whereas questions on the DM scale follow a 3-point format. For all forms except the ECGI, responses must be entered and scored using computer software. Results are provided in an assessment report, which contains a scoring table that links the results to potential eligibility under the Individuals with Disabilities Education Improvement Act of 2004.

DEVELOPMENT. Conners offers a fairly detailed description of the three phases of development, followed by comprehensive information on several types of reliability and validity data gathered during development. During Phase 1, preliminary scales were developed containing large item pools. Items were reviewed for clinical significance and clarity, and readability was maintained at or below the fifth grade reading level. During Phase 2, the pilot study, 155 parents and 157 teachers rated the respective participants, which included children with and without diagnoses for a variety of disorders. Following factor analysis, the pilot data revealed five content areas: Inattention/Hyperactivity, Oppositional Behavior, Emotional Regulation/Defiance, Anxiety, and Social Functioning. Conners also retained the Mood and Affect, Physical Symptoms, and Atypical Behaviors scales based upon theoretical and clinical concerns.

For Phase 3, the normative phase, 204 items were selected for the Parent form and 197 items were selected for the Teacher/Childcare Provider form (hereafter referred to as the Teacher form). Eight hundred children were rated by both a parent and a teacher. This distribution was representative of the general population according to race/ethnicity, based on the 2000 U.S. Census, and was evenly distributed across gender and 6-month age levels. The final EC forms were created with 190 items on the Parent version and 186 items on the Teacher version. Short forms were created at this point, to provide abbreviated scales that correlated with the corresponding full-length form.

TECHNICAL. To standardize the EC, 1,655 Parent and 1,626 Teacher forms were completed. Parental education level and geographic region were varied across the sample, but these data were not compared to the U.S. Census report in the manual. Following multivariate analyses, Conners found significant differences for gender on the Inattention/Hyperactivity scores, with males more frequently displaying problems. Additionally, race/ethnicity had a small significant effect on several of the scales, not listed here for space reasons.

Reliability. Conners provides evidence of reliability for the EC through examination of the instrument's internal consistency, test-retest reliability, and the standard error of measurement (*SEM*). Based on results for internal consistency, the EC-Parent form produced total alpha coefficients from .64 to .94 for the Behavior scales and from .89 to .96 for the Developmental Milestone scale. Total alpha coefficients for the EC-Teacher form ranged from .75 to .96 for the Behavior Scale and .91 to .96 for the Developmental Milestone scale. Specific reliability coefficients tended to be smaller for the younger age groups, particularly for ages 2 and 3. We urge assessment professionals to be aware of the generally lower reliabilities at younger age levels and to interpret results with caution.

Test-retest reliability was very strong, based on ratings from 72 parents and 68 teachers using a 2-to-4 week retest interval. Adjusted *r*'s range from .73 to .92 for the EC-P, and from .86 to 1.00 for the EC-T across the Behavior scale. For the Developmental Milestone scale, the adjusted *r*s ranged from .93 to .98 and from .88 to .97 for the EC Parent and Teacher forms, respectively. Conners provides a table of target values for a Reliable Change Index (RCI) based partly on these results. The RCI can be used to evaluate change following interventions.

Conners presents data for two types of standard error. SEM_1 refers to the variation from the true score that might be attributed to the individual (e.g., states of fatigue or lack of attention). SEM_2 refers to the variations expected due to random error. SEM_1 total results for *T*-scores based on the EC-P range from 2.00 to 5.97 across Behavior and Developmental Milestone scales; SEM_2 results range from 1.58 to 5.15. For the EC-T, SEM_1 total results range from 2.00 to 5.00; SEM_2 results range from 1.84 to 3.76. As in internal consistency, *SEM*s were often larger for lower age groups.

An interrater reliability study was carried out for the EC-P only, based upon a sample of 44 children. Resulting adjusted correlations range from .62 (Physical Symptoms) to .90 (Motor Skills) across the Behavior and Developmental Milestone scales.

Validity. Based on large derivative samples from the standardization group, Conners reports that exploratory analyses resulted in four-factor solutions across the Parent and Teacher report formats: Inattention/Hyperactivity, Social Functioning/Atypical Behaviors, Defiant/Aggressive Behaviors, and Anxiety. Rotated factors accounted for approximately 43% and 47% of the total variance for the EC-Parent and Teacher forms, respectively. Two subscales emerged for the Social Functioning/Atypical Behavior factor for both forms, labeled Social Functioning and Atypical Behaviors. Two subscales also emerged for the EC-P Defiant/Aggressive Behavior factor. Conners subsequently created corresponding subscales, labeled Defiance/Temper and Aggression, on the EC-T, to maintain consistency across the two reporting formats. Conners describes an adequate fit for the four-factor models on both the Parent and Teacher forms, meeting the minimum requirement of several fit indices.

Conners used Analyses of Covariance (ANCOVA) procedures to investigate whether scores discriminate between the general population and specific clinical groups (labeled Cognitive, Communication, Social/Emotional, Adaptive, Behavior, and ADHD). Conners gives a comprehensive description of the statistical procedures used in these analyses. Demographic information (i.e., gender, age, race/ethnicity, geographic region) for the general population and the clinical groups (including primary diagnostic distribution) is available in an appendix.

Conners examined the relevant scales for which differences would be expected between each target clinical group and the general sample, as well as between the target clinical group and other clinical groups (e.g., the ADHD group should score higher on the Inattention/Hyperactivity Scale). Results for all comparisons were supported with one exception: The Social/Emotional group compared to other clinical groups on the EC-P Mood and Affect Scale did not differ significantly. The mean rates for overall classification for the EC-P and EC-T were 86.52% and 86.45%, respectively. For some scales and subscales, particularly associated with social functioning and developmental milestones, the percentage of false positive and false negative classifications fell at or above 10% for some of the clinical groups. For instance, the false-negative rates for the Anxiety scale and the Mood and Affect scale were 17% and 31%, respectively, on the EC-T form, for the Social/Emotional target group.

Conners provides extensive details on convergent and divergent validity. On comparisons with the Behavior Assessment System for Children, Second Edition (Reynolds & Kamphaus, 2004), the Child Behavior Checklist/1 ½–5 (Achenbach & Rescorla, 2001), and the Caregiver-Teacher Report Form/1 ½–5 (Achenbach & Rescorla, 2001) correlations between rationally related scales and subscales were generally strong and supportive of construct validity. For example, the EC Inattention/Hyperactivity scale correlated with similar indexes across behavioral scales in a range from .66 to .93. Generally, across the scales, teacher reports obtained slightly higher correlations with each other than parent reports.

Conners compared the EC Developmental Milestone scale to the Vineland Adaptive Behavior Scales, Second Edition (Vineland-II; Sparrow, Cicchetti, & Balla, 2005; Sparrow, Cicchetti, & Balla, 2006). Resulting correlations for these comparisons were not generally as strong as comparisons between the EC and the Behavior scales discussed above. Among the lowest results was the correlation between the EC Adaptive Skills Scale and the Vineland-II Adaptive Behavior Composite, which fell at -.37, based on parent ratings. Results tended to be highest for the comparison between the EC-T Pre-Academic/Cognitive scale compared to the Vineland-II Academic subdomain (-.77) and the Vineland-II Expressive subdomain (-.78).

Conners also presents results of a comparison of the EC with the Behavior Rating Inventory of Executive Function Preschool Version (BRIEF-P; Gioia, Espy, & Isquith, 2003). It was not obvious to us that the correlation patterns gave a clear picture of convergent validity and divergent validity. We think the purported constructs from the two instruments differ too much to provide strong evidence of construct validity.

Finally, among validity investigations, Conners calculated Pearson *r*s between Parent and Teacher forms (N = 862) to provide an estimate of agreement between informants. Resulting correlations across the Behavior scales and Developmental Milestone scale ranged from .46 (Physical Symptoms) to .87 (Atypical Behaviors).

COMMENTARY. We asked several raters to fill out the EC forms provided with our examination kit. We found the EC to be relatively easy to administer and score. The resulting software reports were fairly comprehensive, presenting the results in several formats, including a circular graph and a traditionally oriented bar graph. We are not sure that the nontraditional circular graph is the best way to present the results. Some test users may be unfamiliar with this format.

We have not evaluated reliability and validity for the short forms for this instrument, nor did we have short forms in our examination kit to try out. We suggest potential users should read the relevant chapters in the manual or look towards other reviews for this evaluation.

SUMMARY. The Conners EC is a comprehensive scale that covers a wide range of behavioral, emotional, social, and developmental concerns for the preschool- or kindergarten-aged child. The Conners EC was easy and quick to administer and score. The manual presents comprehensive evidence for its reliability and validity. The only caveat we might offer is that reliability and validity tends to be higher for the upper age groups for this instrument; examiners of children from 2 to 3 years of age should be cautious in interpreting results for some of the subscales. The Conners EC is a welcome addition to the family of instruments authored by Conners (e.g., Conners 3rd Edition, Conners, 2008a; Conners Comprehensive Behavior Rating Scales, Conners, 2008b), allowing for the evaluation of younger children using similar constructs, but also providing information regarding important developmental milestones as well.

REVIEWERS' REFERENCES

Achenbach, T. M., & Rescorla, L. A. (2001). *Manual for the ASEBA School-Age Forms & Profiles.* Burlington, VT: University of Vermont, Research Center for Children, Youth and Families.

Conners, C. K. (2008a). *Conners 3rd Edition manual.* Toronto, Canada: Multi-Health Systems.

Conners, C. K. (2008b). *Conners Comprehensive Behavior Rating Scales manual.* Toronto, Canada: Multi-Health Systems.

Gioia, G. A., Espy, K. A., & Isquith, P. K. (2003). Behavior Rating Inventory of Executive Function–Preschool Version. Odessa, FL: Psychological Assessment Resources.

Reynolds, C. R., & Kamphaus, R. W. (2004). Behavior Assessment System for Children, Second Edition (BASC-2). Circle Pines, MN: AGS.

Sparrow, S. S., Cicchetti, D. V., & Balla, D. A. (2005). Vineland Adaptive Behavior Scales: Second Edition, Survey Interview Form/Caregiver Rating Form (Vineland II). Livonia, MN: Pearson Assessments.

Sparrow, S. S., Cicchetti, D. V., & Balla, D. A. (2006). Vineland Adaptive Behavior Scales: Second Edition, Teacher Rating Form (Vineland II-TRF). Livonia, MN: Pearson Assessments.

Review of the Conners Early Childhood by JEAN N. CLARK, Associate Professor of Educational Psychology, College of Education, University of South Alabama, Mobile, AL:

DESCRIPTION. The Conners Early Childhood (Conners EC) is an assessment instrument of behavioral difficulties and developmental milestones for children ages 2–6. It is a survey instrument that uses a 0–3 Likert-type annotated scale ("*never, occasionally, often, very frequently*"), completed by teachers or childcare workers and/or parents or caregivers. The Developmental Milestone questions use a 0–2 Likert-type annotated scale ("*no, sometimes, yes*"). Items in the Behavioral section reflect observations within the past 30 days, whereas developmental items reflect overall assessment. The instrument has six formats that can be assessed separately or in conjunction with one another. The full-scale Teacher/Childcare Provider form contains 186 items, of which 112 are behavioral items, 70 are developmental milestone, 2 impairment items, and 2 "additional" questions that are open-ended. The behavioral and developmental sections may be used and analyzed independently; thus each is considered a separate "stand-alone" instrument. There is a behavior short form, containing 48 of the 112 items from the full-length form. There is also an Early Childhood Global Index (ECGI) embedded in each behavioral form, which consists of items from the original (1989, 1990) Conners assessment instruments for children and teenagers. The administration time for the full-length form is 25 minutes; the two stand-alone forms require 15 and 10 minutes; and the behavioral quick form 10 minutes. The Parent/Guardian forms are very similar. The full Parent form contains 190 items (including items about sleep problems), the behavioral section contains 110 items (including the embedded Global Index), the developmental section contains 75 items; there are 3 impairment items, and 2 open-ended items. The behavior short form contains 49 of the 190 items on the full-length form.

DEVELOPMENT. The Conners EC was developed over a 5-year period, in three phases: research, pilot, and norming. Phase 1 included a review of IDEA and other legislation, research related to child development and pathology, and assessment tools currently available. There is no report that the current instrument is based on a single theory or paradigm.

Phase 2 was the pilot study, which included 155 parents/caregivers and 157 teachers/childcare providers (manual, p. 82). Participants with clinical diagnoses in seven categories were included, as well as general population participants. No description of region, facilities, or method of sampling was described in the manual. For the behavioral items, exploratory factor analysis with Maximum Likelihood Estimation and varimax rotation was conducted, and five categories of analysis were created: Inattention/Hyperactivity, Oppositional Behavior, Emotional Regulation/Defiance, Anxiety, and Social Functioning (manual, p. 82). Items for the Developmental Milestones scales were reviewed, but no statistical analyses were offered. The Developmental Scale contained subscale "age of attainment" in Adaptive Skills, Communication, Motor Skills, Play, and Pre-Academic/Cognitive skills. One-item indicators for six clinical indicators were designed, but with no reported statistical analyses (several other one-item categories were added later). Finally, Phase 3 was the normative stage.

TECHNICAL.

Standardization. The norming sample consisted of 800 parents and 800 teachers/childcare providers (manual, p. 84). For the Parent form, data were drawn from 1,315 children from the general population and 340 from clinical samples (manual, p. 227). For the Teacher/Childcare Provider form, the sample was drawn from 1,252 children from the general population and 374 from clinical samples. Sampling for both Parent and Teacher/Childcare Provider forms were aligned with the general U.S. population stratified by age, gender, and race/ethnicity. A total of 204 items (128 behavioral, 76 developmental milestone) were retained for the Parent form. For the Teacher/Childcare Provider form, 197 items (126 behavioral, 71 developmental milestone) were retained. Using subscale data outcomes as guidelines, the five categories found on the final form for both teachers and parents (see above) evolved. From the same analyses the items that comprised the Positive Impressions Scale, the Negative Impressions Scale, and the Inconsistency Index Scales (all measures of validity on the instruments) were formed. For these scales, a preselected 97.5 percentile cutoff was chosen; then a table of raw scores was developed for category cutoffs, with scores at or above 97.5 percentile suggesting "indication." The items for the ECGI were adopted based on former research and review. Finally, the Spanish versions of the Conners EC were developed with the assistance of Spanish-speaking experts in psychology and counseling.

Normative data are provided in the manual, with separate and combined analyses by gender, age, race/ethnicity (Asian, African American, Hispanic, Caucasian, and Other), and geographic region. These data were supplied for the ECGI, the full-scale and short form Behavioral Scale, the Developmental Milestones Scale (using 85th percentile cutoff scores for "age of attainment" in Adaptive, Communication, Play, Motor, and Pre-Academic/Cognitive Skills), the validity scales of Positive Impression, Negative Impression, and Inconsistency Index. Also given were analyses of the duration and familiarity of teachers with the children in the sample.

Reliability. Using alpha coefficients to address internal consistency, the Parent form ranged from .64 (Sleep Problems) to .96 (Pre-Academic/Cognitve skills); statistics on the Teacher form ranged from .75 (Physical Symptoms) to .96 (Inattention/Hyperactivity, Social Functioning/Atypical Behaviors, and Pre-Academic/Cognitive). Test-retest coefficients ranged from .73 (Sleep Problems, Parent form) to 1.00 (Social Functioning/Atypical Behavior, Teacher form), over an interval ranging from 2 to 4 weeks. Standard errors of measurement were typically higher for younger children (2.65 to 7.61 for 2-year-olds), but lower for older children (1.41–7.05 for 6-year-olds) on both Parent and Teacher forms. Interrater reliability coefficients ranged from .62 (Physical Symptoms) to .90 (Motor Skills). All three measures of reliability were strong indicators of consistency.

Validity. Discriminative validity analyses were conducted by a series of ANCOVAs, with large effect sizes (mean effect sizes were 34.1% on the Parent form and 30.4% on the Teacher form). Convergent and divergent validity were assessed by comparing the Conners EC with two or more forms of four other stable instruments: the Behavior Assessment System for Children, Second Edition (BASC-2; Reynolds & Kamphaus, 2004); the Behavior Rating Inventory of Executive Function–Preschool Version (BRIEF-P; Gioia, Espy, & Isquith, 2003); the Achenbach System of Empirically Based Assessment (ASEBA-C TRF; Achenbach & Rescarla, 2001); and the Vineland Adaptive Bahavior Scales, Second Edition (Vineland II; Sparrow, Cicchetti, & Balla, 2005). Correlations ranged from -.78 (Vineland Expressive, Teacher's form) to .92 (BASC-2 TRS-P Negative Emotionality). Exploratory and Confirmatory factor analyses reflected the initial grouping of factors for all behavioral subscales (Inattention/Hyperactivity, Social Functioning/Atypical Behaviors, Defiant/Aggressive Behaviors, and Anxiety). Finally, informant correlations (teacher-parent) were high for each subscale. Similarly, analyses for the stand-alone versions of the behavioral, developmental, and behavioral short forms were consistently acceptable for each subscale, across gender and race/ethnicity. No analyses were offered for the one-item clinical indicators.

COMMENTARY. The test authors demonstrate a successful attempt at developing a comprehensive and useful screening instrument for potential problems in children ages 2–6. Both the computer software and the paper copies of the forms were clear and user-friendly, with short items based on a fifth grade reading level. The instructions for instrument completion, hand-scoring, and interpretation are clear. Online access and report generation are cutting edge. The analyses are detailed and presented in a logical manner. In all facets addressed, the instrument, outcomes, and analytical procedures are true to the descriptions offered by the test developers.

There are four points of concern, some of which may be considered limitations. First, because the instrument serves mainly as a screening device for problem areas, most of the behavioral items are worded negatively. A parent or caregiver may perceive the negative wording as threatening or uncomfortable, and may respond in a manner that attempts to neutralize the perceived threat. On the other hand, the Developmental Milestones items are worded in positive terms, but are revers-scored, so that high scale scores connote higher levels of concern, as is true for the remaining Conners EC scales. Thus, high scores on the Developmental Milestones scale do not reflect "normal" development, but rather abnormal development, which some test users may find confusing given the scale name. Second, there are six items on the validity scale called "Positive Impression," but the items are worded in the form of absolutes ("Behaves like an angel"; "Is perfect in every way"); this may render the scale itself ("*never, seldom*" "*occasionally,*" "*often, quite a bit,*" "*very often, very frequently*") suspect. Third, the items comprising the "Other Clinical Indicators" each represent one category of potential clinical concern. As the test author notes in several places, these items are to be used as part of a system of assessment, in conjunction with other tools and methods as appropriate. Thus, the term "indicators" is an appropriate label for this list of potential clinical problems and test users should not construe these items as single-item scales. Finally, there are two open-ended items at the end of four of the six forms, but no mention of qualitative or other analyses among pilot or norming participants. Although these limitations need attention, they would not deter from use of the instrument when used as instructed.

SUMMARY. Keith Conners brings over 40 years of experience to the development of this instrument. Renowned for his development of the Conners Rating Scales (1989, 1990), he brings his experience and knowledge of child development, assessment and diagnosis of maladaptive behavior, and expertise in instrument development to the important area of early childhood assessment, diagnosis, and intervention. As a screening device for potential problems or challenges among preschool children, it is a user-friendly, well-tested, and documented instrument. The instrument, with corollary instructions for administration, intervention, and application, is aligned with both IDEA standards and World Health guidelines. With online access, and administration and scoring available by either computer or hand, the instrument can be used in a variety of settings and applications.

REVIEWER'S REFERENCES

Achenbach, T. M., & Rescorla, L. A. (2001). *Manual for the ASEBA School-Age Forms & Profiles*. Burlington, VT: University of Vermont, Research Center for Children, Youth and Families.

Conners, C. K. (1989, 1990). *Conner's Rating Scales technical manual*. Toronto, Canada: Multi-health Systems.

Gioia, G. A., Espy, K. A., & Isquith, P. K. (2003). Behavior Rating Inventory of Executive Function-Preschool Version. Odessa, FL: Psychological Assessment Resources.

Reynolds, C. R., & Kamphaus, R. W. (2004). Behavior Assessment System for Children, Second Edition (BASC–2). Circle Pines, MN: AGS.

Sparrow, S. S., Cicchetti, D. V., & Balla, P. A. (2005). Vineland Adaptive Behavior Scales: Second Edition, Survey Interview Form/Caregiver Rating Form (Vineland II). Livonia, MN: Pearson Assessments.

[35]

Conners 3rd Edition.

Purpose: Designed to be an assessment of "Attention-Deficit/Hyperactivity Disorder (ADHD) and its most common comorbid problems and disorders in children and adolescents."

Publication Dates: 1989-2008.

Acronym: Conners 3.

Administration: Individual or group.

Forms, 11: Conners 3–Parent Full, Conners 3–Parent Short, Conners 3–Teacher Full, Conners 3–Teacher Short, Conners 3–Self-Report Full, Conners 3–Self-Report Short, Conners 3 ADHD Index–Teacher, Conners 3 ADHD Index–Parent, Conners 3 ADHD Index–Self-Report, Conners 3 Global Index–Teacher, Conners 3 Global Index–Parent.

Price Data, 2009: $296 per Handscore kit including manual (2008, 470 pages), 25 parent/teacher/self-report QuikScore™ forms, and 25 parent/teacher/self-report short QuikScore™ forms.

Foreign Language Edition: Spanish versions available for Parent and Self-Report forms.

Time: (20) minutes for full length form; (10) minutes for short forms.

Comments: All forms are available in QuikScore™ format; can also be completed and scored online; paper-and-pencil forms can also be scored online; can also be scored using the scoring software program by entering responses from a completed pencil-and-paper administration but cannot be administered through the software.

Author: C. Keith Conners.

Publisher: Multi-Health Systems, Inc.

a) CONNERS 3-PARENT.

Population: Ages 6–18.

Scores, 20: Inattention, Hyperactivity/Impulsivity, Learning Problems, Executive Functioning, Aggression, Peer Relations, DSM-IV-TR ADHD Hyperactive-Impulsive, DSM-IV-TR ADHD Inattentive, DSM-IV-TR ADHD Combined, DSM-IV-TR Conduct Disorder, DSM-IV-TR Oppositional Defiant Disorder, Positive Impression, Negative Impression, Inconsistency Index, Anxiety, Depression, Schoolwork/Grades, Friendships/Relationships, Home Life, Severe Conduct.

Forms, 4: Full, Short, ADHD Index, Global Index.

b) CONNERS 3-TEACHER.

Population: Ages 6–18.

Scores, 20: Inattention, Hyperactivity/Impulsivity, Learning Problems, Executive Functioning, Learning Problems/Executive Functioning, Aggression, Peer Relations, DSM-IV-TR ADHD Hyperactive-Impulsive, DSM-IV-TR ADHD Inattentive, DSM-IV-TR ADHD Combined, DSM-IV-TR Conduct Disorder, DSM-IV-TR Oppositional Defiant Disorder, Positive Impression, Negative Impression, Inconsistency Index, Anxiety, Depression, Schoolwork/Grades, Friendships/Relationships, Severe Conduct.

Forms, 4: Full, Short, ADHD Index, Global Index.

c) CONNERS 3-SELF-REPORT.

Population: Ages 8–18.

Scores, 19: Inattention, Hyperactivity/Impulsivity, Learning Problems, Aggression, Family Relations, DSM-IV-TR ADHD Hyperactive/Impulsive, DSM-IV-TR ADHD Inattentive, DSM-IV-TR ADHD Combined, DSM-IV-TR Conduct Disorder, DSM-IV-TR Oppositional Defiant Disorder, Positive Impression, Negative Impression, Inconsistency Index, Anxiety, Depression, Schoolwork/Grades, Friendships/Relationships, Home Life, Severe Conduct.

Forms, 3: Full, Short, ADHD Index.

Cross References: For reviews by Allen K. Hess and Howard M. Knoff of an earlier edition, see 14:98; see also T5:681 (99 references) and T4:636 (50 references); for reviews by Brian K. Martens and Judy Oehler-Stinnett of the original edition, see 11:87 (83 references).

Review of the Conners 3rd Edition by SHARON ARFFA, Chief of Neuropsychology, The Watson Institute, Sewickley, PA:

DESCRIPTION. The Conners 3rd Edition (Conners 3) rating scales "is a multi-informant assessment of children and adolescents between 6 and 18 years of age" (manual, p. 1). It is a revision of the Conners Rating Scales–Revised (Conners, 1997). The purpose of the Conners 3 is to serve as a thorough and focused assessment of Attention Deficit Hyperactivity Disorders (ADHD) and comorbid conditions of childhood. In addition to supporting diagnoses, the Conners 3 can be used for making decisions about eligibility for special education, to plan and monitor treatment interventions, for research purposes, and for screening purposes. Informants include parents and teachers, as well as a Self-Report form appropriate for children ages 8 to 18. The Parent forms include a full version, a short version, and a version containing the ADHD Index and a Global Index. The Teacher forms include a full version, a short version, and a version containing the ADHD Index and a Global Index. The Self-Report forms include a full version, a short version, and a version containing the ADHD Index. Informants answer questions on a scale from 0 (*Never or Seldom*) to 3 (*Very true or very frequently*). The number of questions vary from 110 (Parent), 115 (Teacher), and 99 (Self-Report) in the full version, to 45 (Parent), and 41 (Teacher and Self-Report) in the short version, to 10 items in the remaining ADHD and Global Index versions.

Reading level required for completion is between third and fifth grade for Self-Report forms and between Grades 4 and 5 for the Teacher and Parent forms. The two administration options include paper-and-pencil administration or online via the internet. The Conners 3 is appropriate for individual or group administration. Parents, teachers, and youth can complete the relevant form with the Conners 3 online program that is accessible from computers with internet access that meet online requirements. Conners 3 forms can be hand scored, scored online via the internet, or through the Conners 3 Software program. During hand scoring, raw scores are automatically transferred from the QuikScore form to a scoring grid. The values in each column are summed and this number is recorded onto a profile form, which contains *T*-scores for the relevant gender and age.

The test author notes that paraprofessionals can calculate raw and *T*-scores although a qualified assessor must be available to oversee accuracy of scoring and interpretation. The test author notes potential Conners 3 users include psychologists, clinical social workers, physicians, psychiatric workers, and pediatric nurses, but all prospective users should have completed graduate level courses in tests and measurement. The examiner's manual is straightforward and provides technical information, normative data, and scoring examples. The Conners 3 scales are meant to focus on ADHD assessment and are not intended to provide a comprehensive evaluation of emotional function. The Conners Comprehensive Behavior Rating Scales (18:33) were developed concurrently with the Conners 3 to serve as a wide range instrument for assessment of emotional, behavioral, social, and academic function.

DEVELOPMENT. The Conners 3 development began with a planning stage where new legislative developments, existing assessment tools, and theory of psychopathology were reviewed. Information was also gathered from focus groups of academicians and practitioners to establish the rationale and structure of the revision of the Conners Rating Scale—Revised. The primary rationale of the Conners 3 was to serve as an in-depth ADHD tool, which would integrate research with clinical opinion, use the most recent diagnostic information, update normative data, and create links to intervention strategies. The test author focused on ADHD in school-aged children and created alternative instruments to address broad range problems in school-aged children and ADHD in young children ages 2 to 6 years (Conners Comprehensive Behavior Rating Scales and Conners Early Childhood Rating Scales). Although the Conners 3 focuses upon ADHD, common co-morbid behavioral disorders (Oppositional Defiant Disorder, Conduct Disorder) are also assessed and a screening is included for internalizing symptoms.

Pilot data were collected from the general population and from a clinical population, and exploratory factor analyses were used to confirm structure of the instrument and to guide item selection. Key content areas selected included Inattention, Hyperactivity, Impulsivity, Learning Problems, Executive Functioning, Conduct Problems, Oppositional Behavior, and Social Problems. The Empirical scales were developed through use of exploratory and confirmatory factor analyses. DSM-IV-TR relevant content included ADHD, Conduct Disorder (CD), and Oppositional Defiant Disorder (ODD) scales. An attempt was made to adopt user-friendly language in the assessment of DSM-IV-TR symptoms and disorders. Because the DSM-IV-TR specifies significant impairment for classification with a disorder, impairment items were added to aid in determining this criteria. The CD and ODD scales replace the Anger Control problems of the previous version. The Executive function measure, anxiety and depression screener items, and the three validity scales (Positive Impression, Negative Impression and the Inconsistency Index) are new additions. The Positive Impression Scale and the Negative Impression Scale reflect extremely positive or extremely negative behaviors that are unlikely to be true most of the time. The Inconsistency Scale was developed by taking 10 pairs with the highest intercorrelations, calculating the difference of the absolute values, and considering scores at or above the 95th percentile on this measure to be probably invalid.

The final version was developed and norms were obtained. Short forms were derived from the full-form data. The short forms do not contain DSM-IV-TR symptom scales, the Inconsistency Index, internalizing screener items, index scales, Severe Conduct Critical items, or Impairment items.

TECHNICAL. The standardization sample for the Conners 3 consisted of 50 males and 50 females in each age group (6-18 years for Teacher and Parent forms and 8-18 years for Self-Report forms) from the general population with an ethnic and racial distribution closely matching 2000 U.S. Census data. The test author drew from various geographic regions and various parental educational levels. Normative data are reported separately by age (each year 6 to 18) and gender. Many of the Conners 3 scales are significantly related to gender, with higher ratings for males, although overall gender accounts for only .6% to 2.9% of the variance on Parent forms and up to 6.6% on Teacher forms.

An additional clinical population of 731 youth with various diagnoses was sampled. Each member of the clinical sample had a primary diagnosis given by a physician, psychologist, or speech pathologist (for language disorders). When possible, a single youth received multiple assessments (such as both parents, multiple teachers), although responses from only one parent or teacher were included in the normative data. Linear *T*-scores and empirical percentiles were used, as the test author did not assume ADHD psychopathology fell along a normal curve. The Conners 3 was co-normed with the Conners Comprehensive Behavior Rating Scales (18:33).

Reliability measures are quite satisfactory. Internal consistency coefficients are .90 or above for Parent and Teacher scales and .85 or above for Self-Report scales. Both test-retest and interrater reliability were appropriately corrected for restriction of range (because there was low variability in the scores). Adjusted test-retest reliability ranges from .82 to .98 for Parent scales except for Executive Functioning (.72) and Peer/Family Relations (.78), from .83 to .90 for Teacher scales except for Executive Functioning (.78), and from .71 to .83 for the Self-Report scale. A Reliable Change Index is available in Tables 11.13 to 11.15, which takes into account the difference in test scores between the two administrations and the Standard Error of Difference.

Validity data include the ability to discriminate between relevant clinical criterion groups. Overall, the Conners 3 can accurately distinguish clinical groups from the general population as well as discriminate between clinical groups of ADHD subtypes, other disruptive behavioral disorders, and learning disorders. Construct validity was established through scale structure validity using first exploratory and then confirmatory factor analyses. A five-factor solution suited the Conners 3 Parent form (Learning Problems, Aggression, Hyperactivity/Impulsivity, Peer Relations, Executive Functioning), a four-factor solution suited the Conners 3 Teacher form (Learning Problems, Aggression, Hyperactivity/Impulsivity, Peer Relations) and a four-factor solution suited the Conners 3 Self-Report form (Learning Problems, Aggression, Hyperactivity/Impulsivity, Family Relations). A moderate level of construct validity was also established by comparing across informants. The mean parent to teacher correlation was .60, the mean parent to youth correlation was .56, and the mean teacher to youth correlation was .48. The convergent and validity calculations included correlations with the earlier Conners version (Conners, 1997), the Behavior Assessment System for Children, 2nd Edition (Reynolds & Kamphaus, 2004) the Achenbach System of Empirically Based Assessment, (Achenbach, 1991), and the Behavioral Rating Inventory of Executive Functioning (Gioia, Isquith, Guy, & Kenworthy, 2000). Overall, there was reasonable evidence of convergent validity.

COMMENTARY. The Conners 3 is a very well-designed, brief instrument with good technical characteristics. It has many advantages over the Conners Rating Scales—Revised (Conners, 1997), but like the Conners Rating Scales—Revised, promises to provide an excellent assessment of ADHD and common co-morbid conditions. Among the advantages is the addition of validity scales to assess responder response bias. The

Conners 3 provides additional information that can be used for making decisions about eligibility for special education, to plan and monitor treatment interventions (including reliable change indices), for research purposes, and for screening purposes. There are several scoring options with a user-friendly online scoring option, a software program contained on a handy zip drive, or the easy QuikScore version. There are several choices of versions, which offer different choices in length of administration and scales yielded. With three informants and two to three options among informants, this makes for 11 different forms. Coupled with the Conners Comprehensive Behavior Rating Scales, which was developed at the same time, the choice of Conners instruments is exceptionally large. This can be troublesome for the clinician who may have to sort through this maze of options, and perhaps develop a decision tree, in order to use the correct form for the correct clinical question.

SUMMARY. The Conners 3 is a well-designed instrument with excellent technical properties that promises to be instrumental in the evaluation, diagnosis, and treatment response of children with ADHD and co-morbid disorders. It has many advantages over its predecessor, yet maintains many of the solid characteristics of the older form. Reliability data are excellent and validity data are substantial, although interinformant ratings are modest. It is highly recommended for clinical use.

REVIEWER'S REFERENCES

Achenbach, T. M. (1991). *Manual for the Child Behavioral Checklist/4-18 and 1991 profile.* Burlington, VT: University of Vermont, Department of Psychiatry.

Conners, C. K. (1997). *Conners' Rating Scales—Revised Technical Manual.* Toronto, Ontario, Canada: Multi-Health Systems.

Gioia, G. A., Isquith, P. K., Guy, S. C., & Kenworthy, L. (2000). Behavior Rating Inventory of Executive Function (BRIEF). Lutz, FL: Psychological Assessment Resources.

Reynolds, C. R., & Kamphaus, R. W. (2004). Behavior Assessment System for Children, Second Edition (BASC-2). Circle Pines, MN: AGS Publishing.

Review of the Conners 3rd Edition by THOMAS M. DUNN, Associate Professor of Psychological Sciences, University of Northern Colorado, Greeley, CO:

DESCRIPTION. The Conners 3rd Edition (Conners 3) is an instrument designed to assess ADHD and other disruptive behavior in children and adolescents. It is the latest update to the venerable Conners' Rating Scales (CRS). Initially introduced in 1989, the CRS became a valuable tool to the clinician concerned about a child who may be suffering from ADHD. The foundation of the CRS was rating scales completed by parents, teachers, and (in most cases) the child to provide multiple sources of information for the completion of an assessment. The Conners 3 continues this tradition with updated norms and item development, consideration of co-morbid conditions, and a number of different forms to aid the clinician in assessment and treatment. Children ages 6 to 18 years of age can be rated by teachers and parents; those youths 8 to 18 years of age can also rate themselves.

There are four different forms of the Conners 3, the full version (the "Conners 3"), an abbreviated format (the "Conners 3 Short"), and two screening forms (the "Conners 3 ADHD Index" and the "Conners 3 Global Index"). All forms of the instrument consist of inventories of face valid questions that are completed by parents, teachers, and by the child if 8 years of age or older. The questions are scored from 0 (*not at all true/seldom/never*) to 3 (*very much true/very often/very frequently*). Scoring the full version reportedly takes 5 minutes of data entry if using the scoring program, whereas hand scoring the instrument takes 20 minutes. A USB flash drive is used to load scoring software (and must be attached to the computer while using the program). There is also reportedly a web-based scoring option. A voluminous 470-page technical manual accompanies the test.

The full length version of the Conners 3 consists of about 100 questions in each inventory and is reported to take approximately 20 minutes to complete. Scores derived from the full version are plotted onto various combinations of six content scales: Inattention, Hyperactivity/Impulsivity, Learning Problems, Executive Functioning, Aggression, and Peer/Family Relations. Scored responses are also loaded onto DSM-IV-TR symptom scales for Inattentive type ADHD, Hyperactive-Impulsive type ADHD, Conduct Disorder, and Oppositional Defiant Disorder. There are three validity scales with the Conners 3: Positive Impression, Negative Impression, and Inconsistency Index. Finally, the full version of the Conners 3 also has critical items for severe conduct and items suggesting impairment, as well as screener items for depression and anxiety.

The Conners 3 Short form, also known as the Conners 3(S), consists of inventories of about 40 questions and reportedly takes 10 minutes to administer with hand scoring or with data entry for computer scoring taking 10 minutes or less.

The Conners 3(S) gives scores across all of the six content scales mentioned previously, as well as scores on the Positive and Negative Impression validity scales.

Both of the screening formats of the Conners 3 reportedly take less than 5 minutes to both administer and to score. The Conners 3 ADHD Index (Conners 3AI) consists of 10 items in each questionnaire and comprises the 10 questions most likely to identify a child with ADHD. The other screener, the Conners 3 Global Index (Conners 3 GI) does not contain a child self-report inventory, and is used to quickly screen for psychopathology. It is also useful in treatment monitoring when the same rater is making repeated observations of the child across time.

User qualifications to administer and score the instrument, provided individuals carefully follow the manual, are modest. Interpreting the Conners 3 is left to professionals with graduate training in tests and measurement and who follow best practices in the ethical use of psychological and educational tests. Raw scores from the inventories are converted into *T* scores. Validity scales are considered and scaled scores of content areas are plotted onto graphs. Symptom scales matching DSM-IV-TR qualifiers are also plotted using *T* scores as well as "symptom counts" to help establish whether the patient meets diagnostic criteria.

DEVELOPMENT. The Conners 3 is the second revision of the CRS (copyright 2008). The original instrument was developed in 1989 with the first revision, known as the Conners Rating Scales–Revised (CRS-R), released in 1997. Obviously, development of this latest edition has built on the first two instruments, and is nearly 50 years in the making, with the original checklists first used by the test author in clinical practice in the 1960s. This update reportedly began with a comprehensive review of clinical and legislative standards of ADHD, as well as focus groups consisting of clinicians, academics, and educators. Special attention was paid to the federal Individuals with Disabilities Education Act (IDEA 2004), and to common diagnostic criteria when establishing whether a child meets educational disability requirements. These efforts resulted in a large item pool that was pilot tested in both general and clinical populations. Exploratory factor analysis drove item selection and scale construction. Experts were asked to comment upon the pilot items. Factor analysis helped construct empirical scales during normative testing.

The resulting scales on the Conners 3 are well conceptualized and thoughtfully cover the complicated symptom presentation for ADHD. The full version gives the clinician an impressive array of diagnostic data, including how the child's symptoms match up to both DSM and ICD-10 criteria and whether the symptoms impair functioning. Validity indices enhance the Conners 3 interpretation and allow test givers to consider whether a rater biased his or her responding on a questionnaire.

TECHNICAL. The normative process for the Conners 3 culminated with an impressive 3,400 individuals in the normative sample. Nearly 7,000 rating forms were completed. Over 100 different sites in North America provided data from a general population group that was meant to parallel the 2000 U.S. Census distribution of gender, ethnicity, and geographical region. More than 800 individuals from a clinical population were also included. There are separate norms for boys and girls.

Alpha coefficients indicate excellent internal consistency (.90 and above) for both the Parent and Teacher forms across both Content and DSM-IV-TR Symptom scales. The self-report form on the Conners 3 also shows very good internal consistency with alpha coefficients of .88 on the Content scales and .85 on the Symptom scales. Test-retest reliability is acceptable and was based on a smaller sample of parents, teachers, and youth over a 2- and 4-week interval. Temporal stability was highest for parent ratings on Content scales (generally .88 or above) and lowest for self-report ratings on all of the scales (ranging from .71 to .83). Finally, correlations across informants (parent, teacher, and child) showed good interrater reliability.

The Conners 3 manual is chock full (47 pages) of validity data that are difficult to distill down to a paragraph or two for this review. In brief, there is strong evidence presented that the instrument has adequate factorial validity with confirmatory factor analysis showing good fit. Convergent validity was demonstrated with significant *rs* using three other instruments: the Behavior Assessment System for Children, 2nd Edition (BASC-2), the Achenbach System of Empirically Based Assessment (ASEBA), and the

Behavior Rating Inventory of Executive Functions (BRIEF). Discriminant validity is high with good sensitivity and specificity, adequate positive-predictive power, and an acceptable classification rate.

COMMENTARY. The Conners 3 is a welcome revision of the CRS-R, an invaluable tool in the assessment of ADHD. The revised instrument contains a normative group of 3,400 individuals and demonstrates strong psychometric properties. The manual is well written and user friendly. The full version of the Conners 3 offers a wealth of data in easy-to-interpret *T* scores on scales that are clinically relevant. The scales concerning Conduct Disorder and Oppositional Defiant Disorder are an excellent addition to this instrument, as many children with disruptive behaviors are often first conceptualized as having the impulsive/hyperactive type of ADHD. Similarly, scales for anxiety and depression may help attribute behavior that is initially thought to be only inattention, but is instead a symptom of a mood or anxiety disorder. The Conners 3(S) seems unnecessary, as the full version takes only 10 minutes longer to complete and yields quite a bit more data. The computer program makes scoring very straightforward and provides a wealth of data making interpretation easy. (Scoring by hand would be a chore, however.) The data afforded from the Conners 3 are especially helpful in the educational setting, with an eye towards helping the provider in determining whether a child meets disability criteria, providing aids in intervention for such youths and help with the formulation of an Individualized Educational Program.

SUMMARY. The Conners 3 is a revision to the 1997 CRS-R, a mainstay in the evaluation of ADHD. The new edition is an effective tool in the evaluation of disruptive behavior in children and adolescents, particularly when assessing for ADHD. It is psychometrically sound, provides clinically relevant data, and will prove to be a leading instrument in both clinical and research settings pertaining to ADHD.

[36]

CPI 260.

Purpose: "The goal of the inventory is to give a true-to-life description of the respondent, in clear, everyday language, in formats that can help the client to achieve a better understanding of self."
Population: Ages 13 and up.
Publication Dates: 2003-2005.
Acronym: CPI 260.
Administration: Group.
Scores, 29: Dominance, Capacity for Status, Sociability, Social Presence, Self-Acceptance, Independence, Empathy, Responsibility, Social Conformity, Self-Control, Good Impression, Communality, Well-Being, Tolerance, Achievement via Conformance, Achievement via Independence, Conceptual Fluency, Insightfulness, Flexibility, Sensitivity, Managerial Potential, Work Orientation, Creative Temperament, Leadership, Amicability, Law Enforcement Orientation, Orientation Toward Others, Orientation Toward Societal Values, Orientation Toward Self.
Price Data, 2009: $21.85 per client feedback report administration; $55.95 per client feedback report and coaching report for leaders administration; $39.50 per client feedback report guide for interpretation (2005, 88 pages); $37.85 per coaching report for leaders administration; $49.50 per coaching report for leaders advanced guide for interpretation (2006, 81 pages); $39.50 per coaching report for leaders user's guide (2005, 42 pages); $89.50 per technical manual (2005, 85 pages); $228.50 per 10 prepaid client feedback report combined item booklet/answer sheets; $194.25 per 5 prepaid coaching reports for leaders combined item booklet/answer sheets.
Time: (25-30) minutes.
Comments: Abbreviated version derived from the California Psychological Inventory (T7:385).
Authors: Harrison G. Gough and Pamela Bradley; Sam Manoogian (Coaching Report for Leaders); Robert J. Devine (Client Feedback Report).
Publisher: CPP, Inc.

Review of the CPI 260 by GARY J. DEAN, Professor and Department Chairperson, Department of Adult and Community Education, Indiana University of Pennsylvania, Indiana, PA:

DESCRIPTION. The CPI 260 is a self-report personality inventory that seeks "to give a true-to-life description of the respondent, in clear, everyday language, in formats that can help the client to achieve a better understanding of self" (manual, p. 1). The CPI 260 was introduced in 2002 in response to requests from businesses and organizations for a shorter, more user-friendly version of the CPI 434, on which the CPI 260 is based. The instrument was shortened to provide a more convenient measure and is oriented toward use in human resources and organizations. The reviewer was supplied with copies of the Client Feedback Form (the 260-item inventory), the CPI 260 manual, and three publications oriented toward using the CPI 260 with leadership development (the CPI 260 Client Feedback Report Guide for Interpretation: Strategies for Use in Business and Organizations, the CPI 260 Coaching Report for Leaders: User's Guide, and the CPI 260 Coaching Report for Leaders Advanced Guide for Interpretation).

The CPI 260 is a forced-choice, self-report inventory in which respondents must agree or disagree with 260 self-descriptive statements. The instrument results in 29 scale scores. Twenty-six of the scales are grouped into five categories and three are higher order measures. The first category is Dealing With Others, which consists of Dominance, Capacity for Status, Sociability, Social Presence, Self-Acceptance, Independence, and Empathy. The second category is Self-Management, consisting of Responsibility, Social Conformity, Self-Control, Good Impression, Communality, Well-Being, and Tolerance. The third category is Motivations and Thinking Style and is made up of Achievement via Conformance, Achievement via Independence, and Conceptual Fluency. The fourth category is Personal Characteristics and includes three scales: Insightfulness, Flexibility, and Sensitivity. Work-Related Measures is the last category and is composed of Managerial Potential, Work Orientation, Creative Temperament, Leadership, Amicability, and Law Enforcement Orientation. The three higher order measures are Orientation Toward Others, Orientation Toward Societal Values, and Orientation Toward Self. These higher order measures, or vectors, result in identifying four lifestyles: Implementers, Supporters, Innovators, and Visualizers. Scale scores of the CPI 260 have a mean of 50 and standard deviation of 10.

Twenty-one of the 26 content scales of the CPI 260 were combined to create 18 measures of leadership characteristics, which were then combined to comprise five "core performance areas" (Advanced Guide for Interpretation, p. 5) of leadership: Self-Management, Organizational Capabilities, Team Building and Teamwork, Problem Solving, and Sustaining the Vision. The leadership characteristics are each composed of two CPI scales, based on conceptual, not empirical, linkages between the CPI 260 scales and the leadership characteristics. Several of the CPI scales are used multiple times in the derivation of the 18 leadership characteristics.

Based on the three publications oriented toward leadership applications, it appears that the CPI 260 was designed to be used primarily to assess leadership potential. The CPI 260 Coaching Report for Leaders: User's Guide contains two sections, one on understanding the report and one on administering the CPI 260 and interpreting the report. This is a practical guide that contains a bare minimum of technical data and is clearly intended to be an introductory work on the instrument. The CPI 260 Client Feedback Report Guide for Interpretation: Strategies for Use in Business and Organizations is a thorough, nontechnical description of the CPI 260, the scales, the report, and applications of the instrument, whereas the CPI 260 Coaching Report for Leaders Advanced Guide for Interpretation is application oriented, having its basis in understanding and using the CPI 260 in a business or organization to identify, assess, and help develop leadership potential.

DEVELOPMENT. All versions of the CPI instruments are based on folk concepts of personality. Folk concepts are described as "a construct about personality that all people, everywhere, make use of to comprehend their own behavior and that of others" (manual, p. 2). The 29 scales of the CPI 260 were derived from the CPI 434 and are virtually the same. The names of four of the scales from the CPI 434 were changed for clarity in the CPI 260: Socialization to Social Conformity, Intellectual Efficiency to Conceptual Fluency, Psychological-Mindedness to Insightfulness, and Femininity/Masculinity to Sensitivity. These changes were made to make the scales more understandable in a business setting.

TECHNICAL.

Norm sample. Norms for the CPI 260 were drawn from four sources: the norm sample reported in the 1996/2002 CPI manual (N = 6,000); a nationwide survey conducted in the U.K. with the CPI 434 in 1998 (N = 2,001); a sample from France (N = 1,424) collected with the CPI 480; and a sample from Italy (N = 1,362) also collected using the CPI 480. The international makeup of the samples reveals some variation by nationality, but overall substantiates that the 29 scales measured by the CPI 260 transcend national boundaries.

Validity. The primary method of validating the scales of the CPI 260 was to run correlations between the CPI 260 scales and the corresponding scales from the CPI 434. Two sets of correlations were used to select items for the CPI 260: external, nontest criteria and correlations with the total score on the CPI 434. The correlations with external, nontest criteria are not described in the

CPI 260 manual. The correlations with the CPI 434 are shown for three different samples: a U.S. sample (N = 6,000), a U.K. sample (N = 2,001), and another sample from the U.S. referred to as the consulting sample (N = 6,000). All items in the CPI 260 were derived from the CPI 434, with the exception of two scales, Communality and Sensitivity. In these cases, items were borrowed from the pool of items used to develop the CPI 434 to bolster the correlations. Medians of the correlations between the CPI 260 scales and the CPI 434 scales range from a low of .81 (Communality) to a high of .97 (Sociability, Self-Control, Achievement via Conformance, and Managerial Potential) for the U.S. sample. Correlations from the U.K. sample and the consulting sample are similar to those of the U.S. sample.

Reliability. Reliability was established using internal consistency estimates (alpha coefficients) from the U.S. sample, the U.K. sample, and the consulting sample. For the U.S. sample, these range from a low of .36 for Law Enforcement Orientation to a high of .86 for Dominance. Correlations from the other two samples are similar to those of the U.S. sample.

COMMENTARY. The CPI 260 is derived from a long line of research and personality instruments. The basis of the CPI scales in folk concepts has been well established. The documentation provided with the instrument is very thorough and detailed, well organized, and conceptually easy to understand with the following two exceptions. First, the information contained in the CPI 260 manual regarding the norm groups and underlying validity of the scales is somewhat sketchy and confusing. No explanation of the external criteria used to validate the scales is provided; the fact that such external criteria exists is mentioned without further reference or explanation. Second, the presentation of the information regarding the norm groups was somewhat confusing, especially with regard to the consulting sample. More information regarding the norm groups needs to be provided in the CPI manuals, rather than leaving the descriptions vague and referring the reader to other references.

Two other areas are potential causes for concern. First, the CPI 260 is a complex and subtle instrument. Its use in business for leadership assessment leaves one to wonder to what degree business people, untrained in the complexities of psychometrics and personality theory, may misconstrue the intent of the CPI 260. For example, it is mentioned that the CPI 260 is not a clinical instrument and does not measure traits (does not measure the extent of dominance, or the characteristics of any of its scales, but rather the extent to which the characteristics measured by the scales correspond with the likelihood that a person would be described as having that characteristic by others). How many human resource directors or management development teams in business will understand that distinction or its implications for use in selecting and training leaders? Second, the connection between the scales of the CPI 260, the leadership characteristics, and core performance areas of leadership need to be explored further empirically. The linkages between the CPI 260 scales and the leadership characteristics and core performances are not based on empirical studies, but rather the judgment of the test authors of the CPI 260. The concepts of leadership characteristics and leadership performance areas need empirical research to substantiate them.

SUMMARY. The CPI 260 comes from a long line of successful instruments in the California Personality Inventory family. The purpose is clearly to expand the use of the instrument in business and organizational settings, primarily as a leadership development assessment. The various manuals contain sound, clear descriptions of the theory and basic concepts of the instrument and have ample practical examples of reports to aid the user in interpretation and application. The instrument should prove a useful tool for leadership assessment, assuming level-headed use and application of it. More information regarding validity and norm samples could be supplied in the CPI 260 manual to help users better understand the derivations of the instrument and the scales.

Review of the CPI 260 by STEPHEN J. FREEMAN, Professor and Chair, Department of Counseling, Texas A & M University-Commerce, Commerce, TX:

DESCRIPTION. The CPI 260 is a shortened version of the California Psychological Inventory (CPI). As the name implies, this version contains 260 items, shortened from 434 with the goal of giving "a true-to-life description of the respondent, in clear, everyday language, in formats that can help the client to achieve a better understanding of self" (manual, p. 1). The test authors intended the instrument to be useful across a wide range of individuals, ages 13 and older. The CPI 260 is self-administered and computer scored by CPP. Administration time is 25–30 minutes.

The CPI 260 contains 20 folk scales, 4 of which (noted with *) were renamed (Dominance, Capacity for Status, Sociability, Social Presence, Self-Acceptance, Independence, Empathy, Responsibility, *Social Conformity [previously called Socialization], Self-Control, Good Impression, Communality, Well-Being, Tolerance, Achievement via Conformance, Achievement via Independence, *Conceptual Fluency [previously called Intellectual Efficiency], *Insightfulness [previously called Psychological-Mindedness], Flexibility, and *Sensitivity [previously called Femininity/Masculinity]), 6 Work-Related Measures (Managerial Potential, Work Orientation, Creative Temperament, Leadership, Amicability, and Law Enforcement Orientation) and 3 Higher Order Measures (Orientation Toward Others, Orientation Toward Societal Values, and Orientation Toward Self).

DEVELOPMENT. The CPI 260 is the fourth edition of the CPI and all 29 scales in it were derived from the 434-item third edition (1995) of the CPI. The manual states one of the goals was to keep the CPI 260 and the CPI 434 as similar as possible.

Materials furnished by the developer included a total of four manuals (CPI 260 Manual, Coaching Report for Leaders User's Guide, Client Feedback Report Guide for Interpretation, and Coaching Report For Leaders Advanced Guide for Interpretation), each providing different information. All items of the CPI 260 were from the CPI 434. Although no new items were developed, some were assigned to different scales.

TECHNICAL. The CPI 260 manual reports normative data on CPI 260 scales for four standardization samples in the U.S. (N = 6,000), U.K. (N = 2,001), France (N = 1,424), and Italy (N = 1,362). Specific information on all sampling procedures, ethnicity, geographic location, education, marital status, and socioeconomic background was not provided. The manual fails to state which edition of the CPI was used with the U.S. sample. The CPI 434 was used with the U.K. sample. Samples in France and Italy received the CPI 480.

Internal consistency reliability (alpha) coefficients were reported for three samples: the U.S., U.K., and an additional sample of 6,000 (3,000 men and 3,000 women) randomly selected (no other demographic information was provided). Values ranged from .70 to .76 for total scores, and individual scale values ranged from .36 to .87. Median test-retest correlations for a 1-year interval conducted on high school students between their junior and senior years were .63 for males and .67 for females. Median test-retest coefficients for a 10-year interval were reported as .78 for males and .77 for females.

The CPI is a good example of the use of empirical keying methodology in scale construction; however, other than the developer's contention that data from the original CPI can be applied to the CPI 260, little psychometric evidence is provided to support the validity of the CPI 260. Atkinson (2003) in reviewing the third edition of the CPI (434) noted the revisions were limited enough that many of the observations about the measures made by previous reviewers were still applicable. With approximately 40% of the items removed or changed, this does not appear to apply to the fourth edition. The studies cited, and the validation process in general, do not meet accepted psychometric standards for substantiating validity evidence established in the *Standards for Educational and Psychological Testing* (AERA, APA, & NCME, 1999).

COMMENTARY. The CPI 260 is the latest edition and the most revised of the four CPI editions. It is a short self-report inventory that, based on previous editions, has potential. In future development, researchers might consider developing better normative data rather than relying on data from prior editions. Critical validity evidence is extremely limited. The four manuals contain a plethora of information; unfortunately, the information (owing to contradictions) can be confusing and casts doubt on inferences made.

SUMMARY. The CPI 260 is the fourth edition of the CPI and was designed "to give a true-to-life description of the respondent, in clear, everyday language, in formats that can help the client to achieve a better understanding of self" (manual, p. 1). Regrettably, most of the psychometric data presented in the manual are from previous editions with inferences made to the CPI 260. Insufficient psychometric information exists to assert that the test consistently or accurately measures any of its associated constructs and, therefore, cannot be recommended for use at this time.

REVIEWER'S REFERENCES

American Educational Research Association, American Psychological Association, & National Council on Measurement in Education. (1999). *Standards for educational and psychological testing.* Washington, DC: American Educational Research Association.

Atkinson, M. (2003) [Review of the California Psychological Inventory, Third Edition]. In B. S. Plake, J. C. Impara, & R. A. Spies (Eds.), *The fifteenth mental measurements yearbook* (pp. 160-161). Lincoln, NE: Buros Institute of Mental Measurements.

[37]

D-1, D-2, and D-3 Police Officer Tests.

Purpose: "Designed to assess the basic abilities identified as being important for successful performance as a police officer."
Population: Candidates for entry-level police officer positions.
Publication Dates: 1999–2006.
Scores: 5 job dimensions: Observation and Memory [Wanted Posters], Ability to Learn Police Material, Police Interest Questionnaire [Non-Cognitive], Verbal and Reading Comprehension (all but D-1), Situational Judgment and Problem Solving.
Administration: Individual or group.
Forms, 3: D-1, D-2, D-3.
Price Data: Available from publisher.
Time: 130 minutes per test.
Comments: D-1, D-2, D-3 are comparable forms; no prior training or experience as a police officer is assumed of candidates taking any of the three forms.
Authors: International Public Management Association for Human Resources and Bruce Davey Associates.
Publisher: International Public Management Association for Human Resources (IPMA-HR).

Review of the D-1, D-2, and D-3 Police Officer Tests by JANET HOUSER, Associate Professor of Health Services Administration, Regis University, Denver, CO:

DESCRIPTION. The Police Officer Tests D-1, D-2, and D-3 are each 100-item tests, administered by paper-and-pencil. The Police Interest Questionnaire (PIQ) is a 30-item test, similarly administered. Items are distributed between multiple-choice items with a single correct answer and interest items that are scaled as "A," "B," or "Cannot decide between A & B." The officer tests have both a cognitive and an attitude scale; the PIQ is solely a measure of interest in dimensions that are characteristic of police work.

There are three methods for scoring the D-series of police officer tests. The tests may be scored manually using hand stencils or an answer key, or the University of Maryland may score them electronically. With the University of Maryland service, the user receives an item analysis. If the test administrator uses an answer key for scoring, the administrator can enter the answer key into his or her own scoring system for scoring on premises.

The tests are intended to assess the ability to learn and remember information, logical reasoning, verbal ability, and personal traits that contribute to success as a police officer. Scoring yields a total score and four subscores, which are intended to reflect basic abilities rather than prior training as a police officer. The four subscores are related to posters, recall from study booklet articles, personal interests, and verbal/reasoning ability. A "Test Information Packet" accompanies each test. The test taker is asked to study the packet for 25 minutes in a controlled testing environment, and then take the questionnaire without referring to the packet. All three versions of the test contain questions that require recall from the posters, questions about the informational passages, interest items, and items requiring reasoning, judgment, and problem solving. The PIQ has 30 items, all rated as "A," "B," or "Cannot decide between A & B."

DEVELOPMENT. The three versions of the Police Officer Tests were developed between 1989 and 1998. Minimal information is provided in the technical manual provided by the publisher regarding initial test development, although appendices in the manual provide clues as to the explicit process used for development. The first appendix is a report of a multisite study that resulted in a detailed description of the knowledge, skills, abilities, and personal traits (KSAPs) most important for success as a police recruit. The key elements of the Police Officer Tests—reasoning ability, interest in police work, ability to learn quickly, and memory—are a subset of the KSAPs identified in this more detailed review. It can be assumed that the Police Officer Tests were intended to address these specific characteristics, but the manual does not make this process explicit. A single figure in Appendix A links a test plan using the subtests of the Police Officer Test D-1 to specific elements of the job analysis, and so it is assumed the test was developed explicitly to measure these dimensions. The specifics of the process for development and testing of individual items is not described in the manual or its appendices.

A second appendix contains a report of a validation study at a single police organization, and a third reports a criterion-related validation study of the D-1 form conducted with a consortium of 13 municipalities. It appears that the Police Officer

Selection Test was developed based on the KSAPs identified in the initial study, the title revised to Police Officer Test D-1 at some point, and then the measure was tested for validity in a single police department, followed by a multisite test. This process is inferred, though, and not directly described in the accompanying materials.

Neither is there an explicit description of the theoretical or conceptual underpinnings of the Police Officer Tests in the supporting materials. No results of a job analysis are provided for selecting this particular subset of KSAPs for the purposes of the development of this specific set of instruments. The developer cites no references to the current research to support the selection of this subset of KSAPs as the most important for these purposes.

TECHNICAL. The technical manual provides in-depth information about the validation procedures, reliability testing, and normative procedures for the Police Officer Test. Specific detail is not provided relative to the Police Interest Questionnaire, but a direct comparison of the items in the PIQ reveals that this test is a compilation of the interest questions from each of the Police Officer Test versions.

The D-1, D-2, and D-3 tests are alternate forms of the Police Officer Test. The scores of the three tests are similar but not identical; the authors provide conversion formulas to convert scores to a single metric. Most of the report provides descriptive data and results of reliability and validity testing on Form D-1 alone. The authors assert that the statistical linkage of the three forms (correlation between forms +.79 to +.81 corrected for range restriction) is of sufficient strength that the validity data for Form D-1 also applies to the alternative forms.

Norm data come from summary descriptive statistics in an applicant database maintained by the test author since inception of the test. The norm sample is from police departments and organizations covering various geographic areas, and appears to match the target population well. Means, standard deviations, and Kuder-Richardson-20 reliabilities for each of the three test forms is available, based on multiple administrations of the test in more than 50 locations. The database manager has compiled test data by unique identifier, so it is possible to track individuals who take more than one form of the tests. These correlations range from +.79 to +.81 after range restriction correction, and so appear to support the conclusion that they measure the same constructs. Norm data have been provided by ethnic group, and a chart that would be of use to Human Resource officers reports the cutoff scores by ethnic group at which the 80% rule is met.

Little emphasis is placed on reliability assessment in the technical manual, but validity testing is reported in such depth that reliability is not a cause for concern. KR-20 reliability values are reported in table form for each test, and range from .86 to .88, so are within acceptable ranges.

Substantial support for the validity of the test is provided in the technical manual. Three types of validity evidence are provided. Criterion-related validity results consist of two studies correlating D-1 scores with job performance ratings and an ongoing study of the correlation between all three test scores and police academy grades. Correlations between the Police Officer Test scores and academy grades were apparently correlated in three locations over several years. When adjusted for range restriction, these correlations were moderately strong, with coefficients between +.51 to +.59. Correlations between job performance ratings and the Police Officer Questionnaire were moderate and ranged from .33 to .61. These lower ratings are not surprising given the sample size was smaller (154 police officers) and interrater reliability among supervisor ratings was not strong.

The authors make no claim of face validity, but in view of the in-depth validity testing, this aspect is not a weakness. The authors refer to several studies linking the D-1 test content and the abilities identified in the analysis of the police officer's job dimensions. The largest study is included as an appendix, but it does little to illuminate the specific linkages between the Police Officer Questionnaire and the job dimensions. A finding that is stronger support for content validity is the provision of "indirect but useful evidence of content validity for these tests...a very high level of candidate acceptance" (manual, p. 8). However, the actual rate is not provided, weakening what would provide support for the usefulness of the tests for candidate screening.

Evidence of construct validity is provided through analysis of test structure via factor analysis and correlations between test scores and variables external to the test. A factor analysis of the subjects indicated two factors that together accounted for more than 77% of test variance. The factors were interpretable as basic general cognitive ability and a noncognitive factor, focusing directly on the interest subtest. Correlation values are also provided between the test and applicants' self-assessment questionnaires (corrected *r* from .022 to .325.) The strongest correlations were between writing ability, integrity, ability to learn laws, memory, and reading ability for the self-assessments. Corrected correlation coefficients for the relationship between the Police Officer Questionnaire and the Wechsler Adult Intelligence Scale were strong, at +.79.

Evidence of validity for the Police Interest Questionnaire is addressed briefly in the manual. Limited to five tests comparing the results of the interest subtest to supervisor ratings of job performance, the results were not convincing. Uncorrected correlation coefficients ranged from a low of +.17 to +.25. Although these are weak correlations, the authors note in the manual that these are "value-added," because they have a lower correlation with cognitive ability measures. The dimensions measured by the PIQ do make a unique contribution to the selection process—albeit one that does not have a clear criterion basis. Conceptually, it would not be expected that interest would predict performance as well as cognitive abilities, and so this result is not a surprising one. The authors did lengthen the questionnaire after the initial validity tests identified its weaknesses; 50% more questions were added in an attempt to improve reliability and overall contribution to decision making.

The technical manual is well organized and presents information in both textual and tabular form so that specific details of the validity analysis can be scrutinized. The validation procedures and results are consistent with acceptable standards and guidelines used for educational, psychological, and employee selection tests (AERA, APA, & NCME, 1999; U.S. EEOC, 1978).

COMMENTARY. Overall, the Police Officer Test D-1 has moderate to strong evidence of validity, using appropriate methods to control for restriction of range. It is acceptable to assume that the two alternative versions (D-2 and D-3) also have acceptable validity, given their strong correlation with the initial version. However, specific testing on these two versions would strengthen evidence of overall validity of the set, as the versions D-2 and D-3 do have some clear differences from D-1, and the variance on these latter tests is greater. The target population is closely approximated by the subjects involved in the validity assessments, and clear normative data are provided for comparison purposes. The test is easy to administer and score. The purpose of the test is straightforward and focused. Overall, the test appears to be a strong one for its stated purposes.

There is less psychometric support for the Police Interest Questionnaire. The lack of a reported theoretical foundation hampers the appraisal of this instrument for fidelity with a conceptual basis. Weak validity statistics do not increase confidence in the capacity of this instrument to reflect specific constructs. The assertions by the author of the manual that the PIQ provides a unique contribution to the assessment of a candidate are not documented with specific statistics, and therefore this claim is not supported by information in the existing technical manual.

Specific information about the procedures used to develop the instrument would be helpful, and its absence hampers a complete appraisal of the test. Particularly relative to the interest survey, a theoretical foundation and supportive literature would help illuminate the foundation of the test and, subsequently, its specific match to a particular application.

SUMMARY. The Police Officer Test D-1, D-2, and D-3 and the Police Interest Questionnaire provide police departments with a means to determine the basic abilities and interest in police work of employment candidates. The tests are easy to administer and score. These tests do appear to appraise many of the elements described in the KSAPs for a police officer, and substantial technical data are provided to support criterion-related, content, and construct validity of the tests. Sufficient evidence of validity is provided that a human resources officer could assume that these tests are indicators of legitimate job requirements, and norm scores (including those supporting the 80/20 rule) are helpful in interpreting the results. The Police Interest Questionnaire is not as well supported. The validity information that is presented demonstrates only weak evidence of criterion-related validity and no evidence of construct or content validity. However, it does appear to provide unique information about the interest of an applicant in the kinds of work that police officers must routinely accomplish.

REVIEWER'S REFERENCES
American Educational Research Association, American Psychological Association, & National Council on Measurement in Education. (1999). *Standards for educational and psychological testing.* Washington, DC: American Educational Research Association.
U.S. Equal Employment Opportunity Commission, Department of Labor, Department of Justice, U.S. Civil Service Commission. (1978). *Federal Register,* 43:38290-38315.

Review of the D-1, D-2, and D-3 Police Officer Tests by CHOCKALINGAM VISWESVARAN, Professor, Department of Psychology, Florida International University, Miami, FL:

DESCRIPTION. The D-1, D-2, and D-3 Police Officer Tests are three parallel forms of a test designed to predict police officer performance. Each form contains about 100 questions and has a mix of items assessing either cognitive skills or interests. It comprises multiple-choice items that assess verbal ability, situational judgment skills, and memory capacity. In addition, there are forced-choice items designed to assess interest in police work as well as personality characteristics such as interest in dealing with and influencing people, a sense of responsibility, community service orientation, and achievement orientation.

The test taker is provided with a candidate study booklet and 25 minutes to familiarize himself or herself with its contents. The study booklet usually contains posters, "articles and facts related to police work," etc. The booklet is then collected and the test form presented to the candidate. A total of 50 items focus on the materials presented in the booklet. The candidates also answer about 30 interest and personality items as well as indicate responses to a situational judgment test. The interest and personality items use a forced-choice technique to minimize socially desirable responding and a warning against faking is also provided with the instructions. Readability analyses are reported in the manual. The Flesch Reading ease formula, Gunning FOG index, and McLaughlin SMOG index are reported. The reading level for the study booklet is at the 12th grade level, the test directions are at the 8th grade level, and the test questions are at the 10th grade level.

DEVELOPMENT. The D-1 form was developed in 1989 and the D-2 and D-3 were developed about a decade later. The technical manual provides observed correlations of .74, .73, and .71 between pairs of the three different forms, which when corrected for range restriction (only a small subset of test takers had taken more than one form) result in substantial correlations between the forms (.80s). Given that the internal consistency reliabilities of the different forms are in the .80s (see Technical section below), these correlations suggest the equivalence of the three forms.

The development of the tests started with a comprehensive job analysis that involved the participation of 596 police officers. The job analysis panel was well represented with minorities and it also had representatives from different geographic regions and police departments of varying size. The job analysts rated the importance, frequency, etc., of 122 job tasks and 13 job duties. There was high agreement across the different police agencies. From these job analyses, 21 knowledge, skills, abilities, and personal characteristics (KSAPs) were identified and linked to the job duties. A test plan was developed to measure KSAPs such as ability to learn police procedures, perceptiveness, ability to learn laws, interest in police work, reasoning ability, learning ability, leadership, persistence, planning skills, problem solving, reading ability, and memorization skills with these three forms of the Police Officer Tests. KSAPs such as speaking and listening abilities were to be assessed in a separate interview.

TECHNICAL. Items were developed to address the above KSAPs. The technical manual reports means and standard deviations based on 3,741 test takers for the D-1 form, 4,270 for the D-2 form, and 3,469 for the D-3 form. However, data on individual item analyses are not provided in the current version of the manual and may be a good addition when the manual is revised. Information should also be provided if any items were deleted or edited based on such item analysis.

The KR-20 reliabilities are reported for the three forms as .88, .89, and .86 (based on sample sizes of 3,741, 4,270, and 3,469, respectively). The intercorrelations among the three subtests (wanted posters, study booklet articles, and reasoning ability) are in the .50s and .60s across the three forms. Consistent with expectations, the correlations between the Police Interest Questionnaire and the three subtests are in the .20s for all three parallel forms. The interest questionnaire score also correlates lower with the total scores (.60s) than the other three subtests (.70s). The correlations between two alternate forms (taken by test takers over a 2-year period) are also in the .70s (and can be construed as a measure of the coefficient of equivalence and stability).

The content validity of the three forms is well documented. A detailed account of the content domain in terms of a job analysis is presented. Further, supervisors were asked to rate the importance of the content dimensions identified in the job analyses (and the ratings suggest that the KSAPs assessed are face valid). A perusal of the items in the three parallel forms also suggests that they are job-related in the opinion of this reviewer.

The criterion-related validity was assessed with respect to two criteria: (a) police academy grades, and (b) supervisor ratings of officer performance. The correlations between D-1 form scores and police academy grades are reported as .61, .87, .41, and .46 in four samples (sample sizes of 41, 14, 34, and 22, respectively). Corrected for range restriction and unreliability in the criterion, these validity coefficients would be higher (and even without these corrections they are substantial). The technical manual also reported three additional criterion-related validity studies (using the criterion of academy grades). The first investigated the D-1 form and reported a validity of .44 (N = 194, corrected validity of .58). The second study investigated the D-2 form and reported a validity of .47 (N = 197, corrected validity of .59). The third investigated the D-3 form and reported a validity of .44 (N = 147, corrected validity of .51).

Two validation studies are reported for the criterion of supervisory ratings of job performance. In the first, based on a sample of 58 police officers, an observed correlation of .61 is found between scores on the D-1 form and supervisory ratings of job performance. The other study comprises a sample of 96 officers and the reported validity is .33. Corrected for criterion unreliability and range restriction, the respective correlations become .73 and .57, respectively. In addition to overall job performance, supervisors also rated performance in 10 subdimensions. Interrater-reliability coefficients for the 10 dimensions were between .51 and .70 and the observed validity (combined across the two samples N = 154) ranged from .19 to .45. D-1 scores were more predictive of situational judgment, knowledge of police work, ability to work under pressure, and written communication skills than they were in predicting job performance dimensions such as physical capacity and cooperativeness. The interest subtest of the D-1 form also correlated well (.23; N = 566) with supervisory ratings of job performance.

The manual also reports demographic group comparisons. Consistent with the literature, mean score difference between White (N = 2,581) and Black (N = 466) candidates was .81 standard deviation units favoring the majority group. Similar White-Black differences were found in the D-2 (3,277 White and 344 Black test takers) and D-3 (2,520 White and 368 Black test takers) forms also. However, no predictive bias was found in the criterion-related validity studies. Hispanic-White differences were in the order of .65 standard deviation units in the three forms. Gender differences were negligible (about .10 standard deviation units). Gender and ethnic group differences were also negligible in the interest section of the three forms. The manual does provide some suggestions about increasing the weight for the interest scores compared to the other sections to reduce potential adverse impact and the resulting loss in validity (to facilitate test users to decide for themselves on the trade-offs). However, in this reviewer's opinion the finding of substantial validity and no predictive bias should suffice for most test users.

Construct validity evidence is also provided. Factor analyses of the D-1 test scores yielded two factors explaining 77% of the variance. The first factor explaining 53% (Eigenvalue of 2.13) of variance had the three subtests assessing cognitive ability loading on it. The relatively minor second factor (24% variance, Eigenvalue of .95) comprised the noncognitive interest items. Test scores also correlated with candidates' education level, report writing exercise, etc. An observed correlation of .63 (.79 corrected for range restriction) was found between test scores and the Wechsler Adult Intelligence Scale.

COMMENTARY. This measure is a well-developed and professionally documented test. It starts with a clear analysis of the job and contents to be tested. It provides data on the equivalence of the three forms. Different types of reliabilities (KR-20 for internal consistency, temporal and parallel-forms reliability estimates) as well as intercorrelations among subtest scores are provided. Criterion-related validity and evidence of no predictive bias have been reported. Group differences (male-female, White-Black,

White-Hispanic) in both the cognitive and noncognitive components have been assessed (and found consistent with extant literature). Construct validity evidence in terms of (a) correlations between test scores and Weschler test scores, and (b) factor analysis of subtests, have been reported. In short, this reviewer cannot criticize the test but provides the following as suggestions for improvement.

The content validity section of the manual could be elaborated. Information on item analyses could also be added to the manual. Because validation is a continuing exercise, more validation studies should be added as data are gathered. In presenting the predictive bias analyses, a table should be added to the technical manual providing the actual results of the moderated hierarchical regression analyses.

SUMMARY. This test assesses situational judgment, ability to work under pressure, ability to learn new information, etc., for police applicants. The test scores have substantial predictive validity and no ethnic or gender biases in prediction have been found. It appears content valid and is likely to generate favorable applicant reactions as the items appear face valid.

[38]

Developmental Profile 3.

Purpose: "Designed to assess the development and functioning of children from birth through age 12."
Population: Ages 0-0 to 12-11.
Publication Dates: 1972–2007.
Acronym: DP-3.
Scores: 5 scales: Physical, Adaptive Behavior, Social-Emotional, Cognitive, Communication, plus General Development Score.
Administration: Individual.
Forms, 2: Interview Form, Parent/Caregiver Checklist.
Price Data, 2007: $199 per complete kit including 25 Interview Forms; 25 Parent/Caregiver Checklists, and manual (2007, 195 pages); $72 per 25 Interview Forms; $72 per 25 Parent/Caregiver Checklists; $76.50 per manual; $348 per kit with unlimited-use scoring and interpretation CD; $249 per DP-3 CD with unlimited-use scoring and interpretation.
Time: (20-40) minutes.
Comments: The Interview form is the preferred method of administration; the Parent/Caregiver Checklist, which contains the same content as the Interview may be used when administering the Interview is not possible because of time constraints or clinical/research needs.
Author: Gerald D. Alpern.
Publisher: Western Psychological Services.
Cross References: See T5:811 (14 references) and T4:764 (1 reference); for reviews by A. Dirk Hightower and E. Scott Huebner of an earlier edition, see 10:90 (3 references); for reviews by Dennis C. Harper and Sue White of an earlier edition, see 9:327; see also T3:698 (5 references); for a review by Jane V. Hunt of the original edition, see 8:215 (1 reference).

Review of the Developmental Profile 3 by ROSEMARY FLANAGAN, Associate Professor, Graduate School of Psychology, Touro College, New York, NY:

GENERAL DESCRIPTION AND INTRODUCTION. The Developmental Profile 3 (DP-3) was designed to assess the functioning and development of children from birth through age 12 years, 11 months. At the upper end of the age range, the instrument's primary use is to identify skills that are below average; thus, the DP-3 can be broadly effective as a screening and diagnostic tool for children from birth to approximately age 9. The DP-3 is a substantial revision of the prior version (Developmental Profile-2; Alpern, Boll, & Shearer, 1986) in terms of test development and psychometric properties. Sampling was greatly improved using a nationally representative norming sample approximating 2005 U.S. Census tract data according to ethnicity, dwelling area, and socioeconomic status. Care was taken to preserve item content that remained relevant.

The DP-3 provides a General Development Score based upon five scales that assess development and functioning: Physical, Adaptive Behavior, Social–Emotional, Cognitive, and Communication. Each scale contains 34 to 38 items for a total of 180 items. The DP-3 may be administered as a Parent/Caregiver Questionnaire or as an Interview; the item content is identical. The uses of the DP-3 now include eligibility determination, educational program development, and measurement of progress.

SCORING AND ADMINISTRATION. The Interview Form is preferred for individual administration; the Parent/Caregiver Checklist can also be used for individual administrations and for group screenings/research. There are age-specific starting points and basals and ceilings are established; thus, a selection of items is given. Each item endorsed adds one point to the raw score. The Parent/Caregiver Checklist is given in its entirety. It is written at a sixth grade reading level, which may not be appropriate for all respondents. Separate normative tables are available for the Interviewer Form and the Parent/Caregiver Form.

The question booklets are user-friendly; directions on the face sheet are clear. There is a place to record demographic information about the child. Scale names are printed on the page(s) to guide the test user. The Scoring/Profile Form contains spaces to record scores and display them graphically.

The DP-3 may also be computer scored. Each response must be manually entered; a computer-based scoring key is necessary to generate the report. The software provides unlimited scoring. Although using the software can limit clerical errors, the hand-scoring procedures are straightforward and readily accomplished.

INTERPRETATION. The importance of obtaining valid data is underscored, yet the test user is left to examine the data for inconsistencies to make such a determination. This is a limitation, given that validity scales are an increasingly common feature of modern tests.

Interpretation of data may be considered on several levels, and begins by comparing the child's scores to normative data. Standard scores are emphasized, although other metrics are available. Extreme scores should be interpreted with caution, as these data may be subject to restricted range. Data should also be inspected for patterns within scales and item analyses should be conducted. A useful feature is a table indicating the age at which each test item is passed by 50% and 95% of children, respectively. Detailed suggestions for intervention based on the individual scales and illustrative case examples are available.

DEVELOPMENT AND STANDARDIZATION. One objective of the author was to retain items from the prior edition that remain useful; 147 users of the DP-II were surveyed to assess their beliefs. Median correlations between the subscales of DP-II and DP-3 ranged from .86–.89 and 105 of 180 items were retained. The test authors also conducted Rasch analyses on a sample of 355 cases to provide information on item difficulty and illuminated gaps in items/item difficulty on each scale. New items were subsequently written to reflect changes in societal expectations for child development and functioning.

Standardization was conducted by 59 interviewers in 21 states. The sampling of children is believed to represent census tract data in regard to gender, race/ethnicity, geographic region, and parental education. The standardization sample for the Interview Form consists of 2,216 children (1,094 boys and 1,120 girls); 318 of the respondents also completed the Parent/Caregiver Checklist. Mothers were interviewed in 85% of the cases, with the remainder of interviewees being fathers or other relatives. The breakdown of the standardization sample according to age cohort is given in the manual; intervals and sampling are not uniform. Sampling was conducted at 3-month intervals from birth through age 2 (N = 878), at 6-month intervals from age 3 through age 6 (N = 774), and at yearly intervals thereafter, through age 12 (N = 564).

The raw scores for the Interview Form and the Parent/Caregiver Checklist were compared. Because the data are sufficiently similar, the data from both forms were combined to increase the sample size for the Parent/Caregiver Form norms and technical data. Inspection of raw score tables in the Appendix indicates that most raw score differences are either 0 or 1 point. This reviewer found it confusing that the manual indicates that 377 individuals (rather than 318) who completed the Interview Form also provided data from the Parent/Caregiver Checklist to generate the Rasch-scaled item difficulty data.

Examination of mean standard scores for the subscales and the General Development Score according to several stratification variables (gender, parent education level, and race/ethnicity) indicates minimal differences. Means ranged from 98.1–101.5 when examined by gender, from 96.4–103.9 according to parent education, and from 93.9–102.4 for race/ethnicity. All of these values are within the standard error of measurement, indicating that the scales are expected to perform equally well across a varied range of individuals.

TECHNICAL PROPERTIES. Internal consistency reliability data are (N = 2,614) reported by 1-year intervals. (How the sample size was determined is unclear.) Median split-half reliabilities for the scales range from .89 (Social-Emotional) to .93 (Physical), and the median split-half reliability for the General Development Score is .97. For a sample of 66 respondents, the test-retest reliability over a period of 13–18 days ranges from .81–.88 for the scales and is .92 for the General Development Score. Median standard errors of measurement for the scales are

4.10 (Physical), 5.08 (Social-Emotional), and 2.40 for the General Development Score. Reliability data and measurement error are within acceptable limits.

Validity data include evidence of construct validity and discriminant validity. Predictive validity is not addressed. Construct validity is reflected in the developmental progression of scores. Construct validity is also reflected in the structural properties of the DP-3; these data include correlations among the scales, exploratory factor analysis using an oblimin rotation, and Rasch analysis. Unfortunately, the details of the exploratory factor analysis are not fully provided and are not convincing because all data loaded onto a single factor with loadings ranging from .61 to .74. It is important that the Rasch analysis demonstrates that the range of item difficulty is similar to the range of person abilities for each scale; the data are in the manual for inspection. Construct validity was further examined through relationships with other tests; scales that are believed to be measuring similar constructs demonstrated substantial correlations. For example, the correlation between the General Development Score and the Adaptive Behavior Composite of the Vineland II (Sparrow, Cicchetti, & Balla, 2005) is .81. Evidence of discriminant validity is provided though group separation. Additional evidence of construct validity for the Parent/Caregiver Checklist is provided though correlation with measures of development that offer conceptually similar parent rating checklists. Although there are weaknesses in the validity data, clear improvements over DP-II are in evidence.

COMMENT. The DP-3 is an improvement over the prior version and should be helpful to practitioners and researchers. It does fall short on test construction and additional research is needed to ensure that the Interview Form and Parent/Caregiver Checklist are truly comparable.

REVIEWER'S REFERENCES

Alpern, G. D., Boll, T. J., & Shearer, M. (1986). *Developmental Profile-II (DP-II): Manual.* Los Angeles: Western Psychological Services.

Sparrow, S. S., Cicchetti, D. V., Balla, D. A. (2005). Vineland Adaptive Behavior Scales, Second Edition. Circle Pines, MN: AGS Testing.

Review of the Developmental Profile 3 by CARLEN HENINGTON, Associate Professor of School Psychology, Mississippi State University, Mississippi State, MS:

DESCRIPTION. The Development Profile 3 (DP-3) assesses parent or caregiver perception of children's development (birth through age 12) and evaluates a range of development (serious delay to average) of children up to age 7 to 9. The DP-3 also can be used to assess significant to severe developmental delays in individuals up to the age of 12. The DP-3 is composed of the following five scales. The Physical scale (35 items) addresses fine and gross motor, stamina, flexibility, strength, and sequential motor abilities, with a focus on gross motor (25 items). The Adaptive Behavior scale (37 items) assesses self-care and survival behaviors (e.g., toileting, eating, dressing, and day-to-day life activities). The Social-Emotional scale (36 items) examines social and emotional competence through questions related to innate personality characteristics often shaped by environmental factors (e.g., expression of needs and feelings, interactions, sense of identity, social mores). The Cognitive scale (38 items) assesses cognitive processes (e.g., perception, memory, concept development). The Communication scale (34 items) assesses receptive (comprehension of verbal or written information) and expressive language (verbal and nonverbal expression), with a focus on expressive skills (26 items).

Two administration forms are available: Interview Form and Checklist Form. The Interview Form is preferred because it can be included in a larger clinical interview and allows clarification of information and evaluation of response validity. The interview takes approximately 20 to 40 minutes to administer to parents or caretakers who are familiar with the child. The goal is to determine whether the child has accomplished each developmental task on the scale. Responses are "yes" or "no," with items arranged in developmental order. Start and stop rules (five consecutive items of yes or no, respectively) facilitate time efficiency. Typically, all five scales are administered and are combined to obtain the General Development score; however, scales of specific concern can be individually administered. The Checklist Form, appropriate in research or when an interview is impractical, is used with individuals who can read/understand the items written at a sixth-grade reading level. The respondent answers all questions on the checklist. For both forms, it is important to answer each administered item because missing responses above the basal on the Interview Form and all missing items on the Checklist Form are assigned a "no" rating.

Scoring is straightforward and similar for both forms, with all "yes" items scored as 1 point (including those below the basal on the Interview

Form). Points are tallied for each scale and the raw score total of all five scales comprises the General Development scale raw score. Raw scores are converted to standard scores (*M* = 100, *SD* = 15) from norm tables. The Scoring/Profile Form provides space for raw score, standard score, confidence interval, descriptive category, percentile rank, and age-equivalents, as well as a graph to plot standard scores. Shaded areas delineate descriptive categories and a referral cutoff line is provided. Interpretation, conducted by professionals with training in measurement and child development, is possible at four levels: (a) comparison to normative data, (b) analysis of scale score patterns and item analysis in which ability is compared to age norms at 50% and 95% pass rates, (c) compilation of multiple information sources, and (d) analysis under the response-to-intervention/remediation model. Case examples are provided in the manual to assist in the understanding of the interpretation process.

DEVELOPMENT. Based on the previous Developmental Profile, the DP-3 is purported to have several improved aspects: (a) a nationally representative normative sample based on U.S. Census figures for ethnicity, and geographic and socioeconomic characteristics; (b) smaller age increments reflecting rapid growth at the younger ages; (c) updated item content reflective of item analyses, including new items related to technology (e.g., computers, video games); and (d) expanded interpretation guidelines. In the development of the DP-3, the authors first obtained feedback about the DP-II. Then, an archival study was conducted to calibrate items by the Rasch one-parameter model using WINSTEPS (Linacre, 2003) to obtain a logit scale (*Z* scores) of item difficulty and personal ability. This provided an analysis of age gaps. Based on the expert input and the archival study, new items were developed and piloted (*n* = 326) in which parents completed the DP-3 Interview Form and the DP-II (318 parents also completed the Checklist Form) for final item development. Correlations between the DP-II and final DP-3 items ranged from .86 to .89 across the five areas.

TECHNICAL. Standardization was conducted with parents (*n* = 2,216, 85% were mothers). Demographic characteristics corresponded to the U.S. Census with multiple ethnicities (e.g., White, Asian, Black/African American, Hispanic/Latino, Native American, Native Hawaiian/Pacific Islander) and were grouped by age (every 3 months for birth through age 2–11, every 6 months for ages 3 through 6–11, and yearly for ages 7 through 12). A comparison of the item difficulty for the two forms showed some difference leading to the two sets (Interview and Checklist) of norm tables. Within the standardization sample, moderator variables were evaluated and showed no clinically meaningful differences for gender. Anticipated differences were found for parent education level (i.e., higher scores were obtained by children of parents with higher education). Small effect size was found for only 4 of 30 comparisons of ethnic groups. Notably, Asians were found to have significantly lower scores on the Social-Emotional scale (*es* = .41). This finding was interpreted by the scale authors as likely due to anomalies within the small sample size (*n* = 100). Based on all analyses, the scale authors concluded that the DP-3 is appropriate for all groups included in the standardization sample.

To assess internal consistency, given the developmental gradient of the DP-3 scales, the split-half method was used with both the standardization and a clinic sample (*n* = 398) and showed all coefficients above .80, with most above .90, using the Interview Form. A smaller sample was used with the Checklist Form, with correlations ranging from .79 to .99. Test-retest of individuals (*n* = 66) conducted with the Interview Form across approximately 2 weeks showed correlations ranging from .81 to .92 for scale scores.

Construct validity was evaluated through interscale correlations, factor analysis, and item response theory analysis. Interscale correlations ranged from .39 (Communication and Physical scales) to a high of .59 (Communication and Cognitive scales) with correlations between individual scales to the General Development scale ranging from .71 to .79. The factor analysis found general development as the first factor for all items. Single factor loadings ranging from .61 to .74 were obtained for the five individual scales. The item response analysis showed that the range of ability extended beyond the range of item difficulty.

Construct validity was also evaluated through comparisons with developmental instruments (i.e., Vineland Adaptive Behavior Scales, Second Edition; Developmental Assessment of Young Children) and domain specific tests (i.e.,

Preschool Language Scales, Fourth Edition; Peabody Developmental Motor Scales, Second Edition). Results showed moderate to high correlations. However, the authors cautioned against overinterpretation of comparison studies due to small sample sizes. Discriminant validity was evaluated with the clinical sample, which was divided into two groups (developmental delays and other problems). The *t*-tests showed lower DP-3 scores in those children with developmental delays than in those with other problems. Additional studies were presented to show separate evidence of construct and discriminant validity for the Checklist Form.

COMMENTARY. The DP-3 is built upon the foundation of the previous instrument (DP-II) and users will find it very familiar with many similarities and will likely welcome this update. Strengths include: (a) the inclusion of a number of ethnic groups to the standardization sample and (b) the administrator computer disk (CD), which allows unlimited assessments to be administered from a computer, leading to easy scoring and report writing. A significant change is that, unlike in previous versions of the DP, the current Cognitive scale does not provide an IQ equivalency score. Although this change is warranted, given advances in intelligence testing, many individuals who have used (or misused) this scale when estimating cognitive abilities of children with delays may regret this change. The main concern about the DP-3 remains the instrument's sensitivity. Although the authors state that the DP-3 has reduced age increments at the youngest ages (for sensitivity to rapid development), sensitivity to developmental gain is still a concern. The ages are grouped in increments of 2 years (i.e., ages 0-0 to 1-11; 2-0 to 3-11), some groupings with only eight items per area. Even fewer items are used at the older ages (4.0 to 5-11) and larger groupings of ages (i.e., ages 6-0 and older) are made.

SUMMARY. The DP-3 is a norm-referenced screening tool used to identify children with potential development delay(s) so that they can be referred for more comprehensive assessment in five commonly identified developmental domains. A variety of scores (e.g., standard scores, percentiles, age-equivalent scores) allow professionals to estimate developmental levels for young children and older children with significant delays. Using the parent or caretaker report, the DP-3 can be administered as either an interview or a checklist. The inclusion of technology items and the updated norms are a strength, as is the addition of the administrator's CD that makes the DP-3 very user-friendly.

REVIEWER'S REFERENCE

Linacre, J. M. (2003). WINSTEPS Rasch measurement computer program. Chicago: Winsteps.com.

[39]

Developmental Scoring System for the Rey-Osterrieth Complex Figure.

Purpose: Designed "to provide developmental guidelines for interpretation of the ROCF," which is a "measure [of] visuospatial ability and visuospatial memory."
Population: Ages 5-14.
Publication Dates: 1986-1996.
Acronym: DSS-ROCF.
Scores: 12 scores, 3 ratings: 4 scores (Organization, Structural Elements Accuracy, Incidental Elements Accuracy, Errors) and 1 rating (Style) per ROCF production (Copy, Immediate Recall, Delayed Recall).
Administration: Individual.
Price Data, 2010: $182 per introductory kit including professional manual (1996, 87 pages), ROCF stimulus card, 25 scoring booklets, and 50 response sheets; $70 per 25 scoring booklets; $50 per 50 response sheets; $15 per ROCF stimulus card; $63 per professional manual.
Time: [35] minutes, including a 15–20 minute delay.
Authors: Jane Holmes Bernstein and Deborah P. Waber.
Publisher: Psychological Assessment Resources, Inc.

Review of the Developmental Scoring System for the Rey-Osterrieth Complex Figure by STEFAN C. DOMBROWSKI, Professor & Director, School Psychology Program, Rider University, Lawrenceville, NJ:

DESCRIPTION. The Developmental Scoring System (DSS) for the Rey-Osterrieth Complex Figure (ROCF) is not a test, but rather a scoring system for the ROCF. The DSS is intended to be used as part of a comprehensive neuropsychological or psychological evaluation. The authors of the DSS claim that the scoring system can differentiate children with learning problems and other clinical populations from those without. The DSS was normed on a total of 454 children from kindergarten (age 5) through eighth grade (age 14). The DSS measures four parameters of the ROCF (Organization, Style, Accuracy, and Errors) and attempts to place a child's performance on the ROCF within a developmental context. The test authors report that the DSS is intended to be interpreted from both a quantitative (i.e., norm referenced) and qualitative perspective (i.e., clinical judgment).

The DSS materials consist of a professional manual, the ROCF stimulus card, response sheets, and the DSS scoring booklet. Examiners will also need five colored felt-tipped pens (e.g., green, blue, yellow, red, black) and a stopwatch. The test authors report that use of felt-tipped pens permits the examiner to track the child's progress throughout the design. The length of time that each colored pen is used is determined by reference to a table in the professional manual. The DSS requires that three trials are administered and scored: copy, immediate recall, and delayed recall. The test authors report that copying the ROCF furnishes information about perceptual and organizational processes, whereas the recall trials reveal encoding and storage processes. The DSS provides three scores (Organization, Accuracy, and Errors) as well as a rating for each of the three DSS trials (i.e., Copy, Immediate Recall, and Delayed Recall). Scoring procedures provided in the manual are detailed and elaborate, requiring considerable examiner familiarity with them. The professional manual provides a useful and well-written discussion of the principles of pediatric neuropsychological theory and diagnosis.

DEVELOPMENT. Thc DSS was created based on the copy and recall productions of the ROCF by 454 children in a single, lower-middle class school district in the northeastern United States. The normative sample ranged in age from 5 to 14 and was composed of 50% females. Kindergarten children were tested individually; all other children were tested in a group setting. Normative scores are presented according to 1-year intervals. The effects of three demographic characteristics on the organization scores were examined by a three-way analysis of variance (age, sex and handedness). Details regarding the development and norming of the DSS were scant and the examiner instead is referred to two Waber and Holmes (1985, 1986) articles. Because the limited normative data do not reflect the U.S. Census and because of the age of the norms, which are nearly a quarter century old, extreme caution should be exercised when attempting to use the DSS as a norm-referenced instrument outside of the school district in which it was originally developed.

TECHNICAL. The DSS was created to provide developmental benchmarks for the ROCF. The data on which the DSS was based were collected in a normative study of 454 lower to middle class children ages 5 to 14. Approximately 50% of these children were female. The original normative study controlled for the demographic characteristics of age, sex, and handedness. Statistical control for additional demographic characteristics is absent. Normative scores are presented by 1-year age groups. Beyond presentation of these data, there is limited information in the professional manual regarding the standardization process of the DSS. Reliability was assessed using only interrater reliability estimates. The professional manual reported that due to clinical considerations as well as familiarity with the figure upon initial exposure, test-retest reliability was not calculated. The reliability estimate for the style ratings was .88 for the copy productions based on a random sample of 50 protocols. The original Waber and Holmes (1985, 1986) study reported a reliability estimate of .95 based on a random sample of 52 protocols. The reliability estimate was .94 for the recall productions. The professional manual reports limited validity evidence based on the original normative sample. Instead, validity evidence reported in the professional manual is predicated upon an accumulation of studies for various conditions including learning disabilities, Attention-Deficit/Hyperactivity Disorder (ADHD), sensory deficits, children treated for leukemia, birthweight, spina bifida and hydrocephalus, closed-head injury, and Fragile-X adult females. According to the professional manual, all studies report that the DSS can discriminate "pathological populations" from the normative sample and other control groups. Unfortunately, additional validity evidence investigating the relationship of the DSS with other measures of visual-motor and cognitive functioning is absent.

COMMENTARY. The DSS creatively attempts to evaluate developmental differences in children's visuospatial and visual memory capacity. Although the professional manual reports that the DSS may be used to score the ROCF quantitatively, the approach to scoring is based upon poor psychometric qualities including a limited normative sample, limited reliability estimates, and a dearth of validity evidence. The normative data do not reflect the U.S. Census, are sorely outdated, and do not meet recommended guidelines for test development (AERA, APA,

& NCME, 1999). As a result, use of the DSS with individuals outside of the normative base is not appropriate. Instead, the DSS might best be characterized as a qualitative, rather than norm-referenced, scoring system. The professional manual devotes considerable space to a discussion of administration and interpretation of the DSS with only a limited amount of space to describing underlying technical properties. Although the DSS is cumbersome to administer and score, it appears useful for enhancing understanding of how an examinee organizes, recalls, and constructs the figures. It is best viewed as a qualitative approach to scoring the ROCF. Considerably less emphasis should be placed on any "quantitative" score that is derived from the tables in the professional manual.

SUMMARY. The DSS attempts to integrate quantitative scoring and a developmental assessment of the reproduction of the figures of the ROCF. The test authors are to be commended for the effort they have put into this project. The scoring approach is creative and detailed, perhaps yielding clinically relevant information when administered in the context of a comprehensive neuropsychological or psychological evaluation. However, the approach to administration and scoring of the ROCF using the DSS is overwhelming and the underlying psychometric properties are inadequate. As a result, the DSS should be considered a qualitative, not norm-referenced, measure of visuospatial and visual memory capacity. Its use as a norm-referenced scoring system to discriminate clinical populations is inappropriate and should be eschewed.

REVIEWER'S REFERENCES

American Educational Research Association, American Psychological Association, & National Council on Measurement in Education. (1999). *Standards for educational and psychological testing.* Washington, DC: American Educational Research Association.

Waber, D. P., & Holmes, J. M. (1985). Assessing children's copy productions of the Rey-Osterrieth Complex Figure. *Journal of Clinical and Experimental Neuropsychology, 7,* 264–280.

Waber, D. P., & Holmes, J. M. (1986). Assessing children's memory productions of the Rey-Osterrieth Complex Figure. *Journal of Clinical and Experimental Neuropsychology, 8,* 563–580.

Review of the Developmental Scoring System for the Rey-Osterrieth Complex Figure by GABRIELLE STUTMAN, Private Practice, Westchester and Manhattan, NY:

DESCRIPTION. The Developmental Scoring System for the Rey-Osterrieth Complex Figure (DSS-ROCF) is a developmental measure of visuospatial ability and visuospatial memory. It utilizes the well-known ROCF drawing originally devised by Andre Rey for use with brain-damaged adults, with normative data later added by Paul Osterreith. The participant first makes a Copy of the design, then a drawing from Immediate Memory, and finally a Delayed Memory representation. The scoring for this test had previously been downwardly normed for, and used with, children. However, the brain-behavior relationships of adults cannot be assumed to have the same diagnostic significance when applied to the dynamic changes of the developing child. The DSS-ROCF was therefore developed via age-grouped observation of children's performance on this task.

The sequence of the child's rendering of the Copy is documented by the use of five standard, medium-point, colored felt-tipped pens (not included in the kit). These are given to the child in a fixed sequence (i.e., green, blue, black, yellow, and red). A fixed period of time for each color is required; the period of time varies inversely with the child's age. The Immediate and Delayed (after about 20 minutes) Memory conditions do not require a sequence of colors.

The manual gives detailed instructions for administration, which is similar to the usual ROCF administrative procedure. Scoring the DSS-ROCF, however, is far more complicated than the standard ROCF. Instead of the usual, rather simple scoring of accuracy and placement, the DSS-ROCF has an Organization score (16–24 features), a Style rating (6–18 features), an Accuracy score (four subscores derived from 12–24 features), and an Error score (four subtypes). The Total Organization score is ordinal, ranging from 1–13, and can be converted to age-corrected percentile ranks. Among the many critical features that are assessed are alignments (that two segments of a line are properly aligned with each other), and intersections (that they intersect accurately). The necessarily detailed procedure for scoring Organization is well described in the manual. The Style rating depends upon the basal Organization score, which must be calculated prior to scoring for Style. Each relevant line must be properly aligned (Organization), but also demonstrate continuity of stroke (Style). The Accuracy score, similar to the scoring with which most neuropsychologists are familiar, requires only that the design elements be recognizable; they do not have to be precisely reproduced or correctly located. Rough age-normed percentile values

(10th, 25th, 50th, 75th, 90th, and 100th percentile groups) are given for this score.

Errors are of four types. The four types of Error include rotation (>45 degrees), perseveration (a defined number of repetitions relevant to each design element), misplacement (relative to the whole figure), or conflation (when one line is used to represent more than one element of the figure). These four subscores are summed to yield a Total Errors score that corresponds to normed percentile values given in the index. The Immediate and Delayed recall conditions are scored along the same lines, but scoring instructions are less complex and drawings have fewer criterial features. Scoring for sample drawings is also provided, along with a section of Frequently Asked Questions to aid understanding of the scoring procedures.

The test authors believe that a given child's clinically observed process and percentile scores "can be used to infer how a child characteristically responds to novel, complex information" (professional manual, p. 41). A chapter on interpretation discusses the complimentary roles of observation and quantitative analysis and the relationship between Copy and Recall performance. Research that relates to specific inferences that flow from the Organization, Style, Accuracy, and Error scores, with regard to the right-left, anterior-posterior, and cortical-subcortical cerebral axes are discussed. The nonlinear nature of developmental change is also discussed.

DEVELOPMENT. The DSS-ROCF is based on the analysis of Copy and Recall drawings produced by 454 children who ranged in age from 5 through 14 years of age. About 50% of the sample was female and 90% were right handed. Children were tested in classroom groups, and blinded protocols were scored by the two test authors. There was a main effect of age, and in every age group right-handed children and those who copied from left to right produced better organized drawings. There was no main effect of sex. The children's drawings were first sorted into five categories of "goodness of organization" (professional manual, p. 65). The alignments and intersections that best discriminated the groups were statistically determined based on clinical ratings, and criterial features were determined for each of the five levels. This procedure was carried out for drawings in each of the five organizational levels to determine how best to discriminate the different Style ratings within those levels. Accuracy and Errors were scored by counting the presence of line segments and errors, respectively. Errors were grouped into the four categories previously defined.

TECHNICAL. Based on a random sample of 52 protocols, interrater reliability regarding Organization was .95 for the Copy productions. Reliability coefficients were .94 for the Recall productions (50 protocols) and .88 and .87 for Style ratings for the Copy and Recall productions, respectively. Reliability of raters' identification of the critical features has ranged from .91 to .96 in a variety of studies. Test-retest reliability is not calculated due to the confounding effects of development upon temporal variables. The correlation between clinical and objective DSS ratings was high (r = .82, p < .00001) indicating good validity. When compared with a sample of learning-disabled children, the DSS normative group "documented substantial differences on all four DSS outcome variables" (professional manual, p. 66). Children with learning disabilities produced drawings that were less well organized with more errors and fewer elements. Organizational deficiency characterizes the performance of the group with Attention Deficit/Hyperactivity, relative to the norm. Interesting distinctions also were found regarding children with sensory and neurodevelopmental disorders, as well as high risk infants and children with acquired head injury.

COMMENTARY. As may be apparent, the DSS-ROCF (relative to the prior ROCF) requires some rather lengthy and thoughtful scoring. This investment of time may be worthwhile when examining a child with an unusual presentation or one for whom previous interventions have been unsuccessful. Certainly it provides an opportunity to get more data than is usually garnered from this instrument. However, under current constraints of time and remuneration, one may prefer to maximize evaluation cost effectiveness by utilizing additional instruments. That said, the DSS-ROCF provides a good diagnostic measure of childhood visuospatial skill and memory, as well as of developing executive functions. Its use by the stated practitioners is appropriate.

SUMMARY. The DSS-ROCF, a developmental measure of visuospatial ability and memory, utilizes the well-known ROCF drawing originally devised by Andre Rey and Paul Osterreith. Its primary benefit is the clear differentiation of different developmental stages as the child progresses in duplicating and remembering the drawing. Distinctions among various clinical groups are also helpful. The manual provides a thorough description of administration and scoring procedures, age-normed percentile scores, a brief summary of test development, and generally acceptable technical data. Its primary weakness is the relatively large amount of time and effort involved in scoring.

[40]

Devereux Early Childhood Assessment for Infants and Toddlers.

Purpose: "Assesses protective factors and screens for social and emotional risks in very young children."
Population: Ages 1 month to 36 months.
Publication Dates: 2007–2009.
Acronym: DECA-I/T.
Scores, 7: 3 Infant scores: Initiative, Attachment/Relationships, Total Protective Factors (composite of previous 2 scale scores), and 4 Toddler scores: Initiative, Attachment/Relationships, Self-Regulation, Total Protective Factors (composite of previous 3 scale scores).
Administration: Group.
Forms, 2: Infant (1 month to 18 months), Toddler (18 months to 36 months).
Price Data, 2009: $199.95 per complete kit including 20 Infant Record Forms, 30 Toddler Record Forms, 5 reproducible Parent/Teacher Profile Masters for 5 different age ranges (1 mo. to 3 mos., 3 mos. to 6 mos., 6 mos. to 9 mos., 9 mos. to 18 mos., 18 mos. to 36 mos.), User's Guide (2007, 111 pages), Strategies Guide (2009, 158 pages), 20 Parent Strategy Guides ("For Now and Forever"), 3 Adult Resilience Journals ("Building Your Bounce: Simple Strategies For a Resilient You"), and Forms CD (including Technical Manual [2007, 51 pages], Reproducible Planning Forms, and Scoring Profiles), all in a poly box carrying case; $19.95 per 20 Infant Record Forms; $29.95 per 30 Toddler Record Forms; $12.95 per 5 reproducible Parent/Teacher Profile Masters; $39.95 per User's Guide; $49.95 per Strategies Guide; $24.95 per 20 Parent Strategy Guides; $9.95 per Adult Resilience Journal; $99.95 per CD Scoring Assistant; technical manual is free to print from publisher's website.
Time: Administration time not reported.
Comments: Ratings by parents, other family members, or childcare providers; scoring completed by hand or with separately sold CD Scoring Assistant; DECA-I/T is "part of an integrated, comprehensive five-step system" that involves implementing strategies and evaluating progress; other tests in the Devereux series include: the Devereux Early Childhood Assessment (DECA; T7:811), the Devereux Early Childhood Assessment–Clinical Form (DECA-C; T7:812), and the Devereux Student Strengths Assessment (DESSA; 18:41).
Authors: Mary Mackrain, Paul A. LeBuffe, and Gregg Powell; Kristin Tenney-Blackwell (Strategies Guide only).
Publisher: Kaplan Early Learning Co.

Review of the Devereux Early Childhood Assessment for Infants and Toddlers by JEAN N. CLARK, Associate Professor of Educational Psychology, College of Education, University of South Alabama, Mobile, AL:

DESCRIPTION. The Devereux Early Childhood Assessment for Infants and Toddlers (DECA-I/T) is a tool to assess "protective factors" in the emotional and social development of infants and toddlers. The tool is a survey instrument to be completed by parent/family/caregivers and/or teachers/child care providers. With a Likert-type 0–4 annotated format ("*never, rarely, occasionally, frequently, very frequently*"), the tool has two forms: the Infant Form (DECA-I; ages 1–18 months) contains 33 items and assesses two named factors: Initiative (18 items) and Attachment/Relationships (15 items); the Toddler Form (DECA-T; ages 18–36 months) has 36 items to assess three factors: Initiative (11 items), Attachment/Relationships (18 items), and Self-Regulation (7 items). Written at a sixth grade reading level, the items are stated in the form of positive attributes or behaviors. Raters are those who have had sufficient contact with the child (described minimally as 2–3 hours per day, 2–3 days per week). The rater is asked to record how often she or he has observed the behaviors in the previous 4 weeks. The responses may be hand coded according to instructions in the user's guide, or be analyzed by the DECA-I/T scoring program, contained in a CD-ROM. Conversion tables with raw scores, *T*-scores, and percentiles are provided, with five age groups (1–3 months; 3–6 months; 6–9 months; 9–18 months; 18–36 months). For interpretation, the scores are divided into three groups: Area of Need (deficit or lower scores); Typical (normal for age); and Strength (above average for age). The items are preceded by a short demographic completion section, with 9 items to identify the child and the rater. No estimate of administration time is provided.

DEVELOPMENT. The development of the instrument began with a review of literature and focus groups of parents and teachers. A list of 112 items was developed, describing specific behaviors that demonstrate developmental capabilities of children ages 1–36 months. A pilot study was conducted in 2005, consisting of 251 participants at 12 sites. According to the theoretical paradigm of the Devereux Institute, there are "risk factors" to which children may be exposed as they develop emotionally and socially; these factors may be found in the environment, family, or within the child and may contribute to the expression of negative behaviors or other developmental obstacles. Likewise, there are "protective factors," which also may be found in the environment, family, and within the child, to assist in the development of resiliency, or the ability to "achieve positive outcomes despite stress and adversity" (user's guide, p. 2). These factors, expressed in behavioral terms, comprise the core items on the assessment instrument; they represent facets in the environment, family, and personal ("within-child") factors. In the pilot study, children with identified special needs scored lower on the "protective factors" that this instrument measures. Based on the paradigm, the instrument was prepared to undergo the standardization process.

TECHNICAL.

Standardization. The standardization sample consisted of 2,183 infants (45%) and toddlers (55%). The rater sample was 48% parents and 52% caregivers/teachers. Data collection came from 29 sites across the U.S., and the sample consisted of Native Americans (2.8%), Asian Pacific Islanders (1.1%), Hispanics (15.1%), African Americans (9%), Caucasians (61.7%), and mixed race (8.8%). Using exploratory factor analysis, two forms (Infant and Toddler) were established. Because of significant differences among raters (parents and caregivers), two separate scales were constructed. Raw scores were converted to *T*-scores and percentiles.

Reliability. Internal reliability coefficients of consistency ranged from .80 to .94 on the Parent Rating Scale for infants, and from .87 to .94 on the Teacher Rating Scale for infants. On the toddler scales, the ranges were from .79 to .94 on the Parent Rating Scale, and from .83 to .95 on the Teacher Rating Scale. Standard errors of measurement for the infant and toddler forms ranged from 2.24 (toddler, teacher scale) to 4.58 (toddler, parent scale). Test-retest coefficients for Total Protective Factors were .84 and .91 among teachers, .91 and .99 among parents, and .85 and .97 overall, for infants and toddlers, respectively. The intervals between testing sessions ranged from 24 to 72 hours. Interrater reliabilities for Total Protective Factors, with the raters split between groups, was .68 for parents and .72 for teachers on the Infant Scale, and .70 for parents and .74 for teachers on the Toddler Scale. Interrater reliability for combined groups was not statistically significant. All four measures suggest good reliability among items and across raters within groups.

Validity. Content validity was derived from a review of literature and other similar or analogous assessment instruments, and an item review by the test authors and Devereux Institute staff. Criterion or predictive validity was determined by two procedures. First, in the pilot study, the instrument was used to assess 15 infants and 69 toddlers who were identified with emotional and behavioral problems, and their scores on the DECA-I/T. Next, their scores were compared with scores from 15 infants and 69 toddlers from the general population. The scores for previously identified children were statistically lower than those from the general population. A second procedure involved calculating the percentage of previously "identified" children who were also found to be in the "Area of Need" level on the DECA-I/T. The infant scores (n = 15) showed a 63.3% match, and the toddler scores (n = 69) showed a 70.3% match. To assess convergent construct validity, 35 toddlers were assessed using the previously developed DECA (1999) and the current instrument. Corresponding subfactor scores were all found to be significant, even though the two scales were developed for children of differing ages. Analyses also showed no significant difference in accuracy of prediction when comparing race/ethnicity. Finally, results from the DECA-I/T were compared with data using the Preschool Major Life Events Checklist (Work, Cowen, Parker, & Wyman, 1990), The Preschool Daily Hassles Checklist (Kanner, Coyne, Schaefer, & Lazarus, 1981), and the Temperament and Atypical Behavior Scale (TABS; Neisworth, Bagnato, Salvia, & Hunt, 1999). As these instruments all assess levels of "high risk," the scores were compared to those labeled "Low Protective Factors" (*T*-scores at or below 40) on the DECA-I/T. There was a high percentage of congruence between those in "low risk" (96.7%) categories or "high risk"

(88%) on the other instruments, compared with those scoring in the "Low Protective Factors" on the DECA–I/T.

COMMENTARY. The DECA-I/T is easy to administer, interpret, and apply in assessing infants and toddlers. There is a separate user's manual and technical manual, which makes both convenient. Each is provided both on a CD-ROM as well as paper copies. Although the user's manual is bound, the technical manual was provided loose-leaf, which was a bit cumbersome to handle; however, the material is both didactic and informative. Three limitations involve technical development and report. First, the review of literature and other assessment instruments predates this decade, and should be updated. Second, the analysis sample sizes (when provided) are small, compared to the total standardization sample (n = 2,183). For example, the test-retest samples consisted of 20 parents and 23 teachers for the Infant Form, and 22 parents and 20 teachers for the Toddler Form; the interrater reliability samples consisted of 45 parents and 63 teachers for the Infant Form, and 49 parents and 60 teachers for the Toddler Form. Testing for criterion validity, data analysis was based on 15 "identified" (labeled as "risk" or "high risk" by professionals) infants and 15 "community" (nonlabeled) infants; the toddler groups consisted of 69 "identified" and 69 "community" participants. Finally, the technical manual (p. 2) suggests that these analyses were from the pilot study; if this is true, no similar results were reported from the larger standardization sample. No sample sizes were reported for any other analyses. With such small samples, and no reported effect sizes, the results may or may not reflect the true attributes of the instrument. Clearly, additional reporting or sampling would be necessary to test the true strength of this instrument.

There are likewise three strengths in considering this instrument. First, it is founded on a clearly illustrated paradigm, and is theoretically true to this model. Second, the overall program–including both hand and computerized administration, scoring, and interpretation–makes the tool useful for institutional accountability, screening for potential risk, and developmental tracking of individuals and interventions. Finally, with the ancillary booklets for intervention and training, as well as access to the Devereux Institute (founded in 1912), the professionals and caregivers have support at any level.

SUMMARY. The DECA-I/T consists of a one-page list of items reflecting protective factors in the emotional, social, and behavioral development of infants and toddlers. Both forms of the DECA-I/T are short, clear, statements that are easy to read and stated in positive phrases. Scoring instructions are clear, by hand or CD-ROM, interpretation is straightforward, and interventions are aligned with the outcome reports.

REVIEWER'S REFERENCES

Kanner, A. D., Coyne, J. C., Schaefer, C., & Lazarus, R. S. (1981). Comparison of two modes of stress management: Daily hassles and uplifts versus major life events. *Journal of Behavioral Medicine, 4,* 1–37.

Neisworth, J. T., Bagnato, S. J., Salvia, J., & Hunt, F. M. (1999). *TABS Manual for the Temperment and Atypical Behavior Scale Early Childhood Indicators of Developmental Dysfunction.* Baltimore: Paul H. Brooks Publishing Co., Inc.

Work, W. C., Cowen, E. L., Parker, G. R., & Wyman, P. A. (1990). Stress resilient children in an urban setting. *Journal of Primary Prevention, 11,* 3–17.

Review of the Devereux Early Childhood Assessment for Infants and Toddlers by MARY J. McLELLAN, Professor, Northern Arizona University, Flagstaff, AZ:

DESCRIPTION. The Devereux Early Childhood Assessment for Infants and Toddlers (DECA-I/T) was published in 2007 and is a downward extension of the Devereux Early Childhood Assessment (DECA; 15:81) that was published in 1999. The Devereux Foundation has a tradition of developing strong psychometric measures relating to identification of behavioral disorders, including the Devereux Behavior Rating Scale School Form (Naglieri, LeBuffe, & Pfeiffer, 1993) and the Devereux Scales of Mental Disorders (Naglieri, LeBuffe, & Pfeiffer, 1994). These measures have provided resources for individuals regarding the identification of children with behavioral disorders within the school-age population. The DECA is suitable for children ages 2–5 and the DECA I/T is appropriate for use with children ages 1–36 months.

The DECA-I/T is part of a system developed by the Devereux Foundation that utilizes prevention from a strength-based perspective. Resilience is the key concept of the DECA and is described as a child's capacity to obtain positive developmental outcomes despite adverse experiences. The identification of characteristics of resilient children played a major role in the development of the DECA-I/T. The system of identification focuses on protective factors and targets individuals with whom to build behaviors associated with healthy emotional functioning. The Devereux Foundation made a commitment to the field of early childhood in 1996 with the launching of the Devereux Early Childhood

Initiative. The core principles of this initiative are based on promotion of social and emotional health for young children.

The measure is administered to parents, caregivers, or care providers who have had extended interaction with the child. The manual specifies that the person completing the questionnaire should have a minimum of 2 to 3 days per week of interaction each comprising at least 2 to 3 hours duration. The responses to the test prompts are based on the last 4 weeks of observed behaviors.

DEVELOPMENT. The description of the literature review for test development identified resilience as a key word. The test authors indicated they reviewed existing measures of infant and toddler social and emotional health, but did not name these measures in the technical manual or user's guide. Focus groups with parents and teachers were utilized to identify behaviors associated with social and emotional health. Directly observable behaviors judged to require little or no inference from the observer were used for item development. During the initial pilot study there were 112 items and after a pilot study in the spring of 2005 the item number was reduced to 68 items. The manual identifies 68 that include 33 items for the 1–18-month form and 36 items for the 18–36-month form corresponding to the Infant Form and Toddler Form, respectively. Factor analysis was utilized to select items and the factors appropriate to each scale. Two factors, Initiative and Attachment/Relationships were found for the Infant Form, and Self-Regulation emerged as a third factor for the Toddler Form.

Parents or care providers complete their ratings of the child's behaviors on a carbonless form and the individual who scores the measure is able to easily add the scores and convert the raw scores to *T*-scores that are then placed on a graph that provides information about the range within which the scores fall. There is a CD-ROM scoring program that can be utilized instead of hand scoring. Scores fall within ranges of strength, typical, or area of need. The DECA system provides information regarding strategies to build positive behaviors associated with resilience and the guides that come with the DECA-I/T provide specific information regarding strategies for caregivers and education professionals.

TECHNICAL.

Standardization. Acceptable standardization practices were followed with representation from gender, geographic, race, and socioeconomic status being distributed in a manner similar to census figures. Early childhood professionals and parents were asked to complete ratings of children in their care. In all, 52% of the ratings were collected from early childhood professionals and 48% from parents. The characteristics of the children were described and the sample of 2,183 children is inclusive of parents and educational professionals who made ratings of different children. Although the size of the sample constitutes adequate representation of these two groups, this reviewer would appreciate a differentiation of the samples within the demographic descriptions.

Reliability. Internal, test-retest, and standard error of measurement reliability coefficients were calculated on the normative sample. The alpha estimates are provided by age ranges of 1–3, 3–6, 6–9, and 9–18 months for the Infant group; the Toddler group required no age distinctions. There is a differentiation between raters on these tables but no individual cell sizes are indicated. Test-retest and interrater reliability samples are described and appear adequate although the sample sizes are quite small.

Validity. The DECA-I/T manual describes content, criterion, and construct validity. The test authors focused on the concept of resilience and directed focus groups with professionals and parents to define positive behaviors associated with resilient children and adults. Factor analysis was utilized to refine test items and create a succinct measure. A sample of children identified with emotional and behavioral challenges was utilized to determine if the DECA-I/T could differentiate between the two groups of children. The test authors were satisfied that the differentiation meets established criteria. To determine convergent validity a small sample of children at the toddler age were given the DECA-T and the DECA. A strong correlation was noted. No other measures were utilized to assess convergent validity.

COMMENTARY. The DECA-I/T is a downward extension of the DECA that has achieved acceptance in the early childhood community. The Devereux Foundation, when developing this instrument, sought to meet the needs of screening for mental health needs within early childhood programs, such as Head Start. The manual makes no mention of other measures available for comparison. The Functional Emotional Assessment Scale (FEAS) by Greenspan, DeGangi, and

Wieder (2001), The Brief Infant-Toddler Social-Emotional Assessment (Briggs-Cowan & Carter, 2001a), and the Infant-Toddler Social-Emotional Assessment (Briggs-Cowan & Carter, 2001b) are measures that assess a similar age span and could have been reviewed by the test authors. In addition, the Vineland Social-Emotional Early Childhood Scales (SEEC; Sparrow, Balla, & Cicchetti, 1998) is another measure that could have been mentioned. Although the SEEC is an older measure, it is worth mentioning. The actual size of the norm groups could also have been more clearly described in the manual.

SUMMARY. The DECA-I/T provides one of the few means of identification of emotional and behavioral challenges for infants and toddlers available today. The test is completed by parents and/or caregivers and consists of 33 items for 3–18-month-old children and 36 items for 18–36-month-old children. Test results can be scored and interpreted by early care professionals and the test kit includes suggestions and guides to help parents and caregivers enhance behaviors associated with resilience. The test authors chose to narrow the concept of social and emotional health to resilience and the behavioral characteristics associated with resilience. As with most new measures, further research related to applicability and utility is strongly recommended.

REVIEWER'S REFERENCES

Briggs-Gowan, M. J., & Carter, A. S. (2001a). Brief Infant–Toddler Social Emotional Assessment. San Antonio, TX: Pearson Assessments.

Briggs-Gowan, M. J., & Carter, A. S. (2001b). Infant–Toddler Social Emotional Assessment. San Antonio, TX: Pearson Assessments.

Greenspan, S. I., DeGangi, G., & Wieder, E. S. (2001). Functional Emotional Assessment Scale. San Antonio, TX: Pearson Assessments.

Naglieri, J. A., LeBuffe, P. A., & Pfeiffer, S. A. (1993). Devereux Behavior Rating Scale School Form. San Antonio, TX: Pearson Assessments.

Naglieri, J. A., LeBuffe, P. A., & Pfeiffer, S. A. (1994). Devereux Scales of Mental Disorders. San Antonio, TX: Pearson Assessments.

Sparrow, S. S., Balla, D. A., & Cicchetti, D. V. (1998). Vineland Social-Emotional Early Childhood Scales. San Antonio, TX: Pearson Assessments.

[41]

Devereux Student Strengths Assessment.

Purpose: "Developed to provide a measure of social-emotional competencies."
Population: Grades K-8.
Publication Dates: 2008-2009.
Acronym: DESSA.
Scores, 9: Personal Responsibility, Optimistic Thinking, Goal-Directed Behavior, Social-Awareness, Decision Making, Relationship Skills, Self-Awareness, Self-Management, Total (Social-Emotional Composite).
Administration: Group.
Price Data, 2009: $115.95 per complete kit including 25 record forms, manual (2009, 161 pages), and norms reference card, all in a vinyl portfolio; $39.95 per 25 record forms; $32.95 per 25 online administration record forms and scoring report; $74.95 per manual; $6.95 per norms reference card; $9.95 per vinyl portfolio; price information for online administration, scoring, and individual student reports available from publisher.
Time: [10] minutes or less.
Comments: Test is part of a series that includes: the Devereux Early Childhood Assessment–Infant/Toddler Version (DECA-I/T; 18:40), the Devereux Early Childhood Assessment (DECA; T7:811), and the Devereux Early Childhood Assessment–Clinical Form (DECA-C; T7:812); ratings "by parents, teachers, or staff at schools and child-serving agencies"; individual and classroom profiles available.
Authors: Paul A. LeBuffe, Valerie B. Shapiro, and Jack A. Naglieri.
Publisher: Kaplan Early Learning Company.

Review of the Devereux Student Strengths Assessment by JEFFREY A. ATLAS, Clinical and School Psychologist, SCO Family of Services, Queens, NY:

DESCRIPTION. The Devereux Foundation, at the forefront of nonprofit residential centers for much of the 20th century, has developed its training and research mission to focus on prevention. Drawing from community and individual psychology trends from the 1960s forward, areas such as resilience, prosocial behavior and positive psychology have been incorporated to produce a measure of social-emotional competencies of children in kindergarten through eighth grade. The Devereux Student Strengths Assessment (DESSA) is an elaboration and upward extension of a series that includes infant/toddler and clinical forms. It should be of interest to school evaluators and social service agencies in identifying the progression of students' strengths.

The test authors submit that low scores on the DESSA "can help identify children who may be at risk for developing behavioral problems" (manual, p. 6). For children already experiencing emotional and behavioral concerns, the DESSA may be used to delineate strengths to be nurtured and target areas for intervention to promote more positive outcomes.

The DESSA is a 72-item, standardized, norm-referenced scale featuring behaviors rated to occur *never*, *rarely*, *occasionally*, *frequently*, or *very frequently*. The scale is designed to be filled out by parenting or teaching figures knowing the child a minimum of 4 weeks. The 10-minute estimate for completion of the scale is reasonable, and the carbonless attached scoresheet eases rapid scoring of the protocol and extensive intratest and cross-rater comparisons. The questions are thought-provoking and are likely to require individual completion during a quiet time of a teacher's or parent's day.

DEVELOPMENT. In developing the DESSA items, the test authors identified 765 potential items in reviewing the resilience literature. They pared down this list by focusing on nonoverlapping, measurable items that did not appear too value-laden, resulting in a pool of 156 items. These were piloted on 428 students in kindergarten through eighth grade, of whom 25% were identified as having significant emotional or behavioral problems. Items showing unsatisfactory reliability (item-total correlations < .60), nondifferentiation of behaviorally disordered children by at least half a standard deviation, or nonapplicability as rated by 20% or more of respondents were eliminated. The resulting set of 81 items was used in the national standardization edition of the DESSA, and ultimately reduced to 72 items after elimination of items demonstrating age trends.

TECHNICAL.

Standardization. Of the 2,494 children comprising the standardization sample, there were 49.5% males, aligning closely with the 51.2% figure for the 5- through 14-year-old age group for the 2006 U.S. Census. Kindergarten youth are somewhat overrepresented (19.8%), with a paucity of seventh (4.9%) and eighth (4.2%) graders; a total of only 23 seventh graders were evaluated in the western region of the country. Athough one may have liked higher *n*s for Grades 6–8, the skewness of the standardization sample towards early grades is consistent with the test authors' interests in primary prevention. Of practical note and in a reflection of the potential generalizability of results, teacher and teacher aides provided ratings of 778 students, parents and other adult relatives in the home provided 1,244, and after-school and other program staff provided the remaining 472 ratings. The DESSA comprises separate norms tables for teachers and parents, taking into account mild dissimilarities across categories in the home and school situations (e.g., students tending to show somewhat better Self-Management in line with demand characteristics of the school milieu).

Although there is slight overrepresentation of African Americans and underrepresentation of European Americans in the standardization sample, overall these and American Indian/Alaskan, Hawaiian/Pacific Islander, and Hispanic versus Non-Hispanic ethnicity percentages all adhere closely to U.S. Census figures.

Socioeconomic status of the DESSA standardization sample reflected slight overrepresentation of children living in poverty, 25% versus 19% in census figures for families whose yearly income was $25,000 or less in 2005.

Effect sizes for racial groups were compared using the d-ratio (difference between mean scores divided by average standard deviation for the two groups). Differences between groups were negligible to small. For male to female comparisons, differences were small, permitting the test authors to maintain unitary norms tables with the expectation that females tend to score several points higher, consistent with Western society mores.

The obtained frequency distribution of each scale was fit to the normal probability standard scores using the obtained percentile ranks through smoothing of irregularities within each scale. The standard score metric utilized for the individual and composite scales were *T*-scores with means of 50 and standard deviations of 10, to ease comparisons within and across student profiles and between different raters.

Reliability. Alpha coefficients were used to examine the internal consistency of each scale; estimates ranged from .82 to .94. The social-emotional composite score demonstrated coefficients of reliability of .98 (parent raters) and .99 (teachers) using a linear combination formula. These estimates are impressive.

Test-retest reliability of test scores was assessed through teacher (n = 38) and parent (n = 54) ratings of the same child in a convenience sample of third to fourth graders tested over 4 to 8 days. All reliability coefficients, ranging from .79 (Parent ratings of Social-Awareness) to .94 (Teacher ratings of Decision Making, Personal Responsibility, and the Social-Emotional Composite) were significant at $p < .01$.

A rather unique feature of the DESSA is its provision on the scoresheet of a *T*-score comparison of scale scores across parent-parent, teacher-teacher, and parent-teacher raters. By referencing the difference scores to Table 5.4 in the manual, one can test for differences at the .05 or .01 significance levels for each scale and the composite scale. Interrater reliability studies of a parent sample of 51 third graders and a separate teacher sample of 51 second graders yielded good respective median reliability coefficients of .73 and .74.

Validity. The DESSA demonstrated good convergent validity with the Behavior Assessment System for Children–Second Edition (BASC-2; Reynolds & Kamphaus, 2004). The DESSA Social-Emotional Composite correlated with the Adaptive Skills Scale of the BASC-2 for 75 parents ($r = .77$, $p < .01$) and 65 teachers ($r = .92$, $p < .01$). The Social-Emotional Composite correlated negatively with the Behavior Symptoms Index of the BASC-2 for both parents ($r = -.64$, $p < .01$) and teachers ($r = -.72$, $p < .01$). The Social-Emotional composite correlated negatively with the teacher-rated School Problems Scale of the BASC-2 ($r = -.70$, $p < .01$).

In examining the predictive validity of the DESSA, the test authors found that 78 third graders in Regular Education had higher scale and composite scores than 78 third graders classified Seriously Emotionally Disturbed. Chi square analysis for group membership, although providing discriminant validity at the $p < .001$ significance level for predicting group membership by a composite score at or below 40 (the "need for instruction" cutoff of the DESSA), eventuated in 24.4% of Regular Education students being misclassified. Two Regular Education parents sampled by the reviewer also yielded misclassification.

COMMENTARY. The DESSA may be useful in monitoring the progress of students whose eligibility for special education already has been determined, particularly students who already receive interventions addressing behavioral or emotional problems. Through biennial administration of the scale to special education students, classes, or schools, a within-subjects design would allow participants to be their own controls for making comparisons in order to assess the impact of interventions.

SUMMARY. The DESSA is an elegant, comprehensive measure of young student social-emotional strengths that may be employed prospectively to assess the progress of children in Grades K–8. The lengthier and more commonly used BASC-2, assessing both behavioral problem and adaptive areas, the latter correlating with the DESSA. Although the BASC-2 is preferable at this time as part of a battery in initial evaluations for special education, the DESSA may be useful in identifying children at risk for developing emotional or behavioral problems.

REVIEWER'S REFERENCE

Reynolds, C. R., & Kamphaus, R. W. (2004). Behavior Assessment System for Children–Second Edition. Minneapolis: American Guidance Service.

Review of the Devereux Student Strengths Assessment by KORESSA KUTSICK MALCOLM, School Psychologist, The Virginia School for the Deaf and Blind, Staunton, VA:

DESCRIPTION. The Devereux Student Strengths Assessment (DESSA) is a 72-item, standardized, norm-referenced rating scale designed to capture the social and emotional competencies of children in kindergarten through eighth grade. he scale is composed of behavioral items that reflect resilient behaviors of children and youth. A total Social-Emotional Composite score, as well as eight subtest scores, can be obtained. The DESSA may be completed by parents, guardians, teachers, and/or other direct care individuals. The DESSA is an upward extension of the Devereux Early Childhood Assessment (DECA; LeBuffe & Naglieri, 1999; T7:811) and reflects the mission statement of the Devereux Center for Resilient Children to promote social and emotional competencies, as well as academic successes, of young children.

The items of the DESSA are presented in a positive behavioral orientation in order to ascertain strengths children have that would lead to resilient, rather than maladaptive, behaviors. These items are categorized into eight subtests of social and emotional competencies. The subtests include Self-Awareness, Social-Awareness, Self-Management, Goal-Directed Behavior, Relationship Skills, Personal Responsibility, Decision Making, and Optimistic Thinking. The Self-Awareness subtest measures a child's understanding of his or her strengths and weaknesses and desires for self-improvement. The Social-Awareness subtest assesses a child's skills in interacting with others through respect, tolerance, and cooperation. The Self-Management scale measures a child's skill in controlling his or her emotions and behaviors, especially in challenging situations. The Goal-Directed Behavior scale assesses the child's ability to initiate and remain focused on presented tasks. The Relationship Skills subtest taps socially appropriate interaction skills that the child uses on a consistent basis. The Personal Responsibility scale assesses the child's ability to reliably contribute to group projects. The Decision Making subtest measures problem solving and personal responsibility in learning. Finally, the Optimistic Thinking subtest taps the child's ability to think in positive terms for his or her current and future life circumstances.

Each item of the DESSA is scored on a 5-point scale based on behaviors the rater observed during a period of 4 weeks from the date of assessment. Raters mark each box corresponding to a 5-point scale that ranges from "Never" to "Very Frequently." Items can be read to raters in the case of suspected or known reading weaknesses of an individual asked to complete the scale.

Scoring of the DESSA is completed by hand by tallying responses in boxes on the inside pages of the record form. Raw scores for each scale are transferred to a score summary table. *T*-scores and percentile information can be obtained from charts on the record form as well as from tables in the manual. An individual student profile is provided on the form to chart *T*-scores for each subtest. Completing this profile enables the determination of strengths, typical behaviors, or areas of weakness according to scores obtained on the various subtests.

DEVELOPMENT. Items for the DESSA were developed from a review of literature noting resilient behaviors of children and youth, social-emotional learning, and positive youth development. From an initial set of 765 items, 156 items were selected through typical scaling techniques to comprise the pilot version of the test. This pilot version was tried out on a sample of 428 students, 106 of whom had histories of behavioral or emotional disorders. Items that did not show item-to-total reliability in discriminating between the identified and nonidentified students, or that were noted to be vague or unclear by raters, were removed from the test. The 81 remaining items comprised the standardization version of the DESSA.

TECHNICAL. Standardization of the DESSA was conducted on a selected sample of 2,494 children. These children represented the usual demographic variables of age, gender, geographic region, race ethnicity, and socioeconomic status of children reflected in the 2006 U.S. Census data. After the standardization data were gathered, the 81 items of the scale were reviewed and reduced to 72 items. These items were then organized into eight social-emotional subtests categorized as core competencies proposed by various curricula that address the teaching of such competencies to children and by the Collaborative for Academic, Social, and Emotional Learning. Items that statistically loaded on each scale were selected for inclusion on that scale.

Reliability of the DESSA was discussed in terms of internal, test-retest, and interrater reliability studies conducted on data obtained during the standardization process. Internal reliability coefficients (using coefficient alpha) ranged from .82 to .98 for parent ratings of each scale and from .89 to .99 for teacher ratings. Test-retest reliability was explored using a group of ratings provided by 38 teachers and 54 parents who rated the same child on two different occasions during a period of 4 to 8 days. Median test-retest reliability coefficients were .86 and .93 for parent and teacher ratings, respectively. Interrater reliability was examined through several studies including having two parents, two teachers, and a teacher/teacher assistant rate the same child in the context of the same environment. Correlations obtained in these studies ranged from moderate to high for the total score, as well as for each of the subtest scores for the parent rater pairs and for the teacher rater pairs.

Validity information for the DESSA was presented in the manual for content-related, criterion-related, and construct-related validity. The test authors noted the degree to which the items of the DESSA reflected skills presented in curricula designed to teach social and emotional competencies as evidence of the content validity of this test. They also noted skills listed in resilient child research that match DESSA items as additional evidence for the content validity of the test. In the criterion-related validity studies the test authors and their associates used data obtained in the standardization of the DESSA to demonstrate that total and subtest scores differentiated between groups of children with and without formal identification of serious emotional difficulties. To establish the construct validity of the DESSA, *T*-scores of this scale were correlated with standard scores from the Behavioral and Emotional Rating Scale–Second Edition (BERS-2; Epstein, 2004) and the Behavior Assessment System for Children–Second Edition (BASC-2; Reynolds & Kamphaus, 2004) for ratings provided on all three scales by parents and by teachers. The DESSA total score correlated significantly (r = .80, p < .01) with the BERS-2 Strength Index as well as with the Adaptive Skills Scale of the BASC-2 (for parent ratings $r = .77$, $p < .01$ and for teachers $r = .92$, $p < .01$). The DESSA Social-Emotional Composite score also was found to correlate negatively with the BASC-2's Behavioral Symptoms Index for both parents and teacher ratings and with the School Problem Scale for teacher ratings. These findings indicated that children who demonstrated strong social competency scores on the DESSA did not show significant levels of problem behaviors on the BASC-2, supporting the notion that the DESSA taps positive behavioral functioning in children.

COMMENTARY. The DESSA is a well-thought-out, appropriately developed test that holds great promise of value for those working with children who face adversity in their lives. The emphasis on identifying positive behaviors is a major attribute of the DESSA. Most rating scales developed to assess the emotional and behavioral functioning of children focus on maladaptive and problem behaviors. The orientation of the DESSA to focus on the adaptive aspects of children's functioning would lend itself well to those efforts that attempt to build a child's appropriate skills in order to help them function successfully in their futures.

The DESSA manual is well organized. The rating scale is easy to complete. The items are written in a straightforward manner that is clear to raters. The test authors attempted to adjust the readability of the test so that most parents and caregivers should have little difficulty in completing the scale without assistance. Allowing the reading of the test to raters who may have limited English proficiency or reading skills is a plus. The length of time a rater needs to have known a child (4 weeks) is one of the shorter periods requested of rating scales and would be of value to professionals who need to obtain measures of a child's functioning early in a school year or intervention process.

The only relative weakness of the DESSA was that its scoring procedures are tedious. Scorer errors could be an issue when adding subtest raw scores and transferring data to the profile chart by hand. The development of a computer scoring system for this test would be of value. [Editor's Note: The test authors advise that a computer administration, scoring, and reporting system is now available.]

SUMMARY. The DESSA is a well-thought-out, norm-referenced, easily administered and interpreted behavior rating scale designed for use with children from kindergarten through eighth grade. It can be completed by parents, teachers, teacher assistants, and others who are providing direct care to children in this age range. Initial reliability and validity information presented in the manual by the test authors and their colleagues is very promising. The developmental processes of the DESSA meet or exceed the standards for test construction set forth by the American Psychological Association. The results of the DESSA would lend themselves well to the process of identification of positive behaviors that could be fostered and supported to help children overcome adversities they have faced or will face in their lives.

REVIEWER'S REFERENCES

Epstein, M. H. (2004). *Behavioral and Emotional Rating Scale examiner's manual.* (2nd ed.). Austin, TX: PRO-ED.

LeBuffe, P. A., & Naglieri, J. A. (1999). *Devereux Early Childhood Assessment user's guide.* Lewisville, NC: Kaplan Early Learning Company Publishing.

Reynolds, C. R., & Kamphaus, R. W. (2004). *Behavior assessment system for Children–Second Edition: Manual.* Circle Pines, MN: American Guidance Service.

[42]

Diagnostic Assessments of Reading, Second Edition.

Purpose: Designed to function as an assessment of individual reading ability for the DARTTS testing and teaching program.
Population: Grades K–12.
Publication Dates: 1992–2006.
Acronym: DAR-2.
Scores, 10: Word Recognition, Oral Reading Accuracy, Oral Reading Fluency (optional), Silent Reading Comprehension, Spelling, Word Meaning, Print Awareness, Phonological Awareness, Letters and Sounds, Word Analysis.
Administration: Individual.
Forms, 2: Form A, Form B (equivalent forms).
Price Data, 2007: $228 per classroom kit (specify Form A or B) including student book (57 pages), 30 response records with directions for administration booklets, teacher's manual (27 pages), 5-user license for Trial Teaching Strategy program; $67.40 per student booklet (specify form); $67.40 per 15 response records with directions for administration booklets (specify form); $25.85 per teacher's manual (specify form); $33.70 per technical manual (2006, 159 pages; CD version also available); $111 per DAR ScoringPro software system.
Time: (40) minutes.
Comments: A component of the DARTTS testing and teaching program.
Authors: Florence G. Roswell, Jeanne S. Chall, Mary E. Curtis, and Gail Kearns.
Publisher: PRO-ED.

Cross References: For reviews by Kevin D. Crehan and Gene Schwarting of an earlier edition, see 12:115.

Review of the Diagnostic Assessments of Reading, Second Edition by TIMOTHY R. KONOLD, Associate Professor of Research, Statistics, and Evaluation, and CAMILLE LAWRENCE, Doctoral Student in Research, Statistics, and Evaluation, University of Virginia, Charlottesville, VA:

DESCRIPTION. The Diagnostic Assessments of Reading, Second Edition (DAR) with Trial Teaching Strategies (TTS) is an individually administered comprehensive diagnostic testing and teaching tool used with school-aged children in Grades K–12. The purpose of the DAR with TTS is twofold: to provide a comprehensive assessment of children's strengths and weaknesses in reading and language, and to inform instructional interventions. Two forms (i.e., A and B) of the DAR were designed to be equivalent short, pre- and post-formal assessments comprising nine tests (i.e., Print Awareness, Phonological Awareness, Letters and Sounds, Word Recognition, Word Analysis, Oral Reading, Silent Reading Comprehension, Spelling, and Word Meaning). Users can expect administration of the battery to take approximately 40 minutes. The TTS is an online teaching component that provides effective informal lessons to improve students' reading and language weaknesses identified through the DAR.

Detailed directions for test administration and scoring are provided in the teacher's manual. In addition, test administrators are provided with a response record with directions for administration, which includes a script for administering the test as well as recording and scoring materials. Benchmarks for mastery are provided for each test and their component parts. Although specific instructions are provided for adequate test administration, evidence concerning the time lapse necessary between the pre- and post-assessments is not provided.

The TTS website contains instructions for accessing the appropriate test for individual students. In addition, each lesson has explicit directions and a list of needed materials. All teaching components also contain a student record form to record student responses. Teachers are given directions for scoring as well as guidelines for interpreting and using the results.

DEVELOPMENT. According to the technical manual, construction of the second edition of the DAR with TTS is based on research supporting the direct assessment of student patterns of strengths and weaknesses in reading. The two theories of the reading process that underlie the testing and teaching procedures assert that reading comprises a diverse set of skills and components, and that qualitative changes occur as reading develops. The construction of the DAR was guided by this theoretical framework as well as additional contemporary research, the authors' earlier work in this area, and a review of previously published instruments. Specific words and reading passages were selected from the original edition of the DAR. These items were compared for grade placement and difficulty based on a combination of standard sources such as reading curriculum materials, word sources, and readability measures. This process led to a revision of Form A and a completely new Form B. The technical manual does not address the construction of the TTS with the same level of specificity as the DAR primarily in terms of detailed pedagogical approaches used for each lesson. However, the general approach underlying the teaching strategies is provided.

TECHNICAL. The standardization sample for the DAR was composed of N = 1,395 students in Grades K–12 for Form A, and N = 1,440 students in Grades K–12 for Form B. Most of the psychometric investigations with the DAR were conducted on Form A. Readers should assume that the information presented below is based on Form A unless otherwise specifically noted. The standardization sample for Form A was selected to be demographically representative of gender, race/ethnicity, and geographic region. In addition, the sample was composed of students from both public and private schools. Raw scores on the DAR can be converted to percentile ranks that are provided separately in 1-year grade intervals. Traditional standard scores are not available.

Reliability. Several investigations into the reliability of scores are presented in the form of internal consistency, classification consistency, and interrater reliability. Internal consistency (split-half based upon Spearman-Brown) estimates for the DAR were generally respectably high (e.g., high .80s and .90s) across many of the subtests and grade levels. One of the purported uses of the DAR is to classify students as "masters" and "nonmasters." Huynh's single administration classification consistency (C) index was implemented on three tests and their component parts for children in Grades K and 1. Results suggested good classification consistency for children in Grade 1 on Print Awareness (C = .87), but a somewhat less favorable value for children in Grade K (C = .66). Consistency estimates were very respectable for the component parts of Phonological Awareness across Grades K and 1 (Cs ≥ .80), and generally good for the component parts of Letters and Sounds (C range = .69–.97). Consistency estimates for other subtests were not provided.

Interrater reliability investigations were conducted on the subtests of Silent Reading Comprehension and Word Meaning to evaluate the consistency of scores applied to open-ended responses by separate judges. Reported estimates were generally favorable (≥ .80) across the limited number of test levels that were examined. Unfortunately, no evidence of test-retest or alternate-form reliability estimates appear to be provided.

Validity. It is widely recognized that validity refers to the accumulation of evidence to support the interpretation of test scores in the context of their purpose. The DAR technical manual reports several investigative validity studies for Form A, the majority of which can be characterized along the lines of content, criterion-related, and construct validity. Content of the second edition of the DAR was largely informed from the blueprint of the original DAR that the authors indicate was already in compliance with recommendations by the National Reading Panel (2000). This second edition of the DAR builds upon the original version through inclusion of revisions to reflect more contemporary reading research. Investigations of differential item functioning were also conducted across gender, race, and ethnic groups to identify items that yield different probabilities of success in answering for members of different groups when matched on ability. Very few items were found to display potential sources of differential item functioning (15 DIF items from the 1,900 investigations). Identified items were further examined and 4 were dropped from the instrument.

Criterion-related validity was examined through correlations among DAR measures and tests located on the Gates-MacGinitie Reading Tests (Macginitie & MacGinitie, 1989). Correlations were generally moderate in size, and reflective of positive results. In addition, DAR scores from ESL students, gifted students, LD students, and Title 1 students were evaluated relative to a matched control group. Groups were matched on the demographics of age, gender, and ethnicity. Results favorably supported the DAR by generally revealing that gifted children performed better than the control group; that ESL children yielded materially lower scores than the control group, particularly in the earlier years (e.g., K–2); differences favored the control group over the LD group; and that differences between Title 1 children and the control group expanded in higher grades.

Evidence of construct validity was somewhat weaker than other forms of validity evidence provided. Although results of DAR subtest intercorrelations were suggestive of reasonable levels of convergent and divergent validity, users would benefit from additional analyses beyond inspection of zero-order correlation coefficients. No evidence is provided in the form of exploratory factor analysis, confirmatory factor analysis, or multigroup confirmatory factor analyses, for example. These are useful analytic tools that provide greater insight into the multidimensional nature of a test's structure than is afforded by bi-variate correlations.

COMMENTARY/SUMMARY. The individually administered DAR consists of a variety of reading measures that hold promise for instructional interventions and are aligned with contemporary theoretical postulates. The measures are relatively easy to administer and require relatively little examination time (i.e., approximately 40 minutes). The breadth of coverage will likely be useful to users for developing a profile of children's reading strengths and weaknesses. Additional strengths include its purported usefulness with a wide age range of children and some strong psychometric properties.

Demonstrating the extent to which scores are free from error (reliability) and that the scores are appropriate for their intended use (validity) is an ongoing process. The technical manual addresses several important psychometric issues relating to the interpretation of scores and appropriateness of use with this population of children. Particularly positive aspects here include the positive internal consistency estimates that were obtained and the criterion-related validity as demonstrated through the ability of the test to separate known groups of children that might be expected to have different levels of reading proficiency. Although there are many positive aspects to this instrument, there remains room for improvement. First, the on-line teaching resources were a bit difficult to locate with no specific Web address indicated in the resources provided. [Editor's note: Test materials provided to the reviewers were published by another company. Between then and publication of the reviews, PRO-ED has taken over publication and distribution and they advise that each customer is now provided an envelope with specific instructions on how to access and activate their account online.] Second, it is not always clear in the technical manual whether the reported psychometrics are based on the second edition of the DAR or the earlier version. Third, although several reliability investigations are provided in the manual for some of the DAR tests, additional investigations are needed for many of the other tests on which limited evidence of reliability is provided. Last, and as indicated above in this review, the use of factor analysis could lead to a better understanding of the internal structure of the instrument.

REVIEWERS' REFERENCES

MacGinitie, W. H., & MacGinitie, R. K. (1989). Gates-MacGinitie Reading Tests. Rolling Meadows, IL: Riverside Publishing.

National Reading Panel. (2000). *Teaching children to read: An evidence-based assessment of the scientific research literature on reading and its implications for reading instruction.* Bethesda, MD: National Institute of Child Health and Human Development.

Review of the Diagnostic Assessments of Reading, Second Edition by NATALIE RATHVON, Assistant Clinical Professor, The George Washington University, Washington DC; and Private Practice Psychologist and School Consultant, Bethesda, MD:

DESCRIPTION. The Diagnostic Assessments of Reading, Second Edition (DAR) is an individually administered norm- and criterion-referenced test designed to diagnose reading strengths and weaknesses and to guide remediation for students in kindergarten through Grade 12. It serves as the assessment component of the Trial Teaching Strategies (TTS), an online set of lessons targeting deficits identified on the DAR. Based on Carroll's (1977) theory of reading comprehension and Chall's stage theory of reading development (1983), the DAR was developed to serve as a single collection of reading and language tests for use by teachers, reading specialists, and others involved in reading remediation. The classroom kit for each form includes a teacher's manual, a student book, 30 response records with directions for administration, and a five-user license for the TTS. Also available are a technical manual, which contains the norms tables, and a software data management program (the DAR ScoringPro).

The DAR consists of nine tests, five of which are leveled by grade: Word Recognition (WR), Oral Reading (OR), Silent Reading Comprehension (SRC), Spelling (SP), and Word Meaning (WM). The other four tests–Print Awareness (PrA), Phonological Awareness (PA), Letters and Sounds (LS), and Word Analysis (WA)–are unleveled, and all but PrA have multiple subtests. Changes to this edition include two new tests (PrA and PA), additional LS and WA subtests, a second parallel form, an oral response comprehension assessment for the first two levels, an optional words-correct-per-minute metric for OR, and newly designed test materials. Changes to the TTS include a Web-based format and new strategies and instructional materials.

Administration. The DAR is untimed and takes about 40 minutes to complete. Kindergarten students and students not achieving mastery on WR Level 1–2 (second half of Grade 1) take PrA, PA, and LS, whereas students in Grade 1 and above begin in WR at their known or estimated reading level. The student's highest WR mastery level provides the starting point for the other DAR tasks except for WM, which is begun at the student's current grade placement. Students scoring at Level 3 or below on WR take WA. The PA subtests should be delivered by audiotape rather than by live voice to enhance interexaminer consistency. For SRC, students read short passages silently and then provide an oral summary (Levels 1–2 and 2) or respond in writing to multiple-choice questions (Levels 3 and above). The oral response format, scored on a 3-point rubric, is optional for Levels 3 and above.

Scoring. Scoring is dichotomous for items on all subtests except for the SRC oral response, which increases scorer consistency but reduces sensitivity on tests such as SP and WM, especially because there are so few items per level (five for SP and four for WM). There is no composite score. Many tasks are highly vulnerable to interscorer variance, especially WM, which requires the student to provide oral definitions for spoken words. Raw scores can be converted to national percentiles using tables in the technical manual. Norms are in 1-year increments for the entire grade range, which is adequate for examinees in Grades 3 and above but too broad for examinees in the early primary grades, when reading and language skills are developing rapidly (Rathvon, 2004). The DAR ScoringPro does not actually score the tests but generates group and individual reports when scores are entered and serves as a database for score aggregation and disaggregation.

Interpretation. Student performance is evaluated in terms of the highest mastery level for the leveled tests and mastery/nonmastery for the unleveled tests, with mastery set at about 70% correct. In the absence of composite scores for skill areas, such as phonological awareness, decoding, and comprehension, comparisons of examinee proficiency must be at the subtest level. The lack of composite scores reduces both interpretability and reliability, especially given the small number of items per task. No case examples are provided in the print or Web-based materials to illustrate how to interpret DAR results or use the data to design remedial instruction. No cautions are offered regarding the importance of considering multiple data sources in diagnosis and treatment planning, such as performance-based assessments, teacher interviews, and classroom observations, in addition to standardized tests.

DEVELOPMENT. The authors developed the DAR and its predecessor to create an instrument that would assess all important reading components, including a measure of reading potential (WM), in less time than that required by administering separate tests. Goals for this edition included adding assessments for young readers and targeting all five components of reading identified by the National Reading Panel (2000). Relatively little information is provided regarding the development of Form B compared with the data provided for Form A.

TECHNICAL ADEQUACY.

Standardization. Standardization for Form A was conducted in fall of 2004 on 1,395 students in Grades K–12 from 24 states. Characteristics are reported by gender, ethnicity, and geographic region by grade, with proportions designed to approximate U.S. 2000 Census data, but because sample characteristics are compared to population data for entire subgroups rather than for each grade, it is not possible to evaluate grade-specific representativeness. Overall, examinees from the Northeast region are overrepresented, and examinees from the Midwest and West are underrepresented. No information is provided regarding other critical variables, such as family income or parental educational level. Also reported are percentages of students in six special groups, but, again, these data are not presented in association with population statistics. Grade group sizes vary widely, with sizes for Grades 9–12 well below the minimum criterion of 100 per norm group interval. Standardization for Form B was conducted in fall of 2005 on 1,440 students in Grades K–12 in 19 states, but examinee proportions are described only in terms of gender and race/ethnicity and only for the entire sample rather than by grade.

Reliability. Corrected split-half reliability coefficients reported by grade are generally in the .90s for the leveled tests, but are much more variable for the unleveled tests. Coefficients reported for consistency of mastery/nonmastery decisions for PrA and for PA and LS subtasks are generally in the .80s and .90s, but no evidence for decision consistency is presented for the WA subtests. Exact agreement for 50 SRC oral responses selected randomly from each of two Form A levels and scored independently by two unidentified raters was 92% for Level 2 but only 80% for Level 7. Consistency between mastery ratings for 50 randomly selected WM responses for two Form A levels scored independently by two unidentified raters was 90% for Level 3 and 88% for Level 6. Because all of these values are based on completed protocols, however, they provide no information about interexaminer consistency during test sessions. Evidence of scoring consistency for the numerous other subtests vulnerable to examiner variance is absent. Evidence of score stability is also lacking. No reliability or validity evidence of any kind is presented for Form B, and no reliability coefficients or raw score means are presented to support the equivalence of the two forms. Given the limited number of items per task and the developmental nature of the skills assessed, it is not surprising that many subtests display floors and ceiling effects. Item gradient violations (Rathvon, 2004) are also pervasive across subtests, reducing the DAR's sensitivity to small differences in performance.

Validity evidence. Specific evidence for the accuracy of the difficulty levels for the leveled tests is provided, but support for item and format selection is limited. No empirical data are presented to support the use of a single page in the student book to assess print awareness rather than the usual illustrated small-book format; the failure to include pseudoword reading tasks, which may be the single most reliable indicator of reading disabilities (e.g., Vellutino, Scanlon, & Tanzman, 1994); or the failure to include higher level phonemic awareness tasks, such as deletion. Evaluation of potential bias included sensitivity reviews and Rasch-based differential item functioning (DIF) procedures, although details are sketchy for Form B. Correlations with the Gates-MacGinitie Reading Tests were generally moderate (.40 to .70s), with the exception of some of the LS subtests. No other evidence is presented to document the relationship of the DAR to other reading or language tests or to contextually relevant measures of reading performance, such as teacher ratings or classroom grades.

Mastery rates for the Form A norm group presented by grade demonstrate the increasing difficulty of the test levels, but there is no evidence that cut scores–a critical component of mastery testing–were reviewed by outside experts to provide additional verification of the selected benchmarks. Form A subtest *p*-values are reported by grade for individual items rather than as subtest medians by grade, making subtest-level analysis difficult. Values for many items on the unleveled tests exceed the criterion level, indicating that they may be too easy to provide an accurate assessment of individual performance. Raw score mean differences between four special groups and matched controls are in the expected direction, with moderate to large effect sizes for students with learning disabilities (LD) and an older Title I group (Grades 3–8). Because examinees with LD are combined into a single group (Grades 3–12), however, generalizations to specific student populations are limited. No predictive validity studies are presented to document the DAR's ability to identify individual students with reading problems (i.e., sensitivity or specificity indices). Research demonstrating the effects of targeted reading instruction on DAR performance (i.e., intervention differentiation studies) is also lacking.

COMMENTARY. Although more technical information is available for the second edition of the DAR compared with its predecessor, this version continues to emphasize usability in general and brevity in particular. Content coverage is abbreviated, making diagnosis and instructional planning tenuous at best. For example, SRC and OR reading passages are a maximum of two paragraphs, with only four questions (some of which are passage independent) per passage for SRC. The suggestion that WM may serve as an estimate of language and cognitive abilities should be disregarded, given the meager number of items per level and vague scoring guidelines. The TTS lessons are very brief, lack evidence of a research base or references to additional resources, and are too limited in scope for effectively addressing higher level reading skills such as comprehension and vocabulary. Other technical shortcomings include standardization samples of insufficient (Form A) or unknown (Form B) size and undetermined representativeness in terms of critical characteristics such as parental educational level. Evidence of interscorer reliability is provided for only two levels for two Form A tests, no evidence of score stability is provided, and no specific reliability or validity evidence is offered for Form B.

SUMMARY. The DAR is likely to appeal to practitioners because of its brevity, ease of administration, alignment with classroom reading tasks, and an online set of lessons addressing identified deficits. Despite its user-friendliness, this edition has numerous technical inadequacies that are likely to result in the overidentification or misidentification of students with reading problems, including a norm group of uncertain representativeness, abbreviated content coverage, and limited support for its proposed uses, especially for Form B. Although there is some evidence that the DAR Form A can discriminate between examinees with reading deficits and typically developing readers, its relationship to other measures of reading is confined to one study with one multiple-choice test, and its utility in identifying poor readers or predicting reading development has yet to be documented. Although this edition is an improvement on its predecessor, an all-in-one, technically sound reading instrument with utility for the full school-aged grade range remains a goal for test publishers and a dream for test users.

REVIEWER'S REFERENCES

Carroll, J. B. (1977). Developmental parameters of reading comprehension. In J. T. Guthrie (Ed.), *Cognition, curriculum, and comprehension* (pp. 1-15). Newark, DE: International Reading Association.

Chall, J. S. (1983). *Stages of reading development*. New York: McGraw-Hill.

National Reading Panel. (2000). *Teaching children to read: An evidence-based assessment of the scientific research literature on reading and its implications for reading instruction.* Bethesda, MD: National Institute of Child Health and Human Development.

Rathvon, N. (2004). *Early reading assessment: A practitioner's handbook*. New York: Guilford Press.

Vellutino, F. R., Scanlon, D. M., & Tanzman, M. S. (1994). Components of reading ability: Issues and problems in operationalizing word identification, phonological coding, and orthographic coding. In G. R. Lyon (Ed.), *Frames of reference for the assessment of learning disabilities* (pp. 279-332). Baltimore: Brookes.

[43]

Diagnostic Test for High School Mathematics.

Purpose: Designed to "provide diagnostic information on the competencies of individual students in various areas of basic, high school math."

Population: High school students.

[43] Diagnostic Test for High School Mathematics

Publication Dates: 2001-2003.
Acronym: DT-HSM.
Scores, 20: Whole Numbers, Common Fractions, Decimal Fractions, Percentages, Signed Numbers, Powers and Roots, Substitution, Setting up Equations, Solving Algebraic Equations, Geometry, Graphs, Tables, Estimation, Probability, Statistics, Order of Operations, Ratios, Math Vocabulary, Word Problems, Miscellaneous.
Administration: Group.
Price Data, 2007: $55 per technical manual (2003, 23 pages); $85 per specimen set including one test, one answer sheet, and sample reports.
Time: (90) minutes.
Author: Joel P. Wiesen.
Publisher: APR Testing Services.

Review of the Diagnostic Test for High School Mathematics by THOMAS P. HOGAN, Professor of Psychology, University of Scranton, Scranton, PA:

DESCRIPTION. As suggested by its title, the Diagnostic Test for High School Mathematics (DT-HSM) purports to provide diagnostic information for individual students and groups of students on competencies required for success in basic high school mathematics or, more specifically, success on the Massachusetts Comprehensive Assessment System (MCAS) statewide testing program for mathematics in Grade 10. The manual also claims that the test can be used for placement of students and for curriculum evaluation.

Materials for the DT-HSM include a 24-page test booklet, a 23-page technical manual, a scannable answer sheet, and several sample score reports. The test contains 60 multiple-choice items, with the unusual feature of offering 10 options per item, in all but a few instances including "none of these." It yields a total score and 20 competency subscores. Seventeen of the subscores are based on 3 items; two are based on 2 items; and one (Miscellaneous) on 5 items. The manual seems conflicted about the matter of time limits for the test, saying in one place (p. 4) that it "may be administered in 90 minutes," but elsewhere (p. 15) that "you may also give the test without a time limit." The manual refers to an online version of the DT-HSM, but it is not clear from the publisher's website (http://www.aprtestingservices.com/educational/dthsm/) exactly how the online version works and the manual contains no discussion of the equivalence of results for the print versus online version.

DEVELOPMENT. According to the manual, the authors based item preparation primarily on examination of the Massachusetts learning standards and released items from the MCAS math test (from 1998–2001), plus "several textbooks ... some other statewide testing programs ... [and] discussions were held with a number of math teachers and math tutors" (p. 9). However, the manual does not lay out the structure of either of the primary sources nor give sufficient detail about the other sources to provide any basis for determining the appropriateness of DT-HSM content coverage for these sources. Further, the manual claims that the 20 competencies represented by the scores "were found to be necessary to answer the MCAS questions" (p. 2). The manual provides no basis for this claim. The manual (p. 15) states that "questions were pilot tested prior to field use." However, it provides no information about the nature of such pilot testing (number of cases, number of items, method of analysis) or about use of the information.

TECHNICAL INFORMATION. The manual presents *norms* based on 1,138 students from four school districts (three in Massachusetts and one in Texas). Other than for state of origin, the manual gives no information about the nature (e.g., demographics) of this group. Crucial information for any meaningful use of the norms would require data on math courses completed, socioeconomic status, ability level, and other such indices. Absent any such information, the norms are meaningless; worse, providing such norms may be misleading if a user assumes some degree of representativeness for the norms. The norms themselves consist simply of means and standard deviations of the raw scores and percentages for the total test and each of the 20 clusters.

Regarding *reliability*, the manual provides an alpha reliability of .89 for the total score, based on the above referenced, undescribed sample of 1,138 students; and a median reliability for the 20 competency area scores of .23, which the manual (p. 16) says is "high enough for the intended purposes for the competency area scores." That is simply not true: A reliability of .23 is not high enough for diagnostic use of scores according to any standard.

The manual considers *validity* under the traditional rubrics of content, criterion-related, and construct validity. Regarding both criterion-related and construct validity, the manual notes that no such studies are available, but acknowledging the need for such studies. Regarding content validity, the manual relies entirely on reference to the authors' efforts to mirror the MCAS math test, as described above. It notes that a potential user from another state would have to conduct a study of that state's math curriculum. Thus, we can conclude virtually nothing about the validity of the DT-HSM for placement or diagnostic purposes.

The publisher's website contains the technical manual used for this review, as well as summary statements on purposes and technical information. Under Reliability and Validity, the website cites only the reliability of the total score (giving .90 rather than the .89 in the manual) and says nothing about validity.

COMMENTARY. A major flaw in the design of the DT-HSM comes in the tradeoff between test length and score detail, that is, between number of items and items per score. Put simply, if you want a lot of information, you need to have a considerable number of items and that takes considerably more test taker time. Computer adaptive testing (CAT) alleviates the conflict somewhat, but this is not a CAT. The DT-HSM manual (p. 14) acknowledges the problem when it notes that "[t]ypically, one constructs a test with 10 or more questions to measure a competency. However, that would result in a test with over 200 questions, and it was thought such a test would be too long to be practical for most users." The obvious conclusion, which the authors seem to disregard, is that if one wants to measure 20 different competencies adequately, then one should develop a test much longer than 60 questions or disclaim any diagnostic utility for the test.

Another serious flaw is the unwarranted assumption that the few items used per area are representative of skill levels in the area. The authors make no attempt to justify the small samples of items per competency as being representative of their respective domains. To say that a student needs remedial work in an area if the student answered, for instance, two out of three items incorrectly in that area requires some evidence that the three items fairly represent competence in that area. If the three items, or even two of them, are very difficult items, then getting only one out of three correct may be quite satisfactory. If the three items are very easy items, then a weakness may exist in that area even if the student achieves a score of 3. For this reason, statements in the various score reports are potentially misleading about strengths and weaknesses.

SUMMARY. The DT-HSM aims primarily to provide diagnostic information about competencies required for success in one state's Grade 10 math test, but also claims usefulness as a placement test and for curriculum evaluation. The DT-HSM fails to provide evidence that it is suitable for any of these purposes. The DT-HSM is not recommended for use and especially not for diagnosing weaknesses in various math areas.

Review of the Diagnostic Test for High School Mathematics by MICHAEL S. TREVISAN, Professor of Educational Psychology, Washington State University, Pullman, WA:

DESCRIPTION. The Diagnostic Test for High School Mathematics (DT-HSM) is a group-administered test designed to assess competencies thought essential for success in tenth grade mathematics. The authors state that the main purpose of the DT-HSM is diagnostic but also suggest that the test could be used for placement of students in pre-calculus classes or the evaluation of a school district's mathematics curriculum. The test is composed of 60 items, with two to three questions per competency area, except the "miscellaneous" area, which is composed of 5 items. Each question is multiple-choice in format, with 10 response options per item. Administration of the test is straightforward with easy-to-follow instructions in the manual. No special professional testing qualifications are required to administer the test. The authors recommend 90 minutes for administration with more if necessary. The test is generally administered without use of calculators. To date, one version of the test exists.

Answer sheets are used with the test and sent to the publisher for scoring. A provision to score the test over the web is also available. Three score reports are generated (individual student, class, and school). These reports provide the number of items correct by competency, number of items correct overall, and corresponding percent. These data are aggregated across students and classes for the class and school report, respectively. A small number of graphic distributions accompany the reports that show, for example, student scores within a class. A spreadsheet with student scores can be obtained upon request.

DEVELOPMENT. The DT-HSM was initially developed by examining the released test items from the 1998–2001 versions of the 10th grade mathematics test from the Massachusetts

Comprehensive Assessment System (MCAS) and identifying competencies essential for success on these items. A sample of some other state tests was also examined. Discussions with several high school mathematics teachers were held to obtain feedback and insight regarding the competencies. Each competency area is deliberately short.

A 10-response option item format is employed for all items. Though unusual, the authors argue that the format reduces the possibility of responding correctly to an item by chance, as well as guards against working the problem backward. Data from another test the publisher developed with 15 options per item showed that students chose each option with similar frequency (Wiesen, 2002). Given these data, the authors maintain that the 10-response option item format is functional and useful.

During the development of the test the items were edited, piloted, and reviewed. Review of items by school personnel, mathematicians, and measurement specialists was conducted. Some items were revised or discarded. Feedback from students while they took the test was also obtained. All items were piloted before actual use.

TECHNICAL. The test was administered to 1,138 high school students in four school districts, three from Massachusetts and one from Texas. Data about important variables from the sample such as grade level, gender, socioeconomic background, or race of the students are not included in the manual.

Reliability (internal consistency) data for the overall test score is respectable, with a coefficient alpha of .89. The median reliability estimate for the competencies is .23 (mean, .27). No other forms of reliability are offered. Interitem correlations, correlations among competency areas, and the correlation between each competency area and the remainder of the test are also provided.

A good deal of content validity evidence is offered through the process of identifying competencies, item development, and feedback from professionals. No other validity evidence is provided for the DT-HSM. The authors state that they are actively seeking research partners (i.e., school districts), offering a reduced price for the test in exchange for appropriate validity data. A brief validity research agenda is outlined in the technical manual.

COMMENTARY. The DT-HSM holds promise as a tool school districts could use to identify strengths and weaknesses in essential mathematics competencies, particularly when readying students for a statewide high school mathematics assessment. The authors have done a nice job of identifying competencies from the MCAS. The authors have stated that the test is a rough guide to determining competency in the identified areas and that other information (e.g., other competency-related tests or classroom assessments) is likely needed. In this way, this reviewer recommends its use. It is not known how well the MCAS aligns with other state-mandated tests. Thus, it is uncertain whether the competencies in the DT-HSM are similar to competencies in other state tests. School personnel from states other than Massachusetts should determine the extent to which the items on the test will provide useful information for identifying their states' high school students' strengths and weakness in mathematics.

In addition, it is recommended that further refinement of the DT-HSM include additional items in each competency area. Although the authors purposefully sought to keep the number of items small to increase use, the low reliability data for the competency areas indicates that there are simply too few items for sound decisions about student competence in any one area, without a significant amount of supporting information obtained from other sources. At this time, the use of the DT-HSM as a placement test is not recommended. Little discussion in the manual is offered concerning its use for placement. Although a norm sample is provided, a larger standardization sample is needed, with differentiation among important variables previously mentioned. The internal consistency reliability estimate for the total test score is fairly good and thus, the authors have a solid basis in which to progress with developing the test for placement.

There is an extensive empirical literature on item writing rules for developing multiple-choice achievement test items (see Haladyna, 1999). Studies concerning the optimum number of response options per item indicate that generally three options per item is sufficient for maintaining reliability and validity of data from achievement tests, though four and five options remains common. The authors have an interesting if not provocative idea in using 10-option items. Yet, there is no empirical study that justifies the use of 10-option items. Impara and Foster (2006) recommend the use of as many as 10 options per item to guard against test fraud, assuming the options are functional. However, Impara and Foster (2006) also acknowledge the existence of item development empirical literature showing that increasing the number of options can make items more difficult. In this reviewer's estimation, the data offered by the authors do not necessarily warrant the claim of item functionality. The data are descriptive in nature, obtained from one test administration, and acquired from another test development effort with even more options per item. An alternative explanation for the relatively even distribution of student responses across options is that students may be confused by the item format and choosing widely across options. In short, the item format may actually be a source of mis-measurement. The low mean score in the standardization data is a concern and may be a further indicator that this item format is problematic. To ferret out these issues a rigorous study to investigate the viability of this item format is recommended. Submission of the findings to a measurement journal for peer review would be important both because the test development community should be keenly interested in these findings and to ensure that claims made by the authors are upheld after professional scrutiny of the work.

The authors employ the choice "none of these" as the last option for most items. Although there is some disagreement in the literature, generally the research studies on this option recommend against its use. Although some maintain that the option can act against working an item backward, the option can unnecessarily confuse students and ironically, get in the way of identifying what students know or do not know. Elimination of this option in future versions of the test is recommended.

SUMMARY. The DT-HSM is designed as a group-administered mathematics diagnostic test for high school students. As a stand-alone test, there is insufficient psychometric information to warrant use. However, with proper support from additional information such as competency-related classroom assessment data, and strong alignment between this test and the specific statewide test students are preparing for, this reviewer is comfortable in recommending its use. The authors should work to increase the length of the test, rigorously investigate the viability of the 10-option item format, and establish broader validity evidence. At this time the DT-HSM is not recommended as a placement test.

REVIEWER'S REFERENCES

Haladyna, T. M. (1999). *Developing and validating multiple-choice test items* (2nd ed.). Mahwah, NJ: Lawrence Erlbaum Associates.

Impara, J. C., & Foster, D. (2006). Item and test development strategies to minimize test fraud. In S. M. Downing & T. M. Haladyna (Eds.), *Handbook of test development* (pp. 99-100). Mahwah, NJ: Lawrence Erlbaum Associates.

Wiesen, J. P. (2002). *Technical manual for the Diagnostic Test for Pre-Algebra Math (DT-PAM)*. Newton, MA: Applied Personnel Research.

[44]

Diagnostic Test for Pre-Algebra Mathematics.

Purpose: Designed to "provide diagnostic information on the competencies of individual students in various areas of basic math."

Population: 8th grade students.

Publication Dates: 2001-2003.

Acronym: DT-PAM.

Scores, 21: Whole Numbers, Common Fractions, Decimal Fractions, Percentages, Units of Measurement, Signed Numbers, Simple Powers, Substitution, Setting up Equations, Solving Equations, Geometry, Comparisons, Graphs, Tables, Estimation, Probability, Statistics, Order of Operations, Ratios, Math Vocabulary, Word Problems.

Administration: Group.

Price Data: Price data available from publisher.

Time: Administration time not reported.

Comments: Available in both print and online administration formats.

Author: APR Testing Services.

Publisher: APR Testing Services.

Review of the Diagnostic Test for Pre-Algebra Mathematics by GEORGE ENGELHARD, JR., Professor of Educational Measurement and Policy, Emory University, Atlanta, GA:

DESCRIPTION. The Diagnostic Test for Pre-Algebra Mathematics (DT-PAM) is a mathematics assessment designed to provide diagnostic information in various areas of basic mathematics. The DT-PAM consists of a single form with 50 items assessing the following 21 areas: Whole Number, Common Fractions, Decimal Fractions, Percentages, Units of Measurement, Signed Numbers, Simple Powers, Substitution, Setting up Equations, Solving Equations, Geometry, Comparisons, Graphs, Tables, Estimation, Probability, Statistics, Order of Operations, Ratios, Math Vocabulary, and Word Problems. Each of these areas is represented by 2–3 items.

The DT-PAM was designed to provide users with a group—administered test closely linked to the mathematics section of the Massachusetts

Comprehensive Assessment System (MCAS). According to the authors, the DT-PAM is intended as a diagnostic math test to pinpoint the strengths and weaknesses of individual students, as well as whole classes and grades. This test may help guide placement decisions, remedial studies, and preparation for statewide exams.

DEVELOPMENT. The DT-PAM consists of multiple-choice mathematics items representing 21 competency areas that the authors identified as underlying performance on the MCAS. The items are in multiple-choice format with 15 response choices. Due to the large number of competencies, there are only two to three items per competency.

TECHNICAL. The authors of the DT-PAM provide a technical manual. Because this is a diagnostic instrument, normative data would not typically be provided. The authors do refer to "normative data" based on eighth-grade students from two school districts (n = 580) obtained in October or November of 2000. The authors suggest that the potential user should contact the publisher for additional normative data. A check of the website did not reveal norms that were more current. These data should be considered a convenience sample, and not used to provide normative information. Because the data were collected in 2000, they are also a bit dated for any useful comparisons.

The authors report the diagnostic scores for the 21 areas. It should be stressed that there are only two or three items for each area. Inferences regarding student strengths and weaknesses are not warranted based upon such a small number of items per academic area.

Reliability information is provided for the total score and for competencies. The reliability coefficient is .934 (coefficient alpha). The internal consistency of the DT-PAM total scores is comparable to similar instruments. No information is provided on test-retest reliability. The median of the reliability coefficients across competency areas is .47 (coefficient alpha) with a range from .12 to 61. The authors do not provide standard errors of measurement with appropriate cautions regarding the interpretation of competency area scores. Validity information is presented in terms of internal evidence based on content analyses and correlations of area scores with total scores. External evidence is presented in terms of correlations of DT-PAM total scores with MCAS scores in mathematics (r = .946, n = 169). Two ACT products (COMPASS and PLAN) were used to provide additional external evidence of score validity. Correlations between DT-PAM and COMPASS were presented for Pre-Algebra (r = .719, n = 35), Algebra (r = .280, n = 48), Reading (r = .460, n = 64), and Writing (r = .383, n = 64). The correlations with PLAN were as follows: Math Score (.756, n = 59), Math Percentile (r = .770, n = 59), Overall Score (r = .671, n = 59), and Overall Percentile (r = .674, n = 59). These validity coefficients are comparable to those obtained with other achievement tests like the DT-PAM.

COMMENTARY. The DT-PAM suffers from many significant problems. First, the number of items is not sufficient to warrant making diagnostic decisions in 21 competency areas. One of the intended uses of the DT-PAM is the identification of relative strengths and weaknesses of students in mathematics. It is unlikely that the DT-PAM would provide additional information that would not already be known to most classroom teachers regarding each student. Second, statewide assessments, such as the MCAS, evolve over time and current content may become dated. According to the MCAS website, "what is important to remember is that each of the curriculum frameworks will always be considered as works in progress, and we will continue to refine them to strengthen them and to keep them current" (retrieved May 10, 2008, from http://www.doe.mass.edu/frameworks/). It is not clear that the DT-PAM matches the current mathematics curriculum frameworks. Third, because the DT-PAM is tightly connected to the MCAS, the utility of the assessment for teachers in other states is not documented. The authors briefly mention analyses of Texas and Florida tests, but potential users should carefully review the items to determine whether or not the content of the DT-PAM matches their local or state curriculum.

The score reports associated with the DT-PAM are also of concern. The individual student report uses a percent scale (0–100), and parents are not sufficiently cautioned about the uncertainty based on the use of only two to three items in each area. The school-wide reports include a ranking of students based on total scores. It is not clear to this reviewer what the recommended uses are for these ranks by school administrators.

The DT-PAM uses a highly unusual format for multiple-choice items with 15 answer choices. This format is quite likely to confuse students who are used to a traditional format with 4 or 5 answer choices. The authors also include "None of these" as a response category for many of the items. Although the authors claim that this format yields higher score reliability and mimics a free-response format, sufficient evidence is not presented to warrant these claims.

SUMMARY. In summary, the DT-PAM cannot be recommended for its intended use as a diagnostic instrument. The small number of items per content area (2–3 items) severely limits the reliability and validity of the diagnostic inferences that can be drawn based on this test. Teachers who do decide to use the test should consider the alignment between the content of the DT-PAM with the curriculum in their school and state. The total score on the DT-PAM may be of some use for predicting future performance on statewide assessments, but users should be very cautious about the degree of curricular alignment.

Review of the Diagnostic Test for Pre-Algebra Mathematics by MARY L. GARNER, Associate Professor of Mathematics, Kennesaw State University, Kennesaw, GA:

DESCRIPTION. The Diagnostic Test for Pre-Algebra Mathematics (DT-PAM) is a paper-and-pencil, 50-item multiple-choice test designed to identify deficiencies in individual eighth-grade students' basic mathematical skills in 21 specific areas. The 21 skill areas were identified as those skills needed for success on the mathematics portion of the eighth grade Massachusetts Comprehensive Assessment System (MCAS). Thus, the purpose of the test is to diagnose student weaknesses in advance of the MCAS, so that the student and teacher know where to focus remediation to improve scores on that test. The 21 skill areas are: Whole Numbers, Common Fractions, Decimal Fractions, Percentages, Units of Measurement, Signed Numbers, Simple Powers, Substitution, Setting up Equations, Solving Equations, Geometry, Comparisons, Graphs, Tables, Estimation, Probability, Statistics, Order of Operations, Ratios, Math Vocabulary, and Word Problems. To minimize the influence of guessing, each item has 15 distractors.

No special skills are required for test administration. The DT-PAM may be administered in one 45-minute class period or in two 45-minute class periods; however, the authors state that scores from different time allotments are not comparable. The answer sheets are returned to the publisher for scoring. A raw score and the percent correct are provided for the total score and for each of the 21 competency areas. A class report, a school-wide report, and an individual score report are provided.

DEVELOPMENT. The development of the test began with a detailed analysis of the skills required to answer questions released by the Massachusetts Department of Education from the 1998 and 1999 administrations of the mathematics portion of the eighth-grade statewide mathematics assessment in Massachusetts, the MCAS. On the MCAS one question may require several competencies but on the DT-PAM competencies are separated for easier diagnosis of specific deficiencies. Twenty-one mathematical competencies were identified as required for success on the MCAS. They include: Whole Numbers, Common Fractions, Decimal Fractions, Percentages, Units of Measurement, Signed Numbers, Simple Powers, Substitution, Setting up Equations, Solving Equations, Geometry, Comparisons, Graphs, Tables, Estimation, Probability, Statistics, Order of Operations, Ratios, Math Vocabulary, and Word Problems. The authors do not indicate exactly who identified the 21 competencies or how those competencies were identified. They state that "discussions were held with a number of math teachers and math tutors concerning the tentative test areas" (technical manual, p. 9).

A multiple-choice format was chosen for ease of administration and scoring. To reduce the influence of guessing and the possibility of students using a guess-and-check strategy, testing all possible answers, each item was written with 15 distractors. The authors do not describe exactly how the items were written or by whom. They make assertions such as "each question is a rather pure test of the competency" and "two or three questions for a competency cover important parts of the competency" (technical manual, p. 13) but do not provide evidence for such assertions. They state that "we wrote some questions to be very basic and others to be more advanced" (technical manual, p. 13). They state that the DT-PAM was reviewed by "diverse subject matter experts" but give no details of the process or of the experts. They also state that the questions were pilot-tested but provide no specifics.

The test is designed so that the first 21 items on the test address each of the 21 competencies, and the next 21 questions ask a second question in each competency. The descriptions of the competencies generally seem broader than the items themselves; for example, there are two items requiring comparisons and both of those items involve comparing numbers in different forms. Competency 12, "comparisons," is described as "compare size of numbers/shapes." No shapes are compared on the test. Competency 13, "graphs," is described as "Understand common types of graphs (i.e., bar, pie, and Cartesian). Find and chart points using X and Y coordinates ... construct a graph from given data" (technical manual, p. 12). However, there are only two such questions on the test, one requires interpretation of a bar graph and the other requires interpretation of a pie graph.

The authors make no mention of the use of calculators in the design of the questions. They state that the DT-PAM was "normed" on groups who did not use calculators but that "the diagnostic value of the test should remain strong even if used with calculators" (technical manual, p. 5). There are no data to support this statement. Indeed, 16 of the test items involve simple calculations of sums, products, and quotients of numbers, so it is unclear exactly what the test would be measuring with calculators versus without calculators.

TECHNICAL. The test has been administered to 972 eighth-grade students from four school districts in Massachusetts. The population of students is not described further. Descriptive statistics—raw score mean and standard deviation and percent correct mean and standard deviation—are provided for 580 students who took the test in one period and 392 students who took the test over two periods. The authors also provide data on the difficulty of the items, in terms of proportion correct, and on the use of the distractors.

Coefficient alpha for the test as a whole was .934. The reliabilities of the individual skill areas, which included only two or three questions, ranged from .12 to .61 with a median of .46. Correlations between scores on the individual skill areas and the total score ranged from .14 to .67.

Evidence for the content validity of the test includes the procedure for the development of the test, comparison with the 2001 eighth-grade mathematics portion of the Florida Comprehensive Assessment Test (FCAT), and comparison with the 2001 eighth-grade mathematics portion of the Texas Assessment of Academic Skills (TAAS). Tables are provided describing what DT-PAM competencies are required for the FCAT and TAAS.

Because the test was originally designed to provide diagnostic information about students who are preparing to take the mathematics portion of the MCAS, the strongest evidence of the validity of the test is provided by comparisons between performance on the DT-PAM and performance on the MCAS. The correlation between performance on the DT-PAM and the official 2001 MCAS for 184 students who took the DT-PAM over a 45-minute period was .80; the correlation for 97 students who took the DT-PAM over a 90-minute period was .90. The correlation between performance on the DT-PAM and performance on the multiple-choice questions from a released version of the 2000 MCAS was approximately .80 and .60 for another group who were given 45 minutes instead of 90 minutes to complete the MCAS. The DT-PAM was also shown to correlate highly with the COMPASS Pre-Algebra (approximately .70, n = 35) and the PLAN Math Score (approximately .80, n = 59).

COMMENTARY. The DT-PAM is a useful tool for sampling very basic pre-algebra skills. The authors present convincing evidence that these skills are associated with success on the mathematics portion of the eighth-grade MCAS. Teachers from any state could certainly use such diagnostic tests to identify student weaknesses and plan remediation, regardless of the presence of state-wide exams.

Because the DT-PAM scores are reported in terms of raw scores, on the test as a whole and on each of the 21 skill areas, the test is very easy to understand by students, parents, teachers, and administrators. The publishers provide a Student Report, a Class Report, and a School-Wide Report. The total score can be used to predict scores on the mathematics portion of the eighth-grade MCAS. Interpretation of the scores in each competency area is ambiguous. The authors suggest that "if a student gets half or fewer of the questions correct for a competency area, there is reason to suggest additional remedial education in that area" (technical manual, p. 32). Because many competency areas have two or three questions, there is really little on which to base a decision.

The authors suggest that the test could be used for class assignment, although they give no indication of the score at which educators should cut students off from the opportunity to study algebra. Although it seems intuitively reasonable to say that success on this test might predict success in an algebra course, research often contradicts intuition. Furthermore, state tests are usually designed to express the minimum requirements for advancement to subsequent grades; they do not necessarily test the higher order thinking or integration of skills that might be most advantageous for study of algebra.

As stated by the authors, the test can be used to identify student weaknesses in isolated, very basic, pre-algebra skills. Although the mathematics portion of the eighth-grade MCAS, as well as other state tests, do require integration of those skills, the DT-PAM does not require such integration. Calculator use does not seem appropriate because so much of the test is straight calculation. Higher order thinking or integration of skills is not tested. Mathematics textbooks traditionally abound with items that test isolated basic skills; teachers do not usually have difficulty quickly making up such tests. For that reason, the DT-PAM would appear to have very limited usefulness. Teachers might be better served by test developers producing tests that identify weaknesses and point to remediation in integration of skills, problem solving, reasoning, making connections, etc. (i.e., areas that are more difficult to assess).

SUMMARY. The DT-PAM is useful for what it was designed to do—give eighth-grade teachers and administrators a way to identify student weaknesses and then plan remediation so that students may succeed on the mathematics portion of the eighth-grade MCAS. The focus is on isolated, very basic pre-algebra skills, not on integration of those skills, not on problem solving, not on higher order thinking. The test is easy to administer. It should be administered over a 90-minute period rather than 45 minutes to avoid testing speed rather than skill. Students should not use calculators. In order to minimize the influence of guessing and other test-taking strategies, there are 15 distractors for each item. The publisher scores the test and provides a total raw score as well as raw scores for each of the 21 skill areas, with a report for the student, class, and school. There is no evidence provided that the test can be used for class assignment or other purposes for which it was not intended.

[45]

Differential Ability Scales–Second Edition.

Purpose: "To profile a child's strengths and weaknesses in a wide range of cognitive abilities."
Population: Ages 2-6 to 17-11.
Publication Dates: 1979-2007.
Acronym: DAS-II.
Subtests: Core, Diagnostic.
Administration: Individual.
Levels, 2: Early Years Battery, School-Age Battery.
Price Data, 2008: $1,120 per complete test kit including administration and scoring manual (2007, 309 pages), normative data tables manual (2007, 165 pages), technical manual (2007, 309 pages), 15 Early Years Battery record forms, 15 School-Age Battery record forms, 10 each of speed of information processing booklets (versions A, B, and C), 4 stimulus books, object recall card, picture similarities cards, phonological process and signed sentences CD, manipulatives, and scoring assistant.
Author: Colin D. Elliott.
Publisher: Pearson.

a) EARLY YEARS BATTERY.

1) *Lower Level Early Years Battery.*
Population: Ages 2-6 to 3-5.
Time: (20) minutes.
Scores, 8: Verbal Ability (Verbal Comprehension, Naming Vocabulary), Nonverbal Ability (Picture Similarities, Pattern Construction), Diagnostic Subtests (Recall of Digits Forward, Recognition of Pictures, Early Number Concepts), General Conceptual Ability.

2) *Upper Level Early Years Battery.*
Population: Ages 3-6 to 6-11.
Time: (31) minutes.
Scores, 19: Verbal Ability (Verbal Comprehension, Naming Vocabulary), Nonverbal Reasoning Ability (Picture Similarities, Matrices), Spatial Ability (Pattern Construction, Copying), Special Nonverbal Composite, School Readiness (Early Number Concepts, Matching Letter-like Forms, Phonological Processing), Working Memory (Recall of Sequential Order, Recall of Digits Backward), Processing Speed (Speed of Information Processing, Rapid Naming), Recall of Objects-Immediate, Recall of Objects-Delayed, Recall of Digits Forward, Recognition of Pictures, General Conceptual Ability.

b) SCHOOL-AGE BATTERY.
Population: Ages 7-0 to 17-11 (and optionally down to age 5-0).
Time: (39) minutes.

Scores, 17: Verbal Ability (Word Definitions, Verbal Similarities), Nonverbal Reasoning Ability (Matrices, Sequential and Quantitative Reasoning), Spatial Ability (Recall of Designs, Pattern Construction), Special Nonverbal Composite, Working Memory (Recall of Sequential Order, Recall of Digits Backward), Processing Speed (Speed of Information Processing, Rapid Naming), Phonological Processing, Recall of Objects-Immediate, Recall of Objects-Delayed, Recall of Digits Forward, Recognition of Pictures, General Conceptual Ability.

Cross References: See T5:837 (14 references) and T4:800 (3 references); for reviews by Glen P. Aylward and Robert C. Reinehr of an earlier edition, see 11:111 (1 reference).

Review of The Differential Ability Scales—Second Edition by ANDREW S. DAVIS, Associate Professor, Department of Educational Psychology, Ball State University, and W. HOLMES FINCH, Associate Professor, Department of Educational Psychology, Ball State University, Muncie, IN:

DESCRIPTION. The Differential Ability Scales—Second Edition (DAS-II) is a revision of the Differential Ability Scales (DAS; Elliott, 1990). The DAS-II is a standardized and norm-referenced instrument that is designed for use with children 2 years, 6 months through 17 years, 11 months of age. Although the DAS-II was not designed as an "intelligence" test, it does yield a General Conceptual Ability (GCA) score that will be useful for practitioners who still use a discrepancy model to determine eligibility for special education. There are two batteries contained within the DAS-II, the Early Years Battery (for children 2 years, 6 months through 6 years, 11 months) and the School-Age Battery (for children 7 years, 0 months through 17 years, 11 months), although children aged 5 years, 0 months to 8 years, 11 months of high or low ability can be administered a battery out of their age range as the two batteries were conormed for individuals of these ages. In addition to the GCA, cluster scores can be determined for all age groups. Cluster scores for young children (ages 2 years, 6 months through 3 years, 5 months) are the Verbal Ability and Nonverbal Ability. Three cluster scores are available for children 3 years, 6 months to 17 years, 11 months of age; they are the Verbal Ability, Nonverbal Reasoning Ability, and Spatial Ability clusters. A Special Nonverbal Composite is a supplemental score that can be derived. Two additional cluster scores are available for children ages 5 years, 0 months to 17 years, 11 months, the Working Memory and Processing Speed clusters. A School Readiness cluster can be calculated for children ages 5 years, 0 months to 8 years, 11 months. In addition to examining the cluster scores and GCA, the test author advocates examining the profile of subtest scores to address diagnostic and ipsative processing issues. This process allows for a hierarchical interpretation of a child's ability at the subtest, cluster, and GCA level. The DAS-II should be easily administered by professionals who have background and training in cognitive assessment and working with children, although extensive review of and practice with the test materials will be essential.

The test author notes that the DAS-II arose from the need to update the standardization sample and "address more fully some of the current trends in cognitive and developmental theory, especially those that are germane to predicting differential responses to intervention" (introductory and technical handbook, p. 1). The DAS-II is not based upon a theory of cognitive processing, although the test author provides interpretive guidelines for linking subtests to the Cattell-Horn-Carroll (e.g., McGrew, 2005) theory of cognitive processing. The selection of subtests seems to have been based upon tasks that would measure a range of abilities in children from a developmental perspective.

DEVELOPMENT. The DAS-II is built upon the research from the DAS and the British Ability Scales (BAS; Elliott, Murray, & Pearson, 1979), both of which underwent rigorous psychometric testing to establish reliability and validity. The DAS-II has added four new subtests to the ones in the DAS. The new subtests are Phonological Processing, Rapid Naming, Recall of Digits Backward, and Recall of Sequential Order. In addition to the new subtests, revisions were made to the subtests retained from the DAS, including adding new items, updating artwork, and improving floors and ceilings. The Math Reasoning, Spelling, and Word Reading subtests were not retained from the DAS.

The test author reports that the development of the DAS-II took place in several phases with consultation with Harcourt Assessment and other experts. The first phase consisted of working with focus groups of school and clinical psychologists, reviewing literature and research, working with experts, and establishing the goals of the revision. The second phase, a national pilot study, examined a nationally representative sample of 300 children (ages 3 years, 6 months to 10 years, 11 months) with 3 potential new subtests, 2 verbal subtests from the DAS, and some matrices items for younger children. The sample included proportional numbers of children in regard to ethnicity. The results of the pilot study were used to assist with the next phase, the National Tryout. During this phase, a nationally representative sample of 900 children (ages 2 years, 6 months to 17 years, 11 months) was assessed with 12 subtests. This included some new subtests and did not use some existing DAS subtests (those for which no new items were added or no psychometric concerns existed). The next phase, Standardization, took place with 3,480 children aged 2 years 6 months to 17 years, 11 months. The standardization sample was representative of the United States population for October 2002 United States Census information and an equal number of males and females were included in the sample. The final phase consisted of eliminating some items, finalizing the scoring, and making slight modifications, although none to the standardized directions. The test author provides an excellent set of tables and graphs demonstrating in great detail the representativeness of the standardization sample. The Rasch model was used to estimate item difficulties and abilities on the various DAS-II subscales. The items were then generally placed in ascending order of difficulty so that test administration could be made appropriate for an individual child, given his or her age and ability level.

TECHNICAL. The test author includes a thorough review of studies detailing the reliability of the DAS-II in the technical manual. Much of this reliability assessment uses modern test theory, which focuses on the accuracy of ability estimates, rather than the more traditional classical test theory, which typically focuses on interitem correlations. In this way, it is possible to report on reliability for samples of children based on their age group and/or ability level, as opposed to simply giving a blanket reliability estimate for an entire group of examinees. With this more detailed information, test users can make decisions regarding the appropriateness of the test for children at specific abilities and ages, rather than having to base a decision on a more general metric that may not apply to a specific case.

The actual reliability values that were obtained from the standardization sample were organized by age group and subtest for the Early Years battery and the School-Age battery. In both cases, they were uniformly above .7 except for several cases where the age was out of level for the subtest. Indeed, for the great majority of subtests, the reliability estimates were greater than .8, and many were more than .9. These values suggest that the DAS-II demonstrated excellent reliability across the standardization sample, regardless of age. In addition to providing reliability evidence for the standardization sample, the technical manual also presents Rasch-based reliability estimates for a number of special examinee subgroups. Again, the values were generally very high, suggesting positive internal consistency for the instrument.

Although the bulk of the reliability analyses relied on the Rasch model framework, there were three additional types of reliability addressed in the technical manual. The test author conducted a test-retest analysis with 369 children who were given the DAS-II at two points in time (with a mean of 23 days between test and retest). A good description of the sample demographics is included, along with a discussion of the batteries and age groupings selected by the test author. Pearson's correlation coefficients were calculated between the two sets of scores as an estimate of temporal stability. Results of these analyses demonstrated that, in general, the subtest scores were consistent over time, with the only possible exceptions being for the Recall of Objects-Immediate for children aged 3 years, 6 months to 4 years, 11 months (r = .54), Matching Letter-Like Forms for children aged 5 years, 0 months to 8 years, 11 months (r = .56), and Recognition of Pictures for children 10 years, 0 months and above (r = .48). All other subtests were correlated over time above .6, with most being above .7.

In order to ascertain the interrater agreement for the DAS-II, a stratified random sample of 60 individuals was selected from the standardization group. Four scorers independently rated each protocol for each subtest, and the intraclass correlation statistic was calculated. The values obtained across ages for each subtest ranged from .95 to .99, indicating extremely high levels of agreement among the scorers for the 60 protocols. Finally, the technical manual also reports on the specificity of the scores (the proportion of score variance that is reliable and unique to the subtest). These specificity values ranged from .17 to .75, with most of the subtests having values between .3

and .6. The test author reports that these results support the specificity of the instrument across subtests and age groups. High subtest specificity enables increased confidence in interpretation at the subtest level.

Validity evidence for the DAS-II was presented in four distinct ways: Correlations among the subtest and composite scores, Confirmatory Factor Analysis (CFA) examining the latent structure being measured by the instrument, correlations between the DAS-II subtests and other measures, and score profiles for special subgroups in the population. Although the tables presenting the correlations among the subtests are somewhat large and unwieldy, with careful examination it is possible to discern from them that many of the subtests are moderately to highly correlated with one another, as would be expected if the instrument were appropriately measuring the constructs of interest.

The CFA models used to assess the validity of the DAS-II were based on the original factor structure associated with the DAS. The test author used the standardization sample described above to evaluate these models for four distinct age groups: 2 years, 6 months to 3 years, 5 months; 4 years, 0 months to 5 years, 11 months; 6 years, 0 months to 12 years, 11 months; and 6 years, 0 months to 17 years, 11 months. Their results generally supported the proposed factor structures, which differed somewhat across age groups. Model fit was assessed using a variety of statistics, including chi-square divided by degrees of freedom, the goodness-of-fit index (GFI) and adjusted goodness-of-fit index (AGFI), the root mean squared residual (RMSR) and the Tucker-Lewis Index (TLI). The instrument's author also compared the fit of several alternative parameterizations of the models to ensure that the generally positive results they obtained represented optimal fit as opposed to merely good fit. For each age grouping, the factor structure proposed by the test author was found to be optimal. Indeed, the results presented for the DAS-II were very similar to those originally reported with the DAS, suggesting that the latent construct remained consistent with the new version of the instrument.

Convergent and divergent validity were assessed using correlations between the DAS-II (total and subtest scores) with a number of other appropriate measures. Given the large number of other scales with which the DAS-II was correlated, it is somewhat difficult to provide a simple summary of results. However, it is clear that the DAS-II generally exhibited good to excellent convergent and divergent validity with these other measures for both healthy individuals and individuals from special populations.

The fourth method for assessing the validity of the DAS-II that was included in the technical manual involved the examination of score profiles for special populations of children. For each of these special groups, a control group (matched on gender, race, parent education level, and geographic region) was drawn from the standardization sample. As with the correlation results presented above, there is a great deal of information for the reader to wade through in order to gain insights into relative group differences on the DAS-II. The test author presents a brief overall summary of these results, as well as good discussions for each of the groups. Nonetheless, the sheer volume of means and standard deviations make interpretation somewhat difficult. For each subscale and each group, *t*-tests comparing the mean subtests scores for the control and special groups were conducted, and an effect size was calculated. Given the obvious problem of Type I error inflation inherent with conducting so many *t*-tests, these results should be read with great care. However, the effect size values do provide useful information regarding the relative performances of the special and control groups. Generally speaking, across subtests, these effect size values buttressed the performance of the DAS-II in accurately differentiating the matched control groups from the others in nearly all cases. The ability to correctly distinguish between groups that are known to differ on one or more of the constructs measured by the instrument provides further support for its validity with these samples.

COMMENTARY. The DAS-II is a revised and updated version of the DAS in which the benefits of the original were retained while updating and improving upon the test materials and standardization sample. Users will enjoy the comprehensive and well-written introductory and technical handbook that accompanies the test battery. This handbook provides a thorough and excellent background on the development, construction, psychometric information, and interpretive guidelines for the DAS-II, as well as good discussion of general issues such as historical aspects of cognitive assessment. Furthermore, a description of each subtest and each cluster includes specific interpretive information. This information will be quite useful for practitioners new to the field of assessment and for experienced examiners as well. Indeed, there is abundant information contained throughout this handbook that would fit in well with an instructional text in a psychological/cognitive assessment graduate course. Despite the comprehensive nature of the test, the administration time is relatively brief, especially for young children. Extensive scoring and administration criteria are contained in the administration and scoring manual. Another strength of the test is the instructions in Spanish provided for subtests that do not require a verbal response from the examinee.

The evidence around the psychometric properties of the instrument was generally well presented and of high technical quality. The psychometric properties of the DAS-II are well documented and quite stellar. The instrument was shown to exhibit high levels of internal consistency across a number of samples, and it demonstrated strong temporal consistency over repeated administrations. Several types of validity were assessed and found to be adequate. The correlations among the subscales were, for the most part, moderate to high, particularly for those thought to measure similar constructs. In addition, the latent variable models posited by the test author were supported by the CFAs, providing further evidence for the construct validity of the scale. In terms of criterion-related validity, both the correlations between the DAS-II subtests and other measures of similar constructs, and the pattern of subtest mean differences between special groups and matched controls support the validity of the instrument with these samples. Finally, the great detail with which the psychometric results are presented, although somewhat overwhelming, will provide the potential user with a great deal of vital information regarding the utility of the DAS-II for assessing children at a variety of age and ability levels.

SUMMARY. The DAS-II represents a valuable addition to the pantheon of tests available to assess cognitive ability in children. The original DAS held the reputation for being particularly useful for young children, and examiners who used the DAS for this purpose will be quite pleased with the revision. Across all age ranges, this revision continues to be child-friendly, psychometrically sound, and of high utility. There is a wealth of technical data, much of which will be excessive for the typical user, but examiners will find that virtually any imaginable psychometric study has been conducted with at least adequate results. Additionally, the development and standardization of the DAS-II set a high standard from which many other tests could benefit. Clearly, the DAS-II has been well studied and the evidence presented in the technical report supports the contention that the instrument was found to be both reliable and valid across a variety of samples. The test manuals are very comprehensive with regard to administration and scoring, and the interpretive guidelines are a significant strength, especially for new users of the DAS series.

REVIEWERS' REFERENCES

Elliott, C. D. (1990). Differential Ability Scales. San Antonio: The Psychological Corporation.

Elliott, C. D., Murray, D. J., & Pearson, L. S. (1979). British Ability Scales. Windsor, England: National Foundation for Educational Research.

McGrew, K. S. (2005). The Cattell-Horn-Carroll theory of cognitive abilities: Past, present and future. In D. P. Flanagan & P. L. Harrison (Eds.), *Contemporary intellectual assessment: Theories, tests, and issues* (2nd ed., pp. 136-181). New York: Guilford.

Review of Differential Ability Scales—Second Edition by GERALD TINDAL, Castle—McIntosh—Knight Professor of Education, College of Education, University of Oregon, Eugene, OR:

DESCRIPTION. The Differential Ability Scales—Second Edition (DAS-II) is a measure of ability (*g*) with materials that involve assessment of verbal, nonverbal, and spatial dimensions; therefore, the test is packaged in a suitcase containing a wide array of materials: (a) an administration and scoring manual; (b) four different stimulus books (for various subtests); (c) several different packets of small toys, cards, and blocks; (d) universal scoring templates for the drawing subtests; (e) record forms (for Early Years and School-Age); (f) response booklets for Speed of Information Processing; (g) a normative data tables manual; (h) an introductory and technical handbook; and (i) two compact discs (one providing an audio for Phonological Processing and video for Signed Standard Sentences and the other providing a Scoring Assistant for Windows® operating systems).

The Early Years battery comprises two levels for children ages 2 years, 6 months to 3 years, 5 months (who take four core subtests) and children ages 3 years, 6 months to 6 years, 11 months who take six core subtests. The School-Age battery is for children ages 7 years, 0 months to 17 years, 11 months who take six core subtests, two of which are in common (noted with an *) across both age groups (the usual age range is included in parentheses after each subtest): Early Years core subtests: Verbal Comprehension (2 years, 6 months to 6 years, 11 months), Picture Similarities (2 years, 6 months to 6 years, 11 months), Naming Vocabulary (2 years, 6 months to 6 years, 11 months), Pattern Construction* (2 years, 6 months to 17 years, 11 months), Matrices* (3 years, 6 months to 17 years, 11 months), Copying (3 years, 6 months to 6 years, 11 months); School-Age core subtests: Recall of Designs (7 years, 0 months to 17 years, 11 months), Word Definitions (7 years, 0 months to 17 years, 11 months), Verbal Similarities (7 years, 0 months to 17 years, 11 months), Sequential and Quantitative Reasoning (7 years, 0 months to 17 years, 11 months); Diagnostic subtests: Recall of Objects-Immediate and Delayed (4 years, 0 months to 17 years, 11 months), Recall of Digits Forward (2 years, 6 months to 17 years, 11 months), Recognition of Pictures (2 years, 6 months to 13 years, 5 months), Early Number Concepts (2 years, 6 months to 6 years, 11 months), Matching Letter-Like Forms (4 years, 0 months to 6 years, 11 months), Recall of Sequential Order (5 years, 0 months to 17 years, 11 months), Speed of Information Processing (5 years, 0 months to 17 years, 11 months), Recall of Digits Backward (5 years, 0 months to 17 years, 11 months), Phonological Processing (5 years, 0 months to 12 years, 11 months), Rapid Naming (5 years, 0 months to 17 years, 11 months).

The test is designed to produce a General Conceptual Ability (GCA) score as well as two or three lower-level composite or cluster scores. A Special Nonverbal Composite (SNC) score that utilizes nonverbal core subtests can also be derived.

The core clusters for ages 2 years, 6 months to 3 years, 5 months include Verbal Ability—Crystallized intelligence (Gc) and Nonverbal Ability—measures of both Fluid intelligence/Reasoning (Gf) and Visual-spatial abilities (Gv). For ages 3 years, 6 months to 17 years, 11 months, the core clusters include Verbal Ability–Crystallized intelligence (Gc), Nonverbal Reasoning Ability—Fluid intelligence/Reasoning (Gf), and Spatial Ability—Visual-spatial abilities (Gv). Finally, diagnostic clusters for ages 5 years, 0 months to 17 years, 11 months include Working Memory—Working memory (MW), Processing Speed—Cognitive processing speed (Gs), and School Readiness (for ages 5 years, 0 months to 8 years, 11 months).

Most children take the subtests appropriate to their age though it is possible for a low ability student to take items from earlier age groups and high ability students to take items from later age groups. Students begin taking the test at an age-specific starting point. If they obtain fewer than three correct responses, they begin taking earlier items; they proceed until reaching a decision point; if they are successful, they may continue until they fail three (to five) consecutive items. The raw score is the total correct, which is then converted to age-referenced normative ability scores. This ability score is converted to a *T*-score with a mean of 50 and a standard deviation of 10. Scores on individual subtests can be expressed as percentile ranks or age equivalent scores. When the core subtests are summed, to a total score for cluster or composite, a standard score is produced with a mean of 100 and a standard deviation of 15.

Test interpretation can occur at three levels: GCA score, cluster scores (Verbal Ability, Nonverbal Ability, Nonverbal Reasoning Ability, and Spatial Ability with only the first two available for the Early Years), and individual subtest scores. GCA reflects *g* as "the general ability of an individual to perform complex mental processing that involves conceptualization and the transformation of information" (introductory and technical handbook, p. 17). At the cluster and subtest levels, test interpretation is described in the following manner. First, core analyses can be made by comparing (a) two cluster means, (b) subtest scores within a cluster, or (c) a subtest score to the mean score of the core subtests. Second, diagnostic analyses can be made by comparing (a) a diagnostic cluster score with the GCA, (b) two subtests within a diagnostic cluster, or (c) an individual diagnostic subtest score to the mean score on the core subtests. Finally, the Wechsler Individual Achievement Test—Second Edition can be used to calculate an ability-achievement discrepancy.

DEVELOPMENT. The DAS-II contains extensive information on its development with several aspects addressed. The basic rationale provides a wealth of information on the theoretical perspectives that drove the development of the test with a key focus on generalization as the purpose for all testing. A broad history of intelligence testing is presented as part of the theoretical background of the DAS-II, including issues prior to and following 1990, noting that the DAS-II is the outcome of research spanning nearly 40 years. Test development concludes with a rather extensive consideration of psychometric versus behavioral assessment methods. In the end, a centrist position is taken in which "the only rational way forward is to consider how the truths fit together compatibly" (introductory and technical handbook, p. 23). Finally, the test author describes the evolution of the DAS-II by describing early predecessors including the first British Ability Scales that began in 1965, the first edition of the Differential Ability Scales that began in 1984, and the second edition of the British Ability Scales (BAS-R) in 1993.

TECHNICAL.

Standardization. Prior to collecting data on a national sample, the test author conducted focus groups and surveys of experts and examiners, conducted a national pilot study, and finally conducted a national tryout with 900 children (ages 2 years, 6 months to 17 years, 11 months). For the final standardization sample, the U.S. Census from 2002 was used to stratify students by age, sex, race/ethnicity, parent education level, and geographic area (Northeast, Midwest, South, and West). A total of 3,480 children were eventually tested as part of the standardization sample including all children with English as their primary language, able to communicate verbally, with normal hearing, and able to take the test in a standard fashion. The percentages of the standardization sample by the stratification variables are presented in a sequence of tables reflecting substantial similarity in proportions for the standardization sample and the U.S. population. Rasch scaling was used in the analysis of items and subtests and to develop item-scoring rules. The norms for each composite (GCA, SNC, and clusters) are based on the distribution of the sums of *T*-scores on the component subtests.

Reliability. The test author addresses the following issues in consideration of reliability: homogeneity, or internal consistency of the test's contents, accuracy of individual items, appropriateness of the item difficulty for groups, temporal stability, and interscorer reliability.

Internal reliability coefficients are reported by age for subtests, clusters, and composites for the Early Years Battery and the School-Age Battery, respectively. For the Early Years, the subtest coefficients range from .79 to .94; most of the coefficients are either excellent (in the .90s) or good (in the .80s). For the School-Age battery, the subtest coefficients range from .74 to .96; most are either excellent (in the .90s) or good (in the .80s). The reliability of the GCA is .95 for the Early Years and .96 for the School-Age; coefficients for cluster scores are somewhat lower than GCA coefficients but high nonetheless. Using these coefficients, standard errors of measurement are reported in each age group for subtests, clusters, and GCA; they range from about 2.5 to 6.0 and are mostly about 3–4 points.

Reliability coefficients of subtests were calculated for special populations, including: attention-deficit/hyperactivity disorder, learning disability, deaf or hard of hearing, expressive language disorder, intellectually gifted, mathematics disordered, reading disordered, reading-writing disordered, limited English proficient, intellectual disability (mild to moderate severity), mixed receptive-expressive language disorder, and developmental risk. The majority of subtest coefficients are higher than those reported for the normative sample.

Test-retest reliability was calculated with 369 children with 109–149 participants from each of the three wide age bands. The mean interval between testing sessions was 23 days. Performances on all subtests are reported for the first and second test along with the correlation between them, corrected *r*, and the standard difference. DAS-II scores have adequate stability across time for all age groups with coefficients of the cluster and composite scores ranging around .73 and many coefficients in good (.70s) or excellent (.80s and above) ranges. In general, scores from the second testing are higher than the first testing, reflecting small to moderate effect sizes.

Interscorer agreement is reported on a stratified sample of 60 protocols, using four independently scored protocols for four subtests that require a significant amount of judgment (Copying, Recall of Designs, Word Definitions, and Verbal Similarities). Using the intraclass correlation, the reliability coefficients for these subtests range from .95 to .99.

Specificity is computed to depict the proportion of score variance attributable to that subtest. "For both the Early Years and School-Age batteries, about 42% of the variance is reliable specific variance. Not surprisingly, the diagnostic subtests have relatively high specificity" (introductory and technical handbook, p. 142). Finally, for 176 children in two early age bands, item response theory

(IRT) estimates of reliability are compared to both alpha and odd-even coefficients; the results reflect values from .85 to .89.

Validity. The author reports several types of validity citing the AERA, APA, NCME Standards (1999) in documenting evidence supporting content, internal structures, and criterion-relations.

Internal validity is documented by displaying the intercorrelations of the subtests and the components to reflect "convergent and discriminant validity" (introductory and technical handbook, p. 149). The test author predicted (and found) that subtests conceptually more highly related to each other (e.g., within the same cluster or core) also were more highly intercorrelated than with other subtests from different clusters or core areas.

Confirmatory factor analysis was conducted to confirm that the items within subtests and clusters could be reduced to a simpler explanatory structure (given that the DAS-II was being constructed from a previous version). "Using the DAS-II normative sample, confirmatory analyses using maximum likelihood procedures were conducted first for the core and diagnostic subtests combined and then for the core subtests only. These separate analyses allowed the team to (a) evaluate the cognitive constructs tapped by the DAS-II and (b) provide evidence for the formation of the DAS-II composite scores" (introductory and technical handbook, p. 153). For the following age groups, the following factor structures were found: (a) ages 2 years, 6 months to 3 years, 5 months had a two-factor solution; (b) for ages 4 years, 0 months to 5 years, 11 months, a five-factor solution was found; (c) for ages 6 years, 0 months to 12 years, 11 months, a seven-factor solution was found; and (d) for ages 6 years, 0 months to 17 years, 11 months, a six-factor solution was found. As the test author notes, the structure of abilities became differentiated with age, as expected.

A series of studies are reported using criterion-related evidence with the following measures of ability and achievement correlated with the DAS-II: Differential Ability Scales (DAS), Wechsler Preschool and Primary Scale of Intelligence—Third Edition (WPPSI-III), Wechsler Intelligence Scale for Children—Fourth Edition (WISC-IV), Bayley Scales of Infant and Toddler Development—Third Edition, Wechsler Individual Achievement Test—Second Edition (WIAT-II); Kaufman Test of Educational Achievement—Second Edition (KTEA-II), Woodcock-Johnson Tests of Achievement—Third Edition (WJ-III), Bracken Basic Concept Scale—Revised, and Ready to Learn. The range of coefficients is reasonably moderate, particularly given the different constructs assessed (from .40s to .70s).

Score profiles are reported on the DAS-II for various special populations, with the expectation that performance would be lower (except for talented and gifted students) than the normative populations. Mean scores are compared for both significance and effect size for matched samples from the normative group and samples of students from the following special populations: Intellectually Gifted, Mild or Moderate Intellectual Disability, Reading Disorder, Reading and Written Expression Disorder, Mathematics Disorder, Attention-Deficit/Hyperactivity Disorder, ADHD and Learning Disorder, Expressive Language Disorder, Mixed Receptive-Expressive Language Disorder, Limited English Proficiency, Developmentally At Risk, and Deaf or Hard of Hearing children who communicate via American Sign Language.

> The results of the various studies reported in this chapter on the internal and external validity of the DAS-II have shown substantial evidence for the hierarchical structure of the battery and for the relationship of the DAS-II composites, clusters, and subtests with other cognitive and achievement measures. In particular, the convergent and discriminant validity of the available DAS-II scores is supported by the consistent interrelationships and patterns of correlations of the DAS-II measures with external measures. Results from the special group studies provide support for the validity and clinical utility of the DAS-II. (introductory and technical handbook, p. 207)

COMMENTARY. The DAS-II is a broad measure of ability that reflects a long tradition in the field of testing. The test is very well developed with a broad range of tasks tapping behaviors that are likely related to general cognitive functioning and that may well be important in performing on school-relevant tasks. Though the test is complex with many subtests and various materials (from manipulatives to stimulus cards), it also is very well organized with these materials clearly packaged and easy to access. The directions for both administration and interpretation are clear, though practice is very necessary, given the complexity of interactions with students.

The test author has preemptively devoted considerable attention to the tension between cognitive and behavioral assessments and, in some ways, oversimplified the issues. No amount of technical information on the content of the test, the criterion-related evidence supporting relations with other measures, or the sophisticated statistical analyses on the internal structures of the behaviors and latent traits they represent, can presuppose the need for scientifically documenting the effect of appropriate classifications and their use in developing effective educational programs.

Should a measure of ability (and as operationalized by the various tasks in this test) be warranted, the DAS-II is probably as good as it gets and could be considered as a very well-developed measure of *g*, with all the assumptions that are made in this effort. However, as the test author also states "the interpretations ... are hypotheses. They are meant to provide us suggestions about how the child's performance might be explained or described. A child's performance on a subtest or cluster would not indicate that *all* of the interpretive statements are applicable. In the tradition of scientific methodology, we should seek further evidence that will support or refute any given hypothesis" (introductory and technical handbook, p. 36). As part of this scientific inquiry, therefore, the effect of diagnosis and placement needs further investigation and documentation, particularly with reference to practical functioning in school-related environments and with school-relevant tasks that have their own unique symbol systems.

SUMMARY. The DAS-II is a very well-developed test of ability and would be a useful tool in a cache of instruments to help place students in appropriate programs. The Standards for Educational and Psychological Testing (AERA, APA, & NCME, 1999) are used to structure the content with theoretical relevance to the construct of ability, criterion-related evidence is systematically documented showing the relation of the test with other similar measures, and the internal structure of the test is documented through a series of confirmatory factor analyses. The standardization sample provides a normative group for making interpretations that are likely quite accurate comparatively. An important caveat, however, needs to be considered in using this test: labeling of conditions, diagnosis of functioning, and placement in programs all need further vindication.

REVIEWER'S REFERENCE

American Educational Research Association, American Psychological Association, & National Council on Measurement in Education. (1999). *Standards for educational and psychological testing*. Washington, DC: American Educational Research Association.

[46]

Differential Scales of Social Maladjustment and Emotional Disturbance.

Purpose: Designed to "differentiate between individuals with social maladjustment and those with emotional disturbances."
Population: Ages 6-0 to 17-11.
Publication Date: 2009.
Acronym: DSSMED.
Scores, 2: Social Maladjustment, Emotional Disturbance.
Administration: Individual.
Price Data, 2010: $133 per examiner's manual (53 pages), 25 summary/rating forms, and 25 scoring overlays.
Time: (5-10) minutes.
Comments: To be completed by a teacher or professional who knows the student well and has observed their behavior in a classroom setting for at least 4 weeks.
Authors: David J. Ehrler, Ronnie L. McGhee, Carol G. Phillips, and Elizabeth A. Allen.
Publisher: PRO-ED.

Review of the Differential Scales of Social Maladjustment and Emotional Disturbance by SHERRY K. BAIN, Associate Professor, and KATHLEEN B. ASPIRANTI, doctoral student in school psychology, Department of Educational Psychology and Counseling, University of Tennessee, Knoxville, TN:

DESCRIPTION. The Differential Scales of Social Maladjustment and Emotional Disturbance (DSSMED) were created specifically to differentiate between children and adolescents with social maladjustment (SM) and those with emotional disturbance (ED). Among professionals who must make the determining decisions about whether a student qualifies for special education services under IDEA (in its various authorizations), making the discrimination between SM and ED has sometimes been very difficult, so instruments that aid in the decision-making process are a welcome addition to the psychologist's arsenal of instruments.

Appropriate for children ages 6 years through 17 years 11 months, The DSSMED is made up of 46 items, 22 items on the ED scale and 24 on the SM scale. Administered in a paper-and-pencil format, the questionnaire is typically completed by a classroom teacher or other professional familiar with the student and can be completed in less than 10 minutes. Scoring is based on a 5-point Likert scale. Although Ehrler and colleagues are fairly specific about the qualifications needed to administer and interpret the DSSMED, they do not list a specific MHS level to qualify. Examiners should be knowledgeable in a number of specific areas (e.g., testing, statistics, general assessment procedures) and should be "trained in the evaluation of students with social maladjustment and emotional disturbance" (examiner's manual, p. 1).

To score the DSSMED, a transparent overlay is placed over the form and response scores are placed in the respective ED or SM column. Raw scores are totaled and used to obtain *T*-scores and percentile ranks. The DSSMED must be scored by hand, and all information can be recorded on the front page of the form. There is a place to record the standard error of measurement (*SEM*) on the record form but *SEM*s are not listed in the appendices of the manual. After a brief search, we did find a table listing *SEM*s at age intervals in the examiner's manual, but not with the scoring instructions.

DEVELOPMENT. We found relatively brief information regarding the test authors' techniques for developing the two scales for the DSSMED. The test authors' rationale for developing their constructs and scales followed an extensive search of the professional literature, examination of professional sources addressing diagnosis and clinical evaluation for the constructs of interest, and examination of factor analytic results for several existing behavioral instruments (e.g., the Revised Behavior Problem Checklist–PAR Edition; Quay & Peterson, 1996). Based on these reviews, the test authors developed a pilot instrument consisting of 25 items for each scale, and administered this instrument to 150 students, randomly selected from public schools in Georgia. An item analysis was carried out based on these results, and four items were deleted to create the final version.

TECHNICAL. The normative sample included 1,337 students residing in 30 states. Demographic distributions of gender, race, exceptionality status, geographic area, educational attainment of parents, and family income were representative of the general population when compared to the 2005 U.S. Census data. Selection of participants was stratified for age across gender, geographic representation, and ethnic groups.

Reliability. Ehrler and colleagues present several types of reliability data in the examiner's manual, including internal consistency results, test-retest results, and interrater reliability. For internal consistency, coefficient alphas for the SM and ED scales ranged from .83 to .98 across 12 age groupings; the average alpha across the two scales was .95. The test authors also present coefficient alphas for subgroups based on gender, ethnic groups, and classification categories (e.g., gifted and talented, ADHD). These alphas also were high, ranging from .88 to .98. Standard errors of measurement (*SEM*) range from 1 to 2 points for the SM scale, and from 2 to 4 points for the ED scale.

For a sample of 156 students across age ranges, the test authors report test-retest reliability based on an interval of about 2 weeks. Corrected for restriction of range, the coefficients for the SM scale range from .90 to .95. For the ED scale, the range is .84 to .97.

Correlation coefficients ranged from .70 to .71 for interrater reliability, based on a study of 47 students rated by four sets of paired teachers. The test authors evaluate these ratings as "very large" (examiner's manual, p. 21) considering external evidence that lower interrater correlations generally occur on behavioral scales than conventionally accepted levels (Achenbach & Edelbrock, 1981).

Validity. Ehrler and colleagues report validity evidence for the DSSMED in several forms, including differential item function analyses (DIF), construct validity, and discriminant validity. To perform the DIF analyses, the authors applied a logistic regression procedure to each item, comparing three dichotomous groups, one based on gender, and two based on ethnic status (African American vs. non-African American, and Hispanic American vs. non-Hispanic). They found 12 item comparisons to be statistically significant, indicating that these items did discriminate between the groups of interest; however, results were deemed to have negligible effect sizes. The 12 specific items were not identified in the examiner's manual.

Concurrent validity was examined by comparing the DSSMED to several scales that purport to measure similar constructs: the Scale for Assessing Emotional Disturbance (SAED; Epstein & Cullinan, 1998), the Behavior Dimensions Rating Scale (BDRS; Bullock & Wilson,

1989), and the McGhee-Mangrum Inventory of School Adjustment (MISA; McGhee & Mangrum, 2007). The comparison groups were small, ranging from 25 to 30 students, and no students above 11 years of age were included in these studies. Results of analyses from these four studies were clearly supportive of construct validity, with 16 of the 18 scales that were expected to correlate across instruments producing correlations in the large to almost perfect range, according to Hopkins's (2002) criteria. The remaining two scales correlated in the moderate range.

The test authors present a table of mean *T*-scores across the entire standardization sample, and mean *T*-scores broken down into gender, ethnic, and clinical groups (including 31 students with emotional disorders and 67 students with disruptive behavior disorders) in order to demonstrate group differentiation. The group with emotional disorders obtained a mean *T*-score of 73 on the ED scale and 53 on the SM scale. The group with disruptive behavior disorders had a mean of 54 on ED and 67 on SM. No other means fell in the significant range. Two discriminant function analyses also confirmed the ability of the DSSMED to discriminate between students with emotional disorders versus no identified disability, and students with disruptive behavior disorders versus no identified disability. Discriminant function classification tables displayed results indicating that there was 86% agreement in classifying students with and without disruptive behavior disorders, and 92% agreement in classifying students with and without emotional disorders. We note that this leaves 14% of students misclassified using the SM scale, and 8% misclassified using the ED scale.

Ehrler and colleagues also present results of a correlational study comparing DSSMED results with academic achievement via scores on the Woodcock-Johnson III Tests of Achievement (Woodcock, McGrew, & Mather, 2001) based on the premise that the DSSMED is designed to measure constructs related to school adjustment. Resulting correlations fell in the -.38 to -.50 range for comparisons of achievement with the SM scale, and -.51 to -.61 for comparisons with the ED scale.

The test authors report that the SM scale and the ED scale correlated at .17 for the entire standardization sample, establishing the independence of the two constructs. Additionally, they reported the goodness of fit based on a single-factor and a two-factor model, using four separate indexes. The goodness of fit for the two-factor model was acceptable for three of the four indexes but was slightly out of the recommended boundary (< .10; obtained index was .12) for the root mean square error method of approximation model.

COMMENTARY AND SUMMARY. The DSSMED is a quick, concise, and easy-to-use scale that is designed to differentiate between students with ED and SM. The examiner's manual is fairly brief and we feel some key elements, such as development of the scale, could have been expanded. The test authors claim that the scale has "broad applicability in the study of students with and without disabilities" (examiner's manual, p. 4), but nowhere are these claims substantiated. In addition, there is only one sample in the examiner's manual of how to fill out and score the form, and case studies or interpretive report models would be welcome additions to the examiner's manual. Nevertheless, reliability and validity seem adequate for the purposes of the instrument, and we believe that psychological examiners who need to gather discriminative evidence for classifying children as ED or SM may find this instrument useful.

REVIEWERS' REFERENCES

Achenbach, T. M., & Edelbrock, C. S. (1981). Behavioral problems and competencies reported by parents of normal and disturbed children ages 4 through 16. *Monographs of the Society for Research in Child Development, 46* (1, Serial No. 188).

Bullock, L. M., & Wilson, M. J. (1989). Behavior Dimensions Rating Scale. Allen, TX: DLM Teaching Resources.

Epstein, M. H., & Cullinan, D. (1998). Scale for Assessing Emotional Disturbance. Austin, TX: PRO-ED.

Hopkins, W. G. (2002). A scale of magnitudes for effect statistics. In *A new view of statistics.* Retrieved June 13, 2002, from http://www.sportsci.org/resource/stats/effectmag.html.

McGhee, R. L., & Mangrum, L. (2007). McGhee-Mangrum Inventory of School Adjustment. Austin, TX: PRO-ED.

Quay, H. C., & Peterson, D. R. (1996). Revised Behavior Problem Checklist–PAR Edition. Odessa, FL: Psychological Assessment Resources.

Woodcock, R., McGrew, K. S., & Mather, N. (2001). Woodcock-Johnson III Tests of Achievement. Itasca, IL: Riverside.

Review of the Differential Scales of Social Maladjustment and Emotional Disturbance by RICHARD F. FARMER, Associate Professor of Psychology, East Carolina University, Greenville, NC:

DESCRIPTION. The Differential Scales of Social Maladjustment and Emotional Disturbance (DSSMED) consists of two rating scales, Social Maladjustment and Emotional Disturbance. The primary purported use of these scales is to "accurately differentiate between individuals with social maladjustment and those with emotional disturbances" (examiner's manual, p. 4). DSSMED items consist of 46 statements that describe observable behaviors, and raters are asked to indicate the frequency with which such behaviors occur on a five-point Likert-type scale, ranging from *never* to *more than once per day*.

Raw scores are obtained by summing item ratings within each scale. Raw scores can, in turn, be converted to *T* scores and percentile ranks based on representative normative data. *T* scores, when derived from aggregated data (i.e., averaged over gender, ages, and scales), are interpreted with reference to one of three descriptive terms: "high risk" (*T* score > 70; includes individuals at or above the 95th percentile), "at risk" (61 ≤ *T* score ≤ 70; includes individuals between the 88th and 95th percentile), and "not at risk" (*T* score < 61; includes individuals at or below the 88th percentile).

Designed for youth between 6 years and 0 months to 17 years and 11 months of age, the DSSMED can be completed in about 10 minutes. This measure is suggested for use as a universal screening measure to identify at-risk youth or as part of a comprehensive evaluation for youth who display possible social or emotional problem behaviors.

The manual describes qualifications of test users, and distinguishes between examiners and raters. Examiners are described as qualified professionals (e.g., knowledgeable in psychometric theory and methods, trained in the assessment of youth with social-emotional difficulties) who are charged with selecting and training the rater to correctly use the DSSMED. Examiners are also responsible for checking the rater's work, scoring the form, interpreting the test's findings, and communicating test results to others. Raters are those who are familiar with the target student's behavior in school settings, and have routinely observed the youth's behavior in such settings for at least 4 weeks. Examiners and raters will typically be school psychologists, counselors, or teachers.

DEVELOPMENT. The DSSMED is described as a "theoretically sound research-based method of evaluating an individual's social-emotional functioning" (examiner's manual, p. 1). Items for the Social Maladjustment and Emotional Disturbance scales were derived from behavioral descriptions of these constructs found in contemporary research and assessment literatures. Twenty-five items per scale (50 items total) were initially developed. Four of these items were subsequently eliminated for failing to meet pre-established thresholds for acceptable corrected item-to-total correlations, resulting in the present 46-item measure. Beyond a brief account of the item retention/rejection and scale refinement processes, there is no substantial discussion of any theory underlying the DSSMED. From the limited descriptions in the manual, it also appears possible that the sample used during the item evaluation and scale refinement process was the same sample on which norms were based.

Two forms accompany this measure. On the Summary/Rating Form, raters record identifying and demographic information and make frequency ratings for each behavior listed. There are also spaces for recording normative scores and listing interpretations and recommendations. The Scoring Overlay is used for recording numerical ratings corresponding to each item in relation to its associated scale and for tallying total raw scale scores.

Because the DSSMED raw score scale distributions were not normally distributed in the normative sample, the test authors used a linear transformation of raw scores to develop corresponding *T* score conversions. As noted in the test manual, this method of standardization places some limits on test score interpretation. Specifically, *T* score values cannot be meaningfully compared across DSSMED scales, nor can they be directly compared with normalized test scores from other measures. Percentile ranks associated with raw scale scores provide additional information and facilitate across-scale comparisons.

Examiners also have the option of referencing raw scores to norms based on the total standardization sample or to norms that are gender-based. The latter set of norms might be particularly pertinent to the interpretation of scores on the Social Maladjustment scale, which has different distribution characteristics as a function of gender and, in the case of male youth, age grouping. Norms for this scale are available for the total sample (males and female youth combined) for two age subgroups (ages 6-0 to 10-11 and 11-0 to 17-11) for male youth within each age subgroup, and for female youth between the ages of 6-0 and 17-11. Norms for the Emotional Disturbance scale are available for the total sample, male youth only, and female youth only, and are based on aggregated data spanning the entire age range of the normative sample (i.e., ages 6-0 to 17-11).

There are no separate sets of norms for people from different ethnic, cultural, or socioeconomic groups. During the scale development and validation processes, however, the test authors attempted to eliminate items that demonstrated any gender or racial bias. They subsequently demonstrated that any bias related to these sources was small and generally nonsignificant. As noted above, however, even with these controls in place during the initial scale refinement process, scale score distributions for the Social Maladjustment scale were substantially different across genders.

TECHNICAL. The DSSMED is norm-referenced, with norms based on a sample of 1,337 youth who were selected to be nationally representative in the areas of geography (e.g., 30 states were represented), gender, race, exceptionality status, parental educational attainment, and family income. Over 100 participants represent each age year between the ages 6-0 and 17-11.

Reliability. Reliability of the DSSMED was evaluated with multiple methods. Internal consistency was indexed by coefficient alpha, with alpha coefficients presented separately for each scale and for each age year. Overall, internal consistency analyses suggest a high level of item reliability (alpha coefficient range for Social Maladjustment: .94 to .98; for Emotional Disturbance: .83 to .96). Alpha coefficients for both scales are also provided for selected subgroups (e.g., various ethnic groups, gifted and talented, learning disordered), and in each instance the reported coefficients are good to excellent.

Test-retest reliability was assessed over an approximate 2-week interval among a subsample of 156 youth from a single township, and estimated by correlating standard scores from both testing occasions. Uncorrected and corrected (for range restriction) reliability coefficients are presented, and were in excess of .84 for both scales for the entire subsample. It is not clear from the test manual, however, if the same rater provided ratings for a given youth on both assessment occasions.

Interrater reliability was evaluated using a sample of 47 students. The manual does not clearly describe the procedures for how interrater reliability was determined. From the information available in the manual, it appears that interrater reliability coefficients are Pearson correlations based on raw scale scores derived from independent ratings from pairs of teachers. Interrater reliability coefficients are reported as .70 for the Social Maladjustment scale and .71 for the Emotional Disturbance scale. Interrater reliability estimates are not provided for ratings of individual test items.

Validity. Evidence in support of the content validity of the DSSMED is provided from item-based analyses (e.g., corrected item-to-total correlations). Criterion-related validity was evaluated with four samples of youth, whereby each sample was administered an additional test or battery that assessed the following domains: emotional disturbance, social maladjustment, school adjustment, and academic achievement. Each of the four samples consisted of 30 or fewer students. A table of DSSMED scale correlations with these external measures is provided. The test authors concluded from these data that there is strong and substantial evidence of criterion-related validity of the DSSMED.

Construct validity was evaluated with multiple methods and approaches, including known-groups contrasts, discriminant function analyses, and a confirmatory factor analysis of DSSMED item sets. Based on the overall pattern of findings, the test authors concluded that, "the DSSMED is a valid differential measure of social maladjustment and emotional disturbance" (examiner's manual, p. 34). The procedures used to identify individuals as belonging to several clinical groups (e.g., disruptive behavior disorder, emotional disorder, attention deficit/hyperactivity disorder) are not specified, however.

COMMENTARY. The DSSMED is suggested to be an accurate and useful measure of social maladjustment and emotional disturbance. The behavioral items are clearly defined and appear to have good face validity given the labels applied to the scales to which they belong. The manual is generally well-written and clear, and essential psychometric data are provided. Procedures used for the development, norming, and evaluation of the DSSMED appear satisfactory, although more information in some areas would have been helpful (e.g., underlying theory, scale development procedures as distinguished from norming procedures, procedural details for some psychometric studies). Preliminary data on the psychometric characteristics of the DSSMED are encouraging, and in the aggregate suggest that the measure's performance is consistent with its underlying assumptions.

As would be expected given a measure of this type, normative data presented in the appendices suggest that the DSSMED is substantially better at discriminating individuals at the higher levels of social maladjustment and emotional disturbance than at the lower levels given the substantial skewness associated with scale raw scores. Interpretive guidelines for scale scores are somewhat sparse and largely limited to scores that fall within the "high risk" category, with descriptive information for individuals who fall within this category closely tied to the content of behavioral items for each scale.

The option to use gender-based and age-restricted norms on the Social Maladjustment scale is a strength of this measure. However, there is no place to indicate on the Summary/Rating Form if the normative scores reported are from the total normative sample or the normative subsample distinguished by gender or age grouping. The descriptive terms provided for *T* scores are based on averages across all genders, ages, and scales. These descriptive labels, however, may not always apply when referenced to specific gender or age subgroups. For example, a raw score of 40 on the Social Maladjustment scale is associated with the following *T* scores (and corresponding percentile ranks) for each norm group: 69 (94th percentile) for the entire sample for ages 6-0 through 10-11; 60 (85th percentile) for the entire sample for ages 11-0 through 17-11; 69 (94th percentile) for males ages 6-0 through 10-11; 58 (80th percentile) for males ages 11-0 through 17-11; 65 (92nd percentile) for females ages 6-0 through 17-11 (there are no separate sets of norms for this scale for females within the age ranges of 6-0 through 10-11 and 11-0 through 17-11). As this example illustrates, age and gender are important considerations in the determination of risk status based on raw scores. A Social Maladjustment raw score of 40 for a female youth aged 12-6 will, for example, be classified differently depending on which norms are used (i.e., as "not at risk" when the total sample norms for her age are used, and as "at risk" when gender-based norms are used). Consequently, greater clarity is needed than what is currently provided on the Summary/Rating Form as to the normative data used and, correspondingly, the basis for score interpretation.

Of the 46 test items, all but 4 items are keyed in the same direction. On the Scoring Overlay provided for this review, the space for recording the youth's score on one item (Item 4, "Hoards items") appears in between the columns for recording scores for Emotional Disturbance and Social Maladjustment items. All other items have corresponding scoring blanks under one of these two scale columns. In the sample Scoring Overlay presented on page 3 of the manual, however, this item is listed as belonging to the Emotional Disturbance scale. It would appear, then, that the placement of the scoring blank for this item represents a production error in the formatting of the Scoring Overlay. Users will need to be cautious when tallying scale items, and include this item in tallies of the Emotional Disturbance scale only. [Editor's Note: The publisher advises that this error has been corrected and replacement materials are being provided to all customers.]

SUMMARY. The DSSMED is a promising and user-friendly measure of Social Maladjustment and Emotional Disturbance among youth aged 6-0 to 17-11. This measure could be of use as a universal screening measure to identify youth at risk, or can be used as part of a comprehensive assessment battery for youth who might be displaying indicators of social maladjustment or emotional distress. The manual provides scoring guidelines that are relatively straightforward and generally easy to follow. Preliminary data that describe the psychometric characteristics of the scales are encouraging. Because scale raw scores are highly skewed and demonstrate some differences in distribution based on gender and age, it would be desirable to have norms based on more restricted age groupings than are currently available. Additional information pertaining to the scale distribution characteristics for youth from diverse ethnic or cultural groups also would be welcomed. Overall, the DSSMED appears to be suitable for use in research and as a screening instrument in school settings.

[47]

ElecTest (Form A, Form A-C, & Form B).

Purpose: For selecting electrical repair and maintenance candidates.

Population: Applicants and incumbents for jobs requiring practical electrical knowledge and skills.

Publication Dates: 1997–2004.

Scores, 9: Motors, Digital & Analog, Schematics & Print Reading and Control Circuits, Basic AC/DC Theory and Electrical Maintenance, Computers & PLC and Test Instruments, Power Supplies, Power Distribution and Construction & Installation, Mechanical and Hand & Power Tools, Total.

Administration: Group.

Forms, 3: A, A-C, B.

Price Data, 2006: $20 per consumable self-scoring test booklet (minimum order of 20); $24.95 per manual (2004, 23 pages).
Foreign Language Editions: Available in Spanish.
Time: (60) minutes.
Comments: Self-scoring instrument; on-line version available; Form B is an alternate equivalent of Form A.
Author: Roland T. Ramsay.
Publisher: Ramsay Corporation.

Review of the ElecTest (Form A, Form A-C, & Form B) by EUGENE P. SHEEHAN, Dean, College of Education and Behavioral Sciences, University of Northern Colorado, Greeley, CO:

DESCRIPTION. The various forms of the Ramsay Corporation Job Skills ElecTest are designed as measures of job knowledge and skill for those in the electrical trades, specifically electricians and electrical technicians, where practical electrical knowledge is critical to job functioning. There are several forms to the test: Form A, Form A-C, and Form B, although this reviewer saw only versions A-C and B. Each of the forms samples from a variety of knowledge areas including Motors, Digital and Analog Electronics, Schematics and Print Reading, etc. All knowledge areas are clearly relevant to the field of electrical work. Job analysis of the work done by electricians and maintenance electricians provided the general background for the identification of the knowledge and skill areas.

Versions A-C and B are very straightforward to administer. Each comprises 60 multiple-choice items. Directions are clear and there are two sample questions. Both versions contain traditional word items and also items referring to schematics or other diagrams. Items are also organized by knowledge area in both versions. In Form B all items have four alternatives (A-D), whereas in Form A-C there is one item with five alternatives. Form B has separate question booklets and answer sheets. Each form comes in a self-contained question and answer booklet in which answer alternatives align with corresponding spaces on a carbon answering sheet. Respondents' answers transfer via pencil pressure onto a sealed answer sheet. The answer sheet can be torn open when the test is completed so that the scorer can easily discern which responses are correct.

The test manual is confusing regarding time for administration, indicating both that the test is untimed but should take no longer than 60 minutes, and that time limits should be observed. No time limit was found on either Form A-C or B.

Three items (3–5) on Form A-C have the same stem and set of alternatives although each pertains to a different motor schematic. A respondent with a modicum of test- taking acumen could answer all three correctly without much knowledge as an electrician. This should be corrected in future versions.

DEVELOPMENT. The test author indicates the ElecTest was developed in consultation with five job experts who independently ranked the various job knowledge and skills for job importance. The job experts also provided information on the percent of items from each area of importance they thought should be in the test. Experts working in pairs then selected from a test bank items to be included in the test. The test manual does not indicate from whence the original items came. The experts were instructed to ensure that each test area included a safety item.

Final item selection came after several hundred individuals had taken an early version of the test. Item selection was based on item point biserial discrimination indices and on item difficulty. This methodology (use of item point biserial discrimination and indices and item difficulty) was used to revise the instrument over time.

TECHNICAL. As mentioned, the ElecTest was initially developed using job experts to prioritize broad categories of the job of Technician Electrical.

The psychometrics behind the ElecTest are generally solid. Internal consistency reliability coefficients are high, ranging from .85 to .92 with three different populations. Correlations between the various subsections of the test are also high and statistically significant. However, given that alternate forms of the test (A-C and B) exist, it is necessary to provide parallel forms reliability. No such information is provided.

The test manual also provides difficulty indices and point biserial correlations for each item on Forms A, A-C, and B.

Several types of validity evidence are described: content-related, criterion-related, and construct. Content validity is assured through the use of job experts during instrument development. Their job experience and knowledge ensures that the test measures critical elements of the job of electrician. The use of job experts in test development also aids with construct validity.

To demonstrate criterion-related validity, the scores of 95 maintenance workers were correlated with ratings provided by managers on several job dimensions. All coefficients were positive and statistically significant indicating the test has the ability to describe or predict job performance. However, the managers' ratings were in broad areas, such as problem solving and technical skills, not in areas specific to the work done by those in the electronics field. Thus, questions can be raised about quality of the criterion-related validity assessment.

Normative data are provided to facilitate the understanding of individual scores and to allow a comparison between groups.

COMMENTARY. The different forms of the ElecTest are easy to administer. It certainly looks like a measure of knowledge for Electricians and Electrical Technicians. With job areas prioritized by job experts, the test demonstrates evidence of content and construct validity. Criterion-related validity shows the instrument has predictive or descriptive powers, although the criterion variables (managers' ratings) may be a little too general for an instrument that measures a skill as specific as job knowledge for Electricians and Electrical Technicians. Reliability coefficients are also strong. However, if alternate forms are to be used then parallel forms reliability also should be addressed.

There is some confusion about the two forms of the test: A-C and B. Form A-C appears more modern and there are no data indicating the relationship between the two forms. There are also three items (3, 4, and 5) in Form A-C that are too similar and that should be revised.

SUMMARY. The ElecTest measures very specialized knowledge and skills for Electricians and Electrical Technicians. Easily administered and easily scored, the different forms of the ElecTest have reasonably good psychometric properties. Estimates of internal reliability and validity indicate the test is internally consistent and measures what it sets out to measure. Given the specificity of the instrument, the ElecTest should only be used to assess knowledge and skills for Electricians and Electrical Technicians.

[48]

Emotional Disturbance Decision Tree.

Purpose: To "assist in the identification of children who qualify for the Special Education category of Emotional Disturbance based on federal criteria."
Population: Ages 5-18.
Publication Date: 2007.
Acronym: EDDT.
Scores, 10: Inability to Build or Maintain Relationships Scale, Inappropriate Behaviors or Feelings Scale, Pervasive Mood/Depression Scale, Physical Symptoms or Fears Scale, Emotional Disturbance Decision Tree Total Score, Attention-Deficit Hyperactivity Disorder Cluster, Possible Psychosis/Schizophrenia Cluster, Social Maladjustment Cluster, Level of Severity Cluster, Educational Impact Cluster.
Administration: Group.
Price Data, 2008: $140 per professional manual (139 pages), 25 reusable item booklets, 25 response booklets, and 25 score summary booklets.
Time: (20) minutes.
Author: Bryan L. Euler.
Publisher: Psychological Assessment Resources, Inc.

Review of the Emotional Disturbance Decision Tree by JONATHAN SANDOVAL, Professor of Education, University of the Pacific, Stockton, CA:

DESCRIPTION. The Emotional Disturbance Decision Tree (EDDT) is based on a set of 156 item statements divided into five sections to be rated by educational or mental health professionals familiar with a target child. The intent is to aid in the identification of children who are eligible for special education services under the Individuals with Disabilities Education Improvement Act of 2004 (IDEIA/IDEA) category *Emotional Disturbance.* The materials include a manual, an item booklet, a response booklet, and a summary form. Section I of the item booklet, Potential Exclusionary Items, consists of four *yes/no* questions addressing factors that might disqualify a child for eligibility. Section II, Emotional Disturbance Characteristics, is made up of 108 statements the rater endorses on a 4-point Likert scale concerning frequency of occurrence over the last few months. Raw scores on this section may be converted into a *T* score and percentile rank on four scales and a total: Inability to Build or Maintain Relationships, Inappropriate Behaviors or Feelings, Pervasive Mood/Depression, and Physical Symptoms or Fears. Performance on each of these scales is also assigned one of five qualitative scores ranging from normal to very high clinical. In addition, the same items yield an estimate, termed cluster score, based on four percentile ranges, of degree of risk for Attention–Deficit Hyperactivity Disorder and Psychosis/Schizophrenia. In Section III, Social Maladjustment, the rater is to choose one of three statements best describing the student in 24 areas. These responses are used to produce cluster scores estimating four degrees of risk for Social Maladjustment, again using qualitative labels based on percentile ranges. Using the same format as Section III, Section IV, based on 9 descriptors, yields estimates of Level of Severity, and Section V, based on 11 descriptors, yields estimates of Educational Impact. The EDDT also provides an Inconsistency score based on discrepancies in the rating of 11 item pairs. No more than 2 items may be missing per scale for a score to be counted (1 per cluster). Each of the EDDT scores, which are related to Federal IDEIA criteria, then are used to assist the rater to consider an eligibility decision for special education.

The EDDT may be rated by an individual or by a group of professionals, such as the members of a multidisciplinary team. There is no parent form. It was developed to evaluate individuals from ages 5 to 18. The test author recommends that raters using the measure be formally trained in psychology or a related field, or have required training and experience in the ethical and competent use of psychological tests. However, qualified graduate level professionals, such as school, counseling, or clinical psychologists, are the only ones to do scoring and interpretation. The examiner's manual is straightforward and provides information about emotional disturbance as defined by IDEIA, technical information, normative data, case studies, and scoring examples.

The EDDT is not intended to be used mechanically to provide a definitive diagnosis. Rather, it is an adjunct to clinical interpretation and an aid to eligibility determinations made by a school-based team.

DEVELOPMENT. The EDDT was created to provide a means for each of the federal special education eligibility criteria to be assessed with one instrument. Other available measures do not explicitly address all of the inclusionary and exclusionary criteria used in educational settings. A school psychologist practicing in the large, multiethnic Albuquerque, New Mexico school district is the test author. The intent was to create a structured and standardized approach to the determination of emotional disturbance in school-aged children. A particular problem the test author sought to address was the role of the presence of social maladjustment in the eligibility determination. After two pilot studies in New Mexico, the measure was refined with the help of the publisher and administered to a normative sample. Following standardization, items were eliminated, modified, and re-assigned to scales based on statistical studies.

TECHNICAL. Norms for the scores on Section II, Emotional Disturbance Characteristics, were based on 601 children obtained from sites in 26 U.S. states. The sample roughly matched the U.S. Census data from 2003 with regard to gender, age, race/ethnicity, and geographical region, although there are some notable exceptions (e.g., West underrepresented and Caucasians overrepresented at older ages). Gender-based norms were produced for four age groups: 5–8, 9–11, 12–14, and 15–18 years. These gender and age brackets were developed from a continuous norming procedure.

The qualitative labels on the test (estimates of risk) were derived from percentiles obtained from a series of samples of children (*N* = 104, 404, 49, 81) identified by the schools as evidencing social maladjustment, emotional disturbance, attention-deficit hyperactivity disorder, and psychosis/schizophrenia, respectively. The demographics of the sample are consistent in terms of gender and ethnicity/race with national demographic data on emotionally disturbed youth, but the Western geographical region was overrepresented. Raw cluster scores converted to percentile ranges were used to determine the four risk levels (less than or equal to 1% = Normal; 2% to 24% = Mild Risk; 25% to 74%, = Moderate Clinical; greater than or equal to 75% = High Clinical).

There is some evidence of internal consistency and stability of the EDDT Emotional Disturbance Characteristic scores. Coefficient alpha estimates for the normative sample for scores at the four age groupings varied from .66 at age 12–14 males on Physical Symptoms or Fears to .95 at age 5–8 for both gender Total scores, with a median value of .83. The alpha estimates for the cluster scores were somewhat higher, the lowest being Level of Severity at .75. The test-retest stability coefficients based on 80 children over approximately 3 weeks were at the same level, from the low .80s for Pervasive Mood/Depression and Physical Symptoms or Fears to .94 for Inability to Build or Maintain Relationships.

For the emotionally disturbed sample, the alpha coefficients and stability coefficients show the same patterns on the Emotional Disturbance Characteristics as the normative sample. The cluster scores derived from this sample have alphas ranging from .80 for Possible Psychosis/ Schizophrenia and Level of Severity to .90 for Social Maladjustment and Attention-Deficit Hyperactivity Disorder. This same pattern of alphas is evident for the cluster scores of the normative sample, although the value for Possible Psychosis/ Schizophrenia is lower at .70 and Level of Severity lower at .75.

Interrater reliability was estimated from ratings of 64 children. Correlations between raters varied from .73 for Physical Symptoms or Fears to .85 for Inability to Build or Maintain Relationships and Pervasive Mood/Depression on the Characteristics scales, and from .67 on the Possible Psychosis/Schizophrenia to .93 on the Level of Severity cluster. The standard errors of measurement vary between 2.24 and 5.83 points for the Characteristics scales, generally falling around 4 points. In all, the estimates of reliability are acceptable and comparable with reliabilities found for other rating scales. Internalizing behaviors and psychotic behaviors are evidently the most difficult to evaluate reliably, and the associated scores should be treated with caution.

The test author provides validity information based on internal structure, on correlation with other measures, and the performance of six samples of children identified as having various, specific special education needs. The intercorrelations of the scores for the two samples show moderate positive correlations and some reasonable patterns. For example, the indicators of internalizing disorders have lower correlations with social maladjustment, and the cluster Level of Severity has a high correlation with Educational Impact. External evidence of validity includes EDDT score correlations with scores derived from other established measures of behavioral adjustment. For both the normative sample and the Emotional Disturbance sample, correlations between the EDDT and the Teacher Forms of the Behavior Assessment System for Children—Second Edition (BASC-2), and the *Clinical Assessment of Behavior* (CAB) yielded moderate positive correlations between the corresponding maladaptive scales and moderate negative correlations between the EDDT and the adaptive scales. For example, for the normative sample, the EDDT Depression score correlated .68 with BASC-2 Depression and .66 with CAB-T Depression. The EDDT Social Maladjustment cluster correlated .72 and .96 with BASC-2 Conduct Problems for the sample with emotional disturbance and the norm sample, respectively, and .65 with CAB-T Social Maladjustment for the norm sample. The pattern of correlations for the Emotional Disturbance sample, who also received the Child Behavior Checklist Teacher Report Form, was similar to the normative sample. In addition, the Emotional Disturbance sample performed as expected on the EDDT Emotional Characteristics scales with significantly higher mean scores, with only 1% falling in the normal category on the EDDT Total, and 88% receiving high or very high clinical scores.

The examiner's manual also presents data on the performance of children with specific learning disability (SLD), speech and language impairment (SLI), mental retardation (MR), attention deficit hyperactivity disorder (ADHD), autism spectrum disorder (ASD), and social maladjustment (SM). This group of children (between 37 and 104 in each group) was administered the EDDT, the CAB, the BASC-2, and measures designed to identify that group. The Clinical Assessment of Attention Deficit—Child was given to a subset of the ADHD group. The Gilliam Autism Rating Scale and the Gilliam Asperger Disorder Scale was given to a subset of the ASD group. The SM group received the Differential Test of Conduct and Emotional Problems, the Conduct Disorder Scale, and the Jesness Inventory—Revised. Moderate correlations in the range of .40 between the EDDT and related scores on these measures were obtained for the ADHD and ASD group, but high correlations were noted between all scores, including the Social Maladjustment cluster (.84–.92) with the measures given to the SM group.

COMMENTARY. As a screening measure and guide, the EDDT is useful and practical for use in the schools, but not necessarily more useful than other measures such as the BASC-2 already in use, assuming users are familiar with the regulations. The norms for the scores are based on relatively small samples of children and samples of convenience were combined to produce them. It is not clear from the manual who the raters were, other than their names, and, most importantly, what qualifications they had in terms of amount of experience and training. Although the manual discusses a group procedure for ratings including parents, it offers no evidence supporting this practice. The issue of fairness to children from different cultures has not been examined in spite of the problem of overrepresentation of various groups in classes for the emotionally disturbed. Because the norms are based on wide age levels, and many scores rendered into qualitative descriptors, the results from the EDDT must be cross validated with other measures and considered merely advisory on their own.

SUMMARY. The EDDT has utility in a particular context, assisting a school-based team to consider all of the factors needed to make a decision about eligibility for special education services. It can be used for rough screening and verifying information from other sources. The norms and the reliability and validity information, although somewhat limited, justify the cautious and judicious use of the test.

Review of the Emotional Disturbance Decision Tree by CHRISTOPHER A. SINK, Professor, School Counseling and Psychology, Seattle Pacific University, and NYARADZO H. MVUDUDU, Associate Professor, Educational Research, Seattle Pacific University, Seattle, WA:

DESCRIPTION. According to the professional manual, the Emotional Disturbance Decision Tree (EDDT) is an individual or group completion rating scale designed to help identify children (ages 5 to 18 years) with "emotional disturbance" (ED), as defined by the federal legislation for special education, including the 2004 Individuals With Disabilities Education Improvement Act (IDEA) and the 2002 Assistance to States for the Education of Children With Disabilities guidelines. It can be used in school and clinical settings as well as in the juvenile justice system as one of many assessment tools to screen children and adolescents for ED.

Consisting of five sections (156 items total) closely linked to the federal ED diagnostic criteria, the EDDT's first section examining potential exclusionary issues (e.g., IQ, hearing-vision, health) has four *yes/no* items. Section II consists of 108 four-point Likert scale items that yield a total score and two subdimensions: Part A—Emotional Disturbance and Part B—Attention-Deficit Hyperactivity Disorder and Possible Psychosis/Schizophrenia Screeners. The total score can be used for research but not for ED screening. For Section III (Social Maladjustment [SM] cluster with 24 items), Section IV (Level of Severity 9-item cluster), and Section V (Educational Impact 11-item cluster), the rater selects one of three choices that best reflects the student's behavior.

The response booklet makes the scoring procedures relatively straightforward and the program manual details the scoring and interpretation procedures. Section II Part A yields raw and *T* scores, percentile ranks, confidence intervals, and qualitative labels. Section II Part B as well as Sections III, IV, and V generate raw scores, percentile ranges, and qualitative classification labels. Raters should know the student well (i.e., have daily contact with the child for at least 4 weeks). Trained and licensed/credentialed professionals (e.g., teachers, social workers, counselors) are the preferable respondents, and only those professionals with extensive testing and special education training, experience, and knowledge (e.g., school psychologists, educational diagnosticians, clinical/counseling psychologists familiar with federal criteria for ED classification) are qualified to score and interpret the scale.

DEVELOPMENT. In developing and validating the instrument, the test author seemed to follow the conventional steps outlined in authoritative psychometric texts (e.g., DeVellis, 2003; Nunnally & Bernstein, 1994). Superficially at least, the measure is grounded in relevant theory, research, and practice, drawing largely from ED-related federal legislation, as well as developmental psychology and special education research. Studies investigating the salient factors impacting the learning processes in students with emotional/behavioral challenges were apparently consulted. In our view, though, foundational publications are not well documented in the test manual.

TECHNICAL. According to the test manual, the initial EDDT item bank used in two pilot studies (sample sizes were not reported) was largely based on the test author's experience and input from practicing school psychologists and clinical diagnosticians from a multiethnic New Mexico school district. As a result, two successive revisions were made, with the final item selection based on acceptable item analytic procedures. Although item-to-scale/cluster total score correlations and the criterion for inclusion-exclusion were not specified, items with low reliability were eliminated. However, in some cases items were retained even if their reliability was inadequate.

Appropriate standardization procedures were followed and the norm sample, albeit undersized (N = 601 children drawn from 26 states, ages ranged from 5 to 18, M_{age} = 11.46, SD_{age} = 3.99, $M_{grade\ level}$ = 6.00, $SD_{grade\ level}$ = 3.81 [range K–12]), appear to be generally representative of key U.S. population Census parameters (e.g., gender = 50.4% female; ethnicity = 66.2% Caucasian; geographic region = 68.4% Northeast and Southern regions). The normative data were presented in the manual for these age groups: 5–8, 9–11, 12–14, and 15–18 years. Percentile ranks for student classification were determined by comparison to clinical samples (N = 104, 404, 49, 81) who met the federal criteria for special education services due to social maladjustment, emotional disturbance, attention-deficit hyperactivity disorder, or psychosis/schizophrenia, respectively.

EDDT reliability evidence was reviewed in the manual as internal consistency coefficients (Coefficient alphas) and stability estimates (Pearson *r*s). Traditionally, alpha coefficients of .70 (Nunnally & Bernstein, 1994) to .80 and above (Anastasi & Urbina, 1997) for rating scales indicate sufficient reliability. For the total normative sample, four of five EDDT scales produced alphas reaching the at least the .80 threshold. With the sample of children exhibiting emotional disturbances (ED), adequate internal consistency coefficients (Mdn_{alpha} = .87) were found for the EDDT scales and clusters. The Physical Symptoms or Fears scale alpha coefficient for the total sample was marginally reliable (.75). For girls aged 12–14 years, the Pervasive Mood/Depression scale's alpha was slightly low (.67), as was the Physical Symptoms or Fears scale alpha for males aged 12–14 years (.66). Standard errors of measurement and confidence intervals based on these reliability estimates were reported by age and gender in the manual.

The test-retest reliability coefficients ($M_{interval}$ = 18.5 days, range 1–44 days) for each of the five scales and five clusters were generally strong, with coefficients ranging from .81 to .94 (Mdn = .91) for the scales. Clusters demonstrated higher values (from .85 to .98, with a median value of .93). Similarly, the interrater reliability coefficients for the EDDT scales were adequate, ranging from .73 (Physical Symptoms/Fears) to .85 (Inability to Build/Maintain Relationships). For the EDDT clusters, interrater reliability estimates ranged from .67 (Possible Psychosis/Schizophrenia cluster) to .93 (Level of Severity).

Validity evidence is relatively well documented in the manual using standard methods (Anastasi & Urbina, 1997). These findings are reported in the manual: (a) intercorrelations ranging from .27 to .92 between EDDT scales and clusters suggest that the measure has a common internal structure; (b) low to moderate positive and negative correlations between EDDT scores and other related behavioral measures (e.g., Clinical Assessment of Behavior Teacher Form and Behavior Assessment System for Children-2 Teacher Form) yielded some support for the measure's convergent and discriminant validity; (c) EDDT scores moderately correlated with ED characteristics as measured by the CAB-T and BASC-2 in various related clinical groups (e.g., children with a specific learning disability, ADHD, or mental retardation); (d) with a moderate level of accuracy, EDDT scores classified children as ED; (e) predictive validity of the EDDT's scales and clusters was also supported by significant (p < .001) t-tests comparing the normative sample to the ED group.

Although not specifically discussed in the manual, the items' content and face validity appeared to be assessed through the constructive feedback from clinical professionals during the EDDT development phase. The ED construct was largely defined in terms of the vague federal classification for ED eligibility. Factorial validity and estimates of factorial invariance across differing samples were not reported in the manual. These data would further establish the measure's construct validity.

COMMENTARY. The EDDT and the test manual have several promising features that clinicians will appreciate. For instance, the manual provides extensive details and examples on how to navigate and interpret the relatively complex scoring procedures. With careful review of respondents' EDDT inconsistency scores, diagnosticians can better assess the utility of students' other scale and cluster scores. By adding ED exclusionary items (Section I), the likelihood of misclassification appears to be reduced. Also noteworthy, the EDDT, when compared to conceptually similar instruments, attempts to be more closely aligned to the federal criteria for ED classification than many other comparable measures. This potential strength may also serve a caveat to administering the EDDT in nonschool settings.

The EDDT poses certain drawbacks for clinicians. The EDDT scales and clusters were largely formulated on the ambiguous and contentious federal IDEA guidelines for classifying students with ED. Nevertheless, the test author strongly contends that the EDDT can readily be used to coherently assess this special education disability category. In our view, because the EDDT's validity has yet to be fully demonstrated, its assessment utility is more modest. To underscore this point, the validity evidence presented in the manual was based on relatively small samples. For instance, to establish the EDDT's convergent validity with conceptually related instrumentation only 11 participant responses were obtained for the Gilliam Asperger Disorder Scale and 22 for the Clinical Assessment of Behavior—Parent Form.

SUMMARY. Overall, the EDDT is user-friendly and reliable and, if deployed with considerable vigilance, a serviceable clinical instrument to estimate children and adolescents at risk for ED. Although the manual suggests the EDDT can be administered in group settings, individual administration is strongly advised. Score interpretations must be made for each section separately. Before using and interpreting the EDDT, test administrators must possess graduate-level education and training in special education, psychological testing, and behavioral disorders. Although further validity data need to be collected, the instrument can be used to tentatively discriminate between the normative sample and various clinical samples. It is prudent to use the EDDT as one of several measures to screen and diagnose children and adolescents.

REVIEWERS' REFERENCES

Anastasi, A., & Urbina, S. (1997). *Psychological testing* (7th ed.). Upper Saddle River, NJ: Prentice Hall.

DeVellis, R. F. (2003). *Scale development: Theory and applications* (2nd ed.). Thousand Oaks, CA: Sage.

Nunnally, J., & Bernstein, I. (1994). *Psychometric theory.* New York: McGraw Hill.

[49]

Employee Wellness Evaluation.

Purpose: Designed to "identify potential problems in several areas of significance for employees" as a clinical aid for referral for counseling or "to provide indications of problem prevalence in a workforce."
Population: Employees seeking counseling.
Publication Dates: 1994-1999.
Acronym: EWE.
Scores, 7: Alcohol, Depression, Stress, Anger, Morale, Management, Family Stress.
Administration: Individual and group.
Price Data, 2008: $52.50 per 25 assessments; $15 per EWE guide (1999, 5 pages).
Time: (10-15) minutes.
Author: Norman G. Hoffmann.
Publisher: The Change Companies.

Review of the Employee Wellness Evaluation by ELIZABETH BIGHAM, Health Psychologist, Lecturer in Human Development, California State University San Marcos, San Marcos, CA:

DESCRIPTION. The Employee Wellness Evaluation (EWE) is an individual or group-administered screening instrument designed to identify potential problems related to employee wellness in the areas of Alcohol, Depression, Stress, Anger, Morale, Management, and Family Stress as well as to identify areas that can be eliminated as potential problem areas. The EWE can also be used as an anonymous measure to estimate the prevalence of these seven problem areas in the workplace.

The EWE is a one-page, two-sided, self-completion assessment with 50 items. It is written in nontechnical English language. The form is self-explanatory and should take no more than 10–15 minutes to complete. After collecting demographic information, 9 multiple-choice items are used to inquire about health-related behaviors, such as how often the employee smokes, drinks alcohol, takes medication, and exercises. This section is followed by 41 true/false items that ask the employee to indicate if a given statement has been true or false during the past year. An example item asks respondents whether they consider their lives complete. The statements are designed to tap into seven areas related to employee wellness, including problems with alcohol, depression, stress, suppressed anger, morale, dissatisfaction with management, and family stress.

Scoring the EWE takes approximately 5 minutes. Two scoring forms are provided with the EWE: The scoring key and the scale summaries. The scoring key is a one-page form designed to calculate scores for each of the seven areas/scales from the employee's responses to the 41 true/false statements. If the employee's response matches the response on the scoring key, the response is circled on the scoring key. The number of circled responses is then totaled for each of the seven scales. The scoring key provides cutoff scores for Moderate and High scores. According to the authors, approximately 5% of employees obtain scores in the High range and less than 20% of employees obtain scores in the Moderate range on any of the seven scales. Responses to the health-related behavior items also provide perspective for interpreting the scale scores. The scale summaries is a one-page, two-sided form that organizes the items by scale. Similar to the scoring key, if the employee's response matches the response on the scale summaries, the response is noted on the scale summaries with a check mark. The format of the scale summaries provides an easy examination of responses within each scale.

DEVELOPMENT. The EWE was published in 1994 with the manual published in 1995 and 1999. The current publisher is The Change Companies of Carson City, NV. The manual does not provide references for the development of the items or cutoff scores; however, it indicates that the content of each of the seven scales is designed to tap into both clinical domains of employee wellness problems, including alcohol, depression, stress, and anger, and job-related domains of employee wellness problems, including morale, problems with management, and family stress. The scales are organized as follows:

1. The Alcohol scale has six items inquiring about preoccupation with use, use to ease emotional distress, loss of memory during use, neglect of responsibilities during use, unintended use, and objections by others. The items related to inability to limit use and loss of memory are DSM-IV criteria for dependence items. The cutoff for substantial risk for abuse or dependence for this scale is an endorsement of three or more items. Additionally, the frequency and quantity questions (Questions 5 and 6) provide additional context for interpreting the Alcohol scale score and clarifying the current situation.

2. The Depression scale has six items inquiring about difficulty sleeping, difficulty enjoying life, frequent feelings of sadness, guilt, or unhappiness, and feeling overwhelmed. The scale again reflects DSM-IV criteria with a score of at least four endorsed items calling for further exploration in this area.

3. The Stress scale has five items inquiring about frequent feelings of anxiety and stress, working under pressure, feeling more stressed than other people and feeling more stressed at the end of the day. An endorsement of four or more items on this scale warrants exploration in this area and possibly stress management.

4. The Anger scale has six items that inquire about suppressed anger, suppressed feelings, feeling about to blow up, being inpatient, and frequent feelings of anger and resentment. The Anger items tap into suppressed anger, which may be helpful in interpreting the Stress scale score. An endorsement of four items from this scale indicates that further exploration is indicated.

5. The Morale scale has seven items inquiring about the employee's feelings and motivations, including whether they have felt unmotivated, unrealistically anxious, afraid, or worried, question their own judgment, or feel that their life is uninteresting. The author indicates that this scale does not correlate highly with depression or other scales but seems to tap into dissatisfaction. An endorsement of four items or more is the criterion for attention for this scale.

6. The Management scale has six items inquiring about the management at the employee's current work environment. Items include whether employees are recognized or publicly criticized, need improvement in working conditions, encounter interference with work, and whether employees' concerns are heard. The scale provides an opportunity to perform comparisons both within and across managerial departments. Scores of four or more are considered elevated for this area.

7. The Family Stress scale has five items inquiring about conflicts between the employee's family and current work, such as how family and personal relationships are impacted by the time and energy demands of their job. High scores may indicate that either the employee is dedicating too much time and energy to their work or that conflicts exist in their home roles. A score for four or more indicates that this area should be evaluated and changes may be explored.

TECHNICAL. Normative data are provided for the EWE from a study of 758 employees in the form of a table of the distribution of scores in the seven scales. No information is provided about the age, gender, race/ethnicity, or employment setting of the sample. Very limited reliability and validity evidence is provided to support the inferences made by the EWE. The author indicates that the scales were factorally derived and examined for internal consistency, citing that the coefficient alphas for the scales ranged from .48 to .80.

COMMENTARY. The EWE is a brief and easy screener that can be administered to an individual or group of employees by office staff. When scored by an appropriately trained professional, the EWE may reveal potential problem areas related to employee wellness. The strengths of the EWE include that the administration and scoring are quick and easy. The manual would benefit from the inclusion of additional normative data for a larger sample, including race/ethnic, age, gender, and workplace information as well as specific results from examination of the reliability of the scales. The author has an extensive history in the assessment of substance abuse and involvement in previous studies of several scales for alcohol problems, depression, and morale issues, and these factors likely contributed to the development of the EWE; however, no references were provided. The brief information regarding the examination of internal consistency did not provide sufficient information to assess the measure; however, it does not appear that the reliability coefficients for the seven scales are likely to be acceptable (i.e., above .70). Although the brevity of the EWE is one of its strengths, it also compromises the reliability and validity of the seven scales, which are merely five to seven items each. The author of the EWE, however, reminds the user several times in the manual in regard to the use of clinical judgment because this measure is only a screening instrument, not a diagnostic tool. The manual would generally benefit from references, such as for evidence supporting the author's indication that the Morale scale does not correlate highly with Depression or other scales and for the Potential Problem Range cut scores.

SUMMARY. The Employee Wellness Evaluation (EWE) is an individual or group-administered screening instrument designed to identify potential problems related to employee wellness in the areas of Alcohol, Depression, Stress, Anger, Morale, Management, and Family Stress as well as to identify areas that can be eliminated as potential problem areas. It is quick and easy to administer and score. Although reliability and validity information is quite limited, the content of the EWE's seven scales seem to have sufficient construct validity for clinician use as a screening instrument to identify areas for further exploration or as an anonymous measure to estimate the prevalence of these problem areas in the workplace.

Review of the Employee Wellness Evaluation by THOMAS M. DUNN, Associate Professor of Psychological Sciences, University of Northern Colorado, Greeley, CO:

DESCRIPTION. The Employee Wellness Evaluation (EWE) is a very brief instrument purported to screen employees in seven areas of potential interest: problem alcohol use, depression, stress, suppressed anger, morale issues, management issues, and job/family conflict. The test is 50 items long and reportedly takes 10 to 15 minutes to administer in a two-page questionnaire. The first 9 items are multiple choice, the remaining are in a true/false format. Scoring is reported to take less than 5 minutes and interpretation is to be done by an "appropriately trained professional who can incorporate the findings of the EWE with other clinical information" (manual, p. 1). Respondents' scores are compared to a template identifying items endorsed in the critical direction. The numbers of items endorsed are counted and compared to either a "high" or "moderate" score. Only 5% of respondents reportedly score in the "high" range, whereas only 20% score in the "moderate" range. In most scales, 4 items endorsed in the critical direction indicate a moderate score, whereas 5 or more items identify a high score. Those employees scoring in a critical range can then be identified and further evaluation can be performed.

The author does not suggest that this instrument is intended for one type of worker over another (e.g., blue vs. white collar employee). In addition to being a clinical tool, the EWE could be taken by workers anonymously (there are forms available without a place for identifying information) and then used as a survey of potential worker-related difficulties. Such a use would be practical when not trying to identify problem workers, but in getting a global sense of a workforce's well-being. A high prevalence of problems found in the workplace (e.g., dissatisfaction with one's supervision) may be a symptom of a dysfunctional organization.

DEVELOPMENT. The EWE presents as being in its second edition with copyright dates of 1995 and 1999; however, there is no specific information indicating that this version is a revision of an earlier test. Information about development of the instrument is quite scarce. There is no mention of the underlying theory that guided test development. Constructs are not defined and there is essentially no discussion of the selection of test items, although the author does suggest that items on clinically oriented scales are tied closely to DSM-IV criteria. There is mention of scales being factorially derived, but there is no description of this process. The manual does not describe pilot testing. It is not clear what type of workers the EWE is intended to evaluate, such as whether the instrument is intended for a factory setting, for example, or an office one. Nor are there any studies listed suggesting theoretical or psychometric underpinnings of the EWE.

TECHNICAL. There is virtually no discussion of the standardization of the EWE. The manual refers only to a "replication study involving 758 employees" (p. 4), but there is no description of this normative group (e.g., breakdown by age, gender, education level). No citation is provided for this study. There is also no indication whether participants from this replication study comprised a single employer, whether the workforce was heterogeneous, what kind of workers were involved, or if the instrument was in its anonymous survey form.

The various scales of the EWE are extremely short (seven areas of interest spread across 50 items), suggesting that reliability will be a potential psychometric limitation. However, the author suggests that internal consistency is good with alpha coefficients ranging from .48 to .80. The manual does not provide the reliability coefficients for individual scales, for example.

Validity data are absent. There is no comparison of this instrument with others purported to identify troubled employees. No studies regarding sensitivity or specificity of the EWE are cited. The manual contains almost no evidence that the instrument measures what it is purported to measure. There is only a brief mention in the alcohol use interpretation that the critical items have been previously shown to be sensitive to problem drinking in other contexts.

Finally, there are no technical data regarding the use of the EWE to assess for the prevalence of workplace problems. For example, it would be helpful to know how many workers need to be sampled to get a sense of the overall level of problems in the workforce. Similarly, it would be valuable to know if a particular employer has an atypically high number of workers reporting problems. Such data could be used to investigate whether worker environment may be detrimental to worker well-being.

COMMENTARY. The EWE is a brief screening instrument used to help identify employees who may be distressed. The content areas of the EWE are certainly of interest to employers, including potential alcohol problems, depression, suppressed anger, and job-family conflicts. Given that it can be completed very quickly (15 minutes or less), its format is ideal for a busy workplace. Scoring the instrument takes a short amount of time, using clerical staff, so screening even a workforce of hundreds could be done in short order. It also has value as an anonymous survey, useful for sampling a worker sentiment. One could envision administering the EWE before and after some intervention (such as a reorganization, or firing of a toxic supervisor) to assess for changes in the prevalence of problem behavior being reported.

Unfortunately, the EWE has significant psychometric limitations. Essentially, the manual contains extremely limited information associated with basic psychometric theory and test construction. The normative group is described only by how large it is. There is no mention of validity. Reliability is described in what appear to be alpha coefficients.

SUMMARY. Used in the strictest sense of a screening device, the EWE has some utility. Administration is very short and can be done in groups. Scoring is neither complex nor time intensive. It probably does identify some workers who warrant a check in with a mental health professional. However, with next to no information about its psychometric properties (particularly validity, including sensitivity and specificity) its utility is limited.

[50]

Executive Dimensions.

Purpose: Designed to assess leadership effectiveness among top-level senior executives.
Population: Senior executives.
Publication Dates: 2004-2006.
Scores, 16: Sound Judgement, Strategic Planning, Leading Change, Results Orientation, Global Awareness, Business Perspective, Inspiring Commitment, Forging Synergy, Developing and Empowering, Leveraging Differences, Communicating Effectively, Interpersonal Savvy, Courage, Executive Image, Learning from Experience, Credibility.
Administration: Group.
Restricted Distribution: Distribution restricted to persons who have completed the publisher's training course.
Price Data, 2007: $395 per survey set including Development Planning Guide (2005, 20 pages), Facilitator's Guide, internet-based surveys, assessment scoring, and 2 printed feedback reports.
Foreign Language Editions: Spanish, French, German, and Dutch versions available.
Time: Administration time not reported.
Comments: Test administered via secure web page.
Author: Center for Creative Leadership.
Publisher: Center for Creative Leadership.

Review of the Executive Dimensions by AYRES D'COSTA, Associate Professor, Quantitative Research, Measurement, and Evaluation in Education, The Ohio State University, Columbus, OH:

DESCRIPTION. Executive Dimensions (ED) is offered by the Center for Creative Leadership (CCL) as one part of its *Assessment Suite,* which has four assessment devices designed to assess leadership effectiveness for top-level executives in business organizations. Based on the CCL website (www.ccl.org), these four devices are: (a) Executive Dimensions, assesses top-level leadership behaviors; (b) Benchmarks (T7:310), measures skills critical for success; (c) Prospector (T7:2062), measures skills for learning and leading; and (d) 360 BY DESIGN, focuses on competencies important to the organization.

ED is claimed to be a 360-degree self-assessment device to enable planning for one's own development as a leader, or as a person. It is not a tool for measuring basic leadership skills/knowledge, and is therefore inappropriate for use in job selection, performance appraisal, or compensation review. Similar leadership assessment programs are being offered on the Internet by the American Management Association (http://www.amanet.org) and by other companies.

In human resources management jargon, a 360-degree system uses multirater feedback to help compare one's self-ratings with similar ratings from superiors, colleagues, and others around an individual in his or her organization. An essential characteristic of such feedback is its confidentiality and anonymity. Typically, it would include ratings from one's immediate boss or supervisor, including members of one's governing board, peers, available direct reports about oneself, and feedback from other persons for whom an individual has direct supervisory or business contact.

The following CCL materials were made available to this reviewer: (a) a brochure titled *Executive Dimensions,* (b) a survey instrument titled Survey for Chris Sample-ED, (c) technical manual v.3.0, (d) (Individual) Feedback Report binder entitled "Prepared for Kim Sample," (e) a development planning guide, and (f) a Group Profile for Executive Dimensions Sample.

ED assessment is based on a 92-item survey with a 5-point rating scale with weights and labels as follows: 1 = *Deficient*; 2 = *Marginally Effective*; 3 = *Effective*; 4 = *Highly Effective*; 5 = *Exceptional.* A sixth response category provided is NA (*Not Applicable*). The 92 items are designed to represent 16 homogeneous leadership competencies, which are further organized into three broad conceptual factors: Leading the business, Leading others, and Leading by personal example.

The web-based survey is requested by and first administered to a prospective self-assessment client, typically a top-level executive. It begins with a very specific Demographics section, seeking information such as gender, date of birth, number of years of education, highest degree earned, type of organization, status/level in organization, job function, race and ethnicity, languages spoken, number of employees, and international management responsibility. The 92 items are then administered, followed by a listing of 16 competencies from which the 5 most important ones must be identified, and finally, an open-ended section asking for written comments about strengths and development needs as a leader.

The client then identifies other raters from his or her immediate group to satisfy the 360-degree assessment process, namely his or her superiors, colleagues, customers, etc. CCL then follows up with similar survey requests and compiles the resulting data. Each rater group may comprise about 5 persons to ensure its representation.

The entire assessment process is automated utilizing electronic media, namely email and web-based approaches, for most communications, data gathering, and reporting (Appendix I of technical manual). The ED assessment results in an individual "Development Planning Guide," and a "Feedback Report" aggregating the various individual assessment data by competency and by rater group.

The Development Planning Guide consists of 10 sections ranging from "How to Use this Guide" to identifying strengths and needs, to articulating and planning for one's developmental goals, including worksheets for self-analysis and follow-up strategies. The Group Profile provides feedback for the organization on its overall performance, its strengths and needs, various rater group summaries, and potential blind spots and unrecognized strengths. A unique comparison provided by ED refers to a normative group based on data from 167 raters who provided feedback on a select group of top executives. This normative index provides a reference point for self-assessment, especially aspiring mid-level executives.

CCL indicates that, because ED is a sophisticated assessment tool and because effective facilitation is critical to its successful use, ED can only be administered by CCL-certified professionals. This reviewer requested but was not provided a copy of the Facilitator Guide. However, information on Facilitator Certification and customizing ED for organizations is provided at the CCL website (www.ccl.org).

Instructions for the administration of the assessment program are outlined in the technical manual. The process is managed via the CCL computer system and by using trained facilitators. All data are treated as confidential and anonymous. Only aggregated ratings are reported to the participant and to the business organization/company. Specialized feedback reports are provided to the individual. The organization has the option of purchasing an aggregated "Group Profile" if they have five or more executives who have taken ED.

DEVELOPMENT. The technical manual provides a somewhat brief (nine-page) summary containing the Development (Section VI) and the Psychometric Background of ED (Section VII). There is no documentation of a broader or more recent research/literature background to this psychometric device, other than the two references, namely, the Borman and Brush (1993) taxonomy, and the Yukl (1989) taxonomy. A modified version of their taxonomy serves as the foundation for this ED assessment.

A Google Scholar (http://scholar.google.com/scholar) search on the keywords "taxonomy managerial performance" by this reviewer did show the Borman and Brush publication as one of four key publications on this topic. The other three taxonomies were linked to Kathuria (2000) and to Johnson, Schneider, and Oswald (1997). However, Google also presented some 13,400 citations, many quite recent, related to the keywords, "taxonomy executive leadership," none of which were cited by CCL, thus suggesting that there may be theoretical limitations of this technical manual. One justification for this might be the targeted business audience for this assessment device.

The two cited taxonomies of leadership performance are the "academic" basis for ED, and they were judgmentally modified with data gathered from senior executives attending CCL courses. "Credibility" is noted as one pragmatic executive competency not included in the two "academic" taxonomies. The technical manual states that 16 scales were identified, and items were written and revised using an iterative process involving subject-matter "experts." Finally, a "pilot version" of ED was pretested using data from 500 executives including 3,000 raters.

TECHNICAL. An expert judgmental process was utilized to develop items for each of the 16 competency areas of the survey. This domain-representation process is fairly standard in the profession and such a process normally provides content validity for the instrument. However, it would be appropriate, based on the professional *Standards* (American Educational Research Association, American Psychological Association, & National Council on Measurement in Education, 1999) of the measurement field, to document this judgment process. No such documentation was available to this reviewer.

Criterion-related validity measures are reported for the 16 scales based on correlation with two concurrent criteria: "ratings of overall effectiveness" of executive and "how likely it is that observers would choose to work" with the executive in the future. Pearson "r" coefficients reported are in the range of .45 to .81 for the first criterion, and .28 to .76 for the second. All correlations are reported to be statistically significant at the .01 level, with $n = 252$. This reviewer would consider these validity results reasonable, although once again, technical documentation of this research work is clearly lacking.

Construct validity is presented, in part, using principal components analysis with equimax rotation. A three-component solution is justified on the basis of the size of the obtained eigenvalues and the conceptual meaningfulness of the factors. The three conceptual factors adopted in the ED instrument (Leading the Business, Leading Others, Leading by Personal Example) correspond reasonably well (but not entirely) to the three factors identified through statistical analyses. The authors observe that such scale development must remain both an art and a science, and this reviewer concurs.

Reliability estimates, computed for each of the 16 scales using test-retest with a 2-month time interval were as follows: For $n = 45$, *r*s ranged from .60 to .85 for the self-ratings and from .81 to .93 for the observer raters. Internal consistency measures for the 16 scales, using coefficient alpha, were as follows: For self-ratings ($n = 392$), *r*s ranged from .68 to .85, whereas for observers ($n = 3{,}032$), *r*s ranged from .74 to .87. In the experience of this reviewer, these numbers appear respectable.

Much of the interpretation based on these survey results must necessarily be situational in that self-assessment comparisons are made on the basis of the individual ratings versus the relevant "other" raters in the 360-degree setting around him/her. This reviewer agrees that this approach is most relevant for the specific purposes of the ED assessment. The leadership development process should begin in the present organizational context and attempt to utilize this learning experience to enhance one's future prospects and skills.

However, there is a normative data-set that CCL uses to provide a reference profile that an aspiring leader can look to as some kind of model. This norm group is based on data collected from product sales and an "exclusive" group of top executives involved with CCL workshops. Although such a reference profile would clearly be an asset in leadership self-assessment and development, it must be recognized that this CCL profile may be biased and should only be utilized with due caution. The development of norms requires a more rigorous norm-group definition/selection process than was apparent in the technical manual, in the opinion of this reviewer.

COMMENTARY. The ED assessment is based on judgmental ratings that are subject to measurement bias and error, regardless of whether these ratings are by self or others. Likert scales are useful devices, but they must be interpreted with caution. Individual differences in self-report bias are not easy to track nor to correct for. Also, as suggested by Item Response Theory (Hambleton, Swaminathan, & Rogers, 1991; Linacre, 1989; Wright & Masters, 1982), Likert scale weights are at best a very tentative basis for generating a scale score. Aggregating ratings from judges with varying degrees of judging severity could render the scale score grossly inaccurate, and compromise the utility of the assessment comparisons. Another major limitation is the lack of a dispersion index for the ratings within each group of raters. An index such as the standard deviation could be provided, along with the statistical mean.

The technical manual is generally weak, not only because of its theoretical deficiencies, but also for other psychometric scale construction considerations. This reviewer strongly recommends adherence to the *Standards* (AERA, APA, & NCME, 1999) of the testing profession in revising the instrument and its technical manual. In general, ED should be a useful assessment device.

The 360-degree feedback approach is a powerful assessment technique in that it attempts to bring together input from various sources that are of critical relevance in one's job setting. However, it has its own cautions and drawbacks. It appears to this reviewer that extra care should be taken so that the selection of significant "others" is not left to convenience or expediency. There is much debate in management circles that the key to the success of such techniques lies in the proper development of assessment instruments, in the careful selection of raters, in the proper presentation and use of the feedback, and in managing and integrating this self-assessment process for the development of individual leaders and the growth of organizational groups. Some useful resources and recommendations are available on the American Management Association website (www.amanet.org).

SUMMARY. The ED is a nicely conceived assessment device, which has great relevance for the development of leaders and top executives in business organizations. Its focus on its use for executive development rather than for selection or job appraisal is appropriate. The need to train and certify facilitators to ensure the proper use of this instrument is justified.

REVIEWER'S REFERENCES

American Educational Research Association, American Psychological Association, & National Council on Measurement in Education. (1999). *Standards for educational and psychological testing.* Washington, DC: American Educational Research Association.

Borman, W. C., & Brush, D. H. (1993). More progress toward a taxonomy of managerial performance requirements. *Human Performance,* 6, 1–21.

Hambleton, R. K., Swaminathan, H., & Rogers, H. J. (1991). *Fundamentals of Item Response Theory.* Newbury Park, CA: Sage.

Johnson, J. W., Schneider, R. J., & Oswald, F. L. (1997). Toward a taxonomy of managerial performance profiles. *Human Performance, 10,* 227–250.

Kathuria, R. (2000). Competitive priorities and managerial performance: A taxonomy of small manufacturers. *Journal of Operations Management, 18,* 622–641.

Linacre, J. (1989). *Many-facet Rasch measurement.* Chicago: Measurement Evaluation Statistics and Assessment Press.

Wright, B., & Masters, G. (1982). *Rating scale analysis: Rasch measurement.* Chicago: MESA Press.

Yukl, G. A. (1998). *Leadership in organizations* (2nd ed.). Englewood Cliffs, NJ: Prentice-Hall.

Review of the Executive Dimensions by MATT VASSAR, Curriculum and Outcomes Assessment Coordinator, Oklahoma State University, Tulsa, OK:

DESCRIPTION. Executive Dimensions is a 92-item 360-degree evaluation tool that measures specific leadership behaviors considered important to job effectiveness at the executive level. The technical manual explicitly notes that the measure is not appropriate for assessing basic skills, job knowledge, or intellectual ability but may be used to provide feedback about leadership competencies. The instrument is administered online and is available in English, Dutch, German, French, and Spanish. All multiple-choice items have five response options: *Deficient*, *Marginally Effective*, *Effective*, *Highly Effective*, and *Exceptional*, along with the inclusion of a *Not Applicable* alternative. Items are said to measure 1 of 16 leadership competencies, which are hierarchically fashioned. A competency rating question and two open-ended items comprise the remaining portions of the assessment. Though not directly stated in the technical manual, it appears that a straightforward mean estimate is calculated for the scoring of each test item. Means are thus obtained for each respondent group (e.g., peers, subordinates, supervisors). For this process, peers and direct reports are considered protected rater groups, and a minimum of three ratings must correspond to an item before its score is printed on the final summary report.

DEVELOPMENT. The content for Executive Dimensions was derived from Borman and Brush (1993) and Yukl (1989) taxonomies of leadership behaviors. It is unclear why the authors chose these particular taxonomies among the extensive literature on leadership theory. Furthermore, a discussion of other leadership measures is not offered to provide differential support for the development of this measure.

TECHNICAL.

Normative sample. It is difficult to determine the sample size of the normative group based on the test's technical manual. The authors note that they collected data from approximately 500 executives and more than 3,000 of their observers on a pilot version of the test. It is unclear whether these data were used during the norming process. The normative sample reported in the manual was composed of 167 top-level executives (29% CEOs, COOs, Presidents, or Managing Directors; 71% Vice-Presidents, Directors, or Board-level Professionals) from firms across various industries. In particular, executives from computer software and services (16.3%), metals and mining (12%), banking (11.4%), and manufacturing (10.2%) comprise the majority of the normative sample. Approximately 61% of executives represented firms with 1,000–4,999 employees, 10% with 5,000–9,999 employees, and 29% with greater than 10,000 employees. Furthermore, the sample was predominately male (81%) and Caucasian (92.7%), with the majority reporting either having obtained a masters (51.5%) or an undergraduate (33.5%) degree. The authors do note that missing data were not included in these calculations. The sample size reported above, however, is incongruent (and noticeably smaller) with the sample sizes reported in both the calculation of coefficient alpha (n = 392) and the principal component analysis of its test dimensions (n = 309). Clarification of this issue is clearly warranted. Based on the provided demographic information, it appears that additional psychometric work needs to be conducted in female and non-Caucasian populations.

Reliability. Two forms of score reliability were reported for the Executive Dimensions instrument. Internal consistency estimates, specifically coefficient alpha, were calculated for each of the 16 dimensions for both the self-report (n = 392) and observer (n = 3,032) samples. Alphas ranged from .74 to .90 for observer ratings and from .68 to .85 for the self-ratings. Across all dimensions, alpha was higher for the observer group. Test-retest reliability was also reported for each dimension over a 2-month period. These correlations ranged from .81 to .93 for the observer ratings and from .60 to .85 for the self-ratings. Both are based on a subsample of 45 respondents. As with internal consistency, test-retest coefficients were higher for the observer group across all 16 competencies. If .70 is used as the benchmark for acceptable estimates of alpha, then only the Sound Judgment and Global Awareness dimensions fall below this standard for the self-report group. It is the opinion of this reviewer, however, that .80 is a more acceptable minimum benchmark, depending upon the use of the measure. In this case, the Global Awareness and Business Perspective dimensions for the observer group, and 14 of the 16 dimensions from the self-report group fell below this standard. In all cases, test-retest coefficients were impressive given the lengthy time period between administrations.

Validity. Validity information of the Executive Dimensions instrument is clearly lacking. The technical manual notes that correlations were calculated between the Executive Dimension ratings and (a) a one-item rating of overall effectiveness and (b) a single-item rating of future intent to work with the individual. Correlations with overall effectiveness ranged from .45 for the Global Awareness subscale to .81 for the Inspiring Commitment subscale. Coefficients with the future intent item ranged from .28 for the Global Awareness dimension to .76 for the Learning from Experience dimension.

Principal components analysis was conducted on a correlation matrix of the 16 leadership dimensions. Three components were reported to represent the final solution. Factor retention was based on the Kaiser-Guttman eigenvalue criterion (eigenvalues > 1.0), interpretability, and expert judgment. In essence, these components appear to be similar to higher order factors with the exception that the first-order factors were not derived factor analytically. Communalities ranged from .57 to .75. A number of dimensions were placed by the scale developers on a particular component even though its factor loadings supported placement elsewhere. In these cases, the technical report notes that expert judgment and conceptual similarity were primary reasons for these placement decisions. It is the reviewer's opinion that additional validation work is needed. Specifically, scores from Executive Dimensions should be examined relative to other leadership measures, or the scale developers should utilize the multitrait-multimethod matrix for additional validation support. Furthermore, it is unclear why the test developers did not perform exploratory factor analysis on the scale items as a means to provide evidence of factor structure. Given that items were derived based on two taxonomies, confirmatory factor analysis using a new sample would also provide needed support for validity.

COMMENTARY. Executive Dimensions is an instrument used to assess leadership competencies at the executive level. Its strengths lie in its 360-degree format, allowing the rating of the executive by multiple respondents including peers, subordinates, and supervisors. Respondents receive a rather impressive, comprehensible report detailing the analysis of findings. By conventional standards, internal consistency estimates were reasonable, and test-retest coefficients were rather impressive. A number of weaknesses or areas of improvement should also be noted. The normative sample appeared to be underrepresentative of both females and non-Caucasians. Furthermore, although the instrument is available in five languages, only validation information is provided for the English version. Measurement invariance or differential item functioning inquiries across cultures/nations are clearly needed. Additional validation work, as previously outlined, is also warranted.

SUMMARY. Executive Dimensions may be a useful tool in the rating of leadership competencies for high-level executives. Its 360 feedback is particularly attractive to those wanting a holistic understanding of a leader's competence. In certain respects, it has been developed based on modern psychometric methods. The reliability and validity information, although limited, may substantiate cautious use of this measure.

REVIEWER'S REFERENCES

Borman, W. C., & Brush, D. H. (1993). More progress toward a taxonomy of managerial performance requirements. *Human Performance, 6,* 1–21.

Yukl, G. A. (1989). *Leadership in organizations* (2nd ed.). Englewood Cliffs, NJ: Prentice-Hall.

[51]

Expressive Vocabulary Test, Second Edition.

Purpose: Designed to assess "expressive vocabulary and word retrieval for Standard American English."
Population: Ages 2:6 to 90+ years.
Publication Dates: 1997-2007.
Acronym: EVT-2™.
Scores: Total score only.
Administration: Individual
Forms, 2: A, B
Price Data, 2008: $390 per complete kit (Forms A & B) including 25 record forms for Form A & 25 record forms for Form B, easel for each form and manual; $45.50 per 25 record forms (specify A or B); $259 per EVT-2 ASSIST™ scoring and reporting software; single form kits also available.
Time: (10–20) minutes.
Comments: Also includes a growth scale value (GSV) to specifically measure progress over time; conormed with the Peabody Picture Vocabulary Test-4 (18:88); EVT-2 and PPVT-4 standard scores allow comparisons between expressive and receptive vocabulary; items are categorized for multiple levels and type of descriptive analysis; scoring and reporting software (ASSIST) allows for multiple types of individual and group reporting, including aggregation and disaggregation options; evidence-based interventions are embedded within the ASSIST.
Author: Kathleen T. Williams.
Publisher: Pearson.
Cross References: For reviews by Frederick Bessai and Orest Eugene Wasyliw of a previous edition, see 14:143.

Review of the Expressive Vocabulary Test, Second Edition by THERESA GRAHAM, Adjunct Faculty, University of Nebraska-Lincoln, Lincoln, NE:

DESCRIPTION. The Expressive Vocabulary Test, Second Edition (herein referred to as EVT-2) is a norm-referenced test that provides a quick assessment of expressive vocabulary and word retrieval for children and adults, ranging from age 2 years 6 months to beyond 90 years of age. In the EVT-2, Expressive Vocabulary is assessed through labeling items and providing synonyms. Examinees are shown a picture and asked to provide a single word to label a picture (e.g., a picture of a cow and the examinee is asked "what do you see?") or to provide a single word synonym for the target word (e.g., a picture of someone cleaning and the examinee is asked to "tell me another word for busy"). Word retrieval is determined by using standard score differences between the EVT-2 and the Peabody Picture Vocabulary Test, Fourth Edition (PPVT™-4; Dunn & Dunn, 2007), which was conormed with the EVT-2.

The EVT-2 was revised to update the stimulus pictures, to create a parallel testing form (Form A and B), to change the record form to include all correct responses and the stimulus question, and to be co-normed with the PPVT-4 to allow for comparison of expressive and receptive language development. The EVT-2 can be used to screen populations of various ages for expressive language problems, to examine labeling in preschool children, and to provide insight into reading difficulties.

ADMINISTRATION AND ITEM SCORING. The materials for the EVT-2 consist of 2 easels, one for Form A and one for Form B, a manual, and record forms for Form A and Form B. The easels are self-standing and very easy to use, including tabs for different age start points. The EVT-2 manual provides an excellent and clear description of the general testing guidelines in terms of standard protocol, scoring information, interpretation, normative studies, and normative and interpretive tables. Two record forms are provided (Record Form A and Record Form B). New to the EVT-2, the record form provides the stimulus question for each item. In addition, a list of all of the correct responses to each item is included on the record form next to each stimulus question. Only the most frequent incorrect responses are provided. A few incorrect responses are tagged with a "P" indicating that the examiner can "prompt" for another answer. The author does not explain fully how it was determined which incorrect answers should be prompted and which should be immediately considered wrong. Without such explanation, the "prompted" responses seem somewhat arbitrary.

The EVT-2 is designed to be administered individually by a trained professional. There are 190 items each on both Form A and Form B. Start points are determined by age and confirmed through establishing a basal level (five correct responses). Ceiling is established by five consecutive incorrect items. The manual provides detailed "administration rules" to assure standard administration. Because the examinee only needs to provide single word responses and because an examinee does not have to start at the beginning of the instrument, administration time is relatively short, ranging from 10–20 minutes.

Because all of the correct responses are written on the record form, scoring is easily done while the test is being administered. A "1" is circled for correct responses, and a "0" is circled for incorrect responses. Space is provided for comments that the examiner may want to record regarding the individual's performance. Detailed scoring rules are provided in the manual.

Total raw score is determined by subtracting the total number of incorrect items from the highest ceiling item. Items that precede the starting point are credited to the examinee and are included in the raw score. Raw scores are noted on the record form. Appendix B, located in the testing manual, provides all of the normative and interpretive tables for Form A and Form B. It includes three tables to convert raw scores to standard scores based either on age, grade (fall), or grade (spring). In addition, tables are provided to convert standard scores to percentiles, normal curve equivalents, and stanine scores. Finally, tables are provided to convert a raw score to a growth scale value (GSV). Although the GSV is not a normative measurement, it is a useful tool to examine vocabulary development across all ages and grades.

Because the EVT-2 and PPVT-4 were conormed with the same sample, comparisons between development of expressive and receptive vocabulary skills can be made. Tables are provided to examine whether differences in standard scores on the EVT-2 and PPVT-4 are significant. An interpretation of the differences in performance on these two instruments is provided in the test manual.

In addition to the quantitative summaries of the raw scores, performance on the EVT-2 can be examined in various qualitative ways. The test manual provides an entire chapter describing qualitative ways to interpret the results. For example, the EVT-2 can be analyzed in terms of home versus school vocabulary (e.g., Does the examinee make more incorrect responses on vocabulary learned at home or at school?) or can be examined in terms of parts of speech (e.g., Does the examinee make more incorrect responses on nouns or adjectives?). Worksheets are provided on the record form and in the manual to help with the qualitative analysis. In addition, a software program can be purchased for electronic scoring and interpretation (EVT-2 ASSIST™).

DEVELOPMENT. The first step in revising the EVT was to survey current EVT users. In addition, a panel of consultants consisting of different cultural groups was convened to assess the cultural sensitivity and fairness of the instrument. Based on these steps, goals for the EVT revision were established, including creating two parallel testing forms, increasing the vocabulary learned in the home environment, including labeling items for older examinees, and dropping items that had become dated.

To create two parallel test forms, 400 items were generated based on existing published word lists. The goal was to find words that are common to standard American English vocabulary and occur with at least high frequency. The manual provides a list of the references used to generate the items. The set included 72 items from the original edition, 113 items from the original edition that were significantly modified, and 220 new items. These items were then categorized in terms of parts of speech and content. Two tryout studies were conducted to pretest the items. Both tryout studies were individually administered to individuals ranging in age from 2–21 years and representing a cross-section of geographic location and mother's education level. A total of 1,451 individuals participated in the first tryout study, and 852 individuals participated in the second tryout study.

Based on the first tryout study, guidelines for scoring were established. Based on frequency of responses given, answers were classified as correct or incorrect. The test manual reports that responses were also evaluated in terms of reference materials although this reviewer would have preferred more elaboration. Item difficulty and item discrimination were determined using a Rasch analysis. In addition, items were assessed for cultural bias by determining if some items were more difficult for certain cultural groups. The pool of items was evaluated by a panel of reviewers representing different cultural and geographical background. Based on the results of the first tryout study, 201 revised or newly created items were administered in a second tryout study. Twenty items were dropped following the second tryout study, resulting in 384 items (192 items for each form). The two forms were balanced in terms of item difficulty, item type, part of speech, content category, and race/ethnicity in the pictures.

TECHNICAL.

Standardization. The sample used to standardize the EVT-2 consisted of 3,540 individuals ranging in age from 2 years, 6 months to over 90 years of age. The sample represented 28 age groups, with 6-month intervals below age 7, one-year intervals for ages 7–14, two-year intervals for ages 15–24, a single 5-year interval for ages 25–30, and 10-year intervals for ages 31 and older. The goal was to test at least 100 individuals in each group. That goal was met or exceeded in all age groups except for the two oldest age groups. Tables are provided in the manual with information regarding distribution of the sample in terms of ethnicity, gender, education level, and geographic region.

Form A and Form B were administered similarly across geographic and demographic characteristics. The PPVT-4 was administered first followed by the EVT-2.

As in the tryout studies, items were analyzed using Rasch procedures. Because Form A and Form B were not fully equivalent, raw scores could not be pooled so that raw scores (for each form separately) were converted to w-ability scores (Rasch scale scores), then these data were pooled, and combined norms provided in this fashion. This conversion allows standard scores between the two forms to be comparable. The test manual provides a table comparing item difficulty between the two forms suggesting that the two forms are similar in item difficulty across the instruments.

Reliability. Reliability was assessed in terms of internal consistency, alternate form, and test-retest reliability. Internal consistency was determined using the split-half method. Reliability coefficients are presented for the 28 age groups and each subtest. Coefficients ranged from .88 to .97, indicating adequate internal consistency. In addition, internal consistency reliability was assessed using a coefficient alpha. In this case, the alpha reliability is measured across the entire instrument. Thus, in the case of the EVT-2, because examinees are not administered the entire instrument, scores for the unadministered items were imputed. The resulting average coefficient alphas were high (.96 for Form A and Form B).

Alternate-form reliability was assessed by counterbalancing Form A and Form B for a subset of the standardization sample (N = 507). The correlation for Form A and Form B ranges from .83 to .91 with consistent reliability across age groups. Test-retest stability was assessed with a group of 348 individuals in five age groups who were given the test twice. The retest occurred anywhere between 2 and 6–8 weeks depending on age group with the average retest time being 4 weeks. The test-retest reliability coefficients ranged from .94 to .97, demonstrating very high stability over time.

Validity. Evidence of validity of the EVT-2 was assessed in terms of content validity, its relationship to other criteria and tests, and its ability to differentiate among special populations of examinees. The author contends that content validity was addressed through the procedures used for item development. In addition, the author states that items were reviewed by a panel of specialists and bias reviewers. Although the author provides a list of the references used to generate the set of items and the guidelines used for item selection, more information regarding what words were not selected would provide additional information concerning how the items were developed. In addition, a discussion of how various word lists were used to generate the set of items would have been helpful.

As expected, in the normative sample, the progression of EVT-2 across the age groups followed an assumed pattern of cognitive development. Vocabulary development rapidly increased in early childhood, gradually increased during adolescence and in early adulthood, reached a plateau in midadulthood, and began to decline in late adulthood. In addition, the EVT-2 was correlated with other measures of vocabulary development and reading skill, including the Peabody Picture Vocabulary Test, Fourth Edition (PPVT-4; Dunn & Dunn, 2007), Comprehensive Assessment of Spoken Language (CASL; Carrow-Woolfolk, 1999), Clinical Evaluation of Language Fundamentals, Fourth Edition (CELF-4; Semel, Wiig, & Secord, 2003), and Group Reading Assessment and Diagnostic Evaluation (GRADE; Williams, 2001). In each of these studies, performance on the EVT-2 and other measures were moderately to highly correlated. In addition, the EVT and the EVT-2 were administered to a group of 377 individuals. A correlation of .81 was obtained, suggesting, as expected, a strong relationship between the two versions.

Finally, studies were conducted in which the EVT-2 was administered to special populations, including individuals with speech impairment, language delay, language disorder, hearing impairment, reading disability, mental retardation, giftedness, emotional/behavior disturbance, and Attention-Deficit/Hyperactivity Disorder. As predicted, results on the EVT-2 of the special population group differ from the general population in varying degrees.

COMMENTARY. The EVT-2 was intended to provide a quick tool to evaluate expressive vocabulary and word retrieval across a large age span (2 years, 6 months through late adulthood). Indeed, the test can be completed in less than 20 minutes. The reliability results suggest that the EVT-2 is a stable measure of expressive vocabulary. In addition, the EVT-2 clearly discriminates among special populations of individuals. However, more information concerning item development in terms of why certain items were included and others were not would add to our confidence in the instrument. Similarly, more information concerning the scoring criteria and determination of prompted responses would be helpful. Given that the EVT-2 is related to independent measures of vocabulary development and reading development, we are given some assurance of its content validity. In addition, although the author provides the list of references used to generate the set of items, it may be wise to explore those references prior to using the EVT-2.

In general, the EVT-2 provides a good overall measure of expressive vocabulary and word retrieval. It is an easy instrument to administer, score, and interpret. It is a helpful tool for professionals who want to assess expressive vocabulary and word retrieval either in a clinical or research setting.

REVIEWER'S REFERENCES

Carrow-Woolfolk, E. (1999). Comprehensive Assessment of Spoken Language. Circle Pines, MN: American Guidance Service.

Dunn, L. M., & Dunn, D. M. (2007). Peabody Picture Vocabulary Test, Fourth Edition. Bloomington, MN: NCS Pearson, Inc.

Semel, E., Wiig, E. H., & Secord, W. A. (2003). Clinical Evaluation of Language Fundamentals, Fourth Edition. San Antonio, TX: Psychological Corporation.

Williams, K. T. (2001). Group Reading Assessment and Diagnostic Evaluation. Circle Pines, MN: American Guidance Service.

Review of the Expressive Vocabulary Test, Second Edition by NATALIE RATHVON, Assistant Clinical Professor, The George Washington University, Washington DC; Private Practice Psychologist and School Consultant, Bethesda, MD:

DESCRIPTION. The Expressive Vocabulary Test, Second Edition (EVT-2) is an individually administered, norm-referenced measure of expressive vocabulary and word retrieval for ages 2 years, 6 months through 90+ years. The EVT-2 was conormed with the Peabody Picture Vocabulary Test–Fourth Edition (PPVT–4; Dunn & Dunn, 2007) to permit comparisons of receptive and expressive vocabulary using the same sample. Applications include (a) screening for expressive language problems, (b) screening preschoolers for language problems, (c) measuring word retrieval, (d) understanding reading difficulties, (e) monitoring growth, (f) research, and (g) evaluating English language acquisition in English language learners. Changes include a second parallel form, a larger sampling of home vocabulary, the addition of early literacy words, and the inclusion of labeling items throughout the test. Each form consists of 190 items arranged in order of increasing difficulty. Materials per form include an examiner's manual, test easel, and 25 record forms. A software scoring program (ASSIST) is available for an additional charge and offers large-scale progress monitoring and data management and a variety of group and individual reports. The EVT-2 consists of two types of items, labeling items and synonym items, both depicted on colored picture plates. In this edition, the record form includes a specific stimulus question for every item.

Administration. The EVT-2 is untimed and takes between 10 and 20 minutes. Basals and ceilings are five consecutive correct and incorrect items, respectively. Starting points are based on age with eight different starting points provided, although there were only two sets of example items given. Although one labeling and one synonym example are provided for the older group, both examples for the younger group are labeling items. Because young children may have trouble understanding the nature of the task, a synonym example should be added to the first entry level. All responses that should be prompted are labeled "P" in the record form, although some of the prompting decisions seem inconsistent. In some cases, seemingly close approximations to the correct response are prompted, but in others, they are not.

Scoring. Items are scored dichotomously. The record form now lists all correct responses, whereas in the previous edition, the examiner had to consult the manual for additional correct and incorrect responses. Again, some of the scoring decisions are perplexing. Responses are summed to yield a single test score. Raw scores can be converted to standard scores (M = 100, SD = 15), percentiles, stanines, normal curve equivalents, age and grade equivalents, and growth scale values (GSVs).

Interpretation. Interpretive guidelines in the manual—sparse in the first edition—have been expanded. The manual includes tables listing receptive/expressive standard score point differences required for statistical significance by age group, as well as differences demonstrated by various percentages of the standardization sample. Five types of qualitative analyses are described, four of which can be completed by the ASSIST program when item responses are entered, but the lack of reliability and validity data for the analyses makes them of questionable value, given the effort required. Although the manual does not offer intervention suggestions, ASSIST individual reports include a set of developmentally appropriate research-based strategies keyed to examinee performance.

DEVELOPMENT. The 5-year revision process included surveys, focus groups, and interviews with EVT users; reviews of research with the EVT; sensitivity reviews; and two national tryouts. Items were selected based on words representing standard American English vocabulary acquired through typical life experiences, using seven word frequency lists and two dictionaries. All of the stimulus pictures were recreated for the new edition. Classical psychometric and Rasch-based analyses were used to examine items for difficulty, discrimination, and differential item functioning after each tryout, with Rasch procedures repeated after standardization. Of the final set of items, 46% were adapted from the original edition and 54% were new. The pictures are generally good representations of the stimulus words, although there are inherent difficulties in depicting non-noun items (such as verbs). Differences between Rasch item difficulty means and standard deviations for consecutive groups of 10 items are minimal across the two forms. Equivalent raw scores for the two forms corresponding to the same Rasch ability value are also similar when plotted on a graph. Standard score means and standard deviations for the two forms are nearly identical for five age groups, but the groups do not include adults over the age of 60.

TECHNICAL ADEQUACY. Standardization data for the final version were collected from fall of 2005 through spring of 2006 for 3,540 examinees sampled to be representative of U.S. 2004 Census data and stratified by gender, age, race/ethnicity, geographic region, parent educational level or examinee educational level, and six special education categories. Sample characteristics are remarkably close to U.S. population data across the age span, although size for the 28 age groups varies considerably (60 to 200 cases). Grade norms, based on 2,003 cases drawn from the age norm group, include 100 to 233 students per grade.

Reliability evidence. Coefficient alpha reliabilities are in the .90s for both forms across age and grade norm groups. Split-half coefficients range from .86 to .97 for age and grade samples, and alternate-form reliability coefficients range from .83 to .91. Test-retest reliability was consistently high (.94 to .97) for periods from 2 to 8 weeks. Given continuing concerns about potential bias in vocabulary measures, reliability coefficients, standard score means, and standard deviations should be reported by gender and racial/ethnic subgroup. As with the previous edition, no evidence of interscorer reliability is presented, a serious omission, given the amount of prompting required and the numerous alternatives for correct and incorrect responses. Floors and ceilings are excellent and item gradients are ample across age groups, making the EVT-2 sensitive to individual differences in expressive vocabulary across the entire range of functioning.

Validity evidence. Items were reviewed by content specialists and bias reviewers, but no empirical evidence is offered to support the single-word format, use of pictorial stimuli, or use of colored drawings rather than photographs. Correlations with two language batteries in preschool and elementary school samples were moderate to high, with stronger relationships with expressive versus receptive measures, as expected. Correlations with a standardized reading battery were moderate to high for vocabulary and comprehension measures and lower for measures not directly assessing vocabulary, although this pattern did not apply across all grades. Compared with the EVT, EVT-2 standard scores are an average of 3.6 points higher. Although the author attributes this improvement to the addition of a stimulus question per item, a slight decline was observed for the youngest age group, and other explanations are possible, such as lower levels of vocabulary ability in the norming sample. Correlations with both forms of the PPVT-4 ranged from .80 to .84, nearly as high as the overall correlation between EVT-2 forms (.87). The vast majority of the criterion-related validity studies included examinees under 21.

Diagnostic validity studies with 12 clinical and special education groups and matched controls from the standardization sample reported statistically significant differences in the predicted direction for all groups except for the two speech-impairment groups, which scored unexpectedly lower. Mean standard scores for school-age language delay and language disorder samples fell within 1 standard deviation of the mean (mean SSs = 88.1) and within the range classified by the EVT-2 as "average." Differences were greater for the adult language disorder sample, which scored about 25 points lower than the norm group.

COMMENTARY. This edition of a widely used vocabulary test demonstrates notable enhancements in usability, including a second form, attractive new artwork, simplified scoring, and strong links to intervention. Psychometric adequacy and evidence for proposed uses vary, however. The EVT-2 has excellent test floors, ample item gradients, and acceptable to high levels of internal consistency, test-retest, and alternate-form reliability, but interscorer consistency has yet to be demonstrated. Moreover, criterion-related validity is limited in scope. The results of diagnostic validity studies are promising, although scores for children with language deficits fell within 1 standard deviation of the mean. No evidence of classification accuracy, such as sensitivity and specificity indices, is presented—a major deficiency in a test designed to screen for language disorders.

SUMMARY. Merits of the EVT-2 include ease of administration, conorming with the PPVT–4, and a software scoring program with evidence-based language interventions. When administered with the PPVT–4, it may be useful in distinguishing word retrieval problems from limited word knowledge, although more studies are needed to demonstrate the utility of these comparisons in diagnosis and treatment planning. Additional evidence supporting the proposed uses of the EVT-2 is also needed, especially for preschool and adult populations. Because the EVT-2 measures only one component of oral language, it should never be used as the only measure to assess language proficiency. Moreover, given the lack of classification accuracy data, it should not be used as the sole instrument to screen for language problems.

REVIEWER'S REFERENCE

Dunn, L. M., & Dunn, D. M. (2007). Peabody Picture Vocabulary Test–Fourth Edition. Minneapolis, MN: Pearson Assessments.

[52]

Firestone Assessment of Violent Thoughts.

Purpose: "Designed to assess the underlying thoughts that predispose violent behavior."

Population: Ages 18+.

Publication Dates: 1999-2008.

Acronym: FAVT.

Scores, 10: Paranoid/Suspicious, Persecuted Misfit, Self-Depreciating/Pseudo-Independent, Overtly Aggressive, Self-Aggrandizing, Total, Theoretical Subscale scores (Instrumental/Proactive Violence, Hostile/Reactive Violence), Validity scores (Negativity, Inconsistency).

Administration: Group.

Price Data, 2010: $125 per introductory kit including professional manual (2008, 148 pages), 25 rating forms, and 25 score summary/profile forms; $60 per 25 rating forms; $20 per 25 score summary/profile forms; $55 per professional manual.

Time: (15-20) minutes.

Comments: Scores normed for Younger Men (ages 18-39), Older Men (ages 40-75), Younger Women (ages 18-39), and Older Women (ages 40-75).

Authors: Robert W. Firestone and Lisa A. Firestone.

Publisher: Psychological Assessment Resources, Inc.

Review of the Firestone Assessment of Violent Thoughts by STEPHEN AXFORD, Assistant Director of Special Services, Falcon School District 49, Adjunct Faculty Member, University of Colorado at Colorado Springs, Licensed Psychologist, Colorado Springs, CO:

DESCRIPTION. The Firestone Assessment of Violent Thoughts (FAVT) is a 70-item, 3-point Likert-type scale (*Rarely/Almost Never*; *Sometimes*; and *Frequently/Almost Always*). It's a self-report measure designed to assess predisposing thoughts associated with violent behavior. As stated by the test authors: "The FAVT is designed to be a brief, efficient indicator of an individual's violence potential" (p. 23, professional manual). Providing *T* scores and percentile ranks, the FAVT is normed on and intended to be used exclusively with adult subjects (at least 18 years old) to discriminate statistically those at risk for committing violent acts. Clinicians should find the FAVT to be an easy to administer and score screening instrument. Because it is a screening instrument, results from the FAVT should be integrated and triangulated with other diagnostic information, as the test authors recognize is best practice, ensuring a systematic, sufficiently comprehensive, and valid approach to threat assessment.

The FAVT materials are well designed, ensuring credible face validity. These materials include: the professional manual, the FAVT Rating Form, and the FAVT Score Summary/Profile Form. The Introduction section of the professional manual provides a comprehensive review of the literature related to assessment of risk for violent behavior, a clear description of the theoretical foundation of the FAVT, provisions for clinical application, and guidelines for intervention and progress monitoring. The professional manual also provides clearly written sections/chapters for Administration and Scoring, Interpretation, Development and Standardization of the FAVT, Reliability and Validity of the FAVT, and Integrating FAVT Scores into Different Treatment Modalities. These technical sections include very useful decision-making flowcharts, samples of completed and interpreted profile forms, and a variety of case studies, all helpful in guiding differential diagnosis, intervention, treatment monitoring, and comprehensive assessment. Similarly, the FAVT Rating Form and FAVT Score Summary/Profile Form are well constructed and easy to use.

DEVELOPMENT. The FAVT is based on Separation Theory (developed by one of the test authors, R. Firestone), grounded in psychoanalytic and existential theory, and focusing on negative internalized thought processes and attitudes theorized as arising from abnormal social development. Initial item development involved soliciting and gathering actual pathological statements from patients with histories of violence and treated in clinical and forensic settings (i.e., incarcerated; anger management). Follow-up factor analyses identified four distinct factors or "Levels": Paranoid/Suspicious, Persecuted Misfit, Self-Depreciating/Pseudo-Independent, and Overtly Aggressive. The test authors chose to add a fifth factor, Self-Aggrandizing, based on their consultation with experts and interviews with offenders. Furthermore, study participants prone to violence exhibited distinct patterns across the levels, and stepwise logistic regression analysis demonstrated that the levels provided significant predictive power. This initial research was followed by separation of the final selected FAVT items into two theoretical categories or subscales: Instrumental/Proactive aggression and Hostile/

Reactive aggression. This was accomplished with the help of an expert panel knowledgeable in the fields of clinical and forensic psychology. Inter-item correlations for each subscale were used to select final items. In addition, the test authors developed two additional scales addressing response bias (i.e., validity scales): the Inconsistency scale, screening for a high degree of inconsistency in responses; and the Negativity scale, screening for a frequent pattern of high ratings (i.e., excessive negative responses).

TECHNICAL. The test authors assembled a body of converging evidence supporting the reliability and validity of the FAVT. In discussing reliability and validity, the test authors reference the *Standards for Educational and Psychological Testing* (AERA, APA, & NCME, 1999), which they very apparently adhered to in developing and standardizing the FAVT. Clear, well-constructed tables tabulating correlation coefficients addressing internal consistency, test-retest stability, and convergent and discriminate factor analyses are provided, along with related detailed and critical discussion. Consistently, sample sizes were sufficiently large, and included proportionate numbers of adult-age subjects with respect to gender and age ranges (18–39 years; 40–75 years) although minority representation was limited for some validation samples (e.g., demographic characteristics of the FAVT test-retest sample). Correlation coefficients are acceptable (e.g., for test-retest stability by level, subscale, and total FAVT, ranging from .61 to .85). In general, the reliability and validity studies reported by the test authors support the psychometric soundness of the FAVT.

COMMENTARY. The FAVT appears to be a well-developed screening instrument for assessing violence potential in adults. As there is a critical need for this type of assessment tool for child and adolescent populations, the test authors are encouraged to develop a similar instrument appropriate for these younger populations. [Editor's Note: The Firestone Assessment of Violent Thoughts–Adolescent (FAVT-A) was published in 2008 and will be reviewed in *The Nineteenth Mental Measurements Yearbook*.] Nevertheless, adhering to the guidelines for appropriate restricted use outlined by the test authors (adult populations), clinicians should find the FAVT to be a useful and well-validated screening tool for assessing dangerousness risk in adults and guiding further action.

SUMMARY. This reviewer recommends the FAVT as a psychometrically and theoretically sound screening instrument for assessing predisposing thoughts and attitudes associated with violent behavior. As the test authors endorse, FAVT results indicating high risk for violent behavior should be followed up with more comprehensive assessment. The FAVT is intended to be used with adult clients (18 years and older) because the standardization sample included only this demographic group.

REVIEWER'S REFERENCE

American Educational Research Association, American Psychological Association, & National Council on Measurement in Education. (1999). *Standards for educational and psychological testing.* Washington, DC: American Educational Research Association.

Review of the Firestone Assessment of Violent Thoughts by M. MEGHAN DAVIDSON, Assistant Professor of Counseling Psychology, University of Nebraska, Lincoln, NE:

DESCRIPTION. The Firestone Assessment of Violent Thoughts (FAVT) is a self-report inventory intended to measure the underlying thoughts that prompt violent behavior, and determine the category and intensity of these thoughts. The measure is based on the premise that thoughts guide behavior. Thought processes are termed "voice" by the test authors and are said to represent a pattern of negative thoughts that are hostile and mistrustful toward others as well as adverse to the self.

The test authors state the measure is appropriate for individuals 18 years of age or older, and may include incarcerated offenders, parolees, inpatient and outpatient clients, and people from the general population. The FAVT was developed to be utilized as (a) a screening tool for violence potential, (b) an indicator of threat assessment, (c) a method of identifying violent thoughts to guide clinical intervention, and (d) an inventory to monitor client progress and change. A total of 15–20 minutes is required to complete the FAVT, and individual and group administration is acceptable.

The FAVT is composed of 70 items with a 3-point response scale indicating the frequency with which a respondent experiences negative thoughts regarding self or others. These 70 items are scored to yield five level scores (i.e., Paranoid/Suspicious, Persecuted Misfit, Self-Depreciating/Pseudo-Independent, Overtly Aggressive, and Self-Aggrandizing), two Theoretical subscale scores (i.e., Instrumental/Proactive Violence and

Hostile/Reactive Violence), and a Total FAVT score. Raw scores are converted to both *T* scores and percentile ranks. Additionally, as indicators of validity of the administration with a respondent, a Negativity Scale score and an Inconsistency Scale score are computed.

The FAVT rating form is a perforated, carbonless booklet composed of an answer sheet for responding to items and a scoring sheet for scoring level, Total scale, and Theoretical subscale raw scores. The FAVT Score Summary/Profile Form is a two-sided single sheet used to transfer the raw scores of the levels, Total scale, and Theoretical subscales to convert them to *T* scores and percentiles. As well, the Score Summary/Profile Form is used to calculate scores for the Negativity scale and the Inconsistency scale. Finally, *T* scores are plotted on a profile graph, which utilizes shaded portions to indicate if *T* scores fall within average, above average, or elevated ranges.

DEVELOPMENT. Separation Theory, described as an integration of psychoanalytic and existential theories, and "Voice Therapy methodology," both conceptualized by the lead author, underscore the FAVT. Items were developed from actual statements made during interviews of clients in both outpatient and forensic settings. More specifically, clients were asked to recall their thoughts before and during a violent incident that had occurred previously. A pilot version of the FAVT with 187 items was culled from these statements and administered to a sample of 576 offenders and parolees. Item response theory (IRT) and exploratory factor analysis (EFA) of these 187 items yielded a 56-item measure with four factors. These factors correspond to the first four levels of the FAVT delineated previously (i.e., Level 1: Paranoid/Suspicious, Level 2: Persecuted Misfit, Level 3: Self-Depreciating/Pseudo-Independent, and Level 4: Overtly Aggressive). The test authors chose to add one item to Level 1, two items to Level 2, three items to Level 3, and four items to Level 4 in an effort to enhance content validity of the levels. In addition, the test authors chose to create Level 5: Self-Aggrandizing by retaining four additional items from the pilot version of the FAVT that did not load on a factor in the EFA analysis. Thus, the final version of the FAVT comprises these five levels.

The two Theoretical subscales were created using a rational-empirical approach, asking clinical and forensic psychology experts to rate the 70 items of the FAVT and to categorize those that represented Instrumental/Proactive aggression and Hostile/Reactive aggression. The 22 items deemed representative of Instrumental/Proactive aggression and the 23 items deemed representative of Hostile/Reactive aggression were administered to a standardization sample (N = 639) and two reference groups (N = 148; i.e., Incarcerated and Anger Management). Based on inter-item correlations, item-total correlations, alpha coefficients, and principal components analyses (PCA), 18 items were retained for the Instrumental/Proactive Violence subscale and 20 items were retained for the Hostile/Reactive Violence subscale.

To assess the validity of the administration, the Inconsistency scale and the Negativity scale were created. Five item pairs with the strongest correlations were selected for the Inconsistency scale from the Incarcerated and Anger Management reference groups. Similarly, items that were endorsed "frequently/almost always" by the Incarcerated and Anger Management reference groups were examined for the Negativity scale. Ten items that were endorsed in this manner by less than 10% of this sample were chosen for the Negativity scale.

TECHNICAL. A stratified sampling technique was employed to garner a standardization sample representative of the U.S. population based on 2003 Census data. The standardization sample excluded individuals who were incarcerated, residing in an inpatient facility, under medical care for schizophrenia or other psychotic diagnosis, had uncorrected vision or hearing loss, and/or could not comprehend or read English. The resulting standardization sample for the FAVT consisted of 639 individuals, aged 18 to 75 years, who closely match the U.S. Bureau of the Census demographics regarding gender, race/ethnicity, educational attainment, and geographic region. Two reference groups, an Incarcerated reference group and an Anger Management reference group, were also examined for standardization purposes. The Incarcerated group included 80 individuals who were currently incarcerated with 56% having a history of violence toward a friend, family member, or someone they cared for. The Anger Management group was composed of 68 individuals who were currently in treatment for anger management and who had a history of arrest; as well, 80% had a history of violence toward a loved one. Demographic variables were analyzed and revealed clinically significant differences regarding gender and age. Thus, separate standard scores are utilized for gender and age (i.e., 18-39 years, 40–75 years).

Estimates of internal consistency are based on a single sample with each normative group (i.e., men 18–39 years, men 40–75 years, women 18–39 years, women 40–75 years) and reference group (i.e., Incarcerated, Anger Management) represented. Sample sizes ranged from 68 to 171. The internal consistency of the levels, total, and subscales for each of the normative and reference groups range from .44 to .97, with the majority falling between .86 and .94. Level 5, Self-Aggrandizing, reduces internal consistency somewhat as alpha coefficients ranged from .44 to .56 for five of the six groups. Test-retest reliability estimates are reported for a subset of the standardization sample (n = 23) with intervals from 73 to 129 days. These estimates range from .61 to .85; however, the majority of estimates range from .69 to .78. Level 4: Overtly Aggressive demonstrates the weakest stability over time.

As indicators of construct validity, FAVT scores were compared to scores on the Maudsley Violence Questionnaire (Walker, 2005), the Blame Attribution Inventory (Gudjonsson & Singh, 1989), the Past Feelings and Acts of Violence Scale (Plutchik & van Praag, 1990), the Inventory of Offender Risk, Needs, and Strengths (Miller, 2006), Personality Assessment Inventory (Morey, 1991), the Firestone Assessment of Self-Destructive Thoughts (Firestone & Firestone, 2006), the Beck Hopelessness Scale (Beck, 1988), and the Trauma Symptom Inventory (Briere, 1995) for a sample including the Incarcerated and Anger Management groups (N = 148), a "normal group" (n = 27), and a control group of internalizing disorder patients (n = 30). A second validity sample (N = 316) was obtained from the San Francisco County Jail and the prisoners were administered the FAVT, the Rosenberg Self-Esteem Inventory (Rosenberg, 1989), the Pride in Delinquency Scale (Shields & Whitehall, 1991), and the Paranoia/Suspiciousness Questionnaire (Rawlings & Freeman 1996). The correlational analyses for both validity samples demonstrate adequate to strong construct validity of the FAVT.

Evidence for criterion-related validity was demonstrated by (a) differences in scores between individuals in the Normal and Internalizing Disorder groups compared to the Incarcerated and Anger Management groups, (b) receiver operating characteristic (ROC) analyses indicating the FAVT Total score as predicting current anger management counseling, and (c) the five level scores, Total score, and two subscale scores adequately classify groups into the normal, elevated, and highly elevated ranges. Regarding predictive validity, race/ethnicity and the Total FAVT in one sample reliably predicted violence toward a loved one, whereas race/ethnicity, educational attainment, and the Total FAVT in another sample reliably predicted arrest.

COMMENTARY. The FAVT is a brief and easy-to-administer measure that has enormous potential in the field of violence assessment. Its primary strength is its item development being so closely tied to clinical data and representing actual statements made by individuals who have perpetrated violence. Similarly, the use of IRT and EFA to evaluate the generated items, along with subsequent pilot testing, are strengths of the measure's development. Other strong areas of the FAVT include (a) the normative sample mirroring broadly the U.S. Census data, (b) the use of validity scales (i.e., the Inconsistency and Negativity scales), and (c) the inclusion of reference groups (i.e., Incarcerated and Anger Management groups). Despite these strengths, the theoretical model of Separation Theory and Voice Therapy upon which the FAVT is based needs further empirical support, particularly by other authors. Additionally, Level 5 demonstrates the weakest psychometric properties and is the only group of items not statistically derived; the measure could benefit from omitting these items in future revisions. Although the use of reference groups is seen as a strength, the smaller sample sizes for these two groups is a limitation. Similarly, the test-retest reliability estimates could be strengthened by inclusion of a larger sample size.

SUMMARY. The FAVT was designed to be a self-report measure of underlying thoughts that prompt violent behavior, as well as a method of determining the category and intensity of these violent thoughts. The assessment meets these intended goals and demonstrates adequate empirical evidence supporting the psychometric properties of the FAVT. The FAVT is likely to be useful in a variety of settings including prisons, residential facilities, and outpatient clinics. Professionals seeking ways to assess threats, potential for violence, and change via clinical intervention and treatment focused on violence reduction would likely find the FAVT a useful measure. Further investigation and evidence of Separation Theory and Voice Therapy would greatly enhance the validity of the FAVT.

REVIEWER'S REFERENCES

Beck, A. T. (1988). Beck Hopelessness Scale. San Antonio, TX: The Psychological Corporation.

Briere, J. (1995). *Trauma Symptom Inventory professional manual.* Lutz, FL: Psychological Assessment Resources.

Firestone, R. W., & Firestone, L. A. (2006). *FAST Firestone Assessment of Self-Destructive Thoughts/FASI Firestone Assessment of Suicidal Intent professional manual.* Lutz, FL: Psychological Assessment Resources.

Gudjonsson, G. H., & Singh, K. K. (1989). The revised Gudjonsson Blame Attribution Inventory. *Personality and Individual Differences, 10,* 67-70.

Miller, H. A. (2006). *IORNS Inventory of Offender Risk, Needs, and Strengths professional manual.* Lutz, FL: Psychological Assessment Resources.

Morey, L. C. (1991). *Personality Assessment Inventory (PAI) professional manual.* Lutz, FL: Psychological Assessment Resources.

Plutchik, R., & van Praag, H. M. (1990). A self-report measure of violence risk, II. *Comprehensive Psychiatry, 31,* 450-456.

Rawlings, D., & Freeman, J. L. (1996). A questionnaire for the measurement of paranoia/suspiciousness. *British Journal of Clinical Psychology, 35,* 451-461.

Rosenberg, M. (1989). *Society and the adolescent self-image* (rev. ed.). Middletown, CT: Wesleyan University Press.

Shields, I. W., & Whitehall, G. C. (1991, December). *The Pride in Delinquency Scale.* Paper presented at the Eastern Ontario Correctional Psychologists' winter conference, Burritts Rapids, Ontario, Canada.

Walker, J. S. (2005). The Maudsley Violence Questionnaire: Initial validation and reliability. *Personality and Individual Differences, 38,* 187–201.

[53]

Fitness Interview Test–Revised.

Purpose: A screening instrument that provides "a structured interview for assessing competency to stand trial."

Population: Juveniles and adults.

Publication Date: 2006.

Acronym: FIT-R.

Scores: Individual item scores only.

Subtests, 3: Understand the Nature or Object of Proceedings, Understand the Possible Consequences, Communicate with Counsel.

Administration: Individual.

Price Data, 2007: $45 per manual (64 pages) and CD-ROM.

Time: Administration time not reported.

Comments: Designed to correspond with case law in the U.S., U.K., and Canada.

Authors: Ronald Roesch, Patricia A. Zapf, and Derek Eaves.

Publisher: Professional Resource Press.

Review of the Fitness Interview Test–Revised by RITA BUDRIONIS, Licensed Clinical Psychologist, Licensed Sex Offender Treatment Provider, Director Dominion Sex Offenders Program, Juvenile and Adult, Virginia Beach, VA, and Associate Professor, Department of Psychology, Old Dominion University, Norfolk, VA:

DESCRIPTION. The Fitness Interview Test–Revised (FIT-R) is a semistructured instrument designed to assist in evaluating individuals regarding their competence to understand the nature of legal proceedings, possible consequences of the proceedings, and their ability to communicate effectively with their legal representative and participate in their defense. This instrument is an assessment procedure that is intended to be administered by a psychiatrist, psychologist, or other professional qualified (depending on the jurisdiction) to perform competency evaluations such as a social worker or nurse practitioner. The test authors report that the FIT-R can be used not only in Canada where it was initially developed, but also can be adapted for use in the United States and Britain for trial competency issues. It is also based on the Dusky (Dusky vs. U.S., 1960) standard requiring factual and rational understanding, and the ability to communicate with counsel as the basis for competency. There were no suggested minimum requirements for training or research use. Items are coded after all information is collected through an interview with the examinee, and the evaluator is charged with making a determination of whether the defendant has a mental disorder and is impaired in any of the three abilities addressed.

DEVELOPMENT. The FIT-R resulted from revision of The Fitness Interview (FIT), which was originally developed in 1984 and focused mainly on legal issues for use in Canada (Criminal Code of Canada: Bill C-30). In the FIT-R, mental status issues were included. The test authors developed three sections that correspond to the Canadian and U.S. standards for competence to stand trial. Each section contains items related to specific abilities, and specific questions that the evaluator should ask the evaluee to determine competency in the areas. The identified factors fall into three general sections: (a) Understand the Nature of Object of the Proceedings (6 items); (b) Understand the Possible Consequences of the Proceedings (3 items); (c) Communicate with Counsel (7 items). The evaluators may probe the answers to certain questions and ultimately rate each item regarding their opinions about the defendant's abilities. Coding sheets are provided through a CD-ROM, and new forms may be printed out without an additional per-use fee.

TECHNICAL. Directions for administering the test are clearly written and generally easy to follow. The estimated time for completion of this procedure is approximately 30 to 45 minutes. The FIT-R uses a 3-point rating scale. A score of 0 indicates no impairment, a score of 1 indicates mild or possible impairment, and a score of 2 indicates serious impairment. The evaluator administers the FIT-R by using a semistructured format, asking questions outlined in the manual, and using a conversational tone. The evaluator is free to probe for more information if the responses to the items are unclear. Following the interview, the evaluator rates the defendant regarding his or her performance on the three general competency issues and makes an overall decision regarding competency. No specialized training is recommended and the test authors state that evaluator training should be defined by the jurisdiction of the court. Scoring is completed on a coding sheet that is provided.

Interrater reliability for most items on the FIT-R fell between .80 and .90, although there is a lack of specific scoring criteria. Interrater reliability was high across different professions ranging from psychiatrists to psychologists to graduate students in psychology. Construct validity of the FIT-R was supported by high agreement with scores on the MacArthur Competency Assessment Tool–Criminal Adjudication (Hoge, Bonnie, Poythress, & Monahan, 1999). There was moderate agreement among scores on "Competence to Plead Guilty" and "Competence to Confess" and positive correlations with intelligence and severity of psychosis. No norms have been published.

The FIT-R has also been used with adults and juveniles ages 11–17. The test authors report that the factor structure of this instrument is consistent for both categories of defendants; however, when evaluating juveniles "evaluators should also assess for cognitive limitations, psychopathology, and developmental immaturity, since these factors could lead to legal impairments" (manual, p. 31).

COMMENTARY. The FIT-R is designed to be best utilized as a screening instrument in forensic settings as a way of identifying both adult and juvenile defendants who show difficulties with competence and may need to be referred for more extensive evaluations. The FIT-R is generally consistent with other measures of competency. It can be used as a screening measure or part of a more broad evaluation of competency.

There are several drawbacks of the FIT-R. Although there is a potential application of the instrument to other countries, the instrument was structured to parallel Canadian law. In addition, there is also a lack of specific scoring criteria and no reported norms.

SUMMARY. In summary, the FIT-R is a semistructured screening interview with demonstrated reliability and validity for assisting with assessment of competency by itself, or within a larger assessment battery appropriate for use with adults and juveniles over the age of 11 years. It facilitates the collection of information relevant to competency issues and assists the evaluator with making recommendations in such situations as competence to waive rights, competence to stand trial, and so forth. The FIT-R can be utilized by a range of mental health professionals to assist in forensic evaluations of competency in Canada and in other jurisdictions such as the United States.

REVIEWER'S REFERENCES

Dusky v. United States, 362 U.S. 402 (1960).

Hoge, S. K., Bonnie, R. J., Poythress, N. G., & Monahan, J. (1999). The MacArthur Competence Assessment Tool-Criminal Adjudication. Odessa, FL: Psychological Assessment Resources.

Review of the Fitness Interview Test–Revised by JOE W. DIXON, Forensic Psychologist and Lawyer, Private Practice, Greenville, NC:

DESCRIPTION. The Fitness Interview Test-Revised (FIT-R) is not a psychometric test, as the name may imply, rather it is a semistructured interview instrument developed to assist in the screening of trial competency early in the judicial process. The FIT-R was developed in Canada and was designed for use with adults and adolescents. The manual describes appropriate users as "mental health professionals, typically psychologists and psychiatrists but also social workers and nurse practitioners in some jurisdictions" (p. 23). The FIT-R strives to capture the essential factors that judges and juries use to adjudicate trial competency in Canadian and American legal systems (trial competency is referred to in Canada as "fitness to proceed").

The FIT-R interview is composed of three sections which represent a three-factor model of competency: (a) understanding and reasoning about legal proceedings, (b) appreciation of case-specific information, and (c) ability to communicate with counsel. These sections capture the two prongs set out in the U.S. Supreme Court's ruling in *Dusky v. United States, 362 U.S. 402* (1960). The Dusky legal test is "whether [the defendant] has sufficient present ability to consult with his lawyer with a reasonable degree of rational understanding–and whether he has a rational as well as factual understanding of the proceedings against him" (manual, p. 1).

The FIT-R is used in a face-to-face interview with a defendant and takes approximately 40 minutes to administer given a cooperative defendant. There are 16 items with key questions for each printed on the interview protocol that is included on the CD-ROM packaged with the FIT-R materials. The items query, for example, such topics as understanding the arrest process; charges against the defendant; appreciation of possible penalties if found guilty; and capacity to relate to counsel, to challenge witnesses, and to testify in a relevant manner. A coding sheet covering each item and the three factors is used to record the clinician's estimation of defendants' status using a 3-point rating scale (0 = *no impairment*, 1 = *mild impairment*, 2 = *serious impairment*). No cut scores or normative tables are provided to assist in reaching a decision on whether or not the defendant is competent or incompetent.

DEVELOPMENT. The FIT-R was developed for use in identifying those pretrial defendants who will require a more in-depth clinical and forensic assessment, presumably because of symptoms of serious mental illness (SMI), from those who are clearly able to proceed. This screening step would save money and time for the criminal justice system by identifying competent defendants early in the judicial process.

The FIT-R represents several modifications of the original instrument, the Fitness Interview Test (FIT), first published in 1984. The FIT was revised in 1998 because of changes made in Canadian law. The current instrument, the FIT-R (2006), reflects only minor wording changes to the questions and items, and the manual was updated to include discussion of U.S. caselaw pertaining to trial competency. The authors of the FIT-R believe that the current instrument is applicable and useful in a forensic context in Canada, the United States, and Great Britain. The manual states that the FIT-R captures key elements of the 1960 *Dusky* standard, as well as the Code of Canada (1985).

The FIT-R focuses upon legal constructs, as it should, and the test authors remind users to also consider clinical issues in the course of any examination for trial competency. The test authors note that each defendant and case is different, and the relative importance of capacity on one element may be more or less important in a different case. The test authors use this as a rationale for not establishing and publishing data to enable comparison of a defendant's total score or a cutoff score useful in the clinician's decision making.

TECHNICAL. The manual reports several empirical studies that demonstrate both reliability and validity for the FIT-R with both adults and adolescents. Zapf and Roesch (1997) demonstrated high agreement on the question of competent/not-competent with institution-based outcomes in a study with 57 males. No false negatives were obtained, an important consideration given the stated purpose of the FIT-R as a screening instrument designed for early identification. Similar results were obtained in two subsequent studies, albeit with slightly lower rates of agreement. In a study with adolescents, acceptable correlations on the three factors assessed with the FIT-R were obtained (Viljoen, Vincent, & Roesch, 2006). Details of these studies are furnished in the manual.

Viljoen, Zapf, and Roesch (2007) in a study of 152 adolescents found the FIT-R to be a useful instrument in assessing basic understanding (knowledge) of the trial process and communication with legal counsel. Similar supportive results were earlier reported in a 2005 study. Nussbaum et al. (2008) reported that the FIT-R and the MacCAT-CA showed good concurrent validity.

In a 2006 survey of the members (n = 152) of the American Psychology-Law Society of the APA and Diplomates in the American Board of Forensic Psychology, Archer, Buffington-Vollum, Stredny, and Handel reported that the FIT-R was the least used "competency or sanity assessment instrument" by those surveyed. In comparison, the MacCAT-CA was the instrument most often used by respondents. However, the MacCAT-CA is a normed instrument designed for pretrial evaluations by clinicians expected to appear in court to proffer testimony, whereas the FIT-R is designed as a screening device, and thus the FIT-R may receive less use with Psychology-Law members and Diplomates in Forensic Psychology.

COMMENTARY. All the specific items that are directly examined with the FIT-R are well-chosen and supported not only by caselaw pertinent to questions of trial competency, but also the items are well-grounded and anchored in historical and contemporary instruments designed to assess trial competency. However, the FIT-R demonstrates several general weaknesses. There are no sample normative data for comparison purposes nor suggested cutscores based upon studies of accurately classified defendants. Further, there are no published scoring reliability data available for either the items or the three factors for adults.

Despite the lack of such reliability and comparison data, my review of the item content of the issues being queried in the 16 items suggests excellent face validity. As a forensic examiner with over 30 years experience and legal training, I found the actual content being queried with the defendant to reflect the substantive areas of knowledge and understanding that judges seek in a competency assessment.

Scores are assigned for each of the 16 items, yet there are no criteria nor is guidance provided for reaching a "Yes-No" decision on any of the three major factors that directly bear on the question of competence. Rather, the user is simply instructed to decide "Yes, Possibly, or No" on the question of impairment for each factor. Thus, despite the well-chosen 16 items, ultimately the competency decision is based solely upon the clinician's subjective judgment.

The FIT-R does serve a useful and worthwhile purpose of ensuring that the clinician queries and actively considers the defendant's knowledge and understanding on each of the 16 items that make up the three cognitive factors that constitute trial competency. Also, users are free to establish their own cutoff scores based upon controlling law in their jurisdiction and standards of clinical practice. In this respect, the FIT-R may act much like a pilot's preflight checklist rather than as a true psychometric instrument.

In 1993, the U.S. Supreme Court in the *Daubert* decision set legal guidelines to consider before admitting scientific evidence into a court of law–falsifiability, peer review and publication, known or potentially known error rate, and general acceptance. Considering these legal guidelines, it is unlikely that the FIT-R would withstand the *Daubert* test if it were used as the basis of competency testimony at trial in federal or state courts that have adopted *Daubert*. There is no adequate basis to determine the FIT-R's falsifiability, nor adequate basis to empirically establish the instrument's error rate. The Archer study argues against general acceptance. However, there exist studies that have favorably examined the FIT-R properties, and it has received favorable peer reviews in recent articles (DeClue, 2006; Grisso, 2003; Nussbaum, 2008). Although these later favorable reviews may argue for general acceptance meeting the *Frye* standard for admissible evidence, the FIT-R may nevertheless be successfully challenged in federal courts and *Daubert* states. Thus, users are likely better advised to utilize the FIT-R as a screening device, the purpose for which it was developed by the test authors.

SUMMARY. As a checklist or screening device, I find the FIT-R to meet its stated purpose of providing "a semi-structured interview to ensure that all important aspects of competence to stand trial are assessed and to increase the uniformity of competency evaluations" (manual, p. 23). The FIT-R meets and exceeds those expectations. It is clearly not a robust psychometric instrument, and it may fall short on *Daubert* criteria, but as a functional and useful forensic screening instrument, I find it thorough and very useful.

REVIEWER'S REFERENCES

Archer, R. P., Buffington-Vollum, J. K., Stredny, R. V., & Handel, R. W. (2006). A survey of psychological test use patterns among forensic psychologists. *Journal of Personality Assessment, 87*, 84-94.

DeClue, G. (2006). Book Section: Essay and reviews of FIT-R: A structured interview for assessing competency to stand trial. *The Journal of Psychiatry & Law, 34*, 371-379.

Criminal Code of Canada, R.S.C., C-46 (1985).

Dusky v. United States, 362 U.S. 402 (1960).

Grisso, T. (2003). *Evaluating competencies: Forensic assessments and instruments, Second edition*. New York: Kluwer Academic/Plenum.

Nussbaum, D., Hancock, M., Turner, I., Arrowood, J., & Melodick, S. (2008). Fitness/competency to stand trial: A conceptual overview, review of existing instruments, and cross validation of the Nussbaum Fitness Questionnaire. *Brief Treatment and Crisis Intervention, 8*, 43–72.

Viljoen, J. L., Vincent, G. M., & Roesch, R. (2006). Assessing adolescent defendants' adjudicative competence: Interrater reliability and factor structure of the Fitness Interview Test-Revised. *Criminal Justice and Behavior, 33*, 467-487.

Viljoen, J. L., Zapf, P. A., & Roesch, R. (2007). Adjudicative competence and comprehension of Miranda rights in adolescent defendants: A comparison of legal standards. *Behavioral Sciences & the Law, 25*, 1-19.

Zapf, P. A., & Roesch, R. (1997). Assessing fitness to stand trial: A comparison of institution-based evaluations and a brief screening interview. *Canadian Journal of Community Mental Health, 16*, 53–66.

[54]

Five-Factor Personality Inventory–Children.

Purpose: Developed to "measure personality dispositions in children and adolescents" in order to "identify children who are at risk for adjustment problems at school and in their community."
Population: Ages 9-0 to 18-11.
Publication Date: 2007.
Acronym: FFPI-C.
Scores, 5: Agreeableness, Extraversion, Openness to Experience, Conscientiousness, Emotional Regulation.
Administration: Group.
Price Data, 2009: $150 per examiner's manual (69 pages) and 25 administration and scoring forms.
Time: (15-40) minutes.
Comments: Descriptive ratings for each of the five scores are provided to aid in the interpretation of personality characteristics as they relate to a child's risk for experiencing adjustment problems.
Authors: Ronnie L. McGhee, David J. Ehrler, and Joseph A. Buckhalt.
Publisher: PRO-ED.

Review of the Five-Factor Personality Inventory–Children by MERITH COSDEN, Department of Counseling, Clinical, and School Psychology, University of California, Santa Barbara, Santa Barbara, CA:

DESCRIPTION. The Five Factor Personality Inventory–Children (FFPI-C) provides an assessment of five personality dimensions in children and adolescents, ages 9 years, 0 months to 18 years, 11 months. These factors are based on a five-factor model of personality identified and replicated in numerous studies on adult populations (Digman, 1990). Four of the five factors on the FFPI-C have the same labels as do those in the adult literature: Agreeableness, Extraversion, Openness to Experience, and Conscientiousness; the fifth factor, Emotional Regulation, replaces the adult label of Neuroticism, as it is seen by the test authors as a more appropriate label for these characteristics in children or adolescents. Each dimension is further defined by six subfacets: Agreeableness encompasses Trust, Straightforwardness, Altruism, Compliance, Modesty, and Tendermindedness; Extraversion is defined by Warmth, Gregariousness, Assertiveness, Activity, Excitement Seeking, and Positive Emotions; Openness to Experience is associated with Fantasy, Aesthetics, Feelings, Actions, Ideas, and Values; Conscientiousness by Competence, Order, Dutifulness, Achievement Striving, Self-Discipline, and Deliberation; and Emotional Regulation is associated with Anxiety, Angry Hostility, Depression, Self-Consciousness, Impulsiveness, and Vulnerability. The stated purpose of the FFPI-C is to describe the five personality dimensions in youth, which can be used for research or to identify problems related to these factors in school or in the community.

The instrument has 75 items, 15 items representing each of the five dimensions. Each item is composed of two opposing anchor statements (example, "I think dogs are nice" and "I think dogs are scary") partitioned by five circles. Respondents are asked to read each statement and to mark their agreement according to the following rules: if they agree with a statement, to mark the circle closest to it, if they somewhat agree with a statement to mark the second closest circle, and if it is hard to chose, to color in the circle in the middle. Respondents are also asked to use the middle circle "as little as possible." This test can be self-administered by a child with a third-grade reading level, or administered by a trained mental health practitioner, and can be administered individually or in groups. Time for completion, including time for the instructions and example, is projected to range from 15 to 40 minutes.

The examiner's manual provides detailed instruction on administering the FFPI-C and on examiner qualifications. The examiner's manual states that any mental health practitioner can administer the instrument provided they have some training in standardized test administration, scoring, and interpretation, as well as some supervised practice in the use of personality assessments. The examniner's manual further indicates that this is the type of training that is available in graduate programs for practitioners. The administration is relatively straightforward, with assessors directed to read the instructions and an example to the client, and to let the respondent complete the rest of the questionnaire on his or her own or to read the rest of the items to him or her if the individual requires assistance with reading. Scoring is completed by opening the perforated edges of the response form and summing the scores inside for items on each scale. Raw scores are then transferred to another part of the form where *T*-scores, percentiles, and descriptive ratings are presented.

The examiner's manual presents tables for conversion of raw scores to *T*-scores and percentile ranks for males and females separately. The examiner's manual also provides a table with the standard errors of measurement (*SEM*) for scores to determine the boundaries of likely scores. In addition, there are descriptive ratings (Very High, High, Average, Low, and Very Low) associated with the *T*-scores and percentile ranks. The source of these descriptive ratings is not fully explained, but each level reflects approximately two standard deviations from the mean or prior rating. Further, the examiner's manual provides guidelines for interpreting subscale scores; these interpretations appear to be, in part, a function of the content of the items in the scales and, in part, based on research (see Validity).

DEVELOPMENT. The FFPI-C, although based on the five-factor model of personality for adults, was developed independently after review of the literature on adults and adolescents and extant assessments. An initial pool of 100 items, 20 for each factor, was created on this basis. These items were generated and approved by an expert committee. In the end, the instrument was designed to have 15 items per scale in order to limit the administration time needed for children and adolescents; specific items were selected based on an item discrimination index analysis, with all selected items correlated at an appropriate level (.35 or higher) with other items on the instrument.

TECHNICAL.

Standardization. The normative sample consists of 1,284 youth in 18 states: California, Colorado, Georgia, Illinois, Indiana, Maine, Massachusetts, Michigan, Minnesota, New York, North Carolina, North Dakota, Ohio, Oklahoma, Oregon, Pennsylvania, Washington, and Wisconsin. To obtain the normative data, the publisher contacted prior test customers and members of the National Association of School Psychologists to find examiners willing to conduct assessments with the test. Each assessor was asked to collect data on at least 20 individuals, attempting in their selections to reflect the demographic characteristics of their communities. Although, to some extent, this process reflects convenience sampling, the final demographic composition of the sample is similar to that of the 2002 national Census in terms of representation of geographic area, gender, ethnicity, and presence of a disability.

Reliability. Several measures of reliability are reported in the examiner's manual. Internal consistency for each subscale is relatively high, with coefficient alphas ranging from .74 for Extraversion to .86 for Conscientiousness. Internal consistency is also presented by age, gender, ethnicity, and disability status. Although the number of scores in each cell is necessarily small in some instances, coefficient alphas typically lie between .71 and .87.

Test-retest reliability was obtained from a sample of 192 individuals in Georgia, with test administrations approximately 2 weeks apart. Correlation coefficients range from .84 to .88 across subscales, further supporting the reliability evidence for this instrument.

Validity. Content validity derives from the manner in which the test was developed, through review of the literature and other scales that measure the five personality dimensions covered in this test, by item analysis finding moderate and significant intercorrelations among items, and by differential item functioning analysis, demonstrating differences in the association of items to the overall construct across different demographic characteristics. Differences were found for gender only, justifying the development of separate norms for males and females.

The examiner's manual presents several studies that support the criterion validity of the FFPI-C in relation to other scales measuring similar constructs. For example, the subscales of the FFPI-C are significantly correlated with corresponding subscales on an adult measure of similar factors, the NEO-Five Factor Inventory (Costa & McCrae, 1991). In addition, the FFPI-C subscales have been correlated with subscale scores on the Behavioral and Emotional Rating Scale (BERS; Epstein, 2004) and the Behavior Dimensions Rating Scale (BDRS; Bullock & Wilson, 1989). However, many of the relationships were not specific to one factor. For example, all five FFPI-C factors were significantly associated with aggression/acting out on the BDRS. The construct validity of the FFPI-C was assessed by examining differences between respondent groups with and without emotional or learning disorders. Differences were found on Emotional Regulation and Extraversion for respondents with emotional disorders and on Conscientiousness and Agreeableness for those with learning disabilities. As well, a specific association hypothesized between Conscientiousness and academic performance was supported.

The interpretation of test scores in the examiner's manual goes beyond current empirical studies on the FFPI-C, however, with some of the provided interpretation based on content validity of the scale or broader research on the five personality dimensions. Although these studies provide direction, care needs to be taken in attributing meaning to higher scores.

COMMENTARY. The FFPI-C, although a relatively new test, relies on an older, established, theoretical and empirical literature base on "big five" personality dimensions to define its importance. Given the large number of studies that have replicated the existence of five personality dimensions in adults and youth, this is an interesting, and potentially important area for further research. The utility of this test will be linked to continued research on its use with youth and adolescents, as well as research on the impact of the "big five" personality factors on school functioning and other youth problems. Further research is needed to determine whether the information on personality factors obtained on this test can inform methods for addressing youth problems in ways not available through other assessments. It is also open for future study whether factor combinations, or dimension profiles, can be used to better understand and address student problems.

SUMMARY. The FFPI-C is used to assess five personality dimensions–Agreeableness, Extraversion, Openness to Experience, Conscientiousness, and Emotional Regulation–in children and adolescents. The test has national norms and strong reliability and validity for measuring those factors. The existence of these personality dimensions has been replicated in the literature for adults and children, with higher and lower dimension scores associated with behavior and academic problems. Research is needed to further delineate the relationship between specific personality factors and youth problems, and to direct appropriate interventions based on these factors.

REVIEWER'S REFERENCES

Bullock, L. M., & Wilson, M. J. (1989). Behavior Dimensions Rating Scale. Itasca, IL: Riverside Publishing.

Costa, P. T., Jr., & McCrae, R. R. (1992). *The NEO Personality Inventory–Revised manual.* Odessa, FL: Psychological Assessment Resources.

Digman, J. M. (1990). Personality structure: Emergence of the five-factor model. *Annual Review of Psychology, 41,* 417-440.

Epstein, M. H. (2004). Behavioral and Emotional Rating Scale–Second Edition. Austin, TX: PRO-ED.

Review of the Five-Factor Personality Inventory–Children by H. DENNIS KADE, Naval Medical Center Portsmouth: Substance Abuse Rehabilitation Program, Norfolk, VA, and Adjunct Assistant Professor, Old Dominion University, Norfolk, VA:

DESCRIPTION. The Five-Factor Personality Inventory–Children (FFPI-C) is a standardized, norm-referenced, self-report inventory designed to measure traits of the five-factor model of personality in children and adolescents. The test authors propose two primary uses: (a) assessment of social adjustment and academic performance difficulties in children and adolescents relying on the correlation with Emotional Regulation and Conscientiousness, respectively, and (b) for personality research on those from age 9 through 18 years.

The FFPI-C was normed on a representative sample of 1,284 individuals between the ages of 9 years 0 months and 18 years 11 months and residing in 18 different states. The test authors suggest that the test can be read aloud to those who cannot read English at a third grade level. The test is untimed, but the 75 items are typically completed in 15–40 minutes. The directions urge the test taker to use the center of the 5-point scale of agreement that ranges between each pair of opposing sentences as little as possible. There is no time range specified beyond "how you feel and think about things from day to day" (examiner's manual, p. 7).

The scoring template is inside the test administration form. With only five scales and sequential items arranged across different factors, the scoring process is very straightforward with little opportunity for error. Note that the inventory cannot be scored if any items are left blank or endorsed with more than one answer. Therefore, the examiner should review the protocol before the respondent leaves and this could limit use of the FFPI-C for group administration. Results yield *T*-scores and percentile ranks based on gender only because age differences were not found in the normative database.

The reporting of results uses five descriptive ranges at elevations from "very low" to "very high" with break points that are different from what is usual. For example, the FFPI-C *T*-score range for "average" is from 43–57 *T*, containing the central 50%, and the 23% in the "high range" have scores from 58–70 *T*. Interpretation of the FFPI-C is based on relatively brief descriptions of characteristics on each scale associated with scores within the five ranges. There are two example case reports in the manual. They include an almost 10-year-old with a conduct disorder who is repeating third grade and a 16-year-old with bipolar disorder who is not consistently taking perscribed medication.

DEVELOPMENT. The FFPI-C is based on the theory that five broad factors account for the majority of variance in personality descriptors: Agreeableness, Extraversion, Openness to Experience, Conscientiousness, and Emotional Regulation (used in lieu of Neuroticism). Test development began with 20 potential items for each of the five factors, generated by a review of the literature on the five factors and their facets. These were reduced to 15 per scale to achieve a relatively brief administration time. Thus, the item pool went from a total of 100 to 75. A committee of experts eliminated 10 items that were possibly biased and 15 more were removed based on item discrimination studies described in the manual.

TECHNICAL. Evidence of content validity, criterion-prediction validity, and construct-identification validity are reviewed in the test manual. Moderate to large coefficients were reported with the NEO Five-Factor Inventory for a sample of 52 adolescents aged 15–18 and with the Junior Eysenck Personality Questionnaire for 184 individuals at ages 9–17. Correlations with self, parent, and teacher ratings of social and emotional functioning are also included in the manual. The FFPI-C scores' ability to discriminate groups with and without emotional disorders or learning disorders is documented along with correlations with academic achievement. Review of the test's validity concludes with confirmatory factor analysis.

Two-week test-retest reliabilities are reported based on a sample of 192 test takers. Across subscales, coefficients ranged from .84 to .88. The test authors are to be commended for reporting coefficient alpha levels for subgroups within the normative samples. The averages for the entire sample are .79 for Agreeableness, .74 for Extraversion, .75 for Openness to Experience, .86 for Conscientiousness, and .80 for Emotional Regulation.

COMMENTARY. The specific limitations of this measure occur within the larger context of the five-factor model's limitations. The authors of the FFPI-C point out that the five-factor model is established across many cultures and languages, but the evidence cited for its existence in the self-report of children is limited to three references in the manual with no discussion of dissenting opinions. Perhaps this argues for the restricted use of the FFPI-C (e.g., in research). Given the presumption that relatively enduring personality traits are being measured, test-retest correlations based on a time period longer than 2 weeks would be informative. The coefficient alphas at the lower end of the range place some limits on making clinical decisions on the basis of these scores, but this use does not seem to be within the scope of the intended uses of the FFPI-C.

SUMMARY. The test authors are to be commended for providing a normed measure of the five factors of personality that extends down to the age of 9 that could prove very useful in research. There has been an increasing interest in the study and treatment of the precursors of personality disorder in children (Bleiberg, 2001). There are signs that clinicians are beginning to return to considering personality traits and a broader perspective than just symptoms in the treatment of adults (Singer, 2005). The FFPI-C could prove potentially useful in clinical practice at the point where these two trends converge by helping the practitioner consider children's symptoms within the context of the five factors of personality.

REVIEWER'S REFERENCES

Bleiberg, E. (2001). *Treating personality disorders in children and adolescents: A relational approach.* New York: Guilford Press.

Singer, J. A. (2005). *Personality and psychotherapy: treating the whole person.* New York: Guilford Press.

[55]

Frenchay Dysarthria Assessment–Second Edition.

Purpose: Designed to provide a "measurement, differential description, and diagnosis of dysarthria."
Population: Ages 15-97.
Publication Dates: 1983-2008.
Acronym: FDA-2.
Scores, 7: Reflexes, Respiration, Lips, Palate, Laryngeal, Tongue, Intelligibility.
Administration: Individual.
Price Data, 2009: $142 per complete kit including 25 rating forms, Intelligibility cards, and examiner's manual (2008, 45 pages); $42 per 25 rating forms; $43 per Intelligibility cards; $68 per examiner's manual.
Foreign Language Editions: Translations available in French, German, Dutch, Norwegian, Swedish, Finnish, Castilian, and Catalan.
Time: (30) minutes.
Comments: Additional items required for administration include: tongue depressor, stopwatch, tape recorder, glass of water, cookie, sterile gloves, and calipers.
Authors: Pamela Enderby and Rebecca Palmer.
Publisher: PRO-ED.
Cross References: See T5:1056 (2 references); for reviews by Steven B. Leder and Malcolm R. McNeil of a previous edition, see 12:154; see also T4:1007 (2 references).

Review of the Frenchay Dysarthria Assessment–Second Edition by JEFF BERRY, Assistant Professor of Speech Pathology and Audiology, and STEVEN LONG, Associate Professor of Speech Pathology and Audiology, Marquette University, Milwaukee, WI:

DESCRIPTION. The second edition of the Frenchay Dysarthria Assessment (FDA-2) is a standardized protocol for the perceptual examination of sensorimotor function of the speech production mechanism. The FDA-2 is intended for use by certified speech pathologists to assess a class of sensorimotor speech disorders (the dysarthrias). Norms for the FDA-2 are reported for the age range of 15–97 years. The test authors contend that the assessment is also appropriate for pediatric patients. The aim of the FDA-2 is to document the performance quality of speech-related behaviors to assist with neurological diagnosis and treatment planning. The test is administered by an individual speech pathologist who rates patient performance on a series of tasks.

Seven of the eight subsections of the FDA-2 use an ordinal rating scale. The number of tasks within each subsection varies, ranging from two to five. For each task, five performance descriptions are provided (denoted a, b, c, d, e). Ratings are intended to encompass the performance range between normal function (a) and no function (e). Performance descriptors associated with the ratings are task specific. Because certain tasks lend themselves to more objective performance criteria (e.g., time of sustained phonation as compared to resonance quality) the objectivity of the rating system varies between tasks. The test authors endorse the use of ratings that fall in between the five performance descriptions (e.g., "b +"), resulting in nine possible ratings for each task. A rating form is used to document all acquired data. This form also includes space for qualitative comments, a summary, and recommendations.

The first six subsections of the FDA-2 organize tasks with respect to different anatomical and physiological subsystems associated with the speech production mechanism. A mixture of nonspeech, quasispeech, and speech behaviors are elicited and judged. Ratings of speech intelligibility in single words, sentences, and conversation are obtained in the seventh subsection. The final subsection directs the speech pathologist to document the potential influences of hearing, sight, teeth, language, mood, posture, speaking rate, and sensation.

DEVELOPMENT. The FDA-2 is the first revision of the original assessment published in 1983. In comparison with the first edition, the test authors eliminate a subsection of jaw assessment tasks, modify the content for speech and speech intelligibility tasks, provide an updated review of literature deemed supportive of the assessment, expand reliability and validity data, provide additional analyses of normative data, and provide additional instructions for administration. The FDA was developed by Dr. Pamela Enderby at Frenchay Hospital in Bristol, U.K. Using practices that are standard for speech and nonspeech assessment of the speech production mechanism (e.g., Darley, Aronson, & Brown, 1975), Enderby sought to standardize and simplify the characterization of dysarthria (Enderby, 1980).

TECHNICAL.

Standardization. The normative sample for the FDA-2 includes 194 typically functioning individuals with an age range of 15 to 97 years. No descriptive statistics regarding the age distribution of the normative sample are provided. However, the test authors divide the norms into "younger" and "older" age groups. The age range of 15 to 59 years includes 111 individuals. The age range of 60 to 97 years includes 37 individuals. More than 90% of the individuals in each group are reported to have scored a top rating of 9. Presumably these results indicate "near normal" performance on all tasks and subsections; however, the derivation of these scores is not explicated and no numeric scoring procedures are described in the examiner's manual. In addition to the data derived from typically functioning participants, the examiner's manual reports performance profiles derived from Enderby (1986). These data show means and standard deviations of FDA-2 task ratings obtained for 107 patients with dysarthria, classified into five groups based on neurological diagnosis (see Construct Validity below). Consistent with the nonnumeric rating system, these data are presented graphically following the conventions suggested for the FDA-2 rating form. For each group, an accompanying paragraph is provided to highlight tendencies that may be pertinent for differential diagnosis.

Reliability. Interrater and intrarater reliability of the FDA-2 were established via five speech therapists and one speech therapy assistant rating a subset of audible tasks recorded from nine patients varying in dysarthria type and severity. Each listener judged the same 42 task examples and then repeated the procedure after a 6-week interval. Reliability coefficients were derived from an analysis of variance with fixed effects. Interrater reliability coefficients ranged from .38 to .79. Only the "raw" scores are presented in the examiner's manual. A post hoc examination of these data reveals interrater reliability coefficients averaging .60 with a standard deviation of .11 and a standard error of .03. Intrarater reliability coefficients are presented for five of the six listeners. The reported coefficients are: .72, .73, .76, .76, and .92. Consequently, interrater reliability may be considered "moderate" and intrarater reliability may be considered "substantial" for the audible portions of the FDA-2. Because fewer than half of the total number of tasks on the FDA-2 can be rated using solely audible criteria, the generalizability of these estimates to the complete FDA-2 is unknown. Details about task-specific reliability are not presented; nonetheless, the test authors report that the "scoring instructions" were revised for individual items that had particularly poor reliability between or within judges. Comparable data to support the assumption that these modifications facilitated improved reliability for individual items are not presented.

The possibility of telehealth application of the FDA-2 is encouraged by the test authors. Theodoros, Russell, Hill, Cahill, and Clark (2003) are cited by the test authors as evidence of the reliability of the FDA-2 across face-to-face and online environments. In an extension of the same internet-based telehealth study, Hill et al. (2006) report mixed results with respect to the reliability of the FDA across environments. Using a "percentage level of agreement" method of comparison, Hill et al. (2006) found 14 of 19 FDA tasks met the clinical criteria indicative of sufficient reliability across environments. However, using the more rigorous Bland and Altman limits-of-agreement method of comparison, Hill et al. (2006) found that only 3 of 19 FDA tasks were sufficiently reliable across environments. Curiously, 2 of these 3 tasks were the "jaw" tasks that were eliminated in the FDA-2.

Validity.

Criterion validity. The test authors of the FDA-2 argue that criterion validity cannot be established because there is no comparable assessment tool. Kent (2009) classifies the FDA-2 as a "composite examination instrument." Although other such instruments are available commercially, numerous comparable tools are also freely available in the published literature (see Kent, 2009).

Construct validity. Based on the results of a study by Enderby (1986), the test authors contend that construct validity for the FDA-2 has been established. Enderby (1986) analyzed a set of task ratings derived from 107 patients with dysarthria. Linear discriminant analysis (LDA) was performed for 85 patients with existing dysarthria-type diagnoses and corresponding neurological diagnoses. LDA classification accuracy ranged from 83.3% to 100% across five diagnostic groups using task ratings from the FDA. LDA classification of the remaining 22 patients was used to demonstrate the potential for differential diagnosis using the FDA in the absence of corresponding neurological diagnoses.

Content Validity. The content validity of the FDA-2 is established primarily through appraisal of the use of the tool in published research literature. The test authors emphasize that the pertinent publications reflect work undertaken in different countries with patients with different severities and types of dysarthria with varying underlying etiologies. McKinstry and Perry (2003) are cited in the examiner's manual as supporting the validity of using the FDA-2 for patients with head and neck cancer. Detailed examination of the results of McKinstry and Perry (2003) suggest weak relationships between speech intelligibility ratings derived from the FDA and performance on tasks within other subsections of the FDA. McKinstry and Perry (2003) report that ratings on 5 of 16 tasks of the FDA correlated significantly with "intelligibility in conversation" ratings. These five measures consisted of three lip tasks and two laryngeal tasks. Consequently, 11 of 15 FDA measures, including all measures of respiratory, soft palate, or tongue function showed no significant correlation with speech intelligibility.

COMMENTARY. The FDA-2 offers a potentially practical solution to the complex challenge of clinical assessment. Unfortunately, the content of the FDA-2 appears to be justified primarily by virtue of the fact that the tool has been used in clinical and research applications for nearly three decades. Given this substantial amount of time for further development, the changes from the first edition to the second edition seem quite insignificant. Given the variety of well-conceptualized, freely available tools to assist the clinician in the assessment of the dysarthrias (Kent, 2009), a substantive and convincing justification for using the FDA-2 remains to be established.

SUMMARY. The FDA-2 is a protocol for the perceptual examination of sensorimotor function for the dysarthrias. The FDA-2 has been used in numerous peer-reviewed research publications for the assessment of patients across the age span and with widely varying underlying etiologies. The FDA-2 requires the administering clinician to use an ordinal rating system to judge performance on a variety of nonspeech, quasispeech, and speech tasks associated with the use of the speech-production mechanism. Speech intelligibility estimates are obtained for single words, sentences, and conversation. Qualitative information pertaining to a variety of "influencing factors" is obtained and documented. A conveniently organized rating form is used to document all acquired data. This form also includes space for a narrative summary and recommendations. As intended by Enderby (1980), this tool standardizes and simplifies a range of complex assessment tasks that have long been used by speech pathologists in clinical settings.

Although these characteristics may bolster the efficiency of clinical assessment, the psychometric foundation for the FDA-2 is quite limited. The structure of the tool and the presentation of the existing norms offer little support for interpreting the results of the FDA-2. Although the content of the FDA-2 reflects a subset of tasks that are routinely used in clinical assessment, the specific tasks used in the FDA-2 have yet to be demonstrated necessary or sufficient for clinical assessment of the dysarthrias.

REVIEWERS' REFERENCES

Darley, F. L., Aronson, A. E., & Brown, J. R. (1975). *Motor speech disorders.* Philadelphia, PA: Saunders.

Enderby, P. (1980). Frenchay Dysarthria Assessment. *British Journal of Disorders of Communication, 15,* 165-173.

Enderby, P. (1986). Relationships between dysarthric groups. *British Journal of Disorders of Communication, 21,* 189-197.

Hill, A. J., Theodoros, D. G., Russell, T. G., Cahill, L. M., Ward, E. C., & Clark, K. M. (2006). An internet-based telerehabilitation system for the assessment of motor speech disorders: A pilot study. *American Journal of Speech-Language Pathology, 15,* 45-56.

Kent, R. D. (2009). Perceptual sensorimotor speech examination for motor speech disorders. In M. R. McNeil (Ed.), *Clinical management of sensorimotor speech disorders* (19-29). New York: Thieme Medical Publishers.

McKinstry, A., & Perry, A. (2003). Evaluation of speech in people with head and neck cancer: A pilot study. *International Journal of Language and Communication Disorders, 38,* 31-46.

Theodoros, D. G., Russell, T., Hill, A., Cahill, L. M., & Clark, K. (2003). Assessment of motor speech disorders online: A pilot study. *Journal of Telemedicine and Telecare, 9,* 66-68.

Review of the Frenchay Dysarthria Assessment–Second Edition by PATRICIA BRAZIER-CARTER, Assistant Professor of Speech Language Pathology, Southern University, Baton Rouge, LA:

DESCRIPTION. The Frenchay Dysarthria Assessment–Second Edition (FDA-2) is a rating scale that is utilized by clinicians to assess a patient's performance on various behaviors related to the functioning of the motor speech system. The FDA-2 can be used as a treatment guide and a tool to assist clinicians in diagnosing specific neurological disorders. The assessment instrument is divided into seven sections: (a) Reflexes, (b) Respiration, (c) Lips, (d) Palate, (e) Laryngeal, (f) Tongue, and (g) Intelligibility. The sections measure the following behaviors: Reflexes: Ratings for cough, swallow, and dribble/drool; Respiration: Ratings at rest and in speech; Lips: Ratings for at rest, spread, seal, alternate, and in speech; Palate: Ratings for fluids, maintenance, and in speech; Laryngeal: Ratings for time, pitch, volume, and in speech; Tongue: Ratings for at rest, protrusion, elevation, lateral, alternate, and in speech; and Intelligibility: Ratings for words, sentences, and conversation.

The Influencing Factors section provides additional information in the areas of hearing, sight, teeth, language, mood, posture, rate, and sensation. These areas provide pertinent information to enable the clinician to provide a diagnosis and develop an effective treatment plan.

The administration time for the FDA-2 is approximately 30 minutes. The test authors suggest that each section be assessed in the order shown on the rating scale. However, the order does not influence the validity of the assessment. Each item within a particular section must be administered in the order as presented.

The patient is either observed, given a set of tasks to perform, or asked questions for each item presented. The task is performed, first by the patient, then by the examiner, and then again by the patient. Only the second attempt at the task by the patient is scored. The rating scale has five "best fit" descriptors ranging from "a" (which indicates normal functioning) to "e" (which indicates no function). These descriptors are very general and allow the examiner flexibility in determining the skill level of the patient. The examiner also may assign half points. The scores are then recorded on the rating form, which provides a clear and concise representation of the patient's performance on each task.

DEVELOPMENT. In developing the FDA-2, the test authors sought to make improvements from the first edition by developing an assessment instrument that would assist clinicians in determining the level and type of neurological deficit, and would assist in determining the diagnosis and also in determining appropriate treatment. The first FDA was published in 1983 subsequent to research in the area of speech production in individuals with neurological disorders/diseases. The FDA-2 was developed as a result of more current research trends and assessment techniques utilized in the diagnosis of various neurological diseases.

A comparison of the original FDA and the FDA-2 revealed four significant improvements: (a) Improved reliability of descriptors. The interrater reliability procedures applied to the FDA revealed that some descriptors were interpreted differently (i.e., voice time). (b) Omission of items that were found to be unreliable or repetitive for treatment purposes (i.e. jaw tests). (c) Improvements in the speech tests specifically in the areas of the use of the lips and tongue in speech. (d) Improvements in the area of intelligibility testing. The FDA-2 consists of 116 words to reduce the probability of the listener becoming familiar with the words. The list is phonetically balanced for types of sounds, position of sounds in words, and word length.

TECHNICAL. The standardization for the FDA-2 initially consisted of 46 normal healthy adults ranging in age from 23 to 64. Then it was administered to an additional 148 normal individuals, 111 ranging in age from 15 to 59 years, with the remaining 37 ranging in age from 60 to 97 years. No information was provided in reference to ethnicity/race, gender, or geographic region of the sample. Interrater and intrarater reliability were established by creating audio recordings of "nine people with a range of types of severities of dysarthria performing the audible tests" (examiner's manual, p. 34). Six speech and language therapists, whose caseloads included adult clients with dysarthria, judged 42 examples of FDA-2 recordings. The intrajudge reliability of the assessment was evaluated by presenting the same 42 tests to the same listeners after a 6-week interval.

"The interrater reliability (reliability coefficient *R*) was calculated using intraclass correlations" (examiner's manual, p. 35). An ANOVA with fixed effects was "performed between the results of two listeners at a time. The mean square of the variances for the listeners (MS listener) and the mean square of the error (MS error) were obtained from the results of the ANOVA and used in the intraclass correlation calculation to produce the reliability coefficient (R) (Streiner & Norman, 1989)" (examiner's manual, p. 35). The interrater reliability between fully qualified speech and language therapists was in all cases moderate or substantial. Intrarater scores were all high, with one having almost perfect reliability (.92). A comparison of the results of all the items indicated that "some of the items were not scored consistently either between or within judges" (examiner's manual, p. 36), which resulted in the revision of the scoring instructions.

Researchers and clinicians have used the FDA for over 20 years, which has influenced the development and improvements for the FDA-2. Input from these aforementioned sources helps establish both face and content validity. In order to ascertain whether patterns of speech disability are reflected by the FDA-2, a study was conducted in which the FDA-2 was administered to 85 patients with a diagnosis of dysarthria. There were five groups, with each group representing a different type of dysarthria. A discriminant analysis was performed on the results. More information on the validity of this instrument would be beneficial.

COMMENTARY. The FDA-2 is a simple assessment instrument that is brief to administer and easy to score. It is a welcome assessment tool to assist clinicians in developing effective treatment plans for various neurological disorders. A weakness of the instrument is that there was no mention of dialect in administration or scoring of any of the tasks. An individual's dialect may impact an individual's ability to produce sounds in words and in sentences that may ultimately directly impact the severity rating and diagnosis.

SUMMARY. The FDA-2 assists with the diagnosis of the types of dysarthria and the neurological impairment associated with the dysarthria. It provides an analysis of each parameter of speech, uses clear descriptors, demonstrates sufficient inter- and intrarater reliability, and includes the necessary word and sentence cards. The test meets its goal and is recommended for use by speech language pathologists treating patients with neurological deficits.

[56]

Functional Evaluation for Assistive Technology.

Purpose: To identify "the most appropriate and effective assistive technology (AT) devices to help individuals with learning problems compensate for their difficulties and meet the demands of specific tasks and contexts."
Population: "Individuals with learning problems (of all ages)."
Publication Date: 2002.
Acronym: FEAT.
Scores: Not scored; "examiner interprets the FEAT on a 'per item' basis."
Administration: Individual and group.
Price Data, 2009: $149 per complete kit including 25 of each of the following forms: Contextual Matching Inventory, Checklist of Strengths and Limitations, Checklist of Technology Experiences, Technology Characteristics Inventory, Individual-Technology Evaluation Scale, and Summary and Recommendations Booklet, and 1 examiner's manual (78 pages); $55 per specimen kit including 1 of each of the following: Contextual Matching Inventory, Checklist of Strengths and Limitations, Checklist of Technology Experiences, Technology Characteristics Inventory, Individual-Technology Evaluation Scale, Summary and Recommendations Booklet, and examiner's manual; $17 per 25 Contextual Matching Inventories; $17 per 25 Checklists of Strengths and Limitations;

$17 per 25 Checklists of Technology Experiences; $12 per 25 Technology Characteristics Inventory; $17 per 25 Individual-Technology Evaluation Scales; $25 per 25 Summary and Recommendations Booklets; $55 per examiner's manual.
Time: Administration time not reported.
Comments: The FEAT should be used by an AT evaluation team rather than a single evaluator; "examiner" is the head of the evaluation team; total number of parts administered depends on "individual's AT needs."
Authors: Marshall H. Raskind and Brian R. Bryant.
Publisher: Psycho-Educational Services.

a) CONTEXTUAL MATCHING INVENTORY.
Purpose: To identify "the tasks in which the individual is typically engaged across settings ... and [to determine] whether the [assistive] technology will be successful across those settings."
Comments: Ratings "based on interviews with... teachers, employers, family members, and/or [the] student or employee" being evaluated.

b) CHECKLIST OF STRENGTHS AND LIMITATIONS.
Purpose: To "provide information concerning academic behaviors associated with listening, speaking, reading, writing, mathematics, memory, organization, physical/motor, and behavior."
Administration: Group.
Comments: Ratings by "teachers, employers, family members, and/or [the] student or employee" being evaluated.

c) CHECKLIST OF TECHNOLOGY EXPERIENCES.
Purpose: "To identify the individual's familiarity with [AT] devices that may be evaluated."
Comments: Ratings based on an interview with the student or employee being evaluated.

d) TECHNOLOGY CHARACTERISTICS INVENTORY.
Purpose: "To evaluate [AT] device-specific characteristics such as its reliability/dependability, operational ease, and so forth."
Comments: Ratings by examiner.

e) INDIVIDUAL-TECHNOLOGY EVALUATION SCALE AND RELATED WORKSHEETS.
Purpose: "To obtain "information about the person's interaction with the AT device that is being evaluated."
Forms: 5 additional worksheets "to be used in conjunction with the Individual-Technology Evaluation Scale:" Optical Character Recognition/Speech Synthesis, Speech Synthesis/Screen Reading Systems, Speech Recognition Systems, Word Prediction Software, Spell Checkers.
Comments: Individual-Technology Evaluation Worksheets are reproducible and found in Appendix B of Examiner's Manual; ratings by examiner.

f) SUMMARY AND RECOMMENDATIONS BOOKLET.
Purpose: "To summarize the assessment information, make recommendations, and arrange for follow-ups to assess for effective implementation."
Comments: Completed by examiner.

Review of the Functional Evaluation for Assistive Technology by MARTA COLEMAN, Instructor, Gunnison Watershed School District, Gunnison, CO:

DESCRIPTION. The Functional Evaluation for Assistive Technology is a standardized assessment instrument designed to "identify the most appropriate and effective device to help individuals with learning problems (of all ages) compensate for their difficulties and meet the demands of specific tasks/functions and contexts" (examiner's manual, p. 7). It can be used "to evaluate single or multiple AT [assistive technology] devices, for single or multiple tasks, in single or multiple contexts" (examiner's manual, p. 7). There are five scales: Contextual Matching Inventory (Parts A and B), Checklist of Strengths and Limitations, Checklist of Technology Experiences, Technology Characteristics Inventory, and Individual-Technology Evaluation Scale with worksheets for (a) optical character recognition/speech synthesis, (b) speech synthesis/screen reading, (c) speech recognition systems, (d) word prediction software, and (e) spell checker. The test authors claim that this assessment tool "can be used by diagnosticians, teachers, disability support service providers, physicians, rehabilitation counselors, therapists, and researchers" (examiner's manual, p. 7). It is advised that a team of Assistive Technology (AT) evaluators be created to conduct the evaluation. Appendix A describes 17 AT devices and brief histories of their benefits and limitations. This is helpful for potential AT users and evaluators. Appendix B provides examples of completed worksheets, as well as blackline masters of worksheets for the Individual-Technology Evaluation Scale.

DEVELOPMENT. In response to several legislative acts on the national level especially during the 1990s such as "Sections 504 and 508 of the Rehabilitation Act of 1973, the Assistive Technology Act of 1998..., the Americans with Disabilities Act Amendments of 1990 and the Individuals with Disabilities Education Act of 1997" (examiner's manual, p. 4), the FEAT was conceptualized as both public and private schools, K-12, began considering AT to support students' learning. The test manual reports that an increase in AT presentations at professional conferences, and an increase in AT products over the past few years influenced the development of this evaluation tool. The test authors cite a dearth of evaluative tools for identifying individuals with learning disabilities who might readily adapt to AT as another reason for the development of this tool. The test authors claim that the FEAT provides a systematic and comprehensive assessment protocol for "determining the most appropriate AT to meet the demands of specific individuals across tasks within particular contexts" (examiner's manual, p. 4). Literature was examined identifying research that investigated the efficacy of AT to ease learning difficulties in a multitude of settings (i.e., educational, governmental, or vocational).

TECHNICAL. The test manual provides a brief discussion regarding how well a student might perform in a classroom using adaptations in order to be successful. The test authors refer to Hammill (1987) who used the term "nonreferenced interpretation" in their description of FEAT, which they claim has been designed "to measure abilities and performance from the perspective of the individual being evaluated and not against a set of norms or mastery criteria" (examiner's manual, p. 40). No total scores or scale scores are produced, but rather information gleaned from the inventories and checklists are interpreted to determine which AT devices might substantially help a student perform better. All subscales of the FEAT have explicit administration procedures. Some subjectivity in rating on the Likert-type scales is required by the rater.

Standardization. Referring to Hammill and Bryant (1991), the test authors refer to two proofs of standardization: reliability and validity.

Reliability. The FEAT uses internal consistency and stability research to indicate reliability. Seventeen normally achieving public school students from Austin, Texas, were involved in the study. Race, age, and gender of these students are described in the manual (pp. 40-41). Another 33 private school students with learning disabilities from Pasadena, California, were also involved in the study, and their race, age, and gender were also described. The private school students' learning disabilities had met the LD criteria described by the National Joint Committee on Learning Disabilities (2001), as reported by the test authors. Internal consistency reliability estimates for each of the five subscales ranged between .80 and .95. Test-retest reliability was examined using a 2-week testing interval and reporting two sources of error variance: content sampling and time sampling. The uncorrected or combined variance for each of the subscales is reported between .74 and .93. The corrected or variance attributed to time sampling alone for the subscales is reported between .80 and .98.

Validity. The test authors discuss content validity through a brief history of the five initial scales' development. A brief history of item development for each scale is discussed in the test manual. For example, items for the first edition of the FEAT were based on the test authors' experiences with the initial behaviors of teachers, students, and employers/employees. Nearly a dozen graduate students with teaching experience were asked to evaluate the initial list of behaviors, which established the foundation for the items on the first edition of the FEAT. The scales were then used with the 50 students previously described. Item discrimination analysis was conducted using a .35 coefficient as a criterion. Median indices of discriminating powers of the five scales are reported between .42 and .65. The test authors report an interruption of validity when comparing results of a silent reading test and reading with an optical character recognition device, because the test authors assume gains are made with that particular technology adaptation, though no data in the manual support this assumption.

The test authors list six cautions in interpreting evaluation results: (a) AT should be used in its own context and not be expected to cure all learning problems, (b) failure to provide a support system for students with learning disabilities via an evaluation team may limit the effectiveness of AT adaptations, (c) users and evaluators of the AT user ought to be trained in the use of the AT device, (d) once AT adaptation is used, continue remedial work, (e) continue evaluation of the AT adaptation(s) for each particular user across a continuum, and (f) AT adaptation is unique to each user; it is not a "one size fits all" tool.

COMMENTARY. The test manual is well-written and easy to follow. An example of how to use the evaluation tool is given in a case study in chapter 3 of the manual, although some examples of how to use each scale are abbreviated to save space. This reviewer recommends providing full examples of how each scale could be used in the case study sample. The time needed to complete the instrument is dependent upon the evaluation team's goals. This evaluator would estimate time needed to complete an evaluation for a single user to be between 20 minutes and 2 hours.

SUMMARY. The FEAT is an instrument designed for use across multiple contexts over time, in evaluating which AT adaptations could be beneficial for students with learning disabilities. The administrative guidelines are well-written and clear. The test authors admit a complex interplay of many factors, and caution thoughtful interpretation of results. This reviewer recognizes utility of this instrument especially in educational settings, though further research is required to satisfy specific uses of AT adaptations for individuals with specific learning disabilities. Theoretical grounding submitted for this instrument is well-documented and lucidly presented.

REVIEWER'S REFERENCES

Hammill, D. (1987). *Assessing the abilities and instructional needs of students.* Austin, TX: PRO-ED.

Hammill, D., & Bryant, B. R. (1991). The role of standardized tests in planning academic instruction. In L. Swanson (Ed.), *Handbook on the assessment of learning disabilities* (pp. 373-406). Austin, TX: PRO-ED.

National Joint Committee on Learning Disabilities. (2001). Learning disabilities: Issues on definition. In National Joint Committee on Learning Disabilities (Eds.), *Collective perspectives on issues affecting learning disabilities* (pp. 33–37). Austin, TX: PRO-ED.

Review of the Functional Evaluation for Assistive Technology by SUZANNE YOUNG, Professor of Educational Research, University of Wyoming, Laramie, WY:

DESCRIPTION. The Functional Evaluation for Assistive Technology (FEAT), published by Psycho-Educational Services, was designed to provide a multidimensional assessment of the use of assistive technology devices for individuals with learning problems. The assessment is made up of five scales that assist an evaluator in determining the appropriateness of specific assistive technologies in a variety of contexts or tasks, considering the strengths and limitations of an individual. The assessment is available only in paper form.

The examiner is primarily responsible for determining who completes this five-scale assessment. The examiner may complete most of the scales but often will rely on a professional team working with the individual. The examiner who completes the scales should be familiar with its administration and technical characteristics, and should have a background in assessing the appropriateness of assistive technologies. In addition, the rater should know the academic behaviors of the examinee well and be able to carefully and thoroughly complete the scales.

The five scales offer the team of evaluators an opportunity to determine the assistive technology device the individual should use for needed tasks in various contexts. The Contextual Matching Inventory is used to evaluate three areas: the tasks an individual person is expected to perform, the setting in which he or she should perform these tasks, and the usefulness of the assistive technology device after it has been applied. The Checklist of Strengths and Limitations allows the evaluators to collect information about a person's abilities, both strengths and limitations, across various academic and cognitive tasks. This scale is used to identify functional dissonance (i.e., the individual does not have the abilities needed to perform certain tasks) as well as whether or not the assistive device can be used to compensate for a learning problem. The Checklist of Technology Experiences is used to assess the individual's familiarity with the specific assistive technology device. The Technology Characteristics Inventory is used to examine the device itself, considering such factors as reliability and technical support. Finally, the Individual-Technology Evaluation Scale (and related worksheets) is used to examine how each device assists the individual when performing various tasks or trying to compensate for certain difficulties.

The FEAT is a comprehensive assessment system that takes into account not only the individual's needs but also allows the examiner to look at them within a variety of settings. In addition, it provides an opportunity to assess the device itself, both for its own characteristics and in specific contexts. The purpose is to find the most appropriate device that will assist an individual in compensating for learning difficulties in different settings or across tasks.

Instructions for administration include a description of the qualifications for both the examiner and the raters who complete the scales. The specific instructions for administering each scale are described in the test manual. The Contextual Matching Inventory should be administered first and is either completed by the professionals who are familiar with the specific settings or by the examiner, after interviewing the professionals. The Checklist of Strengths and Limitations is completed by raters who are familiar with the individual's behaviors in each different environment under consideration. The examiner then evaluates the strengths and limitations that are consistent across the various settings in order to determine the problem areas to be addressed by assistive technology. The Checklist of Technology Experiences is completed by the examiner based on either the examiner's prior knowledge of the individual or on an interview with the individual. The examiner may choose to complete only the sections in this scale that relate to the identified limitations. The Technology Characteristics Inventory is completed after a device has been chosen, but prior to its use. The test authors do not identify the appropriate rater to complete this scale. Finally, the Individual-Technology Evaluation Scale (and related worksheets) is completed for each device and problem area that has been identified. The examiner completes this scale based on an observation with the individual as the device is used in a specific setting or task. Worksheets for five specific technologies can be used along with the evaluation scale so the examiner will be prompted to consider their particular characteristics, operations, functions, and options.

The test authors do not provide information about length of time required to complete the scales but it is clear that it will differ based on the learning problems, the contexts and tasks being evaluated, and the number of assistive technologies being considered. After the scales are completed, the examiner uses the Summary and Recommendations Booklet to assist with interpretation. The examiner summarizes information about the individual, any pertinent background information, raters' names and positions, purpose of the evaluation, and a summary of results from each scale. Recommendations are made based on the overall results and they also include suggestions for support and training needs as well as a plan for re-evaluation.

Overall, the description of the FEAT is thorough and provides an example of an evaluation. The description covers an explanation of the purpose and administration of each scale. Using input from a team of professionals, the system of scales provides a complete assessment of assistive technology uses for an individual with learning problems.

DEVELOPMENT. The FEAT was published in 2002 and this is the first version. Original items for the scales were chosen based on literature, test author experience, and feedback from graduate students. The scale items were then evaluated by experts in the field of assistive technology with a few changes made based on their feedback. The scales were used with two student samples. One sample included 17 normally achieving students from a public school in Austin, Texas. The sample was described as 11 boys and 6 girls, ranging in age from 8.25 to 16.9 years; and with 11 Caucasians, 4 African Americans, and 3 Hispanics (note the total of 18). The other sample included 33 students in a private school for children with learning disabilities in Pasadena, California. They were described as 24 boys and 9 girls, ranging in age from 9.9 to 19.3 years; and including 24 Caucasian, 5 African American, 2 Hispanic, 1 Native American, and 1 Asian student.

The test authors reported item discrimination indices using the two student samples. They correlated each scale item with the total scale score and reported the median as well as the range for each scale. They used a correlation of .35 as their criterion for including an item on the final scale. All median correlations exceeded the criterion but scale ranges for all scales except the Contextual Matching Inventory included items that were below .35. The test authors reported "on the average, the test items satisfy the requirements previously described [criteria of .35]" (examiner's manual, p. 43), suggesting they retained all items in the final version of the FEAT. Reliability and validity are discussed below.

TECHNICAL. In addition to the development of the scales described above, the test authors included information about validity and reliability. Content validity was supported through item choice based on literature and expert opinion. No additional validity evidence was provided. Reliability of each scale, using the development sample of 50 students from Texas and California, was evaluated using internal conistency estimates as well as test-retest correlation coefficients.

Internal consistency estimates, using alpha coefficient, for the scales ranged from .80 to .95, indicating acceptable reliability, according to the test authors. Internal consistency estimates were based on the entire development sample of 50 students.

Test-retest correlations, corrected and uncorrected, were provided based on only the California sample of 33 students with learning disabilities. The scales were completed twice with a 2-week interval between administrations. The uncorrected reliability coefficients ranged from .74 to .93. When reliability was corrected for error due to content sampling, reliabilities were higher for each scale, ranging from .80 to .98.

COMMENTARY. The test authors are to be commended for developing an assessment that provides a multidimensional examination of the use of assistive technology for individuals with learning problems. The five scales together form a system that collects information from varying and important perspectives. Individuals with learning problems will benefit from this careful, detailed, and thoughtful assessment, assuming the technology itself does not lead to additional difficulties. The test authors do account for this possibility though, in their Technology Characteristics Inventory as well as the Checklist of Technology Experiences. Further, the test authors suggest that the initial assessment using the FEAT is followed-up at a later time.

The test authors did not adapt their scale after the item analysis, yet some items had low item discrimination indices. The test authors reported item discrimination for the group and dealt with it as an average. However, item discrimination relates to individual items and not scales so that poorly functioning items can be identified and deleted or replaced.

Content validity was the single type of validity evidence provided by the test authors. Because the test authors had a sample of normally achieving students as well as students with identified learning problems, the authors could have addressed criterion validity. Specifically, the two samples should certainly differ on their needs for assistive technology to compensate for learning problems. This would add strong support for the ability of examiners to use this evaluation system to help individuals with learning problems.

Reliability evidence was found using some or all of the development sample of 50 students, ranging in age from approximately 8 to 19 years. The test authors suggest the FEAT can be used for children and adults but the development sample does not include adults, except for 19-year-olds in the California sample.

SUMMARY. The FEAT is a comprehensive, multidimensional assessment system for assistive technology that supports individuals with learning problems. Although the test authors suggest it is appropriate for all ages, it was developed using school-age children and the test manual refers to school settings, teachers, and school activities more so than tasks outside of school. The test authors make a strong case for the importance of assessing assistive technology for children in schools, particularly because Congress mandated that assistive technology be considered for all students with disabilities when they reauthorized IDEA in 1997. Although the psychometrics could be stronger for the FEAT, the test authors have carefully developed an assessment that appears to be useful and needed. Only one other similar assessment seems to be widely available: the Matching Assistive Technology & CHild (15:145). Its use is limited to children ages 0 through 2. It is similar to the FEAT in that it uses a series of scales. However, reviewers note that no technical information is available (Cohen, 2003; Watson & Doggett, 2003). The FEAT is a much more carefully developed assessment that is useful for children of all ages.

REVIEWER'S REFERENCES

Cohen, L. G. (2003). [Review of Matching Assistive Technology & CHild.] In B. S. Plake, J. C. Impara, & R. A. Spies (Eds.), *The fifteenth mental measurements yearbook* (pp. 541–543). Lincoln, NE: Buros Institute of Mental Measurements.

Watson, T. S., & Doggett, R. A. (2003). [Review of Matching Assistive Technology & CHild.] In B. S. Plake, J. C. Impara, & R. A. Spies (Eds.), *The fifteenth mental measurements yearbook* (pp. 543–544). Lincoln, NE: Buros Institute of Mental Measurements.

[57]

Get Ready to Read!–Revised.

Purpose: Designed as a screening tool to measure preschool students' "understanding of books, printed letters, and words," as well as "the relationship between letters and speech sounds and how sounds can combine to form words" to "determine if they have the necessary early literacy skills to become successful readers."

Population: Ages 3-0 to 5-11.

Publication Dates: 2000-2009.

Acronym: GRTR!.

Scores: Total score only.

Administration: Individual.

Price Data, 2009: $82.95 per complete test kit; $16.55 per 25 child record forms; $1 per summary form; $49.95 per stimulus easel; $25.95 per Early Literacy Manual (2009, 23 pages).

Foreign Language Edition: A Spanish version of the complete test kit is available.

Time: (10-15) minutes.

Comments: Should not be used to screen the same student more than three times in 1 year and at least 3 months should separate screening dates; a summary form is included for administrators to record screening scores at different time points for each student in a particular class or group; the Total score is interpreted using Step Scores or Performance Levels provided in the manual and on the back of the answer sheet; there

are four (1-4) Step Scores (providing information about the student's pre-literacy skill level) that correspond to a range of Total scores.
Author: National Center for Learning Disabilities.
Publisher: Pearson.

Review of Get Ready to Read!–Revised by ZANDRA S. GRATZ, Professor of Psychology, Kean University, Union, NJ:

DESCRIPTION. The Get Ready to Read!–Revised (Revised GRTR!) is an individually administered screening tool to assess the extent to which children have the early literacy skills necessary to learn to read. The scale is to be used with children between the ages of 3.0 and 5.11. A Spanish version of the GRTR! is available (S-GRTR!). The test authors indicate that the Revised GRTR! items measure both print knowledge and phonological awareness although factor analysis and scale cohesion measures did not support the establishment and scoring of two separate sub scales (Lonigan & Wilson, 2008).

The Revised GRTR! contains 25 items administered via a two-sided easel that includes administration directions and one sample question. The child's side of the easel contains four pictures from which the child is to point to an answer. The examiner's side of the easel contains the question and the four response choices with the correct answer highlighted. The easel contains both the Spanish and English versions of the screen. For each item, the examiner marks on the answer sheet a 1 for a correct answer and a 0 for an incorrect answer. Preprinted on answer sheets are the items as well as score interpretation guides.

No prior training is suggested for examiners; the manual is geared toward preschool teachers although information on the web site (www.getreadytoread.org, retrieved 2/9/10) indicates the screener may be administered by parents. It is suggested that 10 to 15 minutes be set aside for testing an individual child. The manual also provides activities aimed at providing the child with experiences that will help to develop prereading literacy. Also on the web site is a short guide for childhood educators and care providers as well as information relative to studies using the screen between 2001 and 2003; however, these materials reflect Get Ready to Read! (GRTR!) and not the Revised GRTR!.

The easel creates a somewhat awkward situation, particularly for the novice examiner. Examiners must sit in such a way that they are able to see both sides of the easel in order to read the question and see to what the child points. Only one sample item is provided; this may not be sufficient for novice test takers and administrators to confirm that the child understands the testing process.

Raw scores are generated by totaling the number of correct answers. Several methods for interpreting scores are offered. Step scores are four score ranges based on the total number correct that describe what the child understands with regard to print and letter-sound associations as well as offering some broad suggestions as to the activities that might benefit the child. Percentile ranks are available at 3-month intervals. Percentile rank data are the basis for Performance Level categories that divide scores into one of three ranges: Below Average, Average, and Above Average. Performance Levels, included in both the manual and answer sheet, depict the raw score obtained by the top 25%, middle 50%, and bottom 25%, respectively, for children in 6-month age groupings (e.g., 3.0 to 3.5 years). Also available are standard scores, which are reported with a mean of 100 and standard deviation of 15.

DEVELOPMENT. The Revised GRTR! is based on the 20-item GRTR! Screener. The GRTR! was developed by researchers at Applied Research Partners, Inc., at the behest of The National Center for Learning Disabilities (Whitehurst, 2001). The GRTR! was developed for use by nonprofessionals to identify children whose experiences, without intervention, would not support the acquisition of reading skills. The premise behind development was that many reading problems are preventable if children have sufficient prereading experiences.

Item selection was based on a series of longitudinal studies that tested 4-year-old Head Start children on emergent literacy skills and then examined their performance at the end of second grade. In particular, based on a series of standardized reading assessments, a group of 124 successful Grade 2 readers and 124 unsuccessful Grade 2 readers were identified. Using discriminant analysis, 14 emergent reading skills from the Developing Skills Checklist (DSC; CTB/McGraw-Hill, 1990), which discriminated between successful and unsuccessful Grade 2 readers, were identified. GRTR! items were developed to capture the emergent reading skills that distinguished between the two groups. An initial pool of 100 items was developed, which was later reduced to 60 by eliminating redundant items. In total, 342 children were administered the 60 remaining items and the 14 emergent reading skills of the DSC. Criteria for inclusion on the GRTR! included items that were highly correlated to the DSC, demonstrated high internal consistency, and had difficulty levels near .50.

The Revised GRTR! sought to increase the overall difficulty of the GRTR! to allow for early literacy screening of children from middle and upper middle socioeconomic backgrounds and to develop national norms. The Revised GRTR! added six new items and eliminated one from the original GRTR!.

Located on the GRTR! web site (www.getreadytoread.org, retrieved 2/9/10) was a technical monograph (Lonigan, 2003) dealing with the Spanish version of the GRTR! (S-GRTR). The Spanish version went through several pilot studies. The first pilot study used translations of the original GRTR! A second field study used the original 20 items plus 6 additional items developed to be phonologically sensitive. The final 20 items were selected from the 26-item pool based on item/total correlations, difficulty level, and correlations with other measures (Preschool Comprehensive Test of Phonological and Print Processing [pre-CTOPPP]). Information relative to the 25-item Revised S-GRTR! was not found.

TECHNICAL. The Revised GRTR! manual presents interpretive information regarding the scoring of Revised GRTR!; little is presented relative to the technical qualities of the measure. Similarly, little is available on the publisher's site (Pearson, retrieved 2/1/10). Rather, information is available from an unpublished report prepared for the National Center on Learning Disabilities (Lonigan & Wilson, 2008).

Normative data. The norm sample for the Revised GRTR! included 866 children between the ages of 3 and 5 years from 20 cities in six states (Lonigan & Wilson, 2008). The sample reasonably replicates that of the population of the United States, with some exceptions when broken down by age group. Across ages, 228 3-year-olds, 398 4-year-olds, and 240 5-year-olds participated. Nothing was found relative to the revision of the Spanish GRTR!.

Reliability. The internal consistency estimate of reliability based on the entire norming sample was .88. By age of child, coefficient alpha estimates of reliability were .77 for 3-year-olds, .84 for 4-year-olds and .83 for 5-year-olds (Lonigan & Wilson, 2008). The reviewer could not find technical information relative to the revision of the Spanish GRTR!. However, some research findings relative to the earlier version (S-GRTR!) were available. In particular, coefficient alpha for the original S-GRTR! was .76 (Lonigan, 2003). No information could be found relative to test-retest reliability regarding the Revised GRTR! or the revised S-GRTR!.

Validity. The Revised GRTR! includes 16 items reported to measure Print Knowledge and 9 items reported to measure Phonological Awareness. These facets have been found to be related to later reading ability (Storch & Whitehurst, 2002). Despite two types of item descriptors, as already noted, factor analysis of the item set failed to suggest the formation of two separate scales (Lonigan & Wilson, 2008). In support of the construct validity of the Revised GRTR!, children's scores on the measure increased with age. In particular, the average item difficulty increased from .42 for 3-year-olds, to .63 for 4-year-olds and .78 for 5-year-olds. A similar pattern in the S-GRTR! was noted (Lonigan, 2003); nothing was found relative to the Revised S-GRTR!.

Lonigan and Wilson (2008) report strong correlations between the Revised GRTR! and longer measures of emergent reading skills (Test of Preschool Early Literacy; TOPEL). In particular, based on a sample of 201 3- and 4-year-olds, the correlations between the Revised GRTR! and the TOPEL Knowledge (r = .76, p < .001), the TOPEL Overall Early Literacy Index (r = .72, p < .001), Phonological Awareness (r = .39, p < .001), and Definitional Vocabulary (r = .44, p < .001) were significant. Other studies were found that confirm significant relationships between the earlier GRTR! and other, relatively long measures of emergent literacy skills (e.g., Molfese, Molfese, Modglin, Walker, & Neamon, 2004) and as a predictor of later reading success (Phillips, Lonigan, & Wyatt, 2009).

With regard to the Revised S-GRTR!, no validity data were found. However, significant correlations between Pre-CTOPP and Preschool Language Scales and the S-GRTR! were reported (Lonigan, 2003).

COMMENTARY. The Revised GRTR! early literacy manual guides the potential user to online resources at www.getreadytoread.org. However, as of the writing of this review, much of the online information, including the technical information, refers to the earlier versions of the GRTR! and S-GRTR!. The only mention of the revised version is an online referral to the test publisher's site. This at best offers little to the potential test user and at worst may confuse the potential user. As a test reviewer, the need to search a variety of online menus and databases to acquire basic technical information was frustrating; a technical manual, offered as an ancillary to the test manual is needed.

Although the manual indicates the Revised GRTR! is geared to "early childhood professionals" the web site indicates the "Get Ready to Read! screening tool was designed for use by parents as well as pre-school professionals" and "is easy to use even if you don't have formal training in education" (www.getreadytoread.org, retrieved 2/8/10). Similarly, the test publisher's site (Pearson) indicates that it is a Level A test, requiring no training to buy. An untrained, nonprofessional may have trouble adhering to unbiased test administration procedures as well as may have difficulty understanding the nature and limitations of a screener.

The premise of the screen is to identify those children who have limited experiences with language or print materials as well as those who may be in need of further testing. It is suggested that more information be provided regarding next steps for assessments of those children who have been offered literacy experiences but do not demonstrate sufficient emergent literacy skills.

The activities listed in the manual might be better marketed to parents who have limited literacy sophistication as a means of helping them help their children acquire the skills necessary to learn to read, independent of the Revised GRTR!. The manual also indicates using "results of the screening to help determine what experiences and activities are appropriate for individual children over the course of the year" (manual, p. 6). In that the evidence suggests that the screen measures only one factor, suggestions that the Revised GRTR! scores be used to determine the specific skills on which to work (e.g., print knowledge, phonological awareness, or emergent writing) are not warranted.

At several junctures the test authors suggest that the test be repeated: "you may also want to repeat the screening in the middle of the year to see how a child is progressing" (manual, p. 6). However, no evidence as to the stability of the measure over time is available. Evidence of test-retest reliability is necessary in order to have confidence in pre/post GRTR! testing.

In summary, the Revised GRTR! is based on research as to the emergent reading skills found to be related to later reading achievement. Although the manual is simple and easy to understand, the screen may not be appropriate for use and interpretation by those not trained in the administration and interpretation of standardized assessments. It would also be helpful if all technical information were amassed into one document. Technical information should be expanded to include estimates of dependability over time of the Revised GRTR! as well as both reliability and validity information relative to the revision of the Spanish version of the GRTR!.

REVIEWER'S REFERENCES

CTB/McGraw-Hill. (1990). Developing Skills Checklist. Monterey, CA: CTB/McGraw-Hill.

Lonigan, C. J. (2003). *Technical report on the development of the NCLD Spanish-language Get Ready to Read! screening tool.* Unpublished manuscript, National Center for Learning Disabilities.

Lonigan, C. J., & Wilson, S. B. (2008). *Report on the Revised Get Ready to Read! screening tool: Psychometrics and normative information.* Unpublished manuscript, Final report prepared for the National Center on Learning Disabilities.

Pearson Get Ready to Read–Enhanced. (2010). Retrieved from http://psychcorp.pearsonassessments.com /haiweb/cultures/en-us/productdetail.htm?pid=P

Molfese, V. J., Molfese, D. L., Modglin, A. T., Walker, J., & Neamon, J. (2004). Screening early reading skills in preschool children: Get Ready to Read. *Journal of Psychoeducational Assessment, 22*, 136-150. doi: 10.1177/073428290402200204

Phillips, B. M., Lonigan, C. J., & Wyatt, M. (2009). Predictive validity of the Get Ready to Read! Screener: Concurrent and long-term relations with reading-related skills. *Journal of Learning Disabilities, 42*(2), 99-110. doi: 10.1177/0022219408326209

Storch, S. A., & Whitehurst, G. J. (2002). Oral language and code-related precursors to reading: Evidence from a longitudinal structural model. *Developmental Psychology, 38*(6), 934-947. doi: 10.1037/0012-1649.38.6.934

Whitehurst, G. J. (2001). *The NCLD Get Ready to Read! Screening tool technical report.* Applied Research Partners, Inc. and the State University of New York at Stony Brook, New York: National Center for Learning Disabilities. (http://www.getreadytoread.org/documan/task.doc_download/gid,14/Itemid,313/)

Review of Get Ready to Read!–Revised by TIMOTHY SHANAHAN, Professor of Urban Education, University of Illinois at Chicago, Chicago, IL:

DESCRIPTION. Get Ready to Read!–Revised (GRTR!) is an individually administered screener for determining whether preschoolers are on track to become successful readers. The test takes 10–15 minutes to administer and includes 25 items aimed at assessing print knowledge and phonological awareness. Print knowledge refers to children's understanding of books, letters, and words, including knowing that print carries a message and the relationship between print and pictures. Phonological awareness refers to the ability to hear words and phonemes (individual language sounds) and to link letters and sounds.

There is both an English and Spanish version, and test results are expressed as standard scores and percentile ranks.

The screener is printed on good quality paper stock and is spiral bound (8.5 inches x 8.5 inches), with an attached easel that folds out as a display stand. This allows the test administrator to show the pictures easily, with answer choices on the child's side and correct answers on the adult's side to facilitate scoring.

Items are multiple-choice, with four picture choices each. The tester asks a question or gives a direction and the child points to one of the pictures in response. Sixteen items ask about print knowledge and 9 about phonological awareness. These different kinds of items are intermingled throughout the test, and no attempt is made to provide separate outcome information about these two types of items. The print knowledge items include a diverse collection of items that ask about children's knowledge of book parts, concepts of letters, numbers, and words, letter names, and that have test takers evaluate which words are "written the best." The phonemic awareness items assess rhyming, phoneme deletion, initial phonemes, sound-letter correspondences, and blending.

The screener provides a criterion-referenced classification of children's performances, as well as normative information that allows comparisons for children ages 3 years 0 months through 5 years 11 months. Information about the test purposes, development, and interpretation, including instructional activities are included in a 23-page manual, and there is an associated website (www.getreadytoread.org).

DEVELOPMENT. The GRTR! was originally developed in 2001 by the National Center for Learning Disabilities. Items included in the original tool were selected from a series of longitudinal research studies of a sample of 700 children. These children were tested using 14 measures of prereading that together predicted second-grade reading achievement with 78% accuracy (these measures included identifying letters and sounds, segmenting sentences, segmenting words, rhyming, identifying how to hold a book, identifying people engaged in reading, differentiating print from pictures and letters from numerals, identifying functions of print, identifying components of written communication, name printing, drawing a person, writing mechanics, and writing quality). Tests with the best predictive powers were then used as a source of potential items for developing the screener. Sixty items from the original tests were selected and transformed into the multiple-choice four-picture format. Then, these 60 items, along with the original 14 prereading measures, were administered to a sample of 342 preschoolers to determine what the final 20 items would be. Items with the best correlations with the original set of measures, a difficulty level near .50, and that had good reliability properties, were selected.

In 2007, a field study was conducted to revise the original screener. The revised instrument includes 19 of the 20 original items, plus 6 new items aimed at making the screener more difficult so it can better distinguish higher performing children. This revised instrument was then validated with 866 children (ages 3-0 to 5-11), leading to adjustments in the normative and criterion-referenced performance levels.

TECHNICAL. The original GRTR! had respectable reliability coefficients (alpha coefficient, .78; split-half reliability, .80), and high correlations with the battery of 14 predictor measures (.69–.70) and a test of letter knowledge (.66). One published study evaluated the reliability and validity of the original instrument (Molfese, Molfese, Modglin, Walker, & Neamon, 2004), and additional, as yet unpublished, studies are discussed in the technical report. Collectively, these studies found that the GRTR! was correlated with knowledge of vocabulary, environmental print, phonological awareness, rhyming, gains in letter knowledge, and word decoding. Given the strong similarity between the two versions of the test, these findings are relevant to any evaluation of the revised instrument.

The Revised GRTR! was normed with a group of 866 children drawn from 20 cities in six states during spring 2007. This sample was representative of the U.S. in terms of sex, region, ethnicity, parent's education, and exceptionality status (e.g., impairments or disabilities). Data indicate that the Revised GRTR! has an internal consistency coefficient of .88, consistent with the high reliability estimates seen in the earlier version of the test.

The Revised GRTR! has obvious content validity, as print knowledge and phonological awareness have been shown to be important precursors of literacy achievement (NELP, 2008), and the test items represent a reasonable sampling of items from these domains. Also, the test correlates well with age, meaning that older students do better on the test than younger students, and it correlates reasonably well (.72) with the Test of Preschool Early Literacy (TOPEL). Given the studies of the original and revised versions of this test, it is evident that the results would be highly predictive of later success in reading. However, these levels of correlation do not preclude the fact that there will be children whose abilities will be mischaracterized by this instrument. Accordingly, the technical report cautions against the use of this test information to make decisions about individual children.

COMMENTARY. Educators need to be able to identify early those children who are likely to struggle in learning to read, as early deficiencies tend to persist without targeted interventions. Early identification allows for a marshalling of resources and opportunities to prevent reading failure. The Revised GRTR! quickly provides such predictions. And, given that many preschool teachers have limited training in literacy, it is imperative that the administrative and interpretive procedures for such a test be easy to use, and with the GRTR! they are.

Predicting success in beginning reading is worthwhile, but it can also misinform teachers and parents. What it takes to succeed in reading initially is a proficiency in decoding print, but later the importance of other abilities, like language, emerge in reading comprehension. To keep making progress in reading, children must have well-developed vocabularies, an understanding of how sentences are interpreted, and solid listening comprehension skills—none of which are measured in the Revised GRTR!. The results are likely to be informative about how well a child will do in Grade 1, but not necessarily in Grade 4. They provide valuable guidance for the child who seems likely to struggle with decoding, but not for students who have other kinds of reading difficulties that tend to emerge later in development.

The original test was offered free on a public website that includes instructional activities and resources for parents and teachers. The revised edition is marketed by Pearson. When this review was written, the online version of the test was still available online. This is confusing because the manual for the revised edition refers to the website for technical information, but the technical information that is there is for the older version of the test not the revised one.

The technical report (Lonigan & Wilson, 2008) was obtained directly from the publisher, and it provides useful information about the norms, reliability, and validity of the test, and includes useful scoring and interpretative information that would be valuable to users, information that is neither included on the website nor in the revised test manual at this time. The technical report and manual each provide scales for interpreting scores, but no practical information about the use of these categories is offered (what should a teacher do if a child is in a particular category?), nor is there any kind of reliability or validity information about these categories. The test itself might be reliable and valid, but the accuracy of placement into these categories might not be.

SUMMARY. Get Ready to Read! Revised is a useful instrument for helping to identify children in preschool and kindergarten who may later have difficulty with beginning reading in Grades 1 and 2. It is an individually administered screener and its results are both reliable and predictive of later achievement. It has been normed on an appropriately representative sample of young children. It does not provide diagnostic information about the print knowledge and phonological awareness that it evaluates, but rather identifies which children might struggle with learning to read. The website that supports this test does not provide technical information about the revised instrument that was reviewed here.

REVIEWER'S REFERENCES

Lonigan, C. J., & Wilson, S. B. (2008). *Report on the revised Get Ready to Read! screening tool: Psychometric and normative information.* Unpublished manuscript, final technical report prepared for the National Center on Learning Disabilities.

Molfese, V. J., Molfese, D. L., Modglin, A. T., Walker, J., & Neamon, J. (2004). Screening early reading skills in preschool children: Get Ready to Read. *Journal of Psychoeducational Assessment, 22,* 136–150.

National Early Literacy Panel (NELP). (2008). *Developing early literacy: Report of the National Early Literacy Panel.* Washington, DC: National Institute for Literacy.

[58]

The Health Sciences Reasoning Test.

Purpose: "Developed for use by educators and researchers to assess the critical thinking skills of health science professionals and health science students".

Population: Health science professionals and students.

Publication Dates: 2006-2007.

Acronym: HSRT.

Scores, 6: Analysis, Evaluation, Inference, Deductive Reasoning, Inductive Reasoning, Total.

Administration: Group.

Price Data, 2008: $60 per manual (2007, 28 pages) and example test booklet; $250 per one-time client online testing set-up fee; $20 each first 50 online testing uses; $15 each 51-500 online testing uses; $10 each online

testing use over 500; $20 each first 50 paper-and-pencil test booklets, answer forms, and scoring sheets; $15 each 51-500 paper-and-pencil test booklets, answer forms, and scoring sheets; $10 each paper-and-pencil test booklets, answer forms, and scoring sheets; discounts available for nonprofit organizations.
Time: (45) minutes.
Comments: This test can be administered online or via paper and pencil.
Authors: Noreen C. Facione and Peter A. Facione.
Publisher: Insight Assessment–The California Academic Press LLC.

Review of the Health Sciences Reasoning Test by BRIAN F. FRENCH, Associate Professor of Educational Psychology (Research, Evaluation, & Measurement), Washington State University, Pullman, WA:

DESCRIPTION. The Health Sciences Reasoning Test (HSRT) is a group or individually administered test designed to assess critical thinking skills of health sciences professionals and students. The HSRT was designed to be used primarily with the postsecondary population. The authors state that the main purpose of the HSRT is to measure only the skills dimension of critical thinking. "Test takers are challenged to form reasoned judgments based on discursive textually presented information" (manual, p. 23). The test is primarily used for group assessment but may be used for program evaluation and individual admission, placement, or advising. The test is composed of 33 multiple-choice, dichotomously scored items, which are intended to assess five subdomains of critical thinking (i.e., Analysis, Inference, Evaluation, Deductive Reasoning and Inductive Reasoning). Each multiple-choice question has three or four distractors.

Test administration can occur in either paper-and-pencil or computer-based format. The test form has quality color photos that accompany many items and some items require use of these images. Administration is straightforward with detailed instructions provided in the manual. No special professional testing qualifications are required to administer the test or interpret the results. The authors recommend 45 minutes for test administration with additional time (i.e., 5–15 minutes) permitted if there is a plan to develop local norms.

Answer sheets are used with the paper-and-pencil form and sent to the publisher for scoring. In the case of the computer-based form, scoring is completed online in a secure environment with results available immediately. Scores (1 total and 5 subscale) can be returned via email. Two score reports are generated (individual and group). Upon request, a file (e.g., Excel, SPSS, Text) on a PC-formatted disk can be sent to the user containing score information. It should be noted that the test publisher will assist with adding other assessments to the online system, which could be useful for research purposes.

DEVELOPMENT. The HSRT was developed by examining items from other critical thinking tests produced by the test publisher (i.e., Insight Assessment). The test is constructed on the theoretical conceptualization of critical thinking skills, supported by a body of literature (e.g., American Philosophical Association, 1990) that proposes critical thinking as a "process of purposeful, self-regulatory judgment. This process gives reasoned consideration to evidence, context, conceptualizations, methods, and criteria" (manual, p. 5). The 33-item test is a sample of a 200-item pool that has been developed based on 20 years of research. It is not clear how item exposure or rotation is controlled. The items were tested in a variety of settings with college- and professional-level audiences, with a majority of the samples being composed of nursing students. No other information was given concerning the samples or item refinement in the development process. Anecdotal information from college students exiting the exam was obtained. The items comprise five subscales including Analysis (6 items), Inference (6 items), Evaluation (6 items), Deductive (10 items), and Inductive (10 items). There is no explanation as to which 33 items of these 38 are used for scoring.

TECHNICAL. The HSRT appears to have been administered to at least two validation samples (n = 444, n = 223). However, there is no information about these samples concerning major characteristics (e.g., gender, race/ethnicity, region) in the manual. Other samples are mentioned, yet the information presented was insufficient for evaluating representativeness of the samples. A table of norms for suggested percentile rankings is presented based on data from a similar critical thinking skills test, yet the test is not identified.

Reliability (internal consistency) data for the overall test score and the five subscale scores is presented with a coefficient alpha of .81 for the total score and a range of .52 to .77 for the subscales. Items were selected based on item discrimination values from item analysis. However, no information is provided concerning these values beyond selected items having a high item-total correlation. No other forms of reliability information are offered.

Very limited score validity evidence is presented to support the use of the HSRT scores in the manner advocated in the manual. Content validity evidence is offered through the process of identifying critical thinking skills and selecting items to match the five domains identified by experts, including interpretation, analysis, evaluation, explanation, and inference. Construct and criterion validity evidence are both discussed but no direct evidence is provided for the HSRT scores. A table of correlations is provided which displays correlations between a criterion (e.g., GRE, ACT, college GPA) and another measure of critical thinking. The authors state that they are expecting other correlations to be available as large cohorts use the instrument. The authors argue against the need for a factor analysis to provide validity evidence of the internal structure of the instrument. However, factor loading estimates are presented with no discussion of this information. The claim also is made that the test will not have differential validity across many groups (e.g., gender, race/ethnicity). Again, no empirical evidence is provided to support this claim. Further score reliability and validity work is warranted for the HSRT. Prior evidence based on other critical thinking measures is insufficient to support the HSRT scores.

COMMENTARY. The HSRT holds some promise as a tool that researchers may use in a battery of assessments to identify an adult's level of critical thinking in the health sciences domain. The authors are commended for developing the assessment grounded in theory that is documented in the literature. The authors have stated that the test's primary purpose is to provide reliable and valid information on the assessed skills for groups. Secondary purposes include information for program evaluation as well as individual admission, placement, and advising. This reviewer would not recommend the HSRT at this time for these stated purposes in the absence of the necessary reliability and validity information.

The manual does advocate for scores to be used at the individual level, in combination with other information of sources. This recommendation is a warranted caution. However, time is spent in the manual discussing how the subscale scores could be used to develop profiles or to identify strengths and weaknesses of examinees (e.g., p. 20). Such use is not supported by the evidence presented in the manual. Furthermore, the claim is made that the internal consistency reliability data are adequate for the stated purposes of the test, supported by Nunnally (1978). The authors (and interested readers) are encouraged to read Nunnally and Bernstein (1994) for revised standards. The values reported in the HSRT manual are not adequate for the stated purposes, especially at the individual level. Work to improve internal consistency reliability and report additional forms of score reliability (e.g., test-retest) is encouraged.

Although a norm sample is discussed and development of local norms is encouraged, little information is offered as to the characteristics (e.g., age, sex) of the samples employed during development. This reviewer also questions how many users will have the technical training, data sources, and time to develop local normative data.

A major weakness of the measure is a lack of psychometric evidence, especially score validity evidence, to support the instrument's use for the stated purposes. It appears a factor analysis was conducted to examine the internal structure of the test. However, insufficient details (e.g., type of factor analysis, handling of dichotomous data) are presented for this information to be useful. Additionally, providing more technical information on the development and functioning of the HSRT and reference to how the testing program is in accord with the *Standards for Educational and Psychological Testing* (AERA, APA, & NCME, 1999) would be beneficial. Including information in the technical manual on the systematic collection of validity evidence, for example, is a must-do task for testing programs (Downing, 2006), regardless of size of the program.

SUMMARY. The HRST is designed to be a group or an individually administered critical thinking assessment for use with a postsecondary population of health sciences professionals and students. With the appropriate psychometric information, such a measure could be used in a variety of ways (evaluation, planning) as stated in the manual. Unfortunately, very little score reliability and validity information is provided in the manual to support the inferences from the HSRT scores advocated by the test maker. The authors are encouraged to gather the necessary data to support the intended use of the overall score and its scales. In the absence of such data, the HSRT is not recommended for use for decision making about individuals or groups at this time.

REVIEWER'S REFERENCES

American Educational Research Association, American Psychological Association, & National Council on Measurement in Education. (1999). *Standards for educational and psychological testing.* Washington, DC: American Educational Research Association.

The American Philosophical Association. (1990). *Critical thinking: A statement of expert consensus for purposes of educational assessment and instruction ("The Delphi Report").* ERIC Doc. No. ED 315-423, p. 80.

Downing, S. M. (2006). Twelve steps for effective test development. In S. M. Downing & T. M. Haladyna (Eds.), *Handbook for test development.* (pp. 3-26). Mahwah, NJ: Lawrence Erlbaum Associates.

Nunnally, J. C. (1978). *Psychometric theory* (2nd ed). New York: McGraw-Hill.

Nunnally, J. C., & Bernstein, I. H. (1994). *Psychometric theory* (3rd ed.) New York: McGraw-Hill.

Review of the Health Sciences Reasoning Test by SANDRA D. HAYNES, Dean, School of Professional Studies, Metropolitan State College of Denver, Denver, CO:

DESCRIPTION. The Health Sciences Reasoning Test (HSRT) is designed to test the critical thinking skills of health science professionals and students. The instrument can be used to assess individuals, groups, or programs. Although health sciences content is used in the questions, neither discipline-specific knowledge nor practical experience is presumed. Instead, the questions are designed to assess whether or not someone is able to use critical thinking skills. The skills identified by the authors are drawn from the Delphi Report (American Philosophical Association, 1990). These are interpretation, analysis, inference, evaluation, and explanation. When these skills are purposefully engaged, the process of critical thinking occurs. The authors stress the HSRT is not designed to assess one's predisposition or willingness to use critical thinking; only the skills necessary for such behavior.

The HSRT is composed of 33 questions in a multiple-choice format with one correct answer and three distractors. The questions are discursive text, which may include diagrams and charts. The questions are deemed by the authors as comparable to information found in textbooks, newspapers, and businesses. The HSRT can be administered to individuals or to groups online or using paper and pencil. In either testing situation, strict instructions are articulated in the user manual to ensure test integrity when used and the security of the test materials in general. When using e-testing (i.e., computer administration) scoring is automatic and descriptive statistical analysis of the group tested is included. Other analytical comparisons can be made through Excel or other spreadsheet software by the user. When using the paper-and-pencil format, answer sheets must be returned to Insight Assessment (the publisher) for scanning and scoring. Scores are then returned to the user with descriptive statistics of the group. A diskette with a database may also be requested to enable further analysis by the user. No data were presented on the comparability of the different methods of administration or scoring.

The HSRT contains five subscales. Each subscale has an associated score and there is also an overall score. The five subscales are as follows: Analysis, Evaluation, Inference, Deductive Reasoning, and Inductive Reasoning. The first three scales are based on the Delphi Report findings and the last two are based on a "traditional conceptualization of reasoning" (manual, p. 9). The analysis subscale measures the comprehension of inputs, internal and external, and also the ability to critically examine the ideas presented. The evaluation subscale includes the ability to assess the credibility and strength of ideas and to state and justify one's own reasoning and arguments. The inference subscale measures the ability to identify relevant information and draw reasonable conclusions. For the HSRT, deductive reasoning "means the assumed truth of the premises purportedly necessitates the truth of the conclusion" and inductive reasoning "means [that] an argument's conclusion is purportedly warranted, but not necessitated, by the assumed truth of its premises" (manual, p. 10).

The subscales in these two groupings are scored using a slightly different numeric scale but the scores are interpreted in a similar fashion. For the first three subscales, a 0–6 scoring scale is used. In the last two subscales, a 0–10 scoring scale is used. In all instances, a low score (0–2 and 0–3, respectively) indicates weakness in the construct being measured, midrange scores (3–4 and 4–7, respectively) indicate average strength in the construct being measured, and a high score indicates strength in the construct being measured. There was no mention of how the overall score was weighted or otherwise impacted by the differential scoring including a theoretical rationale for using such scoring.

DEVELOPMENT. The items in the HSRT were based on a pool of approximately 200 questions developed and tested over a 20-year research program by Insight Assessment designed to test critical thinking. Items in the pool represent the five domains identified by the Delphi group: interpretation, analysis, evaluation, explanation, and inference. The authors describe the pool as discipline neutral. It is unclear whether the items were modified for subject matter consistency in the HSRT or if they were selected from the pool based on skill representation and content specificity. Items for possible inclusion were piloted "in a number of college level and professional employee settings ... [and] an international conference of health care providers of mixed professional field" (manual, p. 23). The items were then analyzed within and across samples and selected based on representation of one of the subscales. Little other information is given about test development.

TECHNICAL.

Standardization. The authors present a sample of norms for the HSRT. The norms are based on a sample size of 223 individuals. Other information about the sample is not reported. The authors suggest using this set of norms as a comparison group but recommend that users develop norms based on their own populations to determine the strength of critical thinking skills relative to other groups that have been previously tested by the user.

Reliability. Estimates of internal consistency (Kuder Richardson-20) indicate that the HSRT is internally consistent (KR-20 = .81). KR-20 coefficients for the subscales were lower to slightly lower ranging from .52–.77. The authors aknowledge that reliability estimates were based on a sample of 444 subjects from a 2004–2005 validation study. No other information regarding the sample was given.

Validity. Content, construct, and criterion validity measures were used to assess the validity of the HSRT. Content validity, described as identification of the pertinent domain and obtaining agreement on it and as using "'sensible' methods of test construction" (manual, p. 24), was cited by the authors as being met. The authors assert that each of the items was carefully selected for its theoretical relationship to the Delphi group's conceptualization of critical thinking.

The authors justify the use of multiple-choice tests by citing expert opinion that thinking can be measured with this test format. They reference two studies of critical thinking conducted in the late 1980s and 1990s using the California Critical Thinking Skills Test (CCTST). A footnote contains pretest and posttest measures indicating that gains in reasoning ability were found after taking a course in critical thinking with no apparent test effects. The authors use this information to justify construct validity of the HSRT. Presumably, the CCTST contains similar if not exactly the same questions of the HSRT as a subset of the CCTST items. If these items are from the same pool, how the results of a validation study comparing scores on the HSRI to the CCTST indicates construct validity of the HSRT is a mystery to this reader of the test manual, as no other studies of the HSRT were cited.

Criterion-related validity for the HSRT was likewise presumed to be similar to the CCTST. The authors cite several studies in which CCTST scores were correlated with predictive measures of college success such as the GRE, ACT, Watson-Glaser, SAT, and GPA. Correlations ranged from .20–.72. Whether or not these results will hold true for the HSRT remains to be seen.

COMMENTARY. The HSRT has the face validity and presumably a great deal of research to back the claim of the test authors that it is an excellent test of reasoning ability. The efficacy of these claims needs further research or specific explanation of research cited by the authors to back their claims of test efficacy. Best practices in test construction dictate that this information is included in the test manual and not left to the test user to track down. Administration, on the other hand, is straightforward, and the ability to administer the HSRT to individuals or to a group is a plus. Understanding how the exam is scored is left out of the manual as all scoring, whether for paper-and-pencil or computerized administration, must be accomplished by the test development company. Although the authors reason that the test user needs to define norms for their individual purposes, leaving out established norms is disappointing. The need to establish norms for each group is time-consuming to the test user.

SUMMARY. The Health Sciences Reasoning Test is designed to test the critical thinking skills of health science professionals and students. The authors present a sample of norms for the HSRT but few other supporting statistics that would help the user decide on the efficacy of the test or viability of its use. The instrument appears to have great potential that at present is not well documented.

REVIEWER'S REFERENCE

The American Philosophical Association. (1990). *Critical thinking: A statement of expert consensus for purposes of educational assessment and instruction ("The Delphi Report").* ERIC Doc. No. ED 315-423, p. 80.

[59]

InQ: Assessing Your Thinking Profile.

Purpose: Designed to "measure individual preferences in the way people think...it is a wide-ranging tool for both individual and group development, and for planning for more effective contacts with others."
Population: Business and industry.
Publication Dates: 1997-2001.
Acronym: InQ.
Scores, 5: Synthesist, Idealist, Pragmatist, Analyst, Realist.
Administration: Group.
Price Data, 2007: $16.95 per Manual of Administration and Interpretation (2001, 73 pages); $69.95 per set of 10 questionnaires.
Foreign Language Edition: Spanish edition available.
Time: (20) minutes.
Comments: Self-administered version of the Inquiry Mode Questionnaire (12:189), which is the trainer-administered version.
Author: InQ Educational Materials, Inc.
Publisher: InQ Educational Materials, Inc.

Review of the InQ: Assessing Your Thinking Profile by PATRICIA A. BACHELOR, Emeritus Professor of Psychology, California State University, Long Beach, Long Beach, CA:

DESCRIPTION. The InQ: Assessing Your Thinking Profile (InQ) was designed to identify an individual's preferred mode(s) of thinking when approaching challenges, making decisions, and solving problems. It is not a test of cognitive skills, intelligence, or personality. The InQ was developed to facilitate the decision-making process for business applications, management consultants, and building management teams. The five thinking modes identified on the InQ are: Synthesist, Idealist, Pragmatist, Analyst, or Realist. No thinking style is right or wrong; rather one's thinking style indicates an expression of preference(s). Those who prefer the *Synthesist* mode use an integrated approach; are creative, curious, place value on the meaning of things (especially words); seek affirmation of worth and admiration. *Idealists* expect much of themselves and others; need to be appreciated and worthy of trust; are supportive and helpful; are especially adept in complex verbal situations. *Pragmatists* provide optimism and motivate people to solve problems; are eager to get tasks done; have a high tolerance for ambiguity and need less structure and predictability; do not have a stake in the issue so anything that will "sell" a solution is fine. *Analysts* see the world as having logical and rational structure; hence, it is most important to them to find the one "best" way to solve a problem. A *Realist* views the world as what can be substantiated; seeks concrete results in a "real world" setting. The accompanying materials include extensive descriptions, characteristics, liabilities, strengths, behavioral cues, techniques for enhancing or minimizing one's thinking style and techniques to use one's thinking style for more effective communication with others.

The InQ is composed of 18 hypothetical problems/items that are each followed by five forced-choice responses (each of which describes one of the five thinking styles); hence, the completed InQ generates 90 (18 x 5) responses/scores. For each problem/item, the examinee is instructed to rank each of the five responses by first anchoring the response *most like you* (5), then *least like you* (1), and then to fill in the remaining responses using 4, 3, and 2, as appropriate. Each thinking style, therefore, has a minimum score of 18 (1 x 18) and a maximum score of 90 (18 x 5). Instructions for self-administration and self-scoring, as well as graphing of one's responses, are clear as are the interpretations and implications of the results. For every thinking style, a score of 60 points and above reveals a preference for the associated thinking style. Approximately 50% of people who took the InQ prefer to use one style of thinking, whereas 35% of people prefer to use two styles of thinking. Two percent use three types, and 13% have flat profiles (all style scores fall between 49 and 59).

DEVELOPMENT. Item development of the InQ was based on the content of a series of seminars presented to business professionals and managers interested in decision strategies outside educational settings in the United States. The first version of the InQ, consisting of 24 items, "was administered to over 400 professionals from the western United States" (Bruvold, Parlette, Bramson, & Bramson, 1983, p. 485). To reduce test-taking time, the test was reduced to 18 items. The 18-item version was administered to more than 2,000 professionals in various business-related occupations. An item analysis was conducted to determine if high scorers for each thinking style assigned a high score (4 or 5) to its associated response. If not, the item response was rewritten so this process continued until all items met this criterion for each of the five thinking modes. Then essentially the opposite criterion was applied. If low-scoring examinees on a thinking style assigned the related response a high score (4 or 5), the response was rewritten. The revised versions were analyzed until a consensus was reached. The final version was administered to 460 persons and an item analysis was performed on these data. Item-total correlations and *t*-tests were computed on the items for the highest and lowest scoring examinees. All but five of the correlations were statistically significant and *t*-tests confirmed these findings, as would be expected.

TECHNICAL.

Standardization sample. The standardization sample used to assess the test-retest (stability) reliability of the InQ was 63 respondents from three university classes who were administered the InQ with approximately 6 weeks between administrations. Factor analysis was utilized to determine the factor structure of the InQ. Profile analysis was used to determine if the InQ possessed construct validity. Two sets of three groups of employees were identified of sufficient size and significant difference in employment type. The profiles of the InQ for the three groups of "occupational" employees: insurance staff workers (n = 18), personnel staff (n = 17), and administrators (n = 30) were compared to the profiles of three groups of "professional" employees: engineers (n = 96), social workers (n = 15), and natural scientists (n = 13) (Bruvold et al., 1983). Combining the three "occupational" and the three "professional" employee groups would yield groups comprising adequate sample size so that meaningful comparisons could be permitted.

Reliability. Test-retest reliability was assessed by correlating the scores of a sample of 63 university students who had taken the InQ twice with approximately 6 weeks between test administrations. The correlations obtained were: Synthesist .75; Idealist .62; Pragmatist .65; Analyst .70; Realist .61. A broader range of samples that were tested over a longer period of time would most certainly lead to higher coefficients than those attained. However, the reported coefficients do provide preliminary support for test-retest reliability of the five thinking styles/modes (subscales) of the InQ. The intercorrelations among the subtests (thinking modes) reveal statistically significant correlations across most subscales, even with the small sample size. The test-retest reliability was not sufficiently high for the subscales to permit individual subscale score interpretation. However, profiles of subtest scores were judged to possess stability necessary for individual score interpretation. Spearman rank difference coefficients were computed by ranking the first test administration of subscale scores from high (5) to low (1) and similarly for the second administration of the InQ for each of the 63 pairs of individuals who took the InQ. These coefficients lend additional support for the stability of the profiles.

Validity. Profile analysis was utilized to detect if the InQ was able to discriminate between profiles of groups of persons in different occupations. More specifically, construct validity can be assessed by using two sets of three different occupational groups to contrast InQ profiles of the five thinking styles to determine if profiles reveal differences across employment tasks. InQ profiles of three groups of "occupational" employees: insurance staff workers (n = 18), personnel staff (n = 17), and administrators (n = 30) were compared to the profiles of three groups of "professional" employees: engineers (n = 96), social workers (n = 15), and natural scientists (n = 13). The mean score for each of the five thinking styles for each of the six different employment groups was graphed. The graphs revealed two basic patterns of strengths and weaknesses in the thinking styles for the "occupational" groups and for the "professional" groups (Bruvold et al., 1983). Hence, the InQ appears to possess adequate construct validity. However, as with all correlational studies, these data were collected after people found their way into occupations. It is impossible to determine causality—that is, did working in an occupation help develop the thinking skill or was the occupation chosen because of the strength of thinking style. Factor analysis revealed support for five distinct subscales and the item composition of the scales.

COMMENTARY. The InQ assesses one's preferred thinking style(s) among business professionals using a self-administered questionnaire. Scant information was provided about the standardization samples used to assess stability reliability, construct validity, or item development. Profile analysis was offered to support construct validity, and factor analysis of item data provided support for five theoretical factors/subscales. Factor analysis was used to increase confidence regarding the five thinking modes on the InQ alone as well as item membership on each thinking style. The assessment of crucial psychometric qualities of the InQ is not adequate at this time, especially as the data presented were almost 30 years old. It is strongly suggested that an updated manual describe participants in sufficient detail to provide important demographic and other descriptive information. Currently, the InQ is a research tool with promising support for construct validity and test-retest reliability (however, a longer time period would have been more conclusive). Demographic data would be essential to assess the gender and cultural/ethnic makeup of the standardized samples in the development of the InQ. Items comprising the InQ were clever, novel, and brief. Hence, the InQ is a promising research instrument.

SUMMARY. The thinking style InQ questionnaire is a tool to aid in the understanding of one's preferred mode of thinking in solving problems that can be used with groups or individuals. The InQ identifies five thinking styles (Synthesist, Idealist, Pragmatist, Analyst, and Realist) that individuals or groups can use to deal with a situation, interact with people, solve a problem, build teams, and select and incorporate new members. The standardization samples used to establish the psychometric qualities were not adequately described and a revision is certainly overdue. Item selection and the participants used in the item analyses were not sufficiently described, unfortunately. Stability (test-retest) reliability was determined by correlating the scores of two administrations of the InQ to 63 university students; correlations were sufficient to warrant a conclusion that the subscales of the InQ possess moderate stability reliability. Profile analysis of two sets of three different occupational groups was presented in an effort to demonstrate the construct validity of the thinking modes of the InQ. Both approaches led to the conclusion that the questionnaire is stable over time and that different occupational groups reveal different thinking profiles on the InQ.

REVIEWER'S REFERENCE

Bruvold, W. H., Parlette, N., Bramson, R. M., & Bramson, S. J. (1983). An investigation of the item characteristics, reliability, and validity of the Inquiry Mode Questionnaire. *Educational and Psychological Measurement, 43,* 483-493.

Review of InQ: Assessing Your Thinking Profile by AYRES D'COSTA, Associate Professor, Quantitative Research, Measurement, and Evaluation in Education, The Ohio State University, Columbus, OH:

DESCRIPTION. The InQ: Assessing Your Thinking Profile (InQ) claims to measure "How you think," thus helping to make the best use of one's competence and to work well with others. It measures thinking styles rather than personality styles such as measured by the Myers-Briggs Type Indicator (see http://www.discoveryourpersonality.com/MBTI.html). Five thinking styles are identified in the Manual of Administration and Interpretation (p. 4) as descriptive of most human thinking: Synthesist (S): Challenging, integrative, process-oriented; Idealist (I): Receptive, assimilative, need-oriented; Pragmatist (P): Adaptive, incremental, pay-off oriented; Analyst (A): Prescriptive, logical, method-oriented; and Realist (R): Empirical, objective, task-oriented.

This review is based primarily on the set of four materials provided by the publisher to this reviewer. These will be described below. However, given current easy access to the Internet, this reviewer will use the Commentary section to present other materials related to the InQ that should be of interest to prospective users.

The first document, InQ: Assessing your Thinking Profile, includes the InQ instrument, its self-scoring rubric, and some basic interpretation and follow-up suggestions. The five styles, coded SIPAR for convenience, are assessed using a forced-choice technique (ipsative rating scale) with 18 sets of 5 items, 1 item for each of the five styles, in each set. The rating system ranges from 1 = *Least like you* to 5 = *Most like you.* Ratings 2, 3, and 4 have appropriate intermediate meanings. In keeping with the psychometric forced-choice technique, each of these five ratings must be utilized within the set. Given 18 sets, the InQ has a total of 90 items. In effect, each of the five styles is assessed using a measurement subscale with 18 items. Each set provides five options, each representing a specific way of thinking, that relate to the five styles and may be randomly ordered.

The self-scoring approach is quite simple in that the candidate can tear out the three sheets with the 18 sets of items, which reveals the scoring rubric (key). The instructions provide a simple check to ensure that the responses are valid (total of all responses must equal 270), and one can then proceed to calculate the raw scores for each of the five styles.

A quick interpretation is based on these raw scores that can range from as high as 90 (5 points x 18 items), or as low as 18 (1 point x 18 items). Specific interpretations suggested are: 72 or higher = dominant approach; 66 to 71 = strong preference; 60 to 65 = moderate preference; 49 to 59 = neutral; 41 to 48 = moderate inclination against; 35 to 40 = strong inclination against; and 34 or lower = predisposition against.

Further interpretation is based on "preference for using two or more thinking styles in combinations: not as a blend but rather using one with another, for whatever reasons" (test booklet, p. 14). Some combinations of styles are common (e.g., Idealist-Analyst, Analyst-Realist, Synthesist-Idealist) but "all combinations can create some element of internal conflict within the person, when the contrasting values are brought together, and all can be of great value when the complementary values are emphasized" (test booklet, p. 14). The InQ then proceeds to present specific ways to augment each style and implications for working with others.

The second document, InQ Your Thinking Profile: Manual of Administration and Interpretation, includes a detailed guide on using and interpreting the instrument. This manual provides an "Agenda" for a seminar to introduce and discuss the InQ. There are some supplementary follow-up materials and exercises to utilize thinking strategies to augment one's thinking style and to influence others, including use in business settings for team-building.

This booklet also doubles as a skeletal technical manual with a few research notes showing item analyses, and test-retest correlations. These will be discussed in the Technical section of this review. The graphic profiles designed to show different occupational norms (in terms of the five InQ styles) for some 14 miscellaneous job types (pp. 68–70) look identical and appear to reflect a printing error.

The third document, Occupational Norm Profiles, is a four-page leaflet showing the style profiles of the 14 selected job types and is obviously an errata sheet for the relevant section of the manual, although not indicated as such. It is not clear how these 14 jobs would be representative of jobs in the business world. The small sample sizes and the job titles suggest a norms list of convenience. Given the specificity of interpreting profiles, it is not clear how one interprets profiles based on the five styles.

The fourth document is a copy of the journal article by Bruvold, Parlette, Bramson, and Bramson (1983), entitled "An Investigation of the Item Characteristics, Reliability, and Validity of the Inquiry Mode Questionnaire," published in *Educational and Psychological Measurement*. As suggested by the title, this article provides some limited technical information about the development of the instrument, which will be discussed in the Technical section of this review.

TECHNICAL. The rationale for the InQ is not provided in the manual, which is essentially a guide for using the instrument. However, the rationale is somewhat sketchily presented in the Bruvold et al. (1983) article. It suggests that the InQ "grew out of an interest in the apparent disparity between intelligence and decision-making competence" (p. 485) in business. One useful reference supporting this idea but not found in the manual is Sternberg (1999).

No instrument suitable for business application was apparently found through the literature search that was conducted by the test authors, and Kolb (1974) is mentioned in the Bruvold et al. article as a typical classroom application. However, a Google search did find at least one other four-scale instrument (see http://www.thelearningweb.net/personalthink.html).

Some sources from Western philosophy (e.g., Hegel, Kant, Singer, Leibniz, and Locke) are referenced in the introductory text of the article but not discussed. Also Bruner, Goodman, and Austin (1956) are cursorily mentioned, but again not discussed. There is a suggestion that the inquiry modes articulated by Mitroff and Pondy (1974) might have resulted in the InQ. The journal article states that a basic assumption underlying the InQ is that there are a limited number of ways of thinking, which influence how one attends to data, assesses problems, and chooses alternatives.

The InQ began with 24 items, was pretested on 400 professionals, and was subsequently reduced to 18 items and administered to 2,000 persons. The journal article presents a "correlational item analysis" using the 18 items as its basis. An item-scale 18 x 5 correlation matrix is presented. Apparently each item score (18 per scale) is correlated with its own scale score and the other 4 scale scores. It would appear to this reviewer that the 18 items would be different for each of the 5 scales, although referencing the same set of 18 themes. Regardless, the interpretation of these data, typically used to justify item-scale assignment, is not possible with this matrix, other than to note that almost all of the *r*s are reported to be statistically significant.

The Bruvold et al. (1983) article also presents test-retest reliabilities (the interval between testing sessions was 6 weeks) in the .61 to .75 range (*N* = 63), which appear low or moderate. The among-scales intercorrelation coefficients are all negative, ranging from -.02 to -.49, suggesting that the five styles are relatively different or independent. Spearman rank correlation coefficients are used to suggest the stability of the SIPAR profiles. Validity was presumably checked by using profile analysis and factor analysis. No statistical results are presented, and the reader is invited to write the test authors for such details. This reviewer was reassured because the test authors noted serious psychometric deficiencies for all except six job titles, because of small sample sizes. Also factor analysis problems are noted because of the ipsative nature of the data and the weak reliability of the scales. Super (1973) noted such problems with his Work Values Inventory. Ipsative ratings tend to artificially exaggerate score ranges, while at the same time rendering them unstable when different sets of specific items are combined into the ispative sets. In other words, the ipsative ratings tend to become dependent on the specific items in the set, and thus compromise both reliability and validity.

COMMENTARY. This reviewer sought additional technical materials from the Internet using a Google Scholar search for "thinking styles." To my surprise, I found an identical instrument at http://web.mit.edu. It has almost the same five SIPAR styles, 18 item sets, and 90 items in total. It is recommended for team-building, but it does not appear to reference the InQ. No scoring key is provided at this site, but the responses may be sent for free scoring.

In searching for a more in-depth discussion of the theoretical underpinnings of the InQ, this reviewer found the presentation on "Cognitive Style" by Wikipedia most useful (see http://en.wikipedia.org/wiki/CognitiveStyle). One is tempted to contrast the InQ multidimensional model with existing personality models, such as the MBTI, which uses a bipolar model based on Carl Jung's theory. Such linkages are needed, as they would provide theoretical meaning and justification for this tool. Furthermore, the psychological terms utilized by InQ, namely its thinking styles, would become more clear if correlated with existing psychological terms prevalent in the personality styles and cognitive styles literature.

An article by Harrison and Bramson (1987) includes the five SIPAR styles, plus a sixth style, "Spiritually-Guided," that is not mentioned by the InQ. Another interesting find on the InQ is the article "I think I am, therefore.... An Inquiry into the thinking styles of IT executives and professionals" by DeLisi and Danielson available at the website: http://www.org-synergies.com/Thinking-Styles.htm. This article discusses the advantages of the InQ thinking-styles approach for IT executives over a personality-styles instrument such as the Myers Briggs Type Indicator (1980), suggesting that the latter would create defensiveness and misunderstanding. An interesting study based on 19 IT groups (*N* = 339) is presented, along with a list of references.

It seems clear to this reviewer that InQ-type assessments are much needed in the business world, and that the InQ has supported some developmental efforts at the university level. The lack of psychometric support for the InQ is obvious, indicating a coherent technical manual following the guidelines prescribed by joint *Standards for Educational and Psychological Testing* (AERA, APA, & NCME, 1999) an immediate necessity.

REVIEWER'S REFERENCES

American Educational Research Association, American Psychological Association, & National Council on Measurement in Education. (1999). *Standards for educational and psychological testing*. Washington, DC: AERA.

Bruvold, W. H., Parlette, N., Bramson, R. M., & Bramson, S. J. (1983). An investigation of the item characteristics, reliability, and validity of the Inquiry Mode Questionnaire. *Educational and Psychological Measurement, 43*, 483-493.

Harrison, A. F., & Bramson, R. M. (1987). *The art of thinking*. Berkeley, CA: Berkeley Publishing Group.

Sternberg, R. J. (1999). *Thinking styles*. London, UK: Cambridge University Press.

Super, D. E. (1973). The Work Values Inventory. In D. G. Zytowski (Ed.), *Contemporary approaches to interest measurement* (pp. 189-205). Minneapolis: University of Minnesota Press.

[60]

Instruments for Assessing Understanding & Appreciation of Miranda Rights.

Purpose: Designed for use in forensic settings to assess an individual's ability to waive their Miranda Rights in a "voluntary, knowing, and intelligent" manner.

Population: Juveniles and adults.

Publication Date: 1998.

Scores, 4: Comprehension of Miranda Rights, Comprehension of Miranda Rights–Recognition, Comprehension of Miranda Vocabulary, Function of Rights in Interrogation.

Administration: Individual.

Price Data, 2007: $99.95 per complete kit including testing easel, 20 test forms, and manual (104 pages); $64.95 per testing easel; $20 per 20 test forms; $26.95 per manual.

Time: 50(60) minutes.

Author: Thomas Grisso.

Publisher: Professional Resource Press.

Review of Instruments for Assessing Understanding & Appreciation of Miranda Rights by JOE W. DIXON, Forensic Psychologist and Lawyer, Private Practice, Greenville, NC:

DESCRIPTION. The Instruments for Assessing Understanding & Appreciation of Miranda Rights by Thomas Grisso is a set of four instruments that assist clinicians in conducting an assessment of a defendant's competency to have waived his Miranda rights. The stated purpose of the instruments is to provide forensically trained mental health professionals with a standardized instrument to aid in the assessment of a criminal defendant's cognitive capacity to understand and appreciate his or her legal rights under Miranda.

The Miranda decision (Miranda v. Arizona, 384 U.S. 436 (1966)) identified specific legal rights afforded to criminal suspects who are taken into custody that must be presented to the suspect before questioning by the police. Typically, these rights are simply read to the suspect by the police. These rights are sometimes not fully understood or appreciated by the suspect, and when that occurs, lawyers subsequently may challenge the admissibility of statements given during custodial interrogation, usually a confession. The central legal issue then becomes whether or not the suspect had the mental capacity to understand and appreciate his or her rights, and whether the waiver of his or her rights was valid. When this legal challenge occurs, more and more frequently lawyers and the courts are turning to mental health professionals to assist in addressing these challenges.

The four instruments developed by Grisso are administered face-to-face with the examinee. The first instrument, Comprehension of Miranda (CMR), assesses understanding of the Miranda warning by having the examinee paraphrase the actual warnings typically read by the police. The four warnings are read one at a time to the examinee, and the examinee is asked to tell, in his or her words, what the warning means. Rules provided for scoring responses are: 2 points if adequate, 1 point if questionable, and 0 points if inadequate. Normative data are provided in the comprehensive examiner's manual for both adolescents and adults.

The second instrument, Comprehension of Miranda Rights-Recognition (CMR-R), presents three interpretations to each of the four warnings and asks the examinee to decide if the interpretation is the same or different from the actual warning. In this manner, examinees who lack sufficient language to validly complete the CMR can demonstrate comprehension of the warnings. One point is given for each correct answer to the 12 interpretations. Again, normative data are supplied in the manual for comparison purposes.

The third instrument, Comprehension of Miranda Vocabulary (CMV), asks the examinee to define six key words that appear in the warnings. Each word is first stated and then read in a sentence. Rules for awarding points are the same as in the CMR, and results are compared with normative data furnished in the manual.

The fourth and final instrument, Function of Rights in Interrogation (FRI), seeks to assess the examinee's comprehension or appreciation of the significance of the Miranda rights in the context of a police interrogation. The FRI attempts to determine three key issues: (a) if the examinee knew he or she could stop the interrogation and ask for a lawyer, (b) if the examinee appreciated the legal jeopardy associated with the interrogation, and, (c) if the examinee knew he or she had the right to not say anything. The FRI uses picture stimuli with several brief stories and the examinee is asked a set of questions (n = 15 for each picture and story set) about the stories in an effort to ascertain the level of appreciation. Scoring rules are the same as in the CMR, and again, normative comparative data is furnished are the manual.

The instruments include a story-board in easel format for ease of use with the FRI instrument, a comprehensive 94-page manual, and a package of 4-page scoring protocols (n = 20) for recording the examinee's responses and the examiner's notes. The test author provides in the well-written manual a rationale for the instruments in the context of the history of the Miranda decision, as well as pointing out strengths and weaknesses of the instruments. The manual contains normative data on adults and adolescents and a detailed description of the instruments and their use. Thus, an experienced examiner who is well trained in forensic examinations for the courts can become well versed and prepared to conduct Miranda examinations with these instruments.

DEVELOPMENT. Each of the four instruments was developed independently, and then were combined into the Instruments fo Assessing Understanding and Appreciation of Miranda Rights.

The test author asserts that primary evidence for the validity of the Miranda instruments derives from the original NIMH research study for which the four instruments were developed. For a discussion of the NIMH study and detailed results, see Grisso (1981) and Grisso (1986).

Reliability data are provided for the CMR (interscorer agreement ranged from .92 to .94 for total CMR scores), CMV (agreement ranged from .97 to .98 for total CMV scores), and FRI (agreement ranged from .94 to .96 for total FRI scores). The test author explained that no tests of reliability were necessary for the CMR-R because scoring is totally objective and requires no subjective judgment. Content validity was established by using the police Miranda warnings; however, actual wording of the warnings varies by jurisdiction throughout the U.S. Users will need to give this careful consideration. Results indicated that total scores for all four instruments were significantly and positively correlated with age and IQ. Overall, reliability findings are excellent.

TECHNICAL. The instruments were originally validated in a study funded by the NIMH. The NIMH funding process subjects the research methodology, data acquisition, and analysis to close scrutiny. Thus, the instruments and the original normative data received rather stringent peer review from the inception. Subsequent to publication of the instruments, numerous studies have utilized the instruments and reported favorable findings (e.g., Fulero & Everington, 1995, 2004).

Juvenile subjects for the original NIMH study were 431 youths ranging in age from 10 to 16 years, approximately 60% were male, 73% were white, and all had been arrested and detained. Adults were 260 subjects ranging in age from 17 to 50 years including 203 male and female volunteers on probation or parole. About 80% were male, and 40% were white. For the nonoffender adults, 57 volunteers who had no legal status were obtained from a variety of settings in the St. Louis, Missouri area.

The normative data in the manual provide for comparison with juvenile, adult offender, adult nonoffender, and total adult groups for each of the four instruments. In total, there are 12 tables providing means by group, correlations with IQ and age, and graphical plots of the data. Also useful for examiners are the normative data broken down by age and IQ level.

In a study of use patterns of forensic psychologists, Ryba, Brodsky, and Shlosberg (2007) reported a perceived weakness of the Grisso instruments due to outdated norms. Apparently, the original norms collected in the NIMH study (circa 1980) are published in the current manual. This was a criticism also made by Rogers et al. (2004), and acknowledged by Grisso (2004). Goldstein, Condie, and Kalbeitzer (2005) reported that a revision of the instruments with more comprehensive and current norms is underway.

Most commentators find the instruments to be acceptable and endorse their use (Frumkin, 2000; Goldstein et al., 2005; Oberlander, Goldstein, & Goldstein, 2003). In a survey of forensic experts, Lally (2003) reported that 88% of respondents found the instruments acceptable, and 55% recommended the instruments in Miranda evaluations. In a survey of forensic psychologists' test usage patterns, Archer, Buffington-Vollum, Stredny, and Handel (2006) reported Grisso's instruments to be the fourth most frequently utilized out of 10 instruments surveyed (34 of 86 respondents reporting use at some level). This use level was considered very favorable because Miranda evaluations are not as common as Competency to Stand Trial evaluations or Insanity evaluations (Ryba et al., 2007).

COMMENTARY. Miranda warnings vary in their wording by jurisdiction, but they all must contain four essential elements: (a) one has the right to remain silent, (b) any statements one makes can be used in court, (c) one has the right to an attorney, and (d) an attorney will be appointed if one cannot be afforded. The Miranda court held that when a suspect waives these rights, he must do so "voluntarily, knowingly, and intelligently" (West v. U.S., 1968). Voluntarily is more of a question for the circumstances under which statements of a confession were made arguably outside the purview of a forensic examiner; however, knowingly and intelligently are clearly cognitive capacities for which the Grisso instruments are well suited to assess. Other factors are also included in a retrospective Miranda evaluation, such as intelligence, age, and suggestibility, but these are outside the scope of the Grisso instruments. The instruments properly focus upon the cognitive capacity of the examinee to have current understanding and appreciation of his or her constitutional rights, and the examiner must then use best clinical judgment as to whether or not the present level of understanding was extant at the time of the waiver. The manual explains that prior training and experience of the examiner must be relied upon to achieve the reconstructive aspect of the Miranda evaluation.

These instruments provide a standardized methodology for assessing cognitive capacity to have waived constitutional rights. Scoring is rather straightforward and objective with examples of correct responses provided. The instruments offer a structured framework to describe examination results to the court, and they provide an empirical basis for opinions and conclusions formulated by the examiner. Also, an examiner may spot inconsistencies in responses, that is, answering correctly in one instrument but incorrectly in another instrument on the same information or concept. This may provide insight into the degree the examinee may be attempting to manipulate the examination process.

Scores on the four instruments have not as yet been subjected to external criteria for legal competency to have waived Miranda, which can only be determined by a court of law. The test author argues that such an outcome comparison would be illogical because the instruments measure cognitive capacity to understand and appreciate at the time of the evaluation and not at some prior time when the waiver of Miranda was actually given to the police by the examinee. Nonetheless, this is a relative weakness because the examinee's current understanding and appreciation is relied upon by the examiner to formulate the reconstructive mental state upon which testimonial opinion is based. Rogers, Jordan, and Harrison (2004) have criticized the instruments because of this lack of validity testing, as well as negligible documentation regarding test construction, ecological validity, and reliability for use in forensic practice. Grisso (2004) explains that such criticisms are unwarranted because the purpose of the instruments is to simply assess current understanding and appreciation and not understanding and appreciation at some prior time. The nature of a Miranda evaluation, however, is reconstructive in nature and the concerns expressed by Rogers et al. (2004) are justified.

In 1993, the U.S. Supreme Court rendered a decision that set out guidelines for the admissibility of scientific evidence, which was later elaborated upon in a subsequent decision to include technical and other evidence (Daubert, 1993; Kumho Tire, 1999). These guidelines include falsifiability, peer review and publication, known or potentially known error rate, and general acceptance. Considering these admissibility guidelines, it is apparent that the Grisso instruments have been peer reviewed and have received wide general acceptance in the field. The instruments are not intended to absolutely determine competency to have waived rights in a yes-no fashion, but are rather intended to assist the forensic examiner in reaching a conclusion on that question. As such, the test author argues rather convincingly that the "error test" of Daubert does not apply. Finally, there remains the question of falsifiability–can the test be fooled by a clever examinee? There are no built-in, validated validity scales. The ultimate reconstructive opinion is that of the examining clinician, based in part upon the results obtained with the instruments and other data collected. The manual cites numerous appellate courts that have taken notice of the instruments and found the results relevant and reliable when questions of waiver of Miranda rights were raised.

As with all forensic examinations conducted for the courts, mental health professionals must be specially trained in forensic issues and have received supervised experience in conducting forensic examinations. This is especially important in conducting retrospective evaluations such as competency to have waived Miranda rights. Professionals with the prerequisite training and experience will find great utility in the Grisso instruments.

A revised version of the instruments is reportedly under development, but as yet has not appeared. The revision is expected to contain updated, more comprehensive normative data, as well as a fifth instrument (Goldstein et al., 2005). The fifth instrument will assess Perceptions of Coercion in Holding and Interrogation Procedures, to assess the examinee's probability of having provided a false confession. If this latter task can, indeed, be accomplished, it will be warmly received by the forensic community.

SUMMARY. Grisso's Instruments for Assessing Understanding and Appreciation of Miranda Rights provides the only standardized test available to forensic examiners to assist in Miranda evaluations. Fortunately, the four Grisso instruments are functional in that they achieve their stated purpose, they are easy to use, and they are very useful in the examination of current cognitive capacity to understand and appreciate Miranda rights. These instruments will have even greater utility when the revised version is published.

REVIEWER'S REFERENCES

Archer, R. P., Buffington-Vollum, J. K., Stredny, R. V., & Handel, R. W. (2006). A survey of psychological test use patterns among forensic psychologists. *Journal of Personality Assessment, 87,* 85-95.

Daubert v. Merrell Dow Pharmaceuticals, Inc., 113 s. Ct. 2786 (1993).

Frumkin, B. (2000). Competency to waive Miranda rights: Clinical and legal issues. *Mental & Physical Disability Law Reporter, 42,* 326-331.

Fulero, S. M., & Everington, C. (1995). Assessing competency to waive Miranda rights in defendants with mental retardation. *Law & Human Behavior, 19,* 533-543.

Fulero, S. M., & Everington, C. (2004). Assessing the capacity of persons with mental retardation to waive Miranda rights: A jurisprudent therapy perspective. *Law & Psychology Review, 28,* 53-69.

Goldstein, N. E. S., Condie, L. O., & Kalbeitzer, R. (2005). Instruments for Assessing Understanding and Appreciation of Miranda Rights. In T. Grisso, G. Vincent, & D. Seagrave (Eds.), *Mental health screening and assessment in juvenile justice* (pp. 357-369). New York: Guilford.

Grisso, T. (1981). *Juveniles' waiver of rights: Legal and psychological competence.* New York: Plenum.

Grisso, T. (1986). *Evaluating competencies: Forensic assessments and instruments.* New York: Plenum.

Grisso, T. (2004). Reply to "A critical review of published competence-to-confess measures." *Law & Human Behavior, 29,* 719-724.

Kumho Tire Co. v. Carmichael, 526 U.S. 137 (1999).

Lally, S. J. (2003). What tests are acceptable for use in forensic evaluations?: A survey of experts. *Professional Psychology: Research & Practice, 34,* 491-498.

Miranda v. Arizona, 384 U.S. 436 (1966).

Oberlander, L. B., Goldstein, N. E., & Goldstein, A. M. (2003). Competence to confess. In A. M. Goldstein & I. B. Weiner (Eds.), *Handbook of psychology, Vol. II: Forensic psychology* (pp. 335–357). New York: John Wiley.

Rogers, R., Jordan, M. J., & Harrison, K. S. (2004). A critical review of published competency-to-confess measures. *Law & Human Behavior, 28,* 707-718.

Ryba, N. L., Brodsky, S. L., & Shlosberg, A. (2007). Evaluations of capacity to waive Miranda rights: A survey of practitioners' use of the Grisso instruments. *Assessment, 14,* 300-309.

West v. U.S., 399 F.2d 467 (1968).

Review of the Instruments for Assessing Understanding & Appreciation of Miranda Rights by MARC JANOSON, President, Forensic Psychology PC, Manhasset, NY, and THOMAS LAZZARO, Forensic Psychologist in Independent Practice, Syracuse, NY:

DESCRIPTION. The Instruments for Assessing Understanding & Appreciation of Miranda Rights offers a direct, norm-based assessment of criminal defendants' capacity for understanding and appreciating Miranda Warnings. The abilities measured are related to the legal concepts of a "knowing and intelligent" waiver. The instrument is much less relevant to the issue of "voluntariness" of the waiver of rights, that is, whether or not a defendant's waiver was or was not the product of coercion.

Four subscales were developed by Thomas Grisso to assess whether a defendant can accurately perceive and appreciate the functions and significance of the Miranda Rights:

Comprehension of Miranda Rights (CMR) is a 4-item subtest that presents each element of the Miranda Warnings and requires the defendant to explain in his or her own words the meaning of each Miranda element.

Comprehension of Miranda Rights–Recognition (CMR-R) is a 12-item subtest that asks the defendant to identify whether statements are the same as or different from the elements of the warnings. The CMR-R was developed to provide a less verbally expressive measure of Miranda understanding.

Comprehension of Miranda Vocabulary (CMV) is a 6-item subtest that asks the defendant to give definitions for 6 key words that appear in this (an outdated St. Louis County, Missouri) version of the Miranda Warnings. The CMV is often considered the least helpful of the four subtests due to the many local variants of the Miranda Warnings and the fact that the actual Miranda waiver form defendants typically sign often contains fewer than four of these six words.

Function of Rights in Interrogation (FRI) utilizes hypothetical police interrogation vignettes to determine whether the defendant understands the function of rights in the context of arrest and interrogation. The FRI is the only subtest that addresses the issue of appreciation (the intelligent prong) of the Miranda Rights Waiver. CMR, CMR-R, and CMV are more relevant to the issue of understanding (the knowing prong) of the Miranda Rights Waiver.

DEVELOPMENT. The original version of the four subtests first appeared in an appendix in the book *Juveniles' Waiver of Rights: Legal and Psychological Competence* (Grisso, 1981). The formal version of the Grisso test was published in 1998. The published version has an examiner's scoring manual, record and scoring forms, and an easel-style book that presents the test items.

All four subtests have scoring guidelines presented in the manual. The manual has normative data derived from Grisso's research in the 1970s on the performances of 431 youth and 260 adults (Frumkin, 2000). Tables providing mean scores across different age and intelligence levels are provided.

Rogers, Jordan, and Harrison (2004) and Rogers and Shuman (2005) have published highly critical reviews of the tests. They assert that the Grisso tests purport to assess the legal construct of Miranda competency. However, the manual explicitly states that "The Miranda measures are a helpful adjunct in Miranda waiver evaluations when combined with other assessment data" (manual, p. 4). The validity of a Miranda waiver is based on the "Totality of the Circumstances" present during police interrogation (Frumkin, 2000).

Rogers and Shuman (2005) state that the Grisso tests do not meet the scientific requirements of forensic psychology (the Frye and Daubert standards) because, in their opinion, the Grisso tests are not generally accepted by the scientific community. However, the Grisso tests are generally accepted by the community of forensic psychologists performing Competence to Waive Miranda (CWM) evaluations as suggested by Lally (2003), who surveyed a sample of diplomats in forensic psychology and found that the Grisso tests were rated as accepted by the majority of the diplomats (88%) who perform Competence to Waive Miranda (CMW) evaluations. Most Miranda experts have endorsed the use of Grisso's Miranda instruments in CMW evaluations (Frumkin, 2000; Goldstein, Condie, & Kalbeitzer, 2005; Oberlander, Goldstein, & Goldstein, 2003).

TECHNICAL.

Standardization. Juvenile subjects included 431 youths, ages 10 to 16. Adult subjects included 260 individuals from age 17 to age 50.

Reliability. Grisso indicates in the test manual that interscorer reliability is quite good for evaluators who are trained scorers. He reports correlation coefficients for total CMR ranging from .92 to .96.

"To examine test-retest reliability, a sample of youths was administered the CMR during their first day in a detention center and again during the third day" (manual, p. 10). The Pearson *r* coefficient was .84 for the 24 youths in the study. In a series of tests of interscorer reliability of the FRI scoring system, Pearson *r* coefficients were between .94 and .96 for the FRI total scores.

Validity. Content validity is suggested by the fact that the "CMR, CMR-R, and CMV take their content from warnings that police officers" (manual, p. 14) actually administer. Construct validity is reflected in the fact that "all four measures are significantly and positively related to age and IQ" (manual, p. 14).

Concurrent validity is reflected in that the CMR correlates with the CMV (r = .67) more substantially than either of these measures correlates with IQ. The CMR correlates with the CMR-R (r = .55) more substantially than either of them correlates with IQ. The results suggest that similar abilities contribute to performance on all three measures. It appears that the common content of the three measures results in performances that are not solely an artifact of general cognitive ability.

COMMENTARY. The Grisso tests should continue to be used as one part of an overall comprehensive assessment in Miranda Comprehension Waiver evaluations. The test manual describes the measure as a "helpful adjunct in Miranda waiver evaluations when combined with other assessment data" (manual, p. 4). The test is an objective, standardized instrument relevant to an individual's ability to comprehend and appreciate the Miranda Warnings and Rights at the time of interrogation.

Many of the criticisms of the Grisso tests offered by Rogers and Shuman (2005) are valid. The generic Miranda Warning presented in the Grisso tests is outdated. In addition, there are numerous variations of the Miranda Warnings in use in the U.S. which means that the defendant's performance on the Grisso Miranda Warning diminishes in relevance as a function of how different the Grisso Miranda Warnings are from the actual warnings administered to defendants. Questions about the validity of generalizing from the Grisso Miranda Warnings to the actual warnings are often raised.

Rogers and Shuman (2005) are correct in opining that the statistical foundation of the Grisso test is limited and somewhat inadequate. Updated and expanded normative data are sorely needed. A more comprehensive statistical analysis of the updated and expanded data also would be appropriate.

The current reviewers note that the Grisso test has no scale specifically designed to assess or detect malingering. Therefore, the forensic evaluator must also administer psychological tests that assess malingering of cognitive and/or psychological impairments in any Comprehension of Miranda Warning evaluation.

SUMMARY. The Grisso test continues to be a useful part of a Competence of a Miranda Waiver Evaluation. Forensic evaluators are urged to use the Grisso measures in a manner consistent with the cautions noted by Grisso and others who have published protocols for conducting CMW evaluations (DeClue, 2005; Frumkin, 2000; Heilbrun, Marczyk, & DeMatteo 2002). A revision of the measure with more contemporary Miranda

Warnings; updated, expanded, and more statistically robust norms; and with another test relevant to the voluntary prong of the waiver would signal substantial improvements.

REVIEWER'S REFERENCES

DeClue, G. (2005). Psychological consultation in cases involving interrogations and confessions. *Journal of Psychiatry and Law, 33,* 313-358.

Frumkin, I. B. (2000). Competency to waive Miranda rights: Clinical and legal issues. *Mental and Physical Disability Law Reporter, 24,* 326-331.

Goldstein, N. E. S., Condie, L. O., & Kalbeitzer, R. (2005). Instruments for Assessing Understanding and Appreciation of Miranda Rights. In T. Grisso, G. Vincent & D. Seagrave (Eds.), *Mental health screening and assessment in juvenile justice* (pp. 357-369). New York: Guilford.

Grisso, T. (1981). *Juveniles waiver of rights: Legal and psychological competence.* New York: Plenum Press.

Heilbrun, K., Marczyk, G. R., & DeMatteo, D. (2002). *Forensic mental health assessment: A casebook.* London: Oxford University Press.

Lally, S. J. (2003). What tests are acceptable for use in forensic evaluations?: A survey of experts. *Professional Psychology: Research and Practice, 34,* 491-498.

Oberlander, L. B., Goldstein, N. E., & Goldstein, A. M. (2003). Competence to confess. In A. M. Goldstein & I. B. Weiner (Eds.), *Handbook of psychology, Vol. 11: Forensic psychology* (pp. 335-357). New York: John Wiley.

Rogers, R., Jordan, M., & Harrison, K. (2004). A critical review of published competency-to-confess measures. *Law and Human Behavior, 28, 707-718.*

Rogers, R., & Shuman, D. (2005). *Fundamentals of forensic practice: Mental health and criminal law.* New York: Springer.

[61]

Inventory of Offender Risk, Needs, and Strengths.

Purpose: Designed "to identify static, dynamic, and protective factors related to offender risk, treatment need, and management."
Population: Ages 18 and older.
Publication Date: 2006.
Acronym: IORNS.
Scores, 28: Overall Risk Index, Static Risk Index, Criminal Orientation, Psychopathy, Intra/Interpersonal Problems, Alcohol Drug Problems, Aggression, Negative Social Influence, Dynamic Need Index, Personal Resources, Environmental Resources, Protective Strength Index, Favorable Impression, Procriminal Attitudes, Irresponsibility, Manipulativeness, Impulsivity, Angry Detachment, Esteem Problems, Relational Problems, Hostility, Aggressive Behaviors, Negative Friends, Negative Family, Cognitive/Behavioral Regulation, Anger Regulation, Education/Training, Inconsistent Response Style.
Administration: Individual or group.
Price Data, 2008: $142 per professional manual (129 pages), 25 response forms, and 25 scoring summary/profile forms.
Time: (20) minutes.
Author: Holly A. Miller.
Publisher: Psychological Assessment Resources, Inc.

Review of the Inventory of Offender Risk, Needs, and Strengths by SHERI BAUMAN, Associate Professor, Department of Educational Psychology, University of Arizona, Tucson, AZ:

DESCRIPTION. The Inventory of Offender Risk, Needs, and Strengths (IORNS) is a 130-item self-report measure that provides information about offender risk that is useful in "assessment, treatment and management" (professional manual, p. 29). The inventory yields scores on four indices, 8 scales, 14 subscales, and two validity scales. According to the test author, respondents typically complete the inventory in between 15 and 20 minutes. The inventory is written at a third grade reading level and has been standardized on both male (ages 18 through 75) and female (ages 18 through 60) offenders and community adults of both genders (the female community standardization sample included individuals through age 75). Respondents record answers (*True* or *False*, with 5 items having an additional *Not Applicable* response option) on a carbonless response form. Directions and examples are provided on the cover, with the items printed on the two inner facing sheets. Scoring is accomplished using the schematic provided on the response form. A scoring summary form is then used to record the scores, *T* scores, percentiles, normative group used, and classification of risk level (low, average, high, or very high) by individual scales. An Overall Risk Score is calculated by summing the risk scores and subtracting protective strengths. An Inconsistent Response Scale score is also obtained and recorded on the summary form. The reverse side of the form provides a graphic representation of the respondent's profile. There are three indices: Static Risk, Dynamic Need, and Protective Strength. The scales that comprise the Dynamic Need Index are Criminal Orientation (subscales: Procriminal Attitudes and Irresponsibility), Psychopathy (subscales: Manipulativeness, Impulsivity, and Angry Detachment), Intra/Interpersonal Problems (subscales: Esteem Problems and Relational Problems), Alcohol/Drug Problems, Aggression (subscales: Hostility and Aggressive Behaviors), and Negative Social Influences (subscales: Negative Friends and Negative Family). The Protective Strength Index includes Personal Resources (subscales: Cognitive/Behavioral Regulation, Anger Regulation, and Education/Training) and Environmental Resources.

DEVELOPMENT. The manual presents a compelling case for the need for this inventory. The self-report method was selected for efficiency and ease of use, but the author emphasizes that inherent limitations of self-report instruments make it imperative that this instrument not be used as the sole determinant of risk status of any offender. In addition, the potential for problematic response styles to influence scores is noted, but the inclusion of a measure of such styles provides useful clinical information. To manage social desirability, negatively worded items were minimized and several items are keyed in the opposite direction from the majority of items in an attempt to minimize the tendency to respond to all items in one direction.

Development of this inventory proceeded systematically, beginning with a review of the literature to identify potential constructs associated with offending behaviors. From the list of constructs, an initial item pool of 201 items was generated, and then piloted on 308 college students, 163 incarcerated male general offenders, and 55 male incarcerated sex offenders. Initial analyses resulted in the elimination of 27 items. The reduced version was re-administered to an additional 115 offenders, and this sample was combined with the previous offender samples for the next phase of the analysis. The factor analysis of the items (excluding the validity items) resulted in the development of scales; two additional factor analyses were conducted on the Dynamic Need/Risk items, and revealed six factors (scales). Those factors were then each subjected to factor analysis to identify subscales.

Five different offender samples, including males and females, were utilized in development of normative data; a community sample was also included for comparative purposes. The manual provides complete demographic information about those samples. The manual presents means and standard deviations by age groups for both offender and community samples.

TECHNICAL. Internal consistency coefficients are provided for all scales and subscales for both offender and community samples. The coefficient for the Overall Risk Index is .88 for both male and female offender samples, and .90 and .85 for male and female community samples, respectively. Coefficients for the three main indices (Static Risk Index, Dynamic Need Index, and Protective Strength Index) range from .76 to .90 for male offenders and .64 to .91 for female offenders. For community samples, coefficients for these indices ranged from .68 to .90. For most scale and subscale scores (20 of 26 for male offenders and 15 of 26 for females), coefficients were above the recommended .70, with similar outcomes with the community samples. Test-retest reliability was computed for a sample of 100 college students with a 21-day interval between administrations. Correlations range from .42 for Irresponsibility to .89 for Aggressive Behaviors. The data presented provide sufficient evidence of the reliability, both internal consistency and stability, of this measure.

Content validity determination relied on the systematic identification of constructs, which was based on a comprehensive literature review. In addition, expert review was used to evaluate the content validity of items. Construct validity was considered by correlating the scores obtained on the IORNS with the extent of respondents' criminal history. IORNS scores were more strongly correlated with number of nonviolent crimes and number of times in jail or prison than with a history of violent or sexual crimes. In addition, correlations were reported between IORNS scores and scores on the LSI-R (Level of Service Inventory—Revised), the PAI (Personality Assessment Inventory), several measures of psychopathology (Levenson's Self-Report Psychopathy Scale and the Self-Report Psychopathy Scale), a measure of substance abuse (Substance Abuse Subtle Screening Inventory; SASSI-3), depression (Center for Epidemiological Studies-Depression; CES-DI) and anxiety (State-Trait Anxiety Inventory). The number of correlations reported in the manual is extensive, and there is considerable variation among them. The totality of these analyses provides evidence of good convergent and discriminant validity with other measures and history. The author acknowledges the need for further psychometric studies with specific groups of offenders (e.g., perpetrators of domestic violence) and further study with female offenders. There is also a need for future studies of predictive validity.

COMMENTARY. This inventory shows promise as part of an assessment protocol for offenders when it is necessary to estimate comparative risk for re-offense. The inclusion of both static and dynamic risk factors, along with protective factors, provides a more complete picture of the risk potential profile than assessment tools that focus on only one set of factors. The test author provides ample evidence of sound development practices, and the number of validity studies reported in the manual is impressive. The test author's caveats are important; any such measure should be used in conjunction with other assessments to make critical decisions about risk and treatment. Nevertheless, forensic evaluators should welcome this new tool because of its comprehensive approach and the initial evidence of reliability and validity. There is a great need for such measures in the field.

SUMMARY. The IORNS is a self-report inventory to assess static and dynamic risk factors and protective factors. It can be completed by respondents in less than 20 minutes, and the reading level (third grade) is such that most offenders will be able to complete it independently. The scoring summary form and profile form provide easy-to-understand data about the respondent that will be useful as part of a comprehensive risk assessment. The measure includes two scales to assess the validity of the responses and also provides an overall risk index that combines the scores on all other scales. The profile will be useful to clinicians for treatment planning in addition to risk assessment.

Review of the Inventory of Offender Risk, Needs, and Strengths by GEOFFREY L. THORPE, Professor of Psychology, and LINDSAY R. OWINGS, Doctoral Candidate, University of Maine, Orono, ME:

DESCRIPTION. The Inventory of Offender Risk, Needs, and Strengths (IORNS™) was designed (a) to assess risk factors (static and dynamic need-related) and protective variables in predicting violent behavior or criminal recidivism, and (b) to monitor changes in these behaviors over time or as a result of treatment in identifying specific interventions or management methods. The IORNS is a 130-item true/false self-report measure intended for use with male (18–75 years old) and female (18–60 years old) general, violent, and sexual offenders in correctional or community environments. The package of materials received from the test publisher consists of a vii + 136-page professional manual, a response form, and a scoring summary/profile form.

The 130 items of the IORNS produce scores on 2 validity scales, 4 indexes, 8 scales, and 14 subscales, as follows. *Validity Scales:* Inconsistent Response Style (10 item pairs) and Favorable Impression (13 items). *Indexes*: Overall Risk Index (a composite of the following three indexes, giving a global risk estimate); Static Risk Index (12 items); Dynamic Need Index (79 items); and Protective Strength Index (26 items). *Scales*: Within the Dynamic Need Index, the 6 scales are Criminal Orientation (19 items), Psychopathy (22 items), Intra/Interpersonal Problems (13 items), Alcohol/Drug Problems (7 items), Aggression (11 items), and Negative Social Influence (7 items). Within the Protective Strength Index, the 2 scales are Personal Resources (19 items) and Environmental Resources (7 items). *Subscales*: Drawn from the items of 6 scales, the 14 subscales are: Procriminal Attitudes and Irresponsibility (from the Criminal Orientation scale); Manipulativeness, Impulsivity, and Angry Detachment (from the Psychopathy scale); Esteem Problems and Relational Problems (from the Intra/Interpersonal Problems scale); Hostility and Aggressive Behaviors (from the Aggression scale); Negative Friends and Negative Family (from the Negative Social Influence scale); and Cognitive/Behavioral Regulation, Anger Regulation, and Education/Training (from the Personal Resources scale). All indexes, scales, and subscales may be designated by three-letter abbreviations supplied by the test author.

The Overall Risk Index score indicates the general risk of re-offending, and is considered clinically significant if it falls at or above the 75$^{th.}$ percentile for the normative group appropriate to the offender's age and gender. The other indexes are best interpreted through the *T* scores and percentile ranks for each scale, as significant discrepancies between scales could distort overall index scores. Respondents' subscale scores are qualitatively designated from percentile ranges as *Low, Average, High,* and *Very High,* because truncated raw score ranges attenuate subscale reliabilities and do not permit the computation of dependable *T* scores. Many of the scales and subscales are designed to provide information useful in planning therapeutic interventions and assessing treatment outcomes.

The test author issues appropriate caveats about the professional qualifications needed for administration and interpretation of the IORNS. Test items were written at a third-grade reading level, and the instrument is administered and scored in paper-and-pencil format. The author estimates that the test usually takes about 15 to 20 minutes to complete.

DEVELOPMENT. The IORNS was developed as "a time-efficient and easily administered measure" for use in "offender risk assessment, treatment, and management" (professional manual, p. 29). The self-report format was chosen for convenience and ease of administration, but because of potential distortions attributable to unhelpful response styles the author included validity scales to assess faking good and inconsistency. Items were designed to minimize the influence of social desirability and of yea-saying and nay-saying. The author noted that the IORNS was not intended to be used alone, and was rather constructed to serve as an adjunct to traditional clinical interviewing and a detailed review of the offender's personal history.

Test development began in 2002 with the designation of 16 pertinent constructs and 201 potential test items drawn from a comprehensive literature review. The author proceeded with two phases of item selection and first- and second-order factor analytic work. A preliminary version of the test was administered to 308 students and 218 incarcerated male offenders, and the 174 test items that survived internal consistency and item-scale correlational analyses were administered to a further 115 offenders. Combining the data from the two offender samples produced a set of 333 responses to the 174 items for further analysis. The indexes, scales, and subscales of the IORNS were derived from further refinement of the constructs and a progressive distillation of the test items following a series of three-factor analyses.

TECHNICAL. Five offender samples and a community group, all adults, provided the normative data for the IORNS. The 218 members of the community sample consisted of 107 men and 111 women. They were recruited from multiple geographic regions, and their demographic statistics were similar to the proportions reflected in U.S. Census data. The 482 offenders consisted of 383 men and 99 women. The five offender samples were 163 male incarcerated general offenders from a private prerelease treatment facility in New Jersey; 68 probated general offenders, 111 incarcerated sexual offenders, and 41 probated sexual offenders, all male, in Texas; and 99 incarcerated female general offenders in Washington. Compared with general population norms, there was a disproportionately high number of African American and Latino/Latina individuals in the offender sample; however, those proportions are commensurate with those in typical jail or prison populations.

The professional manual provides detailed norms and sociodemographic statistics for all samples. Four tables present age-stratified mean IORNS raw scores and standard deviations for men and women in the offender and community samples. The manual also appends a series of 48 *T*-score and percentile conversion tables with 90% confidence intervals.

Concerning internal consistency, the values for coefficient alpha for the index scores ranged from .76 to .90 in male offenders and .64 to .91 in female offenders, and from .82 to .90 in the male community sample and .68 to .87 in the female community sample. Scale and subscale reliability statistics are also reported in detail. In general, the indexes, scales, and subscales of the IORNS demonstrated satisfactory internal consistency, but the Inconsistent Response Style scale gave very low values for alpha (.33 in male offenders; .17 in female offenders; .43 in the male community sample; and .13 in the female community sample).

Test-retest stability in a sample of 100 undergraduate students tested on two occasions, 21 days apart, was viewed as "good" for indexes and scales and "quite reasonable" for subscales (ranging from r = .68 to r = .86 for indexes, r = .53 to r = .84 for scales, and r = .42 to r = .89 for subscales) (professional manual, p. 44).

Construct validity was assessed by correlating the IORNS with criminal history variables and with scores on the Level of Service Inventory—Revised (LSI-R) and the Personality Assessment Inventory (PAI). The correlations between the IORNS indexes, scales, and subscales, on the one hand, and specific criminal history variables, on the other, ranged from low to modest in male offenders in New Jersey. The strongest relationship was between the Dynamic Need Index and Times in jail/prison (r = .37).

The IORNS also showed a level of construct overlap with certain LSI-R and PAI scales. For example, in the New Jersey male offender sample the IORNS Overall Risk Index correlated .41 with the LSI-R Total score, and .57 with the PAI Antisocial Features scale.

Data on predictive validity are lacking.

COMMENTARY. This new measure has several attractive qualities, such as the inclusion of various subtypes of offenders, the representation of relatively high proportions of offenders from ethnic minority groups in the normative samples, and the provision of standardization data from adult female offenders. The IORNS allows one to compare results to normative data not only from offenders but also from community samples, with the potential to help inform decisions regarding probation/parole or treatment. The test author acknowledged her commitment to appropriate ethical and professional standards, advising test users to use a multimodal approach to assessment and to use this self-report measure as corroborating information to be used in conjunction with empirically supported assessment methods for determining risks, needs, and protective factors. The suitability of the IORNS as a measure of treatment outcome with suggestions for management is a significant strength; outcome measures are always important, but especially so in an area traditionally associated with disappointing findings for treatment efficacy.

One commentator has called attention to the instrument's lack of demonstrated predictive validity in the context of sex offender evaluations: "The IORNS is designed to collect data that could be relevant to a risk assessment, but at present there are no data showing how an evaluator could use scores . . . to enhance the prediction of future sexual violence. I do not see how the IORNS could be considered acceptable for use in a current [sexually violent predator] evaluation, as part of an assessment related to either the initial civil commitment trial or a review hearing" (DeClue, 2007, p. 57).

The test author included protective strength variables in the IORNS because of their initial plausibility and her desire to seek empirical support for their relevance, because—in her view—they have been somewhat neglected in measures designed for adult populations. It has to be noted that the Level of Service/Case Management Inventory (Andrews, Bonta, & Wormith, 2004) also includes offender strengths in its protocol, and this instrument has the benefit of a huge normative data base of nearly 150,000 respondents. Nonetheless, the IORNS may have an advantage in economy of administration time and ease of use.

The IORNS was designed to include static and dynamic risk factors in an attempt to increase the utility of the measure and provide more information regarding treatment and management. Although certain static risk factors have been identified as important in predicting recidivism (e.g., Quinsey, Harris, Rice, & Cormier, 2006), dynamic factors have not always shown the same utility (e.g., Philipse, Koeter, van der Staak, & van den Brink, 2006).

SUMMARY. The IORNS is a paper-and-pencil self-report instrument for use in correctional and criminal justice settings to determine the level of an offender's static risk, dynamic risk/needs, and protective factors. The 130-item measure provides scores on several indexes, scales, and subscales, all potentially informative, that may be assigned more or less weight according to clinicians' preferences. The test developer has provided a professional manual with extensive documentation of the test's psychometric properties and tabulations of data from 700 offenders and community individuals in the United States. This standardization sample includes a high proportion of ethnic minority offenders and norms for female offenders as well. Test scores provide valuable information regarding protective and dynamic factors that can be useful to therapy providers in determining treatment efficacy and management strategies. The author encourages researchers to seek more data on the predictive validity of risk assessment prior to utilizing this measure for that purpose.

REVIEWERS' REFERENCES

Andrews, D. A., Bonta, J. L., & Wormith, J. S. (2004). *Level of Service/Case Management Inventory (LS/CMI™): An offender assessment system: User's manual.* North Tonawanda, NY: Multi-Health Systems.

DeClue, G. (2007). Inventory of Offender Risks, Needs, and Strengths (IORNS) review. *The Journal of Psychiatry and Law, 35,* 51–60.

Philipse, M. W. G., Koeter, M. W. J., van der Staak, C. P. F., & van den Brink, W. (2006). Static and dynamic patient characteristics as predictors of criminal recidivism: A prospective study in a Dutch forensic psychiatric sample. *Law and Human Behavior, 30,* 309–327.

Quinsey, V. L., Harris, G. T., Rice, M. E., & Cormier, C. A. (2006). *Violent offenders: Appraising and managing risk* (2nd ed.). Washington, DC: American Psychological Association.

[62]

Iowa Gambling Task.

Purpose: Designed to detect impaired decision making that is mediated by the prefrontal cortex.
Population: Ages 18 and over.
Publication Dates: 1992-2007.
Acronym: IGT.
Scores, 4: Block Net, Total Money, Deck Selection Frequency, Net Total.
Administration: Individual.
Price Data, 2008: $499 per complete testing kit including professional manual (2007, 71 pages), administration card, quick start guide, and administration software program; $50 per professional manual.
Time: [15-20] minutes to administer and score.
Comments: Test administered and scored via personal computer.
Author: Antoine Bechara.
Publisher: Psychological Assessment Resources, Inc.

Review of the Iowa Gambling Task by ANITA M. HUBLEY, Professor of Measurement, Evaluation, and Research Methodology, University of British Columbia, Vancouver, British Columbia, Canada:

DESCRIPTION. The Iowa Gambling Task (IGT) is an individually administered computerized measure of decision-making capacity. The goal of the task is to win as much money as possible or, barring that, avoid losing as much money as possible. The examinee is given a $2,000 credit and is presented with four decks consisting of 60 cards each (30 red, 30 black) on the computer screen. Using the mouse, the examinee selects a card from one of the four decks. A message appears indicating the amount of money won and/or lost and a green bar at the top of the screen lengthens or shortens according to the gain or loss. When instructed on-screen, the examinee selects another card. The standard administration consists of 100 selections or trials, although the examinee is only told that at some point the game will stop. In the long run, two decks are disadvantageous with large immediate gains followed by large losses at unpredictable points whereas the other two decks are advantageous with small immediate gains followed by small losses. The decks differ in terms of the frequency of punishment and the average loss per punishment. Although use of the default settings is recommended, the examiner can easily change the intertrial interval, number of trials, and starting amount of money.

Administration of the IGT is straightforward and takes 10 to 15 minutes. The examiner reads a detailed set of instructions about the goal of the task, what the examinee will see on the computer screen, that losses are not at random or based on previous card selections, that some decks are worse than others, that the color of the cards is unrelated to which deck is better, and to treat the money won or lost as though it is real money. Balodis, MacDonald, and Olmstead (2006) demonstrated that it is critical that the instructions be read in full for optimal performance. The following scores are provided by the computer software: (a) total net score (number of cards taken from advantageous decks C' and D' minus the number of cards taken from disadvantageous decks A' and B'), (b) block net scores (computed the same way as the total net score but provided for each block of 20 cards), (c) number of cards selected from each deck, (d) total money (total amount of money won minus the amount borrowed), and (e) reaction time (amount of time it takes an examinee to make a card choice on each selection).

DEVELOPMENT. The development of the IGT stemmed from a desire to measure, in the lab, the decision-making difficulties of patients with damage to the medial orbitofrontal and ventromedial prefrontal cortex. Originally, the 100 trials of the IGT were administered manually using four custom-made decks consisting of 40 cards each (half red, half black; Bechara, Damasio, Damasio, & Anderson, 1994). Facsimile American paper money was used. In computerizing the task, the key changes made were to increase the number of cards per deck and alter the frequency and magnitude of the delayed punishment relative to the immediate reward. As noted in the manual, studies have shown that the use of real money versus facsimile money, varying intertrial intervals, and manual versus computerized administration does not significantly affect IGT performance. More details about the development of the IGT would be helpful, such as the rationale for the default settings selected, the order of each deck, and the selected frequency and magnitude of the delayed punishment relative to the immediate reward for each deck.

TECHNICAL. Demographically corrected normative data were derived from 932 participants aged 18 to 95 years whose education ranged from 3 to 22 years. Although referred to as "normal" participants, no details are provided about the recruitment process, sites, or testing process. Given the percentages of the normative group whose scores are in the impaired range, clearly "normal" does not refer to a strictly unimpaired sample. Although it is claimed in the manual that the normative sample was well-matched to the U.S. population (for gender, age, and education), the ≤12 years of education group and men in the 80+ age group are undersampled whereas other groups (e.g., 17+ years of education group) are oversampled. Demographically corrected norms were developed using the method of continuous norming and the variables of age and education. Evidence for the incremental validity of such norms for the IGT would be useful. Although regression analyses on the normative sample suggested little influence of gender, age, or education on IGT scores, norms were provided for 16 combined age (18–39, 40–59, 60–79, and 80+ years) and education (≤12, 13–15, 16, and 17+ years) groups based on uncited research. Group sizes range from 15 to 104, but several of the group sizes are unacceptably low for norms. In addition to the demographically corrected norms, norms are also provided based on a subsample (N = 264) that was matched to the 2003 U.S. Census. For both sets of norms, the method of continuous norming was used and norms were provided in the form of *T*-scores and percentiles for the total net score and each of the five block scores. Norms for the total number of cards selected from each deck were presented in five percentile categories: >16, 11–16, 6–10, 2–5, and ≤1. Raw score and demographically corrected *T*-score profiles are produced and may reveal particular patterns of performance over trials. An additional table shows the deck choice, amount won, amount lost, total money, and time for each of the 100 trials. Four case examples are provided in the manual but no other guidance or suggested interpretations for different IGT test patterns are given.

The IGT manual does not address reliability at all. Meaningful estimates of reliability are difficult to obtain because the IGT does not consist of items in the conventional sense used with internal consistency methods and both the set format of the IGT and likely practice effects make accurate test-retest reliability estimates difficult. Nonetheless, reliability is a measurement issue that needs to be addressed and consideration given to the development of alternate forms of the IGT.

Although it is claimed that poor decision making has been demonstrated using the IGT with a wide variety of conditions, including pathological gambling, obsessive-compulsive disorder, Huntington's disease, chronic pain, and affective disorders, the evidence for validity in the manual is limited to only a handful of studies on (a) the relationship of IGT scores to the Wisconsin Card Sorting Test and Tower of Hanoi test, (b) IGT performance in a few relevant clinical groups (i.e., focal brain lesions, substance-dependent individuals, and cognitively intact older adults), and (c) neural activation during IGT administration. Tables showing typical IGT performance by specific clinical groups would be useful. The presented validity evidence also relies heavily on the test author's own research even though much work also has been done by others. Good evidence for the validity of inferences to be made from IGT scores seems to be available in the literature, but it is not well covered in the manual. Moreover, there is considerable discussion in the literature about the IGT as a test of the somatic marker hypothesis, the role of test design specifics in the pattern of findings, and the role of personality characteristics and mood states in IGT performance, none of which are addressed in the manual.

COMMENTARY. The IGT is a brief and easily administered computerized test that appears to meet its goal of capturing decision-making capacity in a lab setting. It is admirable that the test author has attempted to provide norms for the entire adult age range, but the norms would be strengthened by the addition of substantially more individuals with education levels of 12 years or less, more older adults, and more non-Caucasian individuals. The IGT manual could be improved significantly with greater detail provided about test development decisions (e.g., rationale for defaults such as intertrial interval and number of trials), more information about the recruitment process and sites as well as the testing process for these "normal" individuals, evidence for test score reliability, more extensive coverage of validity evidence and consideration of contributing factors to IGT scores, and, subsequently, greater guidance in interpreting test scores and patterns. One issue that is not addressed in the manual is how to deal with the possible trigger effect that this test may have for gambling addicts, whose addiction may or may not be known to the clinician.

SUMMARY. Given the importance of being able to document impaired decision making, the IGT should be a welcome addition in many psychological assessments. This measure, in its current or previous versions, is well-cited in the literature and appears to stand alone as a readily available measure of decision-making capacity. Research on the IGT is promising but, without greater attention paid to reliability and validity evidence as well as possible contributing factors to IGT performance, caution should be exercised in making clinical inferences about IGT scores that extend beyond general statements about decision-making capacity.

REVIEWER'S REFERENCES

Balodis, I. M., MacDonald, T. K., & Olmstead, M. C. (2006). Instructional cues modify performance on the Iowa Gambling Task. Brain and Cognition, 60, 109-117.

Bechara, A., Damasio, A. R., Damasio, H., & Anderson, S. W. (1994). Insensitivity to future consequences following damage to prefrontal cortex. *Cognition, 50,* 7–15.

Review of the Iowa Gambling Task by MATTHEW E. LAMBERT, Clinical Assistant Professor of Neuropsychiatry, Texas Tech University Health Sciences Center, Department of Neuropsychiatry, Lubbock, TX:

DESCRIPTION. The Iowa Gambling Task (IGT) is a computer-administered assessment of decision making, purportedly the first neuropsychological test to assess the decision-making impairments of patients suffering damage to the medial orbitofrontal and ventromedial regions of the prefrontal cortex bilaterally. It was designed to assess decision-making deficits in individuals who generally perform normally on neuropsychological measures of memory, language, intellect, or concentration and attention while demonstrating judgment impairments in work, behavior, and interpersonal relationships.

The IGT is designed to mimic a card game that represents a real-life activity involving decision making to maximize rewards and minimize punishments. The results of an individual's IGT decision-making pattern are used to indicate "impaired," "less than average," or "average" decision-making capacities. Judgement is then required, in comparison with other neuropsychological tests, to decide whether the impairments are due to prefrontal cortex damage or other cerebral damage. The IGT can be used with adults 18 years of age and older. In older adults, the IGT may be used to assess decision-making abilities that may reflect inordinate deterioration sometimes noted in healthy geriatric individuals. Apparently, the IGT has been used with wide-ranging populations including those with focal cerebral damage, wider cerebral impairment, and psychiatric disorders.

IGT administration requires an individual to sit before a computer monitor depicting four decks of cards. General instructions are read aloud, with an instruction printed on the screen to "Pick a Card!" At the top of the screen, a green bar indicates the amount of money won and a red bar indicates how much money was borrowed to play the game. The instructions describe the task, game procedures, and types of feedback, provide guidance for interpreting feedback, and offer encouragement to play the game as if the individual was using his or her own real money.

Each card is selected by moving and clicking the mouse, and results in a monetary reward being displayed accompanied by sounds that supposedly replicate the sounds in a casino and a smiley face. But for some cards the monetary rewards are followed by monetary losses symbolized by an adverse sound and a frowning face.

Standard IGT administration is completed once 100 cards are selected from a combination of the decks. Each deck contains 60 cards. Nonstandard administrations can be conducted by varying the interval between consecutive card selections, the total number of card selections to be made, and monetary parameters. The four decks differ in terms of rewards and punishments based on groups of 10 cards for each deck. Deck "A" has a pattern of increasing monetary values for rewards and punishments, and frequency of unpredictable punishments, although the average loss per punishment remains consistent throughout the card groups. Deck "B" has a similar pattern except that the average loss per punishment increases but punishment frequency remains the same. In contrast, Deck "C" is similar in format to Deck "A" and Deck "D" to Deck "B" except for a pattern of increasing reward to punishment ratios. The first two decks have higher monetary values rewards and punishments as compared to the latter two decks, but can result in a net monetary loss and the latter decks can result in net gains.

A $2,000 loan is given to start the game as signified by both the red and green bars indicating the same amount. As money is won or lost the green bar lengthens or shortens. Each $2,000 increment lost results in a new $2,000 loan automatically granted, and the red bar lengthens by an equivalent amount.

Upon IGT completion a Score Report is generated based on measures of NET TOTAL (difference between total number of cards from the advantageous and disadvantageous decks) and Block Net Scores (difference between cards selected from advantageous and disadvantageous decks over five blocks of 20 card selections). Demographically corrected and U.S. Census-matched *T*-score standardizations for each raw score are provided to assess performance. The demographically corrected *T*-scores are recommended to be used in diagnostic determinations, whereas the U.S. Census-matched scores can be used to infer "capacity for everyday functioning" (professional manual, p. 7). *T*-scores below 40 are considered "Impaired," 40 to 44 "Below Average," and greater than 44 are "Nonimpaired." Visual evaluation of plotted Block Net Scores allows for determination of a random, normal, or abnormal performance based on the perceived learning slope. Other descriptive measures provided include the total number of cards selected from each deck, total money (won minus lost), and reaction time.

DEVELOPMENT. The basis for selecting a card game gambling task to assess decision making is not discussed in the manual other than identifying the IGT as a real-life decision-making task that is risky with no obvious indication of how, when, or what to choose. The original IGT consisted of four "custom-made" card decks with 40 cards per deck, with 20 each black and red faces, and facsimile U.S. currency used. Cards were selected manually. In order to improve speed and accuracy in scoring, the IGT was converted to a computer version with 60 cards per deck to avoid deck depletion. Studies conducted during the developmental process, however, indicated participants believed the computer was generating reward and punishment schedules and that winning the game was impossible. This resulted in a reinforcement schedule change to insure computer version scores were identical to those obtained from the original version.

No information is provided to understand the rationale for the various scores or the impact of changing from a 40- to 60-card deck. IGT performance was noted to be consistent regardless of whether real money was used, there were differing time delays between task trials, or using the manual versus computerized task.

TECHNICAL. Data were compiled from multiple sites from 932 normal participants (45.3% male) ranging in age from 18 to 95 years and 3 to 22 years of education to create the demographically corrected norms. A subsample of 264 participants was selected to create U.S. Census-matched norms. Descriptive data regarding these samples are provided in the manual.

Regression analyses were used to assess the relative variance contribution for age, gender, and education with gender demonstrating the least contribution resulting in it not being included for creating demographic norms. Based on the score distributions, four age and four education groups were established. A continuous norming method was used to obtain predicted means and standard deviations for the demographic and U.S. Census samples. Non-normalized *T* scores were derived for each of the 16 groups. Categorical norms were also created for both normative data sets based on rank ordering of raw scores so that five categories were constructed for scores above the 16th percentile to those less than or equal to the first percentile. These categories are used to characterize degrees of decision-making functioning. These data are presented as extensive tables in the test manual.

Although the manual presents information concerning the IGT development, standardization, and validity procedures, it offers no information concerning reliability. This omission raises major questions about the underpinnings of the validity evidence presented.

The test manual presents numerous validity studies that have demonstrated that poor IGT performance is related to impairment in the medial orbitofrontal or ventromedial regions of the prefrontal cortex. Other studies have noted, however, that IGT deficits were present in individuals suffering damage to other cerebral regions involving the dorsolateral prefrontal cortex, amygdala, and parietal cortex involving the insula and adjacent somatosensory cortex. Similarly, IGT deficits have been found in a variety of populations, including substance abusers, pathological gamblers, chronic pain patients, patients with suicide attempts, cognitively intact older adults, and Huntington's disease patients. Yet, the uniqueness of the IGT as a specific executive and frontal lobe function measure is primarily based on comparisons with the Wisconsin Card Sorting Test (WCST), which has been noted to be not closely associated with IGT performance. The basis for the WCST being a pure measure of executive or frontal lobe functioning has not been supported by its underlying body of research, however. As such, it may be that the IGT is a more general assessment of specific decision-making abilities that requires the evaluation of other neuropsychological data to infer specific prefrontal cortex damage.

Probably the greatest support for IGT performance being associated with frontal lobe functioning is based on functional imaging studies. Many IGT studies have involved normal unimpaired individuals demonstrating activation of the medial orbitofrontal or ventromedial prefrontal cortex structures during task completion. Yet, some studies involving Positron Emission Tomography have demonstrated activation of right-sided prefrontal and posterior cortical regions while completing the task. This result was viewed as consistent with findings from studies involving individuals with impaired parietal regions.

COMMENTARY. The IGT provides a reasonable task to assess decision-making abilities that may be used to help identify impairment in prefrontal cortex structures. Unfortunately, the instructions are rather long and may result in a loss of focus or be confusing for some patients. Older patients with no computer experience may also have difficulty managing the mouse as a response tool without some practice. Although the casino sounds are designed to be instructive, they also can be distracting as there are several different sounds used for rewards and they do not seem to accompany any specific reward pattern. Using a standard set of sounds may improve this problem. Assessing whether sounds are actually an integral part of the task experience may determine if they are necessary for a valid administration. (The online software manual does include information on how to turn off the sounds.)

The manual presents information regarding IGT development, standardization, and validity but is silent about performance reliability. Clearly this is a weakness in the manual. Similarly, the underlying basis for selecting and changing schedules of reinforcement and punishments is not discussed in such a way that aspects of the task related to specific prefrontal functions can be determined. A fuller discussion of the theoretical bases for task parameters would permit an assessment of whether the task actually contributes to understanding cerebral behavior.

Finally, although the IGT seems highly related to prefrontal cortex integrity, its use as a sole measure of such integrity is inappropriate. The finding that impaired IGT performance is related to other cerebral deficits and across numerous patient populations necessitates that it be interpreted in light of a comprehensive neuropsychological test battery. Without it being part of such a battery its interpretation is rendered invalid.

SUMMARY. The IGT provides an innovative measure to assess prefrontal cortex integrity in the context of a comprehensive neuropsychological evaluation. It can be used effectively in this manner. Although there appears to be an adequate basis for interpreting IGT performance related to cerebral structures, there is little discussion of the measure's reliability. The manual also lacks in discussion of the task's theoretical underpinnings related to its development as well as understanding structurally based cerebral behavior. Resolution of these issues can lead to wider research with the task and a greater understanding of cerebral functioning.

[63]

KeyMath-3 Diagnostic Assessment.

Purpose: Designed to assess understanding and applications of mathematics concepts and skills.
Population: Ages 4-6 to 21-11.
Publication Dates: 1971-2007.
Acronym: KeyMath-3 DA.
Scores, 14: Basic Concepts (Numeration, Algebra, Geometry, Measurement, Data Analysis and Probability, Total), Operations (Mental Computation and Estimation, Addition and Subtraction, Multiplication and Division, Total), Applications (Foundations of Problem Solving, Applied Problem Solving, Total), Total.
Administration: Individual.
Forms, 2: A, B.
Price Data, 2008: $699 per complete kit including manual (2007, 371 pages), Form A and Form B test easels, 25 Form A & Form B record forms, and carrying bag; $399 per single form (specify form) kit including manual, test easels, 25 record forms, and carrying bag; $76 per 25 record forms (specify form); $259 per KeyMath-3 ASSIST scoring software.
Time: (30-40) minutes Grades PK-2; (75-90) minutes Grades 3 and up.
Author: Austin J. Connolly.
Publisher: Pearson.
Cross References: For reviews by G. Gage Kingsbury and James A. Wollack of a previous edition, see 14:194; see also T5:139 (15 references) and T4:1355 (5 references); for reviews by Michael D. Beck and Carmen J. Finley of an earlier edition, see 11:191 (26 references); see also T3:1250 (12 references); for an excerpted review by Alex Bannatyne of an earlier edition, see 8:305 (10 references).

Review of the KeyMath-3 Diagnostic Assessment by THERESA GRAHAM, Adjunct Faculty, University of Nebraska-Lincoln, Lincoln, NE:

DESCRIPTION. The KeyMath-3 Diagnostic Assessment (herein referred to as KeyMath-3 DA) is an untimed, norm-referenced test that provides a comprehensive assessment of key mathematical concepts and skills, for individuals ranging in age from 4 years, 6 months through 21 years. The KeyMath-3 DA is composed of two parallel forms (Form A and Form B) with 10 subtests. The subtests, based on National Council of Teachers of Mathematics (NCTM) *Principles and Standards for School Mathematics* (NCTM, 2000) include the following areas: Basic Concepts (Numeration, Algebra, Geometry, Measurement, Data Analysis and Probability), Operations (Mental Computation and Estimation, Addition and Subtraction, Multiplication and Division), and Applications

(Foundations of Problem Solving, Applied Problem Solving).

The KeyMath-3 DA was revised to update test items to correspond with the NCTM standards and to create parallel testing forms (Form A and B), which allow educators to monitor the progress of an individual by taking alternating forms. In addition, the KeyMath-3 DA was designed to provide a link to the KeyMath-3 Essential Resources (KeyMath-3 ER). KeyMath-3 ER is an instructional program that includes lessons and activities directly related to the 10 subtests included in the KeyMath-3 DA. Finally, the KeyMath-3 DA provides updated normative and interpretive data.

ADMINISTRATION AND SCORING. The materials for the KeyMath-3 DA consist of two easels for each form, a manual, and record forms for both forms. The easels are self-standing and very easy to use, including tabs for the different subtests and instructions on start points and establishing basal and ceiling. The KeyMath-3 DA manual describes the general testing guidelines and scoring information. Answers and score summaries, including raw score, scale score, standard score, confidence-interval value, confidence interval, grade/age equivalent, and percentile rank can be recorded on the record form.

The Numeration subtest is always administered first with the start point determined by the grade level. The start points for the other subtests are determined by the ceiling item on the Numeration subtest. Stop points are determined by the ceiling set and ceiling item.

It is generally recommended that all subtests be administered in the order that they are presented. However, the test author notes that there may be reasonable circumstances in which a specific area (e.g., the Basic Concepts area) would be given. According to the manual, average test times for the inventory range from 30–40 minutes for younger examinees to 75–90 minutes for older examinees. Both of these estimates seem very conservative given the number of subtests and breadth of items included. It may be that the estimates do not include rest breaks, which may be necessary for examinees of any age. Test fatigue may become an issue for some examinees.

Because all of the correct responses are written on the test easel, scoring is easily done while the test is being administered. A "1" is circled for correct responses, and a "0" is circled for incorrect responses. Detailed scoring rules are provided in the manual.

A subtest raw score is determined by subtracting the total number of incorrect items from the highest ceiling item. Appendices in the testing manual provide all of the normative and interpretive tables for both testing forms to convert a raw score to a standard score and to assess score profile, subtest comparison, and functional range. Additional tables are provided to convert a raw score to a growth scale value (GSV) using the optional ASSIST scoring and reporting software. Finally, because the KeyMath-3 DA was developed simultaneously with the KeyMath-3 ER, results on the KeyMath-3 DA can be linked to instructional programs included in the KeyMath-3 ER. Although all of the scoring can be done easily by hand, examiners may want to purchase the ASSIST scoring and reporting software, especially if they plan to follow examinee progress over time or if they plan to make an instructional plan using the KeyMath-3 ER. The software reportedly provides progress reports and graphical displays of performance over time.

DEVELOPMENT. The development of the KeyMath-3 DA consisted of surveying relevant professionals regarding the content, administration, and use. In response to survey results, five NCTM content standards (Number and Operations, Algebra, Geometry, Measurement, Data Analysis and Probability) and five process standards (Problem Solving, Reasoning and Proof, Communication, Connections, and Representation) were used to frame the 10 subtests and to generate about 550 new items. These items were initially piloted on a group of 250 students in Grades 1 through 8. From the pilot, many items were modified, the number of extended response items was scaled back, and start points and sequencing was determined.

Prior to the standardization studies, two tryout studies were conducted to pretest the items for item difficulty, grade level-performance, and gender/ethnicity bias. In the first tryout study, there were 1,238 participants ranging from prekindergarten through ninth grade. Although the author notes that the "samples were also controlled by race/ethnicity" (manual, p. 45), no information was given regarding socioeconomic status. Moreover, the sample did not include participants in grades higher than ninth grade. In the administration, the subtests were divided into two forms to reduce testing time.

Item difficulty, item fit, and item discrimination were determined using the Rasch analyses. In addition, item distractors for the multiple-choice items were evaluated. Finally, a panel of reviewers representing different cultural and geographical backgrounds reviewed the test for cultural sensitivity. Based on the results of the first tryout study, the test author states that some items were added, modified, and dropped from the analyses and review performed. However, examples of specific changes and exact number of changes are not provided

A second tryout study was conducted with items from only two of the subtests (Foundations of Problem Solving and Applied Problem Solving) because the test author noted that many of the items in these subtests had been modified as a result of the first tryout study. In this study, 1,196 individuals were included (again ranging in age from prekindergarten to ninth grade). A separate smaller tryout study (*N* = 199, kindergarten through second grade children) was performed to assess the wording of items in the Mental Computation and Estimation subtest. Although the test author states that changes were made as a result of these studies, specific results are not provided.

For the standardization study, two forms (Form A and Form B) were developed, each consisting of 444 items. A few of the items were the same between the two forms (the exact number is not noted). The rest of the items were similar in content but differed slightly in specific numbers used. The example given is an item from the Mental Computation and Estimation subtest, which simply changed the numbers in a simple subtraction.

The standardization study consisted of two administrations, spring and fall. In the spring administration, about half of the sample took Form A and 280 examinees took both Forms A and B. Rasch analyses assessed item difficulty and item fit. In addition, the parallel forms were compared for similarity in difficulty. As a result, 74 items were dropped after the spring administration either for poor fit (19 items), difficulty difference between the two forms (14 items), or reduction of item concentration at the higher end of the assessment (41 items), resulting in 372 items. No mention was made as to how many (if any) of the remaining items were altered.

TECHNICAL.

Standardization. The sample used to standardize the KeyMath-3 DA consisted of 3,630 individuals ranging in age from 4 years, 6 months through 21 years (1,565 in the spring administration; 1,540 in the fall administration). The author's goal was to test at least 110 individuals in each grade level in each season. The sample was recruited to represent ethnic, mother's educational level, geographic region, and special education distributions in the United States. Tables are provided in the manual with information regarding distribution of the sample in terms of ethnicity, gender, education level, and geographic region.

Generally, examinees were given either Form A or Form B. A sample of 280 were administered both forms. Because Form A and Form B were not equivalent, raw scores could not be pooled and these data were considered to be separate normative data. Raw scores for examinees who took both forms were converted to *w*-ability scores via a joint Rasch calibration of the two forms. This procedure allows standard scores between the two forms to be compared.

Reliability. Reliability was assessed in terms of internal consistency, test-retest reliability, and alternate-form reliability. Internal consistency was determined using the split-half method with appropriate adjustments made because examinees at the same grade or age may take different sets of test items. Reliability coefficients are presented for the different age groups and grades for fall and spring. Coefficients ranged from .86 to .99 for the total test scores depending on age group. The data from each form (A and B) were pooled to provide an estimate of the population variance for each age and grade. The pooled variance was used to adjust the reliability for each form to better approximate the reliability of the population.

Alternate-form reliability was assessed by counterbalancing Form A and Form B for a subset of the standardized sample (*N* = 280, see above). The median alternate-form reliabilities are .82 and .85, suggesting that similar scores would be obtained if taking Form A or Form B. Finally, test-retest reliability was assessed with a group of 103 (ranging in grade from Pre-K to Grade 12 and divided into two grade ranges). However, little information is given regarding the exact distribution of ages of the examinees included. The retest occurred anywhere between 6–28 days. The median subtest test-retest reliability coefficients ranged from .86 to .88, demonstrating high stability over time.

Validity. Content validity was established in several ways. First, the KeyMath-3 DA was created using the NCTM principles and standards, utilizing NCTM materials. In addition, over 400 educators and professional consultants provided feedback regarding the content of the assessment.

Construct validity was assessed by demonstrating that raw scores on the KeyMath-3 DA increase rapidly among the younger ages and begin to plateau in high school. However, raw scores only increased an average of 2 points in the high school grades, a finding that may suggest the test does not adequately measure higher mathematical knowledge as taught in the high school grades.

KeyMath-3 DA was shown to be related to a number of different measures of mathematical achievement, including the KeyMath Revised, Normative Update: A Diagnostic Inventory of Essential Mathematics (KeyMath-R/NU; Connolly, 1998), Kaufman Test of Educational Achievement, Second Edition (KTEA-II; Kaufman & Kaufman, 2004), the Iowa Test of Basic Skills (ITBS; Hoover, Dunbar, & Frisbie, 2001), the Measures of Academic Progress (MAP; Northwest Evaluation Association, 2006), and the Group Mathematics Assessment and Diagnostic Evaluation (GMADE; Williams, 2006). For both the KeyMath-R/NU and the KTEA-II, administration was counterbalanced with a test interval average of 9–11 days. For the other inventories, data were gathered from school records with an average test interval of 31–44 days. Tables summarizing the demographics of the study sample used are provided in the test manual. The correlation of the total test scores on the KeyMath-3 DA and the KeyMath-R/NU averaged .92, with the correlation of the subtests ranging from low .70s to low .90s. However, average standard scores from these two measures differed such that the scores should not be considered interchangeable. For the other measures, performance on the KeyMath-3 DA was moderately to highly correlated with the other measures of mathematics achievement.

Finally, analyses were performed to assess whether performance on the KeyMath-3 DA distinguished between examinees representative of special populations, including examinees identified as gifted, diagnosed with ADHD, diagnosed with a Learning Disability (with math alone, reading alone, and math and reading combined), and identified with a mild intellectual disability. As expected, no differences were found between examinees identified with ADHD and what would be expected in the general population. However, performance on the KeyMath-3 DA differed significantly among the rest of the special population groups and the general population group. All three of these assessments of validity suggest that KeyMath-3 DA is a sufficiently valid instrument of mathematical achievement.

COMMENTARY. The KeyMath-3 DA was designed to provide a comprehensive measurement of mathematics achievement that mirrored the standards and principles outlined by the NCTM among individuals in prekindergarten through high school. Indeed, the author did a good job in relying on the NCTM framework and assessing not only procedural knowledge, but also assessing problem-solving ability and conceptual knowledge. However, because the test takes a long period to administer, and it must be administered individually, it may not be useful in a general setting. It may be better suited for cases where a deficit is suspected. It may also be useful if discrepant abilities are suspected in order to identify strengths and weaknesses. In addition, the test seems to have a significant ceiling effect and may not be as useful for high school students who are performing at or above age/grade level.

At the younger end of the continuum, the connection between the KeyMath-3 DA and the KeyMath-3 ER is a great tool for educators who are looking for instructional programs to augment and/or instruct in areas of deficit or strength. The KeyMath-3 DA materials are easy to use, and the manual instructions make it an easy instrument to administer, score, and interpret. It is a reasonably reliable and valid tool to assess comprehensive understanding of mathematics and can also be used to pinpoint and monitor special areas of mathematical knowledge. It may also be useful for program evaluation.

REVIEWER'S REFERENCES

Connolly, A. J. (1998). *KeyMath Revised, normative update manual.* Circle Pines, MN: AGS Publishing.

Hoover, H. D., Dunbar, S. B., & Frisbie, D. A. (2001). Iowa Test of Basic Skills (ITBS). Rolling Meadows, IL: Riverside Publishing.

Kaufman, A. S., & Kaufman, N. L. (2004). KTEA II: Kaufman Test of Educational Achievement (2nd ed.). Circle Pines, MN: AGS Publishing.

National Council of Teachers of Mathematics. (2000). *Principles and standards for school mathematics.* Reston, VA: Author.

Northwest Evaluation Association. (2004). Measures of Academic Progress (MAP). Lake Oswego, OR: Author.

Williams, K. (2004). The Group Mathematics Assessment and Diagnostic Evaluation (GMADE). Parsippany, NJ: Dale Seymour Publications.

Review of the KeyMath-3 Diagnostic Assessment by SUZANNE LANE, Professor of Research Methodology, and DEBRA MOORE, Ph.D. Candidate, University of Pittsburgh, Pittsburgh, PA:

DESCRIPTION. The KeyMath-3 Diagnostic Assessment (KeyMath-3 DA) is a norm-referenced, individually administered measure of mathematical concepts and skills for prekindergarten through Grade 12 students (ages 4 years, 6 months through 21 years). The test's purpose is to provide diagnostic information that can be used to tailor intervention programs for students and to monitor student performance over time. The assessment is designed for use with the KeyMath-3 Essential Resources (KeyMath-3 ER) instructional programs. The KeyMath-3 DA is a revised version of the KeyMath Revised (KeyMath-R; 14:194). An algebra subtest has been added as well as other new content so that it is aligned with the standards outlined by the *Principles and Standards for School Mathematics* (NCTM, 2000). There are also new normative and interpretative data.

The test consists of two parallel forms (Form A and Form B), each with 372 items divided across three content areas: Basic Concepts, Operations, and Applications. These three content areas are divided into 10 subtests ranging from Numeration to Applied Problem Solving. Items are presented one at a time on an easel. The test administrator reads the directions and the item and then records the examinee's answer. Items within each subtest are arranged in order of increasing difficulty. The first subtest, Numeration, has a starting point determined by grade level. Successive subtests have starting points based on the ceiling item from the Numeration subtest. The test is untimed, but the author estimates 30 to 40 minutes for elementary grades and 75 to 90 minutes for secondary grades.

After administration, the examiner can create score reports by hand or with the use of an optional software package that creates the same score reports plus some additional reports. The reports refer the examiner to tables in the technical manual that provide scale scores, standard scores, percentile ranks, grade equivalents, and age equivalents, as well as five descriptive categories referring to the level of student performance.

DEVELOPMENT. The *Principles and Standards for School Mathematics* (NCTM, 2000), state math standards, and the KeyMath-R guided the revisions. A test blueprint that delineates the 10 subtests, and math topics and objectives within each subtest formed the basis of item development. A pilot study was conducted in the spring of 2004 and the results were used to modify items, order items by difficulty, and to determine the starting points for each grade for the tryout.

A tryout was conducted during the fall and winter of the 2004–2005 (October-January) school year. A random sampling procedure, stratified by grade and gender, was used in obtaining the tryout sample of over 2,400 students in prekindergarten through Grade 9. A total of 496 items were divided into subtests across two forms. The data were analyzed using the Rasch model. The item difficulty distribution for each subtest was examined and items were added to fill gaps in the distribution and items were removed in dense areas of the distribution. No information, however, is provided on the targeted item difficulty distribution and the extent to which the targets were achieved. Analyses of item fit, differential item functioning, and reliability were also conducted. Finally, fairness reviews were conducted and the results were used in decisions regarding item modifications and deletions. A second tryout was conducted for two subtests that had considerable modifications as a result of the first tryout.

TECHNICAL.

Standardization. A nationally representative sample of 3,630 individuals aged 4 years, 6 months to 21 years, 11 months participated in the standardization of Forms A and B in both the spring and fall of 2006. The norm sample was chosen using a stratified random sampling procedure with geographical region, gender, SES, race, and special education status as stratifying variables. Sample percentages within each stratifying category matched closely the 2004 U.S. Census data. Students with a verified "specific learning disability" (manual, p. 61) were slightly overrepresented and Hispanics in the low socioeconomic status category were somewhat underrepresented in the norm sample.

Item difficulty, item fit, and DIF values were used from the spring standardization results to determine the final item set and item order. A table identifying the number of items dropped due to various reasons (e.g., poor fit, difficulty difference) is provided. Methods used to determine optimal start points, determine basal and ceiling set rules, and examine the accuracy of the scoring rules are also described clearly in the manual.

To evaluate the comparability of Forms A and B, means and standard deviations of the subtest, area, and total test raw scores by grade and season are provided. The majority of the subtest means across forms are within 2 points and the standard deviations are similar. To develop the norms, half of the norm sample was administered Form A and the other half was administered Form B. The two forms were then calibrated jointly, with a sample of 280 examinees who were administered both forms serving as the link. A linear transformation of the ability estimates for each examinee from the joint calibration was conducted to obtain *w*-ability scores. Subtest age norms were developed for each of the 17 age groups using normalizing translations that converted *w*-ability scores to scale scores. For each of the subtests, a growth curve for each odd-value score (scores range from 1 to 19) was plotted against age and then smoothed. These procedures were used to calculate the *w*-ability score values for the 62 age groups reported in the final norm tables. Using linear interpolation, scale score equivalents for intervening *w*-ability scores were obtained. Finally, *w*-ability scores were converted back to their corresponding raw score values. Grade equivalents were obtained for K–9 and age equivalents were obtained for ages 4 years, 6 months through 15 years, 11 months.

Reliability. The split-half method was used to estimate internal-consistency reliability. Internal consistency coefficients for subtests, areas, and total test across Forms A and B for both the fall and the spring administration are presented by grade level and by age. The coefficients range from .60 to .95 with the large majority of estimates in the .80s. The lowest coefficients were for primary grades.

To obtain alternate-forms reliability, the sample was divided into two subgroups, K–5 and 6–12. The test forms were administered, using a counterbalanced design, to 280 examinees at intervals averaging 10 days. Alternate-form reliabilities for subtests for both samples range from the middle .70s to the low .90s, and alternate-form reliabilities for areas were in the high .80s to mid .90s.

To obtain test-retest reliability coefficients, the sample was again divided into two subgroups. The test forms were administered, on average, 17 days apart to 103 examinees. Test-retest reliabilities for subtests in the K–5 subgroup range from .65 to .95 with the majority in the middle .80s. Test-retest reliabilities for the subtests in the 6–12 subgroup range from .70 to .92 with the majority in the high .80s.

Validity. Validity evidence provided pertains to the test content, adequacy of detecting performance growth, internal structure of the test, external structure of the test, and adequacy of potential decisions based on the test scores. Content validity evidence is provided by a well-defined test blueprint that specifies objectives within the 10 subtests and was informed by the *Principles and Standards for School Mathematics* (NCTM, 2000), state math standards, and information provided by educational practitioners and math curriculum consultants. Items were also reviewed for content and bias.

Performance growth across grades was verified by several methods. First, mean raw scores on subtests, areas, and total test showed an increase across grades. As expected there was more rapid growth during the early grades and less growth at the upper grades. Second, the median growth scale value (GSV) corresponding to the total test raw score was plotted for each grade and the median GSV increased from K through 12.

To provide internal structure evidence, correlations among subtest scores were obtained as well as correlations among the subtests and area and total standard scores. It was expected that the correlations between subtests in the same area would be higher than correlations between subtests in different areas. However, correlations between subtest scores were similar regardless of area, with most exceeding .60. For the K–2 group, for example, the correlations between areas range from .72 to .83 and the correlations between area and total test range from .84 to .97.

External validity evidence was obtained by examining the relationship between the KeyMath-3 DA test and the earlier edition of the test (KeyMath-R/NU), the individually administered Kaufman Test of Educational Achievement, Second Edition (KTEA-II), and three group-administered mathematics tests. The results indicated that the subtest, area, and total test is related to these other measures and in some cases there is an expected differential pattern of correlations when using the subtest and area scores.

KeyMath-3 DA is often used with special populations so the average standard scores were obtained for six groups that represent different diagnoses or special education classifications (e.g., attention-deficit, giftedness, math learning disability). Expected differences between the weighted means for the special populations and the general population were obtained. For example, weighted means for the math learning disability group were generally 1 standard deviation lower than the general population means.

COMMENTARY. The KeyMath-3 DA is an individually administered test that provides valuable diagnostic information to teachers regarding students' strengths and weaknesses. This latest edition better reflects the mathematics being taught in schools by the addition of the problem-solving subtests, the linkage of items to the NCTM process standards, and use of calculators at the upper grade levels. Because the revision for this test was based heavily on the NCTM process standards, the use of external reviewers to verify the link between the items and the NCTM standards would have been a welcome addition. However, there is ample information about the content of the test to help potential users determine if it is appropriate for their purposes. The inclusion of items that ask students to explain their procedures and understanding is noteworthy. For some of these items, additional follow-up questions are provided to the examiner in order to prompt students to provide fuller explanations, which is an attractive feature for an individually administered test.

The manual provides an excellent overview of the available normative scores and the way in which to interpret and use these scores. The score profile clearly displays information that will aid the user in identifying instructional needs for the individual student. The confidence band for each of the scores is drawn on the profile, aiding in accurate interpretation by considering measurement error. Further, a 68% confidence band is used for the subtest scores, whereas a 90% or 95% confidence band is used for the area and total scores. The use of different confidence bands depending on the nature of the interpretation and potential decision reflects the care of the test author in providing the most appropriate information to the test user.

The manual provides a clear and comprehensive description of the design and the technical quality of the test. The procedures and samples for the standardization were well documented. It should be noted, however, that the spring standardization sample was used to determine the final item set and item order. It was assumed that because the Rasch item difficulties are not dependent on characteristics of the sample, values obtained from the spring standardization would generalize to the entire data set. Theoretically, the difficulty estimates should be invariant across samples; however, this finding does not always occur in practice. An examination of the invariance of item parameters across the spring and fall samples could have provided evidence to support this assumption. Reliability coefficients for subtest scores are moderate to high and are generally high for the area and total scores, indicating that users can have confidence in using the area and total scores for making relatively high stakes decisions and using the subtest scores in examining a student's strengths and weaknesses.

Overall, the validity evidence supports using the test for its intended purpose. The author, however, may want to explore the extent to which each subtest measures something unique so that patterns of performance on the subtests can better inform the design of individual student intervention programs.

SUMMARY. The KeyMath-3 Diagnostic Assessment is an individually administered test that is well developed and provides scores that can inform the design of individual student intervention programs and monitor performance over time. The manual is well written and provides clear guidelines for administering, scoring, and interpreting the scores. The technical information provided in the manual is comprehensive, clearly presented, and supports the use of the instrument for its purpose.

REVIEWERS' REFERENCE

National Council of Teachers of Mathematics. (2000). *Principles and standards for school mathematics*. Reston, VA: Author.

[64]

Kindergarten Readiness Test [Scholastic Testing Service, Inc.].

Purpose: Designed "to assist in determining a student's readiness for beginning kindergarten."
Population: Preschool-kindergarten students.
Publication Date: 2006.
Acronym: KRT.
Scores, 8: Vocabulary, Identifying Letters, Visual Discrimination, Phonemic Awareness, Comprehension and Interpretation, Mathematical Knowledge, Full Battery Total, Readiness Classification.
Administration: Group.
Price Data, 2008: $48.50 per user's manual (30 pages), 20 test booklets, 1 answer key, 1 class record sheet, and 1 class summary report; price data for Development and Standardization manual (11 pages) available from publisher.
Foreign Language Edition: Spanish edition available.
Time: (30) minutes.
Authors: O. F. Anderhalter and Jan Perney.
Publisher: Scholastic Testing Service, Inc.

Review of Kindergarten Readiness Test by KATHLEEN M. JOHNSON, Psychologist, Lincoln Public Schools, Lincoln, NE:

DESCRIPTION. The Kindergarten Readiness Test (KRT) is an assessment tool intended to assist in determining a student's readiness for beginning kindergarten (user's manual, p. 3) and is a downward extension of the School Readiness Test (T7:2260), previously published by Scholastic Testing Service. The stated purpose of the KRT is to determine the extent to which underlying competencies for kindergarten have been developed so that instruction can be modified to meet the needs of each student (development and standardization manual, p. 1). The readiness skills included on the KRT are listening vocabulary and comprehension, lower-case letter recognition, visual matching of numbers, letters and geometric designs, phonemic awareness, and early math skills. The test authors, Anderhalter and Perney, recommend that it be administered in two brief, small group or individual testing sessions by a classroom teacher. Although they suggest using two sessions on different mornings (15–20 minutes for Subtests 1 through 4, then 10 minutes for Subtests 5 and 6), the entire test can be administered in about 30 minutes with a short break after Subtest 4. According to the test authors, the KRT is intended to be used at the end of preschool or before the third full week of kindergarten, as a measure of kindergarten readiness. The testing materials include: the user's manual, the development and standardization manual, student test booklets, an answer key, and class summary sheets. The examiner also needs the following items for each administration: a stopwatch and a pencil, marker, or crayon for each student.

The test is composed of six short subtests: (a) Vocabulary (circle one of four pictures to correspond with a word read aloud by the teacher), (b) Identifying Letters (circle one of four or five lower-case letters that correspond to a letter read aloud by the teacher), (c) Visual Discrimination (circle one of four figures in a row that matches the figure at the beginning of the row), (d) Phonemic Awareness (circle one of four pictures that rhymes with or has the same beginning sound as that of a word read aloud by the teacher), (e) Comprehension and Interpretation (circle one of four pictures that corresponds to a short "story" or direction read aloud by the teacher), and (f) Mathematical Knowledge (circle the numeral or figure specified by directions read aloud by the teacher). At the beginning of the KRT, a page of common pictures is presented, and each student practices the expected response of drawing "a ring around" each picture named by the examiner. Each subtest also begins with one sample item, for which feedback is given if a student does not respond correctly. Students are also instructed about how to cross out and change answers.

In the user's manual, the test authors provide a description for the teacher/examiner as to how to prepare for the testing (e.g., scheduling the sessions, space and supervision considerations, the materials needed) and other general directions. The specific test administration directions are printed in boldface print and are easy to read and follow. The directions and all of the items are read aloud to the students. Students are allowed 10 to 15 seconds for making each answer, depending on the subtest. The students mark their responses directly in the multipage test booklet (two pages per subtest) and items are scored as either correct or incorrect. The last page of the booklet is reserved for recording the subtest and total raw scores, as well as the corresponding readiness ratings and the total test percentile rank. The raw score for each subtest is used to identify one of three readiness ratings: Low (-), Marginal (?), or Adequate (+). According to the manual, the Low (-) readiness level indicates that the subtest skill assessed is "lower than desirable" for beginning kindergarten and corresponds to approximately the lowest 10% of students. The Marginal (?) readiness level indicates "some question of adequacy" (user's manual, p. 27) regarding the subtest skill for beginning kindergarten and reportedly corresponds to next lowest 15% of students. The Adequate (+) readiness level corresponds to the upper 75% of students, according to the test authors. The total raw score is used then to identify one of four overall readiness ratings: NR (not ready without attention), MR (marginally ready), R (average degree of readiness), and R+ (above average degree of readiness). Percentile ranks are provided for the total score; the two lower levels represent the lowest quartile and the two upper levels represent the upper three quartiles of the norm group. The process of organizing the KRT data for a class of students is also provided in the user's manual, so that the results can be examined in terms of overall readiness and subtest readiness levels. A Spanish edition is also available.

DEVELOPMENT. The purpose of developing the Kindergarten Readiness Test was to assess competencies that are prerequisite to the formal academic instruction that begins in kindergarten. The KRT is a downward extension of Scholastic's School Readiness Test (the SRT assesses first grade readiness skills). The readiness skills assessed in the KRT represent six of the eight readiness skills contained in the SRT. No information was included in the manual about the SRT or about the subtest or item selection process for the KRT, and no differential item functioning data were presented. The primary rationale for subtest selection for the KRT was to include measures of specific prerequisite early learning skills: vocabulary, comprehension, decoding, and basic math/number concepts. In the development and standardization manual, the test authors describe the rationale for including each subtest in the KRT and caution users that this instrument is only one component of a complete assessment of readiness.

TECHNICAL. The standardization sample included 606 beginning kindergarten students from 18 schools in 12 states. No data are presented in the manual on the degree to which it was a representative national sample or stratified by any specific variables (e.g., gender, SES, ethnicity). No preschool students were included in the normative sample. The normative data are presented as percentile ranks and as readiness levels based on cutscore ranges (for the entire sample as one group with no age differentiations based on the time of testing). Some reliability and validity evidence is summarized by the test authors in the development and standardization manual. Internal consistency reliability coefficients were calculated for each subtest and for the total readiness score for the normative sample. The coefficient values for the subtests cluster near .70 and thus the use of the individual subtest scores is not recommended. The individual subtests have adequate floors but inadequate ceilings in terms of item difficulty, whereas, the total score appears to have floor and ceiling ranges to allow the use of the KRT for screening purposes. The internal consistency for the total readiness score is moderately strong (.86). Factor analyses support the validity of the overall readiness construct; all six subtests had moderate to strong loadings (.62–.77) on a single factor identified by the test authors as Total Readiness. In the development and standardization manual, the test authors include a content description of each subtest (as related to overall readiness as a construct) and some internal structure data (subtest intercorrelations) as validity evidence. The relatively low subtest intercorrelations (ranging from .24 to .53) indicate that each subtest provides independent, but positive, contributions to the overall readiness measure. No data are presented by the test authors regarding concurrent or predictive validity between the KRT and other similar instruments or decision-making criteria. The KRT data are not even compared, for predictive purposes, to data from the SRT (the first grade readiness test) on which the KRT is modeled.

COMMENTARY. The Kindergarten Readiness Test is a downward extension of the existing School Readiness Test (designed for first grade readiness assessment). The skills assessed by the KRT are aligned with essential academic skills as identified in current research (e.g., vocabulary, phonemic awareness, number concepts). The directions for administration of the test and the scoring procedures are effectively detailed in the manual. The subtests appear to be easy to administer and to score. The test authors acknowledge that the KRT is only one part of a process for determining a student's readiness for kindergarten instruction. The technical qualities of the KRT do not support its use as a measure of specific kindergarten competencies, but may be useful as a brief screening to indicate the extent to which prerequisite, early kindergarten skills are already in place for students. Although the test authors state that the students were part of a representative national sample, no data regarding the sample were included in the manual and thus it is unknown how the findings might generalize in common use. In terms of applied use, most teachers and schools typically already have a variety of baseline assessments for documenting beginning kindergarten skill levels and for subsequently identifying the needs of some students for additional, early intervention. The KRT may provide a method of universal screening but it lacks the progress monitoring component essential to evaluating intervention effectiveness so other readiness measures could be more useful. The KRT may be useful for preschool teachers as one piece of data gathered to advise parents about a student's general readiness for kindergarten. However, no preschool students were included in the standardization sample so it is unknown whether the scores accurately reflect the skills of this group (at an age when growth and development of skills can be quite rapid within a time period of several months).

SUMMARY. The Kindergarten Readiness Test is a brief, small group or individually administered screening instrument and it is intended for use with students at the end of preschool or before the third full week of kindergarten. According to the test authors, the KRT is designed to assess a student's readiness for a kindergarten curriculum so instruction can be modified to meet the needs of each student. The readiness skills included on the KRT are listening vocabulary and comprehension, lower-case letter recognition, visual matching of numbers, letters and geometric designs, phonemic awareness, and early math skills. It can be administered in about 30 minutes by a classroom teacher. The overall test score is assigned one of four overall readiness ratings (based on cutscore ranges): NR (not ready without attention), MR (marginally ready), R (average degree of readiness), and R+ (above average degree of readiness). Percentile ranks are also provided for the total score. Although the content of the KRT as a readiness screening instrument seems appropriate, the technical data presented in the manual are limited and, if used, only the total test score should be interpreted.

Review of the Kindergarten Readiness Test by MARK E. SWERDLIK, Professor of Psychology, and KATHRYN E. HOFF, Associate Professor of Psychology, Illinois State University, Normal, IL:

DESCRIPTION. The Kindergarten Readiness Test (KRT) is a group-administered measure of a student's readiness for beginning kindergarten. The test authors note that when entering kindergarten, students differ in the development of the underlying competencies that are critical for early school learning. The KRT is intended to assess the degree to which these fundamental competencies have been developed so that "instruction can be modified to meet the needs of each student" (Development and Standardization Manual, p. 1). The KRT is to be administered at the end of preschool or before the third full week of kindergarten and includes an assessment of six readiness skills. These six readiness skills include Vocabulary (circling one of four pictures for each word read aloud by the examiner), Identifying Letters (circling "one of four or five lower-case letters that corresponds to a letter read" [user's manual, p. 3] by the examiner), Visual Discrimination (circling one figure of the four pictures presented that is identical to the fifth figure presented at the beginning of the row), Phonemic Awareness (circling one of four pictures that has the same initial sound or rhymes with the word read aloud by the examiner), Comprehension and Interpretation (circling one of four pictures that is related to a short story read aloud by the examiner), and Mathematical Knowledge (circling a numeral or figure corresponding to the directions read aloud by the examiner). Each skill area includes one practice or sample and six test items. All test items are printed in black and white in a separate test booklet. Administration and scoring instructions are clear and easy to follow. No specific qualifications are given for the examiner. Nonetheless, the KRT is typically administered in a group by the classroom teacher, but also can be given individually. Test materials for the examinee include a test booklet, a pencil, and at least one crayon, and the examiner requires the separate manual of directions, a copy of the test booklet, and a timing instrument. Students are instructed to turn over the pages of the test booklet so they are looking at only one page at a time. The test authors note, "Many students will need help with this, at least during the early part of the administration" (user's manual, p. 4). If necessary, tests can be administered in one sitting with a rest period after Test 4 (Phonemic Awareness), and total testing time should not exceed 25–30 minutes. However, it is recommended that the KRT be administered in two sittings in the morning with the administration time of Tests 1–4 of approximately 15–20 minutes followed by the remaining two tests, 5 and 6, lasting another 10 minutes.

Three types of assessments are yielded by the KRT. These include a standards-based assessment of the six readiness skills, a standards-based assessment of the overall readiness for beginning instruction in kindergarten based on the sum of the number of correct items for each of the six individual readiness skills, and a norm-referenced assessment of overall readiness providing a comparison with the standardization sample. The total number of items correct for the Total score yields a national percentile and a national stanine corresponding to the percentile rank range. A Standards-Based Readiness Rating is also provided for both the Total Readiness score and each of the six individual subtests. No specific information is provided on how the national percentiles were computed (i.e., based on the distribution of scores from the standardization sample or if a normalization process occurred). Individual Readiness Ratings corresponding to the number correct in each of the six skill areas include: + = Adequate; ? = Marginal; and - = Lower than desirable. Qualitative descriptors for the Overall Readiness Rating corresponding to the Total Readiness score include R+ = Above Average Degree of Readiness; R = Average Degree of Readiness; MR = Marginally Ready; and NR = Not Ready without Attention. Instructional implications, although very broad, are specified for each classification. For example for the NR classification, "The student would require special attention both before and during early instruction. Review of separate skills is essential" (user's manual, p. 28). More detailed instructions are provided related to recording test scores for all students in the class.

DEVELOPMENT. A separate Development and Standardization Manual is provided. The KRT represents an extension of the School Readiness Test (SRT; T7:2260), which was developed to assess readiness for first grade and has been in use for more than 30 years. According to the manual, the KRT includes an assessment of the same readiness skills found on the SRT and also uses the same rating classifications. The KRT test authors note that that the "ratings for the assessment of individual readiness skills utilized a standard-setting model developed by Richard Jaeger for use with the North Carolina High School Competency Test," and involved the "use of judges analyzing test items in making first assessments, to be reevaluated when empirical evidence became available" (Development and Standardization Manual, p. 8). The final scale was applied to the SRT standardization sample of 1,600 students, and distributions of ratings were provided for each subtest for each classification (Low, Marginal, and Adequate). Information is also provided for the development of the standards-based overall rating scale including how the test authors determined the raw score cutoffs for each of the four ratings (Above Average Degree of Readiness, Average Degree of Readiness, Marginally Ready, and Not Ready without Attention).

TECHNICAL. Limited descriptive information is provided related to the standardization sample. The KRT standardization sample was collected during the first 3 weeks of school in the fall of 2004 and consisted of "606 students from 18 schools across 12 states (California, Georgia, Idaho, Illinois, Indiana, Michigan, Minnesota, Missouri, New Hampshire, Pennsylvania, Texas, and Wisconsin)" (Development and Standardization Manual, p. 2). No information is provided regarding gender, age/grade level, race/ethnicity, social class, or IQ of those comprising the standardization sample. Although the test authors describe the standardization sample as a "representative national sample of students" (user's manual, p. 27), no data are presented as to how the characteristics of the KRT sample compare to the U.S. population as a whole.

Internal consistency estimates of reliability for the six individual subtests are satisfactory for screening but not individual diagnostic decisions. Specifically, KR-20 estimates range from .63 (Vocabulary) to .75 (Comprehension and Interpretation) and KR-21 estimates range from .49 (Visual Discrimination) to .75 (Comprehension and Interpretation). The Total Readiness score estimates include .86 (KR-20) and .83 (KR-21) with these levels also more appropriate for screening than individual decisions. Although the test authors note that a "complete assessment of readiness should involve not only readiness scores, but other factors such as classroom behavior, emotional development and parental input, as well as the child's curiosity, determination, and motivation" (Development and Standardization Manual, p. 2), they do not elaborate on using the KRT for screening versus individual decision making. The standard error of measurement of just over 2 points is provided for the total scores and the test authors note the "part-score assessments range between .70 and .99 raw score points" (Development and Standardization Manual, p. 6), which is unclear as some of the reliability estimates for individual subtests are as low as .49. The test authors do not indicate which reliability estimates are used to determine these *SEM* statistics. Item difficulty and item discrimination indexes also are provided for items included on each of the six subtests. For individual subtests, item difficulties tend to be high (with most above .70 suggesting easier items) but item discrimination indexes appear satisfactory, clustering between .26–.56. No other reliability evidence is presented such as test-retest or reliability studies using different samples other than the standardization sample.

Related to content validity, the rationale for choosing the six readiness skills included in the KRT is presented in the Development and Standardization Manual. These six readiness skills are commonly found on published kindergarten readiness tests (e.g., phonemic awareness and visual discrimination). Intercorrelations between the six skill areas are low to moderate (.24–.53) supporting the assessment of separate subskills. The six individual tests have limited "ceilings" with average scores ranging from 57%-83% of the items answered correctly with a median of 76% correct. Despite these limited ceilings, the test authors do not acknowledge this as a limitation because the KRT is concerned primarily with identifying students who have inadequate skills, implying a more diagnostic purpose for the KRT. No specific information is presented by the test authors related to item-tryouts to choose particular items that have the greatest discriminating power to include on each of the six subtests. A principal factor analysis using a Varimax orthogonal rotation of resulting factors produced a single factor supporting the use of a KRT Total Score as a measure of total readiness. Unlike the scores for the separate readiness skill areas, the test authors suggest with an average total score of 27.1 (or 75% of the 36 items) the Total Readiness score has a degree of differentiation at the upper (25% of score points) as well as the lower levels. To support the validity of the qualitative classifications, only the percentage of the standardization sample falling into each category is presented. The test authors report that for the KRT standardization sample, approximately 10% of the students were rated as "Lower than desirable," another 15% were rated as "marginal," and 75% were rated as Adequate. It is not clear that these percentages support the validity of the KRT scores.

The test authors fail to present validity evidence to support the suggested uses of the KRT. There is a specific lack of evidence related to identifying students who will have difficulty in early school learning so that instruction can be modified to meet the needs of each student. For example, no data are presented as to the number of "hits" and "misses," related to identifying students having difficulty in the kindergarten curriculum or how the individual readiness skill ratings or those for overall readiness can be translated into curricular modifications.

COMMENTARY. The exact purposes of the KRT are somewhat unclear in terms of use as a screening test versus a test that can be used for individual decision making related to curricular modification. The stated purpose of the test is to determine the extent to which competencies critical for early school learning are developed so instruction can be individualized. However, at times the test authors seem to suggest it can be used for more diagnostic purposes in terms of modifying instruction. Although possessing ease of administration and scoring, a number of weaknesses compromise the value of the KRT. These weaknesses include a lack of descriptive information about the participants included in the standardization sample (e.g., gender, SES, racial/ethnic) and the degree of representativeness of the sample, reliability data are limited to internal consistency estimates appropriate for screening purposes only, and validity data do not address the specific purposes of the test (determining specific areas of weakness that can be translated into curricular modifications). Qualitative ratings for both the total score and scores yielded by individual subtests tend to be more ambiguous and the manual does not provide adequate examples of how the test results can be used to modify instruction to meet the needs of individual students. At this time, the KRT cannot be recommended as an assessment of readiness for beginning kindergarten.

SUMMARY. The Kindergarten Readiness Test represents an easily administered and scored group screening test intended to be used with all students during the end of preschool or by the third week of kindergarten enrollment. The lack of descriptive information about the standardization sample, together with limited reliability and validity information to support the intended uses of the KRT, does not justify its use at this time.

[65]

Klein Group Instrument for Effective Leadership and Participation in Teams.

Purpose: Designed "to assess a range of behaviors that are essential for effective leadership and teamwork."

Population: Team and group participants of ages 14+.

Publication Date: 2008.

Acronym: KGI.

Scores, 13: Leadership (Assertiveness, Group Facilitation, Initiative, Total), Negotiation Orientation (Perspective Taking, Constructive Negotiation Approach, Total), Task Focus (Task Analysis, Task Implementation, Total), Interpersonal Focus (Positive Group Affiliation, Feeling Orientation, Total).

Administration: Group.

Price Data, 2008: $30 per individual online administration including a downloadable User's Guide and Individual Profile of results; $50 per group online administration (plus $25 per group member) including a downloadable User's Guide, Individual Profile, and Group Profile per group member, and 1 downloadable administration manual per group; $50 per administration manual (138 pages).
Time: (25-30) minutes.
Comments: Available for online and paper-and-pencil administration.
Author: Robert R. Klein.
Publisher: Center for Applications of Psychological Type, Inc.

Review of the Klein Group Instrument for Effective Leadership and Participation in Teams by PHILIP G. BENSON, Professor of Management, New Mexico State University, Las Cruces, NM:

DESCRIPTION. The Klein Group Instrument for Effective Leadership and Participation in Teams (KGI) is premised on the theoretical views of leadership and group dynamics as found in Jungian psychology and the Myers-Briggs Type Indicator (MBTI). The KGI proposes to assess leadership, negotiation, task, and interpersonal skills, scores that can be combined with results from the MBTI. The KGI is intended to allow people to use their MBTI information to enhance their skills in group work.

The KGI has four major scales, each with two or three subscales. The scales and their specific subscales are the Leadership Scale (subscales: Assertiveness, Group Facilitation, Initiative), the Negotiation Orientation Scale (subscales: Perspective Taking, Constructive Negotiation Approach), the Task Focus Scale (subscales: Task Analysis, Task Implementation), and the Interpersonal Focus Scale (subscales: Positive Group Affiliation, Feeling Orientation).

DEVELOPMENT. The KGI was developed over a period of many years, and is theoretically based on the Myers-Briggs Type Indicator (MBTI; 14:251) and models of group processes developed initially by R. F. Bales (1950). Fundamentally, Bales was concerned with the opposing processes of task-related behavior and socioemotional behavior in group or team contexts, and the KGI is designed to measure relevant aspects of both of these polarities.

This reviewer believes that the actual development process for the KGI could have been better described in the manual. Details are at times sketchy, but the preface to the manual does indicate that an initial set of 500 potential items was reduced to 86 for the initial model. The final set of items represents a slightly shorter instrument, but details on how the final items were derived are not clear in the manual.

TECHNICAL. The manual provides a number of indicators for the reliability and validity of the KGI. The standardization was performed with a student sample, based at Western New England College (Springfield, Massachusetts, U.S.A.). The students were drawn from undergraduate programs in education, psychology, and engineering, and a subset of graduate students working toward a master of business administration (MBA) degree. The manual suggests that these individuals are from areas where group activities are critical in employment settings, which is likely to be true, but it is still the case that the sample is skewed to a younger group of test takers (mean age of 24.2, although the range is up to 52 and as low as 17). For understanding group processes in significant work and organizational settings, at least partial inclusion of nonstudent samples would add to the value of the manual.

The sample used was a total of 311 respondents, and the group was almost perfectly split between men and women. The largest subsample, over a third of the total, was the MBA cohort. With the possible exception of the MBA cohort, samples were clearly young overall.

Gender differences were found in mean scores. Women tended to have higher scores on Perspective Taking, Interpersonal Focus, and Feeling Orientation; men had higher scores on the Task Analysis subscale. The Leadership scale, including its two subscales, did not show significant gender-based differences.

Reliability for the KGI seems to be adequate to good. As a measure of constructs, internal consistency reliability seems most relevant. Alpha coefficients range from .70 to .86 for the full sample of 311 respondents used as the normative sample. When alphas are computed separately for the male and female respondents, the smaller sample sizes result in a slightly wider range of values, as would be expected. These alphas range from .65 to .88.

Test-retest reliability is reported for a sample of 74 undergraduate student respondents, at an interval of 30 days. The resulting scale reliabilities ranged from .78 to .92. Overall, the reliability of the KGI seems reasonably well supported.

The validity of the KGI is suggested by several lines of evidence. First, because the KGI is presumed to be theoretically related to the MBTI, and to a lesser extent, the Fundamental Interpersonal Relations Orientation-B (FIRO-B), KGI scores were correlated with scores from these other instruments. For the MBTI comparisons, a relatively large sample of 1,051 respondents was used; for the FIRO-B analyses, samples were much smaller, with a total sample of 85 individuals. Although many more details are provided in the manual, overall it seems that theoretically meaningful relationships can be found between the KGI and these other, well-established measures.

A second line of evidence for the validity of the KGI is found in samples of students who were working in groups in classes. Given feedback on the KGI profiles, students evaluated their perception that the KGI was a reasonably accurate predictor of their interactions with other students in their groups. A third group of MBA students was asked to evaluate the relevance of their KGI profiles in the context of on-the-job group activities. Finally, management teams in business settings who were going through team-building exercises were asked the degree to which the KGI accurately described their behavior in group settings, and whether the information could prove useful in developing improved group skills.

All of these validation efforts seem very much focused on the construct, or possibly content, validity of the KGI. Little in the manual is suggestive of the extent to which the KGI is useful in terms of predictive validity.

COMMENTARY. The KGI seems to be a promising measure for use in a wide variety of group interventions, team building, and individual performance counseling. Indeed, the KGI appears more useful in counseling and employee development than for use as a selection instrument. The KGI manual suggests the measure could be used in selection, but notes that "the respondent remains the owner of the responses and results. Research with instruments similar to the KGI does not support the use of an individual instrument as the sole criterion for selection in a hiring process" (p. 7).

In addition, information presented in the manual (pp. 82–83) suggests that individuals can distort their responses on the KGI. In such a case, the use of a measure for counseling rather than selection is always at least partially indicated.

It is also notable that the KGI was developed on the basis of psychological theory, and not based on a particular job setting. For this reason, it would be incumbent on any user of the KGI in staffing decisions to show clear theoretical connections to a particular job, and these constructs and connections may be abstract enough to prove difficult for this measure. In short, without substantial additional data, data of a form not currently reported in the manual, use of the KGI as a staffing measure is not recommended. With additional supporting data, this position could be reversed.

Although the KGI has been developed in the context of extant models of group dynamics, one can raise the question of its suitability for the changing nature of group work in modern organizations. Increasingly, modern groups and teams are virtual in nature, often composed of individuals who are located across vast geographical distances and time zones. Little in the manual or other documents can be found to address the nature of modern groups and the applicability of the KGI in such contexts. On the other hand, this expansion could prove a useful area for further investigation.

The KGI manual does distinguish between groups and teams, and chiefly distinguishes between the two concepts based on mutual goals, accountability, and mutually shared interdependencies. Such a definition of a team does not require the actual face-to-face dynamics of traditional teams and groups. However, it would subjectively appear that KGI dimensions such as the Leadership scale (subscales of Assertiveness, Group Facilitation, and Initiative) have relevance in virtual teams, whereas such scales as Task Focus (subscales of Task Analysis and Task Implementation) are not as clearly applicable. Of course, all of this speculation is hypothetical and would require serious theoretical analysis and empirical investigation.

SUMMARY. The KGI is an interesting new measure for potential application and research in the development and investigation of group dynamics and interpersonal skills in groups. Perhaps its greatest strength is the extent to which it is based in a strong theoretical model, which allows it to be meaningfully related to a variety of contexts and applications.

Practitioners who engage in career counseling, team development, or individual performance coaching may find this instrument to be a useful addition to their approaches. Those who are getting feedback on their skills and group styles may well find the KGI to be thought provoking. Overall, it has clear potential.

REVIEWER'S REFERENCE

Bales, R. F. (1950). *Interaction process analysis: A method for the study of small groups.* Chicago: University of Chicago Press.

Review of the Klein Group Instrument for Effective Leadership and Participation in Teams by MYRA N. WOMBLE, Associate Professor of Workforce Education, University of Georgia, Athens, GA:

DESCRIPTON. The Klein Group Instrument for Effective Leadership and Participation in Teams is a self-report instrument designed to identify critical behaviors for operating effectively, as leaders or participants, in groups or teams. The Klein Group Instrument for Effective Leadership and Participation in Teams, hereafter referred to as KGI, is accompanied by an individual profile designed to identify a group or team member's group behavior, strengths, and areas where improvement might be needed. This profile provides definitive suggestions for how to improve effectiveness and a group profile is also available that allows a group or team to scrutinize its processes and modify them as necessary. The KGI provides a means of blending individual uses of psychological type with applications for groups and teams. The KGI manual states that those who take the KGI need to have the cognitive capacity to self-reflect and compare their scores to their actual group experiences and that the KGI is appropriate for adolescents ages 14 and over and for adults. It is a self-report instrument that takes from 25–30 minutes to administer. It can be administered online through the Center for Applications of Psychological Type, Inc. (CAPT) website or using a paper-and-pencil method. If administered online, an individual profile is available as soon as the KGI is scored. The website provides basic information about the KGI itself, the KGI for individuals, the KGI for groups, how to take the KGI, sample KGI profile reports, how to purchase the KGI, and how to use results in conjunction with Myers-Briggs Type Indicator (MBTI; 14:251) results. The KGI can be administered to groups online and group members are able to receive a group and individual profile. If the paper-and-pencil KGI is administered, the answer sheets must be sent to CAPT for scoring and individual and/or group profiles can be returned.

DEVELOPMENT. Development of the Klein Group Instrument for Effective Leadership and Participation in Teams involved close examination of both quantitative and qualitative empirical evidence over 12 years. It is grounded in Jungian psychology and the work of Isabel Briggs Myers and Katharine Briggs, best known for the Myers-Briggs Type Indicator instrument (MBTI) which served as its foundation. It is the work of Robert R. Klein, who suggests that its origins lie in experiences over 30 years–from his early years as a trainer and consultant to his dissertation research. After having discussed type and group behavior over time with the director of the Center for Applications of Psychological Type (CAPT), it was suggested that CAPT would be interested in supporting the development of a group instrument that could be used in conjunction with the MBTI. This suggestion resulted in a project to create an instrument that could achieve two goals: to be used as an independent test as well as to complement the MBTI.

Klein began with a list of 500 group behaviors, from which 86, said to represent a cross section of the total list, were selected for use in the first instrument administered to 400 college and high school students. Findings from a factor analysis showed a four-factor solution with the following four factors: assertiveness, initiative, leadership, and perspective-taking and negotiation behaviors for small groups. Each factor yielded high coefficient alphas. These positive results led Klein to consult his own dissertation work and the work of Bales (1950). Klein observed a connection between the task and socioemotional construct and the leadership and perspective-taking negotiation factor. Klein's interpretation of this relationship resulted in the integration of leadership and effective memberships into one model. From the master list of 500 group behaviors, task and interpersonal behaviors were added to the instrument making the four major scales: Leadership, Negotiation Orientation, Task Focus, and Interpersonal Focus. Klein consulted the work of Fisher (Fisher, Ury, & Patton, 1991) and others with regard to negotiation and used these findings to expand the negotiation scale and complete the instrument.

Klein administered the completed instrument to a cross section of 1,300 students (undergraduate education, psychology, engineering, and graduate business) who were receiving professional training in areas where group skills were especially relevant. More than 400 interviews with a variety of students from this group were conducted as a method to evaluate further the responses to the KGI. The cofounder of CAPT, Mary McCaulley, began to monitor Klein's further development of the instrument and CAPT scored the KGI and MBTI so results could be compared and a determination of how the two instruments might complement one another could be made. Findings showed meaningful connections and Klein concluded that the KGI was a feasible complement for the MBTI. From this point, CAPT managed the final phase of the instrument's development. The instrument was shortened for greater focus and time efficiency, a computerized scoring system was developed, and additional field tests were conducted to obtain reliability and validity estimates using similar graduate and undergraduate samples. Final data analyses consistently revealed coefficient alphas of .70 or above on all scales and subscales.

CAPT conducted a final round of field testing with more than 100 business and professional people. Most participants were part-time MBA students at Western New England College (WNEC) and worked full-time jobs, whereas 40 of them were involved in the Springfield Leadership Institute (SLI) sponsored by the WNEC School of Business. All of the SLI participants found that the KGI gave them practical insights that helped them increase their leadership and groups skills, as did the remaining MBA students. The final round also included use of the KGI in two intervention studies with business management teams. Both studies showed the ability of the KGI to help teams refine and improve their performance. As the participants used their results to expand their leadership and group skills in their job settings, Klein held executive coaching sessions to oversee their progress. He included training with the MBTI to inform them about their psychological type and found that use of the MBTI type information with the KGI data helped them gain a deeper understanding of their personalities, which helped them make meaningful changes as leaders and group members. The instrument currently in use includes four major scales and nine subscales based upon a total of 60 item statements on a 5-point scale.

TECHNICAL. The guide for administering the KGI includes a chapter focused on the normative sample. The guide states, "the normative sample for the Klein Group Instrument (KGI) assessment tool came primarily from the key representative subgroups that had been involved in the larger research study with the instrument" (manual, p. 53). The normative sample is identified in text as 311 WNEC students. A table provides data referred to as "essential characteristics" (manual, p. 53) for the normative sample and subsamples as: n = 24 (7.7%) undergraduate education, n = 83 (26.7%) undergraduate engineering, n = 35 (11.3%) undergraduate psychology, and n = 112 (36%) graduate business. However, these numbers represent n = 254 (81.7%) instead of the size of the normative sample n = 311 (100%) as given in text.

When contacted about this discrepancy, the Director of Marketing at the Center for Applications of Psychological Type explained that the four categories are not exhaustive as indicated by the following statement from the guide, "In addition to the subgroups mentioned, there was also a sprinkling of undergraduate arts and sciences students included in the study, both traditional college students and older, nontraditional students, majoring in criminal justice, English, history, and sociology" (manual, p. 53). The Director of Marketing also referenced the guide as presenting "information on the essential characteristics of the total sample and the important subgroups" (manual, p. 53). Finally, the guide also explains the rationale for focusing on these groups with the following statement: "The subgroups represented business and professional communities that have had a practical interest in group processes and in group training" (manual, p. 53). The Director reported that some groups were too small a number to meaningfully group. Finally, the Director reported that data from 57 undergraduate students were drawn from both traditional, and older, nontraditional student populations from several different major areas of study" (R. Rothschild, personal communication, June 11, 2009).

Based on the explanations the norming group would be identified as: n = 24 (7.7%) undergraduate education, n = 83 (26.7%) undergraduate engineering, n = 35 (11.3%) undergraduate psychology, n = 112 (36%) graduate business, and n = 57 (18.3%) additional undergraduate arts and sciences for a total of n = 311 (100%). The undergraduate education and psychology students were arts and sciences students as were the 57 students not identified in the table. The guide also shows the age and gender "essential characteristics" (manual, p. 53) which include the 13 male and 44 female arts and sciences students. Therefore, the norm group was almost equal in terms of the male/female essential characteristic with n = 156 (50.16%) males and *n* = 155 (49.84%) females. The students ranged in age from 17 to 52 and, assuming that the ages of the 57 arts and sciences students fell within this range, the mean age for the entire sample was about 24.2 years. The racial breakdown, apparently not considered an essential characteristic for this normative group, was presented and indicated that the majority of students were Caucasian American (94%), whereas only 3% were Hispanic American, 2% African American, and 1% Asian American.

Results of two general classes of reliability estimates for the KGI are provided. The internal consistency reliability estimates were based on the *n* = 311 sample, which apparently includes the 57 undergraduate students majoring in criminal justice, English, history, and sociology. Coefficient alpha was used for the four major scales and ranged from .82–.86. The range for coefficient alpha on the nine subscales was from .70–.80. Coefficient alphas were provided for both genders to examine the patterns of performance on the KGI. For men, these analyses resulted in a range of .81–.84 on the four major scales and .65–.77 on the nine subscales and for women a range of .82–.88 on the four major scales and .71–.81 on the nine subscales. Similar data were not provided for age to examine the patterns of performance on the KGI. Test-retest reliability was accomplished using 74 students from WNEC who were not a part of the original *n* = 311 sample used for the internal consistency reliability tests. Pearson correlations ranged from .87–.92 on the four major scales and .78–.89 on the nine subscales over a retest period of 30 days.

Validity of the KGI was examined using four strategies. First, scores on the KGI were examined to determine if they correlated with scores on the MBTI (*n* = 1,051 WNEC) and the Fundamental Interpersonal Relations Orientation-Behavior (FIRO-B; *n* = 85 WNEC) instruments as one might predict for these theoretical constructs. Results of the KGI and MBTI correlation study showed no correlations above .40, which the test authors interpreted to indicate "that the KGI does not simply measure psychological type, but performs as an independent instrument that has a number of significant and meaningful correlations with the MBTI instrument" (manual, p. 73). Results of the KGI and FIRO-B study showed significant relationships between the EI, EC, WC, and EA scales and the KGI scales.

Second, MBA students (*n* = 67) enrolled in two courses (Team Leadership and Organizational Behavior) were given personal profiles and self-assessed the accuracy of their results with other students in the courses with whom they had been doing group work. Results showed a majority of the students felt the KGI provided them with accurate information about their group behaviors on the four main scales and nine subscales. Third, MBA students in the two courses previously mentioned wrote reflection papers based on having used their KGI profiles to refine their job performance. These papers were examined and results indicated that the students made meaningful adjustments in their group behaviors based on their KGI results. The final validation effort was performed through an analysis of two intervention studies where the KGI was used with management teams for team building. Results indicated that in both studies, those who received their KGI results, confirmed the accuray of the results, and made adjustments based on the results, subsequently increased their personal and team effectiveness. It was concluded that positive outcomes based on modifed behavior would not have been possible if the scores had not been accurate.

COMMENTARY. The KGI's theoretical background includes theories of group behavior offered by key theorists such as Robert Bales and Wilfred Bion at Tavistock. Such theories are widely accepted and provide a worthwhile framework for the examination of group behavior. The KGI has undergone reasonably significant testing and evaluation in a preliminary fashion using a variety of techniques to help ensure the accuracy of its scores and subsequent profiles. However, if the characteristics of a norm group are not specific, relevant, and well-defined, it is possible for the composition of the group to promote or hamper different types of diagnostic interpretations. Therefore, it is important to consider the characteristics of those included in the normative sample for the KGI. Even if the students in the norm sample were in proportion to the demographics of the regional population, use of the KGI on a broader population could be inconclusive.

The characteristics of the norming group that were considered essential for the KGI were age and gender. The KGI manual appropriately suggests that those who take the KGI need to have the cognitive capacity to self-reflect and compare their scores to their actual group experiences. However, it also suggests that the KGI is appropriate for adolescents as young as 14, whereas the youngest in its norming group were age 17 and patterns of performance for age were not provided in the manual. Also, an important characteristic in today's diverse landscape, race/ethnicity, was not considered an essential characteristic. The small number of students from racial groups other than Caucasian American suggest that although the norming sample may be representative of the larger regional population, it may not be representative of the broader population using the KGI. For example, Caucasian Americans accounted for 94% of the KGI norm sample, but only 75.1% of the total population was identified as Caucasian American in the most recent U.S. Census. African Americans accounted for only 2% of the KGI norm sample yet African Americans accounted for 12.3% of the population in the most recent Census (McKinnon, 2001). These examples suggest that the appropriateness of the KGI with different ethnic and/or cultural groups is unknown.

SUMMARY. It appears that the KGI assessment may be able to provide valuable information for managers seeking to engage specific employees in examining behaviors that are critical for effective team or group work as well as leadership and participation. It can also serve as a quality assessment for specific individuals. However, further research to provide evidence of its appropriateness for those younger than 17, specifically 14–16-year-olds, is needed to clarify that those adolescents generally have the cognitive capacity to self-reflect and compare their scores to their actual group experiences. Overall, employing the KGI with groups younger than 17 may not provide useful results. Ordinarily, those considering an assessment tool such as the KGI would select a tool where the demographic composition of the norm group presents characteristics that approximate those of the group to which the instrument is to be given. Further research to include substantive samples of persons from racial and ethnic groups other than Caucasian Americans would enhance its appropriateness for use with such groups or individuals. Again, employing the KGI with groups or individuals of racial and ethnic groups other than Caucasian Americans may not produce useful results.

REVIEWER'S REFERENCES

Bales, R. F. (1950). *Interaction process analysis: A method for the study of small groups.* Cambridge, MA: Addison-Wesley.

Fisher, R., Ury, W. L., & Patton, B. M. (1991). *Getting to yes: Negotiating agreement without giving in.* New York: Penguin.

McKinnon, J. (2001). The black population: 2000. Washington, DC: U.S. Census Bureau.

[66]

Koppitz Developmental Scoring System for the Bender Gestalt Test, Second Edition.

Purpose: Designed "to document the presence and degree of visual-motor difficulties in individual examinees."
Population: Ages 5–7, 8–85+.
Publication Dates: 1963–2007.
Acronym: KOPPITZ-2.
Scores: Total score only.
Administration: Individual.
Levels, 2: Ages 5-7, 8-85+.
Price Data, 2009: $227 per complete kit including 25 examiner record forms ages 5-7, 25 examiner record forms ages 8-85+, 25 emotional indicators record forms, Bender Gestalt II stimulus cards, examiner's manual (2007, 192 pages), scoring template; $42 per 25 examiner record forms (specify ages 5-7 or 8-85+); $26 per 25 emotional indicators record forms; $53 per Bender Gestalt II stimulus cards set; $86 per examiner's manual (2007, 200 pages); $9 per scoring template.
Time: (6-20) minutes.
Comments: An update of the Bender Gestalt Test for Young Children; current edition utilizes drawings from the Bender Visual-Motor Gestalt Test, Second Edition (16:30).
Author: Cecil R. Reynolds.
Publisher: PRO-ED.

Review of the Koppitz Developmental Scoring System for the Bender Gestalt Test, Second Edition by JOSEPH C. KUSH, Associate Professor, Duquesne University, Pittsburgh, PA:

DESCRIPTION. The Bender-Gestalt remains one of the most popular yet controversial tests available to psychologists. Over time, the Bender has become associated with several distinct practices within the field of assessment: as a projective personality test, a measure of brain impairment, and more recently as a test of visual-motor development.

The Koppitz Developmental Scoring System for the Bender Gestalt Test, Second Edition (KOPPITZ-2) is a revision of the original Koppitz Bender Gestalt Test for Young Children. The KOPPITZ-2 is composed of 16 stimulus cards taken from the Bender Visual-Motor Gestalt Test, Second Edition (Bender-Gestalt II; T7:311) and is used to assess visual-motor integration skills. Children ages 5 through 7 years complete the first 13 cards, and examinees 8 through 85+ years complete Cards 5 through 16. Each of the 16 cards contains a geometric design consisting of dots, lines, angles, and curves combined in a variety of relationships.

The KOPPITZ-2 is individually administered and untimed. Stimulus cards are presented to examinees one at a time, in numerical order, until all age-appropriate cards have been presented. Using a pencil, the examinee is simply told to copy the drawings onto a sheet of paper and to "try to make your drawings look just like the drawings on the card" (examiner's manual, p. 15). Initially, examinees are provided with a single sheet of unlined, white paper but additional sheets of paper may be provided if requested. Administration normally takes between 6 to 20 minutes.

Scoring is relatively straightforward—the raw score for the KOPPITZ-2 is the sum of the scores for each of the Bender cards. Children ages 5 through 7 are scored on 34 separate items, whereas older children and adults receive scores on 45 items. Descriptive criteria are provided to guide the scoring that is recorded in the respective examiner record form. Examinees receive a "0" if their drawing fails to meet the criteria described in the scoring rubric and a "1" if their drawing is satisfactory. A description of the scoring guide is provided in the examiner's manual as are scoring guides and examples. Raw scores can then be converted into standard scores including *T*-scores, *z*-scores, percentiles, stanines, and normal curve equivalents. A separate table in the examiner's manual allows for the calculation of age equivalent scores.

The KOPPITZ-2 also provides 12 Supplemental Emotional Indicators (EIs) using the drawings as a projective test. Errors (e.g., confused order, wavy lines) score 1 point with a total score range of 0 to 12. No normative data are provided for interpreting the total score; however, the test author states that a score of greater than "3" is unusual and may be a sign of emotional disturbance. The examiner's manual does caution that interpretations of EIs are the primary responsibility of the individual examiner.

DEVELOPMENT. The Bender-Gestalt was first developed in 1938 and originally consisted of nine geometric figures. Despite the fact that for the first 20 years of the test's existence there was no formal system for scoring the test, the Bender was used as a projective technique and to diagnose intelligence, emotional disturbance, brain impairment, and visual-motor coordination, and the majority of individuals who used the test scored it using very subjective "clinical judgment." Following Meehl's warnings about the practice of clinical prediction, the next 20 years saw the development of as many as six different methods for scoring the Bender-Gestalt. These scoring systems required from 20 seconds to several hours to complete. Although Lauretta Bender developed a rough scoring method for her test, the method subsequently developed by Koppitz is the one most frequently utilized today by clinicians.

The original Bender was revised in 2003, as the Bender-Gestalt II, and included additional designs, a recall phase, supplementary motor and perception tests, and an observation form. Perhaps the most important component of the Bender-Gestalt II revision was the creation of a normative sample stratified to match the 2000 U.S. Census.

Although the Bender-Gestalt and Bender-Gestalt II has been administered to children and adults, perhaps its greatest current popularity exists in the assessment of the perceptual-motor skills of children. Theoretically, visual-perceptual skills are thought to be related to, yet distinct from, visual-motor skills. Historically, the Koppitz Developmental Bender Test Scoring System became known as the scoring method best suited for assessing visual-motor skills.

The KOPPITZ-2 uses the same standardization sample of 3,535 individuals as the Bender-Gestalt II. Standardization data were collected in 2001 and 2002 and the data were subsequently licensed by the Riverside Publishing Company to PRO-ED for the development of the KOPPITZ-2 scoring. Stratification variables included age, gender, race/ethnicity, geographic region, and educational attainment (socioeconomic level). Additionally, several clinical and special populations were also oversampled. The overall standardization sample, however, is more than adequate and includes more than 1,000 additional examinees than were included in the standardization of the most recent edition of the Beery-Buktenica Developmental Test of Visual-Motor Integration (VMI; 17:20).

TECHNICAL. The KOPPITZ-2 examiner's manual provides information regarding the reliability of the scale. Coefficient alpha reliabilities are reported across age, gender, and race/ethnicity. Coefficient alphas are reported for 20 age ranges, and as would be expected, the lowest coefficients occur for young children. Overall alpha reliability is acceptable at .88; however, coefficients do not reach this level until approximately 10 years of age.

This limitation is pointed out in the examiner's manual (p. 48), "At ages 5 years to 7 years, the alpha values range from .77 to .81, values considered barely adequate for individual applications, but satisfactory nevertheless." Coefficient alphas of .84 to .93 are reported for individuals ages 8 and older. This variability in alpha reliabilities appears to reflect the developmental nature of the measured construct and these reliabilities are comparable with similar tests of visual-motor skills (e.g., Beery-Buktenica; VMI).

The stability of the scale is also reported in a study using 202 examinees who were tested on two occasions following an interval of approximately 18 days. Test-retest reliabilities are reported separately across four age groups and ranged from .75 to .84, with an average coefficient of .78. These scores are lower than were reported for retest scores of the Beery, which produced coefficients of .89 for the VMI, .85 for Visual Perception, and .86 for Motor Coordination. Finally, following an examination of 60 archived KOPPITZ-2 protocols, interrater reliability is reported at .91 for the 5-through 7-year-old sample and .93 for a sample of older examinees.

Taken together, this reliability information is limited. Given the legacy of poor reliability, historically associated with previous versions of thc Bender, greater attention to the stability of the scale was expected. Of course, when measuring a construct that is influenced by developmental maturation, changes in scores across time are to be expected. However, the test-retest interval of the single study mentioned in the examiner's manual was just over 2 weeks, hardly enough time for significant developmental changes to have occurred. Additionally, coefficients are only reported for four age groups; test-retest coefficients across gender, race/ethnicity, and education level are absent entirely. Equally unfortunate is the lack of test-retest reliability data for clinical or special populations.

Psychometric properties of the KOPPITZ-2 with regards to validity are even more wanting. Correlations of the KOPPITZ-2 with a variety of measures of intellectual ability are presented in the examiner's manual. As would be expected, the KOPPITZ-2 correlates much higher with Performance IQ than Verbal IQ; however, the correlations are lower than this reviewer would expect (WISC-III Performance IQ = .63; WAIS-III Performance IQ = .38; Stanford-Binet 5 Nonverbal IQ = .40). Clearly, the constructs of visual-motor ability and nonverbal cognitive ability should be related. However, these data indicate that clinicians should not use the KOPPITZ-2 as even a brief screening measure of intellectual ability.

The examiner's manual also provides the results of two concurrent validity studies comparing the KOPPITZ-2 with measures of academic achievement. Specifically, the examiner's manual presents validity data comparing the KOPPITZ-2 with the Woodcock-Johnson—Third Edition (*N* = 149) and the Wechsler Individual Achievement Test-II (*N* = 61). As mentioned in the examiner's manual (p. 62), "The corrected correlations are small for the most part, although it is interesting to note that the highest correlations are with the areas of reading." With regard to the WJ-III, correlations range from .07 to .46 with a median correlation of .23. Correlations were higher with the WIAT-II, ranging from .20 to .52 with a median correlation of .37.

Relatedly, with a sample of 45 children, the KOPPITZ-2 was compared with a second measure of visual-motor skills, the Beery-Buktenica Developmental Test of Visual-Motor Integration–Fourth Edition. The concurrent validity correlation, corrected for restriction of range, was a moderate .46, indicating that the two measures overlap or possess approximately 21% shared variance. Given the perceived similarities between the two tests, this statistic is surprisingly low.

Additionally, the examiner's manual compares mean scores from seven samples of exceptional students with demographically matched samples of nonexceptional students. Means and standard deviations for each of these groups aare presented in the examiner's manual; as would be expected, in almost all instances, individuals with disorders demonstrated lower mean performance than the matched control sample. In most instances these differences were relatively small.

Finally, the examiner's manual contains an entire chapter describing how the KOPPITZ-2 can be used to assess emotional problems. Unfortunately, this practice is supported by absolutely no psychometric data. The author does caution (p. 87) that, "An interpretation of EIs should be limited to underlying tendencies and attitudes; one should merely use the EIs to develop hypotheses, which then need to be checked against other psychological data and observations." Despite the caution, the chapter continues with multiple unsubstantiated claims for emotional interpretations (e.g., "Increase in size on designs is associated with low frustration tolerance and explosiveness," and "Small size in drawings is associated with anxiety, withdrawal, constriction, and timidity." This practice of armchair hypothesizing perpetuates psychology at its worst and ignores a wise and essential caveat taught to most first-year graduate students, "In God we trust, all others must have data."

COMMENTARY. With the stature and widespread usage of the Bender-Gestalt test, many psychologists have been eagerly awaiting the revision of the KOPPITZ-2 scoring system. Unfortunately, the results of the recent revision are disappointing. The instrument fails to address many of the criticisms of the instrument that have been leveled for over 50 years. Specifically, the KOPPITZ-2 continues to evidence modest short-term, test-retest reliability, particularly for children at young ages. Concurrent validity is the only type of validity addressed in the examiner's manual (no predictive data are presented) and correlations with tests of intelligence, achievement, and even other measures of visual-motor skills are somewhat low.

The author does attempt to put a good face on the limited psychometric data by writing (p. 68), "A test manual can only present a summary or a snapshot of validity evidence at a specific point in time," and later (p. 69), "Rather, users of any test should follow the accumulated literature of the ongoing process of validation of test score interpretations." This premise is supported in the *Standards for Educational and Psychological Testing*, which note that "validation is the joint responsibility of the test developer and test user" (AERA, APA, & NCME, 1999, p. 11). Although the psychometric data presented in the examiner's manual do meet the letter of this law, they fail to meet the spirit. Additional reliability and validity studies, with larger populations, conducted prior to the publication of the scale could have greatly improved the integrity of the instrument. Relatedly, additional research with clinical or exceptional populations would also have served to increase the generalizability of the KOPPITZ-2 scores.

In addition to greater attention to more adequate scale development, the scale could also have addressed the issue of incremental validity, the information a test provides above what is already known. Perhaps in the context of multiple regression analyses, the author could have examined how much predictive power the inclusion of KOPPITZ-2 scores would add to an existing test battery. Additionally, the limited psychometric properties of the scale might have been reframed if the author had demonstrated that the information derived from the KOPPITZ-2 could be done in less time or by examiners with less training. However, data in support of either of these claims are not provided.

The fundamental limitation of the scale, however, relates to validity; what exactly does the KOPPITZ-2 measure? It demonstrates low to moderate correlations with tests of intelligence and academic achievement. It produced only moderate correlations (.46 and .51) with another scale that measures the same construct, visual-motor skills. And despite cautions from the test author, and no psychometric data whatsoever, the scale still produces a score purported to be associated with emotional problems.

SUMMARY. Psychologists have known for many years that statistical prediction rules consistently outperform subjectively derived clinical predictions. In fact, 35 years ago Paul Meehl warned that "if we [psychologists] do not take strong steps to clean up our act, some smart lawyers and sophisticated judges will either discipline or discredit us" (Meehl, 1997, p. 98).

The publication of the recently derived KOPPITZ-2 scoring system for the Bender-Gestalt test had the opportunity to provide data that would allow for defensible statistical predictions. Not only does the KOPPITZ-2 miss the mark as a psychometrically sound measure of visual-motor skills, the decision to include examples of how the scale can be used to assess emotional problems will only perpetuate inconstancy and inaccuracy in clinical decision-making. In its use primarily as a diagnostic indicator, the KOPPITZ-2 also fails to generate any type of treatment validity, that is, information about how the scale provides knowledge beneficial to treatment outcome.

Perhaps when used as a research instrument, the KOPPITZ-2 will stimulate a more rigorous validation process. In its current version the KOPPITZ-2 possesses many psychometric shortcomings that significantly limit the usability of the instrument. Additional research should examine the diagnostic accuracy of the scale including the rate of identified false positives and false negatives. However, until more extensive reliability and validity studies are completed, great caution should be undertaken when using the scale. It is hoped that the generation of expanded empirical findings, generated by independent researchers, will inspire the development of a more psychometrically sound KOPPITZ-3.

REVIEWER'S REFERENCES

American Educational Research Association, American Psychological Association, & National Council on Measurement in Education. (1999). *Standards for educational and psychological testing*. Washington, DC: American Educational Research Association.

Meehl, P. E. (1997). Credentialed persons, credentialed knowledge. *Clinical Psychology: Science and Practice, 4* (2), 91–98.

Review of the Koppitz Developmental Scoring System for the Bender Gestalt Test, Second Edition by KATHARINE A. SNYDER, Associate Professor of Psychology, Methodist University, Fayetteville, NC:

DESCRIPTION. The Koppitz Developmental Scoring System for the Bender Gestalt Test, Second Edition (KOPPITZ-2), assesses the capacity to associate motor responses with visual stimuli through figure copying. Reportedly, the KOPPITZ-2 can evaluate visual-motor deficits, identify individuals for referral, document intervention effectiveness, and assist research. Evaluating visual-motor skills within the context of copying is often utilized in rehabilitation program planning activities for brain-injured adults and children, particularly those with constructional dyspraxias.

Administered individually (6–20 minutes), participants are instructed to copy Designs 1–13 (ages 5–7 years) or Designs 5–16 (ages 8–85 years) in a room free of distractions and with adequate lighting. Examinees are allowed up to one piece of 8.5 by 11-inch paper per drawing. Examinees are not permitted to move the paper from the portrait position, but may place as many drawings per page as they wish and erasure is allowed. No time limits are given, but mean completion times as a function of age are provided in the manual. Stimulus cards are aligned with the top of the paper and all designs must be administered in the prescribed order. When examinees finish a drawing, the next card is placed on top of the previous one. Design cards are in front of examinees throughout the entire test and no component of the test involves memory. It is recommended that examiners be alert to physical and emotional well-being (e.g., fatigue, affect, attention) on the part of an examinee, and there is room on the record form to note potential confounds. An emotional indicators form is included, which records items such as confused order, wavy lines, dashes for circles, progressive increases or decreases in size, etc. However, it must be noted that there are no reliability or validity data presented on these indicators.

Through summing the number of specific criteria met (e.g., the design is composed of circles) for each of the designs, a raw score is obtained, which can then be converted into percentiles and standard scores (mean of 100 and *SD* of 15). Individuals scoring at or below 1.3 *SD*s are considered mildly impaired, whereas individuals scoring at or below 2 *SD*s are considered to be significantly impaired. However, the utility of these impairment distinctions is limited because "it remains the examiner's responsibility to review other test data and the examinee's history to determine the source and meaning of the impairment" (examiner's manual, p. 26). A transparency template is provided to speed the scoring process and eliminate the need for rulers and protractors. *T*-scores, *z*-scores, normal curve equivalents, stanines, and age equivalents are also given. A brief discussion of the problematic nature of the use of age equivalents is provided. Authors note the need to assess fine motor coordination and visual perception independently prior to drawing inferences from the KOPPITZ-2. It is recommended that examiners be formally trained and knowledgeable of the *Standards* of the American Educational Research Association, American Psychological Association, and the National Council on Measurement in Education (1999). It is also recommended that there be additional training if the test is to be administered to older adults.

DEVELOPMENT. The KOPPITZ-2 is a significant revision of the original Koppitz scoring system. Because the original Koppitz norms, from 1963, were based on 5–10-year-olds, the revision updates and extends the norms to older individuals (5–85 years of age) as well as incorporates the seven new designs in the Bender-Gestalt II (Brannigan & Decker, 2006). Other than to emphasize that visual skills and fine motor skills should be assessed independently, there is minimal discussion about the adequacy of utilizing copying as the only measure of visual-motor integration. Item selection information is limited. The original Koppitz scoring system was derived by assessing the errors that young children would make on the original nine Bender cards. Initially there were more than 100 items for the KOPPITZ-2 assessment of the Bender-Gestalt II. When it became apparent that separate scoring elements would be needed for the youngest age group (5–7 years) and the other group (8–85 years), 34 items were retained for the younger group and 45 items were retained for the other group. Scores seem to reach a ceiling fast and do not exhibit a pattern of decline until very late in life. This decline very late in life is mainly related to the three-dimensional items (Card 14 and Card 16). Evaluators must obtain a copy of the Bender-Gestalt II for information on design selection.

TECHNICAL.

Standardization. "The KOPPITZ-2 uses the same standardization sample as the Bender Gestalt II" (examiner's manual, p. 31), which consists of a normative sample of 3,535 individuals ranging in age from 5 years to over 85 years of age. Reportedly, this is representative of the U.S. Census 2000 with regard to age, sex, race/ethnicity, geographic region, and socioeconomic level (inferred by years of education).

Reliability. Because visual motor integration is believed to be a stable construct, KOPPITZ-2 scores should be reliable. To establish test-retest reliability, a sample of 202 individuals ranging in age from 5 years to 85 years received the test twice within 14 to 21 days. Uncorrected test-retest coefficients were as follows: .73 (5–7 years), .75 (8–17 years), .85 (18–49 years), .75 (50+ years), and .77 (total sample). Coefficients "following correction for any *SD*s that were not exactly 15 as in the normative sample" (examiner's manual, p. 50) are also provided, but vary little from the uncorrected values. To establish interrater reliability, two evaluators (the author and a school psychologist) scored 30 protocols for the 5–7-year-old group (with a resultant correlation of .91) and 30 protocols for the 8–47-year-old group (with a resultant correlation of .93). This reviewer would prefer to see the interrater reliability correlations extended to include more older adults and the disability/exceptionality samples.

Validity. Given that copying is the only measure of visual-motor integration, the KOPPITZ-2 is limited with respect to construct validity. The KOPPITZ-2 shows a developmental pattern similar to other tests of copying (e.g., the Full Range Test of Visual Motor Integration), in that skills increase rapidly in early childhood and show modest decline in late adulthood. This pattern is offered as support for construct validity. However, it should be noted that this is presented as "theory-based evidence" (examiner's manual, p. 57) and hypothesis testing is not undertaken.

Content validity assessments were undertaken to ascertain the representativeness of the items in measurement of the visual-motor integration construct. Coefficient alphas (internal consistency) ranged from .77 to .93. Because only one age group had a coefficient alpha less than .80 (the 5-year-olds), the KOPPITZ-2 appears to exhibit internal item consistency across 20 age levels. Coefficient alphas ranged from .73 to .92 for the gender and race/ethnicity subgroups of the sample. Because only three subgroups (females, White, African American) were less than .80, the KOPPITZ-2 again appears to exhibit internal item consistency across these two subgroups. For all but the speech-language disordered category of the Disability/Exceptionality subgroups for ages 5–7, "N/A" is given because there were not enough cases to calculate the coefficient alphas (examiner's manual, p. 50). This paucity is likely the result of the difficulty of assessing the disability categories at such young ages.

Criterion-related validity is assessed through comparisons of examinees' scores on the KOPPITZ-2 with the Wechsler Intelligence Scale for Children (WISC-III; n = 58), Wechsler Adult Intelligence Scale (WAIS-III; n = 80), Stanford-Binet Intelligence Scales (SB-5; n = 387), Woodcock-Johnson Achievement Test (WJ-III; n = 151), Wechsler Individual Achievement Test (WIAT-II; n = 61), and the Beery-Buktenica Developmental Test of Visual-Motor Integration (Beery VMI; n = 45). The Disability/Exceptionality sample was made up of individuals primarily labeled as having "no exceptionality/disability" (examiner's manual, p. 61). Many of the categories have zero participants (e.g., mental retardation, emotional disturbance, autism). Correlations corrected for "range restriction and reliability attenuation" (examiner's manual p. 62) are presented throughout. A summary of the largest uncorrected correlations within each test is as follows: WISC-III Performance IQ (.50), WISC-III Full IQ (.47), WISC-III Perceptual Organization Index (.51), WAIS-III Verbal IQ (.48), WAIS-III Performance IQ (.45), WAIS-III Full Scale IQ (.49), WAIS-III Perceptual Organization Index (.46), SB-5 Full IQ (.31), SB-5 Nonverbal IQ (.33), SB-5 Visual Spatial Index (.30), SB-5 Quantitative Reasoning Index (.32), WJ-III Reading Passage Comprehension (.30), WIAT-II Math Reasoning (.36), WIAT-

II Spelling (.35), WIAT-II Written Expression (.34), WIAT-II Written Language Composite (.39), WIAT-II Pseudoword Decoding (.35), and WIAT-II Reading Composite (.32).

A separate series of studies was undertaken to assess the utility of the KOPPITZ-2 in assessing visual-motor integration within the exceptionality/ disability categories. These categories were as follows: Attention Deficit Hyperactivity Disorder (*n* = 42), Learning Disability–Written Expression (*n* = 30), Learning Disability—Reading (*n* = 118), Learning Disability—Math (*n* = 26), Mental Retardation (*n* = 55), Autism (*n* = 55), and Giftedness (*n* = 109). Because no statistical findings are reported for these studies (only means and *SD*s are provided), conclusions concerning the disability categories cannot be made.

COMMENTARY. Evaluations of perceptual-motor skills in general are difficult because of the lack of construct validity that has historically affected tests of this nature. It is problematic to conceptualize and therefore not easy to assess, yet many educators believe it underlies reading ability (Salvia, Ysseldyke, & Bolt, 2007). Copying tests are known to have little relationship to academic success (Salvia, Ysseldyke, & Bolt, 2007). When construct definitions of perceptual-motor integration are limited, there is a danger of circular reasoning (e.g., if all autistic individuals have perceptual-motor deficits and a particular individual exhibits a deficit, this student is therefore autistic). The test authors stress that deficits in Visual-Motor Integration create problems for everyday functioning, yet this link is not clearly explicated. To the credit of the test authors, it is emphasized throughout the manual that the KOPPITZ-2 is not to be utilized for diagnostic purposes in any way. There is space to record motivation, fatigue, and attention-related factors, but the precise relationship to the construct of visual-motor integration remains unclear. The test authors assert that the unstructured format promotes the assessment of emotional indicators, yet no validity data are presented for these, and the clinical insight gained from them is very limited.

SUMMARY. The KOPPITZ-2 is a well-done assessment of visual-motor integration, within the domain of copying, for children and adults, which may have utility in many settings. To the credit of the authors, the assessment can be administered, scored, and evaluated reasonably quickly. The scoring system appears to have good interrater reliability and allows for generalizations to the U.S. Census, but not the clinical samples. As with the Bender-Gestalt II, the KOPPITZ-2 scoring system does not enable evaluators to determine the causes of deficits in Visual-Motor Integration, and it cannot be used to distinguish clinical groups. Nevertheless, the test authors assert that assessment of copying skills is necessary in and of itself. When given in association with measures of visual perception and motor integrity, the KOPPITZ-2 can be a useful tool if copying skills alone are the sole purpose of the assessment.

REVIEWER'S REFERENCES

American Educational Research Association, American Psychologist Association, & National Council on Measurement in Education. (1999). *Standards for educational and psychological testing*. Washington, DC: American Educational Research Association.

Brannigan, G. G., & Decker, S. L. (2006). The Bender-Gestalt II. *American Journal of Orthopsychiatry, 76*(1), 10-12.

Salvia, J., Ysseldyke, J. E., & Bolt, S. (2007). *Assessment: In special and inclusive education* (10th ed.). Boston, MA: Houghton Mifflin Company.

[67]

Leadership Versatility Index.

Purpose: Designed to measure "versatility on two complementary pairs of leadership dimensions: forceful and enabling, and strategic and operational."

Population: Managers, executives.

Publication Dates: 2001-2007.

Acronym: LVI.

Scores, 7: Overall Versatility, Forceful-Enabling Versatility, Strategic-Operational Versatility, Specific Leadership Behavior Items, Team Productivity, Team Vitality, Overall Effectiveness.

Administration: Group.

Forms, 2: Standard LVI 360, LVI 360-plus.

Restricted Distribution: Special authorization from publisher is required to use the LVI.

Price Data, 2008: $275 per complete Standard LVI 360 test kit; $350 per LVI 360-plus kit including open-ended questions.

Time: (20) minutes.

Comments: The Standard LVI 360 includes only numerical feedback and the LVI 360-plus includes open-ended questions.

Authors: Robert E. Kaplan and Robert B. Kaiser.

Publisher: Kaplan DeVries Inc.

Review of the Leadership Versatility Index by MARK A. STAAL, Operational Psychologist, U.S. Special Operations Command, Ft. Bragg, NC:

DESCRIPTION. The Leadership Versatility Index (LVI) comes in two forms, a 67-item instrument which takes 15–20 minutes to complete, and an enhanced version (LVI 360-plus) with 72 items that requires about 40 minutes to complete. Both 360-degree feedback instruments are administered, scored, and reported over the Internet and are divided into several sections: (a) six questions to assess the strength of relationship between the respondent and subject as well as capturing basic demographic data, (b) four sets of 15 questions assessing different leadership dimensions (Forceful, Enabling, Strategic, and Operational Leadership), (c) seven questions concerning perceived effectiveness, and (d) five qualitative/open-ended questions (enhanced version only). The middle 60 questions are uniquely formatted on a 9-point scale. The response options include *too little, the right amount, and too much.* There are also seven effectiveness questions that follow a "more traditional 5-point Likert scale format common to traditional Likert-type scales." What distinguishes the LVI from other instruments is its unique curvilinear Likert-type format. Many tests use a linear Likert methodology that simply measures a given dimension along a continuum; one either has a little bit, a moderate amount, or a lot. Such instruments fail to capture when more is too much and less is too little. By way of analogy, the LVI attempts to measure leadership versatility—"porridge" that is just right opposed to that which is too cold or too hot, an analogy provided by the authors of the instrument.

The authors argue that the LVI rests on two pillars of leadership, each with a distinct opposite: Forceful versus Enabling, and Strategic versus Operational. One pillar represents how one leads (social/interpersonal), and the other represents what one leads (functional/business). Within each dimension lies an optimal midpoint (the "just right porridge"). The test generates a Versatility score calculated for each pillar suggesting the degree to which the individual makes optimal use of both dimensions in a given pair. The LVI was developed for use with managers and executives to aid them in understanding their own leadership repertoire and to assist them in developing their leadership versatility. The instrument authors state that the LVI's development is based on 20 years of reflection and consulting to senior managers and over a decade of statistical research. The manual points out that professionals interested in using the LVI must receive authorization from Kaplan DeVries Inc. Moreover, there are a number of prerequisites for this authorization, including education, training, and experience. Furthermore, individuals interested in using the LVI must attend a training and certification workshop.

As for the 360-degree nature of the instrument, the LVI manual recommends a minimum of seven feedback surveys be completed for each targeted individual manager/executive (direct reports, peers). Superiors may also provide ratings, with a minimum of four superiors preferred. The instrument authors provide at least two reasons for this minimum. The first concerns the reliability of reporting (the more reports, the greater the reliability) and the second concerns ensuring the anonymity of those surveyed. LVI feedback is aggregated and therefore no single individual respondent is identifiable. This requirement makes prudent sense given the desire for honest feedback. However, the fewer the feedback sources, the less the anonymity.

DEVELOPMENT. The authors designed a prototype of the test in 1993 and the first technical manual appears to have been published in 2001. (The most recent facilitator's guide is dated 2007.) As stated earlier, the instrument is based on the notion that leadership falls along four dimensions. These four dimensions were derived from content analyses, literature review and an iterative series of exploratory factor analyses, Item Response Theory (IRT) methodology, and finally, a confirmatory factor analysis. The results indicated that factor loadings were adequate (ranging between .56 and .84) across all items examined. Only loadings on the Forceful and Enabling leadership dimensions were provided for this review.

According to the 2001 technical manual the normative sample used to validate the LVI consisted of 107 senior executives, reflecting primarily a demographic of 40- to 60-year-old White males from various U.S. firms. In addition, there were 1,036 co-workers, 165 superiors, 362 peers, and 509 subordinate surveys completed on the target sample. The homogenous nature of this sample should be kept in mind when considering the instrument's use with a more diverse management population (e.g., cross-cultural use, ethnic, age, or gender-diverse sample). In a more recent, but undated Appendix to the LVI manual, the authors indicate subsequent analyses have been conducted with a total sample size of 562 managers (5,334 co-workers). No further demographic data were provided about this secondary sample.

TECHNICAL. The LVI technical manual provides a description of the instrument's psychometric properties as well as what procedures were used to validate its use, as does the more recent

Facilitator's Manual. Following a split-half procedure (development and holdout validation halves), the two halves were combined in order to establish reliability and interrater agreement. The LVI's internal consistency was calculated using coefficient alpha. The results of these analyses were mixed. The LVI exceeded .70 coefficient alphas for all four scales, although in its previous version only three scales did so. Moreover, according to the 2001 technical manual, the LVI might be seen as deficient on measures of average factor loadings when examining Forceful and Enabling scales (.66 for Forceful/.63 for Enabling) as well as on measures of average variance extracted (.43 for Forceful/.40 for Enabling). The latter two results suggest that what the LVI may be measuring is something other than its intended constructs. These values have been shown as improved in the more recent Facilitator's Manual. In response, the test authors provide a rather lackluster endorsement for their own instrument by stating, "we still believe that it is a useful tool" and future work should "more adequately map the respective construct domains" (Kaiser & Craig, 2001, p. 5). Both statements appear to reflect the instrument authors' realization that such psychometric results are problematic, and again, these values were shown to be improved in the 2006 Facilitator's Manual. The results of the IRT analysis revealed a difference in the measurement precision between Forceful and Enabling scales. Specifically, Enabling scales showed greater standard errors than Forceful scales. Furthermore, both scales performed better at their measurement tails (i.e., the hot and cold porridge) than they did measuring optimal response levels. In other words, the test appears to be better at "selecting-out" or identifying problematic styles than it does at "selecting-in" or identifying optimal styles. The instrument fared better on measures of interrater reliability and interrater agreement.

Several aspects of the instrument were examined to determine its validity. The LVI appears to have good face and content validity; its question pool appears appropriate to the stated task (assessing leadership versatility). The LVI was examined in relation to other measures of managerial flexibility and found to correlate well with these instruments. Using the various rating sources (superiors, peers, subordinates, self) the degree to which the LVI demonstrates good convergent validity (across groups) was also examined. The result of this analysis suggests general convergence among raters. However, when individuals' versatility indices were correlated with their effectiveness ratings (across rating sources), a different picture emerged. The most consistent disconnect was between self-ratings and all others. Leaders tend to see themselves very differently than others see them. However, the authors of the LVI primarily use perceived effectiveness as a measure of effectiveness. It is regrettable that they were unable to use a more objective measurement to establish effectiveness (e.g., a measure of criterion-related concurrent validity). Although perceptions of the effectiveness of a leader may have value, they are not nearly as valuable if the goal is to measure productivity or material success (e.g., number of widgets made, number of contracts landed). Moreover, there is no question that measures of effectiveness may mean very different things based on the rating source, ultimately confusing what is meant by being "effective." For example, both a subordinate's ability to assess his or her boss's effectiveness as well as a clear idea of what a subordinate uses to define such success is unclear and likely to be very different from his or her superior's assessment of self-effectiveness. This fact makes comparing perceptions difficult and combining them into an index of effectiveness nearly impossible.

The theory behind the LVI presumes a negative relationship between each dimensional polarity (e.g., Forcefulness should not be positively correlated with Enabling). However, when analyzed, the Strategic and Operational dimensions were unrelated, although a negative relationship was found between Forceful and Enabling leadership. The former finding is counter to expectation (they should be negatively related, not absent of a relationship). The authors provide some speculation for this finding; however, the results remain poorly understood and the implications for the theory are also unclear.

COMMENTARY. As with many instruments used in the field of leadership development, the LVI has several appealing features as well as several detractors. The test is built on the notion that versatility is a key element in leadership, which can be characterized by two pillars (each in polarity with an opposite). Using a quadrant model, one's leadership versatility can be calculated in space relative to an optimal point of versatility. The LVI uses the unique characteristic of curvilinear Likert-type scaling that allows for the capture of "too much" and "too little" across the various dimensions examined. This aspect represents some of the LVI's unique contributions to the measurement of leadership style. Unfortunately, there are potential problems to note as well. First, underlying the entire theory is the notion that there is an optimal versatility associated with leadership within specific situations. Moreover, it seems implied that versatility is somehow fixed in space relative to degrees of forcefulness, enabling, operational, and strategic dimensions, at least for specific situations. Certainly, reason would suggest that "optimal versatility" (based on a style of interaction) is relative to the nature of the task under consideration. Therefore, one's forcefulness versus enabling style must be calibrated with respect to the task in question and not simply balanced relative to one another. If this assumption is correct, then one would not necessarily expect source ratings to converge given that each point of optimal versatility must logically be relative to difference points of reference (e.g., different tasks require different approaches to achieve an optimal outcome).

There are some concerns associated with the psychometric properties of the LVI. For example, data on the instrument's reliability (as measured by average factor loadings and the internal consistency of the operational scale) need clarification given their apparent increase in the last decade. Although it performed adequately in interrater reliability, continued review of the form's reliability is needed. Also, the lack of negative correlation between Operational and Strategic scales is confusing and it may call into question the entire dimensional duality.

SUMMARY. The developers of the LVI have invested significant experience and research in constructing a somewhat unique 360-degree leadership style index. It is innovative in theory (measuring leadership versatility) and in question methodology (using a curvilinear Likert-type scale). The LVI is founded on the notion of two pillars of leadership style, each with a distinct opposite: Forceful versus Enabling leadership and Strategic versus Operational leadership. Each dimension is posited to hold an optimal midpoint (the "just right" porridge, using the story of Goldilocks as an analogy). Although the LVI offers some unique features, until recently, its psychometric properties were not what one might hope; recent data appear better to be sure. However, it remains an instrument of promise and it provides a number of advantages over traditional leadership style measures.

REVIEWER'S REFERENCE

Kaiser, R. B., & Craig, S. B. (2001). *Leadership Versatility Index technical report: Item selection and validation*. Greensboro, NC: Kaplan DeVries Inc.

Review of the Leadership Versatility Index by MATT VASSAR, Curriculum and Outcomes Assessment Coordinator, Oklahoma State University, Tulsa, OK:

DESCRIPTION. The Leadership Versatility Index (LVI) is a 67-item, 360-degree evaluation used to measure four dimensions of leadership behavior. These dimensions include Forceful, Enabling, Strategic, and Operational Leadership, of which the Forceful-Enabling and Strategic-Operational dimension pairs are diametrically opposed. Specifically, 12 items comprise each dimension. Following items from the four subscales, there are 6 items designed to measure the performance of the team for which the leader is responsible as well as 1 item addressing the overall effectiveness of the leader. Open-ended questions are also available to detail the leader's specific strengths and shortcomings. The items designed to measure the four leadership dimensions are based on a 9-point scale ranging from *Much Too Little* (-4) to *Much Too Much* (+4). Hence, the zero scale point is deemed the "right amount" on the trait being measured. For additional clarification, a negative score on an item indicates that the leader underperforms on a particular behavior; a positive score indicates overperformance. The scoring procedure for the LVI is complex and consists of deriving a Versatility score (ranging from 0–100), which represents the optimal use of opposing behaviors rather than exhibiting excess or deficiency in such behaviors. Three Versatility scores are noted on the final report: an overall Versatility rating, a Forceful-Enabling Versatility rating, and a Strategic-Operational Versatility rating. The mathematical computation for Versatility scores is derived using geometry, specifically the Pythagorean theorem. A Versatility score computed for each pair of items is computed separately for each rater. The average of these values is calculated across all relevant item pairs, yielding an overall Versatility score for a particular rater. Next, the average Versatility score across all raters in the rating group is computed. This index reflects how close the leader's scores are to the "right amount." Scores are then evaluated in comparison with a normative database.

DEVELOPMENT. The LVI was developed in response to the "more is better" structure of most employee rating scales. The test developers correctly noted that many performance issues are the result of leaders going overboard or pushing too hard for results. Additionally, the scale was created due to a deficit in leadership measurement related to versatility. The test developers designed a prototype instrument for assessing forceful and enabling dimensions in 1993. Subsequent editions based on psychometric analysis and emerging research have since been introduced. The LVI is heavily grounded both theoretically and empirically, having drawn from the works of Bass (1990), House (1971), and many others.

TECHNICAL.

Normative sample. The LVI appears to have extensive psychometric work over a period of many years and across many iterative versions of the scale. To discuss all such work is outside the scope and length requirement of this review. Some reports on technical information of the LVI are not based on what is believed to be the latest scale version; more recent data are based on smaller sample sizes. The overall normative sample was composed of seven independent samples from data collected between 1994 and 2004. Respondents included executives, superintendents, and middle managers. Overall, 562 targets and 5,334 raters were included in different aspects of psychometric analysis. No further demographic is provided about these samples, making it impossible to provide further comment.

Reliability. Two forms of score reliability were reported for the LVI. First, internal consistency estimates (coefficient alpha) were calculated from scores for each of the four dimensions. In the 2001 Technical Manual, coefficient alpha was .82 for the Forceful subscale, .81 for the Enabling subscale, .79 for the Strategic subscale, and .53 for the Operational subscale. In the 2007 Facilitator's Guide, these values were all over .70. The technical report notes that these calculations are based on average values across six independent samples. It appears that these coefficients were derived by aggregating the superior, peer, and subordinate ratings in each of the six samples. Second, convergence among multiple raters was assessed though interrater reliability and interrater agreement statistics. Intraclass correlation coefficients (ICC), used to determine interrater reliability, were calculated for a single rater, and across multiple raters (k = 2 and 4 for superiors, k = 4 and 7 for peers and subordinates). Single rater ICCs ranged from .25 to .53 for the superior ratings, .22 to .38 for the peer ratings, and .20 to .31 for the subordinate ratings across dimensions. Multiple rater ICCs generally fell in the .50 to .90 range across subsamples and dimensions depending on the number of raters. Interrater agreement coefficients ranged from .89 to .93 for superiors, .85 to .89 for peers, and .85 to .89 for subordinates across leadership dimensions. If .70 is used as the benchmark for acceptable estimates of alpha, then only the earlier version of the Operational dimension fell below this standard. It is the opinion of this reviewer, however, that .80 is a more acceptable minimum benchmark. In this case, both Strategic and Operational fell below this standard, although later indices appear more promising. Clearly, additional psychometric work is needed on the Operational dimension. In most cases, interrater reliability and agreement coefficients fell within appropriate ranges (>.70) based on the number of raters.

Validity. A number of steps were taken to examine validity of the leadership dimensions. First, based on theoretical considerations of a polarity effect between opposing dimensions (Forceful-Enabling and Strategic-Operational), test developers hypothesized a negative relationship between these converse subscales. Their hypothesis was supported for the Forceful-Enabling pair; however, the Strategic-Operational pair produced no correlation. Examination of test data revealed a range restriction for strategic leadership, possibly contributing to this unexpected finding. The structural model was next tested. A series of exploratory and confirmatory factor analyses were conducted. Based on results from exploratory analysis, 17 items were selected to represent the leadership dimensions. Test developers found adequate model fit from the confirmatory analysis and provide fit statistics within recommended ranges. Furthermore, both Forceful-Enabling Versatility and Strategic-Operational Versatility were significant predictors of perceptions of overall effectiveness, with roughly half of the variance in overall effectiveness being accounted for by versatility on both dualities. Evidence of convergent and discriminant validity is also noted. The LVI correlates with other measures of managerial flexibility and employee vitality.

COMMENTARY. The LVI is an interesting measure of leadership behaviors based on emerging developments in leadership theory. The length of the LVI is comparable, if not shorter, than other leadership assessment tools making it a user-friendly choice when considering other available options. The iterative development of the LVI over a period of many years to improve psychometric properties is to be commended. The reviewer is also interested in the unique scoring procedure derived for this instrument as well as the interpretation of these scores. Psychometric weaknesses include very low internal consistency estimates for the Operational subscale, at least until the most recent analysis and the absence of correlation between the Strategic-Operational dimension pair. Other psychometric analyses of the LVI were generally favorable.

SUMMARY. The LVI may be used to identify prominent or deficient leadership qualities for employees. Its 360-degree feedback is particularly attractive to those wanting a holistic understanding of a leader's competence. Given the promising psychometric characteristics of scores produced by this instrument, researchers or organizations may want to consider the use of the LVI as a primary or supplemental leadership measure.

REVIEWER'S REFERENCES

Bass, B. M. (1990). *Bass and Stogdill's handbook of leadership: Theory, research, and managerial applications* (3rd ed.). New York: Free Press.

House, R. J. (1971). A path-goal theory of leader effectiveness. *Administrative Science Quarterly, 16*, 321–338.

[68]

Level of Service/Risk, Need, Responsivity.

Purpose: "Designed to assist professionals in management and treatment planning with adult and late adolescent male and female offenders in justice, forensic, correctional, prevention, and related agencies."

Population: "Male and female offenders 16 years of age and older."

Publication Date: 2008.

Acronym: LS/RNR.

Scores, 9: Criminal History, Education/Employment, Family/Marital, Leisure/Recreation, Companions, Procriminal Attitude/Orientation, Alcohol/Drug Problem, Antisocial Pattern, Total (General Risk/Need Factors).

Administration: Individual.

Parts, 2: Interview Guide, QuikScore; Sections, 8: Specific Risk/Need Factors, Prison Experience-Institutional Factors, Other Client Issues, Special Responsivity Considerations, Risk/Need Summary and Override, Risk/Need Profile, and Program/Placement Decision.

Price Data, 2010: $146 per complete kit including 25 interview guides, 25 QuikScore forms, 25 ColorPlot forms, and scoring guide (63 pages); $75 per 25 interview guides; $45 per 25 QuikScore forms; $23 per 25 ColorPlot forms; $29 per scoring guide.

Time: [40–120] minutes.

Comments: Test is part of the LSI family of instruments including the Level of Service Inventory–Revised (LSI-R; 17:107), the Level of Service Inventory–Revised: Screening Version (LSI-R:SV; T7:1449), the Youth Level of Service/Case Management Inventory (YLS/CMI; 17:108), and the Level of Service/Case Management Inventory (LS/CMI; T72842); the Interview Guide is a semi-structured interview used to obtain ratings for the QuikScore form; Sections 2 through 8 provide additional information that is not numerically scored.

Authors: D. A. Andrews, James L. Bonta, and J. Stephen Wormith.

Publisher: Multi-Health Systems Inc.

Review of the Level of Service/Risk, Need, Responsivity by JEFFREY A. JENKINS, Associate Professor, Roger Williams University, Bristol, RI:

DESCRIPTION. The Level of Service/Risk, Need, Responsivity (LS/RNR) is based on a series of instruments developed by the publisher, including the Level of Service Inventory–Revised (17:107), the Level of Service Inventory–Revised: Screening Version (T7:1449), the Youth Level of Service/Case Management Inventory (17:108), and the Level of Service/Case Management Inventory (LS/CMI; T7:2842). Each of these instruments is used for the evaluation, treatment, and management of adult or adolescent offenders. These "level of service" instruments are risk assessment tools used in criminal and juvenile justice settings to allow screening and determination of an appropriate course of action for management of individual offenders. As with all of these instruments, the LS/RNR examines and summarizes characteristics of offenders that relate to intervention and treatment decisions. Indeed, the items on the LS/RNR are identical to those on the LS/CMI, but the LS/RNR does not include the Case Management Plan, Progress Record, and Discharge Summary sections of the LS/CMI. By excluding these latter sections, the LS/RNR was developed for "users or organizations who want to have access to the most current research when conducting their level of service risk assessment but already have in place an offender history management/case management process with which they are comfortable" (LS/RNR scoring guide, p. 4). Thus, it is intended for use as a classification and placement instrument that can augment an organization's existing case management process.

The LS/RNR consists of an interview guide, QuikScore form, ColorPlot profile, and scoring guide. The interview guide allows the administrator to gather relevant information from institutional files and by interviewing the offender in five areas: Section 1: General Risk/Need Factors (43 items), Section 2: Specific Risk/Need Factors (35 items), Section 3: Prison Experience—Institutional Factors (14 items), Section 4: Other Client Issues (Social, Health, and Mental Health; 21 items), and Section 5: Special Responsivity Considerations (11 items). Section 1: General Risk/Need Factors consists of questions relating to the offender's Criminal History, Education/Employment, Family/Marital situation, Leisure/Recreation, Companions, Alcohol/Drug Problem, Procriminal Attitude/Orientation, and Antisocial Pattern. Section 2: Specific Risk/Need Factors examines Personal Problems with Criminogenic Potential and History of Perpetration, which includes Sexual Assault, Nonsexual Physical Assault and Other Forms of Violence, and Other Forms of Antisocial Behavior. Section 3: Prison Experience—Institutional Factors considers History of Incarceration (past and present) and Barriers to Release. Section 4: Other Client Issues (Social, Health, and Mental Health) consists of questions relating to the three areas indicated, and Section 5: Special Responsivity Considerations includes a variety of questions relating to motivation, anxiety, attitudes, intelligence, communication, mental disorders, or psychopathy.

Data gathered from each of the five sections are transferred to the QuikScore form as Yes/No responses or ratings on a 4-point scale made by the interviewer from the offender's responses (3 = A satisfactory situation with no need for improvement, 0 = A very unsatisfactory situation with a very clear and strong need for improvement). Responses to items comprising subsections in Section 1 yield eight subcomponent scores and a total score. These scores are entered on the QuickScore form. Responses to items from Sections 2 through 5 can be used to guide case management. The administrator can use the guidelines in the scoring guide to make a risk assessment and, using the ColorPlot profile, compare the offender to other inmates or community offenders based on normative samples (see Ciampi, 2007, and Cox, 2007, for reviews of the latest norms).

In addition to the five sections summarized above, the LS/RNR, like the LS/CMI, also contains a Risk/Need Summary and Override (four administrator decision items), Risk/Need Profile, and Program/Placement Decision. Unlike the LS/CMI, the scoring for all of these sections is performed on a single QuikScore form. This ease of scoring is one of the justifications for creation of the LS/RNR.

DEVELOPMENT. Because the LS/RNR was developed using items from the LS/CMI, the development process used for the LS/CMI is applicable. Because that process has been discussed previously (Bauman, 2007; Thorpe, 2007), a brief summary here will suffice. The LS/RNR's immediate predecessor, the LS/CMI, was based on "a broad social learning perspective on criminal behavior" (LS/RNR Scoring guide, p. 2). Using areas of offender risk identified in the research literature and from consultation with practitioners, the test authors constructed items in the areas identified earlier, relying on the well-accepted theory that an increase in these risk factors for an offender increases the likelihood of reoffending. Moreover, responsivity to human services programs was identified as a function of a variety of offender characteristics (e.g., motivation, gender, ethnicity, and learning style). The result is an instrument that reflects a comprehensive model of the relationship among risk/need, responsivity, and intervention applicable to a variety of offender populations.

TECHNICAL. The technical characteristics of the LS/RNR are the same as those of the LS/CMI. These are discussed in the LS/CMI user's manual (Andrews, Bonta, & Wormith, 2004), which includes separate chapters on reliability and validity and norms. Users wishing more information about reliability and validity are therefore required to purchase the LS/CMI manual separately. The norms are the subject of two earlier reviews (Ciampi, 2007; Cox, 2007) and are not discussed here.

The reliability for Section 1 of the LS/RNR is reported in terms of each of the most common measures of reliability: internal consistency, test-retest, parallel forms, and interrater. The test-retest, parallel forms, and interrater estimates were derived from a number of different studies exploring the measurement characteristics of the LS/CMI but, as the test authors point out in the LS/CMI user's manual (Andrews et al., 2004, pp. 114-115), they suffer from a variety of potentially confounding effects that make them less useful. However, analysis of data from the norm sample of approximately 76,000 Canadian offenders and 48,000 offenders in the U.S. yielded internal consistency estimates for Section 1. Reliability is sufficiently high for the instrument's intended purposes, and is reported separately for each of the scored subsections. Alpha coefficients were found to be .92 for the total scale, and subscale estimates ranged from .50 to .87. Separate internal consistency estimates are also reported by gender, country (U.S. and Canada), and setting (community and institutional). These do not vary markedly from the total norm sample estimates. Alpha coefficients were also reported for Sections 2 through 5 based on the Canadian norms alone. These were found to range from .24 (Section 3) to .72 (Section 4) for incarcerated offenders, and from .37 (Section 2.2) to .70 (Section 4) for offenders in community-based programs.

As with reliability, the LS/CMI user's manual (Andrews et al., 2004) also provides various sources of evidence of validity for the LS/RNR. Of particular importance for a classification instrument such as the LS/RNR is its predictive validity. Several studies of predictive validity examining the relationship between the LS/CMI and various outcomes (e.g., rearrest, reincarceration) are summarized by the publisher. Validity coefficients for Section 1 and its subsections were found to range from .04 to .63 in samples from the United States, Canada, the United Kingdom, and Singapore. For the most part, the moderate correlations between Section 1 of the LS/CMI and recidivism measures indicate that the LS/RNR possesses adequate validity for correctional classification decision making.

COMMENTARY. As a "repackaging" of the LS/CMI, the LS/RNR is a more "user-friendly" version of its predecessors. It offers a concise risk assessment for offender classification without the case management tools of the LS/CMI. The interview guide and QuikScore form allow users to gather the comprehensive information needed to make informed decisions about an offender's needed level of service. Because the items of the LS/RNR duplicate items from the LS/CMI, the LS/RNR scoring guide is a shortened version of the LS/CMI user's manual. Unfortunately, the LS/RNR scoring guide includes very limited information about the psychometric characteristics of the instrument, and no discussion of the instrument's reliability and validity, which is extensively reported in the LS/CMI user's manual. Given the value of this information to potential users of the LS/RNR, a summary of technical characteristics reported in the LS/CMI user's manual should be included in the LS/RNR scoring guide.

SUMMARY. Like the earlier Level of Service instruments offered by the publisher, the LS/RNR is an excellent assessment tool. The items that comprise the LS/RNR are research-based and have been used and studied extensively in a variety of populations over an extended period of time. The LS/RNR also reflects a sound approach to instrument development, and possesses the technical characteristics that allow users to confidently rely on its scores when used in the intended manner. It offers clearly presented score reports and profiles, is easy to administer and score, and may be confidently used with a variety of offender groups.

REVIEWER'S REFERENCES

Andrews, D. A., Bonta, J. L., & Wormith, J. S. (2004). *Level of Service/Case Management Inventory user's manual.* Toronto, Canada: Multi-Health Systems.

Bauman, S. (2007). [Review of the Level of Service/Case Management Inventory: An Offender Assessment System.] In K. F. Geisinger, R. A. Spies, J. F. Carlson, & B. S. Plake (Eds.), *The seventeenth mental measurements yearbook* (pp. 483-485). Lincoln, NE: Buros Institute of Mental Measurements.

Ciampi, D. F. (2007). [Review of the Level of Service Inventory—Revised [2003 Norms Update]]. In K. F. Geisinger, R. A. Spies, J. F. Carlson, & B. S. Plake (Eds.), *The seventeenth mental measurements yearbook* (pp. 479-480). Lincoln, NE: Buros Institute of Mental Measurements.

Cox, A. A. (2007). [Review of the Level of Service Inventory—Revised [2003 Norms Update]]. In K. F. Geisinger, R. A. Spies, J. F. Carlson, & B. S. Plake (Eds.), *The seventeenth mental measurements yearbook* (pp. 480-483). Lincoln, NE: Buros Institute of Mental Measurements.

Thorpe, G. L. (2007). [Review of the Level of Service/Case Management Inventory: An Offender Assessment System]. In K. F. Geisinger, R. A. Spies, J. F. Carlson, & B. S. Plake (Eds.), *The seventeenth mental measurements yearbook* (pp. 485-487). Lincoln, NE: Buros Institute of Mental Measurements.

Review of the Level of Service/Risk, Need, Responsivity by MARK H. STONE, Adjunct Professor, Aurora University, Aurora, IL:

DESCRIPTION. The Level of Service/Risk, Need, Responsivity (LS/RNR) is an interview/treatment planning instrument deemed appropriate for male and female offenders 16 years of age and older. The interview schedule, LS/CMI, is designed to assess and subsequently guide treatment/placement decisions in forensic settings. The test authors identify the "big eight" factors as the essential elements of the instrument. They provide "concrete, quantitative guidelines" for determining level of risk/need in each of the eight subcomponents, and "strength" notations to supplement the often negative elements that frequently accompany assessment of this population.

DEVELOPMENT. The current instrument evolved from earlier versions described and referenced in the scoring guide. The integration of assessment and intervention within the LS/RNR follows a model presented in the last section of the scoring guide. The model's targeted risk factors, and client noncriminal needs and strengths are further specified by reference to the test authors' studies, and those of others marshaled to organize the LS/RNR model into an integrated approach for the comprehensive assessment of offenders. The LS/RNR is the latest version in a collection of instruments since the 1980s with the Level of Service/Case Management Inventory (LS/CMI) evolving from the Level of Service Inventory–Revised (LSI-R). The general risk/need level is defined by eight LS/CMI subcomponents and (items): Criminal History (8), Education/Employment (9), Family/Marital (4), Leisure/Recreation (2), Companions (4), Alcohol/Drug Problem (8), Procriminal Attitude/Orientation (4), and Antisocial Pattern (4). The items were originally developed by identifying the key elements critical in determining offender assessments. These details are not fully described. Instead, a matrix table provides the correlation coefficients between the LS/CMI and LSI/R for a sample of 340 individuals. The total score correlation was .96, and the subcomponent coefficients ranged from .17 to .68 with a median of .59. Two additional tables using large U.S. standardization samples produced higher subcomponent correlations, but the median and range of subcomponents were much lower than the total score. Other tables provide the user with information about other studies and samples, but the values reported above were the highest ones overall.

The interview guide is a 28-page form that directs a structured interview, and facilitates recording and collating information from the interview. The test authors suggest using this guide, but indicate that users may "develop their own semi-structured interview."

The QuikScore form has eight sections comprising the eight subcomponents. A Yes/No or 0-1-2-3 rating scale summarize the collected data culminating in a Risk/Need profile including each of the eight subcomponents, total score, risk rating, and override conditions for extenuating circumstance. The ColorPlot profile permits immediate conversion of raw scores to cumulative frequency values for over 3,000 female inmates and over 17,000 female community offenders from North America. The reverse side provides the means to convert raw scores similarly for over 35,000 male inmates and/or over 79,000 male community offenders. The gradation from a white background for lower scores to higher scores with a red background indicates high risk/needs. A Gender-Informed Assessment supplement offers two pages of information and references supporting the LS/CMI appropriateness for female offenders.

Chapter 2 of the LS/CMI manual provides 25 pages of detailed instructions for scoring the instrument. The test authors caution against using the QuikScore form without first completing the full administration of the instrument. Their caution is prudent because using only the QuikScore would risk a less comprehensive evaluation. The test authors also caution that acquaintance with the instrument materials is not sufficient: "The LS/CMI require[s] a considerable amount of preparation and training. Without careful, systematic training, reliability suffers accordingly" (LS/CMI manual, p. 116). The importance of carefully assessing offenders makes comprehensive interviewing a necessity. These assessments should be made or be supervised by a competent and licensed professional. Chapter 3 provides almost 60 pages of additional interpretation information with numerous case studies to assist in the appropriate interpretation of the instrument.

TECHNICAL. The LS/RNR provides norms for a large (N = 135,791) North American sample of offenders. Further subgroup samples give data for Canadian, U.S., institutional-placed, and community-placed offenders as well as data from special studies. A variety of target populations allow the selection of appropriate norms by which to evaluate scores.

The reported alpha reliability for a correctional female sample was .91, and close to the reported .89 coefficient for males. The reported alpha for the normative community female sample was .94 compared to .93 for males. A supplemental table permits scores from the earlier LSI-R, to be converted to the current LS/RNR assessment system. The test authors do not recommend a prorating of the scores but offer recommendations for how to address conversion in Appendix B of the scoring guide. This section includes a table providing an item-by-item comparison of both editions.

Reliability information is given in Chapter 5 for the LS/CMI. Internal consistency estimates using alpha coefficients are provided for sample sizes ranging from 124,000 to over 135,000. The total score reliability estimates for North American offenders, by institution/community and female/male ranged between .88 and .93. Reliability estimates for the eight subcomponents of the LS/

CMI ranged from .48 to .87 with a median of .70. Lower reliability estimates were associated with the five subcomponents that have only two or four items. Five studies with samples ranging from about 300 to 900 reported total score alpha estimates of .87 to .91. The subcomponent alpha estimates ranged from .32 to .87 with a median of .67. A small sample of 18 unidentified individuals participated in a test-retest study. The test-retest ranged over an average of 26 days with a total score correlation of .88. The subcomponent coefficients ranged from .16 to .91. Lower estimates were from the subcomponents containing two or four items. Consequently, subcomponent scores should be interpreted with caution. Standard error of measurement values were reported for North American offenders by institution/community and female/male. These values were all similar with a *SEM* estimate of 3 raw score points for the total score. Subcomponent estimates ranged from about one raw score point to .5 points over a smaller range of possible values.

Predictive validity is moderate. Recidivism is the dependent variable for many tables. The correlation of the LS/CMI Section 1 Total score to "any recidivism" was .44 for 561 probationers and .34 for 923 inmates according to Table 6.1. The Section I Total score correlated -.48 to "outcome." These two values (.44 and .48) are the highest in the entire table with lower subcomponent values. Section 1 Total score correlated .63 for recidivism with a sample of 441 female offenders. Subcomponent values were lower ranging from .04 to .59 with a median of .34. The correlations between the LS/CMI Section 1 total score for a male sample to Parole Success were r = .26 (N = 203), to General Recidivism r = .40 (N = 340), to Violent Recidivism r = .30 (N = 340), and to Re-Incarceration r = .38 (N = 324). Subcomponent values were all lower. Concurrent validity was assessed by comparing the LS/CMI Total Score for N = 340 to the SIR (Rettinger, 1998) r = .57, and SFS (Rowe, 1999) r = .44 for general risk/need total. Both estimates were judged highly correlated by the test authors. Mean differences and statistics were given for various offender groups. The problem with these tables is that the large size of the samples looks impressive, but makes all but the slightest difference statistically significant. The 95% confidence intervals are provided so that users can draw their own conclusions from these data. Additional tables provide the user with more information, but nothing is presented that provides more convincing data than the information already reviewed.

COMMENTARY AND SUMMARY. The LS/CMI is "based upon a social learning theory of criminal behavior. It is a general theory of criminal behavior that explains criminal conduct regardless of the setting, the offense and the person" (LS/CMI manual, p. 143). The test authors argue that the LS/CMI and "its derivatives" are expected to function irrespective of setting, offense, and person. The logic driving this statement rests upon accepting a social learning theory sufficient to explain, support, and defend LS/RNR validity. These quotes, and "20 years of validity research" appear insufficient for presenting such a conclusion. Nor are the data sufficient for these generalizations.

The suggestion that test users may elect to create their own semistructured interviews is an invitation to potential problems. It assumes interviews will be conducted by trained and experienced persons. Inviting users to follow their own course encourages interviewers to wing-it and short-cut a full evaluation. The consequences for anything less than thorough interviewing risks less than valid evaluations, jeopardizes the process, and can have later repercussions in studies of reliability and validity. Exposure to the materials is also not sufficient for competency in using the LS/RNR as the test authors indicate.

The strength of this instrument lies in the development of the interview schedule that is provided. Administration and interpretation information are ample and clearly explained. The reliability studies indicate the instrument has utility. Its validity is suggestive, but not strongly supported by the data. I remain hesitant to accept these data as conclusive for more than modest indications in the direction of validity. However, I recommend using the LS/RNR.

REVIEWER'S REFERENCES

Rettinger, J. (1998). *A recidivism follow-up study to investigate risk and need within a sample of provincially sentenced women.* Unpublished doctoral dissertation, Carleton University, Ottawa, ON.

Rowe, R. C. (1999). *The prediction of recidivism in a parole sample: An examination of two versions of the Level of Service Inventory.* Unpublished report. Carleton University, Ottawa, ON.

[69]

Light's Retention Scale.

Purpose: Developed to assist in determining if grade retention will have a positive or negative outcome for a particular student.

Population: Grades K-12.

Publication Dates: 1981-2006.

Acronym: LRS.

Scores: Total score only.
Administration: Individual.
Price Data, 2007: $95 per complete kit including 50 recording forms, 50 parent guides, and manual (2006, 96 pages); $35 per 50 recording forms; $25 per 50 parent guides; $25 per 50 Spanish parent guides; $35 per manual.
Time: (10-15) minutes.
Comments: A nonpsychometric instrument used as a counseling tool with a specific retention candidate; Spanish parent guides available.
Author: H. Wayne Light.
Publisher: Academic Therapy Publications.
Cross References: For reviews by Bruce K. Alcorn and Frederic J. Medway of the 1991 Revision, see 11:208 (2 references); for reviews by Michael J. Hannafin and Patti L. Harrison of an earlier edition, see 9:622, see also T3:1328 (1 reference).

Review of the Light's Retention Scale [2006 Edition] by LORAINE J. SPENCINER, Professor of Special Education, University of Maine at Farmington, Farmington, ME:

DESCRIPTION. Light's Retention Scale [2006 Edition] is a rating scale to use in making decisions regarding a student's retention or promotion. Teachers, school psychologists, school counselors, or other individuals may complete the rating scale that is designed for students in kindergarten through high school. This assessment includes a manual, recording forms, and parent information sheets that provide information about retention and why retention may be beneficial. Parent forms are available in English and Spanish.

Light's Retention Scale [2006 Edition] consists of 20 categories that appear to predict student success if retained, according to the manual. These 20 categories include: Preschool Attendance, Current Grade Placement, Student's Age, Physical Size, Gender and Grade Progress of Student, Previous Grade Retention, Student's Knowledge of the English Language, Immature Behavior, Emotional Disorders, History of Conduct Disorder and/or Defiance, Experiential Background, Siblings, Parents' Participation in School Activities, Student Mobility, School Attendance, Present Level of Academic Achievement, Student's Attitude about Possible Retention, Motivation to Complete School Tasks, History of Learning Disabilities, and Estimate of Intelligence. The manual discusses each of these categories and provides a description of research that supports the use of the category areas. Many of the research studies cited are over 10 years old.

An individual completes the Retention Scale Recording Form by reading statements under each category and marking the sentence that most accurately describes the student. Each statement carries a numerical score. Some categories, such as "Gender and Grade Progress of Student," consist of statements that range in scores from 0 to 3; whereas other categories, such as "History of Learning Disabilities" and "Estimate of Intelligence," consist of statements with higher scores, ranging from 0 to 5. The scale takes about 10 minutes to complete. Afterwards, the examiner totals the scores on all 20 categories and then refers to a table in the manual to interpret the sum of scores. According to the table, students with low scores (sums 0-8) are considered "excellent retention candidates" (manual, p. 24).

DEVELOPMENT. This edition represents the fifth edition and the fourth revision of this scale, first published in 1981. The previous edition was published in 1998. The manual states that the 2006 Edition includes revisions, additions, and improvements in both the manual and recording forms. The manual further states that the category areas were "derived after a careful analysis of a multitude of quality research studies" (p. 5). The author does not include specific information regarding how Light's Retention Scale [2006 Edition] was revised.

TECHNICAL. The manual reports extremely limited classical and contemporary information related to the technical quality of this instrument.

COMMENTARY. Light's Retention Scale [2006 Edition] seems to be a dusted-off relic, dug up from a different era of time. Much of the research cited is over 10 years old and outdated.

The manual provides no technical information regarding the development and the revision of this edition. No information is provided as to how numerical ratings are assigned to specific statements and why some categories are assigned a specific higher or lower score than others. The lack of technical information is a serious problem and individuals using the instrument have no assurance regarding either the validity or the reliability of the information.

Although the author attempts to eliminate students with disabilities such as those with emotional or learning problems from being identified, the assessment instrument could be discriminatory to other groups of students. For example the category "Physical Size" is cause for concern. One statement says "Student is significantly smaller than others the same age." A second statement says, "Student is slightly smaller than most others the same age." The first statement is rated a zero; the second is rated 1. Students of small stature would regularly score low on this area and be potential candidates for retention.

SUMMARY. Light's Retention Scale [2006 Edition] is an attempt to provide school staff with a tool that could be used to identify a student who would benefit from retention. The scale has been revised several times since the first edition in 1981. The manual provides no information regarding technical characteristics of this instrument and there is no quality assurance regarding assessment results. Furthermore, the manual reports little information about the tool's development and revisions. Much of the data that support the categories used to identify students are outdated. This scale has limited use and value.

Review of the Light's Retention Scale [2006 Edition] by HOI K. SUEN, Distinguished Professor of Educational Psychology, Pennsylvania State University, University Park, PA:

DESCRIPTION. The Light's Retention Scale (LRS) is a checklist designed specifically for school personnel as a decision aid when considering grade retention/promotion for a student, and for use as a counseling tool to help clarify problems during parent conferences. The scale consists of 20 items, ranging from "preschool attendance" to "immature behavior" to "physical size," "siblings," and to "motivation to complete school tasks." Each item provides three to six different descriptive categories. The school professional is to select the single category within each item that best describes the child in question. A score value ranging between 0 and 5 is assigned to each category; and the score associated with the selected category would be the score for that child on that item. Some items have fewer score options than others. Scores are summed across all 20 items to obtain a total score. Guidelines are provided for the interpretation of the total score and for possible retention decisions. The author of the instrument reports that the scale takes 10 to 15 minutes to complete.

DEVELOPMENT. The 20 items used in this instrument were derived based on the instrument author's relatively thorough and comprehensive review of pertinent research literature on variables related to successes after retention/promotion. Variables beyond the more common factors of academic achievement or maturity were considered. These include physical, cultural, developmental, and other factors. No central, unidimensional psychological construct is being measured. Instead, the 20 variables were chosen on the basis of whether they were known predictors of academic success after retention.

TECHNICAL. There is no information provided regarding the scaling process, including how the individual item numerical scales were determined or how the total score interpretation guidelines were derived. No information on score reliability was provided, and there does not appear to have been any psychometric analyses conducted to evaluate either item quality, score reliability, rater reliability, decision reliability, standard error of measurement, or any of the numerous other aspects of reliability directly relevant and important to support the recommended use of the scores.

Two pieces of evidence to support validity based on relations with other variables were reported. First, a doctoral dissertation by Hedstrom (1996) was cited and was described as having concluded that LRS is a good predictor of whether a child will benefit from, or possibly be harmed by what is termed "horizontal placement" (manual, p. 7). A second piece of evidence is based on the author's own examination of the records of 49 cases, most of whom were the author's own clients. The author did not report how the 49 cases were chosen. Of the 49 cases, the author found that 22 were recommended for retention whereas 27 were not. Of those who were recommended for retention, the mean LRS total score was 21 points; the mean total score for those who were not recommended was 49. The difference seems to show that LRS scores are consistent with retention recommendations. The author did not report whether the LRS scores were obtained prior to or after the retention recommendations had been made; and if they were obtained prior to the recommendations, whether the LRS scores were part of the profile used to determine retention recommendations. Another important piece of information also not reported is whether the LRS scores were assigned by someone with the knowledge of whether the child has been recommended for retention.

Although no formal content validation exercises were reported, the author provided very comprehensive research literature reviews to support the choice of each of the 20 item areas. These literature reviews provided cogent theoretical evidence that the chosen items were correlates of success after grade retention; as such they constitute the strongest piece of validity evidence to support the use of the LRS to guide retention decisions.

There is no other additional evidence to support clinical utility, classification accuracy, or any other facet of validity. Nor is there any evidence to ensure that the results are free of unintended biases or that the use of the results for retention decisions lead to fair outcomes.

COMMENTARY. The author repeatedly cautioned throughout the manual that this scale should be viewed strictly as a counseling tool and not a "psychometric" test in that there is no central psychological construct being measured. Instead, the 20 items can best be viewed as a checklist of variables to consider when one needs to make a determination of whether to promote or retain a child in a grade. When used as a checklist, in a manner not too different from that of an everyday "to do" list, the instrument can indeed be quite useful. The thorough literature support provides sound justification that these 20 items are important issues to review prior to making important retention/promotion decisions.

The list of 20 variables by itself would have been a very useful tool to aid decisions. However, that provides no guidance as to how much weight to place on each of the 20 factors while making a decision. These weights have been left to the ad hoc and perhaps arbitrary decisions of the user. Perhaps due to this limitation, a scoring scheme was added that is to lead to a total score. Additionally, a score interpretation guide is provided to aid the user in making retention/promotion decisions.

Unfortunately, by adding the scoring method and interpretation guidelines, the author has introduced a host of problems. Unlike the choice of the 20 items, which was guided by research literature, there was no particular theoretical or empirical basis for the particular scoring method or interpretation guidance besides the author's personal extensive professional experience. Given that there is no central psychological construct being measured, the summing of the item scores to form an overall total score upon which decisions are to be made can only be viewed as a linear combination of predictors of success after retention. The fact that items are given different possible scores within the range of 0 to 5 is analogous to assigning prediction weights. The combined effect is that the scoring scheme is analogous to a linear prediction equation and that weights assigned to the individual items are analogous to regression weights. Yet, the values of these weights and the particular linear combination were not derived from data analyses, but were based on the author's own professional judgment. The score interpretation guidelines were similarly determined based on the professional judgment of the author. Other than the author's own professional experience, there is little assurance that these values and guidelines are any more meaningful than the ad hoc professional judgments that would have been made by school professionals without these scores or guidelines.

There is a large host of reliability and validity questions regarding the precision of the scores, the margin of scoring error, the appropriateness of the weights, the predictive accuracy of the total scores regarding retention effectiveness, and many other questions of score-related reliability and validity that remain unanswered. The validity study in which the author examined 49 cases revealed some promising trends regarding the scores, but the same data also raised questions of possible high levels of false positives and false negatives.

The author is quite aware of the limitations of the scoring method and went so far as to caution the user that "the sum (i.e., total score) is not comparable with a score derived from a standardized test instrument" (manual, p. 23). In this case, the question is why assign scores at all? Why add the scores to form a total score? What is the meaning of this total score? Unfortunately, in spite of these repeated cautions to take these scores only as general guides and not as numerically precise or meaningful, the scores are being treated as precise numerical values by the author. The score interpretation guidelines are constructed based on a general notion that these scores do form some order along some dimension. An additional problem of using these scores is that to a typical user, a numerical score provides the implicit meaning of relative precision, objectivity, impartiality, and comparability, when there is no evidence of any of these characteristics in this case.

SUMMARY. Overall, when used strictly as a checklist in a manner not too different from a "to do" list, the Light's Retention Scale is well supported and will provide a valuable guide to a school professional who needs to sort through a rather unwieldy and bewildering array of variables and factors to consider prior to a grade retention decision. However, this positive recommendation is the case only if the scale is used strictly as a checklist to make sure that important variables are not overlooked but without following any of the scoring schemes used in this scale.

There is little evidence that the scoring scheme leads to scores that are meaningful, reliable, or useful. Additionally, the guidelines for score interpretation seem to be arbitrary and without any theoretical or empirical support. Therefore, the effect of using the scores and the scoring guidelines to make grade retention decisions is unknown and can be potentially harmful to the child being evaluated. Therefore, the use of the scores should be avoided.

REVIEWER'S REFERENCE

Hedstrom, S. D. (1996) *A study on the validity and use of the Light's Retention Scale.* Unpublished doctoral dissertation, University of Southern California, Los Angeles.

[70]

The Listening Inventory.

Purpose: Developed as an initial screener for students "who may be at risk for having (Central) Auditory Processing Disorder."
Population: Ages 4–17.
Publication Date: 2006.
Acronym: TLI.
Scores, 7: Linguistic Organization, Decoding & Language Mechanics, Attention & Organization, Sensory-Motor Skills, Social & Behavioral Skills, Auditory Processes, Total Score.
Administration: Individual.
Price Data, 2007: $85 per complete kit including 25 listening inventory forms, 25 profile forms, and manual (64 pages); $50 per 25 listening inventory forms and 25 profile forms; $35 per manual.
Time: 15 minutes.
Authors: Donna Geffner and Deborah Ross-Swain.
Publisher: Academic Therapy Publications.

Review of The Listening Inventory by TIFFANY L. HUTCHINS, Lecturer of Communication Sciences, University of Vermont, Burlington, VT:

DESCRIPTION. The purpose of The Listening Inventory (TLI) is to screen students (ages 4–17) who may need further evaluation for (Central) Auditory Processing Disorder [(C)APD] and to assist in differentiating this diagnosis from behaviors associated with comorbid conditions (i.e., Attention Deficit/Hyperactivity Disorder [AD/HD] and language and learning problems). The TLI is an informant measure to be completed by teachers and parents/caregivers for interpretation by a speech-language professional. The TLI yields a total score based on six subtest (often called "index") scores that assess the following areas of functioning: Linguistic Organization, Decoding and Language Mechanics, Attention and Organization, Sensory-Motor Skills, Social and Behavioral Skills, and Auditory Processes. Relatively low scores are construed as reflecting few symptoms, whereas relatively high scores are taken to indicate more problematic auditory behaviors.

The TLI consists of 103 statements (98 of which are completed by teachers, 102 of which are completed by parents). Statements are rated using a 0- to 5-point scale to indicate the applicability and frequency of a particular behavior or characteristic. Specifically, each statement is rated as follows: 5 if the behavior occurs *more than twice* a day; 4 if the behavior occurs about *once or twice* a day; 3 if the behavior occurs about *once* a day; 2 if the behavior does not occur each day, but does occur *once or twice a week*; 1 if the behavior is *not ever seen*; or 0 if the behavior *does not apply* due to the child's age or circumstance.

This response arrangement combines an ordinal scale (scores of 1–5) with a categorical response option (score of 0) and is cumbersome insofar as accuracy requires the respondent to revisit the scale frequently. Although many items are well-constructed in that they are easy to understand and respond to in light of this response scale, several items are not. For example, several items employ the word "frequently" (e.g., "Frequently does x"), but the use of this word is confusing given that the scale itself is designed to assess frequency. Another poorly construed item asks about the absence of a behavior (i.e., singing); but how does one judge the frequency of an absent behavior? Finally, some items do not tap discrete behaviors but rather enduring characteristics (e.g., self-esteem), which are awkward to judge in terms of frequency. In a related vein, the instructions are underdeveloped in that they do not frame how respondents should approach items. More specifically, it is unclear whether respondents should consider the number of opportunities available to observe certain behaviors and whether difficulty is expected given the child's age and developmental level. Treatment of these concerns in the instructions and revision of the response arrangement and item wording/content may address these problems.

Often, an item is believed to tap more than one domain. As such, a matrix of shaded and unshaded boxes accompanies the statements on the TLI. Respondents are asked to place the appropriate value in the white box/es next to each statement while making sure they do not leave any white boxes blank. Values in each of six columns corresponding to the six aforementioned areas of functioning are then summed. Using a separate profile form/score summary sheet, the six subtest scores and total score are recorded and compared to their corresponding criterion-based cutoff scores "to determine clinical significance" (examiner's manual, p. 5). Scores from the normative sample of teachers and parents were combined resulting in a single cutoff score (i.e., the 70th percentile) for each age group. Age groups are sometimes collapsed and are as follows: 3 to 5 years, 6 years, 7 years, 8 years, 9 years, 10 years, 11 to 13 years, and 14 to 17 years. The scoring and determination of whether a score exceeds a cutoff is simple and straightforward. The TLI takes approximately 15 minutes to complete and score.

DEVELOPMENT. Development of the TLI was prompted by the need for a validated screen for use in the classroom and therapy room. The developers imagine that this tool is useful to begin a dialogue with teachers and parents/caregivers to address areas of concern. As stated above, another purpose of the TLI is to assist in differential diagnosis. Thus, items on the TLI were developed to tap not only (C)APD but also a wider range of behaviors that may indicate concomitant difficulties with attention, motor skills, and social behaviors. Interpretation of the subtest scores are intended to provide the clinician with information about a student's relative strengths and challenges and to assist in making decisions about whether and in what areas there is a need for further evaluation.

TECHNICAL.

Standardization. The TLI was developed on 375 parents and 385 teachers resulting in 760 observations of 385 children (375 children were rated by both their parents and teachers and 10 children were rated by either their parents or teachers). Both children with and without known auditory processing difficulties were included; however, procedures for identifying children as having auditory problems are not described and the number of children in this clinical group and their distribution by age is not given. As a criterion-referenced measure, the inclusion of children with auditory difficulties in the normative sample is questionable and has the potential to compromise accuracy of classification (Peña, Spaulding, & Plante, 2006). Because it is the age range when children are typically seen in clinic for assessment, "slightly more than 86% of the children in the standardization sample were between the ages of 5 and 12" (examiner's manual, p. 19). By contrast, few participants were ages 3 to 5 years, 11 to 13 years, and 14 to 17 years, and only the number of individuals for the collapsed age ranges is given. Without further clarification, the representativeness of the sample and the appropriateness of this measure for use with individuals from these age ranges remains an open question.

No information is provided about the socioeconomic characteristics of the sample. Data regarding region (i.e., North Central, Northeast, South, West), sex, ethnicity (i.e., Asian, Black, Hispanic, Native American, other, and White), and residence (i.e., urban vs. rural living) are reported and are generally (meaning there are exceptions) close to U.S. Census statistics.

Reliability. Very limited evidence is offered to support the reliability of the TLI. Estimates of internal consistency were high for the subtests and total score using both the Spearman-Brown (range = .87–.98) and coefficient alpha (range = .86–.94) methods. Interrater reliability was evaluated by examining whether parent and teacher ratings of the same children differed significantly. Only four of a total of 56 *t*-tests (for each age group, subtest, and total score) demonstrated significant differences, leading authors to conclude that the TLI "can be scored consistently by different examiners" (examiner's manual, p. 37). The problem with this appraisal is that a lack of statistical significance for tests of differences should not be taken to indicate acceptable consistency or agreement between raters and a series of correlation coefficients is needed to address this. No information about the test-retest reliability of the TLI is offered.

Validity. Arguments for content validity are provided by the authors who attempted to develop items capturing a wide variety of (C)APD characteristics as well as several conditions that often overlap with (C)APD. Construct validity was examined using factor analysis and a contrasting-groups method. Factor analysis was used to confirm the placement of several items into categories and to reposition a few items to other categories. Clinical judgment and descriptions in the literature were also used to place items into categories and were the only bases upon which items were selected into the Auditory Processes subscale. To explore construct validity, the combined teacher and parent ratings of children identified as having (C)APD were compared to those of age-matched children who were identified as not having (C)APD. Across subscales and the total score, the scores for the clinical sample were significantly different and nearly twice the scores of the comparison group. Although these data are encouraging, it is difficult to evaluate their importance because the procedures for identifying children as having (C)APD and their representation in the normative sample are underspecified. In a related vein, the comparison for only one age group (age 9 years) was reported. It is important to determine whether the TLI distinguishes children on the basis of diagnostic category across ages. More compelling evidence for construct validity would also involve comparisons of the subscales of the TLI with other measures of constructs believed to be tapped by each subscale. Discriminant validity is also particularly important given the goals of the measure, which are to inform follow-up evaluation procedures and assist in differential diagnosis.

COMMENTARY. Given the purpose of the TLI to screen for (C)APD and help identify areas of relative strengths and challenges for children's auditory behaviors, the strengths of the TLI involve its breadth of content and ease in scoring. Weaknesses of the TLI involve the fact that it combines an ordinal scale (scores of 1–5 to tap frequency) with a categorical response option (score of 0 to indicate not applicable). As such, items deemed not applicable have the effect of lowering scores. Moreover, TLI data are typically treated as interval in nature. When comparing teacher and parent ratings, authors noted that "parents rated their children a bit more severely than did teachers" (examiner's manual, p. 37). However, this interpretation is flawed because the TLI uses a greater number of items for parents, thus giving them more opportunities to increase their scores relative to teachers. For this reason, averaging teacher and parent scores to generate cutoffs increases the likelihood that parents' scores will overestimate problem behaviors whereas teachers' scores may have a tendency to underestimate them. As noted above, scant evidence is offered in support of the reliability and validity of the TLI. In particular, an evaluation of test-retest reliability and concurrent and discriminant validity are sorely needed. Future versions of the test should also provide an estimate of standard error of measurement as well as the confidence intervals to help professionals make decisions about obtained scores in relation to cutoffs. Although a case study is offered to illustrate how this test can be used, the case is one in which the parents' and teacher's scores approach or exceed the cutoff score for every subtest so that for each domain a decision is made to "refer for evaluation." A more helpful case scenario would be one where scores on the TLI's subtests diverged so as to illustrate how this measure might assist in differential diagnosis.

SUMMARY. The TLI is an admirable attempt to develop a screen for (C)APD, inform further evaluation efforts, and assist in differential diagnosis. Although the TLI seemed to be designed to enhance the amount of information necessary to meet these purposes, revision and further development of the measure are needed before it can be recommended for use as either a screen or as a tool to help make decisions about follow-up evaluations. Although not designed to distinguish (C)APD from comorbid conditions, the Children's Auditory Performance Scale (CHAPS; Smoski, Brunt, & Tannahill, 1998) makes use of parent and teacher informants and appears to be a superior alternative for the screening of (C)APD.

REVIEWER'S REFERENCES

Peña, E. D., Spaulding, T. J., & Plante, E. (2006). The composition of normative groups and diagnostic decision making: Shooting ourselves in the foot. *American Journal of Speech-Language Pathology, 15*, 247-254.

Smoski, W., Brunt, M., & Tannahill, C. (1998). Children's Auditory Performance Scale. Tampa, FL: Educational Audiology Association.

Review of The Listening Inventory by SANDRA WARD, Professor of Education, The College of William and Mary, Williamsburg, VA:

DESCRIPTION. The Listening Inventory (TLI) is an informal criterion-based behavioral observation screening measure completed by parents and teachers and developed to help with the identification of students who may be at risk for having (Central) Auditory Processing Disorder ([C]APD). The authors assert that TLI can be used to identify children between 4 and 17 years of age who may be at risk for a listening disorder, to determine whether further evaluation is necessary, and to help differentiate listening/auditory disorders from other co-existing conditions.

According to the manual, TLI can be used by speech/language pathologists, audiologists, and psychologists. The parent questionnaire includes 102 questions, and the teacher rating scale includes 98 questions (97 items overlap both inventories). Student behaviors are rated across six categories including Linguistic Organization, Decoding and Language Mechanics, Attention and Organization, Sensory-Motor Skills, Social and Behavioral Skills, and Auditory Processes.

For each category there are Likert scale items that the respondents rate from 1 (*behavior is not ever seen*) to 5 (*behavior occurs more than twice a day*). A score of 0 can be given on an item if the behavior does not apply due to the child's age or circumstance. However, the authors do not provide any guidance to when items are not age appropriate nor do they provide any scale validation rules for the appearance of numerous 0 ratings.

Specific instructions for completing TLI are printed on the record form. The instructions are straightforward and easy to follow. Additionally, the definitions for the numerical ratings of the Likert scale are printed at the top of each page of the record form for easy reference. Although the directions for TLI are clear, the authors provide no data on the reading level of the directions or the actual items. Although not specifically stated in the manual, it is apparent that the responding teacher and parent (guardian or caregiver) should have daily contact with the student. Completion time for TLI is not specified. It is reasonable to expect teachers and parents to spend an average of 20 minutes completing this measure.

The scoring procedures for TLI are uncomplicated and well-explained. The sum of the ratings in each column is the raw score for that category. A total inventory raw score also is computed. Higher raw scores indicate a higher incidence of problem behaviors. The authors do not provide directions for scoring scales when one or two items are not completed. The raw scores are compared to cutoff scores for interpretation. Cutoff scores were derived from frequency analysis of the scores from the age groups in the standardization sample. Raw scores that fall at or above the 70th percentile are considered severe. The profile form/score summary of TLI provides a concise summary of scores from the parent and teacher, as well as cutoff scores by age across categories.

DEVELOPMENT. According to the authors, TLI assesses behaviors in six categories that are associated with skill weaknesses in auditory processing. The items for TLI were drawn from a review of the literature and the authors' clinical observations. A set of statements was developed to describe the linguistic and auditory processing characteristics of children who are referred for evaluation of auditory processes. The authors also included statements that describe the behaviors of children with disorders of attention and learning. These statements were included due to the comorbidity of (C)APD weaknesses with learning and behavioral problems. It remains unclear how the authors arrived at the six categories of behavior included in the measure. The authors do not cite specific research studies to support the categories of TLI, and specific information about the development of the instrument is not provided.

TECHNICAL. The standardization sample included 385 children with known auditory processing difficulties and nonreferred children between the ages of 3–17 years. Most children (375) were observed by both parents and teachers, whereas 10 children were observed only by a parent or teacher, resulting in 760 sets of observations. The authors treated the parent and teacher ratings of a single child as separate individuals in the sample. For example, Table 2.1 in the examiner's manual shows the age distribution of the sample accounting for 759 children, when only 385 children actually were in the sample. Essentially, this process counts most children twice and inflates the number of children that appear to be in the sample.

Although the authors contend that the norm sample is representative of the U.S. population based on region, gender, ethnicity, and residence (rural/urban), the Northeast region is overrepresented, whereas the South region is underrepresented in the sample. Furthermore, with respect to ethnicity, White children were underrepresented. In terms of age, 86% of the sample was between 5–12 years old. Only 6.6% of the sample fell in the 14–17-year age range, and 11.2% of the sample fell in the 3–5-year age range. In order to collect TLI data on children with known auditory processing difficulties, the examiners recruited parents from their clinical caseloads. The authors do not specify how the parents of nonreferred children were recruited. Additionally, they do not provide data with respect to the percentage of the sample that had auditory difficulties. The balance of clinical children and general education children in the sample impacts the placements of the percentiles used to set the cut scores.

Internal consistency coefficients of TLI were computed for each of the six categories. The internal consistency reliability coefficients reported in the manual are sufficient for the intended purpose of TLI. The average coefficient alphas ranged from .86 (Sensory-Motor Skills) to .96 (Attention and Organization) across age levels. With the exception of a coefficient alpha of .78 in the Sensory-Motor Skills category for ages 14–17, all other values were equal to or greater than .80.

Interrater reliability of TLI was based on the differences between the parent and teacher ratings of the same children. Although parents' ratings were generally higher than the teachers' ratings, these differences were not significant in all but four cases. Due to the consistency of ratings from parents and teachers, the ratings from both sources were combined to produce one set of cutoff scores.

An issue that is not addressed in the presentation of the reliability information is the impact of item number differences for parent and teacher scales. The authors found no difference between the ratings of parents and teachers for most of the scales, yet four of the scales have different numbers of items for parents and teachers. TLI scales are based on raw scores, so differences in the number of items impact the scale scores and the comparison of parent-to-teacher ratings. Additionally, the correlations between parent and teacher ratings are important information to consider for interrater reliability that the authors do not present.

The authors cite the procedures followed in the development of TLI as evidence of content validity. This information is insufficient to judge the adequacy of the content. The content validity of the test would be strengthened by specific details of the development of the instrument, including a blueprint, rationale for particular categories, and any expert reviews.

A factor analysis was computed to provide support for the construct validity of TLI. The results yielded a weak six-factor solution that accounted for approximately 45% of the total variability. Initially, items for each factor were identified by loadings equal to or greater than .40. Inspection of these factors showed two factors that had items related to social behaviors. The authors combined these two factors into a Social and Behavior Skills Category, despite the factor-analytic evidence that they were separate factors. The factor analysis also revealed that several statements loaded on more than one factor, so the authors allowed those items to appear on both. Some items were added to factors if they seemed a "good fit" according to the test authors' clinical experience. The empirical evidence was overridden by the judgment of the authors. Finally, the 6 items that are unique to the parent or teacher forms were placed into the categories by the authors, based on their clinical judgment.

The authors created a sixth group of items that described characteristics of children with known (C)APD. This category of items was derived from descriptions in the literature and the authors' judgments. These 25 items are repeated items from the other five factors. There is no factor-analytic evidence for this scale, and its creation results in several items belonging to three of the six subscales.

The authors provide results of a group differentiation study to support the use of TLI to discriminate between children with (C)APD and a regular education sample. Each group included 103 observations (parent and teacher ratings were combined), and the two groups were matched on age. A series of *t*-test comparisons revealed that the scores of the (C)APD group were significantly higher than those of the regular education sample across all categories. The authors do not specify any effort to control for error with many comparisons that could have been accomplished with a multivariate test.

COMMENTARY. TLI is a brief behavior rating scale for parents and teachers that is easy to complete and score. The authors of the instrument contend that TLI assesses critical behaviors in six categories related to (C)APD; however, the theoretical model for the instrument is weak and validity evidence is inadequate. The authors do not adequately reference or describe the source of the six categories or the items they constructed. The authors use statistical or quasi-statistical analyses (factor analyses) to support the structure of the scale, but they ignore empirical data in favor of clinical judgment. The six categories of the scale are not supported as measures of distinct behaviors associated with (C)APD. Consequently, the meaningfulness and utility of these categories to help identify (C)APD and differentiate (C)APD from other learning/behavioral problems is severely limited. Further support for the validity of TLI could be garnered from convergent validity studies with other instruments that measure the same construct.

SUMMARY. TLI is a criterion-based behavioral observation screening measure completed by teachers and parents intended to help with the identification of students between the ages of 4 and 17 years, who may be at risk for having (C)APD. The authors repeatedly caution against using TLI as a sole criterion for identifying (C) APD and encourage its use as part of a screening process only. Based on the data provided on the technical adequacy of TLI, users should use the instrument cautiously, even for screening purposes. Reliability data are questionable due to item number differences in the parent and teacher scales. Evidence for construct validity is insufficient and suggests that there is considerable overlap among the six categories of the instrument. As a result, only the total score should be interpreted, and the test user cannot differentiate listening/auditory disorders from other co-existing conditions based on TLI results.

[71]

Massachusetts Youth Screening Instrument—Version 2.

Purpose: "To identify youths with potential mental, emotional, or behavioral problems at entry points in the juvenile justice system."
Population: Ages 12-17.
Publication Dates: 1998-2006.
Acronym: MAYSI-2.
Administration: Individual.
Forms, 2: Male, Female.
Restricted Distribution: To use the MAYSI-2 one must be registered with the National Youth Screening Assistance Project.
Price Data, 2009: $194.95 per manual and MAYSIWARE software; $20 per set of 7 screening forms.
Foreign Language Edition: Spanish language paper-and-pencil version is available, plus the software (MAYSIWARE) version also presents the MAYSI items in Spanish, on screen and audio.
Time: (15) minutes.
Authors: Thomas Grisso and Richard Barnum.
Publisher: Professional Resource Press.

a) MALE.

Scores, 7: Alcohol/Drug Use, Angry-Irritable, Depressed-Anxious, Somatic Complaints, Suicide Ideation, Thought Disturbance, Traumatic Experiences.

b) FEMALE.

Scores, 6: Alcohol/Drug Use, Angry-Irritable, Depressed-Anxious, Somatic Complaints, Suicide Ideation, Traumatic Experiences.

Review of the Massachusetts Youth Screening Instrument-Version 2 by RANDY G. FLOYD, Associate Professor of Psychology, The University of Memphis, Memphis, TN:

DESCRIPTION. The Massachussetts Youth Screening Instrument–Version 2 (MAYSI-2) is a 52-item, broad-band self-report inventory for adolescents ages 12 to 17. Its purpose is to facilitate screening for internalizing and externalizing problems and substance use displayed by adolescents who have entered the juvenile justice system. It is available in both English- and Spanish-language editions. In its standard administration, respondents must read each question and mark whether the item is true for them across recent months. Items are totaled using a scoring key and subsequently plotted in a profile. Software called MAYSIWARE is available to present items auditorily to the respondent via a computer, and respondents must respond using a mouse to select "yes" or "no." Responses are then also summarized by this software.

The MAYSI-2 produces six scales for females: Alcohol/Drug Use, Angry-Irritable, Depressed-Anxious, Somatic Complaints, Suicide Ideation, and Traumatic Experiences. For males, it produces each of these scales as well as a Thought Disturbance scale. Scoring profiles are provided in the manual. Standardized scores, such as *T*-scores, are not yielded for each scale, but raw scores are classified, based on norms for each gender and age group (ages 12 to 14 or 15 to 17), into three categories. The categories include a category with no label that represents normative levels of functioning, a Caution category, and a Warning category.

DEVELOPMENT. The MAYSI-2 authors describe an impressive, decade-long series of steps to develop, refine, and provide reliability and validity evidence for the instrument and its scores. These steps include drafting and piloting of items; identifying scales, developing norms, understanding item and scale properties, and developing cut scores (Traumatic Expiriences Scale does not have a cutoff score); and refining scales and cut scores through analysis of additional data sets. Most recently, the initial regional norms were replaced by national norms.

Most MAYSI-2 items were developed based on review of the literature focused on psychopathology prominent during adolescence and consideration of psychopathology common to youth seen in juvenile justice centers. A small subset of items was adapted from other scales (i.e., the Weinberg Screening Affective Scales; Emslie, Weinberg, Rush, Adams, & Rintelmann, 1990). The content, format, and wording of items were reviewed by national experts and regional consultants, and they also evaluated the items for bias. Items were revised based on reviewers' feedback, and items were reviewed again by other regional consultants and by youth in juvenile justice centers. After these additional reviews were considered, readability analysis of items was completed. Dichotomous and dimensional response formats for items were piloted, and the final set of items was piloted with more than 150 youth. Subsequent analysis of internal consistency, item-total relations, item distributions, and scale relations were completed. Convergent and divergent relations between MAYSI-2 scales and those from the Minnesota Multiphasic Personality Inventory-Adolescent (MMPI-A; 12:238; Butcher et al., 1992) were also examined after piloting.

TECHNICAL. MAYSI-2 norms were collected during 1997. The norming sample included more than 1,279 racially diverse youth who were assessed at probation departments, detention centers, and assessment centers in Massachusetts. Based on analysis of this sample as a whole and by gender, most corrected item-total correlation coefficients and alpha coefficients for each scale appear to be acceptable. Only alpha coefficients for Thought Disturbances and Traumatic Experiences for boys were below .70. Test-retest reliability coefficients obtained from relatively small samples (< 45 of each gender) who completed the MAYSI-2 twice across 5 to 14 days indicated evidence of short-term stability across most scales for each gender. For boys, only Somatic Complaints, Thought Disturbances, and Traumatic Experiences and, for girls, only Angry-Irritable, Somatic Complaints, and Traumatic Experiences demonstrated coefficients less than .70. Exploratory factor analysis was conducted using item scores for each gender and for the total sample to ensure the optimal formation of each scale. Based on these results, some items were included on more than one scale, and other items were excluded from scales. Interscale correlations revealed uniform positive relations between scales (which is facilitated by shared item content across a few scales).

Because a sizeable portion of this norm sample also completed both the Millon Adolescent Clinical Inventory (MACI; 12:236; Millon, 1993) and the Youth Self-Report (YSR; Achenbach, 1991) concurrently with the MAYSI-2, these two instruments were used as criterion measures to identify cut scores for the MAYSI-2. Scores from the MAYSI-2 that paralleled "clinically significant" levels of problem behaviors on related scales from the MACI and YSR (e.g., T = 75 and T = 67, respectively) were labeled as being in the Caution category. Cut scores for this category were formed using receiver operating characteristics analysis. The other score category, Warning, was determined using percentile ranks from the initial norm sample. More specifically, scores associated with approximately the highest 10% of those in the sample were identified as the Warning cut scores. Based on data from the norm sample, the convergent and divergent relations between the MAYSI-2 scale scores and those from the MACI and YSR also provided validity evidence. However, no evidence of external relations between MAYSI-2 scores and those from home caregiver and teacher rating scales was presented.

In recent years, a national norm sample of more than 70,000 racially diverse youths across 19 states and four regions of the United States was constructed to evaluate further the initial MAYSI-2 cut scores. As a result of several additional analyses, some modifications were made to the MAYSI-2, such as reducing the Warning cut score for Alcohol/Drug Use by 1 point. Additional factor analysis of items was conducted with the national sample and another large sample from California, but the instrument authors determined that no changes to scale composition seemed to be warranted. Substantial effort was also taken to examine external relations between the MAYSI-2 scores and age group, gender, ethnicity, and legal status—using both the initial and the national samples. Results appeared to support the norm group divisions by age group and gender.

COMMENTARY. The MAYSI-2 manual was well organized, and its provision of evidence supporting the use and interpretation of its scores seemed to be strong. This reviewer believes that its strengths are its brevity (compared to the MMPI-A, YSR, etc.), its focus on problems commonly seen by adolescents in juvenile justice centers, and its reliance on normative data from adolescents in such settings. The MAYSI-2 seems to have been developed and normed for a very specific population. Whereas other self-report inventories may be more applicable for school and clinic settings with children and may be more aligned with symptoms of DSM-IV psychiatric disorders, the MAYSI-2 has demonstrated a network of validity evidence supporting its use with the targeted population of adolescents in juvenile justice centers.

Only a few design limitations of the MAYSI-2 are apparent. First, all items are scaled in the same direction (with Yes responses indicating problem behaviors), which likely decreases careful responding to items. Second, the MAYSI-2 does not include embedded validity scale items, which may be used to indicate malingering, social desirability and acquiescence, reading problems, inconsistent responding, and other response patterns that may be facilitated by having all items scaled in the same direction. Third, due to the relatively low reliability of a few scales, such as Thought Disturbances and Traumatic Experiences, the authors could consider adding items to or refining the item content of these scales. Perhaps future editions of the MAYSI-2 will remedy these concerns.

SUMMARY. The MAYSI-2 is a broad-band self-report inventory for adolescents ages 12 to 17. It stems from many years of active development and refinement, and it seems to have sufficient validity evidence supporting its use and interpretation with adolescents in juvenile justice centers. It should be noted that the MAYSI-2 manual and MAYSIWARE may be purchased from Professional Resource Press. After purchasers register with the National Youth Screening Assistance Project (without fee), they can administer the MAYSI-2 indefinately without per-case costs.

REVIEWER'S REFERENCES

Achenbach, T. M. (1991). *Integrative guide for the 1991 CBCL/4–18, YSR, and TRF profiles.* Burlington, VT: University of Vermont, Department of Psychiatry.

Butcher, J. N., William, C. L., Graham, J. R., Archer, R. P., Tellegen, A. P., Ben-Porath, Y. S., & Kaemmer, B. (1992). *Minnesota Multiphasic Personality Inventory-Adolescent: Manual for administration, scoring, and interpretation.* Minneapolis: University of Minnesota.

Emslie, G., Weinberg, W., Rush, J., Adams, R., & Rintelmann, J. (1990). Depressive symptoms by self-report in adolescence: Phase I of the development of a questionnaire for depression by self-report. *Journal of Child Neurology, 5,* 114-121.

Millon, T. (1993). *Millon Adolescent Clinical Inventory: Manual.* Minneapolis: National Computer Systems.

Review of the Massachusetts Youth Screening Instrument–Version 2 by RENÉE M. TOBIN, Associate Professor of Psychology, and CORINNE ZIMMERMAN, Associate Professor of Psychology, Illinois State University, Normal, IL:

DESCRIPTION. The Massachusetts Youth Screening Instrument–Version 2 (MAYSI-2) is a 52-item, self-report questionnaire designed to assess the social-emotional functioning of adolescents involved in the juvenile justice system. The yes/no formatted questionnaire provides scores for seven scales: Alcohol/Drug Use, Angry-Irritable, Depressed-Anxious, Somatic Complaints, Suicide Ideation, Thought Disturbance (assessed in boys only), and Traumatic Experiences. Each scale includes 5 to 9 items. Respondents are instructed to reflect on their experiences within the last few months for the first six scales. For Traumatic Experiences, respondents report their entire life history of traumatic events. The questionnaire was developed to allow any juvenile justice staff member, even personnel without clinical training, to administer it to the adolescents. As a self-report measure for 12- to 17-year-olds, the MAYSI-2 was written at the fifth-grade reading level. It is also available in Spanish.

Unlike many other measures aimed at assessing mental/emotional disturbance in youth, the MAYSI-2 is strictly a screener. The primary goal is to identify youths who may be in need of additional assessment and/or intervention when they first come in contact with the juvenile justice system. It is not intended to classify/diagnose disorders, to predict future behavior, or to prescribe intervention. Ideally, the measure is administered within 24 to 48 hours of admission to a juvenile justice facility. This timing allows for the assessment of both chronic mental/emotional disturbance and current distress in response to the youth's recent experiences including involvement with the juvenile justice system. Although the MAYSI-2 generates scale scores, it does not provide an overall mental health composite score. Recommended "Caution" and "Warning" cutoff scores identify youth who may be at risk or are clinically significant for problems; however, the authors of the instrument encourage users to determine facility-specific policies establishing when follow-up is required. Specifically, they recommend that each administrator choose which cutoff level (Caution or Warning) to use on each scale and the number of elevated scales (e.g., two scale scores falling in the Warning range) that will be used to indicate a need for follow-up at a particular facility. The MAYSI-2 provides second screening interview forms for each of the scales when following up on elevated scores produced from responses during first screening.

The MAYSI-2 is available in paper-and-pencil and computerized versions. The paper-and-pencil version takes approximately 15 minutes to complete and should be administered individually. Staff may provide assistance by defining words or by reading items aloud. When items are read aloud, administrators are encouraged to provide a separate blank form on which the youth marks his or her responses to increase the likelihood of honest responding. In the computerized version, items are presented on the computer screen while a male voice reads them aloud. The MAYSIWARE software scores the measure and generates a report. Scoring the paper-and-pencil version involves the use of a straightforward scoring key to calculate a sum score of Yes responses for each scale.

DEVELOPMENT. The MAYSI-2 was developed in four phases. From 1994 to 1996 (first phase) the authors developed items and conducted pilot testing. In the second phase (1996 to 1998) efforts focused on finalizing scale content, establishing norms from a large sample in Massachusetts, examining psychometric properties, and identifying cutoff scores. In the third phase (1998 to 1999) the authors reexamined the data from the normative sample and produced the first manual for the MAYSI-2. The final phase (2000–2002) centered on dissemination, assisting its implementation, and further research studies.

Initial item development was informed by the empirical and clinical literature in adolescent psychopathology. Items and scales were developed by a research team with the exception of items assessing depression, which were taken (with permission) directly from the Weinberg Screening Affective Scales (Weinberg & Emslie, 1988). Initial items were reviewed by experts in adolescent psychopathology, and revisions were made before a small sample of youth provided additional suggestions to make items more comprehensible to the target population. This process generated the final set of 52 items. The authors also administered the measure to 50 youth using two different formats (yes/no and 5-point Likert-type scales) and determined that the dichotomous format was adequate for alerting personnel to urgent needs in this population. Pilot testing with 176 Massachusetts adolescents provided further evidence of internal consistency.

With data from a large normative sample from Massachusetts, the authors subjected the nine scales derived from theory to factor analysis. Although an eight-factor solution was found, only seven factors were retained with slightly different items included on a few scales for boys than for girls, and the omission of one entire scale (Thought Disturbance) for girls. Similar factor-analytic results were obtained with a California sample. From 2002 through 2005, the authors spearheaded the National Norms Study in which they compiled MAYSI-2 data collected by others throughout the United States. The psychometric properties of the measure were examined across several demographic variables including type of setting, gender, race/ethnicity, and age using meta-analytic and factor-analytic techniques (Vincent, Grisso, Terry, & Banks, 2008). Data sets from facilities across the country were included if the site administered the MAYSI-2 on a consecutive case basis, was able to transmit the data, released the data to the authors, provided details about how the data were collected, and provided case-based item responses and demographic information. Analyses of this new national sample yielded similar results, with only a few recommendations for changes in cutoff scores. In the case of Warning cutoff scores, the authors opted to adjust only the Alcohol/Drug Use score to match the top 10% of respondents nationally. Thus, all items from the original MAYSI have been retained, although they do not all contribute to the calculation of scale scores.

Since its inception, a growing body of literature is available supporting its use. Updated at least quarterly, the National Youth Screening Assistance Project (NYSAP) website (www.umassmed.edu/nysap) provides access to new research publications, citations, and abstracts on the MAYSI-2. It is in use in 46 states (42 of which rely on it statewide as a juvenile justice screening tool in probation, detention, and correction programs) and five other countries.

TECHNICAL. In the initial normative sample, data were collected in Massachusetts from a total of 1,279 youths between the ages of 12 and 17 years at two intake probation offices, six pretrial detention centers, and two secure assessment centers. Of this total, 749 youths also completed valid protocols on both the Millon Adolescent Clinical Inventory (MACI) and the Child Behavior Checklist—Youth Self-Report (CBCL—YSR). In 94.4% of cases, the measure was administered within 10 days of admission, with the majority (79%) assessed within 48 hours of admission. Within this sample, girls were oversampled (about one-third of the sample). Non-Hispanic White youths made up two-fifths of the sample, with African American, Hispanic, and Asian/Other each comprising one-fifth of the sample. A second large sample of data with better racial/ethnic representation was collected from 3,766 boys and 238 girls in California. The National Norms Study for the MAYSI-2 includes data from 70,423 cases from 283 sites. Because of the scope of data collection, it appears that the normative sample for the MAYSI-2 matches the target population well.

The reliability of the MAYSI-2 scales was examined several ways at each of the different phases of development with details provided in the MAYSI-2 manual. With the initial Massachusetts sample, the item-total correlations (ranging from .37 to .63), the alpha coefficients (ranging from .61 to .86), the interscale correlations (ranging from .24 to .61), and the test-retest stability (ranging from .53 to .89 over a 5–14-day period) are all comparable to or better than other respected measures of similar constructs.

As discussed in the manual, the MAYSI-2 is intended to serve an alerting function, not as a diagnostic or predictive tool. The scales correspond well with theory from the adolescent psychopathology literature. When MAYSI-2 scales from 749 youths (561 boys, 198 girls) were examined in relation to self-reports on the MACI and the CBCL—YSR, results generally indicated strong relations (ranging from .40 to .65) between theoretically relevant constructs on these measures. Efforts to examine the MAYSI-2 in relation to overt behaviors or emotional states are not described in the manual but are available at www.umassmed.edu/nysap.

The authors focused considerable efforts on examining the validity of the measure across age, gender, race, ethnicity, and juvenile justice settings. These efforts resulted in different for boys and girls Traumatic Experiences scales and the omission of a Thought Disturbance scale for girls. The website for the instrument provides additional tables to assist in identifying cutoff scores for different groups.

COMMENTARY. Compared with other mental health instruments containing hundreds of items, the 52-item MAYSI-2 is an easy test to complete, administer, and score. It is presented on two sides of a single sheet of paper (or in a user-friendly computerized format). Its primary strengths are that it requires no clinical training to administer; it is free beyond the low cost of the manual (and the software, for computer administration); it has a strong research backing; and it has a clear, comprehensive manual. MAYSI-2 users need only register their manuals to gain access to unlimited use of the measure. Registration requires agreement to use the MAYSI-2 in its original format without distributing it for profit, to use it for its intended purposes, and to share experiences and research results with the MAYSI-2 authors. This arrangement benefits both the users who are provided with a solid, no-cost screening measure and the test authors who are provided with ongoing access to data from diverse sites to improve the measure and inform the psychological literature.

The authors are to be applauded for their approach to test development. Since its inception in 1994, the MAYSI-2 authors have investigated the measure's use and updated the item content and cutoff scores for the scales based on empirical study. They provide a thorough examination of these scales overall and broken down by demographic variables (e.g., race, age, gender). Their arrangement with users will allow them to continue to build on the strengths of the measure. Ideally, future research efforts will also address how the MAYSI-2 relates to overt behaviors and emotional states.

The measure also includes less-studied secondary screeners for follow-up on each of the scales. These forms appear to be useful, but their utility has not been demonstrated empirically and their format makes them unlikely candidates for such study. Another minor limitation is the lack of a lie scale. Perhaps future versions of the measure will include a lie scale, which might be especially important with the MAYSI-2's target population.

SUMMARY. The MAYSI-2 is a screening test for mental/emotional disturbance in youth within the juvenile justice system. It is designed to serve an alerting function identifying problems in need of triage for the seven scales of Alcohol/Drug Use, Angry-Irritable, Depressed-Anxious, Somatic Complaints, Suicide Ideation, Thought Disturbance (assessed in boys only), and Traumatic Experiences. A growing body of literature on the MAYSI-2 provides evidence of validity and reliability of its scales. As a low-cost, high-quality, brief measure, it is used extensively throughout the United States and in other countries. In its present form, this measure is strongly recommended for research and clinical purposes with this target population.

REVIEWERS' REFERENCES

Vincent, G. M., Grisso, T., Terry, A., & Banks, S. (2008). Sex and race differences in mental health symptoms in juvenile justice: The MAYSI-2 national meta-analysis. *Journal of the American Academy of Child and Adolescent Psychiatry, 47*(3), 282-290.

Weinberg, W., & Emslie, G. (1988). Weinberg Screening Affective Scales (WSAS and WSAS-SF). *Journal of Child Neurology, 3*, 294-296.

[72]

Matrix-Predictive Uniform Law Enforcement Selection Evaluation Inventory.

Purpose: Designed to "assess the future job-performance liabilities of law enforcement officer candidates."

Population: Law enforcement officer candidates.

Publication Date: 2008.

Acronym: M-PULSE.

Scores, 18: Interpersonal Difficulties, Off-Duty Misconduct, Property Damage, Motor Vehicle Accidents, Inappropriate Use of Weapon, Excessive Force, Sexually Offensive Conduct, Potential for Reprimands/Suspensions, Potential for Resignation, Potential for Termination, Chemical Abuse/Dependency, Procedural and Conduct Mistakes, Misuse of Vehicle, Discharge of Weapon, Unprofessional Conduct, Racially Offensive Conduct, Lawsuit Potential, Criminal Conduct.

Administration: Individual or group.

Price Data, 2009: $45 per 10 item booklets; $30 per 50 data entry sheets; $30 per mail-in/fax-in profile report; $25 per online profile report; $60 per technical manual (58 pages).

Time: (60-80) minutes.

Comments: Can be administered online or via paper and pencil.

Authors: Robert D. Davis and Cary D. Rostow.

Publisher: Multi-Health Systems, Inc.

Review of the Matrix-Predictive Uniform Law Enforcement Selection Evaluation Inventory by J. M. BLACKBOURN, Associate Professor of Education, University of Mississippi, University, MS, CONN THOMAS, Professor of Education, West Texas A&M University, Canyon, TX, and JENNIFER G. FILLINGIM, Doctoral Candidate, University of Mississippi, University, MS:

DESCRIPTION. The Matrix-Predictive Uniform Law Enforcement Selection Evaluation Inventory (M-PULSE) consists of 455 items designed to measure 18 liability conduct areas among preservice law enforcement candidates. The Inventory also measures 4 content areas or empirical scales, derived from factor analysis, that relate to on-the-job performance and liability. In addition, the instrument includes 2 validity scales for evaluation of a respondent's response style.

The instrument yields a profile with subscores for each the 18 liability conduct areas, 4 empirical scales, and the validity scales, which allow for a determination concerning the respondent's attitude toward the testing process itself, his or her tendency to fake good on test items (validity scales), areas for potential serious officer liability or misconduct (liability conduct areas), and psychological/personality traits that related to increased officer liability (empirical scales). Each of the subscores on the liability conduct areas has a table indicating where the respondent's score falls among the categories of "low risk," "average," "some concern," or "at risk." Each of the empirical scales has a table that lists a range of scores among the categories of "Positive," Mid-Range," and "Negative." High scores on any of the individual subareas indicate increased chances of problematic officer behavior from the respondent. The authors emphasize the importance to the validity scale as a crucial measure, due to its ability to identify attempts to provide erroneous or misleading information. High scores on this measure indicate that scores on the liability conduct areas and empirical scales are likely misleading and therefore invalid.

DEVELOPMENT. The M-PULSE was developed to address the need of local, state, and federal law enforcement agencies to select officers who possess the lowest levels of risk in relation to acting in an inappropriate or destructive manner. It is based on the assumption that psychological/personality traits are predictors of future behavior. The items included in the M-PULSE target officer misconduct and aggression. Predictive validity is therefore at the center of the instrument's developmental process. The M-PULSE is one example of numerous instruments that attempt to predict future outcomes or potential based on current performance. The work of Binet, Terman's Longitudinal Studies on Giftedness, and the current "Dispositions Movement" in teacher education all share the assumption of predictive validity associated with the M-PULSE. The M-PULSE was designed and developed to be race and gender fair.

TECHNICAL. The normative sample for the M-PULSE consisted of 2,000 officer candidates who were given the instrument between 2003 and 2007. The average age of this sample was 29.1 with a standard deviation of 7.7 and a range of 18–73. The group was 83% male and varied in ethnicity with

53.5% being Caucasian (n = 1,070), 16.5% African American (n = 329), 9.3% Hispanic (n = 185), and 7.5% multiracial (n = 149). Data were drawn from multiple sites across the nation with representation that reflected U.S. Census figures.

The full sample was also drawn from individuals who were administered the M-PULSE between 2003 and 2007. This sample included both the normative sample of police officers and an additional 3,348 individuals. The demographics of this sample included an average age of 29.9 with a standard deviation of 8.5 and a range of 16–78. Males made up 83.7% of this sample, and 61.1% of the sample were Caucasian (n = 3,268), 18.5% were African American (n = 987), 3.9% were Hispanic (n = 206), and 1.6% were multiracial (n = 88).

Reliability estimates calculated via coefficient alpha ranged from .67 to .97 on the empirical scales. Calculation of coefficient alpha was considered inappropriate for the liability scales, as these metrics included actual scales, not simply an item base. The liability scales involved the use of a forward stepwise regression analysis over the 18 different liability areas and 455 items that were included on the scales. For each liability area, the F and p values were highly significant and accounted for a sizable portion of the variance in the scores.

Validity information was available for the empirical scales only. Data were drawn from the full sample and were calculated via factor analysis. The initial run included all 455 items in which any items that did not load at .30 or better were eliminated. The process was repeated until all items loaded at .30 or higher. The factor labeled "Negative Self-Issues" accounted for 9.1% of the variance, the factor labeled "Negative Perceptions Related to Law Enforcement" accounted for 4.5% of the variance; the factor labeled "Impression Management" accounted for 3.3% of the variance; the factor labeled "Unethical Behavior" accounted for 2.3% of the variance; and the factor labeled "Unpredictability" accounted for 2.0% of the variance.

T-scores were used with each of the scales to ease interpretation of the M-PULSE. T-scores for each scale had a mean of 50 and standard deviation of 10. Sixty-eight percent of those candidates taking the M-PULSE scored within 10 points of the mean. Scores within this range are considered acceptable for law enforcement work. Scores below the 40–60 point spread were considered highly desirable for law enforcement work. Scores above 60 indicate less desirable attitudes, behaviors, or predispositions related to successful law enforcement work. Interpretive guidelines for the T-scores on the M-PULSE are provided in the instrument's technical manual.

COMMENTARY. The samples associated with the development of the M-PULSE make up a normative group that includes most of the critical national demographics. The size of the combined samples was appropriate and consistent with national demographics. The regional breakdowns associated with the samples is a helpful addition for better understanding of the instrument's applicability for state and local agencies in different parts of the nation. Weaknesses in the norms include a preponderance of male respondents and a larger percentage of African American respondents as compared to those who were Hispanic. The recent emergence of the Hispanic ethnic group as the largest national majority would necessitate the inclusion of a higher percentage of such respondents if the norms are to accurately reflect national demographics. Although the gender disparity may reflect the existing makeup of law enforcement personnel, a distribution closer to 50% male-50% female might add strength to the instrument and it might more accurately reflect the national demographics in relation to gender. Conversely, this disparity does, as noted above, parallel typical applicant pools for law enforcement positions. Additionally, information on the percentages of "False Positives" and "False Negatives" identified would be helpful.

Validity and reliability values for the M-PULSE are within acceptable limits. Although a few of the reliability scores fell below the .80 level, these were associated with scales that had low numbers of response items. In general, M-Pulse scores do not differ by gender or ethnicity of the respondents. Although two of the subscales (Negative Perceptions Related to Law Enforcement and Overly Traditional Officer Traits) were sensitive to the ethnicity of the test takers, the impact on M-PULSE scores was negligible.

SUMMARY. The authors of the M-PULSE Inventory have developed an instrument that addresses a central concern of all public and private agencies. In today's litigious society, the need to avoid liability and litigation requires a proactive stance. The M-PULSE is an additional tool to aid law enforcement in providing a higher quality of services to the community. It seems to be a sound, reliable, and valid instrument developed and normed in a psychometrically appropriate manner.

Review of the Matrix-Predictive Uniform Law Enforcement Selection Evaluation Inventory by GARY J. DEAN, Professor and Department Chairperson, Department of Adult and Community Education, Indiana University of Pennsylvania, Indiana, PA:

DESCRIPTION. The Matrix-Predictive Uniform Law Enforcement Selection Evaluation Inventory (M-PULSE) is a 455-item self-report instrument designed to aid in the selection of law enforcement personnel. The test authors state that the purpose is to assess the future job performance liabilities of law enforcement officer candidates. The items on the instrument are statements that are rated on a 4-point scale of *strongly agree, agree, disagree,* and *strongly disagree*. Administration takes between 50 and 90 minutes and should be accomplished in a single sitting. Administration is either via a paper-and-pencil version (which must be mailed to the publishers for scoring and interpretation) or an online version with immediate feedback.

The M-Pulse results in a variety of scale scores. There are 2 validity scales: Impression Management and Test Attitude. There are 18 liability scales: Interpersonal Difficulties, Chemical Abuse/Dependency, Off-Duty Misconduct, Procedural and Conduct Mistakes, Property Damage, Misuse of Vehicle, Motor Vehicle Accidents, Discharge of Weapon, Inappropriate Use of Weapon, Unprofessional Conduct, Excessive Force, Racially Offensive Conduct, Sexually Offensive Conduct, Lawsuit Potential, Criminal Conduct, Potential for Reprimands/Suspensions, Potential for Resignation, and Potential for Termination. In addition, there are 12 empirical scales divided into four general areas. The first area is Negative Self-Issues, which consists of Negative Emotions, Egocentrism, Inadequate Views of Police Work, and Poor Emotional Controls. The second area is Negative Perceptions Related to Law Enforcement, which consists of Inappropriate Attitudes About the Use of Force, Overly Traditional Officer Traits, and Suspiciousness. The third empirical scale area is Unethical Behavior, which comprises Lack of Personal Integrity, Negative Views of Department/Leadership, and Amorality. The last area is Unpredictability consisting of Risk Taking and Novelty Seeking.

The inventory is scored using *T*-scores. Scores within one standard deviation (10 points) of the mean ($T = 50$) indicate acceptable behavior. Scores lower than $T = 40$ are indicative of even more desirable traits, whereas scores over 60 are indicative of problematic areas. Scores over 70 are indicative of potentially very problematic behavior.

DEVELOPMENT. The authors began with a pool of 1,100 items, which were developed through the authors' knowledge of police culture and a review of the MMPI-2 and the PAI. These items were then sorted into the 18 liability outcomes that the authors had identified as most critical for police work. The pool of items was subsequently narrowed to 621 "after some initial research, further examination, and expert review" (technical manual, p. 20). Data were next collected on "several thousand law enforcement" recruits "whose job performance was tracked over several years" (technical manual, p. 20). The final pool of 455 items resulted from deleting 166 items based on either poor item correlations or the questionable legality of items.

TECHNICAL.

Norm sample. The norm sample for the M-PULSE consisted of 2,000 officer candidates from whom data were collected between 2003 and 2007. The authors report that the sample is representative of gender and race/ethnicity: 83% male, 53.5% Caucasian, 9.3% Hispanic, 9.3% African American, 16.5% Asian, 4.1% multiracial, and 7.5% other racial/ethnic groups. In addition, different geographic areas of the country were represented in the sample: 19.04% from the Northeast, 22.88% from the Midwest, 35.62% from the South, and 22.46% from the West. There were additional officer candidates included for some analyses resulting in a total of 5,348 individuals used for research and development providing the authors with a very robust sample size.

Validity. A series of statistical analyses were used to determine item placement in each of the 18 liability scales. Multiple regression analysis was used to identify items most predictive of each of the 18 liability scales. All statistics showed multiple *R* values from .45 (Lawsuit Potential) to .73 (Motor Vehicle Accidents). The models that resulted were used to determine the predictive validity of the scales. The resulting analysis showed that the scales were accurate in predicting liability behavior from a low of 65.9% (Procedural and Conduct Mistakes) to a high of 99.2% (Racially Offensive Conduct).

The empirical scales were developed through factor analysis (Varimax orthogonal rotation). This process resulted in the four empirical scales of Negative Self-Issues, Negative Perceptions Related to Law Enforcement, Unethical Behavior, and Unpredictability and their various subscales. Gender and ethnicity studies indicated that the M-PULSE showed no statistically significant differences in identifying persons with risk between men and women and among the various race/ethic groups for any of the scales. Readability of the M-PULSE was established using the Dale-Chall formula and was determined to be at the sixth-grade level.

In addition, the M-PULSE has established correlations with the 10 personality characteristics identified through the California Peace Officer Standards and Training (POST) studies. Although the POST studies state the personality characteristics in the positive, the scales on the M-PULSE have been reversed (stated in the negative) so that high scores on the M-PULSE are associated with potentially negative behavior. The correlations for these scales range from a low of .64 for Substance Abuse to a high of .93 for Emotional Instability/Stress Intolerance.

Reliability. Reliability for the validity and empirical scales was established with coefficient alpha. For the validity scales the values were .75 for Impression Management and .66 for Test Attitude. For the empirical scales, the alpha coefficients ranged from a low of .67 (Novelty Seeking) to a high of .97 (composite score for Negative Self-Issues).

COMMENTARY. The M-PULSE appears to be a well-developed inventory for aiding in the selection of law enforcement officers. Although it shares the drawbacks of any self-report measure, the authors have taken care to develop an item pool that appears to be viable in predicting potentially inappropriate behavior. The inventory is easy to take and administer. The online version offers the better administration procedure with immediate feedback. The test manual is clearly written and provides adequate information with a few exceptions noted below. Especially helpful in the manual, from a user's standpoint, are the detailed administration procedures and example profiles with suggestions for interpretation. Also, care was taken by the authors to ensure a large, robust, and representative sample for the reliability and validity studies.

One area of concern in the manual is the lack of complete description of the development and narrowing of the item pool. The authors refer to experts reviewing the item pool but do not specify the qualifications of the experts or the procedure used by them to narrow the item pool. Another area of concern is the lack of information on how job performance of the officers was measured. The authors allude to the fact that the liability scale scores were correlated with job performance, but they do not report how liability on the job was measured.

SUMMARY. The M-PULSE appears to be a well-designed instrument very suited for its purpose of aiding in the selection of law enforcement personnel. The instrument is easy to administer and the profile report easy to understand and interpret. The authors offer appropriate cautions regarding using the results of the instrument in combination with other data and not overrelying on data from the instrument by itself. Some additional information regarding the development of the item pool and validation procedures needs to be included in the manual for a more complete understanding of the uses and limitations of the instrument.

[73]

Measures of Academic Progress.

Purpose: Designed to provide "educators the information they need to improve teaching and learning" in the areas of reading, language usage, mathematics, and science as well as develop instructional strategies and promote school improvement.
Population: Grades 3–10.
Publication Dates: 2003–2005.
Acronym: MAP.
Administration: Group.
Restricted Distribution: To administer the MAP, professionals must have completed the MAP training requirements.
Price Data, 2008: Prices are available for administration training and MAP licensing on a sliding scale depending on district size; for administration training, prices range from $2,700 to $3,700 and for MAP licensing, prices range from $1,850 to $3,700 for districts of up to 750 students to more than 3,000 students, respectively.
Foreign Language Edition: MAP for mathematics with Spanish audio voice translations is available.
Time: Untimed (approximately 75 minutes).
Comments: MAP tests are computer administered and adaptive.
Author: Northwest Evaluation Association.
Publisher: Northwest Evaluation Association.

a) LANGUAGE.
Scores, 6: Writing Process, Composition Structure, Grammar/Usage, Punctuation, Capitalization, Total.
b) MATHEMATICS.
Scores, 9: Number/Numeration Systems, Operations/Computation, Equations/Numerals, Geometry, Measurement, Problem Solving, Statistics/Probability, Applications, Total.
c) READING.
Scores, 5: Word Meaning, Literal Comprehension, Interpretive Comprehension, Evaluative Comprehension, Total.
d) SCIENCE CONCEPTS.
Scores, 3: Concepts, Processes, Total.
e) GENERAL SCIENCE.
Scores, 4: Life Sciences, Earth/ Space Sciences, Physical Sciences, Total.

Review of Measures of Academic Progress By GREGORY J. CIZEK, Professor of Educational Measurement and Evaluation, University of North Carolina-Chapel Hill, Chapel Hill, NC:

DESCRIPTION. The Measures of Academic Progress (MAP) are computer-adaptive tests designed to measure achievement of elementary and secondary school students in five areas: Reading, Language, Mathematics, General Science, and Science Concepts. Paper-and-pencil, fixed-form versions of the MAP, called the Achievement Level Tests (ALTs), are also available. This review focuses only on the MAP tests and, because technical documentation is available only for the Reading, Language, and Mathematics tests, the General Science and Science Concepts tests are not reviewed here.

The MAP tests are available for students in Grades 2–10. Although they are intended primarily for English-speaking students in traditional school settings, the MAP manual includes information for users who wish to include home-schooled students in an assessment or to adapt the MAP for Spanish-speaking students. Beyond the information provided in the manuals, the Northwest Evaluation Association (NWEA), publisher of the MAP, provides support materials on its website (www.nwea.org), including information to assist educators in preparing to administer the MAP and to interpret results as well as a downloadable PowerPoint presentation to aid students in preparing to take a MAP test. Handbooks with information for test coordinators and proctors are also available. These resources provide step-by-step guides to prepare for MAP administrations, and detailed information on allowable accommodations for English Language Learners and students with special needs. Assessment of Spanish-speaking students is possible on MAP mathematics tests where the test questions appear on screen in English but are accompanied by Spanish audio.

Scores on MAP tests are reported in what are called "RITs"–shorthand for "Rasch units." The testing model underlying the MAP tests is a one-parameter IRT (Rasch) model, and the RIT scale is simply a transformation of the Rasch ability estimates; the scale on which scores are actually reported ranges from approximately 140 to 300. Data warehousing is a prominent feature of the MAP program; students are assigned unique identifiers that permit their scores to be entered into a data base of MAP results (across numerous years and states) and their progress to be tracked.

A typical MAP test has approximately 40–50 multiple-choice items. Reading and Language items have four options; Mathematics items have five options. Each of these subject areas is divided into narrower goal areas. For example, the four goal subareas for Reading comprise Word Meaning, Literal Comprehension, Interpretive Comprehension, and Evaluative Comprehension. Mathematics is divided into eight goals: Number/Numeration Systems, Operations/Computation, Equations/Numerals, Geometry, Measurement, Problem Solving, Statistics/Probability, and Applications. Each goal is tapped by a minimum of 7 items. Abbreviated versions of MAP tests called MAP Surveys are also available. The Survey tests for each subject area consist of 20 items and only overall scores (not goal subarea scores) for a subject area are reported. The publisher of the MAP and MAP users such as a school district collaborate to determine the exact specifications for the MAP tests that will be implemented in a district, including the specific goals to be included, alignment to the district's curriculum, test length, and percentage of items allocated to each goal and subgoal.

MAP tests are computer-administered and adaptive, meaning that each student taking a MAP test receives a set of items that is optimal for the student's ability level. MAP tests for each grade level are created from large item pools (1,500, 1,200, and 1,200 items for Mathematics, Language, and Reading, respectively). Tailoring a test for an individual student is accomplished by selecting an initial item that is 5 RITs below the student's current ability estimate from a previously administered MAP in that subject or, if no previous score is available, the first item will be one that is 5 RITs below the mean of the student's grade-level norm group. The student's performance on the first item provides an improved estimate of the student's ability level and subsequent items administered to the student are chosen in a similar fashion to obtain as precise an estimate as possible of the student's ability level, and to ensure appropriate coverage of goal subareas. The computerized format also facilitates monitoring of student response times. A score is considered invalid if an examinee completes a test in less than 6 minutes or if the conditional standard error of measurement associated with a student's ability estimate exceeds specified thresholds.

Although it provides enhanced efficiency of measurement, the adaptive, computer-administered feature of MAP tests also has some drawbacks. For one, students cannot skip any questions and they cannot go back to review or change responses to a previously answered item. MAP tests are untimed, which may create difficulty for computer scheduling. Potential users of the MAP system will also need to ensure technological infrastructure and availability of testing stations. The MAP technical manual (Northwest Evaluation Association, 2005a) specifies technical requirements, but system testing procedures are not included and the tests cannot be administered via a wireless network. The actual testing interface that the student sees is spartan, but straightforward. A couple of oddities were noted. For example, some tests use letters for answer choices, others use numbers. In the Mathematics test, an on-screen calculator pops into view for some questions for which it would not seem appropriate (e.g., items about identifying geometric shapes) but not for others where it would seem relevant (e.g., calculation items). Overall, however, taking a MAP test via computer seemed to be uncomplicated and not to interfere with sound measurement.

Numerous score reporting options are available. In addition to individual, class, and system reports, users can aggregate student performance in customized ways. Student performance can be summarized in standards-referenced terms using scaled scores, percent correct, achievement categories (e.g., Low, Medium, High) or other systems. Achievement can also be summarized in norm-referenced terms, using familiar percentile ranks and standard scores. Finally, achievement progress or growth can be monitored via cross-grade (i.e., vertical) scales.

Overall, abundant information is provided such that users can extract meaningful information about student achievement for instructional, evaluation, or accountability uses. One caution is in order, however, regarding the student score reports and the listing of "Skills and Concepts to Develop" for individual students. The specific skills and concepts listed are tied to the overall RIT ability level of the student. Thus, the recommended remedial activities will be appropriate for students at that RIT level generally, but may not be relevant to a specific student. Additionally, individual scores are reported for goal areas for individual students although these should be used with extreme caution because they are based on relatively few items.

DEVELOPMENT. Limited information about the content development of the MAP tests is provided. The manual reports that the domains covered were determined using a process by which "a variety of content structures from different agencies for the domain of interest are reviewed and joined" (NWEA, 2005a, p. 19) and that all items developed to sample the domains were written and reviewed by classroom teachers who participated in multi-day item-writing workshops. The teachers are instructed to write items to broad areas such as "computation" or "algebra" and to provide an initial content classification. Items are assigned specific objective classifications at a later time by the publisher when items are officially classified according to a major goal, and to one of 150–200 content categories in a subject area. Information is not provided on the specific curriculum guides, state content standards, professional association recommendations, or textbook series used to circumscribe the domains, or on the qualifications and representativeness of the item writers.

Items were then field-tested with 300–400 examinees and reviewed for fit to the Rasch model and assessed for unidimensionality. The manual also reports that, after field testing, a screening for potential bias is conducted in which "many of the items in the item banks are reviewed by a panel of stakeholders from a variety of racial and ethnic backgrounds" (NWEA, 2005a, p. 22). Additional information on the representativeness of the field test samples and the qualifications of the bias review panels, as well as updated procedures for detecting dimensionality, incorporating procedures for detecting differential item functioning (DIF), and expanding bias and sensitivity reviews to include characteristics such as gender, SES, native language, or other relevant variables would strengthen the development process.

TECHNICAL. Technical information related to the MAP assessments includes information on standardization provided in a norms document (NWEA, 2005b) and information on reliability and validity provided in the technical manual (NWEA, 2005a).

Norms. The norm group data for the MAP assessments were collected between Spring 2001–Fall 2004 and involved approximately 2.3 million students from 5,616 schools in 794 districts across 32 states. However, norm data were not collected exclusively for the MAP; rather, data were combined from students who took MAP or ALT tests, with 77% of the eventual norm group having taken a MAP test. Little information is provided for users to judge the appropriateness of the norms. Essentially, the information is limited to a list of the participating educational institutions, a table showing the percentages of each state's total enrollment that was included in the norm group, and information showing that the grade-level mean scores of a stratified (by proportion of ethnicity at each grade level) random sample taken from the total norm group deviate by only a small amount from the total group means.

Two types of norm information are available: status norms (similar to those reported for typical large-scale norm-referenced tests [NRTs], which portray a student's standing with respect to a comparison group from a single test administration) and growth norms (that yield normative information about students' pre- to posttest score differences). Whereas the technology of status norming is highly refined, the assumptions and procedures for creating growth norms are less advanced. Growth norming for MAP tests is accomplished by compiling the simple differences in RIT scores over time (e.g., fall-to-spring, or spring-to-spring across one or more grade levels) to obtain distributions of these differences. Of potential value to MAP users are what the publisher terms *virtual comparison groups* (VCGs). VCGs allow users to request norms data that are customized and especially relevant to specific users. VCGs are constructed using an individual student matching procedure and the extensive test score database to create a comparison group that is highly similar to the local students of interest.

The manual indicates that the samples used to create regular MAP norms (that is, not VCG norms) were much larger than those taken for the National Assessment of Educational Progress (NAEP) or the Trends in International Mathematics and Science Studies (TIMSS). Although true, readers familiar with those assessments will know that their smaller *n*-counts were enabled by highly precise sampling strategies to ensure representativeness. In addition, both NAEP and TIMSS developers provide abundant information about the demographic and other relevant characteristics of the test-taking groups, so that users can assess the degree to which the norms represent an appropriate comparison group. Little such information is provided for MAP norms. Proportions are indicated by state and student ethnicity, but basic information such as relative composition of males/females, public/private, urbanicity, special needs students, and so on is not provided. Oddly, the norms manual notes that "the NWEA RIT scale norms are not based on samples of students drawn to match national demographic patterns" (NWEA, 2005b, p. 107) and argues that it is "extremely unlikely that any organization could collect data that would allow it to create national norms" (p. 107). Although some supporting rationale for the argument is presented, it is likely that users will either want or assume that any norms provided will at least support typical interpretations.

Overall, in this reviewer's opinion the most supportable conclusions regarding the MAP norms are suggested in the manual where it is noted that a defensible interpretation would be: "If a fourth grade student's RIT score is equivalent to the 50th percentile on these norms, one can say with confidence that this student scored better than 50 percent of the other *fourth grade students who use NWEA testing systems*" (NWEA, 2005b, p. 107, emphasis in original).

Reliability. Three types of reliability evidence are reported. A procedure called marginal reliability (Samejima, 1994) yielded reliability estimates for total scores ranging from .92 to .96 across Grades 2–10 in each subject area. Data for these reliability estimates are based on the varying numbers of students across the grade levels (ranging from approximately 1,600 at 10th grade to approximately 40,000 at 5th grade) and were collected as part of the 1999 MAP norming study. Test-retest reliabilities are also reported based on data collection from 2002. Because the time points for data collection were fall-to-spring or spring-to-spring, the design essentially compared pre- and postinstruction scores. Across all grades and subjects, stability estimates were never lower than .77 (Grade 2 Mathematics) and were as high as .94 (Grade 7 Mathematics) and generally increased across the grades. Finally, conditional standard errors of measurement (*CSEMs*) are reported in RIT units; the *CSEMs* are generally small across most of the effective range of the RIT scale. Overall, it would appear that users can count on MAP scores to be quite reliable.

Validity. Validity evidence for MAP score interpretations comes from two primary sources. First, the comprehensive test development and administration procedures and documentation support conclusions that MAP scores differentiate between students' levels of ability in tested subjects. Although lacking details about the specific content standards, curricula, or alignment processes used, the MAP technical manual indicates that "the manner in which the goals and objectives for each test are developed promotes a high degree of alignment between the curriculum and the test content" (NWEA, 2005a, p. 52). Indeed, because the content of MAP tests results from extensive input on the part of users, it is likely that customized MAP test specifications reflect the curricular goals and objectives of the districts involved and, thus, enhances validity vis a vis those outcomes.

A second source of validity evidence consists of criterion-related and concurrent evidence. The primary source of validity evidence for MAP scores consists of correlations between the ALT assessments and other measures. This is somewhat odd, in that MAP scores are not involved but scores from the publisher's other series, the ALT, are used exclusively. However, the manual documents a consistently high correlation between MAP and ALT scores—this would be expected in that they draw from the same item banks–which affords some confidence that ALT-Criterion relationships are a reasonable proxy for MAP-Criterion relationships.

Relevant validity coefficients reveal that ALT scores in Reading, Mathematics, and Language are fairly strongly related to scores on the Iowa Tests of Basic Skills (ITBS) and the Stanford Achievement Tests, 9th Edition (SAT9). The validity data for the ITBS comparison were drawn from approximately 1,400 examinees each in Grades 3, 5, and 7 in the fall of 1999. No other information about the groups is provided. The correlations range from .77 to .84 in all grades and subjects. Similar results were observed for samples of between approximately 4,000 and 7,000 examinees in Grades 2 through 9 who were administered ALT assessments and the SAT9 in the spring of 2001. Concurrent validity coefficients ranged from .78 to .88. ALT scores were also correlated with scores on various state-level assessments in Wyoming, Colorado, Indiana, and Washington with similar results. Again, no descriptive information is provided to help the reader in judging the representativeness of the samples, but all reported correlations showed uniformly strong relationships. Finally, a study of ALT and MAP scale drift reported by the publisher found a high degree of stability. According to the publisher: "The measurement scales have not drifted by more than 0.01 standard deviations over the quarter of a century in which they have been used" (NWEA, 2005a, p. 27). This finding supports a desirable validity-related property; namely, that MAP scores do not have differing interpretations over time.

COMMENTARY. Overall, MAP tests provide straightforward measurement of foundational knowledge and skills in mathematics, reading, and language usage. The computer-adaptive format permits testing that is tailored to individual students, and the test design process facilitates tight alignment to the educational outcomes judged to be important to users of the MAP system (e.g., school districts). In some respects, the MAP system can be seen as "no frills" measurement. Although advanced in terms of its adaptive nature, the MAP interface is uncluttered, the only item format used is multiple-choice (i.e., there are no constructed-response items), and the length of reading passages is modest.

Advantages of MAP assessments include increased measurement precision for most students, increased efficiency in terms of testing time, and the availability of rich individual and aggregated feedback that supports a range of standards-based, norm-referenced, and growth interpretations. Additionally, the MAP assessments are linked to the Lexile Framework (MetaMetrics, 2008) that, for reading tests, provides teachers, parents, and students with a wealth of resources for matching readers to text. It would appear that users can have confidence in the reliability of MAP scores, and the available validity evidence suggests that those scores can be interpreted as intended indicators of knowledge and skill mastery in core subject areas, as well as indicators of relative standing and relative growth with respect to a comparison group.

A number of enhancements would strengthen the MAP technical documentation. Reliability should be demonstrated for the MAP, not just its stablemate, the ALT. For all reliability and validity evidence, additional descriptive information should include data on gender representation, inclusion of special needs and limited-English proficient students, school type (i.e., public/private), location (urban/suburban/rural), and other demographic characteristics. Considerably more information must be provided on topics such as the content foundation of the assessments, DIF procedures used, and how scores reported on the RIT scale compare to the cross-grade Lexile scale. Some updating and adjustments to the computer interface would be desirable.

SUMMARY. According to the publisher's website, over 3 million students have taken over 24 million NWEA assessments (Northwest Evaluation Association, 2008). There are good reasons for the popularity of MAP assessments and there is much to commend about the MAP assessment system. Available evidence suggests that MAP tests can be used with confidence by school districts to gauge student learning, relative standing, and growth with respect to educational objectives deemed central to the curricular emphases of those districts. The computer-adaptive format yields advantages in precision of scores, efficiency, and flexibility of both individual and aggregate score reporting. NWEA data warehousing provides a strong foundation for research on the MAP and insights for future test development. Some aspects of the MAP would benefit from additional attention. To the extent that the next generation of MAP tests attends to these, the MAP could well transition from being a sound assessment system to a highly defensible and rigorously undergirded leader in student achievement testing.

REVIEWER'S REFERENCES

MetaMetrics, Inc. (2008). *The Lexile framework for reading.* Retrieved December 10, 2008 from http://www.lexile.com

Northwest Evaluation Association. (2005a). *Technical manual for use with Measures of Academic Progress and Achievement Level Tests.* Lake Oswego, OR: Author.

Northwest Evaluation Association. (2005b). *RIT scale norms for use with Measures of Academic Progress and Achievement Level Tests.* Lake Oswego, OR: Author.

Northwest Evaluation Association. (2008). *About us.* Retrieved December 10, 2008 from http://www.nwea.org/about/index.asp

Samejima, F. (1994). Estimation of reliability coefficients using the test information function and its modifications. *Applied Psychological Measurement, 18*, 229-244.

Review of the Measures of Academic Progress by MARK J. GIERL, Professor and Canada Research Chair, Centre for Research in Applied Measurement and Evaluation, Department of Educational Psychology, University of Alberta, Edmonton, Alberta, Canada, and CECILIA B. ALVES, Ph.D. Graduate student, Centre for Research in Applied Measurement and Evaluation, Department of Educational Psychology, University of Alberta, Edmonton, Alberta, Canada:

DESCRIPTION. Measures of Academic Progress (MAP) is a series of computerized adaptive tests developed by the Northwest Evaluation Association (NWEA) for assessing academic achievement from Grades 2 to 10 in the content areas of Reading, Language Usage, Mathematics, and Science. Each MAP test is composed of units called curricular "goals" or objectives. These curricular goals are intended to align with state academic standards. Each goal yields a MAP subscore which, in turn, can be aggregated to produce a total test score. In Reading, curricular goal subscores are provided in the areas of Word Meaning, Literal Comprehension, Interpretative Comprehension, and Evaluative Comprehension. In Language Usage (also called Language, at times, in the technical manual), subscores are provided in the areas of Writing Process, Composition Structure, Grammar/Usage, Punctuation, and Capitalization. In Mathematics, subscores are provided in the areas of Number/Numeration Systems, Operations/Computation, Equations/Numerals, Geometry, Measurement, Problem Solving, Statistics/Probability, and Applications. In Science, two different areas are evaluated: Science Concepts, which has subscores in the areas of Concepts and Processes and General Science, which has subscores in the areas of Life Sciences, Earth/Space Sciences, and Physical Sciences.

The MAP technical manual provides an excellent overview of the design, development, administration, scoring, and maintenance procedures required to support an operational computerized adaptive testing system (see Fischer & Molenaar, 1995; van der Linden & Glas, 2000). Items in each content area of the MAP are administered using this adaptive system where the first item selected is based on the examinee's past MAP performance. If no previous score is available, then the first item selected is based upon the mean performance for students in the same grade. After answering the first item, the examinee's achievement level is estimated. The next item is chosen to match this achievement estimate. If the examinee answers an item incorrectly, then an easier item is presented. Conversely, if the examinee answers the item correctly, then a more difficult item is presented. The algorithm is designed to repeatedly administer items and update the estimate of achievement until a prescribed stopping rule is reached. Once the test is finished, the examinee's overall achievement score in each subject as well as the curricular goal subscores are calculated and reported. Computerized adaptive testing, as implemented with MAP, has many well-documented benefits including shortened tests without a loss of measurement precision, enhanced score precision for low and high ability examinees, improved test security, testing on demand, and immediate test scoring and reporting. MAP tests can be simultaneously administered to as many examinees as there are computers available at the testing site. Because the test is tailored to the performance of the examinee throughout the assessment, it is unlikely that any two examinees will be exposed to the same set of items.

NWEA scale development and computerized adaptive testing procedures are guided by the principles and practices in item response theory (IRT). MAP scoring employs the one-parameter logistic IRT model, which places examinees and items on the same scale. IRT also permits the construction and maintenance of item banks that extend beyond a single grade making it possible to develop measurement scales that range from elementary to high school (in the case of the MAP, Grades 2 to 10), thereby allowing test users to monitor student growth.

DEVELOPMENT. Test development, the MAP authors claim, is guided by the *Standards for Educational and Psychological Testing* (American Educatinal Research Association, American Psychological Association, & National Council on Measurements in Education, 1999). The MAP technical manual contains a detailed and instructional description of the test development processes and procedures associated with IRT-based computerized adaptive testing. MAP test development is characterized as a two-phase process. In the first phase, measurement scales are developed and in the second phase, measurement scales are maintained.

Phase I (Development of Measurement Scales)–To develop the initial scales, many steps are required. To begin, scale boundaries are set by choosing the domain and content of interest. Content structures are developed by NWEA staff and by content specialists. The MAP contains approximately 150 to 200 categories in each content area. Field testing occurs after the items have been written, reviewed, and assigned to a category. Each item is then administered to a sample of 300–400 examinees. The model-data fit between the IRT model and the examinees' item response data are evaluated using tests of dimensionality as well as item-fit statistics (e.g., adjusted point-biserial correlation and adjusted Root-Mean-Square Fit). Item difficulties are then estimated and scaled in logit units and transformed into a Rasch Unit (RIT) scale, which has a mean of 200 and standard deviation of 10. In addition to an overall RIT score, examinees also receive their RIT score range using the standard error of measurement, goal performance, percentile rank, percentile range, and lexile score (for Reading only).

Phase II (Maintenance of Measurement Scales)–With the completion of Phase I, MAP measurement scales can be used to design tests, evaluate student performance, and monitor growth. The existing scales must also be maintained by updating the content structures of the item bank when new content is introduced and by replenishing the bank by adding new items. The process of adding new items to the bank is a sophisticated technical process where newly developed items are combined with operational items in a field test so a "one-step estimation procedure" can be conducted with proprietary item calibration software (see NWEA technical manual, 2005, p. 20) to place the new items onto the operational score scale. The process of item development and banking is ongoing because the MAP adaptive testing process requires many items. As a result, MAP item banks are relatively large ranging from 692 in General Science to 8,461 in Mathematics.

TECHNICAL.

Standardization. A comprehensive norming study was conducted to generate the RIT scale norms for the MAP. The norming sample included more than 2 million students. The majority of these students took the test on one or more occasions in the Fall and Spring of 2003 and/or 2004. All four testing sessions were used to create the status norms, whereas information for the students who took a test in a content area more than once was used to create the growth norms. The sample was drawn from 5,616 schools in 794 districts in 32 states (as well as two schools from outside the

U.S.A.). The geographical range of the samples was diverse and the ethnic characteristics of the samples were comparable to the American population for most ethnic groups. Students' results from Grades 2 to 10 were used to create both status and growth norms in Reading, Language Usage, and Mathematics. Smaller samples were drawn in Science leading to more limited norming results in this content area (see NWEA RIT Scale Norms manual, 2005, p. 7).

Reliability. The reliability of the MAP is evaluated using the marginal reliability estimate as described by Samejima (1994), test-retest reliability, and score precision using standard error of measurement (*SEM*). Marginal reliability, as described in the MAP technical manual, uses the test information function to determine the expected correlation between the scores of two hypothetical tests taken by the same student. Marginal reliability coefficients, computed using 1999 data, ranged from .92 in Grade 2 (Fall) Mathematics and Grade 9 (Spring) Language Usage to .96 on Grades 8 and 9 (Spring) Mathematics. Test-retest reliability is calculated as the correlation between scores on two different test administrations (e.g., Fall and Spring) taken by the same student. Test-retest reliability, computed using 2002 data, ranged from .77 in Grade 2 (Fall to Spring) Mathematics to .94 Grade 7 (Fall to Spring) Mathematics. Score precision is also reported using standard errors of measurement (*SEM*). The *SEM* is consistently low across the majority of the score scales in Mathematics, Reading, and Language Usage demonstrating that MAP efficiency is high. Surprisingly, no evidence is presented to support the reliability of MAP Science. This omission is noteworthy.

Validity. In the MAP technical manual, validity is defined as "the degree to which an educational assessment measures what it intends to measure" (p. 51). This conceptualization of validity is dated and inconsistent with the *Standards for Educational and Psychological Testing* (AERA, APA, & NCME, 1999), where validity is defined as the degree to which accumulated evidence and theory support specific interpretations of test scores entailed by proposed uses of a test (p. 184). Moreover, the evidence presented in the validity section of the MAP technical manual is limited, as it focuses on concurrent validity studies where the correlation between other NWEA assessments (the Achievement Level Tests [ALT]) and other measures of academic achievement are reported across select content areas and grade levels. Correlations between ALT and the Stanford Achievement Test (9th Edition), Colorado State Assessment Program, Iowa Tests of Basic Skills, Indiana Statewide Testing for Educational Progress–Plus, Washington Assessment of Student Learning, and Wyoming Comprehensive Assessment System are reported. The lowest correlation was .60 between the ALT and the Wyoming Comprehensive Assessment System in Language Usage at Grade 4. The highest correlation was .91 between the ALT and the Colorado State Assessment Scale in Mathematics at Grade 8. Across all concurrent validity studies reported in the technical manual, we computed the average correlation for Reading as .85, for Language and Language Usage as .81, and for Mathematics as .85. But, as with the reliability section, no evidence is presented to support the concurrent validity of MAP Science.

COMMENTARY AND SUMMARY. The MAP is a computerized adaptive test system that can be used to measure student achievement from Grades 2 to 10 in the content areas of Reading, Language Usage, Mathematics, and Science. The MAP technical manual provides an excellent description of the design, development, administration, scoring, and maintenance procedures required to support an operational computerized adaptive testing system. This description, as the authors note in their overview of the validity section in the technical manual, provides some evidence to support the valid use of the MAP. The test authors' description of their measurement scale development and maintenance procedures is particularly strong. Some aspects of the technical features in the MAP are also well described. For example, a comprehensive study provides a strong foundation for RIT scale norms that supports both interpretations of students' performances at a single time as well as growth over time. The reliability evidence is also comprehensive, as it includes three measures of score consistency. Unfortunately, this evidence is limited to content areas of Reading, Language Usage, and Mathematics–we received no reliability evidence for Science. The validity evidence, on the other hand, is limited. The authors focus, in the validity section of the technical manual, on the correlation between the ALT and six measures of academic achievement. The focus, again, is on Reading, Language Usage, and Mathematics, to the exclusion of Science. We contend that the omission of Science in both the reliability and validity sections serves as an important limitation of MAP generally, and of the Science content area, specifically.

REVIEWERS' REFERENCES

American Educational Research Association, American Psychological Association, & National Council on Measurement in Education. (1999). *Standards for educational and psychological testing*. Washington, DC: American Educational Research Association.

Fischer, G. H., & Molenaar, I. W. (1995). *Rasch models: Foundations, recent developments, and applications*. New York: Springer.

Northwest Evaluation Association. (2005, May). *Technical manual for use with Measures of Academic Progress and Achievement Level Tests*. Lake Oswego, OR: Northwest Evaluation Association.

Northwest Evaluation Association. (2005, September). *RIT scale norms for use with Measures of Academic Progress and Achievement Level Tests*. Lake Oswego, OR: Northwest Evaluation Association.

Samejima, F. (1994). Estimation of reliability coefficients using the test information function and its modifications. *Applied Psychological Measurement, 18*, 229-244.

van der Linden, W. J., & Glas, C. A. W. (2000). *Computerized adaptive testing: Theory and practice*. Dordrecht, The Netherlands: Kluwer

[74]

Miller Function and Participation Scales.

Purpose: Designed "to determine if a child has a developmental delay in the functional motor abilities needed to participate in early school years."
Population: Ages 2.6-7.11.
Publication Date: 2006.
Acronym: M-FUN.
Administration: Individual.
Parts, 2: Performance Assessment, Participation Assessment.
Price Data, 2008: $369 per complete kit with manipulatives.
Time: (40-60) minutes.
Author: Lucy J. Miller.
Publisher: Pearson.

a) PERFORMANCE ASSESSMENT.

Levels, 3: Ages 2.6-3.11, Ages 4.0-5.11, Ages 6.0-7.11.

Forms, 2: Ages 2.6-3.11, Ages 4.0-7.11.

1) *Ages 2.6-3.11.*

Scores, 21: Follow the Path, Flying Birds, Clouds, Hidden Forks, Find the Rabbits, Copying Shapes, Writing, Visual Motor Behavior Rating, Clay Play, Penny Bank, Origami, Snack Time, Fine Motor Behavior Rating, Statue, Throw and Catch, Soccer, Jumping, Gross Motor Behavior Rating, Visual Motor, Fine Motor, Gross Motor.

2) *Ages 4.0-5.11.*

Scores, 22: Amazing Mazes, Race Car, Hidden Forks, Find the Puppies, Draw a Kid, Writing, Go Fishing (1-4), Visual Motor Behavior Rating, Go Fishing (5-7), Clay Play, Penny Bank, Origami, Snack Time, Fine Motor Behavior Rating, Statue, Ball Balance, Soccer, Jumping, Gross Motor Behavior Rating, Visual Motor, Fine Motor, Gross Motor.

3) *Ages 6.0-7.11.*

Scores, 23: Amazing Mazes, Race Car, Hidden Forks, Find the Puppies, Draw a Kid, Writing, Go Fishing (1-4), Visual Motor Behavior Rating, Go Fishing (5-7), Clay Play, Penny Bank, Origami, Snack Time, Fine Motor Behavior Rating, Statue, Ball Balance, Bouncing Ball, Soccer, Jumping, Gross Motor Behavior Rating, Visual Motor, Fine Motor, Gross Motor.

b) PARTICIPATION ASSESSMENT.

Scores, 3: Home Observations, Classroom Observations, Test Observations.

Population: Ages 2.6-7.11.

Review of the Miller Function and Participation Scales by ABIGAIL BAXTER, Associate Professor, Department of Leadership and Teacher Education, University of South Alabama, Mobile, AL:

DESCRIPTION. The Miller Function and Participation Scales (M-FUN) is a developmental assessment of children's functional motor behaviors and participation in everyday contexts. The purpose of the M-FUN is to help therapists and others assess if "a child's motor competency affects his or her ability to engage in home and school activities and to participate socially in his or her world" (examiner's manual, p. 1). It can be used to understand the neuromotor foundations of functional motor skills and monitor progress in attaining such skills. The M-FUN consists of a series of "games" in which the child demonstrates his or her skills. Caregiver, teacher, and examiner checklists provide qualitative information about children's participation at home, in school or daycare, and during the assessment period, respectively. The M-FUN was developed for children ages 2 years, 6 months through 7 years, 11 months. It can be administered to older children, but normative comparisons cannot be made. The M-FUN kit consists of the examiner's manual, administration directions, workbooks and record forms (including the Test Observations Checklist) for children in two age groups (2:6–3:11 and 4:0–7:11), Home Observations Checklists, and Classroom Observations Checklists. Manipulatives can be purchased with the test or provided by examiners. Examiners will need to supply 10 pennies, napkins, a bottle of water, snack crackers, and a sealable plastic bag for each administration.

The M-FUN can be administered by occupational and physical therapists, educators (adapted physical education or special), and early childhood interventionists with experience using, scoring, and interpreting standardized assessments and knowledge of motor development and sensory processing. Administration takes 40–60 minutes; directions and verbal prompts are included in the administration directions book. Some items are timed. All items are administered for most games; discontinue rules are explained where relevant. The checklists take 5–10 minutes for caregivers, teachers, and examiners to complete.

The test items are scored for performance and the qualitative aspects of the child's response. The manual provides examples of different performance levels and their score values. Raw scores are available for each game. Raw scores are compiled to form three performance scales: Visual Motor, Fine Motor, and Gross Motor. Scaled scores, percentile ranks (with confidence intervals), and age equivalents are available for each performance scale. Progress scores for Fine Motor and Gross Motor are available for ages 2.6-7.11. Progress scores for Visual Motor are available for ages 4.0-7.11. Scaled and progress scores can be plotted. The Neurological Foundations Profile analyzes items that were not passed and provides information on areas of weakness for intervention. The checklists' weighted total scores are compared to cut scores indicating average, below average, or far below average performance.

DEVELOPMENT. The M-FUN focuses on competencies and qualitative aspects of children's functioning leading to an understanding of the neurological underpinnings of the behaviors based upon the World Health Organization's International Classification of Functioning, Disability, and Health (ICF), and the American Occupational Therapy Association's Practice Framework (PF). The M-FUN's items are important functional activities, not isolated skills within different developmental domains. Like the PF it focuses upon visual, fine, and gross motor performance skills; process skills (e.g., organization, adaptation, attention, sustained effort, knowledge); and communication skills. It addresses children's performance patterns, internal and external context factors, activity demands, and individual differences.

M-FUN development began with therapist focus groups describing the type of motor assessment they needed and specifications for such a test. This led to the development of performance items to assess the child's abilities (the games) in a reasonable amount of time, and the rating scales to assess participation in everyday contexts. A review of the previous research on motor skills and their development, the ICF and PF, and information from the focus groups led to the games in the M-FUN. Subject matter experts reviewed all planned items and delineated the developmental skills that the M-FUN should assess. Clinical experience and preschool and early childhood curricula were used to develop a list of tasks. These tasks were then divided into items that could be performance items and those to be assessed on checklists. The performance items were analyzed for underlying motor skills and the development of scoring rubrics. This resulted in a tryout version with 33 games and 205 items that was reviewed by content reviewers who suggested changes before the tryout phase. The tryout phase involved 118 typically developing children and 22 children with a motor impairment without brain involvement. The tryout revealed problems with procedures, directions, stimuli, and record forms that were addressed before standardization.

TECHNICAL.

Standardization. The standardization sample for the performance assessment included 414 children in the test's age range, almost 7% of whom received services "for motor impairment impacting educational performance" (examiner's manual, p. 91). The sample was stratified based on gender, race/ethnicity, and parent education level and was drawn from different regions of the country. Comparison data for race/ethnicity and parent education level to the 2002 U.S. Census are provided but such data for geographic regions, gender, and age are not. The standardization sample underrepresents children of parents with less than a college education and overrepresents those whose parents attained a college degree or higher. Standardization information was used to determine the final number of games for the two age groups. Standardization samples for the Home, Classroom, and Test Observations checklists included 325, 183, and 360 children, respectively, who had also taken the M-FUN. These samples, too, are biased by including disproportionately more children of relatively well-educated parents.

Reliability. Test-retest, internal consistency, and interrater reliability data are presented. Test-retest reliability estimates are from 27 children (or N = 28 from Table 5.1 on page 102 of manual) from the standardization sample who were given the M-FUN 0–21 (M = 14.5) days after the first administration by the same examiner. The two genders were equally represented and half of children's parents had a college or higher degree. They were all White and geographic location is not reported. There is moderate test-retest reliability. Internal consistency was assessed with coefficient alpha across ages for the Visual, Fine, and Gross Motor scaled scores as well as the Home, Classroom, and Test Observations Checklists for the children in the standardization samples. Results varied by age and scale or checklist but were within acceptable ranges. Acceptable internal consistency estimates are also available for a clinical sample of children with motor impairments without cognitive impairments. There is also evidence of a high degree of inter-rater reliability based on a sample of 29 protocols. Information on the standard errors of measurement for the norm-referenced Performance scaled scores and the criterion-referenced Observations scores are presented.

Validity. Validity of the M-FUN was established "based on content, internal structure, relationship to other variables, and ... diagnostic accuracy" (examiner's manual, p. 108). Evidence of content validity comes from the development of the test based on early childhood curricula, reviews of the literature, and the input of subject matter experts. Face validity is evidenced by the M-FUN asking children to engage in specific motor behaviors. There is evidence of convergence and divergence in the scores for the three motor areas as well as the observations in the three separate settings. The M-FUN scores are correlated with scores on the Miller Assessment for Preschoolers (T7:1623), another motor assessment. The M-FUN was also administered to children with motor delays and normal intelligence and their scores were compared to a matched sample of children from the standardization sample. Significant differences ($p < .01$) in M-FUN scores were found between typically developing children and children with identified visual, fine, and gross motor delays. The examiner's manual also presents specificity, sensitivity, and predictive power estimates for diagnostic accuracy. These numbers suggest that the M-FUN is capable of accurately identifying children with and without motor delays.

COMMENTARY. The M-FUN plays an important role in providing assessment information about children's motor skills within functional contexts by assessing actual performance as well as participation. It is built on a solid theoretical foundation. Administration rules and scoring examples, although complex, seem clearly written. However, an apparent lack of attention to detail in the examiner's manual is a concern. For example, references in the text are not on the reference list (e.g., Dunn, 1991), references to parts of the record form are inconsistent (pp. 6, 10), descriptions of some of the samples do not account for all participants (pp. 97, 101, 102), and some references to tables are inaccurate (p. 109). Additionally, standardization samples are biased toward children of relatively well-educated parents and exclude children with cognitive delays who also have motor delays.

SUMMARY. The M-FUN provides useful information for individuals working with young children with motor impairments. Instead of assessing developmental milestones it provides information about children's functional behaviors in real-life contexts. The games are engaging and the checklists easy to complete. Scoring is complex but clear examples are given. The M-FUN provides useful information about children's visual, fine, and gross motor abilities and differences among them. It identifies problems in underlying neurological functioning. The Checklists (Home, School, and Test) provide information about children's level of participation in different contexts. The M-FUN also provides a way for professionals to develop functional goals and a mechanism to monitor children's motor development and assess the influence of interventions.

Review of the Miller Function and Participation Scales by C. DALE CARPENTER, Associate Dean, College of Education and Allied Professions, and Professor of Special Education, Western Carolina University, Cullowhee, NC:

DESCRIPTION. The Miller Function and Participation Scales (M-FUN) is an individually administered assessment for ages 2 years 6 months to 7 years 11 months to measure motor competency and the ability to engage in home and school. M-FUN is organized into Performance Assessment and Participation Assessment. Performance Assessment is a set of standardized games yielding norm-referenced scores, and Participation Assessment consists of observations at home and school yielding criterion-referenced scores.

Performance Assessment is divided into three areas: visual motor, fine motor, and gross motor. Visual motor assessments involve tasks such as tracing a path from the beginning to the end of a maze (Amazing Mazes) and drawing a person (Draw a Kid). Fine motor assessments include tasks of making a clay ball (Clay Play) and folding paper into simple origami patterns (Origami). Gross motor assessments involve such things as throwing and catching a small ball (Throw and Catch) and kicking a small ball (Soccer). Most items within a game are scored using a rubric of 0 to 3. A raw score and scaled score result for Visual Motor, Fine Motor, and Gross Motor. For each of the three areas, the examiner rates behavior during the games and this rating contributes to the participation assessment.

The participation components of the assessment are observations by a caregiver in the home of the child's participation in daily living activities, a teacher or examiner in the school of the child's participation in classroom activities, and during the performance assessments. Examples of home observation items include "opens and closes doors" and "cleans up room." Classroom observations include "follows classroom and school rules" and "maneuvers around obstacles." Observers rate whether the behavior occurs "almost always" to "seldom." There is an opportunity to indicate that the behavior is "not seen" or "not observed." Points are awarded for behaviors that occur successfully some of the time (at least 25%) to almost always (better than 75%). Raw scores result in an age-based criterion rating of average, below average, or far below average indicating mild, moderate, or severe motor delays in body function, activity, and participation. The individual record form also includes a table to record results of three test administrations and to monitor progress.

DEVELOPMENT. The test author states that the International Classification of Functioning, Disability, and Health (ICF), Occupational Therapy (OT) Practice Framework, literature review, and experts helped to determine the domains from which the test was developed. Furthermore, expert focus groups of mostly occupational therapists provided foundational and practical advice on the overall development of M-FUN. The test author also used her previous work with earlier instruments (Miller, 1982, 1993).

Specific items were developed from a blueprint that attempted to identify motor skills that positively impact a child's ability to participate in home and classroom activities. Pilot and tryout testing included 118 typically developing children and 22 children with identified motor impairments in Colorado. Feedback resulted in improvements including scoring procedures. Based on standardization sampling and item analyses, some items were deleted and others were changed so that they were not included for certain age groups.

TECHNICAL.

Standardization. The M-FUN standardization sample included 414 children or about 50 children per age group in 6-month intervals through 4 years, 11 months and in 1-year intervals through 7 years, 11 months. The sample approximated 2002 U.S. Census data for race/ethnicity. Children whose parents were at the upper end of the education continuum (high school diploma and college degree) are overrepresented in the sample compared to national census data.

Reliability. The manual reports test-retest reliability, internal consistency, and interrater reliability. Test-retest reliability coefficients are above .75 for the performance assessment on a sample of 28 children. Alpha coefficients generally exceeded .85 for a sample of 414 children on the performance tests and were over .95 for a sample of over 300 children on two of the observations and a sample of 183 children on the classroom observation. Interrater reliability was studied using a sample of 29 children on the performance assessments and raters agreed on categories of assessment as average or having a motor impairment over 90% of the time.

Validity. The test author presents matrix data showing that the construction of the M-FUN is based on a review of literature, theory, and information from practitioners regarding the content assessed and the way in which it is assessed. Intercorrelation coefficients among the M-FUN norm-referenced scales ranged from .47 to .58 for the performance measures and from .41 to .58 for the observation checklists. Criterion referenced validity is presented showing correlation with the Miller Assessment for Preschoolers (MAP) and correlation with a target group of children with identified motor delays and with typically developing children. Correlation coefficients for relationship of M-FUN to MAP scores are .47 for M-FUN Gross Motor to MAP, and .83 and .62 for Fine Motor and Visual Motor, respectively. In a study of 60 or more typically developing children and children with motor delays, there were significant differences in mean scores on the M-FUN scales between the groups.

COMMENTARY. The M-FUN draws appropriately on the experience of the test author in designing assessment tools for motor functioning among young children. The M-FUN is an instrument that can be administered in a reasonable amount of time yielding norm-referenced and criterion-referenced scores. The observation checklists add a functional component that helps diagnosticians to provide more complete and potentially useful information to educators, therapists, and parents regarding the developing motor abilities of children.

The information presented about the development of the test thoroughly covers the constructs upon which the M-FUN is based and the process for gathering expert data on content and format. A larger standardization sample that more closely approximates national data would add to the confidence users have about the test results; however, reliability and validity data appear adequate for the purposes intended.

SUMMARY. The M-FUN is a potentially useful norm-referenced tool for educators and therapists to identify children who have developmental motor delays that may cause them to experience delays in participating in home and classroom environments. In addition, the diagnostic utility offers help in identifying the nature of motor delays and the areas likely to be affected.

REVIEWER'S REFERENCES

Miller, L. J. (1982). *Miller Assessment for Preschoolers manual.* San Antonio: The Psychological Corporation.

Miller, L. J. (1993). First STEp: Screening Test for Evaluating Preschoolers. San Antonio: The Psychological Corporation.

[75]

Millon College Counseling Inventory.

Purpose: Designed to "help counselors identify, predict, and understand a broad range of psychological issues that are common among college students seen primarily in college counseling settings."

Population: College students ages 16–40.

Publication Date: 2006.

Acronym: MCCI.

Scores, 36: Personality Style Scales (Introverted, Inhibited, Dejected, Needy, Sociable, Confident, Unruly, Conscientious, Oppositional, Denigrated), Severe Personality Tendencies Scale (Borderline), Expressed Concerns Scales (Mental Health Upset, Identity Quandaries, Family Disquiet, Peer Alienation, Romantic Distress, Academic Concerns, Career Confusion, Abusive Experiences, Living Arrangement Problems, Financial Burdens, Spiritual Doubts), Clinical Signs Scales (Suicidal Tendencies, Depressive Outlook, Anxiety/Tension, Post-Traumatic Stress, Eating Disorders, Anger Dyscontrol, Attention [Cognitive] Deficits, Obsessions/Compulsions, Alcohol Abuse, Drug Abuse), Response Tendency Scales (Validity, Disclosure, Desirability, Debasement); plus 7 Noteworthy Responses (Risky Behaviors, Homesickness, Expectation Pressures, Escapist Distractions, Minority Prejudice, Somatic Concerns, Reality Distortions).

Administration: Group or individual.

Price Data, 2009: $206 per hand-scoring starter kit, including 50 answer sheets with test items, answer keys, and manual (2006, 115 pages); $46.50 per 50 answer sheets for hand-scoring; $53.50 per audio CD; $33.50 per manual; $66.50 per computer (Q-Local) starter kit, including manual, 3 answer sheets with test items, and 3 Q Local administrations (does not include Q Local software); $27.50 per 25 Q Local answer sheets; $18 per administration for Q Local interpretive report; $76.05 per mail-in starter kit with interpretive report including 3 answer sheets, manual, and all materials necessary to conduct 3 assessments and receive interpretive reports using the mail-in scoring service; $21 per mail-in interpretive report (price includes answer sheet and scoring).

Time: (20-25) minutes.

Comments: Self-report personality inventory; paper-and-pencil and online administration available; computer (Q-Local), mail-in scoring, and hand-scoring option.

Authors: Theodore Millon, Stephen N. Strack, Carrie Millon, and Seth Grossman.

Publisher: Pearson.

Review of the Millon College Counseling Inventory by MARK A. ALBANESE, Professor of Population Health Sciences, University of Wisconsin School of Medicine and Public Health, Madison, WI, and GEORGIA HINMAN, CEO, Hinman Consulting, Madison, WI:

DESCRIPTION. The Millon College Counseling Inventory (MCCI) is designed as an aid to counselors to "identify, predict, and understand a broad range of psychological issues that are common among college students (ages 16–40)" (manual, p. 3). It is part of a series of instruments derived from Millon's biosocial-learning theory of personality (Millon, 1983) and reflects the view that clinically significant psychological problems are often grounded in expressions of stable personality traits. The MCCI is a 150-item instrument administered in 20–25 minutes via paper or computer producing scores for 11 Personality Styles and Severe Personality Tendencies, 11 Expressed Concerns, 10 Clinical Signs, and 4 Response Tendencies. Scores are expressed as prevalence scores and there are four scales designed to determine whether or not responses are valid.

DEVELOPMENT. Millon's biosocial-learning theory of personality conceptualizes behavior as a product of three polarities: active-passive, pleasure-pain, and self-other. "The *active-passive* polarity refers to whether [or not] an individual takes the initiative in shaping his or her environment to meet his or her needs.... The *pleasure-pain* polarity refers to how an individual is motivated toward events that are attractive and positively reinforcing and away from events that are aversive or painful. The *self-other* polarity refers to whether an individual finds primary gratification in the self or is motivated toward pleasure from external sources" (manual, p. 5). Normal and abnormal personalities are thought to lie along a continuum with no sharp line dividing the two. Normal personality is a balance of the three polarities, whereas abnormal is rigid and maladaptive. The MCCI assesses primarily normal traits common in a college student population.

Development of the MCCI began with 41 initial constructs identified for potential inclusion as scales. Some 177 items were created with from 3 to 5 items for each construct plus 8 items assessing response validity. Each item had five options (0 = *statement never applies or is never true*, to 4 = *always applies or is always true*).

Normative data came from 33 of approximately 455 college and university counseling centers (7.3%) responding to a solicitation letter. Responses to the Beck Depression Inventory-II (BDI-II), The State-Trait Anxiety Inventory (STAI), and the Alcohol Use Inventory (AUI), and a Counselor's form were also obtained for validation purposes. The counselors' task was critical because they: (a) selected and recruited the students for participation whose "psychological traits and problems they knew reasonably well" (manual, p. 23); (b) chose the student's three most prominent personality styles, expressed concerns, and clinical signs (three each for a total of nine student qualities); (c) administered the MCCI and one of the three supplemental forms; and (d) returned the materials to the researchers. Complete data were received for 564 students. Development (*N* = 364 cases) and cross-validation samples (*N* = 200 cases) were randomly created. The development sample was used to create the final scales, whereas the reliability and validity of the final scales were estimated from the cross validation sample.

TECHNICAL.

Scoring. Computer administration of the MCCI provides automatic scoring and graphical reporting of results. Scoring the MCCI by hand takes approximately 20 minutes. The MCCI reports percentiles and prevalence scores for each of 32 scales. The raw score to prevalence score and percentile score conversion charts are provided in the user's manual. Scores above 65 on any scale are considered dominant. Scores on four response scales (Validity, Disclosure, Desirability, and Debasement) have individual criteria to determine response validity. Additionally, if all of the prevalence scores for the Personality Styles scales are below 60 and all of the other scales are below 65, it is considered a flat profile and cannot be interpreted. Finally, if 8 or more items have no response or multiple responses, the results are considered invalid.

Standardization. Standardization is based upon 564 students from 33 college and university counseling centers. Each center averaged 17 students and ranged from 2 to 92. The sample was predominantly female (77.9%), average age = 21.6 (*sd* = 3.6), mostly white (86.3%), and mostly full-time students (93.8%). College year was distributed fairly uniformly ranging from 85 (15.2%) freshman to 141 (25.1%) seniors with an added 86 (15.3%) in graduate or professional school. The number of counseling sessions students had experienced averaged 10.7 (*sd* = 12.5).

Reliability. Data from the 200 cross validation subjects were used to compute coefficient alpha reliability estimates for all 32 scales. The scales contained from 3–9 items and produced alpha coefficients that ranged from .58 to .87 (median = .79).

Validity. Validity data reported were exclusively Convergent/Discriminant. Counselor rating correlations with MCCI scores (convergent validity) were based upon the cross validation sample and ranged from .03 to .40 (median = .23). All but 4 of 32 correlations were statistically significant. Correlations with the BDI-II, STAI, and AUI addressed both convergent and discriminant validity. Because administration of the supplemental tests was optional, relatively few were returned: BDI-II: *n* = 89; STAI: *n* = 52; AUI: *n* = 44. Of the BDI-II correlations with the 32 MCCI scales, all but 5 were statistically significant and 9 were ≥ .60 (ranged from -.37 to .72, median = .42). Statistically significant negative correlations were found for the more positive MCCI scales: Sociable (-.37) and Confident (-.24); supporting the MCCI discriminant validity.

For the STAI, separate correlations were computed for the State and Trait scales. Trait correlations were substantially larger than the State correlations (in absolute value) for 25 of 32 statistically significant correlations. Trait score correlations with the MCCI scores ranged from

-.48 to .74 (median = .48). The corresponding State score correlations ranged from -.41 to .59 (median = .33). The correlations of MCCI scales with the AUI were less strong, with only 10 of 32 being statistically significant and with values ranging from -.30 to .65 (median = .19). Again, the negative correlations were found for the more positive MCCI scales, supporting the discriminant validity claim.

Intercorrelations among the MCCI scales are reported in an appendix and generally conform to expectations. Analyses of gender differences showed males were higher than females by a statistically significant margin on Introverted, Confidence, Oppositional, Peer Alienation, Career Confusion, Attention (Cognitive) Deficits, Unruly, and Alcohol Abuse scales but lower on Conscientious, Anxiety/Tension, and Eating Disorders scales.

The gender differences noted are consistent with results that have been reported in the literature, providing support for the validity of the instrument. The correlations with the other self-report instruments were also consistent with what would be expected from both a rational analysis of such constructs and results reported in the literature. The correlations with counselor ratings provide the strongest validity evidence.

COMMENTARY. The MCCI has a number of strengths, chief of which is its derivation from a theory of personality that has withstood the test of time for over 40 years. Having counselors assess students using the Millon definitions was an important validation step. Further, having the counselors rate subjects before having the students complete the MCCI avoided data contamination.

The random assignment of individuals to development and cross validation samples is a major strength as the reliabilities and validity estimates will be more consistent with those obtained by users. The use of prevalence scores for reporting results is a unique aspect of this instrument. Such scores appear to anchor the percentiles to the frequency of occurrence of the different types of characteristics in the norming sample. Finally, the reliability and validity data support the constructs relatively well.

On the negative side, the instrument's greatest strength may be a weakness. If one does not believe that Millon's biosocial-learning theory of personality is sufficiently well-developed or supported by empirical research, then the rest is pretty much moot. Although the reliability and validity evidence supports the structure of the MCCI, it is not definitive. It is also limited by being based upon concurrent measures as opposed to providing an assessment of stability over time, nor does it provide any evidence supporting its use in predicting psychological issues common in college students. A factor analysis would provide construct validity evidence; however, the norming sample is relatively small for this purpose.

Even though the norming sample is national in how it was sampled, the 33 centers that participated are only 7% of the total solicited. Without more information about how the 33 compare to the national population of colleges and universities in terms of public-private breakdown, size of student body, regional representation, and so on, nothing can be said about its representativeness. This has implications for both how the MCCI is structured as well as how to interpret the results. Because nine scales were deleted due to low correlations with counselor ratings and low prevalence, anomalies in the sample could have a bearing on the validity of the instrument for some populations. For example, one of the scales that was deleted was Minority Prejudice. Because the norming population consisted of only 13.7% minorities, it cannot be determined whether the deletion is a function of the composition of the norming sample or that minority prejudice is a relatively unimportant issue for students being counseled in the college population. The other issue pertaining to the representativeness of the norming sample is that the prevalence scores are based upon how prevalent the different qualities are in the norming sample. If the norming sample is not representative of the particular student body with which one is working, the results from the MCCI could be misleading.

The use of prevalence scores is innovative and maintains the link between the percentiles and actual prevalence in the sample, but it is not clear how the prevalence scores were actually computed. A more detailed explanation and having more than one example would help. Prevalence scores are a sufficiently novel concept that their derivation should be described more clearly.

The lack of information about the counselors who provided data is a concern. Counselors were the most critical link in the data collection chain. They recruited participants, rated participants, administered the MCCI, and returned the completed materials. It would be helpful to give a profile of who they are such as the percentage of the counselors at each center who provided data and their overall gender and racial/ethnic makeup.

An issue that is never really addressed is the comparability of results from paper versus computer administration. Some personality types may feel better working with a machine, others may find it not to their liking. Given the nature of the instrument, computer versus paper administration might be an issue that could affect the results.

There are two practical issues that need to be considered. First, scoring the MCCI by hand is cumbersome. Each subscale score must be individually calculated, requiring the use of a template for each subscale where addition, subtraction, and reversal of score scales must all be done mentally. There are 32 subscale templates in addition to two templates for Validity, Desirability, and Debasement. The manual recommends that each inventory be scored twice. Scoring one respondent's answers took one of the reviewers (GH) approximately 20 minutes; rescoring would double this number. Computer administration and scoring is strongly recommended.

The second concern is the number of factors that render a student's responses invalid and the instrument unscorable. Counselee's responses are invalid if there are more than eight questions unanswered, if the validity score is a 2 or higher, or if the student produces a flat profile. Each of these validation criteria include recommendations for an intervention by the counselor to either clarify results or to re-administer the MCCI. Although there may be valuable information in the reasons for a counselee making invalid responses, the counselor needs to be prepared to investigate, taking time and energy.

Given the concerns with scorability, validity, and time, the MCCI is best used with stable counselees in the initial phases of problem identification. Further, given the small number of minority participants in the data used for instrument development and in the norming sample, care needs to be exercised in using the MCCI with minority counselees.

SUMMARY. The Millon College Counseling Inventory (MCCI) is designed to aid counselors to identify, predict, and understand a broad range of psychological issues that are common among college students (ages 16–40) seen primarily in college counseling settings. It reflects the view that, among college students, clinically significant psychological problems are often grounded in expressions of stable personality traits. The MCCI is a 150-item instrument administered in 20–25 minutes via paper or computer versions that produces scores for 11 Personality Styles and Severe Personality Tendencies, 11 Expressed Concerns, 10 Clinical Signs, and 4 Response Tendencies. Scores are expressed as prevalence scores. In addition, there are four response validity scales. The norming sample came from 33 counseling centers responding to a solicitation sent to a national sample. Derivation of the MCCI from a larger set of items was based upon a subset of the norming sample. Internal consistency reliability estimates range from .58 to .87 for the 32 scales based upon a 200 subject cross validation sample. Concurrent and discriminant correlations with counselor ratings and three supplemental instruments produced values as high as .40 for the counselor ratings and .74 for the supplemental instruments. The patterns of correlations with other instruments and also intercorrelations among the different MCCI scales were generally consistent with what would be logically expected.

Given the heavy reliance on Millon's biosocial-learning theory of personality, users need to familiarize themselves sufficiently with its concepts and level of empirical support in determining their choice. Although the reliability and validity evidence supports the structure of the MCCI, it is not definitive and is limited by being based upon concurrent measures.

REVIEWERS' REFERENCE

Millon, T. (1983). *Modern psychopathology.* Prospect Heights, IL: Waveland Press.

Review of the Millon College Counseling Inventory by ANDREW A. COX, Professor of Counseling and Psychology, Troy University, Phenix City, AL:

DESCRIPTION. The Millon College Counseling Inventory (MCCI) is a multidimensional self-report inventory for use with college-age populations ranging in age from 16 to 40. The inventory is only appropriate for use with individuals enrolled in a college or university environment and participating in college/university counseling center services. It can usually be completed in 20 to 25 minutes. The inventory extends the clinical application of the Millon clinical inventories and is designed to identify examinee personality styles and clinical issues that are typically found among a college population. The test authors contend that measuring personality dimensions is important as clinically significant psychological problems among college students "are often grounded in expressions of stable personality traits" (manual, p. 3). A strength for the inventory is that it is grounded on a comprehensive theory of personality (Millon & Grossman, 2006). This common theoretical foundation promotes continuity among the various Millon inventories spanning adolescence to adulthood.

The Millon College Counseling Inventory consists of 150 items. A response format using a five-choice Likert scale is used ranging from 0 (*never applies or is never true)* to 4 (*always applies or is always true).* The inventory can be scored by computer or through the use of hand scoring templates. Hand scoring is straightforward but tedious; it appears that scoring errors could be made due to the number of calculations required on the part of the scorer. The test authors caution against the use of the MCCI as the sole source of treatment information and planning, advocating the use of information from multiple sources.

Thirty-two profile scales are grouped into three sets: 10 Personality Styles scales and a Severe Personality Tendency scale, 11 Expressed Concerns, and 10 Clinical Signs scales. Response tendencies scales are also provided to assess test taker response validity. Prevalence scores are reported for each scale to depict the prevalence of characteristics that are measured through the inventory.

DEVELOPMENT. In initial scale development, the test authors developed items identifying 41 target constructs that included Personality Styles, Severe Personality Tendencies, Expressed Concerns, and Clinical Signs that were later used in developing the final inventory form. A research form entitled MCCI Form R was developed with 177 items. A solicitation letter was mailed to 455 college and university counseling centers requesting their participation. Centers that indicated willingness to participate in the process were sent additional materials including the MCCI Research Form, supplemental self-report test, and Counselor's Form. Participating centers were asked to administer the MCCI Form R to selected counselees with "psychological traits and problems they [the counselors] knew reasonably well" (manual, p. 23). The Counselor's Form inventoried counselor's ratings for the MCCI Research Form test taker regarding the respondent's prominent personality styles, expressed concerns, clinical signs, and demographic information to include number of treatment sessions, age, gender, and ethnic identification information. Other self-report inventories for completion by research participants included the Beck Depression Inventory-II, State-Trait Anxiety Inventory, and the Alcohol Use Inventory. The final 150-item MCCI inventory was developed from test data submitted through this protocol solicitation.

TECHNICAL. A standardization sample of 564 cases from 33 college counseling centers was obtained through the above-noted solicitation process. The standardization sample was in the age range 17–18 to 36–45 with the majority being age 19 to 23 with a mean age of 21.6. Females comprised 77.9 of the sample with 22.1% being male. The sample's ethnicity included 86.3% Caucasian, 7.1% Hispanic/Latino, 4.8% African American with the remaining percentage composed of other ethnic groups.

"Random assignment was used to divide the total research sample of 564 cases into a development sample of 364 cases and a cross validation sample of 200 cases" (manual, p. 24). The development sample was used to produce final items and scales for the inventory, and the cross validation sample was used to compile validation statistics. The development and cross validation subsamples were similar in noted characteristics to the overall standardization sample. *T* tests and Chi-square tests were used to compare age, gender, number of counseling sessions, enrollment status, average grade (A, B, C, D, or lower) campus residence, fraternity/sorority membership, and employment status for the development and cross validation samples. Findings from these analyses were nonsignificant. Counselor ratings on the Counselor Form were compared for Personality variables, Expressed Concerns, and Clinical Signs for each participant in the standardization sample using assigned ratings ranging from 1 to 3. This analysis was used to determine the similarity of the research sample's psychological characteristics as viewed by their counselors and their inventoried profiles. The two samples were comparable relative to Personality Styles, Expressed Concerns, and Clinical Signs. As described within the inventory's manual, similarity in counselor ratings and inventoried results are noted.

The test manual does not specifically describe the location of participating counseling centers and institutions, other than to list the institution and city and sate of each of the contributing college counselors in the Acknowledgments. However, it appears from the acknowledgments section that the preponderance of participating institutions were from the Northeastern and Southeastern geographical regions of the United States, with limited numbers from the Western, Southwest, or Midwestern regions.

Reliability estimates are provided for the 200 participants comprising the cross validation sample. Coefficient alpha internal consistency coefficients ranged from .58 on the Career Confusion scale to .87 on the Dejected scale. Twenty-six of the 32 scales had internal consistency coefficients of .70 or above with a mean value of .77. Other reliability estimates are not reported. The manual reports that test-retest reliability data are still needed.

Validation for the MCCI is of two types. Convergent validation data are reported between ratings on the before-mentioned Counselor Form completed by counselors submitting an examinee's test protocol and prevalence scores for the 200 cross validation sample cases. The average correlations across the three sets of scales are reported to be comparable: .23 for Personality scales, .21 for Expressed Concerns scales, and .25 for Clinical Signs scales. The manual reports that this "pattern provides support for the validity of the MCCI scales against an independent evaluation of the counselee's traits, problems, and symptoms" (p. 37). Similar convergent validation evidence comparing gender differences is described via *T* test comparisons with significant male and female differences indicated for 11 of 32 scales. These data are reported to be consistent with gender differences for psychological variables.

Concurrent type validation is the second type of validation reported for the MCCI. As completion of the supplemental tests was optional, about a third of the total research sample completed the supplemental tests with 89 completing the Beck Depression Inventory-II, 52 completing the State Trait Anxiety Inventory, and 44 the Alcohol Use Inventory. Though the MCCI is a broad-based assessment (Corcoran, 2004) measuring multiple traits, individual subscales have moderate to high correlation with the above narrow-band assessments (Corcoran, 2004) administered as supplemental measures. This information is described within the manual as support for the construct validity of the MCCI.

The manual devotes a chapter to Millon's model of personality development and the implications of this theoretical perspective to the MCCI scales. Statistical analyses relevant to the inventory's relationship to this model to support construct validation are not provided. There is a need for further research relative to construct validation of the MCCI as is found for other Millon inventories such as that described in Strack and Millon (2007).

COMMENTARY. The MCCI is a useful addition to the Millon family of clinical assessment inventories. It would be useful in assessing clinical issues and dynamics associated with mental health practice within a college/university counseling center. Scoring can be effectuated through computer or hand scoring though the potential for computational errors exists when hand scoring is used. A relatively novel approach was used in relating inventory results to counselor ratings in inventory development and validation. However, a more broadly representative sample of counseling centers from a wider range of geographical regions should be a future research direction for this measure. The standardization sample is predominantly Caucasian and female. Future validation and standardization efforts should focus upon widening the diversity of the standardization sample. Finally, efforts should be directed towards strengthening the construct validation of the inventory as well as obtaining additional reliability data.

SUMMARY. The MCCI was designed to be an inventory to assess clinical issues and clinical dynamics associated with a college-age population participating in treatment through a college counseling center. The inventory appears to assess those clinical issues typically encountered within this practice setting. Material provided within the manual proves useful to practitioners in interpreting inventory results. Future revisions of Strack (2002) should include interpretative information for the MCCI that will augment scale interpretation. Though additional work is needed in scale validation and widening the diversity of the standardization sample, the MCCI should prove to be a useful assessment for this specialized practice setting.

REVIEWER'S REFERENCES

Corcoran, K. (2004). Locating measurement tools and instruments for individuals and couples. In A. R. Roberts & K. R. Yeager (Eds.), *Evidence-based practice manual: Research and outcome measures in health and human services* (pp. 463-470). New York: Oxford University Press.

Millon, T., & Grossman, S. D. (2006). Millon's evolutionary model for unifying the study of normal and abnormal personality. In S. Strack (Ed.), *Differentiating normal and abnormal personality* (2nd ed., pp. 3-49). New York: Springer.

Strack, S. (Ed.). (2002). *Essentials of Millon inventories assessment* (2nd ed.). Hoboken, NJ: Wiley.

Strack, S., & Millon, T. (2007). Contributions to the dimensional assessment of personality disorders using Millon's model and the Millon Clinical Multiaxial Inventory (MCMI-III). *Journal of Personality Assessment*, 89, 56-69.

[76]

Mind Body Wellness Geriatric Rehabilitation and Restorative Assessment System.

Purpose: Designed to "assess pathology and general quality of life for residents who need assisted living or nursing home care based on their levels of behavioral, emotional, and illness symptoms."
Population: Ages 55 and up.
Publication Date: 2008.
Acronym: GRRAS.
Administration: Individual.
Scores: 3 subtests: Psychological Resistance to Activities of Daily Living Index, Geriatric Multidimensional Pain and Illness Inventory, Geriatric Level of Dysfunction Scale.
Price Data, 2008: $205 per introductory kit including professional manual (117 pages), 25 PRADLI rating forms, 25 GMPI rating forms, 25 GLDS rating Forms, and 25 GRRAS profile forms in a soft-sided attaché case; $70 per professional manual; $25 per 25 profile forms.
Authors: P. Andrew Clifford, Kristi D. Roper, and Daisha J. Cipher.
Publisher: Psychological Assessment Resources, Inc.

a) PSYCHOLOGICAL RESISTANCE TO ACTIVITIES OF DAILY LIVING INDEX.
Acronym: PRADLI.
Price Data: $40 per 25 PRADLI rating forms; $125 per PRADLI kit including professional manual, 25 PRADLI rating forms, and 25 profile forms.
Time: (15) minutes.

b) GERIATRIC MULTIDIMENSIONAL PAIN AND ILLNESS INVENTORY.
Acronym: GMPI.
Price Data: $40 per 25 GMPI rating forms; $125 per GMPI kit including professional manual, 25 GMPI rating forms, and 25 profile forms; $299 per unlimited-use CD-Rom scoring system.
Comments: The Mind Body Wellness Geriatric Rehabilitation and Restorative Assessment System Software Portfolio (GRRAS-SP) is available to score and generate reports for all three forms of the GRRAS; the GRRAS-SP requires Windows 2000/XPLVista, NTFS file system, CD-Rom drive for installation, and internet connection or telephone for software activation.
Time: (15) minutes.

c) GERIATRIC LEVEL OF DYSFUNCTION SCALE.
Acronym: GLDS.
Price Data: $45 per 25 GLDS rating forms; $130 per GLDS kit including professional manual, 25 GLDS rating forms, and 25 profile forms.
Time: (15) minutes.

Review of the Mind Body Wellness Geriatric Rehabilitation and Restorative Assessment System by JOHN J. BRINKMAN, Assistant Professor of Psychology and Counseling, University of Saint Francis, and AMBER CARTER, Graduate Assistant, University of Saint Francis, Fort Wayne, IN:

DESCRIPTION. The Mind Body Wellness Geriatric Rehabilitation and Restorative Assessment System (GRRAS) is a comprehensive assessment system of individually administered tests that provide normative data on a broad range of behaviors for adults aged 55 years and older. The system facilitates the assessment of patients in rehabilitation, restorative care settings (e.g., geripsychiatric hospitals), and long-term care facilities. The assessment system consists of three separate tests that evaluate level of independence and cooperation, pain and discomfort, and dysfunctional or disruptive behaviors.

The GRRAS is written in English and takes approximately 15 minutes to complete. Administration and interpretation of the assessment system should be conducted by professionals working in the field of geriatrics including, but not limited to, psychologists, psychiatrists, psychiatric nurse practitioners, and clinical social workers. Additionally, the test authors state that these professionals should possess knowledge of geriatric psychology and behavioral disturbances associated with medical conditions as well as training in psychological assessment and interpretation.

The GRRAS consists of three separate tests: the Psychosocial Resistance to Activities of Daily Living Index (PRADLI); the Geriatric Multidimensional Pain and Illness Inventory (GMPI); and the Geriatric Level of Dysfunction Scale (GLDS). The assessment system was designed to provide a comprehensive evaluation of emotional and behavioral difficulties utilizing a common normative sample; however, each test can be administered individually. Below is a short description of each test organized by their contribution to the overall assessment system.

The Psychosocial Resistance to Activities of Daily Living Index (PRADLI) is the first test in the system. The PRADLI consists of an 8-item form that looks at behaviors associated with functional independence and cooperation as they relate to the Activities of Daily Living (ADL). Each of the ADLs is assessed on a 7-point Likert-type scale (i.e., 1 = *Max assist* to 7 = *Independent*). Additionally, behavioral anchors provide a descriptive category for each point on the scale. For example, a numerical rating of "7" on Item 2 under Eating Habits, has a behavioral anchor of: "Independent. Cooks and is motivated. Resident/patient prepares and eats food independently; requires no assistance or cueing."

The second test in the assessment system is the Geriatric Multidimensional Pain and Illness Inventory (GMPI). The GMPI consists of a 14-item form that assesses the patient's rating of pain, as well as illness behaviors associated with pain or discomfort. Each item is assessed on a 10-point Likert-type scale (e.g., 1 = *mild* to 10 = *excruciating*). This test also provides behavioral anchors with descriptive categories for each point on the scale. The GMPI is composed of three scales: Pain and Suffering, Life Interference, and Emotional Distress. Items from each of the three scales provide for an overall GMPI Total score.

The third test in the assessment system is the Geriatric Level of Dysfunction Scale (GLDS). The GLDS consists of a 20-item form that assesses dysfunctional or disruptive behaviors. Each item is assessed for both frequency and duration on an 8-point Likert-type scale (i.e., 0 = *No frequency, No duration* to 7 = *Continuous, > 6 hr/day*). This test also provides behavioral anchors with descriptive categories for each point on the scale. The GLDS is composed of three scales: Aggressive Agitation, Irrational Agitation, and Dysfunctional Illness Behaviors. Items from each of the three scales provide for an overall GLDS Total score.

Scoring for the three tests requires a combination of clinical observation and collateral information from a record review, other professionals working with the patient, and family members. Scoring for all three tests is done by hand to obtain overall raw scores and raw scores for each domain being measured. Scores can then be interpreted within the context of several comparison groups. The comparison groups include the following: general unaffected group, general affected group, dementia group, and pain group. Based on the comparison group chosen, raw scores can be converted to percentile ranks, a clinical range of raw scores, and a qualitative descriptor. The GRRAS profile form is also provided for a visual comparison among the three test scores. Additionally, the GRRAS Software Portfolio (GRRAS-SP) is available to facilitate scoring.

DEVELOPMENT. The GRRAS was designed to provide for the quantification of behavioral problems that arise in the long-term care setting. Additionally, having quantifiable data allowed for measurable outcomes that can be tied to referral questions. The GLDS was designed to assess behavioral problems in long-term care settings. Item development for the GLDS utilized behavioral problem checklists that the test authors were already using. The PRADLI was designed to assess client cooperation and/or ADLs. Item development for the PRADLI proceeded from referral requests from long-term care staff who needed assistance with client cooperation. Noting that most of the uncooperative behaviors were due to a chronic medical condition that included pain and discomfort, the GMPI was developed. Item development for the GMPI was loosely based on the West Haven-Yale Multidimensional Pain Inventory. After the initial items were chosen, the test authors sought out input from professionals working in the field of geriatrics to assess the clinical utility, usability, and validity. Once items and scales were established, the GRRAS underwent a 2-year pilot study. During that time, test items were refined allowing for more precise terminology including making minor changes in the behavioral anchors in an attempt to increase interrater reliability. Additionally, attempts were made to provide a sample that was more representative of the U.S. population in terms of age, race, and gender while at the same time utilizing specific geriatric groups (e.g., nursing home residents and patients with Alzheimer's disease).

TECHNICAL. The GRRAS was normed using a standardized sample of 512 adult participants with a mean age of 81.2 years. The standardized sample consisted of two groups, referred to as Sample 1 and Sample 2. Sample 1 consisted of 392 participants and represented data collection for all three of the GRRAS measures. Sample 2 consisted of 120 participants and represented data collected after some adjustments were made to the GRRAS as well as collection of additional validity data. This combined sample consisted of both male and female participants from diverse racial and ethnic backgrounds.

Reliability was estimated using internal consistency, test-retest reliability, and interrater reliability. Internal consistency was estimated using the alpha coefficients. The estimates obtained ranged from .71 (GMPI Pain and Suffering) to .93 (i.e., PRADLI Total score). Test-retest reliability was assessed utilizing the initial data collection of Sample 1. Coefficients for the PRADLI ranged from .83 to .98. The GMPI Total and Clusters scores yielded coefficients that ranged from .62 to .96. The test-retest estimates used for the GLDS were obtained on the strongest behavioral complaints for each sample as the cluster scores had not been established. As such, estimates ranged from .86 to .96 for intensity, frequency, and duration. Interrater reliability was assessed using eight examiners during a 3-month to 3-year period of care. Intraclass correlation coefficients ranged from .87 (i.e., Dysfunctional Illness Behavior Cluster) to .96 (i.e., PRADLI Total).

Validity was estimated including concurrent validity, content validity, and construct validity. Test item development for all of the measures proceeded with concurrent validity as a primary consideration. The test authors describe how scoring rubrics were created for each assessment tool and how these enhanced the concurrent validity. Additionally, strong content validity was suggested by the observation that test items provided similar content to already existing measures. For example, test items on the PRADLI provided both convergent and divergent validity with the Independent Index of Activities of Daily Living.

Construct validity was measured by convergent and discriminate validity, comparisons to global and focused measures, factor analysis, and comparisons to clinical groups. Evidence of convergent and discriminant validity was provided for the GRRAS Total and Cluster scores. The coefficients ranged from -.72 (i.e., PRADLI total and Life Interference Cluster) to .01 (i.e., GMPI Pain and Suffering and GLDS Irrational Agitation). Although some high correlations were observed, there also were lower scores that were not statistically significant (e.g., r = -.11 for GLDS Dysfunctional Illness Behaviors and GLDS Aggressive Agitation). The test authors reported that they expected lower scores due to the lower activity levels for the illness behaviors compared to aggressive behaviors.

Construct validity studies also compared the GRRAS to global measures including the Mini-Mental State Examination (MMSE), Reisberg's Global Deterioration Scale (RGDS), the Independent Living Scales (ILS), the Dementia Rating Scale-2 (DRS-2), and the Geriatric Depression Scale (GDS). Coefficients for the GRRAS and the MMSE ranged from -.63 (i.e., GLDS Aggressive Agitation Cluster) to .36 (i.e., PRADLI Total). The RGDS and GRRAS correlations ranged from -.54 (PRADLI Total) to .68 (GLDS Total). Correlations between the ILS and GRRAS ranged from -.67 (GMPI Total and ILS Social Adjustment) to .53 (PRADLI Total and ILS Total Summary). Of note, all comparisons for the MMSE, the RGDS, and the ILS with the GRRAS provided statistically significant results. Correlations between DRS-2 and the GRRAS range from -.61 (GMPI Emotional Distress, GLDS Total, and DRS-2 Total) to .53 (PRADLI Total and DRS-2 Initiation/Perseveration). All but two of the comparisons (i.e., GLDS Dysfunctional Illness with DRS-2 Attention and Conceptualization) between the GRRAS and the DRS-2 provided statistically significant results. GDS and GRRAS correlations ranged from -.39 (GMPI Emotional Distress Cluster and GDS Satisfied with Life) to .46 (GMPI Emotional Distress and GDS Total Score). Many of the correlation coefficients between the GRRAS and the GDS were too low to reach statistical significance. The test authors explain that lower correlations may be due to the method of assessment. The GRRAS assessment is based on observation whereas the GDS is based on self-report in which patients may underreport symptoms of depression.

Construct validity studies also compared the GRRAS to focused measures including the Katz ADL, the Non-Communicative Patient's Pain Assessment Instrument (NOPPAIN), the Cohen-Mansfield Agitation Inventory (CMAI), and the Neuropsychiatric Inventory-Nursing Home Version (NPI-NH). Correlations between the PRADLI and the Katz ADL ranged from .30 (e.g., PRADLI Up-time and Katz ADL Bathing and Toileting) to .98 (PRADLI Dressing and Toileting and Katz ADL Toileting) with all values showing statistical significance. Correlations between the GMPI and the NOPPAIN ranged from -.15 (GMPI Moving About and NOPPAIN Rubbing) to .92 (GMPI Pain Now and NOPPAIN Pain Response Maximum). Although not all of the coefficients demonstrated statistical significance, more robust values were obtained with a majority of the values demonstrating statistical significance. Correlations for the CMAI and GLDS ranged from -.01 (e.g., GLDS Activity Level Dysfunctional Illnes/ Pain and CMAI Factor 1 and GLDS Depressed/ Whithdrawn and CMAI Factor 2) to .85 (GLDS Aggressive Agitation and CMAI Total). Correlations for the GLDS and NPI-NH ranged from -.01 (e.g., GLDS Hoarding/Stealing and NPI-NI Elation and Aberrant Motor Behavior) to .87

(e.g., GLDS Delusional/Psychotic and NPI-NH Delusions). The test authors also report that factor analysis, which was used in test development to separate test items into appropriate clusters, should be included in a discussion of validity as the factor structure was based on existing theory. Finally, clinical group comparisons were made between demographic information and the GRRAS validity groups (i.e., nursing home, assisted living, elopement risk, and independent). Chi square and ANOVA analyses found no differences between the groups and gender, race, age, or marital status. However, significant differences were found between the groups and education. The assessment manual also discussed the frequency of medical and psychiatric diagnoses for each group measured. Pain and illness groups were measured using the GRRAS. The PRADLI, GLDS, and GMPI totals demonstrated higher behavioral disturbances in the pain group compared to the illness group.

COMMENTARY. The GRRAS is a well-designed and comprehensive measure of geriatric pathology and quality of life. The GRRAS is composed of three assessment tools that are easy to administer and interpret. The test kit is attractive and includes the test manual, 25 GLDS clinician rating forms, 25 PRADLI clinician rating forms, 25 GMPI clinician rating forms, and 25 profile forms in a soft carrying case. Scoring is straightforward and takes about 15 minutes per assessment to complete. The test manual offers many benefits including clear examples of scoring procedures, interpretive results, and treatment implications as well as case studies.

There are several advantages to using the GRRAS for the assessment of geriatric populations. First, the ability to administer all of the tests together or to utilize each test individually is of practical importance. Although it would be ideal to administer all measures to each patient for a comprehensive assessment, many times that is not possible. Therefore, the ability to use one measure independent of the comprehensive assessment system may facilitate the assessment of a patient. Additionally, should a clinician need only one piece of information (e.g., pain assessment), the clinician may choose the measure to administer depending on the individual needs of the patient. Another advantage of the assessment system is that all measures utilize common normative samples. The common normative samples allow for comparisons between data from each test. Further, the test authors offer several normative groups for comparison providing an accurate interpretation of test data. Finally, a visual representation of the results for a comparison of all measures is available by filling out the profile form.

Although the GRRAS is a well-designed test of geriatric pathology and quality of life, there is one area that could be developed. Despite the adequate reliability estimates, the validity for the GRRAS has not been well-established. For example, validity studies reported low correlations between scales on the GRRAS and the NOPPAIN and NPI-NH. Many of these coefficients did not reach significance. Regardless, the test authors report that the data collection is ongoing and they will continue to provide data for establishing the test's psychometric properties.

SUMMARY. The GRRAS was designed to be an individually administered measure of pathology and general quality of life for geriatric patients in medical or long-term care facilities. The assessment system adequately measures psychosocial domains of ADLs, pain and illness, and associations of dysfunctional behaviors. The GRRAS is easy to administer and takes about 15 minutes to complete. The GRRAS is also easy to score and may be facilitated by scoring software. Reliability has been adequately established; however, data collection is ongoing to provide well-established validity. The strength of the GRRAS lies in its ability to accurately provide a comprehensive assessment of behaviors seen in geriatric populations. More importantly, the GRRAS provides for an assessment measure that may even improve the patient's quality of life for those who suffer from psychiatric and medical conditions.

Review of the Mind Body Wellness Geriatric Rehabilitation and Restorative Assessment System by TIMOTHY J. MAKATURA, Adjunct Professor of Psychology, Capella University, Minneapolis, MN:

The Mind Body Wellness Geriatric Rehabilitation and Restorative Assessment System (GRRAS) is a recently published instrument that was developed to assess "dysfunctional moods and behaviors associated with psychiatric and medical comorbidities" (professional manual, p. 1). Although this measure can be used for any person over the age of 55, it is designed to be used with residents within long-term care facilities and inpatient medical settings. The test authors argue that a specialized instrument is necessary because psychological assessment and treatment of this population is likely to be complicated by comorbidities, systemic and social-cultural pressures, and the intense emotional influence of patients' family members.

The test authors present a good deal of evidence that supports the contention that persons with chronic medical conditions, pain syndromes, and cognitive impairments demonstrate a higher prevalence of psychiatric disorders than the general population. There seems to be an incremental increase in the prevalence of psychiatric disorders as medical illnesses move from acute to chronic. This increase is further exacerbated by pain. The prevalence of psychiatric disorders in a population with chronic pain and chronic illness is estimated at 50% to 75%. In addition, an estimated 67% to 94% of residents entering or residing in a nursing home have a psychiatric diagnosis. Some level of cognitive impairment is reported in the majority of this population and a significant number of these persons demonstrate concomitant behavioral disturbances. A final consideration is that there is an increasing likelihood that persons 65 years of age and older will spend some time in a nursing home. These statistics support the test authors' contention that a specialized evaluation instrument is necessary.

DESCRIPTION. The GRRAS is composed of three separate assessment instruments: the Psychosocial Resistance to Activities of Daily Living Index (PRADLI), the Geriatric Multidimensional Pain and Illness Inventory (GMPI), and the Geriatric Level of Dysfunction Scale (GLDS). The items that comprise these instruments were drawn from behavioral problem checklists, referral requests from nurses and rehabilitation therapists, and the West Haven-Yale Multidisciplinary Pain Inventory (WHYMPI).

The Psychosocial Resistance to Activities of Daily Living Index (PRADLI) is an eight-item instrument that is rated by a clinician on a 7-point Likert scale. This scale specifically measures the resident's time out of bed as well as his or her ability and willingness to engage in tasks related to eating, dressing, toileting, bathing, participation in medical treatments, participation in rehabilitation therapy, and participation in personal hygiene/social and recreational activities. Each item is rated from "1," which represents the need for maximum levels of assistance to "7," which represents independent completion of the task. Behavioral anchors are provided for each rating. The total score is calculated by summing the scores for each of the eight items. This summary score may be compared to one of four comparison groups.

The Geriatric Multidimensional Pain and Illness Inventory (GMPI) is a 14-item instrument designed to assess pain and other noxious illness symptoms. This instrument provides a section to specify the resident's activities during the observations as well as a listing of common pain-related behaviors. The specific items involve rating of pain, activity limitations resulting from pain, factors that influence pain, emotional symptoms, and active coping. Each item is rated by the clinician on a 10-point scale from 1, indicating limited or mild difficulty to 10, indicating intense or extreme difficulty. Behavioral anchors are provided for each rating. The specific rating is based on clinician observations, reports from the resident, and reports from the resident's family and health care providers. These ratings are used to generate a total score and three symptom clusters scores. The cluster scores include Pain and Suffering, Life Interference, and Emotional Distress. It is noted that 33% of items are common to the Life Interference and Emotional Distress clusters. Once again, the four summary scores may be compared to one of four normative groups.

The Geriatric Level of Dysfunction Scale (GLDS) is a 20-item instrument that was designed to measure dysfunctional behaviors associated with pain, dementia, physical disability, medical conditions, and psychiatric disorders. The GLDS was modeled after a behavioral problem checklist used by the test authors during the referral process. Each of the 20 dysfunctional behaviors categories is given three separate ratings for intensity or level of danger, frequency, and duration. Each of these dimensions is rated on an 8-point scale from zero (0) indicating no significant behavior, no frequency, and no duration to 7, indicating immediate danger, high frequency, and extended duration. The specific rating is again based on clinician observations, reports from the resident, and reports from the resident's family and health care providers. Behavioral anchors and numeric values are provided for each rating. These ratings are used to generate a total score and three cluster scores. The cluster scores include Aggressive Agitation, Irrational Agitation, and Dysfunctional Illness Behaviors. Once again, the four summary scores may be compared to one of four normative groups.

The raw scores from each of these instruments are summed to determine the total and summary scores for each instrument. Summary scores are then converted to percentile ranks derived from one of four comparison groups. The four groups include: (a) the General Unaffected group, which consists of 109 individuals who scored less than Stage 4 on the 7-stage Riesberg Global Deterioration Scale (RGDS) and less than 5 on a 10-point analog pain scale; (b) the General Affected Group, which consisted of 316 individuals who scored greater than or equal to Stage 4 on the RGDS and/or greater than or equal to 5 on a 10-point pain analog scale; (c) the Dementia group, which consisted of 258 individuals who scored greater than or equal to 4 on the RGDS; and (d) the Pain group, which consisted of 166 individuals who scored greater than or equal to 5 on a 10-point pain analog scale. The normative groups allow an individual's performance to be compared to persons with similar cognitive level, pain, and activity level. Cutoff scores and clinical ranges are also provided for each summary score to indicate level of impairment/severity. Individuals in all groups were derived from a sample of 425 individuals. Members of the General Unaffected group were exclusive to that particular group. However, there was significant overlap between the other three normative groups. Statistical analysis revealed no significant group differences on the basis of race or gender.

DEVELOPMENT. The test authors report that the pilot versions of the PRADLI, GMPI, and GLDS were tested with approximately 400 individuals, and each of these measures was found to be reliable and valid although the statistics that support these contentions were not presented. Following the pilot studies, one item was added and the wording of two items was modified to broaden the scope of these items. The final GRRAS measure was administered to a combined sample of 512 individuals that consisted of two separate samples: Sample 1 with 392 members and Sample 2 with 120 members. It is unclear if the participants in Sample 1 were part of the pilot study. Participants in Sample 2 were selected to make the combined sample representative of the U.S population in terms of age, race, and gender. These individuals also provided a broader sampling of various living arrangements and levels of cognitive functioning.

The 8 items on the PRADLI were factor analyzed for 432 individuals. This resulted in a single-factor solution that accounted for approximately 63% of the variance. The 14 items on the GMPI were factor analyzed for 446 individuals. This resulted in a three-factor solution that accounted for approximately 64% of the variance. Interestingly, 2 items loaded on two separate factors. The frequency, duration, and intensity ratings were summed for each of the 20 items on the GLDS. These summed ratings were factor analyzed for 446 individuals, yielding a three-factor solution that accounted for approximately 31% of the variance. The cluster scores were derived from the means and standard deviations of each group of items in the cluster.

TECHNICAL. Measures of internal consistency are provided based on 120 individuals for the total PRADLI score and the total and cluster scores for the GMPI and the GLDS. Coefficients ranged from .68 to .93. Test-retest reliability is based on 22 individuals, but the interval between testing is not stated. Test-retest reliability coefficients ranged from .83 to .98 for the PRADLI individual items and was .97 for the PRALDI total score. Test-retest reliability coefficients ranged from .62 to .96 for individual items on the GMPI. The coefficient for the Pain and Suffering cluster score was .68, but all other GMPI summary scores were greater than .93. Test-retest reliability for the GLDS is limited to a comparison of intensity, frequency, and duration ratings for the three strongest behavioral complaints for each participant. Coefficients ranged from .86 to .96. Interrater reliability is based on ratings of seven residents by eight clinicians at 2 to 3 points during the residents' course of care. There were a total of 20 assessment points in the analysis over the course of 3 months to 3 years. Intraclass correlation coefficients were calculated and ranged from .87 to .97.

Concurrent validity is considered for each of the measures that comprise the GRRAS and is reportedly enhanced by relating this to an external criterion (i.e., level of cognitive impairment, level of pain) and four separate groups. Cutoff scores and clinical ranges also contribute to this validation. The test authors provide logical arguments for content validity.

The test authors present comparisons of the GRRAS to other global and specific measures. It is noted that the raw total and cluster scores were first converted to standard scores to allow for comparison on a common metric. Correlations between the GRRAS and the Mini Mental Status

Examination (MMSE) ranged from .19 to .63. Correlations between the GRRAS and the Reisberg Global Deterioration Scale (RGDS) ranged from .35 to .68. Correlations between the GRRAS and the Dementia Rating Scale-2 (DRS-2) ranged from .11 to .61. Correlations were highest between the GRRAS and Initiation/Perseveration and Total scores from the DRS-2. However, no other pattern of correlations could be identified. Correlations between the Independent Living Scales (ILS) and the GRRAS on 72 individuals ranged from .24 to .67. The GRRAS seems to have the highest correlations with the Social Adjustment Scale and the Total Summary Score, which ranged from .36 to .67. The Geriatric Depression Scale (GDS) and the GRRAS were administered to 392 individuals; correlations ranged from .00 to .46. It is noted that higher correlations were generally noted between the GDS and the total and cluster scores of the GMPI; however, these correlations were modest.

The test authors also present more focused comparisons between the individual components of the GRRAS and similar instruments. The Katz ADL was compared to the PRADLI on 404 individuals and correlations ranged from .30 to .98. The items on both measures were significantly correlated and domains (i.e. Feeding, Dressing, Toileting, Bathing) were correlated .95 to .98. Based on 20 observations of seven residents, correlations were derived between the GMTI item and cluster scores and a six-item measure of pain that involved pain words, pained faces, bracing, pain noises, rubbing, restlessness, and summary scores. Correlations between these measures varied from .04 to .92. High correlations were noted between the specific pain ratings on both instruments, and moderate correlations were noted between pain symptoms and the Emotional Disturbance and Life Interference clusters. Correlations were derived between the GLDS item and cluster scores and the total and three-factor scores of the Cohen-Mansfield Agitation Inventory based on 120 individuals. These correlations varied between .01 and .85 but tended to be in the low to moderate range. Correlations were derived between the GLDS item and cluster scores and the Neuropsychiatric Inventory-Nursing Home version, a measure of psychiatric symptoms in long-term care settings. Correlations between these instruments varied between .00 and .84. Correlations were generally in the low to moderate range.

SUMMARY. The GRRAS is a recently developed, multidimensional instrument that has met the objectives of the test authors to assess moods and behaviors associated with psychiatric and medical conditions in the geriatric population. This instrument provides an effective mechanism for the evaluation and ongoing monitoring of older persons in hospital-type environments. The strength of the instrument is the comprehensive nature, the focus on critical behaviors and symptoms that will likely influence overall care, and the provision of four comparison groups. There are some concerns regarding limited validity but these should be resolved as investigators conduct further research using the GRRAS.

[77]

Multiaxial Diagnostic Inventory–Revised Edition.

Purpose: "Developed to serve as a criterion-referenced diagnostic screening instrument designed to assess personality disorders and clinical syndromes."
Population: Children, adolescents, adults.
Publication Dates: 1989-1994.
Acronym: MDI-R.
Administration: Individual or group.
Levels, 4: Personality Scales, Adult Clinical Scales, Adolescent Clinical Scales, Child Clinical Scales.
Price Data, 2008: $74.95 per manual and 10 copies of each scale.
Time: Administration time not reported.
Comments: "Criterion-referenced."
Author: William F. Doverspike.
Publisher: Professional Resource Press.

a) PERSONALITY SCALES.
Population: Adults.
Scores, 12: Paranoid, Schizoid, Schizotypal, Borderline, Histrionic, Narcissistic, Antisocial, Avoidant, Dependent, Obsessive-Compulsive, Passive-Aggressive, Depressive.

b) ADULT CLINICAL SCALES.
Population: Adults.
Scores, 13: Dysthymic Disorder, Major Depressive Disorder, Bipolar Disorder, Psychotic Disorder, Dissociative Disorder, Posttramautic Stress, Anxiety Disorder, Panic Disorder, Somatoform Disorder, Anorexia Nervosa, Bulimia Nervosa, Alcohol Abuse, Substance Abuse.

c) ADOLESCENT CLINICAL SCALES.
Population: Ages 10-12.
Scores, 12: Attention-Deficit/Hyperactivity Disorder, Oppositional Defiant Disorder, Conduct Disorder, Alcohol Abuse, Substance Abuse, Dysthymic Disorder, Major Depressive Disorder, Anxiety,

Separation Anxiety, Psychotic Disorder, Anorexia Nervosa, Bulimia Nervosa.

d) CHILD CLINICAL SCALES.

Population: Children.

Scores, 12: Attention-Deficit/Hyperactivity Disorder, Oppositional Defiant Disorder, Conduct Disorder, Alcohol Abuse, Substance Abuse, Dysthymic Disorder, Major Depressive Disorder, Anxiety, Separation Anxiety, Psychotic Disorder, Anorexia Nervosa, Bulimia Nervosa.

Review of the Multiaxial Diagnostic Inventory–Revised Edition by ASHRAF KAGEE, Professor of Psychology, Stellenbosch University, South Africa:

DESCRIPTION. The Multiaxial Diagnostic Inventory–Revised Edition (MDI-R) is a criterion-referenced diagnostic screening instrument designed to make determinations of personality disorders and clinical syndromes. Rather than being a standardized test, the MDI-R is a symptom checklist consisting of 110 items organized into 13 subscales on the Adult version. These are: Dysthymic Disorder (7 items), Major Depressive Dissorder (9 items), Bipolar Disorder (8 items), Psychotic Disorder (5 items), Dissociative Disorder (4 items), Posttraumatic Stress (6 items), Anxiety Disorder (8 items), Panic Disorder (10 items), Somatoform Disorder (20 items), Anorexia Nervosa (4 items), Bulimia Nervosa (5 items), Alcohol Abuse (12 items) and Substance Abuse (12 items).

Clinicians using the MDI-R checklist are required to integrate information provided by the scale with other sources of information such as the patient's history, interview data, and other test results. An important advantage of the MDI-R is its flexibility. It may be used as a self-report inventory, clinician rating scale, or a combination of the two. However, at the same time it may be used only as a screening procedure. Thus, information yielded by the scale that appears clinically interesting should be investigated further, for example, in the context of a clinical interview.

Test takers are provided with an MDI-R (revised edition) four-page form, which comes in four versions, namely, Personality Scales, Adult Clinical, Adolescent Clinical, and Child Clinical Scales. The first page of each form provides space for recording identifying information, test-taking directions, and some examples of endorsed items. On the second, third, and fourth pages the items are listed, with yes and no response options corresponding to each item.

The test author suggests that professionals who use the MDI-R have training and experience in a mental health field that includes graduate coursework in assessment, advanced diagnostics, and psychopathology. The manual further indicates that ideal qualifications include a doctorate in psychology, with courses in psychological assessment, tests and measurements, and diagnostic classification.

DEVELOPMENT. The MDI-R is based on DSM-IV criteria. The test author states in the test manual that the original goal of the instrument "was to develop a simple screening procedure to facilitate structured interviews focused on differential diagnostic referral questions" (professional manual, p. 1). The original version of the instrument used a series of diagnostic checklists developed for common clinical syndromes and personality disorders. These checklists were first developed as structured clinical interviews and later were developed for patient self-report. The checklists were then selected on the basis of specific referral questions. In the development of the final version of the MDI, the checklists have been combined into a single larger inventory, divided into three versions. Thus the original version of the scale took shape as separate Personality Scales, Adult Clinical Scales, and Adolescent Clinical Scales.

The revised version of the MDI followed the publication of the *Diagnostic and Statistical Manual-IV* in 1994 and represents an effort "to reproduce adapted diagnostic descriptors from the DSM-IV" (professional manual, p. 2). The test author indicates in the test manual that he obtained permission from the American Psychiatric Association to reproduce these descriptors from the DSM-IV. The test manual states that the scale has been referred to as a "DSM IV Checklist," although the official title is the Multiaxial Diagnostic Inventory (Revised Edition).

TECHNICAL.

Standardization. An important point to bear in mind with the MDI-R is the fact that the scale is not based on normative statistical foundations. The test manual uses the term "idiographic" rather than "nomothetic" to describe the information provided by the instrument. Further, as a symptom checklist lacking validity indicators, the scale is susceptible to response sets biased by distortion, denial, and exaggeration of symptoms, a point rightfully acknowledged in the test manual.

Reliability. The test manual gives no indication that any reliability analyses have been conducted.

Validity. The MDI-R is a criterion-referenced instrument. The test manual states that a "qualitative assessment of item content is more important than a quantitative analysis of scores" (professional manual, p. 22). The test author argues that "individual item endorsements may have more clinical significance than scale scores or psychometric profiles" (professional manual, p. 22). Thus no analyses of scale validity have been conducted.

COMMENTARY. The MDI-R is simple to use and may be administered in either a written or oral manner. Its chief purpose is to elicit and organize symptoms from respondents. This simplicity is simultaneously a limitation, as the instrument is vulnerable to client response sets of denial and exaggeration, as well as demand characteristics of the assessment context. The manual suggests that one way to address this limitation is to build client rapport and establish an appropriate response set before administering the MDI-R. It is unlikely that such procedures will be sufficient to gain a truly accurate assessment of some patients who are bent on misrepresenting their psychological experiences, such as incarcerated or malingering persons. This may also be true for persons with substance disorders and personality disorders. It is unlikely that comparing self-report data with clinician-administered data, as the manual suggests, will be a feasible way of dealing with this limitation.

Another limitation of the scale is the likelihood of high rates of positive diagnoses yielded by the scale, as is common with self-report measures. The manual cautions that the scale is best used "as a screening procedure which requires further follow-up assessment" (professional manual, p. 26). Yet, it is unclear that screening is useful if follow-up assessments are needed. One may as well conduct a proper assessment with appropriate probes to identify instances of denial or exaggeration.

As an overall comment, it is unclear that a general diagnostic assessment is a useful approach to patient evaluation. Thus, the MDI-R is appropriate for only a subset of any typical population of patients seeking psychological treatment.

SUMMARY. The MDI-R is quite limited in terms of its potential usefulness. Although it is simple and easy to administer, it is vulnerable to limitations in terms of reliability and validity. It is also limited in terms of the possibility that respondents may misrepresent their symptoms, either by denial or exaggeration. For clinicians interested in gaining a rapid sense of a patient's salient psychological symptoms, this instrument may be useful, under limited conditions. However, for those clinicians who wish to gain an understanding of a patient's symptoms in order to make an accurate diagnostic assessment this instrument is unlikely to be useful. For such purposes a structured interview schedule is likely to be more useful, such as the Structured Clinical Interview Schedule (Spitzer, Williams, Gibbon, & First, 1992) or the Composite International Diagnostic Interview Schedule (Kessler, Andrews, Mroczek, Ustun,& Wittchen, 1998).

REVIEWER'S REFERENCES

Kessler, R. C., Andrews, G., Mroczek, D., Ustun, T. B., & Wittchen, H-U. (1998). The World Health Organization Composite International Diagnostic Interview Short Form (CIDI-SF). *International Journal of Methods in Psychiatric Research, 7,* 171-185.

Spitzer, R. L., Williams, J. B., Gibbon, M., & First, M. B. (1992). The Structured Clinical Interview for DSM-III-R (SCID). I: History, rationale, and description. *Archives of General Psychiatry, 49,* 624-629.

Review of the Multiaxial Diagnostic Inventory–Revised Edition by ROBERT WRIGHT, Professor, Measurement & Statistics, Widener University, Chester, PA:

DESCRIPTION. The Multiaxial Diagnostic Inventory–Revised Edition includes four different measures. One is a measure of personality type, and the other three are clinical diagnostic inventories: one for adults, one for adolescents, and one for children.

The Multiaxial Diagnostic Inventory–Revised Edition (MDI-R) Personality Scales is a checklist answered using a binomial response, Yes or No, to 95 items. The items consist of a stem or stimulus statement that is self-descriptive. Each statement begins with the pronoun "I" followed by one of several qualifiers. The 95 statements can be scored and reported as measuring longstanding personality features.

The MDI-R Personality Scales provide a battery of 12 personality scales clustered in three groupings. Names for these clusters and the personality dimensions included were borrowed from the DSM-IV-TR (American Psychiatric Association, 2000). Cluster A (24 items) is described as measuring "odd or eccentric personalities" (professional manual, p. 3). This cluster includes three subscales: Paranoid, Schizoid, and Schizotypal. Cluster B (34 total items) is described as measuring "dramatic, emotional or erratic personality" (professional manual, p. 3) types. This cluster consists of four subscales: Borderline,

Histrionic, Narcissistic, and Antisocial. Cluster C (37 items) is described as measuring "anxious or fearful" (professional manual, p. 3) personalities. This cluster is composed of five subscales: Avoidant, Dependent, Obsessive-Compulsive, Passive-Aggressive, and Depressive.

The MDI-R Adult Clinical Scales employ the same format with a total of 110 self-descriptive statements answered by clients as Yes or No. The instrument provides 13 subscale scores including measures of: Dysthymic Disorder (7 items), Major Depressive Disorder (9 items), Bipolar Disorder (8 items), Psychotic Disorder (5 items), Dissociative Disorder (4 items), Posttraumatic Stress (6 items), Anxiety Disorder (8 items), Panic Disorder (10 items), Somatoform Disorder (20 items), Anorexia Nervosa (4 items), Bulimia Nervosa (5 items), Alcohol Abuse (12 items), and Substance Abuse (12 items).

The MDI-R Adolescent Clinical Scales use another 110 self-descriptive items derived from the DSM-IV-TR to define 12 subscales. About 40% of the items on the Adolescent Clinical Scales are taken from the adult scale. The subscales of the MDI-R Adolescent Clinical Scales provide 12 subscale scores including: Attention-Deficit/Hyperactivity Disorder (18 items), Oppositional Defiant Disorder (8 items), Conduct Disorder (14 items), Alcohol Abuse (12 items), Substance Abuse (12 items), Dysthymic Disorder (7 items), Major Depressive Disorder (9 items), Anxiety (8 items), Separation Anxiety (8 items), Psychotic Disorder (5 items), Anorexia Nervosa (4 items), and Bulimia Nervosa (5 items).

The MDI-R provides two approaches for the administration of the instrument: oral administration and the standard written format for administration. The standard directions ask respondents to check (Yes or No) on a list of statements that are self-descriptive. It also asks respondents to write a list of any personal characteristics not covered by the 95 items on the checklist. No indication is given as to what the clinician should do with these additional data.

The manual provides for an oral administration in two contexts of use. One is as a follow-up interview to establish the clinical significance of the client's original set of responses or statement of symptoms. The second is for clients who are illiterate, or with low levels of cognitive functioning. Simple explanations of the stimulus questions are permitted (professional manual, p. 19).

DEVELOPMENT. The original self-descriptive item stems were selected by the test author from a collection of symptom checklists he developed from his clinical practice experience. The clinical checklists were combined and aligned with the third edition of the *Diagnostic and Statistical Manual, 3rd edition Revised* (DSM-III-R), and published as the original version of the MDI. The second edition (1999) was revised to align with the DSM-IV (1994). The test author makes the point that there is true concordance between the MDI-R and the diagnostic criteria of the DSM-IV.

TECHNICAL. Most technical reviews begin with an analysis of the appropriateness of the normative population and statistical assumptions used in setting a population frame, conducting the sampling, and standardizing the measure. The MDI-R cannot be addressed for these dimensions. The test author has judged it not to be necessary to employ statistics or provide a sample, "While the determination of the appropriateness of a psychometric procedure relies heavily on one's own professional judgment" (professional manual, p. v). He makes the case that the instrument is for clinical application purposes, and is criterion based. However, without data no determination of the stability or consistency of scores is possible. No test-retest analysis was done by the author, and no demonstration of interrater agreement was reported.

In designing criterion measures the test author is obligated to establish cut scores using a scientifically appropriate system that can withstand legal challenge and that meets the ethical requirements spelled out by the Joint Committee on Testing Practices (2005). No validation method was employed beyond taking elements of the DSM-IV and turning them into self-descriptions and posing them in a questionnaire. The test author argued that there is no need to study gender differences.

A problem of reliability for the MDI-R is the lack of consistency in the administration. The MDI-R may be self-administered in written form by the client, or it may be administered orally. During oral presentations it may be augmented by an undefined number of prompts by the examiner (professional manual, p. 19).

Problems of validity for the MDI-R can be seen in the scoring model developed by the test author. Subtest items are arranged on the printed form in diagnostic blocks. Each block provides all the items of the subscale. For example, the subscale measuring Panic Disorder on the Adult Clinical Scales has a block of 10 items all starting with the phrase "Panic attacks with…" These 10 items are grouped together making the focus of measurement conspicuous to the client. The down side of that approach is that the MDI-R is subject to denial, exaggeration, and distortion.

Interpretations of the meaning of the scores derived from the MDI-R clinical checklist are quite simple. After each clinical block of questions the questionnaire has a place to record the total number of "Yes" answers. Next to that total is a number representing the cut score between normal and psychopathological performance. The test author determined the cut score by counting the diagnostic symptoms required in the DSM-IV (1994) to make a clinical diagnosis of psychopathology.

Problems with the test author's approach to establishing a cut score can be seen in the case of Attention Deficit/Hyperactivity Disorder. The DSM-IV provides a list of 8 symptoms, 6 of which must be present to label a child as having "AD/HD, Predominant Inattentive Type." There are another 9 symptoms listed in the DSM-IV, 6 of which are required for a diagnosis of "AD/HD Predominant Hyperactive-Impulsive Type." Finally the DSM-IV criteria require 12 symptoms of the previous possible 17 for a diagnosis of "AD/HD Combined Type." Thus, a reasonable reading of the test author's professed allegiance to the DSM-IV as the criterion upon which the MDI-R is based would require a total of 12 of the MDI-R questionnaire items measuring AD/HD be answered "Yes."

The MDI-R children's diagnostic scale has 18 self-description statements related to attention deficit/hyperactive disorder. For the most part, these items are either a verbatim copy or slightly paraphrased wordings of the original in the DSM-IV. As AD/HD often presents in a comorbid pairing with reading disabilities, it is unlikely an elementary age child can read and understand the diagnostic statements on the MDI-R. To be diagnosed with AD/HD a child must only respond with 6 "Yes" responses to the list of 18 possible symptoms. The items describe common characteristics present in most children from time to time. To be indicative of a mental illness such as AD/HD, the DSM-IV requires symptoms must have been present as a dense cluster for at least 6 months. This is not explained on the MDI-R.

By making the list long, the test author increased the likelihood of a positive diagnosis. Using the DSM-IV list of symptoms, the MDI-R set the cut score at a far lower standard than is used in the DSM-IV. As there is no statistically verified criterion validity analysis, these cut scores are hypothetical at best. They have no independently derived foundation as a construct, and are merely self-perceptions expressed by a child or reported by a parent. In either case great caution should be used in deriving any meaning from the "ADD" scale of the MDI-R.

In contrast to the MDI-R approach to attention deficit/hyperactivity disorder (AD/HD), the diagnosis of Anorexia Nervosa (ANO) is made based on the client's response to four questionnaire items. The DSM-IV also has four standards for diagnosing Anorexia Nervosa. The author of the MDI-R made an effort to summarize four clinical descriptions into four "Yes" or "No" questionnaire items.

To have a diagnosis of Anorexia Nervosa the child or adolescent must answer "Yes" to all four items of the "ANO" subscale. An argument can be made that the Anorexia Nervosa subscale as designed is not appropriate on a children's assessment. One of the four items focuses on missed periods of the menstrual cycle. A logical argument can be posed that it is impossible for a premenstrual girl or a boy ever being given a diagnosis of Anorexia Nervosa as they can score a maximum of only three of four possible.

As Anorexia Nervosa involves faulty self-perception by the client, self-perception questions of the MDI-R do not constitute an appropriate measurement approach. This same criticism can be made of most other subtests of the adolescent and children's scales. On the adult scale the same problem occurs when asking clients about their self-perceptions when faulty self-perception, repression, and denial are diagnostic hallmarks of the disorder being diagnosed.

The Multiaxial Diagnostic Inventory, Revised Personality Scales consists of 12 of the personality types described in the DSM-IV-TR (2000). Missing is the five-axis approach defined in the DSM-IV as an organizing system for mental disorders and personality types. This is odd in view of the fact that the test author elected to use the word "Multiaxial" in the instrument's title.

COMMENTARY. The test author and publisher claim that the MDI-R is an "attempt to standardize an assessment format based on some of the more frequently encountered diagnostic categories" (professional manual, p. v). The MDI-R uses some of the diagnostic categories from the DSM-IV, but provides no proof that the categories selected are central to the study of human psychopathology. It provides no evidence the instrument's self-descriptive questionnaire items are valid statements about the individual's mental condition. There are no valid data to document that the cut scores are more than the personal musings of the test author. The publisher has not met the obligation to provide evidence of the instrument's utility and the defensibility of diagnostic statements made based on its scores.

SUMMARY. The author provides no framework for understanding personality and what constitutes a disorder of personality. Without an integrated framework, the instrument provides the therapist with only a list of self-identified possible problems. It does not provide the other dimension of human personality and adjustment. Specifically, it lacks any indications of areas of ego-strength, coping-mechanisms, and psychological resiliency normally included in a complete clinical description of psychological status.

There is no indication that a normative sample of subjects was used in the development of the MDI-R. The test manual offers no statistical evidence to demonstrate that it is reliable or truly valid. The only thing the test's author claims is that he based the scales of the MDI-R on the 1994 edition of the DSM, and called it criterion-referenced. This is in part true, but the diagnostic criteria (cut scores) are hypothetical and speculative at best. We have no way to know if the checklist responses of clients are as salient as the clinical perception of therapists using the DSM-IV diagnostic profiles.

REVIEWER'S REFERENCES

American Psychiatric Association (APA). (1994). *Diagnostic and statistical manual of mental disorders* (4th ed.). Washington, DC: Author.

American Psychiatric Association. (2000). *Diagnostic and statistical manual of mental disorders DSM-IV-TR, Fourth edition, Text revision.* Washington, DC: American Psychiatric Association.

Joint Committee on Testing Practices. (2005). Code of fair testing practices in education (Revised). *Educational Measurement: Issues and Practice, 24*(1), 23-26.

[78]

Murphy-Meisgeier Type Indicator for Children® [Revised].

Purpose: "Intended to help students develop greater awareness of their preferred ways for processing information, making decisions, and forming relationships."
Population: Grades 2-12.
Publication Dates: 1987-2008.
Acronym: MMTIC™.
Scores, 4: Extraversion or Introversion, Sensing or Intuition, Thinking or Feeling, Judging or Perceiving.
Administration: Individual or group.
Price Data, 2008: $67 per online assessment including scoring and a personalized student report; $3 per additional professional report (designed for counselors); $25 per year for access to the MMTIC Facilitator Interface, which allows quantity purchases, set up and management of different groups and individuals, report generation, data management, and free downloadable support materials (including MMTIC manual, 2008, 96 pages).
Time: (15–20) minutes.
Comments: Each report provides the indicated preference for the respondent on the four bipolar dichotomies that are scored.
Authors: Elizabeth Murphy and Charles Meisgeier.
Publisher: Center for Applications of Psychological Type, Inc.
Cross References: See T5:1750 (1 reference); for reviews by Joanne Jensen and Norman Constantine and by Hoi K. Suen of an earlier edition, see 12:249.

Review of the Murphy-Meisgeier Type Indicator for Children [Revised] by JOYCE MEIKAMP, Professor of Special Education, and JEANETTE LEE-FARMER, Associate Professor of Special Education, Marshall University Graduate College, South Charleston, WV:

DESCRIPTION. The Murphy-Meisgeier Type Indicator for Children [Revised] (MMTIC) is a self-report instrument designed to identify personality preferences of children Grades 2 through 12. Grounded in Carl Jung's personality type theory, the MMTIC extends the premise of the Myers-Briggs Type Indicator® (MBTI; T7:1710) to children. Psychological type is used to explain how people process information and make decisions about that information. Measuring personality preferences on four bipolar dimensions, including Extraversion-Introversion, Sensing-Intuition, Thinking-Feeling, and Judging-Perceiving, the MMTIC classifies a child into 1 of 16 possible psychological types. Personality types are identified based on the combination of the four dichotomies.

Written on an early second grade reading level, the MMTIC is a two-option forced-choice questionnaire consisting of 43 items. The child selects an answer from one of two options based on what is preferred. The untimed MMTIC takes approximately 15–20 minutes to complete and can be administered to a group of children or individually. In addition, the instrument can be completed online or via an assessment booklet with paper-pencil answer sheet. If completed online, it must be finished in one sitting. Otherwise, it can be completed over a period of time as needed.

The MMTIC must be submitted either online or via mail for scoring. Only the publisher, Center for Applications of Psychological Type, Inc. (CAPT), can score the MMTIC. The test authors justify this by suggesting the complicated algorithms generated by the items necessitate scoring via computer through CAPT. Then upon scoring, a student report, professional report for education professionals, or class type table report can be generated. Different reports are available for the elementary, middle school, or high school levels. Each report specifies the child's scored type preference, as well as percentage response consistencies for each of the dichotomous pairings. The higher the percentage the more consistently the student chose a response for that type preference.

DEVELOPMENT. Originally developed in 1987 as an extension of the MBTI to children, the MMTIC authors undertook a 6-year revision with the understanding the process is inherent to psychological instrument development. As such, extensive psychometric revision was undertaken in at least five different areas. For example, in the original version, if children could not be placed in a type preference, they were placed in the U-band, reflecting an undecided preference. In the revised MMTIC, the U-band or undecided area has been eliminated as a type preference. The test authors suggested their work and resulting statistics indicated children could consistently select a type preference. Thus, the need for the U-band was negated.

Revisions were also made in the number of items, streamlining and reducing the MMTIC from 70 to 43 items. Latent class analysis (LCA) was utilized to determine the consistency of individual items and to reduce the MMTIC to 43 items. Originally designed for children from Grades 2 to 8, the newer version has been extended to accommodate high school students. Moreover, the student report form has been expanded in an attempt to provide students with a greater explanation of type preferences. Finally, support materials, aimed at helping teachers to explain type preferences and provide student feedback, have been developed to accompany the revised MMTIC.

TECHNICAL. Data for standardization were collected from a sample of 3,949 children, representing various ethnicities, locations, and school district sizes. However, caution should be noted as ethnic breakdown information was provided only for individual schools, not the total research sample. Moreover, sample sizes for individual grade levels varied widely. For example, Grade 2 had but 42 students in the total sample, whereas 1,013 Grade 6 students were included.

The test authors reported alpha coefficients for preferences and gender ranged from .61 to .71 for the revised MMTIC. Reliability coefficients by grade were much more variable, ranging from .46 for the S-N scale for Grade 10 to .78 for the E-I scale for Grade 9.

Split-half reliability estimates for the revised MMTIC ranged from .57 for the J-P scale to .69 for the T-F scale. Test-retest reliability coefficients, based on a period from 3 to 6 months, ranged from .69 to .78 for the four scales. However, results were based upon a limited sample of 311 students, Grades 7 through 12 only.

Grounded in the theoretical work of Carl Jung related to psychological type, the MMTIC seeks to identify type preferences of children. Evidence offered in support of construct validity examined the internal structure of the instrument itself. Utilizing LCA, data were examined to determine if students could be classified into one of four type dichotomies. Results suggest the instrument can consistently classify children into type preferences. For each dichotomy the expected percentages correctly classified were all higher than 85%.

As a measure of criterion-related validity, students were asked prior to receiving their results on the MMTIC to self-assess their preference types. Results indicated the percentage of agreement between students' self-assessment and MMTIC scores ranged from 76%–81%. Moreover, the older the child the higher were the percentages of agreement.

In a separate study related to validity, the test authors compared rank orders of personality type frequencies for both adults and two different samples of children. Utilizing the adult normative sample of the MBTI and the MMTIC with children, results indicated the distribution of types for both children and adults was significantly related. Although the findings relative to validity are supportive, they were all based on studies conducted by the test authors and are limited in number.

COMMENTARY. Most assuredly the MMTIC continues to be a quickly administered measure of personality type for children. Extending the theoretical work of Carl Jung and the MBTI to children, the revised MMTIC has been shortened from 70 to 43 items. Evidence presented in the manual related to split half reliability suggests the reliability of the instrument was only slightly lowered by shortening it. The revised version expanded the age range to include high school students. Alpha reliability estimates by grade suggest the MMTIC might be slightly more reliable with students in higher grades.

Having the instrument readily available online for administration certainly makes it appealing for ease of access. In less than an hour's time, the online version of the MMTIC can be administered, scored, and results generated via three different types of reports—all factors that make it desirable to professionals and parents. However, for future revisions of the MMTIC, the test authors might consider including a comparison of the paper-and-pencil versus online delivery.

Although the student report form was expanded to provide greater detail about type preferences, caution is warranted with the Elementary School Report. This 11-page format is lengthy and the language complicated, suggesting extensive explanation and adaptation is required by the teacher. Although a separate teacher's guide is available to help with the verification of types, the lesson plans are brief. Moreover, the teacher's manual would benefit from differentiating lesson plans, activities, and materials for elementary, middle, and high school level students. [Editor's Note: The publisher advises that a teacher resource book, *The Chemistry of Personality*, was published after test materials were provided to this reviewer.]

Future revisions might carefully control the demographics of participating students as to number at each grade level. In addition, it is suggested that instructions and procedures followed prior or following administration of the MMTIC be identical for all participating students. In the current version, some schools participated in a 10-week verification process, others a 5-week process, and still others chose not to participate at all.

SUMMARY. The revised MMTIC is a self-report instrument designed to identify personality preference types of children. Grounded in the work of Carl Jung as a theoretical base, the MMTIC can be administered relatively quickly via paper and pencil or online. Although reliability of the instrument is adequate, research evidence related to validity is not conclusive in its breadth and depth.

Review of the Murphy-Meisgeier Type Indicator for Children [Revised] by DAVID MORSE, Professor, Counseling, Educational Psychology and Special Education, Mississippi State University, Mississippi State, MS:

DESCRIPTION. The Murphy-Meisgeier Type Indicator for Children [Revised] (MMTIC) is an instrument for identification of the familiar Jung-based psychological type dimensions for students in Grades 2-12. The MMTIC has been expanded in age scope to include high school grades and reduced in length from 70 to 43 items. Items are two-option, forced-choice stimuli; a stem is followed by two statements, the examinee selects one as being most like him or her. The results suggest the student's classification on each of four bipolar dimensions: Extraversion-Introversion (I-E); Sensing-Intuition (S-N); Thinking-Feeling (T-F); and Judging-Perceiving (J-P). The MMTIC is available as an online (web-based) or a paper-and pencil version, and may be given to one or many students at once.

The intended uses of the MMTIC, according to the manual, include helping students "develop greater awareness of their preferred ways for processing information, making decisions, and forming relationships" (p. 3). Teachers may be able to use psychological type information to "adjust instruction, especially for individual tutoring" (p. 3). Parents may be helped to better understand how one child might respond differently to various stimuli than another.

Administration of the MMTIC requires no special training, but it is recommended that the person giving feedback—which requires familiarity with and understanding of psychological type principles—be the one to administer the instrument. Thus, the MMTIC is not the kind of measure that should be administered by clerical personnel, teacher aides, or persons unfamiliar with type theory. The complete process involves giving the student(s) background about what is being assessed and how the results will be reviewed, administration, verification by student of the results, and feedback. Students are said to be able to complete the MMTIC in about 20 minutes.

Due to the way items are differentially weighted, scoring must be completed by the test publisher. Scoring and reporting are included in the instrument cost. Reports include a child's report, professional report, and group or classroom type table report and classroom manager report.

Materials from the publisher include the instrument; three versions of a student type verification activity, *I am a Good Student*; a teacher's manual, *Verifying Type with Students*; and the MMTIC manual that covers development, administration, and suggested uses of results. [Editor's Note: Publisher advises that a teacher resource book, *The Chemistry of Personality*, was published after test materials were provided to this reviewer.]

DEVELOPMENT. The MMTIC is a revised edition (2008 copyright) of the original instrument developed by the test authors, published in 1987. The item format has been retained, though many new items were developed and tried out for the revised version. Of the original version, 24 of the 70 items were retained as is or with slight modification. From a field trial, a 64-item version, having 16 items for each of the four scales, emerged for tryout with a research sample. One ending item, asking for perceived clarity of the instrument, was added for the research sample. Approximately 3,900 students, from 19 schools in 10 states, participated in the research study. Both online and paper-pencil versions were used, though how many used each format was not indicated. Eight schools participated in the verification phase. From the results, 43 items were retained for the final version; the E-I scale has 10 items whereas the other three scales have 11 items each. Items differ as to which of the response options (e.g., the "S" option or the "N" option) appears first, to reduce response bias.

Readability checks of MMTIC items, via Fry's method, show an approximate early second grade level. About 85% of research study students indicated that the items were "clear," about 15% said "confusing." A statistically higher fraction of elementary grade (2–6) students identified the instrument as confusing than upper grade (7–12) students (18% vs. 14%, $p < .01$). Explicit screenings—judgmental or statistical—of items for possible bias due to language, region, ethnicity, or gender are not mentioned.

TECHNICAL. The research study, wherein participants responded to a 64-item version, is the source of the majority of data presented. About 300 students were followed up 3–6 months later for test-retest reliability estimates.

The manual offers classical reliability estimates. Internal consistency values in the form of coefficient alphas are in the low .60s, except for the T-F scale (.71). Split-half estimates are similar, ranging from .57 (J-P scale) to .69 (T-F). From a much smaller sample (about 300 students from Grades 7–12), test-retest reliability estimates are somewhat better, ranging from .69 (J-P) to .78 (E-I). Such values are below the usual guidelines for making decisions about individuals (Cronbach, 1990). However, these methods all involve correlations of scale scores, not consistency or accuracy of classification within or across scales. Within-scale classification consistency for the test-retest sample ranged from 77% (T-F) to 83% (E-I) over a 3–6-month period. Within scales, accuracy of classification, as indicated by the rate of student affirmation of the MMTIC-indicated type, ranged from 76% (S-N) to 81% (E-I, T-F). These numbers are statistically better than chance; the question is whether they are good enough to warrant noneducational classification and potentially differential treatment of students.

A problem with the previous version, the "U-band," was examined. When students' scores were not clearly favoring one end of the scale over the other, the original MMTIC reported an Undetermined type for that scale. Among verification phase participants, only about 5–6% of students could not classify themselves as having a preference for a given scale. This result convinced the test authors to eliminate an indication of Undetermined from the MMTIC, no matter how close the response consistency—the degree to which an examinee selects options favoring one end of a scale over the other—is to 50%, the no-preference value.

Validity information mostly stems from the latent class analysis (LCA) used to both prune the 64-item research version to the 43-item final version and judge the quality of the resultant scales. This approach, using field test data to "clean up" the scales and then asserting the validity of the resultant measure without a new sample, is similar to what Cureton (1950) warned against. The LCA analysis of scale structure apparently presupposed that items for a scale measured just that scale. Scale score correlations suggest that to be mostly a reasonable judgment, except for the relation of S-N and J-P scores ($r = .43$). Individual item correlations are presented in an appendix rather than in the chapter on validity. A strict confirmatory structure analysis presented that includes all scales simultaneously is not presented. Future validity evidence should include a new sample taking the final version.

Does the MMTIC accurately identify student type preferences? Based on the verification data, students agree with the identified type far more often than they disagree, but a substantial fraction of students will not agree or will not identify a type preference. Therefore, results of the MMTIC should not be considered definitive.

COMMENTARY. For purposes of initiating conversations with students, parents, or teachers about possible personality-based differences in how people behave, the MMTIC could be useful. The manual gives concrete suggestions how teachers might use type information to structure lessons and activities so as to not overlook any of the types in their class. The manual also outlines some very good suggestions, admonitions, and limitations associated with the administration and use of the MMTIC. The three main concerns regarding the MMTIC are utility, interpretation, and reliability and validity evidence.

Most examples of MMTIC use given in the manual or teacher's guide center on classroom lessons and activities. The manual states that teachers "can use [type information] to adjust instruction, especially for individual tutoring" (p. 3). Yet, the manual also states "in the classroom, teachers can generally assume that all types are represented and [therefore] design instruction and assessment accordingly" (p. 3). The goal is "not to teach solely to each student's dominant function, but to develop teaching methods that do not ignore any child's dominant function" (manual, p. 52). If that is the case, then there may be less need to assess individual students and instead focus on addressing the preferences of all types (e.g., "no type left behind"). Implementing the proposed 5- or 10-lesson sequence about type differences would require a substantial belief in the utility of type preferences to justify the allocation of so much class time. It would be interesting to see whether students, who are given MMTIC information about themselves and of type differences generally, adapt better in school or at home. For teachers choosing to invest the time and effort to modify their class activities to address type differences, evidence that such classes result in better achievement, adjustment, or both would be helpful. Neither type of evidence is mentioned in the manual.

The score reports give many pages about specific type preferences that are to be shared with the student. Unfortunately, the interpretations in the sample reports do not appear to be tempered in any way for examinees whose consistency scores for a scale are not high (e.g., close to 50%). That seems a poor practice, and does not honor the uncertainty associated with the resulting classifications.

Though online and paper-pencil formats of the MMTIC are available, no evidence is offered as to their psychometric comparability, a serious omission. Whether the MMTIC is suitable for special education students questionable. Accommodations are not addressed, other than reading items in a neutral voice to students having poor reading skill. Given the nature of the instrument, this last point is probably a minor issue. The most pressing concern is that the majority of the technical evidence comes from a sample that took one version of the MMTIC, from which the shorter, final version was derived after analysis of the results.

In the manual, there were several instances of missing information—sentences or paragraphs, portions of tables, an entire page from the acknowledgements, as well as a few errors of fact. Careful proofreading would be helpful.

SUMMARY. The MMTIC is a shorter, more quickly administered version than the original that can be used to determine psychological type preferences of students in Grades 2–12. Actual testing time is brief, though the time needed to inform students about the purpose of the measure, administer, give feedback, and obtain student verification of type is more substantial. For those who find utility in or have affinity for the Jung-type profiles, the MMTIC offers a fairly easy path to obtaining such information about students. Potential users should be aware that some students will find the MMTIC to be confusing; some will not affirm the indicated type; indicated type can change over time; and that the reliability and validity information furnished, though helpful, is at present incomplete.

REVIEWER'S REFERENCES

Cronbach, L. J. (1990). *Essentials of psychological testing* (5th ed.). New York: Harper Collins Publishing.

Cureton, E. E. (1950). Validity, reliability and baloney. *Educational and Psychological Measurement, 10*, 94-96.

[79]

Music Apperception Test.

Purpose: Designed for application in "clinical, educational, organizational and neuropsychology, art and creativity, and language and cognition."

Population: Ages 8 to 45.
Publication Date: 2007.
Acronym: MAT.
Scores, 39: Response Latency, Fluency (Compositional Fluency, Post-Compositional Fluency, Run-on Fluency, Total), Content Categories (Human, Human Mythic, Human Group, Participant Observer, Total Human, Animal, Animal Mythic, Total Animal, Natural, Man Made, Abstract, Morbid, Total Other), Interaction (Solitary, Mutual, Conflict, Detach), Tangential Response (Self, Music Centered, Other, Total Non-Story Reference), Affective Fit (Hedonic Tone, Affect Expressed, Common Theme, Common Interaction, Common Setting, Total), Narrative Style (Logical, Balanced, Kinetic/Imagistic, Disorganized/Other), Morbid Content, Adaptive Response to Change, Time to Termination.
Administration: Individual.
Forms, 4: Standard, Extended, Short Form (A, B).
Price Data, 2007: $189 per starter kit including manual (2007, 125 pages), manual supplement (2007, 115 pages), 20 record forms, administration CD, and carrier bag; $32 per 20 record forms; $40 per manual; $30 per manual supplement; $89 per administration CD; $18 per carrier bag; $30 per administration email coding and interpretation.
Time: (8-25) minutes.
Comments: Test administered via CD; requires the use of a tape or digital recorder to record examinee response.
Author: Leland van den Daele.
Publisher: Psychodiagnostics, Inc.

Review of the Music Apperception Test by MARY L. GARNER, Associate Professor of Mathematics, Kennesaw State University, Kennesaw, GA:

DESCRIPTION. The Music Apperception Test (MAT) is an individually administered test. The examiner plays a series of recordings of music that are approximately 1 minute in duration and are designed to elicit certain emotions. Each recording is followed by a 30-second silent period. Using prerecorded instructions, during which an example is provided of telling a story to music (a narration from "Peter and the Wolf"), the participant is asked to "tell a story to the music." The participant's responses are recorded and later analyzed. The analysis involves coding and analyzing the following variables: (a) Response Latency (RL): the number of seconds from onset of a composition to the beginning of response; (b) Compositional Fluency (CF): the number of words prior to conclusion of the music; (c) Post Compositional Fluency (PCF): the number of words after the conclusion of the music and before the next composition begins; (d) Run-on Fluency (RF): the number of words after the next composition begins (and referring to the previous composition); (e) Total Fluency (F): the total number of words in response to a piece of music (CF+PCF+RF); (f) PACE: the ratio of Compositional Fluency to length of composition in seconds; (g) Time to Termination of Response (TT): the amount of time response extends after termination of the composition; (h) Adaptive Response to Compositional Change (ARC): scored 0 or 1 for whether adaptive responses do not or do exist; (i) Content: each 25 word segment of a response—designated as a response unit (RU)—is coded human, animal, or other; (j) Percent Content: the number of response units coded for human is expressed as a percent of the total number of response units, the number of response units coded for animal is expressed as a percent of the total number of response units, and the number of response units coded other is expressed as a percent of the total number of response units; (k) Interaction: each 25 word segment is coded solitary, mutual, conflicted, or detached; (l) Tangential Reference: each 25 word segment is coded nonstory self-reference, nonstory music-centered reference, or other; (m) Affective Fit: the response as a whole is coded for hedonic tone (positive, negative, neutral), affect expressed (coded as appropriate or inappropriate), and conventional reference (type of interaction, theme, and setting); and (n) Narrative Style: the response as a whole is coded logical, kinetic/imagistic, balanced, disorganized, or other.

The first version of the test appeared in 1967. The current version of the test differs significantly from previous versions in the musical compositions used. The current version of the test uses musical compositions by Israeli composer Elan Gore; these were written specifically for the test in collaboration with the author of the test, Leland van den Daele, and guided by literature on the influence of properties of music on affect and emotion. As asserted by the test author, the MAT has potential as well as some research evidence for being useful in evaluating emotional intelligence, adaptability and creativity, language skills, interaction with others, leadership, executive function, neuropsychological function, and psychological pathology.

There are three versions of the test: a standard version that includes 10 musical recordings and takes 20 minutes; an extended version that includes 12 recordings and requires 25 minutes;

and two alternative short versions that include 4 recordings and require 8 minutes each. The manual and supplement provide a wealth of examples of responses and coding of those responses. Administration, analysis, and interpretation of the test requires professional psychological training.

DEVELOPMENT. The test was developed by Leland van den Daele during his time as a graduate student at Purdue University. Noticing his own rich response to a concert at the Elliot Hall of Music, van den Daele speculated on the possibility of analyzing individuals' reactions to music:

> In contrast to the tests that employed true or false questions, blots or pictures, music directly engaged my feelings and imagination. I reasoned that music stimulates different and perhaps deeper strata of mental function. Since music was not "fixed" as an item on a questionnaire or static like a blot, it provided a wider range of potential responses and invited a wider range of individual differences. (MAT Supplement, p. 2)

The first version of the test was created from a stratified random selection of music from Purdue University's music archives, and included such selections as Puccini's "La Boheme," Gershwin's "American in Paris," and Mozart's "Eine Kleine Nachtmusik." The second, third, and fourth versions of the test included a greater variety of music including jazz, electronic, Asian, blues, Indian, and African music. The first version was tested on 20 patients hospitalized with schizophrenia and 20 controls matched for age, sex, and intelligence; this study is described in the MAT Supplement. The second version of the test was administered to 20 children, from 4 to 10 years old, enrolled in schools in the New York City area. The third version was used in a study involving patients in psychoanalysis and psychoanalytic psychotherapy. The fourth version was used in two studies: one involving Asian children and adults, and another involving executive judgment.

As a result of these studies, the author concluded:

> Experience with different versions of the test revealed the desirability for systematic selection of compositions. Since emotion and affect serve as general organizers of experience and interpersonal behavior, compositions were created for the MAT that endeavored to evoke primary emotions. Construction of the compositions was guided by the available literature on the influence of tempo, key, melodic line, and essentic form, along with generally accepted conventions for expression of affect and emotion. (MAT Supplement, p. 25)

The compositions, created by Israeli composer Elan Gore, can be grouped into light lyrical compositions (interest, joy, love), descending minor compositions (desire, shame, guilt), marshal tempo compositions (excitement, anger), cacophonous compositions (distress, fear), and variable and irregular compositions (terror, disgust). Depending on the emotion the music is designed to elicit, the music may include a variety of instruments and animal sounds.

TECHNICAL. Norms are provided for response latency, total fluency, and content as defined above in "Description." The norms for response latency and fluency are reported for all 12 of the compositions. The norms for content are based on percent content across all compositions. All norms are reported according to the following age groups: 8- to 10-year-olds, 11- to 13-year-olds, 14- to 15-year-olds, 16- to 20-year-olds, and 21- to 45-year-olds. The norms are based on a study by Quinn (1999) that included 168 respondents: 56 children 8 to 10 years old, 56 children 14 to 15 years old, and 56 adults from 21 to 45 years old, with all samples evenly divided between males and females. Note that the norms reported for ages 11 to 13 and for ages 16 to 20 are based on linear extrapolation of the results for 8- to 10-year-olds, 14- to 15-year-olds, and 21- to 45-year-olds. The children were from private schools in the San Diego area and the adults were volunteers from the San Diego community. Seventy-nine percent of the participants were Caucasian. The test author states that professional musicians and those pursuing a career in music were excluded from the study.

Guttman split-half reliabilities for Response Latency ranged from .85 for one of the short forms to .93 for the extended form and .92 for the standard form. Guttman split-half reliabilities for Fluency ranged from .89 for the short forms to .92 for the standard form.

A study separate from Quinn (1999) was conducted to evaluate interrater reliabilities (defined as the average correlation among raters). Raters were seven graduate students in a course in psychological assessment. The raters coded 15 responses. The average correlation among raters was .95 to .99 for Response Latency and Fluency. The average correlation for PACE and TT varied from .92 to .98, and for ARC from .75 to .82. Interrater reliability for content ranged from .85 to .95; for types of Interaction, from .71 to .94.; for Affective Fit, Hedonoic Value, and Affect Expressed, 100%; for Conventional Reference, .81 to .92; and for Narrative Style, .81 to .83.

In the MAT manual, the test author provides an example of a response for each one of the compositions, along with the analysis and interpretation of that response. Additional examples are provided in the MAT Supplement. Also provided in the MAT Supplement is a discussion of results of studies from previous versions of the test, which provide some support for the validity and reliability of the current version.

COMMENTARY. The Music Apperception Test is a very intriguing, creative, and innovative assessment. It has the potential to assess psychological stability, personality, language skills, creativity, emotional maturity, leadership, adaptability, sociability, and response to stress. Many applications of the test, particularly those in an educational setting, have yet to be explored.

The biggest drawback of the test is that, although it has great potential, it needs validation. The current version of the test has only two studies establishing its validity and reliability—one involving 112 children from private schools in San Diego and 56 adults from the San Diego area, and the other involving seven graduate students. The norms provided involve linear extrapolation of a small amount of data. Studies involving the previous four versions of the test, beginning with the first version in 1967, provide some evidence of the validity and reliability of the test but that evidence is based on small samples and not focused on any one group.

The test is relatively quick to administer, from 8 minutes for the short versions to 25 minutes for the extended version. The guidelines provided for coding responses are clear and quite extensive, involving at least 7 continuous variables and 10 categorical variables as well as measures derived from those observed variables. It is not clear, in fact, that the test author has exhausted all the ways to analyze responses. Scoring sheets provide a very clear guide for coding each of the variables.

SUMMARY. In summary, a professional is needed to administer, score, and evaluate the test. The administrator plays a series of one-minute musical recordings and has the respondent tell a story to each of the recordings. The responses are recorded and evaluated according to response latency and fluency, music responsiveness, appropriateness of content, interactions described, tangential responses, conventionality of the response in terms of affect and emotion, and narrative style. The short versions of the test include 4 compositions and require 8 minutes to complete; the standard version includes 10 compositions and requires 20 minutes; and the extended version includes 12 compositions and requires 25 minutes. The compositions advance from light lyrical compositions that elicit emotions of joy or love to more challenging compositions that elicit terror or disgust.

The MAT provides a veritable playground for the psychological, organizational, or educational researcher. The test is a very attractive alternative to paper-and-pencil tests or other static measures of personality, creativity, emotional maturity, leadership, adaptability, sociability, and response to stress.

REVIEWER'S REFERENCE

Quinn, K. S. (1999). *Developmental responses to the Music Projective Test.* Unpublished doctoral dissertation, California School of Professional Psychology, San Diego, California.

Review of the Music Apperception Test by JEFFREY K. SMITH, Professor of Education, University of Otago, Dunedin, New Zealand:

DESCRIPTION. The Music Apperception Test (MAT) is designed to provide a basis for assisting psychologists in assessing individuals in a broad range of applications, including clinical, educational, and organizational settings, as well as in neuropsychological evaluations. The instrument is designed to provide both objective information and the basis for projective assessment. The MAT is administered in a one-to-one setting; a technician may administer the test under supervision, but interpretation of the results requires a trained psychologist.

The MAT consists of a set of 10 relatively short compositions of music to which respondents tell a story. An extended version has 12 compositions, and there are two "short form" versions of the test. The musical compositions were designed for the MAT to elicit certain types of emotional responses: interest, joy, love, desire, shame, guilt, excitement, anger, distress, and fear. In the extended version, there is also terror and disgust. Respondents are told to listen to the music and to "tell a story" about what they are hearing. They may start at any time during the composition and have up to one-half of a minute following the end of the composition before the next composition begins.

They may continue telling their story through the beginning of the subsequent composition.

The responses are analyzed in a variety of ways, producing a large number of scores grouped into categories: general performance (including Response Latency and Fluency of Response), Music Responsiveness, Content, Interaction (of characters in the stories told), Tangential Reference (comments made not directly related to the story being told), Affective Fit (including Hedonic Tone and Affect, among other measures), Narrative Style, and ratios calculated from Fluency and Length of Response. Norms are provided for several of the variables including Latency and Length of Response. Examples of responses and their scoring are provided.

DEVELOPMENT. The MAT has been in development since 1967. It was originally called the Music Projective Test. In a supplement to the MAT, the test author details the background and development of the MAT, including extensive discussions of the theoretical rationale and origins of the measure. After having originally used extant compositions for the measure, a new set of compositions was created for the MAT using fundamentals of music theory and research on psychological response to music. The relationship of the compositions to the intended emotional responses (joy, desire, terror, etc.) was tested with a small sample of graduate students. Factor analytic studies of responses further confirmed the general ability of the compositions to engender the desired emotions. As the test author points out, responses to the compositions are complex and the boundaries between the emotional responses are not clear-cut.

TECHNICAL. The MAT comes with a manual for administration and a second manual for background, theory, and interpretation. Each of these manuals contains information that addresses the technical qualities of the MAT. Details are presented on internal consistency reliabilities for measures such as Latency (time between the beginning of the playing of the composition and beginning of the story being told by the respondent), Fluency (number of words in the story told), and elaborations on these ideas. These reliabilities are acceptably high across the measures for which they exist. But they do not exist for all of the scores that the MAT yields. Norms based on a small sample of respondents are provided for Latency, Fluency, and the degree to which the content of the responses refer to humans, animals, or other content. The MAT manual for administration also contains a number of exemplars of responses, complete with scores and discussions of the scoring. The discussions often involve clinical interpretation of the response, the projective part of the MAT. These interpretations may vary from one clinician to another.

The test author does not provide a lot of information concerning the validity of the MAT in the classical sense of the term validity. In the hands of a clinician experienced in projective techniques, the MAT may well provide a highly useful tool, but there is no evidence presented to support that contention. Specifically, MAT results are not compared to other projective measures or to clinical diagnoses of individuals that have been confirmed. The user has to take on argument that responses to music provide valid indicators of important underlying psychological traits.

COMMENTARY. The MAT is an innovative approach to tapping into basic emotions and personality characteristics through the use of music. But it seems a bit of a work in progress. The current status of the MAT raises a number of questions. The basic question is: What is this instrument for and how should it be used? To flesh out these concerns, one might ask the following: What psychological traits are being measured here? What is one to make of the Latency, Fluency, and Content scores? For example, the test author argues that response latency is a universal in the psychological literature and has been shown to correlate with mental ability, alertness, and a wide variety of other variables. True enough, but when response latency is measured in these studies, it is usually under the instruction to work as quickly as possible, and the interpretation of the latency is contextualized in the theoretical constructs under consideration. It is not clear for the MAT just what the Latency score measures. Fluency presents a similar concern. Fluency is often associated with creativity. Should it be considered a measure of creativity here, and if so, what is the evidence that this is what is being measured? The same problem holds for the other objective measures of the MAT.

As a projective technique, the MAT is only as good as the clinician interpreting the responses. In this regard, this instrument is no different from other projective techniques. Thus, the clinician is part of the instrument itself. No studies are presented that address the quality of the interpretations that clinicians make. Are they difficult to make? How are they to be combined with other information? And finally, is music a good vehicle for engendering the types of responses that would be useful to the clinician, and does it generalize to personality traits beyond response to music?

As a reviewer, and as a measurement specialist who also works in the fields of aesthetics and creativity, this reviewer finds the MAT a highly promising assessment approach that needs more clarity in terms of defining the scores obtained and establishing an empirical basis for the validity arguments associated with those scores.

SUMMARY. The MAT is a projective and objective instrument assessing emotional reaction to a set of music prompts. It has been carefully and thoughtfully developed, and the supporting materials are quite detailed. The idea of using music to engender emotional response is creative, and the theoretical rationale for the use of music is well-developed in the manuals. It is argued that the MAT has a wide variety of interpretations and uses, but it is not clear from the manuals how such uses would be realized. In the hands of a dedicated professional clinician, the MAT may be a useful adjunct used in combination with other information in evaluation work. The MAT appears to be a promising tool, but needs more information on how to use it and more research concerning validity issues.

[80]

NEPSY-II—Second Edition.

Purpose: "Designed to assess neuropsychological development."
Population: Ages 3-0 to 16-11.
Publication Dates: 1998-2007.
Acronym: NEPSY-II.
Scores, 32: Attention/Executive Functioning (Animal Sorting, Auditory Attention and Response Set, Clocks, Design Fluency, Inhibition, Statue), Language (Body Part Naming and Identification, Comprehension of Instructions, Oromotor Sequences, Phonological Processing, Repetition of Nonsense Words, Speeded Naming, Word Generation), Memory and Learning (List Memory, Memory for Designs, Memory for Faces, Memory for Names, Narrative Memory, Sentence Repetition, Word List Interference), Sensorimotor (Fingertip Tapping, Imitating Hand Positions, Manual Motor Sequences, Visuomotor Precision), Social Perception (Affect Recognition, Theory of Mind), Visuospatial Processing (Arrows, Block Construction, Design Copying, Geometric Puzzles, Picture Puzzles, Route Finding).
Administration: Individual.
Forms, 2: Ages 3-4, Ages 5-16.
Price Data, 2007: $845 per complete kit including administration manual (2007, 183 pages), clinical and interpretive manual (2007, 290 pages), 2 stimulus books, 25 record forms (ages 3-4), 25 response booklets (ages 5-16), 25 response booklets (ages 3-4), 25 response booklets (ages 5-16), administration cards, scoring templates, manipulatives, and training CD; $49 per 25 record forms (ages 3-4); $59 per 25 record forms (ages 5-16); $49 per 25 response booklets (ages 3-4); $59 per 25 record forms (ages 5-16); $20 per scoring template; $50 per set of administration cards; $30 per memory grid; $105 per set of 12 blocks; $85 per administration manual; $120 per clinical and interpretive manual; $130 per stimulus book; $100 per training CD.
Time: (45-90) minutes for ages 3-4; (60-180) minutes for ages 5-16.
Comments: Also contains optional qualitative behavioral observations and supplemental scores; earlier edition entitled: NEPSY: A Developmental Neuropsychological Assessment.
Authors: Marit Korkman, Ursula Kirk, and Sally Kemp.
Publisher: Pearson.
Cross References: For reviews by Sandra D. Haynes and Daniel C. Miller of an earlier edition, see 14:256.

Review of the NEPSY-II—Second Edition by RIK CARL D'AMATO, Professor and Head of the Department of Psychology at the University of Macau, Macau SAR, China, and JONATHAN E. TITLEY, University of Macau, Macau SAR, China:

DESCRIPTION. The NEPSY-II is an individually administered assessment battery designed to assess the neuropsychological development of children and adolescents ages 3 to 16. The NEPSY-II was developed to allow for a flexible assessment of six theoretically derived functional domains (i.e., Attention and Executive Functioning, Language, Memory and Learning, Sensorimotor, Social Perception, and Visuospatial Processing). Depending on the purpose of the evaluation and referral question, subtests may be selected to provide a general overview of neuropsychological functioning, a diagnostic measure specific to the referral question, a selective assessment to determine specific information about cognitive abilities, or a comprehensive neuropsychological investigation (D'Amato & Hartlage, 2008). Scoring Assistant and Assessment Planner software is available to assist the examiner in selecting the most clinically useful subtests and scoring the subtests following administration. A useful training CD is also included that provides instructions for the administration and scoring of all subtests.

Subtests are arranged alphabetically in both the record form and administration manual and the flexible battery approach allows the examiner to determine the best order of administration. The administration rules vary by subtest and are provided on the record forms of each subtest, including materials, starting points, reversal rules, discontinue rules, stop points, and time limits. The NEPSY-II uses several different types of scores, including primary, combined, process, and contrast scores. Primary scores provide information on main abilities measured for each subtest. Combined scores are derived from two scores within a subtest and describe performance across two variables. The process scores allow for the examination of specific skills related to a task. Contrast scores assist in determining an examinee's ability on a higher level skill while controlling for performance on a lower level skill (e.g., delayed memory ability controlling for immediate memory). The subtest scores are arranged into six domains, but unlike the first version of the NEPSY, domain scores are no longer calculated or used. Instead, patterns of subtest scores within domains are interpreted. Some may argue that this change is a fatal flaw.

DEVELOPMENT. The development of the NEPSY-II combined neuropsychological theory of Luria with the most current research in neuropsychology and child development (D'Amato, Fletcher-Janzen, & Reynolds, 2005). Luria (1973) believed that behaviors such as language, learning, movement, and memory were the result of an interaction of simple and complex brain systems, and this viewpoint is reflected in the construction of the NEPSY-II. Some of the subtests assess basic subcomponents of neuropsychological domains; other subtests tap into neuropsychological functions that require contributions and interactions between the functional domain areas. Many of the subtests on the NEPSY-II were adopted from traditional, well-researched neuropsychological tasks, but have been adapted to be more child-friendly and easier to administer.

The NEPSY was originally published in Finnish in 1980 by Korkman for children ages 5 to 6 years old (Ahmad & Warriner, 2001). The first English version was published in 1998 for children ages 3 through 12. The NEPSY-II was released in the summer of 2007 and there have been many notable updates and improvements from the first English version. The four major research phases for the development of the NEPSY-II included a pilot phase, a tryout phase, a standardization phase, and a final production and evaluation.

Eleven of the subtests on the NEPSY-II have been expanded from the first version with additional items, creating improved floors and ceilings. The age range was extended through 16 years. Ten new subtests were added in order to provide better domain coverage, and a new domain (i.e., Social Perception) was introduced for the NEPSY-II. Due to limited clinical validity compared to other subtests, four subtests were dropped from the NEPSY-II, including three from the Attention and Executive Functioning domain (i.e., Knock and Tap, Tower, and Visual Attention), and one from the Sensorimotor domain (i.e., Finger Discrimination). Moreover, one must wonder if items developed for very young children are neurodevelopmentally appropriate for 16-year-old adolescents.

TECHNICAL.

Standardization. The standardization of the NEPSY-II included a stratified random sample of 1,200 children and adolescents ages 3 to 16. The sample was representative of the United States population for race/ethnicity, geographic region, and parent education level based on 2003 U.S. Census data. Six of the 26 subtests retained from the 1998 version of the NEPSY were not renormed or modified in any way (i.e., Design Fluency, Imitating Hand Positions, Manual Motor Sequences, Oromotor Sequences, Repetition of Nonsense Words, and Route Finding). These subtests measured constructs that were less likely to be affected by the Flynn effect (Flynn, 1984), which is the rise of intelligence test scores over time.

Reliability. The Clinical and Interpretive Manual for the NEPSY-II provides detailed information concerning subtest reliability estimates for all subtests at the various age levels. The test authors have included evidence of internal consistency reliability using split-half, alpha coefficients, and test-retest methods. Test-retest interval ranged from 12 to 51 days with a mean of 21 days. Approximately 80% of the reliability coefficients reported were above .70 for subtest scores. Some subtests had low reliability within a specified age range, including Design Fluency Total Score for ages 5 to 12 (.59), Word Generation Semantic Total Score for ages 3 to 4 (.59), Memory for Designs Content Score for ages 3 to 4 (.47), and Design Copying Local Score for ages 7 to 12 (.57).

A consistency of classification criteria was used for subtests that had highly skewed and limited score ranges using a test-retest method. To obtain the consistency of classification, the percentage of the standardization sample who scored at the 10th percentile or less, at the 11th to 75th percentile, and above the 75th percentile on both administrations of the same subtest was calculated. The consistency of classification scores for Oromotor Sequences (.50 to .73), Manual Motor Series (.46 to .63), and Route Finding (.58 to .75) indicate that these subtests may not be reliable for certain age groups of children and adolescents when identifying neuropsychological deficits.

Validity. The NEPSY-II Clinical and Interpretive Manual provides evidence of content, concurrent, and construct validity. The development of the NEPSY-II subtests involved multiple revisions of test content based on a review of the research literature, the test authors' clinical and research experience, expert analysis, pilot studies, and qualitative analysis of individual responses to test items. Evidence for construct validity was generally strong, but there was no evidence of a factor analysis to confirm the structure of domains. The manual does include correlations of each subtest with all other subtests by age group. Although the subtests generally correlated well within the same domain, several subtests appeared to correlate better with subtests from other domains. Subtests with low correlations within the same domain included Animal Sorting (.08 to .24 for ages 7–12), Narrative Memory (.05 to .17 for ages 7–12), and Visuomotor Precision (-.07 to -.02 for ages 7–12). The test authors account for the low correlations between subtests in the same domain by indicating that various subtests may measure different neuropsychological functions within a single domain and that a single subtest may measure functions from several domains. Corrected correlations of the NEPSY-II with the 1998 version of the NEPSY ranged from .35 on the Auditory Attention Task to .83 on Sentence Repetition. As would be expected, subtests with less revision of items had higher correlations. The relationship between NEPSY-II subtests and other measures of cognitive, neuropsychological, academic, adaptive, and behavioral functioning supported the concurrent validity for assessing children's and adolescents' neuropsychological development.

COMMENTARY. The NEPSY-II addresses a wide breadth of developmental domains and the flexible administration approach allows the test to be adjusted to the referral question. One of the greatest strengths of the NEPSY-II is the recent and comprehensive standardization of 1,200 children and adolescents that closely approximates the demographics of the U.S. population based on 2003 U.S. Census data. Despite the many strengths of the NEPSY-II, the removal of domain scores makes interpretation difficult. This significant change is problematic because domain scores are typically more psychometrically sound than individual subtests. Examiners should be careful to determine the degree and type of reliability of the specific subtests they are using to draw conclusions. This is an obvious problem given that some of the scores fall below .50. The lower reliability coefficients often appear on the low or high end of the age ranges. Given these data, one must question if some of these subtests should have been deleted from the measure. Despite this difficulty, the various scores provided (i.e., primary, combined, contrast, and process scores) may provide a tremendous amount of information regarding children's neuropsychological development when interpreted properly. Evaluation results should be interpreted in light of everyday observations by the child's parents, teachers, and other professionals, and other available psychological data, because even a normally developing child or adolescent may display below average performance on some of the NEPSY-II subtests (D'Amato et al., 2005). Special group studies reported in the NEPSY-II manual support the clinical usefulness of the NEPSY-II in distinguishing between some developmental and neuropsychological disorders. However, further independent research is needed to confirm the validity of the NEPSY-II for making diagnostic decisions. Interpretation of the NEPSY-II should be a multifaceted process, the depth of which will depend on the user's familiarity with neuropsychology and the underlying paradigm that flows from the theoretical constructs on which the NEPSY-II was based.

SUMMARY. The NEPSY-II may be used to assess neuropsychological development or functioning in the domains of Attention and Executive Functioning, Language, Memory and Learning, Sensorimotor, Social Perception, and Visuospatial Processing. Few contemporary neuropsychological batteries have been designed to meet the needs of children and adolescents. The NEPSY-II is a child-friendly, flexible, and more educationally focused measure than traditional neuropsychological instruments. This measure has many strengths, including a broad and representative standardization sample, excellent clinical utility, and a variety of different scores that can be obtained to help interpret performance. The instrument's integration of qualitative and quantitative evidence from a Lurian perspective allows an in-depth consideration of a child's or adolescent's ability to process information. The NEPSY-II appears to be an excellent instrument that will provide relevant and useful information regarding the neuropsychological functioning of children and adolescents.

REVIEWERS' REFERENCES

Ahmad, S. A., & Warriner, E. M. (2001). Review of the NEPSY: A developmental neuropsychological assessment. *The Clinical Neuropsychologist, 15*, 240-249.

D'Amato, R. C., Fletcher-Janzen, E., & Reynolds, C. R. (2005). *Handbook of school neuropsychology.* Hoboken, NJ: Wiley.

D'Amato, R. C., & Hartlage, L. C. (Eds.). (2008). *Essentials of neuropsychological assessment: Treatment planning for rehabilitation* (2nd ed.). New York: Springer.

Flynn, J. R. (1984). The mean IQ of Americans: Massive gains 1932 to 1978. *Psychological Bulletin, 95*, 29-51.

Luria, A. R. (1973). *The working brain.* Harmondsworth, UK: Basic Books.

Review of NEPSY-II—Second Edition by SCOTT A. NAPOLITANO, Psychological and Academic Success Services, P.C., Lincoln, NE:

DESCRIPTION. The NEPSY-II—Second Edition (NEPSY-II) is the first revision of the original NEPSY, which was published in 1998. The NEPSY-II is an individually administered assessment tool developed to evaluate the neuropsychological development of children from ages 3 to 16. The test's name is not an acronym, but a shortened version of the word "neuropsychology."

The NEPSY-II is a large assessment battery, consisting of multiple subtests that span six domains of neuropsychological functioning: Attention and Executive Functioning, Language, Memory and Learning, Sensorimotor Skills, Social Perception, and Visual and Visuoperceptual Processing. The NEPSY-II may be administered in its entirety to obtain a comprehensive overview of functioning across all domains. The manual also describes multiple specialized batteries that may be administered to answer specific questions without having to administer the entire test battery (e.g., attention/concentration). Additionally, the NEPSY-II has the unique feature of allowing the evaluator to design a battery of his or her own by choosing different combinations of individual subtests.

The NEPSY-II is generally well organized and the materials are well designed and user friendly. Given the large scale of the battery, it does take some practice to become proficient in administering all of the subtests. Additionally, it is essential to be familiar with all components to help in choosing the subtests that will be needed to answer the assessment questions. Although there is definitely a need to spend time learning the NEPSY-II before administering it, the materials are so well organized that the process is very efficient. Administration time is dependent upon how many subtests are actually administered, with the entire battery taking up to 3.5 hours for older children.

The NEPSY-II test scores include four major types of scores: primary scores, process scores, contrast scores, and behavioral observations. Scores are expressed as scaled scores, percentile ranks, percent performance, or cumulative percentages. The variety of test scores allows for each subtest to be broken down into different tasks, each of which yields a separate score. These scores may then be combined or contrasted to allow for further specific interpretation.

DEVELOPMENT. The original NEPSY and the NEPSY-II were inspired by A. R. Luria's work and assessment philosophy, which emphasized the role of multiple brain systems in cognitive functions. Development of the NEPSY and NEPSY-II was also influenced by the fields of developmental psychology and neuropsychology. The test authors report that the tests and scoring were designed with the goal of being able to measure the development of functions over the course of childhood.

The NEPSY-II manual identifies four major goals for the present revision: Improve domain coverage, enhance clinical utility, improve psychometric properties, and enhance usability. One of the most obvious and clinically useful changes from the NEPSY to the NEPSY-II is that the age range for many subtests has been extended up to age 16. The revision process for developing the NEPSY-II included three primary phases that included a pilot study, a tryout phase, and the final national standardization and validation phase. The revision process was guided by both empirical research reviews and clinical experience gained through pilot testing and tryout testing.

TECHNICAL. The standardization sample for the NEPSY-II consisted of 1,200 individuals ranging in age from 3 to 16. The test authors report using a stratified random sample based on U.S. Bureau of the Census data from 2003. The sample was stratified for age, race/ethnicity, geographic region, and parent education level, and this information is reported clearly in the manual. Sample sex was split 50/50 so each group consisted of half males and half females.

The NEPSY-II manual has a detailed section describing the reliability of the subtests. Given the diverse nature of the NEPSY-II subtests and the functions that they measure, the test authors utilized several different methods for calculating reliability. For many subtests, internal consistency reliability was calculated with split-half and alpha methods. In addition, test-retest reliability and decision consistency reliability were utilized for subtests that the test authors report were not appropriate for split-half and alpha methods. These situations involved subtests with a higher level of item interdependence or memory tests that require repeated trials with the exact same items. The test-retest interval ranged from 12 to 51 days, with a mean of 21 days. Overall, most subtests from the NEPSY-II demonstrated adequate to high reliability and adequate stability. The test authors provide a thoughtful discussion of why certain domains such as the memory domain produced lower reliability.

Evidence regarding the validity of the NEPSY-II subtests is thoroughly presented in the manual, and it includes a discussion of content, construct, and concurrent validity. The content validity of the NEPSY-II was established through a review of research literature, the test authors' clinical and research experience, customer feedback, and a review of pilot studies. Based on this information, the subtests were modified and new subtests developed. The test authors note that the NEPSY-II subtests, as well as items within the same subtest, often measure very different abilities. Therefore, there is often a low correlation between subtests and even between items within the same subtest. Given this situation, evidence of construct validity focused on concurrent validity with other measures of specific functions and on a group of studies utilizing special populations. Descriptions are provided for the relationship between the NEPSY-II and other widely used measures of general cognitive ability, measures of academic achievement, measures of neuropsychological functioning, and measures of behavior functioning. Overall, there is acceptable evidence of convergent and discriminant validity. In addition, a set of special group studies is presented utilizing the NEPSY-II with children with Attention Deficit Hyperactivity Disorder, specific learning disorders, language disorders, intellectual disabilities, autism spectrum disorders, neurological disorders, and other clinical groups such as hearing-impaired and emotionally disturbed children.

COMMENTARY. The NEPSY-II is a well-developed neuropsychological assessment tool that is well grounded in theory and appropriately influenced by developmental and practical considerations. There is good evidence for reliability and validity of the NEPSY-II subtests. In addition, the NEPSY-II provides something for practitioners at all levels. The ability to selectively choose to administer different combinations of subtests depending on the presenting concerns is one of the NEPSY-II's greatest strengths. The large scale nature of the NEPSY-II makes it an instrument that requires a fair amount of preparation and practice prior to being able to administer the entire battery efficiently. Therefore, test users should be prepared to spend time learning and practicing this instrument. Additionally, the interpretation of the NEPSY-II is not a simple process and requires some background in the field of neuropsychology.

SUMMARY. Overall, the NEPSY-II represents a positive contribution to the field of neuropsychological assessment of children and adolescents. This well-designed and standardized test battery will be a welcome addition for clinicians working with a wide range of child and adolescent populations.

[81]

Neuropsychiatry Unit Cognitive Assessment Tool.

Purpose: Designed to "assist in the diagnosis and management of cognitive disorders and serve as a guide to more in-depth formal neuropsychological testing."
Population: Ages 18+.
Publication Date: 2008.
Acronym: NUCOG.
Scores, 6: Attention, Memory, Executive Function, Language, Visuoconstructional Function, Total.
Administration: Individual.
Price Data, 2008: A$136.95 per kit including manual (64 pages), 10 Interview Schedule/Cognitive Profiles, and 10 Subject Completion Sheets; A$119.96 per manual.
Time: (20) minutes.
Authors: Mark Walterfang and Dennis Velakoulis.
Publisher: Australian Council for Educational Research Ltd. [Australia].

Review of the Neuropsychiatry Unit Cognitive Assessment Tool by ANTHONY T. DUGBARTEY, Psychologist, Forensic Psychiatric Services Commission, and Adjunct Associate Professor of Psychology, University of Victoria, Victoria British Columbia, Canada:

DESCRIPTION. The Neuropsychiatry Unit Cognitive Assessment Tool (NUCOG) is an individually administered cognitive screening instrument designed to discriminate between cognitively intact and impaired adult neuropsychiatric patients. It comprises 21 clusters of items grouped under five broad cognitive domains: Attention, Visuoconstructional, Memory, Executive, and Language functions. It takes healthy, well-educated individuals about 20 minutes to complete the NUCOG, but empirical studies suggest that it can take up to twice as long for dementia patients (see Walterfang, Siu, & Velakoulis, 2006). Although the NUCOG can be administered by trained clinicians, appropriate interpretation of the test data requires considerably more advanced knowledge of neuropsychiatric disorders, functional neuroanatomy, and psychometrics.

The NUCOG authors assert that the decision to use this instrument must depend entirely upon the clinical situation. But there are several conditions under which it would not be prudent to apply it, such as with nonliterate populations and individuals with moderate to severe developmental intellectual disability. The intended uses of the NUCOG include investigation of suspected cognitive and/or adaptive functional decline, assessment of baseline cognitive functioning, and monitoring of response to treatment interventions.

The test developers propose that a number of features of the NUCOG set it apart from other currently available cognitive screening tools like the Mini-Mental State Examination (MMSE; 15:166). These include the NUCOG's multidimensional format (where data are provided on separate cognitive domains) and the inclusion of an Executive Function subscale. Other putative advantages listed by the test authors include instrument portability and relative brevity in administration (Walterfang, Velakoulis, Gibbs, & Lloyd, 2003).

The NUCOG yields six composite scores. Performance on each of the five cognitive domains can be measured with a summary score (out of 20), and the summation of these five subscale scores produces an overall total NUCOG score with a maximum of 100 points. A stopwatch (not included in the test kit) is required for the administration of one item on the NUCOG. The administration and scoring chapter in the manual is well written, with clear description of illustrative criteria for scoring the examinee's responses. Provision of the specific test instructions on the Interview Schedule Form also makes it highly user friendly for the test administrator.

The Attention domain includes three clusters of items that measure orientation to time and place, forward and reverse auditory digit span, and mental control via recitation of an overlearned sequence in reverse order. These constituent items essentially render the domain a measure of orientation and brief attention span. The five clusters of items that make up the Visuoconstructional domain are quite diverse, and include design reproduction, praxis, somatosensory discrimination, and arithmetic calculation items. One would be unable to make inferences about lateralization of impairments simply by looking up the summary score on this domain: This determination can be done only by qualitative observation of the examinee's test performance and by error analysis. The Memory domain includes a three-item episodic verbal list learning and recall task, as well as items that measure visual design recall and remote (semantic) memory functions. The Executive domain incorporates semantic verbal fluency and verbal abstract conceptualization tasks, as well as Alexander Luria's serial hand sequences. The Language domain includes brief items that survey the broad areas of object naming, oral repetition and comprehension, writing, and reading skills.

DEVELOPMENT. The impetus for the development of the NUCOG arose, in part, from the test authors' dissatisfaction with the diagnostic insensitivity of such extant omnibus tests as the MMSE in clinical psychiatric populations (Walterfang et al., 2003). The NUCOG was originally developed in 2000 and validated at the Royal Melbourne Hospital, Australia. Items comprising the NUCOG were collated and adapted from other psychometric tests that the test developers had found to be clinically useful in bedside assessments at a tertiary referral neuropsychiatric service (Walterfang et al., 2006). The items had to receive full consensus of the test authors before they were included in the test, and they were also specifically chosen to be diverse enough "to minimize the amount of task overlap between items and domains" (Walterfang et al., 2003; p. 326). Although the test authors indicate that the items within each subscale progress in increasing order of difficulty, no empirical psychometric data are provided about the item difficulty levels, either in the technical manual or in a pilot study of the NUCOG's construction (Walterfang et al., 2003) to support this claim. Moreover, the NUCOG does not appear to be based on a clearly articulated theoretical model of cerebral and neurocognitive functioning. One may infer, however, that the NUCOG is heavily influenced by the process approach to neuropsychological testing.

Pilot testing of the NUCOG was conducted with 33 neuropsychiatric patients (67% of whom were hospitalized inpatients), with an average education of 10 years. The test authors interpreted the correlation between total MMSE and total NUCOG scores (.78) as evidence of the NUCOG's "strong construct validity" (Walterfang et al., 2003; p. 327). A deep methodological flaw of this pilot study, however, was that order of administration of the MMSE and NUCOG was not counterbalanced, as all participants first completed the NUCOG, followed by the MMSE the next day. As such, the likelihood of practice effects causing spuriously high MMSE scores was not appropriately controlled. The NUCOG standard errors of measurement are not provided in the pilot study, nor are recommended confidence intervals for various subscale and total scores on the NUCOG provided in the test manual.

TECHNICAL. The NUCOG was validated with a mixed clinical group of 265 neuropsychiatric patients and 82 community-dwelling healthy controls (technical manual indicates 85 controls but source article says 82). The standardization sample for the NUCOG is from Australia, with most of the participants residing in the state of Victoria. No information is provided about the ethno-cultural background of the validation sample, which was approximately evenly distributed by gender. No estimates of the intellectual ability levels of the validation sample were provided.

Cutoff scores are employed as the primary indicator of cognitive impairment, with a NUCOG Total score less than 70 considered to be "highly predictive of a dementing illness, although not all scores of less than 70 are indicative of dementia" (manual, p. 50). This suggested cut score was derived from a receiver operating characteristics (ROC) analysis with 65 patients with and 277 patients without a diagnosis of dementia. The test authors also reported on an empirical study that showed 80% of 122 healthy individuals achieved a total score above 90 on the NUCOG. Another method of interpreting NUCOG scores is by way of subscale pattern analysis using an ipsative approach. Here, visual inspection of the graph plot of the patient's NUCOG subscale scores is used to determine areas of relative cognitive strengths and weaknesses.

Normative data are provided separately by age group (18–40, 40–60, 60–70, and 70+ years) for the NUCOG Total scores, but not for the five separate NUCOG subscales. This lack of age-related normative data of the NUCOG subscales is a major drawback, particularly in light of the test authors' claim of subscale multidimensionality being an advantage of the NUCOG over the MMSE. Because IQ scores were not obtained from the standardization group, it is difficult to tell whether the norms can safely be applied for individuals with IQs in the above average or below average range.

Reliability. Internal consistency reliability, estimated with Cronbach's alpha analysis, yielded a reliability coefficient of .92. Although the test authors correctly interpret this index as indicating strong internal consistency, experts have cautioned against uncritically accepting very high values of alpha, which may reflect nothing more than a high level of item redundancy on the test instrument (Streiner & Norman, 2008). Interrater reliability, derived from the independent ratings of two trained "blind" raters with 10 examinees, yielded a coefficient of .91. The authors did not specify, however, whether these 10 examinees were healthy participants or clinical patients.

Validity. Differences in NUCOG Total scores for the normal controls versus the psychiatric, neurologic, and dementia clinical groups were used to establish the NUCOG's construct validity. As well, the correlation (.69) between the NUCOG Total scores and MMSE scores was used as evidence of the NUCOG's construct validity.

Criterion-oriented validity was appraised by the use of ROC curve analysis to demonstrate that with a NUCOG Total score cutoff at .80, sensitivity and specificity were .84 and .86, respectively, for a diagnosis of dementia. It would have been helpful for the test authors to present ROC data with different clinical populations (such as schizophrenia, depression, and mild cognitive impairment), and include confidence intervals. Evidence from the NUCOG validation study (Walterfang et al., 2006) culminated in the test authors' recommendation that earning a total NUCOG score "greater than 80, but with scores of 16 or less on two or more domains is suggestive of cognitive impairment" (p. 1001). Comparisons between the NUCOG and selected neuropsychological tests were used to establish concurrent validity of the NUCOG, the results of which showed rather modest correlations.

COMMENTARY. The NUCOG is a cognitive screening instrument that is fairly quick and relatively easy to administer. It shows considerable promise for use by busy clinicians who are interested in a brief cognitive screener but are dissatisfied with the MMSE. Unfortunately, reliability and validity data are incomplete. Future validity studies should include larger clinical samples across more specific diagnostic groupings (and not simply "psychiatric," "neurologic," and "dementia"). No mention, for example, is made about the sample composition for the construct validity study that would help the reader determine severity of dementia diagnosis, or even whether the dementia patients were of a primary cortical or subcortical presentation. Also, although the NUCOG developers contend that one of the test's main functions is to help monitor response to treatment, they concede in their main validation study that "we cannot comment on its [in reference to the NUCOG] capacity to detect change" (Walterfang et al., 2006; p. 1001). In fact, change data are reported in the NUCOG manual on only one patient with Alzheimer's dementia. The lack of an information processing domain is a major limitation of the NUCOG, particularly given the clinical utility of processing speed in cognitive assessments. There is more to attention than the NUCOG Attention domain actually measures. With its longest string being seven digits, the Digit Span subtest has a very low ceiling. Working memory is incompletely defined by the test authors, who conceptualize it as a "system of memory responsible for the immediate recall of small amounts of verbal or spatial material" (manual, p. 21). This, of course, is at odds with contemporary definitions of working memory that have both replaced the older concept of short-term memory, and emphasize a more dominant role of the central executive (Baddeley, 1986; 1992). The test authors did not include items that measure prospective memory in this brief screener. The lack of a cued recall adjuvant to the delayed spatial recall test on the NUCOG would make it difficult to determine whether visual memory difficulties are due to a primary retrieval or recall defect. This distinction is especially important in cognitive assessments of memory function. The NUCOG praxis item does not include a test of ideational apraxia. There appears to be some heterogeneity in the items that make up the Visuoconstructional subscale, which includes verbally mediated mental arithmetic calculation tasks. Moreover, the reverse digit span items could arguably be more appropriately placed under the Executive Function domain. No description is provided about the clinical diagnoses of the 22 patients who underwent the neuropsychological tests against which the NUCOG was validated. Moreover, the 22 patients did not all receive the same battery of neuropsychological tests.

SUMMARY. The authors of this instrument have produced a brief cognitive screening measure that, in some respects, appears to be an improvement over the MMSE. It yields separate scores by cognitive domain and also includes an Executive Function subscale. Although the NUCOG is fairly easy to administer and score, its psychometric soundness has yet to be demonstrated. The presentation of inadequate psychometric information about the test (e.g., item analysis, reliability, validity) in the manual, as well as the apparent heterogeneity of items subsumed under some of the subscales, make it difficult to understand exactly what constructs the test assesses. The absence of separate age-related norms for the various cognitive domains severely limits the clinical applicability of the NUCOG. The NUCOG manual is incomplete, and does not include pertinent information about the instrument's pilot and validation studies that are more fully described in other publications (i.e., Walterfang et al., 2003, and Walterfang et al., 2006), but should have been included in the test manual. Although its shortcomings preclude routine clinical use, the NUCOG may be useful to thoroughly trained neuropsychologists or neuropsychiatrists as a method for generating hypotheses about cognitive functioning.

REVIEWER'S REFERENCES

Baddeley, A. D. (1986). *Working memory*. Oxford, England: Clarendon.

Baddeley, A. (1992). Working memory. *Science, 255*, 556-559.

Streiner, D. L., & Norman, G. R. (2008). *Health measurement scales: A practical guide to their development and use* (4th ed). New York: Oxford University Press.

Walterfang, M., Siu, R., & Velakoulis, D. (2006). The NUCOG: Validity and reliability of a brief cognitive screening tool in neuropsychiatric patients. *Australian and New Zealand Journal of Psychiatry, 40*, 995-1002.

Walterfang, M., Velakoulis, D., Gibbs, A., & Lloyd, J. (2003). The NUCOG: Construction and piloting of a cognitive screening instrument in a neuropsychiatric unit. *Australasian Psychiatry, 11*, 325-329.

[82]

Otis-Lennon School Ability Test®, Eighth Edition.

Purpose: "Designed to measure those verbal, quantitative, and figural reasoning skills that are most closely related to scholastic achievement."
Population: Ages 4-6 to 18-2.
Publication Dates: 1977-2003.
Acronym: OLSAT® 8.
Scores, 3: Verbal, Nonverbal, Total.
Administration: Group.
Levels, 7: A, B, C, D, E, F, G.
Forms: 5.
Restricted Distribution: OLSAT 8 is sold only to accredited schools and school districts.
Price Data, 2009: $7.90 per directions for administering for the practice test (Form 5, Levels A-F); $9.70 per 10 practice test packs (Form 5, Levels A-F); $19.70 per directions for administering (Form 5, Levels A, B, C, and D and E/F/G combined); $54.60 per 10 machine-scorable test packs (Form 5, Levels A-D); $45.35 per 10 reusable test packs (Form 5, Levels E-G); $43.85 per 30 machine-scorable answer documents (Form 5, Levels E/F/G combined); $8.50 per class records (Form 5, Levels A-D and E/F combined); $26.25 per response keys for hand scoring (Form 5, Levels A-G); $68.25 per norms book (specify spring [2003, 94 pages] or fall [2003, 94 pages]); $50.40 per technical manual (2003, 65 pages).
Time: (77) minutes over 2 sessions for Levels A-B; (72) minutes over 2 sessions for Level C; 50 (60) minutes over 1 session for Level D; 40 (60) minutes over 1 session for Levels E-G.
Comments: Administered orally at Levels A-B; Level C is partially self-administered; Levels D-G are self-administered; originally titled Otis-Lennon Mental Ability Test.
Author: Pearson.
Publisher: Pearson.
Cross References: For reviews by Lizanne DeStefano and Bert A. Goldman of the Seventh Edition, see 14:271; see also T5:1866 (45 references) and T4:1913 (8 references); for reviews by Anne Anastasi and Mark E. Swerdlik of an earlier edition, see 11:274 (48 references); for reviews by Calvin O. Dyer and Thomas Oakland of an earlier edition, see 9:913 (7 references); see also T3:1754 (64 references), 8:198 (35 references), and T2:424 (10 references); for a review by John E. Milholland and excerpted reviews by Arden Grotelueschen and Arthur E. Smith of an earlier edition, see 7:370 (6 references).

Review of the Otis-Lennon School Ability Test®, Eighth Edition by CLEBORNE D. MADDUX, Foundation Professor of Counseling and Educational Psychology, University of Nevada, Reno, Reno, NV:

DESCRIPTION. The Eighth Edition of the Otis-Lennon School Ability Test (OLSAT 8) is the most recent version of a series of instruments, the first of which was published in 1918. The purpose of the test is "to measure those verbal, quantitative, and figural reasoning skills that are most closely related to scholastic achievement" (technical manual, p. 5). The test is designed to measure the thinking and reasoning abilities that are most important in school achievement. The manual states that the title of the test includes the words "school ability" to emphasize the school-related nature of the abilities that are assessed and to avoid overinterpretation of what is measured. Prior to the Sixth Edition, the title of the test made use of the words "mental," or, originally, "intelligence." The technical manual states that "OLSAT 8 is based upon the same theory of the nature and organization of cognitive ability and seeks to serve the same purposes as earlier editions in the Otis series" (p. 5).

The technical manual notes that the theory upon which the instrument is based posits general intelligence as consisting of two factors: (a) verbal-educational abilities and (b) practical-mechanical abilities. It goes on to state that OLSAT 8 is intended to measure only some of the abilities in the verbal-educational group, and that all of these are learned or developed abilities in "the abstract manipulation of verbal, numerical, and figural symbol systems" (technical manual, p. 6).

The test is in multiple-choice format and yields a variety of Verbal, Nonverbal, and Total scores and requires from 60 to 77 minutes to administer in either one or two sessions, depending on test takers' age. All three scores can each be converted to scaled scores (no information on mean and *SD*), School Ability Indexes (SAI; mean of 100, *SD* of 16), percentile ranks by age, stanines by age, percentile ranks by grade, stanines by grade, and normal curve equivalents by grade.

The OLSAT 8 consists of seven levels (A through G) for use with students from kindergarten through Grade 12. The first four levels (A through D) are for use with children in kindergarten through Grade 3. The manual states that each of these grades requires a separate level because of the rapid rate of intellectual growth in young children. There is one level (E) for children in Grades 4 and 5, one level (F) for Grades 6, 7, and 8, and one level (G) for all four high school grades. The test is completely dictated to students at Levels A and B. The first two parts of Level C are self-administered, and the rest is dictated. The entire test is self-administered at Levels D through G.

Like the OLSAT 7, the OLSAT 8 makes use of 21 multiple-choice item types designed to tap five content clusters, two in the Verbal area and three in the Nonverbal area. The content clusters and item types are (a) Verbal Comprehension, measured by Following Directions, Antonyms, Sentence Completion, and Sentence Arrangement item types; (b) Verbal Reasoning, measured by Aural Reasoning, Arithmetic Reasoning, Logical Selection, Word/Letter Matrix, Verbal Analogies, Verbal Classification, and Inference item types; (c) Pictorial Reasoning, measured by Picture Classification, Picture Analogies, and Picture Series item types; (d) Figural Reasoning, measured by Figural Classification, Figural Analogies, Pattern Matrix, and Figural Series item types; and (e) Quantitative Reasoning, measured by Number Series, Numeric Inference, and Number Matrix item types. All of these item types are not found in any one level. For example, Levels A through C (for the youngest children) contain no items from the Quantitative Reasoning content cluster, whereas Levels D through G (for the older children) contain no items from the Pictorial Reasoning content cluster.

Levels A, B, and C of the test are each divided into three parts. Part I includes the Figural and Picture Classifications items, Part II includes the Figural and Picture Analogy items, and Part III includes the other test items that make up these levels: Aural Reasoning, Arithmetic Reasoning, Following Directions, Pattern Matrix, and Picture and Figure Series. The technical manual states that there are two reasons for this arrangement: (a) All items with dictated stems are in Part III, and (b) all items involving a particular task are together. Within each of these three parts, difficulty scores are used to spiral the items with harder items placed next to easier ones in order to prevent children from sensing that the items are increasing in difficulty. Levels E, F, and G make use of an arrangement in which item type and difficulty is rotated, rather than being arranged by item type only. Level D has one section with figural and verbal items spiraled by difficulty, followed by the rotated arrangement of Levels E, F, and G for the balance of the test.

The test can be hand scored or machine scored, and the directions for administration and scoring are clear and easy to understand and follow, although directions and response keys for each level are found in separate, color-coded booklets. Optional practice tests are available for all levels. What is needed is a variety of sample results with a discussion of each. In fact, the various manuals and technical reports contain no examples or discussions of sample test results and no samples of either computer-generated or hand-generated protocols.

DEVELOPMENT. The OLSAT 8 contains items from both OLSAT 6 and 7 plus newly developed items. No information is provided as to which items came from older editions and which are new. To arrive at OLSAT 8 items, an Item Tryout Program was conducted with 40,000 students from across the country in September and October of 2001. All potential items from the OLSAT 6 and all proposed new items were included in this selection process. Stratified random sampling was used to select school districts using geographic region, SES, urbanicity, and ethnicity as the stratifying variables. Items were reviewed for bias by an advisory panel. Final selection of items was made if they survived the bias review panel and "only if they met certain statistical criteria including appropriate difficulty for the recommended grade levels, biserial correlation coefficients within a range of .30–.70 insofar as possible, and a suitable spread of the examinees across distractors" (technical manual, p. 15). All items were subjected to Mantel-Haenszel procedures to examine differential item functioning by gender, ethnicity, and regular versus special populations. The technical manual states that biased items were eliminated unless it was necessary to retain them to maintain test specifications, and that in such cases, efforts were made to include an equal number of items biased in favor of the contrasting group.

These items seem to show extensive efforts in item selection for OLSAT 8. However, the manual should include details about the number of new versus older items selected as well as more complete details about the functioning of the bias panel. Names and professional affiliations are listed, but there is, for example, no information about their recommendations and which of these were implemented. Nevertheless, the test makers are to be commended for their efforts in minimizing bias.

The technical information that accompanies the test does not adequately discuss the reason for undertaking a new edition, and does not do a good job of describing specific uses for the test and how the results differ from those obtained from widely used intelligence tests.

TECHNICAL.

Standardization. Normative data are presented in two separate booklets entitled "Fall Multilevel Norms" and "Spring Multilevel Norms." Standardization took place in the Spring and Fall of 2002. Sample sizes were very large. There were 275,500 students from 725 school districts for the Spring standardization and another 20,000 from 340 school districts in a study equating levels and another equating OLSAT 8 to OLSAT 7. Fall standardization and the two equating programs involved 135,000 in the standardization and another 15,000 in the equating programs. The standardization was conducted concurrently with that for the Stanford Achievement Test Series, Tenth Edition. School districts were picked by stratified random sampling by state geographic region with SES, urbanicity, and ethnicity as stratification variables. Urbanicity was defined by three categories and SES by five categories. Districts were invited to participate and 20% of the Spring and 30% of the Fall invitations were accepted. An appendix in the technical manual lists all participating school districts. The technical manual states that a weighting procedure was employed to attain a better representation to national characteristics of those variables that have the highest relationship to test performance, but details of the procedure are not presented.

The equating of levels program involved students in Grades K, 1, 2, 3, 5, 7, and 10 who were administered both of two adjacent levels of the OLSAT 8 in counterbalanced order. The equating of the OLSAT 7 and the OLSAT 8 program involved administering both versions to students with the order of administration counterbalanced. The number of students in the equating of levels studies was 7,800, but this number is not consistent with much larger numbers presented earlier in the technical manual regarding students participating in the Spring and Fall Standardization and equating programs.

Reliability. Grade-based and age-based Kuder-Richardson Formula 20 coefficients are presented for Total, Verbal, and Nonverbal scores for the Spring standardization sample. These Reliability coefficients are good, as all are in the .80s or .90s. Kuder-Richardson Formula 21 coefficients are presented for Total, Verbal, Nonverbal, and Cluster (subtest) scores. The Cluster coefficients are predictably lower than the more global scores, but are also adequate. Standard errors of measurement for the SAI scores (mean of 100, *SD* of 16) are presented for each level for Total, Verbal, and Nonverbal scores. All range between 5.5 and 5.8 points.

The test has adequate internal reliability and precision. No information was found on test-retest reliability.

Validity. Face and construct validity was addressed by having all items in the final form reviewed and edited by editorial staff, measurement specialists, and psychologists, although no specific information is presented about this procedure beyond the statement that the review took place. A number of correlational studies are presented as evidence of content, criterion-related, and construct validity. Correlations between OLSAT 7 and 8 are presented for Total, Verbal, and Nonverbal scores for each of the seven levels. The Total score correlations for Levels A through G are .85, .83, .79, .84, .83, .85, and .74, respectively. Correlations for Verbal scores range from .64 (Level G) to .80 (Level D), and correlations for Nonverbal scores range from .71 (Levels C and G) to .80 (Levels A and F). Although these are definitely significant, correlations for Total scores that represent only 55% to 72% shared variance seem low for two versions of a test, each based on the same theory and constructed with similar methods. The technical manual does not discuss the magnitude of these correlations except to maintain that they demonstrate the two versions have a "solid relationship" (technical manual, p. 37).

Criterion-related validity is addressed through correlations between scores on the OLSAT 8 and scores on the Stanford Achievement Test Series. These were calculated for Forms A and D for Total, Verbal, and Nonverbal scores with Total Reading and Total Mathematics scores on the Stanford Achievement Test Series. These correlations demonstrate that these scores are indeed related with most in the mid .50s to lower .70s. This is to be expected, because school ability should certainly be different from, but related to, school achievement. Studies with other indicators of school success should be undertaken. The manual does present a table of mean difficulty values for each level of the OLSAT 8 for each grade in the Spring of the year. These numbers show that the OLSAT 8 tasks are progressively easier for students in higher grades. This constitutes some indirect evidence that the tasks measure school abilities.

Construct validity is addressed by item reviews undertaken by various specialists and by presenting correlations between all pairs of adjacent levels of the OLSAT 8 for Total, Verbal, and Nonverbal scores. These are substantial with correlations for Total scores ranging from .77 to .87, correlations for Verbal scores ranging from .71 to .80, and correlations for Nonverbal scores ranging from .71 to .80. The technical manual also lists correlations between Verbal scores and Nonverbal scores at each OLSAT 8 level and school grade. All are in the .70s with the exception of Level C, Grade 2, which is .68, and Level F, Grade 7, which is .80. There is an overall trend of increasing relationship as students get older. No information about predictive validity is provided.

COMMENTARY. The OLSAT 8 is a multiple-choice test of school abilities appropriate for children in Kindergarten through Grade 12. Normative efforts were extensive, made use of a very large standardization sample, and included intensive procedures to minimize bias. A wide variety of different scores can be generated by reference to clear and easy-to-use tables in Spring and Fall normative booklets.

Directions for administration and scoring are clear and easy to follow, but there are several separate administration manuals, two separate books of norms, a technical manual, and separate response keys. This makes for an unwieldy collection of brief, separate booklets. Technical information, norms, directions for administration, and response keys should be combined into one or two volumes. More importantly, the technical information provided lacks a comprehensive description of the purpose of the test and presentation and discussion of a variety of sample results. The test is based on an early conception of intelligence that posits a general intelligence factor made up of more specific factors, a view no longer shared by all experts. The technical information should deal with this problem and does not do so. In fact, the manual is deficient with regard to detailed discussions of the purpose of the test and does not include a discussion of what the test can tell us that cannot be determined through use of more widely used intelligence tests.

SUMMARY. The OLSAT 8 is a well-standardized, multiple-choice test of school ability for school-age children from kindergarten through 12th grade. It has undergone rigorous screening and editing to eliminate bias. However, it is based on an early conception of intelligence, a fact that is not sufficiently discussed in the manual. Internal reliability of the test is adequate, but there are no data on test-retest reliability. Validity evidence needs to be strengthened. Factor analytic studies are especially needed to confirm the claimed factors. Technical information needs to be expanded and the various technical details now found in a variety of booklets should be combined into one or two volumes. However, the test takes only about 1 hour to administer and is quick and easy to score. Therefore, the OLSAT 8 may be useful as a quick screening instrument to locate those who might profit from more extensive testing. This conclusion is the same one espoused by one of the reviewers of the earlier OLSAT 7 (DeStefano, 2001).

REVIEWER'S REFERENCE

DeStefano, L. (2001). [Review of the Otis-Lennon School Ability Test, Seventh Edition]. In B. S. Plake & J. C. Impara (Eds.), *The fourteenth mental measurements yearbook* (pp. 875–879). Lincoln, NE: Buros Institute of Mental Measurements.

Review of Otis-Lennon School Ability Test®, Eighth Edition by DAVID MORSE, Professor, Counseling and Educational Psychology, Mississippi State University, Mississippi State, MS:

DESCRIPTION. The Otis-Lennon School Ability Test®, Eighth Edition (OLSAT® 8) is a group-administered test available in seven levels, covering Grades K–12. The levels include A—D (Grades K–3, respectively), E (Grades 4–5), F (Grades 6–8), and G (Grades 9–12). The OLSAT 8 measures "those verbal, quantitative, and figural reasoning skills that are most closely related to scholastic achievement" (technical manual, p. 5). Based on Vernon's (1961) hierarchical model of human abilities, in which major factors clustered under a Spearman-type "g," or general, ability have more focused minor and specific factors, the OLSAT 8 covers aspects of the group factor "v:ed," verbal-educational abilities. The purposes for which the OLSAT 8 is said most useful include: (a) measuring students' ability to handle school learning tasks, (b) assisting educators in making pupil placement decisions, and (c) measuring talents so that judgments of achievement versus ability may be made (technical manual, p. 5). The OLSAT 8 contains Verbal and Nonverbal tasks; the distinction depends on "whether knowledge of language is requisite to answering the items" (Directions for Administering, p. 6).

Major content clusters of the Verbal tasks are Verbal Comprehension and Verbal Reasoning. Nonverbal content clusters are Pictorial Reasoning, Figural Reasoning, and Quantitative Reasoning. Each cluster is subdivided into 3–7 specific item types or tasks, which may then have from 1–12 individual items in the test level. Different content clusters and item types appear in OLSAT 8 levels, though each contains equal numbers of Verbal and Nonverbal items (60 total for Levels A–C, 64 for D, 72 for Levels E—G).

Items are multiple-choice format with either four or five options. Item layout on test booklet pages is consistent and easy to follow. One ink color, with occasional shading, is used for items. Each level includes some practice items. There is a practice test available for each test level except Level G. The practice test should be given 1 week prior to taking the OLSAT 8.

The administration of the OLSAT 8 requires no special training, though a proctor for every 25 students is recommended. Administration directions are straightforward and should present no difficulty for school faculty or staff. For Levels A and B, the test is dictated by the administrator, who must pace the students from item to item. Level C is partly dictated and partly timed with students working on their own. Levels D—G are timed; students work on their own after hearing directions. Levels A—C have a recommended testing schedule of 2 days, with administration times of 32–37 minutes (Day 1) and 40 minutes (Day 2). Levels D–G require approximately 40 minutes of test time and about 60 minutes for administration time. Levels A–D use consumable test booklets; Levels E–G use separate answer sheets. Tests may be scored locally, with the aid of the response key and appropriate norms booklet, or sent to the publisher for off-site scoring and reporting.

Norms are given for Total, Verbal, and Nonverbal scores. Age-based normative scores include percentile ranks, school ability indexes (SAIs), and stanines. SAIs use an IQ-type scale (mean = 100, standard deviation = 16). Grade-based normative scores include percentile ranks, stanines, normal curve equivalents (NCEs), and three "cluster performance categories" that broadly group students into the lowest (1–3), middle (4–6), or highest (7–9) stanines. Fall and Spring norms are available.

DEVELOPMENT. The OLSAT 8 is the newest version (2003 copyright) of an ability series initiated by Arthur Otis, first published in 1918. The OLSAT has apparently changed little since the Sixth Edition. The OLSAT 8 incorporates a mixture of items from the Sixth and Seventh Editions, as well as items developed for the new edition. The format and structure (clusters and item types) of the test have been consistent going back through at least the Fifth Edition (Anastasi, 1992). National item tryouts were conducted in Fall 2001 prior to the final standardization in April-May and September-November 2002. Items taken from the Sixth Edition were included in the item tryout process; those from the Seventh were not. Item sensitivity reviews were conducted by panel members who inspected items for concerns based on gender, race/ethnicity, geographic region, socioeconomic status, and disability. Statistical comparisons for differences from the item tryouts across selected groups, matched by test scores, were also conducted using the Mantel-Haenszel procedure. The extent to which this process resulted in items being modified or culled is not explained.

Materials available from the publisher include Fall multilevel norms, Spring multilevel norms, a technical manual, practice tests, response keys, test booklets, answer sheets (for Levels E–G), and directions for administration.

TECHNICAL. Standardization for the OLSAT 8 was conducted in conjunction with the Stanford 10 achievement battery. Overall, the Spring 2002 standardization sample mirrors the 2000 U.S. Census figures closely for geographic region, socioeconomic status, urbanicity, disability status, ethnicity, and inclusion of nonpublic schools. The largest discrepancies were an underrepresentation of urban students and an overrepresentation of rural students. Weighting procedures were applied to adjust for such differences. The Spring standardization involved approximately 275,000 students and the Fall standardization about 135,000. OLSAT 7 and OLSAT 8 scores were equated; about 6,400 students took both. For vertical equating of the OLSAT, about 7,800 students took their target level of the OLSAT 8 and the level below that. These last two samples included Grades K, 1, 2, 3, 5, 7, and 10. It is not clear how kindergarten students participated in the vertical equating, as no lower form is available. Age norms are provided in 3-month intervals for ages 6–18. Overall, the standardization process appears to have been done well.

The technical manual offers a limited, traditional presentation of classical information at the total, subtest and, in some cases, the content cluster levels. Item-level information includes median point-biserial correlations (item-subtest) and mean item *p*-values; both are given by test level only for the Spring standardization sample. Estimates of score reliability are reported only from the spring standardization sample. We do not know whether score reliability might be different, especially for

Levels A–C, in the Fall. Internal consistency reliability estimates for Total, Verbal, and Nonverbal scores are given by grade and by age using the Kuder-Richardson Formula 20. Kuder-Richardson Formula 21 (KR-21) estimates are given for grade-based results down to the content cluster level (e.g., Verbal comprehension) as well. The KR-21 estimates were unexpected, as these assume equal difficulty for all items in a (sub)test–an inappropriate assumption for the OLSAT 8. Standard errors of measurement (*SEM*s) are available only in classical theory form, and represent overall values only, not conditional values which vary by score. The technical manual incorrectly describes the precision of total SAI scores as having an *SEM* of approximately 5 points (p. 35); reported values (p. 36) round to 6 points for all levels and ages. Estimates of score stability (test-retest reliability) are not furnished. Key decision points associated with evaluating items via the Rasch model (e.g., which measures of model-item fit were used, what threshold for a mean square fit index was used to cull items) are not discussed.

Reliability estimates for total scores are adequate for making judgments about individual examinees, according to guidelines like Cronbach's (1990). These values tend to be in the low .90s. Estimates of Verbal and Nonverbal subtest score reliability are typically in the low to mid .80s, and are consistent with what one would predict due to having half as many items as the total test. KR-21 estimates for cluster scores were often far too low, in the .50s–.60s, to warrant consideration for making judgments about individuals. Estimates of reliability appear high enough to make judgments about groups of examinees.

Validity evidence is somewhat sparse. Authors of the technical manual show evidence of having consulted the 1999 *Standards* (AERA, APA, NCME, 1999), but evidence of relationships to external variables (whether convergent or discriminant) involves only OLSAT 7, correlations among subtests on OLSAT 8, and correlations with Stanford 10 subtests. Correlations of total OLSAT 8 and OLSAT 7 scores vary from .74 (Level G) to .85 (Levels A, F). These are taken by the test authors as partial evidence for test content validity. It is not obvious how these results affirm that test content corresponds to the intended construct, unless one assumes that the OLSAT 7 was a valid measure. The OLSAT 8 is somewhat easier than the OLSAT 7 for lower grades (Levels A and B, mean raw score difference of about 5 points), and more difficult than OLSAT 7 for higher grades (Levels D–F and G show mean raw score differences of about 3 and 11 points, respectively). Implications of this finding are not discussed.

Validity evidence for internal test structure includes correlations of raw scores across adjacent test levels, correlations of Verbal and Nonverbal scores, and median item point-biserial values. Given the purported hierarchical structure of the OLSAT 8, confirmatory analyses of the factor structure of the instrument would offer useful and more compelling evidence. Correlations of spring total OLSAT 8 scores with Stanford 10 subtest scores generally range from the .50s–.70s, with the majority of values in the .60s or below. The technical manual rightly points out that this shows overlap, but that the OLSAT 8 is distinct from the Stanford Achievement Test in what it measures. Because these measures were jointly normed, the correlations may be somewhat higher than what users will see if OLSAT 8 is given in the Fall of the school year and an achievement battery in the Spring.

For the three expressed purposes of the OLSAT 8–measure ability to learn, facilitate pupil placement, and to judge achievement versus ability–additional validity information would be helpful.

COMMENTARY. As lengthy a pedigree the OLSAT 8 has, there are some serious concerns and limitations that potential users should know. Most of these points have been noted by previous reviewers (see MMY 9:913, 11:274, 14:271). These include test use, validity, reliability, and utility.

What is appropriate use of OLSAT 8 scores? That is a question that is yet to be satisfactorily answered by the documentation that accompanies the test. Because the test is said to "measure those verbal, quantitative, and figural reasoning skills that are most closely related to scholastic achievement" (technical manual, p. 5), educators and even parents may be tempted to apply the scores in ways that are unwarranted. For example, should OLSAT 8 scores be used in deciding which students are ready for an algebra course in the eighth grade? Should a kindergarten student be retained based on OLSAT 8 scores? It would be helpful to have specific examples of decisions or judgments for which the OLSAT 8 scores would and would not be appropriate. Can the OLSAT 8 be used with students for whom English is not their primary language? Though the Nonverbal portion of the

OLSAT is said not to require language mastery to answer questions, it requires sufficient receptive vocabulary to comprehend the directions. Can it be used with students having visual impairments? What sorts of testing accommodations can be made that do not change the meaning or usefulness of the scores? As it stands, it is up to the user to figure out the answer to the question of appropriate use.

Additional validity evidence should be made available. The test authors assert that correlations of OLSAT 8 and OLSAT 7 scores help make the case for test content validity. Because the OLSAT 8 borrows some unknown but likely substantive fraction of items from the OLSAT 7 (and 6), the fact that the scores correlate may reflect more this degree of item overlap across editions than anything else. Evidence of independent affirmation that items do indeed measure the purported Vernon-type factors is not presented. Confirmatory factor analysis would be a logical procedure to help make the case that the OLSAT 8 measures higher order factors of school-related ability. Data to show OLSAT 8 scores are indeed related to school attainment (beyond concomitant scores on the Stanford 10) would be helpful, as would other discriminant validity information. Is the OLSAT 8 a speeded test to any degree? The upper levels (part of D, and E–G) have fixed time limits for items and administration directions that imply possible speededness. No data are presented to show that students routinely attempt most items within the allotted time. The use of SAI scores invites potential misunderstandings due to their resemblance to IQ-type scores; the test authors used to call them deviation IQ scores and refer to this in the current documentation, while correctly asserting that these are not IQ scores.

Additional reliability information would be helpful. Score stability data would assist potential users. Conditional standard errors of measurement should be furnished. Aside from stanine scores, users are not encouraged strongly enough to take into account the potential imprecision of obtained scores as an indicator of a student's true level of ability. Reliability information is presented only from the Spring standardization sample; Fall administration data should be similarly documented.

Utility must also be considered. At a time when school personnel feel burdened by mandatory achievement testing in order to satisfy local, state, and federal requirements, what is the payoff of adding another type of test to the mixture, thereby usurping even more instructional time? If grades, achievement scores, and teacher recommendations are available, should an ability test be used in preference (or in addition) to these other sources when making decisions about students? Past grades generally do a better job of predicting future grades than do test scores. Past achievement test scores typically correlate as well or better with future achievement test scores than do ability test scores. The unique role that an ability measure can play must be judged sufficiently important to justify the additional testing time and costs involved. Second, instances of identifying students for exceptionalities or handicapping conditions may more often call for individually administered measures given by qualified examiners. Third, for middle school and beyond, placement issues tend to hinge more on course sequences and prior course performance than on ability test scores. Fourth, converting scores to age norms locally requires users to complete three separate conversions after having scored the test: (a) raw to scaled scores, (b) scaled to SAI scores then, (c) SAIs to age-based percentile ranks or stanines. That is a lot of effort, and assures that many may prefer to pay to have the tests scored by the publisher.

SUMMARY. The OLSAT 8 is easily administered, may be scored locally or sent to the publisher, can be used for small or large groups of examinees (with sufficient proctors), includes practice items, and practice tests may be purchased as well. Past users of the OLSAT series will find the updated version to be a familiar package. Vertical equating allows for a common score scale across all levels of the test, though the scaled scores generally take a back seat to the SAIs, percentile ranks and stanines. National norms are relatively recent and based on substantial samples; Fall and Spring norms are available. Those considering adoption of the OLSAT 8 are cautioned to consider whether the utility of the test offsets the concerns raised here and by reviewers of earlier editions.

REVIEWER'S REFERENCES

American Educational Research Association, American Psychological Association, & National Council on Measurement in Education. (1999). *Standards for educational and psychological testing*. Washington, DC: American Educational Research Association.

Anastasi, A. (1992). [Review of the Otis-Lennon School Ability Test, Sixth Edition.] In J. J. Kramer & J. C. Conoley (Eds.), *The eleventh mental measurements yearbook* (pp. 633-635). Lincoln, NE: Buros Institute of Mental Measurements.

Cronbach, L. J. (1990). *Essentials of psychological testing* (5th ed.). New York: Harper Collins Publishing.

Vernon, P. E. (1961). *The structure of human abilities* (2nd ed.). London: Methuen & Co. Ltd.

[83]

Overall Assessment of the Speaker's Experience of Stuttering.

Purpose: Designed to "provide clinicians with a measure of the overall impact of stuttering on a person's life."
Population: Individuals 18 and over who stutter.
Publication Date: 2008.
Acronym: OASES.
Scores, 4: General Information, Your Reaction to Stuttering, Communication in Daily Situations, Quality of Life.
Administration: Individual or group.
Price Data, 2008: $70 per starting kit including technical manual (41 pages) and 25 record forms; $25 per 25 record forms; $65 per Q local scoring and reporting software starter kit including technical manual, 3 record forms, and 3 Q local administrations; $25 per local scoring record forms; $8 per profile report; $72.50 per mail-in scoring service starter kit including technical manual, 3 record forms, and 3 interpretive reports; $12 per mail-in scoring interpretive report; $9.50 per mail-in scoring profile report.
Foreign Language Edition: Record Forms are available in Spanish.
Time: (15-20) minutes.
Authors: J. Scott Yaruss and Robert W. Quesal.
Publisher: Pearson.

Review of the Overall Assessment of the Speaker's Experience of Stuttering by SANDRA D. HAYNES, Dean, School of Professional Studies, Metropolitan State College of Denver, Denver, CO:

DESCRIPTION. The Overall Assessment of the Speaker's Experience of Stuttering (OASES) is designed to assess how an individual with a stuttering disorder experiences their symptoms including "perceptions of observable stuttering behaviors, reactions to stuttering, and difficulties in performing daily activities involving communication" (manual, p. 1). The end goal of this assessment is to provide clinicians with a measure of the overall impact of stuttering on a person's life. The test can be used throughout treatment to assess progress. The test can also be used in research settings. Assessing the overall impact of stuttering on an individual's life makes the OASES a unique measure among tests of stuttering.

The OASES is composed of 100 questions. For each question, the test taker is asked to identify how much the statement applies to him or her on a Likert-type scale with 1 meaning *not at all* and 5 meaning *completely*. The questions are divided into four sections, each correlating to a specific component of stuttering disorders as classified by the *International Classification of Functioning, Disability, and Health* (ICF; World Health Organization, 2001). The ICF is designed to help assess the impact of symptoms on a person's activities of daily living and ability to participate fully in life. The sections include: General Information, assessing the speaker's perception of impairment; Your Reactions to Stuttering, assessing the individual's affective, behavioral, and cognitive reactions to stuttering; Communication in Daily Situations, assessing the difficulties that the speaker has when communicating in daily life; and Quality of Life, assessing environmental and contextual factors involved in stuttering and any participation restrictions the person experiences. All questions were written for easy comprehension.

Each subscale has an associated score and there is also an overall score. The manual contains five tables, one for each subscale and one for the overall rating, to guide the clinician or researcher in interpretation of scores. Score ranges are listed along with associated impact ratings. Score ranges are identical for the subscales as well as the overall score. Scores are determined by summing the Likert number associated with answers given within a subscale and dividing by the number of items answered in that section. The overall score is simply calculated by adding the total number of points for all items answered and dividing by the total number of questions answered.

Number of items answered is an important factor in scoring of the OASES. The administrator must determine whether or not an omitted item was a "legitimate skip" or not. Some of the items on the OASES will not apply to all test takers. These include items regarding marriage, children, employment, or therapy. The items that may be legitimately skipped are listed in the manual and are also identified on the scoring sheet for ease of identification. Other omitted items or otherwise unscoreable responses, such as marking two answers, should be addressed with the client whenever possible.

Impact ratings range from mild to severe and are determined by identifying the range in which the numerical score falls. Impact scores help identify the extent to which a person's stuttering disorder affects his or her life. Detailed descriptions for each severity level are given for each impact score, enabling the clinician to better establish a treatment plan and to assess progress. Answers to individual items can be examined, too, for development of a more detailed and individualized treatment plan.

The test authors are careful to detail administration protocol including the need to build rapport with the client despite the lack of necessity for being with the individual or group when test taking occurs. The test authors recommend a quiet setting, provision of a number 2 pencil or a computer, and 15 to 20 minutes for testing. The OASES has simple and clear instructions that can be read by the client or by the clinician.

DEVELOPMENT. Early development of the OASES was based on the World Health Organization's (WHO) *International Classification of Impairments, Disabilities, and Handicaps* (ICIDH; World Health Organization, 1980) description of stuttering. In addition to using the ICIDH criteria, two additional criteria, speaker's reactions to stuttering and environmental reactions to stuttering, were added. After extensive literature and test instrument review, these broad categories were divided into three scales that approximate three of the four scales that were included in the final version of the OASES. The initial item pools were evaluated by two focus groups, speech-language pathologists and people with a stuttering disorder. The OASES was then revised and pilot testing was conducted on each of the three scales as separate tests. The final version was developed after WHO released the ICF. Based on this foundation, the three scales were combined into one instrument and the general information section was added.

TECHNICAL.

Standardization. Norms were based on a sample of 173 individuals with a stuttering disorder. Participants' ages ranged from 18–78 with a mean age of 51. The ratio of males to females was 3:1, closely mirroring the distribution of gender in the population of persons who stutter. No information was provided on ethnicity or other characteristics. Items were subjected to item analysis to determine if each item has the appropriate distribution. On all but four items, the range of answers was 1 to 5.

Reliability. Estimates of internal consistency (split-half) indicate that the OASES has a high degree of internal consistency with scale scores ranging from .94 to .98 and an overall score rating of .99. Test-retest reliability confirms this with scores ranging from .89 to .95. The test-retest interval was 10 to 14 days.

Validity. Content and construct validity measures were used to assess the validity of the OASES. Content validity was assessed in test development by following the WHO classifications and descriptions, both ICIDH and ICF, of stuttering disorders. Additionally, giving the initial test to experts and patients further supports content validity.

Construct validity was assessed by examining internal consistency within and between sections. Internal consistency was much higher within sections (.94 to .98) than between sections (.66 to .82), demonstrating that items have good internal consistency although there are relationships among the subscales.

Comparison to another measure of stuttering disorders, the Erickson S24 (Andrews & Cutler, 1974), was also used to assess construct validity. The Erickson S24 is designed to assess interpersonal communication attitudes about stuttering in adolescents and adults. Given the uniqueness of the OASES, a perfect match could not be made and the Erickson S24 was the closest approximation found. The study was conducted with an earlier version of the OASES with 71 participants. The highest correlation was .83 between the S24 and the speakers' reactions to stuttering scale.

COMMENTARY. The OASES is a well-developed test based on solid test construction practices, research, and theoretical foundation. The manual is thorough and easy to navigate. Likewise, the test booklet is user friendly, as are the scoring and interpretation protocols. The OASES was adequately assessed for validity and reliability and the outcomes of these studies support that this instrument is indeed valid and reliable. Further research on the differences among people of different ethnicities and between genders would be useful in interpretation and treatment planning. The OASES is a unique measure among tests of stuttering disorders and should prove very useful to clinicians and researchers alike.

SUMMARY. The Overall Assessment of the Speaker's Experience of Stuttering (OASES) is designed to assess how an individual with a stuttering disorder experiences his or her symptoms. The OASES is a well-developed test based on solid test construction practices, research, and theoretical foundation. The OASES is a unique measure among tests of stuttering disorders and should prove very useful to clinicians and researchers alike.

REVIEWER'S REFERENCES

Andrews, G., & Cutler, J. (1974). Stuttering therapy: The relation between changes in symptom level and attitudes. *Journal of Speech and Hearing Research, 34,* 312–319.

World Health Organization. (1980). *International classification of impairments, disabilities, and handicaps (ICIDH).* Geneva, Switzerland: Author.

World Health Organization. (2001). *International classification of functioning, disability, and health (ICF).* Geneva, Switzerland: Author.

Review of the Overall Assessment of the Speaker's Experience of Stuttering by JEANETTE LEE-FARMER, Associate Professor of Special Education, Marshall University, South Charleston, WV, and JOYCE MEIKAMP, Professor of Special Education, Marshall University, South Charleston, WV:

DESCRIPTION. The Overall Assessment of the Speaker's Experience of Stuttering (OASES) is an instrument presented on a trifold record form. It is composed of 100 questions that are to be completed by a person (aged 18 or older) who stutters. Items that are not relevant may be skipped. Clients respond to each question by circling 1 of 5 points on a Likert rating scale, where the larger number represents the most negative response. The diagnostic is untimed, and usually takes between 15 to 20 minutes to complete. It can be completed individually or in groups. It is recommended that clients use either a ballpoint pen or pencil (rather than a felt-tip). Completion via computer is an option. The self-report generates information related to the speaker's attitudes regarding his or her oral language experiences.

The cover of the protocol includes instructions to the client and requests a limited amount of demographic data that can be helpful for research purposes, such as marital status, children, status of employment, and speech therapy received. The manual includes further information such as when to use the test, test setting and conditions, notes on establishing rapport, and how to introduce the test.

The main questions on the OASES are organized into four categories: General Information, Your Reactions to Stuttering, Communication in Daily Situations, and Quality of Life. Descriptive statistics are presented to help a clinician assess how a client responds to situations in comparison to others who stutter. An item analysis can readily reveal particular issues of concern that are unique to each client. The categories measure the impact that dysfluency has on the person's life, making the OASES a comprehensive assessment that can aid clinicians and educators in making appropriate decisions regarding a multidisciplinary treatment plan.

DEVELOPMENT. The development of the OASES spanned close to 10 years, including consultation with the National Stuttering Association (NSA) Research Committee, the World Health Organization (WHO), individuals at Pearson, educational colleagues, researchers, clinicians, graduate students, and others. Item pools were submitted to speech-language pathologists, revised, presented to focus groups, and revised again. Three different trial instruments were administered and evaluated in two tryout studies. The pilot studies involved over 300 individuals with language dysfluency. The three trial instruments were combined into a single instrument, originally called the Comprehensive Assessment of the Speaker's Experience of Stuttering (CASES). Further changes occurred before a final version was developed. Standardization measures were completed with a diverse sample before the OASES was presented. Participants for the standardization process included members of the National Stuttering Association (40%), nonmembers who contacted the organization for information, and others who were recruited by the test authors and their colleagues. The age range was 18–78, with 51 years as the mean age (*SD* = 13.5). The ratio of males to females was 3:1. According to Bloodstein (1995), this ratio reflects the distribution of the larger population of adults who stutter. The OASES includes updated descriptors for the disorder as promoted by WHO.

This new instrument is designed to provide information from the speaker's perspective regarding the impact of stuttering on one's daily state of being. Prior research studies have related that stuttering frequently impacts the life of the speaker by causing high levels of anxiety (e.g., Ezrati-Vinacour & Levin, 2004; Prasse & Kikano, 2008).

TECHNICAL. Each question on the OASES underwent an analysis using standardization data to make certain there was appropriate distribution of scores. The mean, mode, standard deviation, skew, and kurtosis for each item are presented in four tables, with summary statistics for each section of the test.

Test-retest reliabilities are high ranging from .89 to .95, using test-retest intervals between 10 and 14 days. Additionally, internal consistency is strong for each section (.94, .97, .96, and .98 for sections I, II, III, and IV, respectively). The overall reliability for internal consistency is .99, with a *SEM* of .08.

Likewise, content validity of OASES scores was assured as the test authors based the questions entirely on the World Health Organization's framework for describing the human health experience, with reference to the *International Classification of Impairments, Disabilities, and Handicaps* (ICIDH; World Health Organization, 1980) and *The International Classification of Functioning, Disability, and Health* (ICF; World Health Organization, 2001). Construct validity was measured, with only moderate correlations between sections (desirable), and higher correlations regarding internal consistency. In comparison with the Erikson S24 instrument (Andrews & Cutler, 1974), which measures interpersonal communication attitudes about stuttering in adolescents and adults, the OASES had correlations ranging from .68 to .83.

COMMENTARY. Scoring is made simple for the clinician. On the front sheet of the protocol, space is provided for recording raw score points, for indicating the number of items completed for each section, and for calculating by simple division the "Impact Score" for each section of the test. A conversion chart is presented in the same space for determining if a client's self-report indicates that one's stuttering has a mild, mild/moderate, moderate, moderate/severe, or a severe impact on one's inclusive life experience. The clinician simply refers to a range of scores beneath each Impact rating, and places a check in a box corresponding to the Impact Score. An OASES overall test score can be determined that summarizes the inclusive life experience affected by the client's oral communication patterns.

For each section of the test, the overall Impact rating score is not only ranked, but also presented with a thorough interpretive description to aid the clinician in determining the matching "overall characteristics and experiences" for the speaker (Tables 3.2, 3.3, 3.4, and 3.5 in the product manual). Similarly, an interpretive description for each ranking of the overall Impact ratings is provided (Table 3.1).

Numerous tests and investigations have focused on the physiological aspects of stuttering. Some have investigated the related attitudes of the clients. The test authors (Yaruss & Quesal, 2006) note the Speech Situation Checklist (SSC), Self-Efficacy Scale for Adults Who Stutter (SESAS), Erickson's S-Scale, the Inventory of Communication Attitudes (ICA), the Subjective Screening of Stuttering (SSS), and the Wright-Ayer Stuttering Self-Rating Profile (WASSP). Although each of these tools has strengths, the OASES integrates elements regarding the totality of the disorder into a compact, single instrument that reliably examines the effect of treatments, based on the self-reported anxiety levels of the speaker.

SUMMARY. The OASES is a self-administered survey for adults who stutter. It is easy to complete, and easy for a clinician to score. Clients rate their feelings about how their oral language skills impact their lives. Domains of examination include overall feelings of the client in response to stuttering, along with emotional reactions, perceptions regarding one's own communication skills in specific places (e.g., work, home, social situations), and the sense of well-being (quality of life) the client feels. The instrument can be used to pinpoint areas in need of attention by a treatment team. It can be readily administered several times, providing comparative data regarding a client to clinicians prior to, during, and following a treatment period. Although it offers no recommendations for treatment exercises, devices, programs, medication, and so forth, it does offer an easy to use gauge that measures progress in current action plans.

REVIEWERS' REFERENCES

Andrews, G., & Cutler, J. (1974). Stuttering therapy: The relation between changes in symptom level and attitudes. *Journal of Speech and Hearing Research, 34,* 312–319.

Bloodstein, O. (1995). *A handbook on stuttering* (5th ed.). San Diego, CA: Singular.

Ezrati-Vinacour, R., & Levin, I. (2004). The relationship between anxiety and stuttering: A multidimensional approach. *Journal of Fluency Disorders, 29,* 135–148.

Prasse, J. E., & Kikano, G. E. (2008). Stuttering: An overview. *American Family Physician, 77,* 1271, 1278.

World Health Organization. (1980). *International classification of impairments, disabilities, and handicaps (ICIDH).* Geneva, Switzerland: Author.

World Health Organization. (2001). *International classification of functioning, disability, and health (ICF).* Geneva, Switzerland: Author.

Yaruss, J. S., & Quesal, R. W. (2006). Overall Assessment of the Speaker's Experience of Stuttering (OASES): Documenting multiple outcomes in stuttering treatment. *Journal of Fluency Disorders, 31,* 90–115.

[84]

P-BDQ Police Officer Background Data Questionnaire.

Purpose: Assesses backgrounds and personal characteristics of entry-level police officer candidates.

Population: Candidates for entry-level police officer positions.

Publication Dates: 1999–2000.

Acronym: P-BDQ.

Scores: 5 biodata subtypes: Background, Lifestyle, Interest, Personality, Ability.

Administration: Group.

Price Data: Available from publisher.

Time: 30 minutes.

Comments: "It is recommended that this test be used in conjunction with one of IPMA-HR's other entry-level police officer tests."

Author: International Public Management Association for Human Resources and Bruce Davey Associates.
Publisher: International Public Management Association for Human Resources (IPMA-HR).

Review of the P-BDQ Police Officer Background Data Questionnaire by THOMAS R. O'NEILL, Psychometrician, National Council of State Boards of Nursing, Chicago, IL:

DESCRIPTION. The P-BDQ Police Officer Background Data Questionnaire (P-BDQ) is a pencil-and-paper, self-report questionnaire that is designed to supplement a battery of cognitive tests for the purpose of screening police officer candidates. Although the literature submitted by the publisher indicates that candidate selection procedures should have a high degree of validity, the publisher never provides a clear description of either the construct or the screening mechanism upon which the P-BDQ is based. This review is based upon a copy of the questionnaire, a technical report (Davey & Jacobson, 1999), and information found on the publisher's website.

The questionnaire consists of 50 multiple-choice questions of which three are optional, unscored, biodata and demographic items (gender, age, and race). On each question, the candidate is asked to select one answer from the response options listed below it. Every question has a set of three to five response options. The response options are typical of biodata inventories and are likely empirically keyed. There is only one form of the questionnaire.

The questionnaire can be administered by the human resources staff that is recruiting and screening officer candidates, but the scoring of the questionnaire can only be performed by the publisher. The publisher's website indicates that there is a 30-minute time limit for the administration of this biodata survey and that survey administrator smust sign a security agreement, which requires them to keep the content of the survey secure to prevent providing a subset of candidates an unfair advantage. The catalogue on the publisher's website also indicates that each P-BDQ survey costs $6, plus a $75 administration fee for each batch ordered. There is also an additional scoring charge of $45 per batch plus $.50 per answer sheet. Typical turn-around time for receiving scored results was not included in the provided literature. The manner in which the results are reported back to the agency screening the candidates is unclear, too. In particular, it is unclear if the results are reported back as a decision, a single score, or subtest scores.

DEVELOPMENT. The 1999 release of the P-BDQ is a revised version of the original 1992 release. The intent behind the P-BDQ was to identify the characteristics (knowledge, skills, abilities, and personal traits) that contribute to successful performance of the activities engaged in by entry-level police officers. The position of "patrol officer" was selected because new officers are routinely assigned to that role. Attempts were also made to identify characteristics that would contribute to successful performance across diverse U.S. jurisdictions. Because the authors envisioned this questionnaire as part of a battery of tests, cognitive traits such as learning ability, reading ability, and basic reasoning were not the focus of the survey. Instead, the survey focused on Background items (education, work experience, past achievements, etc.), Lifestyle items (social activity, exercise, etc.), Interest items (which activities do you prefer?), Personality test-type items, and Ability items. Efforts were made to link these characteristics to the successful performance of patrol officers. Despite this attempt, however, it is unclear what this set of questions represents as a construct. Some biodata inventories are construct-oriented and may be considered like psychological instruments. Others are purely actuarial. This instrument is clearly one of the latter grouping.

TECHNICAL. Although the 1999 P-BDQ technical report contained a substantial amount of information, it was difficult to read. The technical report could be substantially improved by improving the writing to help the reader follow the logical flow of the test development process. Better labeling for the figures would be especially helpful. The technical report describes rationale for item development and the pilot testing; however, a problem arises in the process. The initial development of the 1999 P-BDQ contained 107 questions of which 5 were demographic, yet the linking of questions back to a job analysis, the pilot testing, the validation procedures, the adjustment for "social desirability," the tests for adverse impact upon minority groups, and so on were all based upon the 107-question survey, but the final version of the survey contained only 50 questions. The technical manual reports the reduction in the number of items as the last step. Of the 107 initial survey items, 50 were retained on two criterion-keys, with 12 additional items kept for research purposes. All data for the final form of this instrument are based upon the two 19-item, empirically derived scales. Because the scoring key for the survey is proprietary, it was not available for the review. This omission made trying to understand how scores are generated impossible, although one may still focus on its concurrent or predictive validity.

Despite these drawbacks, the authors have attempted to do some interesting and commendable things. First, the authors have attempted to adjust for social desirability. The authors identified a set of items that might be susceptible to inflation due to a "social desirability" factor and compared them with a set of items that have "less subjective" response options. The authors point out that inflation on the "more subjective" subtest should not be interpreted as the candidate deliberately trying to distort their responses but rather it is just a tendency to elevate (or depress) their ratings in a systematic manner. It is unclear whether this matter is really an issue for the consumer of the questionnaire because it does not seem that the results on this subtest are reported.

Another commendable aspect was the effort to show that the questionnaire was not biased against protected classes such as ethnic minorities or women. An analysis does show that there is a statistically significant performance difference between white and black subsamples, although this analysis was based on more than 2,500 candidates, so the power of the test was quite high. Moreover, the differences between groups was much smaller than those typically found on cognitive tests. There were also differences in some of the comparisons between white and Hispanic subsamples as well as between the male and female subsamples. The authors include some tables as guidelines for where to set the cutscore that would be unlikely to trigger the 4/5th rule (80% rule). It is assumed that any user of this questionnaire would be familiar with this aspect of the Uniform Guidelines on Employee Selection Procedures (1978).

With regard to construct validity, the authors have approached the problem from the perspective of predicting an outcome rather than clearly articulating a construct. As a result, there is little evidence of traditional construct validity. For this reason, the content validity is somewhat lessened, but one can see that the questions on the survey might be related to successful performance as a patrolman and the job analysis does support these notions to some extent. The concurrent validity is the strongest of the types of validity presented in the technical report. It demonstrates that the P-BDQ results are correlated with supervisor's ratings. Although the results were statistically significant, the magnitude of the correlation was less than .35. Although these correlations may seem low to some, it is important to keep in mind that many factors beyond "background data" are at work in patrol duties, citizen interactions, traffic enforcement, crime scene duties, accident scene duties, handling disturbances, investigation and interviewing, apprehension & arrest, court preparation and testimony, etc. Such correlations are quite typical of many tests evaluated via predictive validity.

COMMENTARY. A clear description of exactly how this instrument should be used and what it is purported to measure would help the consumer understand how to use it. Clearly, this product should not be used by itself for police candidate selection and the publisher seems to agree with that opinion in the technical report. The added benefit that it brings to the selection process likely has value as an aid to the interviewing process, but not as a defendable psychometric instrument with great predictive power. This questionnaire would be more useable to consumers if it had an administrator's manual that was written for the human resources staff member who would be deciding which battery of tests to purchase or the staff member who will actually administer the tests. Examples of what the scored questionnaire results look like would be helpful, especially if they had suggested interpretations by the authors.

A more clearly written technical manual also would help psychometricians understand exactly how the questionnaire works and would be helpful in the event of fending off a legal challenge to an employment decision made partially from the results of this survey. A clear description of the scoring key would be helpful, although that information need not be made available to every administrator.

Caution should be exercised in using the P-BDQ. There may be special concerns about making decisions about the employability of candidates on the basis of characteristics other than a clearly articulated ability. It would be prudent to run a questionnaire like this by an experienced human resources professional or labor attorney in one's own state before using it in a substantive way to make employment decisions.

If the purpose is to screen out a large number of inappropriate applicants who might take legal action, it might be better to use a standardized interview with questions that can be used as red flags such as the following: Have you been convicted of a felony? In the past, have you been chronically tardy for work? Can you hold down a job? Hopefully, working together, human resources and legal counsel could devise some questions for such an interview. Of course, this empirically derived questionnaire could also be used in conjunction with such an interview.

If the purpose is to rank the candidates that one believes to be generally appropriate, then this questionnaire might be helpful, especially if a company has a large number of applicants. It may be economical to use this measure if the candidate pool is large because although the per unit cost of the survey remains constant, the scoring charge and the order handling fee can be spread out over a large number of candidates.

SUMMARY. The content in the questionnaire seems similar to what might be asked in an interview. The advantage of the P-BDQ is that the same prompts are provided to all candidates and the responses are all scored the same way. There are no rater effects. Although the questionnaire seems to have predictive power, like many biographical inventories, the existing documentation does not make it easy to explain how it works, which could be an issue if one had to defend it in court or to the media.

REVIEWER'S REFERENCES

Davey, B., & Jacobson, L. S. (1999). *Development and validation of the background data questionnaire (BDQ) for police officer selection* (Technical report). Alexandria, VA: International Personnel Management Association.

U. S. Equal Employment Opportunity Commission, Department of Labor, Department of Justice, U. S. Civil Service Commission. (1978). Adoption by four agencies of Uniform Guidelines on Employee Selection Procedures. Federal register, 43:38290-38315.

[85]

P-Det 1.0 and 2.0 Police Detective Tests.

Purpose: Developed "to assist law enforcement departments ... in promoting qualified candidates to the detective position."

Population: Candidates for promotion to the police detective position.

Publication Dates: 2004–2006.

Acronym: P-Det 1.0; P-Det 2.0.

Scores: 3 knowledge areas: Police Investigation Procedures, Laws Related to Police Work, Concepts for Writing and Completing Reports/Records and Paperwork.

Administration: Individual or group.

Forms, 2: P-Det 1.0, P-Det 2.0.

Price Data: Available from publisher.

Time: 120 minutes per test.

Comments: P-Det 1.0 and P-Det 2.0 are comparable forms [the publisher advises that the form now available is the P-DET 2.1 (released in 2007), but it was not yet available when this review was written]; reading lists are available to help candidates prepare for the exams.

Author: International Public Management Association for Human Resources.

Publisher: International Public Management Association for Human Resources (IPMA-HR).

Review of the Police Detective Examination P-Det 1.0 and P-Det 2.0 by KARL N. KELLEY, Professor of Psychology, North Central College, Naperville, IL:

DESCRIPTION. The Police Detective Tests (P-Det 1.0 and P-Det 2.0) were developed in 2004 to aid in the selection of police officers seeking promotion to the rank of detective. The test is intended to measure three primary dimensions: (a) Police Investigation Procedures, (b) Laws Related to Police Work, and (c) Concepts for Writing and Completing Reports, Records, and Paperwork. The test can be administered to individuals or to groups with a total testing time of 2 hours.

Three different types of items are included on this test. This reviewer considers most of the questions to be situational judgment items where applicants read a specific scenario and select the most appropriate response among the provided options. Other items are objective, content questions asking for specific information. A third group of questions requires candidates to determine the accuracy of a report. The test publisher, on the other hand, maintains that although some questions are written in a scenario format, they are all based upon content knowledge.

DEVELOPMENT. The developers followed a rigorous multistep procedure in creating items for this test. In the first phase, developers conducted a job analysis of the police detective job. Strategies for collecting data for the job analysis included the observation of detectives on the job and structured interviews with detectives from four different departments. Based on this information, a list of specific job tasks and necessary KSAOs (knowledge, skills, abilities, and other) were created. This information was then distributed, in the form of a job analysis questionnaire, to 16 different departments varying in size and location. Police detectives rated each of the tasks in terms of importance (1 meant of little importance to 5 meant critically important) and frequency (1 connoted very low to 5 meant very high). A task was dropped if more than 40% reported that they did not perform this task. Tasks were retained only if their mean importance rating was greater than 2.5. A total of 96 specific tasks and 39 KSAOs were retained following this process.

Based on this structure, test developers then created specific test questions including content and accuracy items. Item content was derived from incidents described in the job analysis and from a collection of standard law enforcement reference books (a reading list of these books is provided to all applicants). The items were reviewed by a group of Subject-Matter Experts (SME) who rated the importance of each item on a scale from 0 (*not important*) to 3 (*very important*). Any item with an average score less than 1 was eliminated from this test. A total of 95 items were retained for both versions of this test.

An important goal for the developers was to create a selection test that could be applied to any law enforcement department across the country. Because of this goal, KSAO correlations were computed by department size (serving small < 25,000, medium 25,001–75,000, and large > 75,000 populations) and location (West, Midwest, and East/South East). Correlations ranged from .75 to .99 and all were statistically significant ($p < .01$).

TECHNICAL. The technical manual accompanying this test provides a comprehensive overview of the test development process. Specific information about participating police departments and item development was clearly explained.

This test has high face validity—applicants taking this test would likely view it as meaningfully related to the job they are seeking. Subject-Matter Experts rated 78% of the test items as important for the job. Thus, the content validity of the test is supported. Unfortunately, few additional psychometrics are provided for this test. There is no information on either the criterion-related validity or the reliability of the test. Normative information was not given to this reviewer, but some normative data have been provided in a separate document subsequent to the conduct of this review. Finally, although the manual provides a reading list for applicants, no testing protocols were provided to this reviewer. [Editor's note: The test publisher has informed Buros that they are made available to those who order this instrument.]

COMMENTARY. Based on the information provided in the technical manual, the developers of this test have done an outstanding job of developing the items on the test. Items on the test are engaging and relevant. The authors present items ranging from interrogation of suspects to the appropriate use of grammar. Particularly interesting is the incident description and the accompanying completed investigation report where participants seek out possible errors.

There are many strong components of this test; however, the lack of important psychometric information makes it difficult to evaluate its effectiveness more fully. Specifically, this test could have good predictive validity, but no information on this concern was provided. The manual also neither suggests using criteria nor within-group norms to evaluate the test.

Finally, although the items have strong face validity, the test developer does not address some of the current issues in some of both types of questions used in this testing. The stem content of the items appears relevant, but the developers do not address issues concerning either response instruction or different scoring methods (Weekley, Ployhart, & Holtz, 2006).

SUMMARY. The test developers are clear that these tests can assist in the selection of Police Detectives. No claim is made that this test is a more effective predictor than other selection techniques but it could be a component of a comprehensive selection process. Based on the information provided, that likely would be an appropriate use of these tests. With additional supportive research, more weight could be given to test scores.

REVIEWER'S REFERENCE

Weekley, J. A., Ployhart, R. E., & Holtz, B. C. (2006). On the development of situational judgment tests: Issues in item development, scaling, and scoring. In J. A. Weekley & R. E. Ployhart (Eds.), *Situational Judgment Tests: Theory, measurement, and application* (pp. 157–182). Mahwah, NJ: Lawrence Erlbaum Associates, Inc.

[86]

P-1SV and P-2SV Police Officer Tests.

Purpose: Developed to "assess the competencies that new police officers need to perform successfully on the job."
Population: Candidates for entry-level police officer positions.
Publication Dates: 2003–2006.
Acronyms: P-1SV; P-2SV.
Scores: 5 job dimensions: Ability to Learn and Apply Police Information, Ability to Observe and Remember Details, Verbal Ability, Ability to Follow Directions, Ability to Use Judgment and Logic.
Administration: Individual or group.
Forms, 2: P-1SV, P-2SV.
Price Data: Available from publisher.

Time: 130 minutes per test.
Comments: P-1SV and P-2SV are parallel forms; no prior training or experience as a police officer is assumed of candidates taking the tests.
Author: International Public Management Association for Human Resources.
Publisher: International Public Management Association for Human Resources (IPMA-HR).

Review of the P-1SV and P-2SV Police Officer Tests by DENIZ S. ONES, Professor and Hellervik Professor of Industrial Psychology, University of Minnesota, Minneapolis, MN, and STEPHAN DILCHERT, Assistant Professor of Management, Baruch College, City University of New York, New York, NY:

DESCRIPTION. The P-1SV and P-2SV Police Officer Tests are alternate-form measures intended to assess some characteristics required to perform entry level police officer jobs successfully. Each test form contains 100 multiple-choice questions, which are dichotomously scored (correct/incorrect), and each test yields a single overall score. The knowledge, skills, abilities, and personal characteristics (KSAPs) that the tests assess are specified in the technical manual as: (a) Reasoning Ability, (b) Observation/Perceptiveness, (c) Ability to Learn Proper Police Procedures, (d) Speaking Ability, (e) Ability to Learn Laws to be Enforced, (f) Writing Ability, (g) Problem Solving, (h) Memory, (i) Learning, (j) Reading, and (k) Planning/Organizing. To measure these KSAPs, six subtests are used on each test form: Ability to Learn and Apply Police Information (25 items on both forms), Ability to Observe and Remember Details (12 items on both forms), Verbal Ability (Vocabulary and Reading Comprehension) (23 items on P-1SV; 31 items on P-2SV), Ability to Follow Directions (20 items on both forms), and Ability to Use Judgment and Logic (20 items on P-1SV; 12 items on P-2SV). The time limit for each test is 1 hour and 45 minutes. The target individuals are entry-level police officer job applicants. The tests are designed for use as part of personnel selection and screening *systems*, rather than as the sole instruments on which hiring decisions are based. No prior knowledge or experience in law enforcement is assumed. Prior to testing, applicants are provided with an information packet/guide to examine and study for 25 minutes in a controlled setting. Many items on the tests are based on or refer to these study guides.

DEVELOPMENT. The tests are considered to be two new forms of previously developed police officer exams (Davey, 1992; International Personnel Management Association, 1998). The competencies to be assessed by the tests were based on extensive job-analytic information.

Job-analysis. Test development relied on detailed job analyses conducted by Davey (1992) and updated by IPMA (1998). The goal of the job analyses was to define the entry-level police officer job and to determine how similar job requirements were from department to department in order to develop a common test. In the initial job-analytic data collection effort, 44 police departments from 13 states gathered data from 596 police officers with 1–5 years of experience. For the supplemental job analysis conducted to update the original job analysis, 45 police departments from 27 states and regions of the U.S. convened subject matter expert (SME) panels consisting of two police officers and one first line supervisor. SME panels provided consensus-derived ratings for each job duty on importance and time spent as well as importance of broader competences. There was a high degree of correspondence between the findings from the two job analyses. Furthermore, analyses revealed that job duties, their importance, time spent performing them, and broad competencies required to perform the duties were highly similar across different regions of the country. There were few differences between departments serving areas with small, medium, large, and very large populations. Based on these findings, the test developers concluded that the same 21 KSAPs are likely needed for effective job performance across departments and regions, enabling the development and use of the police officer tests.

Item development and selection. Eleven of the 21 KSAPs were determined to be measurable by using a multiple-choice exam format and six subtests were written to assess them. Given the goal of 100 test questions for each form, a greater number of items were written (154) for inclusion on each form, with 31 questions common to the two forms. Information manuals to be studied by the applicants as part of the testing process were designed to consist of "what must be learned by police recruits and applied on the job" (technical report, p. 36). Based on research with 40 undergraduate students using previous versions of the police officer tests, the amount of time applicants are allotted to study the information manuals under controlled conditions was limited to 25 minutes. For each form, an initial pool of 45 questions was based on the information/study guides. The remainder of the questions were similar in type to those used on their previous versions of the police officer tests.

Items were finalized after staff members of the test developer took the tests (four individuals taking P-1SV and three taking P-2SV). This pilot process was followed by data collection for a concurrent validation study from 98 (for P-1SV) and 97 (for P-2SV) police officer incumbents from 14 agencies. Item analyses based on data from these samples focused on item difficulty (overly easy items were dropped) and inter-item relationships (to ensure high internal consistency). Practical considerations, such as having parallel content for the two alternate forms, also played a role in finalizing the test content. Twenty-five anchor items were retained on both forms of the test.

The test manual as well as the website of the test publisher indicate that the corresponding subsections of the two test forms consist of the same number of items. However, after an inspection of the two test booklets (which include tables of contents with sections by item number) and the actual test items, this statement appears to be incorrect. Two subsections (Verbal Ability and Ability to Use Judgment and Logic) are made up of differing numbers of items on the two test forms. This fact further complicates direct comparisons between attributes of the two purportedly alternate forms.

TECHNICAL.

Normative information. Normative information is provided for the respective concurrent validation samples of 98 and 97 police officer incumbents for the two forms of the test. No normative data are reported for police officer applicants, the intended population.

Reliability. Based on data from the concurrent validation study samples, internal consistency reliability estimates (KR-20) were reported as .89 for both forms. No other reliability estimates are provided, including the correlation between the two forms of the test indicating alternate form reliability. The latter is crucial for computing the correct standard error of measurement of two tests that are used as alternatives for each other. The standard errors of measurement reported for the two forms (a) rely on the internal consistency reliability and (b) use in their computation the standard deviations of the job incumbents tested. The latter is very likely smaller than the standard deviation among job applicants and likely contributes to the low *SEM*s, which were thus computed using inappropriate data.

Validity. The validity evidence offered to support the use of the tests is a concurrent validation study with subsets of the incumbent samples described above for whom job performance information could be gathered from two supervisors (*N*s = 97 and 96 for the two forms, respectively). The observed validities for the two forms are reported as .206 and .230 for ratings of overall performance, and .293 and .296 for a composite of 10 dimensions of officer performance. Operational validities computed after correcting for unreliability in the criterion using interrater reliabilities found in these samples (.50 to .59) are .50, .52, .42, and .41, respectively. No data are reported to indicate predictive validity. However, previous research on cognitive ability test criterion-related validities indicates that in this domain, concurrent validities tend to estimate predictive validities accurately (Barrett, Phillips, & Alexander, 1981).

The question remains which constructs are assessed by the overall score of the police officer tests. The content of the scales and the criterion-related validities reviewed above suggest that P-1SV and P-2SV overall scores assess general mental ability. It is odd that no data are offered examining the nomological networks of the tests, including convergent validity with other measures of cognitive ability. Such evidence would have allowed the test developers to draw on findings and conclusions from the broader literature on personnel selection (e.g., validity generalization).

Also lacking is an examination of subgroup differences (mean and variability) among groups protected under the Civil Rights Acts as well as an examination of predictive fairness. Again, if the test developers had reported the necessary evidence to establish their tests as measures of general cognitive ability, they could have relied, at least to some extent, on the literature on test fairness and bias for cognitive ability tests in general (e.g., predictive fairness).

COMMENTARY. The P-1SV and P-2SV police officer tests contain content that closely matches some competencies required for effective performance as entry-level police officers. The tests are based on thorough job analyses that have been most recently updated in 1998. Given the apparent content validity of the measures and their high face validity, the test authors are to be commended.

However, there are a number of weaknesses in the data used to support the reliability, equivalence, and validity of test scores. There is little normative information provided for the tests, and data reported are for small samples of incumbents, rather than applicants. The test publisher should gather and report more extensive normative data for the measures.

Different types of measurement error need to be investigated with both measures' scores. Of particular interest is the alternate-form reliability of these tests. In the technical manual, the equivalence of the scores on the two tests is inferred by pointing to the same content coverage of the measures, the equal number of items on each form, similarities of score distributions, and similarities of criterion-related validities. Also, a set of regression analyses using the common set of items on both tests are offered. Contemporary psychometric analyses of test score equivalence are currently lacking and highly recommended.

A single concurrent validity study is used to support the validity of the tests for predicting job performance. In the concurrent validity study, a number of features are to be commended. These included the gathering of job performance data for validation purposes only (rather than using performance ratings collected for administrative purposes) and the use of two supervisors to rate the performance of each officer. The latter increases the reliability of ratings and allows for computations of interrater reliability for job performance as well as appropriate corrections for attenuation to estimate operational validity. Unfortunately, without evidence of construct (i.e., convergent) validity, the question whether the overall test scores are indicators of general mental ability remains open. Also, regarding criterion-related validity, the concurrent validity evidence from two small samples is not sufficient. Either the test developers should present large-scale predictive validity evidence for their measures or empirically establish that the tests assess general cognitive ability. In the latter case, massive meta-analytic evidence for such measures and their fairness (see Ones, Viswesvaran, & Dilchert, 2005) could be brought to bear on the validity of the present tests.

SUMMARY. The content of the police officer tests is based on solid job-analytic data. The test developers point to 11 separate KSAPs that are assessed by the instruments. However, the resulting overall score likely assesses general cognitive ability, which is a construct predictive of performance in any domain of work. There are some important gaps in the data offered to support test use. These measures are very likely useful in the selection of entry-level police officers across various agencies across the U.S. However, such a conclusion is not yet firmly and fully established by the data offered by the test publisher.

REVIEWERS' REFERENCES

Barrett, G. V., Phillips, J. S., & Alexander, R. A. (1981). Concurrent and predictive validity designs: A critical reanalysis. *Journal of Applied Psychology, 66*, 1-6.

Davey, B. (1992). *Development and validation of the 375.1 and 375.2 police officer examinations.* Alexandria, VA: IPMA.

International Personnel Management Association. (1998). *Development and validation of the A-4 police officer examinations.* Alexandria, VA: IPMA.

Ones, D. S., Viswesvaran, C., & Dilchert, S. (2005). Cognitive ability in personnel selection decisions. In A. Evers, O. Voskuijl, & N. Anderson (Eds.), *Handbook of selection* (pp. 143-173). Oxford, UK: Blackwell.

[87]

Parenting Relationship Questionnaire.

Purpose: Designed to "capture a parent's perspective of the parent-child relationship."
Population: Parents of children ages 2–5, 6–18.
Publication Date: 2006.
Acronym: PRQ.
Scores, 7: Attachment, Communication (child and adolescent only), Discipline Practices, Involvement, Parenting Confidence, Satisfaction with School (child and adolescent only), Relational Frustration.
Administration: Individual.
Levels, 2: Preschool, Child and Adolescent.
Forms, 3: Parent Feedback Report, Preschool, Child and Adolescent.
Price Data, 2009: $133 per hand-scored starter set including 25 of each hand-scored form (preschool, child/adolescent, and parent feedback), and manual (104 pages); $356 per PRQ Assist starter set including 25 of each form (preschool, child/adolescent, and parent feedback), manual, and Assist computer scoring software; $32 per 25 hand-scored forms (specify preschool or child/adolescent); $27 per 25 computer-entry forms (specify preschool or child/adolescent); $44 per 25 scannable forms (specify preschool or child/adolescent); $27 per 25 parent feedback report forms; $64 per manual; $36 per test item audio CD; $267 per Assist scanning software.
Time: (10-15) minutes.
Comments: For use in conjunction with the Behavior Assessment System for Children, Second Edition (BASC-2; 17:21) or as a stand-alone instrument; alternative starter sets and upgrades available for current BASC-2 users, contact publisher for details.
Authors: Randy W. Kamphaus and Cecil R. Reynolds.
Publisher: Pearson.

Review of the Parenting Relationship Questionnaire by MARY M. CLARE, Professor of Counseling Psychology, Lewis & Clark College, Portland, OR:

DESCRIPTION. The Parenting Relationship Questionnaire (PRQ) is a four-point (*Never, Sometimes, Often, Almost Always*) self-report scale completed by parents or other primary caregivers to reflect the nature of a parent/caregiver-child relationship. The questionnaire has two forms: a 45-item Preschool scale (PRQ-P; ages 2–5) and a 71-item Child and Adolescent scale (PRQ-CA; ages 6–18). The items of the PRQ have been written to be easily readable (third-grade level) and the questionnaire requires approximately 10–15 minutes to complete. The test authors indicate the utility of this instrument for use in child-focused "clinical, pediatric, counseling, school, and other settings" (manual, p. 1) where the nature of the parent/caregiver-child relationship is germane to assessment and intervention in support of the child client's well-being.

Upon completion, the PRQ-CA yields seven scaled scores describing the parent/caregiver-child relationship relative to empirically established dimensions of Attachment, Communication, Discipline Practices, Involvement, Parenting Confidence, Satisfaction with School, and Relational Frustration. The PRQ-P yields five scaled scores, all of which are in common with the PRQ-CA; however, Communication and Satisfaction with School are not part of the PRQ-P. In addition the test authors have successfully embedded four indices to assist clinicians in discerning the validity of respondents' engagement with the questionnaire. These metrics reflect defensiveness (overly positive response bias), unusual negativity, response consistency across items generally answered similarly, and invalidating response patterns that indicate lack of attention to item content. The latter two indices may be generated solely with use of the PRQ scoring and reporting software, which also affords comparisons between parents/caregivers and analyses to track relationship changes over time. Finally, the test authors point out several critical items and related responses that would warrant particular attention. As such, these particular items provide indicators of areas in which additional assessment is advisable.

DEVELOPMENT. Based on their identification of the need for assessing the relationships between children and their parents/caregivers, the PRQ authors reviewed the research literature on these relationships to extract and examine essential constructs (Attachment, Communication, Involvement, Parenting Confidence, and Satisfaction With School). These constructs then served to establish the conceptual limits within which items would be pooled, selected for final inclusion, and ultimately interpreted.

Items were written by the test authors and staff toward the development of two pilot forms. In a pilot study, employees of a publishing company, who met criteria of having children between the ages of 4 and 18, responded to these forms. Based on the data from these responses (n = 215, 106 for one form, 109 for the other), factor analyses guided the selection of items fitting with the seven theoretical constructs. Between January 2003 and October 2005 the test authors pursued thorough standardization toward finalization of questionnaire content and norms. In their manual, the test authors provide instructive description of their use of covariance structure analyses (CSA), which they summarize as allowing "theoretical considerations to guide (but not determine) scale structure ... [and specification of] items unduly influenced by other dimensions" (p. 33).

The standardization sample for the PRQ includes children from five age groups (2–5, 6–9, 10–12, 13–15, 16–18), four ethnic categories (African American, Hispanic, White, Other), four regions of the U.S. (including AK but not HI; successfully drawing from rural and urban communities), and four levels of maternal education (≤11th grade, HS graduate/GED, 1–3 years college or technical school, 4+ years college or technical school). The sample was also representative of "children and adolescents diagnosed with or classified as having emotional, behavioral, or physical problems" (manual, p. 41). Based on analyses of standardization data, the test authors concluded that valid score interpretation could be accomplished based on age-group norms aggregated across the above categories. A single statistical exception led to the derivation of a second set of norms based on reported sex of the respondent (i.e., male and female raters).

TECHNICAL. As mentioned above, the test authors employed a CSA approach (also known as confirmatory factor analysis) to move their initial item pool into its final form. Employing incremental analyses across standardization groupings by construct and by item, this approach offers strong evidence for construct validity (i.e., fitting item clusters with predefined dimensions of healthy parent/caregiver-child relationships) and to initial verification of internal reliability among items. Subsequent exemplary analyses of psychometric properties reported in the manual produced strong quantitative evidence of reliability (internal consistency, test-retest, and articulation of standard errors of measurement) and validity (internal and external convergent and divergent validity). Limitations to cultural/logical validity are discussed below.

COMMENTARY. In any endeavor based in traditional scientific methodology, several points of subjectivity are generally overlooked (in particular, the articulation of hypotheses and the interpretation of statistical data). Hypothesis formation requires a narrowing of focus to make a specific prediction of the way variables will interact toward measurable outcomes. This narrowing is necessarily a subjective process, identifying what to attend and what to ignore. In psychometrics, the process of item development is similarly subjective.

In the case of the PRQ, the test authors selected items to fit within the bounds of their a priori identification of seven constructs. This focusing process is essential to the process of developing psychometric tools. It is also unavoidably mediated by the knowledge and worldviews of the test authors. The PRQ authors drew carefully on their career-long attention to the practical and empirical knowledge related to parent/caregiver-child relationships. They were also guided explicitly by deep review of relevant and established psychological literature. Nonetheless, the seven constructs and related items of the PRQ are limited to the cultural and circumstantial conditions represented in the professional literature and filtered through the experiences and interpretations of the test authors.

The PRQ has its normative basis in a national sample carefully representative of all regions of the U.S., rural and urban. The test authors also took care to ensure representation of historically marginalized groups. However, standardization data for the published PRQ were collected using penultimate versions that had been winnowed down based on responses to pilot questionnaires completed by employees "of a major publishing company" (manual, p. 31); that is, people with jobs and education who live in cities (one in CA, one in MN). Before the PRQ was taken through the norming process, the content of the instrument was already significantly culturally limited.

Cultures exist in significant part to care for and socialize children. Respected childcare practices and standards vary by culture, and a child's sense of security is thus cued by culturally specific signifiers. Although the PRQ provides norms based on age of the child and reported sex of the caregiver/respondent, there are no explicit normative referents for children by cultural context be that ethnic, socioeconomic, linguistic, religious, or by caregiver sexual orientation or physical ability status. Admittedly, such fine-grained analyses would strain psychometric conventions. However, the cost of aggregation is the disappearance of culturally specific variables. The risk is misinterpretation and subsequent mistreatment based on flawed data. Even with statistical justification for the representative generality of aggregate scores, the PRQ's basis in a priori constructs and responses of publishing professionals may miss crucial indicators of healthy parent/caregiver-child relationships in cultures outside those represented by the test authors and early respondents.

SUMMARY. The subjectivity described above does not disqualify the PRQ as a useful tool. With clinical awareness and great attention to cultural nuance in what children recognize as signs of comfort and security, the general indicators available from the PRQ can be helpful for guiding support of children and their families. Nonetheless, it remains vital for the test authors and publisher to go beyond addressing limitations and to provide specific interpretive guidance relative to the PRQ's conceptual source in a particular worldview. This challenge represents one of the classic and pressing conundrums of contemporary behavioral science. Serious attention to the realities of human diversity will persist in guiding improvements in both knowledge and practice and remain a central ethical responsibility.

As a final comment, this review would be incomplete without an expression of appreciation of the PRQ authors, Drs. Randy Kamphaus and Cecil Reynolds; both consummate psychometricians who have given their careers to the careful development of technically exemplary assessment instruments for use in supporting the well-being of children and youth. In the acknowledgements section of the PRQ manual, Kamphaus eloquently honors Reynolds, and I join him in the appreciation of Reynolds' extensive and tireless contribution to the disciplines of psychology and education. Further, I extend this appreciation to include

Kamphaus, no less influential in the consistency of his contributions over recent decades.

The function of a psychometric review is to offer perspectives outside those available in the instrument or its manual. As mentioned above, the PRQ is based in exemplary technical conventions. The PRQ thus resides among the strong psychometric tools available for guiding responsible and responsive support of real children and youth.

Review of the Parenting Relationship Questionnaire by SANDRA WARD, Professor of Education, The College of William & Mary, Williamsburg, VA:

DESCRIPTION. The Parenting Relationship Questionnaire (PRQ) is a norm-referenced instrument developed to obtain the parent's perspective of the parent-child relationship. Such information can be used to select appropriate interventions. The Preschool level (ages 2–5; PRQ-P) consists of 45 items, and the Child and Adolescent level (ages 6–18; PRQ-CA) consists of 71 items. The scales of the PRQ-P include Attachment, Discipline Practices, Involvement, Parenting Confidence, and Relational Frustration. The PRQ-CA includes these five scales plus Communication and Satisfaction with School. The test authors provide a succinct description of each scale. The items are written at a third grade reading level, and the instrument takes an average of 10–15 minutes to complete. Additionally, the PRQ includes an audio-recording of the items that can be used with parents with limited ability to read English, but who can understand spoken English sufficiently.

The test authors provide specific instructions for administration, scoring, and interpretation of the PRQ. The PRQ is completed by the parent/caregiver. It may be useful to have more than one respondent, and up to five raters can be compared using the PRQ scoring software. The PRQ includes three types of record forms: hand-scored, computer-entry, and scannable. The directions in the manual are specific to using the hand-scored form, but they are applicable to the other two forms.

Scoring of the PRQ is straightforward and uncomplicated. The hand-scored forms of the PRQ allow the questionnaire to be administered and scored with a single form. The parent/caregiver reads each item and circles N (*Never*), S (*Sometimes*), O (*Often*), or A (*Almost Always*). Upon completion, the examiner separates the two parts of the form to reveal an inner page with the items already scored. This inner page also includes a summary table and graphical profile. The test authors provide directions for situations when items are not completed or are multiply answered. The raw score for each scale is converted to a *T* score (mean of 50, standard deviation of 10) and a percentile rank. *T* scores are based on a linear transformation of raw scores that preserves the shape of the raw score distribution. Consequently, scales may differ in their ranges of *T* scores. Standard scores and percentile ranks can be determined based on a female norm sample or a male norm sample determined by the gender of the respondent. Sample scoring pages are helpful to illustrate the scoring process.

The test authors are commended for their inclusion of four validity scales to identify problematic response sets. The F ("faking bad") index measures the respondent's tendency to rate the parent-child relationship in an excessively negative manner. The D ("defensive") index measures the respondent's tendency to give excessively positive ratings of the parent-child relationship. The Response Pattern index detects careless responding or inadequate comprehension of item content. The Consistency index measures the degree to which responses are inconsistent. The Response Pattern index and the Consistency index are only available with the PRQ computer software. The test authors clearly explain the use of cutoff scores and interpretation of the validity indices.

For interpretation, the test authors recommend use of norm-referenced scores and the integration of PRQ data with other information. Clear interpretation guidelines are provided for each scale, including the meaning of high and low scores and their relevance to the child's functioning. All interpretations are supported by cited research.

DEVELOPMENT. An initial list of constructs for the PRQ was derived from a literature review. Items were developed based on the definitions of these constructs. These items were refined based on feedback from internal and external reviewers. A tryout study was conducted with two forms created from the initial 184 items. The 215 obtained surveys were subjected to a series of factor analyses to evaluate the loading of each item on its corresponding scale. Items with standardized loadings <.30 and/or high modification indexes were dropped. The corresponding scale items from the two tryout forms were combined to develop the item set used in the standardization study.

The final selection of PRQ items and scale construction were based on data collected during standardization and submitted to confirmatory factor analysis. The test authors' intent in test development was to maximize the psychometric properties of the PRQ while keeping the questionnaire length as short as possible. Furthermore, the test authors investigated item bias through differential item functioning and partial correlations between items and demographic groups.

TECHNICAL. The data for standardization of the PRQ were collected between January 2003 and October 2005. The norm sample included 4,130 cases from 41 states. Based on the large raw score differences between male and female raters, the test authors created separate norms for gender of rater. Due to small differences in raw scores across the age range of the PRQ-P, separate norms were not created. At the PRQ-CA level, separate norm groups for age levels were based on score differences between age groupings. Normative data are provided for the following age groups: ages 6–9, ages 10–12, ages 13–15, and ages 16–18. Sample sizes for age groups range from 500–750 for the female rater group (total N = 3,500), and 100–150 for the male rater group (total N = 630). The gender of the child was balanced for each norm group. The standardization sample closely matches the 2001 U.S. Census data for socioeconomic status (parent education), race/ethnicity, geographic region, and classification in a special education program.

The internal consistency reliability coefficients reported in the manual are sufficient for the intended purpose of the PRQ. The median coefficient alphas for each scale across age groups exceed .80. On the one scale (Parenting Confidence) where the internal consistency reliability dropped below .80, the median values were still equal to or greater than .76. Test-retest reliability for the PRQ was computed on 74 cases at the PRQ-P level and 159 cases at the PRQ-CA level. The test-retest interval averaged from 33 days for the PRQ-P and 35 days for the PRQ-CA. The correlations ranged from .78 (Parenting Confidence scale) to .89 (Discipline Practices scale) for the PRQ-P level and from .72 (Discipline Practices scale) to .84 (Communication scale) for the PRQ-CA level. The lower test-retest coefficients on the PRQ-CA (median = .79) raise some concerns about the consistency across caregivers' ratings of the same child over time.

The test authors provide strong evidence to support the validity of the PRQ. Support for the test's content validity is demonstrated in the purposeful and thorough approach to item development and selection. Furthermore, the moderate intercorrelations in expected directions among the PRQ scales suggest a consistent internal structure.

The test authors provide evidence to support the convergent and discriminant validity for the PRQ. The individual scales of the PRQ-P and PRQ-CA were correlated with other measures of parent-child relationships. In most instances the appropriate scale(s) of the PRQ correlated highest with corresponding scale(s) of the instrument being used as the criterion. However, some correlations between the criterion measure scales and other scales of the PRQ were similar to the correlations with the appropriate scale used as a criterion. These results provide evidence for convergent validity, but they call into question the separateness of the individual scales of the PRQ.

In order to support the use of the PRQ to provide information relevant to the treatment of children's emotional and behavioral difficulties, the test authors provided correlations between PRQ ratings and ratings of behavior and emotions. The PRQ-CA Relational Frustration scale correlated strongly with ratings of externalizing problems in children, and it correlated moderately with ratings of depression. The PRQ-CA Parenting Confidence scale correlated moderately with Adaptability and Resiliency scales of the criterion measure. These findings generally support the use of the PRQ as an indicator of emotional problems in children.

The results of several criterion group studies provide support for the criterion-related validity of the PRQ-CA. These studies used data collected during standardization from parents who reported that their child was identified as having an emotional or behavioral problem. The clinical groups included all conditions (AC), attention-deficit/hyperactivity disorder (ADHD), emotional/behavioral disturbance (EBD), mental retardation or developmental delay (MR/DD), learning disability (LD), and speech or language disorder (SLD). Different PRQ-CA T-score profiles were obtained for the AC, ADHD, EBD, and MR/DD groups. Profiles for the LD and SLD groups were undifferentiated. It is unclear how the test authors established that the profiles were different except through inspection. Additionally, it should be noted that the sample sizes for these studies were relatively small, and the results may not be generalizable to the larger population without further research. Profiles were not examined for the PRQ-P due to difficulties in precise diagnoses at the preschool level.

A confirmatory factor analysis supports the separate scales of the PRQ-P and PRQ-CA. Median factor loadings of items on their designated scale were .58 and .64 for the PRQ-P and PRQ-CA, respectively. The test authors provide the factor loadings of each item with its corresponding scale; however, they do not provide information on the factor loadings of items on other scales. This information would be helpful to determine any overlap between the scales and to support their individual interpretation.

COMMENTARY. The PRQ is a useful instrument to obtain the parent/caregiver's perspective of the parent-child relationship. The test authors adhered to rigorous procedures and standards in the instrument's development. The PRQ is well standardized at both the preschool and adolescent levels. The reliability data support the use of the instrument as a screening measure of parent-child relationships to be used in conjunction with other information for selecting appropriate interventions. The lower test-retest reliability coefficients suggest some inconsistency in parent/caregiver ratings over time. Validity data for the PRQ-P and PRQ-CA are adequate.

SUMMARY. The PRQ is a user-friendly instrument that is completed by parents/caregivers to provide information on the parent-child relationship. The PRQ is easy to administer and interpret. The technical adequacy of the instrument, including standardization and reliability, is robust. The content validity and convergent validity of the instrument is adequate. Confirmatory factor analysis supports the scales of the PRQ. The PRQ can be used as a screening measure as part of a comprehensive assessment to determine appropriate interventions for students.

[88]

Peabody Picture Vocabulary Test, Fourth Edition.

Purpose: Designed for use as a measure of receptive vocabulary for Standard American English.
Population: Ages 2:6 to 90+ years.
Publication Dates: 1959-2007.
Acronym: PPVT-4.
Scores: Total score only.
Administration: Individual.
Forms, 2: A, B.
Price Data, 2008: $390 per complete kit (Forms A & B) including administration easels, 25 record booklets Form A & 25 record booklets Form B, and examiner's manual; $40.50 per 25 record booklets (specify A or B); $259 per PPVT-4 ASSIST™ scoring and reporting software; single form kits also available.
Time: (10-15) minutes.
Comments: Also includes a growth scale value (GSV) to specifically measure progress over time; conormed with the Expressive Vocabulary Test-2 (18:51); PPVT-4 and EVT-2 standard scores allow direct comparisons between receptive and expressive vocabulary; items are categorized for multiple levels of descriptive analysis; evidence-based interventions are embedded in the scoring and reporting software (ASSIST) and allow for multiple individual and group reports with aggregation and disaggregation options.
Authors: Lloyd M. Dunn & Douglas M. Dunn.
Publisher: Pearson.
Cross References: For reviews by Frederick Bessai and Orest Eugene Wasyliw of the third edition, see 14:280; see also T5:1903 (585 references) and T4:1945 (426 references); for reviews by R. Steve McCallum and Elisabeth H. Wiig of an earlier edition, see 9:926 (117 references); see also T3:1771 (301 references), 8:222 (213 references), T2:516 (77 references), and 7:417 (201 references); for reviews by Howard B. Lyman and Ellen V. Piers, see 6:530 (21 references).

Review of the Peabody Picture Vocabulary Test, Fourth Edition by JOSEPH C. KUSH, Associate Professor, Duquesne University, Pittsburgh, PA:

DESCRIPTION. The most recent revision of the Peabody Picture Vocabulary Test, Fourth Edition (PPVT-4) represents an important update to an already well-established instrument. Like previous versions of the instrument, the test is designed to assess the receptive English-language skills of both children and adults. In its original version, the PPVT (Dunn, 1959) was developed with the intent of being a test of verbal intelligence for school-aged children. Over 20 years later, the publication of the Peabody Picture Vocabulary Test—Revised (PPVT-R; Dunn & Dunn, 1981) added adult norms for individuals up to 40 years of age. With the publication of the third edition of the scale (PPVT-III; Dunn & Dunn, 1997) the age range was expanded to provide norms for individuals between the ages of 2.5 and 90+ years of age.

The current version of the scale consists of two parallel forms: Form A and Form B. Both forms consist of 228 items, each containing four colored pictures arranged on a single page. The examinee points to the picture that best describes the meaning of a word spoken verbally by the examiner. Raw scores are converted to standard scores, typically a mean of 100 and standard deviation of 15, and can be converted to percentile ranks, normal curve equivalents, stanines, and age and grade equivalents. Testing time averages approximately 11 to 12 minutes.

The PPVT-4 is an individually administered, untimed measure of receptive vocabulary. The test authors instruct examiners to allow examinees ample time to respond, but recommend providing a verbal prompt if no response is given within 10 seconds. Because examinees are only administered items of appropriate difficulty for their developmental or intellectual level, the test can be completed in a very brief amount of time; the test manual indicates that 90% of the standardization sample completed the scale in 20 minutes or less.

Despite the relative simplicity of the instrument's administration, user qualifications specify that the instrument "may be administered by individuals with a range of educational backgrounds, provided that they are thoroughly familiar with the test materials, have received training in procedures for individual test administration, and have been taught the methods for computing PPVT-4 raw scores and using the norm tables in this manual to obtain derived scores" (manual, p. iv). The PPVT-4 examiner's manual provides information to assist examiners in establishing rapport and in testing individuals with special needs.

The actual administration of the PPVT-4 items is relatively simple and straightforward—the examiner speaks the stimulus word and asks the examinee to point to the corresponding picture. Acceptable prompts include, "Show me [word]," "Point to [word]," "Put your finger on [word]," "Find [word]," or "Where is [word]?" Once it becomes clear that the examinee understands the task, the examiner can simply state the stimulus word without any prompt. A pronunciation guide is provided for the examiner to assist with items of greater difficulty. If necessary, a word may be repeated, or if the examinee has a motor impairment, the examiner may point to each of the four possible pictures and ask the examinee to nod or blink to indicate his or her response. This accommodation greatly expands the utility of the instrument by allowing for participation by very young children, or individuals with severe motor impairments. Although individuals are not penalized for guessing, examiner "coaching" is not permitted.

In most instances, the initial test questions begin at a point appropriate for the examinee's chronological age. The manual clearly outlines rules for where to begin the test as well as how to establish basal and ceiling sets. Easy to understand figures, taken from the scoring booklet, are also presented and provide clear, pictorial directions for beginning and discontinuing the test. Practice scoring exercises are also included.

DEVELOPMENT. The development of the PPVT-4 incorporates almost 50 years of previous scale development. The technical manual indicates that the test authors had two primary goals in mind with this revision, replacing all black-and-white picture stimuli with full-color illustrations, and the addition of more, very easy items for more accurate measurement of young children and examinees with low ability levels.

Consistent with previous revisions, data from the previous standardization sample (PPVT-III) were reviewed to identify items that needed to be replaced or updated. In addition to the need for additional items at the low end of the scale, the authors also determined that an increase in items was necessary in the categories of body parts, clothing, emotions, fruits and vegetables, musical instruments, and toys and recreation, along with a reduced representation of action words and adjectives. This revision resulted in the creation of 1,700 color pictures (some newly created and some adapted from the third edition and colorized) that served as the initial item pool of the PPVT-4 standardization sample.

The standardization process was comprehensive and should serve as an exemplary model for future instruments of this type. Initially, the face validity of the scale was established by asking educators from the United States, Canada, Great Britain, and Australia to examine the items and identify any that did not have similar applicability and usage across cultures. Next, a series of national tryouts occurred that resulted in the refinement of the scale (e.g., by eliminating words that were found to be commonly mispronounced by the examiner, or that had become outdated). Additionally, several special populations (e.g., ethnic minorities, children with special needs) were also oversampled to produce large enough data sets that would allow for appropriate statistical analyses. Item difficulty and discrimination indices were then calculated, as were Rasch difficulty estimates. Twenty-seven items were subsequently found to be biased and were eliminated from the scale. Attention also was given to the frequency with which distractor items were selected, and unsound items were modified or replaced.

The final standardization of the PPVT-4 occurred between the fall of 2005 and the spring of 2006 at 320 sites throughout the United States. The standardization sample included 3,540 participants ages 2 years, 6 months through 90+ years to create age norms and a subsample of 2,003 cases (Grades K–12) to create grade norms. The test included 228 items, derived from the national tryouts, arranged in increasing difficulty. As with previous editions, two parallel forms were created (Forms A and B); 75% of the items were adapted from the third edition and 25% were newly created. Males and females were represented equally in the items and race/ethnicity illustrations were approximately proportionally represented. Although these characteristics are to be expected of a scale at this point in time, it is interesting to remember that the original PPVT was standardized on a restricted sample of approximately 4,000 white individuals, all living near Nashville, TN. Equally interesting is the fact that the original PPVT contained only one picture of an individual from a minority background—a Black train porter.

Considerable attention was given to the standardization of the PPVT-4 and the norms will generalize to most segments of the United States population. The sample was matched to percentages of the stratification variables in the most recent United States Census. The norming sample was stratified into 28 age groups, by gender, by race/ethnicity (White, African American, Hispanic, and Other), and by SES (education level). Additional PPVT-4 stratification variables included four geographic regions (Northeast, North Central, South, and West) and educational placement. Children receiving special education services included representation from the following categories: attention deficit/hyperactivity disorder, emotional/behavioral disturbance, specific learning disability, developmental delay, mental retardation, speech language impairment, and autism. Comprehensive tables describing the stratification representation across each of these classification variables are provided on pages 39–48 of the technical manual.

TECHNICAL. Chapter 5 of the PPVT-4 technical manual provides extensive evidence supporting the reliability of the scale. Spearman-Brown corrected, split-half, and alpha reliabilities are reported across age, grade, and season (fall and spring) and consistently fall above .95, reflecting solid internal consistency evidence. Alternate form reliability (based on a subsample of 508 examinees) is also reported across five age groups and ranged between .87 and .93 with a mean of .89, suggesting that Forms A and B will, in fact, yield comparable scores. These scores are all comparable to those produced by the previous version of the scale (PPVT-III). Finally, as part of the standardization process, 340 examinees were retested with the PPVT-4 following an approximate interval of 4 weeks. Test-retest reliabilities are reported separately by age and ranged from .92 to .96. Corresponding standard errors of measurement (*SEM*) are also adequate, with a mean score of 3.6 reported across the 28 age levels.

Two summary comments should be made regarding the reliability of the PPVT-4. First, as would be expected of a scale of this importance, the test authors completed a comprehensive series of reliability analyses as part of the standardization process rather than wait to have the analyses completed by independent researchers following the publication of the scale. However, the sample sizes used by the publisher were relatively small and will necessitate subsequent empirical replication. Of course, future research should examine PPVT-4 constancy across longer intervals of times and with additional clinical populations. Despite the limited sample sizes used by the publishers, the reliability of the PPVT-4 is quite solid across all demographic subsamples. Even with very young children (ages 2–4) the reliability of the scale is impressive and users of the instrument can be confident that outstanding stability will be evidenced across all ages, ethnic backgrounds, and with alternate forms.

Acceptable detail is provided in the technical manual describing the validity of the scale. Regarding content validity, all items included in the scale were drawn from the most recent editions of the *Merriam-Webster Collegiate Dictionary* and *Webster's New Collegiate Dictionary*. As with reliability studies, a series of detailed validity studies are carefully presented on pages 59–67 of the technical manual. The majority of this research describes the criterion validity of the scale, that is, correlations with other measures of achievement. These studies used subsamples from the standardization sample and each of the studies utilized a counterbalanced approach such that the order in which the instruments were completed was randomized to counterbalance practice effects. Additionally, each of the calculated correlations was statistically corrected for restricted range.

With regard to achievement, the PPVT-4 correlates well with measures of expressive vocabulary and with measures of oral language. These correlations are uniform across age and are all in the moderate to high range. Additionally, the scale demonstrated moderate correlations with a measure of group reading achievement (mean correlation .63) and stronger (as would be expected) correlations with the PPVT-III (mean correlation .84).

The test authors should be commended as well for the series of studies performed with special populations. These studies included an examination of individuals with speech impairments, language disorders, hearing impairments, specific learning disabilities, mental retardation, emotional/behavioral disturbance, attention deficit/hyperactivity disorder, and with a population of gifted children and adolescents. As would be expected, extreme variability among these populations was evidenced, and although additional studies with larger sample sizes are necessary, the studies included within the technical manual provide preliminary evidence that clinicians who work with these populations will find helpful.

COMMENTARY. Although the test manual describes the theoretical relationship between vocabulary and verbal ability, the manual also indicates, "it is important to remember that vocabulary is acquired knowledge or achievement and that, despite its strong empirical relationship to cognitive abilities, it is conceptually distinct from them" (p. 4). As a result, no correlations between the PPVT-4 and measures of cognitive ability are presented in the technical manual. Perhaps the most significant limitation of the standardization process is that no exploratory or confirmatory factor analyses were conducted, as were no predictive validity studies. Although the theory underlying the instrument would suggest the presence of a single unitary construct (receptive vocabulary), this conclusion has yet to be supported by empirical data. Similarly, it remains unclear how accurately the scale will be able to predict future academic achievement. These findings are critical and will await future researchers.

SUMMARY. This revision of the most popular scale of receptive vocabulary represents a solid improvement upon an already outstanding scale. The most obvious improvement that will be noticeable to examiners is the larger, colored and updated illustrations. A more subtle, but significant improvement is the increased stability of the scale with very young children and for children with special needs. Although additional, independent research remains to be conducted, extending the psychometric properties of the scale, psychologists, speech clinicians, and educators can immediately use the scale with confidence for both screening and diagnostic purposes in the assessment of receptive English vocabulary.

Review of the Peabody Picture Vocabulary Test, Fourth Edition by STEVEN R. SHAW, Assistant Professor of Counselling and Educational Psychology, McGill University, Montreal, Quebec, Canada:

DESCRIPTION. The Peabody Picture Vocabulary Test, Fourth Edition (PPVT-4) is a measure of receptive (hearing) English vocabulary of children and adults. English vocabulary has implications for language competence, selecting instructional content, measuring learning, as part of a neuropsychological assessment battery, as part of reading assessment, and a correlate of general mental ability. The PPVT-4 is a norm-referenced, individually administered, and untimed instrument for persons aged from 2 years, 6 months to 90 years and older.

The PPVT-4 is designed to be administered by a Level B examiner (i.e., Bachelors degree with coursework in principles of measurement, administration, interpretation of tests, and formal training in the content area). The process is that the examiner reads aloud a single word and the examinee selects from four picture options. Administration requires only a pointing response. Examinees are tested over a critical range of approximately 60 items that represent items of the appropriate level of difficulty. Forms A and B each have 228 total items. Seventy-five percent of the items on the PPVT-4 were adapted from the PPVT-3 and 25% are new for the fourth edition. These items are divided into 19 sets of 12 words each. The basal set is the lowest set that contains zero or one errors. The ceiling set is the highest set of items containing eight or more errors. Testing is discontinued upon reaching the ceiling set. Rules for establishing basal and ceiling sets of items are clear and well-described. Testing time usually requires 10 to 15 minutes.

The PPVT-4 yields the following normative scores: standard scores, percentile ranks, normal curve equivalents, age equivalents, grade equivalents, and stanines. In addition, there is a new score called the growth value scale (GVS), which provides a standard transformation of raw scores. This non-norm-referenced metric can be used to make statistical comparisons of the amount of examinee change in scores over time.

There are several potential purposes and approaches to interpretation for the PPVT-4. Some of the uses described in the manual are: to build rapport as the initial component of an assessment battery, to use with preschool students, to use for children with expressive language disorders, to use for children with cerebral palsy or motor impairment, and to use for children who perform poorly on group tests. Because the PPVT-4 is available in two parallel forms it also can be used to assess improvement over time. The test authors emphasize the value of vocabulary as one of the five major components of reading ability. Therefore, special emphasis is placed on the use of the PPVT-4 as part of a reading assessment battery. The test authors also warn against overgeneralization of the PPVT-4 to general intelligence or overall language abilities.

The ASSIST Scoring and Reporting System for the PPVT-4 is the computerized scoring and interpretation system. Although the PPVT-4 is relatively easy to score using the tables provided in the test manual, computerized scoring reduces the probability of errors in scoring. This software is easy to use. The report generated from the software provides all of the different types of scores. Moreover, the ASSIST System provides a computer-generated report, qualitative analysis of responses, information about vocabulary development, and suggestions for instructional approaches to improve vocabulary. Although not required for scoring or interpretation, the ASSIST System adds significant value to scoring and interpretation.

DEVELOPMENT. The PPVT-4 is the latest in the venerable line of receptive vocabulary measures. The test authors sought opinions from the National Speech-Language Advisory Board and the American Speech-Language-Hearing Association. The results of these opinions led to the following changes: larger and full color artwork; increasing the number of easy items; updating words used; providing a framework for qualitative interpretation by the parts of speech of words; addition of the growth value scale (GVS); and additional materials such as form letters to parents in English and Spanish, improved scoring and interpretive software, and streamlined administration of training items.

Yet, much remains the same. In a sample of 322 participants, the mean scores for the PPVT-III and PPVT-4 are the same (i.e., 100.8). Thus, some clinics and schools may find it unnecessary to readjust cutting or eligibility scores due to the inclusion of a new instrument. Although inclusion of impressive color artwork is a major point in the revision of the PPVT-4, the manual reports that color versus black-and-white artwork has little to no effect on scores.

TECHNICAL. The PPVT-4 manual provides detailed evidence on standardization, reliability, and validity.

Standardization. The standardization sample consisted of 3,540 participants. The sample was selected to be representative of the U.S. Census on the basis of gender, race/ethnicity, educational level of participants or their parents, geographic region, and special education status of school-aged students. The sample was divided into 28 age groups. The age groups vary in age range from 6 months (from ages 2 years, 6 months to 6 years, 11 months) to 10 years or more (ages 31 to 81+). There were 60 to 200 participants in each age group. Other than a slight underrepresentation of the Western geographic region, all other variables appear to be very closely aligned with the U.S. Census figures.

Reliability. The PPVT-4 manual provides reliability information on split-half reliability, coefficient alpha, stability, and alternative forms reliability. Split-half reliabilities ranged from .90 to .97 with an average of .94. Alpha coefficients ranged from .93 to .98 with an average of .97. The standard error of measurement is 3.6. Alternate form reliability data on Forms A and B were collected on a sample of 508 participants. The results show alternative forms reliability ranging from .87 to .93 with an average of .89. Stability data were collected on a sample of 340 participants with an average of a 4-week span between testing. Test-retest coefficients ranged from .92 to .96. There is strong evidence provided for several different types of reliability.

Validity. Evidence for validity is described in terms of content, correlations with other measures, and differences among special populations and the standardization sample. Validity support according to the *Standards for Educational and Psychological Testing* (American Educational Research Association, American Psychological Association, & National Council on Measurement in Education, 1999) is based on test content, response process, relationship to other variables, internal structure, and evidence based on consequences of testing. Reported evidence for the PPVT-4 does not take into account response process, internal structures, or evidence concerning the consequences of testing.

The strongest evidence of validity for the PPVT-4 is the correlations with other instruments. The PPVT-4 was conormed with the Expressive Vocabulary Test (Second Edition). The PPVT-4 was also studied with the Comprehensive Assessment of Spoken Language, Clinical Evaluation of Language Fundamentals: Fourth Edition, Group Reading Assessment, and Diagnostic Evaluation. These correlations are all in the moderate to high range, indicating appropriate and expected agreement with tests of similar constructs.

The PPVT-4 was also administered to samples of persons with hearing impairment, speech impairment, language delay, mental retardation, learning disabilities, giftedness, emotional and behavioral disabilities, and attention deficit hyperactivity disorder. Generally, these samples show differences in the expected directions. However, it is notable that the speech impairment sample earned scores near the mean of the nonclinical reference group. This lends support for the use of the PPVT-4 for persons with speech impairment.

COMMENTARY. Although the scope of the PPVT-4 is narrow (i.e., receptive [hearing] language), vocabulary remains a core feature of the assessment of reading, speech and language, and general intelligence. The result is that the PPVT-4 is widely used by educators, neuropsychologists, psychoeducational specialists, psychologists, and speech and language therapists. There are many tests and subtests that assess vocabulary. In many ways it is unclear why the PPVT-4 is so widely used when there are already subtests within many tests of intelligence, academic achievement, and neuropsychological functioning that seem to be adequate measures of receptive vocabulary. Yet, there is always room in an assessment battery for a test as well-designed, technically sophisticated, relatively inexpensive, and quick and easy to administer as the PPVT-4. However, the rather old-fashioned reporting of validity does not respond to important modern conceptions of validity that include description of the response process, internal structures, and evidence on the consequences of testing.

SUMMARY. The PPVT-4 continues the line of excellent measures of receptive language. Among the important and productive features of the PPVT-4 are ease of administration and interpretation, well-developed ASSIST Scoring and Reporting System for computerized scoring, short administration time, and the simple required examinee response (pointing). For these reasons, the PPVT-4 remains one of the most commonly administered tests in psychoeducational and speech and language assessment. Given the high quality of the technical features, detailed examiner's manual, and flexibility of uses and interpretations, the PPVT-4 deserves to remain a popular component of assessment batteries.

REVIEWER'S REFERENCE

American Educational Research Association, American Psychological Association, & National Council on Measurement in Education. (1999). *Standards for educational and psychological testing*. Washington, DC: American Educational Research Association.

[89]

Pediatric Attention Disorders Diagnostic Screener.

Purpose: Designed to assist clinicians in diagnosing children with ADHD by using multiple sources and multiple types of assessments.

Population: Parent- or school-referred children ages 6-12.

Publication Dates: 2000-2008.

Acronym: PADDS.

Scores, 22: 4 scores per SNAP-IV form (Parent/Guardian, Teacher): ADHD–Inattention, Hyperactivity/Impulsivity, ADHD–Combined Type, Total (calculated as likelihood ratio); Total count of behavioral responses (Redirection/Re-instruction, Fidgeting, Emotional Reaction) per Target Test; Raw score and likelihood ratio per Target Test (Target Recognition, Target Sequence, Target Tracking); 5 cumulative, Post-test probabilities of being diagnosed with ADHD (calculated each time additional assessment is entered into PADDS system).

Administration: Individual.

Parts, 4: SNAP-IV Rating Scale, Computer Administered Diagnostic Interview, Structured Assessment of Testing Behaviors, Target Tests of Executive Functioning.

Price Data, 2008: $695 per PADDS full version including Clinical Manual (66 pages), Software Installation and Use Manual (30 pages), and CD-ROM (Version

1.0.45) with unlimited uses; $395 per PADDS standard version including Clinical Manual, Software Installation and Use Manual, and CD-ROM (Version 1.0.45) with 5 pre-loaded uses; $100 per 10 additional uses; quantity discounts available.
Time: (35-45) minutes; (25-30) minutes to administer all three Target Tests of Executive Functions; (10-15) minutes to input data from previously completed CADI and SNAP-IV forms.
Comments: Also called Pediatric ADHD Screener; testing software is Windows compatible and requires Adobe Reader (included) for viewing of summary reports.
Authors: Thomas K. Pedigo, Kenneth L. Pedigo, and Vann B. Scott, Jr. (Clinical Manual).
Publisher: Targeted Testing, Inc.

a) SNAP-IV RATING SCALE.
Purpose: Identifies "Parent and teacher ratings [of the child] of the behavior criteria for ADHD based on criteria set by the [DSM-IV-R]."
Publication Date: 1992.
Acronym: SNAP-IV.
Scores, 8: 4 scores per form: ADHD–Inattention, Hyperactivity/Impulsivity, ADHD–Combined Type, Total (calculated as likelihood ratio).
Administration: Group.
Forms, 2: Parent/Guardian, Teacher.
Foreign Language Editions: Available in Spanish; contact publisher for availability of other languages.
Time: Administration time not reported.
Comments: Separate ratings by parent/guardian and teacher.
Authors: James M. Swanson, W. Nolan, and W. E. Pelham.

b) COMPUTER ADMINISTERED DIAGNOSTIC INTERVIEW.
Purpose: Screens for "possible co-morbid conditions that can mimic or exacerbate ADHD symptoms."
Acronym: CADI.
Scores: Not scored; Clinical feedback may be provided for 6 possible domains: Medical History/Systems Review, Developmental History, Social/Emotional Functioning, Depression/Anxiety, Attention/Hyperactivity, Behavior/School History.
Administration: Group.
Foreign Language Editions: Available in Spanish; contact publisher for availability of other languages.
Time: Administration time not reported.
Comments: Interview can be computer administered and completed during child's session, or interview and protocol can be printed out and completed prior to child's session. Ratings by Parent/Guardian.

c) STRUCTURED ASSESSMENT OF TESTING BEHAVIORS.
Purpose: Designed to "help assess and quantify behavior changes in subjects across administration as in pre-medication and post-medication challenges."
Scores, 3: Total count of behavioral responses (Redirection/Re-instruction, Fidgeting, Emotional Reaction) per Target Test.
Administration: Individual.
Time: (25-30) minutes.
Comments: Ratings by administrator of Target Tests.

d) TARGET TESTS OF EXECUTIVE FUNCTIONING.
Purpose: Computer presented tasks "aimed at providing objective assessment of a subject's ability to employ various but not all executive processes: (planning, attending, organizing input, storing and retrieving information, modulating emotions and sustaining effort)."
Acronym: TTEF.
Scores, 6: 2 scores (Raw score and likelihood ratio) per Target Test (Target Recognition, Target Sequence, Target Tracking).
Administration: Individual.
Time: (25-30) minutes to administer all three Target Tests.

Review of the Pediatric Attention Disorders Diagnostic Screener by RAMA K. MISHRA, Neuropsychologist, Department of Psychiatry, Medicine Hat Regional Hospital, Medicine Hat, Alberta, Canada:

DESCRIPTION. The Pediatric Attention Disorders Diagnostic Screener (PADDS) is designed to assist in the diagnosis of Attention Deficit Hyperactivity Disorder (ADHD) in children between 6 and 12 years of age (Pedigo, Pedigo, & Scott, 2008). This system uses multiple measures including a computer-administered diagnostic interview (CADI); the Swanson, Nolan, and Pelham–IV (SNAP-IV) parent rating scale and teacher rating scale; and three computer-administered objective tests (viz., Target Tests of Executive Functioning [TTEF]). The executive functioning tests focus on target recognition, target sequencing, and target tracking. The program calculates diagnostic likelihood ratios that are graphed on a nomogram to provide incremental validity when results are combined from multiple measures. The results also provide traditional standard scores, *T*-scores, *z*-scores, and percentile ranks compared to clinical and nonclinical reference groups.

It takes about 25 to 30 minutes to complete the Target Tests of Executive Functioning. The data from previously completed CADI and SNAP-IV ratings can be entered for analysis in 10 to 15 minutes. Thus, all tests can be completed in less than an hour for analysis and interpretation.

DEVELOPMENT. The test authors have identified the importance of multiple sources of information including assessment of executive operations and working memory for identification of ADHD in children. Accordingly, the authors of the PADDS tested 395 children between the ages of 6 and 12 years with ADHD and 330 non-ADHD peers from seven states in the United States with the Target Tests of Executive Functioning. Identification of ADHD was made by clinical interview, intelligence testing, cognitive testing for short-term auditory and visual memory, and performance on either the Conners' Continuous Performance Test (CPT-II) or the Test of Variables of Attention (TOVA). All ADHD children were tested in the morning prior to taking their stimulant medication during the day. The non-ADHD children were drawn from elementary schools in the same states and were screened with the Conners Rating Scale-Teacher Version.

TECHNICAL. Psychometric properties of the PADDS have been reported for internal consistency, test-retest reliability, concurrent validity, convergent validity, discriminant validity, and construct validity. The test authors have also reported receiver operator characteristics (ROC) for sensitivity and specificity as well as positive and negative predictive power in the clinical manual.

The internal consistency coefficient has been reported to be .86 and test-retest stability coefficient has been reported to be .85. The test-restest interval was 1 to 2 years. Concurrent validity has been reported by correlation coefficients of -.39 to .43 between three PADDS tests (viz., Target Recognition, Target Sequencing, and Target Tracking), and four subscales of the TOVA (viz., Omission, Commission, Response Time, Variability, and Multiple Response). The PADDS scales and CPT-II subscales were also reported to be in the range of -.52 to .00 for a second sample. Finally, correlation coefficients of PADDS executive functioning tests with the Behavior Rating Inventory of Executive Function (BRIEF) scales were reported to be in the range of -.30 to .12. Convergent validity was reported by a correlation coefficient of .38 between the PADDS and the Test of Variable Attention (TOVA). The hit rate was reported to be 94% for PADDS Target Tests, 66% for the Brown ADD Scales, and 68% for the Conner's CPT-II for a sample of 38 children. Discriminant validity indices were reported by the relationship of the PADDS with IQ and memory. It was reported that the PADDS tests were not related to Full Scale IQ, Verbal IQ, and Performance IQ measured by the Wechsler Abbreviated Scale of Intelligence (*p*s > .05). PADDS tests were also unrelated to visual memory and verbal memory measured by the Children's Memory Scale and the Wide Range Assessment of Memory and Learning II (*p*s > .05). The test authors claim that positive and significant correlations with the executive operations of the Brown ADD scales demonstrate construct validity of the PADDS. However, the study used only 35 participants and the correlations were modest (-.41 to .12). Finally, the test authors have used receiver operator characteristics (ROC) to report a Sensitivity Index of .88 and Specificity Index of .89.

COMMENTARY. The PADDS is quite clearly a new type of test that is highly useful for many frontline clinicians, particularly due to the fact that it combines three objective measures of executive functioning, a diagnostic interview, and parent/teacher rating scales (Reddy, Fumari, Pedigo, & Scott, 2008). The test results provide incremental validation of information from all sources so that the clinician can evaluate the strength of a positive or negative diagnosis.

The normative sample and validations study samples on which the PADDS has been developed are quite limited. It would be helpful to use the PADDS on large scale studies or multiple studies to determine additional information on the sensitivity and specificity of this screening test on a broad range of children with attentional difficulties. The criterion measure against which the PADDS needs to be evaluated continues to be problematic due to the complexities of attentional disorders. It might be necessary to divide the criterion groups into subtypes based on specific characteristics. Clinicians and researchers would likely be interested to see how the PADDS measures are related to other established tests such as the Cognitive Assessment System (Naglieri and Das, 1997; 14:109), which has three subtests in the Attention domain and three subtests in the Planning domain in addition to two other processing-related domains. In the future, older children need to be included in studies on the PADDS so that it can be used for children older than 12 years of age, particularly for adolescent onset of ADHD, which is expected to be a new category in DSM-V (Barkley, 2006; Kupfer & Regier, 2008).

SUMMARY. In summary, the PADDS is a very useful tool for assessment of attention deficit hyperactivity disorder in younger children. The clinicians in particular will benefit from the comprehensive approach to assessment that combines multiple sources of information. More research is obviously needed to establish validity of this approach to make a positive diagnosis of ADHD or rule out ADHD in children with greater accuracy from the available probability indices.

REVIEWER'S REFERENCES

Barkley, R. (2006). *Subtypes of ADHD: Implications for clinicians.* Continuing Medical Education (CME) presentation in Calgary on April 25, 2006.

Kupfer, D. J., & Regier, D. A. (2008). *Current activities: Report of the DSM-V task force (November 2008).* From the American Psychiatric Association website, http://www.psych.org/MainMenu/Research/DSMIV/DSMV/DSMRevisionActivities/DSMVTaskForceReport.aspx

Naglieri, J. A., & Das, J. P. (1997). Cognitive Assessment System. Itasca, IL: Riverside Publishing.

Pedigo, T. K., Pedigo, K. L., & Scott, V. B. (2008). Pediatric Attention Disorders Diagnostic Screener. Okeechobee, FL: Targeted Testing Inc.

Reddy, L. A., Fumari, G., Pedigo, T. K., & Scott, V. (2008). Pediatric Attention Disorders Diagnostic Screener for children at-risk for attention-deficit/hyperactivity disorder. *The School Psychologist, 62*(3), 93-98.

Review of the Pediatric Attention Disorders Diagnostic Screener by JANET REED, Senior Staff Neuropsychologist, Henry Ford Behavioral Health, Division of Neuropsychology, Detroit, MI:

DESCRIPTION. The Pediatric Attention Disorders Diagnostic Screener (PADDS) represents a multimethod approach to identifying symptoms associated with attention disorders in children 6–12 years of age. The stated goal of the PADDS is to use an evidence-based approach to the assessment of attentional problems in children. Base rates and cut scores from parent and teacher report (SNAP-IV) of symptoms and child performance on three computer-administered continuous performance tasks (Target Tests of Executive Function; TTEF) are used to establish a probability of a diagnosis of ADHD along with local base rates. The PADDS consists of four components: An observation rating form for behaviors observed during the continuous performance task (Structured Assessment of Testing Behaviors); a background and diagnostic checklist that can be administered by computer or paper-and-pencil (Computer Administered Diagnostic Interview; CADI); Parent and Teacher report of symptoms (SNAP-IV); and three different trials of a continuous performance task (TTEF). The Report for the Cognitive Tests and SNAP-IV consists of a summary of SNAP-IV rating scores, a Fagan Nomogram that plots the pre- and posttest probabilities, and Likelihood ratios for each TTEF. Each subsequent calculation uses the previous test result's posttest probability as the pretest probability to produce a cumulative posttest probability of a diagnosis of ADHD. A PADDS Predictive Index Score in the 90th–99th percentile is considered to "clearly support a diagnosis of ADHD" (clinical manual, p. 17); whereas a score in the 80th–90th percentile is considered "suggestive of ADHD" (clinical manual, p. 17); and scores below the 80th percentile are "not deemed adequate to support a clinical diagnosis of ADHD" (clinical manual, p. 17).

The Computer Administered Diagnostic Interview (CADI) consists of 113 questions covering Medical History and Systems Review, Developmental History, Social/Emotional Functioning, Depression/Anxiety, Behavior, and School History. The SNAP-IV parent and teacher versions (adapted from Swanson, Nolan, & Pelham, 2002) each consist of 20 statements rated on a 4-point Likert scale (0 = *Not At All*, 1 = *Just a Little*, 2 = *Quite a Bit*, 3 = *Very Much*). The SNAP-IV yields four scores: Inattention, Hyperactivity/Impulsivity, ADHD-Combined Type, and a Total score (calculated as a likelihood ratio). The Likelihood Ratio of 9 (based on the reported sensitivity and specificity of .90) for each scale was established and combined into a single probability. The Structured Assessment of Testing Behaviors is a form for recording the number of times during administration of the TTEF the child requires redirection or re-instruction, fidgeting, and emotional reactivity. The CADI and SNAP-IV can be administered on the computer or provided on paper with scores entered by the examiner. Scores from the Structured Assessment of Testing Behaviors are entered by the examiner.

Administration of the TTEF takes 25–30 minutes, with another 10 minutes to enter data from Parent and Teacher Reports, diagnostic checklist information, and behavioral observations. The TTEF consists of three computer-administered tasks. Stimuli are colorful and attractive nonlexical figures (squares, circles, and other shapes). Each task is preceded by instruction and practice that need to be completed before the program will allow continuation of the task. Feedback is provided, with the words "correct" or "wrong" printed on the screen after each response. If the participant does not respond within 5 seconds, the program will time-out and display a STOP command and score the trial as a miss. The tasks are Target Recognition, Target Sequencing, and Target Tracking. Scoring is performed automatically by the computer program.

DEVELOPMENT. The TTEF were developed by a pediatric psychologist based on current research indicating the need for assessing greater aspects of children's executive functioning and working memory. The test authors cogently note that with the potentially low base rate of 4% in the general population, a measure with 90% sensitivity and 90% specificity has only a 25% positive predictive index in making a diagnosis. Each of the subtests was designed to tax both inhibitory and cognitive controls. Tasks were developed to be non-language-based and to lend themselves to cross-cultural uses, with consideration for behaviors relevant to classroom demands.

TECHNICAL. The standardization sample for the TTEF consists of 240 females and 485 males ranging in age from 6 to 12 years, which included 395 ADHD and 330 non-ADHD matched controls (Typical group) in seven states across 10 test sites. Hispanic race (7%) was underrepresented relative to the 2006 U.S. Census population estimates (20%), with Caucasian (70%) and African American (20%) races relatively well represented relative to population estimates (76% and 15%, respectively). ADHD children were identified through clinical assessment using interview, history, cognitive testing, measures of short-term auditory and visual memory, continuous test performance results, and review of criteria met for ADHD. The Typical group was recruited from elementary schools in the same states as the ADHD group. Those with clinically significant signs of depression, anxiety, or emotional disorders were excluded from the sample.

Cut scores were developed for each of the TTEF based on the lower performance of the ADHD versus the Typical group on all measures. Two of the three TTEF scores had to fall in the predicted direction to be considered a classification "hit." Thus, those in the ADHD group would need to perform at or below the cut point on two TTEF to be considered accurately classified by the measure. Across age groups, sensitivity ranged from .80 to .91; specificity ranged from .84 to .92; positive predictive power ranged from .75 to .95; and negative predictive power ranged from .72 to .94. Raw scores for each TTEF were used to determine individual test sensitivity and specificity, from which likelihood ratios were calculated.

Internal consistency, test-retest, and interrater reliability were assessed for the TTEF. Internal consistency reliability for the three TTEF ranged from alpha = .80 to .92. Stability of the diagnostic classification on a subsample 6 months after initial testing yielded a stability coefficient of .94. Phi and kappa coefficients were .70 and .90, respectively. On a second sample (n = 27) over 1 to 2 years, 23 were correctly classified, for a stability coefficient of .85, phi of .70, and kappa of .73.

Separate validity studies were conducted using the Test of Variables of Attention (TOVA) and the Conners' Continuous Performance Test, Second Edition (CPT-II). Correlations between TOVA variables and PADDS subtest scores ranged from .02 (p = n.s.) to .43. Correlations between CPT-II scores and individual TTEF scores ranged from .00–.52. A third sample (n = 59 participants 6–12 years) was administered the Behavior Rating Inventory of Executive Function (BRIEF), Teacher and Parent forms. Correlations between composite scores on the BRIEF and the TTEF ranged from -.01 for Parent Report of Working Memory to -.30 ($p < .05$) for Teacher Report of Emotional Control.

COMMENTARY. The developers of the PADDS have attempted to capitalize on recent trends in assessment of evidence-based evaluation of psychiatric disorders in children using Bayesian Theory and methods to determine the probability of a diagnosis of ADHD given known values of base rates of the disorder, individual performance, and collateral reports on behavior. This approach, along with the nonverbal nature of stimuli, represents a novel approach to differentiating children with ADHD from nonclinic-referred children. The TTEF clearly assess distinct constructs from existing continuous performance tests as evidenced by their low correlations with specific indices.

One caution for users is that the model of cumulative posttest probabilities likely overestimates posttest probabilities due to intercorrelations between measures (most especially the TTEF; Frazier & Youngstrom, 2006). The PADDS possesses adequate reliability, but evidence for construct validity is limited. Adequate discriminant validity is demonstrated for differentiating those with ADHD from those without clinical disorders. However, there is no demonstrated validity for differentiating ADHD from other clinical disorders. Low construct validity, based on correlations between the TTEF and collateral report measures, is consistent with low correlations between widely used CPT measures and behavioral reports (Edwards et al., 2007), and this should not be considered to indicate lack of evidence for construct validity. The administration time for the PADDS (30 minutes) is considerably longer than that of other continuous performance tests (14 minutes) and possesses a limited age range.

SUMMARY. The PADDS represents a meritorious attempt at using evidence-based evaluation of test characteristics (sensitivity and specificity), population characteristics (base rates), and multiple sources of data (individual performance, teacher report, and parent report) in an attempt to improve the diagnostic accuracy of ADHD. The main advantage is the approach to establishing prior and posttest probabilities. The primary disadvantage is the length of test administration time relative to well-established tests with substantially shorter administrations and a greater range of norms across age ranges.

REVIEWER'S REFERENCES

Edwards, M. C., Gardner, E. S., Chelonis, J. J., Schulz, E. G., Flake, R. A., & Diaz, P. F. (2007). Estimates of the validity and utility of the Conners' Continuous Performance Test in the assessment of inattentive and/or hyperactive/impulsive behaviors in children. *Journal of Abnormal Child Psychology, 35*, 393–404.

Frazier, T. W., & Youngstrom, E. A. (2006). Evidence-based assessment of attention-deficit/hyperactivity disorder: Using multiple sources of information. *Journal of the American Academy of Child and Adolescent Psychiatry, 45*, 614–620.

[90]

Pediatric Behavior Rating Scale.

Purpose: "To assist in the identification of serious emotional dysregulation and related disorders—most notably early onset bipolar disorder."
Population: Ages 3-18.
Publication Date: 2008.
Acronym: PBRS.
Scores, 10: Atypical, Irritability, Grandiosity, Hyperactivity/Impulsivity, Aggression, Inattention, Affect, Social Interactions, Total Bipolar Index, Inconsistency Score.
Administration: Group.
Forms, 2: Parent (PBRS-P), Teacher (PBRS-T).
Price Data, 2010: $235 per introductory kit including professional manual (128 pages), 25 reusable Parent item booklets, 25 reusable Teacher item booklets, 25 Parent response booklets, 25 Teacher response booklets, 25 Parent score summary/profile forms, and 25 Teacher score summary/profile forms; $31 per 25 reusable Parent item booklets; $31 per 25 reusable Teacher item booklets; $47 per 25 Parent response booklets; $47 per 25 Teacher response booklets; $21 per 25 Parent score summary/profile forms; $21 per 25 Teacher score summary/profile forms; $52 per professional manual.
Time: [15-20] minutes.
Comments: Pediatric Behavior Rating Scale Scoring Program (PBRS-SP) offered separately.
Authors: Richard M. Marshall and Berney J. Wilkinson.
Publisher: Psychological Assessment Resources, Inc.

Review of the Pediatric Behavior Rating Scale by JANET REED, Senior Staff Neuropsychologist, Henry Ford Behavioral Health, Division of Neuropsychology, Detroit, MI:

DESCRIPTION. The Pediatric Behavior Rating Scale (PBRS) is a standardized Parent (PBRS-P; 102 items) and Teacher (PBRS-T; 95 items) report scale to assess symptoms associated with early onset Bipolar Disorder (BPD) in children and youth from 3 to 18 years of age. The PBRS is considered appropriate for use by school psychologists, clinical psychologists, pediatricians, psychiatrists, and other professionals to aid in the identification of early onset bipolar disorder and in the differentiation of early onset bipolar disorder from other psychiatric disorders of childhood with similar behavioral characteristics.

Instructions are to rate each item on a 4-point Likert scale indicating the frequency of each behavior in the past month: *Never, Sometimes, Often*, or *Always*. Raters for the PBRS-T (e.g., teachers, school social workers, school psychologists) are required to know the child a minimum of 4 weeks, with at least daily contact; or more than 4 weeks of contact several days per week. Scaled scores consist of an Inconsistency Index to judge validity of the report, a global symptom rating index (Total Bipolar Index), and eight subscales. The respondent reviews questions from the item booklet and records responses in the self-scoring response booklet. The examiner uses the template (scoring sheet) on the response booklet to total scores from each subscale. Raw scores are transferred to the score summary along with responses to particular items to calculate the Inconsistency Index. Critical items that require immediate attention are also transferred to the score summary form. Raw scores are converted to *T*-scores (mean = 50, standard deviation = 10) using age- and gender-based normative tables in the appendices of the professional manual. A cutoff score of 11 or greater on the Inconsistency Index indicates Questionable/Inconsistent responding.

Names of the eight clinical scales are: Aytpical, Irritability, Grandiosity, Hyperactivity/Impulsivity, Aggression, Inattention, Affect, and Social Interactions. The Atypical Scale reflects "behaviors frequently associated with psychotic disorders (e.g., bizarre beliefs, auditory hallucinations, delusions, self-harm behaviors, excessive fears)" (professional manual, p. 21). The Irritability scale was designed to reflect persistent and chronic irritability leading to severe emotional dysregulation and behavioral/emotional outbursts. The Grandiosity scale consists of items regarding sense of self and mood, bullying, intimidation of others, stealing, and failing to take responsibility for actions. The Hyperactivity/Impulsivity scale inquires about difficulty sitting still, overactivity, and impulsivity. The Aggression scale includes items to gauge aggression towards others, objects, or animals. The Inattentive scale assesses inattentiveness, distractibility, and difficulty focusing. The Affect scale consists of items assessing suicidal ideation, mood disturbance, and cognitive distortions. The Social Interactions scale is composed of items assessing "the ability to make friends, relate to others, and engage in social interactions" (professional manual, p. 21). There are 17 critical items on the PBRS-Parent form and 15 on the PBRS-Teacher form, which reflect self-abusive behavior, vindictiveness, expression of violent themes, norm-violating behavior, atypical experiences, and suicidal ideation. Interpretation involves examining the consistency of responses (Inconsistency Index), total symptoms (Total Bipolar Index; TBX), symptom profile (PBRS scales), comparison of forms across raters, evaluation of critical items, and integration with other relevant data. Scores equal to or below 59 are considered Within Normal Range; between 60 and 69 At-Risk, and greater than or equal to 70 are Clinically Significant.

DEVELOPMENT. Items for the PBRS were developed based on the test authors' experience, with the aim of including items specific to bipolar disorder as items reflective of comorbid disorders and disorders with similar symptoms. Three experts (all psychologists) independently reviewed and grouped the scales into five categories that comprise the rationally derived scales of the PBRS. Modifications were made after review by a school psychologist and after item-total correlations were examined. The test authors are careful to point out that like most single sources of clinical information, the PBRS does not render a clinical diagnosis and is not an omnibus behavior rating scale. The test authors state that the PBRS is for symptom and profile identification, support of diagnostic impressions, facilitation and identification of behavioral interventions in educational settings, a research tool for definition of the disorder, differentiation from other disorders, and evaluation of the efficacy of interventions.

TECHNICAL. The normative sample consisted of 541 parents and 610 teachers of children 3 through 18 years of age through direct recruitment of data sites. The sample is reported to be well-matched to the U.S. population by age and gender, based on U.S. Census Data from 2007, with the exception of oversampling of Caucasian parents in the Parent-report sample (89.6%). The combined clinical sample (diagnosed with Bipolar Disorder, Attention Deficit/Hyperactivity Disorder, Oppositional Defiant Disorder, Conduct Disorder, and Pervasive Developmental Disorder) consisted of 224 parents and 194 teachers of children identified through direct recruitment of data sites. The Inconsistency score cutoff was determined by the use of seven item pairs. Correlations between the items in each pair were calculated and frequency distributions were developed.

Internal consistency, test-retest, and interrater reliability were calculated. Coefficient alphas for scales and the Total Bipolar Index in the normative group ranged from .60 to .89 for the PBRS-P, and .75 to .97 for the PBRS-T with ranges from .79 to .95 and .83 to .96 for the combined clinical sample on the PBRS-P and PBRS-T, respectively. Median test-retest reliability over 6–44 days was .82 and .93 for PBRS-P and PBRS-T, respectively. Median interrater reliability coefficients for PBRS-P with the PBRS-T, and between parents on the PBRS-P were .83 and .81, respectively.

Construct validity was examined using intercorrelations between scales and the Total Bipolar Index correlations with other behavioral measures and examination of mean differences across clinical groups. Intercorrelations between scale scores and the Total Bipolar Index ranged from .33 to .86 for the normative sample and .01 to .82 for the combined clinical sample on the PBRS-P. Intercorrelations on the Teacher version range from .47 to .92 for the normative sample and from .03 to .82 for the combined clinical sample. Correlations among informants on other behavioral measures were calculated for the normative sample (Teacher and Parent ratings on the Clinical Assessment of Behavior Rating form and the Behavior Assessment System for Children, Second Edition) and the combined clinical sample (Child Mania Rating Scale, Conduct Disorder Scale, and Conners' Teacher Rating Scale–Revised: Short Version). Correlations between the PBRS-P and the Child Mania Rating

Scale ranged from .07 to .63 for the Parent report, and -.23 to .70 for corresponding Teacher report forms in a mixed clinical sample (ADHD, ODD, CD, Bipolar Disorder). Correlations were from .16 to .74 between the teacher forms on the Conduct Disorder Scale. The PBRS-T correlated .16 to .69 with the Conners' Teacher Rating Scale-Revised: Short Version. *T*-tests between the ADHD and Bipolar groups were significant on most scales and on the Total Bipolar Index for the PBRS-P and PBRS-T.

COMMENTARY. The PBRS is a brief Parent and Teacher report rating scale that is easy to administer and score. It is also an inexpensive adjunct to existing scales assessing a wide range of internalizing and externalizing symptoms. Its greatest strength lies in its ability to differentiate those with ADHD and those with high levels of emotional dysregulation and risky behaviors as evidenced by significant differences between mean scores of those with ADHD and those with Bipolar Disorder. Double negative wording of some items is confusing to raters and may result in limited validity. Although the reliability of the scale is adequate, validity is somewhat limited. In further refinement of the PBRS, factor analysis of items is recommended, to validate the scale construction. Discriminant function analyses are recommended to assess the ability of the PBRS to differentiate among disorders with symptom overlap (e.g., Conduct Disorder, Oppositional Defiant Disorder, other mood disorders), especially because this is a stated goal. The current state of the art for evidence-based assessment of Bipolar Disorder consists of developmentally appropriate assessment of symptoms of grandiosity, euphoria, and mania and the use of Likelihood ratios based on the sensitivity and specificity of measures for making diagnostic decisions about pediatric Bipolar Disorder (Youngstrom & Youngstrom, 2005).

SUMMARY. The PBRS is a parent and teacher report measure assessing symptoms of emotional dysregulation in the past month, and may be useful as an adjunct to other broad-band behavioral measures in a clinical setting, or as an initial screening tool. Overall validity is modest, with the PBRS differentiating normal and clinically diagnosed participants, but not differentiating well among clinical groups. Although its ability to differentiate those with bipolar disorder from those with similar or comorbid conditions is limited, it holds promise as a tool assessing the severity of these symptoms and monitoring them over time. Further, it may help to identify rapid cycling episodes and/or medication efficacy. The use of this instrument is not advised for individuals without proper clinical training to differentiate Bipolar Disorder from other clinical disorders.

REVIEWER'S REFERENCE

Youngstrom, E. A., & Youngstrom, J. K. (2005). Evidence-based assessment of pediatric bipolar disorder, Part II: Incorporating information from behavior checklists. *Journal of the American Academy of Child & Adolescent Psychiatry, 44,* 823–828.

Review of the Pediatric Behavior Rating Scale by TONY C. WU, Faculty, College of Social and Behavioral Sciences, Walden University, Minneapolis, MN:

DESCRIPTION. The Pediatric Behavior Rating Scale (PBRS) is an individually or group administered questionnaire for parents and teachers to complete, designed for aiding diagnosis and treatment planning for childhood onset bipolar disorders. The test authors indicate it will be advantageous to mental health and allied health professionals interested in the differential diagnoses of early onset bipolar disorder from other similar childhood emotional and behavioral disorders. The PBRS was intended for use with parents and teachers of children ages 3 to 18 years, with a normative sample from diverse ethnic and racial groups, geographic regions, and residential communities in the U.S.

The PBRS materials include Parent and Teacher version item booklets and response booklets, along with score summary/profile forms. The Parent and Teacher questionnaires generate a Total Bipolar Index score, as well as scale scores for Atypical (symptoms often associated with psychotic disorders), Irritability, Grandiosity, Hyperactivity/Impulsivity, Aggression, Inattention, Affect (mood changes), and Social Interactions. The administration instructions are easy to follow; the test authors claim that it takes approximately 15–20 minutes to complete each version of the questionnaire, and an additional 15–20 minutes to hand score it. In addition, the test authors note that the Pediatric Behavior Rating Scale scoring software program is available. Scoring, computing, and recording of the scales and Total Bipolar Index are not complicated. In fact, it is straightforward. For hand scoring, a calculator might be needed, but it is not necessary, as scoring involves only addition of items. Once the raw scores are computed for each scale, conversion tables grouped by gender and age are used to determine corresponding *T* scores and percentile ranks. In terms of interpretation, the test authors claim that the Total Bipolar Index score is the most robust score that may help to distinguish between clinical and nonclinical groups. Additionally, the test authors recommend the analysis of critical items and inconsistency score to aid in differential diagnosis and treatment planning.

DEVELOPMENT. In the development of the PBRS, the test authors desired a test that would be a functional tool for school and clinical psychologists, pediatricians, psychiatrists, and mental health professionals to detect symptoms associated with early onset bipolar disorder and to differentiate bipolar disorders from other severe childhood mental health disorders. The test authors trace the origins of the PBRS to the emerging consensus among practitioners regarding the existence of two variations of pediatric bipolar disorders although the current DSM-IV-TR (American Psychiatric Association, 2000) criteria are used to diagnose children and adolescents.

The standardization sample of the PBRS included 541 parents and 610 teachers of children ages 3 through 18 years. Besides the normative sample, data were aggregated on a combined clinical sample of 224 parents and 194 teachers of children ages 3 through 18 years, including Bipolar, ADHD, ODD, CD, and PDD samples. The standardization sample also represents ethnically diverse groups, such as Caucasian, African American, Hispanic, and Other.

TECHNICAL. Overall, meaningful estimates of reliability and validity are provided by the test authors. Available data provide adequate evidence to support inferences made from the PBRS. Specific to reliabilities, internal consistency coefficients for the PBRS Parent form ranged from .60 for the Atypical Scale to .89 for the Irritability Scale. Similarly, it was reported that the alpha coefficient of the Total Bipolar Index for the PBRS Parent form was .95. With regard to test-retest stability, coefficients for the PBRS Parent form were strong, as evident by coefficients ranging from .74 to .90. Similarly high coefficients were obtained for the PBRS Teacher form. Test-retest coefficients ranged from .81 to .96. It was also reported that overall interrater reliability was high. For instance, "median reliabilities were .83 and .81 for the Parent-Teacher and Parent-Parent samples, respectively" (professional manual, p. 41).

Likewise, validity evidence is provided by the test authors to support conclusions drawn from the PBRS. The test manual reveals that intercorrelations for the normative sample were .33 for the Hyperactivity and Affect scales and .86 for the Irritability scale and the Total Bipolar Index, respectively. The intercorrelations for the combined clinical scale were .01 for the Social Interaction and Grandiosity scales and .82 for the Aggression scale and the Total Bipolar Index. Furthermore, convergent validity is reported as higher for the PBRS Teacher version than for the Behavior Assessment System for Children: Second Edition (BASC-2 TRS; Reynolds & Kamphaus, 2004), along with moderate to high correlations among scale scores.

COMMENTARY. The PBRS is a succinct and straightforward test that has clinical utility in the differential diagnosis of severe childhood emotional and behavioral problems. It features test items that specifically tap into the construct of childhood onset bipolar disorders, which other existing tests do not offer. Moreover, recording, scoring, and interpreting are concise and easy to follow. Norms are based on a nationally representative sample, with both nonclinical and clinical individuals. Sound validity and reliability evidence is provided to support the inferences drawn from the results. Nonetheless, in future PBRS revisions, the test authors might want to consider specifying the "Other" ethnic group (i.e., Asian American) in order to clarify the construct with specific cultural groups. Additionally, the test authors might want to think about combining the item and response booklets into one form to assist in the ease of testing process in situations where test administration space is limited. Finally, the development of a self-report form might be beneficial to capture the overall symptomatology of this multifaceted mental illness, as a child's internal states might be difficult for others to capture and discern.

SUMMARY. The Pediatric Behavior Rating Scale (PBRS) is a norm-referenced and standardized tool that can facilitate the diagnosis and treatment of children ages 3 to 18 years who have severe emotional and behavioral problems. The key feature of the PBRS is to assist in the detection of early onset bipolar disorder and subsequent treatment planning. Although the construct of childhood bipolar disorders is rather controversial, the PBRS was developed in an attempt to ascertain the symptoms and/or syndromes of this highly complex disorder. The test administration and psychometric property are supported by the evidence. Given the data provided, this test is recommended for clinical use, as a part of a comprehensive psychological assessment. The PBRS would be of particular use for mental health professionals and allied health partners in evaluation and treatment of children and adolescents with challenging emotional or behavioral issues.

REVIEWER'S REFERENCES

American Psychiatric Association. (2000). *Diagnostic and statistical manual of mental disorders* (4th ed., text rev.). Washington, DC: Author.

Reynolds, C. R., & Kamphaus, R. W. (2004). *Behavior Assessment System for Children: Second Edition manual.* Circle Pines, MN: American Guidance Service.

[91]

Performance Perspectives Inventory.

Purpose: "A general-purpose measure of normal personality [based on the Big Five structure] designed for business settings."

Population: "[Job] candidates across a broad range of positions."

Publication Dates: 2001–2009.

Acronym: PPI.

Scores, 37: 5 Major Scales based on 22 Component Scales: Agreeableness (Caring, Helpful, Complying, Considerate, Trusting), Conscientiousness (Thoroughness, Achievement Focus, Diligence, Initiative, Organization), Stability (Even Tempered, Self-Confidence, Optimism, Composure), Extraversion (Influential, Likes Attention, Sociable, Lively), Openness (Inventiveness, Flexibility, Curiosity, Quick Thinking); 8 Occupational Scales grouped into 3 categories: Associate (Implementing, Providing Service), Leadership (Establishing, Managing), Specialist (Analyzing, Creating, Selling), no category (Loyalty); 2 Special Scales: Careful Responding, Impression Management.

Administration: Group.

Price Data, 2009: $32 per online test per quantity of 5-99 tests purchased (includes overall PPI scoring report, but not PPI Caregiver Profile); $18 per online PPI Caregiver Profile per quantity of 5-24 Profiles purchased; $24 per online PPI Caregiver Profile with optional Problem Solving Index per quantity of 5-24 Profiles purchased; quantity discounts available; contact publisher for pricing information regarding paper-and-pencil version; Technical Manual (Version 8, 2009, 104 pages), Caregiver Profile: Administrator's Guide (Version 8, 2008, 27 pages), and Caregiver Profile: PPI Manual Supplement (Version 8, 2008, 24 pages) can be downloaded free of charge with authorization from publisher.

Foreign Language Editions: Spanish and Chinese editions available online.

Time: Online administration: (20-25) minutes, (15) additional minutes for optional component of the Caregiver Profile; paper-and-pencil administration: (25-30) minutes, (20-25) additional minutes for optional component.

Comments: Distributed under the title "ViewPoint General Personality Survey (GPS); available online or in paper-and-pencil format; optional PPI Caregiver Profile is a special method of scoring the PPI and is distributed under the title "Careview."

Authors: Joseph D. Abraham and John D. Morrison, Jr. (PPI Technical Manual [Version 8] and PPI Caregiver Profile: Administrator's Guide [Version 8]).

Publisher: A & M Psychometrics, LLC; sole distributer: PSI Services, LLC.

a) PPI CAREGIVER PROFILE.

Purpose: "A special method of scoring the PPI [that provides] a targeted assessment of candidates for Direct Support Professional and other caregiving positions."

Population: "Applicants for the position of Direct Support Professional and closely related jobs."

Scores, 5: Nurturing (i.e., PPI Agreeableness), Dependable (i.e., PPI Conscientiousness), Positive Attitude (i.e., PPI Optimism), Performance/Retention Index (i.e., mean of first three scores), Problem Solving Index (optional score based on the Numerical Ability (EAS2) subtest).

Comments: Numerical Ability (EAS2) is a subtest of the Employee Aptitude Survey (EAS) published by PSI Services, Inc.; the EAS2 is offered in conjunction with the PPI by A & M Psychometrics, LLC (a certified PSI partner company).

Review of the Performance Perspectives Inventory by MICHAEL D. BIDERMAN, Professor of Psychology, University of Tennessee at Chattanooga, Chattanooga, TN:

DESCRIPTION. The Performance Perspectives Inventory (PPI) copyrighted by A & M Psychometrics is a 155-item personality questionnaire designed for business settings. It measures the Big Five personality dimensions, 22 facets (called components in the PPI manual) of these dimensions, and seven occupational scales designed to "predict job performance, satisfaction, and fit in several broad occupational categories" (technical manual, p. 7). Specifically, the questionnaire can be scored for the Big Five dimension of Stability (S) with components Self-Confidence, Optimism, Composure, and Even-Tempered; Extraversion (E) with components Influential, Likes Attention, PPI Sociable, and PPI Lively; Openness (O) with components PPI Inventiveness, PPI Flexibility, PPI Curiosity, and PPI Quick Thinking; Agreeableness (A) with components PPI Caring, PPI Helpful, PPI Complying, PPI Considerate, and PPI Trusting; and Conscientiousness (C) with components PPI Thoroughness, PPI Achievement Focus, PPI Diligence, PPI Initiative, and PPI Organization. In addition, scores are provided for Establishing,

Managing, Analyzing, Creating, Selling, Implementing, and Providing Service. The questionnaire also includes two special scales–Impression Management and Careful Responding. A third special scale, Loyalty, consists of the means of Agreeableness, Conscientiousness, and Stability, and is available for persons using the PPI Scoring Web Service.

Items are short declaratory phrases of 2 to 10 words. Respondents indicate how accurately they are described by the phrases using a 1 (*Very Inaccurate*) to 5 (*Very Accurate*) response scale. Scales scores are calculated as stens, defined as "((raw score – distribution mean)/distribution standard deviation*2) + 5.5" (technical manual, p. 19) rounded to the nearest whole number, with values less than 1 set equal to 1 and values greater than 10 set equal to 10. Interpretive reports provided in the scoring process use the descriptors "Low" for sten values less than 4, "Average" for values between 4 and 7, and "High" for values larger than 7.

A scoring report presents scores graphically on a percentile scale with the respondent's scores represented by a diamond-shaped symbol on a horizontal linear scale within regions named "Low," "Average," and "High." The scoring report presents the above summary results for A, C, E, and O and their components on one page and the results for S and the Occupational Scales on a second page. Following the two-page summary are eight pages of verbal descriptions presumably appropriate for the respondent's scores on the Big Five dimension scales, the component scales, and the occupational scales. A separate report called the "PPI Caregiver Profile" targeted for assessment of candidates for Direct Support Professional and other caregiving positions is available. This report presents respondent scores on A, C, and Optimism, the score on an index combining those three scales, and an optional score on the Employee Aptitude Series (EAS) Numerical Ability scale.

The test is available online or in paper-and-pencil format. English, Spanish, and Chinese language versions are available, the last two only online. Time to administer is 20–30 minutes with 15 25 extra minutes required for the optional component of the Caregiver Profile.

DEVELOPMENT. The majority of test items were selected from the International Personal Item Pool (IPIP; Goldberg, 1999a). Items with content that seemed appropriate for a scale were identified and assigned to that scale. Goals in the item assignment process were to have 8 or fewer items per scale, to have an approximately equal number of positively and negatively worded items, and to include as many "business friendly" (technical manual, p. 9) items as possible. The item selection process yielded a preliminary questionnaire of 167 items defining 22 scales. Initial estimates of reliability and convergent and discriminant validity were assessed using a data set of 989 respondents provided by the Oregon Research Institute (Goldberg, 1999b). Based on reliability estimates, item-total correlations, and principal components analyses of the preliminary questionnaire, the collection of items was refined including the addition of some items written specifically for the questionnaire, and a second assessment was performed using a sample of 247 respondents. The refinement process resulted in the final questionnaire of 155 items, 144 of which are used to define the component scales, with 11 items used for special scales and/or future revisions. Of the 144 items, 82 are positively worded. No information is given concerning which items were included in each scale, nor is information on how many items were included in each scale provided in the manual.

TECHNICAL.

Standardization. Means, standard deviations on the original 1-5 response scale, and percentiles associated with sten values of 4, 5.5, and 7 are provided for several norming samples. The first table provides information for the Big Five dimensions and 22 component scales based on the refinement sample, (N = 247). Other tables provide information on the Big Five dimensions and 22 component scales, on the seven occupational scales and on two special scales–Impression Management and Loyalty–for a general/occupational sample of 2,800 cases "balanced to include approximately equal numbers of job applicants and non-applicants, and weighted to approximate March 2008 U.S. Census population demographics" (technical manual, p. 19), a development sample of "1426 cases, comprising individuals completing the PPI for self-insight or development purposes" (technical manual, p. 20), a selection/promotion sample "of 6054 adults who completed the PPI primarily for selection, promotion, or other job-related administrative purposes" (technical manual, p. 20), a China sample of "1240 job applicants–primarily university graduates–seeking employment with major technology firms" (technical manual, p. 21), and an India sample of "578 employed adults in India who have completed the PPI for selection, placement, or development purposes" (technical manual, p. 21).

Across all norming samples, means of scales on the 1–5 response scale ranged from 3.06 to 4.75, with more than half the means larger than 4.0 in each sample. Percentiles of sten scores of 4, 5.5, and 7 are also presented for all the samples. The fact that means were generally above the response scale midpoint of 3 suggests that the scales may be subject to ceiling effects, whereas the fact that the percentiles of the sten midpoint of 5.5 were generally less than 50 suggests that the distributions were slightly negatively skewed.

In the "refinement" (technical manual, p. 11) sample, females had significantly higher scores on Agreeableness, Implementing, and Providing Service (differences in standard deviations (d) such that d = .41, .26, and .32, respectively) with males significantly higher on Analyzing (d = .40). No other male/female differences in Big Five or occupational scale means were significant and no other standardized difference (d) was larger than .23. No differences between whites and blacks in the refinement sample were significant, with the largest d = .23. No gender or ethnic group comparisons of PPI component scores were available. In the refinement sample, age was positively correlated with Agreeableness, Impression Management, and Implementing and negatively correlated with Openness, Creating, and Analyzing. All correlations were less than .22. Educational level was positively correlated with Conscientiousness, Extraversion, Stability, Openness, Impression Management, Establishing, Managing, Creating, Analyzing, and Selling. All correlations were less than .24.

Reliability. Coefficient alpha reliability estimates for the Big Five scales ranged from .78 to .88 for the refinement sample with coefficient alphas for the component scales ranging from .72 to .87 (Median = .795). Test-retest reliability estimates based on a 32 day interval for a 73-case subset of the refinement sample were comparable. The coefficient alphas obtained from the preliminary sample were comparable to those obtained from the refinement sample. No reliability estimates for the seven occupational scales or the two special scales are given.

Validity. Convergent validity was assessed in several ways. From the preliminary sample, convergent validity correlations of the Big Five scale scores with corresponding NEO-PI-R (Costa & McCrae, 1992) scale scores were .73, .75, -.85, .83, and .65 for A, C, S, E, and O. (The NEO reports Neuroticism, which is treated here as the inverse of S.) These correlations were based on samples of 430 to 456 respondents. Convergent validity correlations with ratings by peers using the Mini-Marker Adjective Checklist (Saucier, 1994) were .59, .44, .41, .36, and .46 for E, A, C, S, and O. Similar correlations were .59. 45, .41, .49, and .53 with ratings by peers using the Big Five Inventory (John, Donahue, & Kentle, 1991). Both sets of ratings were based on samples ranging from 219 to 291 pairs of respondents. From a sample of 43, convergent validity correlations of the final self-reported PPI Big Five scale scores with corresponding self-reported BFI scores were .78, .62, .83, .87, and .73 for the dimensions listed above. Convergent validity correlations with BFI peer ratings involving 51 pairs of respondents were .61, .24, .60, .35, and .33. The BFI "Neuroticism" scores were reverse-coded to represent stability in these analyses. The Spanish version of the PPI was administered to 36 bilingual adults who completed the English version first and then the Spanish version about 5 months later. Convergent validity correlations were .78, .70, .77, .77, and .68 for A, C, E, S, and O.

There is also some evidence on discriminant validity. Based on analyses of subsets of the preliminary sample with the numbers of subjects ranging from 238 to 333, off-diagonal discriminant validity correlations between self-report PPI Big Five dimension scores ranged from .044 to .53 with mean .33. In a sample of 133 caregiver incumbents responding under instructions "to respond as if they were applying for the direct support position" (manual supplement, p. 6), discriminant validity correlations between A, C, and S ranged from .48 to .63. From the peer ratings based on the Mini-Marker checklist and BFI, correlations of peer ratings with self-ratings of different dimensions ranged from -.09 to .28, with a mean of .09. For a sample of 43 who took both the BFI and the PPI, correlations between self-report measures of different dimensions from different instruments ranged from .08 to .59, with a mean of .32. For the sample of 51 pairs of raters, correlations between measures of different dimensions from different raters ranged from -.19 to .32 with a mean of .10.

Principal components analyses of 22 component scale scores of the preliminary sample found five factors with eigenvalues greater than 1. For that solution, the largest loading of each PPI component was on the appropriate factor. A similar principal components analysis of the refinement sample yielded similar results, with each PPI component having its largest loading on the appropriate Big Five dimension. A third principal components analysis of the data of the selection/promotion norming sample resulted in all but one of the PPI components having the largest loading on the appropriate Big Five dimension.

Results of several studies present evidence of criterion-related validity. In a sample of 55 concierges and lobby officers, the PPI Implementing scale correlated .30 with a job performance index based on 14 performance rating items and .36 with a single-item rating of overall job performance. For 55 security guards the correlation of PPI C was .29 with a job performance index and .27 with a single-item rating of overall job performance. For 40 real estate agents, the correlation of PPI Selling scale with supervisory ratings of job performance was .37. The ratings correlated .35 with PPI E, .33 with Social, .31 with Achievement Focus, .38 with Diligence, and .39 with Initiative. The correlation of average gross revenue of 31 quick service restaurant managers was .37 with PPI Establishing. PPI Managing correlated .44 with average profitability and -.42 with average labor costs for the same sample. The success rate in gaining agreement of call recipients by 359 incumbent outbound call center representatives correlated .23 with C, .22 with S, and .15 with A. Instructor ratings of new hire training performance of 81 new hires correlated .28 with C, .26 with S, .25 with E, and .42 with O.

"In a study of 132 in-home caregivers" (technical manual, p. 18) a Loyalty scale, computed as the mean of PPI A, C, and S, correlated .20 with satisfaction with work performed, .18 with satisfaction with coworker and peer relations, .20 with overall satisfaction with the job, and .20 with the total of six facet satisfaction items.

COMMENTARY. The PPI is one of several instruments that measure the Big Five personality dimensions. The evidence described above suggests that the PPI measures of the Big Five exhibit good convergent validity with other measures of the Big Five including the NEO-PI, Mini-Markers, and the BFI. The fairly large self-report discriminant validity correlations suggest that responses to this instrument might be affected by common method bias. Recent evidence suggests that responses to the IPIP 50-item sample scale, drawn from the same pool of items as the PPI, are affected by such bias (Nguyen, Biderman, Cunningham, & Ghorbani, 2008). The reliability, construct validity evidence, and criterion-related validity evidence presented suggest that the PPI Big Five measures are no better and no worse than other Big Five measures. Some of the other Big five questionnaires are shorter than the PPI (Mini-Markers, BFI; NEO-FFI; the IPIP Sample questionnaires) and one is longer (the NEO-PI). Choices between them might involve length and cost. Currently, the IPIP sample questionnaires are available without charge for researchers or practitioners who are willing to create instruments from them and score them.

There is less evidence concerning the validity of the PPI component scales than there is for the Big Five scales. Several tables of correlations of the PPI components with NEO-PI facets were provided in the manual. However, it is difficult to arrive at a firm conclusion concerning their convergent validity based on these because they were not created to match NEO-PI facets. No information (e.g., off-diagonal correlations) was provided concerning discriminant validity of the components.

Lack of information also characterizes the situation with respect to the occupational scales. No information is available for them regarding reliability or convergent or discriminant validity. The little criterion-related validity information that is available appears promising, but more information is needed before it could be recommended that personnel decisions could be made using those scales.

It is disappointing that the actual items for each scale are not presented in the manual. For example, one cannot be certain whether some items appear in more than one component, how the questionnaire could be shortened if a practitioner wanted only a subset of the scales, or if a practitioner wished to form his or her own judgment concerning the content of items in a particular scale.

SUMMARY. It appears that the PPI measures the Big Five personality dimensions as well as other measures that are available. The data provided in the technical manual suggest that the

PPI measures of the Big Five are reliable with acceptable construct validity, and that they possess criterion-related validity that is about what would be expected from measures of the Big Five. The PPI also provides a number of other predictive scales and two special scores. It appears that they were carefully developed. However, there is little evidence at the present time concerning the psychometric characteristics of the component and occupational scores.

REVIEWER'S REFERENCES

Costa, P. T., Jr., & McCrae, R. R. (1992). *Professional manual, Revised NEO Personality Inventory (NEO-PIR) and NEO Five-Factor Inventory (NEO-FFI).* Odessa FL: Psychological Assessment Resources.

Goldberg, L. R. (1999a). A broad-bandwidth, public domain, personality inventory measuring the lower-level facets of several five-factor models. In I. Mervielde, I. Deary, F. De Fruyt, & F. Ostendorf (Eds.), *Personality psychology in Europe* (vol. 7; pp. 7–28). Tilburg, The Netherlands: Tilburg University Press.

Goldberg, L. R. (1999b). The Eugene-Springfield Community Sample: Information available from the research participants. *ORI Technical Report, Vol. 39*, No. 1. Oregon Research Institute.

John, O. P., Donahue, E. M., & Kentle, R. L. (1991). *The "Big Five" Inventory—Versions 4a and 54.* Berkeley: University of California, Berkeley, Institute of Personality and Social Research.

Nguyen, N. T., Biderman, M. D., Cunningham, C. J. L., & Ghorbani, N. (2008). *A multi-sample re-examination of the factor structure of Goldberg's IPIP 50-item Big Five Questionnaire.* Symposium presented at the 2008 Academy of Management Annual Meeting, Anaheim, CA.

Saucier, G. (1994). Mini-markers: A brief version of Goldberg's unipolar Big-Five markers. *Journal of Personality and Social Psychology, 73,* 1296-1312.

Review of the Performance Perspectives Inventory by CHOCKALINGAM VISWESVARAN, Professor, Department of Psychology, Florida International University, Miami, FL:

DESCRIPTION. The Performance Perspectives Inventory (PPI) is a measure of the Big Five factors of personality with items chosen for relevance to workplace settings. The PPI was constructed to avoid references to mental illness or abnormality, assessments of which are legally prohibited prior to a job offer in many occupational assessments. The English version has both an online and a traditional paper-and-pencil administration format whereas Spanish and Chinese translations are available as online versions only. In addition, users can add a numerical ability test. A combination of personality factors and numerical ability is presented for selecting successful health care workers (i.e., the Caregiver Profile). The administration manual provides detailed descriptions and scripts to be read for online and paper-and-pencil administrations. Instructions are clearly spelled out if users are interested in collecting demographic information for Equal Employment Opportunity analyses as well as if they want to add a numerical ability test to assess a caregiver profile.

DEVELOPMENT. The authors started by compiling a list of personality components relevant to the workplace. Psychological terminology and components with negative connotations for employees such as depression were avoided. After selecting 5–7 components for each of the Big Five factors of personality, the authors reviewed the 1,699 self-reported items in the International Personality Item Pool (IPIP) and selected up to 20 items for each of the components. Some components were eliminated due to excessive conceptual overlap or because too few items were available in the IPIP pool for that component. Care was taken to include both positively and negatively worded items. A total of 22 components were selected. Using the data provided by the Oregon Research Institute, component scores were constructed for 989 respondents. This sample was 98% Caucasian and the mean age was 51 years. Principal component analysis was done to cluster the components into the five factors. The five factor scores thus derived were correlated with scores from other established measures of the Big Five to check the construct validity. In addition Occupational scales (7 categories to assess functions such as leadership) were constructed from these components and they were correlated with interest scales and occupational scales from other inventories such as the Hogan Personality Inventory. An impression management scale was also constructed and found to have substantial correlations with other measures of social desirability.

This preliminary version of the PPI was composed of 167 IPIP items, was also augmented with an additional 25 items, and was then administered to 247 respondents. The mean age of the sample was 37 years (more appropriate for organizational use than the mean age of 51 in the Oregon sample used in the development of the preliminary version) and the sample was 39% male and 83% Caucasian (still unrepresentative of most organizational samples, but more representative than the 98% Caucasian Oregon sample). The scales were refined to include only work-relevant items, again balancing positively and negatively worded items, aiming for a minimal internal consistency of .65 for scales, and keeping the number of items to no more than 8 for each component. Factor analyses of the refined scales supported the Big Five structure with the 22 component scales loading on the hypothesized five factors. Factor-analytic results on a normative sample of 6,000 cases also supported the hypothesized factor structure.

The PPI Caregiver Profile was constructed with a thorough job analysis of the "Habilitation

Training Specialist" position. Job descriptions and related documents were studied and 13 supervisors provided assessments of the importance and level of work activities in a job analysis questionnaire. The important work activities and abilities, skills, and attitudes needed for successful performance were identified. Based on the importance and level of work activities, support professionals include the occupations of home health aides, personal and home care aides, etc. A sample of 133 incumbent health aide workers were given the PPI and three tests from the Employee Aptitude Series (EAS) to assess Verbal Comprehension, Numerical Ability, and Verbal Reasoning. Correlations of the scales with supervisory ratings of job performance and self-reported job satisfaction were analyzed. Agreeableness, Conscientiousness, and Optimism from the PPI and the numerical ability scores from the EAS were found to be predictive of the criteria. As such, five scores (one of which is optional) were included in the Caregiver Profile Report: Nurturing (PPI Agreeableness), Dependable (PPI Conscientiousness), Positive Attitude (PPI Optimism), caregiver performance/retention index (which is an average of the above three), and an optional Problem Solving Index (Numerical Ability score, corrected for guessing).

TECHNICAL. For the PPI, the norm sample comprises 2,800 cases including both applicants and nonapplicants. The test publishers also give the option of using organization-specific norms. Users can also opt for developmental norms (based on 1,426 cases) when the assessment focuses on development and training programs. Finally, separate selection/promotion norms (based on 6,054 adults) are also available. The norms for the Caregiver Profile are currently based on the norm samples for the PPI and EAS tests. The test publisher also provides separate normative data for Chinese samples (based on 1,240 job applicants) and Indian samples (n = 578).

The coefficient alphas for the five factors and the 22 components were above .70 in the sample of 247 respondents. Test-retest reliabilities (with an average time interval of 32 days) were also above .70 for all the scales. Reliability estimates for the five scores in the Caregiver profile were not provided in the manual.

Criterion-related validity data for PPI scales are reported in six samples. In a sample of concierge/lobby officers, PPI Implementing scores correlated .30 with a job performance index (average across supervisory ratings on 14 dimensions of performance) and .36 with supervisory ratings of overall performance. This first study was a concurrent validation study with a sample of 55. In a second concurrent validation study involving 55 security guards, the PPI Conscientiousness scale was reported to predict supervisory ratings of performance. In a third sample of 40 real estate agents completing the PPI for developmental feedback, PPI scales of Selling, Extraversion, Sociable, Achievement Focus, Diligence, and Initiative had positive correlations with supervisory ratings of performance. The criterion-related validity of the PPI Establishing and Managing scale was assessed in a sample of 31 restaurant managers. The PPI leadership scale correlated .37 with an objective measure of restaurant performance (gross revenue over 3 years), and PPI Managing correlated .44 with profitability and -.42 with average labor costs. In another sample of incumbent call center representatives (N = 359), PPI scores of Conscientiousness, Agreeableness, and Stability correlated .23, .15, and .15, respectively with a measure of the representative's success rate in gaining agreement from individuals to participate in a research study. Additionally, Conscientiousness, Extraversion, Stability, and Openness correlated with performance (as measured by instructor ratings) in a new training program for a subsample (n = 81) of the call center representatives. Finally, the PPI scales and the numerical ability test have been correlated with job satisfaction and supervisory ratings of job performance for health care aides.

PPI scale scores have been reported to have good construct validity. PPI scores correlated with peer ratings of personality (n = 51) as well as scores on another measure of Big Five (n = 43). The English and the Spanish versions of the PPI had correlations of .73 to .82 (corrected for transient error) in a sample of 36 bilinguals who took both versions over 5 months. Finally, managerial samples scored higher in PPI managing scales compared to nonmanagers (d =.48).

Ethnic and gender differences were also explored. The gender and ethnic differences in PPI scores are small in magnitude and unlikely to cause adverse impact in personnel decisions. However, if numerical ability scores are used in constructing the caregiver profile (Problem Solving), a difference of six tenths of a standard deviation is found between ethnic groups. However, no evidence of predictive bias was found in the analyzed sample.

COMMENTARY. The PPI appears to be a well-developed measure of the Big Five factors of personality specifically suited for workplace assessments. The normative data, explorations of group differences, and convergent validity evidence with other measures, etc., are detailed and impressive. The authors have provided an informative technical manual and clear administration instructions. Criterion-related validity evidence seems to be mostly based on incumbents. It would be interesting to see if criterion-related validity holds in applicant situations where faking may play an important role. Group differences (ethnic, age, and gender) are negligible but it would be interesting to see if that pattern holds in applicant selection situations.

SUMMARY. The PPI was designed to assess personality in organizational settings. The test appears to assess the Big Five adequately and ample reliability and validity (construct and criterion-related validity in incumbent samples) evidence are provided. Given the importance of personality in explaining organizational behavior, and the scarcity of personality inventories developed specifically for workplace assessments, this instrument is likely to be useful for organizational researchers.

[92]

Personality Assessment Inventory—Adolescent.

Purpose: An "objective test of personality designed to provide information on critical client variables in professional settings."
Population: Ages 12–18.
Publication Dates: 1990-2007.
Acronym: PAI-A.
Scores, 53: Somatic Complaints (Conversion, Somatization, Health Concerns, Total), Anxiety (Cognitive, Affective, Physiological, Total), Anxiety-Related Disorders (Obsessive-Compulsive, Phobias, Traumatic Stress, Total), Depression (Cognitive, Affective, Physiological, Total), Mania (Activity Level, Grandiosity, Irritability, Total), Paranoia (Hypervigilance, Persecution, Resentment, Total), Schizophrenia (Psychotic Experiences, Social Detachment, Thought Disorder, Total), Borderline Features (Affective Instability, Identity Problems, Negative Relationships, Self-Harm, Total), Antisocial Features (Antisocial Behaviors, Egocentricity, Stimulus-Seeking, Total), Alcohol Problems, Drug Problems, Aggression (Aggressive Attitude, Verbal Aggression, Physical Aggression, Total), Suicidal Ideation, Stress, Nonsupport, Treatment Rejection, Dominance, Warmth, Inconsistency, Infrequency, Negative Impression, Positive Impression.
Administration: Group.
Price Data, 2008: $295 per complete kit including professional manual (2007, 190 pages), 2 reusable item booklets, 2 administration folios, 25 hand-scored answer sheets, 25 profile forms-adolescent, 25 critical items forms-adolescent, and 1 professional report service answer sheet in a soft-sided attaché case; $32 per reusable item booklet; $34 per 10 soft cover item booklets; $48 per 25 hand-scored answer sheets; $30 per 25 profile forms-adolescent; $35 per 25 critical items forms-adolescent; $70 per professional manual.
Time: 45(55) minutes.
Comments: Designed to complement its parent instrument, the Personality Assessment Inventory (18:93).
Author: Leslie C. Morey.
Publisher: Psychological Assessment Resources, Inc.

Review of the Personality Assessment Inventory—Adolescent by H. DENNIS KADE, Naval Medical Center Portsmouth: Substance Abuse Rehabilitation Program, and Adjunct Assistant Professor of Psychology, Old Dominion University, Norfolk, VA:

DESCRIPTION. The Personality Assessment Inventory—Adolescent (PAI-A) is a self-report personality questionnaire for clinical assessment at ages 12 to 18 years. It was developed as an extension of the adult Personality Assessment Inventory (PAI; 18:93) for adolescents. The manual states that the PAI-A is not appropriate for comprehensive assessment of normal personality domains. Analysis of the test instructions and items shows reading comprehension at a 4.0 grade level is required. The Flesch Reading Ease score is 80.9, suggesting a fifth grade level. This is within the easy range, perhaps harder to read than a comic but easier than a teen magazine.

The test manual indicates there are 264 items that take adolescents 30–45 minutes to complete and examiners 10–15 minutes to score, yielding 22 nonoverlapping scales. Each item is answered on a 4-point scale ranging from *false/not at all true,* to *slightly true, mainly true,* or *very true.* The written instructions for the adolescent are succinct, but contain no example item. The question booklet and answer sheet items are arranged in columns. Breaks in one do not correlate with breaks in the other, but the answer sheet layout facilitates scoring without keys. Alternating colors are used to help the adolescent visually separate the rows on the answer sheet. A critical item sheet facilitates inspection of 17 answers with space for notes from subsequent queries. With no age or gender differences, only one profile sheet is needed to convert raw scale and subscale scores to *T*-scores.

Reference to normative tables in the manual is unnecessary. The examiner's manual is well organized with a detailed table of contents that facilitates its use as a reference.

Hand score and optical scan score answer sheets are available; the latter are also used for the publisher's mail-in scoring service. Computer-based administration, scoring, and interpretive report software is available. Though its purchase price is more than the PAI-A test kit itself, additional per-use fees are charged only for on-screen administrations. Hand scoring is quite straightforward and a scoring example is included in the manual. Guidelines for interpretation included in the manual extend beyond single scales at different elevations to suggest profiles based on cluster analysis. Unfortunately, no example clinical cases are supplied that might illustrate integration of the interpretive guidelines. The manual states that PAI-A interpretation requires training in psychometric assessment and psychopathology.

The four validity scales included in the PAI-A support decisions about the validity of an individual's protocol. There are 10 pairs of items in the Inconsistency scale; completely random responding produced an average *T*-score of 82 on this scale and scores above 77T render the protocol invalid. The 7 items of the Infrequency scale were rarely endorsed in the normal and clinical samples; random responding produced an average *T*-score of 82, and scores above 78T indicate invalid protocols. The 8 items of the Negative Impression scale were infrequently endorsed in the clinical and particularly in the normal samples; random responding produces an average *T*-score of 77, and a sample instructed to malinger averaged 108T. Scores above 84T indicate invalid protocols. The 8 items of the Positive Impression scale were endorsed most frequently by a sample instructed to respond with positive impression enhancement (average score of 68T), least often by clinical cases, with the normal sample falling in between. Scores above 71T indicate invalid protocols. The manual states that protocols with more than 13 unanswered items are problematic and scales or subscales with more than 19% unanswered should not be interpreted.

DEVELOPMENT. Both the structure and most of the items from the PAI were retained in the PAI-A. Thus, constructs relate to the diagnostic categories of mental disorder and the experience of symptoms and other factors relevant to treatment (e.g., Aggression, Suicidal Ideation, Stress, Nonsupport, Treatment Rejection) that occur across the life span. A few items had to be reworded to make them more age-appropriate (e.g., changing "work" to "school"), but new items were not introduced because the PAI-A was not intended to assess psychopathology unique to adolescents. Pilot testing used 275 clinical cases who were 65% male, 54% from forensic (juvenile detention) settings, 26.7% from inpatient mental health, and 22.8% from outpatient mental health. Internal consistency and mean interitem correlations within scales were used to eliminate 80 items. One item was omitted from scoring on the Infrequency scale because adolescents endorsed it too often. The PAI-A item pairs used to score the Inconsistency scale were selected empirically, rather than using the PAI items.

TECHNICAL. The test manual provides information on the PAI-A's empirical structure such as scale intercorrelations, exploratory factor analyses, confirmatory factor analyses of subscales, and cluster analyses. Normative data for the U.S. Census-matched standardization sample and (for comparison purposes) the clinical sample are included in appendices, as well as data on item means and standard deviations in both samples, scale and subscale correlations with the validation measures in the community sample, and frequency distributions of clinical scale codetypes across nine diagnoses plus the entire clinical sample.

T-scores are based on a community sample of 707 students in junior and senior high school and college who were between the ages of 12 and 18 years from 21 states stratified by race/ethnicity and gender within age bands to match the 2003 U.S. Census. Analysis showed only two scales had more than 5% of their variance accounted for by ethnicity, gender, or age: higher scores for males on Antisocial Features and higher scores for non-Caucasians on Paranoia. These differences are about 5 *T*-Score points.

Data were also gathered on 1,160 representative clinical cases from 78 sites: outpatient mental health (49.7%), juvenile/correctional (33.3%), inpatient mental health (12.7%) and other settings. The clinical sample data were used to generate a clinical "skyline" on the profile form that exceeds 98% or is 2 standard deviations above the mean. Evidence is provided that the most common diagnoses in treatment are represented, but there are fewer than 5% with an anxiety disorder.

Standard error of measurement values for scales in the community sample average 4.68 *T*-score units (range of 3.3 to 5.9) and subscales average 4.94 (range of 3.42 to 6.42). Coefficient alpha internal consistency values are reported in community and clinical samples for scales and subscales. Internal consistency for scales (except Inconsistency and Infrequency) averaged .79 for the community standardization sample and .80 for the clinical sample. Except for Dominance in the clinical sample, all scale values meet or exceed the .70 traditionally considered acceptable for research use, but only Aggression in the community sample and Suicidal Ideation in the clinical sample reach the .90 standard for making decisions about individuals. Only 13 of the 31 subscales meet or exceed .70 in the community sample and 18 in the clinical sample; none reach the .90 standard. These results are not surprising given the brevity of the scales and subscales. The test author is to be commended for addressing the stability of profiles, though the only datum reported was a median inverse correlation of .84 for the relative position of scale scores within the profiles of test-retest cases. The latter 100 participants were reassessed to yield an average test-retest stability coefficient of .78 for the scales (except Inconsistency and Infrequency) after a mean of 18 days (range from 9 to 35 days).

Six validity studies with clinical and community samples ranging from 77 to 1,160 are reported that provide a wealth of support for criterion-related validity. Only clinical diagnosis and symptom checklist were used in the largest sample, but other samples used multiple measures of personality and psychopathology: Minnesota Multiphasic Personality Inventory—Adolescent (MMPI-A), Adolescent Psychopathology Scales (APS), Personality Inventory for Youth (PIY), NEO Five-Factor Inventory (NEO-FFI), Symptom Assessment-45 (SA-45), College Adjustment Scales (CAS), Clinical Assessment of Depression (CAD), Adolescent Anger Rating Scale (AARS), Beck Depression Inventory (BDI), and State-Trait Anxiety Inventory (STAI). Exploratory factor analysis using a principal components approach with orthogonal rotation produced four factors accounting for 41%, 10%, 9%, and 6% of the variance with the first interpreted as representing psychological distress.

COMMENTARY. Like other tests linked to diagnostic nosology, the adequacy of the theoretical model behind the PAI-A is limited by the adequacy of the diagnostic model itself. The test's focus on core characteristics of diagnoses without directly attempting to replicate all diagnostic criteria may prove advantageous if more peripheral criteria change over time or are unimportant to decisions made by the user. As the manual points out, research continues to evolve on some diagnoses such as bipolar mood disorder in adolescents, so that there is no current gold standard by which to judge the PAI-A for some disorders. It would be useful if more information was presented showing the PAI-A's power to discriminate constructs and diagnoses, such as depression/mood disorders and anxiety/anxiety disorders. In the clinical sample, less than 4% had diagnoses of posttraumatic stress disorder or mania/hypomania, and less than 2% had borderline personality disorder (the only Axis II diagnosis tabulated). Current clinical practice with adolescents often requires a differential between these and other diagnoses, particularly when serving a population with a history of early maltreatment and trauma. Future editions of the manual would also benefit from data on the scales' sensitivity to treatment effects, the relationship of PAI-A scores to diagnoses made by research criteria, gender/racial/ethnic/cultural differences by diagnosis such as males versus females with Attention Deficit Hyperactivity Disorder, and on profile stability in adolescents 18 years of age and older who complete the PAI after the PAI-A.

SUMMARY. The PAI-A achieves its stated purpose of providing a parallel form that extends the PAI to adolescents. More information on discriminative validity and on the ability to detect more subtle denial and malingering is needed. The PAI-A provides an attractive option to the growing number of other self-report measures available for this age group in clinical decision-making (many summarized in Sattler & Hoge, 2006; extensive reviews of several are in Reynolds & Kamphaus, 2004). Self-report measures that parallel parent and teacher ratings typically lack validity scales. The Millon Adolescent Personality Inventory has significant shortcomings (Sattler & Hoge, 2006), and the other Millon scales for this age group have only clinical norms. The PAI-A has the advantage of ease and economy of scoring over the MMPI-A, another downward extension of an adult test of psychopathology. Also, the MMPI-A takes 60–90 minutes to complete and a seventh grade reading level is recommended, but many items are even more difficult (Sattler & Hoge, 2006). The PIY might be considered as an alternative to the PAI-A when empirical scales rather than diagnosis-based scales are acceptable (see review by Sattler & Hoge, 2006). If not, then the APS is a good alternative, but clinical experience has shown the APS has difficulty detecting cases of sophisticated denial. When there is an anticipated need to reevaluate an adolescent over the age of 18, then a clear advantage to the PAI-A is allowing future testing to be based on a very similar measure, the PAI.

REVIEWER'S REFERENCES

Sattler, J. M., & Hoge, R. D. (2006). *Assessment of children: Behavioral, social and clinical applications* (5th ed.) San Diego: Jerome M. Sattler.

Reynolds, C. R., & Kamphaus, R. W. (Eds.). (2003). *Handbook of psychological and educational assessment of children: Personality, behavior and context* (2nd ed.). New York: Guilford Press.

Review of the Personality Assessment Inventory—Adolescent by JONATHAN SANDOVAL, Professor of Education, University of the Pacific, Stockton, CA:

DESCRIPTION. The Personality Assessment Inventory—Adolescent (PAI-A) is an extension to 12- through 18-year-olds of the Personality Assessment Inventory (Morey, 1991). Both measures may be used with 18-year-olds. The self-report personality measure consists of 264 items that generate 4 Validity scales, 11 Clinical scales, 5 Treatment Consideration scales, and 2 Interpersonal scales. Nine of the 11 Clinical scales and the Aggression Treatment Consideration scales have from three to four subscales based on 5 to 6 items each. Other scales typically are derived from about 8 items. In total there are 22 scales and 31 subscales expressed as linear *T* scores. On the PAI-A, a respondent indicates if a statement is *False, Not At All True; Slightly True; Mainly True;* or *Very True* about himself or herself. The intent is to measure constructs relevant to the presence of mental disorder. It is not intended to be a general measure of personality in normal individuals. The materials include a professional manual, an item booklet, hand-scored and optical scan answer sheets, a Critical Items form, and a Profile form. Computer administration and scoring options are available from the test publisher. The Critical Items form consists of 17 items from the PAI-A suggesting behavior or psychopathology demanding immediate attention, such as Suicidal Ideation. The form permits a follow-up interview to explore the critical response. The profile form permits the examination of patterns of scores across the 22 areas, particularly 10 clusters of modal scores identified by statistical analysis that are associated with particular groups such as substance abusers.

The test author states that the interpretation of profiles and test score patterns must be done by qualified and experienced clinical professionals. The examiner's manual is straightforward and provides information about administration considerations, administration procedures, scoring procedures and options, and test feedback to test-takers. Included is a chapter on interpretation that discusses the rationale and construct underlying each scale and subscale and possible meanings of high scores. The PAI-A is not intended to be used mechanically to provide a definitive diagnosis but is rather to provide information relevant to clinical diagnosis, treatment planning, and screening for psychopathology. The information from the PAI-A should supplement information from multiple sources such as case histories, clinical interviews, and other mental tests.

DEVELOPMENT. The test author designed the PAI-A to retain the structure and most of the item content of the adult inventory. A few items were reworded to fit adolescent experience. Items were carefully selected based on 15 criteria involving expert opinion, discriminant validity, reading level (fourth grade), positive and negative response sets, and item statistics such as differential item functioning. A total of 344 items were pilot tested with 275 adolescents with mental health diagnoses. Some 80 items with different statistical characteristics for adolescents and adults or other problems were eliminated from the standardization version.

TECHNICAL. Norms for the scores were based on 707 adolescents obtained from sites in 21 states in the U.S. The norm sample closely matched the U.S. Census data from 2003 with regard to gender, age, race/ethnicity, but not geographical region, although all regions were represented as well as urban and rural areas. Participants were recruited in a variety of ways including through schools in targeted areas. The sample was not random, but purposive, and data were collected on 1,032 adolescents to create the demographic match. Norms are not broken down by age, ethnicity, or gender, as observed group differences were typically within the range of measurement error and account for less than 5% of the variance in scores.

Normative data of a different sort were obtained from a clinical sample of 1,160 adolescents identified by clinicians working in 78 institutions such as inpatient or outpatient mental health settings and juvenile correctional settings as having a mental illness or emotional disturbance. The clinical sample was 58.4 % male and 72.3% Caucasian, 19.8% African American, 4.5% Hispanic, and 4.4% other with a pattern of diagnoses comparable to those found in another large-scale study, with the exception that depression was somewhat overrepresented and anxiety disorder underrepresented, compared to the other study.

Evidence of internal consistency and stability of the PAI-A indicates the test has reasonable reliability. Coefficient alpha estimates for the normative sample scores on the 20 substantive scales range from .70 for the Positive Impression Scale to .90 for Aggression with a mean of .79. A similar pattern of alpha values was found for the clinical sample, with remarkable consistency across ages, genders, and ethnicities. The values for the subscales, based on fewer items, was lower, ranging from .47 for Anxiety-Related Disorders-Phobias to .85 Anxiety-Related Disorders-Traumatic Stress, with a mean of .69 for the normative sample. Again, the same pattern and levels of alpha was true of the clinical sample. Test-retest stability over a 9- to 35-day interval based on 100 adolescents in the normative sample for the substantive scales ranged from .65 for Positive Impression to .89 for Somatic Complaints with a mean of .78. Coefficients for the subscales ranged from .59 for Mania-Irritability to .88 for Aggression-Physical Aggression with a mean of .76. The manual also reports stability of PAI-A profiles over time.

The test author provides validity information based on a number of studies correlating the PAI-A scores with clinician ratings and with related scores on other commonly used diagnostic measures such as the Minnesota Multiphasic Personality Inventory—Adolescent and the Beck Depression Inventory. Also examined were differences in performance between the normative and clinical samples and the level of performance of the clinical sample on particular scales. The validity scales of Inconsistency, Infrequency, Negative Impression, and Positive Impression were also studied by computer modeling and experimentation with groups of adolescents instructed to "fake bad" or "fake good." In general, correlations with scales from other measures were in the expected moderate range of .40 to .70. The highest correlations were found for measures of Anxiety and Depression. More modest correlations were found for the Suicidal Ideation, Stress, Treatment Rejection, and Dominance Scales of the PAI-A and parallel measures. In general, patterns of scores of groups from the clinical sample were consistent with their identified disorder. An impressive amount of validity data from studies by the test author and others is provided in the manual and indicates the measures are as valid as other comparable tests. Studies of the internal structure of the PAI-A include an examination of scale intercorrelations, exploratory and confirmatory factor analysis, and cluster analysis. The pattern of intercorrelations is similar for the standardization sample and the clinical sample and related scales have moderate to high correlations within expected domains such as Anxiety, Antisocial Behavior, and Psychosis. A factor analysis of the scales in both samples yielded four orthogonal factors related to internalization, externalization, substance abuse, and social alienation. These factors are consistent with the findings on other measures. The confirmatory factor analysis validated the subscale structures of the PAI-A scales indicating excellent goodness of fit between the subscales and their assigned scales. The manual discusses the method of cluster analysis used to identify 10 profiles on the PAI-A, and to the extent that these profiles make sense, provides some support for the validity of the test.

COMMENTARY. Given the vague description of how the normative and clinical samples were obtained, it is difficult to know what biases may have crept into the norms. This is not a critical issue, but should be taken into account in interpreting the test. In any case, because of the developmental variability of adolescents, care should be taken to consider the measurement error around an obtained score. Otherwise, the test was carefully developed using modern psychometric techniques. The issue of test-fairness for minority groups was considered in test development, but more validity work in this area would be welcome. Clearly the test shows promise in clinical applications and may be considered a viable option to other traditional self-report measures for adolescents. The fourth grade reading level and somewhat fewer self-report items are an advantage in soliciting cooperation.

SUMMARY. The PAI-A is a well-designed downward extension of the PAI. This self-report inventory, with good measures for detecting uninterpretable results, should aid in clinical diagnosis when used in conjunction with information from other sources. The norms, reliability, and validity information justify the careful and judicious use of the test by qualified clinicians.

REVIEWER'S REFERENCE

Morey, L. C. (1991). *Personality Assessment Inventory professional manual.* Odessa, FL: Psychological Assessment Resources.

[93]

Personality Assessment Inventory [2007 Professional Manual].

Purpose: Designed to provide information relevant to clinical diagnosis, treatment planning, and screening for psychopathology.
Population: Ages 18 and over.
Publication Dates: 1991-2007.
Acronym: PAI.
Scores, 54: Somatic Complaints (Conversion, Somatization, Health Concerns, Total), Anxiety (Cognitive, Affective, Physiological, Total), Anxiety-Related Disorders (Obsessive-Compulsive, Phobias, Traumatic Stress, Total), Depression (Cognitive, Affective, Physiological, Total), Mania (Activity Level, Grandiosity, Irritability, Total), Paranoia (Hypervigilance, Persecution, Resentment, Total), Schizophrenia (Psychotic Experiences, Social Detachment, Thought Disorder, Total), Borderline Features (Affective Instability, Identity Problems, Negative Relationships, Self-Harm, Total), Antisocial Features (Antisocial Behaviors, Egocentricity, Stimulus-Seeking, Total), Alcohol Problems, Drug Problems, Aggression (Aggressive Attitude, Verbal Aggression, Physical Aggression, Total), Suicidal Ideation, Stress, Nonsupport, Treatment Rejection, Dominance, Warmth, Inconsistency, Infrequency, Negative Impression, Positive Impression.
Administration: Group.
Price Data, 2009: $295 per complete kit including professional manual (2007, 385 pages), 2 reusable item booklets, 2 administration folios, 25 hand-scored answer sheets, 25 adult profile forms-revised, 25 critical item forms-revised, and 1 professional report service answer sheet; $36 per 10 item booklets; $33 per reusable item booklet; $50 per 25 hand-scored answer sheets; $36 per 25 adult profile forms-revised; $33 per 25 college profile forms; $30 per 25 critical item forms-revised; $70 per professional manual; $33 per administration folio.
Time: 55(75) minutes.
Author: Leslie C. Morey.
Publisher: Psychological Assessment Resources, Inc.
Cross References: See T5:1959 (8 references); for reviews of a previous edition by Gregory J. Boyle and Michael G. Kavan, see 12:290 (8 references); see also T4:1997 (3 references).

Review of the Personality Assessment Inventory [2007 Professional Manual] by ANDREW A. COX, Professor of Counseling and Psychology, Troy University, Phenix City, AL:

DESCRIPTION. The Personality Assessment Inventory (PAI) was developed in 1991. It is a multidimensional objective inventory designed to measure psychopathology in adults age 18 and over. It provides information related to the screening and diagnosis of psychopathology and treatment planning for various psychopathological conditions. The current PAI form is not a revision of normative data, test form, or interpretative guidelines from the original 1991 edition. The reader is referred to Boyle (1995) and Kavan (1995) for reviews of this instrument. The current version reflects the revision and publication of a second edition of the PAI professional manual to describe research related to the instrument since the original manual publication in 1991.

The PAI includes 344 items to which test respondents provide answers on a 4-point scale: F = *False, Not At All True*, ST = *Slightly True*, MT = *Mainly True*, and VT = *Very True*. Twenty-two nonoverlapping scales are provided to include 4 validity scales, 11 clinical scales, 5 treatment scales, and 2 interpersonal scales. Ten scales are subdivided into 31 subscales. Clinical syndromes measured by the PAI were selected on the basis of historical importance within the nosology of mental disorders and their implications in current clinical practice. An average fourth grade reading level is required to respond to the inventory. An audio CD administration mode is available for test takers with reading or psychomotor deficits. A Spanish translation of the inventory is available. The manual also reports that the inventory has been translated into other languages. Test takers can respond on a handscored answer sheet or optical scanning answer sheet. A profile form allows translation of test raw scores into linear *T*-scores for all scales, subscales, and supplemental indexes. Profile forms are available for adults and college students. The adult profile form has been revised from earlier editions. A revised critical items form is available to identify response tendencies to facilitate review of inventory critical items that may be useful for assessment purposes. A structural summary form was also revised for supplemental scoring and interpretation.

The publisher has a scoring and report service available for use with the scannable answer sheet as well as onsite optical scoring capability. Computer administration, scoring, and interpretative reports are also available via software. Various specialized interpretative reports are available to compare PAI scores to specific normative groups of interest to law enforcement, public safety, or correctional settings.

DEVELOPMENT. The manual describes the initial development of the PAI item pool, development of research alpha and beta versions of the inventory, inventory field testing, and selection of the final item pool. The standardization sample is a U.S. Census—matched standardization sample consisting of a stratified gender, ethnic origin, and age sample of 1,000 adults selected from the community, a sample of 1,265 adult patients selected from various clinical settings, and a college student sample consisting of 1,051 students. U.S. Bureau of Census 1995 population projections were used for sample selection. Details describing characteristics for each of the above samples are provided within the manual.

TECHNICAL. The professional manual provides chapters detailing internal consistency and test-retest reliability for the instrument. Boyle (1995) and Kavan (1995) describe the original reliability studies. The revised manual reports subsequent reliability studies ranging from 1994 through 2005. Most internal consistency coefficients for these studies ranged from .70 to .80. Internal consistency estimates were lower for a Spanish version of the PAI suggesting that issues in comparability of English and Spanish versions exist with a need for additional research in this area. Earlier test-retest correlations are reported in Boyle (1995) and Kavan (1995). The revised manual reports subsequent test-retest reliability studies that have been conducted with other samples with a mean correlation of .76.

Validation data are reported in the second edition of the manual. Earlier validation efforts are described in Boyle (1995) and Kavan (1995) as well as summarized in the manual. Subsequent validation studies consisting of construct, convergent, and discriminant validation data are reported in the revised manual for the validity, clinical, treatment consideration, interpersonal, and supplemental indexes scales. Validation studies typically involve comparisons between criterion groups and control groups, as well as various correlational studies. Descriptive data for the various validation studies are reported within the manual. These data further illuminate the inventory's use as a clinical measure with a range of clinical populations and clinical settings. These data suggest that the PAI is adequate for the purposes purported for the inventory.

The revised manual presents data describing factor analyses for the inventory. It is indicated that the inventory is not based on an "overarching, well-articulated classificatory theory," but on clinical constructs. Factor analytic studies since publication of the original test manual are described. General distress, acting out, egocentricity and exploitation, and social detachment factors are indicated. Factorial loadings and intercorrelations are reported within the manual. These data reflect an initial basis for further research into the factor analysis of the inventory.

COMMENTARY. The PAI is a well-researched inventory for assessing psychopathology. The manual provides comprehensive discussion of the use, development, technical characteristics, and continuing research associated with the development of this instrument. The manual provides interpretative information for the instrument although additional resources such as Morey (1996, 2003) may be needed for comprehensive interpretation of results for use in clinical practice. The software available for use with the PAI would be a good investment for clinicians using the inventory on a consistent basis. Reliability and validity appear to be acceptable for the inventory's use in clinical and research settings. Ongoing research is taking place that continues to highlight the measure's psychometric characteristics.

A review of recent literature suggests that the PAI is generating a considerable amount of research. Research into the use of the inventory within international settings (Anderson & Ones, 2007; Groves & Engel, 2007; White, 1996) are reported. Additionally, research with diverse client populations and clinical settings is also described in the literature (Edens & Ruiz, 2008; Hopwood, Creech, Clark, Meagher, & Morey, 2007; Kurtz & Blais, 2007; Mullen & Edens, 2008). The revised manual describes a short form of the inventory with research literature highlighting the utility of such a short form (Frazier, Naugle, & Haggerty, 2006). Such research continues to highlight the technical characteristics of the measure as well as promote its utility in diverse clinical settings.

SUMMARY. The Personality Assessment Inventory is an individually or group-administered multidimensional self-report measure for assessing psychopathology with examinees age 18 and older. Norms are available for an adult stratified standardization sample, college students, and adult clinical patients. The inventory was developed in 1991. The current edition does not reflect a revision of the actual instrument or normative sample. Available materials reflect a revised second edition of the inventory manual updating the reader with more recent research involving the PAI, and revision of the adult profile, critical items, and structural summary forms to improve their interpretation and usability in clinical practice. As the inventory itself has not been revised, reviews by Boyle (1995) and Kavan (1995) continue to be pertinent to the current inventory. A review of current literature by this reviewer suggests that the PAI has generated a considerable amount of research. Such research will continue to promote the use of the PAI as noted by Kavan (1995) as an alternative and competitor to the MMPI-2 (Ben-Porath, Tellegen, Butcher, Graham, & Dahlstrom, 1989; T7:1655) and other broad-based clinical measures. The PAI appears to be a good instrument for use in clinical practice as well as psychological research.

REVIEWER'S REFERENCES

Anderson, N., & Ones, D. S. (2007). The construct validity of three entry level personality inventories used in the UK: A cautionary case study. *European Journal of Personality, 22,* 147-150.

Ben-Porath, Y. S., Tellegen, A., Butcher, J. A., Graham, J. R., & Dahlstrom, W. G. (1989). Minnesota Multiphasic Personality Inventory-II. Bloomington, MN: University of Minnesota Press.

Boyle, G. J. (1995). [Review of the Personality Assessment Inventory.] In J. C. Conoley &J. C. Impara (Eds.), *The twelfth mental measurements yearbook* (pp. 764–766). Lincoln, NE: Buros Institute of Mental Measurements.

Edens, J. F., & Ruiz, M. A. (2008). Identification of mental disorders in an in-patient prison psychiatric unit: Examining the criterion-related validity of the Personality Assessment Inventory. *Psychological Services, 5,* 108-117.

Frazier, T. W., Naugle, R. I., & Haggerty, K. A. (2006). Psychometric adequacy and comparability of the short and full forms of the Personality Assessment Inventory. *Psychological Assessment, 18,* 324-333.

Groves, J. A., & Engel, R. R. (2007). The German adaptation and standardization of the Personality Assessment Inventory (PAI). *Journal of Personality Assessment, 88,* 49-56.

Hopwood, C. J., Creech, S. K., Clark, T. S., Meagher, M. W., & Morey, L. C. (2007). The convergence and predictive validity of the Multidimensional Pain Inventory and the Personality Assessment Inventory among individuals with chronic pain. *Rehabilitation Psychology, 52,* 443-450.

Kavan, M. G. (1995). [Review of the Personality Assessment Inventory.] In J. C. Conoley & J. C. Impara (Eds.), *The twelfth mental measurements yearbook* (pp. 766–768). Lincoln, NE: Buros Institute of Mental Measurements.

Kurtz, J. E., & Blais, M. A. (2007). Introduction to the special issue on the Personality Assessment Inventory. *Journal of Personality Assessment, 88,* 1-4.

Morey, L. C. (1996). *An interpretative guide to the Personality Assessment Inventory.* Odessa, FL: Psychological Assessment Resources.

Morey, L. C. (2003). *Essentials of PAI assessment.* Hoboken, NJ: Wiley.

Mullen, K. L., & Edens, J. F. (2008). A case law survey of the Personality Assessment Inventory: Examining its role in civil and criminal trials. *Journal of Personality Assessment, 90,* 300-303.

White, L. J. (1996). Review of the Personality Assessment Inventory: A new psychological test for clinical and forensic assessment. *Australian Psychologist, 31,* 38-40.

Review of the Personality Assessment Inventory [2007 Professional Manual] by GEOFFREY L. THORPE, Professor of Psychology, and RACHEL D. BURROWS, Doctoral Candidate, University of Maine, Orono, ME:

DESCRIPTION. The Personality Assessment Inventory (PAI) is a 344-item, multiscale self-report inventory for use in the clinical assessment of adults. Respondents select an answer to each item from a 4-point scale: F = (*false, not at all true*), ST = (*slightly true*), MT = (*mainly true*), and VT = (*very true*). The typical administration time is 40 to 50 minutes. The test produces scores on 22 discrete scales: 4 validity scales, 11 clinical scales, 5 treatment scales, and 2 interpersonal scales. The validity scales assess for inaccuracies in and distortions of responding attributable to Inconsistency, Infrequency, Negative Impression, and Positive Impression. Six supplemental validity indicators include a Rogers Discriminant Function, drawn from weighted combinations of 20 scale scores, designed to distinguish genuine from simulated profiles.

The clinical scales assess Somatic Complaints, Anxiety, Anxiety-Related Disorders, Depression, Mania, Paranoia, Schizophrenia, Borderline Features, Antisocial Features, Alcohol Problems, and Drug Problems. Most of the clinical scales also yield subscale scores reflecting recognized components of the syndromes. For example, the Antisocial Features scale encompasses the subscales Antisocial Behaviors, Egocentricity, and Stimulus-Seeking. The Treatment Consideration Scales address features important to treatment planning that overlap across diagnostic categories: aggressive attitudes and behaviors, thoughts and ideas related to death and suicide, current life stressors, perceived lack of support, and attitudes toward treatment—including "unwillingness to participate actively in treatment, a refusal to acknowledge problems, and a reluctance to accept responsibility for problems in one's life" (professional manual, p. 46). The Interpersonal scales assess the levels of dominance and warmth that respondents display in their relationships with others.

Test users may also examine critical items and interpret various supplemental indexes, profile codetypes, and modal cluster profiles. The first 160 items of the PAI have received a level of validation as a short form of the instrument.

Raw scores on the PAI scales and subscales are plotted on a multi—sided profile form that indicates the corresponding *T* scores. These values were derived from the standardization sample of 1,000 U.S. Census-matched adults from the general community. The test author suggests that

T scores of 70 and above may indicate clinically significant problems.

The PAI inventory itself still bears only the original copyright dates 1990 and 1991 and thus has not been changed, but the professional manual (2007) is a second edition that provides "updated information about the technical aspects of the test norms, reliability, and validity" (professional manual, p. 1).

DEVELOPMENT. The PAI scales were selected to reflect five constructs that the developer believed were "most pertinent to a broad-banded assessment of mental disorder ... (a) validity of an individual's responses, (b) clinical syndromes, (c) interpersonal style, (d) treatment complications, and (e) characteristics of the individual's environment" (professional manual, p. 106). Potential test items were generated by a team of researchers, faculty members, practitioners, graduate students, and others drawing from the research literature, classic texts, diagnostic manuals, and clinical experience. The resulting item pool of over 2,200 was eventually distilled into the 344 items of the PAI.

Item selection and scale development of the PAI took place in two stages. In the first stage, each of the potential items was evaluated for the conceptual meaning of its content. This evaluation consisted of: (a) ratings of the quality of the item and appropriateness of the subscale assignment by members of the research team, (b) a sorting study of item content by experts in the specific fields, and (c) a review of item content to eliminate those that could be offensive to male or female respondents or to those with particular racial, religious, or ethnic group identifications. The second stage was a two-tiered empirical evaluation of the 776 items that survived the first stage. In the first tier, the alpha version of the test was administered to a sample of college students for the purposes of "evaluating item distributions, item social desirability, possible gender effects, and studies of the manipulations of response set to investigate the effects of malingering or faking on item responses" (professional manual, p. 123). This process resulted in a beta version of the test with 597 items, next administered to a heterogeneous sample of individuals from community and clinical settings to examine the items' internal consistency, specificity, and internal validity in addition to differential responding by groups varying in age, gender, race, or ethnicity. The 344 items that constitute the PAI itself were those that demonstrated the optimal psychometric properties and appeared to best reflect the constructs that the test was intended to measure.

TECHNICAL. The PAI was standardized on three samples of respondents: the general community sample noted earlier (*N* = 1,000), a sample of patients from 69 clinical sites (*N* = 1,265), and college students from seven universities (*N* = 1,051).

Reliability. The data for internal consistency showed that the median alpha coefficients for PAI scales and subscales were .81 (general community sample), .86 (clinical sample), and .82 (college student sample). Test-retest reliability was assessed with additional community and college samples who were retested after 24 or 28 days. Taken together, those two groups produced test-retest correlations ranging from .79 to .92 for the clinical scales.

Validity. At 133 pages, the chapter entitled "Validity Studies" is by far the longest in the professional manual. The test author emphasizes convergent, construct, and discriminant validity, and has amassed data not only from his own validation studies but also from hundreds of others that have appeared in print since the PAI was first issued in 1991. Validity data are presented for all five groups of scales and indexes. The chapter documents the correlations of PAI components with other well-known inventories and structured clinical interview protocols, and presents studies of various criterion groups and their differential responses to the PAI elements. For example, among clinical participants, PAI Depression correlates .66 with the MMPI D scale (Scale 2), and PAI Schizophrenia correlates .55 with the MMPI Sc scale (Scale 8).

Modern test theory methodology was used in concert with classical test theory procedures in some applications. In a *tour de force* of documentation, the test author provides in this chapter 26 figures and 50 tables that, among other things, delineate the relationship between the indexes and scales of the PAI and dozens of external instruments as responded to by thousands of individuals in a variety of settings.

Standardization. Tables for converting raw scores to T scores are found in six of the manual's appendixes. The U.S. Census-matched community sample of 1,000 respondents is the standardization sample proper. Similar tables for clinical, African American, senior (age 60 or over), and college student samples are provided for comparison purposes only. Test users in many settings and with a diversity of respondent populations are likely to find the raw and *T* scores of appropriate comparison groups tabulated within these appendixes and in the chapter on validation.

COMMENTARY. The test author paid elaborate attention to detail in developing and validating the PAI, which has also been extensively researched by others. The most cursory of informal surveys revealed half a dozen articles on the PAI in a handful of recent issues of *Psychological Assessment,* the topics being short versus full forms of the PAI, clinician-assessment versus self-assessment using the PAI, predicting sex offender adjustment, assessing antisocial personality disorder, and back irrelevant responding (completing later test items in a less valid manner than earlier items) as a PAI validity indicator (two articles). As the test author notes (professional manual, p. 1), the PAI is ranked among the top four personality tests in terms of its general popularity and widespread professional acceptance. Recent citations attest to its utility in assessing critical clinical variables in a broad spectrum of populations in clinical and forensic settings (e.g., Caperton, Edens, & Johnson, 2004; Guy, Poythress, Douglas, Skeem, & Edens, 2008).

The level of detail involved in scoring supplemental indexes can be excessive. To take the most extreme example, calculating the Rogers Discriminant Function involves multiplying each of 20 scale and subscale scores by a different weighting, the value of which is expressed to eight places of decimals—in effect, working at the level of a 100 millionth of a raw score unit. In the example provided in the professional manual (Figure 2.4, p. 17), this results in a sum of -1.35172, which is then interpolated on the profile form between the values of -1.25 and -1.50 to give a *T* score of 47. When we performed the same calculation after rounding the weighting values to 2 places of decimals we obtained a sum of -1.34 and the same *T* score.

A final quibble—the test's label as the Personality Assessment Inventory may mislead some professionals who do not follow the early tradition of the Minnesota Multiphasic Personality Inventory (MMPI0; Hathaway & McKinley, 1943) in drawing parallels between (if not even equating) personality and psychopathology. Many would expect a personality inventory to consist of scales measuring extraversion, neuroticism, and at least the other components of the familiar "big five" traits rather than a list of constructs with names similar to those of mental disorders. Yet, with his typical thoroughness, the test author provides a table of correlations between the PAI scales and the NEO Personality Inventory (NEO-PI) domains for a community sample (professional manual, Table H.9, p. 358), and the relationships seem consistent with expectation: For example, PAI Anxiety correlates .75 with Neuroticism, PAI Paranoia correlates -.54 with Agreeableness, and PAI Borderline Features correlates -.31 with Conscientiousness.

SUMMARY. The PAI is a self-report inventory assessing personality and psychopathology that is convenient to administer, psychometrically sound, extensively researched, and suitable for use in clinical, forensic, and other applied settings. It can be recommended as an alternative to the MMPI-2 (Butcher, Dahlstrom, Graham, Tellegen, & Kaemmer, 1989; T7:1655) for its relatively short administration time and its inclusion of scales directly measuring a respondent's amenability to treatment.

REVIEWERS' REFERENCES

Butcher, J. N., Dahlstrom, W. G., Graham, J. R., Tellegen, A., & Kaemmer, B. (1989). *Minnesota Multiphasic Personality Inventory-2: Manual for administration and scoring*. Minneapolis: University of Minnesota Press.

Caperton, J. D., Edens, J. F., & Johnson, J. K. (2004). Predicting sex offender institutional adjustment and treatment compliance using the Personality Assessment Inventory. *Psychological Assessment, 16,* 187-191.

Guy, L. S., Poythress, N. G., Douglas, K. S., Skeem, J. L., & Edens, J. F. (2008). Correspondence between self-report and interview-based assessments of antisocial personality disorder. *Psychological Assessment, 20,* 47-54.

Hathaway, S. R., & McKinley, J. C. (1943). The Minnesota Multiphasic Personality Inverntory (rev. ed.). Minneapolis: University of Minnesota Press.

[94]

Picture Interest Career Survey.

Purpose: "Provides an easy way for people with limited reading ability or special needs to explore their career interests and find a job that fits."
Population: Ages 10-65.
Publication Date: 2007.
Acronym: PICS.
Scores, 6: Realistic, Investigative, Artistic, Social, Enterprising, Conventional.
Administration: Group.
Price Data, 2008: $42.95 per 25 tests.
Time: (15) minutes.
Author: Robert P. Brady.
Publisher: JIST Publishing, Inc.

Review of the Picture Interest Career Survey by SHERI BAUMAN, Associate Professor, Department of Educational Psychology, University of Arizona, Tucson, AZ:

DESCRIPTION. The Picture Interest Career Survey (PICS) is a brief self-report paper-and-pencil vocational interest instrument that is "essentially language free" (administrator guide, p. 1). It is based on the well-known Holland codes (RIASEC) and the interest categories of "people, data, things, ideas." It is suitable for both individual and group administration. According to the test author, the survey can be used with individuals ages 10–65, and is useful for persons who have limited literacy skills, and who are not English speakers. It can be used with visually impaired clients by providing verbal descriptions of the illustrations. "Suggested" directions are provided in English only.

The PICS contains 36 items, each of which consists of three line drawings of a person doing a work task. The client circles the drawing that is most interesting to him or her. Scoring is straightforward and can be accomplished in about 5 minutes by either the client or the administrator. Each of the RIASEC codes is included in the same number of items as primary and secondary codes. The result of the survey is an Occupational PICS Code (RIASEC) that quantifies relative interest in each of the occupational themes. To relate the code to potential careers, the user can access the Career Locator and Career Planning Worksheet that accompany the survey and are also available for free online download. In addition, many other resources for this purpose are widely available, such as the *O*NET Dictionary of Occupational Titles* (JIST Works, 2004) and the *Enhanced Occupational Outlook Handbook* (JIST Works, 2007).

DEVELOPMENT. Development of the survey began in 2003. Absent from the administrator's guide (the only manual) is any rationale for the need for such a survey, given the number of career assessments based on the RIASEC codes that are already available. The author does not present a case for the need for a "language-free" version, although an argument surely could be constructed based on data from career service agencies.

Written items (descriptions of job tasks) were developed first, although the process of item selection or the number of items in the initial item pool is not described in the administrator's guide. For each item, three written descriptions of the task were created, with each of the three tasks representing a different RIASEC primary code and all three tasks having the same secondary code. The pictorial version was developed from the written version after initial psychometric studies had been completed. The author opted to produce a single version, rather than separate male and female versions, based on the research with gender-specific forms.

TECHNICAL. Validity was assessed by comparing the codes obtained on the PICS with those obtained on another interest inventory using the RIASEC codes. To his credit, the test author calculated the degree of congruence using a sophisticated statistical method devised to assess congruence between person codes and environment codes (Brown & Gore, 1994). The sample in the initial study was quite small (n = 30); no demographic information about the sample is provided. It is also not clear how closely in time the two inventories used for the calculations were completed. That is, were they taken on the same day, and if not, how much time had elapsed between administrations? The description of the study used to determine the test-retest reliability also lacks specific information about the time interval. It is interesting that the author used the *C* index (Brown & Gore, 1994) to compare the RIASEC codes obtained from two different assessment instruments in one study, but not for other studies. Evidence of content validity is based upon the equal distribution of items associated with each of the RIASEC letters and the equal number of items in each of the people, data, things, and ideas categories.

To demonstrate that the survey exhibits concurrent and criterion validity, the author reports results of three studies. In each, the codes obtained on the PICS were compared to the codes for the careers in which participants were currently interested, training for, and/or working in. Unfortunately, the test author did not use the *C* index for this comparison. Instead, he presents the judgments of expert raters on whether there was a match (yes/no) between the PICS code and the criterion career. The justification for this statistical strategy is not given. As each career's code can be found in any of a number of sources, it is problematic that the *C* index was not used for these studies; this is the type of comparison for which that index was designed. The sample sizes for the three studies were 42 (adults ages 20–59), 25 (high school students), and 70 (students from a residential vocational training school in Jamaica, West Indies).

Two studies of construct validity were conducted with samples of 12 individuals (Study 1, age not provided) and 11 individuals (no ages given) who completed both the PICS and the SDS (Self-Directed Search), Holland's widely used process for obtaining one's RIASEC profile. Spearman's coefficient was used as a measure of correspondence, and adequate, statistically significant correlations were obtained. Finally, test-retest reliability was assessed using the rank orders of the RIASEC codes on both administrations. Three small samples were used: a "random sample of [18] adults" (administrator's guide, p. 11), a sample of 8 adults attending professional school, and a sample of 13 high school seniors. The median correlation coefficient for the combined samples was .83.

The test author does not provide demographic information about the samples used in survey development, with the exception of age (and location of one of the samples). It is not clear how a random sample of 18 adults was recruited. The educational levels for the adults are not given. An apparent justification for the absence of data on race/ethnicity of the samples, or other discussion of multicultural applications, is given in a brief paragraph stating that vocational personality typologies, such as the RIASEC codes, have been found to be similar across racial and ethnic groups and gender, based on previous research. However, the study cited in support of the similarities across groups used a different measure and the sample consisted of college-bound high school students only (Day & Rounds, 1998).

COMMENTARY. This new survey of career interests using the RIASEC model provides a method for determining the career interests of individuals who have limited English or literacy. However, although the three job tasks from which respondents choose are presented visually as line drawings, there are a number of drawings in which the minimal text is critical to understanding what the job task is. Thus, it is not entirely language-free, as the author contends. In addition, the quality of the line drawings is not high. In some cases, the task portrayed is not clear. Although figures of both genders are included, the absence of any racial/ethnic diversity is a significant limitation. A further concern regarding cross-cultural applicability is the absence of any directions in languages other than English. If individual administrators create their own version of instructions, there is no assurance that all users will have a clear understanding of the task.

The administrator's guide claims that the PICS is appropriate for use with individuals ages 10–65, yet it does not appear that the samples upon which the survey was tested included that entire range of ages. No samples included children below high school age, for example, and when age information was given about the samples, no participants were older than 68. Without testing the survey on all ages in the range, this claim of suitability appears premature.

The size of the samples on which the psychometric properties were determined is problematic. The varied statistical techniques used to determine validity is also puzzling. Finally, the absence of demographic information about the samples in the validation and reliability studies leaves questions about the representativeness of the sample. As noted above, the fact that high school students had similar RIASEC structures regardless of race or gender using another survey is not sufficient evidence of the cross-cultural applicability of the current survey; further study is warranted.

SUMMARY. The PICS is a brief pencil-and-paper screening survey based on the Holland codes. The survey uses line drawings rather than verbal descriptions of worker tasks so that clients with limited language or literacy can use it. Scoring is straightforward and the results provide a summary code that can then be matched with careers for which demands and environment are consistent with that code. Although easy to administer and score, there are questions about the psychometric attributes given the small samples used in validation studies and the absence of demographic information about the samples. Further studies using samples representative of the clients for whom the survey might be used would increase the utility of the survey. The quality of the line drawings may also be problematic for some users, especially those in which the minimal text is crucial to understanding the task being depicted. Further research is needed to establish the overall value of this measure.

REVIEWER'S REFERENCES

Brown, S. D., & Gore, P. A. (1994). An evaluation of interest congruence indices: Distribution characteristics and measurement properties. *Journal of Vocational Behavior, 45*, 310-327.

Day, S. X., & Rounds, J. (1998). Universality of vocational interest structure among racial and ethnic minorities. *American Psychologist, 53*, 728-736.

JIST Works. (2004). *O*NET dictionary of occupational titles* (3rd ed.). Indianapolis, IN: JIST Publishing.

JIST Works. (2007). *Enhanced occupational outlook.* Indianapolis, IN: JIST Publishing.

Review of Picture Interest Career Survey by JULIA Y. PORTER, Associate Professor of Counselor Education, Mississippi State University-Meridian, Meridian, MS:

DESCRIPTION. The Picture Interest Career Survey (PICS) is a 36-item picture interest inventory based on John Holland's RIASEC occupational coding system (Holland, 1992) and Prediger's interest categories and work tasks (1982). For each of the 36 items, test takers are presented with three drawings that represent different work activities for a total of 108 pictures. For each item, the test taker selects the drawing that is the most interesting to him or her by circling that picture. An Occupational PICS Code is determined based on the test taker's responses. This code can be used with any of the RIASEC system occupational materials to assist the test taker with career exploration and planning.

The PICS is designed to be used with individuals ages 10 to 65 years and may be administered individually or in group settings. Scoring options include self-scoring or administrator scoring. Estimated scoring time is 5 minutes. Scoring results in a three-letter code (tied scores will result in more than one code) called the Occupational PICS Code, which is based on scores from six vocational personality areas: Realistic, Investigative, Artistic, Social, Enterprising, and Conventional. The maximum score on each of the six vocational personality areas in the code is 18. This code can be explored in more depth using the PICS Career Locator that covers 600 jobs listed from the *O*NET Dictionary of Occupational Titles*. Education and training level information is provided for each of the 600 jobs listed. After the test taker has narrowed his or her job interests, the PICS Career Planning Worksheet guides the test taker through realistic job exploration and building a job profile. The PICS Career Planning Worksheet and PICS Career Locator are both available online and may be downloaded at no extra charge.

DEVELOPMENT. The first studies on the development of the PICS began in 2003 on a 36-item written inventory with each item presenting three written choices, which were examples of one of the six RIASEC vocational personality types. Two pictorial versions of the inventory were then developed from the written version. One version portrayed female workers and the other version male workers doing the same work tasks. Research studies indicated that the congruence level remained significantly high ($C = 16.3, p < .0001$) when the instrument version with opposite-gender workers was administered. Based on these findings, a follow-up study was conducted ($n = 37$) comparing combined single form results with a same-gender form. A significantly high relationship was found between the two instruments using Spearman (r_1) rank order correlations ($Mdn\ r_1 = .90, p < .001$).

The current version of the PICS was published in 2007 and contains 108 pictures. There are 18 pictures representing each of the vocational personality types in RIASEC (Realistic, Investigative, Artistic, Social, Enterprising, Conventional) and 27 pictures representing each of the four areas of Prediger's interest categories and work tasks (people, data, things, ideas).

TECHNICAL. A series of research studies begun in 2003 that ranged from $n = 8$ to $n = 70$ resulted in a standardization sample of 199 (91 adults; 108 adolescents).

A construct validity study conducted with adults ($n = 26$) in 2003 on the written version of the PICS examined the congruence between the Occupational PICS Code and Career and Life Explorer codes. Data analysis resulted in a C index of 12.03 ($mn\ C = 12.03$, $SD = 3.9$). After the revision to a pictorial interest inventory, additional construct validity studies were conducted on the PICS ($n = 12$, $n = 11$) comparing the PICS and Holland's Self-Directed Search (SDS). Results from these studies yielded a combined Spearman (r_1) median of .71 (.755; .66, respectively; $p < .01$), which was statistically significant.

Content validity was established by examining item validity and sampling validity. For each of the RIASEC vocational personality types there are 18 pictures for each primary letter code and 18 pictures for each secondary letter code. For each of the 4 Prediger interest categories (people, data, things, ideas), there are 27 pictures for each category. The test developer reports that item and sampling validity criteria were met. The PICS administrator's guide includes a detailed table of the content validity comparisons. Concurrent criterion-related validity was established through three studies ($n = 42$; $n = 25$; $n = 70$) that resulted in a combined result of 784 affirmative matches out of 822 comparisons made (95.37%).

Reliability studies conducted in 2003 on the written version of the PICS ($n = 21$) used a test-retest design that resulted in a Spearman (r_1) correlation coefficient of .87 ($p < .01$). Three test-retest reliability studies ($n = 18$, $n = 8$, $n = 13$), each with a retest interval of approximately 1 month, were conducted after the PICS was revised to include pictures instead of a written format that resulted in a combined median Spearman (r_1) correlation coefficient of .825 ($p < .001$).

Multicultural concerns of ethnicity, race, culture, gender, and age were addressed in two ways:

a) Racial and ethnic validity were established by examining the RIASEC system of coding because correlations were established between PICS and RIASEC. RIASEC normative data support the use of RIASEC with individuals from different racial and ethnic minorities. b) A gender study with adults ages 22–68 (n = 30) compared each study participant's Occupational PICS Code with their RIASEC career code for their current job. Study data returned a C index of 16.3 (t = 10.09, p < .0001).

Although data results for validity and reliability were statistically significant, sample sizes were too small to be able to generalize results. Additional data about the characteristics of the norm groups used would help test administrators determine if the PICS is appropriate for use with a particular group of individuals being assessed. Additional studies with larger samples also need to be conducted to verify results reported in early studies.

COMMENTARY. The Picture Interest Career Survey addresses a need to provide alternative instruments for individuals who may not do well on traditional paper-and-pencil interest inventories because of challenges such as language or ability levels. Strengths of the PICS include the ease of administering and scoring the PICS and its compatibility with the RIASEC system. Another strength is the PICS Career Planning Worksheet, an easy-to-read and easy-to-use career exploration worksheet, which is provided free to PICS users.

Although preliminary findings indicate that the PICS is an instrument with adequate evidence of reliability and validity, additional research studies are needed with larger sample sizes to be able to generalize research findings. A more detailed description of the characteristics of the sample used in each of the validity and reliability tests would also help test administrators determine if the PICS would be appropriate for the population they plan to survey (American Educational Research Association, American Psychological Association, & National Council on Measurement in Education, 1999; Whiston, 2004).

The PICS sample test item for administrator demonstration purposes includes a brief written picture description, which the test administrator reads to the test taker. Including a table with a brief written description of each of the picture items would help test administrators better standardize the testing procedures. Some of the pictures are easy to identify but other pictures are complex and might result in misinterpretation or multiple interpretations.

The PICS administrator's guide includes a brief primer on RIASEC vocational personality types (p. 3). The guide also includes a diagram of the hexagonal circumplex model showing the relationship between Holland's vocational personality types and Prediger's interest categories and work tasks (p. 12), which is a good review for test administrators and can also be used in explaining the test purpose and results depending on the age and ability level of the test taker.

SUMMARY. The Picture Interest Career Survey was designed to identify occupational interest areas for individuals aged 10–65 for whom traditional interest inventories might not be appropriate because of language or ability barriers. Items on the PICS include 108 drawings of work tasks related to RIASEC and Prediger's four interest categories and work tasks. The 36 survey items are presented in groups of 3. Survey responses result in a PICS Occupational Code that can be used with other RIASEC system materials such as the *O*Net Dictionary of Occupational Titles* (JIST Works, 2004), *Enhanced Occupational Outlook Handbook* (JIST Works, 2007), and the *Dictionary of Holland Occupational Codes* (Gottfredson & Holland, 1996) to explore career options. The PICS should be used with caution and in conjunction with other researched instruments because reliability and validity data are limited and additional standardization tests are needed to verify the appropriateness of the PICS with diverse populations.

REVIEWER'S REFERENCES

American Educational Research Association, American Psychological Association, & National Council on Measurement in Education. (1999). *Standards for educational and psychological testing.* Washington, DC: American Educational Research Association.

Gottfredson, G. D., & Holland, J. L. (1996). *Dictionary of Holland occupational codes.* Lutz, FL: Psychological Assessments Resources, Inc.

Holland, J. L. (1992). *Making vocational choices: A theory of vocational personalities and work environments.* Odessa, FL: Psychological Assessment Resources, Inc.

JIST Works. (2004). *O*NET dictionary of occupational titles.* (3rd ed.). Indianapolis, IN: JIST Publishing.

JIST Works. (2007). *Enhanced occupational outlook handbook.* Indianapolis, IN: JIST Publishing.

Prediger, D. J. (1982). Dimensions underlying Holland's hexagon: Missing link between interest and occupations? *Journal of Vocational Behavior, 21,* 259-287.

Whiston, S. C. (2004). *Principles and applications of assessment in counseling* (2nd ed.). Belmont, CA: Wadsworth/Thomson Learning.

[95]

PL-1 and PL-2 Police Administrator Tests (Lieutenant).

Purpose: Developed as knowledge-based tests suitable for the command level and to assist police departments in promoting qualified candidates to a higher rank.

Population: Candidates for promotion to the police administrator position.
Publication Dates: 1998–2006.
Acronyms: PL-1; PL-2.
Scores: 4 knowledge areas: Police Procedures: Patrol and Investigation, Laws Related to Police Work, Concepts of Supervision, Concepts of Administration.
Administration: Individual or group.
Forms, 2: PL-1, PL-2.
Price Data: Available from publisher.
Time: 150 minutes per test.
Comments: PL-1 and PL-2 are comparable forms; reading lists are available to help candidates prepare for the tests.
Author: International Public Management Association for Human Resources.
Publisher: International Public Management Association for Human Resources (IPMA-HR).

Review of the PL-1 and PL-2 Police Administrator Tests (Lieutenant) by RUSSELL W. SMITH, Senior Psychometrician, Alpine Testing Solutions, Henderson, NV:

[Editor's note: The publisher has informed the Buros Institute that the PL-2 is no longer in circulation due to its age. The PL-1 was updated and became the PL-1.2. The reviewer did not have access to this revision. The test publisher now provides users with some normative information. This normative information for the PL-1.2 is based upon data from 469 job candidates including 36 African Americans, 23 Hispanic Americans, and 3 Asian Americans. A list of the police forces where these officer candidates took the test is also provided. No evaluation of the adequacy or representativeness of this sample is made by either the publisher or Buros. This information was not made available to the reviewer by the test publisher.]

DESCRIPTION. The Police Administrator Test (Lieutenant/Section Head) is a knowledge-based exam designed to be used as an aide for selecting candidates for promotion within police departments. The exam is designed to measure five content areas: (a) Knowledge of Concepts of Supervision, (b) Knowledge of Concepts of Administration, (c) Knowledge of Standard Police Procedures, (d) Knowledge of Laws Related to Police Work, and (e) Knowledge of Police Investigative Procedures.

The exam is designed to measure knowledge related to administrative and supervisory positions within police departments across the United States. The content measured by the examination is meant to be general to administrative and supervisory positions across the country. It is not designed to be exhaustive of all the knowledge and skills necessary for such jobs. For example, the examination does not cover state- or department-specific procedures and laws. The authors suggest that the examination be used in conjunction with other selection methods and that users develop a "sub-test concerning local rules, policies, laws, etc." (Addendum PL-1, p. 4).

There are two 100-item selected-response versions of the examination (PL-1 and PL-2) administered via paper-and-pencil. Each form consists of four subtests based on the content areas: Police Procedures (standard and investigative), Laws Related to Police Work, Concepts of Supervision, and Concepts of Administration.

DEVELOPMENT. This test is based on a thorough job analysis conducted in 1998. The job analysis began by observing and interviewing police lieutenants on the job. Efforts were made to have an appropriate geographically and demographically representative sample, including observing both day and night shifts. Documentation, including copying forms and reports completed by the lieutenants, was collected. A list of tasks/duties, knowledge, skills, and abilities was created and reviewed during the observations and interviews.

Two job analysis questionnaires were developed based on the list, one for incumbents and one for supervisors, and sent to a demographically diverse sample of police departments throughout the country. The questionnaires asked the participants to rate the importance and frequency of each of the tasks at the time of promotion, not what would be learned on the job. Demographic information, including race and gender, are reported in the technical report (Technical Report, pp. 6-7). The importance and frequency ratings were reviewed and compared between the two groups. Decision rules were created for selecting the knowledge skills and abilities to be measured by the examination. The importance data were used to create a preliminary test blueprint by dividing the average of the importance ratings within each of the four subtest areas and dividing by the sum of the averages.

Thirty item writers from 14 police departments across the country wrote items using the list of reading resources included in the study list (Technical Report, pp. 41-42). The items were reviewed and psychometrically edited. Additional items were selected from the previous version of the examination based on their statistical difficulty and discrimination. The subtests were then sent to subject-matter experts (SMEs) in 26 police departments across the country to rate the importance of each. Items were eliminated from the bank based on importance ratings key disputes. The same SMEs were also asked to review the blueprint that resulted from the job analysis and job analysis questionnaire. The result was a final blueprint with 100 items mapping to that blueprint. This version is referred to as PL-2.

A second form of the examination was developed in 2003. This version is referred to as PL-1. The purpose and content is designed to parallel the original in content. A total of 138 items were reviewed using a process similar to that used for the PL-2 items. These items were either from the previous version of the exam, selected based on their statistical difficulty and discrimination, or from an item bank maintained by the publisher, or newly written. The newly written items were based on content from the updated versions of a subset of the original reading list books.

TECHNICAL. The job analysis and job analysis questionnaire are well described in the Technical Report and PL-1 Addendum. Comparisons between the ratings of the incumbents and supervisor offer good evidence that the content is appropriate. Particular attention is given to the sample representation of the participants and subject matter experts who contributed to the development of the examination blueprint and item development. However, the content validity rests entirely on how well the results of this job analysis align with the tasks the specific department considering use of the examination would be attempting to measure. This alignment should be a critical consideration for those considering the use of this examination.

No other specific empirical evidence is offered regarding the development of this examination. No evidence of concurrent validity is offered. No information is provided regarding the geographies, demographics, and performance of actual candidates taking the examination. With the exception of item statistics from the previous version of the exam used to select items to be used on the newer versions of the examination, no empirical item or test level performance information is provided. No norming information is provided. No reliability information is provided. No information regarding performance standards is provided.

COMMENTARY. It would be prudent for the publisher to provide empirical evidence regarding the performance of the examination. This evidence should include, at the very least, evidence of reliability and evidence that the items do not perform differentially between various subgroups. Although sufficient evidence is offered that the content of the two versions of the exam, the PL-1 and PL-2, are parallel with respect to content, no evidence is provided that they are equivalent in difficulty.

This examination has been purposefully built to be generalizable to police departments across the country and to multiple supervisory and administrative positions within those departments. This examination does not measure all the objectives deemed important for promotion within any one department. It may prove useful for departments that wish to use it to measure the concepts and knowledge that it has been designed to measure. It would likely prove more useful if norming data were available so departments might compare the performance of their candidates to that of candidates nationally.

Departments considering using this examination should be cautioned that an interdepartmental job analysis should be conducted. The Police Administrator examination could then be used to measure its designated content areas that align with the content areas resulting from the interdepartmental job analysis. As the publishers suggest, it should only be used as a part of a battery of selection criteria. Additionally, if using this test for selecting candidates for promotion, the burden of providing evidence such as reliability and setting appropriate performance standards will fall on the user. Further, the different versions of the examination should not be used interchangeably without evidence of their equivalence. Local validation is important.

SUMMARY. The Police Administrator examination was developed as a knowledge-based test to be included as one of many selection criteria in promoting police officers to supervisory or administrative positions. It is designed to measure some, but not all, important knowledge and skills necessary for promotion. It is based on a thorough job analysis generic to such positions throughout all police departments. No empirical evidence of the examinations (e.g., reliability or construct validity) has been provided. No norming information and no performance standard information have been provided. Potential users of this exam should consider this instrument if they are willing to provide evidence that the objectives are in alignment with their own and report on the reliability and performance standards.

[96]

Primary Test of Nonverbal Intelligence.

Purpose: Intended for "assessing [nonverbal] reasoning abilities in young children."
Population: Ages 3-0 to 9-11.
Publication Date: 2008.
Acronym: PTONI.
Scores: Total score only.
Administration: Individual.
Price Data, 2009: $208 per complete kit including picture book, 25 record forms, and examiner's manual (84 pages); $95 per picture book; $47 per 25 record forms; $74 per examiner's manual.
Foreign Language & Other Special Editions: Test directions are available in eight foreign languages: Spanish, French, traditional Chinese (Mandarin), simplified Chinese, German, Tagalog, Vietnamese, Italian, Japanese; alternate directions for children with hearing impairments can be administered using American Sign Language, Manually Coded English, Aural/Oral English, and Sign-Supported Speech/English.
Time: (5-15) minutes.
Comments: Children respond to items by pointing to the correct picture in the picture book.
Authors: David J. Ehrler and Ronnie L. McGhee.
Publisher: PRO-ED.

Review of the Primary Test of Nonverbal Intelligence by CONNIE THERIOT ENGLAND, Professor, Graduate Education, Lincoln Memorial University, Knoxville, TN:

DESCRIPTION. The Primary Test of Nonverbal Intelligence (PTONI) is an individually administered measure of a "variety of reasoning abilities" (examiner's manual, p. 2) of children ages 3 years, 0 months to 9 years, 11 months. The complete PTONI kit consists of an examiner's manual, picture book, and 25 examiner/record forms.

Persons familiar with other versions of the Test of NonVerbal Ability (CTONI, CTONI-II, etc.) will be familiar with test procedures. To administer, the examiner asks the child to point to the *one*, of a set of pictures or geometric designs, which does not belong with the others. The PTONI provides training items that model the targeted unlike picture/geometric design "pointing response"; thus, ensuring comprehension of task requirements.

DEVELOPMENT. The PTONI was designed specifically to measure the intellectual ability of young children for whom other traditional assessment tools may be inappropriate, to "predict future outcomes for these children" (examiner's manual, p. 2), and for "research concerning intelligence and related topics" (examiner's manual, p. 2).

The manual provides a thorough description of administration procedures, alternate administration procedures for those with hearing impairments, and translated directions for administration in eight different languages (Spanish, French, Traditional Chinese, Simplified Chinese, German, Tagalog, Vietnamese, Italian, and Japanese). Data for normative scores–nonverbal indexes (standard scores) and percentile ranks are provided in descriptive terms ranging from "very superior" for nonverbal abilities above 130 to "very low" for scores below 70. Developmental scores–age equivalences, are also provided. Normative sampling information provided age-norm confidence intervals at the 68%, 90%, and 99% levels, with a mean 4-point *SEM* across age groups.

TECHNICAL. The standardization sample consisted of 1,010 children, ages 3-0 to 9-11 years. Each selected child was representative of the normative population for the "nation as a whole" (examiner's manual, p. 21). Reference to the selection process used for the translation subgroup was unavailable. The manual did, however, state that the sample for persons with hearing impairments was a clinical sample and may not be representative of the nation's hearing-impaired population as a whole. Demographic characteristics of the sample are reported by age, gender, ethnicity, and geographic regions of the United States.

The entire normative sample was used to determine coefficient alphas that met or exceeded the .90 criterion set for Nonverbal Indexes. The test authors report that commensurate means and standard deviations for both foreign and English language administrations provide evidence that language differences had no effect on the overall results. However, separate alpha coefficient data for foreign language translation results of the PTONI were not reported in the manual.

Information on test-retest reliability is based on a subgroup of 94 students from California and Georgia who were reassessed after a 2-week period. Combined time sampling data revealed a .97 correlation between test administrations providing ample support for time sampling reliability.

Interscorer reliability was examined by having four professionals, two school psychologists, and two speech-pathologists judge four videotapes: a 4-year-old black male with no known disability; an 8-year-old white female previously diagnosed with Down's Syndrome; a 7-year-old Hispanic with no known disability, assessed in Spanish; and a 9-year-old male previously classified as having a specific language disability. Interscorer reliability for this group of judges was .99, supporting the authors' conclusion of little test error in assessment data.

Validity data provided in the PTONI manual include "content-description, criterion-prediction and construct identification" (examiner's manual, p. 33). The test developers state that although varying terms are used to describe validity data, writers of current educational and psychological textbooks generally assert that test developers should show content validity, criterion-prediction validity, and construct validity.

The test authors' operational definition of "content-description" validity consists of five criteria employed for item selection. The first two of these criteria are a "detailed rationale for the selection of item content" (examiner's manual, p. 33), and a correlation of items measuring behaviors typically used to define intelligence. The test developers provide specific guidelines, gleaned from in–depth analyses of various assessment instruments purported to measure nonverbal intelligence, to provide them appropriate item selection strategies: oral instructions followed by a pointing response; "visualization, analogical thinking, perception of spatial relations, sequential recount and categorical formulation" (examiner's manual, p. 34); and abilities "measured in both pictured object and geometric design contexts" (examiner's manual, p. 34). A caveat of the PTONI is that directions are specifically intended to be given in a "language" other than gestures. The test authors, quoting studies by Oller, Kim, and Choe (2001), contend that using pantomime alone to administer complex, nonverbal items to a young population of subjects may not be adequate to ensure true understanding has occurred.

Furthermore, the test authors clearly stipulated the term *nonverbal intelligence* had not been empirically supported as a unique construct in "any influential model of cognition" (examiner's manual, p. 34). The statement seemingly is intended to clarify the test's name indicating that a nonverbal test of intelligence was basically a test that measured certain cognitive abilities nonverbally. Whereas, the term "nonverbal intelligence" was an unsupported hypothetical construct. It is interesting to note, however, that the UNIT (Universal Nonverbal Intelligence Test) demonstrated the strongest correlation with the PTONI (r = .92). And, despite the PTONI's emphasis on being a performance test requiring nonverbal responses, these two assessment tools measure many of the same cognitive constructs related to intelligence.

The third criterion used to identify test selection items was that PTONI results concur with current theories of intelligence. The test developers provide their theoretical framework for the PTONI as most closely aligning with those of the Cattell-Horn-Carroll Model of cognitive abilities (McGrew, 1997) and Das's model (Das, Naglieri, & Kirby, 1994). According to the developers, three broad factors of the CHC theory, *Fluid Reasoning*, *Comprehension-Knowledge*, and *Visual Processing*, are included to a greater or lesser degree in each of the PTONI items. The test authors also refer to Salvia, Ysseldyke, and Bolt's (2007) description of behaviors associated with cognition (examiner's manual, pp. 35, 36) to support the PTONI's content description validity. They conclude that with the exception of those abilities obviously associated with language, the PTONI's content description validity is supported and is able to test for both higher and lower order cognitive abilities.

"Conventional item analysis methods" (examiner's manual, p. 33) were implemented to determine item discrimination coefficients and item difficulty for the PTONI. Using the results of the 1,010 children in the normative sample, the developers state that the final 75 selected items clearly distinguished seven age groups: 3, 4, 5, 6, 7, 8, and 9 years of age.

The final criterion for "content description" analysis used differential item functioning analyses to demonstrate the lack of bias in test items. Using a significance level of .001, the test authors conducted 225 comparisons for three focus groups. Unfortunately, whether these focus groups included children from the foreign language translation groups is unclear.

"Criterion-Predictive Validity" (examiner's manual, p. 40) was accomplished by comparing the PTONI with five other measures: the Comprehensive Test of Nonverbal Intelligence–Second Edition (CTONI-2); the Universal Nonverbal Intelligence Test–Abbreviated (UNIT); the Detroit Tests of Learning Aptitude–Primary: Third Edition (DTLA-P:3); the Bracken Basic Concept Scale–Revised (BBCS-R); and the Learning Disabilities Diagnostic Inventory (LDDI). The magnitude of correlations for these independent samples resulted in large to very large coefficients.

To support the "construct-identification validity" (examiner's manual, p. 41) of the PTONI, the test authors used academic performance and school-related ability. In addition to "mid-year semester report card grade averages in the areas of reading, English, spelling, and mathematics" (examiner's manual, p. 46), the test authors employed the Young Children's Achievement Test (YCAT) and the Academic Skills cluster from the Woodcock-Johnson III Tests of Achievement (WJ-III) for correlation with the PTONI. Based on statistically significant coefficients, the test developers suggest the PTONI is strongly related to scholastic abilities.

COMMENTARY AND SUMMARY. The PTONI appears to be a psychometrically sound measure of nonverbal ability as demonstrated by its high correlations with other measures of nonverbal intelligence. The PTONI is intended to be quick (5–15 minutes), accurate, and cost-efficient for measuring cognitive abilities of children ages 3 through 9, nonverbally. The test authors question the legitimacy of a "nonverbal" intelligence stating no empirical evidence appears in the literature to support this construct. However, because the PTONI and the UNIT had the highest correlations (higher than the PTONI and the CTONI), it appears that regardless of the terminology, both assessments provide the option of measuring upper and lower level cognitive skills in a format that requires no oral response from the child. Further discussions on this point may be needed.

REVIEWER'S REFERENCES

Das, J. P., Naglieri, J. A., & Kirby, J. R. (1994). *Assessment of cognitive processes: The PASS theory of intelligence.* Needham Heights, MA: Allyn & Bacon.

McGrew, K. S. (1997). Analysis of the major intelligence batteries according to a proposed comprehensive Gf-Gc framework. In D. P. Flanagan, J. L. Genshaft, & P. L. Harrison (Eds.), *Contemporary intelligence Assessment: Theories, tests, and issues* (pp. 151–180). New York: Guilford.

Oller, J. W., Kim, K., & Choe, Y. (2001). Can instructions to nonverbal IQ tests be given in pantomime? Additional applications of a general theory of signs. *Semiotica, 133,* 15-44.

Salvia, J., Ysseldyke, J. E., & Bolt, S. (2007). *Assessment: In special and inclusive education* (10th ed.). Boston: Houghton Mifflin.

Review of the Primary Test of Nonverbal Intelligence by KORESSA KUTSICK MALCOLM, School Psychologist, The Virginia School for the Deaf and Blind, Staunton, VA:

DESCRIPTION. The Primary Test of Nonverbal Intelligence (PTONI) is an individually administered test of intellectual ability designed for children ages 3.0 to 9.11 years. Examinees are required to view a set of three to five drawings of objects or geometric patterns on a page and then point to the one item that is not like the others. The test can be administered in 5 to 15 minutes. A single raw score is obtained for the test, which can be converted into percentile ranks, standard scores, and age equivalencies. Standard scores range from 46 to 149. Tables are also provided to convert percentiles and standard scores to *T*-scores, *z*-scores, and stanines. Psychologists and others trained in the measurement of intellectual assessment can administer the PTONI.

In constructing the PTONI, the test authors maintain they focused on developing a test that would limit cultural, language, and motoric factors that could adversely influence a child's performance on a test of intellectual functioning. To this end, they decided upon procedures that minimized verbalizations to convey directions for the test. They also selected a pointing response mode that could be accomplished by touch, light beam, head pointers, and so forth. The verbal directions presented to the child are simple, straightforward, and common to children's educational games and television activities. Directions can be given in eight languages in addition to English. These eight languages include Spanish, French, Traditional Chinese (Mandarin), Simplified Chinese, German, Tagalog, Vietnamese, Italian, and Japanese. Directions also may be presented in American Sign Language, Manually Coded English, Aural/Oral English, and Sign-Supported Speech/English. Sample items are available in the initial presentation of the test and instructions are provided to correct any errors on these samples so that the child is given a good opportunity to understand the task at hand.

DEVELOPMENT. The development of the PTONI was undertaken by the test authors in order to provide an unbiased assessment of intellectual functioning, especially for young children and those children who face developmental challenges such as autism, language delays, and motor difficulties. They traced the history of assessment of intelligence through nonverbal means. They noted this history as a basis for the PTONI. The test authors, however, do not provide a clear rationale for the development of this test in light of other similar tests they reviewed. The authors mentioned reference to earlier nonverbal measures of abilities, such as the Columbia Mental Maturity

Scale (Burgemeister, Blum, & Lorge, 1972) as a basis for their test items. They did not, however, provide a description of how specific items were written or selected for the PTONI.

TECHNICAL. The PTONI was normed on a sample of 1,010 children who were selected from sites identified in 38 states across the United States. These children attended educational programs in school systems that reportedly matched demographic characteristics of the region in which they lived. It did not appear that participants in the norming of the PTONI were randomly selected. The test authors provided information regarding the degree to which the sample matched the major demographic variables on the 2007 U.S. Census. Normative information is provided at 3-month increments for ages 3.0 to 4.0 and then by 2-month increments to age 9.11.

Reliability information provided in the manual includes the test authors' reports of high alpha coefficients (.90 to .95) and small standard errors of measurement values (3 to 5 points) across age levels of the normative sample at each age year from 3 to 9. Test-retest reliability was noted in three studies. In each, 30 to 33 children were given two administrations of the PTONI with a 2-week interval between evaluation sessions. Resulting correlation coefficients ranged from .96 to .97. Scorer reliability was reported as being very consistent (r = .99 to 1.0), based on a very small sample (n = 4) of professionals scoring four videotaped administrations of the test.

Validity for the PTONI was presented in the manual in terms of construct and criterion-related predicted validity. The test authors provided detailed reviews of statistical information related to these concepts, but little actual information from studies they conducted on their own test. The studies they did conduct examined the correlations between the PTONI and other similar tests. In general, strong positive correlations were obtained in these studies. When the PTONI score was compared to the Nonverbal Intelligence Quotient of the Comprehensive Test of Non-Verbal Intelligence–2 (Hammill, Pearson, & Wiederholt (in preparation) the resulting correlation coefficient was .88. When compared to the Universal Nonverbal Intelligence Test (Bracken & McCallum, 1998) the coefficient was .92. And when compared to the total score of the Bracken Basic Concept Scale–Revised (Bracken, 1998) the resulting coefficient was 85. Correlations between the PTONI and individual subtest scores for all of these tests also yielded strong positive correlations. Moderate to strong positive correlations were obtained when the PTONI total score was correlated with the total and subtest scores of the Woodcock-Johnson III: Tests of Achievement (Woodcock, McGrew, & Mather, 2001) and with reported academic grades available for the older children in the samples.

COMMENTARY. The PTONI is a simple to administer test of nonverbal intelligence for children 3.0 to 9.11 years of age. The test authors provided a comprehensive review of literature related to the rationale for the basis of a nonverbal test of intelligence, but did not indicate why their test would be any better than others similar to it that are on the market. Some positive features of the PTONI include the short time for administration, which would lend itself well to use in screening programs. The lower age limit of the test (age 3) would also be of value to professionals who are working with preschool-aged children. The range of standard scores includes values above and below two standard deviations from the mean of the test that would be useful for examiners working with children who show advanced or significantly delayed development to aid in placement and programming decisions. The inclusion of directions in other languages such as Spanish and American Sign Language is a positive feature of the test, which would lend itself well to the evaluation of children from diverse cultural populations. Likewise, the provision that the PTONI can be administered through the use of American Sign Language and other manually supported communication systems is a positive feature of the test. It would have been valuable, however, if the test authors had taken steps to examine any performance differences that might result from these alternative administrations prior to the publication of the PTONI. Future studies in this area would be important. Likewise, additional information regarding the reliability and validity of the PTONI, especially in terms of its use with low-incident populations, would be in order before the test can be used with confidence for these populations.

SUMMARY. The PTONI is an easily administered and scored test of nonverbal intelligence that would be appropriate for use with young children, especially those who face challenges in their social, language, or motoric functioning. The test would be of most value for screening programs that require a measure of intellectual assessment. It also would hold value as a secondary measure of intellectual functioning when assessing high needs populations, especially for preschool and primary aged children. Additional information regarding the reliability and validity of this test would be of value, particularly in terms of use of this test with children of low-incident disability conditions. Studies examining the validity and reliability of the PTONI when alternative languages are used to administer the test (e.g., given in Spanish or ASL) would be of value. Examiners looking for tests of nonverbal intelligence might also consider reviews of the Comprehensive Test of Nonverbal Intelligence (Hammill, Pearson, & Wiederholt, 1997; a revision is in development), the Test of Nonverbal Intelligence (Brown, Sherbenou, & Johnsen, 1997), and the Universal Nonverbal Intelligence Test (Bracken & McCallum, 1998).

REVIEWER'S REFERENCES

Bracken, B. A. (1998). The Bracken Basic Concept Scale–Revised. San Antonio, TX: Psychological Corporation.

Bracken, B. A., & McCallum, R. S. (1998). Universal Nonverbal Intelligence Test. Itasca, IL: Riverside.

Brown, L., Sherbenou, R. J., & Johnsen, S. K. (1997). Test of Nonverbal Intelligence (3rd ed.). Austin, TX: PRO-ED.

Burgemeister, B. B., Blum, L. H., & Lorge, I. (1972). Columbia Mental Maturity Scale. San Antonio: Harcourt Assessment.

Hammill, D. D., Pearson, N. A., & Wiederholt, J. L. (1997). Comprehensive Test of Nonverbal Intelligence. Austin, TX: PRO-ED.

Hammill, D. D., Pearson, N. A., & Wiederholt, J. L. (in preparation). Comprehensive Test of Nonverbal Intelligence (2nd ed.) Austin, TX: PRO-ED.

Woodcock, R. W., McGrew, K., & Mather, N. (2001). Woodcock-Johnson III. Itasca, IL: Riverside.

[97]

Process Assessment of the Learner–Second Edition: Diagnostic Assessment for Math.

Purpose: "Designed for measuring the development of math processes in children."

Population: Grades K-6.

Publication Date: 2007.

Acronym: PAL-II M.

Scores: 48 scores across 17 subtests: Numeral Writing (Automatic Legible Numeral Writing at 15 Seconds [NWAL], Legible Numeral Writing [NWL], Total Time [NWTT], Reversals [NWR], Omissions [NOW], Transpositions [NWTR]), Oral Counting (Oral Counting [OC]), Numeric Coding (Numeric Coding [NC]), Fact Retrieval: Look and Write (Addition [FRLW-A], Subtraction [FRLW-S], Mixed Addition and Subtraction [FRLW-AS], Multiplication [FRLW-M], Division [FRLW-D], Mixed Multiplication and Division [FRLW-MD]), Fact Retrieval: Listen and Say (Addition [FRLS-A], Subtraction [FRLS-S], Mixed Addition and Subtraction [FRLS-AS], Multiplication [FRLS-M], Division [FRLS-D], Mixed Multiplication and Division [FRLS-MD]), Computation Operations (Task A-Spatial Alignment [CO-SA], Task B-Verbal Explanation [CO-VE], Task C-Problem Solution [CO-PS], Computation Operations Composite [COC]), Place Value (Oral [PVO], Written [PVW], Problem Response Written [PVPW], Place Value Composite [PVC]), Part-Whole Relationships (Part-Whole Concepts [PWC], Part-Whole Fractions and Mixed Numbers [PWF], Part-Whole Time [PWT], Part-Whole Relationships Composite [PWRC]), Finding the Bug (Finding the Bug [FB]), Multi-Step Problem Solving (Multi-Step Problem Solving [MSPS]), Quantitative Working Memory (Quantitative Working Memory [QWM]), Spatial Working Memory (Oral [SWMO], Drawing [SWMD]), RAN: Digits (Single Digits Total Time [RAN-DTT], Single Digits Rate Change [RAN-DRC]), RAN: Double Digits (Double Digits Total Time [RAN-DDTT], Double Digits Rate Change [RAN-DDRC]), RAN: Digits and Double Digits Total Scores (Digits + Double Digits Rate Change [RAN-D-DDRC], Digits + Double Digits Total Errors [RAN-D-DDTE], Digits + Double Digits Total Time Composite [RAN-D-DDC]), RAS: Words and Digits (Words and Digits Total Time [RAS-WDTT], Words and Digits Rate Change [RAS-WDRC], Words and Digits Total Errors [RAS-WDTE]), Fingertip Writing (Fingertip Writing [FW]).

Administration: Individual.

Levels, 5: Kindergarten, Grade 1, Grade 2, Grade 3, Grades 4-6.

Price Data, 2009: $338 per Math Kit including 10 Response Booklets, 10 Record Forms, Stimulus Book, Stimulus Booklet, Administration and Scoring Manual (141 pages), and Comprehensive User's Guide CD; $74 per 25 Response Booklets; $54 per 25 Record Forms; $109.20 per Stimulus Book; $78 per Stimulus Booklet; $104 per Comprehensive User's Guide CD.

Time: (60-120) minutes to administer all subtests; time limit varies across individual subtests.

Comments: The PAL-II M has three applications: (a) "Tier 1: universal screening for early intervention and prevention," (b) "Tier 2: problem-solving consultation and progress monitoring," (c) "Tier 3: differential diagnosis and treatment planning;" number and type of subtests administered depends on grade level and application.

Author: Virginia Wise Berninger.

Publisher: Pearson.

Review of the Process Assessment of the Learner–Second Edition: Diagnostic Assessment for Math by LAURA HAMILTON, Senior Behavioral Scientist, RAND Corporation, Pittsburgh, PA:

[Disclaimer: The opinions expressed in this review are those of the review author and should not be attributed to the RAND Corporation.]

DESCRIPTION. The Process Assessment of the Learner–Second Edition: Diagnostic Assessment for Math (PAL-II M) is an individually administered assessment of mathematics skills and processes for students in kindergarten through sixth grade (ages 5 through 13 years). It also can be used for older students who are performing at the sixth grade level or lower. It is designed to be administered by skilled personnel such as school psychologists. The user's guide describes several purposes: screening to identify students who may be at risk for low achievement, progress monitoring for struggling students, and diagnosis regarding processing problems. The PAL-II M includes 14 subtests, some of which focus on concepts and skills whereas others measure cognitive or neurodevelopmental processes that research suggests are related to a student's ability to learn math. Not all subtests are given at every grade level. Administrators may also choose to use only one or a few subtests that are relevant to specific concerns about a child's math learning. Administration of the full test generally requires between 60 and 120 minutes.

For most subtests, scoring can be completed after test administration has ended, though a few require scoring to be done during administration. Item responses are scored either dichotomously or using a partial-credit model in which the maximum score is 2 or 3. Scoring is mostly objective but three subtests involve subjective scoring. A few subtests require the administrator to record the time it took for the student to complete each item, and some have discontinue rules that indicate when to stop testing based on the number of consecutive incorrect item responses. The administration and scoring manual provides clear and detailed instructions for recording and scoring students' responses and for calculating raw and derived scores. The manual also provides guidance regarding what subsets should be administered to address specific concerns about students' math learning, as well as recommended interventions for students identified as having various skill deficits.

DEVELOPMENT. According to the test author, the development of the PAL-II M was motivated by a perception that existing intelligence and achievement tests fail to provide information on why a student may fail to demonstrate a skill or what can be done to address students' specific instructional needs. The assessment draws on research on math processes and their relationships with achievement, as well as on the test author's teaching and clinical experiences. Its development was guided by a conceptual framework that includes low- and high-level procedural skills and concepts. The PAL-II M was subjected to several stages of testing during its development, including a tryout phase that involved 400 students distributed across Grades K through 6.

TECHNICAL. The standardization was conducted using 225 examiners from across the U.S. who were selected based on experience and access to students in the relevant grade levels. The standardization sample included 700 students, with 100 drawn from each relevant grade level. A stratified random sampling procedure was used, with stratification variables including race/ethnicity, sex, age, region, and parent/guardian education level. Students with certain types of diagnoses, including learning disabilities or language disorders, were excluded. The user's guide presents tables that demonstrate that this sample closely resembles the U.S. Census figures. The administration and scoring manual provides several tables of norms by grade level, including scale score equivalents of raw scores for each subtest.

The test author acknowledges the difficulties inherent in estimating score reliability for tests that have floor or ceiling effects, which is the case for some subtests at some grade levels. In addition, the application of specific approaches to estimating reliability, such as the calculation of internal consistency estimates, is more appropriate for some subsets than for others. The test author has provided extensive information about reliability estimation for each subtest and uses appropriate approaches given the content and scoring systems used in each subtest. For subtests for which internal consistency was deemed appropriate, split-half and alpha coefficients were calculated. For other measures, test-retest stability was estimated using data from a sample of 129 students who participated in two testing sessions ranging from 2 to 34 days apart. Stability coefficients are correlations between scores obtained from the two sessions and were calculated separately for two groups: Kindergarten through Grade 3 and Grades 4 through 6. The user's guide also includes standard errors of measurement and guidelines for creating confidence intervals, which can be helpful for communicating the degree of uncertainty associated with each score.

Internal consistency coefficients of at least .80 were obtained for a majority of subtest and composite scores, though coefficients for a few subtests were slightly lower. Ceiling effects appear to be responsible for low internal consistency estimates for some subtests at some grade levels. Most of the stability coefficients are higher than

.70, again with some exceptions. Average scores were higher in the second testing session than in the first session for most subtests, which suggests some practice effects, but the differences tended to be small.

Measures of rater agreement were calculated for each subtest and were found to be high for subtests that involved objective rules with minimal interpretation but were lower in cases that required subjective judgment. It is important to point out that the training that the scorers in the standardization process received may have led to higher levels of agreement than would be obtained in operational testing situations.

The user's guide presents several sources of validity evidence. It mentions the relevance of consequences to evaluating the validity of test scores, but does not provide any evidence related to consequences of using the PAL-II M.

The discussion of content evidence starts with a discussion of the fact that the content of the PAL-II M is drawn from extensive research linking math processes with student achievement, but it does not provide explicit information about the quality and content of the studies on which the assessment is based. Similarly, it states that evidence of children's response processes was gathered to provide additional information about content evidence, but it does not include details about the collection of these data (numbers and ages of students, methods for coding transcripts, etc.).

Evidence of construct validity consists of intercorrelations among subtest scores for each grade. In general, correlations within domains are higher than correlations across domains. There are several examples of near-zero correlations that appear to be consistent with the expectations of the test author and the nature of the skills measured. For example, Oral Counting and Numeral Writing show no relationships with other subtests in the upper grades, which is not surprising given the fact that most students in the upper grades have obtained a reasonably high level of proficiency on these subtests. Most of the correlations are moderate, suggesting that the various subtests tend to capture different skills, though the correlations are also affected by score reliability, which is lower at the subtest level than for composites or the test as a whole. Concurrent evidence was provided based on correlations between PAL-II M scores and scores on two measures of general cognitive ability: the Differential Ability Scales–Second Edition (DAS–II) and The Wechsler Nonverbal Scale of Ability (WNV). The magnitudes of the correlations varied by subtest and in some cases were fairly low, but because the PAL-II M was designed to measure something other than general ability, these low correlations should not necessarily be viewed as evidence of lack of validity. The test author also presents correlations with the NEPSY-II, a measure of neuropsychological functioning. These correlations varied substantially but tended to be low and in many cases near zero.

COMMENTARY. The PAL-II M appears to a well-researched measure that can provide educators with information that cannot be easily obtained through other sources. The administration and scoring procedures used in the PAL-II M are designed to uncover the processes in which students engage as they attempt each item rather than focusing exclusively on the end result. For example, students use pencils without erasers so that if they make a mistake that they want to correct, they must cross it out rather than erasing it, thereby providing a written record of errors and corrections that can be scored. The user's guide provides clear, detailed information on all aspects of administration and interpretation and offers guidance for working with teachers and others to address students' needs. It also provides various record-keeping forms that can be useful for documenting performance and communicating with teachers, parents, and others who are involved in a child's educational planning, as well as interview guides, questionnaires, and structured observation forms that can be used to collect supplemental information about student performance.

Although extensive information about score reliability and validity is presented, some additional analyses would be helpful. For example, the standardization sample excluded students with certain special needs but schools may benefit from evidence regarding the appropriateness of the test for these students. It also would be useful to have more information on how score reliability and validity might be affected by the level of training and experience of the administrator. Moreover, given the length of the test and the often limited amount of time available for testing, users would benefit from analyses to explore whether administering a portion of the assessment would produce useful information about students' skills and areas of need. Additional guidance on how the PAL-II M scores should be combined with other information to design appropriate interventions would be useful. Finally, evidence of the extent to which appropriate use of PAL-II M leads to better decision making would be extremely useful for evaluating the validity of test scores and utility of the measure.

SUMMARY. The PAL-II M provides potentially useful information to help educators and clinicians understand the sources of students' difficulties in learning math and could be a valuable tool when used in combination with other information to design interventions. The administration and scoring guidelines are clearly written and relatively straightforward, and the technical information presented in the user's guide suggests that use of the test with students in Kindergarten through Grade 6 is probably justified, though other information should be incorporated into instructional decision making. Prospective users would benefit from additional validity evidence, particularly regarding the consequences of PAL-II M use for students' educational experiences and future achievement.

Review of the Process Assessment of the Learner–Second Edition: Diagnostic Assessment for Math by KATHERINE RYAN, Associate Professor, and MICHAEL J. CULBERTSON, Illinois Distinguished Fellow, Department of Educational Psychology, University of Illinois–Urbana-Champaign, Urbana, IL:

DESCRIPTION. Broad measures of achievement and aptitude yield little insight about the particular hindrances students encounter when learning mathematics, because mathematics integrates a host of component skills, which single-dimensional tests typically confound. When students show difficulty in mastering math content, educators need detail-rich tools to identify the particular deficiencies in math-related skills that hinder student progress, in order to provide efficient, effective, targeted interventions to put students on the track toward math achievement. Virginia Wise Berninger created the Process Assessment of the Learner (PAL) to provide the kind of detailed measurement of low-level mathematical processes teachers need to diagnose problems in students' math learning. The second edition (PAL-II) consists of refinements to the original PAL, based on developments in the test author's broader clinical research program on learning difficulties.

The PAL-II Math battery consists of 14 subtests covering math-related processes shown to be the best predictors of math achievement, including measures of number sense, numeral coding/decoding, basic computation, multi-step problem solving, and self-monitoring. Administering the whole battery is estimated to take one to 2 hours, but the PAL-II provides educators with the flexibility of administering only those subtests that are relevant to a student's particular needs. Moreover, the PAL-II is embedded in a three-tiered approach to math assessment: screening, monitoring, and diagnosis. Consequently, the single assessment system can support educators at all stages of an intervention program. The administration and scoring manual and accompanying user's guide provide suggestions for how the PAL-II can be used in each tier to diagnose a number of typical presenting symptoms for common math learning difficulties, along with suggested intervention strategies.

DEVELOPMENT. The research behind the PAL-II began with the goal of empirically identifying variables that explained underachievement in reading, writing, and math and that could be linked to evidence-based interventions that target the learning deficiencies. The original PAL was published in 2001 as a collection of the measures Berninger had developed during her research program. The refinement of these measures leading to the publication of the PAL-II proceeded in three phases: a small pilot study (2000), a trial period (2004–2005), and national standardization and validation (2006). Modifications to item content, administration directions, and scoring rules were made between each phase in response to student responses and examiner feedback.

TECHNICAL. The PAL-II was standardized on a nationally representative sample of 700 normally developing English-proficient students based on an October 2003 U.S. Census Bureau survey. The sample was stratified by grade (K–6), sex, race/ethnicity (White, African American, Hispanic, and other), Census Bureau geographic region, and parent/guardian education (0–11 years, high school graduate or equivalent, some post-secondary), with 100 students (50 boys and 50 girls) in each grade. The marginal distributions of the standardization sample along each stratification variable closely match the population distributions from the Census Bureau survey. The technical description in the user's guide indicates that students were randomly selected, but does not provide recruitment details or participation rates.

Most subtests exhibited strong internal consistency as measured by split-half and alpha methods

(r > .85), as well as fairly strong test-retest reliability (r = .70–.90). All standardization cases were double-scored by independent raters. Most subtests involve highly objective scoring, with correspondingly very high interrater agreement (r = .95–.99). Interrater agreement for subtests with more-subjective scoring, which involved assessment of legibility and drawings, was also high (r = .88–.98).

With respect to validity, the PAL-II benefits from the substantial body of research on the underlying cognitive processes related to math achievement that were translated into psychometric measures. Mathematics is a highly integrated and cumulative subject–even seemingly simple math tasks can require the application of a number of different processes or competencies. The lack of mastery of any of these component processes can result in a barrier to learning of more-integrated tasks and concepts. The PAL-II user's guide includes an overview of the research that links the processes the PAL-II measures with math achievement, along with references to studies that establish these links. Because the PAL-II is intended to measure a set of diverse math-related processes instead of broadband math achievement, subtests should ideally have low to moderate correlations (most were < .5). Moreover, PAL-II subtests exhibited low to moderate correlations with other measures of math and cognitive ability (most r < .4, many r < .3), suggesting that the PAL-II provides additional diagnostic ability beyond these existing measures.

COMMENTARY. The PAL-II standardization is limited by its rather small sample size, particularly relative to the total sampling frame with over 600 cells. Each of the seven sets of grade-level norms was derived from only 100 students, and sampling did not take into account community size or type. Testing accommodations may be necessary for students with physical impairments. The test author notes that although the norms are not valid under these modifications, the PAL-II may still provide useful qualitative information about the strengths and weaknesses of physically impaired students. Furthermore, several of the PAL-II subtests are highly language-laden in their instructions or content, which could pose particular difficulties for students with limited English proficiency or for struggling readers.

The PAL-II administration materials benefit from very clear visual presentation and detailed instructions. Key information, such as start points, discontinue rules, and timing, is repeated in both the administration manual and the record booklet for quick reference. Overall, the subtests are very easy to score, and the administration manual provides full scoring examples for each subtest. Within each subtest, items are arranged in order of increasing difficulty with rules for discontinuing administration after a set number of errors so that students are not required to attempt too many items that are beyond their ability.

SUMMARY. The great strength of the PAL-II lies not in national standardization but in the rich diagnostic information provided by its many subtests of basic math-related processes. In the end, educators care less about how a student compares with national norms than about what specifically hinders a student's progress in learning and how to target interventions to overcome students' individual difficulties. The significant contribution of the PAL-II to the psychometric and educational communities is its many subtests that disentangle the highly integrated basic processes of mathematics in order to determine specific causes of students' learning difficulties, which can be particularly useful in the middle grades, when students may not have achieved fluency in basic skills, but mathematics instruction has progessed beyond basic to higher level skills. The PAL-II has been designed from the beginning to assist educators in identifying the right interventions for struggling students, and has great potential for helping all students succeed.

[98]

Process Assessment of the Learner–Second Edition: Diagnostic Assessment for Reading and Writing.

Purpose: "Designed for measuring reading and writing skills and related processes in children."

Population: Grades K-6.

Publication Dates: 1998-2007.

Acronym: PAL-II RW.

Scores, 83: Alphabet Writing Automatic Legible Letter Writing (AWAL), Alphabet Writing Legible Letter Writing (AWL), Alphabet Writing Total Time (AWTT), Copying Task A Automatic Legible Letter Writing (CPAAL), Copying Task A Legible Letter Writing (CPAL), Copying Task A Total Time (CPATT), Copying Task B Legibility (0-30 seconds) (CPBL-30), Copying Task B Legibility (0-60 seconds) (CPBL-60), Copying Task B Legibility (0-90 seconds) (CPBL-90), Copying Task B Copy Accuracy (CP-BCA), Handwriting Total Automatic Letter Legibility Composite (HWGTALC), Handwriting Total Legibility Composite (HWGTLC), Handwriting Total Time

Composite (HWGTTC), Handwriting Total Reversals (HWGTRC), Handwriting Total Inversions (HWGTI), Handwriting Total Omissions (HWGTO), Handwriting Total Repetitions (HWGTRP), Handwriting Total Transpositions (HWGTTR), Handwriting Total Case Confusions (HWGTCC), Handwriting Total Format Confusions (HWGTFC), Receptive Coding (RC), Expressive Coding (EC), Orthographic Coding Composite (ORC), Rhyming (RY), Syllables (SY), Phonemes (PN), Rimes (RI), Phonological Coding Composite (PLC), Are They Related? (RR), Does It Fit? (DF), Sentence Structure (ST), Morphological/Syntactic Coding Composite (MSCC), Pseudoword Decoding Fluency at 60 seconds (PDF-60), Pseudoword Decoding Accuracy (PDA), Find the True Fixes (FF), Morphological Decoding Fluency Accuracy (MDFA), Morphological Decoding Fluency (MDF), Morphological Decoding Composite (MDC), Word Choice Accuracy (WCA), Word Choice Fluency (WCF), Sentence Sense Accuracy (SSA), Sentence Sense Fluency (SSF), Compositional Fluency Total Number of Words (CFTW), Compositional Fluency Total Correctly Spelled Words (CFCSW), Compositional Fluency Total Complete Sentences (CFCST), Expository Note Taking Accuracy (NTA), Expository Note Taking Fact Errors (NTFE), Expository Report Writing Quality (RWQ), Expository Report Writing Organizational Quality of Report Writing (RWO), Expository Report Writing Irrelevant Thoughts Added (RWITA), Cross-Genre Compositional and Expository Writing Total Number of Words (CGWTW), Cross-Genre Compositional and Expository Writing Total Correctly Spelled Words (CG-WCSW), Cross-Genre Compositional and Expository Writing Total Complete Sentences (CGWCS), Letters (WML), Words (WMW), Letters and Words Composite (WML-WC), Sentences: Listening (WMSL), Sentences: Writing (WMSW), Sentences: Listening and Sentences: Writing Composite (WMSL-SWC), Verbal Working Memory Composite (WMVC), RAN-Letters Rate Change Raw Score (RAN-LRC), RAN-Letters Total Time (RAN-LTT), RAN-Letter Groups Rate Change Raw Score (RAN-LGRC), RAN-Letter Groups Total Time (RAN-LGTT), RAN-Words Rate Change Raw Score (RAN-WRC), RAN-Words Total Time (RAN-WTT), RAN-Letters -Letter Groups and -Words Total Rate Change Score (RAN-L-LG-WRC), RAN-Letters -Letter Groups and -Words Total Errors (RAN-L-LG-WTE), RAN-Letters -Letter Groups and -Words Total Time Composite (RAN-L-LG-WC), RAS-Words and Digits Total Time (RAS-WDTT), RAS-Words and Digits Rate Change Raw Score (RAS-WDRC), RAS-Words and Digits Total Errors (RAS-WDTE), Oral Motor Planning Total Time (OMT), Oral Motor Planning Total Errors (OME), Finger Repetition-Dominant Hand Total Time (FSRP-DTT), Finger Repetition-Non-Dominant Hand Total Time (FSRP-NTT), Finger Succession-Dominant Hand Total Time (FSS-DTT), Finger Succession-Non-Dominant Hand Total Time (FSS-NTT), Finger Succession Total Errors (FSSTE), Finger Sense Frequent Motoric Overflow (FSFMO), Finger Sense Occasional Motoric Overflow (FSOMO), Finger Localization (FSL), Finger Recognition (FSRC).

Administration: Individual.

Levels, 5: Kindergarten, Grade 1, Grade 2, Grade 3, Grades 4-6.

Price Data, 2009: $468 per complete kit including 10 Response Booklets, 10 Record Forms, Stimulus Book, Stimulus Booklets (A and B), administration and scoring manual for Reading and Writing (2007, 225 pages), and Comprehensive User's Guide CD; $74 per 25 Response Booklets; $79 per 25 Record Forms; $109.20 per Stimulus Book; $78 per Stimulus Booklet–A; $78 per Stimulus Booklet–B; $104 per Comprehensive User's Guide CD.

Time: (60-120) minutes to administer all subtests; time limit varies across individual subtests.

Comments: The PAL-II RW has three applications: (a) "Tier 1: universal screening for early intervention and prevention," (b) "Tier 2: problem-solving consultation and progress monitoring," (c) "Tier 3: differential diagnosis and treatment planning"; number of subtests administered depends on grade level and application; "designed to complement the Wechsler Intelligence Scale for Children-Fourth Edition (WISC-IV) and the Wechsler Individual Achievement Test-Second Edition (WIAT-II Update)"; previous edition entitled Process Assessment of the Learner: Test Battery of Reading and Writing.

Author: Virginia Wise Berninger.

Publisher: Pearson.

Cross References: For a review by Karen E. Jennings of an earlier edition, see 16:199.

Review of the Process Assessment of the Learner–Second Edition: Diagnostic Assessment for Reading and Writing by S. KATHLEEN KRACH, Associate Professor, Troy University, Montgomery, AL:

DESCRIPTION. The test author describes the purposes of the Process Assessment of the Learner–Second Edition: Diagnostic Assessment for Reading and Writing (PAL-II RW) as an instrument "for measuring (a) reading and writing skills and related processes in children in Kindergarten (K) through Grade 6, and (b) linking assessment results with instructional interventions" (administration and scoring manual, p. 1). She goes on to describe how the PAL-II RW can be used in a multitiered approach; for example at Tier 1 it could be used as a screener, at Tier II it could be used for progress monitoring, and at Tier 3 the PAL-II RW could be used for diagnostic purposes.

The test is designed to accompany the Wechsler Intelligence Scale for Children–Fourth Edition (WISC-IV; Wechsler, 2003) and the Wechsler Individual Achievement Test–Second Edition (WIAT-II; Wechsler, 2005). The test author states that although the WISC-IV provides predictive data (what will happen) and the WIAT-II provides data on learning outcomes (what is happening), neither provide the rationale for a child's performance (why it is happening). The PAL-II is designed to provide those additional data.

Contained in the test kit are the stimulus materials, blank record forms, and the administration and scoring manual, as well as a CD-ROM entitled "User's Guide." The CD provides specific information about how to interpret the scores for each of the three tiers. In addition, it provides information about the test development and psychometrics of the instrument. Finally, the CD provides extensive lists of resources and references in the area of written language. These resources include handouts, example forms, bibliographic references, case studies, instructional models, and other helpful materials.

DEVELOPMENT. The PAL and the PAL-II RW subtests were derived from research on children's language learning spanning three decades. Each subtest is linked back to specific data collection models. Although many of the subtests from the PAL-II RW are the same as those from the PAL, the test author reiterated appropriate item analysis. Specifically, the PAL-II RW was developed across three phases. The first phase was a pilot, the second a "tryout," and the third was a national standardization and validation. Data from the third phase were collected in 2006.

TECHNICAL. The normative sample for the PAL-II RW included 700 students, 100 students from each grade (K–6). These 700 students were derived as part of a stratified sampling procedure used to collect data across variables similar to those found in the U.S. Census data. These variables included grade, gender, parental education, geographic location, and race/ethnicity.

Reliability studies were performed using measures of internal consistency. Although in general the subtest and composite scores demonstrated acceptable internal consistency, some individual subtests at certain ages may need to be reconsidered before interpretation (Krach & McCreery, 2010). For example, the AWAL reliability coefficient for Kindergarten, first, second, and third grade is .58. Test-retest statistics range from .07 to .89; overall, these statistics are lower (and more variable) than would be expected of a test this size. This is a similar problem to the original PAL as described in the Jennings (2005) review.

The test developers address content, construct, and concurrent validity in the user's manual. Much of the content validity is addressed through the previous studies that began prior to the creation of the original PAL. It was from these studies that the current items were generated; therefore, the test author argues that the content validity of the items is already established. Intercorrelational data found within the PAL-II RW indicate that intradomain correlations are high and interdomain are more moderate. This is expected for tests with high construct validity.

In addition, content and concurrent validity were evaluated based on comparisons to cognitive and neuropsychological tests. The test author adds that a moderate correlation between the PAL-II RW and these measures would indicate that the instruments are related while each still measures something unique. Correlations between the WNV and the PAL-II RW as well as the NEPSY-II and PAL-II RW fell in the test author's expected range in all areas. Correlations between the DAS-II and the PAL-II RW were modest across most areas.

COMMENTARY. The PAL-II RW is an update of the PAL (Berninger, 2001). In Karen Jennings' (2005) review of the original PAL, she described the instrument as a good test to use for the coordination of assessment data and intervention planning. These same comments hold true for the current version of the test. The need for an instrument such as the PAL-II RW has grown considerably since it was originally published. This is in part due to a need for instruments that may be used in intervention planning as well as multitiered data collection. Therefore, a test such as the PAL-II RW is not only a good test to have, but may be an essential one for many educator's toolkits.

For example, a multitiered model that would benefit from the data provided by the PAL-II RW might be the Response to Intervention (RTI) diagnostic model (Bradley, Danielson, & Doolittle, 2005) that is currently used in the schools due to changes in federal law. Specifically, IDEA (2004) describes a learning disability as "a disorder in one or more of the basic psychological processes involved in understanding or in using language" and that one method that can be used for assessing a specific learning disability is by evaluating a child's response to a scientific, research-based intervention. Therefore, many assessment specialists are looking for an instrument that can measure the processing components that comprise the skills needed to understand written language.

Given this need, designing the PAL-II RW as a multitiered test of processing skills to be used with the more traditional diagnostic tools such as the Wechsler Intelligence Scale for Children–Fourth Edition (WISC-IV; Wechsler, 2003) and the Wechsler Individual Achievement Test–Second Edition (WIAT-II; Wechsler, 2005) was a smart move on the part of the test author and the publisher. To accomplish this collaboration between the different instruments, the test author provides an extensive CD-ROM with valuable tools. These tools provide valuable suggestions, research, and practical application materials that would be helpful to most educators. The information on the CD is well planned and extensive.

Unfortunately, the information on the CD is also difficult to access. The CD must be installed on a machine (PC-only); therefore, if that machine is not with the user, neither are the additional materials. With the proliferation of information on the internet, a much better way of providing the materials (most of which are just documents) could be through a Website that can be accessible from almost anywhere without taking up room on the user's hard drive (and requiring Macintosh users to have a second machine). In addition, the file structure within the CD was somewhat congested and confusing. The current organization of the information on the CD made it difficult to access some of the better parts. In addition, it forced the user to read the same materials over and over again in order to gain a complete understanding of the instrument.

Apart from the CD, the main concern for the reviewer is the claim by the test author that the PAL-II RW can be used for "progress monitoring" (administration and scoring manual, p.1). Given that the majority of the subtests have only one version, there is the strong possibility that test-retest effects could influence score changes instead of actual change in the test taker's skills. In addition, the CD materials for Tier II intervention monitoring strongly encourage the user to seek additional tests to track changes in the child's abilities over time. Therefore, it does not seem as if the PAL-II RW could be seen as a stand-alone Tier II progress-monitoring tool no matter what the publisher's claims may be.

One final note, in her review of the original PAL, Jennings' (2005) main concern focused on the psychometric properties (e.g., sampling, interrater reliability, and validity) in the development of the instrument. The test's author (Berninger, 2007) states that the psychometric properties of the current version are an improvement on the previous version. Based on a review of the psychometric data provided in the PAL-II RW user's guide, this statement appears to be true.

SUMMARY. The PAL-II RW can be a tool for educators who need additional processing data in the areas of reading and writing that other tests cannot provide. It examines aspects of written language that most other tests do not. And, using these data, an educator can make clear decisions to plan future interventions for the child in question. In general, the PAL-II RW appears to be a solid test and an improvement on the original PAL. The main concern for the test is to remind any educational specialist using it to focus on its diagnostic and intervention planning strengths instead of trying to use the PAL-II RW as a progress-monitoring tool.

REVIEWER'S REFERENCES

Berninger, V. W. (2007). Process Assessment of the Learner: Diagnostic Assessment for Reading and Writing (PAL-II). San Antonio, TX: Psychological Corporation.

Bradley, R., Danielson, L., & Doolittle, J. (2005). Response to intervention. *Journal of Learning Disabilities, 38*, 485-486.

Individuals with Disabilities Education Improvement Act of 2004 (IDEA), Pub. L. No. 108–446, 118 Stat. 2647 (2004). [Amending 20 U.S.C. §§ 1400 et seq.].

Jennings, K. (2005). [Review of the Process Assessment of the Learner: Test Battery for Reading and Writing (PAL).] In R. A. Spies & B. S. Plake (Eds.), *The sixteenth mental measurements yearbook* (pp. 834–837). Lincoln, NE: Buros Institute of Mental Measurements.

Krach, S. K., & McCreery, M. (2010). Use of reliability data in score interpretation: or, why to use the technical data when making diagnostic decisions. *The School Psychologist, 64*, 8-12.

Wechsler, D. (2005). Wechsler Individual Achievement Test–Second Edition. San Antonio, TX: The Psychological Corporation.

Wechsler, D. (2003). Wechsler Intelligence Scale for Children–Fourth Edition. San Antonio, TX: The Psychological Corporation.

Review of the Process Assessment of the Learner–Second Edition: Diagnostic Assessment for Reading and Writing by JENNIFER N. MAHDAVI, Associate Professor of Special Education, Sonoma State University, Rohnert Park, CA:

DESCRIPTION. The Process Assessment of the Learner–Second Edition: Diagnostic Assessment for Reading and Writing (PAL-II RW) is a standardized, norm-referenced measure designed to identify cognitive and neurodevelopmental processes related to the acquisition of reading and writing skills of children in kindergarten through Grade 6. The test battery is extensive, consisting of 26 subtests in 12 domains such as Phonological Decoding, Verbal Working Memory, and Rapid-Automatic-Naming, with many of the subtests yielding more than one score that can be used in error-analysis of a child's performance. The entire test may be given in about 2 hours; however, in most cases only subtests related to areas of concern are required.

This assessment is geared toward use at three tiers of intervention as related to Response to Intervention (RTI); at the first tier, children might be screened to determine whether they appear to be at risk for reading/writing failure; at the second, the assessment is best used as part of the problem-solving consultative process; and at the third, it may be used as one measure to diagnose disabilities. A section of the manual lists possible areas of concern that would cause a child to be referred for assessment, such as "child cannot figure out how to decode (pronounce) unknown words" (administration and scoring manual, p. 148) and goes on to suggest the most appropriate subtests to be used, broken out by grade level. A table summarizes which subtests and items within subtests might be used at the different grade levels.

The variety of assessments and response types (oral, written, tactile) make this a complicated test to administer and score. Each subtest has slightly different rules for starting points, discontinuing, timing, and required materials; these rules are delineated on the record form. A user's guide CD-ROM supplements the manual and record form with additional guidance on administering and scoring each subtest. This guide is particularly necessary to analyze the more subjective subtests, such as "Expository Note Taking and Report Writing."

With no computerized scoring package available, the test administrator must transfer raw scores and so on to charts in the front of the record form, then use tables in the appendix of the manual to convert to derived scores. All raw scores are converted to derived ones by grade level only; there are no tables based on chronological age. Percentile ranks and standardized scaled scores, with a mean of 10 and standard deviation of 3, are available for most subtests. For subtests with very skewed distributions, cumulative percentages are given in percentage bands so that students may be compared to others by levels of performance. Base rates are provided for categorical scores in subtests related particularly to writing, in which rubrics are used to evaluate work against a standard rather than students against others. Composite scores for domains with more than one subtest are based on equally weighted scaled scores for those subtests, not on raw scores.

The user's guide CD-ROM contains information about how the PAL-II RW may be used in planning and implementing instruction at three tiers. Suggestions about how to interpret a child's performance on the various subtests and lesson plans to address areas of weakness are included as well as a bibliography of relevant research for each area addressed.

DEVELOPMENT. The guiding theory of the PAL-II RW is that the learning processes of each individual will affect how instruction is received and new material learned. Dr. Berninger's research and clinical experience in cognitive, linguistic, and neuropsychological theories of learning have shaped this assessment; the many subtests are designed to tap smaller, more precise learning processes, such as working memory and executive function, to better identify the best instructional methods. The use of problem-solving consultation by professionals engaged in teaching children is a key component of making the PAL-II RW an instructionally relevant assessment tool.

The subtests that comprise the PAL-II RW are said to be based on extensive published or in-progress research, references for which are available in an appendix on the user's guide, but not provided in the text describing the development of new subtests. As well, subtests from the previous version were expanded to cover more content. The test author conducted a tryout phase of these subtests in the field, with 369 students without disabilities and 31 more with LD or ADHD and made changes to items based on results of this pilot.

The varying rules for administering the assessment were developed during piloting. Some subtests were designed to be administered in their entirety, regardless of the grade of the child. Start points for other subtests were selected by skipping items that 95% of children in grade answered correctly during piloting; discontinue rules by the number of items that 95% of children missed in a row. This procedure means that the discontinue rules range between two and seven items missed. Detailed information about the development of the items for each subtest is not provided.

TECHNICAL.

Standardization. The PAL-II RW was normed with 700 children, 100 each from kindergarten through Grade 6; half of the children were female. The sample was adequately stratified according to 2003 U.S. Census data for age, grade, race/ethnicity, parent education, and geographic region. Excluded from the norming sample were children who had been referred for special education services or assessment, children with cognitive, emotional, or mental health disabilities, and those taking any medications that might interfere with performance on the assessment. As one stated purpose of the PAL-II RW is to make differential diagnoses of whether children have disabilities in reading and writing and another is to screen children who might need more intensive instruction, it is a concern that such children were excluded from the standardization sample.

Reliability. Test-retest reliability data were reported for a sample of 129 children stratified into K–3 (n = 81) and 4–6 (n = 48) grade groups. African American and Hispanic children were oversampled within this group, as compared to 2003 U.S. Census data. Retesting occurred 2–34 days later (mean = 15 days). Reliability coefficients were reported for scaled/composite scores, where available, and raw scores for subtests in which cumulative percentage values were reported. There was greater test-retest reliability for the younger group of children, with coefficients mainly in the range of .70 and greater and only a few falling at .50 or below. For the older group of students, nearly half of the reliability coefficients for the subtests fell below .70. The handwriting measures, which are the most subjectively graded and also subject to significant range-restriction in items and possible scores, had the lowest test-retest reliability. Reliability coefficients reported for the cumulative percentage scores were low; most fell below .50 for both the younger and older groups of students. Range-restriction of items and skewness of the distribution of the sample were blamed for these low coefficients.

Validity. The manual defines the content validity of the PAL-II RW primarily by what it was not designed to test; not academic achievement, nor intellectual ability, but the cognitive process tested may overlap with such tests. The test author states that the PAL-II RW is designed to measure developmental processes in five domains: cognitive/memory, receptive/expressive language, fine and gross motor, attention/executive function, and social/emotional. Validity is determined partially by observing the strategies a child uses in responding to test items and through analysis of errors made.

Intercorrelations of selected subtest scores are provided by grade. As expected, subtests with skills in similar domains of processing (Receptive and Expressive Coding correlated at .47 to .58 across the grades) had higher values than did those in domains not expected to be related (at sixth grade, there was .00 correlation between Oral-Motor Planning and Expository Report Writing Quality). With a plethora of subtests reported by seven grade levels, it is difficult to evaluate the content validity of the PAL-II RW as a whole based on intercorrelations; even the discussion of validity in the manual is more of a defense of the reason for low intercorrelations than it is of how this assessment validly measures academic processes.

In examining convergent validity, the PAL-II RW is compared to the Differential Ability Scales–Second Edition (DAS-II) and the Wechsler Nonverbal Scale of Ability (WNV) as well as the NEPSY-Second Edition (NEPSY-II), although these are all normed by age and the PAL-II RW is normed by grade, which makes comparisons more difficult. Moderate correlations between the DAS-II verbal cluster and several coding/decoding and working memory composites on the PAL-II indicate that the processes are similar. The WNV and the PAL-II RW were not correlated in most areas, highlighting the difference between the nonverbal nature of the former and the level of verbal performance required on the latter. Comparisons between the NEPSY-II and the PAL-II RW show that the latter assesses a more narrow set of processes than the former, allowing for more precise analysis of student performance.

Differential performance of children along gender, ethnic, and culture lines was not discussed, although sampling in these areas appears to be adequate. However, the validity of the PAL-II RW as a measure to select students who are at risk for academic failure or to diagnose learning disabilities is questionable, given that these children were excluded from all norming of the test.

COMMENTARY. The PAL-II RW is a lengthy tool for measuring very specific academic processing skills. The ability to examine the particular strengths and needs a child exhibits in relation to learning to read and write can be quite valuable to professionals such as psychologists, special educators, and speech and language pathologists working together in problem-solving consultation. There is also a wealth of research cited to support the theoretical construct of process assessment, much of it published by the author of the PAL-II RW.

The provision of a user's guide with information about how to interpret the results of PAL-II RW testing, how to use it as one piece of information in multidisciplinary assessment, and basic suggestions of instructional strategies that may benefit students with a particular learning profile is a strength of this measure. It is unfortunate that the user's guide has been supplied as a Windows only program that must be installed on the computer to be used. The PDF format supplied is difficult to navigate, runs slowly, and does not include hotlinks, a searchable index, or an easy way to locate information. Although an indispensable component of the PAL-II RW package, the user's guide will be inaccessible or frustrating for many people.

The number of subtests, with their varying rules for starting, discontinuing, and scoring is quite complicated. Also, with so many scores to record, transfer, and manipulate, the absence of a computerized scoring program is sorely felt. Although anyone with graduate level training in the administration and scoring of individualized, standardized assessments is qualified to use the PAL-II RW, additional training or assistance may be required to fully understand all of its intricacies.

SUMMARY. The wide variety of assessments of processing in reading and writing in the PAL-II RW may provide a more nuanced look at children's performance in these areas than other tests. However, it is unwieldy to administer, score, and interpret. The user's guide must be consulted, but it is not accessible to all users. A serious weakness of the test is the exclusion of students with or perceived to be at risk for reading or writing failure from the norming group and all tests of reliability and validity. This is puzzling in an assessment that the manual repeatedly claims is designed to identify such students and diagnose their problems.

[99]

Profile of Creative Abilities.

Purpose: "Designed to measure the creative abilities of students."
Population: Ages 5-0 to 14-11.
Publication Date: 2007.
Acronym: PCA.
Scores: Creativity Index, Drawing (New Elements, Originality, Orientation, Perspectives, Total), Categories (Fluency, Flexibility, Total), Home Rating Scale Total, School Rating Scale Total.
Price Data, 2009: $158 per complete kit including 25 Home Rating Scales, 25 School Rating Scales, 25 Student Forms, 25 Summary and Scoring Booklets, Picture Booklet, and examiner's manual (2007, 97 pages); $27 per 25 Home Rating Scales; $27 per 25 School Rating Scales; $27 per 25 Student Forms; $27 per 25 Summary and Scoring Booklets; $9 per Picture Booklet; $49 per examiner's manual.
Author: Gail R. Ryser.
Publisher: PRO-ED.

a) PCA SUBTESTS.
Purpose: Designed to "measure two aspects of divergent production."
Scores: Creativity Index, Drawing (New Elements, Originality, Orientation, Perspective, Total), Categories (Fluency, Flexibility, Total).
Subtests, 2: Drawing, Categories.
Administration: Group (Drawing) and individual (Categories).
Time: (30-40) minutes.

b) PCA RATING SCALES.
Purpose: Designed to "measure creative abilities, domain-relevant skills, creativity-relevant skills, and intrinsic task motivation."
Scores: Total score only for each scale.
Administration: Group.
Forms, 2: Home Rating Scale, School Rating Scale.
Time: Administration time not reported.
Comments: Home ratings by parents/guardians; school ratings by teachers/educators.

Review of the Profile of Creative Abilities by STEVEN I. PFEIFFER, Professor of Educational Psychology and Learning Systems, College of Education, Florida State University, Tallahassee, FL:

DESCRIPTION. The Profile of Creative Abilities (PCA) consists of two subtests (Drawing and Categories) and two rating scales (a Home and a School form) that are purported to measure "creative abilities, domain-relevant skills, creativity-relevant skills, and intrinsic task motivation of students between the ages of 5-0 and 14-11" (examiner's manual, p. 5).

The Drawing subtest includes eight stimuli with instructions for the child to use each stimulus to create a picture. To encourage a creative element to the task, the child is specifically instructed to "draw a picture that no one else would think of" (examiner's manual, p. 5). Scoring of this subtest is based on Guilford's (1959) ideas on creativity and assesses the following elements: number of new elements added to the picture, originality, whether the drawing is transformed through location or position, and whether the child's drawing provides perspective. This task is untimed.

The Categories subtest consists of two matrices of 20 animal pictures and 20 shapes. The child is instructed to form groups of at least three objects and to tell the examiner the reason for the grouping. This task is timed: the child is allowed 3 minutes for each form to name as many categories as possible. Scoring of this task is also based on Guilford's (1959) ideas; scoring consists of the number of student responses generated ("fluency") and the number of different categories ("flexibility").

The Home and School rating scales are identical 36-item forms employing a 4-point Likert scale based on how often the child exhibits each behavior or characteristic. The examiner's manual states that the PCA was designed for three purposes: to assist in identifying students as gifted, to monitor progress in a creative-thinking class, and to serve as a research tool.

DEVELOPMENT. Development of the PCA was guided by Guilford's (1959) structure of intellect model and Amabile's (1996) theorizing on creativity. The test author sought to incorporate, in the two subtests and rating scale, the following components of creativity: sensitivity to problems, fluency, flexibility, originality, redefinition (the ability to transform an object or idea), and penetration (the ability to see more than what is apparent on the surface). The rating scale also rates intrinsic motivation.

The test manual does not provide information on item development or beta testing of the PCA. It is unclear how the items on the Drawing subtest, Categories subtest, and the Home and School rating scale were developed. No information is provided on whether any revisions, item pruning, or pilot testing were part of test development. There is also no information on whether experts were consulted as part of item development.

TECHNICAL. The PCA was normed on a sample of 640 children across 11 states. The sample was stratified by three age intervals (5-0 to 8-11; 9-0 to 11-11; 12-0 to 14-11). Because the standardization sample was not very large, there are a small number of students at some ages, a concern in terms of the representativeness of the standardization sample (e.g., at age 5 there were 43 students; at age 12 there were 32 students).

The test manual states that the standardization sample closely approximates the U.S. population. The sample does appear to closely match the U.S. Census in terms of geographic region, race and Hispanic ethnicity, and parent education level. However, the standardization sample does not closely match the U.S. Census in terms of gender (e.g., 46% of the standardization sample are male whereas 51% of the U.S. school-age population are male), and family income (30% of the sample have a family income of $75,000 and over whereas 19% of U.S. families have an income in this upper range).

The manual reports split half, alternate form, and alpha coefficients to support reliability of the PCA. Split-half reliability was used for the Drawing Subtest 1; alternate forms reliability was used for Drawing Subtest 2, and coefficient alpha was applied to the 36-item Home and School rating scale. The manual does not explain the rationale for why different approaches to assessing test reliability and consistency were applied across the different subtests of the PCA. The highest reliability coefficients were for the Home and School rating scale (all in the .94–.98 range). Overall, reliability coefficients ranged from .76 to .98, with the majority in the .80s (10 of 20 reliability coefficients range from .82–.87). The average standard error of measurement across age intervals is 1.0 for Subtests 1 and 2 Drawing and Categories, respectively, 6.0 for the Creativity Index, 5.0 for the Home rating scale, and 2.0 for the School rating scale. Test-retest reliability over a 2-week time period, involving 48 students, was .70 for Subtest 1, .74 for Subtest 2, .73 for the Home rating scale, and .86 for the School rating scale. Finally, the test author and a trained rater independently scored 38 protocols to yield an index of interrater agreement for Subtest 1 (Drawing) and Subtest 2 (Categories). Interscorer agreement was high for both subtests.

Development of the PCA was guided by the work of Guilford and Amabile. As an index of content validity, the manual depicts how PCA items match Guilford's model of creative abilities and Amabile's model of creative skills and processes. Evidence in support of criterion-predictive validity is provided by comparing the PCA with the Torrance Test of Creative Thinking–Figural (TTCT–Figural; Torrance & Ball, 1998) and the Scales for Identifying Gifted Students (SIGS; Ryser & McConnell, 2003). The TTCT–Figural is a popular and widely used measure of creativity and consists of three drawing subtests. The SIGS is a less well known scale; likely it was selected as a criterion measure because of convenience and familiarity–the first author of the SIGS is the author of the PCA. Overall, the correlations between the PCA and the TTCT (.43–.60) and the SIGS (.33–.55) were, at best, moderate, and in some instances low (e.g., the PCA Drawing subtest correlated .43 with the TTCT: Creativity Index; yielding only 18% shared variance on very similar creativity tasks). The PCA Home and School rating scale correlated more highly with the SIGS (.35–.86).

Evidence in support of construct validity was provided by examination of group differentiation across different cohorts. The mean standard scores for the total sample used to norm the PCA (the "mainstream" nongifted students) were compared to a cohort of gifted students (n = 61), and a group of students who participated in a "creative thinking" class (n = 59). The IQ scores of the gifted sample (and the comparison group of "mainstream" nongifted students is not reported. The mean PCA score for the gifted cohort was about 2/3 standard deviation higher than the normative sample; the mean PCA score for the group of students who participated in the creative thinking class–who had training in creativity, was almost 1 standard deviation above the mean of the normative sample. The creative thinking class were not administered the PCA pre-intervention, so it is impossible to know whether the test was measuring changes in creative skills or reflecting latent group differences independent of the intervention. Further, it is unclear from a theoretical perspective, and not discussed in the manual, why PCA scores for a group of apparently nongifted students provided with a creativity training experience should score higher than a group of gifted students.

The manual provides a correlation between teachers' and parents' ratings as further evidence of test validity (.45, statistically significant). Finally, the manual reports that the PCA was compared to two tests of intelligence (Comprehensive Test of Nonverbal Intelligence, Geometric Nonverbal Subtests and the Wechsler Intelligence Scale for Children–Third Edition). Correlations ranged from .26 (PCA Subtest 2: CTONI) to .68 (PCA Creativity Index: CTONI). Correlations with the WISC-III Performance Scale were as follows: .54 (PCA Subtest 1: Drawing), .21 (PCA Subtest 2: Categories), .48 (PCA Creativity Index), all in the moderate range.

The samples used in the validity studies do not closely approximate students across the U.S. (too few Black/African American and Asian American/Pacific Islander students, and no American Indian or Hispanic students in the studies). Overall, the manual does not provide enough details on the recruitment of samples or the methodology and design of the validation studies.

COMMENTARY. The PCA is designed to fill a void in the gifted field, and to provide practitioners in the schools with a relatively quick and easy-to-use, reliable and valid measure of creative abilities. The PCA is an attractive instrument and easy to administer. Scoring, particularly of the Drawing subtest is difficult and can be challenging for the practitioner. The manual does not provide enough research data to support validity and, therefore, use of the PCA in individual decision making cannot be recommended at this time.

Validity studies lack detail and rigor, and would not pass muster if submitted to peer review journals. What is most needed are a series of validation studies that examine how well the PCA predicts to real-life (in-the-classroom and out-of-school) creative products and ideas. Plucker and Barab (2005) and Runco (2005) remind us that high scores on tests of creativity typically do not predict to any real world creative behaviors in the natural environment. If the PCA is to become a useful diagnostic and educational tool, then it will be important to demonstrate its utility in predicting to real-world creative skills and competencies.

SUMMARY. The PCA was developed as a test of creative thinking abilities. The test is designed for students ages 5-0 to 14-11 and consists of two subtests and two rating scales. Development of the test was guided by Guilford's (1959) structure of intellect model and Amabile's (1996) theorizing on creativity. The test is easy to administer, and students will enjoy the two subtests, Drawing and Categories. Similarly, parents and teachers will find the 36-item rating scale easy to complete. Scoring of the two subtests, particularly the 8-item drawing task, can be challenging and requires a good deal of instruction and practice to master.

Based on the research reported in the manual, there is not enough validity evidence at this time to support the use of the scale for gifted identification or to monitor a student's progress in a gifted program (two of the stated purposes of the scale). However, the scale is appropriate for use as a research tool (the third stated purpose of the scale). The limited number of validation studies lack conceptual and methodological rigor. The PCA may yet prove to be a useful instrument to assist in the screening and identification of gifted children; however, before it can be recommended for use in individual decision making, more carefully designed validation studies are needed.

REVIEWER'S REFERENCES

Amabile, T. M. (1996). *Creativity in context.* Boulder, CO: Westview Press.

Guilford, J. P. (1959). Three faces of intellect. *American Psychologist, 14,* 469-479.

Plucker, J. A., & Barab, S. A. (2005). The importance of contexts in theories of giftedness. In R. J. Sternberg & J. E. Davidson (Eds.), *Conceptions of giftedness* (pp. 201-216). New York: Cambridge University Press.

Runco, M. A. (2005). Creative giftedness. In R. J. Sternberg & J. E. Davidson (Eds.), *Conceptions of giftedness* (pp. 295-311). New York: Cambridge University Press.

Ryser, G. R., & McConnell, K. (2003). Scales for Identifying Gifted Students. Waco, TX: Prufrock Press.

Torrance, E. P., & Ball, O. E. (1998). The Torrance Tests of Creative Thinking Streamlined Scoring Guide-Figural A and B. Bensenville, IL: Scholastic Testing Service.

Review of the Profile of Creative Abilities by JOHN F. WAKEFIELD, Professor of Education, University of North Alabama, Florence, AL:

DESCRIPTION. According to the examiner's manual, the Profile of Creative Abilities (PCA) was designed primarily to identify "gifted students in the area of creative thinking" (p. 7). Alternate uses include monitoring progress in creative-thinking classes and conducting research. The contents of the PCA include two subtests of divergent thinking and two rating scales (Home and School). The rating scales have identical items. The examiner's manual instructs a school psychologist or other qualified test administrator how to administer and score the four measures that make up the PCA. Tables at the back of the manual allow the user to convert raw scores to standard scores and percentile ranks, and to derive a standardized "creativity index" from combined total scores on the two divergent-thinking subtests.

DEVELOPMENT. In developing the PCA, the test author used two models of creativity, one based on J. P. Guilford's concept of divergent (vs. convergent) thinking and the other based on Teresa Amabile's inclusion of social and environmental factors in creativity. Following Guilford, the test author defines divergent production as "the generation of alternatives to satisfy specified broad requirements" (examiner's manual, p. 2). The two divergent-thinking subtests apply Guilford's concept by calling for the student to (a) complete eight pictures based on incomplete figures, and (b) on two separate exercises of 20 geometric figures, identify as many categories of three or more figures as possible based on some common feature. The eight completed drawings are each scored for four out of six divergent operations identified by Guilford (sensitivity to problems, originality, redefinition, and penetration). The two lists of categories generated on the other subtest are scored for the other two divergent operations (Fluency and Flexibility).

Following Amabile, the test author defines social and environmental factors in creativity as "domain-relevant skills, creativity-relevant processes, and intrinsic task motivation" (p. 4). The rating scales for educators and parents quantify these factors through 13 of 36 items. Each item asks the adult to decide how often the child being rated exhibits a behavior (from "*never*" to "*much more than peers*"). Domain-relevant skills and creativity-relevant processes are each assessed by 4 items, and intrinsic task motivation (how often a child finds an activity motivating in itself) is assessed by 5 items. The other 23 items assess how often the child exhibits a behavior related to one of Guilford's six divergent operations.

TECHNICAL. The standardization sample for the PCA in 2005 consisted of 640 children assessed in the United States from 11 geographically diverse states. Their gender, ethnicity, parental education, and ages reflected the distribution of the school-age population. Whether or not the sample reflected the SES distribution of the population in 2005 is unclear from the data provided.

Evidence of interscorer reliability on the divergent-thinking subtests is minimal (the test author and one trained scorer with 38 protocols), but the resulting coefficients are high (.95 or higher for each divergent subtest and the Creativity Index). Reliability of scores on the Drawing subtest increases with age (from .76 at 5–7 years to .84 at 12–14 years) and is higher for the Creativity Index (.86) than for separate divergent-thinking measures. Internal reliabilities of scores on rating scales are very high (.94 for ratings by parents and .98 for ratings by educators), but interrater reliabilities within the same environment (home or school) are not reported. Evidence of PCA test-retest reliability (or stability) of scores over 2 weeks for a sample of 48 students (ages 5–14) is acceptable for the subtests and Creativity Index (.70 to .75), but no assurance is given that different raters were involved at different times to provide an accurate assessment of rating scale score stability.

The test author used complementary models of creativity in the design of the instrument, but these models were not systematically integrated. Consequently, the content validity of each PCA measure for the identification of creative abilities has to be judged independently. Most of the PCA tasks are modifications of existing tasks used to assess creative abilities. The test author compares specific tasks on the PCA to tasks on the Structure of Intellect Learning Abilities Test (SOI-LA), the Torrance Tests of Creative Thinking (TTCT), and her own Scales for Identifying Gifted Students (SIGS). The PCA Drawing task resembles the TTCT-Figural exercise called Picture Completion, for example, but there are specific differences in the Drawing subtest. The stimulus lines are angular, the test is not timed, fluency and flexibility are not calculated, titles of drawings are not scored, and few opportunities exist for bonus points (e.g., for humor or movement). Whether these modifications enhance or diminish the relation of scores to creative abilities is significant, but the issue is not discussed.

Evidence of criterion-related validity is lacking. The correlation between the PCA Creativity Index and the TTCT Creativity Index is reported to be substantial (.56), but the acknowledgment of the Drawing subtest as a variant of Picture Completion suggests that the criterion was not independent. Similarly, correlations between PCA Home and School rating scales and corresponding SIGS Creativity subscales are very large (.74 to .86), but coefficients of this magnitude suggest overlap between the instruments and raise doubts as to whether different raters filled out the rating forms on the different instruments. To minimize such overlaps and doubts, independent criteria should be used to validate the PCA. Peer nominations, self-reports, and consensual assessments of creative products by expert judges are all suitable to assess creative abilities in children (Shaughnessy & Wakefield, 2003), and they all represent independent validation criteria. The newness of the PCA excuses the absence of correlations that would substantiate predictive validity over time.

Evidence of construct validity is also lacking. Indications that gifted children perform better than average on PCA measures do not validate the instrument as a tool to assess creative abilities. Nor do indications that children taught in a creativity class perform better than average on the PCA.

Common conceptions in the fields of gifted and creative education, such as the distinction between convergent and divergent thinking, suggest that correlations between intelligence tests and creativity tests should reflect this distinction. The test author reports one study of 61 children, ages 5 to 14, who took multiple measures of intelligence and the PCA. The PCA Creativity Index correlated .54 with scores on one measure of nonverbal intelligence and .43 with full-scale Wechsler Intelligence Scale for Children–Third Edition (WISC-III) scores (IQs). These correlations are at the high end of what one would expect. Correlations of PCA scores with both divergent- and convergent-thinking subtests of the SOI-LA might yield more information with respect to what the PCA measures vis-à-vis divergent and convergent thinking.

COMMENTARY. The title of the test can lead the user to expect a profile of scores, each measuring a different creative ability, but this profile is not the information that the test supplies. The instrument is composed of different measures that combine indices of different creative abilities into total scores. PCA scores were standardized on what appears to be a nationally representative sample, and standards of reliability for the Creativity Index have been met. Evidence of the interrater reliability of scores on the rating scales, however, is missing. Given the correlation reported between Home and School scales (.43 [uncorrected correlation]), interrater reliability is probably not high, signaling that raters require training. Practical obstacles to training classroom teachers and parents as raters are considerable, limiting the value of high rating scale scores to that of a structured teacher or parent nomination. This value is significant, but users need to interpret high rating scale scores carefully.

Content validity is adequately demonstrated for each measure, but standards of criterion-related and construct validity have yet to be met. For example, evidence that instruction in creative thinking increases PCA scores of an experimental group (vs. a control group) would support construct validity, but this evidence has yet to be supplied. In particular, validation criteria need to be chosen that are independent of PCA tasks. More evidence of reliability and validity needs to be gathered before the PCA should be used for gate-keeping decisions in gifted or creative education.

SUMMARY. The PCA is a new instrument to help identify creative children. Its technical strengths include standardization of scores on a representative sample of the school-age population in the United States, evidence of subtest score reliability, and similarity of content to existing instruments. Its technical weaknesses are lack of evidence of interrater reliability on the rating scales and lack of evidence of criterion and construct validity. Its current form should be regarded as a research edition.

REVIEWER'S REFERENCE

Shaughnessy, M. F., & Wakefield, J. F. (2003). Creativity: Assessment. In N. Piotrowski & T. Irons-Georges (Eds.), *Magill's encyclopedia of social science: Psychology* (pp. 459-463). Pasadena, CA: Salem Press.

[100]

The ProfileXT Assessment.

Purpose: "Multi-purpose assessment that is used for selection, coaching, training, promotion, managing, and succession planning."
Population: Present and potential employees.
Publication Dates: 1999–2007.
Acronym: PXT.
Scores: 21 scores in 4 subgroups: Thinking Style Scale (Learning Index, Verbal Skill, Verbal Reasoning, Numerical Ability, Numeric Reasoning), Behavioral Trait Scales (Energy Level, Assertiveness, Sociability, Manageability, Attitude, Decisiveness, Accommodating, Independence, Objective Judgment), Occupational Interests Scales (Enterprising, Financial/Administrative, People Service, Technical, Mechanical, Creative), Distortion Scale.
Administration: Group or individual.
Forms, 2: Online, Paper and Pencil.
Price Data: Available from publisher.
Time: (50–70) minutes.
Comments: Web-based administration available; 8 result reports: Placement Report, Coaching Report, Individual Report, Succession Planning Report, Candidate Matching Report, Job Profile Summary Report, Job Summary Graph, and Job Analysis Report. [Editor's Note: The publisher provided a revised 2007 technical manual that was not available at the time the reviewers completed their initial evaluations. The 2007 technical manual was subsequently sent to the reviewers, and they revised their reviews to reflect this new manual. After reading the revised reviews, the test publisher informed us that additional information existed (e.g., the actual formulas used to compute percent match to a pattern) in a format that is considered proprietary. An offer was extended to share such information with our reviewers in a confidential manner so that the reviews would contain a maximum amount of information, but the test publisher chose not to provide this information prior to publication.]
Authors: Profiles International, Inc.
Publisher: Profiles International, Inc.

Review of The ProfileXT Assessment by CAROLINE MANUELE ADKINS, Professor Emeritus, Hunter College, School of Education, City University of New York, New York, NY:

The primary purpose of the ProfileXT (PXT) is for "evaluating how an individual fits into a particular job" (technical manual, p. 1-1). The PXT consists of four separate parts, which include (a) Behavioral Traits (182 items), (b) Occupational Interests (55 items), (c) Thinking Styles (77 items), and (d) Distortion Scale (uses items from the Behavioral Traits Scale). The items are in forced and multiple-choice formats and each of the sections reports scores for varying numbers of scales.

DESCRIPTION. The PXT is computer administered and scored with special PXT software. Scores are reported on 20 individual STEN scales with scores ranging from 1 (*low*) to 10 (*high*) with raw scores "normed so that the distribution of scores for the United States working population will fall on each scale with a normal distribution" (technical manual, p. 1-4). Scores are also reported on "specific job match patterns," which compare an individual's (employee's) score to characteristics of other people in the organization who are effective in a position or challenged by the position.

To put this "job match" scoring in place, organizations that use the PXT must build their own job match patterns. According to the manual the software provides methods for inputting a given organization's job performance criterion measures, correlating this information with PXT scales to identify high and low performers, creating job matching patterns for this information, and, finally, determining an individual employee's degree of fit to these patterns.

The PXT is intended for use with the general working population of the United States, who would be employees and applicants for employment in a variety of diverse organizations. The manual notes that the target populations for the PXT are similar to those used for norming the measure. Specifically, the PXT was normed on more than 600,000 employees in 25,000 client organizations with mixed educational levels, and age, gender, and ethnicity representative of the U.S. population in general.

Data from the PXT's use in all these organizations are combined and used in studies to demonstrate the effectiveness of the Job Pattern Matching Process and to study whether the process contributes to any adverse impact against minority groups. The large numbers in these combined groups contribute to generally positive conclusions about the egalitarian nature of the PXT. To understand how the measure really works with different groups, however, one needs to go beyond the combined data studies and examine studies in the manual that include more refined subgroups. In general, the nonspecificity of the target populations and mixing of all ages, skilled and unskilled occupations, diverse educational levels, and work roles tend to make score interpretation quite problematic (e.g., what do specific scores on the different scales in the PXT really mean?). [Editor's Note: The meaning of the test scores for a particular job at a particular company may and likely do acquire meaning, but the manual combines data across jobs and companies in a manner that makes such a discernment one of considerable difficulty.]

DEVELOPMENT. The PXT is constructed as a "test battery" and each section of the PXT has its own developmental history. The Behavioral Traits section was derived from measures previously known as The Personality Survey-I (PS-I) and The Personality Survey-II (PS-II) with both instruments designed to measure "normal personality traits." Items for these measures were all "selected by a panel of psychologists without reference to a particular theory" (manual, p. 2-1), with later revisions based on the results of factor-analytic studies.

The current Behavioral Traits section consists of nine scales, which are intended to assess traits that relate to job performance, employee turnover, promotion potential, training success, and conscientious behavior. The personality scales are: Accommodating, Assertiveness, Attitude, Energy Level, Independence, Objective Judgment, Sociability, Manageability, and Decisiveness. The manual for the PXT defines the meaning of these individual scales in descriptive terms but there is little to no reference to personality theory or constructs. Determining the relationship of high and low scores on these scales to job performance is difficult for the user who must sort through pages of concurrent validity studies. Consolidating these data with tables of norms for various occupational settings, positions, roles, and demographic characteristics would be extremely helpful for ease of, and confidence in, the interpretation of scale scores.

The Occupational Interests section is said to "parallel" the underlying theory found in Holland's Vocational Preference Inventory and there are obvious similarities between Holland's six occupational themes and the six occupational interest scales of the PXT. In the PXT these are labeled: Enterprising, Financial/Administrative, People Service, Technical, Mechanical, and Creative. Interests on these scales are measured by the selection of preferences between paired comparisons of common activities. Items for these scales were selected again by a panel of psychologists who were experienced in occupational assessment. This section of the PXT also produces three letter codes such as EFP, MTE, and FPE, which are supposed to be compatible with Holland's Dictionary of Occupational Codes. The manual indicates that this part of the PXT can be used as a "guide to vocational and career exploration" (p. 2-11), but it is unclear how this fits into the interpretation of PXT scores, uses, and applications (e.g. what does an employee do with these results?). Are they used to counsel a poor performing employee out of the organization or into another position or to explore other career choices? And finally, how do results in this section relate to job performance, turnover, promotion prospects, etc.? Clarification in the manual as to proposed uses would be helpful.

The Thinking Style section of the PXT "refers to the ability to use old learning applied to new experiences" (manual, p. 2-12). Originally developed as a test of general learning and a measure of general abilities, the 77 multiple-choice items are now divided into five scales: Verbal Skill (Vocabulary), Verbal Reasoning (Analogies), Numerical Ability (Math and Fractions), Numerical Reasoning (Reasoning and Problem-Solving), and Learning Index (composite score of other four sections). Development of these scales was based on creating a large pool of numeric and verbal learning questions with the best questions selected by item analysis for type and level of difficulty. Absent from the development information in the manual for this section of the PXT is also any reference to theoretical constructs for item derivation.

TECHNICAL. Reliability studies are presented for each of the sections in the form of coefficient alpha analyses for measures of internal consistency and a 7-week test-retest administration for 83 manufacturing company employees. Internal consistency correlations for the Behavioral Traits scales range from .73 to .87, for the Occupational Interest scales from .74 to .84, and for the Thinking Style scale from .79 to .84. The moderate to moderately high reliability figures suggest that the scales are fairly homogenous with individuals responding consistently to many items in the test. Results from the test-retest study in a work setting demonstrate good score stability with correlations for each of the three parts respectively ranging from .75–.91, .67–.78, and .66 to .80.

It would appear that content validity issues for the most part may have been ignored in the sense that little attention has been paid in the manual to identifying how items were constructed or why they were included in the measure other than that experts selected them. Construct validity studies are presented for each of the three sections. Scores on the Behavioral Traits section are correlated with scores achieved on three other measures of adult personality including the Guilford-Zimmerman Temperament Survey, with positive correlations for 6 out of 10 scales; the Gordon Personal Profile and the California Psychological Inventory with 5 significant scale correlations each. It appears that there is evidence for the fact that the PXT is measuring a substantial number of traits similar to those in these well-established measures. Evidence for studies correlating the Occupational Interests scale with Holland's Self-Directed Search range from .43 to .65, also reflecting a substantial commonality of content.

Because this test is used for job selection and promotion, the issue of criterion-related validity is of special interest. A series of studies done in different employment settings examined the relationship of PXT scores and various performance criteria. The majority of these studies support the ability of this measure to differentiate between high and low performing employees. In a series of other studies, Occupational Interest patterns were also found to be related to expected occupational groups (e.g., higher scores on the Enterprising and People Service scales for people in sales). The presentation of criterion-related validity studies for the Thinking Style scale appears confusing in the manual, and they are difficult to interpret. For example, one study uses the criterion of educational achievement with ninth grade through graduate-level students mixed in the sample. The correlates of test scores with job performance grouped by occupational titles are not particularly strong suggesting that the Thinking Style scale is not that useful for predicting job performance in specific occupational groups.

COMMENTARY. A major issue for the PXT is that the technical manual does not include a theoretical rationale for the development of items and scales in all sections of the measure. In effect, it appears to have no theory or research base except for its obvious reference to Holland's organization of interests and modal personality patterns. This deficiency relates to not only what is being measured but also to why we are measuring it. For example, why is there a Decisiveness scale, how is the trait defined, and what does research or theory say about how or why it is related to different types of job performance?

The reliability information provides support for the use of the test and some of the validity studies presented indicate serious concern by the authors to provide evidence that the measure is doing what it is supposed to do. More attention to content validity studies is needed to address how the test relates to performance in specific jobs, especially in the Thinking Style scale.

The manual is not particularly well written; the language is often obtuse and convoluted. The manual also needs to offer more information about critical aspects of administering and interpreting the PXT. The use of the instrument could be improved by including more specific target population norm tables and providing examples for the user as to how to interpret test profiles. It is possible that this information has been left out of the manual in the sense that the expected use of the PXT may be dependent on the Profiles International Group (the test's developers) to administer, score, and interpret the test for a specific company that hires them according to profiles for successful employees for successful employees for specific jobs at that company. Moreover, their norms tables may be so inclusive as to render use for specific occupations relatively meaningless.

SUMMARY. The PXT is a measure that has a variety of technical information and studies supporting it that substantiate some of its psychometric characteristics. It provides gross evidence (in large combined data samples) for the measure's nondiscriminatory nature and for its ability to distinguish between high and low job performance. A potential user would need to examine in depth whether or not the software in the PXT has the ability to provide localized data for the "job matching" part of the measure. Of most discomfort to this reviewer is the technical manual's absence of theory in the development of the measure, which limits one's ability to interpret scores effectively and to understand what is really being measured. The presentation of additional studies also focused on smaller, more representative and targeted norm groups in the manual would be quite useful.

Review of The ProfileXT Assessment by RICHARD T. KINNIER, Professor, and NICOLE L. NIESET, Ph.D. Candidate, Counseling Psychology Program, Arizona State University, Tempe, AZ:

DESCRIPTION. The ProfileXT Assessment (PXT) is designed to "facilitate achieving the best possible fit for positions in the working world" (technical manual, 2007, p. 1-1). Results are used to make effective job placements, develop effective work teams, and design optimal training programs. The PXT consists of three sections: Behavioral Traits, Occupational Interests, and Thinking Style. Resulting scores can also be used to "match" test-takers to specific jobs, according to the authors.

Behavioral Traits includes 182 statements referring to the test-taker's traits or opinions, answered by marking either "yes" or "no." This section yields scores on nine scales (e.g., Energy Level, Assertiveness) and a Distortion scale designed to measure "a person's tendency to create an exaggerated or potentially false positive impression"(technical manual, p. 2-5). Each scale is scored on a STEN scale of 1 (*low*) to 10 (*high*).

Occupational Interests includes 55 items, each presenting two activities. The test-taker is instructed to choose which activity he or she strongly or probably prefers. This section yields scores on six scales or interest areas (e.g., Enterprising, People Service). Each scale is scored on a STEN scale of 1 (*least interested*) to 10 (*most interested*). Similar to the Strong Interest Inventory, the test-taker's interests can also be rank-ordered.

Thinking Style includes 77 multiple-choice items and five scales. According to the manual, "Thinking style refers to the ability to use old learning applied to new experiences in order to measure the flexibility of thinking required to grasp concepts in a job or training setting" (technical manual, p. 2-15). The scales are: a Learning Index, Verbal Skill (18 vocabulary words), Verbal Reasoning (20 analogies), Numerical Ability (22 arithmetic calculations), and Numerical Reasoning (17 math problems). Each scale is scored on STEN scales (scores range from 1-10 with a mean of 5.5 and a standard deviation of 2).

Results can be presented in different report formats (e.g., Job Profile, Placement Report, Coaching Report). Some formats use verbal descriptors only. Others display STEN scores on bar graphs along with verbal descriptors. Some reports include "Job Match" scores expressed as percentages to which the test-taker presumably matches with specific jobs.

DEVELOPMENT. Each of the three sections of the PXT was developed independently. In the opinion of these reviewers, a major problem in regard to the description in the manual of the development of all the scales is a pervasive vagueness and lack of specific information on item construction, refinement, and validation, as well as the omission of much relevant data. For example, in the Behavioral Traits section, the manual authors claim it is based on their first Personality Survey (PS-I), in which items were derived from factor and item analyses. No details or data are presented on how the item pool was created and refined. In the Occupational Interests section, the authors discuss Holland's Vocational Preference Inventory and compare their six themes to Holland's, but they are vague about how they developed their almost identical themes. The authors report that they used factor analysis to identify independent themes, but the data presented are quite incomplete (i.e., these reviewers believe that all of the loadings and the number of subjects in the study should be included, for example). The Thinking Style section consists of four tests of verbal and numerical abilities. Thus, the term "style" is inaccurate. According to the manual (p. 2-15), the tests were initially developed in 1988. Item analyses were conducted on a "large pool of questions" (technical manual, p. 2-16), and two resulting scales were divided into the current four. More details (e.g., the number of initial items, the rationale, and precise procedure for dividing the scales) should be provided in the technical manual. Perhaps the most innovative but questionable part of the PXT is the procedure for matching test-takers to specific jobs. The manual fails to describe adequately the precise psychometrics of such "job match patterns," although perhaps the test publisher provides this information to clients or potential clients. The test authors do discuss general ideas and refer to specific studies, but the presentation in the technical manual is somewhat vague and disjointed.

TECHNICAL. The manual presents rather extensive data on norms, reliability, and validity studies on all of the scales. The authors of the manual claim a norm sample of over 600,000 individuals, which would be an extremely large sample. For the reliability and validity studies most sample sizes were typical for these types of tests with the exception of one huge sample of over 206,000 test-takers that was used for several of the studies. The *Test Standards* require that the authors should describe the origins, composition, and nature of such an unusually large sample. Reliability studies consisted of internal consistency (alpha coefficients) and test-retest studies. For the Behavioral Trait scales, alpha coefficients ranged from .73 to .87 (M = .79). For the Occupational Interest scales, alpha coefficients ranged from .74 to .84 (M = .77). For the Thinking Style scales, alpha coefficients ranged from .79 to .84 (M = .81). All of these can be considered reasonably strong. The test-retest results are mixed. As noted in an earlier version of the technical manual, in a study with 157 university students, retested at 3 months, coefficients across all scales ranged from .37 to .77, with a median of about .50. These coefficients are low. In a more recent study with 83 employees from a manufacturing company, retested at about 7 weeks, coefficients across all scales ranged from .66 to .91, with a median of about .75. These coefficients can be considered reasonably good.

The authors conducted a variety of validity studies. For the Behavioral Traits, they examined intracorrelations of the scales, intercorrelations with other personality tests, and criterion-related studies (e.g., relationships between scores and sales performance, employee evaluations, and employee turnover). Generally, the data support validity of the scales. However, the studies were conducted on an earlier version of the PXT (the PTP), rather than the current one. Validity of the Occupational Interest scales was estimated by scale intracorrelations, intercorrelations with other tests (e.g., the SDS [Self-Directed Search] and PTP [earlier version of the PXT]), and criterion-related validity studies (e.g., the scale scores of different professionals). All of the intracorrelations were low but significant, which is difficult to interpret. The high correlations with the SDS scales can be considered supportive of validity. Comparative scores of different professionals also support validity. The four Thinking Style scales consist of a relatively small number of items (specifically 17, 18, 20, and 22 items). Such small numbers of items sometimes raise a concern about validity. Validity of the scales was estimated by correlating scores with overall GPA, math and English and science grades, as well as with job performance. The correlations were supportive of validity. Finally, the presentation of data on the Distortion scale, the Adverse Impact Analysis, demographic comparisons, the meta analyses of predictive utilities, and "Job Match patterns" was impressive but is also described in the manual in a somewhat vague and confusing manner. The flowchart in the manual was clear but the rest of the text was not as precise and clear as it could be.

COMMENTARY AND SUMMARY. On the positive side, the PXT is an easy, brief test to take and administer. Results are presented in clear, easy-to-understand STEN bar graphs. The reports are descriptively rich. Unfortunately, some conclusions appear to go too far beyond the data. For example, on a "Sample Individual Report" several comments about the test-taker's ability to communicate are written on the basis of a short vocabulary test. Other comments similarly seem to overgeneralize from the test results. We are especially concerned about data on "Adverse Impact" and the "Job Match Pattern" (technical manual, p. D-1). The authors must more clearly describe how the Job Match Pattern was validated and how the percentages are obtained. Until they do we are skeptical about the validity of the scores. The individual scales do appear to be fairly reliable and valid, though some test-retest correlations were low. All of the scales in the PXT may be better measured by already well-established personality, interests, and abilities tests, in our opinion. The advantage in using the PXT is its brevity and its easy-to-understand STEN bar graphs. As long as interpretation does not go beyond straightforward interpretation of the specific scales, followed by tentative and broad discussions about apparent patterns and possible job matches, then the test could be useful.

[101]

PST-100SV and PST-80SV Public Safety Telecommunicator Tests.

Purpose: Designed to assess critical abilities required for entry-level public safety telecommunicator positions

Population: Candidates for entry-level public safety communicator positions.

Publication Date: 1995.

Acronyms: PST-80SV; PST-100SV.

Scores: 5 knowledge areas: Listening Skills, Reading Comprehension, Ability to Learn and Apply Information, Reasoning Ability, Ability to Use Situational Judgment.

Administration: Individual or group.

Forms, 2: PST-80SV, PST-100SV.

Price Data: Available from publisher.

Time: 144 minutes for PST-100SV; 120 minutes for PST-80SV.

Comments: The two versions contain exactly the same questions with the exception of the Listening Skills subtest, which has an audio component and so the PST-80SV version of the exam is available for those jurisdictions that do not have the audio equipment needed to administer the Listening Skills subtest.

Author: International Public Management Association for Human Resources.
Publisher: International Public Management Association for Human Resources (IPMA-HR).

Review of the PST-100SV and the PST-80SV Public Safety Telecommunicator Tests by MYRA N. WOMBLE, Associate Professor of Workforce Education, University of Georgia, Athens, GA:

DESCRIPTION. The PST-100SV Public Safety Telecommunicator Test is a 100-item entry-level test designed to assess critical abilities on these content area subtests: Listening Skills, Reading Comprehension, Ability to Learn and Apply Information, Reasoning Ability, and Ability to Use Situational Judgment. The PST-80SV Public Safety Telecommunicator Test is an 80-item entry-level test designed to assess critical abilities on the same content area subtests as the PST-100SV except Listening Skills. Because both tests are designed for the entry-level, candidates are not required to have prior training or experience. Both tests are multiple-choice whereby candidates must decide on one of four possible answers and record responses by blackening a circle on an answer sheet. Candidates are allowed 24 minutes to complete the 20-item Listening Skills portion of the PST-100SV, then 2 hours to complete the remaining 80 questions. Candidates are allowed 2 hours to complete the PST-80SV test. Establishment of a passing point for these tests is the responsibility of the jurisdiction administering the test. Assistance is offered to jurisdictions in setting passing points through a test response data report for each test. This report presents test data gathered from jurisdictions that use the publisher's tests and includes information on passing points, score distributions, and adverse impact data. It is updated annually and each update reflects the previous 5 years of test response data.

DEVELOPMENT. The 1995 technical report contains detailed information about test development. Primarily, the PST-100SV and PST-80SV were developed using two strategies involving a consortium of interested, volunteer jurisdictions. First, a job analysis was conducted to define the job of Public Safety Telecommunicators (PSTs); identify critical duties and tasks performed by PSTs; identify the knowledge, skills, abilities, and other characteristics (KSAOs) needed to perform the duties and tasks successfully; and determine if the job is similar across jurisdictions. Second, a concurrent validation study was conducted using data collected in two phases: (a) administering the PST tests to PSTs, and (b) having supervisors evaluate the PSTs' job performance.

Job analysis involved the development and review of preliminary (a) tasks and (b) KSAO lists. Next, on-site visits with 10 jurisdictions across the country were made to conduct job observation sessions, collect resource materials, and conduct subject matter expert (SME) interviews. The SMEs reviewed preliminary tasks and KSAO lists, provided comments on how accurately the tasks and KSAOs reflected the job, and advised as to the accurate categorizing of tasks under each duty. Each task and KSAO was reviewed, discussed, and reworded or eliminated. Three job analysis questionnaires were developed, one completed by incumbent PSTs and designed to obtain ratings pertaining to importance of each task and the frequency with which the tasks are performed; another completed by first-line supervisors/lead workers to gather information on the link between the duties and the KSAOs needed to perform them effectively; and a third was sent to a subgroup of first-line supervisors/lead workers to gather information on the link between individual tasks and KSAOs needed to perform them effectively.

Data collected from a sample of 443 PSTs resulted in development of 191 test questions for five KSAOs (Listening Skills—40, Reading Comprehension—41, Concept Memory—46, Reasoning Ability—28, and Situational Judgment—36). Based on item analysis data and preliminary subtest correlations with performance ratings, 100 questions were selected for inclusion on the final test. The report clearly documents removal of test items from analysis and provides detailed information about flaws or problems discovered in the item analysis phase such as item difficulty, clarity, and bias.

TECHNICAL. This section is divided into three categories—standardization, reliability, and validity—and addresses findings from the concurrent validation study.

Standardization. The concurrent validation study sample consisted of 347 PSTs who had been on the job for at least 6 months, had up to 8 years experience on the job, and were from 49 jurisdictions, combined law enforcement and fire and solely law enforcement. A majority of the PSTs were white (85.3%) females (70.9%). In terms of generalizing, the report suggests that PSTs in the sample with less time on the job (i.e., approximately 67%, 6 months–4 years) tend to be more similar to the applicant pool than long-term employees. However, these tests were developed using data from volunteer PSTs in 40 states, thus limiting ability to generalize. The passing scores are subjective in nature because they are set by jurisdictions; as such, their appropriateness for different ethnic or cultural groups is unclear. For example, it is possible to set passing scores in a way that maximizes or minimizes the number of minority candidates who fail the tests. Although a small change in the passing score would likely not change the meaning of the test scores, it could greatly increase or decrease minority pass rates.

Reliability. Data collected from 347 PSTs rendered a KR-20 reliability coefficient of .88 for the 100-item exam and .85 for the 80-item exam, both acceptable levels of reliability by general standards. KR-20 reliability coefficients are also provided for each subset, but are not presented in this review due to space limitations. However, the KR-20 reliability coefficients are considerably lower for the subsets, ranging from a high of .74, which is adequate, to a low of .60, which may indicate limited applicability. With the Listening subtest eliminated, the mean score for the PST 80SV (67.48) is considerably lower than the mean score for the PST 100SV (85.57). To assess the degree to which different raters gave consistent estimates, the Spearman Brown formula was used to determine the interrater reliability coefficient of .69, also adequate, on the overall performance rating. These results indicate a dependable rating process considering interrater reliability coefficients are typically lower than other types of reliability estimates. However, as raters' training improves, interrater reliability is likely to improve. Data were also examined to determine the relationship of each dimension to the overall performance rating and the composite performance rating. Reliability coefficients for overall and composite performance are both reported as .93 (n = 347), indicating very good reliability of scores obtained on these tests.

Validity. Developers used the mean performance rating to compute a composite rating using the mean performance rating for PSTs rated by one supervisor and for PSTs rated by two supervisors. The composite rating was used as the primary criterion measure in the study because it was considered the most dependable criterion measure. The relationship between the scores on both tests and the composite performance ratings rendered a validity coefficient of .22 on both tests, both statistically significant at the .001 level. With regard to fairness, the regression equations were tested with regard to their intercepts and slopes. Composite performance scores were used to compute validity coefficients for the PST-100SV for males (.221, n = 101) and females (.237, n = 246) and for Whites (.205, n = 296) and Blacks (.333, n = 29). Validity coefficients for the PST-80SV were also computed separately for males (.228, n = 101) and females (.241, n = 246) and for Whites (.212, n = 296) and Blacks (.311, n = 29), also using composite performance scores. Fisher's z comparisons were used to test for differences between validity coefficients and none were found. Other groups had insufficient numbers of subjects to test for statistical analysis. These results indicate fair to adequate usefulness of both tests as predictors of performance.

COMMENTARY. The value of these tests as measures of critical abilities for PSTs is adequate; however, the following three concerns suggest potential users give careful consideration prior to adoption. First, developers purport that the tests are fair predictors of PST performance for males, females, Whites, and Blacks. However, fairness to other ethnic groups has not been established, and no documentation was provided to indicate that potential users are made aware of this possible limitation. There is also no evidence that other variables such as language have been considered. Second, the manner in which jurisdictions are provided assistance in determining passing scores for these tests could make their use more difficult or time-consuming than might be initially expected. As mentioned earlier, some assistance is available through test response data reports. Third, considerable change has occurred in the U.S. since the development of these tests more than a decade ago, particularly in demographics and technology. Further, validity was established in accordance with the 1985 *Standards for Psychological and Educational Testing*, which were revised significantly in 1999 to reflect changes in federal law and measurement trends affecting validity, testing individuals with disabilities or with different linguistic backgrounds, new types of tests, and new uses of existing tests (APA Online, para. 1, 2003). Consequently, a thorough reexamination of these tests to address updated standards and other types of societal changes that impact this entry-level position is needed.

SUMMARY. Materials provided for review include empirical evidence that the PST-100SV and PST-80SV tests yield consistent results and measure the same way each time. The validity and reliability of these tests are supported by an assiduous process that included a job analysis and a concurrent validation study. Positive aspects of the tests include clear instructions for candidates, candidates are not required to have prior training or experience in the target job, and candidates are allowed to review their responses if time remains upon completing the tests. Information about how the tests are scored was not provided for this review; however, concerns for potential users of these tests will likely be making judgments about test fairness, establishing a passing point, and determining if the tests are right for their agency.

REVIEWER'S REFERENCE

APA Online. (2003). *Testing and assessment: The standards for educational and psychological testing*. Retrieved October 12, 2006, from http://www.apa.org/science/standards.html

[102]

PSUP 1.1, 2.1, and 3.1 Police Supervisor Tests (Corporal/Sergeant).

Purpose: Designed as "a promotional test for the police supervisor."
Population: Candidates for promotion to the police supervisor or corporal/sergeant position.
Publication Dates: 2003–2006.
Acronyms: PSUP 1.1; PSUP 2.1; PSUP 3.1.
Scores: 5 knowledge areas: Laws Related to Police Work, Police Field Operations, Investigative Procedures, Supervisory Principles and Concepts & Reports, Records and Paperwork.
Administration: Individual or group.
Forms, 3: PSUP 1.1, PSUP 2.1, PSUP 3.1.
Price Data: Available from publisher.
Time: 150 minutes per test.
Comments: PSUP 1.1, PSUP 2.1, and PSUP 3.1 are comparable forms; reading lists are available to help candidates prepare for the tests.
Author: International Public Management Association for Human Resources.
Publisher: International Public Management Association for Human Resources (IPMA-HR).

Review of the PSUP 1.1, 2.1, and 3.1 Police Supervisor Tests (Corporal/Sergeant) by JAY R. STEWART, Director and Associate Professor, Rehabilitation Counseling Program, Division of Intervention Services, Bowling Green State University, Bowling Green, OH:

DESCRIPTION. The PSUP 1.1, 2.1, and 3.1 Police Supervisor Tests (Corporal/Sergeant) are comparable test forms designed as promotional tests for assessing candidates seeking the rank of police supervisor or corporal/sergeant positions. Each of the three tests is a 100-item achievement test. The items are multiple choice with number of choices ranging from two to five. PSUP 1.1 and PSUP 2.1 are alternate forms to be used by a police department that gives promotional tests at least annually. PSUP 3.1 is intended for use by a police department that gives promotional tests less often than annually. The test versions are all composed of the following topic areas: Laws Related to Police Work (24 items), Police Field Operations (24), Investigative Procedures (15), Supervisory Practices (27), and Reports, Records, Paperwork (10). The publisher reports that an updated manual is being developed.

Each test version can be administered individually or to a group. The tests are time limited to 2½ hours. The test packet is composed of a sheet of general instructions, followed by 21–24 pages of questions with an answer sheet. The answer sheet can be scored in three ways: (a) hand-scored with a provided stencil that is laid over the answer sheet, (b) an answer key is supplied, which can be used with optical scanning devices, or (c) the answer sheet can be mailed to International Public Management Association for Human Resources (IPMA-HR) for scoring. IPMA-HR works with agencies that may need to provide accommodations under the Americans with Disabilities Act.

DEVELOPMENT. The development of the Police Supervisor Test began with a national job analysis of first-line police supervisor positions by IPMA-HR and Bruce Davey Associates. The two groups obtained information from 119 municipal units across 39 states on police supervisor tasks, duties, and competencies. Municipal units (represented by 637 police supervisors) rated the competencies needed for newly promoted first-line police supervisors throughout the country. Statistical analysis of these results indicated that a uniform national testing procedure was appropriate for needed competencies.

IPMA-HR's test was developed to measure competencies in the above listed topic areas by drawing 250 questions from IPMA-HR's test bank of questions for promotion to police supervision, which were linked to job analysis competencies, reading lists, psychometric soundness, police supervisor candidate feedback, and item validity data previously gathered on test bank items. A number of questions from the test bank were updated in 2003 to reflect recent Supreme Court decisions on police activities. From the 250 questions, the PSUP 1.1 and PSUP

2.1 were created as alternate tests; both had 100 items. The 100-item PSUP 3.1 was developed by drawing one-half of the best rated questions from both the PSUP 1.1 and PSUP 2.1.

TECHNICAL.

Standardization. At present, there is no reported norm sample; however, IPMA-HR has gathered data on 6,000 police supervisor candidates regarding scores that individual departments report. The data include scores by race and by gender. IPMA-HR reports that it is also collecting what the departments are using as cutoff scores for promotion. The data-gathering process appears to have potential as the basis for identifying a proper norm group, and IPMA-HR reports that they intend to establish scoring norms.

Reliability. Reliability was estimated through the KR20 (PSUP 1.1 = .86 [n = 94], 2.1 = .84 [n = 95], 3.1 = .87 [n = 98]). This reliability measure is considered excellent for all three tests.

Validity. Content validity would seem to be adequate. Point-biserial r, correlations between individual item performance and total test score, had been performed on most of the items. Average point-biserial correlation coefficients and the number of test items of the entire test are as follows: PSUP 1.1 = .24 (n = 94), 2.1 = .23 (n = 95), 3.1 = .25 (n = 98). Criterion-related validity had also been established for most of the test items—though not for the tests as a whole—through correlating the individual test item performance with supervisor ratings of applicants' current job performance. Average item validity coefficients and number of test items of the entire test are as follows: PSUP 1.1 = .14 (n = 72), 2.1 = .15 (n = 72), 3.1 = .16 (n = 89). These indicate a moderate positive correlation between answering the item correctly and having a positive current rating by one's supervisor. Construct validity could be implied through the heavy use of police supervisors to determine topic areas and those competencies covered by test items and relative competency importance.

COMMENTARY. The PSUP tests are the result of a major undertaking, which provides a national service: an aid in promoting qualified personnel to police supervisors. Because effective police work is highly dependent upon the guidance of line police supervisors in following laws and departmental procedures, this exam reflects the areas of laws, procedures, and practices related to evidence gathering and arresting offenders. The tests reflect the need for practical knowledge of applying theory to likely situations. The six books that are suggested for test preparation are the source books for the questions and answers. The source books are up-to-date and excellent test preparation books. The examples used in the test questions are clearly stated and examples appear common to everyday police work. Even though police departments are fairly uniform in their application of law and proper procedures, assembling and using a norm group to determine cutoff scores and report on items such as gender and race differences, if any, may not be appropriate for all police departments because of the varying sociopolitical demands among independent departments across the country. But, it does appear that the tests have captured the essence of both basic law and procedural knowledge needed in competently supervising police work.

However, because it is imperative to meet testing standards (Kline, 2000), additional reliability and validity studies need to be performed on these tests. Test-retest and split-test reliability levels should be determined, as well as additional concurrent and predictive validity levels. Fundamental to these investigations would be to differentiate between needed achievement-levels of newly hired police supervisors and longer term supervisors who have benefited from on-the-job supervision.

SUMMARY. The PSUP 1.1, 2.1, and 3.1 Police Supervisor Tests are thoroughly founded in the practical application of police supervision theory to actual police work. These tests are a work in progress, which can benefit from additional confirmation of its applicability to police promotional processes. Many of the individual test items have been tested, refined, and updated over the years. It appears that the test can be of significant use for assessing achievement levels in knowledge of police supervision work. The three tests are recommended for use in police departments that are attempting to improve the work relevance and objective measurement of police supervision promotional criteria.

REVIEWER'S REFERENCE

Kline, P. (2000). *Handbook of psychological testing* (2nd ed.). London: Routledge.

[103]

PsychEval Personality Questionnaire.

Purpose: "Measures both normal personality and pathology-oriented traits to provide a multidimensional profile of the individual."

Population: Ages 16 and over; adults.
Publication Dates: 2002-2007.
Acronym: PEPQ.
Administration: Individual or group.
Price Data, 2010: $84 per interpretation introductory kit including manual (2006, 133 pages), test booklet, answer sheet, and pre-paid mail-in processing certificate; $59.75 per manual; $24.75 per 10 reusable test booklets; $22.25 per 25 answer sheets; publisher scoring rate varies by quantity ($24.25 to $36 per report); $83 per Protective Services Report Plus introductory kit including manual (2007, 116 pages), questionnaire, answer sheet, and pre-paid mail-in report processing certificate; $59.75 per Protective Services Report manual; $23.50 to $35 per Protective Services Report Plus (volume discounts available).
Time: (75-90) minutes.
Comments: Computer administration and scoring available; Reports: Protective Services Report Plus available for post-offer selection and fitness for duty evaluations for personnel in high-risk, public safety professions; PEPQ Interpretation available for use in both personal and vocational counseling.
Authors: Raymond B. Cattell, A. Karen S. Cattell, Heather E. P. Cattell, Mary T. Russell, and Scott Bedwell.
Publisher: Institute for Personality and Ability Testing, Inc. (IPAT).

a) RESPONSE STYLE INDICES.
Scores, 3: Impression Management, Infrequency, Acquiescence.
b) NORMAL PERSONALITY SCALES.
Scores: 16 Primary Factors: Warmth, Reasoning, Emotional Stability, Dominance, Liveliness, Rule-Consciousness, Social Boldness, Sensitivity, Vigilance, Abstractedness, Privateness, Apprehension, Openness to Change, Self-Reliance, Perfectionism, Tension; 5 Global Factors: Extraversion, Anxiety, Tough-Mindedness, Independence, Self-Control.
Comments: Items and norms from the 16PF Fifth Edition (T7:2346).
c) PATHOLOGY ORIENTED SCALES.
Scores, 12: Psychological Inadequacy, Health Concerns, Suicidal Thinking, Anxious Depression, Low Energy State, Self-Reproach, Apathetic Withdrawal, Paranoid Ideation, Obsessional Thinking, Alienation and Perceptional Distortion, Thrill-Seeking, Threat-Immunity.
d) INDICES.
Scores, 4: Quick-Eval, Depressive Characteristics, Distorted Thought Patterns, Risk-Taking.
e) OCCUPATIONAL INTEREST SECTION.
Scores, 6: Realistic Theme, Investigative Theme, Artistic Theme, Social Theme, Enterprising Theme, Conventional Theme.

Review of the PsychEval Personality Questionnaire by EUGENE V. AIDMAN, Senior Research Scientist, DSTO, Adelaide, Australia, and Visiting Professor, Kingston University, London, UK:

DESCRIPTION. Practitioners familiar with the 16PF and IPAT's range of factor-analytically derived instruments will recognize the PsychEval Personality Questionnaire (PEPQ) as an updated and enhanced version of the Clinical Analysis Questionnaire (CAQ; Krug, 1980; T7:540). As with the original CAQ, it combines normal personality assessment (with the latest edition of the 16PF forming its front end) and pathology screening (with clinical scales at the back end).

According to the test developer, the PEPQ is intended for normal personality assessment and screening for psychopathology in the contexts of (a) general clinical evaluation and clinical research, (b) counseling, (c) forensic assessment, and (d) post-offer selection.

DEVELOPMENT. Part I is the familiar 185-item self-report (16PF, 5th Ed.; Cattell, Cattell, & Cattell, 1993), and Part II contains 140 items for pathology-oriented scales that have been expanded and refined using both traditional reliability enhancement and Item Response-Theoretic scale development strategies. As with the original CAQ, all PEPQ items have a three-choice response format, with the middle choice usually representing an "uncertain" category.

Standardization of the PEPQ pathology-oriented scales has been conducted on an impressive sample of about 5,000 individuals, which resulted in substantial improvements over the original CAQ. The resulting Part II contains 12 scales; 6 comprise the Depressive Characteristics Index (Health Concerns, Suicidal Thinking, Anxious Depression, Low Energy, Self-Reproach, and Apathetic Withdrawal); 5 were developed on the basis of an item pool derived from a factor analysis of the MMPI to make up the Distorted Thought Patterns Index (Paranoid Ideation, Alienation and Perceptual Distortion, and Obsessional Thinking) and the Risk-Taking Index (Thrill-Seeking and Threat-Immunity scales); the Quick Eval Index contains 1 scale (Psychological Inadequacy).

TECHNICAL. Psychometric properties of the PEPQ Part I are well known–they can be found in the numerous reviews of the 16PF, 5th Edition. The rest of this review will focus on the PEPQ Part II. The *reliability* of the PEPQ's pathology-oriented scales was evaluated on a general population sample

(N = 1,763) and a clinical sample (N = 529). Estimates for the general population range from .68 to .87, with a mean of .79 and standard deviation of .07. Internal consistency estimates reported in the manual are slightly but invariably higher for the clinical sample.

Test-retest reliability of PEPQ pathology-oriented scales ranged from .59 to .81 for a 4-week interval (with a mean of .67, n = 67).

Validity. Evidence for the validity of PEPQ pathology-oriented scales presented in the test manual derives from (a) studies of gender, age, and race differences; (b) correlations with existing measures such as CAQ and MMPI-2; and (c) the known-group analysis.

Group (a) data reported in the test manual are largely trivial, with very few gender, age, or race comparisons exceeding the $d > .50$ criterion for nontrivial differences. Correlations between PEPQ pathology-oriented scales and the corresponding CAQ scales range between .59 and .92, indicating generally good correspondence between the two versions.

Intercorrelations between the PEPQ pathology-oriented scales range from .04 to .77 (with a good majority between .60 and .70), which indicates a considerable variance overlap between most of these scales. Unfortunately, the manual does not report any attempt to reveal latent variable structures indicated by this variance overlap. Thus, the argument for grouping the scales into depression, distorted thought, and risk-taking remains incomplete. Correlations with the MMPI-2 reported in the manual (Table 26 on p. 50) support *convergent validity* of PEPQ's depression cluster by consistently higher correlations between this cluster's scales and MMPI's Depression/Psychasthenia complex relative to MMPI's Paranoia/Schizophrenia scales. The same correlational evidence for PEPQ's Distorted Thought Patterns cluster is not as convincing: Scales in this cluster correlate equally well with MMPI's Depression/Psychasthenia complex and their MMPI equivalents–Paranoia/Schizophrenia scales. Further, almost all PEPQ's pathology scales (except the risk-taking pair) showed correlations ranging between .45 and .66 (N = 132) with MMPI's Infrequency and Correction scales, which indicate their significant contamination by impression management and jeopardizes their *discriminant validity*.

The known-group analysis was conducted by identifying DSM diagnostic groups (Tier I and Tier II) within the clinical sample (N = 529) by experienced CAQ users and treating mental health professionals and comparing PEPQ profiles for these diagnostic groups. The ad hoc nature of these groups and large variation in their size (from n = 189 for Depressive Disorder to n = 7 for Bipolar II and Paranoid) do not amount to a convincing argument for construct validity of the PEPQ's individual, pathology-oriented scales. In particular, although generally confirming the expected trends in the directions supporting *convergent validity* of PEPQ pathology-oriented scales, the test manual does not discuss issues *of discriminant validity*–an important omission, especially given the subscale overlap mentioned above.

Protective Services Reports. An important new feature of the PEPQ is Protective Services Reports (PSRs) of Emotional Adjustment, Integrity/Control, Intellectual Efficiency, and Interpersonal Relations. These four dimensions are composites of 16PF (5th ed.) primary factors identified earlier (IPAT Staff, 1987), but with new factor weights empirically derived during PEPQ development. Simultaneous reliability estimates for these linear composites, computed from the known reliabilities of 16PF (5th ed.) primary factors, range from .76 for Emotional Adjustment to .89 for Interpersonal Relations. Temporal stability of the composites is also impressive, with 7-month test-retest correlations ranging from .71 to .83. Evidence of the PSR's validity is not as compelling, however. Intercorrelations among PSRs indicate substantial variance overlaps between the dimensions, raising doubts about discriminant validity that are not addressed in the manual. For example, correlation between Integrity/Control and Emotional Adjustment is .64 for the PEPQ sample and .54 for the general population sample–both are high enough to indicate a degree of convergent validity. Detailed examination of the composites reveals that only two primary factors (G and Q3) contribute to the Integrity/Control dimension, and they also happen to be a subset of the Emotional Adjustment composite. This suggests that discriminant validity between these two factors is unlikely to be supported. In fact, based on the data available to date it seems more appropriate to treat Integrity/Control as a subfactor of Emotional Adjustment rather than a separate dimension.

Further, the Protective Services sample scores are significantly higher than general population scores on all PSRs except Intellectual Efficiency.

The latter is interpreted as reflecting a lower average level of education in the law enforcement samples; the former (e.g., substantially higher Emotional Adjustment scores) as reflecting job requirements in protective services. The two interpretations are not particularly consistent with one another, which does not help clarify an intriguing observation: Is lower Intellectual Efficiency indicative of positive outcomes in protective services occupations? Similar observations are known in high-stakes military selection, when mid-range cognitive ability becomes more preferable than high-end ability. To this reviewer's knowledge, however, these observations have not filtered through into the open literature.

Criterion validity of PSRs has been examined on four different protective services samples, against a range of performance criteria. One of these samples was re-analyzed from literature and the other three represent test developer's original research. Although Emotional Adjustment shows predictable associations with positive work behaviors (r = .39) and job-specific knowledge (r = .33) among corrections officers, with completion of military security training (Cohen's d = .87), being hired for a deputy sheriff's job (d = .74), and with metropolitan patrol officers' history of disciplinary action (d = .44), the only notable associations for both Integrity/Control and Intellectual Efficiency dimensions are moderate ones (d = .55 and d = .50, respectively) with being selected for a deputy sheriff's job. Similarly, the limited support for the Interpersonal Relationships dimension comes from its associations with success in military security training (Cohen's d = .70) and with peer preference for joint service/collaboration after this training (particularly pronounced for unit commanders). Overall, with the exception of Emotional Adjustment, evidence of the PSR's criterion validity remains inconclusive.

Evidence of PSR-related criterion validity for PEPQ's pathology scales is derived from known-group comparisons: Participants from the protective services standardization sample scored consistently lower than the general population on all seven PEPQ depression scales (Cohen's ds range from .52 to .79) but much higher on Threat Immunity scale (Cohen's d = -1.07). Interestingly, no meaningful differences were observed on Thrill Seeking or any Distorted Thought Pattern scales. The same comparisons were more convincing on a more tightly defined sample of civilian police officers (N = 236) applying for peacekeeping jobs (Jones & Newhouse, 2006): The applicants scored consistently lower than either general population or PEPQ clinical sample on all PEPQ's pathology scales (except Threat Immunity scale where the pattern is reversed). Although these results are encouraging, the lack of replication is not.

COMMENTARY. The PEPQ continues the long-standing tradition of CAQ in combining normal and clinical personality assessment. With regard to the latter it leaves a lot to be desired. Although the PEPQ's clinical scales have demonstrated good reliability, evidence of their validity is rather limited. Their groupings into depression, distorted thought, and risk-taking clusters has face validity but lacks empirical support in the form of a latent variable analysis. Validation strategies deployed to date remain tentative. Known-groups validation is acceptable as an initial strategy but needs to be complemented by stronger criterion studies to support claims of criterion validity. This requirement is even more relevant in the protective services reporting applications (a key novelty of the new instrument): Demonstrating better emotional adjustment and lower levels of pathology among protective services personnel compared to the general population is not sufficient to claim PEPQ's validity for these applications–simply because the same is likely to hold true for other occupational groups (e.g., Aidman, 2007).

SUMMARY. The PEPQ appears to be a solid instrument, with a strong conceptual foundation and considerable empirical justification. However, evidence of its validity, as currently documented, is incomplete–particularly in its key application areas of selection into protective services occupations. Caution is recommended in using it as a standard clinical or selection instrument until more validation data become available.

REVIEWER'S REFERENCES

Aidman, E. V. (2007). Attribute-based selection for success: The role of personality attributes in long-term predictions of achievement in sport. *Journal of the American Board of Sport Psychology, 1, 1-18.*

Cattell, R. B., Cattell, A. K., & Cattell, H. E. P. (1993). Sixteen Personality Factor (Fifth Edition) Questionnaire. Champaign, IL: Institute for Personality and Ability Testing, Inc.

IPAT Staff. (1987). *Law Enforcement Assessment and Development Report manual.* Champaign, IL: Institute for Personality and Ability Testing, Inc.

Jones, J. W., & Newhouse N. K. (2006, October). *Normal and clinical personality profiles of international peacekeepers and team leaders.* Paper presented at the annual convention of the Military Testing Association, Kingston, Ontario, Canada.

Krug, S. E. (1980). *Clinical Analysis Questionnaire manual.* Champaign, IL: Institute for Personality and Ability Testing, Inc.

Review of the PsychEval Personality Questionnaire by FREDERICK T. L. LEONG, Professor of Psychology, Michigan State University, East Lansing, MI:

DESCRIPTION. The PsychEval Personality Questionnaire (PEPQ) is one in a long line of clinical measures such as the Minnesota Multiphasic Personality Inventory-2 (MMPI-2; T7:1655) and the Millon Clinical Multiaxial Inventory-III (MCMI-III; T7:1639). However, it is unique in two aspects. It is based on Cattell's Sixteen Personality Factor Questionnaire (16PF; T7:2346) as well as the Clinical Analysis Questionnaire (CAQ; T7:540). It consists of 185 items measuring normal personality traits derived from the 16PF Fifth Edition Questionnaire and 140 items measuring psychopathology derived from the CAQ. Second, the PEPQ is unique in combining a measure of normal personality and a measure of psychopathology. The authors of the PEPQ suggest that a flat profile on the MMPI-2 conveys little information of the individual being assessed beyond the fact that he or she does not appear to be suffering from any psychopathology. The PEPQ on the other hand can provide information on both pathology and normal traits in one relatively short instrument that requires about 75–90 minutes to complete. It was designed to be used for clinical evaluations, counseling, and forensic applications as well as clinical research.

DEVELOPMENT. Beginning in 1999, the authors of the PEPQ revised the CAQ into Part 2 of their new measure. They also incorporated the 16PF into Part 1 of their measure, representing an assessment of normal personality traits. Part 1 of the PEPQ, as a measure of normal personality, consists of the 16 personality dimensions from the Cattell 16PF, namely Warmth, Reasoning, Emotional Stability, Dominance, Liveliness, Rule-Consciousness, Social Boldness, Sensitivity, Vigilance, Abstractedness, Privateness, Apprehension, Openness to Change, Self-Reliance, Perfectionism, and Tension. Consistent with recent developments in the Five Factor Model (FFM) of personality, the PEPQ also provides five higher order Global Scales that parallel the FFM. These Global Scales consisting of Extraversion, Anxiety, Tough-Mindedness, Independence, and Self-Control, roughly overlap with Extraversion, Neuroticism, Openness, Agreeableness, and Conscientiousness of the Revised NEO Personality Inventory (NEO-PI-R; Costa & McCrae, 1992). The pathology scales of the PEPQ consist of the following: Health Concerns, Suicidal Thinking, Thrill-Seeking, Anxious Depression, Low Energy State, Self-Reproach, Apathetic Withdrawal, Paranoid Ideation, Threat Immunity, Alienation and Perceptual Distortion, Obsessional Thinking, and Psychological Inadequacy.

Through a special scoring procedure, the PEPQ is also able to provide a profile of occupational interest based on Holland's model of vocational personality type. These types include Realistic, Investigative, Artistic, Social, Enterprising, and Conventional. Holland's model is the dominant occupational classification system in the field currently and this addition to the PEPQ clearly extends its applications for the counseling domain. However, further research is needed to determine the extent to which the PEPQ derivation of Holland themes is comparable to other measures that were expressly designed as vocational interest measures.

Therefore, unlike other measures that have either followed a rational or empirical method to scale construction, the PEPQ is really a refinement of two existing instruments and a combination of those two measures into a single instrument that is useful for a comprehensive psychological evaluation of an individual. As a refinement and combination of two previous measures, the PEPQ inherits the strengths and some of the weaknesses of these two measures. A detailed review of either the 16PF and the CAQ is not possible here and the reader is referred to previous reviews of these two instruments (Guthrie, 1985; McLellan, 1995; Rotto, 1995).

Normative data for Part 1 of the PEPQ were based on a stratified sample of 10,261 individuals, whereas Part 2 was based on a sample of 1,763 individuals. When compared to the U.S. national population as reflected in the U.S. Census, both normative samples of the PEPQ tended to be younger and more educated than the national population.

TECHNICAL. The authors of the PEPQ reported good reliability and validity data for their measure. In terms of internal consistency, alpha coefficients ranged from .68 to .87 with a median value of .76 for the normal personality scales. For the clinical research sample, the alpha coefficients ranged from .73 to .91 with a median value of .82. Test-retest reliability over a 2-week period yielded coefficients that ranged from .69 to .87 across the scales with a mean coefficient of .80. The 2-month interval test-retest reliability also yielded acceptable coefficients, ranging from .56 to .79 with a mean coefficient of .70.

In terms of evidence of validity, the authors of the PEPQ conducted analyses to compare across sex, age, and racial groups. Finding only a few differences was interpreted as representing some evidence of the validity of the PEPQ. In addition, convergent validity was examined by comparing the PEPQ with the MMPI-2. The pattern of results revealed the theoretically expected convergence of scales across the two measures. Scale by scale comparisons were also conducted and revealed the expected correspondence. Further validity evidence for the PEPQ came from an analysis of diagnostic groups where raters arrived at a 90% agreement between the PEPQ clinical scale scores and the diagnoses that were provided by some of the clinicians who helped collect the clinical sample data. However, this convergence was only true for Tier 1 groups where only the primary diagnoses were used.

Response style measures are available for the normal personality portion of the PEPQ. These measures include Impression Management, Infrequency, and Acquiescence. However, it was surprising that no parallel response style measures were included for the pathological scales where faking good is more likely to occur. Instead, the authors emphasize the importance of establishing rapport as a counter to this tendency.

COMMENTARY. The authors of the PEPQ have followed standard test development procedures to construct a psychometrically sound instrument. The PEPQ also has the advantage of being based on two well-established instruments with considerable supporting empirical studies. Although providing evidence of both reliability and validity of the PEPQ, there is some concern raised regarding the normative samples for both the normal personality scales as well as the clinical scales. In having used a younger and more highly educated normative sample, questions remain as to whether social class will likely become a confound in the various applications of the PEPQ. Further research that is targeted to this question will have to determine if the PEPQ, as it is currently normed, will inadvertently classify those who are less educated and from lower social classes as either more pathological or lacking the prototypical set of "normal" personality traits.

The authors of the PEPQ have also claimed that a major advantage of their instrument is the combined measure of normal and pathological dimensions. Although this seems like a logical argument, it does require further supporting evidence. It appears that the best construct for evaluating this claim is that of clinical utility. Clinical utility refers to the ease and effectiveness of an assessment instrument as well as the usefulness of the information provided by such an instrument. In other words, having a combined measure should increase the clinical utility of the instrument above and beyond just using either a clinical measure (such as the CAQ) or a measure of normal personality (such as the 16PF). The higher clinical utility of the PEPQ as a combined measure should result in enhanced clinical decision making and/or improved clinical outcomes when the target measure is used. However, the authors of the PEPQ do not provide such evidence of the increased clinical utility of their instrument along these lines. Although clinical utility is not a traditional psychometric construct, it should nonetheless be critically evaluated if the authors of psychological tests claim that is one of the major advantages of their instrument.

A couple of other minor problems with the PEPQ include the fact that there is not a strong correspondence between several of the derived five factors and the typical measures of the FFM of personality. For example, Neuroticism in the FFM is more general than the PEPQ measure, which seems highly loaded in terms of anxiety components. Similarly, in the clinical scales of the PEPQ, there is no separate measure of depression as is typical of most clinical instruments (e.g., MMPI-2). Instead, the PEPQ equivalent of that dimension is the Anxious-Depression scale, which once again is loaded with the anxiety component. This lack of a separate measure of depression, unconfounded with anxiety, remains a problem.

SUMMARY. The PEPQ was developed as an extension and combination of two previously developed and validated measures of personality, namely the 16PF and the Clinical Analysis Questionnaire. As such it inherits most of the strengths and weaknesses of these two measures. In addition, the PEPQ's normative sample is younger and more educated that the U.S. population, which serves as a problem. The lack of response style measures for the pathological scales is also problematic. The authors claim that a major advantage of the PEPQ is that it is a combined measure of normal and pathological personality dimensions but no evidence for the increased clinical utility of this combination in a single instrument was provided.

REVIEWER'S REFERENCES

Costa, P. T., Jr., & McCrae, R. R. (1992). *Revised NEO Personality Inventory (NEO-PI-R) and NEO Five-Factor Inventory (NEO-FFI) professional manual.* Odessa, FL: Psychological Assessment Resources.

Guthrie, G. (1985). [Review of the Clinical Analysis Questionnaire.] In J. V. Mitchell, Jr. (Ed.), *The ninth mental measurements yearbook* (pp. 340–341). Lincoln, NE: Buros Institute of Mental Measurements.

McLellan, M. J. (1995). [Review of the Sixteen Personality Factor Questionnaire, Fifth Edition.] In J. C. Conoley & J. C. Impara (Eds.), *The twelfth mental measurements yearbook* (pp. 947–948). Lincoln, NE: Buros Institute of Mental Measurements.

Rotto, P. C. (1995). [Review of the Sixteen Personality Factor Questionnaire, Fifth Edition.] In J. C. Conoley & J. C. Impara (Eds.), *The twelfth mental measurements yearbook* (pp. 948–950). Lincoln, NE: Buros Institute of Mental Measurements.

[104]

Psychological Processing Checklist—Revised.

Purpose: Designed to assess processing deficits by differentiating "between learning disabilities, under-achievement and other disabling conditions" to inform intervention development.
Population: Ages 5–10.
Publication Dates: 2003–2008.
Acronym: PPC-R.
Scores, 7: Auditory Processing, Social Perception, Visual Processing, Organization, Visual-Motor Processing, Attention, Total Score.
Administration: Individual or group.
Price Data, 2010: $95 per complete test kit; $67 per technical manual (2008, 84 pages): $46 per 25 QuikScore forms.
Time: (15) minutes.
Comments: To be completed by the student's regular or special education teacher.
Authors: Mark E. Swerdlik, Peggy Swerdlik, Jeffrey H. Kahn, and Tim Thomas.
Publisher: Multi-Health Systems, Inc.
Cross References: For reviews by Bruce A. Bracken and Keith F. Widaman of the earlier edition, see 16:204.

Review of the Psychological Processing Checklist–Revised by JOYCE MEIKAMP, Professor of Special Education, Marshall University Graduate College, South Charleston, WV and JEANETTE LEE-FARMER, Associate Professor of Special Education, Marshall University Graduate College, South Charleston, WV:

DESCRIPTION. The Psychological Processing Checklist–Revised (PPC-R) is a screening device used to identify and assess classroom behaviors related to psychological processing difficulties in children from kindergarten through fifth grade. Specifically, its purpose is to provide a quick screen to aid in the identification and diagnosis of children who may have a learning disability. Consisting of 35 items, grouped into six processing categories, the entire instrument can be completed and scored in less than 30 minutes. Designed for completion by a student's regular education teacher, the rating scale may be completed by a special educator or other education professional having regular contact with the child. The test authors caution the form should be completed only by education professionals having observed the child in the classroom for at least 6 weeks.

For ease of administration and scoring, raters respond directly onto the PPC-R form; respondents react to and rate the child on a series of classroom-oriented statements related to six areas of processing abilities. Potential processing deficits are assessed in the areas of Auditory Processing, Visual Processing, Visual-Motor Processing, Social Perception, Organization, and Attention. The frequency of these specific processing behaviors are rated on a scale from 0 to 3, with 0 being *Never*, 1 *Seldom, once to several times per month*, 2 *Sometimes, once to several times per week*, and 3 *Often, once to several times per day*.

Once completed, the form itself is separated to reveal a scoring grid from which raw scores are easily generated. In addition to a total score, separate raw scores are obtained for each of the six processing scales. Via plotting of raw scores on the PPC-R Profile sheet, *T*-scores and percentile ranks are derived for the total score and six processing scales. On the last page of the QuickScore form, the assessor can compare each of the scores to determine whether or not differences are statistically significant.

DEVELOPMENT. Other than renorming, the earlier version of the Psychological Processing Checklist (PPC) and the PPC-R are indistinguishable from one another. The PPC-R is a restandardization of the PPC with expansion of the norming sample in size, geographical, and ethnic representation. The 35 items themselves from the PPC remain unchanged on the PPC-R.

Although the PPC was developed with only Illinois students, the PPC-R sample included 2,654 students from across North America with 171 of those being Canadian. Both regular education (n = 2,107) and learning disabled students (n = 606) were included. Approximately an equal number of males and females were in this sample. Apparently only 62 students from the western United States participated. Neither students nor school districts were randomly selected in the standardization process. No mention is given as to how the students or data sites were actually selected. Although the racial and ethnic diversity was increased and more representative, the test authors extended a cautionary note when the PPC–R is used with ethnically diverse groups.

Originally developed in 2003, the six processing categories were developed from the Illinois State Board of Education's (1990) criteria for identifying specific learning disabilities. As such, the PPC began in response to a local Illinois school system's desire to simplify the identification of processing deficits as a part of a multidisciplinary assessment. No mention is made in the technical manual of any theoretical basis for the PPC-R. One has to wonder with the ongoing interest in information processing models and assessment, why the test authors of the PPC-R did not provide a theoretical link.

TECHNICAL. Relative to reliability and internal consistency, in particular, strong estimates of coefficient alpha were reported for both the PPC-R scale scores and the Total Score. Reliability for the standardization sample, including regular education and students with learning disabilities, ranged from .82 to .95.

Interrater reliability also was reported, based on data collected on the PPC as early as 2001. In fact, two of the three studies cited in the technical manual were from unpublished master's theses. The third study's findings were reported at a poster session of a national convention (Kahn, Swerdlik, Swerdlik, Cody, & Dambek, 2003). Because the items for the PPC-R were not changed from the PPC, it was noted the results were applicable to the PPC-R. Correlations on the six processing scales ranged from .40 to .92. Interrater reliability values from the total score ranged from .70 to .99. All three studies rated small numbers of students (n = 30 to 36) to establish interrater reliability. In each study, 2 to 4 teachers provided ratings of the students' processing behaviors to determine interrater reliability.

Several types of validity were addressed in the technical manual. Content validity was established by having a panel of teachers and school psychologists review the PPC items and scale areas. A comparison of students with learning disabilities (n = 821) and regular education students (n = 2,385) was used to investigate known-groups validity. Results from seven separate t-tests comparing PPC-R scores indicated students with learning disabilities were rated as having significantly more processing difficulties for all six scales and the total score.

To address construct validity, a series of confirmatory factor analyses were conducted to determine whether the PPC-R measured multiple areas of processing and if individual items were strong measures of specific processing areas. Results indicated a six-factor model fit the data better than a single factor model. However, factor analyses indicated correlations between the Organization and Attention scales were 1.00. As noted by the test authors, differentiation between Organization and Attention processing difficulties could be problematic and classroom interventions based on the PPC-R should be monitored for effectiveness.

In support of convergent validity, two studies investigating correlations with intelligence tests were described. Correlations between the Woodcock Johnson Tests of Cognitive Ability–Revised (WJ-R; Woodcock & Johnson, 1989) and PPC scores were offered by the test authors in support of convergent validity. Based on data from 42 regular education children, 5 to 11 years of age, several of the correlations were significant, but not all were as hypothesized. For example, it had been anticipated the PPC Visual Processing scale would correlate significantly with WJ-R Visual Matching. Contrary to expectations, although the PPC Visual Processing correlated significantly with the WJ-R Visual Matching (-.38), it demonstrated no relationship with Visual Closure (-.03) or Picture Vocabulary (-.07).

In the second study with 30 first graders, when the PPC was correlated with the Cognitive Assessment System (CAS; Naglieri & Das, 1997) similar results in the expected direction were reported. The PPC total score correlated significantly with the CAS Full Scale score (-.41).

More recently, the test authors examined the use of the PPC-R for planning classroom interventions. Although data were collected on only three students, findings suggested the PPC-R might be helpful for academic interventions.

COMMENTARY. Like the PPC, the relative strengths of the PPC-R continue to be ease of administration and scoring, as well as its use as a quick screening device. Much of the inherent attraction of the PPC-R is its promise to aid in classroom interventions for processing difficulties and potential learning disabilities. However, research supporting its use for classroom interventions is extremely limited.

Like the PPC, the PPC-R continues to lack a theoretical basis for its development. A missing link for construct validity continues to be the theoretical basis and connections to the PPC-R.

The test authors are to be commended for expanding the norming sample in size, geographical, and ethnic representation. Despite the fact the PPC-R is a restandardization of the PPC, without changes to the actual items, one has to ask if the time has not come to expand the sphere of technical adequacy to include more recent instruments measuring psychological processing. The majority of studies investigating reliability and validity were conducted on the PPC in 2003 and prior to its original publication. Future studies could certainly, at the very least, increase the sample size and expand the populations investigated.

Moreover, investigating convergent validity with actual measures of psychological processing rather than measures of intelligence only, are warranted for future revisions. The field of psychology and education is moving in the direction of understanding how children process information rather than obtaining a standard score on a measure of cognitive functioning. Once the how is understood, classroom interventions will naturally follow.

SUMMARY. The PPC-R is a quick screening device used to identify and assess classroom behaviors related to psychological processing difficulties. Specifically, its intent is to aid in the identification and diagnosis of children who may have a learning disability. Restandardized, the PPC-R has an increased sample size, geographical, and ethnic representation. A theoretical connection and additional analyses of reliability and validity are encouraged for future revisions.

REVIEWERS' REFERENCES

Illinois State Board of Education. (1990). *Criteria for determining the existence of a specific learning disability: Recommended procedures for identification and assessment.* Springfield, IL: Author.

Kahn, J. H., Swerdlik, M. E., Swerdlik, P., Cody, H., & Dambek, L. (2003, April). *A new instrument for the assessment of and planning interventions for* learning *disabilities/processing deficits: A review of the psychometric evidence supporting the use of the Psychological Processing Checklist (PPC).* Poster presented at the annual conference of the National Association of School Psychologists, Toronto, Ontario, Canada.

Naglieri, J. A., & Das, J. P. (1997). Cognitive Assessment System (CAS). Itasca, IL: Riverside.

Woodcock, R. W., & Johnson, M. B. (1989). Woodcock-Johnson Psycho-Educational Battery–Revised. Allen, TX: DLM Teaching Resources.

Review of the Psychological Processing Checklist–Revised by TAWNYA J. MEADOWS, Assistant Professor of Pediatrics, Munroe Meyer Institute, University of Nebraska Medical Center, Omaha, NE, and NATASHA SEGOOL, Post-Doctoral Fellow, Munroe Meyer Institute, University of Nebraska Medical Center, Omaha, NE:

DESCRIPTION. The *Psychological Processing Checklist-Revised* (PPC-R) is a brief rating scale that functions as a screener for a teacher's perceptions of a student's psychological processing. The Individuals with Disabilities Education Act (IDEA) and other professional organizations define specific learning disabilities as deficits in one or more basic psychological processes that impair learning. The PPC-R was developed as a standardized measure of six of the nine processing dimensions identified by the Illinois State Board of Education (ISBE) for identification of learning disabilities. The test authors provide operational definitions for all nine processing dimensions. The PPC-R is unique in that it allows teachers to provide input on students' classroom behaviors in combination with a multisource diagnostic evaluation (e.g., intelligence tests, achievement tests, and Response to Intervention).

The PPC-R consists of 35 items in which the teacher rates students in Kindergarten through Grade 5 on a 4-point frequency scale. The use of multiple raters working as a group or individually is encouraged. Regardless of who completes the PPC-R, the rater should know the child for at least 6 weeks to ensure a valid description of the child's classroom behavior. PPC-R ratings can be completed in 15–20 minutes or less, and scoring requires an additional 10 minutes.

Raw scores on each of the six dimensions and the total score can be converted into standardized scores on a *T*-score metric and percentile ranks. *T*-scores are based upon gender norms with *T*-scores higher than 60 indicating a potential processing difficulty. In addition, percentile ranks of a sample of students in special education are provided to compare overall processing abilities. Scale difference scores also can be calculated for each possible pair of *processing* deficit areas and the total score, resulting in 21 possible paired scale contrasts to examine if there are significant differences among the processing dimensions. However, the instrument does not account for Type I error due to multiple comparisons through the use of a Bonferroni adjustment and assessors should be cautious when interpreting these differences.

DEVELOPMENT. The PPC-R is a normative update of the original PPC published in 2003. The PPC was initially developed for one Illinois school district that wanted to better identify the *processing* deficits of children assessed for learning disabilities. The initial version included 85 items distributed across nine *processing* areas, and included two forms based upon grade level (i.e., Kindergarten–5th grade and 6th–12th grade). The test authors note that the second form was eliminated because it was difficult for upper-level teachers to reach agreement on students' behaviors. Following a pilot study, the PPC was reduced to 35 items that assess six processing dimensions, including Auditory *Processing* (7 items), Visual *Processing* (7 items), Visual-Motor *Processing* (6 items), Social Perception (5 items), Organization (5 items), and Attention (5 items). Three processing dimensions were eliminated: Monitoring, Conceptualization, and Automaticity and Speed of Mental Processing. The PPC-R maintained the same items as the original version.

Most PPC-R items clearly appear to be related to *processing behaviors*; however, there are items on the instrument that may be related to physical limitations and not perceptual-motor processing difficulties. Therefore, it is unclear if the PPC-R items differentiate between behavioral deficits that result from either physical or *processing* difficulties. Additionally, some item examples appear developmentally inappropriate and were perhaps designed for Form II and were inappropriately retained, for example late for school. For younger elementary students, punctuality may be more related to parent factors than the child's ability in managing time.

TECHNICAL. The PPC-R was restandardized in 2007 to expand the standardization sample to provide greater sampling across geographic regions, racial/ethnic samples, and to increase overall normative sample size. The PPC-R was normed on 2,107 general education students and 606 special education students with learning disabilities in kindergarten through fifth grade from all regions of the United States and a small sample of students from Canada. Forty-three percent of the normative sample came from the Midwest, whereas other regions were greatly underrepresented (i.e., West, 2% and Canada, 6%). The general education sample was used as the normative sample, and the special education sample's raw scores at the 25th, 50th, and 75th percentiles were provided as a reference. The sample size was adequate and roughly equally distributed across grades, although kindergarten students were somewhat underrepresented. Gender representation was fairly even across all grade levels. The ethnicity of the general education students was representative of the U.S. population, but ethnicity was not presented as a function of gender or grade level and socioeconomic status and characteristics of the school districts (i.e., size, public or private, rural versus urban) are not reported. At times, the technical manual is unclear, with the test authors referencing different sample sizes when reporting descriptive statistics, reliability, and validity data, with some tables reporting a larger sample size than the normative sample.

An examination of the descriptive statistics of general education students across grade levels suggest that processing difficulties partially follow a developmental progression (i.e., the fewest processing difficulties were reported in fifth grade students). However, there were multiple exceptions that were not explained. Third grade students were rated as having the most processing difficulties on four of six scales. In addition, African American students were rated as having significantly more processing difficulties than either Caucasian or Hispanic students on all scales except for the Visual-Motor Processing scale. The test authors conclude that the grade and ethnicity patterns may be due in part to nonrandom sampling and corresponding confounding effects of school districts. It remains unclear whether or not these findings represent "real" differences between students at different grades and between different ethnicities.

The PPC-R had strong internal consistency for both the normative general education sample and the special education sample, with alpha coefficients ranging from .86 to .93 (Total Score .95) for the general education sample and .82 to .91 (Total Score .94) for the special education sample. Three small studies of the PPC suggest moderate to strong interrater reliability, ranging from .70 to .99 for the Total Score, with lower subscale correlations that ranged from as low as .40 to as high as .92.

Validity of the PPC-R was documented by examining for differences in *T*-test scores between students in general education versus those in special education. The two groups were found to differ across all subscales and the Total score, providing evidence of validity because students with diagnosed learning disabilities should have greater processing difficulties than general education students.

Additionally, the test authors report convergent and divergent validity on the basis of correlations between the PPC-R and two intelligence tests (Woodcock-Johnson Test of Cognitive Ability–Revised [WJ-R; Woodcock & Johnson, 1989] and

Cognitive Assessment System [CAS; Thorndike & Hagen, 1993]) and two standardized achievement tests (Iowa Test of Basic Skills [ITBS; Hoover, Dunbar, & Frisbie, 2001] and Cognitive Abilities Test [CogAT; Naglieri & Das, 1997]). Evidence for convergent validity was mixed as a result of each PPC-R subscale correlating moderately with multiple WJ-R subtests that theoretically do not involve that form of processing. For example, the Visual Processing scale correlated significantly with the WJ-R Memory for Sentences (-.31), Visual Matching (-.38), Analysis-Synthesis (-.32), and Broad Cognitive Ability (-.33) scales. Although the significant correlation between WJ-R Visual Matching was expected, the scale did not correlate significantly with two other WJ subscales that theoretically involve visual processing–Visual Closure (-.03) and Picture Vocabulary (-.07). Similarly, evidence of discriminant validity is mixed, as the WJ-R Memory for Sentences theoretically involves auditory processing rather than visual processing. Finally, the validity of the visual-motor processing and social perception scales remains largely unexamined because none of the intellectual or educational tests specifically involved tasks requiring these processes.

COMMENTARY. The test authors appear to have made significant attempts to improve the psychometric properties of the instrument compared to the last version, particularly in the form of a significant increase in the size of standardization sample and the inclusion of students outside of the state of Illinois. However, it is unclear why the test authors continue to retain a six-subscale model of psychological processing when factor analysis suggested a five-factor model given the perfect correlation between the Organization and Attention factors. Similarly, all six factors are moderately to highly correlated with one another (range .58 to 1.0). Further attention to the relationship between psychological processes should be provided within the technical manual to caution assessors from overcompartmentalizing these related processes. The PPC-R was developed as a screening instrument and for only that use should it be used. However, in the manual the case studies provided stress the use of PPC-R as providing information for intervention. No empirical support for the use of the PPC-R in guiding intervention is provided in the manual nor could any be found after a review of the literature. Therefore, further evidence of validity (e.g., instructional validity) is needed. A review of the literature was conducted and no peer-reviewed publications were found. It appears that the research involving the PPC-R has been solely in the form of a few master's theses and posters at national conferences.

SUMMARY. The PPC-R is a 35-item teacher rating form designed to screen *processing* deficits along six dimensions. The scale is quick to complete and score, allowing for comparisons between the rated student and special education sample, as well as for norm-referenced interpretation. The test authors have made significant efforts to improve the psychometric strength of the instrument, improved norm sample, and provided adequate evidence of internal consistency and interrater reliability, but validity evidence is somewhat less supportive. Its weaknesses include items that that may involve multiple processes, unexplained variation in scores across grade levels, and developmentally inappropriate examples. For its intended purpose as a screening device to identify possible bases for learning disabilities, the PPC-R appears to be a useful option.

REVIEWERS' REFERENCES

Hoover, H. D., Dunbar, S. B., & Frisbie, D. A. (2001). Iowa Tests of Basic Skills. Itasca, IL: Riverside Publishing Company.

Naglieri, J. A., & Das, J. P. (1997). Cognitive Assessment System (CAS). Itasca, IL: Riverside Publishing Company.

Thorndike, R. L., & Hagen, E. P. (1993). Cognitive Abilities Test. Itasca, IL: Riverside Publishing Company.

Woodcock, R. W., & Johnson, M. B. (1989). Woodcock-Johnson Psycho-Educational Battery–Revised. Allen, TX: DLM Teaching Resources.

[105]

PsychProfiler.

Purpose: Assists in the "identification and treatment of disorders in children, adolescents and adults."

Scores, 54: 22 "Positive Screen Cutoff" conclusions (YES/NO) per population level: Generalised Anxiety Disorder, Obsessive-Compulsive Disorder, Post-Traumatic Stress Disorder, Attention-Deficit/Hyperactivity Disorder (Hyperactive-Impulsive Type, Inattentive Type, Combined Type), Conduct Disorder, Oppositional Defiant Disorder, Expressive Language Disorder, Mixed Receptive-Expressive Language Disorder, Phonological Disorder, Dysthymic Disorder, Anorexia Nervosa, Bulimia Nervosa, Disorder of Written Expression, Mathematics Disorder, Reading Disorder, Asperger's Disorder, Autistic Disorder, Tic Disorder-Motor, Tic Disorder-Vocal, Tourette's Disorder; 1 additional conclusion unique to Child and Adolescent level: Separation Anxiety Disorder; 4 additional conclusions unique to Adult level: Panic Disorder, Specific Phobia, Major Depressive Disorder, Antisocial Personality Disorder; 1 "Reliability Measure" per form per population level (Parent-Report, Self-Report, Teacher-Report [Child and Adolescent]; Self-Report, Observer-Report [Adult]).

Administration: Group.
Price Data, 2008: A$775.01 per Adult PsychProfiler (APP) Kit including manual (2007, 174 pages), APP software, 10 APP Self-Report Forms, and 10 APP Observer-Report Forms; A$795 per Child and Adolescent PsychProfiler (CAPP) kit including manual, CAPP software, 10 CAPP Parent-Report Forms, 10 CAPP Self-Report Forms, and 10 CAPP Teacher-Report Forms; A$1,385 per complete kit including APP kit and CAPP kit; A$59.50 per 10 APP Self-Report Forms; A$59.50 per 10 APP Observer-Report Forms; A49.50 per 10 CAPP Parent-Report Forms; A$49.50 per 10 CAPP Self-Report Forms; A$49.50 per CAPP Teacher-Report Forms; A$495 per APP software; A$495 per CAPP software; A$199.95 per manual.
Comments: Available for computer or paper-and-pencil administration; software is Windows compatible.
Authors: Shane Langsford, Stephen Houghton, and Graham Douglas.
Publisher: Australian Council for Educational Research Ltd. [Australia].

a) CHILD AND ADOLESCENT PSYCHPROFILER.
Population: Ages 2-17.
Publication Dates: 1999-2007.
Acronym: CAPP.
Forms, 3: Parent Report, Self-Report (only administered to children ages 10+), Teacher-Report.
Time: (15) minutes per form.
Comments: Formerly called Child and Adolescent Disorder Screening Instrument (CADSI).

b) ADULT PSYCHPROFILER.
Population: Ages 18+.
Publication Date: 2007.
Acronym: APP.
Forms, 2: Self-Report, Observer Report.
Time: (25) minutes per form.

Review of the PsychProfiler by MARK E. SWERDLIK, Professor of Psychology, and W. JOEL SCHNEIDER, Assistant Professor of Psychology, Illinois State University, Normal, IL:

DESCRIPTION. The PsychProfiler is a collection of rating scales that serve as screening tools for the assessment of a large number of the most common mental health disorders of children, adolescents, and adults. Those clients who meet screening criteria then require follow-up or extensive diagnostic assessment and formal diagnosis. More specifically, the test authors suggest that use of the PsychProfiler can facilitate early identification and intervention by providing objective and reliable data, lead to a more efficient use of interviewing time, improve the process of differential diagnosis by differentiating between various disorders that share common characteristics and assist with the diagnosis of co-morbidity, lead to improved communication particularly with regard to sensitive issues with parents and clients, be used for the evaluation of the effectiveness of particular interventions, and result in improved referral services.

The PsychProfiler comprises two rating scale systems based on age. Items included in the forms that comprise these two systems represent restatements of the DSM-IV diagnostic criteria specified for each of the disorders. One system, the Child and Adolescent PsychProfiler (CAPP), represents a revision of the Child and Adolescent Disorder Screening Instrument (CADSI) and includes a self-report form (SRF) administered to children older than 10 and a parent report form (PRF) each comprising 111 items, and a teacher report form (TRF) consisting of 91 items. The CAPP is appropriate for children and adolescents ages 2–17 years and screens for 20 of the most common disorders of childhood and adolescence based on DSM-IV criteria. The Adult PsychProfiler (APP) is administered to adults ages 18 and older, and includes both a self-report form (SRF) with 190 items and an observer report form (ORF) composed of 190 items. The APP screens for 23 of the most common mental health disorders in adults and is also based on DSM IV criteria.

The test authors propose that special qualifications are not required to administer the PsychProfiler as it represents a screening instrument and not a diagnostic tool. Those interpreting the rating scales should have mental health training such as psychologists and psychiatrists. The examiner can either read the instructions to the rater or have the rater read them from the rating form.

The CAPP requires approximately 15 minutes for raters to complete and can be administered individually or in a group such as in a classroom (for the SRF). The APP can be completed in approximately 25 minutes. Differential times were not provided for each individual rating scale (e.g., self-report vs. parent form).

The PsychProfiler includes both paper-and-pencil and computer-based administration options in which the examinee can respond to each item that is presented individually on-screen and use a mouse to respond using a Likert scale. No data are presented investigating the equivalency of the paper-and-pencil versus computer-administered formats for either the CAPP or APP. Using the scoring and interpretation software provided with the PsychProfiler, reports can be generated as hard copies or saved as PDF or RTF files. Currently only a PC version of the software program is available but a Macintosh version may become available in the future.

The appendices of the test manual include examples of the adult and child/adolescent reports generated by the software as well as the complete software manuals, including depictions of computer screens for computer administration, for both the CAPP and APP. Data can be entered from completed pencil-and-paper forms into the PsychProfiler software program in about 5 minutes. An option also exists for forms completed as part of large scale testing programs to be mailed to a designated social research company (in Australia) that will enter the data, produce reports, and return within 5 days. However, the length of time to provide the reports for test users in the United States is not specified.

Ratings are made based on the frequency of various behaviors. The Likert Scale options of *Never*, *Rarely*, *Sometimes*, *Regularly*, *Often*, and *Very Often* are recoded as *Never* = 0, *Rarely* = 0, *Sometimes* = 0, *Regularly* = 1, *Often* = 1, and *Very Often* = 1 (for a few more serious behaviors and low frequency behaviors, *Sometimes* is recoded as a 1 not 0). "These values were chosen because although many people with and without disorder may exhibit similar behaviors, it is the frequency of the behavior" (manual, p. 46) that is critical to diagnosis. Summing items within each disorder yields a screening score. Scores above the respective cutoff score indicates a "positive screen" for that particular disorder. The software generates a report that includes which disorders the client was rated as a "positive screen" and from which form; an "identification of which specific items led to the positive screen cutoff" (manual, p. 46) being reached, and the total number of positive screens that were reported by each rater. For each form, the reliability statistic, Omega, must be higher than .07 for results to be considered reliable. The Omega statistic serves as a validity check by identifying respondents who answered the scale in a random or logically inconsistent manner. Respondents with low Omega statistics may not have given valid answers to the questions. Although the use of Omega seems reasonable in this instance, no empirical data were presented to support the use of the Omega statistic.

In the current form of the measure, the scoring metric boils down to a binary response form (0 or 1). Thus, the Omega statistic is simply the proportion of item pairs in disagreement subtracted from the proportion in agreement. This statistic has some well-known flaws. Specifically, the statistic is inflated whenever one of the response categories is less frequently endorsed (Cohen, 1960), as may be the case with psychiatric symptoms. Until evidence supporting of the use of Omega is produced, its value is not known with precision and must be used with caution.

The primary interpretations resulting from ratings from the PsychProfiler includes whether or not the client exhibits behaviors at such a level of intensity (frequency) as to suggest the need for further assessment or follow-up related to a particular disorder; provides information as to differential diagnosis between disorders that share similar symptoms such as anxiety and depression; and to assess for co-morbidity of disorders. Examples of further assessments and follow-up for particular disorders or combinations of disorders are provided as part of the case studies as are illustrations of the steps in interpretation. Examples of follow-up assessment include clients being asked to expand upon their ratings for particular items as part of clinical interviews, administration of additional more narrow band rating scales (e.g., Beck Depression Inventory for those who have "positive screens" for depression), and other cognitive, educational, or personality tests.

DEVELOPMENT. Test development occurred over the course of several decades and began with the publication of a previous version of the CAPP, the Australian Child and Adolescent Screening Inventory, which was based upon the doctoral dissertation of one of the test authors, which was then revised and renamed as the Child and Adolescent Disorder Screening Instrument (CADSI). As part of the revision process for the PsychProfiler, additional wording changes were made to the CADSI to clarify language and the scale was extended from a 4-point Likert scale to a 6-point scale. The instrument was developed through a series of studies to first determine which child and adolescent disorders to include in the CADSI. These studies sampled teachers and a small number of school psychologists then cross-validated the list generated with a larger sample of school psychologists (72 corresponding to a return rate of 53%) who rank ordered the most common referrals. The researchers determined relative prevalence "by summing the cross product of the number of school psychologists assigning each rank by the value of the rank" (manual, p. 29). These development studies were limited in sample size and generalizability (all occurred in Western Australia). No cross validation studies occurred in different geographical regions outside of Western Australia. The test authors then focused on the construction and validation of the CADSI, to identify the 21 disorders based on the results of the surveys of teachers and school psychologists. The items constructed were composed of expanded wording of DSM-IV disorder criteria. Items were also adapted from other rating scales and seven items were randomly selected and reworded to assess rater reliability.

Item readability statistics were generated by Microsoft Word. The readability statistics take into account objective features of the text such as words per sentence, syllables per word, and so forth. The Flesch-Kincaid Grade Level for the CAPP is 4.6 and for the APP it is 8.1. As is the case for most rating scales, no empirical studies of children's and adults' understanding of the text of the items is presented. After many years of use, the test authors note that the CADSI underwent some refinement including wording changes to further improve reliability and validity and was renamed the Child and Adolescent PsychProfiler in 2007.

The adult rating scale (APP) represents an upward extension of the child/adolescent form and is theoretically, conceptually, and developmentally similar to the CAPP. However, no test development activities were conducted or described specifically in the test manual for the APP.

TECHNICAL. There are no comparison groups (standardization sample) for either the child/adolescent or adult scales. Rather, screening cutoff criteria for each of the disorders was based on those specified in the DSM-IV.

The test authors note that in order to ensure the validity and reliability of the PsychProfiler, its first version was subjected to a series of rigorous psychometric analyses over the past 8 years. Reliability studies were limited to interrater reliability. Specifically for the CAPP, reliability was assessed using agreement across seven repeated items and pair-wise agreement in ratings between three groups of raters (self-report, parent, and teacher) for 823 students in Years 5, 7, 9, and 11 and ages 10–18 from four government primary schools and six secondary schools from diverse areas. Another interrater reliability study was conducted using both the adult and child/adolescent rating scales. Matching forms were used for participants who completed them in a clinical setting. For the APP, 46 participants had their matched forms (self-report and observer-report). "For the CAPP, 40 participants had three matched forms (i.e., self-report, parent-report, and teacher-report)" (manual, p. 43).

Although interrater reliability was described by the test authors as "very high" for both adults and children, the method of determining the reliability of the test was unusual and difficult to interpret. For each pair of raters, all the matched 6-point item pairs were correlated for each individual respondent. This procedure has several flaws. The correlations can be inflated simply due to the variability of endorsement rates. In addition, the Pearson correlation coefficient used is not appropriate for ordinal data, as noted previously in the test manual itself. Most problematic, this procedure does not inform the user about the reliability of the measure at the proper level: the scale. It may be of passing interest to note the average reliability of an item. However, most clinical decisions are made at the level of scales. No attempt is made to clarify how reliable any of the scales are (or better yet, the reliability of the decision-rule that tells the user whether to investigate the problem more systematically).

Construct validity was assessed by having the scale completed by children and adolescents who were formally diagnosed by pediatricians and then assessing the sensitivity of the instrument for each disorder by comparing the formal clinical diagnosis of each child with the screening cutoff for that disorder based on DSM IV criteria. There also was no investigation of these cutoff scores using independent samples.

Content validity evidence included that the items were based on the diagnostic criteria of the DSM-IV; items were also adapted from the Child Symptom Inventory-4 and were compared to other rating scales (Adolescent Symptom Inventory-4, ASI-4). In order to ascertain that items were appropriate for their intended age range, two primary school principals, without mental health training, were asked to identify items they thought included inappropriate content for young children. Several items were identified including those relating to forced sexual activity, breaking and entering, and deliberate lighting of fires. Using a small sample of 9–10-year-old Australian pupils, a readability analysis was also conducted on the CADSI, including computerized analysis of items and focus groups identifying the most difficult words to understand. A readability analysis was also conducted on the APP. Results indicated that the rating scale is appropriate for adults with a reading level of Year 9 and above. Australian law mandates compulsory schooling though Year 10 so the APP is appropriate for most adults in Australia. However, the appropriateness of the APP for many U.S. adults with reading levels below this level is more questionable.

For any screening test, evidence of sensitivity (Schaughency & Rothlind, 1991) is critical and can be measured by the percentage of true positives and negatives. Weaker evidence of the sensitivity of the CADSI, which can be applied to the CAPP, was presented and included comparing the rates of agreement of screening decisions (i.e., positive screens) based on parent and self-rating scales and diagnoses of Australian pediatricians for restricted samples (i.e., limited age ranges of ages 10–17 and geographically limited to Australia). Further validity evidence presented includes the prevalence rates from these validity studies being compared to those presented in the DSM-IV manual. Overall, sensitivity for the parent form (72% agreement) was satisfactory whereas the self-report form is weak (only 50% agreement). Some diagnostic categories reached 100% agreement and others had extremely low sensitivity. Limited validity data are provided for different cultural groups and for the evidence that is provided, limited descriptive information about the sample is available. No additional reliability or validity studies are provided for the adult scale (APP).

COMMENTARY. The PsychProfiler is easy to administer, either by raters completing scales using pencil and paper or computer administered, scored, and interpreted. It allows for a multisource assessment by including forms for the client (for ages 10 and older), parent, observer, and teacher to complete. The PsychProfiler covers a wide age range with a child/adolescent rating system (CAPP) for children and adolescents ages 2–17 and an adult system (APP) appropriate for ages 18 and older. Some item vocabulary may make use in the United States more questionable.

Reliability and validity evidence for the CAPP is based primarily on previous versions of the rating scale (CADSI) and limited evidence is available for the APP. Of the reliability and validity data presented for both scales, the reliability (only interrater reliability) and validity study criteria are weak. Sample sizes were small and drawn from geographically restricted areas with questionable generalizability to the United States and perhaps even Australia itself. Item development and positive screen cutoffs are based on DSM-IV diagnostic criteria.

SUMMARY. The PsychProfiler consisting of both adult (APP) and child/adolescent (CAPP) systems and multiple forms (self-rating, observer, parent, and teacher) is easy to administer, score, and interpret. The use of the PC software, included with the purchase of the PsychProfiler test kit, facilitates the administration, scoring, and interpretation process. The validity evidence for the stated purposes such as screening and determining the effectiveness of intervention program are both limited in terms of scope and generalizability for use with individuals in the United States and perhaps parts of Australia as well. Limited reliability and validity information to support the intended uses of the PsychProfiler does not justify its use, as better options do exist.

REVIEWERS' REFERENCES

Cohen, J. A. (1960). A coefficient of agreement for nominal scales. *Educational and Psychological Measurement, 20,* 37–46.

Schaughency, E. A., & Rothlind, J. (1991). Assessment and classification of attention deficit hyperactive disorders. *School Psychology Review, 20,* 187-202.

[106]

Report Completion Exercise for Firefighter, Police Officer, and Correctional Officer.

Purpose: "Video-based test designed to assess observation and listening skills as well as written communication skills."

Population: Candidates for entry-level firefighter, police officer, and correctional officer positions.

Publication Date: 2005.

Scores: Total score only.

Administration: Individual or group.

Price Data: Price data available from publisher (administration fee is waived if ordered with another testing product).

Time: (30) minutes.

Comments: Departments choosing to administer one of the tests must develop their own scoring criteria with the assistance of scoring guidelines provided by publisher; administered via videos; joint technical report available for all three tests.

Author: International Public Management Association for Human Resources.

Publisher: International Public Management Association for Human Resources (IPMA-HR).

a) FIREFIGHTER REPORT COMPLETION EXERCISE.

Population: Entry-level firefighter candidates.

Publication: 2005.
Acronym: F-RCE.
b) POLICE OFFICER REPORT COMPLETION EXERCISE.
Population: Entry-level police officer candidates.
Publication: 2005.
Acronym: P-RCE.
c) CORRECTIONAL OFFICER REPORT COMPLETION EXERCISE.
Population: Entry-level correctional officer candidates.
Publication: 2005.
Acronym: C-RCE.

Review of the Report Completion Exercise for Firefighter, Police Officer, and Correctional Officer by CHOCKALINGAM VISWESVARAN, Professor, Department of Psychology, Florida International University, Miami, FL:

DESCRIPTION. The Report Completion Exercise is designed to assess written communication, observation, and listening skills. Videotaped scenarios are presented to the test-takers and different scenarios are developed for the three firefighter, police officer, and correctional officer jobs. For firefighter and police applicants, scenarios are depicted that would typically arise in each of the public safety areas. The test publisher provided copies of one evaluation report form for each job along with a technical manual for evaluation. The forms include (a) a cover page, (b) a page where factual information (e.g., names of parties, vehicle number) can be noted, and (c) blank pages for the test taker to write a summary report. Test takers are allowed to take notes while viewing the videotapes. The manual provided merely states that scoring guidelines are provided but the description of the test provides a statement that the departments choosing to administer one of the tests must develop their own scoring criteria. It is also reported that the administration of this measure can be either individual- or group-based, and that the total time allotted is 30 minutes.

DEVELOPMENT. The videotapes were developed based on careful job analysis. For the police officer test, the frequency and importance of 122 police officer job tasks were evaluated by incumbents. The job analysis panel also evaluated 13 police duties in terms of (a) what percent of time was spent on each, and (b) how important each was to perform correctly. Next, the job analysis panel reviewed 21 knowledge, skill, ability, and personal characteristics (KSAPs) and rated how important each was for successfully performing the job of a police officer. Finally, the KSAPs were rated as to their importance for the 13 duties. A similar strategy was used with firefighter and correctional officers. For all three jobs, the three KSAPs—observation, listening, and written communication—were deemed important and videotaped scenarios were developed for their assessment.

TECHNICAL. The technical report presents evidence of a survey-based job analysis that was performed to support the content validity of the examination. This job analysis includes information on Task Frequency; Time Spent; Importance; Knowledge, Skills, and Abilities Needed; and the perceived linkages between the knowledge, skills, and abilities on one hand and the job duties on the other. These data were presumably used to support the use of the exercises for selecting candidates for the target jobs. The technical manual provides no other validity information (i.e., criterion-related validity), and it provides no reliability or norming data.

COMMENTARY. This reviewer believes that considerably more information should be made available than is currently provided in the technical manual. Comments are organized below in three sections. First, comments on the job-analytic information are presented. Second, some of the additional technical data that should be gathered in the coming years are identified. Finally, some general comments on these assessments are made.

In presenting the job-analysis data, the report mentions that originally ratings were obtained from 569 officers on duty time spent, importance, task frequency, and importance of KSAPs. It is also stated that the lists of duties, tasks, and KSAPs were developed from job descriptions, observation, interviews, etc. More information on how these lists were compiled would be useful in the technical report. The test publisher suggests that more detailed information on job analysis is available in other reports that they did not make available to this reviewer. The manual gives a breakdown of the panelists based on demographic data (e.g., gender and race) but it should be made clear whether there were group differences in importance or criticality ratings.

Second, information on what guidelines are provided to individual departments to develop scoring guides should be included. The reliability of the scores across scorers, time, etc. needs to be provided. More importantly, the correlation between these scores and job performance assessments are needed. Also necessary are data on demographic group differences to check for bias and adverse impact, especially if these tests are used in high-stakes employment decisions. Furthermore, if the test is to measure three skills (listening, observational, and written communication), the total score should be supplemented with three-dimensional scores, and evidence of discriminant validity across the four scores should be provided.

Finally, given the description of the tests, it appears that they measure language ability as much as writing, listening, and observational skills. In this reviewer's opinion, the description of the test also suggests a high component of general mental ability. Revisions of the manual should provide the correlation between these scores and measures of general mental ability. In fact, evidence that these tests have incremental validity over general measures of ability would enhance the applicability of the tests.

SUMMARY. Assessing written communication, observational, and listening skills in police officer, firefighter, and correctional officer applicants is important. The tests present a good initial attempt and it is hoped that over the years the necessary technical data will be accumulated.

[107]

Resiliency Scales for Children & Adolescents.

Purpose: Designed to assess "core characteristics of personal resiliency in children and adolescents."
Population: Ages 9-18.
Publication Dates: 2006-2007.
Scores, 13: Sense of Mastery (Optimism, Self-Efficacy, Adaptability, Total), Sense of Relatedness (Trust, Support, Comfort, Tolerance, Total), Emotional Reactivity (Sensitivity, Recovery, Impairment, Total).
Administration: Individual or group.
Price Data, 2009: $99 per complete kit including manual (2007, 183 pages) and 25 combination scales booklets; $64 per 25 combination scales booklets; $47 per manual.
Time: (10-25) minutes.
Comments: A downward extension of the Resiliency Scales for Adolescents.
Author: Sandra Prince-Embury.
Publisher: Pearson.

Review of Resiliency Scales for Children and Adolescents by CHRISTOPHER A. SINK, Professor, School Counseling and Psychology, Seattle Pacific University, and NYARADZO H. MVUDUDU, Associate Professor, Educational Research, Seattle Pacific University, Seattle, WA:

DESCRIPTION. According to the test manual, the Resiliency Scales for Children and Adolescents (Resiliency Scales) are composed of three self-report questionnaires (Sense of Mastery [MAS], Sense of Relatedness [REL], and Emotional Reactivity [REA]) designed to identify resiliency factors in children and adolescents aged 9–18. The MAS has 20 items divided into three subscales: Adaptability, Optimism, and Self-Efficacy. The REL's 24 items comprise four subscales: Comfort, Support, Tolerance, and Sense of Trust. The 20-item REA scale represents three subdimensions: Impairment, Recovery, and Sensitivity. Items use a 5-point Likert scale (*never*, *rarely*, *sometimes*, *often*, and *almost always*) and require only an elementary-age reading proficiency.

Scoring procedures are relatively straightforward. Item scores for each scale are summed to yield a raw score, which is then converted into a T score (M = 50, SD = 10). T scores are compared with the relevant norm group (age groups 9–11, 12–14, 15–18 years) T scores. Higher MAS and REL T scores suggest the client has more resiliency resources and less vulnerability, whereas lower REA T scores suggest less vulnerability and more resiliency.

Two overall indices are calculated: Resource Index (RI; the mean standardized MAS and REL subscale T scores; scores range from 10–90), and Vulnerability Index (VI; REA T score minus RES T score; scores range from 20–90 for children and from 22–85 for adolescents). For developmental reasons two subscales are not interpreted for certain age groups (MAS: Adaptability subscale for 9–11 and 12–14 age groups; REL: Tolerance subscale for the 9–11 age group). Subscale raw scores are transformed into scale scores (M = 10, SD = 3, range 1–19). Based on the normal curve, T and scale scores (ss) are interpreted as *high* (e.g., $T \geq 60$, ss $\geq$ 16), *above average, average, below average* and *low* (e.g., $T \leq 40$, ss $\leq$ 4).

The Resiliency Scales are administered by trained examiners (individuals knowledgeable of and experienced in clinical assessment procedures and psychological testing). Scores aid in developing intervention plans that focus on clients' personal strengths and vulnerabilities. When group-administered, the scales are utilized for prevention screening. For younger children, the items can be read aloud. Test administration is relatively short (children, 15–25 minutes; adolescents, 9–15 minutes). Although not specified in the test manual, the time needed for scoring and interpretation seems workable even for a busy clinician.

DEVELOPMENT. The manual outlines four phases that roughly correspond with accepted scale development processes (Netemeyer, Bearden, & Sharma, 2003; Nunnally & Bernstein, 1994). The test author describes the scales' theoretical foundation, drawing from social learning theory, psychosocial theory, and developmental psychopathology. The resiliency research literature is also cited. The scales' key constructs relate to the personal attributes that contribute to a child's/adolescent's resiliency to adversity and underlying protective factors. Expert psychologists were consulted during the item development phase.

The organization and presentation of the sampling and psychometric data are inadequate. For the MAS and the REL scales, the manual discusses the pilot reliability research conducted with nonclinical (*n* = 106) and unspecified clinically diagnosed (*n* = 90) adolescent samples. To pilot the REA scale, 89 clinically diagnosed (disorders: mood, conduct, anxiety, and unspecified) and 101 nonclinical adolescents were assessed. Initial data produced adequate internal consistency (alpha coefficients) and stability coefficients (Pearson *r*s) for the Resiliency Scales.

To determine the underlying dimensionality of the scales (10 subscale scores) with younger respondents, confirmatory factor analyses with a fairly large sample (*N* = 450, age range 9–14) were conducted. The three-factor model was largely substantiated. Although the results are underreported in the manual, the items comprising the MAS, REL, and REA scales were then factor analyzed largely revealing the subscales listed above.

TECHNICAL. The scales were standardized with nine norm groups (total sample, females, males, respondents divided into four age strata). Children (*n* = 450) and adolescent (*n* = 200) standardization samples were purposively drawn from community sources (school and professional contacts). To match the general population samples, the norm group included participants (5%) with clinical diagnoses but not in treatment. Although less than ideal, the overall sample was matched to the general population on race/ethnicity and caregiver education level. There were no significant adolescent gender differences in scale and subscale scores. However, when the younger age sample was examined, significant gender effects for several scales and subscales were reported.

For each age group and gender, the three scales and two general indices were internally consistent (total sample alpha coefficients ranged from .83 to .93). However, for the 9- to 11-year age group, three subscales (Adaptability, alpha = .56; Optimism, alpha = .69; Tolerance, alpha = .68) did not meet either the .70 (Nunnally & Bernstein, 1994) or .80 (Anastasi & Urbina, 1997) threshold for adequate reliability. When the data were disaggregated by gender, the Adaptability scale (12–14 age group) failed to meet the .70 threshold (alpha = .61). The older group (ages 15–18) revealed at least passable reliability for both genders across all subscales (alphas ranged from .79 to .97). Standard errors of measurement (*T* score units) were generally small (about 2–3 for scale scores and about 1 for subscale scores).

A mean 12-day test-retest period (range = 5–61 days) was used to determine scale stability. Pearson correlations were adjusted to address the time period variability. For the 9- to 14-year age group (*n* = 49), all scale and index scores generated acceptable stability coefficients (*r*s ≥ .79). Three subscales showed low-moderate test-retest reliability (Adaptability, *r* = .62; Optimism, *r* = .68; Support, *r* = .69). Certain subscale stability coefficients for the female (Tolerance, *r* = .60; Support, *r* = .64) and male (Adaptability, *r* = .65; Sensitivity, *r* = .57) samples were also less stable. For the 15- to 18-year age group (*n* = 65), all resiliency scores yielded satisfactory test-retest coefficients (scale *r*s ≥ .86; subscale *r*s ranged from .74 to .88). Subscale stability coefficients for the late adolescent female group ranged from .71 to .94, and for the older males, *r*s ranged from .70 to .91.

To determine convergent validity and divergent validity, the Resiliency Scales were correlated with other conceptually similar instruments. For example, Reynolds Bully Victimization Scale (Reynolds, 2004) was significantly correlated to various resiliency subscales (e.g., male Sensitivity and Impairment subscale scores ranged from .48 to .64; female Adaptability, Self-Efficacy, Comfort, Trust, and Support scores ranged from -.58 to -.77). Further, the Brown ADD Scales for Children (Brown, 2001) was significantly correlated with the

Adaptability and Tolerance subscale scores. With the exception of Anxiety, Beck Youth Inventories' (BYI-II; Beck, Beck, Jolly, & Steer, 2005) Negative Affect and Behavior subscales were significantly correlated with MAS and REL (9–14-year age group, *r*s = -.31 to -.38). MAS and REL subscale scores were significantly related to the BYI-II's Self-Concept scale (*r*s =.74 and .70, respectively), as was the RI (*r* = .78). REA was correlated with the BYI-II's Disruptive Behavior, Anger, Depression, and Anxiety (*r*s = .43 to .70) scales, and the VI was significantly correlated with BYI-II's Anxiety (*r* = .36) and Disruptive Behavior (*r* = .71) scales.

For the late adolescent (15–18 years) group, using nonclinical samples as respondents, the three resiliency scales were significantly correlated to various related inventories. For example, all BYI-II Negative Affect and Behavior scales correlated with various resiliency scores (e.g., MAS: *r*s = -.51 to -.61; REL: *r*s = -.45 to -.57; REA: *r*s = .65 to .76). The Resiliency Scales' VI was significantly related to BYI-II Anxiety (*r* = .65) and Disruptive Behavior (*r* = .66) scale scores. The RI was significantly associated with the BYI-II's Anxiety, Depression, Anger, Disruptive Behavior (*r*s = -.51 to -.62), and to Self-Concept (*r* = .79) scale scores. For this older age group, the Piers-Harris Children's Self-Concept Scale (PHCSCS-2; Piers, 2002) scores also significantly correlated with various resiliency measures (e.g., MAS scale, *r* = .60; MAS subscales: Optimism, *r* = .62; Self-Efficacy, *r* = .51). Finally, the REA and REL resiliency scales and their subscale scores were significantly correlated with all scores on the Conners' Adolescent Symptom Scale: Short Form (CASS:S; Conners, 1997; e.g., REA: *r*s = .48 to .65; REL: *r*s = -.48 to -.64).

To establish criterion validity for the Resiliency Scales, various clinical samples were compared (*t* tests) to matched nonclinical groups. For the 9- to 14-year age group, the two samples were significantly different across all resiliency scores, producing relatively large effect sizes (*d*s = .67 to -1.84). However, when comparing 14 individuals with Bipolar Disorder with the nonclinical sample, nonsignificant group differences in REL scale and subscale scores were found. Similarly for the 15- to 18-year age group, the clinical and matched nonclinical groups differed across all scales and subscales (*d*s ranged from .44–2.27). For the 15- to 18-year-old sample, group (clinical [Bipolar Disorder] vs. nonclinical respondents) resiliency subscale score differences were nonsignificant.

COMMENTARY. As an intake screening tool, clinicians should find the Resiliency Scales functional for several reasons. Trained psychologists and other mental health professionals will find it easy to administer and relatively uncomplicated to score and interpret. The booklet used to graph a respondent's Resiliency Profile and VI scores should aid in intervention planning. The scales may also diminish the bias (i.e., the influence of response descriptors) inherent in self-report measures by incorporating on the response booklet acronyms and numbers rather than full labels to identify scales and subscales. Because particular items refer to activities in which respondents typically participate, the stigmatization potential may be lessened. There are multiple examples in the manual to guide the examiner through the interpretation process.

As with most new scales, this measure has significant limitations as well. For example, the factor analytic method used for subscale development was unspecified and the associated results were underreported. The range of *T* and standard scores for each clinical classification is indicated in the manual, but it is unclear if the descriptors (e.g., *high, low*) reflect actual functioning levels of clinical populations. Scale suitability with clients from underrepresented groups requires further study. Although initial psychometric outcomes were promising, the research sample sizes were far too limited to posit any firm conclusions about the scales' validity and reliability.

SUMMARY. The Resiliency Scales adopt a strengths-based approach to the clinical screening of personal resiliency and vulnerability characteristics in children and youth. Because this user-friendly measure is relatively new, its long-term psychometric properties unconfirmed, and its norms restricted, the scales should be administered and interpreted with caution by trained clinical professionals. Any definite conclusions about respondents' resiliency resources and threats to their mental health should be avoided. With additional research, this instrument may become a valuable adjunct for mental health screening and intervention planning.

REVIEWERS' REFERENCES

Anastasi, A., & Urbina, S. (1997). *Psychological testing* (7th ed.). Upper Saddle River, NJ: Prentice Hall.

Beck, J. S., Beck, A. T., Jolly, J. B., & Steer, R. A. (2005). Beck Youth Inventories—Second Edition. San Antonio, TX: Pearson.

Brown, T. E. (2001). Brown Attention-Deficit Disorder Scales for Children and Adolescents. San Antonio, TX: Pearson.

Conners, C. K. (1997). *Conners' Rating Scales—Revised technical manual.* Toronto: Multi-Health Systems, Inc.

Netemeyer, R. G., Bearden, W. O, & Sharma, S. (2003). *Scale procedures: Issues and applications.* Thousand Oaks, CA: Sage.
Nunnally J., & Bernstein, I. (1994). *Psychometric theory.* New York: McGraw Hill.
Piers, E. (2002). Piers-Harris Children's Self-Concept Scale (2nd ed.). Los Angeles: Western Psychological Services.
Reynolds, W. (2004). Reynolds Bully Victimization Scale. San Antonio, TX: Pearson.

Review of the Resiliency Scales for Children & Adolescents by JOHN J. VENN, Professor, Department of Exceptional Student and Deaf Education, College of Education and Human Services, University of North Florida, Jacksonville, FL:

DESCRIPTION. The Resiliency Scales for Children & Adolescents: A Profile of Personal Strengths (Resiliency Scales) assess significant personal characteristics associated with resiliency. The scales predict how well children and youth successfully recover from significant distress, adversity, and trauma. The age range of the scales is 9–18 years, and they may be given to individuals or to groups using a self-report format. The instrument measures resiliency using three scales: Sense of Mastery, Sense of Relatedness, and Emotional Reactivity. The Sense of Mastery scale has subscales for assessing Optimism, Self-Efficacy, and Adaptability. The Sense of Relatedness scale includes measures of Trust, Support, Comfort, and Tolerance. The Emotional Reactivity Scale evaluates Sensitivity, Recovery, and Impairment.

Administration takes about 5 minutes per scale, and the items are completed using a pencil-and-paper form in which the individual chooses one of five responses from 0 (*Never*) to 4 (*Almost Always*) for each item. The Resiliency scales are written at a third grade reading level. Available scores include *T* scores for the three global scales and scaled scores for the 10 subscales. A Resource Index score based on the Sense of Mastery and Sense of Relatedness scales may be calculated along with an overall Vulnerability Index score derived from all three scales.

The Resiliency Scales are useful in a variety of clinical settings as a screening tool for functions such as intake evaluation and as an intervention guide for treatment planning and related purposes. Because the scales are so brief, they should be used together with additional assessment data and clinical information when making diagnostic, staffing, intervention, and placement decisions.

DEVELOPMENT. The Resiliency Scales are a downward extension of the Resiliency Scales for Adolescents (Prince-Embury, 2006). The original scales were developed for youth from 15–18 years of age. A normative study was conducted with the original scales along with reliability and validity research designed to establish the consistency of the scores and the effectiveness of the instrument. When the scales were expanded to include ages 9–14, a second normative study was conducted with children and adolescents in this age group. The revised scales also introduced two overall scores: a vulnerability index and a resource index. As part of the revision process, scoring and interpretation of the scales was divided into three age ranges: 9–11, 12–14, and 15–18 years. Although the overall scoring procedures are similar for each age group, there are some differences in the scoring procedures at different age levels. For example, not all subscales are used with younger children.

TECHNICAL. Information in the manual about the process used to develop the norms is vague. The total norm sample included 650 children and adolescents. The first sample from the original scales consisted of 200 children ages 15–18. When the scales were extended downward to ages 9–14 a separate normative study was conducted with a sample of 450 children. During the norm development process this second sample was split into two age groups because significant differences were identified among the scores of children from 9–11 and 12–14 years of age. The manual describes investigations of three aspects of the reliability of Resiliency Scale scores. These included an internal consistency study and an investigation of the standard error of measurement. The coefficients in the internal consistency studies ranged from .56–.92 for the 10 subscales, from .85–.97 for the three scales, and from .93 to .97 for the resource and vulnerability indexes. The coefficients are in the acceptable range for the three scale scores and the two indexes, but they fall below acceptable levels for the subscales. As a result, examiners and practitioners should use the subscale results very cautiously, if at all, keeping in mind the poor reliability of these scores. A separate test-retest stability investigation was conducted with small groups (49 children; 65 adolescents) of children (9–14 years) and adolescents (15–18 years) who took the scales over various periods of time. Mean intervals were 12 and 8 days for the children and adolescents, respectively. The manual reports several studies evaluating the validity of Resiliency Scales scores including factor analysis, concurrent validity with five other instruments, and criterion-related validity using clinical groups of children and adolescents from the normative samples. These studies provide initial evidence regarding the reliability and validity of the instrument.

COMMENTARY. The Resiliency Scales feature straightforward administration and scoring procedures along with useful interpretation guidelines, and the instrument was designed with a great deal of flexibility. It may be used with individuals and groups, and the three scales may be used alone or in any combination. The previously noted concerns about the subscales should be taken into consideration in the interpretation and clinical application process. The norm sample may be compromised in several ways including a lack of details about the development process and the development of norms over time rather than as one unit. Despite these drawbacks, the scales have utility as a tool for estimating the capacity to overcome significant life impediments. The scales appear to be a highly effective tool for screening. They also may be used in conjunction with other data and information to develop individual psychoeducational and therapeutic interventions. The scales hold much promise for use in research studies as a vehicle for gathering further insight into the qualities and dimensions of resiliency.

SUMMARY. The Resiliency Scales are a new tool for predicting the capability of children and adolescents to rebound from major life trauma and significant adversity. The scales can be given and scored efficiently and interpreted in a flexible manner. This is valuable in the process of responding to the personal strengths and weaknesses and the varied and often unique needs of children and adolescents as they deal with significant life obstacles. Clinicians, teachers, and parents can all benefit from the data and information provided by the Resiliency Scales.

REVIEWER'S REFERENCE

Prince-Embury, S. (2006). Resiliency Scales for Adolescents: A Profile of Personal Strengths. San Antonio, TX: Harcourt Assessment, Inc.

[108]

Revised Children's Manifest Anxiety Scale: Second Edition.

Purpose: "Designed to assess the level and nature of anxiety in children and adolescents."
Population: Ages 6-19.
Publication Dates: 1985-2008.
Acronym: RCMAS-2.
Administration: Group.
Scores, 6: Inconsistent Responding Index, Defensiveness, Total Anxiety, Physiological Anxiety, Worry, Social Anxiety.
Price Data, 2008: $99.50 per kit including 25 autoscore forms, one audio CD, and one technical manual (2008, 83 pages); $44.50 per 25 autoscore forms; $59.50 per technical manual; $15.50 per audio CD; $49.50 per Spanish version including 25 English autoscore forms and 25 Spanish item sheets.
Foreign Language Edition: Spanish version available.
Time: (10-15) minutes.
Comments: The revised edition includes the addition of an inconsistent responding index.
Authors: Cecil R. Reynolds and Bert O. Richmond.
Publisher: Western Psychological Services.
Cross References: See T5:2214 (140 references) and T4:2257 (47 references); for a review by Frank M. Gresham of an earlier edition, see 10:314.

Review of the Revised Children's Manifest Anxiety Scale: Second Edition by GYPSY M. DENZINE, Associate Dean and Professor of Educational Psychology, Northern Arizona University, Flagstaff, AZ:

DESCRIPTION. The Revised Children's Manifest Anxiety Scale: Second Edition (RCMAS-2) has a long history dating back to Taylor's 1951 Manifest Anxiety Scale (MAS) that was designed to measure manifest anxiety in adults based on items from the Minnesota Multiphasic Personality Inventory (MMPI; Hathaway & McKinley, 1943). Castaneda, McCandless, and Palermo (1956) later revised the MAS to create a children's version of the scale (CMAS). After using the CMAS for more than a decade in clinical practice, Bert Richmond saw the need to make substantive changes to the CMAS. With his colleague Cecil Reynolds, Richmond and Reynolds originally presented their measure of children's anxiety in a 1978 *Journal of Abnormal Child Psychology* article. Since the Revised Children's Manifest Anxiety Scale (RCMAS; Reynolds & Richmond, 1985) became available through Western Psychological Services in 1985, the RCMAS has been extensively used by educators, psychologists, other helping professionals, and researchers for understanding and treating children's anxiety problems. According to the test authors, the RCMAS can be used to diagnosis overall anxiety in children, as well as characterize its nature. They also claim their scale can be used to determine eligibility for special education services.

The RCMAS-2 represents Reynolds and Richmond's changes in the second edition of their scale. Similar to the RCMAS, the revised scale provides a Total Anxiety score, as well as Physiological Anxiety, Worry/Oversensitivity, and the Lie subscales. The Lie scale has been renamed to the Defensiveness scale and it no longer contains double-negative worded items. Another change is the RCMAS-2 Social Anxiety subscale has replaced the RCMAS Social Concerns/Concentration scale. The RCMAS-2 contains three significant changes from its previous version. First, the test authors added an Inconsistent Responding index composed of nine pairs of RCMAS-2 items. Second, the latest version of the scale contains a 10-item Short Form for assessing anxiety in children. The Short Form is based on 3 Physiological Anxiety, 4 Worry, and 3 Social Anxiety items. A third change is the 10-item content cluster developed to measure children's performance anxiety.

Administration. The RCMAS-2 is a paper-and-pencil, 49-item self-report scale that takes respondents about 10 to 15 minutes to complete. The 10-item Short Form Total Anxiety scale can be completed in less than 5 minutes. The RCMAS-2 is most appropriate for children aged 6 to 19 and norms are available for the following stratified age groups: 6 to 8, 9 to 14, and 15 to 19.

The scale "may be administered either to an individual or to a group of respondents" (manual, p. 3). The individual responds to each answer giving a "yes" or "no" answer based on how he or she thinks and feels about themselves. The directions inform the respondent that there are no right or wrong answers.

Scoring and interpretation. The manual contains two parts: Part I–Administration, Scoring, and Interpretive Guide and Part II–Technical Guide. The manual also contains a useful Appendix of studies using the RCMAS sorted by topic listing with full citations provided in the reference section.

The scale uses the AutoScore™ Form (WPS Product No. W-467A) that is easy to use and utilizes an age-appropriate profile sheet for scoring. According to the test authors, RCMAS-2 scores are to be interpreted in a four-step process: (a) review of the validity of the responses given, (b) examination of Total Anxiety score, (c) evaluation of the scale scores, and (d) examination of the specific content of the items that have been endorsed. The RCMAS-2 contains two validity scores–the Inconsistent Responding (INC) Index and the Defensiveness (DEF) score. Validity scores are useful for determining if a respondent may have been noncompliant, careless, experiencing vision problems or other health issues, completed the items in a random manner, or attempted to answer questions in a way to look good in the eyes of others. INC and DEF scores are not available for the Short Form. The INC score is based on inconsistent responding to paired items with nearly identical content. Discordant responses are associated with an increased likelihood that the examinee responses are not valid indicators of his or her functioning. The DEF score is based on nine items that measure the extent to which the respondent willingly admits to everyday imperfections. According to the test authors, younger children may be more likely to have DEF scores of 5 or higher but we should expect low DEF scores for older children and adolescents.

Scores can be interpreted in a normative manner and the manual contains norms for several groups of individuals. For example, adjusted *T*-scores are presented separately for males and females and several ethnic groups (Asian/Pacific Islander, Black/American, and Hispanic/Latino). Norms also are presented for children and adolescents between the ages of 6 and 17–19. Norms are based on the full reference sample that contained a total of 3,086 children with approximately equal numbers of male and female respondents. The test authors obtained a standardization sample (n = 2,368) from the full reference sample (n = 3,086) that would more closely match the demographic composition of the U.S. population. Because there were no major or meaningful differences between the two samples based on different genders or ethnic groups, the test authors used the full reference sample.

DEVELOPMENT. According to the test authors, the scale maintains its original foundation in trait theory. Although brief, the manual does provide a summary of theoretical and empirical literature they relied on throughout the evolution of the RCMAS-2, including the most recent findings from studies designed to investigate the relations between brain behavior and anxiety.

The manual also provides detailed information regarding changes at the item and scale levels between the RCMAS and RCMAS-2. The test authors began the revision process by adding new items and changing the wording of some RCMAS items. In total, 40 new or reworded items were tested using a sample of 308 children and adolescents. The same group of respondents also completed the RCMAS and a version of the newly revised scale with a rating scale rather than a yes/no response option. The pilot RCMAS-2 with a rating scale used the following response options: *Never, Sometimes, Often,* and *Always*. Because the scores from the two rating scale approaches were not reliably equivalent, the test authors chose to retain the *yes/no* format so that the scale could be completed in a shorter amount of time and would be easier for young children to comprehend.

After completing typical statistical analyses, the test authors retained 33 of the original 37 RCMAS items for the RCMAS-2. Three items on the RCMAS Lie scale were reworded to eliminate the use of double-negative worded items. The four scales of the RCMAS-2 contain more items compared to the RCMAS: Total Anxiety–40 items (increased from 28 in the RCMAS); Physiological Anxiety–12 (increased from 10); Worry–16 (increased from 11); Social Anxiety–12 (increased from 7).

The raw scores were transformed using a normalization process described by Angoff (1984). Simple linear transformations of the normalized raw score distributions were performed to obtain the standard scores. As a result, the *T*-scores correspond with the same percentile ranks for the scales. For both males and females, the average *T*-score of 50 described the average scores for both groups. The small effect sizes (ranging from .07 to .18) indicate the gender differences in RCMAS-2 scale scores do not have practical significance. The only meaningful difference for various demographic groupings was the higher than average Social Anxiety scores for Asian/Pacific Islander respondents (effect size .31). There were some age differences observed, with younger children having higher amounts of self-reported anxiety and notably higher scores on the Defensiveness scale.

The Short Form scale is new to the revised instrument and yielded a .90 correlation with the full-form Total Anxiety score. The correlations between the RCMAS and RCMAS-2 ranged from .96 for the Total Anxiety scale and .88 for the Social Anxiety scale (renamed Social Concerns/Concentration scale). The test authors note the interform correlations are higher than the alpha coefficients and the test-retest reliability estimates. Therefore, the test authors suggest there is sufficient evidence to justify the claim that the RCMAS and RCMAS-2 are equivalent and the abundance of previous research conducted on the original scale can be imported to the RCMAS-2.

TECHNICAL. Evidence for the reliability and validity of the RCMAS resides in the results of many empirical studies (see Ryngala, Shields, & Caruso, 2005; Seligman, Ollendick, Langley, & Baldacci, 2004, as examples), many of which are summarized in the Reliability and Validity sections of the manual. To date, there has been little research conducted on the psychometric properties of the RCMAS-2 other than the studies conducted by Reynolds and Richmond that are presented in the manual.

Overall, the manual contains important information about the samples utilized for establishing reliability and validity of the constructs. The RCMAS-2 manual provides a thorough discussion of the appropriateness of this scale for different demographic groupings and empirical data are presented in tables for gender and ethnic groupings.

Reliability. Internal consistency reliability for the RCMAS-2 indicates the scale has content homogeneity and the alpha estimates are adequate and improved over the RCMAS. Coefficient alpha estimates ranged from .92 (Total Anxiety) to .75 (Physiological Anxiety) for the full reference sample (N = 3,086). Similar coefficient alpha reliabilities were found across different gender, age, and ethnic groups. The test authors reported adequate alpha estimates ranging from .92 (Total Anxiety) to .70 (Physiological Anxiety) in a clinical sample of children with one of the following anxiety disorders: attention deficit disorder (n = 57), autism spectrum disorders (n = 36), anxiety disorders (n = 32), depression (n = 101), oppositional defiant disorder (n = 42), conduct disorder (n = 73).

Evidence of test-retest reliability of the scales was obtained from a sample of 100 school children, who completed the RCMAS-2 on two occasions with a 1-week delay. The highest test-retest correlation was for the Total Anxiety scale (.76) and the lowest test-retest correlation was for the Short Form Total Anxiety scale (.54). The internal consistency estimates for each scale are higher than any of the scale intercorrelations, so there is empirical justification for interpreting separate scales as opposed to one global anxiety score.

The standard errors of measurement expressed as *T*-score units ranged from ±3 for Total Anxiety to ±5 for Physiological Anxiety and Defensiveness for the full reference sample.

Validity. The manual contains evidence for the establishment of content and construct validity for the RCMAS-2; however, the test authors note they mostly refer to previous empirical evidence gathered for the RCMAS. For example, they reference previous research findings demonstrating the relative stability of RCMAS scores, which provide theory-based evidence for the construct of trait anxiety. The RCMAS-2 item-to-total correlations provide evidence of sufficient item-to-construct coherence.

There is a long history of factor analytic studies that can be traced back to a study conducted in 1974 on the CMAS factor structure (Finch, Kendall, & Montgomery, 1974). The manual contains detailed information about the factor analysis procedures conducted on the RCMAS-2, which ultimately resulted in the interpretation of a five-factor solution. Similar to factor analytic studies on RCMAS scores, the Defensiveness items divided into two factors for the RCMAS-2. The clearest and most interpretable factor was the Total Anxiety scale. The Social Anxiety factor was less clear and several items had significant overlap with items on the Worry scale (correlation between the two scales was .73). The test authors chose to retain the scale structure; however, they recognize the need for future research with different samples to clarify the relations between the Social Anxiety and Worry scales.

Further evidence of the validity of the scale's scores comes from a study investigating the relations between RCMAS-2 scores and scores obtained from the Children's Measure of Obsessive-Compulsive Symptoms (CMOS; Reynolds & Livingston, in press). The CMOS contains three scales: Obsessions, Compulsions, and Outcomes (effects on everyday functioning). As predicted, the highest correlations were between the Obsessions and Total Anxiety (r = .52) and the Obsessions and Worry scales (r = .47; n = 2,550). Stronger associations were found for a clinical sample of 341 children (Obsessions and Total Anxiety, r = .73; Obsessions and Worry scales, r = .74). Similar to the RCMAS, the RCMAS-2 scores were moderately correlated with Conners' Rating Scales (CRS; Conners, 1989) for both parent and teacher ratings. The higher correlation (-.37) was found between Worry scores and CRS teacher ratings of Cognitive Problems/ Inattention.

COMMENTARY AND SUMMARY. The RCMAS-2 is straightforward in its administration, scoring, and interpretation. Overall, the manual provides sufficient evidence to demonstrate that the RCMAS-2 is a psychometrically sound measure of children's and adolescents' anxiety. Given the research to date, the RCMAS-2 can be recommended for use with children to understand and diagnosis anxiety in school-aged students.

The manual contains three brief case studies based on the following individual situations: (a) perfectionism and underachievement, (b) academic problems and family discord, and (c) Asperger's Syndrome and disruptive behavior. For each case, the test authors discuss the presenting problems, provide a detailed description of the presented RCMAS-2 profile sheet, and make specific recommendations for intervention and treatment. The test authors make the point that when considering the case studies it is imperative to recognize that high anxiety scale scores do not necessarily mean there is an anxiety disorder present. The test authors also address the necessary qualifications for who can administer and interpret RCMAS-2 scores.

The potential limitations of the RCMAS-2 may be more related to missing information in the manual rather than the psychometric properties of the scale. First, the discussion of DEF scores could be expanded to provide more information. For example, the test authors refer to concerns about "low" and "high" DEF scores but no specific values or theoretical justifications are provided for determining what is "low" or "high." Second, although the scale is available in Spanish and audio CD, the manual does not contain detailed information about the psychometric properties for these alternative forms. Nor are separate norms available for respondents who completed the Spanish or audio editions.

In conclusion, because there is 89% overlap of items between the RCMAS and the RCMAS-2, and the scale structures are equivalent, researchers and clinicians familiar with the earlier version should be pleased with the newly revised scale. The RCMAS-2 retains the strengths of the earlier scale while offering numerous improvements such as the addition of a Short Form Total Anxiety Scale and the elimination of double-negative wording in Defensiveness items. The updated norms and data from studies that provide evidence that support the interpretation of RCMAS-2 scores are notable contributions to the study of measuring anxiety in children and adolescents.

REVIEWER'S REFERENCES

Angoff, W. H. (1984). *Scales, norms, and equivalent scores.* Princeton, NJ: Educational Testing Service.

Castaneda, A., McCandless, B. R., & Palermo, D. (1956). The children's form of the Manifest Anxiety Scale. *Child Development, 27,* 317-326.

Conners, C. K. (1989). Conners' Rating Scales (CRS). North Tonawanda, NY: Multi-Health Systems.

Finch, A. J., Kendall, P. C., & Montgomery, L. E. (1974). Multidimensionality of anxiety in children: Factor structure of the Children's Manifest Anxiety Scale. *Journal of Abnormal Child Psychology, 2,* 331-336.

Hathaway, S. R., & McKinley, J. C. (1943). Minnesota Multiphasic Personality Inventory (MMPI). Minneapolis: University of Minnesota Press.

Reynolds, C. R., & Livingston, R. B. (in press). *Children's Measure of Obsessive-Compulsive Symptoms (CMOCS): Manual.* Los Angeles: Western Psychological Association.

Reynolds, C. R., & Richmond, B. O. (1978). What I Think and Feel: A revised measure of children's manifest anxiety. *Journal of Abnormal Child Psychology, 6,* 271-280.

Reynolds, C. R., & Richmond, B. O. (1985). Revised Children's Manifest Anxiety Scale (RCMAS). Los Angeles: Western Psychological Services.

Ryngala, D. J., Shields, A. L., & Caruso, J. C. (2005). Reliability generalization of the Revised Children's Manifest Anxiety Scale. *Educational and Psychological Measurement, 65,* 259-271.

Seligman, L. D., Ollendick, T. H., Langley, A. K., & Baldacci, H. B. (2004). The utility of measures of child and adolescent anxiety: A meta-analytic review of the Revised Children's Manifest Anxiety Scale, the State-Trait Anxiety Inventory for Children, and the Child Behavior Checklist. *Journal of Clinical Child and Adolescent Psychology, 33,* 557-565.

Taylor, J. A. (1951). The relationship of anxiety to the conditioned eyelid response. *Journal of Experimental Psychology, 41,* 81-92.

Review of the Revised Children's Manifest Anxiety Scale: Second Edition by MARGOT B. STEIN, Clinical Associate Professor, University of North Carolina at Chapel Hill, Chapel Hill, NC:

DESCRIPTION. The Revised Children's Manifest Anxiety Scale: Second Edition (RCMAS-2) by Cecil R. Reynolds and Bent O. Richmond is a full revision of the Revised Children's Manifest Anxiety Scale (RCMAS), a self-report questionnaire designed to assess the nature and level of anxiety in children and adolescents from 6 to 19 years. The RCMAS-2 takes 10–15 minutes to administer and may be given either individually or in a group setting. It now comprises 49 items, 12 more than on the RCMAS. Each of these items requires a *Yes* or *No* answer and is written at a mid-second grade reading level. If the child has difficulty reading, an Audio CD is available for audio presentation of the items. The RCMAS-2 yields scores for six scales: Total Anxiety, Physiological Anxiety (PHY), Worry (WOR), Social Anxiety (SOC), Inconsistent Responding Index, and Defensiveness.

Goals for revising the RCMAS were to update the standardization sample, improve the scale's psychometric properties, and broaden content coverage while retaining the brevity, elementary reading level, and content-based item clusters of the RCMAS. The test authors felt it desirable to replace the Social Concerns/Concentration scale from the RCMAS with the Social Anxiety scale and a cluster of items related to the experience of performance anxiety has been added. The RCMAS Lie scale has been renamed the Defensiveness scale and the items on the Lie scale that were confusing to students because of the double-negative phrasing have been reworded. An Inconsistent Responding Index has been added. Further changes included a 10-item Short Form, an updated and ethnically diverse standardization sample, and improved support for the interpretation of RCMAS-2 results. Qualifications for administering, scoring, and interpreting this instrument are formal course work in psychological tests and measurements, understanding of basic psychometrics that underlie test use and development, and supervised experience in administering and interpreting clinical tests. For those using the RCMAS-2 for clinical use, course work in developmental psychopathology and supervised experience in the use of personality tests in the diagnosis and treatment of childhood emotional and behavioral disorders is expected.

The test protocol includes an "AutoScore" Form with a scoring worksheet that facilitates rapid calculation of the scores. A section of the scoring instructions has a work area for calculating the Inconsistent Responding index score. Scoring for most items involves placing a check mark in a box to the right of each item for which *Yes* is circled, then tallying the check marks in each column, and entering the sum at the bottom of the scoring worksheet. The Total raw score comprises the PHY, WOR, and SOC scales only. For the Short Form, one simply counts the number of *Yes* responses for the first 10 items. The user selects the Profile Sheet corresponding to the respondent's age (e.g., 6 to 8, 9 to 14, or 15 to 19), transfers the raw score to the Profile Sheet, and records the appropriate *T*-score and corresponding percentile rank.

DEVELOPMENT. The well-written and organized manual of the RCMAS-2 provides a succinct history of the development of its predecessor, the RCMAS, and its earlier versions, the MAS (Taylor, 1951) and the CMAS (Castaneda, McCandless, & Palermo, 1956). The RCMAS was standardized on 4,972 children between the ages of 6 and 19 and its standardization sample contained 44% white males, 44% white females, 5.8% black males, and 6% black females. The sample (1985) was obtained in 13 states, over 80 school districts from all major geographic regions in the United States but was not stratified according to SES. Reliability estimates ranged from .42 to .87. It is noteworthy that no Hispanic/Latinos were included in the standardization sample. Collapsed across the 12 age levels, reliability estimates had a median of .82. Of the 48 alpha coefficients reported across age, race, and sex, 17 fell below .80, suggesting caution in using the RCMAS for these groups given the low internal consistency estimates. In addition, most of the alpha coefficients reported for the three anxiety subscales and the Lie scale fell below .80, and some far below, indicating poor domain sampling and the unreliability of individual subscales for interpretive purposes. On the other hand, the Total Anxiety score was determined to be reliable, though its stability remained an open question.

In the RCMAS most items were retained and the RCMAS-2 scales correlate highly with its predecessor. The only statistically significant score differences on the same items suggested that children and adolescents in the most recent sample seemed to describe themselves more "defensively," that is, more in the direction of socially desirable responses but reported a somewhat higher overall anxiety level than those in the 1985 sample. Several of the "never" items on the RCMAS were changed; for example, "I never get angry" became "I get angry sometimes." Six new items were added to the Worry/Oversensitivity scale and six new items to the Social Concerns/Concentration (renamed Social Anxiety scale), designed to reflect the apparent increase in social and performance anxiety of children in contemporary American society, as documented by new research. Consequently, prior research using the RCMAS should extend equally to its revision version.

TECHNICAL.

Standardization. The RCMAS-2 standardization sample included 2,368 children from the full reference sample of 3,086 children, with approximately equal males and females aged 6 to 19. Generally reflecting the U.S. population, it included 61.5% white, 17.1% Hispanic/Latino, 14.8% Black/African American, 3.5% Asian/Pacific Islander, 1.0% Native American, and 1.9% "Other." Addressing the absence of stratification according to SES for the RCMAS standardization sample, that of the RCMAS-2 included the number of years of completed education of the head of household as an index of socioeconomic status. Those who did not complete high school were oversampled (twice the percentage of the U.S. population) whereas "some college" and "college graduates" were somewhat undersampled. In terms of geographical region, the standardization sample roughly approximated percentages for the U.S. population. Raw score distributions for all RCMAS-2 scores were "normalized."

The moderator variables examined for effect on RCMAS-2 scores were gender, ethnic background, and age. Subgroups were formed to examine whether the average scores of the entire sample provided a satisfactory reference point for the performance of each subgroup. The meaningful differences found for various demographic groupings indicated that the expected mean of 50*T* characterized the scores of males and females, Asian/Pacific Islanders, and Hispanic/Latinos equally well. However, as a notable exception, the Asian/Pacific Islanders showed a higher than average Social Anxiety score, representing a moderate difference. As noted for the RCMAS, the RCMAS-2 continued to show relatively high scores on all scales for the youngest children, particularly with regard to Defensiveness, whereas adolescents continued to obtain lower scores than younger children, particularly on the Defensiveness scale.

Reliability. Reliability estimates refer to the consistency and relative accuracy with which scores taken from a measuring instrument estimate the amount of some trait or other variable that the test is intended to measure. Coefficient alpha for the Total Anxiety score (.92) of the RCMAS-2 was better than reported for the RCMAS. As with the RCMAS, the Worry/Oversensitivity subscale scores were associated with the highest subscale reliability estimates (.86). Alpha reliability estimates for other individual scales were as follows: .75 for Physiological Anxiety, .80 for Social Anxiety, and .79 for Defensiveness. Similar internal consistency estimates were obtained for groups differing in gender, age, and ethnic background, and no age trends were apparent. There was a particularly strong correlation between WOR and SOC scores. Retest reliability estimates were obtained for a sample of 100 school children who completed the RCMAS-2 once and then for a second time 1 week later. Reliability estimates ranged from .76 for Total Anxiety to .64 for Social Anxiety and a low of .54 for the Short form, though this is not surprising given its brevity and heterogeneous nature. The Standard errors of measurement varied from +/- 3 for Total Anxiety to +/- 5 for Physiological Anxiety and Defensiveness. The test authors acknowledge that, as with its predecessor, comparisons across RCMAS-2 scales in an individual protocol should be made cautiously, and "only as an aid to hypothesis generation" (manual, p. 44). As this test is a brief measure, and anxiety and its functional impact is complex, additional information is essential to render an accurate diagnosis.

Validity. Much of the information provided in the RCMAS-2 manual is taken from the RCMAS manual and the subsequent research presented in chapter 6 is related to RCMAS scores. As is its predecessor, the RCMAS-2 is derived from a theory of trait anxiety, which is distinct from state anxiety in that trait anxiety is a more lasting predisposition to experience anxiety in a variety of settings. The accompanying manual relies on correlations between the RCMAS and the State-Trait Anxiety Inventory for Children (STAIC) to examine concurrent validity and, to a lesser extent, convergent and discriminant validity. Indeed, only the STAIC State (rather than the STAIC Trait) showed an above-average score relative to the standardization sample of the various scales consisting of IQ, RCMAS, Walker Problem Behavior Identification Checklist, and STAIC. Consistent with expectations, correlations between the RCMAS-2, Children's Depression Inventory, and the Parent and Teacher forms of the Conners Rating Scales (CRS) are quite low, with the highest correlations between the Anxious-shy scale of the CRS completed by parents and the RCMAS-2 Total Anxiety scale (.34) and the Anxious-shy scale and the RCMAS-2 Worry scale (.38). Another high correlation was between SOC and the teacher report of ADHD symptoms on the CRS (.43).

Like the RCMAS, the RCMAS-2 employs a five-factor solution to describe the factor structure of the scale. The factor loadings for each of the three anxiety factors on the RCMAS-2 are only slightly higher (.32 to .58) than on its predecessor (.26 to .61).

ANOVA methodology for examining item bias based on culture/ethnicity (African American, White, other) and gender in the RCMAS-2 provided significant ($p < .001$) between and within effects. For male participants, 25 instances of item bias were identified across three ethnic groups: 9 for the White group; 10 for the African American group; and 6 for the "Other" group. Among the findings, for White male children, 5 items were identified as biased against the group and 4 biased in favor of the group. Seven items were determined to be biased against the African American males and 3 showed a bias favoring the African American male participants. For female participants, 38 instances of item bias were found: 14 for White participants, 14 for African American participants, and 10 for the "Other" participants. For both White and African American females, 8 items were identified to function in a negative manner and 6 showed a positive bias. For the "Other" female group, 7 items were negative and 3 showed positive bias. No consistent theme or similarity of content was found to occur within any group that would indicate a characteristic type of item that was likely to be determined as biased. The test authors state that the only "characteristic" of consistently biased items is that they are psychometrically weaker items, with less reliability and more ambiguity than other items.

COMMENTARY. The RCMAS-2 seems to be a well-standardized self-report measure of anxiety among children and adolescents. It uses a large and representative standardization sample and has added much-needed new demographic categories for ethnicity as well as parental educational background that provide useful information about SES. As with its predecessor, the Total Anxiety score of the RCMAS-2 is adequate for individual interpretation but the reliabilities of the anxiety subscales remain too low for separate subscale interpretation. Data on the stability of the RCMAS-2 also remain sparse and the factor analysis does not seem substantially better than that of the RCMAS. Nevertheless, the RCMAS-2 represents changes to better identify and meet the current needs of children and adolescents. Distinguishing between worry and social anxiety and including a performance anxiety cluster facilitates a more effective clinical diagnosis. Removing double negatives from some test items and renaming the "Lie scale" as "Defensiveness" reduces error through ambiguity and confusion and more closely reflects the social desirability factor it aims to measure. The new Short Form will be useful in certain situations despite its limitations.

SUMMARY. The RCMAS-2 represents a highly useful tool for a multitrait-multimethod investigation leading to accurate and effective diagnosis and treatment of the social-emotional problems of children and adolescents today. The RCMAS-2 should not be used as a stand-alone assessment of anxiety and it does not distinguish state and trait anxiety. However, the construct of anxiety has been further refined to better recognize performance and social anxiety. A large and well-designed standardization sample now includes much-needed broader demographic variables for ethnicity (Hispanic/Latino, Native American, Asian/Pacific Islander, and Other in addition to

White and Black/African American, as well as level of parental education that can serve as an indicator of SES. The revised scoring format makes administration more efficient. The RCMAS-2 manual is well-written and organized and there now is a Short Form.

REVIEWER'S REFERENCES

Castaneda, A., McCandless, B., & Palermo, D. (1956). The children's form of the Manifest Anxiety Scale. *Child Development, 27*, 317–326.

Taylor, J. A. (1951). The relationship of anxiety to the conditioned eyelid response. *Journal of Experimental Psychology, 41*(2), 81–92.

[109]

Reynolds Adolescent Depression Scale—2nd Edition: Short Form.

Purpose: "Designed as a brief screening measure for the assessment of depression in adolescents."
Population: Ages 11-20.
Publication Dates: 1987-2008.
Acronym: RADS-2:SF.
Scores: Total score only.
Administration: Group.
Price Data, 2010: $79 per introductory kit including professional manual (2008, 91 pages) and 25 test booklets; $40 per 25 test booklets; $45 per professional.
Time: (2-3) minutes.
Comments: Abbreviated version of Reynolds Adolescent Depression Scale—2nd Edition (16:211); self-report measure; may be administered aloud.
Authors: William M. Reynolds.
Publisher: Psychological Assessment Resources, Inc.

Review of the Reynolds Adolescent Depression Scale–2nd Edition: Short Form by MICHAEL G. KAVAN, Professor of Family Medicine and Professor of Psychiatry, Associate Dean for Student Affairs, Creighton University School of Medicine, Omaha, NE:

DESCRIPTION. The Reynolds Adolescent Depression Scale-2nd Edition: Short Form (RADS-2:SF) is a 10-item self-report instrument "designed as a brief screening measure for the assessment of depression in adolescents" (professional manual, p. 1) between the ages of 11 and 20 years. The RADS-2:SF is meant to be used by clinical psychologists, school psychologists, counselors, social workers, psychiatrists, other mental health professionals, and researchers who have limited time available for the assessment of depression, and its results provide mental health professionals with information for making decisions about a patient's affective status. The test author is careful to point out that the RADS-2:SF "does not provide a formal diagnosis of depression" (professional manual, p. 3), but instead provides an indication of the clinical severity of depression in adolescents. In fact, the RADS-2:SF provides only a Total score, which acts as a global assessment of the severity of depressive symptomatology in adolescents. Additional interviewing with the adolescent and possibly parents and others is necessary in order to make a formal diagnosis.

The RADS-2:SF may "be administered individually or in a group setting" (professional manual, p. 3). It is typically self-administered, but may be read aloud to adolescents with reading problems or developmental delays. The RADS-2:SF takes approximately 2 to 3 minutes to complete. The test items have a Flesch-Kincaid grade level of 1.2 and a Flesch Reading Ease index of 95.6%. Based on the Simple Measure of Gobbledygook (SMOG) Index, items were written at the 3.0 school grade level. The Coleman-Liau Index suggested a reading index at the 2.29 grade level and the Gunning Fog Index at the 2.75 grade level.

The test author suggests that any mental health professional, researcher, or other professionals such as physicians or nurses who have been trained to administer self-report measures to individuals and/or groups may administer the RADS-2:SF after becoming familiar with the manual. Test materials include the RADS-2:SF manual and a two-part carbonless test booklet. Examinees are asked to circle the number under *Almost never, Hardly ever, Sometimes,* or *Most of the time* that "best describes how you really feel" (professional manual, p. 23) for each of the 10 items. No alternative language versions of the RADS-2:SF are available, and investigations of performance in adolescents whose first or native language is not English have not been conducted by the test author or others.

Scoring of the RADS-2:SF is easily accomplished by separating the answer sheet from the scoring sheet. Scores are tabulated and placed into a Score Summary Table that includes Total raw score, *T* score, and percentile rank information. Scoring takes approximately 1 minute.

Interpretation is based on cutoff scores and percentile ranks provided within the manual. These are meant to "identify individuals who demonstrate a clinical level of depression symptom severity" (professional manual, p. 33) and who warrant further evaluation. The test author suggests that positive scores also occur in adolescents who manifest "other forms of psychopathology or a generalized level of psychological distress" (professional manual, p. 34).

DEVELOPMENT. The RADS-2:SF is an abbreviated version of the Reynolds Adolescent Depression Scale–2nd Edition (RADS-2; 16:211), which was published in 2002. The original Reynolds Adolescent Depression Scale (RADS) was published in 1987. The 10 items of the RADS-2:SF were drawn from the RADS-2. Items for the RADS were selected based on the DSM-III diagnostic criteria for major depressive disorder and dysthymic disorder as well as symptoms specified by the Research Diagnostic Criteria as assessed by the Schedule for Affective Disorders and Schizophrenia. In developing the RADS-2:SF, the six critical items from the RADS-2 were selected for inclusion "based upon their excellent ability to discriminate between clinically depressed and nondepressed adolescents" (professional manual, p. 5). The remaining items were included because they were specific to dysphoric mood, loss of interest, and irritability/anger. Other criteria for the selection of these items included their ability to demonstrate homogeneity with the RADS-2 Total scale based on item-total correlations with and coefficient alpha reliability of the Total scale. A factor analysis resulted in a single factor. Nine of the 10 RADS-2:SF items showed "strong" item-total scale correlations with the other item being included due to a desire to retain a reverse-scored item on the instrument.

TECHNICAL. The school standardization sample included 9,052 adolescents from seven states and one Canadian province. Ages ranged from 11 to 20 years (mean = 14.99) and adolescents were grouped into early adolescence (i.e., ages 11–13), middle adolescence (i.e., ages 14–16), and late adolescence (i.e., ages 17–20) groups. There were more females than males and 23% of the sample reported membership in a non-Caucasian ethnic group. A sample of 3,300 adolescents were drawn from this group and served as a normative comparison sample reflecting the 2000 U.S. Census proportions on ethnicity. This sample had equal numbers of males and females and equal numbers of adolescents in each previously mentioned age grouping. Two clinical samples included 101 adolescents with one or more DSM-III-R or DSM-IV Axis I diagnoses, 27% of which were for major depressive disorder; and 70 adolescents identified by a school-based screening for depression. Both clinical samples were highly represented by Caucasians. Raw score means and standard deviations by gender are provided for the total standardization and school samples, and *T*-scores are provided for the total standardization sample by age group. *T*-score means and standard deviations are also provided for the total standardization sample as well as by gender and by ethnic group. The test author recommends that the total standardization sample be used as the primary normative group for identifying adolescents with depression.

Internal consistencies (coefficient alpha) and standard errors of measurement were determined for various adolescent samples. Internal consistency was .86 for the total school sample (n = 9,052) and .84 for the total standardization sample (n = 3,300). For the clinical sample of 101 adolescents with DSM-III or DSM-IV diagnoses, internal consistency was .90 with item-total scale correlations ranging from .54 to .70. Internal consistency for "a sample of 50 adolescents who met criteria for special class placement" (professional manual, p. 43) due to intellectual disability was .85. Item-total scale correlation coefficients for the total standardization sample ranged from .28 (Reduced Affect) to .67 (Helplessness). Item-total scale correlations for males and females within the total standardization sample ranged from .26 (Reduced Affect for the male sample) to .69 (Helplessness for the female sample).

RADS-2:SF test-retest reliabilities over an "approximately" 2-week time period were computed for several samples. A test-retest reliability coefficient of .81 was found on a sample of 1,765 adolescents recruited from the total school sample, .82 for a subsample of 676 adolescents from the total standardization sample, and .82 for a clinical sample of 70 adolescents. The test author notes that very little difference in mean *T* scores (range from 1.36 to 1.57) was noted over the two testing periods, providing further evidence for high test-retest reliability.

In terms of content validity, the test author stresses the importance of symptom sampling and the degree to which each item relates to the overall test. In regards to symptom sampling, the test author indicates that symptom content is consistent with several mental health taxonomies including the DSM-IV. However, a review of the RADS-2:SF items and DSM-IV-TR (APA, 2000) diagnostic criteria shows that the RADS-2:SF items cover only four of the nine diagnostic criteria for major depressive disorder. The median item-total correlation for the RADS-2:SF is .55 with a range from .28 (Reduced Affect) to .67 (Helplessness) suggesting that, for the most part, individual items do contribute to the RADS-2:SF total score. The test author also reports strong score equivalence between the RADS-2:SF and the RADS-2 based on average item means and mean score differences.

In support of criterion-related validity, the RADS-2:SF was shown to correlate .80 with the Hamilton Depression Rating Scale (HDRS) in a sample of 485 junior high and senior high school students. It should be noted that the HDRS was once thought to be the "gold standard" for the assessment of depression, but is now considered to be significantly flawed (Bagby, Ryder, Schuller, & Marshall, 2004). The RADS-2:SF also has been shown to correlate with various other mental health instruments including the Beck Depression Inventory (.80 in a clinical sample of 70 adolescents) and with the Major Depression scale and the Dysthymic scale from the Adolescent Psychopathology Scale (.73 for both scales in the school validity sample of 485 students with a mean age of 14.56 years). The RADS-2:SF also correlated .94 (corrected correlation coefficient of .89) with the RADS-2 in the total school sample of 9,052 adolescents, .96 (corrected correlation coefficient of .91) in the school validity sample of 236 students in Grades 6, 7, and 8 (mean age = 12.18 years) and .96 (corrected correlation coefficient of .92) in the clinical sample of 70 adolescents with mean age of 17.48 years. An examination of other studies regarding the convergent validity of the RADS-2:SF demonstrated that it correlated .57 with the Hamilton Anxiety Scale, .73 with the Revised Children's Manifest Anxiety Scale, .67 with the Suicidal Ideation Questionnaire, and .64 with the Suicidal Behaviors Interview in a school sample of 485 students between the ages of 12 and 19. In a study with 236 middle-school students, the RADS-2:SF correlated .58 with the Beck Hopelessness Scale and mirrored closely correlations that the RADS-2 had with several other mental health measures.

With regard to discriminant validity, the RADS-2:SF correlated -.69 with the Rosenberg Self-Esteem Scale, -.62 with the Academic Self-Concept Scale-High School Version, and -.38 with the Marlowe-Crowne Social Desirability Scale–Short Form in the school-based validity sample (n = 485). Contrasted groups validity was demonstrated by significant and predicted score differences between "a sample of 27 adolescents drawn from the total school sample who were matched by age and gender with a clinical sample of 27 adolescents" (professional manual, p. 55) with major depressive disorder.

Additional evidence for the validity of the RADS-2:SF is based on a principal axis factor analysis that resulted in a one-factor solution, consistent with the test author's intent for the RADS-2:SF to be a one-dimensional screening measure for depression in adolescents. Factor loadings ranged from .38 to .75 in the total school sample (n = 9,052). A RADS-2:SF cutoff score of 61 (*T* score), which corresponds to a raw score of 26, is meant to "identify individuals who demonstrate a clinical level of depression symptom severity" (professional manual, p. 33) and who warrant further evaluation. The cutoff score was empirically determined by examining the discriminative ability of various RADS-2:SF scores in their ability to differentiate between a sample of 27 adolescents with major depressive disorder and gender- and age-matched adolescents drawn from the total standardization sample. A *T* score of 61 corresponds to a percentile rank of 86, which is slightly more than one standard deviation above the mean for the study sample. The cutoff score has a sensitivity of 96.3, a specificity of 74.1, and a hit rate of 85.2. Cutoff scores are also provided to assist in determining the severity of depressive symptomatology; however, these were based only on percentile rank ranges.

COMMENTARY. The RADS-2:SF was developed as a brief screening measure to assist in identifying adolescents who are depressed and may need treatment. The test author designed the measure for use by both researchers and clinicians in school, clinical, and other settings who have limited time available for such screening. It is based on its predecessors (the RADS and the RADS-2) and, thus, has strong psychometric lineage. The test author states that the "RADS-2:SF demonstrates high levels of reliability, validity, and clinical utility" (professional manual, p. ix).

In general, studies do support the contention that the RADS-2:SF has strong reliability. Although item-total correlations vary from the low to moderately high range, internal consistencies with various school and clinical samples are high. Test-retest reliability is also appropriate for an instrument measuring depression, and validity appears to be generally strong as well. Factor analyses support a one-dimensional instrument for measuring depression. Convergent and discriminant validity also appear appropriate with the RADS-2:SF demonstrating positive correlations with measures of depression, anxiety, suicidal ideation/behavior, and hopelessness, and negative correlations with measures of self-esteem and self-concept. Although the test author reports that item symptom content is consistent with several mental health taxonomies including the DSM-IV, an examination of RADS-2:SF items and DSM-IV-TR diagnostic criteria shows that the RADS-2:SF covers only four of the nine diagnostic criteria (i.e., depressed mood, diminished interest or pleasure in activities, feelings of worthlessness, and recurrent suicidal ideation) for major depressive disorder.

In regards to clinical utility, the RADS-2:SF does provide both clinicians and researchers with an easy to use and very quick way to screen for depression in adolescents. With its generally strong reliability and validity, the RADS-2:SF can be used confidently to screen for this disorder. However, further research is necessary to assess the clinical utility of the cutoff scores provided within the manual to determine whether these provide truly meaningful gradations of adolescent depression or are just statistical conveniences. In addition, as the test author admirably points out throughout the manual, the RADS-2:SF should only be used as a screening measure and not as a diagnostic indicator for major depressive disorder. A positive score on the RADS-2:SF must be followed by a clinical interview by a trained professional that covers all DSM-IV-TR diagnostic criteria for depression along with the consideration of data from a variety of other sources.

It should be noted that whereas a recent U.S. Preventive Services Task Force (2009) reported that there was inadequate evidence that screening tests accurately identify major depressive disorder in children, they did note that adequate evidence *does* exist for screening adolescents. In fact, they "recommend screening of adolescents (12–18 years of age) for major depressive disorder (MDD) when systems are in place to ensure accurate diagnosis, psychotherapy (cognitive-behavioral or interpersonal), and follow-up" (U.S. Preventive Services Task Force, 2009, p. 1223). Therefore, to assure proper diagnosis and mitigate any harm associated with screening and certain treatments, positive screening results must be followed by more thorough diagnostic evaluation (AACAP, 2007). Anything less would be a disservice to our adolescents who are intended to benefit from screening instruments.

SUMMARY. The RADS-2:SF is a 10-item self-report instrument designed to screen for depression in adolescents. As a brief version of the RADS-2, the RADS-2:SF is a technically strong instrument that is easily administered to adolescents individually or in group settings. The cutoff score for depression is empirically based; however, additional research is necessary on the clinical utility of using scores to differentiate depression severity in adolescents. Overall, this is an excellent screening instrument that ranks with other strong screening measures for adolescent depression including the Beck Depression Inventory (T7:275), the Beck Depression Inventory for Primary Care (Beck, Guth, Steer, & Ball, 1997) and the Reynolds Adolescent Depression Scale–2nd Edition (16:211).

REVIEWER'S REFERENCES

American Academy of Child and Adolescent Psychiatry. (2007). Practice parameters for the assessment and treatment of children and adolescents with depressive disorders. *Journal of the American Academy of Child and Adolescent Psychiatry, 46*, 1503-1526.

American Psychiatric Association. (2000). *Diagnostic and statistical manual of mental disorders* (4th ed., text rev.). Washington, DC: Author.

Bagby, R. M., Ryder, A. G., Schuller, D. R., & Marshall, M. B. (2004). The Hamilton Depression Rating Scale: Has the gold standard become a lead weight? *American Journal of Psychiatry, 161*, 2163-2177.

Beck, A. T., Guth, D., Steer, R. A., & Ball, R. (1997). Screening for major depression disorders in medical inpatients with the Beck Depression Inventory for Primary Care. *Behaviour Research and Therapy, 35*, 785–791.

U.S. Preventive Services Task Force. (2009). Screening and treatment for major depressive disorder in children and adolescents: U.S. Preventive Services Task Force recommendation statement. *Pediatrics, 123*, 1223-1228.

Review of Reynolds Adolescent Depression Scale–2nd Edition: Short Form by RAMA K. MISHRA, Neuropsychologist, Department of Psychiatry, Medicine Hat Regional Hospital, Medicine Hat, Alberta, Canada:

DESCRIPTION. The Reynolds Adolescent Depression Scale–2nd Edition: Short Form (RADS-2:SF) is a screening measure of severity of depression in adolescents, 11 to 20 years of age. This screening measure has only 10 items and takes about 2 to 3 minutes to complete either individually or in a group. It is written in simple language at a third grade reading level. The items on this test are drawn from the 30-item Reynolds Adolescent Depression Scale–Second Edition (RADS-2; Reynolds, 2002; 16:211). The degree of depression is determined from the total score. Further assessment can be done using the RADS-2 for in-depth analysis.

The RADS-2:SF uses a 4-point Likert-type response format (e.g., *almost never, hardly ever, sometimes*, or *most of the time*). The respondents are asked to indicate how they usually feel. Items are worded in the present tense to capture current symptoms.

DEVELOPMENT. The test author has identified that the main goal for this short form was to create a version of the previously published Reynolds Adolescent Depression Scale–Second Edition (Reynolds, 2002) with one-third or 10 items. The goal was to maintain adequate reliability and validity, but create a short version for quick screening purposes. All 6 critical items and 4 additional items from the RADS-2 were selected based on their level of discrimination between depressed and nondepressed adolescents. Additional criteria in the item selection also included the magnitude of correlation with the RADS-2 total score as well as type of symptoms (e.g., dysphoria, loss of interest, and irritability/anger). The original RADS was field tested more than 8,000 adolescents and the RADS–2 has been used in hundreds of empirical studies.

It was not adequately explained why it was decided to have 10 items, or why only 1 item was worded in the positive direction and was reverse scored. The test author found strong correlations between all but 1 item with the total score, but decided to keep the item due to the fact that it was the only reverse-scored item on the test and also due to the content of the item with respect to depression.

TECHNICAL. The standardization of the RADS-2: SF involved more than 9,000 adolescents from eight U.S. states and one Canadian province (i.e., British Columbia). The sample for this short version included the original sample used for developing the RADS-2 and additional data collected since the RADS-2 was published in 2002. The total sample was divided into three age groups, 11 to 13 years, 14 to 16 years, and 17 to 20 years to reflect early adolescence, middle adolescence, and late adolescence. Approximately 44% of the total sample were male and 56% were female. Approximately 23% of the sample were non-Caucasian. The average socioeconomic status of the sample was 8.53 (*SD* = 3.32, range 1–18) based on the Hollingshead Occupational Index applied to both parents.

The standardization sample consisted of 3,300 adolescents from the total sample, which reflected the 2,000 U.S. Census proportions with respect to gender, ethnic background, and age group distribution. Additionally, two clinical samples were used. The first clinical sample consisted of 59 females and 42 males with a total of 101 adolescents with one or more DSM-III or DSM-IV diagnoses based on a standardized clinical interview. The second sample consisted of 45 females and 25 males with a total of 70 adolescents with Axis-I diagnoses and used for test-retest reliability study and in validity studies. Separate groups of adolescents were used from the school and standardization samples for test-retest reliability, criterion-related validity, convergent and discriminant validity, contrasted groups validity, and clinical validity. Norms for the RADS-2:SF were based on the standardization sample of 3,300 adolescents. Raw scores were converted to *T*-scores for each sample.

The reliability estimates of RADS-2:SF are fairly high. Internal consistency reliabilities were reported in the range of .84 to .90 for the school, standardization, and clinical samples. Test-retest reliabilities were slightly lower, but quite good with a range of .81 to .82 for these groups, based on a retesting interval of about 2 weeks. Validity estimates have been reported for criterion-related validity and construct validity. As expected, the RADS–2:SF demonstrated high correlation with the RADS-2 with a correlation coefficient of .96 and .80 with the Hamilton Depression Rating Scale. The correlation of RADS-2:SF with the Major Depression scale and Dysthymic Disorder scale of the Adolescent Psychopathology Scale (Reynolds, 1998) were .73 each. Both convergent and discriminant validity estimates have been reported to establish construct validity. The correlation of RADS-2:SF with related scales from the Beck Hopelessness Scale (Beck, Weissman, Lester, & Trexler, 1974), the Hopelessness Scale for Children (Kazdin, French, Unis, Evseldt-Dawson, & Sherick, 1983), and the Bully-Victimization Scales (Reynolds, 2003) were reported to be in the range of .29 to .82, respectively. Several scales from the Adolescent Psychopathology Scale that are unrelated to depression showed weak relationship with RADS-2:SF. For example, correlation coefficients ranged from .22 to .37 with conduct disorder, substance abuse, and mania subscales.

In one of the large independent studies reported by Milfont et al. (2008), the RADS-2:SF was reported to have a strong correlation with other measures of depression. They found that with a cutoff score of 26, the RADS-2:SF classified a higher percentage of students as having depressive symptoms compared to the RADS in a large New Zealand sample.

It has not been explained adequately the usefulness of a school-based sample that was almost three times the standardization sample. It was also not explained how the standardization sample was selected from the larger school-based sample. Also it was not clear if the total sample was a combination of several studies conducted using the RADS-2 and RADS-2:SF.

COMMENTARY. The RADS-2:SF is a 10-item depression scale, suitable for screening purposes. This test has been normed on a large sample with U.S.-Census-matched diverse samples and provides similar reliability and validity estimates as the 30-item RADS-2. However, it has not been explained why the test author chose to use a sample from one of the western provinces of Canada. It was not clear from the information provided in the manual whether the short form was derived from the 30-item RADS-2 standardization data or developed independently. In any case, the technical foundation for this test is quite strong and therefore recommended for clinical use, particularly when the clinician has other tests to consider for overall assessment. However, three issues need to be considered by prospective users, including clinicians and researchers. In terms of time, the 30-item version RADS-2 does not take much longer than the 10-item RADS-2:SF. The RADS-2 provides four subscales and a total score to help interpret subclinical levels of depression from elevations on subscales. Finally, the "multiple gate screening procedure" flow chart provided by the author of the RADS-2:SF recommends that the RADS-2 be used if the score obtained by an individual is above the cutoff to reduce false positives. Therefore, the use of the RADS-2:SF is limited to situations in which only a very brief screening is required or feasible.

SUMMARY. The RADS-2:SF is a brief measure of depression in adolescents between the ages of 11 and 20 years. It is most ideal for clinical screening and referral service. However, for diagnostic assessment, monitoring treatment effectiveness, and research, the 30–item RADS-2 is a better choice. Increased false-positives and absence of any subscales make the RADS-2:SF less attractive for the frontline clinician and researcher.

REVIEWER'S REFERENCES

Beck, A. T., Weissman, A., Lester, D., & Trexler, J. (1974). The measurement of pessimism: The Hopelessness Scale. *Journal of Consulting and Clinical Psychology, 42,* 861–865.

Kazdin, A. E., French, N. H., Unis, A. S., Evseldt-Dawson, K., & Sherick, R. B. (1983). Hopelessness, depression, and suicidal intent among psychiatrically disturbed inpatient children. *Journal of Consulting and Clinical Psychology, 51,* 504–510.

Milfont, T. L., Merry, S., Robinson, E., Denny, S., Crengle, S., & Ameratunga, S. (2008). Evaluating the short form of the Reynolds Adolescent Depression Scale in New Zealand adolescents. *Australia and New Zealand Journal of Psychiatry, 42,* 950-954.

Reynolds, W. M. (1998). *Adolescent Psychopathology Scale psychometric and technical manual.* Lutz, FL: Psychological Assessment Resources.

Reynolds, W. M. (2002). Reynolds Adolescent Depression Scale–2nd Edition. Lutz, FL: Psychological Assessment Resources.

Reynolds, W. M. (2003). *Reynolds Bully Victimization Scales for Schools: Manual.* San Antonio, TX: Psychological Corporation.

[110]

Roberts-2.

Purpose: Designed to provide an "assessment of a child's or adolescent's level of social cognitive understanding."
Population: Ages 6–18 years.
Publication Dates: 1982–2005.
Scores, 28: 2 Theme Overview scales (Popular Pull, Complete Meaning), 6 Available Resources scales (Support from Self—Feeling, Support from Self—Advocacy, Support from Other—Feeling, Support from Other—Help, Reliance on Other, Limit Setting), 5 Problem Identification scales (Recognition, Description, Clarification, Definition, Explanation), 5 Resolution scales (Simple Closure or Easy Outcome, Easy and Realistically Positive Outcome, Constructive Resolution, Constructive Resolution of Feeling and Situation, Elaborated Process with Possible Insight), 4 Emotion scales (Anxiety, Aggression, Depression, Rejection), 4 Outcome scales (Unresolved Outcome, Nonadaptive Outcome, Maladaptive Outcome, Unrealistic Outcome), 2 Unusual or Atypical Responses scales (Unusual—Refusal/No Score/Antisocial, Atypical Categories).
Administration: Individual.
Editions, 3: Set of Test Pictures Featuring White Children and Adolescents, Set of Test Pictures Featuring Black Children and Adolescents, Set of Test Pictures Featuring Hispanic Children and Adolescents.
Price Data, 2008: $180 per complete kit including manual (2005, 171 pages), Casebook, Quick Scoring Guide, Set of Test Pictures Featuring White Children and Adolescents, and 25 record forms; $49.95 per manual; $59.95 per Set of Test Pictures Featuring White, Black, or Hispanic Children and Adolescents; $34.50 per 25 record forms; $55 per Continuing Education Questionnaire and Evaluation Form; $55 per Casebook (including 1 Quick Scoring Guide).
Time: (30–40) minutes.
Comments: Previous version entitled Roberts Apperception Test for Children.
Authors: Glen E. Roberts (test and manual) and Chris Gruber (manual only).
Publisher: Western Psychological Services.
Cross References: For reviews by Merith Cosden and Niels G. Waller of an earlier version, see 14:322; see also T5:2242 (8 references) and T4:2285 (5 references); for a review by Jacob O. Sines of an earlier edition, see 9:15054.

Review of the Roberts-2 by FREDERIC J. MEDWAY, Professor of Psychology, University of South Carolina, Columbia, SC:

DESCRIPTION. The Roberts-2 is an updated and technically improved version of the widely used Roberts Apperception Test for Children. Though having administrative features of a projective test such as the Thematic Apperception Test (T7:2645), the Roberts-2 is presented as a measure of children's social understanding of common, everyday experiences and is intended for youth between ages 6 (Grade 1) and 18 (Grade 12). The assessment of social understanding or social cognitive competence occurs through the presentation of 16 pictorial stimulus cards. These black-and-white pictures show interpersonal situations involving parents and peers. For each picture the examinee is asked to tell a complete story (one with a beginning, middle, and an end) about the pictured situation. These descriptions are then transcribed and a comprehensive scoring system is applied to the responses. Administration should be under an hour; however, it is unclear how long scoring and interpretation may take. Social understanding is described as "greater awareness of conventional social meaning, differentiated themes, and ... resolution of story themes and conflicts" (manual, p. 3). The measure is intended for use with children referred for adjustment problems and for use in research studies. The Roberts-2 specifically avoids the label of a projective test and the association with underlying internal states and unconscious processes. There are separate versions of the test pictures for White, Black, and Hispanic children.

The Roberts-2 has seven major scales, each with several subcategories that seek to capture two assessment functions: developmental adaptive function (changes over time in social perception) and clinical function (unusual or atypical social perception). The seven scales are: Theme Overview Scales, Available Resources Scales, Problem Identification Scales, Resolution Scales, Emotion Scales, Outcome Scales, and Unusual or Atypical Responses. A coding protocol assists the examiner in coding responses into categories within each of these scales. For example, a transcribed picture response might be coded in terms of how most children would view the picture, in terms of the resources that story characters use to deal with or cope with various situations and emotions, in terms of how well a problem is articulated, in terms of how well problems are successfully resolved and insight into future situations is gained, in terms of the expression of four emotions (anxiety, aggression, depression, and rejection), in terms of adaptive story outcomes, and in terms of nine various atypical responses that range from refusal to respond to themes of violence, abuse, death, and sexuality.

DEVELOPMENT. As noted, the Roberts-2 updates and presents several new features beyond the original test published in 1982. The major changes include updated drawings; improvements in the scientific aspects of the test, including standardization, sampling, reliability, and validity information; providing a new manual that clarifies the coding categories and interpretation; adding cards representing ethnic group members; and redesigning the scoring sheet. The 171-page user's manual covers administration, scoring, interpretation, and various technical features. It is designed to take the original Roberts measure and subject the thematic content to better and more well-articulated objective scoring. It presents numerous examples of responses to make it easier for the user to score the narrative content, and do to so in a reliable way. It is designed to further establish the psychometric properties of the measure which, in the original measure, were not always positively reviewed.

TECHNICAL. In response to criticisms of the original measure and consistent with best practices in narrative assessment (Esquivel & Flanagan, 2007), the Roberts-2 presents standardization data based on a national sample, new test-retest reliability data, validation evidence showing "a developmental progression of social cognitive skills" (manual, p. 4), and discriminant validity evidence demonstrating differences among children with varying degrees of emotional disturbance. There are two test development samples. There is a standardization or normative sample of 1,060 children (48.8% male) tested in 15 states in the four major geographic regions of the U.S. The ethnic background of the sample is 3.4% Asian, 12.8% Black, 10.4% Hispanic, and 72.7% White. Descriptive statistics for this sample are presented for each of the seven major scales and subcontent areas. Data analyses on this sample demonstrated the need to differentially report norms by age but not by gender. Also, there is a referred clinical sample of 467 children drawn from seven clinics and special education facilities. This sample was 68% male and had a higher percentage of Black and Hispanic students (60%) than the standardization sample.

The test manual reports a study of interscorer agreement using data from both the standardization and clinical samples. Interscorer reliability coefficients across both samples and all scales is high (median = .92). Test-retest reliability is reported for subsamples within the standardization and clinical sample using subgroups of 30 children each. Test-retest reliabilities for both samples are respectable (median values of .71 and .75 for nonreferred and clinical samples respectively), although not higher than other narrative measures. The interval between test administration was not specified. Validity evidence is presented in terms of "power to document developmental differences" and "power to document different performance in nonreferred and referred groups" (manual, p. 135). Results are presented that support both functions of the Roberts-2 with only 1 of 28 scales (Depression) not differentiating across age or clinical status. The manual presents information on the various scales across developmental levels, showing clear developmental trends on some scales but not others. There also are some clear trends in comparing the standardization and clinical samples. For example, children in the former sample much more often bring their stories to a successful resolution compared to children in the clinical sample.

COMMENTARY. Great care and thought have gone into improving the Roberts-2 as the authors have done an excellent job responding to past criticisms and limitations of the original version, which itself took years to develop. The stimulus pictures have been updated and appear more modern, administration continues to be straightforward, and examinees will be engaged by the task and identify with the common situations portrayed. The Roberts-2 clearly has moved away from a projective test with objective scoring to one that attempts to use social perception and reasoning to make clinical interpretations, cautioning rightly that the test is designed to be part of a comprehensive battery. Although test administration is straightforward, test interpretation and scoring is relatively complex given the many different scales and subscale scores that may be derived. It is reported that experienced users of the original scale can use the revision following a 2-hour workshop. However, scoring appears fairly difficult for a novice user and new users would also likely need a structured workshop and considerable practice to feel comfortable with many of the scoring categories. Although the test manual provides many examples, it is recommended that novice users check their scoring and interpretation with someone experienced with the measure. The manual also might be improved with examples of how the Roberts-2 might be used as part of a comprehensive testing battery. Such an example could show how this measure could be used in conjunction with other tests (both cognitive, affective, and behavioral) to yield both diagnostic data and specific recommendations for intervention. In short, although examiners may be expert in test interpretation the existing manual provides little help in suggesting ways to actually modify or address deficits in social understanding.

SUMMARY. The Roberts-2 is a welcome revision and improvement of a widely used storytelling test. The revision updates the original version, presents needed technical data, and has a comprehensive manual to aid in scoring. The measure, however, remains time-consuming and complex to score, and examiners will require considerable training and practice to score a number of the categories.

REVIEWER'S REFERENCE

Esquivel, G. B., & Flanagan, R. (2007). Narrative methods of personality assessment in school psychology. *Psychology in the Schools, 44,* 271-280.

Review of the Roberts-2 by RACHEL J. VALLELEY, Associate Professor, Munroe-Meyer Institute and Pediatrics, University of Nebraska Medical Center, Omaha, NE, and BRANDY L. CLARKE, Pediatric Psychology Intern, Munroe-Meyer Institute, University of Nebraska Medical Center, Omaha, NE:

DESCRIPTION. The Roberts-2 is intended for children and adolescents between the ages of 6 and 18 (Grades 1–12) referred for mental health or special education services for social or emotional adjustment concerns. The Roberts-2 is designed to serve two functions: (a) a developmental adaptive function and (b) a clinical function for children experiencing social and emotional problems. The Roberts-2 includes 16 pictures of children and adolescents in common social situations (e.g., peer and parent-child interactions). Cards are selected by the examiner based on appropriate gender and ethnicity (White, Black, or Hispanic) for the examinee. Examinees are asked to tell a story about each image that has a beginning, middle, and end, as well as describe emotional responses. Test examiners transcribe the examinee's responses verbatim during the testing session or from audiotape to identify the presence of statements reflecting various social cognitive themes.

Examinee statements are scored across seven scales made up of 2–6 subscales. The Theme Overview scales include Popular Pull (POP) and Complete Meaning subscales (MEAN). Popular Pull refers to how the majority of nonreferred children and adolescents perceive what is represented in each card. Complete Meaning refers to the child or adolescent's ability to develop a comprehensive story following the instructions given. The Available Resources scales are made up of six subscales designed to assess the resources (internal and external) that characters in the respondents' stories are able to access. The five Problem Identification subscales are made up of a hierarchy of problem-solving skills from Recognition to Explanation. The Resolution scales are also viewed as a hierarchy of adaptive problem-solving skills related to how the story is resolved. The Emotion scales are made up of Anxiety, Aggression, Depression, and Rejection. Outcome scales identify responses given by children who have difficulty in resolving the stories in a successful manner. The Unusual or Atypical Response scales are used "to identify responses that denote a disturbance in functioning or serious pathology" (manual, p. 53), such as refusing to respond and giving antisocial or unusual responses.

Responses are coded according to whether the response falls into each scale for a card by placing a check mark for represented scales. Checks are added up for each scale to provide a total raw score. Total raw scores are calculated and converted into *T* scores for each of the subscales and compared against standardized and clinical sample norms. Profiles are created on a developmental/adaptive and clinical scale. Developmental/adaptive scale profiles indicate possible areas of social cognitive strength or weakness. Clinical scale profiles indicate areas of clinically significant differences on the Outcome and Unusual or Atypical scales.

DEVELOPMENT. The Roberts-2 is a revision of the Roberts Apperception Test for Children (RATC; McArthur & Roberts, 1982). Improvements of the Roberts-2 were intended to enhance the technical adequacy of the assessment, as well as update and improve the test materials. To accomplish these goals, the test authors developed more quantitative scores versus qualitative projective analyses; tested the measure on a large, representative standardization sample; and provided stronger reliability and validity evidence. Improvements to test materials included: (a) updating test pictures, (b) including ethnically representative card sets, (c) clarifying and differentiating coding categories, (d) providing an extensive sample of coded sample responses, (e) redesigning the scoring sheet to promote efficiency, and (f) providing a scale-by-scale discussion of score meaning to aid in interpretation. The test manual also states that the Roberts-2 was developed out of research related to social competence. However, a description of the theory or research supporting the development of the test was not provided. Additionally, no mention was made in the test manual of pilot-testing or other methods used to develop the scoring procedures or selection of test items.

TECHNICAL. The normative sample consisted of 1,060 children recruited from frequently attended agencies (e.g., schools, church groups, sports clubs), across 15 states from the four major geographic regions of the U.S. However, a higher percentage of children from the South (48%) were represented in the sample as compared to U.S. Census data (35.1%). The sample size for each age ranged from 39 to 98 with ethnicity (i.e., Asian, Black, Hispanic, and Caucasian) and parent's educational level closely matched to the U.S. Census. Data were also collected on a referred clinical sample that consisted of children being seen in seven clinics. A higher percentage of boys encompassed this sample and the sample size for each age ranged from 5–59 for each age group. However, information was not provided on the types of clinics nor diagnoses for the referred sample.

Given that examinees provide open-ended responses, interscorer agreement is extremely important. Interscorer agreement was calculated on 10 complete transcripts (5 clinical and 5 nonclinical) for children ages 6–16. The test author scored the protocols to provide a criterion after which 10 clinicians with experience with the RATC also scored these protocols. These clinicians attended two, 2-hour workshops based on materials from the manual. The median interscorer reliability coefficient across all scales reported in the manual was .92 with a range of .43 to 1.00. However, most scales were above .80. Test-retest reliability data were collected on a referred (N = 30) and nonreferred sample (N = 30). The length of time between test-retest was not provided in the test manual. Correlation coefficients for scales were as follows: Theme Overview Scales ranged from .77–.84, Available Resources Scales ranged from .46–.94, Problem Identification scales ranged from .57–.86, Resolution scales ranged from .57–.86, Emotion scales ranged from .17–.88, Outcome Scales ranged from .69–.86, and the Unusual or Atypical Responses scales ranged from .45–.85. Finally, reliability data were presented regarding the *SEM* for each scale according to raw scores and *T*-scores. *T*-score *SEM*s range from 2.49

(Support Self-Feeling) to 8.01 (Rejection) with most *SEM*s falling above 4.0.

Interpretation of each scale is broken into technical and clinical notes. Technical notes provide a summary of the psychometric properties of each scale. Clinical notes provide impressions of what the scale may mean but give no data to support determinations made. For example, the authors of the test manual interpret that for the Popular Pull scale "Inaccurate or deviate [*sic*] perceptions prevent the accurate reading of ordinary social cues and lead to inappropriate responses" (p. 115). Yet, there are no data presented on the relationship between the stories told and how children perceive and respond to real life situations.

Validity information in the manual is based upon expected developmental differences across age groups and differences between referred and nonreferred samples. Each of the scales, with the exception of one (Depression), showed a significant difference according to age or clinical status. The test manual provides details as to which scales have validation support for developmental and/or clinical status.

COMMENTARY. The usefulness of this measure for assessing emotional and social functioning of children and adolescents is of limited value for a variety of reasons. First of all, there is a lack of information provided to assist a test user in determining the merit of the test. Specifically, there is no information on the underlying theory, how items were selected, how the example responses were developed, whether items and responses were piloted, a detailed description of the clinical sample, and how ethnicity may or may not impact responses and interpretation of the test. Furthermore, no estimate is given for how long it takes to administer, transcribe, and score the test. Transcribing detailed responses may take an extended amount of time and would be impractical for many clinicians on a routine basis.

The author purports that a major improvement to this version is stronger reliability and validity evidence. However, reliability evidence appears to be minimal with interscorer agreement being calculated only for examiners who received training. Furthermore, test-retest data were calculated using a small sample and incomplete information was provided on the amount of time between testing sessions. Finally, the *SEM*s for many of the scales are at least 4.0, which results in a large variability of *T*-scores.

In addition, the test manual appears to neglect many areas pertaining to the validation of this scale. For example, the test manual does not provide information discussing content-description validation procedures. It is unclear if these items were piloted on a sample to determine the scales or factors, as well as whether the scales were cross-validated on a second sample. Thus, the scales' predictive ability could be spuriously high due to random sampling errors and not true differences according to developmental or clinical status. Furthermore, no data are presented regarding how this test compares to measures assessing similar constructs or the previous version of this test.

Finally, the utility of the information gained from using this assessment tool is not addressed in the manual. There is no information showing that the scores ascertained would be helpful diagnostically nor in designing treatment plans based upon social dysfunction. Thus, the clinical utility of this measure is called into question.

SUMMARY. The Roberts-2 is a revision of the Roberts Apperception Test for Children designed to measure social cognitive functioning for children ages 6 through 18. With this revision, the authors provide detailed examples of possible responses to aid in the scoring and interpretation of the measure. These examples may allow for more reliable scoring of responses across examiners. However, important information regarding the validation and clinical utility of the measure is lacking. Additionally, the amount of time required to administer and score the test using detailed transcriptions may make it impractical for routine clinical use. Based on these considerations, this measure is not recommended for the assessment of child and adolescent social cognitive functioning.

REVIEWERS' REFERENCE

McArthur, D. S., & Roberts, G. E. (1982). *Roberts Apperception Test for Children (RATC) manual.* Los Angeles: Western Psychological Services.

[111]

SCAN-3 for Adolescents and Adults: Tests for Auditory Processing Disorders.

Purpose: "Designed to identify auditory processing disorders in adolescents and adults."
Population: Ages 13-50.
Publication Dates: 1986-2009.
Acronym: SCAN-3:A.
Scores, 21: 4 screening test scores: Gap Detection, Auditory Figure-Ground 0 dB, Competing Words-Free Recall, Total (P/F); 5 diagnostic test scores: Audi-

tory Processing Composite (Filtered Words, Auditory Figure-Ground 0 dB, Competing Words-Directed Ear, Competing Sentences, Total); 3 supplementary test scores: Auditory Figure-Ground +8 dB, Auditory Figure-Ground +12 dB, Time Compressed Sentences; ear advantage summary score for each of the following: Auditory Figure-Ground 0 dB, Competing Words-Free Recall, Filtered Words, Competing Words-Directed Ear-Directed Right Ear, Competing Words-Directed Ear-Directed Left Ear, Competing Sentences, Auditory Figure-Ground +8 dB, Auditory Figure-Ground +12 dB, Time Compressed Sentences.
Administration: Individual.
Price Data, 2010: $255 per complete kit including 25 record forms, manual (2009, 120 pages), and Audio CD; $57 per 25 record forms; $97 per manual; $107 per Audio CD.
Time: (10-15) minutes for the screening tests; (20-30) minutes for the diagnostic and supplementary tests.
Comments: Screening test scores are "criterion-referenced"; Auditory Figure-Ground 0 dB test is identical across the screening and diagnostic levels; all scores (except for Gap Detection) are calculated as a composite of the participant's right ear score and left ear score, and the ear-advantage score is the difference between the right and left ear scores; additional materials required: "CD player with a track display or a two-channel audiometer" or access to a computer, two sets of stereo headphones, and a stereo Y-adapter if necessary; revision of SCAN-A: A Test for Auditory Processing Disorders in Adolescents and Adults.
Author: Robert W. Keith.
Publisher: Pearson.
Cross References: For reviews by William R. Merz, Sr. and Jaclyn B. Spitzer of the earlier edition entitled SCAN-A: A Test for Auditory Processing Disorders in Adolescents and Adults, see 13:274.

Review of the SCAN-3 for Adolescents and Adults: Tests for Auditory Processing Disorders by JERRELL CASSADY, Professor of Psychology, Department of Educational Psychology, Ball State University, Muncie, IN, and CATHERINE WAGNER, Graduate Student in School Psychology, Department of Educational Psychology, Ball State University, Muncie, IN:

DESCRIPTION. The SCAN-3 for Adolescents and Adults: Tests for Auditory Processing Disorders (SCAN-3:A) is designed to "evaluate auditory processing abilities in the areas of: temporal processing, listening in noise, dichotic listening, and listening to degraded speech" (manual, p. 2). This assessment can be used to determine whether or not an individual is at risk for an auditory processing disorder (APD). The results can be used along with additional observations and information to diagnose an APD.

The SCAN-3:A is an individual test administered by a trained professional (e.g., audiologists, speech-language pathologists, school psychologists) for use with individuals aged 13–50 years. The test requires 10–15 minutes to administer three screening tests and an additional 20–30 minutes to administer four diagnostic and three supplementary tests. All of the tests are administered by using the provided auditory CD, which contains recorded test directions, practice items, and test items. The examinee and examiner must wear headphones because words are presented separately in the right and left ears. A general explanation of the assessment is given by the examiner to the examinee before testing begins. The examiner then interrupts the CD only to correct inaccurate responses to practice items. All test scores are divided into separate right ear and left ear scores so that an ear advantage score can be determined. The importance of the ear advantage score is that it may be an indication of hemispheric dominance for language or neurologically based language or learning disorders.

Screening tests. The examiner must first administer the three screening tests (Gap Detection, Auditory Figure-Ground at 0 dB Signal-to-Noise Ratio, and Competing Words-Free Recall). Failure on any of the screening tests indicates the examinee needs to be referred for more detailed assessment for specific auditory processing disorders. The diagnostic tests should be administered to provide additional diagnostic background information.

Gap Detection measures temporal processing by presenting two tones separated by a gap. The gap varies from 0 milliseconds to 40 milliseconds. The examinee must determine if he heard one tone or two. If the examinee cannot distinguish two tones as the gap increases, a temporal processing disorder may be indicated.

Auditory-Figure-Ground 0 dB measures the examinee's ability to process speech in the presence of background noise. Some children with learning disabilities have difficulty with auditory figure-ground tasks because they have problems attending to relevant stimuli when there is competing noise. In this test, the target speech and background noise are presented at the same decibel level.

Competing Words-Free Recall is the final screening test. This is a dichotic listening task that measures the maturation of the auditory system. The examinee hears one word in each ear at the same time and repeats them in any order. If the examinee has difficulty with this subtest, it may indicate that auditory pathways are still maturing or there is damage present.

Diagnostic tests. The first diagnostic subtest is Filtered Words, which measures the examinee's auditory closure skills. The examinee hears part of a word at different Hz levels and must fill in the missing information to complete the word. An examinee who scores low on this subtest may have difficulty understanding speech when part of the signal is distorted. The Filtered Word low-pass criterion was changed from 500 Hz in the SCAN-A to 750 Hz in the SCAN-3:A based on data that indicated 750 Hz to be more discriminative in identifying APDs.

The second diagnostic test is the Auditory-Figure Ground to 0 dB Signal-to-Noise Ratio test, which also serves as a screening measure. If given as a part of screening, it does not need to be repeated. If performance on this scale is low, the supplementary Auditory-Figure Ground measures (see below) can be administered to produce more fine-grained analysis of performance ability.

The third diagnostic subtest is Competing Words–Directed Ear. This is another dichotic listening task that measures auditory system maturation. In this subtest, the examinee hears one word in each ear at the same time. They must then recall the words in a specified order. Half the trials ask for the right ear word first and half ask for the left ear word first. Low scores on this subtest suggest delayed maturation of the auditory system, reversed cerebral dominance for language, or a neurological disorder. This diagnostic subtest is more difficult conceptually than the Competing Words-Free Recall screening measure (discussed earlier). In the Directed Ear test the examinee must repeat the words in the directed order, presumably requiring a greater degree of working memory use in the task.

The fourth diagnostic subtest is Competing Sentences. This is a dichotic listening task that measures auditory system maturation and hemispheric specialization. In this task, two sentences are presented to the examinee at the same time, one in each ear. In half the trials the examinee must repeat only the right ear sentence and in the other half they repeat only the left ear sentence. Poor performance may indicate the presence of an APD.

Supplementary tests. The SCAN-3:A includes two more Auditory Figure-Ground tests, Auditory Figure-Ground 8 dB Signal-to-Noise Ratio and Auditory-Figure Ground 12 dB Signal-to-Noise Ratio. These two subtests are supplementary and can be given if the examinee scores low on Auditory Figure-Ground 0 dB. These tests present the target speech at 8 decibels and 12 decibels louder than the background noise, providing evidence for the examinee's needs for auditory intensity to ensure optimal listening conditions.

The final subtest is the third supplementary test, Time Compressed Sentences. This subtest measures the examinee's ability to process speech presented at a rapid rate. The examinee hears one sentence and then must repeat what was said word-for-word. Scores on this subtest provide information on degraded speech perception and temporal processing abilities. A low score indicates that the examinee has problems perceiving the changing acoustic features of speech.

Scoring and interpretation. Scoring and interpretation are standardized and facilitated with the Score Summary sheet and detailed interpretation tables in the manual. The manual also includes an interpretation section that provides a description of how scaled scores should be interpreted for each test. Each test also includes a section on ear advantage interpretation, noting which ear advantages are normal and which may be cause for concern. The interpretation section also makes recommendations for interventions and provides case studies as examples for examiners to reference while scoring and interpreting results.

DEVELOPMENT. The SCAN-3:A is a revision that was developed by using feedback from clinicians trained in assessing APDs, a review of the current literature, a nationwide pilot study, and a nationwide standardization study. Five new tests were added and the original four from the SCAN-A were revised based on suggestions from professionals and to replace outdated items.

ASHA certified and state-licensed speech-language pathologists and audiologists were used as the examiners during the field research studies on the new and changed items in the SCAN-3:A. Each record form was scored by two scorers and the average agreement between the two was 97%. The pilot research was conducted on 156 nonclinical adolescents and 34 clinical adolescents between the ages of 12 and 15 years. This research addressed the ease of administration, appropriateness of content, and clarity of instructions. This process gathered data from 75 certified speech-language pathologists, audiologists, and educational diagnosticians who provided strong support that the test was easy to follow and administer.

TECHNICAL.

Normative data. The normative sample for the SCAN-3:A was developed in a study including 250 individuals ages 13–50, drawn from a sample including examinees in 32 states by examiners who met predetermined qualifications. The normative sample was stratified to match 2004 U.S. Census targets for race and ethnicity, geographic region, and education level of the examinee or the examinee's primary caregiver. Based on the prevalence rates of APDs in adults and adolescents, 2% of the examinees in the normative sample had been previously diagnosed with an APD.

Reliability. Test-retest reliability was reported for all tests and composite scores, with Pearson product-moment correlations ranging from .54–.80. The overall composite test-retest coefficient was .78 (corrected). The test-retest evaluation included 58 adolescents and adults who were tested over an interval of 1–29 days. Internal consistency estimates were generated using a split-half method, with the primary subtests used in the calculation of the Auditory Processing Composite Score ranging from .71 to .96. Finally interscorer reliability on the SCAN-3:A was very strong in the normative sample study ($r > .98$).

Validity. Evidence demonstrating validity was limited, but included estimations of content and construct validity. Content validity was addressed by comparing SCAN-3:A tasks to the American Speech-Language-Hearing Association Technical Report on Auditory Processing Disorders. Correlational analyses among the subtests and the composite scores were provided as evidence of construct validity with supporting data. Diagnostic utility was demonstrated to be strong and effective, though when comparing the normative sample and the known APD participants completing the SCAN-3:A.

COMMENTARY/SUMMARY. The SCAN-3:A appears to be a very useful screening and diagnostic tool that is based on a sound theoretical and empirical base. The revision from the earlier version was driven by both research and practical matters. The administration, scoring, and interpretation are quite simple and supported by an excellent and easy-to-follow manual. Some confusion may arise for new examiners related to the distinction between screening and diagnostic measures, but careful review of the manual and testing materials should resolve those initial difficulties.

Review of the SCAN-3 for Adolescents and Adults: Tests for Auditory Processing Disorders by RICK EIGENBROOD, Professor in Education, Seattle Pacific University, Seattle, WA:

DESCRIPTION. The SCAN-3 for Adolescents and Adults: Tests for Auditory Processing Disorders (SCAN-3:A) is a battery of tests intended for use with adolescents and adults ages 13 years through 50 years. It is a revision of the SCAN-A: A Test for Auditory Processing Disorders in Adolescents and Adults (SCAN-A). The test is individually administered with a relatively short administration time for the three screening tests (10–15 minutes), plus varying additional time (20–30 minutes) for the four diagnostic and three supplementary tests depending on which supplemental tests are administered and the ability of the individual being tested. According to the manual, the revisions for the SCAN-3:A reflect increased evidence-based research in the field that resulted in improvements in approach, content, scoring, and interpretation of the test battery. Revisions include the addition of a test of temporal processing, improved scoring of the Competing Sentences test by allowing credit for partial responses, a free recall response mode for Competing Words, scoring changes for the Competing Words–Directed Ear by allowing credit only for responses in the directed order, redesigning the SCAN-A into a battery of tests to include screening tests with criterion scores, and additional tests of differing signal-to-noise ratios in an effort to help "the clinician to better understand the ratio at which individuals perform well or poorly" (manual, p. 4).

The test kit includes the examiner's manual, a record form (protocol), and an audio compact disk (CD). In addition, the examiner must have access to either a CD player or an audiometer with two channels and CD capability, and stereo headphones. Specific requirements for the CD player/audiometer are described in the manual. Directions for administering and scoring each component of the test battery are clearly presented in the manual with additional directions provided on the record form and CD for ease of administration.

Three screening tests are those first presented on the record form and CD–Gap Detection, Auditory Figure-Ground, and Competing Words-Free Recall. The manual states that all three screening tests must be passed, and if the examinee fails to pass even one of the screening tests, that the diagnostic tests should be administered. However, it is unclear whether or not the screening tests need to be administered before moving to the diagnostic tests, because the manual states that diagnostic tests should be administered to those who fail the screening, or have been identified by other means as being at risk for an Auditory Processing Disorder (APD). The manual also states that one of the screening tests and one of the diagnostic tests could be used as supplementary tests. The manual indicates that if the examinee fails one or more of the screening tests, then the diagnostic tests should be administered, and goes on to make other recommendations regarding failure on specific screenings. The diagnostic tests include Filtered Words, Auditory Figure-Ground at 0 dB Signal-to-Noise Ratio, Competing Words-Directed Ear, and Competing Sentences. The supplementary tests include Auditory Figure-Ground +8 dB Signal-to-Noise (AFG +8) which is suggested if the examinee does not pass the AFG 0 diagnostic tests, and the Auditory Figure-Ground at +12 dB Signal-to-Noise Ratio +12 dB (AFG +12), which can be administered to determine "more about the optimal listening condition the examinee requires" (manual, p. 28).

According to the SCAN-3:A manual, the instrument comprises a "battery of tests designed to identify auditory processing disorders in adolescents and adults (13–50)" (manual, p. 2). Results may be used to identify whether or not the examinee has an APD, and the results can then be used to make recommendations for individualized management and remediation.

The test manual specifies that the test should be administered only by those who have training and experience in administering and scoring standardized tests. Additionally, test administrators should have experience testing individuals of similar age, cultural and linguistic backgrounds, and with comparable clinical histories. The person giving the tests should be familiar with the instrument and practice administration of the tests before administering them for clinical purposes. The directions in the manual reflect standardized and typical requirements for the administration of standardized assessment. The manual states that it is important to accept dialectical variations during the testing process. Additionally, the manual states that "the examinee should pass a hearing screening at 1,000, 2,000, and 4,000 Hz bilaterally before administration of any SCAN-3:A tests" (manual, p. 6).

Scores reported for the SCAN-3:A include scaled scores (*M* = 10, *SD* = 3, Range = 1–19) and percentile ranks for the diagnostic and supplementary tests. All scaled scores are reported with confidence intervals. An Auditory Processing Composite (APC) score (*M* = 100, *SD* = 15) is also reported for adolescents and adults. According to the manual, the APC score provides information in the areas of "degraded speech, listening in the presence of background noise, and dichotic listening" (manual, p. 34).

In addition to the scaled and standard scores, the ear advantage is also calculated for each test (except Gap Detection) by comparing the raw scores of the left and right ear. The test authors state that a mathematical difference between scores is a strong indicator of "hemispheric differences" between the right and left ear that are not "normal," or indicative of "neurologically-based language/learning disorders" (manual, p. 33).

DEVELOPMENT. The development of the SCAN-3:A was based largely on professionally accepted test development standards (see, e.g., Gall, Gall, & Borg, 2007). Steps in the development of the test included online survey feedback from those who had used the previous edition (SCAN-A), phone interviews with those who provided contact information on the online survey, a review of current literature, an initial tryout study, and a national standardardization of the instrument. In addition, online survey responders who indicated that they used the SCAN-A were invited to be part of a panel (User's Group) to provide more extensive feedback during the development of the SCAN-3:A. The User's Group included eight audiologists and speech-language therapists. The results of the survey prompted several changes between the SCAN-A and the SCAN-3:A.

The revised test was then evaluated through a pilot study with a sample of 156 adolescents (ages 12:0 through 15:11), and a clinical study with 34 participants who had been previously identified as having an APD. The makeup of the samples should be considered adequate for a pilot study.

Based on analysis of the pilot sample, additional changes were made.

TECHNICAL. The final version of the SCAN-3:A was standardized on a sample of 250 adolescents and adults, with 110 and 65 adolescents in the 13:0 to 15:11 and 16:0 to 19:11 age groups, respectively, and 50 and 25 in the 20:0 to 39:11 and 40:0 to 50:11 age groups, respectively. Though the manual provides evidence that the standardization sample was representative of the U.S. population in terms of gender, racial and ethnic background, geographic region, and primary-caregiver education, the sample size does not meet accepted standards for effective standardization. There was also no evidence that the sample included appropriate representation of students with special needs (i.e., children receiving services for special education).

The theoretical grounding for the SCAN-3:A is not well developed, and is limited to a brief narrative defining auditory processing disorders, and very brief rationale for the testing of auditory processing disorders.

The SCAN-3:A manual reports three types of evidence for reliability–test-retest, internal consistency, and interscorer reliability. Reported test-retest corrected correlations across an interval of 1–29 days for all ages ranged from a high of .80 for Competing Words–Directed Ear and Competing Sentences to a low of .54 for Auditory Figure Ground +8 dB. A number of the correlations do not meet the recommended test-retest reliability correlations expected of a screening instrument and all of the correlations fall below the recommended correlations for a diagnostic instrument (Salvia, Ysseldyke, & Bolt, 2007).

The manual also reports evidence for internal consistency by reporting split-half reliability corrected correlation coefficients for the standardization sample for each of the tests and the Auditory Processing Composite score. Average reliability coefficients across all ages for the standardization sample ranged from a high of .93 for Competing Sentences and the APC to a low of .53 for Auditory Figure Ground +8 dB. A review of the reliability coefficients for the various tests and age categories indicated that some were unacceptably low (e.g., Auditory Figure Ground +12 dB = .43 for ages 13.0–15:11 and Auditory Figure Ground +8 dB = .45 for ages 16.0–19:11). The reported split-half reliability coefficients indicated a similar pattern for internal consistency. Average internal consistency evidence was strong for some of the tests (Filtered Words, Competing Sentences) and the APC with correlations of .91 or higher.

The test manual provides acceptable evidence for interrater reliability.

The test author provides various forms of evidence in an effort to support the validity of the SCAN-3:A. First, evidence of the instrument's content validity is discussed in terms of how the test was designed to include items that are consistent with measurement of auditory processing skills, and how the revised test included additional items that were not included in the previous version. However, there is no detailed discussion of how the various test and composite scores are linked to scientifically based research literature. In brief, the evidence for SCAN-3:A content validity is inadequate.

The manual also provides a brief discussion of Response Processes that also seems inadequate as evidence for validity of the instrument. Although the test author states that such evidence of validity "was accumulated through empirical and qualitative examination of response processes" (manual, p. 66), there is no systematic reporting of those examinations beyond a couple of examples.

Evidence for construct validity for the SCAN-3:A is presented across all ages due to the small sample size at each age. Results of the intercorrelation analyses indicate that some of the tests are moderately to highly correlated (e.g., Competing Words–Directed Ear and Competing Words–Free Recall = .71), whereas others are weakly correlated. As the manual states, most of the low correlations are for the dichotic listening tests that might be expected to have low correlations because they assess very different components of auditory processing in comparison to other tests in the battery. The moderate to high subtest intercorrelations between each of the tests in the battery and the composite score provides evidence of acceptable internal structure. Overall, though the sample size used to analyze internal structure of the instrument seems inadequate, the intercorrelation results presented would suggest adequate internal consistency as one indicator of validity.

Finally, evidence for criterion-related validity was examined through the use of a "special group study," and an analysis of "diagnostic accuracy." Results from a "special group study" that compared individual test and composite scores of a sample of 61 adolescents and adults diagnosed with an APD with a matched control group found a statistically significant difference for each test (except filtered words) and composite score. A thorough analysis of test results to correctly identify those with or without an APD purports to provide support that the tests have diagnostic utility depending on the cutoff selected for the scaled scores. However, the evidence provided by the manual suggests that the SCAN-3:A is more accurate in identifying those with an APD than in identifying those without an APD. For example, when the cutoff score is ≤ 8, SCAN-3:A diagnostic tests correctly identified 93% of those with an APD, but only 49% were correctly identified as not having an APD. This should raise serious doubts about the use of the instrument as a diagnostic measure.

COMMENTARY. The relationship between an APD and learning and behavioral disabilities continues to be controversial in special education. Though the belief persists that auditory processing deficits related to learning difficulties can be identified and remediated, research supporting this position has not been established (Cacace & McFarland, 1998), though Kavale and Forness (2000) found some evidence for a connection between reading and perceptual skills when visual and auditory processes were considered together. However, even if there was a clear relationship between auditory processing skills and learning (especially reading) there is a general consensus among researchers that it is not possible to assess central APDs directly (Kavale & Forness, 2000). The author of the SCAN-3:A does not address these concerns in the description of the measurement's development.

The usefulness of the SCAN-3:A to accurately identify auditory processing deficits is questionable for at least three reasons. First, validity of the assumption that there exists a relationship between APDs and learning problems has not been established in the research, and the test author has not provided any significant support or evidence that the skills assessed in the SCAN-3:A are, in fact, related to learning difficulties. Second, the battery's underlying construct(s) are not well developed or connected to any substantial research base. Third, the psychometric characteristics of the battery are marginal at best. Though the evidence for criterion-related validity is adequately established, evidence for content and construct validity are weak. Reliability data presented in the manual indicates lower than acceptable reliability for most of the tests (Salvia, Ysseldyke, & Bolt, 2007).

SUMMARY. The SCAN-3:A is a norm-referenced assessment battery of Auditory Processing that can be administered and scored in a relatively efficient manner. However, its usefulness as either a screening or diagnostic measure is questionable due to the concerns expressed earlier. Evidence for reliability falls short of accepted standards, and without adequate construct validity, it cannot be recommended as a diagnostic tool.

REVIEWER'S REFERENCES

Cacace, A. T., & McFarland, D. J. (1998). Central auditory processing disorder in school-aged children: A critical review. *Journal of Speech, Language, and Hearing Research, 41,* 355-373.

Gall, M. D., Gall, J. P., & Borg, W. R. (2007). *Educational research: An introduction.* San Francisco: Pearson.

Kavale, K. A., & Forness, S. R. (2000). Auditory and visual perception processes and reading ability: A quantitative reanalysis and historical reinterpretation. *Learning Disability Quarterly, 23,* 253-270.

Salvia, J., Ysseldyke, J. A., & Bolt, S. (2007). *Assessment: In special and inclusive education* (10th ed.). Boston, MA: Houghton Mifflin.

[112]

SCAN-3 for Children: Tests for Auditory Processing Disorders.

Purpose: "Designed to identify auditory processing disorders in children."
Population: Ages 5-12.
Publication Dates: 1986-2009.
Acronym: SCAN-3:C.
Scores, 21: 4 screening test scores: Gap Detection (ages 8-12 only), Auditory Figure-Ground +8 dB, Competing Words-Free Recall, Total (P/F); 5 diagnostic test scores: Auditory Processing Composite (Filtered Words, Auditory Figure-Ground +8 dB, Competing Words-Directed Ear, Competing Sentences, Total); 3 supplementary test scores: Auditory Figure-Ground +12 dB, Auditory Figure-Ground 0 dB, Time Compressed Sentences; ear advantage summary score for each of the following: Auditory Figure-Ground +8 dB, Competing Words-Free Recall, Filtered Words, Competing Words-Directed Ear-Directed Right Ear, Competing Words-Directed Ear-Directed Left Ear, Competing Sentences, Auditory Figure-Ground +12 dB, Auditory Figure-Ground +0 dB, Time Compressed Sentences.
Administration: Individual.
Price Data, 2010: $255 per complete kit including 25 record forms, manual (2009, 124 pages), and Audio CD; $57 per 25 record forms; $97 per manual; $107 per Audio CD.
Time: (10-15) minutes for the screening tests; (20-30) minutes for the diagnostic and supplementary tests.
Comments: Screening test scores are "criterion-referenced"; Auditory Figure-Ground +8 dB test is identical across the screening and diagnostic levels; all scores (except for Gap Detection) are calculated as a composite of the participant's right ear score and left ear score, and the ear-advantage score is the difference between the right and left ear scores; additional materials

required: "CD player with a track display or a two-channel audiometer" or access to a computer, two sets of stereo headphones, and a stereo Y-adapter if necessary; revision of SCAN-C Test for Auditory Processing Disorders in Children–Revised.
Author: Robert W. Keith.
Publisher: Pearson.
Cross References: For reviews by Annabel J. Cohen and Jaclyn B. Spitzer and Abbey L. Berg of an earlier edition entitled SCAN-C Test for Auditory Processing Disorders in Children—Revised, see 16:217; for an earlier edition, see also T5:2300 (1 reference); for a review by Sami Gulgoz of the original edition, see 11:341 (2 references).

REVIEW of the SCAN-3 for Children: Tests for Auditory Processing Disorders by GARY L. CANIVEZ, Professor of Psychology, Department of Psychology, Eastern Illinois University, Charleston, IL:

DESCRIPTION. The SCAN-3 for Children: Tests for Auditory Processing Disorders (SCAN-3:C) is a revision of the SCAN-C Revised and is an individually administered test using a standard compact disc of audio recordings of instructions and stimuli played through headphones to purportedly measure "auditory processing disorders" (APD) in children ages 5–12. The definition for APD provided in the manual is that of the American Speech-Language-Hearing Association (ASHA, 1996, 2005). Robert W. Keith, the test author, implies that APD is related to academic and behavioral difficulties and that information from the SCAN-3:C will provide information about functional abilities and auditory system neuromaturation. Precious little theoretical background information and theoretical support for the construct of auditory processing is provided in the manual.

The SCAN-3:C is divided into three screening tests (Gap Detection [GD], Auditory Figure Ground +8 dB [AFG8], and Competing Words–Free Recall [CWFR]), four diagnostic tests (Auditory Figure Ground +8 dB [AFG8], Filtered Words [FW], Competing Words–Directed Ear [CWDE], and Competing Sentences [CS]), and four supplementary tests (Competing Words–Free Recall [CWFR], Auditory Figure Ground 0 dB [AFG0], Auditory Figure Ground +12 dB [AFG+12], and Time Compressed Sentences [TCS]). The manual is a bit confusing in that Keith notes there are four diagnostic tests (one supplementary test is also included among the diagnostic tests) but notes there are only three supplementary tests when one of the screening tests is also included as a supplementary test (Competing Words–Free Recall). Those not passing *all* screening tests (two for ages 5–7, three for ages 8–12) are then administered the diagnostic tests. The manual notes that performance on diagnostic tests is to be used "in combination with observations and other information" (p. 2) to make a diagnosis of APD but specific examples of observations or behaviors and other information to be used in diagnosing of ASD were not delineated.

DEVELOPMENT. Goals for revision noted inclusion of temporal processing tests; increasing difficulty of the Filtered Words subtest to improve ceiling; including tests with different signal-to-noise ratios; modifying the Competing Sentences subtest to allow partial credit; modifying scoring for Competing Words to allow only direct order correctness; include screening, diagnostic, and supplementary tests with scaled scores; and providing ear advantage prevalence for all tests. Changes from the SCAN-C and item development were presented in the manual, as were summaries of field research and pilot research before standardization. Test instructions are included on a professionally recorded compact disc and extensive information is provided regarding equipment needed to present the SCAN-3:C. Examiner qualifications indicate who may administer the SCAN-3:C but there is no guidance as to who or what qualifications are needed to interpret the scores. Detailed description and examples for administration and completion of the record form are provided.

NORMS AND SCORES. The standardization sample (N = 525) was obtained using a stratified national sampling across variables of race/ethnicity, geographic region, and education level of the child's primary caregiver (a likely proxy for SES as reliable income information is difficult to obtain). Tables comparing the standardization sample to 2004 U.S. Census estimates across stratification variables showed a close match on *single* variables. Unfortunately, there are no tables comparing sample proportions and population matches crossing two stratification variables (i.e., race/ethnicity X caregiver education level), so although there is a close match to the Census estimates across single variables, it is not possible to tell from the manual if disproportional representation exists in some cells within the matrix. Such tables are commonly published in other Pearson products such as Wechsler scales of intelligence. There were between 50 and 77 individuals within each age group from

5 through 9 years but 198 within the combined ages 10, 11, and 12. This is consistent with the SCAN-C Revised but there appears to be no information as to why these three age groups were combined. The manual presents standardization sample exclusionary criteria of pure tone hearing screening failure, past or present otitis media (or other illnesses that affected hearing), speech and/or language disorder, intellectual disability, and/or limited English proficiency, which could affect test performance.

Subtest scaled scores (M = 10, SD = 3, range 1-19) within each of the six age groups were obtained using a "method of inferential norming" (manual, p. 64) where means, standard deviations, and skewness were examined from first through fifth order polynomial regressions with comparison to theoretical distributions and growth curves that produced percentiles for raw scores. Although minor irregularities were reportedly corrected through smoothing, the method of smoothing (statistical vs. hand/visual) was not noted. The composite score (M = 100, SD = 15) was generated by summing the four diagnostic subtest scaled scores and normalized with composite score distribution smoothed (method unreported) to eliminate irregularities. Specification of methods to determine criterion-referenced cut scores for determining pass or fail was presented in the manual.

RELIABILITY. The manual contains common errors in a number of places by referring to reliability as a property of the test (i.e., "reliable tests," "test was perfectly reliable," "more reliable the test," p. 37) when reliability and error are properties of test scores obtained on a particular sample at a particular time. Reliability estimates are generally considered to be acceptable for individual clinical decision making when correlation coefficients meet or exceed .90 (Salvia & Ysseldyke, 2001). Reliability of SCAN-3:C scores was estimated with short-term test-retest (stability), internal consistency, and interscorer agreement. Short-term stability (1–29 days) for a small sample (n = 48) of standardization sample participants produced subtest stability coefficients ranging from .47 to .70 (uncorrected) and from .54 to .73 (corrected) and composite score stability coefficients of .78 (uncorrected) and .77 (corrected). These estimates indicated inadequate short-term stability for individual decision making. Internal consistency estimates across the six age groups ranged from .89 to .93 (M_r = .91) for the composite score and from .52 to .94 (M_r ranged .59 to .91) for the subtests. The Filtered Words and Competing Sentences subtests met or approached internal consistency sufficient to allow individual decision making where the other subtests did not. Among the diagnostic subtests, the Auditory Figure-Ground +8 dB had the lowest internal consistency estimate averaging .72 across all age groups. Thus, many subtest scores generally lacked sufficient reliability for individual decision making. Although composite score internal consistency estimates were generally acceptable, short-term stability estimates were not. Finally, all SCAN-3:C standardization tests were independently scored by two scorers, and due to the objective nature of SCAN-3:C scoring, interscorer agreement was very high, ranging from .98 to .99.

Standard errors of measurement are provided based on internal consistency estimates by age group and for the total sample and should be considered best case estimates as they consider only one source of error variance (Hanna, Bradley, & Holen, 1981). Estimated true score confidence intervals (90% and 95%) are provided in the manual for the composite score but test users are required to apply the appropriate standard score confidence interval critical values provided in the raw score to scaled score conversion tables. The formula to produce the increasingly asymmetrical confidence interval the farther the scaled score is from the mean is not provided in the manual. Obtained score confidence intervals also are not provided. When the assessment question is concerned with estimating the true score of the individual at the time of the evaluation (rather than the long-term estimate), the obtained score confidence interval is appropriate (Glutting, McDermott, & Stanley, 1987; Sattler, 2008). Obtained score and estimated true score confidence intervals are close in cases where the reliability coefficient is high but diverge as the estimated true score confidence interval becomes much more asymmetrical the farther the obtained score is from the mean and as reliability estimates decrease.

VALIDITY. The SCAN-3:C manual notes five approaches for examining validity evidence including test content, response processes, internal structure, special group studies, and diagnostic accuracy/utility. Test content appears to relate to characteristics outlined in the ASHA definition for APD. Examination of the SCAN-3:C internal structure was reportedly done by visually inspecting the correlation matrix of subtest intercorrelations.

Some moderate to high correlations were observed along with some low, near zero correlations between subtests. Such description in the manual seemed more like convergent and divergent (discriminant) validity considerations rather than internal structure per se. Factor analysis was apparently not conducted or reported in the manual; it is not always possible to visually inspect a correlation matrix and determine the latent structure of a test. Exploratory factor analysis (EFA) undertaken by this reviewer using the eight-subtest correlation matrix presented in the test manual produced communality estimates ranging from .22 (Filtered Words) to .74 (Competing Words–Directed Ear). Two factors had eigenvalues greater than one and scree analysis (Cattell, 1966) suggested the presence of two factors. Two factors were extracted and rotated with promax (oblique rotation) and factor pattern loadings placed CWDE, CWFR, and CS with Factor I and AFG12, AFG8, AFG0, FW, and TCS with Factor II, although pattern loadings for FW and TCS were not optimal (< .40). The two factors were correlated .39. Also missing but potentially informative are subtest specificity estimates that are noted salient when exceeding subtest error variance and represent *potential* for subtest interpretation beyond composite scores. Only SCAN-3:C TCS, FW, and CS subtests had salient subtest specificity. Further exploration and research regarding the structure of the SCAN-3:C is necessary but these minimal analyses should have been conducted and described in the manual to better describe and understand the structure. Given that the subtest reliabilities for most subtests were inadequate for individual decision making, factor-based scores might provide a useful alternative.

Validity evidence based on distinct group differences for a small (N = 40) sample of 5–12-year-olds "diagnosed" with APD were compared to a matched (race/ethnicity, age, parent education level) control group from the SCAN-3:C standardization sample. The APD group included children so identified by a certified audiologist or speech-language pathologist or "a composite score on a test of auditory processing" ≤ 1 *SD* from the mean (manual, p. 73). There is no indication as to how many children were identified APD by each method or if group differences existed between those different methods of APD identification. Also, there is no indication as to the criteria used by the audiologists or speech-language pathologists to diagnose APD or tests of auditory processing used. Mean SCAN-3:C differences between the APD and normal groups were statistically significant (p < .05) for all subtests (except Filtered Words) and for the composite score. Effect sizes were moderate to large (except Competing Words–Free Recall and Filtered Words). These results are supportive but group differences provide a necessary but not sufficient condition for diagnostic use of a test.

Examination of diagnostic accuracy/utility was also reported in the validity section of the manual and a method that should be used much more often for all diagnostic tests. It was mentioned that a sample of audiologists estimated 2–5% of children have APD (low base rate) and 25–80% of clients referred for evaluation are diagnosed with APD. Epidemiologically based population prevalence estimates were not provided (if they even exist) so the actual population base rate may be unknown. Because diagnostic efficiency statistics and utility are dependent on base rates, substantial differences may occur depending on which base rate one applies. A major problem in the manual is the lack of description of characteristics of the sample used to generate the diagnostic efficiency statistics and how those with APD were so determined and with whom they were compared. Further, although positive and negative predictive power (PPP, NPP) are the more important statistics to report as they are "rule in" and "rule out" statistics, Kessel and Zimmerman (1993) noted that *all* diagnostic efficiency statistics and the observed cell frequencies should be presented in such studies. Two tables in the manual presented varied PPP and NPP estimates by varying base rates and it appears that the statistics presented for the Matched Sample 50% may be from the earlier described group difference study but it is not specifically identified as such. To put the predictive power statistics in perspective, Landau, Milich, and Widiger (1991) suggested a PPP benchmark of .75 for diagnostic purposes and only in the case of base rates of 80% (a most generous assumption) does the SCAN-3:C achieve this benchmark but at a substantial cost in low NPP. Most PPP estimates were not supportive for diagnostic use. When examining presented cut scores at more reasonable population base rates for APD (4% or 25%) PPP estimates are disappointingly low and the SCAN-3:C does not appear useful for classification of APD; however, it does appear to be helpful in ruling out APD (good NPP). Another method that could be used to illustrate the effect of different cut scores on sensitivity and specificity would be to examine ROC curves and estimate the area under the curve (Swets, Dawes, & Monahan, 2000).

CRITIQUE/FUTURE CONCERNS. Compared to the SCAN-C Revised, the SCAN-3:C appears to be an improvement in content but there are very serious psychometric limitations yet present including questionable reliability for all but the composite score and very limited evidence for validity. Many more validity studies should have been conducted and presented in the manual such as comparisons with other tests purporting to measure auditory processing to examine convergent validity. Much greater detail regarding sample characteristics of diagnostic efficiency/utility studies should have been provided. It would also be helpful for the manual to present and summarize empirical studies of reliability, validity, and utility of earlier editions to provide a review of research demonstrating psychometric support. From the SCAN-3:C manual it appears that no empirical studies were published in peer-reviewed journals. It would have been helpful to see how children classified with ADHD perform on the SCAN-3:C in comparison to children with APD (but not ADHD) and, more importantly, whether the SCAN-3:C can distinguish individuals with ADHD from APD. Also, there is no indication nor are there data to suggest how aspects of performance on the SCAN-3:C relate to the construct and measures of attention or how APD differs from ADHD or executive functioning. Also, how do individuals of varying levels of intelligence perform on the SCAN-3:C? Do individuals of higher intelligence perform better than those of average intelligence? Do those with average intelligence perform better than those with below average intelligence or mental retardation? Cohen (2005) remarked in her review of the SCAN-C that "clarification of the theoretical part of the manual is recommended for a next revision and reports of tests of convergent and discriminant validity are needed" (p. 910). Sadly, it appears that this important advice was ignored. Further, the cost of this test appears exorbitant given these psychometric data and the dearth of SCAN-3:C research presented within the manual. A great deal of additional research is required to fully understand the parameters of the SCAN-3:C and it is hoped that Keith (and others) will embark on a mission to further study the reliability, validity, and utility of scores from the SCAN-3:C. It is also hoped that in future revisions greater attention will be paid to the critical psychometric issues noted in this and other reviews. But at present, the SCAN-3:C should not be used in diagnostic decision making.

REVIEWER'S REFERENCES

American Speech-Language-Hearing Association. (1996). Central auditory processing: Current status of research and implications for clinical practice. *American Journal of Audiology, 5,* 41-54.

American Speech-Language-Hearing Association. (2005). *(Central) auditory processing disorders.* Retrieved January 2007, from http://www.asha.org/docs/html/TR2005-00043.html.

Cattell, R. B. (1966). The scree test for the number of factors. *Multivariate Behavioral Research, 1,* 245-276.

Cohen, A. J. (2005). [Review of the SCAN-C: Test for Auditory Processing Disorders in Children–Revised]. In R. A. Spies & B. S. Plake (Eds.), *The sixteenth mental measurements yearbook* (pp. 907-919). Lincoln, NE: Buros Institute of Mental Measurements.

Glutting, J. J., McDermott, P. A., & Stanley, J. C. (1987). Resolving differences among methods of establishing confidence limits for test scores. *Educational and Psychological Measurement, 47,* 607-614.

Hanna, G. S., Bradley, F. O., & Holen, M. C. (1981). Estimating major sources of measurement error in individual intelligence scales: Taking our heads out of the sand. *Journal of School Psychology, 19,* 370-376.

Kessel, J. B., & Zimmerman, M. (1993). Reporting errors in studies of the diagnostic performance of self-administered questionnaires: Extent of the problem, recommendations for standardized presentation of results, and implications for the peer review process. *Psychological Assessment, 5,* 395-399.

Landau, S. R., Milich, R., & Widiger, T. A. (1991). Predictive power methods may be more helpful in making a diagnosis than sensitivity and specificity. *Journal of Child and Adolescent Psychopharmacology, 1,* 343-351.

Salvia, J., & Ysseldyke, J. E. (2001). *Assessment* (8th ed.). Boston: Houghton Mifflin.

Sattler, J. M. (2008). *Assessment of children: Cognitive foundations* (5th ed.). San Diego, CA: Author.

Swets, J. A., Dawes, R. M., & Monahan, J. (2000). Psychological science can improve diagnostic decisions. *Psychological Science in the Public Interest, 1,* 1-26.

Review of the SCAN-3 for Children: Tests for Auditory Processing Disorders by CONNIE THERIOT ENGLAND, Professor, Graduate Education, Lincoln Memorial University, Knoxville, TN:

DESCRIPTION. According to the test manual, the SCAN-3 for Children: Tests for Auditory Processing Disorders (SCAN-3:C) is an individually administered screening test designed to identify auditory processing disorders in children ages 5 years to 12 years. The test kit includes 25 record forms, test manual, and audio CD. Not included in the kit but needed for assessment are a CD player or CD drive, stereo Y-adapter, and an audiometer to calibrate the CD player or CD driver to 50 dB HL. The screening subtests, Gap Detection, Auditory Figure–Ground +8 dB (AFG+8), and Competing Words–Free Recall (CW-FR) take about 10–15 minutes to administer. The Gap Detection subtest is only for children ages 8:0–12:11. Examinees must pass the AFG+8 dB and the CWFR to pass screening. The diagnostic and supplementary tests take 20–30 minutes to complete. The diagnostic subtests include Filtered Words (FW) and AFG+8, Competing Words–Directed Ear (CW-DE), and Competing Sentences (CS). The supplemental subtests include Auditory–Figure Ground +12 dB (AFG+12), Auditory Figure–Ground 0 dB (AFG 0), and Time Compressed Sentences (TCS).

Administration procedures are clearly defined. All subtests are recorded on the provided audio CD. Directions for calibration procedures using an audiometer and CD player or CD driver are also provided.

DEVELOPMENT. The manual defines Auditory Processing Disorders (APD) using skill sets adopted by the American Speech-Language-Hearing Association (ASHA, 1996, 2005), which includes poor performance in one or more of the following skills: Sound localization and lateralization, Auditory discrimination, Temporal aspects of audition, Auditory performance with acoustic signals, Auditory performance with degraded acoustic signals, and/or Auditory pattern recognition.

Quoting ASHA (1996, 2005), the manual states the purpose of SCAN-3:C is "to determine if an APD is present, and if so, to describe its parameters, including functional auditory abilities and neuromaturation of the auditory system. The auditory processing assessment should provide information about developmental and acquired disorders of the central auditory system" (p. 2).

The SCAN-3:C can be used to evaluate a child's skills in temporal processing, listening in noise, dichotic listening, and listening to degraded speech. The test developer's close association with his consumers permitted him to expand and deepen understanding of the concept of APD. A feedback loop between test developer and experts, diagnosticians, and clinicians in the field of auditory processing allows for constant redevelopment and refinement of this type of assessment tool. For example, one suggestion from the consumers was to include ear advantage in the subtests. With the exception of Gap Detection, all subtests include ear advantage. The test manual gives an excellent description of ear advantage and the reader is referred to that section of the manual for further information.

Improvements to the differential diagnostic capability of the SCAN-3:C include: The AFG subtest is administered at the 0 dB, +8 dB, and +12 dB rather than only at +8 dB; the FW subtest is administered at the 750Hz low-pass filter instead of the 1000hz filter used in the earlier SCAN-C; and the revision of the directed ear instructions.

TECHNICAL. Much of the technical information for individual subtests is included within the description of the revision process used in the development of the SCAN-3:C. The SCAN-3:C retains all four of the SCAN-C's subtests (Auditory Figure-Ground, Filtered Words, Competing Words, and Competing Sentences) with Competing Words and Competing Sentences using new scoring procedures. The SCAN-3:C has five additional subtests: Gap Detection, Auditory Figure-Ground 0 dB signal-to-noise ratio, Auditory Figure-Ground +12 dB signal-to-noise ratio, Competing Words–Free Recall, and Time Compressed Sentences.

Normative data were collected through the administration of the SCAN-3:C to 525 children representative of the general population to age, sex, race/ethnicity, geographic region, and primary caregiver's education level. All examiners were properly licensed to conduct the assessments (i.e., audiologists and speech-language-pathologists). Children excluded from the standardization sample were those who failed a pure-tone screening hearing test; presented with ear infections; had an identified speech articulation, rhythm, or language disorder; had an identified intellectual disability; and/or had limited English Proficiency.

The SCAN-3:C gives an ear advantage score that may indicate hemispheric dominance for language as well as provide information on the development of the child's auditory system (e.g., "A child with a typically developing auditory system will have higher right ear scores than left ear scores on the dichotic listening tests," manual, p. 35).

Subtests' raw scores for the SCAN-3:C are converted to standard scores with a mean of 10 and a standard deviation of 3 and a range of 1–19. Average scores fall between 7 and 13. The SCAN-3:C's Auditory Processing Composite (APC) score provides information on the auditory processing skills of children in degraded speech, listening with background noise, and dichotic listening.

To evaluate test-retest reliability, 48 children were tested on two occasions. The interval betweeen testing sessions ranged from 1 to 29 test days. Composite test/retest correlation coefficients averaged .77, with effect sizes ranging from .14 to .75, and with consistent improvement across subtests upon retesting. Confidence intervals, based on the internal consistency reliability coefficients of each test or composite score, are available at the 90% and 95% levels. Percentile ranks and descriptive classifications are given for scale scores of 7 and above (84th percentile) as falling within the normal range, scale scores of 4 to 6 as borderline, and scale scores of 3 or below as disordered. Interscorer reliability data were extremely strong with coefficients ranging from .98 to .99.

Evidence of validity estimates are provided for test content, response processes, and internal structure. The manual's comprehensive coverage of the revision of its earlier version, along with research on the utility of the current SCAN-3:C as an assessment tool for clinicians, supports the test developer's commitment to his consumers.

As stated in the manual, test content validity of the SCAN-3:C represents an improvement in the measurement of temporal processing; adding a different response mode for dichotic listening, and including additional conditions for listening in noise. Evidence based on response processes showed that the frequency of "blends" impacting the scoring system was not statistically significant. Validity evidence based on internal structure reflects the degree to which the pattern of intercorrelations among subtests provides a more complete interpretation of the child's auditory processing abilities (e.g., highest correlation between tests of measuring similar skills).

SUMMARY. The SCAN-3:C appears to be a psychometrically sound assessment instrument for the screening and identification of APD in children aged 5–12. Strengths of the instrument are its firm grounding in ASHA approved "auditory skills processing sets," its commitment to its clinicians in the form of a feedback loop of data to improve or redesign aspects of the instrument, and its strong reliability and validity scores. The SCAN-3:C manual provides theoretical underpinnings, construct descriptions, and intervention strategies for APDs.

Additional research on the SCAN-3:C will provide much information on the use of this tool as a measure of the functional auditory abilities and neuromaturation of the auditory system of young children as well as "provide information about developmental and acquired disorders of the central auditory system" (manual, p. 2). If the examiner's manual is an indication of the test developer's commitment to ongoing research and development, no doubt the needed research will be accomplished.

REVIEWER'S REFERENCES

American Speech-Language-Hearing Association. (1996). Central auditory processing: Current status of research and implications for clinical practice. *American Journal of Audiology, 5,* 41-54.

American Speech-Language-Hearing Association. (2005). *(Central) auditory proessing disorders.* Retrieved January 2007, from http://www.asha.org/docs/html/TR2005-00043.html

[113]

School Motivation and Learning Strategies Inventory.

Purpose: Designed to measure "strategies students actively employ in learning and test taking."
Population: Ages 8-12, 13-18.
Publication Date: 2006.
Acronym: SMALSI.
Scores, 11: Study Strategies, Note-Taking and Listening Skills, Reading and Comprehension Strategies, Writing and Research Skills, Test-Taking Strategies, Time Management (teen only), Organizational Techniques (teen only), Time Management/Organizational Techniques (child only), Academic Motivation, Test Anxiety, Attention and Concentration.
Administration: Group.
Levels, 2: Child, Teen.
Forms, 2: Child Form, Teen Form.
Price Data, 2008: $199 per complete kit including manual (108 pages), 25 child test forms, 25 child profile sheets, child scoring template, 25 teen test forms, 25 teen profile sheets, teen scoring template, and audio CD; $135 per child or teen kit including manual, 25 test forms and 25 profile sheets (specify form), scoring template (specify form), and audio CD; $45 per 25 test forms, $32.50 per scoring template, $28 per 100 profile sheets (specify forms); $16.50 per audio CD; $52.50 per manual; $399 per scoring CD.
Time: (20-30) minutes.
Comments: The same manual is used for both Child and Teen forms.
Authors: Kathy Chatham Stroud and Cecil R. Reynolds.
Publisher: Western Psychological Services.

Review of the School Motivation and Learning Strategies Inventory by CHRISTINE NOVAK, Associate Clinical Professor, School Psychology Program, The University of Iowa, Iowa City, IA:

DESCRIPTION. The School Motivation and Learning Strategies Inventory (SMALSI) is a self-report tool designed to determine student performance across a comprehensive set of behaviors representing learning strategies, academic motivation, and test-taking. This inventory is unique in that it is designed especially for use with school-aged youth. There are two forms: a Child Form for students aged 8–12 years, and a Teen Form for students aged 13–18 years. Both forms consist of over 100 items written at a third grade reading level, which should take from 20–30 minutes to complete. The SMALSI can be administered individually or to a group; the form also can be read to students who have difficulty reading. The

SMALSI is intended for use in both general and special education for the purposes of: (a) screening to facilitate identification of topics for group instruction; (b) prereferral intervention, which may ameliorate learning difficulties and avert the need for special education; (c) special education assessment, which is linked directly to intervention in areas that may exacerbate academic difficulties; and (d) research related to understanding the nature of these skills and to the development of effective interventions for learning strategies, test taking, and academic motivation.

Scoring is straightforward, using either templates or a computer program. Included is an Inconsistent Responding Index, which helps to discern whether responses were affected by carelessness, noncompliance, or lack of understanding; this feature would be helpful when screening groups of students and using computer scoring. The SMALSI yields numerous scale scores rather than a total score in order to examine more easily areas of strength and weakness. Clear guidelines for describing and interpreting the resultant *T*-scores are provided in detail and summarized in user-friendly tables.

DEVELOPMENT. The SMALSI was developed to meet the need for a psychometrically and conceptually sound measure for assessing learning strategies at the elementary and secondary level. According to the authors, existing measures tend to be adaptations of tools for college students or are narrowly defined. The SMALSI identifies 10 constructs relevant to academic achievement: Study Strategies, Note-Taking and Listening Skills, Reading and Comprehension Strategies, Writing/Research Skills, Test-Taking Strategies, Organizational Techniques, Time Management, Low Academic Motivation, Test Anxiety, and Concentration/Attention Difficulties. These constructs were selected because they represent discrete behaviors that can be the focus of intervention and have been demonstrated empirically to relate to achievement. The manual provides a brief overview of each construct, citing literature from 1979–2001.

TECHNICAL.

Standardization. The standardization sample for the SMALSI consisted of over 100 (range 109–558) students at each year level and grade level. The sample compared favorably overall to the 2000 U.S. Census with regard to gender, race, ethnicity, region, and parental education. In both the child and teen samples there were more than twice the percentage of Black/African American students in the sample than in the population, whereas White students were undersampled at about the same proportion. The child sample included 17% more students from the South than the U.S. population, and for the teens, there was a lower representation from the Midwest (10%) compared to the population percentages. The sample was drawn primarily from public schools; the extent to which students in special education were included is not reported.

Average *T*-scores were reported for select groups to determine whether clinically significant differences might emerge that would warrant alternative score interpretations or separate norms. Moderate effect sizes (.30–.47) were noted in some instances. Deviations were particularly apparent for Grade 8 (lower average strengths in Study Strategies, Writing, Test-Taking and Organization; higher than average difficulties with Motivation). Further, the Writing/Research average for American Indian/Alaska Native was lower for both the child and teen groups as well as Hispanic/Latino teens, whereas the Reading/Comprehension average was higher than expected for Black/African American teens. The authors respectfully indicate that more research is needed to clarify what implications derive from these differences.

Reliability. Only one form of reliability was reported for the SMALSI (i.e., internal consistency). The lack of interrater reliability probably should not be an issue given that the test is objectively scored. Stability was omitted with the rationale that "the primary interest is in the accuracy of measurement at the time of assessment and not necessarily the longer-term stability" (manual, p. 58); however, if one of the main purposes of the SMALSI is to assess change over time due to intervention effects, then an estimate of the amount of error that can be expected simply due to the passage of time is critical.

Coefficient alpha for the child and teen scales ranged from .69–.91. The lowest estimate was for Writing in the child sample; in fact, for the 8–9-year-olds, this coefficient drops to .60–.64, which raises concern about the consistency of behavior in response to items at this level. The Writing/Research scale overall evidenced the weakest reliability coefficients, whereas the Test Anxiety scale produces the strongest correlations. Another curious finding reported by the authors is the higher reliability coefficients overall for the American Indian/Alaska Native subgroup.

Validity. Evidence of content validity was presented in terms of expert review in the development of the items and item analysis used in the selection of final items. To investigate the theoretical basis for score interpretation, several investigations were described. Interscale correlations showed generally predictable patterns of relationship, such as negative to near zero correlations between scales representing desirable skills and those representing liabilities. Of note was the level of shared variance for the Study Skills and Note-Taking scales with almost every other scale for both the child and teen samples, which suggests that these skills may be highly dependent on the quality of other skills such as Organization, Time Management, and Reading Comprehension. The authors did not clearly specify a model of Learning Strategies; skills were viewed as multidimensional rather than subsumed by one overarching construct. Factor analyses would be an interesting adjunct for examining how these constructs relate, especially at different age levels.

Correlations with tests measuring related-but-not-identical constructs also followed expectation, such as a high degree of correspondence between the SMALSI index of Low Motivation and the School Maladjustment scale of the Behavior Assessment System for Children. Correlations with the measure selected to demonstrate the association between competence in learning strategies and academic achievement were somewhat disappointing due to limits imposed by the restriction of range of scores on the criterion measure. As the authors note, further research with broader measures may provide more convincing evidence.

Finally, in an attempt to show that the test could differentiate identified groups, two studies were reported. In the first, the mean scores from 23 students identified as Gifted and Talented showed mean scores on 8 of 10 of the Teen scales that were substantially higher than expected, as were 3 of 10 of the Child scales. Perhaps surprisingly, the Writing/Research scale had the highest effect size on both forms. In another study, 32 students attending a special school focusing on developing academic skills in students from disadvantaged backgrounds were shown to perform significantly better on the Study Strategies, Reading Comprehension, and Writing/Research scales, but reported significantly lower motivation and test anxiety. The authors suggest that these results support their claim that those areas assessed by the SMALSI can be increased through training and instruction; however, this conclusion could be questioned because it is unclear whether these students, who were selected because of their academic promise, already had these skills before entering the school program.

COMMENTARY. The SMALSI has been carefully developed with school-aged students and shows remarkable consistency for the elementary student (particularly age 9 and up). The flexibility for determining group performance as well as that of individual students is a useful feature for screening. Further, the specification of multiple skill areas provides a fairly comprehensive assessment. Given the limited understanding of the development of learning strategies and related concepts, the SMALSI would provide an excellent foundation for further research because it measures similar aspects for children as well as teens. In terms of practice, there is no direct evidence that identification of strengths and weaknesses according to SMALSI results will eventually lead to improved academic skills with intervention. The authors provide exceptional resources for interventions, which should assist in designing studies to affirm this link. Relatedly, there is no direct evidence to suggest that using the SMALSI as part of a comprehensive assessment battery will help to differentiate Learning Disabilities from low achievement related to poor learning strategies. Again, studies measuring academic outcomes as a result of training in areas constituting weaknesses on the SMALSI would strengthen this claim.

SUMMARY. The SMALSI is a useful tool for school personnel to identify discrete skills that MAY boost achievement following intervention; outcome studies are necessary to determine to what extent the SMALSI can aid in prereferral assessment or special education decision making.

Review of the School Motivation and Learning Strategies Inventory by CLAUDIA R. WRIGHT, Professor Emerita, California State University, Long Beach, Long Beach, CA:

DESCRIPTION. The School Motivation and Learning Strategies Inventory (SMALSI)—Child Form (ages 8–12) and Teen Form (ages 13–18) are self-report measures that serve as diagnostic tools for students who apply ineffective study skills and/or experience low levels of motivation, test anxiety, and/or concentration problems when engaged in academic activities. The 147-item, 9-scale SMALSI-Child and the 170-item, 10-scale SMALSI-Teen yield scores dealing with "student strengths" and "student liabilities." "Student strengths" encompass 7 learning strategies scales: (a) Study Strategies (STUDY)—selecting, relating, and encoding new with previously learned information; (b) Note-Taking/Listening Skills (NOTE)—discriminating key points and note-taking efficiency; (c) Reading/Comprehension Strategies (READ)—utilizing previewing, monitoring, reviewing, and self-testing methods; (d) Writing/Research Skills (WRITE)—applying self-checking skills and using various approaches when researching topics; (e) Test-taking Strategies (TEST)—applying techniques to enhance test performance; (f) Organizational Techniques (ORG)—organizing study materials for assignments; and (g) Time Management (TIME)—planning and completing assignments in a timely manner. For SMALSI-Child, TIME and ORG scales are combined forming the Time Management/Organizational Techniques (TIMORG) scale. "Student liabilities" information is obtained from three scales: (a) Low Academic Motivation (LOMOT)—lacking internal motivation to engage in school-related tasks; (b) Test Anxiety (TANX)—experiencing excessive worry related to test taking; and (c) Concentration/Attention Difficulties (CONDIF)—problems with focusing, avoiding distractions, or adjusting to academic-related demands. The Inconsistency Responding (INC) Index Score, generated for each form, is derived from the difference in response patterns for selected paired items expected to yield similar values; exceeding the INC criterion flags an examinee as possibly careless or inattentive when responding to test items.

Test administration and scoring. SMALSI item-statements are written at the middle third-grade level for both forms. If students are reading below this level or the examinee has relevant limitations, additional time for test-taking may be required. Either form can be administered to students individually, in intact classrooms, or in large groups using paper-and-pencil templates or computer. A 4-point Likert-type formatted scale employs response options (*N*) *Never*, (*S*) *Sometimes*, (*O*) *Often*, and (*A*) *Almost always*, with values of 0, 1, 2, and 3, respectively. Response forms can be scored manually using templates or by computer (software is available from the publisher). The technical manual provides useful instructions for test administrators and includes a completed sample profile, clear directions for creating profiles, and helpful guides for interpreting all scale scores.

DEVELOPMENT. The development of the SMALSI was predicated on the need to conceptualize learning strategies more narrowly and with a more practical focus on study skills built upon behaviors children recognize and use to acquire and process information and which can help to structure interventions. Conventional content validation procedures were employed including exhaustive literature reviews, detailed rationales for selected constructs, clear operational definitions, close alignment of item content with supporting theoretical frameworks, carefully worded text for each item-statement, expert review, and the application of appropriate statistical methods for item selection and deletion.

TECHNICAL.

Standardization. Data for normative groups were obtained from samples of students enrolled primarily in U.S. public schools in the Northeast, Midwest, West, and South (for which Child and Teen forms were oversampled 52% and 35%, respectively, with no explanation). The SMALSI-Child Form was administered to 1,821 students aged 8 to 12 with 51% females and 49% males. Respondents were classified as White, 48%; Black, 29%; Latino, 8%; Asian, 3%; Native American and Other, each 5%; and nonresponders, 2%. For grade level: Grade 3, 21%; Grade 4, 28%; Grade 5, 31%; Grade 6, 14%; and Grade 7, 6%. For age: 8, 8%; 9, 23%; 10, 29%; 11, 25%; and 12, 15%. The SMALSI-Teen Form was administered to 1,100 students aged 13–18 with 54% female and 45% male. The ethnic breakdown was White, 41%; Black, 26%; Latino, 15%; Asian, 2%; Native American, 8%; Other and nonresponders, each 4%. For grade level: Grade 7, 10%; Grade 8, 11%; Grade 9, 17%; Grade 10, 26%; Grade 11, 15%; and Grade 12, 21%. For age: 13, 13%; 14 and 15, each 18%; 16, 23%; 17, 18%; and 18, 10%.

Each of the SMALSI scale scores from the normative data is approximately normally distributed and converted to standard scores (normalized *T* score, mean of 50*T*) to allow for comparisons of scores across scales and for comparisons of group or individual performances with normative group scores. The technical manual includes a series of tables displaying average *T* scores obtained for each scale stratified by form, gender, ethnicity, age, and grade level.

Reliability. Internal-consistency reliability estimates (coefficient alpha) and standard errors of measurement (*SEM*) were obtained for SMALSI scale scores for the total standardized samples and stratified by form, age, grade level, gender, and ethnicity. SMALSI-Child standardized scale scores yielded acceptable coefficient alphas ranging from .69 to .89 (*Mdn* = .79): STUDY, .77; NOTE, .81; READ, .79; WRITE, .69; TEST, .76; TIMORG, .77; LOMOT, .83; TANX, .89; and CONDIF, .85. For SMALSI-Teen standardized scale scores, alphas ranged from .77 to .91 (*Mdn* = 83.5): STUDY, .86; NOTE, .86; READ, .82; WRITE, .77; TEST, .84; ORG, .79; TIME, .81; LOMOT, .83; TANX, .91; and CONDIF, .88. Comparable alphas were observed across scales for subgroups.

Validity. Differential-group performance on SMALSI scale scores involved the examination of one-sample *t* tests (alpha = .01) and relevant effect sizes for age (8–18; *ns* ranged from 110–519, *mdn* = 203); grade level (Grades 3 to 12; *ns* ranged from 109–558, *mdn* = 229); gender (Child: 894 males, 916 females; Teen: 488 males, 598 females); and gifted and talented (GT: Child, 23; Teen, 33) and academic development (AD: Child, 32) programs. *T* scores remained stable for age and grade with small but statistically significant linear increases reported for CONDIF and LOMOT as a function of age. Although not statistically significant, the Teen data revealed general improvement in skills. Females scored consistently higher than males on the "student strengths" SMALSI scales with statistically significant differences on all comparisons for the Teen Form and on a majority of the comparisons for the Child Form with the exceptions of STUDY, READ, and TIMORG; on the "student liabilities" scales on both forms, males scored higher on LOMOT and CONDIF ($p < .01$ for Child only) and females scored higher on TANX ($p < .01$ for Teen only).

It was hypothesized that students classified as GT would score higher on SMALSI scale scores than those in the fifth grade or in the seventh- and eighth-grade standardization samples on the Child and Teen Forms, respectively. A sample of 23 GT students (Grade 5; 6 males and 17 females) was administered the Child Form and a sample of 33 GT middle-school students (18 males and 15 females) completed the Teen Form. (For these samples, determination of GT status did not include any direct assessment of SMALSI variables.)

As expected, a comparison of average GT SMALSI scale scores with corresponding standardization statistics revealed that GT students' performance was more positive on all scales. For SMALSI-Child, controlling for age and gender revealed that GT group averages were significantly different for the WRITE, TIMORG, and TANX scores yielding moderate to large effect sizes: .70, .60, and .59, respectively. Scale score comparisons on the Teen Form revealed 8 of 10 statistically significant differences, with moderate to large effect sizes: STUDY, .70; WRITE, .94; TEST, .60; ORG, .80; TIME, .81; LOMOT, .93; TANX, .68; and CONDIF, .60 (*mdn* = .75).

The final comparison group was a sample of 32 students from an academic development (AD) school (small classroom instruction and learning skills training emphases), serving disadvantaged youth who have shown academic promise. Of the 32 students who completed the Child Form, 16 were Black; 11, White; and 5, Latino. It was hypothesized that AD students would score higher than those in the standardization sample. Findings indicated that these students scored higher on five of the six "student strengths" scales (with NOTE the exception), and higher on all three "student liabilities" scales. Controlling for age and gender, moderate to large effect sizes were observed for STUDY, .54; READ, (a finding consistent with the curriculum emphasis) .67; WRITE, .55; LOMOT, .80; and TANX, .51 (*Mdn* = .55). These results suggest that although AD students perceived themselves as better prepared, on average, with respect to "student strengths" than the standardized group, they experienced greater challenges with motivation and test anxiety issues—perhaps related to the study skills curricular focus and higher expectations held for academic performance.

Concurrent- and construct-related validity efforts focused on correlations between SMALSI scale scores and personality-related behavior, school adjustment, and academic competence variables. A sample of 23 students completed the SMALSI-Child Form and the Behavior Assessment System for Children (BASC) Self-Report of Personality-Child (SRP-C; 17:21); and 24 students completed the SMALSI-Teen and BASC, Self-Report of Personality-Adolescent (SRP-A; 17:21). The BASC was designed to assess a variety of dimensions dealing with child personality, emotion, and behavior. Scale scores include Attitude to School, Attitude to Teachers, Relations with Parents, Interpersonal Relations, Locus of Control, Self-Esteem, Self-Reliance, to name several; and composite scores are School Maladjustment, Clinical Maladjustment, and Emotional Symptoms, where high scores hold negative connotations, and Personal Adjustment, for which high scores carry positive connotations. In general, SMALSI "student strengths" scale scores were negatively correlated with those BASC SRP scores associated with maladjustment, and SMALSI "student liabilities" scale scores were positively correlated. For the SMALSI-Child sample, the strongest correlations were observed between LOMOT and BASC SRP-C Attitude to School scale scores (.72), Attitude to Teachers (.81), and School Maladjustment (.83). It was concluded that the dimensions assessed by SMALSI "student strengths" scale scores are moderately associated with a student's school adjustment and the attitudes she or he holds toward school and teachers.

To examine the relationship between SMALSI scale scores and achievement, the authors selected the Texas Assessment of Knowledge and Skills (TAKS; Texas Education Agency, 2004), designed to assess minimum attainment of grade-level skills in Reading, Math, Social Studies, and Science. As a mastery test, the distribution of TAKS scores are typically negatively skewed, a circumstance likely to reduce the size of correlations with other measures. One sample of 32 students completed the TAKS and the SMALSI-Child Form, and a sample of 53 students completed the TAKS and the Teen Form. Although coefficients observed for both samples were not strong, the data provided some useful information. Correlations between SMALSI-Child "student strengths" scale scores yielded low to moderate coefficients with TAKS Reading (.25 to .48, *Mdn* = .36), Math (.09 to .41, *Mdn* = .125) Science (.03 to .30, *Mdn* = .12) scores. The strongest relationships were observed between STUDY, NOTE, WRITE, TIMORG, and TANX scale scores and the TAKS Reading scores with median correlations of .38, .34, .48, .45, and -.15, respectively and for WRITE and TANX with TAKS Math scores (.41 and -.39, respectively). SMALSI-Teen scale score correlations with TAKS scores ranged from .01 to .47 with the strongest coefficients observed for the "student liabilities" scale scores, LOMOT and TANX with Reading (-.30 and -.32, respectively), Math (-.26 and -.20, respectively), Social Studies (-.33 and -.47, respectively), and TANX and CONDIF with Science (-.27 and .21, respectively). Overall, coefficients derived from the adolescent data were smaller than those for the child sample. However, patterns revealed TEST, LOMOT, and TANX were stronger for adolescents than for children, suggesting that development of study and learning strategies might be more meaningful for younger students as these skills are related to achievement. For adolescents, motivation and test anxiety factors appeared more important.

Although conceptually and academically relevant variables were identified for investigations seeking to validate SMALSI scale scores, the use of small sample sizes in several studies merits caution in interpreting trends in the data.

COMMENTARY. A compelling argument for SMALSI development addressed two issues: (a) an abundance of research has generated instruments for assessing learning-related and academic-motivation constructs that have been conceptualized in a variety of ways but have used disparate terms interchangeably (e.g., learning styles, learning skills, learning strategies, and so on) creating confusion; and (b) most instruments have been designed primarily for college students but employed derivative revisions of original test items for both elementary and secondary students (e.g., Learning and Study Strategies Inventory [LASSI], 17:105 and Study Attitudes and Methods Survey [SAMS], 14:376). The SMALSI items appear more salient for younger students and, given the scales are conceptually and psychometrically sound, the SMALSI offers a reasonable alternative to other tests.

Application of SMALSI scale scores was discussed regarding prereferral interventions for children with special needs, which would afford a relatively quick, thorough, and cost-effective addition to the arsenal of methods employed for such purposes; however, to this end, no specific study or data base was offered. Appropriate reservations and cautions were raised with respect to CONDIF scale scores—specifically, that these not be used to diagnose ADHD or any other clinical disorder.

It would be informative in future SMALSI research efforts to increase Asian, Latino, and Native American representation as the latter two groups, in particular, have greater numbers of underperformers in academic settings who could benefit from more accurate identification of "student strengths" and "liabilities" that may facilitate implementation of appropriate interventions.

SUMMARY. The SMALSI scales reflect constructs that are distinct, readily operationalized, and easily grasped by students and teachers to enhance instruction, learning, and intervention. Evidence of differential-group performance across relevant subgroups supports the instruments' usefulness. The SMALSI-Child and -Teen Forms provide exceptional diagnostic tools for assessing school-related motivation and learning strategies employed by students and for identifying problem areas for students who are academically low performers in school.

REVIEWER'S REFERENCE

Texas Education Agency. (2004). Texas Assessment of Knowledge and Skills (TAKS). Austin, TX: Author.

[114]

Self-Perceptions of Adolescents.

Purpose: Designed to measure an adolescent's concept of self.
Population: Adolescents.
Publication Dates: 1965-2007.
Scores: 8 scales: Self as a Person (Self Concept, Ideal Concept, Reflected Self, Perceptions of Others), Self as a Student (Self Concept, Ideal Concept, Reflected Self, Perceptions of Others).
Administration: Group.
Forms, 8: Self as a Person Scales (Self Concept, Ideal Concept, Reflected Self/Other, Perceptions of Others), Self as a Student (Student Self, Ideal Concept as a Student, Reflected Self as a Student/Other, Perceptions of Others/Student Self).
Price Data, 2007: $40 per 25 scales (specify form); $40 per test manual (2007, 39 pages); $.40 per scale for scoring; $40 per analysis of profile charts and reports.
Time: (5–20) minutes.
Comments: Developed from the original Self-Perceptions Inventory (15:226) and is part of the SPI series that includes: Self-Perceptions of Adults (18:115), Self-Perceptions of Children (18:116), Self-Perceptions of College Students, Self-Perceptions of School Administrators (18:117), Self-Perceptions of University Instructors (18:118), Self-Perceptions of Teachers, and Self-Perceptions of Nurses.
Author: Louise M. Soares.
Publisher: Castle Consultants.
Cross References: For reviews by Mary M. Clare and Aimin Wang of the 1999 Revision of the Self-Perceptions Inventory, see 15:226; see also T4:2421 (1 reference); for a review by Janet Morgan Riggs of an earlier edition, see 9:1101; for a review by Lorrie Shepard of an earlier edition, see 8:673 (2 references).

Review of the Self-Perceptions of Adolescents by STEPHEN AXFORD, Assistant Director of Special Services, Falcon School District 49, Adjunct Faculty Member, University of Colorado at Colorado Springs, Colorado Springs, CO:

DESCRIPTION. The Self-Perceptions of Adolescents (SPI/Adolescents) is an easy-to-administer and score Likert-type, self-report and other rater (i.e., parent, teacher, sibling, classmate, etc.) multiple survey inventory designed to measure adolescent self-concept. The SPI/Adolescents is one of eight assessment tools comprising the Self-Perceptions Inventory Series (SPI). The SPI Series also includes the following inventories: Self-Perceptions of Adults, Self-Perceptions of Children, Self-Perceptions of College Students, Self-Perceptions of Nurses, Self-Perceptions of School Administrators, Self-Perceptions of Teachers, and Self-Perceptions of University Instructors. Copyright dates for the SPI/Adolescents are: 1965, 1975, 1999, and 2007. Two reviews in the *Fifteenth Mental Measurements Yearbook* (Clare, 2003; Wang, 2003) of the 1999 Revision of the SPI Series both conclude that the SPI should be restricted in use to research, primarily due to lack of validation evidence, although theoretical foundation and construct development were also criticized by the reviewers. Nevertheless, the SPI Series, including the SPI/Adolescents, is commercially available (www.castleconsultants.us), with apparent intended use by consultants for program evaluation (as noted in the 2008 document from the publisher entitled The Market Place), such as in school districts, hospitals, corporate settings, universities, and "other learning environments." However, it is not clear from the information provided by the test author as to exactly how the data provided by the SPI Series, and by the SPI/Adolescents in particular, might be specifically used for program evaluation. Close examination of the survey items and the Interpreting Profiles section point to an emphasis on maladjustment and therefore clinical application, although the Theoretical Background and Development sections of the test manual provide insight allowing inferences about how the data may be used for consultation and intervention.

Apparently assembled for the *Mental Measurements Yearbook* reviewers' examination, the provided SPI/Adolescents materials are neatly organized in a desktop-published compilation of various documents, including: a brief overview of the SPI/Adolescents focusing on the construct of "self," a price list/order form, the test author's résumé, a one-page document highlighting the ongoing development of the SPI and related products, copies of the SPI/Adolescents surveys, and the Self-Perceptions of Adolescents test manual. The test manual includes the following sections: Theoretical Background, Development of the SPI/Adolescents, Technical Information (i.e., validation, administration, scoring, and interpretation), appendices delineating personality trait factors from John W. French's research, and MMPI codes. All these materials are well organized and user friendly.

DEVELOPMENT AND TECHNICAL. The SPI Series, including the SPI/Adolescents, represents a compilation of research conducted by the author and her late husband, Anthony, over decades. Much of the validation research provided by the test author for this review was already considered by Clare (2003) and Wang (2003) in their reviews (MMY 15:226). As these reviewers noted, additional validation of the SPI Series was needed before it could be recommended for clinical application. With the 2007 revision of the SPI/Adolescents, the test author cites a substantial body of research addressing validation concerns noted for the 1999 Revision. These studies enlisted 838 seventh and eighth grade students (428 males/410 females), and 425 high school students (215 males/210 females), although additional demographic information is lacking, thereby limiting generalization of findings. Content validity coefficients based on expert appraisal range from .50 to .83. Construct validity coefficients range from .63 (Middle School Self-Concept) to .79 (High School Self-Concept). Concurrent validity (multitrait multirater matrix) reliability coefficients range from .67 to .89. Reliability coefficients are reported to be .90 for stability over approximately 2-month intervals and .87 for internal consistency. In general, the validation data support the psychometric adequacy of the SPI/Adolescents, but the test author needs to provide more detail in analyzing the results of these statistical tests and related implications for application.

In the Theoretical Background and Development sections of the test manual, the test author provides a detailed overview of the theoretical presuppositions and foundation for the constructs, for example, self, global self-concept, ideal concept, reflected self, and self-perception within a taxonomic model (i.e., multiple intelligences) as considered by the SPI/Adolescents. In general, the theoretical approach is developmental, grounded in the theoretical works of Jean Piaget, David Elkind, and Erik Erikson. This gives a clue as to how the data gleaned from the SPI/Adolescents may be used from an interactionalist/organismic/genetic epistemological view in conducting program evaluation. Viewing programs (i.e., educational settings) as systems, consideration of the reciprocal interaction of individual differences (i.e., traits related to self-perception) within these systems (i.e., "group profiles") may well have importance in determining how to more effectively intervene within these systems. This reviewer recommends further discussion by the test author, exploring the practical application of the SPI/Adolescents.

COMMENTARY. In the interpretive section of the test manual, the test author cautions that SPI/Adolescents test results "should not be used as conclusive foundations for categorizing either individuals or groups" (p. 32, test manual). This seems to be prudent advice, given the complex and elusive nature of the central construct examined by the SPI/Adolescents, the self. Therefore, this reviewer concurs and further recommends that practitioners using the SPI/Adolescents for program evaluation or intervention consider the data it provides within the context of a body of evidence, triangulating the data with other sources of information in gaining a comprehensive, ecological perspective. It is clear that the test author does not advocate using the SPI/Adolescents as a comprehensive clinical evaluation tool. With this in mind, following the precautions outlined by the test author, the SPI/Adolescents should serve as a useful tool within the limited scope of gaining insight into the adolescent's self-perceptions, particularly as related to the educational setting.

SUMMARY. The SPI/Adolescents is a survey instrument designed to measure an adolescent's concept of self from a developmental perspective. Although long acknowledged as appropriate for research use, the SPI/Adolescent also may have utility related to consultation and program evaluation, recognizing adolescent self-concept has theoretical importance when examining educational systems. The test author is encouraged to provide more information considering appropriate application of the SPI/Adolescents.

REVIEWER'S REFERENCES

Clare, M. M. (2003). [Review of the Self-Perceptions Inventory [1999 Revision].] In B. S. Plake, J. C. Impara, & R. A. Spies (Eds.), *The fifteenth mental measurements yearbook* (pp. 808–810). Lincoln, NE: Buros Institute of Mental Measurements.

Wang, A. (2003). [Review of the Self-Perceptions Inventory [1999 Revision].] In B. S. Plake, J. C. Impara, & R. A. Spies (Eds.), *The fifteenth mental measurements yearbook* (pp. 810–812). Lincoln, NE: Buros Institute of Mental Measurements.

Review of the Self-Perceptions of Adolescents by ERIC S. BUHS, Associate Professor of Educational Psychology, University of Nebraska-Lincoln, Lincoln, NE:

DESCRIPTION. The Self-Perceptions of Adolescents (SPA) instruments are drawn from a series of self-perception inventories originally developed by Drs. Louise M. and Anthony T. Soares and are intended to tap aspects of adolescents' self-concept. The inventory contains two sets of scales, Self as a Person and Self as a Student, that each contain four subscales of 25 items each: Self Concept, Ideal Concept, Reflected Self, and Perceptions of Others. All scales are self-reports except for the Perceptions of Others subscales–these are observer ratings to be completed by parents, siblings, relatives, teachers, peers or others familiar with the adolescent. The Reflected Self measure is intended to indicate one's perception of a relevant other's view of the self–the other may be a friend, teacher, or parent.

The scales were designed for use with community samples of middle- and high-school students and items use a forced-choice format where respondents complete items using a 4-point scale indicating how well elements of pairs of "opposite" adjectives describe themselves. Each item response is scored as +2 (very positive), +1 (more positive), -1 (more negative), or -2 (very negative). Item scores are summed across all 25 scale items to yield an overall score for each of the eight subscales (range = +50 to -50). Discrepancy scores also may be calculated to indicate the difference between pairs of scale scores, differences between comparable trait-pairs across scales, and differences between single-item pairs across scales. No specific instructions or pairs of items/sets of items appropriate for discrepancy scores (below the whole-scale level) are indicated or discussed. Raw scale scores may be converted to stanines for standardized comparisons. No specific formal training is required to administer the measures.

DEVELOPMENT. Original development of the test authors' self-perceptions scales occurred in the 1960s and 1970s and the adolescent scales were most recently revised in 2005-2006. The scales are designed to tap aspects of self-concept based on a conceptual framework drawn from work published in the 1940s, 1950s, and 1960s. Authors such as Erik Erikson, Carl Rogers, and Jean Piaget are cited (among others), but specific authors or models are not cited as primary sources for the model presented here. The conceptual framework discussed stresses self-concept as a comparison of positive and negative traits across various domains. The domains are not identified but are broadly described as likely to emerge through brain development, the action of brain enzymes, nutritional factors influencing the "cognitive dimension of self-concept development" (manual, p. 5), and/or through hemispheric specialization of brain function. Sample diagrams indicate "self-pictures" that include family roles (e.g., self as sister), academic domains (e.g., math, reading), future roles (e.g., worker, mother), a social self, and other roles (e.g., volunteer, athlete). The current test author emphasizes that self-concept is developed through social interactions, integration of the social responses of others, internalization and reinforcement of self-perceptions, and from responses to "the challenges and the pressures which the organism encounters in the normal course of living" (manual, p. 2). Self-concept is presented as being maintained by intermittent reinforcement and as constantly evolving over the life-course as part of "a dynamic of infinite diversity" (manual, p. 5). The 25 adjective pairs used in the items are reported as having been drawn from French (1953) and are presented as related to clusters from the Minnesota Multiphasic Personality Inventory (MMPI; see *Validity*, below). An original set of 36 pairs was later reduced to 25, although criteria for the reduction are not presented. The item-pairs used appear to tap a wide range of self-perceptions including affect, sociability/relationships, self-worth/self-esteem, and various personality attributes. The 25 pairs are identical across most scales. The item pairs of the Student as a Self scale are targeted to learning and school issues. No domain-specific subscales are identified within the subscales. Because of the very broad descriptions of the targeted self-concept construct it is unclear whether or not the scales represent the intended construct(s) accurately. Some item-pairs are similar to those in current, widely used measures of child/adolescent self-concept (e.g., Harter, 1982).

TECHNICAL.

Standardization. The measure was renormed in 2007 with a sample of 838 seventh- and eighth-graders (428 males) and with 425 students from Grades 9 through 12 (215 males). Socioeconomic status, age, ethnicity, and/or other demographic data are not presented. Means and standard deviations are presented for males versus females and by grade-level (Grades 9–12 only). Data are also presented from a 1999 data set but, with the possible exception of the Self as a Student scales (treated as a single score, undefined), the measures were apparently an earlier version and contained different item sets (specific information not provided for the 1999 data). Selected scale scores are presented from the Self as a Person measures, but only an overall score (undefined) from the Self as a Student scales is presented. No scores are presented from any of the Perceptions of Others scales. The reported data appear to indicate adequate variability for the scales/scores examined. Some interpretation of possible score differences between groups is also made, but no statistical comparisons of group scores were presented.

Reliability. Estimates of score stability using either 7/8- or 10-week intervals and estimates of internal consistency (alphas) are given for what appear to be data drawn from the entire sample from the 1999 and 2007 administrations (see above). The values presented appear to indicate a high degree of stability and internal consistency but specific scales/scores are not indicated as a source for the single statistics presented as estimates of stability and internal consistency.

Validity. One source of possible validity information for the scales may be examined through associations presented among selected Self-Perception scale scores and selected MMPI scale scores. Dates for the data presented are not given, but they appear to be from the original scale development for the Self-Perception Inventory (perhaps ca. 1967) carried out prior to the development of the adolescent scales. The scale scores presented for Self Concept, Ideal Concept, and Reflected Self display nonsignificant to moderate correlations across 10 MMPI scale scores (undefined) and several unlabelled "validity scales." Content, construct, and concurrent validity statistics are also presented from the 1999 and 2007 samples (overall samples only). No interpretation of the validity data is presented and no detailed description of the external scores with which the current scale scores are compared (specific statistics or the method of comparison) is provided. Concurrent validity estimates apparently present bivariate correlations with overall scale scores (undefined) among self- and selected peers-, teacher-, and parent-ratings. The validity evidence presented is not precisely described and any firm evaluation of the utility of the scales to measure self-concept within specific age-, gender-, or ethnic-groups is not possible.

COMMENTARY. The Self-Perceptions of Adolescents scales are intended to tap broad aspects of self-concept based on conceptual frameworks from early research and theory. It is important to note that the Perceptions of Others subscales gather observer ratings of a subject's behaviors and attitudes, and so on, and should not be represented as self-perceptions. Despite recent revisions, the measure does not appear to incorporate perspectives from more current research and theory (i.e., work published since ca. 1970). The constructs intended to be tapped here are most similar to current constructs labeled global self-concept or self-esteem (overall judgments of self-worth), but they appear much broader and not clearly defined enough to draw firm comparisons to current self-concept constructs. The limited guidance for interpreting the scale scores suggests a relatively complex and subjective evaluation of the self as generally positive versus negative, a comparison of the ideal versus actual self, and comparisons of self-perceptions with those of peers, family, and teachers. These judgments of concurrence and/or discrepancy are broadly tied to possible outcomes such as defensiveness, tendencies toward negative social interactions, and very general motivational orientations toward unspecified goals. No empirical data evaluating possible links to attitudinal or behavioral outcomes are presented and the potential utility of interpretations for research or applied use is questionable. The reliability and validity data provided with the scales evaluated here are not described in enough detail to make any clear, empirically based judgments about the psychometric properties of the scales.

SUMMARY. In order to make decisions about the use of Self-Perceptions of Adolescents, researchers and practitioners face a complicated task and the test materials lack detail that accurately and fully describe the measures conceptually or empirically. The scales reflect theory taken from literature not currently in broad use and they reflect the relatively unique perspective and methods of the test authors–this makes decisions about the utility of the scores even more complex. The scores produced would appear to represent very broad aspects of self-perceptions (and those of others) and it is unlikely that links to adjustment processes or outcomes typically present in current research or in clinical settings would be present or could be meaningfully interpreted.

REVIEWER'S REFERENCES

French, J. W. (1953). *The description of personality measurements in self and others.* Princeton, NJ: Educational Testing Service.

Harter, S. (1982). The perceived competence scale for children. *Child Development, 53*, 87-97.

[115]

Self-Perceptions of Adults.

Purpose: Designed to measure an adult's concept of self.

Population: Adults.

Publication Dates: 1965-2006.

Scores: 8 scales: Self as a Person (Self Concept, Ideal Concept, Reflected Self, Perceptions of Others), Self as a Working Adult (Self Concept, Ideal Concept, Reflected Self, Perceptions of Others).

Administration: Group.

Forms, 16: Self as Person Scales (Self Concept/Adjectives, Self Concept/Sentences, Ideal Concept/Adjectives, Ideal Concept/Sentences, Reflected Self/Adjectives, Reflected Self/Sentences, Perceptions of Others/Adjectives, Perceptions of Others/Sentences), Self as a Working Adult (Self Concept/Adjectives, Self Concept/Sentences, Ideal Concept/Adjectives, Ideal Concept/Sentences, Reflected Self/Adjectives, Reflected Self/Sentences, Perceptions of Others/Adjectives, Perceptions of Others/Sentences).

Price Data, 2008: $40 per 25 scales (specify form); $40 per 50 answer sheets; $.25 per customized booklet; $.40 per profile chart; $40 per test manual (2006, 44 pages); $.40 per scale for scoring.

Time: (5–20) minutes.

Comments: Developed from the original Self-Perceptions Inventory (15:226) and is part of the SPI series that includes: Self-Perceptions of Adolescents (18:114), Self-Perceptions of Children (18:116), Self-Perceptions of College Students, Self-Perceptions of School Administrators (18:117), Self-Perceptions of University Instructors (18:118), Self-Perceptions of Teachers, and Self-Perceptions of Nurses.

Author: Louise M. Soares.

Publisher: Castle Consultants.

Cross References: For reviews by Mary M. Clare and Aimin Wang of the 1999 Revision of the Self-Perceptions Inventory, see 15:226; see also T4:2421 (1 reference); for a review by Janet Morgan Riggs of an earlier edition, see 9:1101; for a review by Lorrie Shepard of an earlier edition, see 8:673 (2 references).

Review of the Self-Perceptions of Adults by NANCY L. CRUMPTON, Part-time Faculty, Troy University; Part-time Faculty, Walden University; Montgomery, AL:

DESCRIPTION. The Self-Perceptions of Adults is one of the forms in the Self-Perceptions Inventory Series, with specific focus on the description of individual self-concept of adults. There are two perspectives of perception measured to include Self as a Person and Self as a Working Adult. Within each area there are four lists of 40 dichotomous trait pairs that define the structure of the inventory. Self Concept, Ideal Concept, Reflected Self, and Perceptions of Others are contained in the Self as a Person. Self as a Working Adult, Ideal as a Working Adult, Reflected Self, and Perceptions of Others are included in the Self as a Working Adult category. There is also an optional format for each section of the inventory, structured in sentence format instead of the one- to two-word adjective in the listing of traits. The sentence format is shorter, with 30 variables. Ratings are structured in four columns to note the descriptive relationship to each set of traits as "very" aligned with one trait or the other, or "more" aligned with one adjective or the other. In the Self as a Person inventory and in the Self as a Working Adult, the ratings of Reflected Self and Perceptions of Others the test taker indicates the perspective of the rating from 1 of 12 groups or by filling in a blank on the form (for the Perceptions of Others only). The blank option was added in the 1999 Revision for test takers to define ratings by any person important to the individual (not represented by a group). If the test taker selects one of the groups from the list, the box noting the specified group is checked. The list includes Supervisors, Partners, Siblings, Neighbors, Roommates, Fellow Workers, Health Specialists, Children, Parents, Friends, Subordinates, and Spouse.

Section instructions for the Adult Form include Administrative Instructions, Scoring, and Profiling Scores. Each section is easily understood. Included is a statement that the test may be read to individuals who have reading problems, learning disabilities, or language difficulties. It is also noted that the sentence format may be preferable to the adjective format for some individuals to better understand the intent of the ratings. The scales may be administered at one time, or over a period of time. Each scale is scored separately with scoring for each response receiving a value of +2, +1, -1, or -2. The sum of all responses is the index score for each scale and adding scores for all scales provides the raw score for the test. Raw scores are converted to stanine scores for standardized comparisons. A group profile can be charted using the means for each scale. Discrepancy scores between the scales of specific item responses provide another method of comparison. Interpretation of the profiles is defined based on ranges of stanine scores of Moderate (4th–6th stanine), Extremely High, and Extremely Low. Larger discrepancies between index scores "may signal trouble spots" (manual, p. 35) and discussion of meaningfulness is presented. The test author states that any interpretations should be made judiciously as the complexities of individuals' self perceptions over time may create change.

DEVELOPMENT. According to the test author, self-concept is a construct, comprising sets of an individual's perceptions in different roles and the interrelationship of these perceptions is the focus of measurement. An individual's experiences in different settings, with certain groups of persons, observing behaviors, determining the effectiveness of her or his own behaviors and how these contribute to quality in relationships, provide the theoretical basis for the structure of the Self-Perceptions of Adults. Information from the 1999 revision was included in the manual to provide perspective to the 2006 Revision.

The 2006 Revision added four dichotomous pairs of traits to the list and one substitution of a pair. These changes are consistent in each list of the Self as a Person. The "Student Self" was deleted from all of the Adult forms. Although following the same format, the list of the item-pairs in Self as a Working Adult are noted by the test author to be more relevant to the working adult. Self as a Person and Self as a Working Adult now have optional forms, using sentence form for the dichotomous traits. Support for the 2006 changes is not documented in the References section of the manual, as references listed appear to be sources for the initial development of the scales. A 1969 reference is the most current listed.

TECHNICAL. Although there is a statement indicating that additional items in the scales, which increased the length of the instrument, "has the tendency of improving the results of the technical evaluation" (manual, p. 20), there was no evidence that technical features were measured or described in the Technical Information section of the manual. No correlations to previous versions of the test were provided. The focus of this revision was noted to be on interactions of the Self Concept as a Person and as a Worker. Six groups contributed to the standardization data of the 2006 Revision including young working adults in an urban setting (50 males, 50 females); full-time office workers and part-time students in area colleges (270 males, 202 females); small business managers and mid-level corporate executives (150 males, 50 females); workers in a factory (225 males, 180 females); university students in Rome, Italy (44 males, 79 females); and young workers in Rome (33 males, 55 females). No specific descriptions of the individuals in these groups (ages, race/cultural representation, educational, occupational, etc.) were available. Why these particular groups were selected and why the results of the standardization sample would be relevant in using the instrument were not provided. Multicultural groups that would be more representative of individuals or groups identified by census data would offer support for use of the test in practical applications.

Discussions of the scores within the groups and between groups focused on differences in scores based on gender and comparisons of American groups (in general) to young Italian workers who had lower Ideal Concept scores and higher Reflected Self/Parents scores. The data set of business managers and middle level executives reportedly had the highest Self scores. What these results would mean to someone using the instrument was not specified.

Comments describing the findings were made as suppositions rather than research-based conclusions (e.g., "perhaps males have more confidence in their work than in themselves as people" (manual, p. 31). Statistical report of validity was presented in coefficients that would represent significant findings at $p < .01$ on all measures. No discussion was available to explain how the coefficients were determined, such as predictive validity of on-the-job success of those taking the test based on scores of Self as Worker. Categories of Information were not descriptive of a particular group, but as scores of all groups combined. All reliability coefficients were reported as .90 or higher without description of the process or the sample used. Although a test-retest process with an 8-week interval was noted for the coefficient of stability, no other information was provided to identify groups that participated in the process. Correlation of MMPI codes to the traits in the rating forms of the Self as a Person are included in the manual, but the example of the rating form is not the 2006 Revision.

COMMENTARY. The Self-Perceptions of Adults is one of the forms of the Self-Perceptions Inventory Series initially developed in 1965. From the information presented in the manual for the 2006 Revision, there are theoretical conclusions made and examples of constellations of possible interactions of persons (family, work relationships, etc.), based on self-perceptions as determined from test results, but confidence in application of the information is not supported. The research accumulated through the years would be useful in the development of a more diagnostic use of the Inventories. Information obtained in the Self-Perceptions of Adults has potential utility in career counseling specifically, if statistical credibility was demonstrated.

SUMMARY. The 2006 revision of the Self-Perceptions of Adults includes the perspectives of Self as a Person and Self as a Working Adult to better understand the individual's self-concept and what impact self-perceptions may have on making choices and meeting challenges within her or his individual context. Instructions for administering and scoring the test are presented clearly; however, the utility of the test in providing understanding of or direction for individuals is not supported. Taking the years of accumulated data and providing evidence of the theoretical conclusions based on the performance of test takers of diverse subgroups, in sample sizes that are adequate for analyses, and presenting statistical evidence that the test meets its intended purposes are needed.

Review of the Self-Perceptions of Adults by RICHARD F. FARMER, Associate Professor of Psychology, East Carolina University, Greenville, NC:

DESCRIPTION. The Self-Perceptions of Adults (SPA) scales are a set of self-report and rating measures purported to assess an adult's concept of self. The SPA is part of a larger series of measures that also includes Self-Perceptions of Adolescents, Self-Perceptions of Children, Self-Perceptions of College Students, Self-Perceptions of School Administrators, Self-Perceptions of University Instructors, Self-Perceptions of Teachers, and Self-Perceptions of Nurses. Collectively, these measures constitute the Self-Perceptions Inventory (SPI) series.

The test manual comes in a three-ring notebook binder, with individual pages inserted within plastic protective sheaths. Tabbed dividers are used to separate main sections within the binder. Included in the test binder is a descriptive overview of the SPI series, a description of underlying theory, copies of the various forms of the SPA, a description of the development of the SPI series, statistical summary tables, administration instructions, and guidelines for profile interpretation. Page numbers are not provided for several of the sheets contained in the binder; consequently, it is not always possible to reference specific information to the pages where it is located.

Designed for adults, the SPA represents a modest revision of the SPA scale from the 1999 revision of the SPI. For each of the major domains measured by the SPA (Self as a Person and Self as a Working Adult), assessments can be performed within each of four subareas: Self Concept (or the respondent's sense of self as a person), Ideal Concept (or the respondent's perception of how he or she would like to be), Reflected Self (the respondent's sense of self as perceived by others), and Perceptions of Others (described as an "observation scale," created "to obtain a constellation of self-pictures," manual, p. 13). The latter scale is to be completed by someone familiar with the target person (e.g., partner, sibling, friend, neighbor). Within the Self as a Person domain (adjectives), the four subscales primarily differ in terms of their associated directions (e.g., "What kind of person do you see yourself at the moment?"; "What kind of person would you like to be if you could change?"; "What kind of person do you thnk [*sic*] others see you?"; "What kind of person do you think this person is?"). The four subscales of Self as a Working Adult similarly differ in terms of the instructions that accompany the bipolar scales.

For this revision of the SPA, four additional adjective pairs were added to the Self Concept as a Person domain, and one additional pair was substituted for a previous pair. The Reflected Self and Perceptions of Others scales also currently allow respondents to indicate which perspective among several groups of persons is reflected in the ratings (e.g., parents, neighbors, siblings, children).

Test items utilize a semantic differential forced-choice format, where respondents are asked to indicate which of four statements best represents the respondent's experience along a bipolar continuum. For example, given the bipolar adjectives "happy" and "unhappy" or the bipolar sentences "I am a happy person" and "I am an unhappy person," a respondent is asked to indicate if they are "very happy," "more happy than unhappy," "more unhappy than happy," or "very unhappy." Each major domain (Self as a Person and Self as a Working Adult) is assessed with 40 item pairs (with the item content different across domains). In most circumstances, the individual forms within the set of SPA measures can be completed within 10 minutes.

It is not clear from the test manual as to what would constitute appropriate uses of this test. The interpretive guidelines provided, however, suggest that scale responses or profiles might variously suggest defensiveness, maladjustment, dissatisfaction with self, or a perception of rejection by others.

DEVELOPMENT. The earliest version of the current revision of the SPA was copyrighted in 1965. Since this time, there have been multiple revisions and modifications of the SPI, with several tailored versions developed for specific groups (e.g., teachers, university undergraduate students, nurses, school administrators).

The theoretical basis for the SPA appears to be largely unchanged from that which guided the development of the SPI series. The test author defines self-concept as "an abstract idea that is generalized from particular instances" and "a system of perceptions which the organism formulates of the self in an awareness of its distinctive existence" (manual, p. 1). Self-perception, in turn, is defined as "the generic 'self concept'" (manual general information page, p. 1), and described as "a number of independent–and in some ways, interrelated–factors contingent upon roles, situations, and areas of success and failure" (manual general information page, p. 1). The test author goes on to speculate that different self-concepts emerge from experiences in different settings, and are further modified by behaviors the individual displays in such settings, the consequences that such behavior produces, how such behavior is perceived by others, and the quality of relationships one has with others. The test author further emphasizes the importance of the interactions of and consistencies in self-perceptions.

Other theoretical issues related to the self, self-concept, and self-perceptions are discussed in the test manual, such as the component features or aspects of the self, the etiology of the self, and an overview of research on the self. The theoretical formulations of Spearman, Thurstone, Guilford, Gardner, Rogers, McCandless, and others are referred to briefly, although it is not entirely clear how these theorists informed the test author's views of self-concept and self-perception. Overall, the empirical bases for the test author's theoretical formulations remain unclear.

Guidelines for test administration and scoring are provided. Raw scale scores can be converted to stanine equivalents for standardized comparisons across scales. Conversion tables are provided. The standardization sample used to generate these tables, however, is not identified. Consequently, it is difficult to determine for whom these scoring guidelines are relevant.

The test author provides interpretive guidelines as well. Extremely high Self Concept scores are suggested as possibly reflecting "defensiveness," "lack of awareness of the self," or "overall satisfaction with the self without yet possessing or demonstrating maturity or sophistication" (manual, p. 34). Extremely low Self Concept scores are suggested to possibly indicate "a tendency toward maladjustment" and a "greater dislike of the self" (manual, p. 34). The empirical bases for these interpretations are not specified.

TECHNICAL. Essential psychometric data on the SPA are either not provided or not sufficiently described. Much of the research presented in the test manual is dated and does not appear to be related to the current version of the SPA. At the end of the chapter on development, for example, three tables of data are provided (ANOVA and correlation tables). These tables, however, refer to research findings obtained 45 years ago with a much earlier version of the SPA.

Similarly, much of the material presented in the chapter describing technical information appears to relate to the 1999 revision. Within this chapter, scale means, standard deviations, and standard errors are presented for different SPA-related scales. Descriptions are very sparse related to the samples on which these data are based as well as the sampling procedures and methods used. Rather, these descriptions are largely limited to brief accounts of the sample size, gender distribution, and vocation (e.g., "urban setting–young working adults," "full-time office workers and part-time students," "small business managers and middle level corporate executives," and "workers in a factory"; manual, pp. 21–22). Descriptive data from an Italian version of the SPI are also presented, as are correlations that SPI adult forms have with MMPI scales and outcomes from a factor analysis on 36 trait pairs. Other relevant and important sample and procedural descriptions are not provided. Later in the chapter, descriptive scale data (means, standard deviations, and standard errors) are presented for the most recent version of the SPA. As before, however, samples and sampling procedures are not adequately described. It is, therefore, not clear what these data reference or how they should be used. A table of coefficients is also presented, with different sections labeled with the following headings: content validity, concurrent validity, predictive validity, coefficient of stability, and internal consistency. Additional details are not provided that would allow readers to determine how these data were obtained and on what measures they are based.

COMMENTARY. Many of the problems noted with the 1999 revision of the SPI (Clare, 2004; Wang, 2004) also apply to the current version of the SPA. These include, but are not limited to: (a) a vague theoretical foundation that does not appear to be substantially influenced or modified by research developments during the last four decades; (b) a poorly written and organized test manual that is frequently unfocused, disjointed, and redundant; (c) the inclusion of obsolete data in the test manual that are based on earlier versions of the SPA; (d) an absence of any indication that ethnic or sociocultural factors were considered in the development, evaluation, and norming of SPA scales; (e) the provision of normative data that appear to be inadequate and unrepresentative of the larger population; (f) the paucity of systematic empirical research and evaluation related to the SPA reviewed in the test manual; and, (g) an absence of compelling interpretive guidelines supported by data.

SUMMARY. The SPA is a collection of measures intended to assess adults' self-concept. Although the SPA has some intuitive appeal, it presently suffers from a variety of concerns that, in the aggregate, suggest extreme caution in the use of the measure. Overall, the use of this measure for purposes other than research is premature.

REVIEWER'S REFERENCES

Clare, M. M. (2004). [Review of the Self-Perceptions Inventory (1999 Revision)]. In B. S. Plake, J. C. Impara, & R. A. Spies (Eds.), *The fifteenth mental measurements yearbook* (pp. 808–810). Lincoln, NE: The Buros Institute of Mental Measurements.

Wang, A. (2004). [Review of the Self-Perceptions Inventory (1999 Revision)]. In B. S. Plake, J. C. Impara, & R. A. Spies (Eds.), *The fifteenth mental measurements yearbook* (pp. 810–812). Lincoln, NE: The Buros Institute of Mental Measurements.

[116]

Self-Perceptions of Children.

Purpose: Designed to assess children's self-concepts and "determine developmental differences in the self during the typical growth periods of childhood."
Publication Dates: 1965-2008.
Acronym: SPI/Children.
Administration: Group.
Price Data, 2009: $40 per 25 scales (specify form); $40 per test manual (2008, 38 pages); $.40 per scoring per scale; $40 per analysis report.
Time: (10) minutes per scale.
Comments: Revision of the Student Forms of the Self-Perceptions Inventory (15:226).
Authors: Louise M. Soares and Anthony T. Soares (test).
Publisher: Castle Consultants.

a) SELF AS PERSON.
Population: Ages 6-8.
Scores, 4: Self-concept, Student Self, Perceptions of Others (Self), Perceptions of Others (Student).

b) SELF AS STUDENT.
Population: Ages 9-11.
Scores, 4: Self-concept, Student Self, Perceptions of Others (Self), Perceptions of Others (Student).

Cross References: For reviews by Mary M. Clare and Aimin Wang of the entire Self-Perceptions Inventory [1999 Revision], see 15:226; see also T4:2421 (1 reference); for a review by Janet Morgan Riggs of an earlier edition, see 9:1101; for a review by Lorrie Shepard of an earlier edition, see 8:673 (2 references). For reviews by Gerald E. DeMauro and Michael R. Harwell of an earlier edition of the Nursing forms, see 11:356.

Review of Self-Perceptions of Children by KATHLEEN D. ALLEN, Associate Professor of Education, St. Martin's University, Lacey, WA:

DESCRIPTION. The Self-Perceptions of Children (SPI/Children) is designed to assess the self-concept of children. The test authors define self-concept as the "system of perceptions" formulated from an "awareness of its distinctive existence" (manual, p. 1). The SPI/Children measures this construct with a compilation of questionnaires in two separate instrument sets. One instrument set is designed for students in Grades 1–3 (Primary Level), and the other for students in Grades 4–6 (Intermediate Level). Each grade level set consists of four questionnaires that respondents can complete in 10 minutes. Two of them, Self Concept and Student Self, are self-report questionnaires. Two questionnaires, Perceptions of Others: Self Concept and Perceptions of Others: Student Self, are filled out by raters familiar with the child, such as friends, parents, teachers, and siblings.

Each Primary Level questionnaire consists of 18 response items and each Intermediate Level has 20 items. For each item, students must make a forced choice on a four-category continuum scale between two opposite terms. Each continuum scale response is given a score between -2 and +2. Responses are totaled to yield a raw score. A chart is provided in the manual to convert raw scores into stanines, which allows the data to be converted to individual and group profiles.

The complete test manual includes testing instruments, order forms, introductory information, theoretical background, and technical information. The technical information includes instructions for standardized test administration.

DEVELOPMENT.

Theoretical framework. The test authors of the Self-Perceptions of Children inventory develop a case for a multiple-dimensional theory of self-concept that is assessed with multidimensional responses. This multidimensional theory is based on the interface between cognitive, social, and physical components of self-perception.

Task development. Historical theoretical background on the selection of the multidimensional semantic differential response scale is provided in the manual. In the original (1965) edition, response items were generated by selecting 36 pairs of bipolar trait pairs from the work of French (1953). These pairs were then connected to the cluster codes of the Minnesota Multiphasic Personality Inventory (Hathaway & McKinley, 1943). The resulting inventory questionnaires were given to 240 undergraduate college students to determine sound and problematic response queries. The original questionnaires from 1965 have been revised several times (1973, 1999, and 2008). For the latest revision, the differences in means and standard deviations of responses of 750 elementary students across grade levels were examined.

TECHNICAL.

Standardization. The test authors gave the Self Concept questionnaires to 425 elementary school students (180 primary and 245 intermediate). The Perceptions of Others inventory was administered to a person familiar with each student. Questionnaires also were administered to secondary and college students. Questionnaires given to the latter two groups of students were from the Self Perceptions Inventory for Adolescents and College Students, developed by the same authors. The main purpose of this type of standardization project was to determine differences between students of different ages. Based on the findings of this project, some of the response items in the Self-Perceptions Inventory for Children were revised to reflect developmental differences.

Evidence of construct validity is provided in the test manual. Scales were given to an "expert pool" of psychologists, psychiatrists, researchers, students, and working adults for evaluation. Using this evaluation, construct validity coefficients between .65 and .79 are reported. The same pool of experts was utilized for evidence of content validity. The coefficients range from .77 to .84 for this measure. The manual does not explicitly describe and name other self-concept inventories for content validity, nor does it provide statistical evidence of validity using other measures.

Concurrent validity is evaluated by using the different forms of questionnaires in the manual. Coefficients ranging from .30 to .93 are reported for comparisons of ratings by students, peers, teachers, and parents.

Reliability is substantiated with a coefficient of stability of .88 after 10 weeks and .90 (alpha) for internal consistency reported in the test manual. Reliability coefficients were highest for student and parent inventory responses.

COMMENTARY. The Self-Perceptions Inventory series has been in existence since 1965 and has gone through four revisions. It is evident that the 2008 revision for the Self-Perceptions of Children has improved the match between the theoretical construct of developmental stages and the response items. It has also provided insights into the differences of the self-concept paradigm between these stages.

The manual provides ample historical discussion of the theoretical construct of the Self-Perceptions of Children, but in many instances citations are not provided. Citations that are provided are at least 40 years old.

New evidence of reliability and validity has broadened the practicality of the SPI/Children for use in research as well as in the classroom. Evidence for construct validity would be strengthened if the case for the theories of self-concept and self-perception was unequivocally stated in a straightforward manner with citations of current as well as seminal theorists in child psychology. Another support for construct validity would be to review the Minnesota Multiphasic Personality Inventory (Hathaway & McKinley, 1943), which was used as a source for development of the Self-Perceptions Inventory series. Because the MMPI has been revised and was designed for adults, it could be worthwhile to determine whether it is still valid for the Self-Perceptions of Children.

The conversion of raw scores into individual and group profiles is well described. This makes possible the use of SPI/Children by teachers and counselors in the school setting. It would be helpful if the manual provided guidelines and suggestions for student metacognitive reflection.

SUMMARY. The 2008 edition of the Self-Perceptions of Children inventory is quick and easy to administer to children. Some evidence of reliability and validity has been well established, but a more thorough revision of construct and content validity is needed for the SPI/Children to be employed as a research instrument. If the underpinnings of the theoretical framework were updated to reflect current psychological research on self-concept, the inventory would have broader application to research, theory construct, and the classroom setting.

REVIEWER'S REFERENCES

French, J. W. (1953). *The description of personality measurements in self and others.* Princeton, NJ: Educational Testing Service.

Hathaway, S. R., & McKinley, J. C. (1943). *Manual of the Minnesota Multiphasic Personality Inventory.* Minneapolis, MN: University of Minnesota Press.

Review of the Self-Perceptions of Children by CHER EDWARDS, Associate Professor and Chair, Department of Counselor Education, Seattle Pacific University, Seattle, WA:

DESCRIPTION. The Self-Perceptions of Children (SPI/Children) instrument is one in a series of inventory instruments designed by the same author. The series includes self-perception inventories for adults and children as well as academic perceptions including primary, intermediate, advanced, and college populations. The SPI/Children includes two assessment inventories–one intended to assess the child's general self-concept (Self Concept scale) and the other to assess the child's concept of self as a student (Student Self scale) at the primary (1–3) and intermediate (4–6) grade levels.

The instrument allows for the child to self-assess as well as for assessment by an outside assessor (e.g., friend, parent, teacher, sibling, or other). The purpose of the instrument is to identify high discrepancies or extreme scores that may indicate areas of concern such as defensiveness, maladjustment, or an unrealistic assessment. Additional benefits including obtaining a group profile and identifying changes over time are also noted.

The instruments employ a forced-choice technique in which the test taker must choose one of four options created by the test taker in between two opposite statements. The primary version of the instrument consists of 18 items for both the assessment of self-concept and school self. The intermediate level consists of 20 items for each assessment inventory.

Administrative instructions are provided although they do not specify who is appropriate to administer the test or if any training should occur. A statement is provided for the test administrator to read to the students. No statement is provided to read to outside evaluators. The test manual indicates that test items may be read to individuals with "reading problems, learning disabilities, or language difficulties" (manual, p. 29).

Scoring is relatively direct–each of the four positions receives a score allocation ranging from -2 to +2 with no zero score. The very positive position receives a score of +2, the more positive position receives a score of +1, the more negative position receives a score of -1, and the very negative position receives a score of -2. The sum of scores yields an index (raw) score that can be converted to stanines for standardized comparisons using a profile chart/conversion table provided by the test author.

DEVELOPMENT. The development of the SPI/Children began with an instrument intended to measure self-concept, ideal-concept, and reflected-self of adults and was piloted with a population of undergraduate students in 1962 and copyrighted in 1965 as the "Self-Perceptions of Adults" inventory. Additional forms were published from 1967 to 1999 in an effort to assess younger students or different groups of adults to evaluate self as a student, self as a partner, self as a teacher, self as a professional nurse or student nurse, cultural identity, and self as a school administrator. In 2005, the test author developed the current instrument by separating the student form into the two children's scales (primary and intermediate).

The initial instrument was developed in consideration of the theoretical works of Lecky (1945), Rogers (1950), and McCandless (1961), indicating the concept of self is related to behavior as well as an existing correlation between poor self-concept and poor adjustment. The SPI/Children is supported by the theories and research of Piaget (1936/1952), Elkind (1967), and Erikson (1950), focusing on developmental issues related to self-concept. The test items were chosen from opposite traits in adjective form from French's (1953) text, *The Description of Personality Measurements in Self and Others* and then related to cluster codes from the Minnesota Multiphasic Personality Inventory (MMPI). The SPI/Children provides detail of piloting for the instrument's predecessors. The development phase for the current version spanned a 3-year period and included 425 elementary school students in Grades 1–6. Limited information was reported regarding this pilot project on the primary and intermediate groups aside from a reported discovery that "elementary students tended to be much more positive about themselves–both in the dimensions of individuals and of students–than the adolescents and the college students" (manual, p. 13). The test author provides a list in the manual of the traits included for each item on the two inventories for each level and reported "the final decision on the layout of the items was consistent with the theoretical base of the construct as well as the technical foundation of assessment that was appropriate to the construct" (manual, p. 11). The connection between the list of what the items were intended to measure with the actual items comprising the instrument was unclear.

TECHNICAL. Although technical information is provided regarding this series of instruments, the results pertaining specifically to the SPI/Children are ambiguous. The SPI/Children test manual indicates the initial test authors piloted the instrument during three revision periods (1999, 2005–2007, and 2007–2008). The 1999 revision project included 569 students in Grades 1–6, the 2005–2007 revision included 425 students (180 students in Grades 1–3; 245 in Grades 4–6), and the 2007–2008 revision project included 750 students in Grades 1–6. In the 1999 data, students were compared by gender and urban or suburban setting and the 2005–2007 as well as the 2007–2008 data specify grade level only.

Given the grade levels assessed, it appears the sample matches the intended population although generalizability is less clear given ethnicity, diverse learning qualities, and English language learners (all appropriate for this instrument according to the test administrator directions) are not identified. The significant difference between the 1999 revision and 2007–2008 revision were the separation of primary grades from upper elementary grades and reduction of both scales from 20 items to 18 items for the primary grades in the latest revision.

It would be interesting to provide a test item analysis comparing ethnic/culture identification of participants as some of the items have the potential to be culture-bound. For example, in many western cultures, identifying self as a "special person" is considered to be appropriate and associated with positive self-esteem whereas in many eastern cultures, identifying self as extraordinary or "special" would be considered offensive. Similarly, on the Student Self scales, the responses to the item regarding whether the respondent likes to work with others or work alone may be impacted by a student's identification as part of an individualistic or collectivist culture.

For the current revision (2007–2008), reliabilities for the self-report form are reported as .88 for coefficient of stability (Pearson *r*s) and .90 for internal consistency (alpha coefficients). Reliability coefficients for outside assessors (peers, teachers, parents) ranged from .69 to .89. Reliabilities between .80 and .90 are considered adequate and sufficiently reliable for most research purposes. The sample for establishing this reliability score included 750 students, with 125 students from each of Grades 1–6. The number of outside assessors (peers, teachers, parents) was not reported.

The validity coefficients reported are within an acceptable range for a self-report instrument. However, there are concerns given the lack of norming data for gender, racial, ethnic, and cultural groups. In addition, the test author refers to an expert pool in the validity testing but does not indicate how the pool was chosen or the basis for their expertise related to the self-concept of children. Although the test author provides an explanation as to how the content of the items was chosen, little evidence is provided to substantiate the relationship between the construct of self-concept and the individual test items.

COMMENTARY. Appendix A of the manual outlines the original traits chosen from French's (1953) work as well as the MMPI codes the traits were clustered with for the SPI/Children. These traits and codes include indications of psychotic tendency, psychopathic deviate, and other psychiatric descriptors, which one would expect requires a specific level of training to administer the instrument and properly refer if indicated. Test administrators may consider liability issues of identifying students with potential deviant personality traits without the necessary education and expertise to appropriately attend to such needs. Although identifying such is not indicated as a specific purpose of this instrument, the test author cites theorists linking poor self-concept with poor adjustment–often considered the basis for many of the diagnostic traits associated with the MMPI.

This instrument addresses the importance of self-concept as it relates to child development. Administration and interpretation directions are relatively simple and require no training. Such a scale has the potential to identify children who may have challenges related to self-concept and to support early intervention.

The instrument itself may be difficult for young children to interpret given the test requires participants create their own midpoint statements for each test item. The test example provides midpoint statements between the opposite statements although each test item does not. This is not a Likert-type scale where each of the four points represents the same term (e.g., strongly agree, agree, disagree, strongly disagree) but rather a variation of the opposite terms (e.g., "I am happy in school," "very happy," "more happy than sad," "more sad than happy," "very sad," and "I am sad in school"). For the actual test items, only the two opposite terms are provided. This requirement would also add potential variability in how younger participants choose to interpret each data point in between the statements provided for each item.

Current literature may provide guidance to support validity and reliability as it relates to cultural, language, and gender issues of test items. Most notably missing is the work of Dr. Susan Harter, from the University of Denver, who has published numerous studies related to self-esteem and self-concept of children and adolescents since 1965.

SUMMARY. Although the SPI/Children addresses the important issue of self-concept for children, additional evidence is needed regarding the validity and reliability of this instrument and recent, scholarly support should be included. The use of the MMPI for clustering purposes should be evaluated given its normative sample composition on an adult population. Gender, cultural, and language considerations should be included and the instrument validated for these populations. It is also recommended that individuals with education and training on the assessment and treatment of children with counseling needs be consulted or identified as those competent to administer this instrument.

REVIEWER'S REFERENCES

Elkind, D. (1967). Egocentrism in adolescence. *Child Development, 38,* 1025-1034.

Erikson, E. H. (1950). *Childhood and society.* New York: Norton.

French, J. W. (1953). *The description of personality measurements in self and others.* Princeton, NJ: Educational Testing Service.

Lecky, P. (1945). *Self-consistency, a theory of personality.* New York: Island Press.

McCandless, B. R. (1961). *Children and adolescents, behavior and development.* New York: Holt, Rinehart, & Winston.

Piaget, J. (1936/1952). *The origins of intelligence in children.* New York: International Universities Press.

Rogers, C. R. (1950). Significance of self-regarding attitudes and perceptions. In M. L. Reymert (Ed.), *Feelings and emotions.* New York: McGraw-Hill.

[117]

Self-Perceptions of School Administrators.

Purpose: Designed to measure a school administrator's concept of self.

Population: Adults.

Publication Dates: 1965-2005.

Scores: 8 scales: Self as a Person (Self Concept, Ideal Concept, Reflected Self, Perceptions of Others), Self as a School Administrator (Self Concept, Ideal Concept, Reflected Self, Perceptions of Others).

Administration: Group.

Forms, 8: Self as Person Scales (Self Concept, Ideal Concept, Reflected Self, Perceptions of Others), Self as a School Administrator (Self Concept, Ideal Concept, Reflected Self, Perceptions of Others).

Price Data, 2008: $40 per 25 scales (specify form); $40 per 50 answer sheets; $.25 per customized booklet; $.40 per profile chart; $40 per test manual (2005, 40 pages); $.40 per scale for scoring.

Time: (5–20) minutes.

Comments: Developed from the original Self-Perceptions Inventory (15:226) and is part of the SPI series that includes: Self-Perceptions of Adolescents (18:114), Self-Perceptions of Children (18:116), Self-Perceptions of College Students, Self-Perceptions of Adults (18:115), Self-Perceptions of University Instructors (18:118), Self-Perceptions of Teachers, and Self-Perceptions of Nurses.

Author: Louise M. Soares.

Publisher: Castle Consultants.

Cross References: For reviews by Mary M. Clare and Aimin Wang of the 1999 Revision of the Self-Perceptions Inventory, see 15:226; see also T4:2421 (1 reference); for a review by Janet Morgan Riggs of an earlier edition, see 9:1101; for a review by Lorrie Shepard of an earlier edition, see 8:673 (2 references).

Review of the Self-Perceptions of School Administrators by MARTA COLEMAN, Instructor, Gunnison Watershed School District, Gunnison, CO:

DESCRIPTION. The Self-Perceptions of School Administrators is part of the Self-Perceptions Inventory (SPI) Series. The thesis on which this instrument is based postulates that self-perceptions "develop independently according to experience, reinforcement, and treatment, and possibly through individualized conceptualizations in the long-term memory system" (manual, p. 5). This instrument attempts to measure the construct of school administrator self from two forms, each with four scales: Self as Person with the scales Self-Concept, Ideal Concept, Reflected Self, and Perceptions of Others; and Self as a School Administrator with the scales Self-Concept, Ideal Concept, Reflected

Self, and Perceptions of Others. The respondent is asked to identify his or her sense of self on a four-point continuum of antonymic adjectives in each scale grounded on a particular question. The continuum provides intensity and direction. Each scale has 40 items of dichotomous, semantic terms in the form of adjectives. In both forms, the scale, Perceptions of Others, requires the respondent to indicate his or her role to the administrator: School Board Member, Community Leader, Supervisor, Assistant, Teacher, Parent, Peer, Student, or Friend. Administration of the instrument may be individual or group. The administrative instructions indicate that "all forms do not have to be administered on the same day," though the respondents are to "work quickly," perhaps finishing in 10 minutes (manual, p. 27). Scoring establishes raw scores and three discrepancy scores: Total Discrepancy, Mean of Discrepancies, and Single-Dimension Discrepancy. Raw scores may be converted to stanines. Stanine scores may then be profiled according to the "Interpreting Profiles" section of the test manual. The appendix holds three lists of traits from (a) John French's 1953 book, *The Description of Personality Measurements in Self and Others*, (b) the code of MMPI scales, and (c) the list of bipolar traits used for this instrument, which is a compilation of the previous two lists. Persons interested in school administrators' self-perceptions may administer, score, and interpret this test.

DEVELOPMENT. The 1962 SPI format was "an experiment to determine what would be the most appropriate format for measuring the concept of self" (manual, p. 8) as it is "inferred from behavior and that evolves from experience" (manual, p. 1). The 1962 SPI format underwent revision in 1999, reportedly in urban and suburban school districts with 32 superintendents, with 36 superintendents, and also with 55 principals. The 1999 format included a list of 36 pairs of leadership traits. The most recent revision of the instrument came in 2005 with the addition of four more pairs of leadership traits, when it was administered to 24 superintendents and 36 principals, both groups being from urban and suburban school districts. No other descriptive information regarding the normative groups is detailed.

The test author establishes a theoretical foundation of the Self-Perceptions of School Administrators by briefly visiting a history of Spearman's "g" and *s* factors, adding terse summations regarding intelligence by other authors such as Thurstone, Thorndike, Harter, Garfinkel, Guilford, and Gardner. The idea of intelligence is paired with the construct of "self" that was established with Lecky's 1945 theory of self-consistency, as the test author notes other researchers with similar views, Carl Rogers (1950) and Boyd McCandless (1961). The test author describes the establishment of an index to measure "self" and the index's historical pitfalls, finally resting with the current state of the instrument, attending to a self-reported full exploration of monadic and dyadic scores. The test author provides a model of the Self, clustered with differentiating self-perceptions intended to provide a visual account of the Self, with the anticipation of further brain research that may illuminate "a dynamic of infinite diversity" (manual, p. 5). Indeed, the test manual is hard to follow.

TECHNICAL.

Standardization. The norm sample of the 2005 revision only indicates job title as either "superintendent" or "principal." No gender identification, work experience, cultural background, age, ethnicity, linguistic, or other human diversity considerations are mentioned. It is not known if the members of the norm group were employed in private or public schools or whether that is necessary to know. It is assumed Superintendents (n = 24) and Principals (n = 36) are from the United States. As is, using these data is limiting, considering generalizability.

Reliability. "The 1999 data were based upon 36 pairs of traits, with a possibility of scores ranging from -72 to +72. The 2005 data are based upon 40 pairs of traits, with a possibility of scores ranging from -80 to +80" (manual, p. 25). The test author reports test/retest reliability at 8 weeks at .92 and internal consistency reliability at .85–.91.

Validity. The test author reports content validity at .62–.73; predictive validity at .57 to .65; and concurrent validity at .59 to .64. Additional validity data for the SPI Series include construct validity at .53 to .66 and the multitrait-multimethod validity at .58 to .74. These latter data are listed under "General Information" of the measurement, with no further discussion in the manual. Means and standard deviation data are listed for each scale in both the 1999 and 2005 data.

COMMENTARY. The manual is difficult to follow as it makes brief historical references to the constructs of intelligence and self, with little reference to research on leadership in schools. There is a dearth of information regarding current brain research and its possible connection to the concept of self. This lack of lucid proposition and explanation in the manual limit the use of this instrument. The paradigms (referred to as "constellations") seems logical in presentation, but are not fully explained for possible utility with this instrument.

SUMMARY. Perhaps best utilized in research and further development, this instrument may not assist in improvement of school leaders. Explanation for the need of this instrument would be very helpful. Though the test manual briefly explains construct development and scale development, it does not explicitly detail the uses for knowing a school administrator's concept of self. The lay person most likely will have difficulty using this instrument and making inferences from results.

Review of the Self-Perceptions of School Administrators by SUZANNE YOUNG, Professor of Educational Research, University of Wyoming, Laramie, WY:

DESCRIPTION. Self-Perceptions of School Administrators was published in 2005 and is part of a series titled Self-Perceptions Inventory (SPI). It consists of two general perceptions measured by eight scales. The instrument measures self-concept as a person and self-concept as a school administrator. For both aspects, scales measure general perceptions of self, ideal perceptions, reflected perceptions, and perceptions of others, with eight scales in all.

The first instrument in the SPI series was published as the Self-Perceptions of Adults in 1965 and was designed to measure self-concept, ideal concept, and reflected self. The instrument was revised over the years, adding and changing items. A new set of instruments was added in 1973, titled Academic Perceptions Inventory, and was designed for students. New scales were added and tested from 1992 to 1995 to assess the perceptions of school administrators, supervisors, and other coordinators in schools; this new set was titled Self-Perceptions Inventory and was published in 1999. Finally, in 2005, a separate scale (Leadership and Management Inventory) comprising of 60 items was designed to assess leadership and management functions. Additional items were develped and added to the remaining scales. The revised instrument was renamed Self-Perceptions of School Administrators and was published in 2005.

The test author discusses the importance of understanding one's own self-concept. The instrument collects information on self-concept that is made up of one's own beliefs of personal self-concept both personally and as an administrator, including ideal beliefs, how one thinks others see him or her, and how others actually do perceive him or her. By examining the overall profile, one would understand discrepancies and consistencies about one's self-concept.

Self-Perceptions of School Administrators can be administered either to individuals or a group. The test manual describes what the administrator should say as well as the order and timing of scale administration. Scoring, profiling, and interpreting results are also described. The instrument is available on paper only. Scoring is done by the test administrator and results can be communicated to the individual or can be used to develop a profile of a group.

DEVELOPMENT. Self-Perceptions of School Administrators was developed as part of a continued progression of the Self-Perceptions Inventory Series, first published in 1965. Since that time, additional assessments have been added, items have been changed or revised, and scales have been added to existing assessments. The school administrator series, first published in 1999, addressed five areas of management and used seven scales. Six groups of people who understood traits and functions of school leaders tested the instrument: superintendents, school principals, assistant superintendents, assistant principals, teachers, and department chairs. In 2006, one additional instrument was added to the Self-Perceptions Inventory Series that examines leadership and management traits. In addition, four new pairs of traits were added to the remaining scales. The new scale was grounded in the current roles and responsibilities of school leaders. Again, the test author consulted an expert pool, although she does not describe the pool nor does she explain how the experts were used in the development of items.

TECHNICAL. The validity and reliability of the Self-Perceptions of School Administrators have each built on previous instruments in the series, likely enhancing the usefulness and confidence that users might have in the current instrument. In the test manual, the test author repeats the technical information from the 1999 instrument and also adds information for the current instrument.

The test author reports correlation coefficients to show evidence of content validity, concurrent validity, and predictive validity. Coefficients ranged from .57 (others' perceptions of on-the-job success) to .73 (perceptions of self, according to the expert pool). Validity coefficients were similar to the 1999 instrument but also generally higher.

Reliability was demonstrated using both test-retest (coefficient of stability, 8-week retest interval) and internal consistency (alpha coefficients). The reliability coefficients were .92 and .91, respectively, with both coefficients higher than in 1999.

COMMENTARY. The Self-Perceptions of School Administrators does not seem to be consistently on solid ground. The instrument was based on the test author's prior work in the series of self-perception inventories, with the assumption that the newest revision would be valid and reliable because of convincing evidence for the previous version. However, in a review of the 1999 version of the series, Clare (2003) pointed to the lack of substantial literature foundation as a concern. In the current manual, the test author added a reference list with sources dating from 1945 to 1969; dated sources such as these are not helpful in providing a convincing argument regarding the theoretical underpinnings of self-concept. Additionally, in this current version, the test author makes note of changes in the concept of "leadership" since the 1999 version, but does not cite sources for this belief except to say that experts suggested university training was lagging behind expectations of leaders in schools. Wang (2003) was more favorable than Clare and described the instrument as easy to administer and to complete and suggested that it should be used only for the purposes of research. The current instrument is very similar; its ease of use is a positive characteristic.

The test manual provides validity (content, concurrent, and predictive) and reliability (stability and internal consistency) coefficients that are moderate to high. However, the test author does not explain the sample used to demonstrate validity and reliability. In addition, coefficients are not provided separately for each scale.

SUMMARY. I recommend the use of the Self-Perceptions of School Administrators to assess self-concept of a person and self-concept as a school administrator for research purposes only. My hope is that in the next revision, the test author will give more attention to current research on self-concept for school administrators. In addition, the validity and reliability coefficients would be much more convincing if the test author would clarify how these coefficients were determined, as well as describe the validation sample and provide validity and reliability coefficients for each scale.

REVIEWER'S REFERENCES

Clare, M. M. (2003). [Review of the *Self*-Perceptions Inventory.] In B. S. Plake, J. C. Impara, & R. A. Spies (Eds.), *The fifteenth mental measurements yearbook* (pp. 808–810). Lincoln, NE: Buros Institute of Mental Measurements.

Wang, A. (2003). [Review of the *Self*-Perceptions Inventory.] In B. S. Plake, J. C. Impara, & R. A. Spies (Eds.), *The fifteenth mental measurements yearbook* (pp. 810–812). Lincoln, NE: Buros Institute of Mental Measurements.

[118]

Self-Perceptions of University Instructors.

Purpose: Designed to measure an adult's concept of self.

Population: University instructors.

Publication Dates: 1965-2008.

Scores: 16 scales: Self as a Person [College Professors] (Self Concept, Ideal Concept, Reflected Self, Perceptions of Others), Self as a Person [Adjunct Faculty] (Self Concept, Ideal Concept, Reflected Self, Perceptions of Others), Self as a College Professor (Self Concept, Ideal Concept, Reflected Self, Perceptions of Others), Self as an Adjunct Faculty Member (Self Concept, Ideal Concept, Reflected Self, Perceptions of Others).

Administration: Group.

Forms, 16: Self as a Person [College Professors] (Self Concept, Ideal Concept, Reflected Self, Perceptions of Others), Self as a Person [Adjunct Faculty] (Self Concept, Ideal Concept, Reflected Self, Perceptions of Others), Self as a College Professor (Self Concept, Ideal Concept, Reflected Self, Perceptions of Others), Self as an Adjunct Faculty Member (Self Concept, Ideal Concept, Reflected Self, Perceptions of Others).

Price Data, 2008: $40 per 25 scales (specify form); $40 per 50 answer sheets; $40 per test manual (2008, 41 pages); $.40 per scale for scoring and profiles; $40 per report for analysis.

Time: (5–20) minutes.

Comments: Developed from the original Self-Perceptions Inventory (15:226) and is part of the SPI series that includes: Self-Perceptions of Adolescents (18:114), Self-Perceptions of Children (18:116), Self-Perceptions of College Students, Self-Perceptions of Adults (18:115), Self-Perceptions of University Instructors (18:118), Self-Perceptions of Teachers, and Self-Perceptions of Nurses.

Author: Louise M. Soares.

Publisher: Castle Consultants.

Cross References: For reviews by Mary M. Clare and Aimin Wang of the 1999 Revision of the Self-Perceptions Inventory, see 15:226; see also T4:2421 (1 reference); for a review by Janet Morgan Riggs of an earlier edition, see 9:1101; for a review by Lorrie Shepard of an earlier edition, see 8:673 (2 references).

Review of the Self-Perceptions of University Instructors by THEODORE COLADARCI, Director of Institutional Research and Professor of Educational Psychology, University of Maine, Orono, ME:

DESCRIPTION. The Self-Perceptions of University Instructors is the latest derivative of the Self-Perception Inventory Series, with which Louise and Anthony Soares have been associated since its origins in 1965. The Self-Perceptions of University Instructors defies easy description. This putative "concept of self" instrument comprises two sets of four scales. In the first set, university instructors rate themselves "as a person" with respect to Self Concept ("What kind of person do you see yourself at the moment?"), Ideal Concept ("What kind of person would you like to be if you could change"?), and Reflected Self ("What kind of person do you thnk [*sic*] others see you?"). The fourth scale, Perceptions of Others, is completed by someone who knows the instructor ("What kind of person do you think this person is?"). All four scales in this first set comprise the same 40 pairs of "bipolar traits (e.g., bold/timid), and the respondent's task is to select one of four choices along the respective item's underlying continuum. Regarding bold/timid, the example, the response options are very bold, more bold than timid, more timid than bold, and very timid.

In contrast to these Self-As-Person ratings, the second set of scales calls for ratings of Self as an Instructor. There are separate forms for "college professors" and "adjunct faculty members." For example, college professors rate themselves with respect to Self as a College Professor ("What kind of instructor do you see yourself at the moment?"), Ideal as a College Professor ("What kind of instructor would you like to be if you could change"?), and Reflected Self ("What kind of instructor do you think others see you?"). Again, the fourth scale, Perceptions of Others, is completed by someone who knows the instructor ("What kind of instructor do you think this person is?"). Substitute "college professor" with "adjunct faculty member" and you have the language for the latter group. These Self-as-Instructor scales similarly comprise 40 trait pairs although, curiously, only 6 are the same as those included on the Self-as-Person scales.

Each item is scored as follows: -2 is assigned to the "very negative position" (e.g., very timid), -1 to the "more negative position" (e.g., more timid than bold), +1 to the "more positive position" (e.g., more bold than timid), and +2 to the "very positive position" (e.g., very bold). Item scores are summed to yield an "index score" for each of the eight scales, each of which can be converted to a stanine (based on normative data, described below). Although the test authors encourage users to examine discrepancies among a respondent's index scores (e.g., Self-Concept versus Ideal Self, or Self-Concept as a Person versus Self-Concept as a College Professor), this is arguably problematic when comparing the Self-as-Person and Self-as-Instructor scales because of the aforementioned nonequivalence of the 40 trait pairs. More on this later.

The testing manual, an unpolished and poorly organized document, also provides instructions for administration and guidance for interpretation.

DEVELOPMENT. As with the Self-Perception of University Instructors scales themselves, the development of this instrument defies easy description. The test authors' account of theoretical background and development takes the reader through a wandering history of self-concept theorizing and measurement (with some intelligence theory thrown in) and, in turn, the test authors' many instrument development activities since 1965 when they introduced their Self-Perceptions of Adults. I found the chronology of, and relationships among, the many instruments difficult–at times, impossible—to follow. Suffice it to say that Self-Perceptions of University Instructors is the latest instrument to directly descend from the original Self-Perceptions of Adults. The latter comprised 36 pairs of bipolar traits which, for reasons that remain undisclosed, the test authors took from a text by French (1953). Over the years, they tweaked these trait pairs a bit, added 4 more, and produced separate forms targeting one group or another (e.g., teachers, nurses, school administrators, and now university instructors).

As I described above, Self-Perceptions of University Instructors asks respondents to differentiate between Self as Person and Self as Instructor (both with respect to Self-Concept, Ideal Concept, and Reflected Self, along with the solicited perceptions of others). But again, only 6 of the 40 trait pairs are identical across the Self-as-Person and Self-as-Instructor forms. In several instances, only half of a trait pair appears on both forms; otherwise, the trait pairs are wholly different across forms. This nonequivalence is odd, particularly in view of the test authors' interest in, and promotion of, comparisons between Self-as-Person and Self-as-Instructor index scores. Absent a compelling equivalence argument (the test authors are inexplicably silent on this matter), Self-as-Person and Self-as-Instructor comparisons simply are inappropriate.

TECHNICAL. To provide a normative context for Self-Perceptions of University Instructors, the test authors report scale means and standard deviations based on 80 faculty "in undergraduate arts and sciences programs," 80 faculty "in undergraduate professional programs" (education, engineering, and nursing), and 80 faculty "in graduate programs" (business, law, and medicine). These statistics are presented separately for college professors and adjunct faculty members, and each statistic is reported separately for males and females. (There is an equal number of college professors and adjunct faculty members for each set of programs, although no *n*s accompany the sex breakdowns.) We are told nothing else about these faculty, their institutions, or how either were selected, which renders these data uninformative. Further, although the test authors presumably used these data for their stanine conversions, separate stanines are not reported for college professors and adjunct faculty members or for males and females.

As for reliability and validity, the adduced evidence appears on a single page and cries out for elaboration. Regarding reliability, we are told only that the Self-Perceptions of University Instructors has a 9-week test-retest reliability of .90 and an alpha coefficient of .88. No other information is provided about the determination of either statistic, nor do the test authors explain why they report a single reliability coefficient for an eight-scale instrument. No additional information accompanies the validity coefficients either. A table entitled "content validity (expert pool)" (manual, p. 28) shows 8 coefficients ranging from .62 to .86. I have no idea how these coefficients were obtained or what they mean. Similarly, I do not know what sense to make of the 2 coefficients in a table entitled "construct validity (expert pool)" (manual, p. 28), the 2 coefficients in a table entitled "predictive validity (on-the-job success)" (manual, p. 28), or the 10 coefficients in a table entitled "concurrent validity (multi-trait multi-rater matrix)" (manual, p. 28).

COMMENTARY. There is little to recommend in Self-Perceptions of University Instructors. First, the nonequivalence of the Self-as-Person and Self-as-Instructor forms arguably renders problematic the cross-form comparison of index scores the test authors encourage. The problem of nonequivalence across forms notwithstanding, as I examined the Self-Perceptions of University Instructors scales and read the accompanying material, I continued to wonder how I, a professor, could partition my sense of self "as a person" and, in turn, "as an instructor." Are not the two hopelessly confounded? Lofty theoretical rhetoric aside, I do not believe the test authors adequately address this fundamental question. Second, the presented information regarding norms, reliability, and validity precludes meaningful use of the test. Indeed, it is unfathomable that authors of a commercially available instrument would report reliability and validity evidence as these test authors have. Third, even if these shortcomings somehow could be ignored, it remains unclear just what an index score from this instrument can tell us. In their guidance for interpretation, for example, the test authors state that "[a]n extremely high Self Concept score may indicate defensiveness since highly self-satisfied people sometimes tend to deny bad traits. On the other hand, an unduly high concept of self may also mean a lack of awareness of the self or an overall satisfaction with the self without yet possessing or demonstrating maturity or sophistication" (manual, p. 31). (I would suggest a third possibility: This person has a justifiably high self-concept.) But which is it, and how is one to know? In short, a score from this instrument seemingly does not permit a useful interpretation.

SUMMARY. Over the years, *The Mental Measurements Yearbook* has included a number of reviews of these test authors' instruments. After constructively pointing to one shortcoming or another, each reviewer almost invariably concluded with the obligatory caution: The instrument can be used for research, but not clinical, purposes. In the case of the Self-Perceptions of University Instructors, I question the value of even using it in research.

REVIEWER'S REFERENCE

French, J. W. (1953). *The description of personality measurements in self and others.* Princeton, NJ: Educational Testing Service.

Review of Self-Perceptions of University Instructors by SANDRA M. HARRIS, Assessment Coordinator, College of Social and Behavioral Sciences, Walden University, Minneapolis, MN:

DESCRIPTION. The Self-Perceptions of University Instructors (SPI/University Instructor) is a group or individually administered measure of an adult's perception of self as a university faculty. The intended population is adults teaching in the university setting. It is not clear whether the intended population includes faculty at community colleges, technical schools, trade schools, or professional schools.

The instrument contains four global factors: Self as a Person/College Professor; Self as a College Professor; Self as a Person/Adjunct; and Self as an Adjunct Faculty. Each factor is divided into four scales: Self-Concept, Ideal Concept, Reflected Self, and Perceptions of Others. Although not explicitly stated, it can be inferred that a respondent would complete items for only two of the four factors. It is expected that a respondent would complete the scales that represents his or her status as a full-time or adjunct faculty member. It is presumed that a person who completes the instrument would receive a total of eight scale scores.

Items on each scale are presented in a forced-choice format that is based on the semantic differential technique. Each scale of the instrument consists of 40 pairs of adjectives that are polar opposites in meaning. Each adjective is placed on opposite ends of a line that is marked in four quadrants. The middle of the line is interpreted as a neutral point. Each quadrant is anchored by the words very or more. Respondents answer each item by marking on the line the quadrant that most reflects the way the individual looks at self as a person.

The administration and instructions are clear and easy to follow. The test authors do not indicate how long it takes to complete the instrument, but it would likely take about 15–20 minutes to complete the eight scales, each of which is scored separately. The scoring for each item is as follows: +2 for a *"very"* positive position, +1 for a *"more"* positive position, -1 for a *"more"* negative position, or -2 for a "very" negative position. Items on each scale are summed to yield a total scale score that ranges from -80 to +80. The test authors give procedures for converting raw scores to stanine scores for the purpose of standardized comparisons. The manual provides instructions for developing and interpreting individual profiles; however, the interpretations are complex or confusing and include interpretations based on moderate stanine scores. Interpretations are given for each of the eight scales, but no instructions are given for calculating a global score. The interpretations are general in nature. The test authors do not discuss how the profiles can be used in a practical context. The manual also gives instructions for calculating a group profile but does not indicate how to interpret such a profile.

DEVELOPMENT. The original Self-Perceptions Inventory was developed during an experiment that was designed to determine the best way to measure self. The test authors suggest that the basis of the items on the instrument was Prescott's theory of self-consistency and the thought that accurate measures of self are rooted in comparisons of positive and negative terms. No details were given regarding how specific principles of self-consistency theory served as the foundational theory for the SPI series.

Development of the SPI/University Instructors is rooted in the development of the Adult Self-Perception scales, which was copyrighted in 1965. The early instrument consisted of three scales (Self-Concept, Ideal Concept, and Reflected Self). The original scales consisted of 36 pairs of bipolar adjectives. The early response format is similar to the current response format. Over time the test authors included the Perceptions of Others scale. The Self as University Instructor was designed in 2008. No information was given regarding theoretical reasons for adding the fourth factor. The current instrument began with 36 pairs of traits and was eventually increased to 40 points. The test authors indicated that the increase in the number of items was implemented to (a) facilitate comparisons with the Self as a Person Scale and (b) increase the reliability of the variables contained in the two scales.

TECHNICAL. The standardization sample for the SPI/University Instructor consisted of 240 full-time and adjunct faculty in a variety of undergraduate and graduate programs. The sample included 40 full-time and 40 adjunct faculty in each group. No details were given on where the study took place. The manual reports means and standard deviations according to gender, but no other demographic information is provided about the sample. The lack of details regarding the demographic characteristics of the normative sample is a limitation of the manual. Due to these limitations, one cannot conclude the sample is representative of the larger population of university instructors, which limits the generalizablity of findings. The issue of generalizability has been addressed in previous reviews of tests from the SPI series (Clare, 2003; Demauro, 1992; Harrell, 1992; Wang, 2003).

Several types of validity were reported for the SPI/University Instructor. However, the test authors did not differentiate whether the data were for full-time faculty, adjunct faculty, or a combination of both. Content validity estimates reportedly ranged from .62 to .86 across various scales. Construct validity estimates were reported for two of the scales and ranged from .64 to .72.

However, no indication was given regarding the specific statistical procedure used to assess content or construct validity. Concurrent validity was reported using the multitrait-multirater method. The manual presents a 4 x 4 correlation matrix that includes ratings for self, students (.35), colleagues (.56), and administrators (.43). However, it is not clear which aspect of self was being rated. Further, it is not clear how the test authors generated the singular scores for the correlations. The test authors also reported predictive validity of .60 for Self as Adjunct Faculty and .69 for Self as College Professor. The criterion variable for the predictive validity was on-the-job-success; however, the construct of on-the-job-success was not defined. The method for operationalizing on-the-job-success was not specified.

The data reported for reliability were weak. The manual reported a single 9-week stability coefficient of .90. Likewise, only a single value of coefficient alpha of .90 was given. The manual did not provide details of how the single reliability indices were generated. One would expect to find separate reliability estimates for each of the 16 scales of the instrument. The limitations regarding the technical merits of the SPI have been noted in previous reviews (Clare, 2003; Demauro, 1992; Harrell, 1992; Wang, 2003).

COMMENTARY. The SPI/University Instructor is a group or individually administered instrument that is easy to administer and score. More extensive data are needed regarding the psychometric properties of the instrument. Data for the normative sample needs to be strengthened and more clearly defined. There are many cultural factors (such as age, length of time teaching, ethnicity, position, and tenure status) that can affect a person's perception of self as a university instructor. Data on these demographic variables need to be collected and included in comparative studies of self-perceptions of university instructors. The limited data on the normative sample have been a long-standing concern with the SPI series (Clare, 2003; Demauro, 1992; Harrell, 1992; Wang, 2003). Additional details are needed on how specific validity indices were obtained, including statistical procedures used to establish validity. These details need to be included in narrative form. In addition, information regarding reliability needs to be expanded. The test authors must provide information regarding reliability for each of the 16 scales included in the instrument.

SUMMARY. The SPI/University Instructor was designed to assess individual perceptions as a university professor. There needs to be an explanation of the practical utility of the instrument. The test authors should discuss how the instrument can be used in a practical setting. Also, more details are needed regarding how the psychometric properties of the instrument were derived. Specifically, information regarding the demographic characteristics of the normative sample needs to be expanded. Also, there needs to be additional information regarding the procedures used to establish the validity and reliability of the instrument.

REVIEWER'S REFERENCES

Clare, M. M. (2003). [Review of the Self-Perception Inventory–1999 Revision.] From B. S. Plake, J. C. Impara, & R. A. Spies (Eds.), *The fifteenth mental measurements yearbook* [Electronic version]. Retrieved October 31, 2009, from http://web.ebscohost.com.

Demauro, G. E. (1992). [Review of the Self-Perception Inventory–Nursing Forms.] From J. J. Kramer & J. C. Conoley (Eds.), *The eleventh mental measurements yearbook* [Electronic version]. Retrieved October 31, 2009, from http://web.ebscohost.com..

Harrell, M. R. (1992). [Review of the Self-Perception Inventory–Nursing Forms.] From J. J. Kramer & J. C. Conoley (Eds.), *The eleventh mental measurements yearbook* [Electronic version]. Retrieved October 31, 2009, from http://web.ebscohost.com.

Wang, A. (2003). [Review of the Self-Perception Inventory-1999 Revision.] From B. S. Plake, J. C. Impara, & R. A. Spies (Eds.), *The fifteenth mental measurements yearbook* [Electronic version]. Retrieved October 31, 2009, from http://web.ebscohost.com.

[119]

Sensory Processing Measure.

Purpose: "Enables assessment of sensory processing issues, praxis, and social participation in elementary school-aged children."

Population: Ages 5-12.

Publication Date: 2007.

Acronym: SPM

Scores, 15: Social Participation, Vision, Hearing, Touch, Body Awareness, Balance and Motion, Planning and Ideas, Total Sensory Systems, Environment Difference, Art Class Total, Music Class Total, Physical Education Class Total, Recess/Playground Total, Cafeteria Total, School Bus Total.

Administration: Group.

Price Data, 2010: $155 per comprehensive kit including 25 Home AutoScore Forms, 25 Main Classroom AutoScore Forms, School Environments Form CD, and manual (102 pages); $125 per School kit including 25 Main Classroom AutoScore Forms, School Environments Form CD, and manual; $99 per Home kit including 25 Home AutoScore Forms and manual; $42 per 25 AutoScore Forms; $32 per School Environments Form CD (unlimited use); $66 per manual; $22 per Continuing Education (CE) Questionnaire and Evaluation Form.

Time: (15-20) minutes each for the Home and Main Classroom Forms; (5) minutes for each School Environment Form.

Comments: The Home and Main Classroom Forms may be used individually or together, but the School

Environments Forms may only be used in conjunction with the Main Classroom Form.

Authors: L. Diane Parham and Cheryl Ecker (Home Form); Heather Miller Kuhaneck, Diana A. Henry, and Tara J. Glennon (Main Classroom and School Environments Forms).

Publisher: Western Psychological Services.

Review of the Sensory Processing Measure by MICHAEL K. CRUCE, Nationally Certified School Psychologist, Special Education Department, Lincoln Public Schools, Lincoln, NE:

DESCRIPTION. The Sensory Processing Measure (SPM) examines the managing of sensory issues, praxis (the ability to plan and organize one's movement), and social participation in elementary school children ages 5 through 12 by way of an integrated system of rating scales. The SPM is based on sensory integration theory, which suggests that the integration and processing of sensory inputs is important in shaping neurobehavioral development. The SPM consists of three forms. The SPM Home Form is a 75-item rating scale completed by parents in 15 to 20 minutes that measures eight constructs (Social Participation, Vision, Hearing, Touch, Body Awareness, Balance and Motion, Planning and Ideas, and Total Sensory Systems) cited by the test authors to be important in determining sensory integration strengths and deficits. The SPM Main Classroom Form takes a student's primary-grade teacher 15 to 20 minutes to complete, consists of 62 items, and measures the same eight constructs at school as the Home Form. In both the Home and Classroom Forms the Total Sensory Systems Score signifies a general dysfunction in sensory processing. The SPM School Environments Form is a short-form measure of sensory issues that may arise in a specific school environment (Art Class, Music Class, Physical Education Class, Recess/Playground, the Cafeteria, and/or the School Bus). Each of the School Environment Forms consists of 15 questions with the exception of the School Bus form, which contains 10 questions. The School Environments Forms may be used in any combination and take under 5 minutes to complete. All forms of the SPM consist of a 4-point Likert-type scale (Never, Occasionally, Frequently, Always). The scales may be used separately or in combination, although the test authors report that the School Environments Form should not be used in isolation from the Main Classroom Form.

The SPM is typically administered to parents and teachers for their completion independently. The forms contain a carbon paper and responses are automatically transferred to the scoring worksheet. The examiner adds up and transfers raw scores to the profile sheet. The Home and Classroom Forms yield *T*-scores for interpretive purposes and fall into three ranges: the Typical range, the Some Problems range, and the Definite Dysfunction range. The School Environments Form uses a cutoff score for each setting that corresponds to significant problems in that location. Scoring for the Home and Classroom Form takes approximately 10 minutes each to complete.

DEVELOPMENT. The instrument was developed with the cooperation of two author groups engaged in separate projects to produce a comprehensive instrument to bridge the gap between home and school environments in the identification of sensory integration problems. The SPM Home Form originated from the Evaluation of Sensory Processing (Parham & Ecker, 2002), and the SPM Main Classroom and School Environments Form evolved from the School Assessment of Sensory Integration (Miller Kuhaneck, Henry, Glennon, and Mu, 2007). The test authors set out to re-analyze data from the original instruments in order to condense the assessments into more user-friendly and efficient packages, as well as to structure the test under a unified theory and to prepare the test for a large standardization pool. Finally, a research version of each instrument was created to be used in the standardization.

The theoretical basis of the SPM was derived from Ayres's theory of sensory integration (1972), which is a widely held framework used by occupational therapists in working with young people who have sensory difficulties. The SPM manual reports that disorders of sensory integration are believed to include: not using sensory information, sensory seeking behaviors, being overwhelmed by sensory stimuli, difficulties with sensory discrimination, and sensory-motor problems. The theory is developmental in nature as early emerging senses provide the foundation for growth of more mature visual and auditory systems (Ayres, 1972). It is suggested that students who exhibit impediments with sensory processing may have impairments in other areas of functioning such as planning and organizing their body movements.

TECHNICAL. The standardization sample consisted of 1,051 children aged 5 to 12 from approximately 76 sites across the United States. No children were included in the standardization sample from full-time special education programs. Demographic characteristics of the sample approximate U.S. Census population estimates for most dimensions of interest. However, the test authors note that Caucasians are slightly overrepresented. Males and females are almost equally represented. The Midwest appears to be significantly overrepresented with the South and West underrepresented. Additionally, parents with college degrees were overrepresented. In addition to the primary teacher rating the students, six additional school environments were rated to assist in the development of the SPM School Environments Form.

A clinical validity study was undertaken to determine the utility of the instruments. This study consisted of 345 children between the ages of 5 and 13 who were being seen by occupational therapists. That sample consisted of mostly white males, whose parents were in the upper socioeconomic status. The data yielded from both the standardization and clinical validity study were used to shape the final scales and item content for all forms.

To assess reliability, internal consistency estimates were examined by the test authors using alpha coefficients. Internal consistency for the scales on each form ranges between .69 and .98. The Vision, Hearing, and Touch scales have some of the lowest internal consistency estimates ranging from .75 to .84 for the total sample. Although acceptable, this is concerning as vision, hearing and touch would be areas where the identification of sensory issues would be most observable. Social Participation, Planning and Ideas, and the Total Sensory Systems Score all demonstrate excellent reliability. Internal consistency for the School Environments Form also was strong. Test-retest reliability data were collected on 77 children ages 5–12 in a 2-week follow-up using both the Home and Main Classroom Forms. As would be expected, stability was high with all composites demonstrating coefficients above .94. Additionally, standard errors of measurement and confidence intervals calculated at 95% appear to be quite acceptable.

Content validity for the instruments was first evaluated using the instruments in their original form. The test authors evaluated items from the original tests and condensed items that were redundant and not aligned with Ayres's theory of sensory integration. The item sets were then subjected to several rounds of expert review where they were retained only if they were judged to adequately represent the intended sensory function. A research version of the new test was then subjected to confirmatory and exploratory factor analyses to examine construct validity. In the confirmatory analysis, the researchers used two competing factor models (sensory systems vs. sensory integration vulnerabilities) on a sample of clinic-referred children. The test authors report that the sensory systems factor was the best fit for the data. The exploratory factor analysis yielded seven factors that do not appear to align closely with the item content of the eight scales that make up the test. The first factor for the Home Form is likely a behavioral factor and the test authors acknowledge that this factor appeared to measure generally problematic behavior. Of the factors that the test authors examined, Vision, Hearing, and Touch were questionable, and Taste and Smell did not load clearly on any of the factors and were included only in the Total Sensory score. Additionally, items on the Home Form appear to hang together in their factors better than items on the Classroom Form. Convergent validity was examined by comparing the SPM to the Sensory Profile (Dunn, 1999) and results indicate adequate overlap in areas where the tests display similar content. Finally, criterion-related validity was addressed by comparing young people from the standardization sample to those in the clinical sample. Results indicated that the instrument was able to distinguish those in the typical sample from those in the clinical group.

COMMENTARY. The Sensory Processing Measure is a comprehensive measure of sensory difficulties in school-aged children. The test authors have quantified sensory integration issues into constructs that can be assessed and measured using observable behavior. This is definitely progress when considering the controversial nature of sensory integration therapies among many psychologists. This instrument would be a good choice if one needs to identify sensory difficulties across environments, and the School Environments Form especially fills a gap seen in most rating scales as it looks at alternate settings where students are likely to struggle. This measure is best used comprehensively, and one should be guarded in interpreting the SPM Main Classroom Form in isolation without the use of the SPM Home Form for comparison. As the item content and scale names are the same on both forms, a quick comparison of behavior can be made. In future versions of the SPM, the test authors may wish to consider examining the item content further as the Taste and Smell factors were not usable as major scales, and the Vision, Hearing, and Touch scales could stand to be strengthened.

SUMMARY. The Sensory Processing Measure was designed to evaluate sensory dysfunction in school-aged children. Although sensory integration interventions are seen as controversial among psychologists, it appears that they are used with some frequency by occupational therapists. This test assists in identifying areas where students display inappropriate behaviors that may be sensory related. There is some concern as to whether these behaviors represent sensory-related deficits or behavioral symptoms associated with various diagnoses (e.g., Autism, ADHD). Nevertheless, the SPM appears to be a usable, structurally sound instrument that attempts to quantify sensory problems in children. The SPM would be a good instrument for occupational therapists to use in planning appropriate empirically validated treatment options.

REVIEWER'S REFERENCES

Ayres, A. J. (1972). *Sensory integration and learning disorders.* Los Angeles: Western Psychological Services.

Dunn, W. (1999). Sensory Profile. San Antonio, TX: Psychological Corporation.

Miller Kuhaneck, H., Henry, D. A., Glennon, T. J., & Mu, K. (2007). Development of the Sensory Processing Measure-School Form: Initial studies of reliability and validity. *American Journal of Occupational Therapy, 61,* 170–175.

Parham, L. D., & Ecker, C. (2002). Evaluation of sensory processing; Research version 4. In A. C. Bundy, S. J. Lane, & E. A. Murray (Eds.), *Sensory integration: Theory and practice* (2nd ed; pp. 194-196). Philadelphia: F. A. Davis.

Review of the Sensory Processing Measure by T. STEUART WATSON, Professor of Educational Psychology, Miami University, Oxford, OH, and MICHAEL F. WOODIN, Assistant Professor of Educational Psychology, Miami University, Oxford, OH:

DESCRIPTION. The Sensory Processing Measure (SPM) is an integrated system of individually administered behavioral rating scales that assess sensory integration and sensory processing issues in elementary school-aged children across home, classroom, and different school environment settings (i.e., art class, music class, physical education class, the playground, the cafeteria, and the school bus). The SPM is used to assess a wide range of behaviors and characteristics in children related to the operation of sensory systems, sensory processing difficulties, social participation skills, and praxis (the ability to plan and organize movement). The test authors claim that the SPM will be useful in determining the types of interventions that would be most appropriate for a child as a means of measuring program effectiveness, building team collaboration regarding intervention strategies, fostering program planning, and developing Individualized Educational Plans (IEPs).

There are eight forms of the test, including the Home Form, Main Classroom Form, and six scale forms for the School Environment Form. The Home and Main Classroom Forms each contain items forming eight different scales, including Social Participation (SOC), Vision (VIS), Hearing (HEA), Touch (TOU), Body Awareness (BOD), Balance and Motion (BAL), Planning and Ideas (PLA), and Total Sensory Systems (TOT). The Home Form, completed by the child's parent or home-based care provider, consists of 75 items. The Main Classroom Form, containing 62 items, is to be completed by the child's primary classroom teacher. Both the Home and Main Classroom Forms take 15 to 20 minutes to be completed by their respective respondents and then 5 to 10 minutes to be scored by the examiner via a carbon copy, automatic score transfer worksheet system. The School Environments Forms comprise six separate rating sheets that are provided to those purchasing the measure on an unlimited-use CD that can be printed by the user on demand. The six school environments assessed include Art Class, Music Class, Physical Education Class, Recess/Playground, Cafeteria, and School Bus settings. Each rating sheet has 15 items with the exception of the School Bus sheet, which has 10 items. Each of the School Environment Forms yields only a Total score. The estimated time for raters to complete each of these forms is 5 minutes. All eight forms use the same response format as each item is rated for the frequency of the behavior via a 4-point Likert scale with the response options of *Never, Occasionally, Frequently,* and *Always.*

Professional and/or allied educational staff members who may administer and score these measures include those "who do not have backgrounds in occupational therapy or psychological testing" (examiner's manual, p. 4). However, to interpret the SPM, it is highly recommended that the individual should be an occupational therapist or other professional (such as a psychologist, counselor, social worker, speech-language therapist, or physical therapist) who has formal training in sensory integration. It is noted that a potential user should read the manual to take into account the theory, development, background information, and technical characteristics of the SPM before administering it. This admonition probably should be heeded given the rather tenuous nature of the data on sensory integration and its relationship to effective treatment.

The AutoScoreTM feature permits transfer of the examinee's responses to a scoring worksheet that allows for easy calculation of the scores. The eight scores yielded by both the Home and Main Classroom are converted from raw scores into *T*-scores as well as their corresponding percentile ranks. The *T*-scores for these two forms are then identified as falling within either the "Typical" range (*T*-score of 40 to 59), the "Some Problems" range (*T*-Score of 60 to 69), or the "Definite Dysfunction" range (*T*-score of 70 to 80). The School Environments Forms yield no *T*-scores. Rather, these forms yield a Total score for each environment that is interpreted against an established cutoff criterion. Those children who score above the cutoff score are said to be "experiencing an unusually high number of sensory processing problems in that environment" (examiner's manual, p. 4). Scoring instructions and norms tables are included with the Home and Main Classroom forms. Cutoff scores for the raw scale scores taken from the School Environments Forms are included in the examiner's manual. Interpretative case studies, intervention suggestions, and guidelines are provided in the manual for examiner reference. The examiner's manual provides an overview of the theory underlying the SPM, as well as clear directions, interpretative guidelines, representative case studies, technical appraisals, and references. The scoring forms provide easy-to-follow instructions, data graphics, and charts.

DEVELOPMENT. The SPM is actually a merger of two previously published measures. The Home Form is a revised version of the Evaluation of Sensory Processing (ESP; Parham & Ecker, 2002), whereas the Main Classroom and School Environments Forms were developed from the school-based rating scale entitled the School Assessment of Sensory Integration (SASI; Miller Kuhaneck, Henry, Glennon, & Mu, 2007). The goals underlying this combination of assessment instruments were to maximize clinical utility of the measures and share a common standardization effort. By so doing, it was the test authors' intent to create an integrated collection of parallel test materials regarding sensory processing and sensory integration that could be used across multiple settings.

TECHNICAL. Norms for this assessment were based on a sample of 1,051 children ranging in age from 5 to 12 years who were recruited from regular education elementary school classrooms. All of the children in the sample were assessed with the SPM Home Form (completed by the child's parent or caretaker) and Main Classroom Form (completed by the child's primary school teacher). Although the students sampled were from regular education classrooms, they were not excluded if they were found to have mild academic or behavioral difficulties. Demographic data about the sample were compared by age and against the 2001 U.S. Census data with regard to gender, race, geographical distribution, and educational attainment of parents. In terms of age, initial analyses of the 5–12 age group conducted revealed a significant effect of age on SPM scale scores with the scores decreasing gradually as age increased. To account for this effect, the standardization sample was split into two groups, 5–8 and 9–12 years of age, and comparisons were run with effect sizes calculated for each scale. Resulting effect sizes were all small (< .25) indicating that the effect of age on SPM scores was not statistically meaningful. As such, the test developers decided to provide norming tables based upon the whole age group encompassing the ages of 5 to 12. With regard to approximation of the U.S. Census data, the distribution of males and females was the only category that approximated the Census figures. All other demographics were found to vary from the Census data. In terms of race, the sample slightly overrepresented Whites and slightly underrepresented African Americans and Asians. Geographically, the South and West regions of the U.S. were underrepresented, whereas the sample drew disproportionately from the Midwest. The highest educational attainment of the parents of children in the sample was assessed and it was determined that the highest category (4-year college or more) was overrepresented in comparison with the Census data. In contrast, the lowest SES category (less than high school education) was found to be close in its approximation to the Census figures. Because of the potential moderating effects of the disproportionate demographic figures identified, effect size analyses were conducted to determine if any clinically meaningful differences between groups were found to exist. Based upon their analyses, all differences yielded small effect sizes (< .25), and the authors concluded that there were no statistically meaningful differences and that the findings were supportive of the use of single norm sets for the primary Home and Main Classroom Forms.

In addition to the development of the Home and Main Classroom Forms with the primary standardization sample, subsamples of children were rated by individuals from the six other school settings assessed through the School Environments Forms. The size of these subsamples was considerably smaller than the primary standardization sample as their number ranged from 171 to 311. The test authors indicated that the practical limitations of finding and coordinating raters across seven different school environments resulted in a realization that it was not possible to attain demographic representativeness for the School Environments Forms. As such, these subsamples were not used to derive normative scores. Instead, cutoff scores based upon clinical judgment were set and indicated in the examiner's manual along with base rates for the percentage of students falling below the cutoff. The School Environments Forms are provided as ancillary rating scales published on a CD and provided in a format that can be downloaded and printed as needed.

Reliability. The internal consistency and stability of both the Main Classroom and Home Forms was found to be within acceptable limits for a behavioral rating scale. All total sample coefficient alpha estimates were at or above .75. Coefficient alphas were at or above the .80 level for seven of the eight Home Form scales and five of the eight Main Classroom Form scales. The Hearing and Touch scales for the 9–10-year-old standardization group from the Main Classroom Form fell below the .70 threshold. As the test developers posited, it is likely that short item length (7–8 items) of those scales may have partially contributed to the lower coefficients. The median internal consistency for the School Form was .86 and for the Home Form was .85 and the median test-retest reliability was .97 with a 2-week interval between testing sessions. The standard errors of measurement varied between 1.29 and 4.40 points.

Validity. The test authors of the SPM indicated the content validity of the instrument stems from its relationship to the theoretical constructs and principles underlying the sensory integration theory upon which it is based and upon which two prior test development efforts were made. Multiple expert reviews resulted in removal or retention of items to reflect their relationship to sensory system functions, social participation, and praxis. Construct validity was addressed through factor analyses. Results of the factor analyses provided support for the basic scale structure of the SPM. Item-scale correlations provided robust support for the Home Form as a measure that can be scored and interpreted according to its separate scales. In contrast, questionable results were attained for the Main Classroom Form in terms of high interscale correlations between the BOD (proprioception) and BAL (vestibular) scales. This finding should be considered when interpreting results from these scales in individual cases.

Convergent validity was reported through comparisons to the Sensory Profile (Dunn, 1999), which is a caregiver-rated measure of a child's sensory processing abilities. Findings indicated that the SPM Home Form yielded strong and consistent relationships with the scores on the Sensory Profile. There was no measure upon which to build convergent comparisons with the SPM Main Classroom Form. As such, the relationship between the Main Classroom Form and the independently completed School Environments Forms scales was assessed. Findings of strong relationships between these forms provide support for the stability of measurement of these forms. Evidence of discriminant validity was provided as it was found that clinically meaningful effect sizes were observed in distinguishing a sample of clinic-referred children to those within the normative sample.

COMMENTARY. In a recent pediatric review of sensory integration (SI) theory and practice, Williames and Erdie-Lalena (2009) concluded that SI represents a potential adjunctive treatment but that efforts to standardize SI diagnosis and treatment in research would be necessary to provide a more definitive assessment of treatment efficacy. Development of the SPM is a step in that direction. This measure can be used by those occupational therapists steeped in SI theory and practice. It also can be used by school and allied professionals who would seek to integrate or use such data within their client populations. The SPM has an adequate normative base, provides data across multiple settings in home and school environments, is easy to administer and score, and provides adequate to moderate evidence of reliability, validity, factor structure, and discriminant validity. One concern is the broad age range of the normative sample in that the scoring of the instrument encompasses age groups from 5–12 along developmental dimensions including social participation, sensory issues, and motor planning abilities. Although statistical analyses yielded no significant differences between the age groups making up this normative sample, it is clinically difficult to understand how so few differences would have been noted across such a large age span. In addition, although effective comparisons were made to two other tests in common use within the SI field, no relationships to measures in other fields were made. It would be useful to examine convergent validity with other measures of social, motor, or sensory function from fields such as neuropsychology, speech-language pathology, and achievement. Further, although the case studies are exemplary in demonstrating the use of the SPM and SI terminology, it would be beneficial to include case studies that integrate other sources of assessment and intervention information from allied fields.

SUMMARY. The test developers have constructed an integrated sensory processing measure within the field of sensory integration that provides norm-referenced, standardized data across settings (Home, Classroom, and School Environments) and multiple raters (Caregiver, Primary Teacher, School Personnel) for children aged 5–12. SI is a field of endeavor that is growing and achieving greater acceptance and understanding within the professional literature of occupational therapy and allied fields in health and education. There is a need for quality assessments that can add to the diagnostic accuracy associated with SI and to increase treatment acceptability and efficacy. Estimates of reliability, validity, and construct structure are adequate to strong and the SPM is easy to administer and score. The interpretive guidelines represent an excellent attempt at providing clear-cut suggestions for understanding a child's sensory profile and its relation to intervention planning, program development, and construction of a child's Individualized Educational Plan (IEP). Further connections to assessments and work in allied fields such as neuropsychology, school psychology, speech-language therapy, and education would help to broaden this instrument's use within different settings and professions. At the present time, we feel that use of the SPM and similar instruments should be restricted to research applications due to the lack of data supporting its use in identifying effective treatments and the ability of the construct to add a significant degree to our understanding of behavioral and social disorders.

REVIEWERS' REFERENCES

Dunn, W. (1999). Sensory Profile. San Antonio, TX: Psychological Corporation.

Miller Kuhaneck, H., Henry, D. A., Glennon, T. J., & Mu, K. (2007). Development of the Sensory Processing Measure—School form: Initial studies of reliability and validity. *American Journal of Occupational Therapy, 61,* 170-175.

Parham, L. D., & Ecker, C. (2002). Evaluation of sensory processing: Research version 4. In A. C. Bundy, S. J. Lane, & E. A. Murray (Eds.), *Sensory integration: Theory and practice* (2nd ed.; pp. 194-196). Philadelphia: F. A. Davis.

Williames, L. D., & Erdie-Lalena, C. R. (2009). Complementary, holistic, and integrative medicine: Sensory integration. *Pediatric Review, 30,* e91-e93.

[120]

Sensory Profile School Companion.

Purpose: Assesses a student's sensory processing abilities and their effect on the student's functional performance in the classroom and school environment.
Population: Ages 3-0 to 11-11.
Publication Date: 2006.
Scores, 13: 4 Quadrant scores (Registration, Seeking, Sensitivity, Avoiding), 4 School Factor scores (School Factors 1, 2, 3, 4), 5 Section scores (Auditory, Visual, Movement, Touch, Behavior).
Administration: Individual.
Price Data, 2007: $140 per complete kit including user's manual (2006, 106 pages), 25 teacher questionnaires, and 25 summary score sheets; $45 per 25 teacher questionnaires; $29 per 25 summary score sheets; $95 per user's manual.
Time: 15(30) minutes.
Author: Winnie Dunn.
Publisher: Pearson.

Review of the Sensory Profile School Companion by ELIZABETH BIGHAM, Health Psychologist, Lecturer in Human Development, California State University San Marcos, San Marcos, CA:

DESCRIPTION. The Sensory Profile School Companion is a judgment-based teacher questionnaire that assesses "a student's sensory processing abilities and their effect on the student's functional performance in the classroom and school environment" (user's manual, p. 1). It is designed to be part of a comprehensive assessment of students 3 years, 0 months to 11 years, 11 months of age and can be combined with the Sensory Profile Caregiver Questionnaire to compare performance in different contexts. The purpose of the Sensory Profile School Companion is to assist interdisciplinary teams in identifying specific responses, clarifying how these responses affect performance, and planning interventions for the classroom. The Sensory Profile School Companion has 62 items divided into three main sections: Environmental Sensations, Body Sensations, and Classroom Behaviors. The Environmental Sensations section asks about the student's responses to, and use of, auditory and visual stimuli in the classroom. The Body Sensations section inquires about the student's responses to, and use of, movement, touch, and personal space as encountered in the classroom or playground. The Classroom Behaviors section assesses behaviors related to the student's behaviors and interactions within the classroom. The Sensory Profile School Companion generates 13 scores reflecting the student's responsiveness to sensory experience, including high or low threshold responses, and how these responses are reflected in the student's classroom participation.

Teachers complete the Sensory Profile School Companion questionnaire, providing information about their experience with the student, including how long and often they have had this level of contact with the student, and a description of any current challenges this student is having in the classroom. The 62 items each ask the teacher to report the frequency of a specific behavior. The response choices are *Almost Always, Frequently, Occasionally, Seldom,* and *Almost Never*.

Questionnaire completion time is approximately 15 minutes and scoring takes approximately 15–30 minutes. Scoring does not require any special training; however, interpretation of the scores should be performed by a professional with expertise in sensory processing, such as occupational therapists or other professionals who have acquired this expertise through post-professional education. To score, the raw scores are transferred to the Scoring Summary, which divides the questions into 13 areas including four quadrants (Registration, Seeking, Sensitivity, and Avoiding), four school factors (need for external support, awareness and attention, range of tolerance, and level of availability for learning), and five sections (Auditory, Visual, Movement, Touch, and Behavior). Raw scores in each area are then totaled and transferred to a grid, which provides a visual comparison of the student's scores compared to the typical distribution of scores for that quadrant, school factor, or section. The user's manual provides a general framework for interpreting the scores, including general features consistent with high or low scores for each area and suggested intervention strategies for each area. Additionally, the manual provides sample case studies, with completed questionnaires, scoring summaries, interpretations, interventions, and intervention outcomes as well as comparison scores for students with ADHD, Asperger's disorder, and autism.

DEVELOPMENT. The Sensory Profile School Companion was developed to extend the original Sensory Profile's use into the school setting. The Sensory Profile (Dunn, 1999; 16:220), Infant/Toddler Sensory Profile (Dunn, 2002; 16:220), and Adolescent/Adult Sensory Profile (Brown & Dunn, 2002; 16:5) assess integration using Dunn's Model of Sensory Processing. This model proposes an interaction of neurological thresholds and self-regulation (Dunn, 1997). Neurological threshold refers to the point in the neurological continuum at which the student generates a response to stimuli from the environment. The level of the student's threshold and whether he or she is able to respond appropriately is determined by his or her ability to organize and balance information simultaneously from different sources within the environment. For example, a high threshold, or habituation, would indicate the need for extra stimulation from that stimulus to generate a response that would be adaptive or maladaptive depending on the situation. Conversely, a low threshold, or sensitization, would indicate that minimal stimulation from that stimulus generates a response. Self-regulation refers to strategies used to manage sensory input on a continuum of passive to active. An example of a passive strategy is to complain but not take action in response to unpleasant sensory input whereas an active strategy would be to hum to control the amount and type of sensory input.

The interaction of level of neurological threshold and passive/active self-regulation is represented in the four quadrants of the Sensory Profile School Companion, as follows: High Neurological Threshold & Passive Self-Regulation = Registration; High Neurological Threshold & Active Self-Regulation = Seeking; Low Neurological Threshold & Passive Self-Regulation = Sensitivity; Low Neurological Threshold & Active Self-Regulation = Avoiding. According to Dunn's Model of Sensory Processing, each student has some amount of each pattern and anextreme score in one pattern does not, in itself, constitute a basis for intervention; however, understanding can lead to appropriate interventions when indicated.

To develop the items for the Sensory Profile School Companion, the author asked 12 teachers to complete as many of the Sensory Profile Caregiver Questionnaire items as possible. The teachers were able to rate students on 49 of the 125 items. Several new items were generated that were relevant to behaviors and activities in school and 118 teachers across the United States completed the revised version, rating over 700 students including 127 with disabilities. The manual includes detailed results from analysis of these responses by teacher characteristics, such as amount of contact with the student, years of teaching experience, and frequency of contact, and by student characteristics, such as by grade level, age, and gender. Among these results was a notable possibility that students whose primary language is Spanish may have different behaviors in Seeking, Sensitivity, and School Factor 2.

The 62 final items were determined through factor analysis of the national study data and elimination of items with weak relationships within the factor structure. The resultant four factors (School Factors 1, 2, 3, and 4) represent sensory processing patterns aligned with Dunn's Model of Sensory Processing, so that two of the four quadrants (Registration, Seeking, Sensitivity, and Avoiding) are represented in each of the school factors. All four quadrants are also represented in the each of the sections (Auditory, Visual, Touch, and Behavior) except for the Movement section, which does not have Sensitivity. The means and standard deviations from the standardization sample are provided and were used to develop cut scores for the four quadrants, four school factors, and five sections.

TECHNICAL. The standardization sample for the Sensory Profile School Companion included 118 teachers' ratings of over 700 students 3 years, 0 months to 11 years, 11 months of age. The manual includes frequency and length of contact, years of teaching experience, and education for the teachers as well as gender, race/ethnicity, primary language, age, disability, and grade for the students in the sample.

Reliability was estimated by calculating internal consistency (coefficient alpha) and test-retest stability. The alpha coefficients for the items in each quadrant, school factor, and section for a sample of 585 students without disabilities ranged from .83 to .95, indicating a high degree of internal consistency. The test-retest reliability coefficients for the items in each quadrant, school factor, and section for a sample of 126 students without disabilities ranged from .80 to .95, indicating a high degree of stability from one rating to a second rating within 21 days of the first rating. Small to moderate variability is indicated by *SEM*s of .24 to .63.

Content validity was established during the development of the Sensory Profile School Companion through interviews and pilot studies using the Sensory Profile Caregiver Questionnaire, which resulted in the research version of the Sensory Profile Teacher Questionnaire. Analysis of responses from 12 teachers across the United States revealed factor groupings and sensory patterns. School Factors 1, 2, 3, and 4 were generated through principal component analysis on ratings from 61 teachers (N = 585) and Varimax rotation. A four-factor solution was most interpretable, accounting for 52.4% of the variance. Given the differences in the contexts, correlations of the Sensory Profile School Companion with the Sensory Profile Caregiver Questionnaire for both students with and without disabilities across the areas were not anticipated, nor obtained, providing evidence of convergent and discriminant validity (48 without a disability, 59 with ADHD, 12 with Asperger's Disorder, and 56 with autism). Psychometric evidence documentation and comparison scores are also included for students with ADHD, Asperger's disorder, and autism (N = 127).

COMMENTARY. The strengths of this measure include the solid theoretical basis, organized structure and scoring, and generous interpretation/intervention guidance. The author's expertise and contributions in this area are extensive and responsive to the needs of educators and therapists in the field. The manual would benefit from the inclusion of data from a larger sample of students with special needs with more racial/ethnic diversity. Interrater reliability of this measure is particularly important as it is dependent on teacher ratings yet was not presented in the manual.

SUMMARY. The Sensory Profile School Companion is a brief and easy to use assessment of sensory processing in the school environment based on teacher report. It is designed for use in combination with other evaluations, observations, and reports. Scoring is simple, and generous guidance for interpretation of scores and suggested interventions is provided.

REVIEWER'S REFERENCES

Brown, C. E., & Dunn, W. (2002). Adolescent/Adult Sensory Profile. San Antonio: TX: Harcourt Assessment.

Dunn, W. (1997). The impact of sensory processing abilities on the daily lives of young children and their families: A conceptual model. *Infants and Young Children, 9* (4), 23–25.

Dunn, W. (1999). *Sensory Profile user's manual.* San Antonio, TX: Harcourt Assessment.

Dunn, W. (2002). *Infant/Toddler Sensory Profile user's manual.* San Antonio: TX: Harcourt Assessment.

Review of the Sensory Profile School Companion by SHAWN POWELL, Instructor of Psychology, Casper College, and private practitioner, Casper, WY:

DESCRIPTION. The Sensory Profile School Companion assesses a student's sensory processing abilities and the resulting effect on school performance. It is intended for use with children ages 3 years, 0 months to 11 years, 11 months. The Sensory Profile School Companion is designed to be administered as a part of a comprehensive student evaluation to gain information about a student's functioning across various environmental settings such as home, school, and community.

The Sensory Profile School Companion is composed of the user's manual, teacher questionnaire, and a scoring summary. It can be scored by hand or by a computer-based program that scores the teacher's questionnaire and generates a report of test results. The teacher questionnaire has 62 items rated on a frequency scale ranging from *Almost Always, Frequently, Occasionally, Seldom,* to *Almost Never.* This scale contains well-defined behavioral anchors for each rating category. The test response pattern can be used to determine if one or more given sensory systems is interfering with a student's sensory processing. School-based programming can then be developed to identify a student's response to sensory situations, to determine how the responses affect a student's school behavior and performance, and to assist educators in developing effective interventions for children with sensory deficits.

Occupational therapists, psychologists, speech-language pathologists, and educators can administer the Sensory Profile School Companion. Professionals from these various disciplines are encouraged to consult with an occupational therapist as they start using this test to gain a firm understanding of sensory processing. The test manual indicates it takes approximately 15 minutes to complete the teacher's questionnaire and 15 minutes to score the questionnaire.

The Sensory Profile School Companion is a norm-referenced test and produces scores for five sections, four quadrants, and four school factors. The five section scores are Auditory, Visual, Movement, Touch, and Behavior. The four quadrant scores are Registration, defined as awareness of all available sensation; Seeking, which measures a student's interest and pleasure in different types of sensation; Sensitivity, defined as the ability to notice all types of sensation; and Avoiding, which measures the need to control the amount and type of sensation available. The four school factors measure the student's need for external support in order to learn, student awareness in the learning environment, student tolerance, and availability to learn. The test manual provides one set of scores that are not age referenced.

A student's responses as rated on the teacher questionnaire can be compared to four groups. These four groups are children without disabilities, children with attention-deficit/hyperactivity disorder, children with Asperger's Disorder, and children with autism. Using raw scores and standard deviations, a child's ratings can be considered in relation to the test's standardization sample. Descriptive categories of Much Less Than Others, Less Than Others, Similar to Others, More Than Others, and Much More than Others are provided to assist in the interpretation of test results.

The Sensory Profile School Companion user's manual provides three examples to assist examiners in learning to administer, score, and interpret the test. The manual also offers guides to intervention planning for students with specific sensory deficits.

DEVELOPMENT. The Sensory Profile School Companion was developed in 2005 and 2006. Its development included a pilot study, standardization, and a factor analysis. The theoretical underpinnings of the Sensory Profile School Companion were derived from the understanding that if students have difficulty with sensory processing, this difficulty will negatively affect their school performance. The test manual emphasizes the importance of the central nervous system's role in monitoring and regulating information to form suitable responses to various types of stimuli. The theoretical foundation of this test is grounded in neuroscience principles such as habituation (being able to ignore familiar stimuli) and sensitization (focusing on a given stimuli that is important to the individual at the time).

TECHNICAL.

Standardization. When the Sensory Profile School Companion was developed, 118 teachers from "schools across the United States" (user's manual, p. 12) provided ratings of 712 students. Of these 712 students, 585 (approximately 82%) were identified as not having a disability and 127 of the students (approximately 18%) were identified as having a disability. Demographic information on the teachers who provided the ratings includes: educational level, frequency of contact, time of contact with the rated students, and years of teaching experience. The test manual demographic information about the students without disabilities in the normative sample includes: age, gender, race/ethnicity, parent education level, grade level, and primary language spoken. The manual also provides demographic information about the age, gender, race/ethnicity, parent education level, grade level, and number of services received for students in the sample identified as having disabilities. Of the 127 students identified as having a disability, the sample included 59 students with attention-deficit/hyperactivity disorder (approximately 46%), 12 students with Asperger's disorder (approximately 9%), and 56 students with autism (approximately 44%). The manual does not provide information about the geographical locations from which the sample was drawn other than the reference to schools across the United States.

Reliability. Two estimates of the Sensory Profile School Companion reliability are provided: alpha coefficients for internal consistency and test-retest stability. Internal consistency estimates for the quadrant, school factor, and section scores ranged from .83 to .95. Test-retest reliability estimates are reported for 126 students taken from 1 to 21 days and ranged from .80 to .95. No information on interrater reliability is presented in the test manual.

Validity. The validity of the Sensory Profile School Companion is provided by a principal component factor analysis. The test manual indicates after data from the pilot study were analyzed a four-factor solution accounted for 55% of the variance in the data. After the standardization data were collected a second factor analysis of the ratings of students without disabilities was conducted that accounted for 70% of the variance in the data.

COMMENTARY. The Sensory Profile School Companion is intended to assess sensory processing abilities and the effect of sensory deficits on the student's school performance. It was developed as a norm-referenced test. It is easy to administer, interpret, and score. The Sensory Profile School Companion test manual contains relevant intervention guidelines that can be applied when specific sensory deficits are observed.

Several factors in the development of the Sensory Profile School Companion warrant consideration. As the test depends on teacher ratings it was surprising that information about its interrater reliability was not present in the test's manual. Information regarding the reliability of what is being reported is paramount in developing a rating scale based on teacher observation.

The test's normative sample has several limitations that reduce its ability to be generalized. One factor that detracts from the test's normative sample is the lack of information regarding the geographic locations of the 712 students who composed the normative sample. The test manual does not specify the locations from which the sample was drawn other than a reference to schools across the United States, not a sufficient description to allow for national comparisons. A second limiting factor is the overall sample size of 712. This sample is considerably smaller than sample sizes used in the development of the majority of modern test instruments designed for use across the United States.

The normative sample was divided into two broad categories, students without disabilities and students with disabilities. No information is provided in the manual to describe the process through which students were placed into one of the two categories. Additionally, the manual indicates that the sample contains a group of only 12 students identified as having Asperger's disorder. A group of 12 students in a national sample is too small to allow actuarial comparisons.

The Sensory Profile School Companion scoring system is problematic. It is not age referenced and one set of scores is designed for use with children from ages 3 to 11. Tremendous differences exist between the sensory abilities of a 3-year-old and an 11-year-old. These differences are not accounted for by the test manual's scoring system.

SUMMARY. The Sensory Profile School Companion is designed to assess a student's sensory processing ability and the effect of this processing on school-based performance. It is well grounded in the principles of neuroscience and assesses a variety of attributes involved with student learning and school behavior. This test was developed following a traditional norm-referenced process that included a pilot study. The Sensory Profile School Companion has several limitations that detract from its usefulness as a true measure of sensory processing. These limitations include a small standardization sample, limited information on the geographical representation of the sample, and the use of a single scoring system for children who range in age from 3 to 11. Nonetheless, when used as intended, as a part of a comprehensive evaluation of student functioning, the Sensory Profile School Companion may provide unique insights in sensory deficits and provide useful intervention recommendations.

[121]

Shipley-2.

Purpose: Measures cognitive functioning and impairment in children and adults, including crystallized knowledge and fluid reasoning.

Population: Ages 7-89.
Publication Dates: 1939-2009.
Scores: 7 scores possible, 4 scores per profile form: Vocabulary, Abstraction, Composite A, and Impairment Index (AQ) for Composite A Form, or Vocabulary, Block Patterns, Composite B, and Impairment Index (BQ) for Composite B Form.
Administration: Group.
Price Data, 2010: $120 per kit including 20 Vocabulary AutoScore forms, 10 Abstraction AutoScore forms, 10 Block Patterns forms, and manual (2009, 148 pages); $35 per 25 AutoScore forms; $80 per manual; $199 per unlimited-use Scoring CD; $33 per Continuing Education (CE) Questionnaire and Evaluation Form.
Time: (20-25) minutes.
Comments: Previous edition called Shipley Institute of Living Scale; earlier versions entitled Shipley-Institute of Living Scale for Measuring Intellectual Impairment and Shipley-Hartford Retreat Scale for Measuring Intellectual Impairment.
Authors: Walter C. Shipley (all forms and manual), Christian P. Gruber (manual, Abstraction form, Vocabulary form, Composite A profile sheet, Composite B profile sheet), Thomas A. Martin (manual, Block Patterns form, Composite B profile sheet), and Amber M. Klein (manual).
Publisher: Western Psychological Services.
Cross References: For information for previous edition see T5:2402 (71 references) and T4:2453 (63 references); for a review by William L. Deaton of the Shipley Institute of Living Scale, see 11:360 (56 references); see also 9:1122 (13 references), T3:2179 (64 references), 8:677 (39 references), and T2:1380 (34 references); for a review by Aubrey J. Yates, see 7:138 (21 references); see also P:244 (38 references), 6:173 (13 references), and 5:111 (23 references); for reviews by E. J. G. Bradford, William A. Hunt, and Margaret Ives, see 3:39 (25 references).

Review of the Shipley-2 by THEODORE L. HAYES, Personnel Research Psychologist, U.S. Office of Personnel Management, Washington, DC:

[All opinions expressed herein are solely and exclusively those of the review author.]

DESCRIPTION. The Shipley-2 is a revision to the Shipley Institute of Living Scale (SILS). The Shipley-2 is positioned by its publisher as a brief measure of crystallized and fluid intelligence that may be administered and scored by personnel ranging from minimally trained paraprofessionals through licensed psychologists for the purpose of determining intellectual functioning [Editor's Note: The publisher advises that the next reprint of the manual for this test will include a correction indicating that use of the Shipley-2 should always be under the supervision of an individual who has the education, training, and experience required for use of cognitive measures in their area of application.] Three test types (verbal, reasoning, and block completion) are included, each with time limits provided. The test is meant to be scored to yield either of two combined scores (verbal plus reasoning or verbal plus blocks), each with a mean of 100 and a standard deviation of 15; additional ratio scores of the test scores yield other indicators of cognitive functioning. The publisher claims that the Shipley-2 can be administered to, and interpreted for, respondents throughout the mental ability range aged 7 through 89 years. Interpretative examples are provided for clinical, educational, and employment scenarios.

DEVELOPMENT. The Shipley-2 has three component scales designed to measure either crystallized or fluid intelligence. The first section, a measure of crystallized intelligence, consists of 40 English vocabulary words. The SILS had 40 vocabulary items, and of these all but eight words (e.g., lissom, tumble) have been retained in the Shipley-2, and others were added based on publication usage frequency (Kucera & Francis, 1964). Rasch analysis models were used to develop the final item set, but no item parameters are provided. Fluid intelligence is assessed through a 25-item measure of eduction, referred to in the SILS and Shipley-2 as "Abstraction," and in a block rotation test. According to the test publishers, the Abstraction test in the SILS was only moderately difficult and had "spotty coverage at the higher end" of the ability continuum (manual, p. 43); the current iteration apparently has more difficult reasoning items than the SILS. The Block Patterns scale is based on original work by Kohs (1920). It is a nonverbal test consisting of 12 items spread between two test parts.

The Shipley-2 can be scored to yield a number of composite measures. Composite A is the sum of the standardized score for Vocabulary plus the standardized score for Abstraction, whereas Composite B is the sum of the standardized score for Vocabulary plus the standardized score for Block Patterns. This approach yields a set of comparable summary measures that either emphasize or de-emphasize verbal fluency. Beyond the composite scores, SILS researchers developed three ratio scores: a "Conceptual Quotient," a ratio of Abstraction to estimated Abstraction based on Vocabulary; an "Abstraction Quotient," the Conceptual Quotient adjusted for education and age;

and a "Block Quotient," essentially the Abstraction Quotient but using Block Pattern score rather than Abstraction. All three "quotients" are referred to within the Shipley-2 manual as indices of cognitive functioning.

Test materials include a manual and paper/pencil-based test stimuli. The spiral-bound manual is replete with case studies that may be useful for clinicians and educators who wish to use the Shipley-2 as a diagnostic assessment. There are also a few dozen pages of intricate scale scores to intelligence percentile interpolation tables to cover the broad age range for which the Shipley-2 might be used.

TECHNICAL.

Standardization. The manual describes normative data collection as relying upon SILS users in various community settings who provided data on occasion. This results in a normative sample of about 1,200 adults and 1,880 children. Adult respondents as a group are disproportionately more likely white, Southern, and non-Hispanic than comparable U.S. Census data from 2005 would suggest, whereas children as a group are more likely American Indian, Northeastern, and non-Hispanic than expected. Although group differences are mentioned and discussed, "normative values" by group are not provided. Finally, no data are presented to indicate the empirical distribution of Shipley-2 scores within age group, which indicates that the manual's percentile tables are based upon a model of expected values within the normally distributed population.

Reliability. Evidence concerning both internal consistency and test-retest stability of the Shipley-2 is presented in the test manual. Internal consistency estimates are very high. For children, the median internal consistency estimate for Composite A (Vocabulary plus Abstraction) is reported as .87 and for Composite B (Vocabulary plus Block Patterns) it is reported as .89. For adults, the corresponding median values are .91 for Composite A and .93 for Composite B. The stability estimates are also quite high: For children (aged 7–12), they are .84 for Composite A and .76 for Composite B; for teenagers (aged 13–19), .89 for Composite A and .92 for Composite B; and for adults (aged 17–87), .94 for Composite A and .93 for Composite B.

The retest period ranged from 1 to 2 weeks. This is too short a time interval. The test publisher acknowledges that item recognition likely influenced retest performance.

The publisher does not provide reliability by specific age cohort even though the publisher frequently notes that cognitive abilities fluctuate over the life span. The overall standard error of measurement (*SEM*) provided in the manual is nearly one-half a standard deviation, which is likely too low for some age cohorts and too high for others–and assumes without empirical support that the *SEM* is equivalent across the ability distribution range within or across age cohorts.

Validity. The publisher presents three types of validation arguments for the Shipley-2. The argument for content validity is based upon the assertion that vocabulary items reflect the content of crystallized intellectual ability, whereas reasoning and/or nonverbal block rotation tasks reflect the nature of fluid intellectual ability. These assertions are plausible given the factor model outlined in Carroll (1993). As expected, the Shipley-2 has a correlation in the mid-.60s with the Wonderlic Personnel Test, in the mid-.60s and .70s with the Wide Range Achievement Test 3, and in the mid-.50s with the Wide Range Achievement Test 4. Correlations with various forms of the Wechsler intelligence tests are also in this range. In all, the data presented for criterion validity show the construct relation of the Shipley-2 but not its association with external nontest criteria.

COMMENTARY. A review of the manual and test content leaves many questions. First, the Shipley-2 is meant to assess intellectual functioning for respondents from ages 7 to 89 across the range of intellectual functioning. This seems *prima facie* to be an extraordinary claim. Moreover, would a geriatric psychologist or a pediatric psychiatrist really believe that a single measure could accomplish this adequately within all populations of interest? The test manual clearly states that the SILS was more adequate at assessing functioning up to an IQ of about 105, and moreover there are no current references addressing the age- and aptitude-continuum question for the Shipley-2. Thus one must consider this contention as an aspiration until studies are published.

It should also be noted that the test materials are intended for use and interpretation exclusively for those with adequate U.S.-English proficiency. Stimulus words comprising vocabulary items were chosen based on word frequency as published in 1964. Relying on a "baby boomer"-era word frequency roster in the "millennial" age seems of dubious value.

In regard to utilization, the publishers state explicitly that the Shipley-2 may be used for clinical evaluation, in educational settings, and for employment testing. The value of the Shipley-2 for the age and ability continuums is empirically unknown, though users of the SILS may not be troubled by this. Also, the probative value of the Shipley-2 for assessment of intellectual functioning is possibly as much a function of clinical skill as test material. However, the value of the Shipley-2 in employment settings is oversold by the publisher, included almost as an afterthought, and this reviewer would be remiss in not strongly dissuading the use of instruments such as the Shipley-2 in a clinical evaluation of intellectual functioning in a work setting, especially by "HR staff" as stated in the manual.

It is probably not unexpected that internal reliability for cognitive ability measures is high, but in this case it is notable that the high value comes from an admixture of putatively distinct "types" of intelligence (Composite A, fluid and crystallized; Composite B, verbal and spatial). One wonders how successfully the test stimuli tap into truly different rivers of intellectual functioning if they are that highly correlated.

As with many tests, its value is largely related to the skill of the test user. Its generalized utility awaits independent empirical validation. Previous SILS users, or those seeking a quick cognitive assessment tool, may not be troubled by the many shortcomings of the Shipley-2.

SUMMARY. The Shipley-2 is an easily administered, easily scored measure of general intelligence. The publisher overextends by claiming to measure too much, too broadly, and in too many domains. The methodology used to create this revision is at best haphazard. Claims of "normative percentile values" across age cohorts and ability ranges strain credulity. No correlations with nontest performance are presented. The publisher is either unaware of these shortcomings or elides them.

REVIEWER'S REFERENCES

Carroll, J. B. (1993). *Human cognitive abilities: A survey of factor-analytical studies.* New York: Cambridge University Press.

Kohs, S. C. (1920). The block-design tests. *Journal of Experimental Psychology, 3,* 357-376.

Kucera, H., & Francis, W. N. (1964). *Brown corpus of standard American English.* Providence, RI: Brown University.

Review of the Shipley-2 by TRACY THORNDIKE-CHRIST, Assistant Professor of Special Education and Educational Psychology, Western Washington University, Bellingham, WA:

DESCRIPTION. The Shipley-2 is a revision and restandardization of the Shipley Institute of Living Scale. It is a brief measure of cognitive functioning and impairment that can be administered easily to individuals or groups. The test produces a quick estimate of cognitive functioning that can be used in a wide variety of educational, clinical, and research settings. Like its predecessor, the Shipley-2 yields estimates of crystallized knowledge and fluid reasoning skills. Crystallized knowledge, gained through education and experience, is measured via a 40-item Vocabulary scale, very similar to the one used in the original Shipley. The Shipley-2 now offers two ways to assess fluid abilities, the capacity to apply logic while learning and solving problems: (a) the Abstraction scale, a revised version of the scale from the original test, includes 25 alpha and numeric puzzles and (b) the new Block Patterns scale, a version of the well known Kohs cube designs using a multiple-choice response format. The latter option has the advantage of being a totally nonverbal measure of fluid reasoning skills. The Shipley-2 can be used with children and adults aged 7 to 89 years. Administration can be completed in 20 to 25 minutes, depending on which measure of fluid ability is used, and takes only an additional 5 minutes to score. Raw scores for each scale are easily converted into standard scores using age stratified normative tables. Standard scores on the Shipley-2 have a mean of 100 and a standard deviation of 15, the most common values used in ability testing, making scores easy to interpret for users familiar with other measures of cognitive functioning. Composite scores can be generated from the combination of the Vocabulary scale score and the score on one of the scales of fluid ability to reflect overall cognitive functioning. For adults, a discrepancy between scores on Vocabulary and Abstraction or Vocabulary and Block Patterns may be indicative of cognitive impairment; the Shipley-2 allows the calculation of Impairment Index scores to reflect the degree of cognitive deterioration.

DEVELOPMENT. The Shipley-2 represents an updated and improved version of an instrument with a long history of use. Development of the new test included revision of the items included on the Vocabulary and Abstraction scales, the addition of a nonverbal option for assessing fluid abilities, and standardization with a large sample broadly representative of the U.S. population and an extended age range. The original Shipley was developed to (a) address a practical need for a quick test of intellectual functioning, and (b) provide separate estimates of crystallized and fluid ability that could be used to gauge degree of cognitive impairment. The test was and is grounded in the assumption that crystallized and fluid abilities, taken together, provide a good estimate of overall cognitive skill and that these abilities are differentially resistant to impairment and cognitive deterioration with crystallized knowledge being more stable than fluid reasoning skills.

A thorough description of the process of the revision of items on the Vocabulary and Abstraction scales and development of the Block Patterns scale is provided in the test manual. Revision of the items on the Vocabulary and Abstraction scales was informed by use of both classical test theory methods and modern item response theory. IRT analyses indicated areas where the original scales could be improved. Multiple rounds of revision, piloting, and refinement, all clearly described in the test manual, were conducted to arrive at the final set of items that make up the Vocabulary and Abstraction scales on the Shipley-2.

The new Block Patterns scale was developed to address criticism that the original Abstraction scale had a sizable verbal component and, therefore, was measuring a combination of crystallized knowledge and fluid reasoning rather than just fluid ability. Block Design tasks have been used for decades as nonverbal measures of intelligence and are included on most individually administered tests; a substantial body of research supports their use for this purpose. The authors of the Shipley-2 designed a Block Patterns scale that could be administered in a paper-and-pencil format with multiple-choice scoring. Items went through extensive piloting and revision informed by both IRT and classical statistical analyses before being included on the new scale for the Shipley-2.

TECHNICAL. The standardization sample consists of 2,826 individuals aged 7 to 89 years and is broadly representative of the demographic characteristics of the U.S. population in terms of sex, education level, parent's education level, and ethnic group membership. The sample was separated into a child sample covering ages 7 to 19 and an adult sample of individuals aged 17 to 89 for all analyses. Because cognitive abilities change very rapidly in childhood, the child norms consist of nine stratified age groups with separate norms provided for each year up through age 12. Norms for adults are stratified by decade. All groups, with the exception of 80–89-year-olds, contained at least 100 individuals. The test manual contains detailed descriptions of the processes used to derive standard scores for each scale, composite, and impairment index.

The reliability of scores on the individual scales and composites was examined separately for the adult and child samples. Internal consistency was estimated using the split-half method with alternating consecutive items, later adjusted with the Spearman-Brown formula to estimate reliability of the full length scales. For the adult sample, alpha coefficients for the Vocabulary scale ranged from .85 to .92 with a median of .90 across all age groups. Values ranged from .66 to .91 with a median of .77 for the Abstraction scale and .74 to .94 with a median of .91 for the Block Patterns scale. Internal consistency values for the composite scores were slightly higher, as would be expected with larger samples of behavior. For the child sample, internal consistency estimates ranged from .82 to .91 with a median of .87 for Composite A and .78 to .94 with a median of .89 with slightly lower estimates for the shorter individual scales. Overall, all values are well within the acceptable range for internal consistency with the exception of the Abstraction scale (.66) for adults aged 50–59 years. The test authors explored but could find no explanation for this anomalous result.

A subset of the standardization sample (N = 296) took the Shipley-2 on two occasions to estimate score stability over time. Composite and Vocabulary scores for the adolescent (ages 13 to 19) and the adult (ages 17 to 87) samples were stable over a 1- to 2-week interval with all test-retest coefficients .89 or higher. Stability estimates for the scales of fluid ability ranged from .82 to .90. The results for children (ages 7 to 12) were lower and more varied though still acceptable, ranging from .74 to .84. Standard errors of measurement were calculated for each score type at each age level and the test manual clearly explains how and why *SEM* values should be used to develop confidence intervals around observed scores.

Multiple sources of validation evidence are provided to support proposed interpretations and uses of scores from the Shipley-2. Interscale correlations substantiate the crystallized/fluid ability distinction that forms the theoretical underpinning of the test. The relationship between age and vocabulary was linear, whereas the relationships between age and the scales of fluid ability were curvilinear; findings were all consistent with those predicted by theory. Item-total correlations confirm the three-scale structure in both adult and child samples. Factor analysis at the scale level showed that all scales had very high loadings on a single factor, thus supporting the assertion that composite scores measure overall cognitive ability. Item response analyses verified that items evenly cover the full range of skills to be measured and are appropriately placed along a difficulty gradient for each scale. Differential performance on the Shipley-2 was evaluated for a number of demographic groups. Mean comparisons showed small differences between males and females but larger differences among the mean scores of the major ethnic groups in the United States. These differences mirror patterns seen on other measures of cognitive ability with Blacks and Hispanics obtaining lower scores and Asians obtaining somewhat higher scores than the White majority. The magnitude of these differences decreased when socioeconomic status was taken into account. These findings are consistent with those observed for other tests of cognitive ability.

Strong evidence of concurrent validity was demonstrated by the strength of relationship between scores on the Shipley-2 and scores on multiple other measures of cognitive ability and several standardized achievement tests. For instance, correlations between WAIS-III full scale IQ and the Composite A and Composite B scores on the Shipley-2 were .86 and .85, respectively. The correlations between scores on the WISC-IV and the Shipley composite scores were lower but still strong as were correlations between the Shipley-2's scale and composite scores with scores on measures of academic achievement. Further, scores on the Shipley successfully distinguished between members of a clinical sample (N = 340 adults and N = 143 children) with known cognitive impairments and those in the standardization sample with moderate to large effect sizes. To document applied utility of scores on the Shipley-2, results of studies using the original test in a wide range of contexts with diverse individuals for a variety of purposes are summarized.

COMMENTARY. The Shipley-2 yields scale scores for crystallized knowledge and fluid reasoning and composite scores that are psychometrically strong enough to stand alone as estimates of overall cognitive ability. The test manual includes detailed information about administration, scoring, and score interpretation presented so clearly that even inexperienced test users should find it easy to understand. New norms are based on a large, representative sample of the U.S. population that included both adults and children. The addition of a nonverbal option for measuring fluid reasoning should increase the utility of the test for certain populations and satisfy critics of the original Abstraction scale. Extensive evidence is provided to support both the reliability of scores and the validity of a wide range of score-based inferences.

SUMMARY. The Shipley-2 is a brief, easy-to-administer test of cognitive functioning and impairment that can be used with adults and children, individually or in groups. The revision and restandardization of the test represent substantial improvements over the original version while retaining those features of the Shipley Institute of Living Scale that are familiar to users and have contributed to the test's long history of continuous use. The new Block Patterns scale offers a nonverbal alternative for measuring fluid reasoning ability in a paper-and-pencil format. The Shipley-2 provides a quick estimate of cognitive functioning that can stand alone or be used as part of a more comprehensive evaluation when a more complex picture of ability is required.

[122]

Situational Outlook Questionnaire®.

Purpose: "Measures the climate for creativity, innovation, and change in an organization, within teams, and can be used for leadership development."
Population: Adult employees or members of a company, organization, or team.
Publication Dates: 1995-2007.
Acronym: SOQ.
Scores, 9: Challenge/Involvement, Freedom, Trust/Openness, Idea-Time, Playfulness/Humor, Conflict, Idea-Support, Debate, Risk-Taking.
Administration: Group.
Restricted Distribution: "The SOQ is only to be administered by those who have completed a qualification program."
Price Data, 2008: $75 per manual (2007, 390 pages).
Time: (25) minutes.
Comments: Includes analysis of narrative comments from open-ended questions; Web-based assessment; manual title is "Assessing the Context for Change, Second Edition"; in addition to computing scores for individual participants, averages for the organization are

also computed for comparison purposes; "The SOQ is only to be administered by those who have completed a qualification program."

Authors: Scott G. Isaksen and Göran Ekvall, with contributions from Hans Akkermans, Glenn V. Wilson, and John P. Gaulin.

Publisher: The Creative Problem Solving Group, Inc.

Review of Situational Outlook Questionnaire by JULIA Y. PORTER, Associate Professor of Counselor Education, Mississippi State University-Meridian, Meridian, MS:

DESCRIPTION. The Situational Outlook Questionnaire (SOQ) is a two-part web-based instrument that assesses individuals' perceptions about the climate (work environment) of an organization, a team, or a leader to be creative and innovative. Estimated administration time for this self-report instrument is 20–25 minutes. Training is required to become an SOQ administrator. Per participant cost for SOQ administration is $55 with an additional sliding scale cost of $12–$16.50 per participant for the qualitative analysis and narrative results report.

The first section of the instrument contains 53 questions that focus on nine dimensions of organizational climate (work environment): Challenge/Involvement, Freedom, Trust/Openness, Idea-Time, Playfulness/Humor, Conflict, Idea-Support, Debate, and Risk-Taking. Responses for each question are reported on a Likert-type scale with possible responses that range from 0–3 with 0 being *Not at all applicable* and 3 being *Applicable to a high degree.* Scores for each of the nine climate dimensions result in a scaled score from 0–300 and are used to assign one of the following designations: innovative organizations, average organizations, or stagnated organizations. Other statistical information included in the data report includes averages, ranges, and standard deviations for each of the dimensions.

The second part of the instrument includes three short answer questions that explore work environment factors that affect creativity and innovation: Whether the environment helps or hinders their creativity and what could be done to improve their creativity within their working environment. Results of this part of the instrument are reported as narrative data in a Microsoft Word document.

Support is offered from the test developers for presenting and utilizing SOQ results. Assessment results are intended to be used to set goals to change or improve the climate of an organization, a team, or a leader.

DEVELOPMENT. The SOQ is based on over 50 years of research that began with Göran Ekvall, a Swedish Industrial Psychologist, working on the concept of creativity in organizations in 1954. Then Ekvall and Isaksen began collaborating on a project to see if the levels of creativity in an organization could be increased. Through their research studies conducted during the 1980s, climate was found to "play the part of an intervening variable" (technical manual, p. 46) and research began on an instrument to measure the organizational climate for creativity and innovation.

The first two-part version of the SOQ was used in 1991. Previous versions had focused on quantitative results and some of the earlier versions had 10 dimensions instead of 9. The current version of the SOQ was revised in 2001. It is based on grounded theory and research design principles.

TECHNICAL. Development of the SOQ began with a quantitative assessment instrument called the Creative Climate Questionnaire (CCQ). The test developers' goal was to identify and assess the organizational conditions that support and encourage creativity and innovation. The first version of the SOQ was a translation of the CCQ from Swedish to English. That version had 50 quantitative questions and was a self-report, pen-and-paper instrument that covered 10 dimensions. The CCQ was normed in the 1980s with a sample of professionals (N = 434) who worked in the fields of education (n = 248) and business (n = 186). The sample ranged in age from 21 to 66. Means and standard deviations were computed for the overall group and for each of the subgroups. Based on this information, the authors determined that climate could be identified for different organizational groups. Additional statistical analyses were not performed to determine levels of significance.

The most recent version of the SOQ was developed in 2001 and was normed with 4,730 individuals whose ages ranged from 17 to 69. Scale means and standard deviations were calculated for the entire sample. Statistical analyses for each of the dimensions using coefficient alpha resulted in alphas that ranged from .76 to .90. Correlation analysis of the SOQ's dimensions and items resulted in a strong level of significance for each correlation ($p \leq .01$). Statistical analyses also showed a difference in climate scores for males and females with females having significantly more positive scores than males. Five of the nine dimensions on the SOQ also showed a significant correlation with age. Studies were also conducted comparing the online form and the paper form. Analysis of variance results indicated that the means are not significantly different and that both versions are consistent on all nine dimensions. Pearson correlations between the two formats also resulted in verification that the formats produce similar results with an overall correlation of .92. Eight of the dimensions (Challenge/Involvement, Freedom, Trust/Openness, Idea-Time, Playfulness/Humor, Idea-Support, Debate, Risk-Taking) are positive in that the higher the score, the better the organizational climate in regard to encouraging innovation and creativity. One dimension (Conflict) is negative with lower scores resulting in higher innovation and creativity.

Because previous research studies had established the validity of the nine dimensions on the SOQ and their intercorrelations, research on the validity for the current version was begun using the Promax method of extraction for factor analysis. The nine dimensions examined accounted for 61.4% of the variance. Data results also showed that "the SOQ can discriminate between productive and unproductive work situations" (technical manual, p. 200). Additional validity evidence is presented in the administrator's manual.

Internal reliability was established using coefficient alpha, which resulted in alphas that ranged from .69 to .89. The dimension of Trust/Openness resulted in an alpha of .69, which was the only dimension that fell below the standard of .70.

Test-retest reliability was established using aggregated scores from four groups of respondents within one organization during a 7-month time frame. No significant differences were identified. Extensive research studies have been conducted on the SOQ and additional detailed information is available in the test administrator manual.

COMMENTARY. The SOQ test instrument and administrator materials are well prepared and easy to understand. The Assessing the Content for Change technical manual, which can be purchased, has an excellent overview of the SOQ that includes test development, general administration information, and an in-depth explanation of the concept of climate and its importance in organizational structure. This manual is helpful for test administrators considering adoption of the SOQ.

Individuals interested in becoming an SOQ administrator submit an application. Test administrator training is a two-part process with the initial training completed through distance learning. It focuses on content and at the end of this training, the prospective SOQ administrator takes a comprehensive exam and must score 80% or higher to continue in the training program. The second part of the training focuses on practical application and administration of the SOQ and may be completed as a course or as a tutorial under the direction of a Qualified SOQ Trainer. The Qualified SOQ Practitioner certificate is valid for 3 years and is renewable.

SUMMARY. The Situational Outlook Questionnaire (SOQ) is an online assessment instrument that provides information for individual leadership development, for team building development, and for organizational improvement based on organizational climate as it relates to creativity and innovation. The current two-part instrument includes a quantitative section with 53 Likert-type items and a qualitative section with three open-ended questions. Strengths of the SOQ include the 50-year research base from which it was developed and the extensive documentation available for it, which includes a 390-page administrator's manual, a brief overview of the SOQ in a 34-page introduction manual, a CD with guidelines and additional content information, a DVD that includes an interview with test developer Göran Ekvall by test developer Scott G. Isaksen, and a CD with additional resources. The administrator manual includes an annotated bibliography on relevant climate and creative strategy research, which is useful for test administrators who are using the SOQ as part of a research study. Training requirements to become an SOQ administrator may be a limitation for the financial and time resources of some test administrators.

Review of the Situational Outlook Questionnaire by JOHN SAMPLE, Associate Professor, Adult Education and Human Resource Development, Florida State University, Tallahassee, FL:

DESCRIPTION. The Situational Outlook Questionnaire (SOQ) is a 53-item climate assessment used to improve creativity, change, and innovation in organizations. The SOQ also includes three open-ended questions that provide additional qualitative insights. For purposes of the SOQ, "climate is defined as the recurring patterns of behavior, attitudes and feelings that characterize life in the organization" (technical manual, p. 23). Climate and creativity are "especially effective predictors of creative performance in turbulent, high pressure, competitive environments" (Hunter, Bedell, & Mumford, 2007, p. 69). Creativity and change are influenced by the organization's climate, which is viewed as an intervening variable within the larger context of an organization. Other factors include the external environment, leadership behavior, organizational culture, management practices, systems, policies and procedures, individual needs, motives, mission and strategy, structure and size, resources and technology, task requirements, individual skills and abilities, and organizational and psychological processes. These factors constitute a Model for Organizational Change for which climate is the central construct. The SOQ is available as an online assessment, although earlier versions of the assessment were administered by pencil and paper. Language options include English, French, Spanish, and Dutch. Internal or external consultants who have been qualified by the Creative Problem Solving Group, Inc. use the measure to focus a variety of interventions that impact leadership and management. Typically, once the assessment has been completed online, the consultant provides a briefing that explains what was measured and how the scores were derived. Scores for the SOQ range from 0 to 300. Six concentric circles are used to display scores. The innermost circle represents a score of "0" and the outer circle represents a score of 300 and circles are added at 50-point intervals. The nine factors making up the SOQ are arranged around the outer circle and lines connect each set of scores. Color coded scores are plotted on a "spider" diagram for each of the nine dimensions. The one-page summary can include a spider plot for an individual score, a plot for the individuals' organization, or a plot for a unit within the organization for each of the nine dimensions, and aggregated plots for 10 innovative and 5 stagnated organizations for each of the nine dimensions. Also included is a review of the three open response questions. Participants also receive *An Introduction to Climate* by Isaksen and Akkermans (2007). The SOQ is used for leadership and team development. Individuals in a leadership development program complete the SOQ and select observers from shared contexts who also complete the SOQ for purposes of comparison. The SOQ is also used for team development and a team version of the SOQ is available. The qualified practitioner would typically provide only aggregated scores for each team. Given individual and team feedback, the consultant assists the organization in planning concrete ways to improve climate, innovation, and creativity.

DEVELOPMENT. The SOQ has a 50-year history of development, beginning with research and practical applications by Dr. Göran Ekvall during the 1950s. Ekvall has collaborated with Dr. Scott Isaksen (Center for Studies in Creativity at Buffalo State College and The Creative Problem Solving Group) and his associates since the 1980s. Ekvall, a Swedish industrial psychologist, focused his early research on personnel practices and improvement strategies, including idea-suggestion tactics (Isaksen, 2007). He concluded that the diffusion of innovative ideas was influenced by organizational climate. Ekvall's 1981 original Creative Climate Questionnaire (CCQ) identified four dimensions measured by 50 items: Mutual Trust, Challenge and Motivation, Freedom, and Pluralism. The CCQ was revised six times over the next 10 years. The 1982 revision resulted in the removal of 12 items and the addition of 6 new items based on factor analysis for a total of 44 items. The 1983 revision focused on innovation in organizations and resulted in the reconfiguration and addition of additional dimensions: Challenge, Support for Ideas, Trust, Freedom in Organizations, Freedom in the Job, Dynamism, Tension, and "global," for a total of 50 items. The 1986 revision resulted in 10 dimensions that appeared to account for the greatest amount of variance when assessing innovation capacity in an organization: Challenge, Freedom, Idea Support, Dynamism, Playfulness, Debate, Trust, Conflict, Risk-Taking, Idea Time (50 items). The Swedish version of the CCQ was translated into English in 1986. The 1989 revision included edited items to improve evidence of reliability and validity, including item order change and the addition of an omnibus item. The 1991 revision resulted in a name change (Climate for Innovation Questionnaire) that clarified the purpose of the survey. Three open-ended questions were added during the 1991 revision making the assessment a multimethod tool. In 1995, the survey was renamed the Situational Outlook Questionnaire (SOQ) to represent better an "ecological function of assessment" (technical manual, p. 51). Dynamism as a dimension was deleted and its items were redistributed across some of the following reconfigured nine dimensions: Challenge/Involvement, Freedom, Trust/Openness, Idea-Time, Playfulness/Humor,

Conflict, Idea-Support, Debate, Risk-Taking (50 items). Conflict is designated as the only negative dimension. Each dimension contains 3 to 7 items, each of which is scored on a 4-point scale (0 = *not at all applicable*; 1 = *applicable to some extent;* 2 = *fairly applicable;* 3 = *applicable to a high degree*). Revisions of the SOQ in 1998 and 2001 focused the use of statistical methods for item analysis. Items were edited for clarity with a major focus on Risk-Taking and Trust/Openness dimensions. Additional analysis led to improved reliability for these two dimensions.

TECHNICAL. The technical analysis of the 2001 version of the SOQ is based on a sample of 4,730 individuals from 27 businesses and organizations during the period September 2002 through February 2006. The sample includes 1,169 individuals from a leadership development program for a global software provider and 1,052 people from a global financial services and accounting firm. "Of the 2,646 individuals who indicated their gender, 1,628 were males and 1,018 females" (technical manual, p. 166). Ages ranged from 17 to 69 years, for an average of 38 years for the 2,864 who reported that data. Forty-six percent of the sample was from North America; the remaining 54% included respondents from the U.K., Germany, Italy, France, the Netherlands, Belgium, and Denmark. Race, ethnicity, or other culture variables were not reported in this sample. Chapter 12 of the SOQ technical manual reports scale means and standard deviations for the entire sample and a standard error of measurement for each of the nine dimensions. Coefficient alpha ranges from a high of .90 for Conflict to a low of .76 for Idea-Support for the complete sample. Interitem correlations and coefficient alpha are reported for each of the nine dimensions. The number of items for each dimension varies between 5 and 7 items. Trust/Openness demonstrates the lowest of the nine dimensions (alpha = .69). Coefficient alpha for the remaining seven dimensions ranges from .89 to .79. Interdimension correlations are strong ($p \leq .01$), demonstrating that dimensions of the SOQ had positive relationships with each other (i.e., the "challenge/involvement dimension is strongly correlated to idea-support, trust/openness, and risk-taking," p. 177). Females score higher on all nine dimensions when compared to males. Age of individuals yielded significant correlations for all but two dimensions (Playfulness/Humor and Idea-Time). Levels of significance for both sex and age may be a function of the "size of the samples, as the *r*s are rather small" (Isaksen, 2007, p. 462). Stability of the SOQ over time was demonstrated in a 7-month study in which individuals and observers completed the SOQ on four different occasions. Scores on all nine dimensions were very close over the time period. A principal component analysis of the nine dimensions using the complete sample was conducted using a Promax rotation. This method accounts for 61.4% of overall variance. Challenge/Involvement accounted for 32.3% of the variance. Additional studies that assess the relationship of creative climate to other variables important to organizations are reported in the technical manual (i.e., suggestion and recognition awards, creative performance, personality, creativity styles, problem-solving style, and teamwork climate). The ability of the SOQ to discriminate positive (best case) and negative (worst case) scenarios was demonstrated with a series of four studies. All nine dimensions demonstrated significant differences across best and worst case scenarios (F test, $p < .0001$, $df = 1$).

COMMENTARY. Ekvall, Isaksen, and associates make a strong argument for the effect of organizational climate on change, creativity, and innovation. The developers of the SOQ provide a solid foundation for the theory, nature, and context for change, including a useful distinction between an organization's climate and culture. The history for the identification of dimensions and items for the SOQ, and its predecessor the CCQ, are supported by more than adequate attention to reliability, validity, and related analysis. Two of the dimensions, Risk-Taking and Trust/Openness, deserve additional editing and improvement. The use of the SOQ may be problematic with culturally diverse groups given that no norms are available for members of those groups.

SUMMARY. The SOQ is used for individual and team assessment of an organization's climate. Qualified practitioners are trained to administer and interpret feedback. These practitioners must agree to the strict ethical use of the SOQ. Fifty years of documented research and development provide a level of confidence for both qualified practitioners and their clients. The SOQ is recommended for its intended purposes.

REVIEWER'S REFERENCES

Hunter, S. T., Bedell, K. E., & Mumford, M. D. (2007). Climate for creativity: A quantitative review. *Creativity Research Journal, 19,* 69-90.

Isaksen, S. G. (2007). The situational outlook questionnaire: Assessing the context for change. *Psychological Reports, 100,* 455-466.

Isaksen, S. G., & Akkermans, H. J. (2007). *An introduction to climate.* Orchard Park, NY: The Creative Problem Solving Group.

[123]

Skills Confidence Inventory, Revised Edition.

Purpose: Designed as part of the process of educational or career exploration to measure the confidence of career professionals in their abilities to successfully perform various work-related tasks and activities.
Population: Ages 15 and up.
Publication Dates: 1996-2005.
Scores, 6: Realistic, Investigative, Artistic, Social, Enterprising, Conventional.
Administration: Group.
Price Data, 2008: $69.50 per technical manual (2005, 54 pages); $11.20 per online profile administration; $17.60 per online interpretive report; $112 per 10 mail-in prepaid combined item booklets/answer sheets; quantity discounts available.
Time: (45-55) minutes.
Comments: This test is to be taken with the Strong Interest Inventory (18:129).
Authors: Nancy E. Betz, Fred H. Borgen, and Lenore W. Harmon.
Publisher: CPP, Inc.

Review of the Skills Confidence Inventory, Revised Edition by JOSEPH C. CIECHALSKI, Professor, Department of Counselor & Adult Education, East Carolina University, Greenville, NC:

DESCRIPTION. The Skills Confidence Inventory was designed to measure skills confidence based on Albert Bandura's theory of self-efficacy (1977). It is administered with the Strong Interest Inventory (18:129). In fact, both inventories are contained in one test booklet. Two editions of the inventory were considered and reviewed. The 1996 edition contained 317 items of the Strong Interest Inventory whereas the 2005 edition contained 291 items of the Strong Interest Inventory. The same 60 items composing the Skills Confidence Inventory were included in both the 1996 and 2005 editions.

The authors of the inventory indicate that when administering the inventory the administrator should, "Allow sufficient time for test administration, scoring, and receipt of results" (manual, p. 21). Testing time is reported as about 45–55 minutes. The test manual provides detailed instructions on administering the inventory as well as information on the use of the inventory for career planning.

Suggestions on how to interpret the Skills Confidence Inventory are also included in the manual. Several tables and figures are presented in the manual to assist in interpreting profiles. A profile is divided into two parts: (a) Levels of Skills Confidence and (b) Comparison Levels of Skills Confidence and Interest. For example, sections on what the scores mean for clients with typical profiles, moderate profiles, and flat profiles are explained in easy-to-understand terms.

The test manual is well written and contains considerable material that clearly presents the essentials of the Skills Confidence Inventory. For example, one chapter includes an overview of the inventory; another contains detailed information on the construction of the inventory; a third contains the directions and instructions for administering the inventory; a fourth includes suggestions for interpreting the inventory; and still another contains five very useful case studies.

DEVELOPMENT. The initial version of the Skills Confidence Inventory consisted of 195 items based upon John Holland's (1985) six General Occupational Themes (GOTs). The six GOTs are Realistic, Investigative, Artistic, Social, Enterprising, and Conventional. These six GOTs are also used in the Strong Interest Inventory. Examinees were requested to respond to each item based on their degree of confidence on a scale of 1 to 5. A "1" indicates "No Confidence," whereas a "5" indicates "Complete Confidence." This version was then pilot tested on a sample of 73 individuals (49 women and 24 men) consisting of working adults, graduate students, and undergraduate students. Based on the results of the pilot study, the number of items was reduced to 151 items. An even larger scale study consisting of 1,147 adults and 706 college students was conducted. The purpose of this study was to reduce the number of items of the Skills Confidence Inventory to 60 items consisting of six 10-item scales for each of the GOT themes. Examples of items from the final version of the Skills Confidence Inventory are included in Table 2.1 in the manual.

TECHNICAL.

Standardization. The normative sample for the Skills Confidence Inventory included 562 employed women, 585 employed men, 261 college men, and 445 college women. Percentile equivalents for this sample are included in tabular form in the manual for employed women, employed men, female college students, and male college students. Although ethnicity and race results are not included in the tables noted above, the manual does provide narrative of ethnicity and gender results of the inventory.

Reliability. Internal consistency coefficients are reported in the manual. The resulting reliabilities ranged from a low of .84 to a high of .87 in the student sample and from a low of .84 to a high of .88 for the adult sample. In a 2002 study, internal consistency coefficients for African Americans ranged from a low of .80 to a high of .88, values comparable to those for White students who had coefficients that ranged from a low of .80 to a high of .87. Test-retest coefficients for a small sample of college students (44 men and 69 women) after a 3-week interval ranged from a low of .83 to a high of .87.

Validity. Concurrent validity values for the Skills Confidence Inventory are reported in the manual. The differences between men and women as employed adults and as college students are also presented. The results indicated that employed adults had higher levels of confidence than college students. A table presented the resulting confidence intervals for the differences between men and women. The results also indicated that in general men are more confident in their confidence skills than women. A detailed discussion of concurrent validity is presented in the manual. Studies of incremental predictive validity were discussed briefly. In general, incremental predictive validity was supported. Several studies are described in the manual to provide evidence of the construct validity of the Skills Confidence Inventory. The resulting correlations of the studies comparing the Skills Confidence Inventory to the Strong Interest Inventory are presented in tables in the manual. In addition, other construct validity studies comparing the Skills Confidence Inventory to other instruments are also included in the manual. All the studies described in the manual provide evidence of the construct validity of the Skills Confidence Inventory.

COMMENTARY. The Skills Confidence Inventory and the data supporting it, like that of the Strong Interest Inventory, are impressive. The instrument is easy to administer and the manual includes an entire chapter devoted to administering the test. Numerous studies were cited that provide evidence for both validity and reliability. The internal consistency reliability and the test-retest reliability of the Skills Confidence Inventory are more than adequate. Likewise, evidence supporting the concurrent, predictive, and construct validities is also more than adequate. Results of the inventory are very easy to interpret. Profiles are described in detail and five case studies presented in the manual enable the user to see how the profiles can be used with clients who differ in age, gender, ethnicity, and education.

Although the norming populations of the adults were sound, this reviewer has a concern with the norming sample of the college students. The college student population was drawn from students from only two universities: Ohio State University and Iowa State University. Perhaps in future editions of the inventory the authors will expand the college norming sample to other colleges and universities. Finally, the authors need to be complemented for enumerating the limits of The Skills Confidence in the manual.

SUMMARY. The manual is very comprehensive. It contains not only administration and technical information, but also detailed descriptions on the use and interpretation of inventory results. The inventory is well organized and easy to use and comprehend. Used together with the Strong Interest Inventory, it will provide career counselors with helpful information to help their clients. Therefore, this reviewer highly recommends its use to career counselors.

REVIEWER'S REFERENCES

Bendura, A. (1977). Self-efficacy: Toward a unifying theory of behavioral change. *Psychological Review, 84,* 191–215.

Holland, J. L. (1985). *Making vocational choices: A theory of careers* (2nd ed.). Englewood Cliffs, NJ: Prentice Hall.

Review of the Skills Confidence Inventory, Revised Edition by GYPSY M. DENZINE, Associate Dean and Professor of Educational Psychology, Northern Arizona University, Flagstaff, AZ:

DESCRIPTION. The authors developed the Skills Confidence Inventory in 1996 based on their belief that the career exploration process can be enhanced by including information about individuals' perceived capabilities with respect to their career interests. The Skills Confidence Inventory parallels and accompanies John Holland's vocational types, as measured by the six General Occupational Themes (GOTs) on the Strong Interest Inventory® assessment.

The authors state the Skills Confidence Inventory can be used by counselors to help college students identify a major and career choice. In addition, scores obtained from working adults can be used to help employees identify their current self-perceived abilities, as well as areas for skills development.

The original 1996 Skills Confidence Inventory has not changed; rather the manual has been revised in response to the 2004 revision of the

Strong Interest Inventory (18:129) assessment. The revised manual contains new research findings and case studies of clients who have taken both the Skills Confidence Inventory and the Strong Interest Inventory. Both scales are organized in terms of the six General Occupations Themes (GOTs): Realistic, Investigative, Artistic, Social, Enterprising, and Conventional that have their origin in John Holland's theory of career choice. Similar to the GOTs, the Confidence Themes can be arranged in a hexagon that specifies their relations and predicts that themes adjacent to each other are more closely related than themes opposite from each other on the hexagon.

The Skills Confidence Inventory is grounded in Bandura's social cognitive theory and the construct of self-efficacy expectations (1977). Although Bandura distinguishes self-efficacy from confidence, the Skills Confidence Inventory developers chose to adopt the term skills confidence rather than self-efficacy in an effort to use a term more familiar to practitioners. The inventory also draws upon Hackett and Betz's (1981) social cognitive career theory (SCCT), which is generally considered to be the first career theory to incorporate Bandura's work on self-efficacy. Self-efficacy beliefs have a prominent role in SCCT in influencing career preferences, choices, performance, and persistence.

Administration. The Skills Confidence Inventory contains two types of items: (a) task and activity items and (b) subject area items. Respondents use a 5-point scale ranging from "No confidence at all" (1) to "Complete confidence" (5). The Task and Activities subscale contains 48 items and the Subject Area subscale contains 12 items, and respondents are asked to rate their confidence in their ability to complete a course in a specific subject area.

Scoring and interpretation. Respondents complete the 60 items on the Skills Confidence Inventory that are analyzed by computer. The inventory is administered in combination with the Strong Interest Inventory assessment®. Clients typically take 45–55 minutes to complete the two inventories "on either the SkillsOne® test administration [web] site or when using the prepaid item booklet/answer sheet" (manual, p. 21) that is mailed in for scoring.

I found the process of reading the instructions and completing the items in the test booklet to be a very straightforward task, which took approximately 30 minutes.

The manual contains a one-page sample Skills Confidence Inventory client profile, as well as the following materials: (a) a blank worksheet for listing client's skills confidence and interest in a quadrant format, (b) a sample Action Steps for High-Priority Themes, (c) a sample Action Steps for Themes That Are Good Options If Confidence Can Be Increased, and (d) a sample Action Steps for Themes That Are Possible Options If Interests Develop. All interpretative documents were professional looking, well-organized and labeled, and clear to understand.

According to the authors, if a client responds to fewer than 57 items, the inventory might be considered invalid. However, no empirical evidence is provided for the recommended fewer than 57 items cutoff score criteria for interpretation. Scores are not intended to be interpreted in a normative manner, and the manual does not contain norms for any groups of individuals.

DEVELOPMENT. In the 1990s, meetings of the Strong Research Advisory Board began to focus on the need to apply Bandura's theory and work on self-efficacy to career behavior. Nancy Betz added to this discussion her expertise of applying social cognitive theory to the theory and assessment of career behavior. The manual contains a very brief discussion of the construct of self-efficacy and social-cognitive theory, which is conceptual rather than empirical.

Item and scale development occurred over several years and led to an initial version that contained 195 items. After item and scale refinement, the inventory was reduced to 60 items based on a sample of 1,147 employed adults and 706 college students. The test developers used the following criteria to determine final item selection: (a) "correlated highly with its own scale," (b) "had relatively low correlations with other scales," (c) "minimized gender differences," and (d) "contributed to representation of all major aspects of its Theme" (manual, p. 7). The manual contains sufficient information regarding who can administer and interpret inventory scores.

TECHNICAL. Evidence for the reliability and validity of the Skills Confidence Inventory resides in the results of numerous empirical studies, which are summarized in the Reliability and Validity sections of the manual. Overall, the manual contains important information about the samples utilized for establishing reliability and validity of the constructs. The manual provides a thorough discussion of the appropriateness of this scale for different demographic groupings, including gender as well as comparative data for college students versus employed adults.

Internal consistency reliability for the inventory has been well established by numerous studies conducted by the scale developers and others. Data from 1,147 employed adults and 706 college students were used to test the final version of the inventory (60 items comprising six 10-item scales based on Holland's six General Occupational Themes). Alpha reliability coefficients ranged from .84 (Enterprising) to .87 (Realistic) for the college student sample and from .84 (Enterprising) to .88 (Realistic) for the employed adults sample. Betz and Gwilliam's (2002) study that is summarized in the manual presents evidence that the inventory has adequate reliability for a sample of 111 African American college students (ranging from .80 for Investigative and .88 for Realistic).

Evidence of test-retest reliability of the scales was gathered by Parsons and Betz (1998), who reported "correlations of .83 for Realistic, .86 for Investigative, .85 for Artistic, .87 for Social, .84 for Enterprising, and .84 for Conventional" in "a sample of 113 college students (44 men and 69 women)" (manual, p. 9) who were tested 3 weeks apart.

The manual addresses three types of validity: concurrent, incremental predictive, and construct. Concurrent validity was established by providing evidence for the hypothesis that working adults should have higher levels of skills confidence as compared to college students (Betz, Harmon, & Borgen, 1996). Additional evidence of concurrent validity was established by examining gender differences in skills confidence (Betz, Harmon, & Borgen, 1996). In a sample of 445 college women and 261 college men, men scored higher than women in skills confidence for the Realistic, Investigative, Enterprising, and Conventional areas. College women scored higher in skills confidence on the Social scale compared to college men. Gender differences were also found within the working adult sample, with men scoring higher on the Realistic and Enterprising scales compared to women.

Betz, Borgen, Kaplan, and Harmon (1998) examined the predictive capability of Skills Confidence Inventory scores for occupational group membership based on Holland's model of vocational types. In general, the probability of occupational family group membership increased in correspondence with increased confidence scores. However, there was stronger predictive ability of confidence scores depending on the occupational family. Forty-seven percent of the women with very high Investigative confidence were employed in Investigative occupations (42% for men). Whereas, differential validity was reported due to the finding that only 10% of the women with very high Artistic confidence were in Artistic occupations. In contrast, 43% of the men with very high Artistic confidence were in Artistic occupations.

Betz and Klein (1996) provided additional support for the concurrent validity of the Skills Confidence inventory when they reported results showing that the scale construct validity has some overlap with scores obtained from the Generalized Self-Efficacy Scale (Sherer et al., 1982). They found the Social and Enterprising scales had the highest correlations (.45 and .53, respectively) with the social scale on the Generalized Self-Efficacy Scale in a sample group of 200 college students.

Donnay and Borgen (1999) investigated the extent to which Skills Confidence Inventory Scales predicted occupational group membership beyond what career interest can measure. Using discriminant analysis, they found statistical incremental validity for self-efficacy scores in predicting occupational group membership beyond the six General Occupational Themes (Holland) of the Strong Interest Inventory assessment. GOTs alone accounted for 79% of the variance in occupational group membership, compared to 91% when both GOT and Skills Confidence Scale scores were used in the model. In another study, Rottinghaus, Lindley, Green, and Borgen (2002) reported that the six Skills Confidence scores added an additional 16% of the variance in predicting educational aspirations after the 10% of the variance accounted for by personality measures (the Big Five scores) was removed from the model. They found the strongest predictors of educational aspiration beyond personality were Investigative and Social Confidence.

Evidence of construct validity was established by Betz and Gwilliam (2002) in a study in which they examined the relations between scores on the Skills Confidence Inventory and the Self-Efficacy Questionnaire (SEQ; Lenox & Subich, 1994). The SEQ also measures self-efficacy for Holland's six career Themes. Unfortunately, Betz and her colleagues do not discuss the similarities and differences between the two scales in the revised Skills Confidence manual. The average correlation between the two scales was .74, which provides sufficient evidence of convergent validity. Solid average correlations (range = .75 to .86) were also found between Skills Confidence Inventory scores and the six activity competency scales of the Personal Globe Inventory (Tracey, 2002).

Two other studies provided evidence of the construct validity of the Skills Confidence Inventory. In one study, Betz et al. (2003) found high and conceptually meaningful correlations between the Skills Confidence scores and the scores obtained from the related 17 Basic Confidence Scales (BCS) (obtained from the Expanded Skills Confidence Inventory, Betz et. al, 2003). The BCS have some expected overlap with Holland's Themes; however, they were constructed to measure more work place domains that are important across a wide range of occupations (e.g., writing, mathematics, public speaking). For example, Betz et al. (2003) found a high correlation between Realistic Skills Confidence scores and the Mechanical scores. In another study with college students, Rottinghaus, Betz, and Borgen (2003) reported correlations ranging from .63 to .92 between the six scales of the inventory and the Basic Confidence Scale scores.

Consistent with Holland's theory, Betz and Gwilliam (2002) found that the average correlation between Skills Confidence scores for nonadjacent themes was .30. This finding provides evidence for discriminant validity of the inventory.

The authors provide basic details about the samples and methodologies used to gather evidence of validity and reliability. My review of the literature revealed several published articles on the psychometric properties of the inventory, as well as numerous empirical studies using the scale.

SUMMARY. Given the research to date on item and scale development, the Skills Confidence Inventory can be recommended for use with nonclinical populations of college students and adults. Although the authors state the scale is appropriate for use with individuals 15 years of age and up, there is insufficient evidence to recommend the scale for a 15- to 18-year-old population.

One of the strengths of the inventory is that it was designed to be a companion measure to the Strong Interest Inventory assessment. As noted in the manual, researchers have found a strong connection between career interest and confidence. For example, Rottinghaus, Larson, and Borgen's (2003) meta-analytic study based on 11 samples (24,289 respondents) revealed a 45% shared variance between Investigative interest and confidence.

In general, the manual contains an adequate description of the procedures and decisions used to develop the items and the inventory. One of the strengths of the manual is the in-depth coverage of gender issues. The five case studies presented in the manual are interesting, relevant, and provide the test administrator with a wide variety of client profiles. The manual does not mention if the inventory is available in multiple languages.

Persons hoping for an in-depth treatment of Bandura's social cognitive theory and self-efficacy research may be disappointed in the manual. It is noticeable that the authors do not address Bandura's criticisms of researchers who measure self-efficacy at the global rather than task-specific level. It seems there is still a great need to correlate scores obtained from the inventory with scores obtained from more specific occupational self-efficacy scales (e.g., teaching self-efficacy, engineering self-efficacy). Also, although the authors briefly mention that they choose to title the scale "confidence" rather than "self-efficacy," the manual could be improved by the inclusion of Bandura's fine distinction between confidence and self-efficacy. According to Bandura (1997):

> Confidence is a catchword rather than a construct embedded in a theoretical system. Advances in a field are best achieved by constructs that fully reflect the phenomena of interest and are rooted in a theory that specifies their determinants, mediating processes, and multiple effects. Theory-based constructs pay dividends in understanding and operational guidance. The terms used to characterize personal agency, therefore, represent more than merely lexical preferences. (p. 382)

One shortcoming was that the materials I received to review did not contain information about how to obtain results or the cost and time line for processing results. Second, although the manual reviews several investigations that examine the psychometric property of the inventory, it is noted most studies cited were conducted by one of the authors. Third, the developers claim the six Skills Confidence scores can be combined to average an overall score that could range from 1.0 to 5.0. The manual does not, however, provide evidence of reliability and/or validity for the global score. The test authors provide overall skills confidence scores for subgroups of the sample that show employed men have the highest overall mean score (3.5) and college women have the lowest mean score (3.1). The authors claim that an overall Skills Confidence score below 2.8 is of concern and may be related to poor self-esteem. Unfortunately, this claim is speculative and no theoretical and/or empirical evidence is provided to substantiate this proposition, and no detailed information is provided to justify the value of 2.8 as a cutoff score. In conclusion, The Skills Confidence Inventory is straightforward in its administration, scoring, and interpretation. Overall, the manual provides sufficient evidence to demonstrate that the inventory is a psychometrically sound measure of one's confidence for various activities and subject areas. The manual contains the basic information recommended by the leading professional associations in education and psychology (American Educational Research Association, American Psychological Association, & National Council on Measurement in Education, 1999).

REVIEWER'S REFERENCES

American Educational Research Association, American Psychological Association, & National Council on Measurement in Education. (1999). *Standards for educational and psychological testing*. Washington, DC: American Educational Research Association.

Bandura, A. (1997). *Self-efficacy: The exercise of control.* New York: W. H. Freeman.

Betz, N. E., Borgen, F., Kaplan, A., & Harmon, L. (1998). Gender as a moderator of the valididy and interpretive utility of the Skills Confidence Inventory. *Journal of Vocational Behavior, 53,* 1–19.

Betz, N. E., Borgen, F., Rottinghaus, P., Paulsen, A., Halper, C., & Harmon, L. (2003). The Expanded Skills Confidence Inventory: Measuring basic domains of vocational activity. *Journal of Vocational Behavior, 62,* 76–100.

Betz, N. E., & Gwilliam, L. (2002). The utility of measures of self-efficacy for the Holland Themes in African American and European American college students. *Journal of Career Assessment, 10,* 283-300.

Betz, N. E., Harmon, L., & Borgen, F. (1996). The relationship of self-efficacy for the Holland Themes to gender, occupational group membership, and vocational interests. *Journal of Counseling Psychology, 43,* 90-98.

Betz, N. E., & Klein, K. (1996). Relationships among measures of career self-efficacy, generalized self-efficacy, and global self-esteem. *Journal of Career Assessment, 4,* 285–298.

Donnay, D., & Borgen, F. (1999). The incremental validity of vocational self-efficacy: An examination of interest, self-efficacy, and occupation. *Journal of Counseling Psychology, 46,* 432-447.

Hackett, G., & Betz, N. E. (1981). A self-efficacy approach to the career development of women. *Journal of Vocational Behavior, 18,* 326–339.

Lenox, R., & Subich, L. M. (1994). The relationship of self-efficacy beliefs and inventoried vocational interests. *Career Development Quarterly, 42,* 302-313.

Parsons, E. & Betz, N. E. (1998). Test-retest reliability and validity studies of the Skills Confidence Inventory. *Journal of Career Assessment, 6,* 1–12.

Rottinghaus, P. J., Betz, N., & Borgen, F. (2003) Validity of parallel measures of vocational interests and confidence. *Journal of Career Assessment, 11,* 355–378.

Rottinghaus, P. J., Larson, L., & Borgen, F. (2003). The relation of self-efficacy and interests: A meta-analysis of 60 samples. *Journal of Vocational Behavior, 62,* 221-236.

Rottinghaus, P. J., Lindley, L., Green, M. A., & Borgen, F. H. (2002). Educational aspirations: The contribution of personality, self-efficacy, and interests. *Journal of Vocational Behavior, 61,* 1–19.

Sherer, M., Maddux, J., Mercandante, B., Prentice-Dunn, S., Jacobs, B., & Rogers, R. W. (1982). The Self-Efficacy Scale: Construction and validation. *Psychological Reports, 51,* 663-667.

Tracey, T. J. G. (2002). Personal Globe Inventory: Measurement of the spherical model of interests and competence beliefs. *Journal of Vocational Behavior, 60,* 113-172.

[124]

The Social Problem-Solving Inventory for Adolescents.

Purpose: Designed to "measure self-reported covert and overt social problem solving behaviors in personal as well as social contexts."

Publication Date: 2003.

Acronym: SPSI-A.

Scores, 13: Automatic Process, Problem Orientation (Cognition, Emotion, Behavior), Problem-Solving Skills (Problem Identification, Alternative Generation, Consequence Prediction, Implementation, Evaluation, Reorganization), Total Score.

Administration: Group.

Forms, 2: Long, Short.

Price Data, 2006: $6 per reproducible Electronic Long & Short versions; $19 per manual (2003, 114 pages); contact publisher for electronic scoring and interpretation pricing.

Foreign Language Editions: Long and Short versions available in English, Spanish, Romanian, and Persian.

Time: Administration time not reported.

Authors: Marianne Frauenknecht and David R. Black.

Publisher: SPSI-A, LLC.

a) LONG VERSION.

Population: Grades 9-10.

b) SHORT VERSION.

Population: Grades 6-7, 9-10, college.

Review of the Social Problem-Solving Inventory for Adolescents by STEPHANIE STEIN, Professor and Chair, Department of Psychology, Central Washington University, Ellensburg, WA:

DESCRIPTION. The Social Problem-Solving Inventory for Adolescents (SPSI-A) is a self-report measure of covert and overt social problem-solving behaviors. The SPSI-A was designed to align with the authors' model of social problem solving (SPS), a "cognitive-affective-behavioral process an individual uses to generate a variety of potential solutions or responses to a problem or stressor encountered in daily living" (manual, p. 2). It is specifically intended for adolescents though no actual age or grade ranges are given.

The instrument is available in both a long version (64 items) and a short version (30 items). The items are on a 5-point Likert-like scale, ranging from *Not at all true of me* to *Extremely true of me.* Negative items are reverse scored so the higher the score, the greater the social problem-solving ability. It can be individually or group administered and is estimated to take between 30 to 45 minutes for the longer version to be completed by young adolescents, though no actual time limit is set. In order to reduce testing fatigue, the authors recommend administering the short form to 6th–8th graders and using the total score, unless both scale and subscale scores are needed. In that case, the longer version would be recommended. Students in Grades 9 and above are recommended to use the long version due to increased reliability.

Mean raw scores are recorded for the total score, three primary scale scores and seven to nine subscale scores. In addition, quartile normative scores are available for the total score on the SPSI-A. The authors claim that the scores can be interpreted holistically (using just the total score) or analytically (using the scale and subscale scores). However, the calculation and interpretation of the scores on the interpretive report form is clumsy and confusing. Theoretically one is supposed to be able to identify an appropriate norm group, locate and record the normative raw scores from that group, and then calculate the raw score averages for the test-taker. Unfortunately, the instructions in the manual for scoring and interpretation are confusing and insufficient for all but the most seasoned test administrators.

DEVELOPMENT. The test authors developed the SPSI-A by modifying the adult measure of Social Problem-Solving by D'Zurilla and Nezu (1990). They started by taking the 70 items from the adult scale and modified them to decrease reading comprehension levels to the 9th grade level. The authors then added an additional 10 new items (from an original pool of 30 items) to measure the three components (facts, rules, and techniques) of automatic processing from the Black and Frauenknecht SPI model. The resulting 80 items were then separated sequentially into the three distinct scales of Automatic Process (APS), Problem Orientation (POS), and Problem-Solving Skills (PSSS). The POS was further broken down into three subscales: Cognition, Emotion, and Behavior. The PSSS was originally broken down into four subscales of Problem Identification, Alternative Generation, Consequence Prediction, and Implementation/Evaluation. The test was administered three different times to samples of 9th grade students enrolled in health education classes. After each administration, some items were dropped because they did not contribute to the internal consistency of the measure and, after two administrations, several additional items were added and some scales were reorganized. The reading comprehension level of the items was further reduced to a 7th grade level on the final version of the instrument. The current final revision of the long version has 64 items, three primary scales and eight subscales (with the addition of Reorganization under the PSSS). The short version has 30 items with 3 items from the APS and 3 from each of nine subscales (Implementation/Evaluation is broken into two subscales on this version).

TECHNICAL. The authors report a standardization sample of 1,433 adolescents for the long version of the SPSI-A and 475 for the short version. In all cases, the adolescents in the norm sample were described as "convenience samples of students enrolled in required health courses in different schools in the Midwest" (manual, p. 56). The normative data for the standardization sample include four referent groups in the long version and another four referent groups in the short version. However, only 371 students from Grades 9 and 10 (mean age of 15.5) were actually administered the current long version of the SPSI-A. The remaining 1,062 adolescents from the first three referent groups were administered earlier versions of the instrument that were used and later modified during the development phase. All of these prior versions included items that are not in the current version of the SPSI-A. It appears that all of the adolescents in the four referent groups for the short version were administered identical instruments.

In all referent groups, the standardization sample was predominantly White. The long version referent groups and two of the short version referent groups had roughly equivalent distributions of males and females, with the two remaining short version samples with a higher representation of females. The short version samples also varied more in age than the long version samples (all 9th and 10th graders). The short version sample consisted of four groups of students in 9th/10th grade (n = 280), 6th grade (n = 75), 7th grade (n = 41), and college (n = 79).

Reliability. Internal consistency and test-retest reliability data are presented in the SPSI-A manual. Alpha coefficients range from .93 to .95 for SPSI-A Total score on the various renditions of the long version. The short version SPSI-A Total score had coefficients that range from .91 to .94. As expected, the long form Total score was generally more reliable than the scale scores (APS from .77 to .88, POS from .92 to .94, PSSS from .89 to .95) and the scale scores were generally more reliable than the subscale scores (POS subscales from .64 to .90 and PSSS subscales from .52 to .92). The APS (no subscales) appears to be the scale with the weakest internal consistency reliability. Within the POS subscales, Cognitive had the lowest reliability (.64) and Behavior had the highest (.89). Within the PSSS subscales, Consequence Prediction had the lowest reliability (.52) and Problem Identification had the highest (.92). In general, the reliability coefficients improved with later versions of the long form, which is expected because the purpose of the revisions was to improve reliability. The scale score internal consistency coefficients for the short form of the SPSI-A were not as strong as the long form with the exception of the PSSS scale (.92 to .95). Subscale scores for the short form were also somewhat lower than the long form (ranging from .51 to .89). Overall, the SPSI-A appears to demonstrate moderate to good internal consistency reliability.

The test-retest reliability data for the SPSI-A came from two administrations of the Revised Version II long form to the same 360 students over a 2-week time interval. Pearson-product moment correlations were .83 for the SPSI-A Total scores, .67 for the APS, .78 for the POS (subscales ranged from .64 to .74), and .77 for the PSSS (subscales ranged from .63 to .72). Matched-pair *t*-tests showed no significant differences between scores on the first and second administration except for the APS and the Emotion and Consequence Prediction subscales. Based on this limited sample, the SPSI-A appears to be a relatively stable instrument.

Validity. The manual for the SPSI-A discusses content, concurrent, and construct validity. Though the authors claim content validity for the SPSI-A, there was actually no content validation on the adolescent version of the SPSI. Instead, items on the original adult version of the SPSI were developed and screened by experts in the field. To establish concurrent validity, the scores on the SPSI-A were compared with the Brief Symptoms Inventory (BSI) Global Severity Index and the nine dimensions, based on the assumption that deficiencies in social problem-solving skills would be related to feelings of distress and other personal problems. The inverse correlations between the SPSI-A Total score and the GSI were all significant for each sample but fairly modest in size (-.31 to -.45). The strongest correlations were with the POS scale (-.61 to -.65) and the three POS subscales (Cognitive, Emotion, and Behavior). There were few significant relationships between the GSI and the PSSS and APS.

Student scores on the Personal Problem Checklist for Adolescents (PPC-A) were also compared with the SPSI-A. Similar to the BSI, a significant inverse, though modest, correlation existed between the Total score on the SPSI-A and the PPC-A. Again, this significant relationship was mostly due to the moderate correlation between the POS and the PPC-A (-.45).

Convergent and discriminant validity, as well as factor analysis and intercorrelations between scales and subscales were all presented in the manual as evidence for construct validity of the SPSI-A. A strong correlation (.82) between the SPSI-A Total score and the total score on the Problem-Solving Inventory was used to support convergent validity. The authors suggest that weak to modest correlations between the SPSI-A Total score and self-reported grade point average provide evidence for the discriminant validity of this scale as measuring something different than academic achievement. An exploratory factor analysis conducted on the data from Version II of the long form indicated that 10 factors accounted for 55.8% of the variance. Finally, comparisons between the scales and subscale indicated that subscales were more strongly correlated with other subscales within the same scale. Furthermore, the three main scales correlated more strongly with the total score than with each other. The authors suggest that these correlations offer support for the multidimensional nature of the instrument.

COMMENTARY. The strengths of the SPSI-A are ease of administration, a diligent record of continual revisions of the instrument to maximize reliability, and then consequently, evidence of good internal consistency reliability. Evidence for validity is not as strong, especially because a test needs to be validated for a specific purpose and the manual does not clearly indicate how these data are to be used. Other significant problems with the instrument are the normative data and the lack of sufficient and clear guidelines for scoring and interpretation in the manual. Not only is the normative sample very homogenous, but the normative data are misleading because most students included in the norm group for the long version were not administered the current form of the instrument. Furthermore, the manual and interpretive report form could both use a major overhaul to make them clearer and more user-friendly. If test administrators referred to the manual to learn about the SPSI-A, they would have to wade through three chapters until the instrument is actually described in the fourth chapter. Even then, they still would not find a clear and concise statement of the purpose of the instrument and its intended uses. I administered the instrument to myself to get a better feel for it. Even though I have more than two decades of experience and training with assessment, I found the scoring clumsy and confusing and the interpretation very murky.

SUMMARY. The SPSI-A is a modification of the SPSI intended for adolescents and adapted to incorporate aspects of Black and Frauenknect's problem-solving model. The theory base and the good internal consistency reliability of instrument suggest that it could make a promising research tool. However, it is not ready for primetime as a tool for making decisions about individual students because of limitations in the norm sample and problems with clarity in the manual. It is recommended that the authors administer the SPSI-A to a larger and more ethnically and geographically diverse norm group and then revise the manual to make scoring and interpretation of the instrument more straightforward and meaningful.

REVIEWER'S REFERENCE

D'Zurilla, T., & Nezu, A. (1990). Development and preliminary evaluation of the Social Problem-Solving Inventory (SPSI). *Psychological Assessment, 2,* 156-163.

Review of the Social Problem-Solving Inventory for Adolescents by CLAUDIA R. WRIGHT, Professor Emerita, California State University, Long Beach, Long Beach, CA:

DESCRIPTION. The Social Problem-Solving Inventory for Adolescents (SPSI-A) is a social skills theory-based, self-report measure designed to help identify strategies adolescents employ when dealing with personal- or social-related challenges and to guide structured interventions for developing new strategies and enhancing problem-solving competence. The purpose of the instrument varies by form. Detailed information is derived from the 64-item SPSI-A with 4 scale and 9 subscale scores: (1) The 8-item Automatic Process Scale (APS) score assesses a tendency to apply strategies that have worked in the past. (2) The 24-item Problem Orientation Scale (POS) measures an adolescent's perceived competence for dealing with issues and yields a total scale score equal to the average of three subscale scores: (a) Cognitive (COG), confidence in one's intellectual ability to engage in the SPS process; (b) Emotion (EMO), a description of feelings one might experience when engaged in SPS; and (c) Behavior (BEH), a willingness to approach rather than avoid the process. (3) The 32-item Problem-Solving Skills Scale (PSSS) emphasizes use of an evaluation process when problem solving and generates a total scale score that is the average of 6 subscale scores: (a) Problem Identification (PID), (b) Alternative Generation (ALT), (c) Consequence Prediction (CON), (d) Implementation (IMP), (e) Evaluation (EVL), and (f) Reorganization (REO). And, (4) Total Scale (TOT), the average of APS, POS, and PSSS scale scores. The 30-item SPSI-A yields a TOT score recommended for examinees younger than 13 or when an overall assessment of an examinee's perceived skills is desired. For both forms, examinees are instructed to think about a recent encounter with an inter- or intrapersonal problem when responding to item-statements and to employ a 5-point Likert-type, response-formatted scale with anchors ranging from 0 (*not at all true of me*) to 4 (*extremely true of me*), circling the number that best describes him or her.

Test administration. The SPSI-A can be administered individually or in groups, under supervision (the 64-item SPSI-A in about 30-45 minutes and the 30-item form in 20). Useful standard test administration guidelines and a checklist cover such topics as informed consent, uniform testing conditions, time keeping, and guided questions and answers to facilitate the testing process. For examinees who are 13 years of age or younger and for those with cognitive or other relevant limitations, it is recommended that the test administrator read aloud test instructions and items.

Scoring. For a fee, test data can be submitted electronically for scoring and interpretation; relevant norms, individual SPSI-A scores, and profile graphics are provided. The technical manual includes simple equations for calculating SPSI-A scores and a sample interpretive report to facilitate data analysis in-house; however, careful note should be taken of reverse-scored items before final calculations are made; facility with statistics and familiarity with profiling in testing are necessary.

DEVELOPMENT. The SPSI-A shares similar constructs, items, and scales with the Social Problem-Solving Inventory (SPSI) published by D'Zurilla and Nezu (1990) and designed for adults and adolescents 11 years of age and older. The two inventories differ with respect to (a) reading level, with SPSI items at Grade 12.4 and the current SPSI-A version at Grade 7; (b) newly created

APS items derived from Black and Frauenknecht's (1990) SPS Model; and (c) newly created REO items, unique to the model. Standard methods for item inclusion and deletion were employed during test development.

TECHNICAL.

Norms. Norm-referent group data reported in the SPSI-A manual are offered for various versions of the SPSI-A during development and should be used with caution, as respondents were predominately White and in Grades 9 and 10. Relevant to this review are the normative data for the 64-item SPSI-A obtained from a sample of 371 adolescents, nearly equally divided between 9th- and 10th-grade students (51.5% and 43.4%, respectively, and 5.1% nonresponders [NR]) with a mean age of 15.5 (SD = .73). Of the total group, 51.5% were male and 48.5% female; 72.8% of the sample was White, 15.4% African American, 2.4% Hispanic, 2.2% Native American, 3.5% Asian, 1.4% Other, and 2.3% NR. To create norm-referent groups for the 30-item SPSI-A, the instrument was administered to four groups. (1) For Grades 9 and 10, a sample of 280 examinees, with a mean age of 14.6 (SD = .81), were enrolled in Grade 9 (91.8%) or in Grade 10 (3.6%), 4.6% NR; 55.2% were male and 44.8% female; 88.9% were White, 3.2% African American, 1.4% Hispanic, 1.8% Native American, 1.4% Asian, and 3.3% Other. (2) For Grade 6, a sample of 75 examinees had a mean age of 11.6 (SD = .53); 50.7% were male and 49.3% female; 96.1% were White, 1.3% each for Hispanic, Asian, and Other. (3) For Grade 7, a sample of 41 examinees had a mean age of 12.7 (SD = .67); 39% were male, 61% female; 80.5% were White, 14.6% African American, and 4.9% Other. (4) For the college-age group, a sample of 79 examinees had a mean age of 22.4 (SD = 4.77); 77.2% were female and 22.8% male; 94.9% were White, 3.8% African American, and 1.3% Asian. For the norm-referent group of 371 examinees, multiple t comparisons for gender and for grade (9 and 10) revealed no statistical differences of any consequence.

Reliability. Appropriate estimates of internal-consistency reliability were obtained for scale and subscale scores on both the 64-item and 30-item SPSI-A. For the 64-item SPSI-A, two samples were employed (Ns = 308 and 371) yielding median alpha coefficients for scale scores TOT, .95; APS, .80; POS, .93; and PSSS, .94; and for subscale scores COG, .77; EMO, .885; BEH, .87; PID, .82; ALT, .87; CON, .85; IMP, .845; and REO, .845. For the 30-item SPSI-A, similar but lower alpha patterns were obtained with two new samples (Ns = 279 and 67). Median alpha coefficients for scale scores were TOT, .925; APS, .77; POS, .785; and PSSS, .935; and for subscale scores, COG, .545; EMO, .585; BEH, .77; PID, .665; ALT, .81; CON, .805; IMP, .73; EVL, .74; and REO, .865. No stability (test-retest) data were provided for either final SPSI-A version.

Validity. There is no independent information supporting the content validity of the SPSI-A items. The authors deferred to the work of their predecessors, D'Zurilla and Nezu (1990) who did use appropriate content validation procedures for SPSI items. Concurrent validity evidence was based on two hypotheses that SPS is related to distress and to unresolved personal problems. Two samples (Ns = 308 and 371) of adolescents aged 14–15 were administered the 64-item SPSI-A and the 53-item Brief Symptoms Inventory (BSI; 15:38), which was designed, in part, to screen for psychological distress. BSI scores used for these comparisons included the Global Severity Index (GSI), and 9 subscales: Anxiety, Depression, Hostility, Interpersonal Sensitivity, Obsessive-Compulsive Behaviors, Paranoid Ideation, Phobic Anxiety, Psychoticism, and Somatization. Scores from the two inventories were correlated resulting in a 10x12 matrix (BSI x SPSI-A where IMP and EVL subscale scores were combined) and yielded moderate, inverse correlation coefficients between GSI and POS scores, r (306; 369) = -.65 and -.61, respectively. Similar patterns with slightly smaller coefficients were observed between all BSI scores and POS, COG, EMO, and BEH subscale scores (all $p < .001$), supporting the notion that some aspects of SPS and distress are related. No other associations were notable.

To examine the relationship between SPS constructs and personal problems, correlations were obtained between scores on the SPSI-A and on Schinka's (1989) Personal Problem Checklist for Adolescents (PPC-A), which is a listing of 240 common "problems" and was used to obtain the total number of problems (PPC) derived from 13 areas: Appearance, Attitude, Crisis, Dating, Emotions, Family, Health, Home, Job, Money, Religion, School, and Social. A moderate correlation was obtained between SPSI-A POS and PPC (r[336] = -.45, $p < .001$), suggesting examinees with higher scores on the SPS measure tend to report fewer personal problems.

COMMENTARY. Validity concerns are threefold. First, the revised SPSI-A item-statements that resulted in the reduction of reading level from 12.4 to 7 were not reexamined for content validity. It is not known what effect, if any, such revisions might have had on the content validity of SPSI-A items for the new target population. Second, although a number of studies are reported in the technical manual supporting the utility of previous SPSI-A versions for assessing the effectiveness of SPS interventions for adolescents, no new data are provided using the most recent version of the instrument. And, third, construct validity evidence, although promising, was based on past versions of the instrument. Finally, because normative data were obtained from predominantly White examinees, additional information regarding how culturally and language-diverse adolescents respond to SPSI-A items would be welcomed.

SUMMARY. For professionals working with adolescents enrolled in Grades 9 and 10 in classroom or intervention settings, the SPSI-A offers a promising, reliable measure of SPS self-efficacy with modest support of its concurrent validity.

REVIEWER'S REFERENCES

Black, D. R., & Frauenknecht, M. (1990). A primary problem-solving program for adolescent stress management. In J. H. Humphrey (Ed.), *Human stress: Current selected research* (Vol. 4, pp. 89–109). New York: AMS Press.

D'Zurilla, T., & Nezu, A. (1990). Development and preliminary evaluation of the Social Problem-Solving Inventory (SPSI). *Psychological Assessment, 2*, 156–163.

Schinka, J. A. (1989). *Personal Problems Checklist*. Odessa, FL: Psychological Assessment Resources.

[125]

Social Skills Improvement System Rating Scales.

Purpose: "Assists professionals in screening and classifying students suspected of having significant social skills deficits."

Population: Ages 3-18 years.

Publication Dates: 1990-2008.

Acronym: SSIS Rating Scales.

Scores, 51: 2 scale scores with 7 and 5 subscales, respectively, per teacher, parent, and student rater: Social Skills (Communication, Cooperation, Assertion, Responsibility, Empathy, Engagement, Self-Control) and Problem Behaviors (Externalizing, Bullying, Hyperactivity/Inattention, Internalizing, Autism Spectrum [not included on Student forms]), 1 Academic Competence Scale score [Teacher form only], and 3 Validity Indexes per rater (F Index, Response Pattern Index, Response Consistency Index).

Administration: Group.

Forms, 4: Teacher, Parent, Student (ages 8-12), Student (ages 13-18).

Price Data, 2010: $245.80 per Hand-Scored Starter Set (English) including Rating Scales manual (2008, 227 pages) and 25 of each rating form; $322.60 per Hand-Scored Starter Set (English/Spanish) including Rating Scales manual and 25 of each rating form; $53.05 per 25 Computer-Entry (English) Teacher, Parent, Student (ages 8-12), or Student (ages 13-18) forms; $42.60 per 25 Hand-Scored (English) Teacher, Parent, Student (ages 8-12), or Student (ages 13-18) forms; $103 per Rating Scales manual; $254 per ASSIST Software CD-ROM (Win/Mac); $600.75 per Rating Scales ASSIST Software for Scanning CD-ROM (Win); additional Starter Sets available with ASSIST Software.

Foreign Language Edition: Spanish edition available for Parent and Student forms.

Time: (15-20) minutes.

Comments: Student form not administered for children age 7 and younger; revision of Social Skills Rating System (T7:2375); SSIS Rating Scales are part of larger Social Skills Improvement System, which includes SSIS Performance Screening Guide, SSIS Classwide Intervention Program, and SSIS Intervention Guide; hand-scored or computer-entry forms available for all Rating Scales; Parent and Student forms available as audio recordings; optional ASSIST Scoring and Reporting System Software available (computer-entry or scanning version).

Authors: Frank M. Gresham and Stephen N. Elliott.

Publisher: Pearson.

Cross References: For information regarding the Social Skills Rating System, see T5:2452 (24 references); for reviews by Kathryn M. Benes and Michael Furlong and by Mitchell Karno of the Social Skills Rating System, see 12:362 (10 references); see also T4:2502 (4 references).

Review of the Social Skills Improvement System Rating Scales by BETH DOLL, Professor, Department of Educational Psychology, and KRISTIN JONES, Graduate Student in Educational Psychology, University of Nebraska-Lincoln, Lincoln, NE:

DESCRIPTION. The Social Skills Improvement System (SSIS) Rating Scales are norm-referenced measures for screening and classifying student social behaviors that are important for school success. Alternative forms can be completed by multiple raters (teachers, parents, and students) across home and school settings. The scales can be administered repeatedly at 4-week intervals to describe changes over time or in response to interventions. Although hand-scored versions of the scales are available, most users will purchase the optional SSIS ASSIST program, which provides a detailed score report that generates visual and statistical analyses of differences across administrations.

The SSIS Rating Scales include four components. The principal measure, the Social Skills Scale, describes students' positive social behaviors while interacting with others. A second measure, the Behavior Problems Scale, identifies negative behaviors that compete with social competence and may be important to address in social skills intervention. The third measure, the Autism Spectrum Subscale, provides a preliminary rating of the symptoms of pervasive developmental disorders. The fourth measure, the Academic Competence Scale, is composed of seven items in which teachers rank students' academic performance relative to that of classmates.

Items are completed using both frequency ratings and importance ratings. Parent and Teacher frequency ratings describe how often the behavior has occurred during the previous 2 months; using the self-report form, students rate how accurately problem statements describe their behaviors. Importance ratings ask parents, teachers, and students (ages 13–18) to rate the importance of each behavior for students' success and can be used to prioritize behaviors to address via interventions. In addition, the SSIS Rating Scales include three useful validity scales that allow examiners to judge the veracity of raters: an F scale that will be elevated when raters describe students as having an unrealistic number of problems; a response pattern index that is elevated if raters provide an unusual pattern of responses (e.g., provides the same response to most of the items or provides a highly variable number of responses); and a response consistency index that is elevated if raters complete similar items in very different ways.

The SSIS Rating Scales are part of a multicomponent system for strengthening students' social skills. Additional SSIS components include a guide for universal screening of social skills across a class or school; a curriculum for strengthening students' social skills in general education classrooms; and an intervention guide that translates SSIS Rating Scale results into social skill intervention units. Only the SSIS Rating Scales are reviewed here.

DEVELOPMENT. The SSIS Rating Scales are a major revision, and not simply a renorming, of the Social Skills Rating System (SSRS; Gresham & Elliott, 1990; T7:2375). Ninety percent of the items were new or substantially revised. Other changes from the SSRS include the addition of the Communication and Autism Spectrum subdomains, addition of the validity scales, alignment of content across teacher and parent forms, the adoption of a 4-point response format to improve scale reliability, improved item content for 3- to 5-year-olds, updated norms, addition of a Spanish version of the parent and student scales, and resources for linking score information to intervention development. The scales' content was selected to be representative of current research on social skills and achievement, to which the SSIS authors have contributed. New items for the Social Skills Scale were written to describe seven domains of social behavior that the test authors identify as important: Communication, Cooperation, Assertion, Responsibility, Empathy, Engagement, and Self-Control. Items for the Problem Behaviors Scale were written to describe students' internalizing, externalizing, and bullying behaviors. Other items were guided by diagnostic criteria for the Autism Spectrum Disorder and Attention-Deficit Hyperactivity Disorder described in the *Diagnostic and Statistical Manual of Mental Disorders, Fourth Edition, Text Revision* (DSM-IV-TR; American Psychiatric Association, 2000).

Items were then subjected to a series of statistical analyses to determine the final forms of the scales. Items were retained if they had an item-total correlation greater than .40 on the Teacher and Parent Forms; item-total correlations for the Student Forms were somewhat lower. Although item-total correlations were also computed for the Academic Competence Scale, these are not described in the manual, and seven of the nine proposed Academic Competence items were retained based on "rational analysis of item content" (manual, p. 51). Differential item functioning analyses showed that a small number of Social Skills scale items functioned significantly differently across gender or ethnic groups. However, because these differences were not observed consistently across all forms, only one item was subsequently excluded from the final form.

Special mention is merited for the development of the Spanish version of the scales. These were translated by psychologists who spoke Spanish as their first language, and translations were then verified by a professional translation service. The Spanish language scales were used during norming of the scale, including one group of respondents who were deliberately recruited because of their ability to speak Spanish and a second group of respondents who were recruited in the normal manner but subsequently identified as Spanish-speaking. Item-total correlations were examined separately for the Spanish-language respondents and were slightly lower than those reported for English-language respondents in the sample. Internal consistency of the Spanish-language subscales was verified to be adequate.

TECHNICAL. The SSIS Rating Scales are technically sound measures. The normative sample of 4,700 students (3- to 18-year-olds) is a close match to the 2006 U.S. Census data for age, gender, ethnicity, geographic region, and educational diagnosis. The norm group included representative numbers of children with a range of educational disabilities and mental disorders such as children with an autism spectrum disorder, developmental delay, emotional/behavioral disturbance, intellectual disability, specific learning disability, and speech/language impairment. To ensure that standardization ratings were thoughtful and accurate, teachers were never asked to rate more than six of their students; to facilitate comparisons across raters, special effort was made to secure multiple raters for each student in the norm group. Analysis of the standardization sample showed that the factor structure of the Social Skills Scale was a modest fit to the seven-factor model of social skills predicted by the test authors, with Comparative Fit Index values in the mid-.80s. Subsequent correlational analyses verified that the structure and interrelations among subscales were consistent with the test authors' conceptual framework.

The rating scales were also carefully constructed to conform with national standards for reliability. Internal consistency reliability was strongest for the scales' total standard scores but is adequate across the subdomains. Coefficient alphas for the Social Skills Scale ranged from .83 to .97 across age groups on the Teacher form, and were slightly lower on the Parent form (ranging from .74 to .96) and the Student form (ranging from .72 to .95). A similar pattern was noted for the Problem Behaviors Scale, where coefficient alphas ranged from .75 to .96 across age groups for the Teacher form, from .76 to .95 for the Parent form, and from .79 to .95 for the Student form. Coefficient alphas for the Academic Competence Scale ranged from .93 to .97 across age groups. The test-retest reliability of the SSIS Rating Scales was also appropriate. The manual describes studies of test-retest reliability for Teacher, Parent, and Student forms. For the Teacher form, results describe median adjusted correlations of .83 across 43-day intervals, with median adjusted correlations of .86 across 61-day intervals for the Parent form, and median adjusted correlations of .79 across 66-day intervals for the Student form. For SSIS Rating Scale standard scores, correlations between two independent teacher raters ranged from .61 to .68, with correlations of .50 to .62 for two independent parent raters. Interrater correlations for subdomain standard scores were lower.

The manual presents extensive construct validity information for the SSIS Rating Scales. For the most part, the pattern of intercorrelations among scales and subscales was consistent with the test authors' predictions. Evidence of the relation of the SSIS to similar and dissimilar measures is also presented including comparisons between the SSIS Rating Scales and the Social Skills Rating System (Gresham & Elliott, 1990), the Behavior Assessment System for Children, Second Edition (BASC-2; Reynolds & Kamphaus, 2004), the Vineland Adaptive Behavior Scales, Second Edition (Vineland-II; Sparrow, Cicchetti, & Balla, 2005; 2006), the Walker-McConnell Scale of Social Competence and School Adjustment (SSCSA; Walker & McConnell, 1995a; 1995b), and the Home and Community Social Behavior Scales (HCSBS; Merrell & Caldarella, 2002). In general, correlations were as expected across the forms with scales measuring similar behaviors correlating more highly than scales measuring dissimilar behaviors.

COMMENTARY. The SSIS Rating Scales hold substantial advantages for examiners. The availability of parallel Teacher, Parent, and Student forms; the option for re-administering the scales at 4-week intervals; and the availability of statistical comparisons across raters and administrations combine to make these a pragmatically useful measure of students' social behaviors. Examiners can use these scales to make dependable comparisons of students' rated social behaviors in different settings, across time, or in response to interventions. Given the very careful standardization of the scales, examiners can be confident that the standard scores provide appropriate comparisons with national, gender-specific groups. Because they were integral to the SSIS Rating Scales' development and standardization, the Spanish Language rating scales are dependable alternatives for many raters who do not speak English well. The manual's explanation of the scales' content, and of the derived scores and indices, is clear and well-stated. Moreover, interpretive guidelines provided in the manual, and supplemental tools within the SSIS multicomponent system, can guide examiners' translation of scale results into useful plans for intervention. Although the conceptual framework for the SSIS Social Skills Scale is strictly behavioral, the test authors are clear in describing what it is. The test authors' behavioral model for linking strengths and weaknesses to intervention is nicely explicit and provides a reasonable strategy for use of scale results in practice.

Still, because the SSIS Rating Scales are strictly behavioral in their orientation, they have less utility for students whose strengths or deficits in social competence are cognitive or affective in orientation. Scale items reflect an "adult perspective" that appropriate social behaviors are those that are well-mannered and prosocial. Scale results are less representative of such strategically important peer interactions as participating in "rough and tumble" play, joining in playful verbal jostling and teasing with friends, judging social situations as these unfold, or identifying varied and innovative responses to social problems. Authentic social competence is more than simply the performance of social behaviors. Examiners will need to extend and elaborate on the SSIS Rating Scales' judgments of social strengths to achieve a full understanding of students' social competence.

In several respects the manual overinterprets the meaning of SSIS Rating Scale results. In particular, the test authors make a conceptual distinction between performance deficits and acquisition deficits, and suggest that a "0" rating presumes an acquisition deficit whereas a "1" rating presumes a performance deficit. In reality, a "0" rating on items only means that the rater rarely sees the student perform this behavior. This might occur if the student disliked the behavior (e.g., some students avoid compromising at all costs), or if the student misjudged the social situations that called for the behavior (e.g., highly aggressive students frequently misjudge accidents as intentional acts of aggression without realizing that compromise is called for), or if the student sees no incentives for the behavior (e.g., students might consider compromise to be walking away from a chance to get their own way). Thus, the items on the SSIS Social Skills Scale are limited in their capacity to distinguish between performance and acquisition problems. Examiners will need to carefully test the limits and probe raters' perceptions to distinguish between the two with confidence.

As a second example, the value added by the SSIS Academic Competency Scale is quite limited. In practical terms, the seven items on this scale are simply teacher judgments about students' relative performance compared to classmates. Most schools and teachers are already aware of these judgments, which are amply captured in most standard report cards. Thus, this scale provides little new information for examiners.

The Behavior Problems Scale poses a different challenge. Despite the scale's name, its item content is limited to behavioral concerns that are related to social interactions. Information included in the manual suggests that the scale's representation of internalizing problems is very narrow, and it correlates more strongly with measures of anxiety and withdrawal than with measures of depression or somatic complaints. Similarly, the newly added Autism Spectrum Subscale is not sufficient for a comprehensive or accurate examination of students' autistic symptoms and its name suggests more than the scale can truly provide. Preliminary information reported in the manual suggests that the Autism Spectrum Subscale was elevated in a sample of children with autism spectrum disorders, but also in a sample of children with generic developmental disabilities.

SUMMARY. In summary, the SSIS Social Skills Scale provides a technically sound and pragmatically useful measure of the positive and well-mannered student social behaviors that parents and teachers appreciate. The scale's usefulness is greatly enhanced by the parallel Parent, Teacher, and Student forms and by the option for systematic comparisons across raters and points in time. Even though the implicit definition of social skills does not include all important components of social competence, those positive social behaviors that are included are nicely assessed and the resulting measures are useful for practice.

The Behavior Problem Scale is less useful. As a collective, the items describe a very narrow range of problem behaviors and key behavioral disturbances are poorly represented. The Autism Spectrum Subscale and Hyperactivity/Inattention Subscale are particularly misleading because they are neither comprehensive nor entirely accurate but carry titles representing specific disorders or symptoms represented within the DSM-IV. Examiners are advised to substitute a comprehensive behavior assessment inventory instead of using the SSIS Behavior Problems Scale or the SSIS Autism Spectrum Subscale. The Academic Competence Scale provides little new information, and can easily be replaced by simple review of students' cumulative academic records or report cards.

REVIEWERS' REFERENCES

American Psychiatric Association. (2000). *The diagnostic and statistical manual of mental disorders* (4th ed., text rev.). Washington, DC: Author.

Gresham, F. M., & Elliott, S. N. (1990). Social Skills Rating System. Minneapolis: NCS Pearson, Inc.

Merrell, K. W., & Caldarella, P. (2002). Home and Community Social Behavior Scales. Eugene, OR: Assessment-Intervention Resources.

Reynolds, C. R., & Kamphaus, R. W. (2004). Behavior Assessment System for Children (2nd ed.). Minneapolis: NCS Pearson, Inc.

Sparrow, S. S., Cichetti, D. V., & Balla, D. A. (2005). Vineland Adaptive Behavior Scales: Parent/Caregiver Rating Form (2nd ed.). Minneapolis: NCS Pearson, Inc.

Sparrow, S. S., Cicchetti, D. V., & Balla, D. A. (2006). Vineland Adaptive Behavior Scales: Teacher Rating Form (2nd ed.). Minneapolis: NCS Pearson, Inc.

Walker, H. M., & McConnell, S. R. (1995a). Walker-McConnell Scale of Social Competence and School Adjustment, Elementary Version. San Diego: Singular Publishing.

Walker, H. M., & McConnell, S. R. (1995b). Walker-McConnell Scale of Social Competence and School Adjustment, Adolescent Version. San Diego: Singular Publishing.

Review of the Social Skills Improvement System Rating Scales by JEANETTE LEE-FARMER, Associate Professor of Special Education, Marshall University, South Charleston, WV, and JOYCE MEIKAMP, Professor of Special Education, Marshall University, South Charleston, WV:

DESCRIPTION. The Social Skills Improvement System Rating Scales (SSIS) is a rating scale intended to identify positive behaviors "social skills" and undesirable actions "problem behaviors" that are presented by students. Separate forms are provided for the following groups to complete: teachers, parents, students aged 8–12, and students aged 13–18. In addition to the version in English, there is a version in Spanish. The protocol is on paper, folded to have 8.5 inch by 11 inch size pages. The inside two pages contain all the statements for the test takers.

On the Student Forms, 46 statements, all beginning with "I," are printed under the category of "Social Skills." Students are directed to fill in a circle with a coded letter following each statement that matches how they perceive themselves: N if they think the statement is "not true" for them; L if they think a statement is "a little true" for them; A if they think a statement is "a lot true" for them; and V if a statement is "very true" for them. For both groups of students, the questions are identical in number, in wording, and in the sequence of presentation. Different colors distinguish the protocols. In addition, the form for the adolescents includes response circles to fill in to rate how important they think each statement is for when they are with others. Statements 47 through 75 on the Student Forms fall under the "problem behaviors" category. For both age groups, again, the statements are identical.

Parents and teachers respond on a 4-point scale to rate the frequency of student behaviors (*never*, *seldom*, *often*, or *almost always*). Parents and teachers rank 46 social skills, most of which are identical, though presented in a different sequence. Additionally, they rate each behavior on its importance to them on a 3-point scale (*not important*, *important*, or *critical*). For problem behaviors, parents rank 33 characteristics, whereas teachers rank 30 on a 4-point scale.

The test is untimed and is estimated to take 15 to 20 minutes to complete. It can be completed individually or in group settings. It is recommended that clients use either a ballpoint pen or pencil (rather than a felt-tip). Scoring can be done by hand or by computer. The hand-scored protocols are printed using NCR papers with corresponding scores for the responses circled on the copy sheet.

The cover of the protocol includes instructions to the client and requests a limited amount of demographic data that may be helpful for research purposes. For students, information gathered includes the full name, birth date, current date, grade placement level, and gender. For adults who complete the rating scales, the researcher additionally gathers the respondent's relationship to the student, and his or her gender.

The manual includes further information such as when to use the test, test setting and conditions, notes on establishing rapport, how to introduce the test, administration, scoring, reliability and validity, and more.

DEVELOPMENT. The SSIS is a revision of the Social Skills Rating System (SSRS), an instrument that has been in use for nearly two decades. The current instrument under review has updated norms based on the 2006 U.S. Census Bureau demographic data. Each age group in the new norms had equal numbers of males and females, and matched the American population ratios of race/ethnicity and socioeconomic status by geographic region. Four thousand seven hundred students, in 36 states at 115 sites participated in the standardization.

Statements were added to cover new subscales of Communication, Engagement, Bullying, and Autism Spectrum characteristics. Furthermore, additions were made to provide greater coverage to existing subscales. Spanish forms are new to the SSIS (revised) version.

TECHNICAL. Ratings were obtained (means, standard deviations) from several exceptional groups (those with developmental delays, with emotional/behavior disorders, autism spectrum disorders, the gifted/talented, specific learning disabilities, speech/language impairments, and intellectual disabilities). Students with attention deficit/hyperactivity disorder were also compared to nonclinical groups. Charts detail the study groups by age range, gender, and race, and also include the mother's educational level. Other tables present the representation of the norm samples, and list raw score means and standard deviations for each social skill and problem behavior measured.

Internal consistency estimates, in the .70s–.90s for each age group, are moderately high to high. Test-retest reliability was confirmed with average scores remaining stable following second administrations of the instrument with teachers, parents and also with the student completers (test-retest interval ranged from 2 to 87 days).

COMMENTARY. School personnel across the nation are frustrated about behavior issues in schools (Simonsen, Sugai, & Negron, 2008). With the SSIS, Gresham and Elliott provide an assessment tool that objectively captures statements that can be presented to teachers, students, and their parents; analyzed quickly; and then used to spearhead a program of social skills remediation. The domain is crucial to the success of students in school and in life, and numerous variables must be taken into account when making assessments and assumptions regarding student actions (Cartledge, 1996). Completing the instrument is user-friendly. On the cover of the protocol, directions are given with a model that illustrates the correct way to mark responses. On both the computer-scored and hand-scored versions, the test taker responds to all the statements on the two inside sheets. Scoring directions to the clinician are provided directly on the inside of the protocol, with a summary page having raw scores converted to standard scores, a confidence interval and percentile rank, and practitioner-ready information such as noting whether the behavior level was below average, average, or above average.

Areas are provided for the scorer to indicate additional assessment information, and for making intervention planning notes on the hand-scored forms. The authors of the SSIS aimed to provide the practitioner with valid information to aid in the development of interventions. Specific interventions, which this reviewer expected, were not found in this instrument's manual. [Editor's Note: Specific interventions may be found in the SSIS Intervention Guide, which is not part of the Rating Scales, which were reviewed, but is part of the larger Social Skills Improvement System. The larger system includes the SSIS Performance Screening Guide, SSIS Classwide Intervention Program, and SSIS Intervention Guide. The review was for the Rating Scales portion of this system only, and the reviewers did not receive the other materials.] Teachers need lots of "how-to" information for the daily routine to be effective. A separate program from the test authors is available with specific plans for remediation of problem behaviors. Gresham and Elliott do provide numerous tables that reveal the characteristics of the samples used, item-total correlates for scales and subscales, reliability coefficients, special populations, and more.

SUMMARY. The SSIS is a straightforward scale to assess a student's behavior. Students, parents, and teachers respond to a mere two pages of statements. Responses analyzed are expected to generate specific information for the clinician regarding the student's social adjustment in the areas of communication, cooperation, assertion, responsibility, empathy, engagement, self-control, externalizing and internalizing behaviors, traits of bullying, hyperactivity, and correlates to autism spectrum disorders. The number of statements used to gauge each area is limited, and caution is raised in making connections to an exceptionality as complex as autism spectrum disorders. The ease of administration and scoring, and the content range of statements, however, makes the SSIS a handy screening tool for teachers to generate an individualized or group intervention plan to promote socially acceptable behaviors.

REVIEWERS' REFERENCES

Cartledge, G. (1996). *Cultural diversity and social skills instruction: Understanding ethnic and gender differences.* Champaign, IL: Research Press.

Simonsen, B., Sugai, G., & Negron, M. (2008). Schoolwide positive behavior supports: Primary systems and practices. *Teaching Exceptional Children, 40*(6), 32–40.

[126]

Spelling Performance Evaluation for Language and Literacy, Second Edition.

Purpose: Designed to analyze "a student's patterns of misspelling."

Population: Grades 2–12 and adults.

Publication Dates: 2002–2006

Acronym: SPELL-2.

Scores, 5: Phonological Awareness, Orthographic Knowledge, Morphological Knowledge, Semantic Relationships, Mental Orthographic Images.

Administration: Individual.

Price Data, 2007: $445 per complete kit including examiner's manual (2006, 138 pages), CD-ROM for single computer use, unlimited administrations; $150 for pay-per-student kit including examiner's manual, CD-ROM for single computer use, single administration credit ($75 per additional test session); volume discounts available.
Time: (30–120) minutes.
Comments: Test is computer adaptive; student performance will determine which of 11 test modules are to be administered.
Authors: Julie J. Masterson, Kenn Apel, and Jan Wasowicz.
Publisher: Learning by Design.

Review of the Spelling Performance Evaluation for Language and Literacy, Second Edition by SHARON deFUR, Professor of Special Education, College of William and Mary, Williamsburg, VA:

DESCRIPTION. The Spelling Performance Evaluation for Language and Literacy, Second Edition (SPELL-2), an untimed computerized prescriptive spelling assessment, generates individualized spelling objectives for children in Grades 2–12. Test respondents should have a developmental age of 7+ years, understand the use of a keyboard/mouse, and be able to follow age-appropriate directions. Specialists working with adult learners can use the SPELL-2 diagnostic assessment to target adult literacy education.

Certified or licensed professionals can administer and use results from the SPELL-2. The SPELL-2 does not require specialized training in administration, scoring, or interpretation as the SPELL-2 software automatically integrates these components. Supervised paraprofessionals can oversee test administration. The examiner's manual urges assessment administrators to familiarize themselves with the assessment, theory, and instructional implications of these criterion-referenced results. The examiner's manual provides educative resources including theoretical overviews, instructional implications, glossaries, frequently asked questions, test items, sample reports, and example letters to parents and teachers.

The SPELL-2 software uses animated figures (fairy or wizard) to guide students through multiple spelling assessments. The process begins with a screening assessment (Selector Module). Completion of the Selector Module automatically generates the start of a Main Test Module (level dependent on screening results). On average, students take 30–60 minutes to complete the Selector and Main Modules. The examiner can choose to have animation breaks throughout the assessment as a way to maintain student attention and task persistence. The program allows stopping the assessment, automatically bookmarking the stopping point. The test authors recommend implementing the SPELL-2 over several days. Selector Test Modules provide pre-assessment practice with corrective feedback; there is no corrective feedback during the Main Test Modules.

Completion of the Main Module generates a Preliminary Analysis report that identifies the need for one or more of six additional Modules. A Final Analysis Module provides diagnostic information and a Reporting Module generates individualized student objectives. The SPELL-2 program generates sample letters to teachers and parents aligned with individual assessment results.

The SPELL-2 provides teachers, students, and parents with a comprehensive evaluation of a student's skills in multiple spelling process areas (phonological awareness, orthographic knowledge, morphological knowledge, semantic relationships, and mental orthographic images). The SPELL-2 is not a norm-referenced assessment and does not generate grade or age equivalents, percentiles, or standard scores. The test authors recommend using other standardized tests when the assessment purpose is to provide norm-referenced comparisons.

The SPELL-2 examiner's manual includes an easily installed CD program. The SPELL-2 software provides an Examiner Preview allowing the user to hear instructions and try practice items for each SPELL-2 Module. The www.learningbydesign.com website offers additional software support.

DEVELOPMENT. The SPELL-2 (2006) is the second edition of the SPELL (2002). The manual does not identify changes from the first edition.

According to the examiner's manual, the SPELL-2 emanated from a theoretical model, spelling research, and a need for an accurate measurement tool in spelling. Wasowicz, Masterson, and Apel (2003) argue that spelling is a complex skill that influences both reading and writing. Furthermore, these authors (and test developers) contend that assessment that discerns specific linguistic deficiency leads to more targeted instruction. Masterson, Apel, and Wasowicz (2003) provide a model of assessment that promotes systematic spelling error analysis and literacy instruction. This model, along with spelling and language theory, guided the development of SPELL (2002) and, presumably, the revised SPELL-2 assessment.

Neither the examiner's manual nor the website provides detailed information on the test development process. Within the Frequently Asked Questions (FAQ) Appendix, one of the FAQ responses indicates that content validity measures were used to select test items that were within the vocabulary level for each Module, although there is no citation of how those measures were gathered. The examiner's manual states that the SPELL-2 assesses 60 of the most common spelling patterns and that the published resources guided pattern inclusion. The examiner's manual includes three sections of citations differentiating them by "helpful resources, assessment resources, and references" (pp. 126–127).

No information was evident regarding field-testing of the SPELL-2, systematic expert reviews, or other external evaluations of the use of the SPELL-2. Several case studies (authored or co-authored by the test developers) exist describing the use of the SPELL assessment process that included testing followed by targeted instruction; each case documented spelling progress. The most extensive documented use of the assessment has been in a homogeneous Midwestern university elementary lab school.

TECHNICAL.

Standardization. The SPELL-2 is a criterion-referenced assessment and is not norm-referenced.

Reliability. No reliability data are available at this time (Mooney, 2006).

Validity. A criterion-validity study conducted by Mooney (2006) reported strong correlations with two subtests of the Woodcock Diagnostic Reading Battery and the Test of Written Spelling. Based on this study, she concluded that the SPELL validly measures students' spelling abilities.

The theoretical base used to develop the content of the SPELL-2 offers support that the items used in the assessment represent the intended construct (various spelling process domains such as phonological awareness). In addition, the test authors contend that the SPELL-2 offers sufficient opportunities to respond to words representative of various linguistic domain(s) or error patterns, thus enabling valid diagnosis and prescriptive recommendations. The SPELL Model of Asssessment (Masterson et al., 2003), a theory-driven assessment practice, was seemingly used to create the software program that analyzes student responses.

COMMENTARY. The SPELL-2 performs a clinical diagnostic spelling/literacy error analysis that, in practice, usually emerges only as specialists (teachers, clinicians, therapists, etc.) develop a deep understanding of the structure of language and spelling process. As language researchers and clinicians, the authors of the SPELL-2 have created a program that performs diagnostically what specialists either cannot do, or may not have the opportunity to do, in their daily work. The model of spelling assessment seems logically and theoretically sound. Professionals interested in developing their understanding of language and the spelling process will find the SPELL-2 examiners manual educative for theoretical underpinnings as well as for practical applications for spelling instruction. In addition, actively taking the assessment and generating a report for analysis helps users make the connection between theory and practice. One might argue that the SPELL-2 assessment removes the diagnostic demand from the specialist; this could prove expedient in identifying instructional strategies. Instructionally, I believe it remains critical that specialists develop the diagnostic understanding of language to create similar hypotheses as those generated by this assessment. Properly studied, the SPELL-2 could contribute to the development of such understanding.

Neither the examiner's manual nor the website discuss how SPELL-2 program design decisions were made. However, the test authors clearly considered student developmental needs in designing this extensive computer-based assessment. To the test authors' and designers' credit, the program's animated characters engage the school-age respondent. The optional animations (short cartoon-like interactive presentations) offer a distraction that breaks up the monotony of responding to spelling prompts. Use of the computer and keyboard to spell may be novel to some students and is much more consistent with current writing practices in adult life (the examiner's manual indicates that research has not found keyboard and mouse use to be a detriment to spelling and is, in some cases, beneficial). The SPELL-2 requires minimal adult facilitation as the program guides give directions and corrective feedback (use of earphones is recommended). I would be interested in the degree to which students require assistance as they take

SPELL-2 tests, and the impact of this assistance on test performance.

The test authors deliberately chose to include sufficient opportunities to respond to spelling prompts as one way to assure reliability and validity of diagnostic items. Consequently, the assessment Modules require sustained attention and time commitment. I created a mock student and responded to prompts using the Selector Test and Wizard as Guide. My mock responses resulted in an assessment starting in Test Module 2. After 30 spelling prompts, I began exploring various "hurry-up" options (testing the various options for pausing, exiting, and resuming) and ended the assessment after 50/141 words. It is important to note that the pause, exit testing, and resume testing worked well; the resume testing feature assumes that the student remembers the original instruction for a particular Module. I am curious as to the impact that test saturation may have on performance. Likewise, although being able to start and stop offer accommodation options, the SPELL-2 literature did not discuss whether such procedures affect student performance or whether it matters if the break is for 10 minutes or for a day or how frequently breaks are taken. The examiner needs to understand that the student must complete an entire Test Module before the program generates an analysis report; the program does offer a feature that allows the examiner to review actual student responses from incomplete tests.

SUMMARY. The SPELL-2 is a promising comprehensive diagnostic spelling literacy tool that supports learning specialists' assessment efforts, potentially guiding systematic and targeted instruction for students who demonstrate persistent written language or spelling deficits. Spelling research literature supports the theory that influenced the SPELL-2 assessment. However, limited information regarding the development of the SPELL-2, implementation evaluation, more extensive and inclusive outcome evaluation, as well as technical adequacy and effectiveness in a wider audience than currently reported limits my recommendation for widespread adoption. Intuitively, the assessment tool provides critical literacy diagnostic data. Less clear is how well learning specialists, teachers, or parents can rely on, or effectively use, these data to improve literacy outcomes for students. Additional research on this assessment will provide feedback for usage by assessment consumers. In the meantime, I suspect that consumers who use this tool will develop a deeper understanding of the complexity of spelling and written language.

REVIEWER'S REFERENCES

Masterson, J. J., Apel, K., & Wasowicz, J. (2003). *SPELL model of assessment* (Technical Publication No. 03-1). Evanston, IL: Learning by Design, Inc.

Mooney, R. (2006). *Criterion validity of the Spelling Evaluation Language and Literacy (SPELL)* (Unpublished master's thesis). Missouri State University, Springfield, MO.

Wasowicz, J., Masterson, J., & Apel, K. (2003). *Spelling performance evaluation for language & literacy* (Monograph No. 1). Evanston, IL: Learning by Design, Inc.

Review of the Spelling Performance Evaluation for Language and Literacy, Second Edition by KAY STEVENS, Associate Dean and Director of Graduate Studies, Texas Christian University, Fort Worth, TX:

DESCRIPTION. The Spelling Performance Evaluation for Language and Literacy, Second Edition (SPELL-2) is an untimed computer-delivered prescriptive instrument designed to identify spelling error patterns and provide instructional recommendations based on assessment results. Administration and scoring procedures are entirely computer managed. An adult is required to monitor the test taker's effort and concentration during the computer-delivered administration to determine when a break from testing may be required. The target population includes students in Grades 2 through 12 and adults. Examinees must know how to use a keyboard and mouse and follow computer-delivered directions. During the main portions of assessment, the examinee listens (preferably with headsets) to dictated words, spells each word via keyboard entry, and clicks the mouse after completing each item. No feedback is provided. The software program analyzes all responses according to "a complex series of proprietary algorithms" (examiner's manual, p. 4) to determine error patterns and recommend instructional objectives and procedures. Animation, consisting of fictional characters that guide the examinee through the program, is optional. Testing time is estimated to be between 30 to 60 minutes for screening and 30 to 60 minutes for the main testing. The examinees' pace and the level of word list(s) administered determine the exact duration of assessment. Administration time may be divided into a series of shorter sessions if the examinees' effort and/or concentration wane.

The SPELL-2 contains 11 modules: (a) The Selector Module is a screening procedure to determine which word list, out of four levels, to administer during the Main Test Module. (b) The Main Test Module contains four lists of words, each list assessing a more complex set of spelling patterns. The examinees begin with the word list selected during screening. (c) The Preliminary Analysis Module recognizes spelling error patterns based on the examinees' performance on the Main Test Module, which determines if further testing is required. (d–i) Six supplementary modules are administered when needed to assess more in-depth skills including phoneme segmentation and discrimination, base-word spelling, and morphological knowledge–administration time per supplementary module ranges from 3 to 12 minutes. The need for administering supplementary modules is determined based on results from the Main Test Module. (j) The Final Analysis Module identifies the "cause" of spelling errors and generates instructional objectives. (k) The Reporting Module provides detailed printed information regarding the examinee's performance including spelling error patterns, recommended instructional objectives, and letters to parents and teachers describing assessment results. SPELL-2 does not use traditional scores, but rather, specific information related to the examinees' error patterns.

Detailed and effective instructions for using the software program are provided in the examiner's manual. Also included is a generous amount of information regarding spelling instruction and remediation as well as an appendix containing frequently asked questions, recommendations for spelling instruction, definitions of spelling terms for parents and teachers, examples of computer-produced letters to parents and teachers describing results of a hypothetical assessment, the four spelling lists, and a glossary of terms.

DEVELOPMENT. The test authors state that the development of the SPELL-2 was based on theoretical advances and empirical findings indicating that a multiple-linguistic approach is more effective than traditional spelling assessment and instruction citing several references that support the underlying theory. Five linguistic skill areas provide the basis for the multiple-linguistic approach. The skills areas include (a) phonological awareness, (b) phonics, (c) vocabulary, (d) morphology, and (e) mental orthographic memory. The test authors clearly define each area and describe the relationship between the skill area and spelling.

Although traditional spelling assessment determines a student's spelling level based on the number or percent of words spelled correctly, the SPELL-2 analyzes up to 60 error patterns related to the five skill areas, reports each problem area, and provides instructional objectives based on the assessment data. Assessing spelling using a multiple-linguistic approach is logical and generally accepted.

Empirical support for SPELL-2 development is questionable. The test authors cite two studies examining the effectiveness of a spelling intervention program titled SPELL Links to Reading and Writing: A Word Study Curriculum (Wasowicz, Apel, Masterson, & Whitney, 2004) based on the multiple-linguistic approach and published by the publishers of SPELL-2. Kelman and Apel (2004) is a case study of an 11-year-old girl whose reading and written spelling accuracy were assessed before and after receiving instructional intervention from *SPELL-Links to Reading & Writing* resulting in improvement in both areas. A second study conducted by Apel, Masterson, and Hart (2004) compared one elementary classroom receiving traditional spelling instruction to a second classroom receiving multiple-linguistic spelling instruction. A 40-word spelling test representing a range of spelling complexity was used to measure effective size. Pre-post data revealed that the class receiving the multiple-linguistic-based spelling instruction demonstrated significant improvement whereas the class receiving traditional spelling instruction did not. Neither of the two studies used the SPELL-2. The empirical support cited in the manual is actually support for a multiple-linguistic approach to teaching spelling. Although there is a logical connection between the multiple-linguistic instructional approach and the SPELL-2, actual research on the development and use of the SPELL-2 is absent.

The examiner's manual states that the SPELL-2 software analyzes error patterns using "a complex series of proprietary algorithms to recognize patterns of misspellings and to determine how much, if any, additional testing must be completed" (p. 4). Without knowledge of algorithm details, the user is faced with accepting the development of the error pattern interpretation and instructional objectives on faith. If, in fact, the algorithms are found to be reliable and valid, the detailed, prescriptive data generated by the SPELL-2 would be a useful basis for explicit spelling instruction. The examiner's manual does include the four word lists (Levels 1–4) in the appendix and a description of the spelling patterns assessed per level in the introduction section. However, no information is provided to justify item selection. No pilot testing using the SPELL-2 was documented. No information regarding the changes from SPELL to SPELL-2 was included.

TECHNICAL. The SPELL-2 is a criterion-referenced assessment instrument; therefore, no standardization related to a normative sample is required. A standardized cutoff score per error pattern was given. Below 60% on any error pattern indicates the need for word-level, explicit instruction whereas 60% to 100% indicates "emerging" patterns, for which the examiner is directed to instructional suggestions provided in "Other Considerations for Spelling Instruction" on page 44 of the examiner's manual. Not included is the methodology needed for determining cutoff scores.

Neither reliability nor validity data were included in the manual for SPELL-2. In the "FAQ" section of the manual's appendix, the test authors reference criterion validity on SPELL (First Edition) and state that a validity study on SPELL-2 is underway. One study of a previous edition and one study underway are inadequate. Criterion-referenced tests require specific types of technical measures. Some examples include content validity, predictive validity, test-retest reliability, interrater reliability, and a rationale for setting the cutoff score. The absence of such measures seriously limits the acceptability of the instrument.

COMMENTARY. The SPELL-2 is purported to be a prescriptive assessment tool that analyzes spelling errors, identifies error patterns, hypothesizes the cause of the pattern, and provides instructional objectives that address the spelling problem areas. The multiple-linguistic approach appears logically sound. Conducting error analysis on written spelling is not an uncommon practice. Detecting error patterns, hypothesizing the cause of the patterns, and providing data-based instructional objectives is commonly recommended, thus offering credibility to the procedures employed in SPELL-2 (Beirne-Smith & Riley, 2009). Teachers typically complete the error analysis process by poring over writing samples and recording errors using pencil and paper. A reliable and valid computer program that conducts the analysis and provides detailed feedback regarding error patterns is certainly preferable.

The SPELL-2 lacks the technical data to fully recommend its use. Highly noticeable was the absence of any type of validity or reliability measures. In addition, generalization from keyboard spelling to hand-written spelling was not established. It has been this reviewer's experience that teachers too often are sold on attractive packaging and face validity rather than technical adequacy. Test developers are responsible for conducting appropriate procedures required for criterion-referenced test development.

SUMMARY. The SPELL-2 provides a computer-delivered criterion-referenced assessment instrument that leads to systematic instruction based on error patterns analyzed and described by a series of algorithms built into the software program. A systematic package of assessment and instructional materials that saves time for busy teachers while providing effective instruction is commendable. The practice of error pattern analysis is critical for the development of efficacious, direct, and individualized instruction. The assessment of spelling abilities based on a multiple-linguistic approach indicates advancement in the science of teaching spelling.

The test authors fail to adequately describe the psychometric and procedural development of the SPELL-2. Too much weight was placed on the superiority of the underlying multiple-linguistic instructional approach, and too little effort was spent on the development of the SPELL-2. Finally, the lack of transparency regarding the "complex series of proprietary algorithms" (examiner's manual, p. 4) used to analyze error patterns and to make instructional recommendations is unacceptable in scientific inquiry.

REVIEWER'S REFERENCES

Apel, K., Masterson, J. J., & Hart, P. (2004). Integration of language components in Spelling: Instruction that maximizes students' learning. In E. R. Silliman & L. C. Wilkinson (Eds.), *Language and literacy learning in schools* (pp. 292–315). New York: Guilford Press.

Beirne-Smith, M., & Riley, T. F. (2009). Spelling assessment of students with disabilities. *Assessment for Effective Intervention, 34,* 170-177.

Kelman, M., & Apel, K. (2004). The effects of a multiple linguistic, prescriptive approach to spelling instruction: A case study. *Communication Disorders Quarterly, 25,* 56-66.

Wasowicz, J., Apel, K., Masterson, J. J., & Whitney, A. (2004). *SPELL-Links to reading & writing: A word study curriculum.* Evanston, IL: Learning By Design, Inc.

[127]

Stanford Reading First.

Purpose: Designed to "identify students in kindergarten through grade three who are at risk of reading below grade level by assessing reading foundation skills and monitoring reading progress."

Population: Grades K.0–K-5, K.5–1.5, 1.5–2.5, 2.5–3.5, 3.5–4.5.

Publication Dates: 2002–2004.

Scores, 10: Sounds and Letters, Word Study Skills, Word Reading, Sentence Reading, Reading Vocabulary, Reading Comprehension, Listening to Words and Stories, Listening Vocabulary, Speaking Vocabulary, Oral Reading Fluency.

Administration: Individual and group.

Levels, 5: Stanford Early School Achievement Test Level 1, Stanford Early School Achievement Test Level 2, Primary 1, Primary 2, Primary 3.
Parts, 2: Multiple-Choice, Oral Fluency.
Price Data, 2009: $53.40 per technical data report (2004, 85 pages); $73.60 per training kit; $35 per 10 machine-scorable test packs (specify level); $13.25 per Oral Reading Fluency reusable booklet (specify level); $14.85 per directions for administering (specify level); $27.55 per response key (specify level); $9 per class record (specify level).
Time: (75) minutes.
Comments: Multiple-Choice component items are taken from Reading and Listening subtests of the Stanford Achievement Test Series, Tenth Edition (16:232), and the Oral Fluency items are new to Reading First.
Author: Pearson.
Publisher: Pearson.

Review of the Stanford Reading First by C. DALE CARPENTER, Professor of Special Education, Western Carolina University, Cullowhee, NC:

DESCRIPTION. The Stanford Reading First is designed to be a group and individually administered assessment of reading foundation skills for learners in kindergarten through third grade and to identify children who may be at risk of falling behind peers in reading. Stanford Reading First is a subset of the Stanford Achievement Test Series, Tenth Edition (Stanford 10; 16:232) including the five reading achievement tests with an additional Oral Fluency test composed of Speaking Vocabulary and Oral Reading Fluency specifically developed for the Stanford Reading First. This review is not intended to duplicate recent reviews of the Stanford 10 (Carney, 2005; Morse, 2005), which cover the multiple choice portion. This review focuses on the Oral Fluency portion.

The multiple choice portion of the test was developed from the Reading and Listening subtests of the Stanford 10. Phonics is measured with Word Study Skills at the primary levels and Sounds and Letters at the lower levels (SESAT 1 and 2). Vocabulary is assessed with Listening Vocabulary, Speaking Vocabulary, and either Word Reading at the first three levels or Reading Vocabulary on the last two of the five levels. Reading fluency is measured through Oral Reading Fluency and Reading Comprehension. Finally, reading comprehension strategies are assessed primarily by listening and traditional reading comprehension passages.

The Oral Fluency portion of the Stanford Reading First, consisting of Speaking Vocabulary and Oral Reading Fluency, is individually administered. At the lowest level, Speaking Vocabulary presents a color illustration of people engaged in an activity and asks the examinee to name the objects in the picture and to tell a story about what is happening in the picture. At the highest level for Speaking Vocabulary, Primary 3, examinees tell a story based on four pictures depicting a sequence of events. Examiners award a score of 0–3 based on a scoring rubric including correct sequence, appropriate ideation, and elaboration. At the lowest level, SESAT 1, Oral Reading Fluency consists of examinees responding to oral questions when presented with visual prompts identifying letters, numerals, and words. At the highest level, examinees are presented with a passage and a picture and are required to read aloud. Examiners award a score of 0–3 based on a scoring rubric for accuracy (correct pronunciation), appropriate rate, and use of expression.

The directions for administering Oral Fluency tests are clearly printed in the manual and on the Oral Fluency test booklet for each level. The examiner reads one side of the test booklet while the examinee sees the other side. Scores are kept in the multiple-choice booklet. Pictures and print are in color and easy to see and interpret. The scoring rubrics are concise and easy to find. However, discontinuation or establishment of ceiling for individually administered Oral Fluency tests are located in the separate Technical Data Report and require careful reading.

The outcomes emphasized with the Stanford Reading First are three performance levels for each of seven subtests, each of two components (multiple-choice and oral fluency), and the overall test. Performance levels are At Grade Level or performance at or above the 40th percentile based on grade comparisons, Needs Additional Intervention or performance at or above the 20th percentile and below the 40th percentile, and Needs Substantial Intervention or performance below the 20th percentile. Other scores for the Reading First Total available are scaled scores, percentile ranks, stanines, and normal curve equivalents.

DEVELOPMENT. Stanford Reading First, as a new edition of Stanford 10, was developed to respond to the No Child Left Behind (NCLB) Act as well as a number of other factors to include better integration with classroom instructional activities and materials through an engaging format and presentation of materials according to the Technical Data Report. Test blueprints were based on national and state standards and recommendations including the International Reading Association, Reading First Academy, and National Assessment of Educational Progress test frameworks.

Test items were developed in accordance with the revised blueprints based on expert reviewer input, and items were piloted in a carefully constructed tryout program. The multiple-choice component was administered to approximately 500 students in each grade. Oral fluency items were individually administered to 20 students in each grade, kindergarten through third grade, in San Antonio, Texas in January 2003. Items were analyzed using a variety of methods including *p*-values, correlation with total scores, Rasch models, and Mantel-Haenszel methods to estimate bias. In addition, advisory panels were convened to review items and materials to eliminate bias.

According to the Technical Data Report (p. 21), the "foremost consideration for selection of items for the final forms was fit of content to the test blueprint." The authors also attempted to balance items measuring the cognitive levels of "basic understanding" and "thinking skills" throughout the multiple-choice items. A unique feature of the Stanford 10 is that items are not sequenced in order of difficulty level to reduce frustration sometimes caused when examinees experience increased failure when items are sequenced by difficulty level. Reviewers noted this feature in reviews for the Stanford 10 (Carney, 2005; Morse, 2005), and it was continued in Stanford Reading First.

TECHNICAL.

Standardization. The norm sample for the Stanford Reading First included 400 students at each of the five test levels for two different testing programs for a total of 3,464 in a sampling procedure that matched demographic characteristics of Stanford 10 standard samples. Both Form A and B from each level of each component were included in the samples except Form B of the multiple-choice portion of the lowest level, SESAT 1, which is not available.

Reliability. Internal consistency coefficients using Kuder-Richardson 20 formula are all equal to or exceed .89 on samples of over 300 students at each level for entire test forms. Alternate form reliability is included through the equating program through descriptive statistics such as means, standard errors of measurement, and standard deviation. Values are similar for both forms where available. Information regarding test-retest or interrater reliability is not provided.

Validity. Content validity data consist of the information provided for creating test blueprints including a review of standards for professional organizations, academic standards for states, and the NAEP test frameworks. The authors refer to experts in content and measurement in the development of items but do not list names or provide detailed explanation. Criterion-related validity data presented include intercorrelations with other subtests and scales of the Stanford Reading First. No data are presented correlating scores on Stanford Reading First with other tests or with other predicted outcomes. Construct validity data show relationships among items to test scores, subtest to subtest scores, and expected increases with grade level placement. These data are within traditionally accepted values.

COMMENTARY. Earlier reviews (Carney, 2005; Morse, 2005) point out strengths and weaknesses of the Stanford 10 that apply to the parts of the Stanford 10 included in Stanford Reading First, because it is an edition of the Stanford 10. The history of the Stanford 10 and earlier versions provides a consistent body of knowledge regarding its use. Revised materials and formatting developed for the Stanford 10 are attractive, engaging, and provide useful organizational aids.

The Oral Fluency portion, specifically developed for the Stanford Reading First, appears to complement the multiple-choice portion. However, more information about the theory on which the subtests were developed and choices of item content, format, and number is needed so that users can make informed decisions about the match of the measure with educational goals. There is little development in the technical manual of the rationale for including the Oral Fluency portion.

The Oral Reading Fluency subtests, Speaking Vocabulary and Oral Reading Fluency, are scored using rubrics, an accepted method of scoring for the content. Interrater reliability showing consistency of users to score student performance according to the rubrics is not presented and was not available by request from the publisher. Sample responses with associated scores in the directions are not included but would be helpful.

The Stanford Reading First is intended to be a diagnostic tool to identify students at risk of not achieving at grade level. However, the Stanford Reading First has not proven to be a useful tool to educators for the purpose it was intended. Although the technical manual provides information about its careful development, the manual does not provide information about the validity or usefulness of the outcome categories: At Grade Level, Needs Additional Intervention, and Needs Substantial Intervention. Information is provided about how these categories were developed, but there is no information about how these outcomes correlate with other measures of reading achievement such as other published tests or even teachers' independent ratings of student reading achievement. Educators who use the instrument are left to judge whether the results actually help decisions regarding students' reading. The data do not indicate whether other means of identifying students who need intervention are as effective as using the Stanford Reading First.

SUMMARY. The Stanford Reading First is a promising edition of Stanford 10 for those interested in identifying students at risk of not achieving at grade level in reading because it provides national norms for a comprehensive assessment of reading skills in an engaging format that is not overly long. The multiple-choice portion can be administered in a group, and the Oral Fluency portion is individually administered. Currently, more technical data are needed for potential users to have more complete confidence in decisions made based on test result.

REVIEWER'S REFERENCES

Carney, R. N. (2005). [Review of the Stanford Achievement Test, Tenth Edition]. In R. A. Spies & B. S. Plake (Eds.), *The sixteenth mental measurements yearbook* (pp. 969-972). Lincoln, NE: Buros Institute of Mental Measurements.

Morse, D. T. (2005). [Review of the Stanford Achievement Test, Tenth Edition]. In R. A. Spies & B. S. Plake (Eds.), *The sixteenth mental measurements yearbook* (pp. 972-975). Lincoln, NE: Buros Institute of Mental Measurements.

Review of the Stanford Reading First by JEFFREY K. SMITH, Professor of Education, University of Otago, Dunedin, New Zealand:

DESCRIPTION AND DEVELOPMENT. The Stanford Reading First is designed to assess foundational reading skills and reading comprehension beginning in kindergarten through the first half of fourth grade. There are two components to the Stanford Reading First: a multiple-choice test that assesses recognition of sounds and words, vocabulary, and either listening or reading comprehension, and an oral fluency measure that assesses the speaking vocabulary and oral reading fluency of students. There are five levels of the measure available, corresponding to the beginning of kindergarten through the first half of fourth grade.

The measure is based on the 10th edition of the Stanford Achievement Tests (Stanford 10; 16:232). The multiple-choice portion of the test comes from items taken from the Stanford 10, whereas the oral fluency portion is new to the Stanford Reading First. The scores available are designed to correspond closely to the requirements of the federal No Child Left Behind Act. The Stanford Reading First provides the usual options for score reporting, including percentiles, stanines, NCEs, and scale scores. Also provided are Performance Levels, which indicate whether a student is at grade level, in need of moderate additional help, or in need of substantial additional help. These levels were determined through the use of an Angoff standard-setting procedure, although the developers then set the 20th percentile and the 40th percentile as cut points for these levels for all forms and levels of the tests, which calls into question the degree to which the Angoff procedure influenced the final determinations.

The multiple-choice tests consist of three-option multiple-choice items that assess word recognition skills, reading vocabulary, and either listening comprehension or reading comprehension. Word recognition skills begin with very rudimentary notions of letters and words at the kindergarten level, and move up to identifying compound words and word endings at the higher levels. Reading vocabulary ranges from calling simple words (at the kindergarten level) to identifying word meanings in context (at the higher levels). Listening comprehension is assessed at the kindergarten level of the test by reading simple stories to children and having them respond to questions. At the upper levels, students read stories and respond to questions.

The Oral Fluency portion of the Stanford Reading First assesses Oral Reading Fluency and what the developers call Speaking Vocabulary. The measures vary according to the level of the assessment. At the lowest level, Oral Reading Fluency is measured by having students call out letters and numbers. At higher levels, students call out words, then simple sentences, then read stories aloud. They are scored by teacher administrators according to a rubric. For Speaking Vocabulary, at the lower levels, students name objects in a picture and then make up a story about the picture. At the higher levels, they make up a story about a sequence of pictures. It is difficult to understand why this second portion of the measure is called "speaking vocabulary." Speaking Vocabulary may be a component of making up stories based on a picture or pictures, but it certainly would not appear to be the ability in its entirety.

TECHNICAL. An extensive technical manual accompanies the tests. The amount and quality of information presented varies considerably. There is ample information on topics such as the reliability of the tests, the performance of students in vertical equating studies, and correlations of the subscales across measures. The internal consistency reliabilities for the tests are quite high, in the .90s for all total scores and most of the subscores. On the other hand, there are no test-retest or parallel-form reliabilities presented, nor any studies of the reliability across raters for those parts of the test that require teachers to make judgments about scores. Furthermore, many of the technical aspects of the development of the measure are discussed, but the details are not presented. For example, there are no data from the standard-setting exercises, nor from the item bias research that was conducted.

Perhaps the most disturbing aspect of the technical manual is that there is little to no validity evidence presented for the tests. Just how much validity evidence is present depends on one's definition of what counts as validity evidence. There are correlations among subscales, which give an idea of the internal structure of the measures, but there is no information provided that would allow one to assess whether the tests measure what the developers contend that they measure. There are no studies that relate the scores to other measures of reading ability, nothing that ties the scores to teacher judgments of reading ability, nor any studies that show how well the tests perform in a longitudinal fashion. The technical manual has a two-page section on validity, but it does little but talk about validity in generalities and refer the reader to appendices that are primarily concerned with reliability issues. The lack of validity information found here is not different from what is found in many technical manuals for tests, but it is wanting nonetheless.

SUMMARY AND COMMENTARY. The Stanford Achievement Tests are a long-established element of American school testing. The Stanford Reading First is very traditional in its approach, which has strengths and weaknesses. On the positive side, much of the measure has been tested over the years and found to be quite usable by schools. On the other side of the equation, the measure leans heavily on traditional approaches to assessment, relying, for example, on the assumption that multiple-choice testing is the best way to assess reading and prereading skills in children as young as 5 years of age. The tests are quite straightforward, if somewhat detailed, to administer. They are presented attractively in full color, with easy-to-comprehend illustrations. Sample items provide clear examples for students to follow. On the Oral Fluency test, the teacher is required to score student performance based on a rubric. These scoring judgments are not complicated, but there are no exemplars presented for teachers to follow, nor is research presented on the ability of teachers to make these judgments.

Given the long history of the Stanford tests in use in American schools, and the straightforward and traditional nature of the measures, it is reasonable to conclude that the Stanford Reading First will provide highly useful measures of reading comprehension, as well as its foundational elements. In particular, the Stanford Reading First strives to present the user with an assessment that is in keeping with the dictates of the No Child Left Behind legislation, and it appears to be successful in this endeavor. But these conclusions are based on the history of the testing program and the appearance of the tests themselves. These are supported by technical data from a reliability perspective, but sadly not from a validity perspective. On that front, there is much work to be done before one can safely conclude that the Stanford Reading First is living up to its promise to assess the five essential components of reading as specified in No Child Left Behind. They *might*, but we do not have the evidence to conclude that they *do*.

[128]

Strong Interest Explorer.

Purpose: Self-scorable assessment intended to help individuals learn more about their interests to help them "define a career direction, select classes or activities," and/ or "choose a major or technical program."

Population: High school and community college students, or early career populations.

Publication Dates: 1933-2001.

Acronym: SIE.

Administration: Group.

Scores, 14: Working with Numbers, Health and Science, Music and Arts, Writing and Mass Communications, Cultural Relations, Helping Others, Teaching and Training, Law and Politics, Office and Project Management, Business/Sales/and Marketing, Working with Computers, Outdoor Environment/Plants & Animals, Construction and Engineering, Protective Services.

Price Data: Available from publisher.
Time: (8-10) minutes.
Comments: It is suggested the SIE be given in a classroom or group setting and led by a teacher or counselor; developed as a simplified alternative to the Strong Interest Inventory (18:129).
Author: Judy Chartrand.
Publisher: CPP, Inc.

Review of the Strong Interest Explorer by BERT A. GOLDMAN, Professor Emeritus, University of North Carolina Greensboro, Greensboro, NC:

DESCRIPTION. The Strong Interest Explorer (SIE) provides an ipsative, self-scorable alternative to the Strong Interest Inventory (SII; 18:129) in which interests in 14 basic areas are measured for high school, community college, and early career populations. This 140-item instrument takes about 8–10 minutes to complete. Each of the 140 items identifies a job, a school subject, or an activity beside which the respondent places an X if that item is liked or the item is left blank to indicate that it is disliked. The 140 items are arranged in 14 columns, each containing 10 items. Each of the 14 columns represents a different area of interest. These 14 areas of interest are grouped under six broader areas of interest such as Investigative, Artistic, Social, Enterprising, Conventional, and Realistic, which are the same six General Occupational themes used in the SII. Two of these six General Occupational Themes, Social and Realistic, are each composed of 3 of the 14 interest areas. The remaining four General Occupational Themes are each composed of 2 of the 14 interest areas. Scoring of the SIE is accomplished by counting the number of X responses for each of the 14 basic areas and recording them on a 1 to 10 vertically placed scale under each of their related General Occupational Themes. Thus, at a glance, respondents can see where their highest interests lie. The next step invites respondents to record their 14 areas of interest scores on the pages containing the corresponding descriptions of each of these 14 interest areas. Thus, for each of the 14 interest areas, there is a brief description of what people do who work in that area and the college majors, technical training programs, occupations, and activities that relate to that interest area. Respondents are then asked to circle any of these descriptors about which they would like more information. Finally, for those areas of interest in which respondents indicate a desire for more information, several resources are suggested. The instrument is intended to be administered by a teacher or counselor in a classroom or group setting.

DEVELOPMENT. Initially, items were selected from the 317 items of the 1994 SII to provide information that did not appear to make a difference for ethnic groups. Added to these items were those from the 2002 revised SII and a pool of new items written by the CPP research staff. Feedback on this pool of items concerning face validity and reading level was obtained from 25 local high school students. A group of experts also reviewed these items. This feedback led to development of a 181-item form which was administered to 321 freshmen (as always, with some missing data) at a midwestern university. This initial set of items was narrowed based upon the feedback from 321 freshmen who completed the form and of whom 55% were female and 45% were male (note: Information provided by the CPP Research Department has the gender percentages reversed) and 65% were Caucasian with the remaining 35% sparsely spread among various ethnicities.

The narrowed version consisted of 154 items administered to 343 high school students of whom 70% were female and 30% were male. Also, 84% were Caucasian and the remaining 16% were sparsely spread among various ethnicities. This version was then narrowed to a final 140-item version containing 93 original items from the 1994 and 2002 SII, 12 modified items from these two SII instruments, and 35 new items written by the CPP research staff.

TECHNICAL.

Three samples were employed to determine internal consistency. Of the three samples, one sample was also used to determine one aspect of validity, and two segments of that same sample were employed to determine two additional forms of validity. Given the ipsative nature of the instrument, individuals compare their interests across the 14 basic interest scales rather than compare their interests with a norm group.

A technical report states that the SIE "is designed to provide students and early career explorers with an estimate of their interests" (p. 1). The manual translates this intended population to mean high school and community college students. However, there is no description of what is meant by early career populations. High school students and freshman college students were used in conducting item selection and for determining internal consistency. Employed adults were also used to compile a measure of internal consistency and they were the only group used to determine 6-week test-retest reliability and validity of the SIE. As to what is meant by employed adults, not the slightest clue is given. There is no information concerning their age, gender, ethnicity, or type of employment.

Reliability. Reliability of the SIE was determined by the relatedness of all items across the 14 basic interest scales (internal consistency) over each of the three samples (i.e., high school students, college freshmen, and employed adults). Across the three samples, 90% of the alphas were at least .80 with three at .90 and one as low as .69. In addition to providing internal consistency, test-retest stability over a 6-week period of time was also provided. However, this measure of stability was determined using only the employed adult sample. All of the correlation coefficients across the 14 basic interest scales were at least .70, with 5 at least .80. However, because the SIE is intended for use with high school students and college students, it is of considerable value to know how stable, over time, are the interests of these target groups rather than that of employed adults for whom the instrument was not specifically designed.

Validity. All validity data were compiled using the employed adult sample from which reliability data were also collected. Validity was examined in three ways (i.e., correlation of SIE scores with: self-expressed interests, current type of work, and type of work to which the employed adult would like to switch). The highest correlations were obtained between the SIE scores and the self-expressed interests, which ranged from .41 (Helping Others) to .68 (Working with Numbers) with a mean correlation of .55 across the 14 basic interest areas. These correlations are positive, but not as high as one might expect given that respondents were asked to indicate their interests on the SIE followed by asking them on a supplemental questionnaire to indicate in which of the 14 basic interest areas they were interested. Also, this reviewer questions the use of employed adults. Why not perform the same validity check using high school students and college freshmen as they comprise the target group for whom the SIE is intended, rather than employed adults?

The other two attempts to provide validity information also used the sample of employed adults. They were asked to write the type of work they do and the type of work they would like if they switched careers. A system was devised for coding both sets of responses so that they could be correlated with the basic interest scores. Due to missing data there were 11 correlations instead of 14 ranging from -.05 to .45 between type of work and SIE scores of which two were significant at $p < .05$ and four significant at $p < .01$. Also, due to missing data there were 11 correlations instead of 14 ranging from -.15 to .34 between type of work they would like if they switched careers and SIE scores of which three were significant at $p < .05$ and one was significant at $p < .01$. However, three correlations were negative ranging from -.06 to -.15. Thus, the attempt to show SIE validity by correlating one's type of work with SIE scores is not very convincing when only 6 of the 14 basic interest scales produced significant correlations. Much less convincing were the data to show SIE validity by correlating SIE scores with type of work if one's career were switched. These data were much less convincing because only 4 of the 14 basic interest scales produced significant correlations along with 3 negative correlations. Instead of producing data from these latter two unconvincing attempts to establish validity using employed adults, why not use a longitudinal study to show correlations between SIE scores of the target groups for whom the instrument is intended and their eventual majors and the work entered by the non-college-bound segment of the target group?

COMMENTARY. The notion of a simplified interest inventory that requires only 8 to 10 minutes of response time, is self-scorable, and is ipsative whereby individuals compare their own 14 interest scores instead of employing normative data with which to compare, sounds very useful, especially because it should be administered under the guidance of an instructor or counselor. Reliability data collected from high school students and college freshmen revealed good internal consistency. In addition, 6-weeks test-retest reliability data are also good; however, these data were collected from employed adults instead of from a target group of high school students and college freshmen. Validity data consisting of correlations between responses to the SIE and expressed interest, although good, as expected, were not determined from target group high school students and college students. The other two sources of validity data (i.e., correlations of SIE scores with current type work and with preferred work pending a career switch) are meager at best, and perhaps should be substituted for data involving what target group respondents ultimately select as their college majors or type of work, instead of using nontarget samples of employed adults.

SUMMARY. If an instructor or counselor working with high school students, college students, or other similar age groups has need to administer a self-scorable, brief, time-consuming instrument that measures current interest in 14 simplified basic interest areas of these target groups, then perhaps the SIE will be of use. However, the professionals using the instrument should be aware of the instrument's good internal consistency and good 6-week test-retest reliability, but that these data were collected from another unrelated target group, and meager validity data were also collected from an unrelated target group. On the other hand, in the opinion of this reviewer, perhaps these instructors or counselors might be better advised to use the Strong Interest Inventory (18:129) upon which the SIE is based, or use such instruments as the Kuder Career Search (T7:1379) or the Kuder Skills Assessment (T7:1382).

Review of the Strong Interest Explorer by EUGENE P. SHEEHAN, Dean, College of Education and Behavioral Sciences, University of Northern Colorado, Greeley, CO:

DESCRIPTION. Intended for use by students and early career explorers, the Strong Interest Explorer (SIE) is designed to provide a broad assessment of vocational interests and how these interests relate to educational programs, careers, and extracurricular and service learning pursuits. The SIE is very easy to administer. Instructions are clear and the vocabulary should be comprehensible to a high school student or even a middle school student. Certainly students at community colleges should find the instrument easy to complete.

The SIE follows a logical order. Respondents first complete a series of 140 items pertaining to jobs (e.g., sales manager, firefighter), school subjects (e.g., English composition, environmental science), and activities (e.g., making a speech, woodworking) in which they indicate whether, regardless of ability or training, they would like the item. Respondents next score their own results by counting and totaling the number of preferences they made in each of 14 columns. They then graph each of the 14 scores into columns representing basic and self-descriptive interest scales (e.g., Enterprising: Business, Sales, and Marketing). Thus the respondents can easily see not only their absolute level of interest in the 14 areas, they can also readily discern their relative interests across the 14 scales. Respondents can learn more about their preferences by reading a general summary of the areas and by reviewing lists of college majors and technical training programs, occupations, and activities (jobs, extracurricular, or volunteer activities). Important for an interest inventory, the final section deals with "Next Steps," which guides respondents in how to gather more information about their interests. Respondents are assisted through a series of steps from identifying areas in which they have an interest to listing classes, schools, and occupations that would help advance their career exploration. Included in these next steps is information about where one can gather more data about jobs, such as library and web resources. Good suggestions regarding other ways to collect career information from job incumbents are provided: informational interviews, job shadowing, and internships. Respondents will derive the most value from this instrument if they take it while under the guidance of a career professional.

The authors indicate it should take no more than about 8 to 10 minutes to complete the 140 preference items. However, respondents could and should devote a good deal of additional time to the development of a deeper understanding of their interests. Indeed, the instrument should foster a lengthy series of follow-up steps in career exploration.

DEVELOPMENT. In a technical report describing the development of the SIE, the authors indicate the instrument was developed as a variant of the Strong Interest Inventory (SII) designed for early career explorers. They list several differences between the two instruments including: more basic items in the SIE, fewer number of interest scales in the SIE, the ipsative nature of the SIE, specific integration with educational and occupational information in the SIE, and that the SIE is self-scored.

Items from the SII served as the basis for the SIE. A series of factor analyses, item revisions and rewriting, including reviews by high school students, resulted in the current version of the SIE. This version does contain some items from previous versions of the SII.

The procedures used in instrument development are appropriate for the instrument. The authors analyzed several iterations of the instrument prior to the development of the final version.

Especially noteworthy is the effort to incorporate high school students into the procedures to develop the SIE.

TECHNICAL. As mentioned, the SIE is based on analyses using high school students: 343 students (70% female and 84% Caucasian) comprised the sample from which the final instrument was derived. Given the ipsative nature of the instrument, no normative data are provided nor, in the opinion of this reviewer, needed.

The psychometrics behind the SIE are solid. The authors provide information on two types of reliability: internal consistency and test-retest. Internal consistency reliability was assessed to be .80 or higher for almost all scales across samples of college students, high school students, and employed adults. Such good reliability coefficients are important because the scales are meant to assess focused constructs.

Measures of test-retest reliability are also strong. Using a sample of 108 employed adults who took the SIE twice over a 6-week period the test-retest reliability was found to be a minimum of .70.

To measure validity, correlations between respondents' scores on the basic interest scale scores and their self-expressed interest in each of these areas was computed and found to be an average of .55. Further, there was a significant relationship between scores on the basic interest scales and both actual areas of work and areas in which respondents indicated they would like to work were they to change employment. The SIE also has strong face validity–those completing the instrument will be in no doubt as to its purpose.

COMMENTARY. The SIE is an easy instrument to administer and one that provides a good entryway into the area of career exploration. Its main strengths lie in the straightforward manner in which it leads respondents to concrete steps they can take to identify their career interests and then to follow up on those interests. That it is self-scoring means respondents can take the SIE and obtain immediate feedback on their scores. Its format (ease of administration and scoring, information on careers, and specific suggestions provided about next steps) makes the SIE especially appropriate for those in the preliminary stages of career exploration. For its purposes, the SIE is psychometrically sound: appropriate procedures and samples were used in its development and it has good reliability and some evidence of validity.

The instrument relies on 140 career-focused items to which respondents express a preference. In some ways these items are fairly traditional. An updated version of the SIE should include examples of new career options such as jobs using technology and new career prospects in the sciences that rely on multidisciplinary knowledge.

SUMMARY. Based on the SII, the SIE is an interest inventory designed for use by those in the early stages of career exploration. The SIE is self-scoring and easy to administer. The instrument certainly affords high school and community college students with a logical entry to the career exploration process and it provides specific suggestions regarding future steps in the vocational identification process. The psychometric data underlying the SIE are robust: Measures of reliability and validity demonstrate the SIE has internal and temporal consistency and measures what it is purported to measure.

[129]

Strong Interest Inventory [Newly Revised].

Purpose: Intended to generate an in-depth assessment of "interests among a broad range of occupations, work and leisure activities, and educational subjects"... "to help individuals match their interests with occupational, educational, and leisure pursuits that are compatible with those interests."

Population: Ages 16 and over.

Publication Dates: 1927-2005.

Administration: Group.

Scores, 290: 6 General Occupational Themes: Realistic, Investigative, Artistic, Social, Enterprising, Conventional; 30 Basic Interest Scales: Realistic (Mechanics & Construction, Computer Hardware & Electronics, Military, Protective Services, Nature & Agriculture, Athletics), Investigative (Science, Research, Medical Science, Mathematics), Artistic (Visual Arts & Design, Performing Arts, Writing & Mass Communication, Culinary Arts), Social (Counseling & Helping, Teaching & Education, Human Resources & Training, Social Sciences, Religion & Spirituality, Healthcare Services), Enterprising (Marketing & Advertising, Sales, Entrepreneurship, Politics & Public Speaking, Law), Conventional (Office Management, Taxes & Accounting, Programming & Information Systems, Finance & Investing); 244 Occupational Scales: Accountant (f, m), Actuary (f, m), Administrative Assistant (f, m), Advertising Account Manager (f, m), Architect (f, m), Art Teacher (f, m), Artist (f, m), Athletic Trainer (f, m), Attorney (f, m), Automobile Mechanic (f, m), Banker (f, m), Biologist (f, m), Bookkeeper (f, m), Broadcast Journalist (f, m), Business Education Teacher (f, m),

Buyer (f, m), Carpenter (f, m), Chef (f, m), Chemist (f, m), Chiropractor (f, m), College Instructor (f, m), Community Service Director (f, m), Computer & IS Manager (f, m), Computer Scientist (f, m), Computer Systems Analyst (f, m), Corporate Trainer (f, m), Cosmetologist (f, m), Credit Manager (f, m), Dentist (f, m), Dietitian (f, m), Editor (f, m), Elected Public Official (f, m), Electrician (f, m), Elementary School Teacher (f, m), Emergency Medical Technician (f, m), Engineer (f, m), Engineering Technician (f, m), English Teacher (f, m), ESL Instructor (f, m), Farmer/Rancher (f, m), Financial Analyst (f, m), Financial Manager (f, m), Firefighter (f, m), Flight Attendant (f, m), Florist (f, m), Food Service Manager (f, m), Foreign Language Teacher (f, m), Forester (f, m), Geographer (f, m), Geologist (f, m), Graphic Designer (f, m), Health Information Specialist (f, m), Horticulturist (f, m), Housekeeping/Maintenance Manager (f, m), Human Resources Manager (f, m), Interior Designer (f, m), Investments Manager (f, m), Landscape/Grounds Manager (f, m), Law Enforcement Officer (f, m), Librarian (f, m), Licensed Practical Nurse (f, m), Life Insurance Agent (f, m), Marketing Manager (f, m), Mathematician (f, m), Mathematics Teacher (f, m), Medical Illustrator (f, m), Medical Technician (f, m), Medical Technologist (f, m), Military Enlisted (f, m), Military Officer (f, m), Minister (f, m), Musician (f, m), Network Administrator (f, m), Nursing Home Administrator (f, m), Occupational Therapist (f, m), Operations Manager (f, m), Optician (f, m), Optometrist (f, m), Paralegal (f, m), Parks & Recreation Manager (f, m), Pharmacist (f, m), Photographer (f, m), Physical Education Teacher (f, m), Physical Therapist (f, m), Physician (f, m), Physicist (f, m), Production Worker (f, m), Psychologist (f, m), Public Administrator (f, m), Public Relations Director (f, m), Purchasing Agent (f, m), R&D Manager (f, m), Radiologic Technologist (f, m), Realtor (f, m), Recreation Therapist (f, m), Registered Nurse (f, m), Rehabilitation Counselor (f, m), Reporter (f, m), Respiratory Therapist (f, m), Restaurant Manager (f, m), Retail Sales Manager (f, m), Retail Sales Representative (f, m), Sales Manager (f, m), School Administrator (f, m), School Counselor (f, m), Science Teacher (f, m), Social Science Teacher (f, m), Social Worker (f, m), Sociologist (f, m), Software Developer (f, m), Special Education Teacher (f, m), Speech Pathologist (f, m), Technical Sales Representative (f, m), Technical Support Specialist (f, m), Technical Writer (f, m), Top Executive (f, m), Translator (f, m), Travel Consultant (f, m), University Professor (f, m), Urban & Regional Planner (f, m), Veterinarian (f, m), Vocational Agriculture Teacher (f, m); 5 Personal Style Scales: Work Style, Learning Environment, Leadership Style, Risk Taking, Team Orientation; 9 Administrative Indexes: Total Percentage, Occupations, Subject Areas, Activities, Leisure Activities, People, Your Characteristics, Total Response Index, Typicality Index.

Price Data, 2008: $112 per 10 prepaid profile combined item booklet/answer sheets; $69.50 per technical manual (2005, 286 pages); $29.50 per user's guide (2005, 72 pages); $89 per technical manual (2005, 276 pages) and users guide set; $11.20 per profile administration; $17.60 per Profile and Newly Revised Interpretive Report.
Time: (40-50) minutes.
Authors: David A. C. Donnay, Michael L. Morris, Nancy A. Schaubhut, and Richard C. Thompson; Judith Grutter and Allen L. Hammer (user's guide).
Publisher: CPP, Inc.
Cross References: For reviews by Kevin R. Kelly and Eugene P. Sheehan of the 1994 Edition, see 15:248; see also T5:1790 (19 references); for reviews by John Christian Busch and by Blaine R. Worthen and Perry Sailor of the Fourth Edition, see 12:374 (43 references); see also T4:2581 (64 references); for reviews by Wilbur L. Layton and Bert W. Westbrook, see 9:1195 (17 references); see also T3:2318 (99 references); for reviews by John O. Crites, Robert H. Dolliver, Patricia W. Lunneborg, and excerpted reviews by Richard W. Johnson, David P. Campbell, and Jean C. Steinhauer, see 8:1023 (289 references, these references are for SVIB-M, SBIV-W, and SCII). For references on the Strong Vocational Interest Blank For Men, see T2:2212 (133 references); for reviews by Martin R. Katz and Charles J. Krauskopf and excerpted reviews by David P. Campbell and John W. M. Rothney, see 7:1036 (485 references); for reviews by Alexander W. Astin and Edward J. Furst, see 6:1070 (189 references); see also 5:868 (153 references); for reviews by Edward S. Bordin and Elmer D. Hinckley, see 4:747 (98 references): see also 3:647 (102 references); for reviews by Harold D. Carter, John G. Darley, and N. W. Morton, see 2:1680 (71 references); for a review by John G. Darley, see 1:1178. For references on the Strong Vocational Interest Blank For Women, see T2:2213 (30 references); for reviews by Dorothy M. Clendenen and Barbara A. Kirk, see 7:1037 (92 references); see also 6:1071 (12 references) and 5:869 (19 references); for a review by Gwendolen Schneidler Dickson, see 3:649 (38 references); for a review by Ruth Strang, see 2:1681 (10 references); for a review by John G. Darley, see 1:1179.

Review of the Strong Interest Inventory [Newly Revised] by KEVIN R. KELLY, Head, Department of Educational Studies, Purdue University, West Lafayette, IN:

[Editor's Note: This reviewer also reviewed the Strong Interest Inventory in 2003 in *The Fifteenth Mental Measurements Yearbook.* Because many of his perceptions and evaluations of that instrument appear largely similar to those of this current version of the Strong Interest Inventory, he has quoted from his previous review numerous times throughout the review. We nevertheless consider the current review as an objective review of the instrument.]

DESCRIPTION. The Strong Interest Inventory [Newly Revised] (Strong) is a 291-item interest inventory designed for use by high school and college students and adults. The five main uses of the Strong are to: Aid educational and career decision making, structure career assessment and counseling, stimulate client self-exploration, assist in personnel decisions, and explore reasons for job dissatisfaction. The reading level is between eighth- and ninth-grade levels; administration time is 35–40 minutes. Respondents report their preferences and perceptions in six sections: Occupations, Subject Areas, Activities, Leisure Activities, People, and Your Characteristics (describing the respondent's characteristics).

The Strong yields five types of results. The six General Occupational Themes (GOTs) are homogeneous scales representing the interests from Holland's hexagonal model: Realistic, Investigative, Artistic, Social, Enterprising, and Conventional. The GOT results are reported to the test-taker in a table describing the interests, work activities, potential skills, and values associated with each theme. The GOT standard scores are displayed with bar graphs with descriptive labels ranging from "*Very Little*" to "*Very High*."

The Basic Interest Scales (BISs) are also homogeneous interest scales; however, they measure more specific interests than the GOTs. For example, Medical Science is a BIS within the Investigative GOT. The top 5 and bottom 3 BISs are reported for each respondent, followed by a section with a bar graph and standard score for each of the 30 BISs within its corresponding GOT area.

There are 244 Occupational Scales (OSs), which reflect the similarity of the test taker's interests to those of satisfied job incumbents in 122 occupations. Each of the scales differs for male and female populations. The OSs are empirically derived from the response profiles of occupational criterion groups. High OS scores indicate that the test taker shares both the likes and dislikes of these criterion groups. The Strong Profile lists the top 10 and bottom 3 OSs; the one-, two-, or three-letter Holland code is reported in parentheses following each OS. The following pages include a bar graph, descriptive label (similar-midrange-dissimilar), and standard score for each OS within its corresponding GOT interest area. For example, the Accountant OS is displayed within the Conventional GOT area. The OSs are listed in rank order from "most similar" to "most dissimilar" within each of the six GOT interest areas. The OS results are based on comparison to same-sex criterion groups.

There are five Personal Style Scales (PSSs): Work Style, Learning Environment, Leadership Style, Risk Taking, and Team Orientation. The PSS results are displayed on graphs anchored by sets of bipolar characteristics. For example, the Work Style score will fall on a continuum between preference for "working alone" and "working with people."

In addition to the GOT, BIS, OS, and PSS components of the score interpretation is a Profile Summary that includes top GOT, BIS, and OS interests and PSS preferences. A final section of the report provides a table with item response percentages for each of the six sections of the instrument. The table also includes item response total, items omitted, and a typicality index (described briefly below); these indices can be used to appraise the validity of the Strong profile.

In addition to the basic Strong Profile, five other report formats are available. These reports for high school and college students incorporate age-appropriate exploration activities as well as internship and job information related to interest results.

Changes in the Strong Interest Inventory [Newly Revised]. Several revisions were made to the 2004 Strong. Of the original 317 items, 193 were retained and 98 new or adapted items were added for a total of 291 items. The previous "Like-Indifferent-Dislike" response option was expanded to five options including "Strongly Like" and "Strongly Dislike."

For the GOTs, computer hardware items were included in the Realistic Theme and computer software items were added to the Conventional Theme items. The BISs were extensively revised. Ten new BISs were added (e.g., Protective Services). The content of four BISs was changed. For example, a combined Nature & Agriculture BIS was formed based on the previous separate Nature and Agriculture scales. Four BISs were also eliminated. Finally, updated names were adopted for 13 scales. For example, Medical Service is now Healthcare Services. There were several changes to the OSs. The new Strong has 244 OSs, compared to 211 in the 1994 version, with separate scoring routines for 122 OSs for women and men. Efforts were made to reduce the number of items for each OS.

Regarding the PSSs, a Team Orientation scale was added. Also, the Risk Taking/Adventure scale title was changed to Risk Taking.

Finally, there were other changes to the Administrative Indexes. The previous Total Response Index was replaced by counts of items completed and omitted. The Infrequent Responses Index was replaced by the Typicality Index, which is "based on consistency of response to 24 item pairs" (manual, p. 4).

DEVELOPMENT. The Strong represents two interest measurement traditions: Empirically developed, heterogeneous and theoretically developed, homogeneous scales. The original Strong Vocational Interest Blank scales differentiated criterion occupational groups from people in general. The OS results are based on the likes and dislikes of occupational criterion groups. Empirically derived interest scales are powerful because a respondent can score similarly to occupational groups that he or she had not "considered previously as career alternatives. However, respondents can be confused as to why they score 'similar' to ... Ministers, [for example,] because there are numerous ways that one can score high–or low–on any given ... scale" (Kelly, 2003; p. 895).

This problem was addressed by introduction of the homogeneous BISs in 1968. Homogeneous scales, which represent responses to items with similar content, are easily understood. A respondent scoring similarly to the Minister OS can see the link to a high score on the Religious & Spirituality BIS. "The homogeneous GOTs were incorporated into the Strong Profile in 1974 to ... organize the reporting of the BIS and OS results. The [Strong combines] the immediacy of criterion-group scaling and the transparency of homogeneous scaling" (Kelly, 2003; p. 895).

TECHNICAL.

Standardization. The test developers constituted a new General Reresentative Sample (GRS) for the 2004 Strong. The 2004 GRS consists of 1,125 women and 1,125 men and represents a total of 373 occupations.

The female GRS had the following racial/ethnic composition: 68.3% Caucasian, 10.3% African American, 6.4% Multiethnic, 6.2% Latina/Hispanic, 4.3% Asian American or Asian, and 3% Other (broken down further in the manual). For men, the composition was: 76.2% Caucasian, 6.5% Multiethnic, 4.4% African American, 3.8% Latino/Hispanic, 2.4% Indian, 2.2% Asian American or Asian, and 2.3% Other (again, broken down in the manual). The average GRS member age was 35.46; average time employed in current occupation was 4.63 years.

Additional volunteers were solicited to form new OSs for the 2004 Strong. The women in these new occupational samples had the following racial/ethnic composition: 81.5% Caucasian, 6.1% Multiethnic, 3.1% African American, 1.7% Asian American or Asian, 1.1% Latina/Hispanic, and 1.4% Other. For men, the composition was: 76.4% Caucasian, 4.9% Multiethnic, 2.3% African American, 2.3% Asian American or Asian, 1.8% Latino/Hispanic, 1.6% Indian, and .9% Other. Average age for the occupational samples was 43.21. There were fewer members of racial and ethnic groups in these occupational samples than in the GRS. Occupational sample members tended to be employed longer in their current position, more satisfied with their work, and more highly educated than GRS members.

Reliability. Coefficient alphas for the GOT, BIS, and PSS scales were calculated using the GRS of 2,250 women and men. The alpha coefficients for the GOTs were in the range of .90–.95. Short-interval (2–7 months) test-retest reliability coefficients were .84–.89 with a median of .86. The median long-interval (8–23-month) test-retest reliability for the GOTs was .84. Alpha coefficients for the BISs were in the range of .80–.92 with a median of .87. Short-interval test-retest coefficients were between .77–.93 with a median of .85–.86.; long-interval test-retest coefficients ranged from .74–.90 with a median of .83–.84. Alpha coefficients for the OSs were not reported. The OS test-retest reliability coefficients were in the range of .71–.93 with a median of .86. For the PSSs, alpha coefficients were in the range of .82–.87. Short-interval test-retest reliability coefficients were between .77–.90 with a median of .89; long-interval test-retest reliability coefficients were .70–.91 with a median of .86. In general, in the opinion of this reviewer, the reliability properties of the Strong scales are impressive.

Validity. There are two forms of convergent and discriminant validity evidence for the GOTs. First, GOTs were correlated with OSs for women and men in the GRS. Predictable patterns were apparent. For example, the female and male Engineering Technician OSs had the highest correlations with Realistic GOT; female and male Buyer OSs had their lowest correlations with Realistic GOT. A similar pattern of results was attained for the other five GOTs. Second, a sample of 879 college students completed the 2004 Strong; they were categorized as belonging to one of 75 college majors. Average GOT scale scores were calculated for each of these 75 major groups; rank-ordered means of these college major groups were arrayed within each of the six GOT areas. Results again corresponded highly with expectations. For example, female Literature majors had the highest Artistic GOT scores. The GOT-OS correlations and GOT profiles of educational majors appeared highly consistent with expectations based on Holland's (1997) theory. The same methods were used to document the concurrent validity of the 30 BISs. These results are also consistent with theoretical expectations.

"The concurrent validity of the OSs was evaluated by calculating the Tilton Overlap, which is the percentage of OS scores in an occupational criterion group ... matched by scores in the GRS distribution. Low overlap indicates that a criterion group is highly distinct from the GRS" (Kelley, 2003; p. 896). The lowest overlap percentage was 17% for female Athletic Trainer and male Medical Illustrator; the interest profiles of these occupational groups were most distinct from the GRS profile. The highest overlap was 62% for female Administrative Assistant and Sales Manager and male Credit Manager, Maintenance Manager, Parks and Recreation Manager, and Nursing Home Administrator. The interest profiles of these occupational groups overlap considerably with the GRS interest profile. The median overlap for the OSs was 44%, indicating a difference of approximately 1.5 standard deviations between the means of the OS criterion groups and the GRS. The OSs appear to represent unique interest profiles of distinct occupational groups.

Concurrent validity is also reflected in the correlations of the OSs within their respective GOTs. For women, the OS correlations within themes were in the range of .39–.57 with a median of .41; for men the range was .27–.58 with a median of .52. These OS correlations within theme follow the predicted pattern. The manual includes a detailed discussion of six predictive validity studies using previous versions of the OSs. There is a moderate-to-excellent correspondence between OSs and subsequent occupational selections. Overall, this evidence constitutes strong support for the validity of the OSs.

The validity of the PSSs was addressed by examining correlations with the GOTs and BISs. The correlations were largely in accord with expectations. For example, Risk Taking was most highly correlated with the Realistic GOT (.71 for women, .68 for men) and Protective Services BIS (.73 for women, .71 for men). Correlations between the PSSs and OSs for the GRS also were examined. The overall pattern of results also was consistent with expectations. For example, the Leadership Style PSS was most strongly correlated with the Elected Public Official OS for women and Operations Manager OS for men. The PSS score distributions of the educational major groups also were in the predicted direction. There was no mention of predictive validity findings for the PSSs.

COMMENTARY. This reviewer believes that the Strong has eight distinct strengths. "First, it provides ... empirical and homogeneous [interest] scale results in an attractive profile. Second, the GOTs represent Holland's hexagonal model better than other popular interest measures (Rounds, 1995). Third, there are no significant differences in the structures of female and male GOTs (Anderson, Tracey, & Rounds, 1997). Fourth, the circular order of the six GOTs [Realistic, Investigative, Artistic, Social, Enterprising, and Conventional] holds for Caucasian, African American, Asian American, and Latino/a women and men" (Day & Rounds, 1998; Day, Rounds, & Swaney, 1998; Fouad, Harmon, & Borgen, 1997; Kelley, 2003, p. 897). Fifth, the updates of the BISs and OSs have maintained the currency and relevance of the instrument. Sixth, the Total Response and Typicality indices enable counselors to interpret profiles accurately. Item Response Percentages provide insight into confusing results. Seventh, the profile encourages users to reference the O*NET to attain complete information regarding the Occupational Scales. Finally, the manual provides extensive technical information and valuable suggestions for interpretation of the Strong.

The Strong also has three weaknesses. First, criterion group data for 104 (43%) of the 244 OSs were collected 25 or more years ago; these OS scores are based on response profiles that may not adequately represent the interests of contemporary job incumbents. For example, the female University Professor criterion group was sampled in 1972 and only 77% of this group had completed a doctorate. It might seem plausible that the characteristics of female university professors have changed over the last 37 years. There is a pressing need for the criterion groups to be updated.

Second, some racial and ethnic group members were not adequately represented in the 2004 GRS, although these are the most broadly representative norm samples to date for this long-standing instrument. Percentages of Africans, Asians (males only), Native Americans, and Latinos/Latinas were underrepresented. There was a similar problem in the new occupational samples. The Strong GRS and new occupational samples do not appear to represent the racial and ethnic diversity of this country. To be fair, it should be acknowledged that the test developers were challenged to find experienced respondents engaged in typical occupational tasks who were satisfied in their work. However, this realistic and operational concern does not diminish the responsibility of test developers to constitute a norm group that reflects the general population.

Third, the manual does not specify the response percentages attained in comprising the occupational samples. It is not clear, for example, how many potential respondents were solicited to attain the final occupational samples. Further, no evidence was presented to describe how these respondents compared to members of their respective occupational groups.

CONCLUSIONS AND RECOMMENDATIONS. The Strong is the best interest assessment available for career counselors. It has many impressive psychometric properties. The Strong has been demonstrated to be highly valid for women and men as well as for various racial and ethnic groups. It provides an impressive and comprehensive profile of interests. This reviewer recommends use of the Strong without reservation.

REVIEWER'S REFERENCES

Anderson, M. Z., Tracey, T. J. G., & Rounds, J. (1997). Examining the invariance of Holland's vocational interest model across gender. *Journal of Vocational Behavior, 50,* 349-364.

Day, S. X., & Rounds, J. (1998). Universality of vocational interest structure among racial and ethnic minorities. *American Psychologist, 53,* 728-736.

Day, S. X., Rounds, J., & Swaney, K. (1998). The structure of vocational interests for diverse racial-ethnic groups. *Psychological Science, 9,* 40-44.

Fouad, N. A., Harmon, L. W., & Borgen, F. H. (1997). Structure of interests in employed male and female members of U.S. racial-ethnic minority and nonminority groups. *Journal of Counseling Psychology, 44,* 339-345.

Holland, J. L. (1997). *Making vocational choices: A theory of vocational personalities and work environments* (3rd ed.). Odessa, FL: Psychological Assessment Resources.

Kelly, K. R. (2003). [Review of the Strong Interest Inventory [1994].] In B. S. Plake, J. C. Impara, & R. A. Spies (Eds.), *The fifteenth mental measurements yearbook* (pp. 894–897). Lincoln, NE: Buros Institute of Mental Measurements.

Rounds, J. (1995). Vocational interests: Evaluating structural hypotheses. In D. J. Lubinski & R. V. Dawis (Eds.), *Assessing individual differences in human behavior: New concepts, methods, and findings* (pp. 177-232). Palo Alto, CA: Davies-Black.

Review of the Strong Interest Inventory [Newly Revised] by NEETA KANTAMNENI, Assistant Professor, and MICHAEL J. SCHEEL, Associate Professor, University of Nebraska-Lincoln, Lincoln, NE:

DESCRIPTION. The Strong Interest Inventory [Newly Revised] (Strong) is an advanced, highly developed inventory that assesses career interests. The purpose of the Strong is to provide individuals with information about themselves and their preferences in order to help them make career decisions; it is intended to match individuals' interests with occupational/educational activities. The Strong is primarily used in educational settings, although it can be used successfully in a range of other settings.

The Strong is composed of six sections for a total of 291 items. A 5-point Likert-type response scale ranging from *Strongly Like* to *Strongly Dislike* is used. Instructions direct respondents to indicate how they feel about engaging in certain kinds of work, subject areas, activities, and leisure activities as well as working with certain types of people.

The Strong provides test takers with several types of information including: (a) their scores on six General Occupation Themes (GOTs) that reflect their overall work/career interests, (b) scores on 30 Basic Interest Scales (BISs) representing the consistency of their interests in 30 specific content areas, (c) scores on 122 Occupational Scales (OSs) reporting the similarity between their interests and interests of people who are employed and are presumably satisfied in specific occupations (because they remain in those occupations), and (d) scores on five Personal Style Scales (PSSs) that represent how they like to learn, work, lead, take risks, and work within teams. Additionally, the Strong provides information about inconsistent and unusual response sets.

TEST DEVELOPMENT. The Strong relates the interest patterns of test takers to the patterns of people working and who might be seen as satisfied in various occupations to determine their career interests; this comparison allows for an understanding of one's career interests. The Strong compares test takers' scores to members from the General Representative Sample, which acts as a normative group. In order to compile interest scales, the Strong examines how closely a test taker resembles the interests of individuals within the General Representative Sample.

Items for the GOTs were created to measure six broad dimensions of interests postulated in

Holland's theory (1973) as *Realistic, Investigative, Artistic, Social, Enterprising, and Conventional* interests. The GOTs provide a complete overview of career interests and occupational orientation. They were developed by selecting approximately 20 items to represent each interest theme based on the descriptions provided in Holland's theory. After being selected, intercorrelations among items, statistical evidence regarding the popularity of items, and item-scale correlations were used to choose items that contributed most to the homogeneity of the scale items.

The items for the 30 Basic Interest Scales were developed using the statistical method of clustering. Initial BIS dimensions were identified through factor analysis. Items were then based on intercorrelations and item content. The items are clustered together because individuals who respond to these questions tend to respond similarly to all of the items, reflecting a similar activity interest. The Occupational Scales were developed by identifying 12 to 45 items for each scale that differentiate the likes and dislikes of individuals in various occupations from the general population. The OSs were normed on a criterion group of people employed within each occupation; these criterion groups were created using the profiles of individuals within specific occupations who had experience in their occupation, who were satisfied with their work, and who pursued typical occupational tasks. Finally, the Personal Style Scales were developed by creating items that examined individuals' work, learning, and leadership style as well as their risk-taking and team orientation. Each of the PSS scales was constructed individually and normed extensively through the General Representative Sample.

The current revision of the Strong includes changes to the assessment structure, item content, and item response options. The most noteworthy changes are the following. Two parts of the 1994 version of the Strong were eliminated, resulting in the current version having only six sections. The 1994 version included 317 items, of which only 193 items were included in the revision; 98 new items were additionally developed or adapted for a total of 291 items. Thirteen new BISs were created or modified while retaining 17 from the 1994 version. Finally, the previous 3-point response option was changed to a 5-point response option using a Likert-type scale.

TECHNICAL.

General Representative Sample (GRS). The GRS is actually two samples, one of women and one of men. The GRS is approximately equivalent in ethnic diversity to the overall population of the United States. Respondents' Strong Profiles are scores on the GOTs, BISs, and PSSs converted to standard scores and then compared to respondents from the General Representative Sample. The comparison to the General Representative Sample uses a combined female and male sample and produces a standard score with a mean of 50. The user's guide does provide separate male and female means, making it possible for test takers to make comparisons between the combined sample and that of the separate genders.

As stated above, the GRS for the newly revised Strong was compiled with the goal of representing the ethnic/racial makeup of the U.S. This goal was generally achieved. For instance, the 2000 U.S. Census reports approximately 75% Caucasians/Whites in the population. In comparison, the GRS consists of approximately 72% Caucasians/Whites. Although generally mirroring the ethnic/racial makeup of the U.S., the GRS does fall short with some ethnic groups. For example, only 1 male and 7 female Native Americans were included. Such a subsample is too small to be a useful comparison for use with Native American respondents. Examples of other low numbers include 7 Hawaiian Natives or Pacific Islanders, 73 Asian Americans or Asians, and 113 Latino/a/Hispanic (5% of sample). Unlike gender, ethnicity/racial means are not reported in the user's guide, making it impossible for users to interpret scores by ethnicity norms.

Also important to note, the newly revised Strong might have limited usefulness with international individuals (i.e., individuals from countries outside the U.S.) because test makers strived to make the GRS representative of only the U.S. Therefore, research is needed to test generalizability to non-U.S. samples.

Reliability evidence. As reported in the manual, of the BISs retained in the new version, the internal consistency (alpha) reliability improved for 14 scales and decreased for 6. The mean alpha was .85 for the 10 new BISs. All BIS alphas were seen by these reviewers as at the acceptable level of .80 or above. Test-retest reliability demonstrates consistency across time as represented through a study reported in the manual of 174 respondents who were evaluated using a short interval (2 to

7 months) and a long interval (8 to 23 months), yielding a range of *r*s from .74 to .93.

Validity evidence. Reported in the manual, the 2004 version represents a major change in content due to technical and economic shifts in the 1990s. Therefore, the compilation of validity evidence for the new version of the Strong is crucial. Despite the reported major shift in content of the 2004 revision, correlations with the 1994 version remain high for the retained BISs ranging from .80 (e.g., Law) to .98 (e.g., Athletics) with a median correlation of .95. Of course, these correlations do not include and cannot consider the 13 BISs new to the revised version.

Concurrent and construct validity evidence is offered in the manual through correlation matrices comprising the 30 BISs and six GOTs. These correlations demonstrate that BISs that fall under a GOT category are more highly correlated within that GOT and less with other GOTs and hence provide some evidence of convergent and discriminant validation. For instance, the Mechanics & Construction BIS has a .88 correlation with Realistic, but a much lower correlation with nonadjacent GOTs of the Holland hexagon (i.e., Artistic = .19; Social = .04; Enterprising = .21), and higher correlations with adjacent GOTs (Investigative = .58; Conventional = .37). Other validity evidence is found when comparing individual occupational scales with BISs. For instance, for both men and women, the BIS, Protective Services, contains the OS of firefighter and as expected its correlation is approximately .77 whereas the OS of Artist has a correlation of about -.30 with this BIS. This difference represents discriminant validity evidence. Although predictive validity evidence from previous versions of the Strong demonstrates an ability to predict occupational choice, no predictive validity evidence is yet available for the 2004 version.

As with previous versions of the Strong, gender differences exist of more than .5 standard deviation units for some gender-traditional areas. For instance, men scored 5+ points higher on average than women for the traditionally male-dominated occupation of Mechanics & Construction, whereas women scored 4+ points higher than men for the traditionally female-dominated occupational area of Counseling & Helping. Hence, gender-specific interpretation of results is encouraged.

COMMENTARY. This revision provides updating and streamlining of the previous version of the Strong and reflects changes in the world of work over the previous decade. The newly revised 2004 Strong underwent extensive item revision with 98 new items contributing to a reduced total of 291 items. The 2004 Strong also has 30 BISs representing an expansion in content with only 17 retained from the 1994 Strong. The response format was also improved going from a 3-point to 5-point scale. Each of these changes is significant and the end result appears to be an updated and more refined instrument than the 1994 version.

Although many improvements have been realized in the 2004 version, challenges exist to be explored through future research. Research findings from the 1994 version cannot be completely generalized to the 2004 version. Studies are needed (a) to validate the predictive capacity of the new version; (b) to investigate the test's ability to generalize results to non-U.S. populations; and (c) to examine the Strong's use with various ethnic/racial groups in the U.S. through collection of larger representative samples for those groups. The new version, although an update and an improvement, still falls short in use with nonmajority individuals. In addition, use within a global context is also unproven, especially because norming was restricted to the U.S.

Despite these challenges, the 2004 version of the Strong retains its place as one of the most if not the most important career interest assessment instrument in existence. The updated 2004 version depicts the world of work in the U.S. well and has provided evidence of successful validation efforts. Its test constructors appear to have succeeded in improving on the already excellent psychometric properties of previous versions of this well established instrument.

REVIEWERS' REFERENCE

Holland, J. L. (1973). *Making vocational choices: A theory of careers.* Englewood Cliffs, NJ: Prentice-Hall.

[130]

Structure of Temperament Questionnaire.

Purpose: Designed to "measure the traits which appear as consistent patterns and dynamics of behavior, more or less independently of the content of the situation."
Population: Ages 15–75.
Publication Date: 2007.
Administration: Group.
Price Data, 2009: $147 per complete Extended STQ or Compact STQ test kits including professional manual, 50 response forms, and 50 scoring summary/profile forms; $77 per 50 Extended STQ or Compact STQ carbonless response forms; $20 per 50 scoring summary/profile forms.

Foreign Language Editions: Complete test kits available in Chinese, Polish, Russian, and Urdu.
Authors: Vladimir M. Rusalov and Irina N. Trofimova.
Publisher: Psychological Services Press.

a) EXTENDED STQ.
Acronym: STQ-E.
Scores, 13: Motor Ergonicity, Social Ergonicity, Intellectual Ergonicity, Motor Plasticity, Social Plasticity, Intellectual Plasticity, Motor Tempo, Social Tempo, Intellectual Tempo, Object-Related Emotionality, Social Emotionality, Intellectual Emotionality, Validity Scale.
Time: (30) minutes.

b) COMPACT STQ.
Acronym: STQ-77.
Scores, 13: Motor Ergonicity, Social Ergonicity, Motor Tempo, Social Tempo, Sensitivity to Physical Sensations, Empathy, Intellectual Ergonicity, Plasticity, Sensitivity to Probabilities, Self-Confidence, Impulsivity, Neuroticism, Validity Scale.
Time: (15) minutes.

c) SHORT STQ.
Acronym: STQ-26.
Scores,13: Motor Ergonicity, Social Ergonicity, Intellectual Ergonicity, Motor Plasticity, Social Plasticity, Intellectual Plasticity, Motor Tempo, Social Tempo, Intellectual Tempo, Object-Related Emotionality, Social Emotionality, Intellectual Emotionality, Validity Scale.
Time: (10) minutes.

Review of the Structure of Temperament Questionnaire by GERALD E. DeMAURO, Managing Educational Assessment Scientist, American Institutes for Research, Voorheesville, NY:

DESCRIPTION. The Structure of Temperament Questionnaire (STQ) is derived from an impressive body of theory and research. It "provides a compact assessment tool and a detailed map to diagnose and differentiate between stable temperamental traits" (manual, p. 100). The comprehensive review in the manual aids the evaluation of the validity evidence.

The STQ can be individually or group-administered with paper-and-pencil, mail-in, faxed paper-and-pencil, or computer-assisted administration and scoring. Examiners do not need formal education if they are supervised by graduate-level professionals. Controlled test practices are observed. Administration instructions are clear.

The STQ has Extended, Compact, and Short versions. It offers raw scores, percentiles, and *T*-scores for each scale of the different versions of the instrument. Scores should be interpreted by trained professionals.

Validity Scales are scored first to assure the examinee's truthfulness. Forms are available to plot *T*-scores for profile analyses across the STQ scales. Special attention is directed to the highest and lowest *T*-scores, especially those equal to or greater than 70 and those equal to or less than 30. Indexes summing various combinations of scores are offered to help interpret Extended STQ performance.

The test authors advise that the STQ might assist job and staff assessment, with special attention given to scales best related to the job. They also advise that the STQ can help identify students with school difficulties. Descriptions supported by research are provided for clinical use of the STQ.

DEVELOPMENT. Consistent with Rusalov's (1997) conclusions, the original Russian STQ assessed eight scales, object-related (motor) and social activities in each of four traits: (a) Ergonicity, or the capacity to sustain an activity; (b) Plasticity, or the ability to respond to environmental changes by moderating behavior; (c) Tempo, or speed of performance; and (d) Emotionality, or emotional sensitivity to discrepancies between expected and actual performance.

In 1988–1990, the eight-scale form was translated into English. Forty-nine male and 55 female psychology students took the instrument in 1993 (Bishop, Jacks, & Tandy, 1993). Factor analysis revealed a factor structure consistent with the Russian version.

The Russian Extended STQ was then developed, containing 150 4-point Likert-like items, in the original two activities plus a third activity area, Intellectual (Rusalov, 1997). The resulting 12 scales had 12 items each plus 6 validity items. The Extended version of the STQ was developed in five main steps followed by age and cross-cultural adaptations: (a) Rusalov composed 20 binary (true-false) items for each of eight scales. About 60% of the items were edited. Twelve items were chosen for each scale that were only related to that scale. Nine validity items brought the total to 105 items; (b) A pool of 30 items per 12 scales was then developed, including the original 105 items and 6 validity items; (c) One-hundred and fifty adults took these items, that were now in a 4-point Likert format. Twelve items each for 12 scales plus 6 validity items were retained; (d) These 150 items were edited for congruity to the temperament construct and then administered to 300 subjects; (e) Five-hundred and eighty-six subjects took these items with other related measures; (f)

Russian Teenager (ages 11–16), Early School (ages 7–11), and Preschool (ages 3–6) versions of the STQ were developed and field tested on samples of 510 and then 208, 200 and then another 112, and 100 subjects and then another 43 children, respectively; (g) The cross-cultural versions of the Extended STQ were developed and field tested in English, Chinese, Urdu, and Polish.

Besides age-appropriate versions, the STQ also has Short (STQ-26), Compact (STQ-77), and Extended versions. The Compact version (STQ-77) was developed in seven steps based on theoretical models, including three dynamical dimensions of life: power, variability, and sensitivity to the environment. These steps were: (a) 44 STQ items with the highest reliabilities, 28 new items and 16 edited STQ items composed the STQ-88; (b) pilot tests were conducted for English and Chinese STQ-88 versions; (c) split-half and test-retest reliabilities, factor analysis, and item-total score correlations were computed; (d) factor analysis of the English STQ-88E confirmed the 12-scale structure. The most reliable six items for each scale and five validity items were chosen for the STQ-77 questionnaire, and Chinese, Polish, and Urdu versions were developed; (e) fifty-two Canadian subjects participated in test-retest reliability studies; (f) special construct validity studies gave evidence of good convergent and discriminant properties of the 12 scales in relation to theoretical models; and (g) development began on the French STQ-77.

Theoretical models and factor analysis were the bases for developing the 12 STQ-77 scales: Motor Ergonicity, Social Ergonicity, Motor Tempo, Social Tempo, Sensitivity to Physical Sensations, Empathy (Social Sensitivity), Intellectual Ergonicity, Plasticity, Sensitivity to Probabilities, Impulsivity, Self-Confidence, and Neuroticism.

TECHNICAL.

Standardization. The normative samples used American, Australian, Canadian, Chinese, Canadian-Urdu, Russian, and Canadian-Polish participants, aged 15–75 for the appropriate forms. Extended versions of the STQ were administered to many samples, including 1,937 Russian and 1,014 Canadian-English participants. The norms collapse performance across different age forms, reporting score conversion tables for men and women less than 30, 30–45, and over 45.

Validity. Rusalov alone and with others conducted several studies describing the relationships between Extended STQ scales and 27 cognitive measures. IQ loaded significantly on the same factor as Intellectual Ergonicity, Intellectual Plasticity, and Intellectual Tempo. Analysis of Variance revealed significant differences in IQ among groups with low, average, and high Intellectual Ergonicity scores. The Intellectual scales of the Extended STQ were significantly correlated with other measures of intelligence.

In several studies the STQ-R (Russian) was administered with the Eysenck Personality Questionnaire (EPQ; Eysenck & Eysenck, 1968) and other instruments. Significant relationships were reported between the EPQ Extroversion scale and various STQ scales and between EPQ Neuroticism and Emotionality scales.

Several STQ scales were predictors of school achievement and differences in factors of semantic space (Trofimova, 1997, 1999). Volkova (2006) found significant relationships between several of 26 verbal characteristics and the Ergonicity scores in Object-Related, Social, and Intellectual activities. Many other studies also found good convergent and discriminant properties of the STQ scales as predicted by theory. The test authors provide a very useful table summarizing these findings.

Performance of monozygotic twins had higher correlations than performance of dizygotic twins on all scales but Intellectual Plasticity, suggesting considerable heritability of these temperament traits (Rusalov & Galimov, 2002). The scales were also correlated with expert opinions given by psychology students about 124 subjects (Rusalov, 1997, 2004).

Principal components with varimax rotation factor analysis decomposed performance into the same four factors for the Russian Extended STQ (STQ-R), and for the American and Canadian samples on the English Extended STQ. These factors were extracted from analyses of the Teenager version of the STQ, and the Russian Early School and Preschool STQs. Four factors were also extracted from the English Compact STQ. Analyses of all of the Compact and Extended versions of the STQ identified factors labeled as Physical, Social, and Intellectual Activity, and Emotionality.

Rusalov (1997, 2004) reported higher scale scores for both male Canadians and male Russians on 8 of 12 Extended STQ scales. In 10 of the 12 scales, the direction of differences for Russians and Canadians agreed (7 favoring men).

A number of studies showed age differences on the age-appropriate STQ forms. These support the use of the age and gender norms provided by the test authors. Developing common scales across age groups would control for any differences in scale properties between forms.

The test authors used half-split (odd/even) factor analytic techniques to examine the factor structure of the Extended and Compact STQs, using samples of 1,014 and 936 participants (Extended and Compact versions, respectfully) who completed English versions of the scale. The factor structures presented in the test manual appear similar to one another, suggesting that the factor structure is stable across the Extended and Compact versions. However, tabulated information should be double-checked for accuracy, as certain lapses in congruity are not easily explained.

Reliability. Test-retest correlations for the Short and Extended Russian and English STQs were respectable. Alpha coefficients on the eight-scale STQ and Extended versions were also respectable. Very few of the item-scale correlations were below .20.

COMMENTARY. The test authors summarize a very large body of research, first defining temperament and all of its dimensions and then demonstrating relationships between STQ scores and theoretical manifestations of temperament. The test authors might consider developing common scales across test versions, conducting formal standard setting studies to aid interpretation, and providing practice questions in administration instructions.

SUMMARY. The test authors provide a comprehensive review of literature and research on the temperament construct. Development and technical studies are consistent with the research and theory. The manual needs editing to assure the appropriate tables are referenced, the tabled material agrees with the discussion, and repeated material is purged.

REVIEWER'S REFERENCES

Bishop, D., Jacks, H., & Tandy, S. B. (1993). Structure of the Temperment Questionnaire (STQ): Results from a U.S. sample. *Personality and Individual Differences, 14,* 485-487.

Eysenck, H. J., & Eysenck, S. B. G. (1968). *Manual for the Eysenck Personality Inventory.* San Diego: Educational and Industrial Testing Service.

Rusalov, V. M. (1997). *Manual for Questionnaire of Formal-Dynamical Properties of Individual.* Moscow: Russian Academy of Sciences. IPAN. (In Russian).

Rusalov, V. M. (2004). *Formal-Dynamical Properties of Individual [Temperament]. Short Theory and Methods of Measurement for Various Age Groups.* Moscow: Russian Academy of Sciences. IPAN. (In Russian).

Rusalov, V. M., & Galimov, R. A. (2002). On heredity of formal-dynamical properties of individuality. *Proceedings of The Second International Luria Memorial Conference.* Moscow.

Trofimova, I. N. (1997). Interconnections of characteristics of temperament with some peculiarities of cognitive activity of human [temperament]. *Questions of Psychology (Voprosi psihilogii), 1,* 74-82.

Trofimova, I. N. (1999). How people of different age, sex and temperament estimate the world. *Psychological Reports, 85*(2), 533-552.

Volkova, D. A. (2006). Analysis of approaches to study activity as temperamental and personality properties of a subject. *Reports of RUDN University (Vestnik RUDN), Psychology and Pedagogics, 1*(3), 74-82.

Review of the Structure of Temperament Questionnaire by STEVEN V. ROUSE, Professor of Psychology, Pepperdine University, Malibu, CA:

DESCRIPTION. The Structure of Temperament Questionnaire is actually the name of a family of tests: the 150-item Extended Form (Extended STQ), the 77-item Compact Form (STQ-77), and the 26-item Short Form (Short STQ). Although the test was designed to "determine the individual style and particularities of performance of normal people" (manual, p. 100), the manual advocates its use for organizational (e.g., applicant selection), clinical (e.g., diagnostic aids), and educational purposes (e.g., identification of cognitive and emotional problems).

The three forms of the test may be administered either in a paper-and-pencil or computerized format. When the paper-and-pencil format is used, the test administrator may either handscore the test or mail in or fax in the answer sheet for a free computer-generated report. The manual estimates that handscoring would take between 8 and 30 minutes, depending on the form being used; this estimate is plausible because the scoring procedure requires transcribing all responses onto a scoring section of the answer sheet. *T*-scores are obtained using one of six profile sheets, depending on the respondent's sex and age (i.e., younger than 30, 30 to 45 years old, or older than 45). When the computer-administered form is used, a computer-generated profile is available.

DEVELOPMENT. Drawing upon theoretical and empirical conceptualizations of temperament in the Russian research literature, the Extended STQ is based on a model that posits three different types of activity: Object-Related (i.e., physical activity), Social, and Intellectual. For each type of activity, there are four different biologically determined characteristics of behavior: Ergonicity (i.e., the tendency to maintain extended energy), Plasticity (i.e., the ability to adjust one's behavior), Tempo (i.e., speed), and Emotionality (i.e., the tendency to be sensitive to failure). Thus, the model proposes 12 distinct temperamental characteristics, such as Object-Related Tempo (i.e., the speed of one's physical movements or manual work) and Intellectual Plasticity (i.e., the degree to which a person engages in flexible, divergent problem-solving).

A multistep process led to the eventual set of 150 items on the Extended STQ. First, a set of 105 Russian-language items were written to measure the eight Object-Related and Social temperaments; Intellectual characteristics were not included in the model at this initial stage. This set of items was expanded to a total of 366 questions, which were then clarified on the basis of item-total correlations, resulting in 12 temperament scales (with 12 items per scale) and a 6-item validity scale.

Having developed a Russian-language version of the Extended STQ, translated forms were created. Although the manual explicitly states that forward and backward translation was conducted for the Chinese, Urdu, and Polish forms, no back-translation was conducted in preparing the English form; rather, a team of researchers revised the translation twice in an effort to attain equivalence.

Following the development of the Extended STQ, the 26-item Short STQ was created by selecting the two items from each scale that had the highest item-total correlation coefficient. Data obtained from one sample showed that the correlation between the short form and long form of counterpart scales ranged from .43 to .84, with a mean of .66.

To create a midsized form of the test, the STQ-77, 60 items were selected from the full form of the test; 44 of these items were selected on the basis of strong internal consistency statistics, and an additional 16 were revised and edited to improve their reflection of the underlying constructs. Additionally, 28 new items were written to measure additional characteristics related to impulsivity and sensation-related activities. However, when these 88 items were factor analyzed, a 12-factor solution differed distinctly from the conceptual basis of the Extended STQ. The final set of 77 items was selected on the basis of having strong internal consistency values for these 12 factors; as a result, some of the scales are conceptualized as being counterparts of scales from the Extended STQ (such as Social Tempo), some reflect amalgamations of scales from the Extended STQ (such as Plasticity, which is largely composed of items from the Object-Related Plasticity and Social Plasticity scales), and some of which are distinct from the Extended STQ scales (such as Self-Confidence and Sensitivity to Physical Sensations).

TECHNICAL. Insufficient information is provided regarding the normative sample used for the standardization of the different forms of the STQ. The manual indicates that the sample included men and women from ages 15 to 75, including respondents from various regions of North America, Australia, and Asia, representing a range of ethnic, socioeconomic, and educational backgrounds. However, no additional details are provided. The manual fails to indicate the proportional representation from different geographical regions, languages, education levels, or age levels; notably, even the sample size of the normative group is absent. Thus, a potential test user is unable to evaluate the extent to which comparisons with the normative sample are appropriate for the population with which he or she anticipates using the test.

The data presented in the manual suggest that a higher level of reliability is obtained among Russian-speaking respondents than among English-speaking respondents. For example, test-retest (2–4-week interval) analyses conducted in Russian resulted in correlations that were at or above .70 for all 12 Extended STQ scales, whereas data from a comparable English-language analysis (6–12-month interval) resulted in correlations at or below .60 for four scales, with a minimum of .43. Alpha coefficent values obtained for a large Russian-language sample were all at or above .75, with 9 of the 12 scales yielding coefficients at or above .80; however, a large English-speaking sample yielded alpha values at or below .75 for 10 of the 12 scales, with only 1 scale having an alpha value above .80. The alpha values reported for the Chinese, Urdu, and Polish (retest interval not provided) forms of the test were also consistently lower than those obtained with the Russian-language test, suggesting that greater measurement precision is attained when the test is used in its original language.

Many forms of evidence that are typically presented in considering validity are absent in the STQ manual. For example, given the model that was used as the basis of the Extended STQ, one would have expected to find intercorrelation matrices to show associations across the three types of behaviors. Although intercorrelations are not provided, results of factor analyses consistently yielded a four-factor solution: three of the factors were primarily defined by the Object-Related, Social, and Intellectual behavior domains, but the fourth factor was defined by the Emotionality scales from each of the three behavior domains. No validation data are provided for the Validity Scale or for the specific cutoff at which protocols are deemed to be invalid. Furthermore, the manual lacks validation data for the recommended applied uses of the test. Numerous bold recommendations (such as the argument that "People with high Empathy scores should not be assigned to middle management position[s]" (manual, p. 92) raise concerns regarding the legality of following these guidelines for selection purposes in the absence of validating support. Similarly, the recommended use of the STQ as a diagnostic aid is hampered by the lack of specific *T*-score cutoffs that represent "high" and "low" levels and the lack of validating evidence that the proposed scales are indeed diagnostic of pathology.

COMMENTARY. The theoretical model of the STQ is a novel conceptualization of personality traits and temperaments, and carries the promise of a distinctly different approach to omnibus personality inventories. Unfortunately, several flaws undermine confidence in this test. For example, a potential strength of this test—the multiple translations—is undermined by the lack of supportive evidence of the equivalence across forms. As noted by Geisinger (2003), linguistic equivalence (which might be attained by an accurate translation and back-translation) is not tantamount to conceptual equivalence, functional equivalence, or metric equivalence. A potentially valuable validity scale is undermined by a lack of information regarding its development and validation. Potentially valuable applied uses are undermined by a lack of empirical support for the interpretive hypotheses. A potentially valuable multinational normative sample is undermined by a lack of descriptive data regarding its demographic characteristics. Finally, the potentially valuable theoretical structure is undermined by the dramatic differences in the scales that comprise the Extended STQ and the STQ-77. In short, the STQ has the promise of providing a new conceptualization of temperament, but in the absence of supporting evidence, one cannot determine whether or not it fulfills its promise.

SUMMARY. Drawing on theoretical and empirical traditions in Russian psychological research, the STQ measures three types of behavior (physical, interpersonal, and intellectual) and four different temperamental traits (activity level, flexibility, emotionality, and speed) for each type of behavior. Three forms of the test (differing in length and scale composition) are available, and the original Russian form has been translated into English, Polish, Urdu, and Chinese. Although numerous empirical studies are described in which STQ scales had substantive correlations with other scales and with psychophysiological variables, sufficient evidence has not been provided to justify its use in applied settings. In the absence of such evidence, the use of the STQ for research purposes would be more prudent than using the test for selection, diagnosis, or guidance.

REVIEWER'S REFERENCE

Geisinger, K. F. (2003). Testing and assessment in cross-cultural psychology. In J. R. Graham, J. A. Naglieri, & I. B. Weiner (Eds.), *Handbook of psychology: volume 10, Assessment psychology* (pp. 95-117). Hoboken, NJ: Wiley.

[131]

Structured Assessment of Violence Risk in Youth.

Purpose: Designed to "assist professional evaluators in assessing and making judgments about a juvenile's risk for violence."
Population: Ages 12–18.
Publication Dates: 2002-2006.
Acronym: SAVRY.
Scores: Total rating only.
Administration: Individual.
Price Data, 2010: $98 per complete kit including professional manual (2006, 97 pages) and 50 rating forms; $62 per 50 rating forms; $46 per professional manual.
Time: [10-15] minutes.
Comments: Completed by a mental health professional utilizing multiple sources to provide accurate estimates of behavior; structured interview questions also included.
Authors: Randy Borum, Patrick Bartel, and Adelle Forth.
Publisher: Psychological Assessment Resources, Inc.

Review of the Structured Assessment of Violence Risk in Youth by CYNTHIA HAZEL, Assistant Professor, Child, Family and School Psychology, Morgridge College of Education, University of Denver, Denver, CO:

DESCRIPTION. The Structured Assessment of Violence Risk in Youth (SAVRY) is an assessment for evaluating the risk of violence and planning interventions for violence risk management in youth, ages 12 to 18 years. The instrument is composed of three domains of risk factors, containing 24 items, and one domain of protective factors, containing 6 items. The rating form provides areas for indicating additional risk and protective factors, specific conditions of concerns, and a Summary Risk Rating. The 24 risk factor items are assessed as low, moderate, or high and the 6 protective factor items are assessed as present or absent. The Summary Risk Rating is scored as high risk, moderate risk, or low risk. The test manual provides explanations for the scoring of each of the 30 items. Information for rating items should come from multiple sources such as youth self-report, parent/caregiver reports, teacher reports, social worker reports, police reports, probation reports, psychological and psychiatric evaluations, school records, juvenile justice records, and mental health and medical records. The evaluator is to weigh the information contained in these sources, while at the same time considering the credibility and reliability of the source, to create a composite answer to each item. The Summary Risk Rating is a cumulative assessment of the youth's violence risk but is "not linked directly to a particular score or range of scores" (professional manual, p. 18). The manual contains case illustrations for Summary Risk Ratings of High Risk, Moderate Risk, and Low Risk. Appendix A of the manual lists general screening questions and detailed questions for inquiry into violence history. No information is provided about how long it takes to administer the assessment.

The test authors intend that the assessment be completed by "professionals in a variety of disciplines who conduct assessments and/or make intervention/supervision plans" (professional manual, p. 12) acting in compliance with all relevant laws, policies, and ethical standards. SAVRY administrators are required to have training and experience in conducting individual assessments, knowledge of child and adolescent development, and experience with violent youth.

DEVELOPMENT. The test authors developed the SAVRY to provide a standard rubric that could be used by a variety of systems that need to assess and manage youth violence. Modeled on structured professional judgment protocols for adult violence risk, the SAVRY utilizes structured professional judgment, an alternative to actuarial formulae and unstructured clinical judgments. The test authors state that "the item content is focused specifically on risk in adolescents" (professional manual, p. 5) and acknowledge the inconsistencies of adolescent violence. However, no empirical evidence is provided for the SAVRY's three risk domains (historical risk factors, social/contextual risk factors, and individual/clinical risk factors), although some evidence is given for the protective factors domain.

TECHNICAL.

Standardization. The SAVRY manual does not give information regarding the population on whom the SAVRY was developed, but refers readers to various validation studies. The test authors note that more investigation is needed into the effects of gender and race, and that few females have been part of the validation samples.

Reliability. To test reliability, item scores were given numeric values and summed to create a Risk Total. Studies have reported internal consistency of .82 to .84 for the SAVRY items with the Risk Total. However, in clinical use, answers on individual items are meant to guide but not determine the assessment of the Summary Risk Rating. Studies have found interrater reliabilities of .72 to .85 for the Summary Risk Rating. A notable lack is that test-retest reliability is not addressed in the manual.

Validity. The manual presents evidence with respect to concurrent validity and criterion validity; however, it fails to address content validity or construct validity. Concurrent validity for the Risk Total was reported with the Youth Level of Service/Case Management Inventory (YLS/CMI; r = .64 to .89) and the Hare Psychopathy Checklist: Youth Version (PCL/YV; r = .48 to .74). Predictive power increased in hierarchical regression analyses when SAVRY data were added to the YLSI/CMI and the PCL:YV with respect to aggressive behavior in institutions and symptoms of serious conduct disorder. With regard to criterion validity, three studies have shown the SAVRY Summary Risk Rating to be significantly correlated with measures of recidivism (.74 to .89). The predictive validity of propensities for violence with nonincarcerated populations is less known.

A recent study (Meyers & Schmidt, 2008) found strong predictive validity for violence recidivism with the SAVRY for juvenile offenders across gender and ethnicity at 1-year and 3-year follow-ups. At the 1-year follow-up, the SAVRY was a better predictor of general recidivism than violence recidivism. Good predictive validity of violence recidivism and general recidivism was demonstrated irrespective of gender and ethnicity at the 3-year follow-up.

COMMENTARY. The SAVRY is a promising tool for assessing violence risk in youth. However, its strengths are also its weaknesses. Understanding that youth violence propensities are situational, multifaceted, and individualistic, the test authors have created a structured tool that still leaves much room for the evaluator's clinical judgment. Thus, it is essential to use a skilled evaluator who must collect extensive information from multiple sources. The test authors are very clear that the SAVRY is an aid or guide to assist professional judgment in the rating of violence risk in youth and not an actuarial instrument or psychological test. The key strength of the SAVRY is the ability of the instrument to assist in making structured clinical judgments based on sound assessment while concurrently preserving leeway for case-specific analysis.

The SAVRY appears to have strong validity; the predictive validity findings for incarcerated youth populations are particularly promising. Much less is known about the validity for nonincarcerated youth. The user would benefit from greater explanation in the manual of the theoretical underpinning of the three risk domains and one protective domain. The reliability of the SAVRY is less well established. The stated evaluator qualifications may not be adequate for reliable evaluation, given that all scoring is dependent on the administrator's professional judgment. Further, in clinical applications, it may be difficult to collect data from all pertinent sources required for comprehensive decisions regarding a youth's violence and resiliency potential. Assessment of test-retest reliability and interrater reliability in various applied settings would greatly strengthen the understanding of the clinical utility of the SAVRY.

SUMMARY. The SAVRY is a novel instrument for assessing violence risk in adolescents, ages 12 years to 18 years. The SAVRY provides structure for an evaluator to analyze evidence from multiple sources in a multifaceted determination of a youth's risk for violence. The instrument is composed of three domains of risk factors and one domain of protective factors. The validity of the SAVRY (especially in its ability to predict recidivism) appears promising, but more evidence of reliability in clinical settings is needed.

REVIEWER'S REFERENCE

Meyers, J. R., & Schmidt, F. (2008). Predictive validity of the Structured Assessment for Violence Risk in Youth (SAVRY) with juvenile offenders. *Criminal Justice and Behavior, 35,* 344-355.

Review of the Structured Assessment of Violence Risk in Youth by SHAWN POWELL, Instructor of Psychology, Casper College, and private practitioner, Casper, WY:

DESCRIPTION. The Structured Assessment of Violence Risk in Youth (SAVRY) is designed to measure the risk for violence in 12- to 18-year-old adolescents. It is intended to be used as an aid in evaluating an adolescent's risk for exhibiting violence toward self and others. A structured professional judgment approach was followed in developing the SAVRY. It is not an actuarial test as it does not produce test scores, include base rate comparisons, or contain cutoff scores.

The SAVRY is intended to assist clinicians in making judgments about an individual's level of risk for violent behavior by directing attention to factors associated with adolescent violence. These factors are Historical Risk Factors, Social/Contextual Risk Factors, Individual/Clinical Risk Factors, and Protective Factors. It also allows additional Risk Factors and other Protective Factors to be considered. The SAVRY can be used to assess an adolescent's level of violence risk in various settings including inpatient psychiatric hospitals, juvenile justice settings, residential treatment facilities, schools, mental health centers, and outpatient clinics.

Formal training in conducting individual evaluations, knowledge of child/adolescent development, and an understanding of youth violence is required to use the SAVRY. The SAVRY manual suggests psychologists, psychiatrists, social workers, and juvenile probation officers with adequate training can competently administer this instrument. The time required to complete the SAVRY varies depending on the manner in which it is completed (via interview and/or record reviews). Another factor that will determine the time required to complete the instrument is the amount of information available about an individual's past, current, and future potential for violence.

As part of a comprehensive assessment of an individual's risk for violence the SAVRY can serve as a guide in conducting adolescent risk assessments. It could be used to guide semistructured interviews with adolescents, peers, staff members, parents, teachers, or administrators, completed through record reviews and observations, and/or used to guide clinical case staffings. Results from the SAVRY may be used to develop treatment recommendations to design safety management programs for adolescents at risk of harming themselves or others based on their assessed level of violence.

The SAVRY contains 24 items rated as low, moderate, or high. It also includes 6 mutually exclusive items rated as present or absent. The rating form contains behavioral rating category anchors for all presented items. It includes a Summary Risk Rating of low, moderate, or high that allows a professional judgment to be made in determining an adolescent's overall level of risk based on the individual's current situation.

The SAVRY manual contains detailed information on the items presented in the rating form.

Each item is linked to specific research relating the item's topic to the assessment of an adolescent's risk for violence. The manual also provides three case illustrations to assist in the administration and interpretation of this instrument.

DEVELOPMENT. The SAVRY was developed to assist in evaluating an adolescent's risk level for committing violent acts. It was modeled after adult violence risk protocols that use structured professional judgment to determine the level of violence risk an individual poses. The test authors indicate they developed the SAVRY with six criteria in mind. The criteria used include risk factors associated with adolescent violence, current research, the unique aspects of adolescent development, obtaining treatment recommendations from the instrument's results, considering individual and research based factors related to adolescent violence, and ease of use.

The SAVRY is founded on the assessment of four factors related to adolescent violence. The first of these factors is Historical Risk. This factor considers an adolescent's past history relative to committing violent acts, exposure to violent acts, parental history, maltreatment, and school achievement. Social/Contextual Risk is the second factor; it measures interpersonal relations, peer influences, levels of personal and parental support, and environmental influences on an adolescent's potential to commit violent acts. The SAVRY's third factor is Individual/Clinical Risk. This factor is intended to assess an adolescent's attitude, behavioral status, and psychological functioning. The fourth factor is Protective, which measures environmental and personal antecedents that could reduce an individual's tendency to act in a violent manner. This factor includes prosocial involvement, social support, attachment, family and school affiliation, and resilient traits.

TECHNICAL.

Standardization. The SAVRY was not developed as a traditional psychometric test and a traditional test development process was not followed when it was designed. The factors it measures were based on numerous independent research studies measuring various risk factors for violence in adolescents. The SAVRY was not administered to a normative group when it was developed. The manual indicates it is appropriate for use with males and females between the ages of 12 and 18. Additional information concerning the characteristics of individuals for whom the SAVRY is appropriate is not included in the manual.

Reliability. The SAVRY manual indicates its internal consistency coefficients range from .82 to .84. Estimates of interrater reliability for the Summary Risk Rating range from .72 to .85. The method used to determine interrater reliability is not presented and the results provided are from three independent studies reported over the course of 4 years.

Validity. Evidence of the SAVRY's validity is provided in the form of criterion validity, concurrent validity, and incremental validity. The instrument's criterion validity was obtained by comparing the SAVRY risk total score to the Youth Level of Service/Case Management Inventory (Hoge & Andrews, 2002) resulting in a .89 coefficient and the Hare Psychopathy Checklist: Youth Version (Forth, Kosson, & Hare, 2003) yeilding a coefficient of .78 for offenders. The SAVRY demonstrated incremental validity as it improved the predictive power when given in addition to either of these two instruments. The SAVRY manual indicates the instrument demonstrated significant correlations with behavioral measures of aggression (.40) and aggressive conduct disorder symptoms (.52) which are given as evidence of its concurrent validity.

COMMENTARY. The test authors' use of structured professional judgment in developing the SAVRY prompts a comparison to actuarial testing. Professional judgment has been found to be as accurate as formal testing in assessing an individual's risk for violence in periods up to 1 year. However, actuarial testing is reportedly superior to professional judgment in determining risk for violence in periods longer than 1 year (Mossman, 1994). This raises questions about the efficacy of structured professional judgment compared to actuarial testing in measuring an adolescent's level of risk for violence.

Several positive aspects of the SAVRY promote its use. The SAVRY's structured professional judgment approach does not preclude the use of actuarial testing in determining an adolescent's level of risk for violence. Its use has been found to increase the accuracy of such evaluations when used in combination with actuarial tests. The SAVRY allows more flexibility than actuarial tests as it may include factors not assessed by actuarial tests. As the SAVRY encourages the use of multiple data collection methods in assessing an adolescent's risk for violence, it serves as a reminder that single test scores should not be used to make clinical judgments.

As the SAVRY is not a formal test, it can be administered numerous times in a short period. It does not have a recommended waiting period between administrations. Thus, it can be used to assess and re-assess an adolescent's risk of committing violent acts without concern for test/retest effects. More information regarding the population to be assessed using the SAVRY would be welcome. Additionally, some behavioral anchors used on the rating form are not entirely mutually exclusive. This makes it difficult to truly rank a given adolescent's risk on specific factors.

SUMMARY. The SAVRY is based on research associated with known factors of adolescent violence. It uses a structured professional judgment approach rather than a traditional actuarial testing approach. It is an appropriate measure to use in the assessment of an adolescent's level of violence risk. It is designed for use with 12- to 18-year-old males and females. More information regarding the specific populations for which it is intended would be appreciated.

The SAVRY provides a comprehensive approach to the assessment of violence risk in adolescent populations and can be used across a variety of settings. When combined with additional information from actuarial testing it produces a more thorough assessment of adolescent risk for violence than when used in isolation. It is a solid contribution to the field of adolescent violence risk assessment.

REVIEWER'S REFERENCES

Forth, A. E., Kosson, D., & Hare, R. D. (2003). The Hare Psychopathy Checklist: Youth Version (PCL:YV, Research Version). Toronto, Ontario, Canada: Multi-Health Systems.

Hoge, R. D., & Andrews, D. A. (2002). Youth Level of Service/Case Management Inventory (YLS/CMI). North Tonawanda, NY: Multi-Health Systems.

Mossman, D. (1994). Assessing predictions of violence: Being accurate about accuracy. *Journal of Consulting and Clinical Psychology, 62*, 783-792.

[132]

Structured Photographic Expressive Language Test-Preschool 2.

Purpose: Designed to "probe a child's ability to generate early developing morphological and syntactic forms."
Population: Ages 3 to 5-11.
Publication Dates: 1983-2004.
Acronym: SPELT-P 2.
Scores: Total score only.
Administration: Individual.
Price Data, 2008: $165 per manual (2005, 79 pages), 37 color photographs, and 50 response forms.
Time: (20) minutes.
Comments: Includes a system of alternative response structures for assessment of the African American population.
Authors: Janet Dawson, Connie Stout, Julia Eyer, Patricia Tattersall, Janice Fonkalsrud, and Karen Croley.
Publisher: Janelle Publications, Inc.
Cross References: See T5:2524 (13 references) and T4:2588 (1 reference); for a review by Joan D. Berryman of an earlier edition, see 9:1198 (2 references).

Review of the Structured Photographic Expressive Language Test-Preschool 2 by TIFFANY L. HUTCHINS, Lecturer of Communication Sciences, University of Vermont, Burlington, VT:

DESCRIPTION. The purpose of the Structured Photographic Expressive Language Test—Preschool 2 (SPELT-P 2) is to identify children (ages 3 years, 0 months to 5 years, 11 months) who may have difficulty in the development of early morphological and syntactic constructions. The SPELT-P 2 is a revision of the SPELT-P (Werner & Kresheck, 1983), which was intended as a screening tool. By contrast, the SPELT-P 2 is designed to provide a more comprehensive measurement for identifying children who perform significantly below their age-matched peers. It is also designed to help clinicians note specific strengths and weaknesses in children's expression of morphosyntactic forms.

The SPELT-P 2 employs a standardized administration procedure to provide a contextual framework for eliciting 40 target structures. The stimulus for each item is one or two color photograph(s). The photographs are effective in portraying familiar objects, activities, and events and improve upon those for the earlier version by including persons from a range of racial backgrounds. Each photograph is accompanied by verbal cues, which appear on the response form. The response form facilitates administration and scoring of the test and, with few exceptions, the cues feel natural and uncontrived. The few cues that seem awkward are arguably unlike those that children typically experience in their everyday interactions. For example, Item 40 (designed to elicit the front embedded clause "After it rains") employs the cue "Before it rained, everything was dry. But it just rained. Tell me what it's like now. Start with 'After.'" In a related vein, Item 37 violates a pragmatic convention by asking the child to direct a question to a character in a photograph.

It is expected that children will respond within the context of their unique experiential frameworks and they are not to be penalized for either unconventional vocabulary or errors in phonology. In the event that cueing is unsuccessful for producing a target, a maximum of three additional prompts may be provided. Any prompting necessary to elicit the correct response is permitted except those that provide the target for imitation. A number of helpful suggestions for additional prompts are provided in the manual's appendix. As Berryman (1985) noted in her review of the SPELT-P, looking back and forth between the response form and the subject (not to mention the prompting suggestions in the appendix) can complicate testing. Presenting the verbal cues and prompts on the back of the photographic stimuli should be considered as a remedy.

All items are scored as correct (1) or incorrect (0; including no response or a grammatically correct but simplified response). The raw score is simply the total number correct. Raw scores are then converted into standard scores (mean = 100, *SD* = 15) for each of six 6-month age groups. Standard scores are accompanied by 90% and 95% confidence intervals. Percentiles and percentile bands (90%) are also given as are age-equivalency ranges for raw scores. The SPELT-P 2 takes approximately 20 minutes to complete.

DEVELOPMENT. The development of the SPELT-P 2 was undertaken to update the photographic stimuli, revise and improve several items from the SPELT-P, add items to assess more comprehensively the ability to produce morphosyntactic forms, and analyze normative data to provide standard scores and percentile ranks. "The total number of items was increased from 25 to 40; 8 items were retained from the SPELT-P, 7 items were revised, and 25 new items were added" (manual, p. 1). Guided by a current review of the literature, a 48-item test was developed and presented to an unstated number of clinicians for their feedback regarding the appropriateness of the photographic stimuli and the elicitation procedures. The 48-item version of the test was also piloted on 80 children (ages 3 years, 0 months to 5 years, 11 months). Although specific details are lacking, results from the pilot along with additional clinician review were used to decrease the number of test items to 40.

TECHNICAL.

Standardization. The SPELT-P 2 was standardized on a sample of 1,747 children ages 3 through 5 years. No information about income is provided for the sample. Data for region (representing 26 states in the Midwest, West, South, and East), gender, maternal education level, age, and ethnicity (i.e., African American, White, Hispanic, and "other") are reported. Only data for ethnicity are compared to U.S. Census statistics. Authors report that whereas the percentages of African Americans and Whites in the standardization sample were close to Census statistics, Hispanics were underrepresented and "other" ethnicities were slightly overrepresented. Although not described in the manual, correspondence with the test authors revealed that all children in the sample were primary speakers of English and that the scoring of tests obtained from African American children followed the guidelines in the back of the manual for evaluating the responses of speakers of African American Vernacular English (AAVE). As the manual states, approximately 2.5% of the sample was identified as language impaired but no information is available regarding the nature of the language impairment. Moreover, given the goals of the SPELT-P 2 to identify children who may have problems with morphosyntax, the inclusion of language-impaired children in the normative sample is questionable and actually has the potential to compromise accuracy of classification (Peña, Spaulding, & Plante, 2006).

Reliability. The test-retest reliability of the SPELT-P 2 was evaluated "with a sample of 35 males and 27 females (median age was 4-0 to 4-5); 8% of the sample was minority" (manual, p. 39). The reliability coefficient was .96. Although this finding is encouraging, only the median age category is identified and so it is unclear whether the test-retest sample adequately surveyed and spanned the age range for which this test is intended. In a related vein, a correlation coefficient can assess consistency of scores but it does not assess agreement between scores. Percent exact agreement for each item may be conducted in the future to address this. The median test-retest interval was 14 days. This time period seems appropriate but again the mean and range for the number of days are not reported. Authors do not report whether the examiners for each administration were the same or different, an important factor.

Interjudge reliability was evaluated with two trained raters who "independently scored verbatim written protocols of 230 children" (manual, p. 39). Correlation coefficients between the two raters ranged from .99 to 1.00 for the six age ranges surveyed. Percent exact agreement was also high and ranged from 97.44% to 100%. It is important to note that for these data, the term "interscorer reliability" is more precise than "interjudge reliability," and no data are offered to evaluate the measure's interexaminer reliability.

Internal consistency of scores for the standardization sample was relatively high and ranged from .798 to .882 for the six age groups. Internal consistency estimates were used to compute the standard error of measurement and confidence intervals.

Validity. Content validity of the SPELT-P 2 is fairly well documented. Some domains are less well tapped, whereas others have been expanded upon. In each case authors provide sound rationales for item selection that are tied to the goals of the test. Guided by the reasoning that scores on a valid test of morphosyntactic abilities should increase with age, construct validity was evaluated by examining the descriptive statistics for SPELT-P 2 scores across the six age ranges. Although mean scores did increase with age, more compelling evidence would involve a correlation to indicate the strength of the relation between scores and age. This demonstration is needed but by no means sufficient given that any developmental construct would be expected to increase with age. Thus, a more convincing demonstration of the measure's construct validity would involve contrasting-groups methodology to determine whether SPELT-P 2 scores distinguish between typically developing children and children identified with specific language impairment. Concurrent validity was explored by examining the relationship between scores on the SPELT-P 2 and another measure believed to tap morphosyntactic abilities (i.e., the syntax construction subtest of the Comprehensive Assessment of Spoken Language; Carrow-Woolfolk, 1999) yielding a correlation coefficient of .86, which is also encouraging.

COMMENTARY. Given the goals of the SPELT-P 2, the strengths of the measure include the content of the test, the response sheet that facilitates administration, and the ease of scoring. The examiner's manual is also user-friendly and should be understood readily by professionals administering the test. The chapter by Nola T. Radford in the manual providing a description of the response variations of speakers of AAVE and her guidelines for administering and scoring the SPELT-P 2 are reasoned and instructive. This discussion is critically important in helping to ensure that credit is given for either standard or equivalent AAVE constructions.

With regard to construct validity, some advanced items on the SPELT-P 2 may be unnecessarily difficult for young children and arguably tap constructs other than morphosyntactic abilities. For example, cues for several items include the word "ask" (e.g., "What does she *ask* her mom?") yet there is compelling evidence that children as old as age 5 years have difficulty understanding "ask' (Chomsky, 1969) and that their comprehension is easily dominated by contextual and interpersonal expectations (Warden, 1981). Anecdotally, this reviewer administered the SPELT-P 2 to a 4.5-year-old girl who routinely, spontaneously, and correctly produced the advanced constructions believed to be tapped by the measure. In line with the cited literature, her responses suggested that she uniformly misinterpreted the word "ask" as "tell." A correct response was secured only when the cue had been reframed and the word "ask" omitted (i.e., What does she *say* to her mom?"). In a related vein, Item 38 employs the cue "What does the boy think?"; however, the difficulty young children have with the understanding of mental state terms (particularly when attributed to others) is well-documented. In the future, authors may reconsider the precise wording and form of such cues to minimize their potential for tapping lexical and pragmatic domains.

Normative scores on the SPELT-P 2 are negatively skewed and skewness increases with age due to progressively smaller standard deviations that reflect the perfect or near perfect performance of older subjects. Because this distribution was expected and observed, a normalizing function was not used in the derivation of standard scores. Therefore, there is great potential for standard scores and their accompanying confidence intervals to be grievously misinterpreted. The same is true for percentiles and percentile bands because, as the test authors note, standard scores do not correspond to the same percentiles as they would in a normal distribution. The test authors caution against interpreting small score differences by recognizing the considerable overlap in the percentile bands, which indicate that "measurement error plays a significant role in the score difference" (manual, p. 37). Similar caution is advised for interpreting age equivalency ranges, which are characterized as an "extremely rough estimate of test-age performance" (manual, p. 37). Although test developers clearly communicate how the complexities in their data limit the usefulness of the scores obtained, this lack of precision remains a serious problem given one of the goals of the SPELT-P 2, which is to "identify children who perform significantly below their age-equivalent peers" (manual, p. 2). By contrast, the other stated goal of the measure (i.e., to assist clinicians in noting specific areas and strength and weakness in children's production of morphosyntactic structures) is better justified.

SUMMARY. The SPELT-P 2 uses an innovative format for assessing children's morphosyntactic abilities and improves upon the earlier version of the test by enhancing the measure's content and stimulus materials. Some encouraging evidence is provided in support of the measure's reliability and validity; however, the validation procedures are underspecified and a contrasting-groups method of construct validation is sorely needed. The form and content of some advanced items may be problematic and the usefulness of all derived scores is questionable. Although further development is needed before the SPELT-P 2 can be recommended as an assessment tool, it may prove useful for clinicians who seek to explore the children's relative morphosyntactic strengths and weaknesses as part of a larger battery of formal and informal measures.

REVIEWER'S REFERENCES

Berryman, J. D. (1985). [Review of the Structured Photographic Expressive Language Test.] In J. V. Mitchell, Jr. (Ed.), *The ninth mental measurements yearbook* (pp. 1490–1491). Lincoln, NE: The Buros Institute of Mental Measurements.

Carrow-Woolfolk, E. (1999). CASL: Comprehensive Assessment of Spoken Language. Circle Pines, MN: American Guidance Service, Inc.

Chomsky, C. (1969). *The acquisition of syntax in children from 5 to 10.* Cambridge, MA: M.I.T. Press.

Peña, E. D., Spaulding, T. J., & Plante, E. (2006). The composition of normative groups and diagnostic decision making: Shooting ourselves in the foot. *American Journal of Speech-Language Pathology, 15,* 247-254.

Warden D. (1981). Children's understanding of ask and tell. *Journal of Child Language, 8,* 139-149.

Werner, E., & Kresheck, J. (1983). Structured Photographic Expressive Language Test-Preschool. Sandwich, IL: Janelle Publications.

Review of the Structured Photographic Expressive Language Test—Preschool 2 by ROGER L. TOWNE, Associate Professor, Department of Communication Sciences and Disorders, Worcester State College, Worcester, MA:

DESCRIPTION. The Structured Photographic Expressive Language Test—Preschool 2 (SPELT–P 2) is a test used to assess the expressive use of morphology and syntax (morphosyntax) of children aged 3 years, 0 months through 5 years, 11 months. The SPELT-P 2 is a revision of an earlier screening test (the SPELT-P) developed by Werner and Kresheck (1983). Through this revision the SPELT-P 2 was expanded to become a more comprehensive normative assessment tool. Its primary purpose is to help identify children who are having difficulty in the early development of expressing certain morphological and syntactic features. In addition, the authors noted that the test can help a clinician identify specific linguistic strengths and weaknesses of a child, and "may be used to test the morphosyntactic development of children who are speakers of African American Vernacular English" (manual, p. 2).

The SPELT-P 2 format is relatively straightforward, making test administration simple and reliable. Test interpretation, however, is a more complex process requiring the examiner to have an in-depth understanding of child language development including the development of morphology and syntax. The test consists of a test manual, a photographic stimulus book, and a response form. The manual contains usual information regarding test development, administration, scoring, and interpretation. In addition, it also includes specific information and guidelines regarding how to score and interpret responses given in African American Vernacular English. The photographic stimulus book contains two practice items and the 44 photographs (4-inches by 6-inches) used to elicit targeted morphological and syntactic structures. The response form includes examiner and child information, verbal prompts for each test item that correspond with the photographs, scoring guidelines, and a summary of test results.

The test is administered by presenting a photographic stimulus item along with the provided verbal prompt(s) designed to elicit a verbal response from the child containing specifically targeted morphological and/or syntactic structures. The child's response is written down and scored as either correct or incorrect relative to guidelines provided on the response form and in the test manual. If a child does not respond, additional prompts may be given in order to elicit a response. Suggestions for additional prompts are provided in the test manual. If there is still no response from the child a score of "no response" (NR) is recorded in the response form. As there are no basal or ceiling criteria, all test items must be administered and scored in order for the results to be reliable and valid.

Scoring is also simple and straightforward. Before scoring it is suggested that the accuracy of responses made by the child at the time of testing be quickly confirmed using the guidelines provided in the test manual when necessary. A raw score is then calculated, which is the total number of correct responses made by the child. Tables are provided in the test manual to convert the raw score to a standard score, 90% and 95% confidence intervals, a percentile rank, a 90% percentile band, and an age equivalent score. These data are then recorded in the test results summary area on the response form. As the authors noted, analysis and interpretation of a child's test performance must go beyond simply reporting these scores in that additional "knowledge of morphology and syntax and understanding of the specific structures targeted in this assessment tool are required to interpret the child's performance" (manual, p. 27).

DEVELOPMENT. As previously noted, the SPELT-P 2 is a revision of the original SPELT-P (Werner & Kresheck, 1983), which was created as a screening tool to be used with young children. Presumably due to the age of the SPELT-P, this revision began with a review of current literature regarding the development of morphology and syntax in children. Based on this review, the revision proceeded with four goals in mind: (a) to update and add new photographic stimuli that more accurately reflected pictured activities and current cultural diversity, (b) to revise original test items to better assess morphosyntactic structures, (c) to add new needed test items, and (d) to develop normative data.

Following this process, a 48-item draft revision was created and distributed to a number of practicing clinicians for their evaluation and feedback regarding the ability of the photographic stimuli and prompts to elicit the targeted morphosyntactic structure. The photographs and prompts were revised again based on this feedback. A pilot study was then initiated using the 48-item test, which was administered to 80 children within the 3 years, 0 months to 5 years, 11 months age range. Results from this pilot testing and additional comments from clinicians were used to reduce the 48 items to the current 40. In so doing, the number of test items in the revised form increased by 15 when compared to the original SPELT-P. This 40-item version was then used for the standardization process. The extent of this revision changed the use of the SPELT-P 2 from being a screening tool similar to the original test to its use as a norm-based assessment tool providing a more comprehensive measurement of children's morphological and syntactic development.

TECHNICAL. Standardization of the SPELT-P 2 took place during a 13-month period in 2004 and 2005. The standardization sample contained 1,747 children between 3 years, 0 months and 5 years, 11 months of age, representing 26 states in the four major geographic regions of the United States. Demographic variables included in the sample were geographic region, gender, ethnicity, and child's age. Although the authors made no mention of attempting to have the standardization sample match current census demographic data, they did report that the sample relative to ethnicity generally reflected national census data for African American and White children. Also from the tables presented in the test manual, it appears that all demographic variables were generally well distributed across the standardization sample. In addition, the authors reported that approximately 2.5% of the standardization sample were identified as language impaired, and reported the educational levels of the mothers of the children in the sample. No discussion of the relevance or significance of these data were provided.

Test reliability was established three ways: test-retest reliability, interjudge reliability, and internal consistency. Test-retest reliability was established by re-administering the test to 62 representative children from the standardization sample within 14 days of the initial administration. Correlation in performance between the initial and second administrations was .96 suggesting strong test-retest reliability. Interjudge reliability was evaluated by having two trained raters independently score the results from 230 representative children from the standardization sample. Interrater correlations ranged between .99 and 1.00 with the two judges disagreeing in only one instance. Estimates of internal consistency for the standardization sample ranged from .798 to .882, whereas standard error of measurements by age group ranged between 2.26 and 2.71. Together these data suggest that the SPELT-P 2 appears to demonstrate very good reliability as well as good internal consistency.

Test validity was also established three ways: content validity, construct validity, and concurrent validity. Content validity of the SPELT-P 2 was established by thoroughly reviewing the current literature on children's development of morphology and syntax in comparison to the items on the original SPELT-P. This process resulted in the revision of many test items and the addition of other items to reflect more closely current knowledge and beliefs of experts in the field. In addition, the SPELT-P 2 test items were compared to those in the Index of Productive Syntax (IPSyn) (Scarborough, 1990), a widely used tool for the analysis of children's language. As the authors noted, this comparison revealed that many of the test items in the IPSyn were represented in the SPELT-2, especially in the area of assessing verb phrases. Construct validity was established by comparing test performance of the standardization sample between the age range groups and confirming that as children aged their test performance got better. This trend is commensurate with the established developmental construct that the use of morphosyntactic structure in expressive language increases with age. Therefore, the intent of the authors that the SPELT-P 2 be developmental in nature was reinforced. Evidence of concurrent validity was established by comparing test performance on the SPELT-P 2 with test performance on the Syntax Construction subtest of the Comprehensive Assessment of Spoken Language (CASL; Carrow-Woolfolk, 1999). Sixty-one children from the standardization sample were administered both tests with the correlation between scores at .86 "indicating a substantial overlap in scores between the two tests as they measure the use of morphosyntactic constructions in expressive language" (manual, p. 41). From the evidence presented, the SPELT-P 2 appears to be a valid test relative to its intended purpose of measuring the developmental acquisition of morphosyntactic structures in young children.

COMMENTARY. The SPELT-P 2 is a revision of the original SPELT-P, a widely used language screening tool for young children. This revision, including its standardization, has resulted in the SPELT-P 2 being more useful than a screening tool in addition to it being a more comprehensive language development assessment tool. However, as with most assessment tools that focus on a specific aspect of language development (in this case the use of morphophonemic structures), it should not be used alone in identifying children with developmental language problems. As the authors noted "It should, of course, be used in combination with informal measures of morphosyntax and both formal and informal measures of the other domains of ... language" (manual, p. 4).

Clinicians familiar with the original SPELT-P will recognize the similar format and structure of the SPELT-P 2 and should easily become comfortable and reliable in its administration. Incorporation of normative data in the revised test allows clinicians not only to measure an individual child's morphosyntactic skills, but to be able to compare those skills to children of a similar chronological age. Also, as the authors intended, the format of the test facilitates identifying a child's relative morphosyntactic strengths and weaknesses. Further, it does provide significant information in the test manual regarding how to adapt the test successfully for children who speak African American Vernacular English. However, it must be kept in mind that the focus of the SPELT-P 2 is limited to expressive morphosyntax and it is not meant to assess other important areas of language development in children such as expressive vocabulary or pragmatics. Likewise, it does not assess any aspects of a child's receptive language skills. Therefore, as the authors noted, a complete assessment of a child's expressive and receptive language skills must include additional test measures in other important developmental areas. It is incumbent upon the clinician to select such tests to meet the child's needs.

SUMMARY. The SPELT-P 2 appears to be a thoughtful and useful revision, which clinicians should find helpful when assessing morphosyntactic development in young children. The test is simple to administer and score, the photographic stimuli are interesting and attractive, and the addition of normative data is especially appreciated. As noted previously, test interpretation is not simple. Interpretation requires broad knowledge in child language development and specific knowledge in developmental morphology and syntax. Although the test is considered comprehensive, it narrowly focuses on a specific area of expressive language development and, hence, should not be used alone in assessing the overall language development and functional level of a child. When used as the authors intend, the SPELT-P 2 should make a useful and welcome addition to a clinician's choice of child language assessment tools.

REVIEWER'S REFERENCES

Carrow-Woolfolk, E. (1999). CASL: Comprehensive Assessment of Spoken Language. Circle Pines, MN: American Guidance Service, Inc.

Scarborough, H. S. (1990). Index of productive syntax. *Applied Psycholinguistics, 11,* 1-22.

Werner, E., & Kresheck, J. (1983). Structured Photographic Expressive Language Test—Preschool. Sandwich, IL: Janelle Publications.

[133]

Structured Photographic Expressive Language Test—Third Edition.

Purpose: Designed to "examine expressive use of morphology and syntax."

Population: Ages 4 to 9-11.

Publication Dates: 1983-2003.

Acronym: SPELT-3.
Score: Total score only.
Administration: Individual.
Price Data, 2008: $165 per manual (2003, 97 pages), 54 color photographs, 30 response forms, and storage box.
Time: (20) minutes.
Comments: Includes a system of alternative response structures for assessment of the African American population.
Authors: Janet I. Dawson, Connie E. Stout, and Julia A. Eyer.
Publisher: Janelle Publications.
Cross References: See T5:2524 (13 references) and T4:2588 (1 reference); for a review by Joan D. Berryman of an earlier edition, see 9:1198 (2 references).

Review of the Structured Photographic Expressive Language Test—Third Edition by JORGE E. GONZALEZ, Assistant Professor, Department of Educational Psychology, Texas A&M University, College Station, TX, and CRAIG S. SHWERY, Assistant Professor, Elementary Education Teaching Programs, University of Alabama, Tuscaloosa, AL:

DESCRIPTION. The Structured Photographic Expressive Language Test—Third Edition (SPELT-3) is an individually administered 53-item assessment tool that measures a child's generation of specific morphological and syntactic structures. The SPELT-3 takes approximately 15 to 25 minutes to administer. It is designed to elicit responses from children through the use of structured familiar visually and auditorily presented stimuli. Developmental in nature, the test is appropriate for both clinical and research settings for children between 4 years and 9 years, 11 months of age. The SPELT-3 is a revision of the SPELT-II and retains the design of previous versions. The revision was undertaken to update photographic stimuli and add new photographs reflecting American cultural diversity, update items to assess morphosyntactic structures more accurately and the addition of more complex structures since standardization was expanded to include older children.

The SPELT-3 is intended for use in identifying children whose performance is substantially below their age-equivalent peers in morphosyntactic structures, to note strengths and weaknesses in individual children, and for use in assessing morphosyntax development of children who may speak an African American English dialect. Examiners using the SPELT-3 are expected to have a thorough grasp of child language development. In particular, a strong emphasis on morphology and syntax, training in evaluation and testing, as well as understanding of test administration, scoring, and test interpretation.

Test materials in the SPELT-3 consist of a 97-page test manual, a photographic stimulus book, and response forms. The photographic stimulus book contains a practice item along with 53 photographs to elicit the targeted responses. Administration is fairly straightforward. The examiner presents a practice item, places the photographic stimulus book in front of the child, reads an eliciting statement for an item (e.g., "Tell me about this picture"), records the child's response, and, if necessary, prompts further, using suggestions found in the manual's appendix. Testing continues until all 53 items are administered. If the child does not respond, the examiner may vary the eliciting statement through further prompting. The manual explicitly notes that there should be no more than three prompting attempts.

Child responses are recorded on the response form. Correct responses are determined on whether the child's response reflects the target structure. The response form includes the most frequently elicited child statements from past standardized norms. Examiners are also encouraged to review the scoring guide in the manual for further guidance. Incorrect responses represent a child omitting the correct target structure, a nonresponse or an "I don't know" statement after three prompts, or an omission of the required target structure despite a grammatically correct sentence. Scores include a raw score of the total number of items scored as correct, standard scores with a mean of 100 with a standard deviation of 15, confidence intervals, percentiles, and age equivalents. The manual recommends interpreting the standard scores derived after calculating the raw score.

DEVELOPMENT. As noted previously, the SPELT-3 reflects updates to the SPELT-II. The revision began with a thorough review of current research on children's development of morphology and syntax. Individual items assessed for content and currency were revised using collaborative input made by practicing clinicians. Items were also revised, deleted, or added to reflect information from a "consensus of experts" (manual, p. 41) who reviewed the photographs for appropriateness. A 58-item pilot of the test was administered to 60 children distributed across 6-month age intervals.

Results of the pilot and additional clinician review reduced the test to its current 53-item format.

TECHNICAL.

Standardization. The SPELT-3 was normed on 1,580 children 4 through 9 years of age from 20 states representing four major geographic areas of the United States: West, South, Northeast, and Midwest. Speech language pathologists working in numerous clinical settings provided recruited the norming sample. Demographically, the distribution of the norming sample reflected closely African American and White children but underrepresented Hispanics. Approximately 7% of the sample was identified as Language Impaired. Scores derived from the norming process included standard scores, percentiles, and age-equivalents. Because standard scores reflected no clear difference between males and females, the authors combined male and female norms for all age groups. The norms are reported for 6-month intervals up to age 7. After age 7, 12-month intervals for older children are employed. Percentile scores corresponding to each raw score were also obtained. Because of the skewed nature of the distribution, the authors recommend great caution in interpreting small score differences, as well as cautioning that any interpretation must take into consideration influencing factors beyond the child's responses (e.g., experiential deficits). The authors also caution interpretation of age-equivalents, especially on raw scores at the upper limits of an age equivalency.

Reliability. Evidence of score consistency is represented in test-retest, interjudge (i.e., rater) reliability, and internal consistency. Test-retest reliability with a median interval of 11 days was .94. Interrater reliability was achieved by having two judges independently score a sample of 85 females and 101 males from eight states. Interrater correlations ranged from .97 to .99. Internal consistency estimates on the standardization sample ranged from .76 to .92, with a median reliability estimate of .86.

Validity. Validity for the SPELT-3 was established using content, construct, and concurrent validity. Content validity relied on reviewing existing research on children's development of morphological and syntactical processes relative to the SPELT-II items. One means of evaluating the content was to compare items in the SPELT-3 to items in the Index of Productive Syntax (Scarborough, 1990), a widely used instrument used to analyze spontaneous language in clinical and research settings. The authors reported relevant overlap as evidence of content validity. Because the SPELT-3 is developmental in nature, the authors posited that an increase in age could be expected to parallel an increase in scores—evidence of construct validity. As expected, on the SPELT-3 test scores increased with age. Concurrent validity was established by using the Comprehensive Assessment of Spoken Language (CASL; Carrow-Woolfolk, 1999) as the criterion measure. The correlation between the two measures was .78, indicating substantial overlap between the measures.

COMMENTARY. With its updated norms and carefully reviewed items, the SPELT-3 arguably sets the standard for measurement of morphosyntax, an important normal oral language development precursor. A strength of the SPELT-3 is that it is grounded in sound theoretical, conceptual, and applied research on what is known about the normal developmental continuum of language and the bases of atypical language development. The SPELT-3 is a must in contributing to documentation necessary for qualifying children for services in schools. Current research clearly supports the need to identify children with early morphosyntax difficulties. In the absence of early identification, these children are a high risk for later word reading and other problems (Carlisle, 2004). The most notable weakness of this measure is the lack of sufficient construct validity and limited concurrent validity. Although providing indirect evidence, construct validity extends beyond demonstrating a mean increase in a standard score as a function of increasing age. Construct validity is best measured using convergent and discriminant validation by the multitrait-multimethod matrix.

SUMMARY. The SPELT-3 is a well-researched and well-developed measure of morphosyntax structures in children. The authors provide compelling evidence of theoretical, conceptual, and applied foundations. Speech and language personnel as well as other related personnel can use this test with confidence in assessment and qualifying decisions. Caution should, however, be used in using this instrument with English-language learners.

REVIEWERS' REFERENCES

Carlisle, J. F. (2004). Morphological processes that influence learning to read. In C. A. Stone, E. R. Silliman, B. J. Ehren, & K. Apel (Eds.), *Handbook of language and literacy* (pp. 318-339). New York: Guilford Press.

Carrow-Woolfolk, E. (1999). CASL: Comprehensive Assessment of Spoken Language. Circle Pines, MN: American Guidance Service, Inc.

Scarborough, H. S. (1990). Index of productive syntax. *Topics in Language Disorders, 8,* 46-62.

Review of the Structured Photographic Expressive Language Test—Third Edition by DARRELL L. SABERS, Professor of Educational Psychology, and HUAPING SUN, Doctoral Student, University of Arizona, Tucson, AZ:

DESCRIPTION. The Structured Photographic Expressive Language Test—Third Edition (SPELT-3) is a revision of SPELT-II. It is designed as an individually administered screening instrument to assess grammatical morpheme development of children ages 4 years, 0 months through 9 years, 11 months. There are no basal or ceiling rules, and thus all 53 items are expected to be administered. The administration of the test takes approximately 20 minutes.

A colored stimulus photograph and verbal statements and/or questions are provided to elicit the target structure for each item. Test responses are recorded on a separate response form. Berryman (1985), in a previous review of SPELT-II, suggested cutting and pasting each verbal stimulus from the response form to the back of the corresponding photograph to eliminate looking back and forth from the response form and the examinee. This suggested improvement was not made in the SPELT-3. We also recommend providing all acceptable responses to a test item on the response form to save the examiner's time in writing down the complete response during the test administration when the examinee's response is acceptable but different from the standard form.

Responses are scored as correct, incorrect, or incorrect-no response. The number of correct items is totaled to give a raw score. Standard scores, percentile ranks, and their confidence intervals are provided at half-year intervals for children ages 4 years, 0 months to 7 years, 11 months and at 1-year intervals for children ages 8 years, 0 months to 9 years, 11 months. Age equivalents may be calculated, and the authors properly warn that if used they should be interpreted with caution. However, the authors do not give any advice on the range of scores that might suggest the possible language impairment and need for further diagnostic assessment. Test users are informed that the complexity of language production could be affected by the child's cognitive, social, and linguistic ability and thus performance should be interpreted with "consideration of influencing factors beyond the child's responses on the test" (manual, p. 39).

Alternative scoring criteria are presented separately for children who use African American Vernacular English (AAVE). However, norms are not developed for this group. Consequently, the score interpretation for AAVE users is criterion-referenced only.

DEVELOPMENT. The SPELT-3 is the updated revision of the SPELT-II. The item revision was based on practicing clinicians' comments on whether the photograph and the elicitation statement are likely to elicit the desired response, whether anything in the picture is likely to produce a negative response, or if anything is culturally insensitive. The resulting 58-item test was then piloted on 60 children of the target ages. The final 53 items were determined from the pilot test results and additional clinician review. The major revision included more complex structures so that the ceiling problem with older age groups in SPELT-II (Berryman, 1985) was alleviated. However, no detailed information about the item analyses of the pilot test and how the decision was made is presented. The reasons why the other 5 items were dropped are unknown.

TECHNICAL. The SPELT-3 was standardized on 1,580 children to whom the test was administered by participating speech-language pathologists from 20 states in four major geographical regions in the United States. One hundred and sixty-three children were excluded because of the incomplete data on the response form. No comparison was made to see whether these children with incomplete data were demographically different from the children included in the standardization procedure. The distribution of the standardization sample by age, region, ethnicity, and gender is listed in the manual. The percentages of the sample in the age-by-region cells are not well-balanced. The U.S. Census figures are not provided in the manual, so we cannot judge whether the unbalance was purposefully made to match the population distribution or resulted from inadequate sampling technique. To the authors' credit, this test successfully identified slightly more than 7% of the norming sample as language impaired, which is comparable to the prevalence rate in the population. This change adequately addressed the issue raised previously in regard to the normative sample for SPELT-II that no children with apparent developmental problems were included and overidentification of children with language impairment was suspected (Berryman, 1985).

A linear transformation was used to compute the standardized scores. As a result, raw scores of

35, 36, and 37 correspond to 10th, 11th, and 14th percentiles for ages 7 years, 0 months through 7 years, 5 months but to 11th, 13th, and 16th percentiles for ages 7 years, 6 months through 7 years, 11 months. The percentiles could be smoothed so that the same raw score would not result in a higher percentile rank for an older age group.

Test-retest reliability was .94 for a sample of 31 girls and 25 boys aged from 4 years, 0 months to 9 years, 11 months. The test-retest interval is not identical for all participants but averaged 11 days. It is expected that test-retest reliability coefficients would be lower if they were reported for each age level because of less variability within each age group. Internal consistency coefficients ranged from .76 to .92 with a median of .86 across age levels. The Pearson correlations between scores assigned by two raters on 188 completed protocols were from .97 to .99 across age levels. The average percentages of exact agreement and 1-point difference were 63% and 27%, respectively. It should be pointed out that there are two errors in a table in the manual (Table 6): Reliability of the SPELT-3 Scores (manual, p. 45). In this table the percent agreement for ages 5 years, 0 months to 5 years, 11 months totals to 110% and the percent agreement for ages 6 years, 0 months to 6 years, 11 months totals to only 90%.

Content validity is supported by the evidence that the SPELT-3 covers 14 of the 17 verb categories and 9 of the 11 categories in the area of question/negation from the Index of Productive Syntax (Scarborough, 1990), even though noun phrases are less well targeted by the SPELT-3. The authors claim that this is appropriate because "children with language impairment have increased difficulty with verbs, not nouns" (manual, p. 46). However, no data are presented to show that verb categories discriminate better than noun categories between children with and without language impairment. A moderate correlation of .78 between SPELT-3 and the Comprehensive Assessment of Spoken Language Syntax Construction Test (Carrow-Woolfolk, 1999) was used to assess concurrent validity of SPELT-3, but the sample size of 34 is small.

Construct validity of the SPELT-3 is based on the expectation that test score means should increase with age whereas standard deviations should decrease with age, and that the rate of development should be higher for younger children. More convincing evidence is needed because any developmentally sensitive skill could follow the same pattern. Besides, the standard deviation was smaller for age 8 than for age 9 for the norming sample, and the rate of score increase was more prominent between ages 5 and 6 than between ages 4 and 5.

COMMENTARY. The SPELT-3 aspires to screen for potential language impairment in the area of morphology and syntax. Its key strength is that it has good coverage of target structures. The manual clearly explains the administration process and the scoring criteria. It also contains some important admonitions for score interpretation such as age equivalents.

A big concern we have is how well the photograph and accompanying auditory stimuli could elicit the target structure. Berryman (1985) pointed out in a review of the SPELT-II that a lack of comprehension of the stimuli should not depress a child's score. We totally agree with that argument, but this problem still persists in the SPELT-3. First, it is cognitively demanding for a young child to pretend to be someone else. We administered the test to a 5-year-old boy. As a result, this 5-year-old boy answered a question as himself instead of pretending to be the mother in the picture to ask the question as demanded by one item. Second, the examinee could produce a pragmatically perfect response to a situation without the target structure, and not get credit for it. For example, the response "Can you please find my shoe" to one item appears no worse than "Where is my shoe." Third, just looking at the picture is sometimes not enough, and children need to pay attention to the elicitation statement/question, too. For example, two pictures portray nearly the same setting but the different prompts require different verbal responses. In the future development of the test, further studies are needed to see how factors other than the ability of language production could affect children's test scores. The validity of the test use is questionable until this issue is resolved.

SUMMARY. The SPELT-3 may have some merit as an additional tool to assist speech-language pathologists in identifying children with potential language impairments. The test users' expertise of morphology and syntax is assumed. The reliability evidence of this test is mostly positive. More effort should be put into justifying the process of eliciting the desired structure.

REVIEWERS' REFERENCES

Berryman, J. D. (1985). [Review of the Structured Photographic Expressive Language Test-II]. In J. V. Mitchell, Jr. (Ed.), *The ninth mental measurements yearbook* (pp. 1490-1491). Lincoln, NE: Buros Institute of Mental Measurements.

Carrow-Woolfolk, E. (1999). CASL: Comprehensive Assessment of Spoken Language. Circle Pines, MN: American Guidance Service.

Scarborough, H. S. (1990). Index of productive syntax. *Applied Psycholinguistics, 11,* 1-22.

[134]

Survey of Pain Attitudes.

Purpose: "Developed to assess a patient's attitudes and beliefs about pain."

Population: Ages 21-80 currently suffering from chronic pain.

Publication Dates: 1987-2007.

Acronym: SOPA.

Administration: Group.

Scores, 7: Adaptive Beliefs (Control Scale, Emotion Scale), Maladaptive Beliefs (Disability Scale, Harm Scale, Medication Scale, Solicitude Scale, Medical Cure Scale).

Price Data, 2009: $175 per introductory kit including technical manual (2007, 52 pages), 25 rating forms, 25 score summary/profile sheets, and 25 pain worksheets; $60 per technical manual; $65 per 25 rating forms; $35 per 25 score summary/profile sheets; $25 per 25 pain worksheets.

Time: (10-15) minutes.

Authors: Mark P. Jensen and Paul Karoly.

Publisher: Psychological Assessment Resources, Inc.

Review of the Survey of Pain Attitudes by J. M. BLACKBOURN, Associate Professor of Education, University of Mississippi, University, MS, JENNIFER G. FILLINGIM, Doctoral Candidate, University of Mississippi, University, MS, and CONN THOMAS, Professor of Education, West Texas A&M University, Canyon, TX:

DESCRIPTION. The Survey of Pain Attitudes (SOPA) is a measure designed to assess attitudes and beliefs of adults experiencing pain. As beliefs are phenomenological assumptions about reality, they have a significant impact on a patient's response to treatment. Therefore, an accurate assessment of beliefs and attitudes in a patient can serve to improve outcomes.

The SOPA consists of a carbonless rating form, a score summary sheet, and an optional pain worksheet. Patients respond to each of the 57 items on the rating form using a 5-point Likert scale with acronyms as the different points (VU = Very Untrue for you; SU = Somewhat Untrue for you; N = Neither true or untrue for you or does not apply to you; ST = Somewhat True for you; & VT = Very True for you) on the scale. The score summary sheet is essentially a protocol that provides a profile of the client as well as measures of the validity (Inconsistency Score) and reliability (Reliable Change Scores) of the client's responses. The reverse side of the summary score sheet provides a profile utilizing the scores obtained on the rating form to indicate the levels of the patient's Adaptive Beliefs (those that tend to relate to positive therapeutic outcomes) and Maladaptive Beliefs (those that tend to contravene positive therapeutic outcomes). The Optional Pain Worksheet is an additional measure that yields a range of the client's pain (from "worst possible pain" to "no pain"), the current level of pain. The reverse side of the Optional Pain Worksheet shows a human figure that allows the patient to indicate the specific area of pain.

Each of the forms is administered individually to the patient using a pencil. The instrument is appropriate for use with persons 21 to 80 years of age. The test authors state that the SOPA may be administered, scored, and interpreted by individuals who have professional training in psychology or a related field or possesses licensure or certification by an organization or agency that requires appropriate training in the ethics and competencies associated with psychological measurement and assessment.

DEVELOPMENT. The Survey of Pain Attitudes was designed and developed to give professionals in the medical field enhanced insight into the psychological functioning of persons experiencing chronic pain. As personal attitudes are a critical component in successful treatment of physical problems, a better understanding of each client's attitudes and beliefs would allow all medical staff to individualize therapy to enhance the chances of successful recovery. The rationale for the SOPA is consistent with current research findings related to the psychological dimension of medical treatment.

TECHNICAL. The normative sample for the SOPA consisted of 415 adult individuals who suffered from various forms of disability. A total of 125 individuals with multiple sclerosis were included in Sample 1, 127 persons with spinal cord injury were included in the second sample, and 163 persons with chronic pain made up Sample 3.

The average age of Sample 1 was 50.79 years with a standard deviation of 10.77 and a range of 24-80. The group was 24.8% male and 93.6% Caucasian with all other racial groups combined making up only 6.4% of the sample.

Sample 2 consisted of 127 persons with spinal cord injury ranging in age from 21-79 years with a mean age of 48.47. Sample 2 was mostly male (72.4%) with Caucasians making up 85% of the group. The standard deviation for this sample was 11.72.

The demographics of the third sample included an average age of 43.2 with a standard deviation of 10.12. Persons in this sample ranged in age from 21-74 years. Only 48.5% of Sample 3 was male, whereas females made up 51.5%. Eighty-nine percent of the sample was Caucasian.

Reliability estimates were provided for all seven of the SOPA's subscales. The SOPA possesses moderate to strong internal consistency as estimated by alpha coefficients ranging between .64 and .84. The available values were drawn from two previous studies and an analysis of the above three samples. Test-retest reliabilities were high to moderate, ranging from .67 to .79. In addition, *T* scores for the SOPA scales reflected a high degree of stability due to the minimal degree of difference.

Validity for the SOPA was considered via intercorrelations among the SOPA scales, correlation analyses between the SOPA scales and related measures, and the use of the SOPA as a measure of treatment outcomes. The three samples described previously were employed in the process (N = 415), as well as previous studies conducted by the test authors.

In terms of validity determined through the intercorrelation of the SOPA scales, all the correlations were significant at either the .01 or .001 levels with the exceptions of the comparisons between the Emotion scale and the Medical Cure scale and the Control and Solicitude scales.

Construct validity of the SOPA was assessed by a comparison of the instrument with similar instruments used to assess (a) Mental Health/Psychological Functioning and (b) Physical Dysfunction/Disability. In the case of the former, the majority of comparisons were found to be significantly related. In the latter instance, comparisons also indicated levels of significance at .01 in one study.

The SOPA possessed strong to moderate predictive validity in relation to treatment outcomes. It was particularly effective as an assessment of treatment effectiveness in relation to therapeutic programs with a cognitive-behavioral orientation. All seven of the SOPA scales demonstrated statistically significant changes from pretreatment to posttreatment with changes maintained for 12 months after termination of therapy for five of the scales. In addition, the test authors state that two scales (Disability and Control) were particularly effective in identifying those patients who were likely to deteriorate following the termination of therapy.

COMMENTARY. The Survey of Pain Attitudes instrument seems to be a valid and reliable measure of patient attitudes and beliefs about their pain. Substantial research supports this contention. The test authors have attempted to provide medical professionals with a psychometric tool that will facilitate the implementation of more effective treatment methodologies and improve therapeutic outcomes.

Although the instrument appears to be sound, the preponderance of Caucasians in the normative samples requires consideration when used with minority individuals. Demographics that mirror the diversity of the nation as a whole enhance an instrument's applicability and utility. It has always been a basic tenet of psychological measurement that applicability of a test was partially dependent on whether or not individuals similar in makeup to the subject were included in the norm group. The low levels of African Americans and Hispanics in the norm sample call the SOPA's applicability for these groups into question. Also, the size of the norm group is a concern (especially in light of the aforementioned low numbers of minority respondents). Although the instrument has important clinical uses and has adequate validity and reliability, a more extensive norm sample would strengthen the SOPA.

SUMMARY. The Survey of Pain Attitudes seems to be a valid and reliable measure of a patient's beliefs concerning the dimensions of their pain. It would seem to be a useful planning and predictive tool for medical professionals related to the prognosis of treatment therapies and the selection and/or modification of intervention methodologies. As with all self report-instruments the examiner should be cautious and judicious in the interpretation and generalization of results.

Review of the Survey of Pain Attitudes by STEPHEN J. FREEMAN, Professor and Chair, Department of Counseling, Texas A & M University-Commerce, Commerce, TX:

DESCRIPTION. The Survey of Pain Attitudes (SOPA) was developed to assess attitudes and beliefs about patients' pain—specifically patients who suffer from pain related to a physical disability and/or psychological functioning (e.g., depression) and in relation to outcomes of cognitive behavioral treatment for such pain. The SOPA is a 57-item self-report inventory in which respondents are asked to indicate their level of agreement with statements on a 5-point Likert scale. Seven scales are divided into two areas: Adaptive Beliefs and Maladaptive Beliefs. The Adaptive Beliefs domain consists of two scales: Control scale and Emotion scale. The Control scale assesses the belief that the patient can control her or his pain. The Emotion scale assesses the belief that her or his emotions have impact on her or his experience of pain. The Maladaptive Beliefs area consists of five scales: (a) Disability scale, (b) Harm scale, (c) Medication scale, (d) Solicitude scale, and (e) Medical Cure scale. The Disability scale assesses the belief that the patient is disabled by her or his pain. The Harm scale assesses the belief that pain is an indication of physical harm and exercise should be avoided. The Medication scale assesses the belief that medication is appropriate treatment for chronic pain. The Solicitude scale assesses the belief that others, especially family members, should be solicitous in response to her or his pain. The Medical Cure scale assesses the belief that a medical cure is possible for her or his pain. An optional pain worksheet containing two components (pain intensity and a pain chart) is included but is not necessary to score the SOPA.

The test authors intended the instrument to be useful across individuals from 21 to 80 years of age. The SOPA is self-administered and takes 10-15 minutes to complete.

DEVELOPMENT. The SOPA was initially developed in 1987 and has evolved in three phases into the current version. The initial version of the SOPA was developed using a dichotomous (true/false) response format containing 74 items measuring five constructs (Medical Cure, Control, Solicitude, Disability, and Medication). In Phase II, three changes were made to the instrument. First, the dichotomous format was replaced with a 5-point Likert scale to better reflect varying degrees of respondent beliefs. Second, additional items were added to the existing scales to increase content validity and reliability. Third, additional items were developed to assess two additional domains: Harm and Emotions. These changes resulted in a 57-item scale assessing seven pain-related beliefs. In Phase III, based on respondent complaints regarding item wording, all items were evaluated and 23 items were rewritten for increased clarity.

TECHNICAL. The SOPA manual reports normative data were derived from 415 adults aggregated from three samples. Sample 1 consisted of 125 participants diagnosed with Multiple Sclerosis the "majority" of whom were randomly selected from a group contacted through the Multiple Sclerosis Association in the western U.S. Sample 2 consisted of 127 participants with spinal cord injury. Sample 3 consisted of 163 participants with chronic pain who were participating in an outpatient pain program.

The SOPA and other measures were mailed to participants in Samples 1 and 2. Response rates were 68% for Sample 1 and 55% for Sample 2. Data from Sample 3 were collected prior to beginning the pain program.

Aggregated demographic characteristics reported an age range of 21–80 with a mean age of 47.10 years. Gender distribution was 48.7% male and 51.3% female. Ethnicity was reported as 89.2% Caucasian, 1.7% African American, 1.9% Hispanic, and 7.2% other or unreported. Participants education level were reported as ≤ 9th grade 2.7%, 10-11 grade 4.1%, high school graduate/GED 13.7%, vocational school 10.6%, some college 31.6%, college graduate 23.4%, graduate school/professional school 14%. Employment status was reported as 30.6% working full- or part-time, 2.6% full- or part-time students, 13.5% retired, 5.5% were homemakers, 46.3% were unemployed due to illness/pain/disability, and 4.1% were unemployed due to other reasons.

Reliability. Internal consistency reliability (alpha) coefficients were reported for SOPA scales for the standardization sample and ranged from .65 to .82. Test-retest reliability coefficients (using a 2-week interval) ranged from .67 to .79.

The manual reports several existing studies examining the convergent validity of the SOPA against other instruments reportedly measuring similar constructs. The SF-36 Mental Health Scale, the Center for Epidemiological Studies Depression Scale, Beck Depression Inventory, Psychosocial Dysfunction and Physical Dysfunction Scales of the Sickness Impact Profile, Roland-Morris Disability Scale, and the Brief Pain Inventory. Pearson correlations were calculated between scales and indices of the other instruments. Values ranged from .72 to -.55.

COMMENTARY. The SOPA is an ambitious undertaking that is in its third phase of refinement and development. For such a complex phenomenon as pain the manual appears rather abbreviated and provides no discussion of the theoretical model used as a guide in developing the instrument.

In the normative sample Caucasians were overrepresented as were those participants with some college, college degrees, and/or graduate or professional school education (69%). A representative sample of minorities would minimize cultural test bias. Similarly, educational status needs to be more representative of the general population. The normative sample could benefit from the inclusion of a broader range of diagnostic categories (e.g., fibromyalgia, diffuse musculoskeletal pain, lumbar and cervical disc disease) and information regarding the duration of pain. Finally, there is a question regarding a possible threat to external validity as all indications point to the standardization of the test using only pain populations and/or disability samples without reference to pain-free "normals" or those having pain who have not required or sought treatment.

Reliability coefficients reported were moderate to strong as were reported test-retest reliability coefficients. Reports of construct validity would be strengthened if information on the theoretical model used to guide instrument development were included.

SUMMARY. Evaluation of pain is one of the most complex phenomena in human experience. We must therefore respect the test developers' impressive efforts and their continuing endeavors and research-based refinements. The nonrepresentativeness of the normative sample creates a threat to external validity, and limits the utility of the SOPA.

[135]

TerraNova, Third Edition.

Purpose: "An assessment system designed to measure concepts, processes, and skills taught throughout the (U.S.) nation."
Population: Grades K-12.
Publication Dates: 1997-2009.
Acronym: SCAN-3:C.
Administration: Group.
Levels, 12: 10 (Grades K-6 to 1-6), 11 (Grades 1-6 to 2-6), 12 (Grades 2-0 to 3-2), 13 (Grades 2-6 to 4-2), 14 (Grades 3-6 to 5-2), 15 (Grades 4-6 to 6-2), 16 (Grades 5-6 to 7-2), 17 (Grades 6-6 to 8-2), 18 (Grades 7-6 to 9-2), 19 (Grades 8-6 to 10-2), 20 (Grades 9-6 to 11-2), 21/22 (Grades 10-6 to 12-9).
Price Data, 2009: Price data for Teacher's Guide (2009, 353 pages) and Technical Report (on CD only, 2008, 384 pages) available from publisher; $61.05 per norms book (specify Fall norms, Winter norms, or Spring norms).
Time: Administration time varies by test and level.
Comments: Earlier versions were called California Achievement Test and Comprehensive Test of Basic Skills.
Author: CTB/McGraw-Hill.
Publisher: CTB/McGraw-Hill.

a) TERRANOVA, THIRD EDITION SURVEY EDITION.
Purpose: Designed to "yield norm-referenced information and some curriculum-referenced information in a minimum of testing time."
Price Data: $151 per 25 consumable Survey test books (Levels 12-13, specify level); $136 per 25 reusable Survey test books (Levels 14-21/22, specify level); $24.65 per Survey Test Directions for Teachers (Levels 12-21/22, specify level); $17.70 per 25 packages of math manipulatives (Levels 13-21/22, specify level); $6.20 per Survey Directions for Practice Activities (Levels 12-18, specify level).
Comments: All items are selected-response items.

1) *Level 12.*
Population: Grades 2-0 to 3-2.
Scores: 4 Survey scores (Reading, Mathematics, Science, Social Studies).
Time: (135) minutes.

2) *Level 13-21/22.*
Population: Grades 2-6 to 12-9.
Scores: 5 Survey scores (Reading, Language, Mathematics, Science, Social Studies).
Time: (170) minutes.

b) TERRANOVA, THIRD EDITION COMPLETE BATTERY.
Purpose: Designed to be "capable of generating precise norm-referenced achievement scores and a full complement of objective mastery scores."
Price Data: $193.75 per 25 consumable Complete Battery test books (Levels 10-13, specify level); $151 per 25 reusable Complete Battery test books (Levels 14-21/22, specify level); $24.65 per Complete Battery Directions for Teachers (Levels 10-21/22, specify level); $17.70 per 25 packages of math manipulatives (Levels 13-21/22, specify level); $24.65 per 25 Complete Battery Practice Activities (Levels 10-18, specify level); $6.20 per Complete Battery Teacher Directions for Practice Activities (Levels 10-18, specify level).
Comments: A combination of the Survey items and additional selected-response items.

1) *Level 10.*
Population: Grades K-6 to 1-6.
Scores: 2 Complete Battery scores (Reading, Mathematics).
Time: (95) minutes.
2) *Levels 11-12.*
Population: Grades 1-6 to 3-2.
Scores: 4 Complete Battery scores (Reading, Mathematics, Science, Social Studies).
Time: (160-180) minutes.
3) *Levels 13-21/22.*
Population: Grades 2-6 to 12-9.
Scores: 5 Complete Battery scores (Reading, Language, Mathematics, Science, Social Studies).
Time: (245) minutes.

c) TERRANOVA, THIRD EDITION MULTIPLE ASSESSMENTS.
Purpose: This edition "combines selected-response items of the Survey edition with sections of constructed-response items that allow students to produce their own short and extended responses."
Price Data: $202.50 per 25 consumable Multiple Assessments test books (Levels 11-21/22, specify level); $24.15 per Multiple Assessments Directions for Teachers (Levels 11-21/22, specify level); $17.70 per 25 packages of math manipulatives (Levels 13-21/22, specify level); $24.65 per 25 Multiple Assessments Practice Activities (Levels 11-21/22, specify level); $6.20 per Multiple Assessments Teacher Directions for Practice Activities (Levels 11-21/22, specify level).
1) *Levels 11-12.*
Population: Grades 1-6 to 3-2.
Scores: 4 Multiple Assessments scores (Reading, Mathematics, Science, Social Studies).
Time: (260-270) minutes.
2) *Levels 13-21/22.*
Population: Grades 2-6 to 12-9.
Scores: 5 Multiple Assessments scores (Reading, Language, Mathematics, Science, Social Studies).
Time: (335) minutes.

d) TERRANOVA, THIRD EDITION PLUS TESTS.
Purpose: Designed to "provide additional in-depth information about students' basic skills.
Price Data: $65.80 per 25 Form C Plus test booklets (Levels 11-13, specify level); $56.70 per 25 Form C Plus test booklets (Levels 14-21/22, specify level); $24.65 per Complete Battery/Plus Directions for Teachers (specify Level 16-18, 19-21/22).
Time: Administration time not reported.
Comments: "Used in conjunction with the Survey, Complete Battery, and Multiple Assessments components."
1) *Level 11.*
Population: Grades 1-6 to 2-6.
Scores, 3: Word Analysis, Vocabulary, Mathematics Computation.
2) *Levels 12-13.*
Population: Grades 2-0 to 4-2.
Scores, 5: Word Analysis, Vocabulary, Language Mechanics, Spelling, Mathematics Computation.
3) *Levels 14-21/22.*
Population: Grades 3-6 to 12-9.
Scores, 4: Vocabulary, Language Mechanics, Spelling, Mathematics Computation.

Cross References: For reviews by Gregory J. Cizek and Robert L. Johnson of the Second edition, see 16:245; for reviews by Judith A. Monsaas and Anthony J. Nitko of an earlier edition, see 14:383; for information on the Comprehensive Tests of Basic Skills, see T5:665 (95 references); see also T4:623 (23 references); for reviews by Kenneth D. Hopkins and M. David Miller of the CTBS, see 11:81 (70 references); for reviews by Robert L. Linn and Lorrie A. Shepard of an earlier form, see 9:258 (29 references); see also T3:551 (59 references); for reviews by Warren G. Findley and Anthony J. Nitko of an earlier edition, see 8:12 (13 references); see also T2:11 (1 reference); for reviews by J. Stanley Ahmann and Frederick G. Brown and excerpted reviews by Brooke B. Collison and Peter A. Taylor (rejoinder by Verna White) of Forms Q and R, see 7:9. For reviews of subtests of earlier editions, see 8:721 (1 review), 8:825 (1 review), 7:685 (1 review), 7:514 (2 reviews), and 7:778 (1 review).

Review of the TerraNova, Third Edition by JOHN O. ANDERSON, Professor, Department of Educational Psychology, University of Victoria, Victoria, British Columbia, Canada:

DESCRIPTION. The TerraNova, Third Edition (TerraNova 3) is an assessment system "designed to measure concepts, processes, and skills taught throughout the nation" (teacher's guide, p. 4). The test battery provides educators with a comprehensive tool to measure and monitor student progress relative to local, state, and national standards in domains of Reading, Language, Mathematics, Science and Social Studies from mid-kindergarten (Level 10) to the end of Grade 12 (Level 22). The tests come in a number of configurations (Survey, Complete Battery, Multiple Assessment, and Plus) that vary in size and the range of scores provided. In addition to the domains noted above, the Plus version adds measures of Word Analysis, Vocabulary, Language Mechanics, Spelling, and Mathematics Computation. Test administration can vary from a low of 15 minutes (e.g., the Plus subtests of Spelling or Vocabulary) to over 6 hours with the Multiple Assessment with Plus configuration at Levels 13 to 22. The Survey configuration offers tests from Level 12 to 22, and consists of selected response items only and requires less time for administration than the Complete Battery or Multiple Assessments forms of the test. The Complete Battery adds more selected response items to the item sets used in the Survey to result in longer tests of higher reliability, and expanded coverage to include Levels 10 and 11. The Multiple Assessments forms add constructed response format items to the Survey configuration and offer coverage of all levels.

The TerraNova 3 tests provide practice items for most levels of the test in the different configurations. McGraw-Hill also offers many additional assessment tools that could be used in conjunction with the TerraNova 3 such as InView, a test of general cognitive abilities that can be used to generate expected scores for students in the reports generated from TerraNova test administration, and *Classroom Connections to Terra Nova, The Second Edition*, which is a four-volume reference set for teachers linking the test to teaching activities, practice items, and learning outcomes.

DEVELOPMENT. TerraNova was developed to meet the requirements of the *No Child Left Behind* (NCLB; U.S. Department of Education, 2002) legislation and appears to be intended for use in state-wide and district-wide testing programs. Test developers consulted curriculum frameworks and content documents from most of the states in the U.S. to align the TerraNova test specifications with the learning domains common in U.S. schools. In developing the tests there was attention paid to compatibility with assessment guidelines and procedures of the American Association for the Advancement of Science, the International Reading Association, National Assessment of Educational Progress, National Council of Teachers of English, and the National Council of Teachers of Mathematics. The tests are composed of a mix of selected and constructed response item formats with a predominance of selected response formatted items. As part of test development, usability analyses were conducted to evaluate student use of the tests and associated materials.

The tests were normed on national (U.S.) samples of age appropriate students with approximately 15,000 students at each level (the exception being the youngest level–10 and 11–which had samples of approximately 4,000 and 10,000 students, respectively). The sample of schools was stratified on the basis of region, community type, socioeconomic status, and special needs. The educational jurisdictions participating in the norming are listed in the technical manual.

TECHNICAL. The scoring and analysis of the item responses of the norming samples was conducted using an item response theory (IRT) approach with a 3-parameter model for the selected-response items, and a 2-parameter partial credit model for constructed responses. A number of score scales were derived for reporting test results: national percentiles, normal curve equivalent scores, stanines, and grade equivalent scores. In addition, users can obtain Anticipated Achievement Scores based on the student's age, grade, and score on a general cognition test (this requires the additional administration of the CTB/McGraw-Hill tests InView or the Primary Test of Cognitive Skills), which would allow for the identification of over/underperforming students. Scores are reported for each domain tested and there is also the possibility of generating a Total Score which combines results from Reading, Language, and Mathematics items.

In addition and in accordance with requirements embedded in the NCLB legislation, TerraNova has developed proficiency levels (Objective Performance Index consisting of five levels: Step 1, Progressing, Nearing Proficiency, Proficient, and Advanced) which are related to learning outcomes measured by the test. The proficiency levels are developed for four age/grade clusters: Primary, Elementary, Middle School, and High School. The test score cutpoints between levels were determined by expert panels using the bookmark procedure–the initial setting of cutpoints was conducted in 1996 and reaffirmed during the development of TerraNova 3. Verbal descriptions of each proficiency level are included in the teacher's guide for TerraNova, Third Edition, but the inclusion of some sample items to illustrate the performance boundaries of each level would help test users to better understand the pragmatic meanings of and differences between the proficiency levels. Full understanding of the cutscores requires users to wade through 70 pages of tables in the technical report listing objectives and scores for each domain for each of the four grade levels.

TerraNova has conducted and reported a number of statistical analyses to evaluate the quality of the test. Differential item functioning

(DIF) procedures were implemented for both ethnicity and gender of respondents and results indicate low to no DIF on the items used in the TerraNova instruments. Item difficulties are tabulated for all items and range from a low of .14 to .98. Although the tables are comprehensive and a useful inclusion in the technical report, it would be helpful to include graphs of the distributions of item difficulties (locations) for each test and level of the TerraNova package. The completion rates for the norming samples are reported and indicate that the time limits for the tests are reasonable for the intended respondents. An evaluation of ceiling effects investigating percentile scores at the maximum score level indicated no substantial ceiling effects were present. Correlations between different tests within each level show moderately positive (.21 to .93) relationships between Reading, Language, Mathematics, and Science.

COMMENTARY. TerraNova 3 is a big comprehensive assessment battery intended to do all testing required by the NCLB legislation. The user will have to devote a substantial amount of time and effort to understand the test and make meaningful interpretation of results. For example, the TerraNova test materials used in this review consisted of 57 documents (test booklets, teacher guides, and practice items) in addition to a 374-page technical report on disk and a 342-page teacher's guide. The test is clearly designed for use in the U.S. context, and a number of the test items would not be appropriate for use outside of the U.S. system with references to U.S. history, currency and nonmetric units, and the national nature of the norms.

The technical work done on generating normed scores is well-described in the technical report and comprehensive in attention to significant measurement issues. The analyses suggest that TerraNova 3 has solid psychometric characteristics. However, given the complexity of the tests, the variety of score scales available and the dependency on CTB for scoring, analysis, and reporting, it would be wise for users to devote sufficient time and effort to thoroughly understand the test, its linkage to local curricular objectives, and the meanings of the proficiency levels within the school context being assessed. The availability of reporting scores as predetermined proficiency levels will tend to devolve into the use of the TerraNova proficiency levels as educational standards. The user is well advised to evaluate explicitly the nature of the cutpoint used by McGraw-Hill and their assignment of items to objectives before using the results generated by the CTB scoring service.

In the manuals there are appropriate cautions embedded regarding fair testing practice–it may be useful to emphasize these cautions to optimize user awareness of issues such as a test is but one source of information about student achievement and school performance; that no single test is equally appropriate for all students; or that teaching to the test is not an appropriate practice (although CTB offers a variety of resources to do just that–practice test items and a four-volume teaching resource linked to TerraNova). In the teachers' guide there is a section that is to an extent at variance with the curriculum focus taken in the development of the TerraNova. Part 5 provides an alternate framework for interpreting test results–Critical Thinking Framework–a 57-page section that could be useful but appears to detract from the primary design elements of TerraNova.

SUMMARY. TerraNova is a widely used test as evidenced by the release of the third edition. The CTB/McGraw-Hill assessment resources appear to be embedded within a number of large educational jurisdictions–the CTB website (CTB.com) lists over 15 state-specific sites that provide access to assessment resources associated with in-state student testing. TerraNova is a central element of the CTB spectrum of tests that offers a comprehensive assessment program that requires users to ascend a rather steep learning curve in order to be fully cognizant of test characteristics and the meanings of scores generated.

REVIEWER'S REFERENCE

U.S. Department of Education. (2002). *No Child Left Behind Act*, Public Law 107–110—Jan. 8, 2002 115 stat. 1425. Retrieved February 2010 from http://www.ed.gov/policy/elsec/leg/esea02/107-110.pdf

Review of the TerraNova, Third Edition by MICHAEL HARWELL, Professor, Department of Educational Psychology, University of Minnesota, Minneapolis, MN:

DESCRIPTION. The seemingly ever-expanding role of standardized achievement tests in education has created a substantial need for assessments that are psychometrically sound, incorporate state and local standards as well as practices recommended by professional organizations, and are packaged in ways that facilitate appropriate interpretation and use of scores. The TerraNova, Third Edition (TerraNova 3) is a strong candidate in this arena. The TerraNova 3 is a revised version of the TerraNova, The Second Edition (2002) and is a comprehensive standardized assessment system designed primarily to assess concepts and skills taught in U.S. schools in Grades K-12. Users generally administer one of three major TerraNova 3 tests (Survey, Complete Battery, Multiple Assessments) within which the content areas Reading, Language, Mathematics, Science, and Social Studies are assessed using a single test form (Form G). Other tests (e.g., Plus Tests) can be administered in conjunction with a major TerraNova 3 test to provide additional information. The tests are also available in Braille, large-print versions, and Spanish.

Both norm-referenced and criterion-referenced scores are provided. Norm-referenced information is available in the form of scale scores, national percentiles, customized percentiles, grade-equivalent scores, and normal-curve-equivalent scores. Scale scores produced by norm-referenced tests for TerraNova 3 are on the same scale as that of previous versions of this test and thus can be compared directly to assess growth over time (e.g., growth in mathematics achievement in a school). Scoring of criterion-referenced tests follows a typical standards-based format, consisting of a small number of discrete categories (e.g., Progressing, Nearing Proficiency, Proficient, Advanced). TerraNova 3 also reports a Lexile score for Reading tests, which serves as a measure of a student's ability to comprehend written materials. There is abundant guidance from supporting materials to facilitate appropriate interpretation and use of scores.

Tests. The three major TerraNova 3 tests are the Survey, Complete Battery, and Multiple Assessments. An important feature of TerraNova 3 tests is the use of page layouts and graphics that were constructed to reflect the kinds of instructional materials students see on a daily basis, which ideally promotes optimal student performance.

The Survey is described as being appropriate when testing time is an important consideration and norm-referenced information is needed, although the test also reports criterion-referenced information. All of the Survey items are multiple choice (called selected response in the test materials). TerraNova 3 uses test levels to link students with tests appropriate for their grade. The first is Level 10 and corresponds to Grades K.6–1.6, where K.6 indicates the sixth month of the school year for kindergarten students, Level 11 corresponds to a grade range of 1.6–2.6, and so on. The last level is 21/22 and corresponds to a grade range of 10.6-12.9. Reading, Mathematics, Science, and Social Studies are available for Levels 12–21/22 and Language for Levels 13–21/22. The numbers of items in the Survey test varies by test level and content area, with the total number of items across content areas ranging from 106 for Level 12 to 142 items for Levels 14, 15, and 17. Total testing time for the Survey is 2:15 (hr/mn) for Level 12 and 2:50 for the remaining levels.

The Complete Battery is a combination of Survey items plus additional items that assess the same five content areas but include kindergarten and first grade students (with the exception of Language, which begins with third grade students). All items are selected-response items. This test is described as being appropriate when "greater precision of measurement and a fuller array of criterion-referenced" (technical report, p. 6) information are needed. The numbers of items vary by test level and content area, ranging from a total across content areas of 70 items for Level 10 to 142 for Levels 14, 15, and 17. Total testing time for the Complete Battery ranges from 1:35 (hr/mn) for Level 10 to 4:05 for Levels 13–21/22. The Complete Battery also provides an Objective Performance Index standards-based score for each student assessing their mastery of specific objectives: Step 1 (Level 1, Low Degree of Mastery), Progressing and Nearing Proficiency (Levels 2 and 3, respectively, Moderate Degree of Mastery), Proficient and Advanced (Levels 4 and 5, respectively, High Degree of Mastery).

The Multiple Assessments test combines selected-response and constructed-response items, and both norm-referenced and criterion-referenced information are provided. The number of items varies by test level and content area, ranging from a total of 136 items for all content areas for Level 11 to 184 items for Level 16. Total testing time for Multiple Assessments is 4:10 (hr/mn) for Level 11, 4:20 for Level 12, and 5:35 for Levels 13–21/22. The number of constructed-response items varies across content areas and levels but is naturally much smaller than the number of selected-response items. For example, Reading Level 11 has 40 selected-response items and 5 constructed-response items, whereas Level 21/22 has 33 and 6, respectively.

The three major tests (Survey, Complete Battery, Multiple Assessments) can also be paired with other tests to obtain additional information. The Plus Tests provide more content-specific information; for example, a Word Analysis test is available for Levels 11, 12, and 13 and consists of 20 selected-response items with a testing time of 15 minutes. The InView Test and the Primary Test of Cognitive Skills assess narrower content and provide information about the expected achievement of students who are similar in age, grade, and month in school.

Cizek (2005) commented that documentation was a strength of TerraNova, The Second Edition, and this is generally the case for TerraNova 3. The teacher's guide provides a well-organized and understandable introduction with a focus on objectives, different kinds of items, and appropriate interpretation and use of scores including a description of test accommodations and interpretations of scores obtained under accommodations. The teacher's guide is a lengthy 343 pages but the presence of an index helps users find the information they need. The technical manual is likewise a fairly thorough description of the technical aspects of test development, standardization, and scoring. The technical manual comes in at a massive 374 pages but unfortunately has no index. This oversight is hard to understand and reduces the accessibility and usefulness of the technical manual. Another apparent oversight is that Lexile scores are described in the teacher's guide but do not appear in the technical manual.

DEVELOPMENT. Many new items were generated for TerraNova 3, a welcome practice in an educational landscape that can change substantially in a relatively short period of time. Another important strength of TerraNova 3 is its incorporation of national, state, and professional organization standards and recommended practices (e.g., National Council of Teachers of Mathematics), National Assessment of Educational Progress (NAEP) documents, textbooks, and curriculum guides to identify common goals and objectives that shaped test specifications. These specifications guided content, grade-level appropriateness, and equity issues reflected in five principles used to guide the development of TerraNova 3: (a) provide valid and equitable assessments of achievement in the content areas, (b) "offer multiple methods of measuring student progress," (c) provide "information useful for improving instruction," (d) "reflect current curricula and national standards," and (e) "engage and motivate students so they will do their best work" (technical support, p. 15). Adherence to these principles increases the likelihood that TerraNova 3 will satisfy local or state testing requirements.

Guided by the test specifications, item writers researched and wrote selected-response and constructed-response test items and developed scoring rubrics for the latter. Tryout studies were conducted using a national sample of approximately 45,000 U.S. students to examine the items in practice. Analyses of item responses were used to check that test specifications and goals were met, and included using differential item functioning to examine whether items were operating similarly in different student groups (e.g., African American, Hispanic, White). Testing materials were also reviewed by educational community professionals representing various groups to help minimize gender, ethnic, region, and age bias.

TECHNICAL.

Norming. A standardization study was used to generate appropriate norms, and there is abundant evidence that test developers did this in a careful and thorough way. A norming sample of approximately 200,000 U.S. students representing ethnic and socioeconomic groups for various geographic regions and community types were sampled. Specifically, "public schools were stratified by region, community type, and socioeconomic status," and "Catholic schools and private non-Catholic schools were stratified by region and community type" (technical report, p. 53). Students were then randomly sampled within strata with a total of 844 schools from 630 school districts participating. Testing was completed in the Fall of 2006 and the Winter and Spring of 2007. Schools participating in the standardization study included students needing testing accommodations (e.g., students with disabilities) as well as LEP and ESL students, helping to improve the generalizability of the norms. This process also yielded time limits for tests.

Reliability. For constructed-response items, intraclass correlations and weighted kappa coefficients were used to assess agreement among raters. These values are reported for content areas and typically exceed .90, suggesting strong agreement. Item difficulties, standard errors of measurement (*SEM*), and KR-20 measures of internal consistency are also reported, and, as expected, these statistics vary across content areas and test levels but on the whole provide evidence of adequate reliability. The total test score statistics provide strong evidence of reliability. *SEM* information for scale scores is provided in a series of figures by content area and test level but unfortunately is not discussed. Descriptive statistics for scale scores are also provided. One missing piece of information is the consistency of scores across test administrations, which was also missing for TerraNova, The Second Edition (Cizek, 2005).

Validity. The technical manual describes various efforts to provide validity evidence, the most impressive being the evidence for test content, that is, evidence that items capture specified content reflected in test specifications incorporating specific objectives. The technical manual also provides construct evidence in the form of correlations between content area scores and correlations of content area scores with InView scores. The construct evidence presented is adequate but would be enhanced if correlations of TerraNova 3 scale scores with NAEP scores were reported, which was also suggested by Cizek (2005). Other validity evidence is reflected in the care taken to ensure items are not biased against particular student groups, which involved following a written process in item development designed to minimize bias, including input from educational community professionals about items, and differential item functioning analyses.

COMMENTARY. The TerraNova 3 is a strong entry in the achievement test arena. Users seeking a comprehensive assessment system that incorporates state and local standards, best practices recommended by professional organizations, strong psychometric evidence supporting test content and score interpretation, and that is packaged in ways that facilitate appropriate use and interpretation of scores, can comfortably turn to the TerraNova 3. The TerraNova 3 has a few flaws but these are relatively minor alongside its strengths.

SUMMARY. The TerraNova 3 is a revised version of TerraNova, The Second Edition (2002) and is a comprehensive standardized assessment system designed primarily to assess concepts and skills (i.e., achievement) taught in U.S. schools in Grades K-12. TerraNova 3 was developed and standardized in a way that helps to ensure items assess carefully specified objectives and that scores can be accurately generalized across a broad group of students. TerraNova 3 also enjoys extensive documentation.

REVIEWER'S REFERENCE

Cizek, G. J. (2005). [Review of TerraNova, The Second Edition]. In R. A. Spies & B. S. Plake (Eds.), *The sixteenth mental measurements yearbook* (pp. 1025-1030). Lincoln, NE: Buros Institute of Mental Measurements.

[136]

Test of Adolescent and Adult Language, Fourth Edition.

Purpose: Designed "(a) to identify adolescents and adults who score significantly below their peers and therefore might need help improving their language proficiency, (b) to determine areas of relative strength and weakness among language abilities, and (c) to serve as a research tool in studies investigating language problems in adolescents and adults."
Population: Ages 12-0 to 24-11.
Publication Dates: 1980-2007.
Acronym: TOAL-4.
Scores, 7: Spoken Language (Word Opposites, Word Derivations, Spoken Analogies), Written Language (Word Similarities, Sentence Combining, Orthographic Usage), General Language.
Administration: Individual or group.
Price Data, 2007: $195 per complete kit including 25 examiner record booklets, 25 written language forms, and manual (2007, 109 pages); $55 per 25 examiner record booklets; $75 per 25 written language forms; $75 per manual.
Time: (60) minutes.
Authors: Donald D. Hammill, Virginia L. Brown, Stephen C. Larsen, and J. Lee Wiederholt.
Publisher: PRO-ED.
Cross References: See T5:2668 (7 references); for reviews by John MacDonald and Roger A. Richards of an earlier edition, see 13:323 (6 references); see also T4:2738 (9 references); for reviews by Allen Jack Edwards and David A. Shapiro of an earlier edition, see 10:365; for a review by Robert T. Williams of an earlier edition, see 9:1243.

Review of the Test of Adolescent and Adult Language, Fourth Edition by AIMÉE LANGLOIS, Professor Emerita, Department of Child Development, Humboldt State University, Arcata, CA:

DESCRIPTION. The Test of Adolescent and Adult Language, Fourth Edition (TOAL-4) was developed to measure "spoken and written language in adolescents and young adults" (examiner's manual, p. 5) between 12 years, 0 months and 24 years, 11 months of age. The test's main purpose is to identify individuals who may need language intervention and to specify the strengths and weaknesses of these individuals' language. The authors also intend for the test to be used for research.

The TOAL-4's six subtests assess spoken and written vocabulary and grammar as well as orthographic usage. Although the authors explain why they selected these features of language, they summarily dismiss the exclusion of items to assess phonology and pragmatics. They contend that assessing phonology requires a "contrived" (examiner's manual, p. 3) approach and that the assessment of pragmatics skills does not lend itself to a testing format; however, they fail to provide evidence to support these contentions. This omission is troubling given the test's title, the authors' claim that the test "was built to measure important communicative abilities" (examiner's manual, p. 1), and the well-established link between phonology, semantics, grammar, and pragmatics.

All the subtests (Word Opposites, Word Derivations, Spoken Analogies, Word Similarities, Sentence Combining, and Orthographic Usage) measure integrative language as well as expressive and receptive language. For each subtest, examinees use receptive language to listen to or read a stimulus, transform the stimulus in some way with integrative language skills, and express the new format in speech or writing. The test provides scaled scores and percentile ranks for all subtests, as well as three composite indexes: Spoken Language, Written Language, and General Language.

Most suitable for individual administration, the TOAL-4 can be completed in an hour. For each subtest, testing begins with the first item and ends when the person being tested has produced three consecutive incorrect responses. The authors state that the written portion can be administered to groups of individuals but do not elaborate under what conditions this approach would be advisable.

The TOAL-4 is easy to learn. It includes an examiner record booklet, a written language form, and an examiner's manual. The record booklet, which the examiner completes for each examinee, provides instructions for administration and scoring as well as practice items for all subtests. It also includes the stimuli for the spoken language subtests and two sections for respectively describing the conditions under which the test was administered (e.g., noise level, examinee's energy level) and writing interpretations and recommendations. The written language form contains the stimuli for the written portion of the test and spaces in which examinees enter their responses. The examiner's manual includes examples for scoring the written responses as well as instructions for reporting results for each subtest in terms of raw scores, percentile ranks, scaled scores, and seven descriptive ratings that range from *very poor* to *very superior*. Additional instructions pertain to reporting composite indexes for spoken and written language and a Composite Index for the entire test. Most clinically useful is the manual's section on interpreting test scores and composite indexes, which includes a description of four clinical patterns that result from comparing spoken and written language indexes. The authors not only discuss the diagnostic implications of each pattern, they also raise issues about interpreting results in terms of confirming them with other observations and relying on clinical skills. To that effect, they emphasize that "only professionals with formal training in assessment [of language skills] should administer the TOAL-4" (examiner's manual, p. 9). They also stress that potential test users should "practice giving the test several times" (examiner's manual, p. 9) before administering it.

DEVELOPMENT. The authors offer a sound rationale for the development of the TOAL-4 and its use. They emphasize that, by heeding critiques of prior editions of the test, they improved this version in 10 different ways from the inclusion of the theoretical model on which it is based, to the collection of new norms with a representative sample, new reliability and validity studies, and the look of the test. In addition, they devote an entire chapter of the examiner's manual to discussing test bias and how they controlled for it in this edition.

TECHNICAL. As opposed to prior versions of the test, the TOAL-4 was standardized with a new group of examinees who comprised 1,671 individuals from 12 to 24 years of age with 65 to 193 individuals per age group. The sample represents the U.S. population with respect to gender, ethnicity, geographic region, Hispanic status, exceptionality status, family income, and parent education level. Seven tables document this information and support four of the improvements of this edition of the test.

The authors evaluated the internal consistency, test-retest, and interexaminer reliability of the TOAL-4. Measures of internal consistency, obtained from the entire standardization sample, revealed alpha coefficients ranging from .94 to .97 for the composite scores and from .83 to .96 for individual subtest scores. These indicate that the test has high internal consistency and that the standard errors of measurement are stable. Alpha coefficients for 10 subgroups representing gender, ethnic, and exceptionality categories are also high, and indicate that test users can make recommendations based on test results with confidence.

A total of 108 individuals divided into three age groups were retested 2 weeks after the original administration. Measures of test-retest reliability yielded high correlations for all age groups' composite scores (.89+) and acceptable (.79) to excellent (.90+) correlations for their individual subtest scores. These coefficients indicate that the TOAL-4 scores remain stable over at least this period of time.

Interscorer reliability was determined by having "two PRO-ED staff members" (examiner's manual, p. 31) score the Word Similarities, Sentence Combining, Orthographic Usage, and the Written Language Composite scores from 50 protocols from the normative sample. Correlation coefficients of .97, .82, .98, and .97 were obtained for each subtest, respectively, indicating that the TOAL-4 has good to excellent interexaminer reliability. Assuming that the two individuals who participated in this study had formal training in language assessment, clinicians can feel confident that results obtained by similarly trained colleagues and/or referral sources reflect an examinee's performance. Nonetheless, to complete this section, the authors should have provided information about the professional backgrounds and experience of these PRO-ED staff members.

The authors attended to content, criterion-related, and construct validity in the development of the test. Evidence of content validity is both qualitative and quantitative. It includes a detailed rationale for item and testing format selection for each subtest, and a discussion that supports the identification of four clinical groups based on the composite indexes. Empirical data on content validity result from a conventional item analysis for item discrimination and difficulty, and from a differential item functioning analysis for test bias. Based on this evidence test users can be confident that the test has met the requirement for content validity.

To determine the criterion validity of the TOAL-4 it was administered to seven groups of students with and without school-related problems. Their scores were then correlated with other valid measures of spoken and written language. The authors provide numerous tables to illustrate their findings, which reveal large and very large coefficients for all subtest scores and composite indexes. These provide convincing evidence of the test's ability to predict an examinee's performance in other activities that involve language.

Construct validity was measured empirically to verify six hypotheses generated from six constructs (e.g., given that language skills are related to age, subtest scores should correlate with age). Results showed that test scores are significantly related to age and intelligence, that the subtests and composite scores contribute a unique variance to the total score, and that the test differentiates among groups of individuals with and without language disabilities. In addition, a confirmatory factor analysis indicates that the General Language composite index reflects both spoken and written language abilities when there is a difference of 7 or less between these scores. Conversely, a discrepancy of 8 or more should lead examiners to place less emphasis on the General Language composite.

COMMENTARY AND SUMMARY. The TOAL-4, as a means to measure spoken and written vocabulary and grammar in adolescents and young adults, has many strengths. First, its standardization with a representative sample of the U.S. population indicates that the test can be used with individuals from multiple backgrounds. Second, the manual provides a useful interpretation section as well as comprehensive information about the revision of the test, its reliability, and its validity. The record forms are easy to follow and provide detailed instructions for administration and scoring that streamline test administration.

However, the test has some weaknesses that should not be ignored. The absence of subtests for the assessment of phonology and pragmatics limits its usefulness; the authors' contention that assessing these two language features cannot be done with this test format is not supported with references. The conditions under which examiners can administer the written portion of the test to a group are not discussed and beg for an explanation. The professional status of the examiners who participated in the test-retest reliability measurement is not provided. However, the strengths of the TOAL-4 override its weaknesses and should lead clinicians who assess adolescents and young adults with language disorders to consider it as a valuable addition to their test library for the assessment of vocabulary and grammar.

Review of the Test of Adolescent and Adult Language, Fourth Edition by DOLORES KLUPPEL VETTER, Professor Emerita, University of Wisconsin-Madison, Madison, WI:

DESCRIPTION. The Test of Adolescent and Adult Language, Fourth Edition was originally designed, and subsequently revised three times, to assess the spoken and written language of adolescents and young adults. This revision was in response to reviewers' concerns, as well as to reflect modifications in the theoretical model on which it was based.

The TOAL-4 is appropriate for individuals, ages 12 years, 0 months to 24 years, 11 months, capable of understanding the instructions and able to produce oral and written responses. Examiners are cautioned against administering the TOAL-4 to anyone who fails the practice items. Examinees are asked to complete six subtests: three measuring aspects of Spoken Language (Word Opposites, Word Derivations, and Spoken Analogies) and three of Written Language (Word Similarities, Combining Sentences, and Orthographic Usage). Composite scores (Indexes) may be obtained for Spoken and Written Language as well as for General Language ability.

Although the Spoken Language subtests must be administered individually, it is possible to administer the written subtests to a group. For all subtests, examinees go through the same process: Listen to or read a stimulus, transform it into a new form, and express the new form orally or in writing. Subtests are initiated with the first item and a ceiling is reached with three consecutive failures. Correct responses for the Spoken Language subtests are provided adjacent to the items; scoring criteria for the Written Language subtests are provided in the examiner's manual. The TOAL-4 typically is completed in about an hour.

Age-referenced tables permit the conversion of subtest raw scores into standard scores (Mean = 10, *SD* = 3), percentile ranks, and associated descriptions. Composite Indexes (Mean = 100, *SD* = 15) and percentile ranks for Spoken Language, Written Language, and General Language may then be determined. Guidance in interpreting scaled subtest scores and Composite Indexes as well as for intraindividual discrepancy analyses for statistical significance and clinical (meaningful) differences are presented. Extensive statistical evidence of reliability (i.e., coefficient alphas, test-retest, and scoring consistency) and validity (i.e., content-description, criterion-prediction, and construct-identification) of the TOAL-4 is provided.

DEVELOPMENT. Two previous versions of the Test of Adolescent and Adult Language were designed to address reviewers' criticisms; the TOAL-4 is another response. It came about for several reasons: a) the original TOAL was developed almost 30 years ago and new research data and conceptualizations of language have emerged, b) reviewers emphasized the need for additional validity evidence, and c) some subtests were criticized because of length and/or format (i.e., they were seen as contrived).

The theoretical structure that underpins the TOAL-4 involves concepts of features, modes, and systems. The features of language are its semantics, grammar, graphology, phonology, and pragmatics. The TOAL-4 is designed to evaluate semantics, grammar, and graphology. Modes refer to the manner in which language is transmitted (i.e., spoken or written). The TOAL-4 has subtests measuring each of these. Systems refer to the comprehension-integration-production aspects of language. The TOAL-4 was designed to assess the individual's ability to integrate language, although obviously some degree of comprehension and production is present for integration to occur.

The TOAL-4 was modified to assess language use more effectively and subtests were changed so that administration and scoring time are shortened. New normative data, keyed to recent U.S. Census data, have been collected. New research evaluating reliability within subgroups (e.g., gender, ethnic identity) and evaluating validity from different perspectives has been conducted.

TECHNICAL.

Standardization. A sample of 1,671 individuals was chosen from 35 states and tested during the fall of 2004 through the fall of 2005. Coordinators at each location were trained using the TOAL-4. Participating schools were selected that reflected the demographic characteristics of the locale. Additional examiners, chosen from customer files of PRO-ED, were each asked to administer the TOAL-4 to 20 children. The authors compared the characteristics of the sample (i.e., gender, region, ethnicity, Hispanic status, exceptionality status, family, income, and educational level of parents) with those reported in the Statistical Abstract of the United States (U.S. Bureau of the Census, 2004) and concluded that it is representative of the population from which it was drawn.

The examiner's manual contains instructions for administering each subtest, for completing the record booklet, as well as the scoring criteria for the Written Language subtests. It also describes in detail the types of scores available and the process of intraindividual discrepancy analyses.

Tables facilitate the conversion of raw scores for each subtest to percentile ranks and scaled scores for 12-month intervals starting with age 12 and extending through age 20; there is a single table for participants aged 21 years through 24 years, 11 months. Additional tables assist in converting the scores for Spoken Language, Written Language, and General Language to percentile ranks and in assigning descriptive labels. Although these labels may be helpful for reporting to lay persons, they do not have statistical meaning.

Internal consistency reliability. Coefficient alphas are presented by age as well as averaged for subtests (i.e., .87 to .95) and indexes (i.e., .95 to .97). However, "at all 13 ages, the SEM for the subtests and composites are 1 and 3, respectively" (examiner's manual, p. 29). Given that coefficient alpha was found to vary in magnitude and that the formula that calculates *SEM* contains alpha, this is puzzling. No explanation is offered of the fixed *SEM*. Coefficient alphas for subtests and composite indexes were also calculated for subgroups (e.g., male, female, African American, gifted and talented) and are similar in magnitude to those previously cited.

Test-retest reliability. Descriptive statistics and test-retest correlations are provided for groups: Ages 12–14 (*N* = 38), 15–18 (*N* = 38), and 19 years and over (*N* = 32) and the combined sample. Correlation coefficients ranged from .83 to .94 for subtests and from .92 to .97 for composite indexes.

Interscorer reliability. Although detailed scoring criteria are presented for the Word Similarities, Sentence Combining, and Orthographic Usage subtests, some judgment by the examiner is still required. In order to speak to the reliability of the scorers, two PRO-ED staff members, working independently, scored 50 protocols taken from the normative sample. The sample included persons who were 13 to 24 years of age, 10 were male and the remaining female; they had a wide range of abilities and resided in the south or the midwest. Using standard scores, the correlations for the three subtests ranged from .82 to .98; it was .97 for the Written Language composite.

Content validity. Four demonstrations of content validity are provided. First, lengthy and detailed rationale is presented for the items and choice of format for each of the six subtests. The arguments presented speak persuasively for the construction and content of the TOAL-4. Second, four clinical groups were identified as diagnostically distinct on the bases of examinees' performance on Spoken (SL) and Written Language (WL). The groups were: (a) SL and WL are average or above; (b) SL and WL are below average; (c) SL is above and WL is below average; and (d) SL is below and WL is above average. The test authors argued that the distribution of the people into groups is consistent with expectations derived from "reason, experience, and statistical data" (examiner's manual, p. 46). However, defense of the last group (WL > SL) is lacking and the authors stated that "future research should be conducted to learn precisely who these people are" (examiner's manual, p. 46).

Validity: Item analysis. Item discrimination and item difficulty were used to delete items that did not meet established criteria as well as to order the items (easy-to-difficult) for the final version of the TOAL-4. Median discriminating powers and difficulty percentages for subtests are presented by examinees' age and for an average. In general, the data are supportive of the content. Differential item functioning (item bias) was assessed for dichotomies of gender, race, and ethnicity. Less than 1% of the comparisons indicated potential bias.

Criterion-related validity. Seven samples were used to determine the relationships among TOAL-4 scores and the total or component scores from seven criterion measures. Data collection for four of the samples was adventitious. The remaining three used data collected by the authors. Some measures are published instruments (e.g., Woodcock-Johnson III, WISC-III) of history and stature; others, however, are listed as still in preparation (e.g., Pragmatic Language Observation Scale, Written Language Observation Scale) and no published description is available. Finally, the number of cases in the samples ranged from 27 to 140, and student characteristics are quite variable; that information, however, is presented in detail. Given these circumstances and the problems associated with each, the evidence of criterion-related validity is difficult to assess. The authors argue that they have presented reasonable evidence that various scores of the TOAL-4 are related to other measures that evaluate similar attributes.

Construct validity. The manual details the process used to evaluate the traits underlying the TOAL-4. Each of six basic premises was seen as integral to performance on the TOAL-4; each resulted in hypotheses that were evaluated logically or empirically. The authors hypothesized that performance on the TOAL-4 should be related to age and to intelligence, and they postulated that different groups of people should achieve different scores (e.g., exceptionality groups should be different than mainstream). Given the way in which subtests were constructed (i.e., items sequenced from easy to hard after item analysis) it would be surprising if such evidence were not found; correlations between age and subtests were .45 to .64.

Some evidence for validity was based on correlations between TOAL-4 scores and scales from the WISC-III and WISC-IV. In this section all potential correlations are provided and their magnitudes and direction are as would be expected.

The authors end the section on validity with a discussion of confirmatory factor analysis and present a model for General Language as well as for Spoken/Written Language. They conclude that when Spoken and Written Language are seemingly comparable, then the General Language composite is best interpreted with a two-ability model (i.e., Spoken Language and Written Language), but when there is a significant discrepancy between Spoken and Written Language, then it would be best to interpret performance on each individually and not emphasize the General Language composite.

COMMENTARY. The TOAL-4 is the latest revision of a test of spoken and written language appropriate for individuals from age 12 through young adulthood. The authors have attempted to respond to every critique of each previous version published. Although their efforts are laudable and undoubtedly produced an instrument that is substantially improved, the resultant examiner's manual is extremely difficult to read and use, and its proofreading leaves much to be desired (e.g., both errors and contradictions). There is redundancy throughout the manual (e.g., more or less elaborate descriptions of the individual subtests can be found in several of the chapters). Tutorials on general statistics and their implications are included in the examiner's manual in addition to the statistical information for this test. Therefore, a large amount of time could be spent reading information already known, prior to finding the information for the TOAL-4. It appears that the extensive reliability and validity data presented responds to the majority of criticisms of previous versions of the TOAL-4. However, because three separate documents are required to administer the TOAL-4, the examiner will likely need to practice juggling these materials.

SUMMARY. The TOAL-4 is an instrument useful in assessing spoken and written language in individuals 12 years to 24 years, 11 months of both genders, and who may have varied ethnic backgrounds. With the exception of individuals with learning disability and/or attention-deficit-hyperactivity disorders, the numbers of individuals in other exceptionality groups (e.g., mental retardation) are very small in the validity studies and examiners should be warned that use of the instrument with these groups could be problematic. The instrument may be used for describing spoken and written language abilities, as well as an overall general language ability.

[137]

Test of Auditory Processing Skills—Third Edition.

Purpose: "To measure a child's functioning in various areas of auditory perception."
Population: Ages 4-0 through 18-11.
Publication Dates: 1985–2005.
Acronym: TAPS-3.
Scores, 9: Word Discrimination, Phonological Segmentation, Phonological Blending, Number Memory Forward, Number Memory Reversed, Word Memory, Sentence Memory, Auditory Comprehension, Auditory Reasoning.
Administration: Individual.
Price Data, 2007: $130 per complete set including 25 test booklets, Auditory Figure-Ground CD, and manual (2005, 102 pages); $65 per 25 test booklets; $20 per Auditory Figure-Ground CD; $45 per manual.
Foreign Language Edition: Spanish version is available.
Time: (60) minutes (untimed).
Comments: Represents a complete reshaping of the Test of Auditory-Perceptual Skills, Revised.
Authors: Nancy A. Martin and Rick Brownell (TAPS-3); earlier editions by Morrison F. Gardner.
Publisher: Academic Therapy Publications.
Cross References: For reviews by Annabel J. Cohen and by Anne R. Kessler and Jaclyn B. Spitzer of the Test of Auditory-Perceptual Skills, Revised, see 13:324 (2 references).

Review of the Test of Auditory Processing Skills—Third Edition by TIMOTHY R. KONOLD, Associate Professor of Research, Statistics, and Evaluation, and REBECCA BLANCHARD, Doctoral Student in Research, Statistics, and Evaluation, University of Virginia, Charlottesville, VA:

DESCRIPTION. The Test of Auditory Processing Skills—Third Edition (TAPS-3) is an individually administered assessment for children ages 4 years, 0 months through 18 years, 11 months. The TAPS-3 was designed to be included in the toolboxes of speech-language pathologists, audiologists, teachers, and other clinicians trained to assess the spectrum of student auditory skills. The TAPS-3 focuses specifically on skills used in developing, using, and understanding spoken language. Although it is untimed, it generally can be administered in 1 hour and scored in approximately 15 to 20 minutes.

The TAPS-3 is composed of nine core subtests and an optional Auditory Figure-Ground Screening measure that can be used to initiate the test session. The test is presented on CD and is useful in screening for hearing loss and/or attention problems but should not, the test authors caution, act as a tool to diagnose attention disorders. Though the screener is optional, students suffering from behavioral or attention problems may not be accurately assessed by the TAPS-3. The nine core subtests include Word Discrimination, Phonological Segmentation, Phonological Blending, Number Memory Forward, Number Memory Reversed, Word Memory, Sentence Memory, Auditory Comprehension, and Auditory Reasoning. These subtests can be combined to measure three broader indices (i.e., Phonological Skills, Memory, and Cohesion) and an Overall measure of auditory processing skills.

Instructions vary somewhat by subtest. Typically, examiners read information aloud to which the student must correctly respond. For example, to test memory, the examiner might read a sequence of numbers and instruct the student to repeat the numbers in the same order. Responses are scored according to the specific rubric given for each item, but examiners can expect that students will earn points—or in some cases partial credit—for correct answers. Scores are available in raw score form, standardized form, percentile ranks, and age equivalents.

DEVELOPMENT. The TAPS-3 is an updated version of Gardner's Test of Auditory Perceptual Skills, Revised (1996). The test authors note that the utility of Gardner's version declined in light of new research suggesting that auditory skills are not used solely after information is received and before it is interpreted. Instead, the test authors draw their theory from Bellis (2002, in TAPS-3 manual) who noted that auditory skills rely upon the "interaction of higher-order cognitive factors with lower-order neurological and/or sensory mechanisms" (manual, p. 11). Many of the subtests located in the TAPS-3 were developed in accordance with these ideas, which also prompted the title change from a test of "Perceptual Skills" to a test of "Processing Skills."

Item construction was based largely upon previous versions of the TAPS and the test authors' reviews of the literature. After practitioners reviewed the items for face validity, item difficulty and discrimination bias were assessed. Differential Item Functioning was used to assess potential sources of bias between gender, race, and residence groups. No evidence of item bias was reported to be present. Final selection of items was based on analysis from normative data, including correlations between item order and item difficulty as well as discrimination indices. The test authors also considered the opinions of test examiners and practitioners. No specific information about pilot testing is offered.

TECHNICAL. The standardization sample for the TAPS-3 was composed of approximately 2,000 children evaluated at over 182 testing sites throughout the United States. The sample was closely stratified in accordance with 2000 U.S. Census data on the variables of gender, race/ethnicity, parent education level, residence, and geographic region. In addition, children were well represented across the intended age range of use, with nearly 100 children represented at each 1-year interval through age 11, and multi-year intervals in later years through age 18.

Normative scaled scores (M = 10, SD = 3) are provided in 3-month intervals for children under 7 years of age, 6-month intervals for children in the middle interval (i.e., 7 years, 0 months through 10 years, 11 months), and 12-month intervals for the upper age range (i.e., 11 years, 0 months through 18 years, 11 months). Percentile ranks and age equivalent scores are also available.

Reliability. Several investigations into the reliability of scores are presented in the form of internal consistency, test-retest, and standard errors of measurement. Internal consistency estimates (alpha and Spearman-Brown) are provided separately by age groups across the nine core subtests. Estimates are reported to range from ".49 to .97 for the various age groups, with medians of .69 to .94 across all ages" (manual, p. 52). Several of these estimates at the lower end of the range fall below acceptable contemporary standards and call into question the test authors' use of the adjective "moderate" to describe these lower values. Users should consult the table of estimates provided in the manual to determine whether the subtests they intend to use demonstrate appropriate levels of internal consistency for the age group with whom they are working. Internal consistency estimates are not provided for the Overall scale or the three indices of Phonological Skills, Memory, or Cohesion.

A test-retest reliability study (*N* = 218) is reported across an average 20-day period between initial and follow-up examination. Estimates are provided separately for each of the nine subtests (range = .64–.93) and the Overall scale (range = .92–.96). No estimates are provided for the three indices. The reported ranges here are across measures and age groups. Test-retest estimates were generally more favorable than the reported internal consistency values. Standard errors of measurement are provided for all subtests, indices, and the Overall scale by age group to facilitate score interpretations. In addition, 90% and 95% confidence interval bands are provided.

Validity. It is widely recognized that validity refers to the accumulation of evidence to support the interpretation of test scores in the context of their purpose. The TAPS-3 examiner's manual reports several investigative validity studies that in the aggregate do a fair job convincing users that the instrument would be appropriate for its intended purpose. Little space is dedicated to content validity, where users are informed of the work that went into ensuring that cross-contamination of other skills was minimized in the test authors' focus on measuring auditory skills. In addition, item discrimination and item bias studies were said to have guided the final selection of items.

Correlations between the TAPS-3 and two earlier versions of the TAPS (-R and –UL) ranged from .21 to .60 across scales for a sample of 23 children of unreported age and other demographics. The use of previous versions of the TAPS for this purpose is somewhat unclear as the test authors note that "the content of the TAPS-3 differs from that of previous editions" (manual, p. 61) and that the correlations were expected to be moderate. Several of the reported correlations were quite low, and fail to provide strong evidence that the different measures are tapping into the same construct of auditory processing.

On a more positive note, evidence is provided to suggest that the TAPS-3 may be useful in discriminating between children with and without auditory processing skill deficits. Children with a previous diagnosis of auditory processing difficulties (*N* = 56) were found to score significantly (both statistically and materially) below typically developing students (*N* = 244) on TAPS-3 measures.

Both principal component and maximum likelihood (ML) exploratory factor analyses were conducted to investigate the underlying structure of the TAPS-3 subtests and to provide support for the advocated scoring structure underlying the three indices (i.e., Basic Phonological Skills, Auditory Memory, and Auditory Cohesion). Reported results suggest a tendency to overfactor, as many of the eigenvalues across age groups were less than 1.0 for the second factor, and all eigenvalues were less than 1.0 for the third factor. Moreover, retention of factors did not appear to be guided parallel analysis, and the amount of variance reportedly accounted for by each of the individual factors was less than 4% across factors and age groups (see pages 68-69 of TAPS-3 manual). Results from ML estimation were more favorable on this point, and essentially confirmed a 3-factor structure.

COMMENTARY/SUMMARY. The TAPS-3 represents somewhat of a material change from its predecessors (TAPS-R and TAPS-UL) in terms of content coverage. It measures a broad array of auditory processing skills, and provides several layers of interpretation through its subscales, indices, and Overall scale that will be useful for developing a profile of children's auditory processing skills and deficits. Its advantages include its purported use with a wide range of children from preschool through Grade 12, the instrument appears easy to administer and score, and perhaps of most importance, there is some evidence to suggest that it does a good job discriminating between children with and without auditory processing problems.

Demonstrating the extent to which scores are free from error (reliability) and that the scores are appropriate for their intended use (validity) is an ongoing process. The examiner's manual addresses several important psychometric issues relating to the interpretation of scores and appropriateness of use with this population of children. Although some of the reported results are promising, there is room for improvement. Several of the internal consistency estimates for some subtests and age groups were below contemporary standards. In addition, much (though not all) of the reported validity evidence is somewhat weak, which will likely limit the confidence users will have in the instrument.

REVIEWERS' REFERENCES

Bellis, T. (2002). *When the brain can't hear: Unraveling the mystery of auditory processing disorder.* New York: Pocket Books.

Gardner, M. F. (1996). Test of Auditory-Perceptual Skills, Revised. Hydesville, CA: Psychological and Educational Publications, Inc.

Review of the Test of Auditory Processing Skills—Third Edition by DOLORES KLUPPEL VETTER, Professor Emerita, University of Wisconsin-Madison, Madison, WI:

DESCRIPTION. The Test of Auditory Processing Skills—Third Edition (TAPS-3) was designed to assess the auditory skills believed to be necessary for the development and use of language. The test manual states that it is an extensive revision of the Test of Auditory Perceptual Skills (TAPS, TAPS-R, and TAP-UL) by Morrison Gardner. It is so different from the original/revised TAPS, however, that it should be considered a new instrument. Its development was judged necessary because of changes in the theory and knowledge base related to auditory processing and how auditory processing relates to the development of language and its comprehension and uses.

The TAPS-3 is appropriate for youth, ages 4 years, 0 months to 18 years, 11 months and provides information in four areas: auditory attention (optional Figure-Ground test), basic phonemic skills, auditory memory, and auditory cohesion. Suspected hearing loss, central processing deficits, or concerns about auditory attention should be ruled out prior to administration because any of these could interfere with an individual's performance. Although the Figure-Ground test is said to be optional, if an examinee makes more than two errors, it is suggested that the examiner stop and determine whether this is typical performance because of the impact of auditory attention on remaining subtest performance.

Examiners must have intact phoneme awareness, be competent in the administration and interpretation of educational or psychological tests, and specifically in administering and scoring the TAPS-3. Materials include the examiner's manual, an audio CD with general instructions, examples, a pronunciation guide, and the optional two-part auditory Figure-Ground subtest and test booklets. Examiners are encouraged to practice presenting the stimuli and to compare their productions with the demonstrations on the CD.

Descriptions of scoring are in the test manual and immediately preceding each subtest. Raw scores, transferred to the test booklet, are converted into scaled scores (mean = 10, *sd* = 3) and percentile ranks through the use of age-based tables (2-month intervals ages 4-6; 6-month intervals ages 7-11; yearly thereafter). Scaled scores are summed and transformed into standard scores (mean = 100 and *sd* = 15) for three indexes, Phonological Skills, Memory, Cohesion, and the Overall. Graphic presentation of the scaled and standard scores and percentile ranks for subtest and indexes is facilitated by a plotting area at the bottom of the page. The test authors caution that the TAPS-3 is not a replacement for audiological testing and should be used in conjunction with other data and observations in forming a diagnosis.

DEVELOPMENT. The Test of Auditory Processing Skills—Third Edition (TAPS-3) is said to be "a very thorough reshaping" (manual, p. 6) of the Test of Auditory Perceptual Skills, Revised (TAPS-R and TAPS-UL), originally authored by Morrison Gardner. The new authors state that the purpose remains the same and that modifications are the result of new data and an updated theoretical perspective: thus, a new name, but the old acronym.

The TAPS-3 is now a single instrument, rather than two, that assesses auditory processing abilities over a large age range. Its aim is to evaluate those aspects of auditory processing that the test authors considered most relevant to the development and use of oral language: Auditory Discrimination, Auditory Memory, and Auditory Cohesion. The optional Auditory Figure-Ground subtest is provided on the CD to screen for auditory attention problems. Items and subtests were revised or added after a review of the current literature as well as comments and concerns from professionals who used or had evaluated the previous TAPS. Items were then subjected to various analyses, including item difficulty and bias. Final item choices "were shown to be highly discriminating, culturally balanced, and sensitive to a wide range of ability" (manual, p. 45). Changes in test structure include: (a) the order reflects an easy-to-hard progression; (b) four new subtests were added; (c) some new items were developed for some of the subtests; and (d) the optional Figure-Ground subtest has been added. In addition, instructions, ceilings, and scoring for most subtests are different from the former TAPS.

TECHNICAL.

Standardization. Standardization was accomplished through the testing of 2004 participants between the ages of 4 years, 0 months and 18 years, 11 months at 182 sites across the continental United States and Alaska. Examiners were contacted through customer files of Academic Therapy Publications (ATP) or from a list of speech-language professionals. Examiners were instructed to choose participants randomly from both regular classrooms and from persons with various disabilities and to provide demographic data as well as any other test scores (for use in validity studies) to the test authors. Test administrations were recorded and the protocols were scored after being received at ATP. Because the normative sample size varied at each age group, a weighting formula was applied that took gender, race/ethnicity, education of the parent, regional location, and rural/urban living into account prior to its comparison with the 2000 U.S. Census and with the U.S. Department of Education for disability status. When comparisons are reviewed, the percentages are very similar.

Raw scores converted to scaled scores from Word Discrimination, Phonological Segmentation, and Phonological Blending are combined to form the Phonologic Index; similarly the scaled scores of four subtests (i.e., Number Memory Forward, Number Memory Reversed, Word Memory, and Sentence Memory) make up the Memory Index; and those from Auditory Comprehension and Auditory Reasoning are combined in the Cohesion Index. All scaled scores contribute to the Overall Index. *Z*-score distributions (M = 100, SD = 15) permit the reading of standard scores for these indexes. In addition, there are tables that permit the conversion of these to other standard metrics (e.g., percentile ranks, *T*-scores, stanines) as well as to age equivalents.

Reliability. Coefficient alphas and Spearman-Brown split-half coefficients were calculated for 11 age intervals and for the total for each subtest. Alpha estimates range from .56 to .96 and split-half coefficients range from .49 to .97 with medians of .69 to .94 across all ages. Test-retest reliability coefficients were calculated for 140 participants between 4 and 9 years of age, for 78 participants between 10 and 18 years of age, as well as for the total (N = 218). Intertest intervals averaged 20 days. Coefficients were .96, .92, and .96, respectively. In addition, standard errors of measurement and 90% and 95% confidence limits are presented for subtests by age, and standard errors of estimation and 90% and 95% confidence limits are provided for the three indexes and the Overall Index.

Validity. Content validity was addressed in the development of the TAPS-3 through the choice of materials and activities that are considered relevant to everyday as well as academic tasks. A rationale stipulates the basic auditory activities the test authors believe are required for an individual to be successful in "the cognitive and communicative aspects of language" (manual, p. 9). It is this rationale that provides the underlying theoretical bases for the TAPS-3 and that makes this instrument substantially different from previous ones with the same basic acronym.

Despite these differences, the test authors state that criterion validity was determined by correlating the scaled scores for the subtests and the TAPS-3 indexes with the TAPS-R and TAPS-UL as concurrent measures. The sample size is relatively small (N = 23) and not surprisingly the correlation coefficients are as well (.21–.58). Although these values reflect the relationship between the measures, they hardly provide much support for the notion of criterion validity. Later these same correlations are suggested to provide evidence for the TAPS-3 measuring "some of the same constructs as previous editions of the test, and some new constructs" (manual, p. 63).

The rationale for construct validity rests upon the test authors' arguments that auditory processing should show a developmental progression in individuals; therefore, there should be a correlation between age and scores on the TAPS-3. When reviewed, age and raw scores yield modest correlations (i.e., .36 to .69). The test authors also posit a relationship between the TAPS-3 and intelligence. Correlations are presented for the standard scores on the three indexes and the Overall with the WISC-3 Full Scale, Verbal, and Performance IQs. Why Performance IQ should be related to auditory processing was not explained and those correlations are .46 and below. As would be expected, correlations are slightly higher for the WISC-3 Verbal Scale and the TAPS-3 indexes (i.e., .44–.60). The mean age of the sample was 9.92, SD = 2.16. This apparently was an adventitious study that resulted from examiners reporting intelligence testing data that were available when they evaluated participants during the standardization process.

Two studies on clinical group differences are provided. Children with auditory processing disorders (N = 56) and children with attention disabilities (N = 110) were compared to same-aged children (N = 244) on the TAPS-3. Although the ages of the children with disabilities were not given, it appears that the same comparison group was used for both studies because the sample size and means (with one exception) are the same. Significant differences between each set of means were reported using two-sample t-tests.

Finally, extensive factor analyses yielded three factors (Basic Phonological Skills, Auditory Memory, and Auditory Cohesion). These analyses provided the best confirmation of the theoretical underpinnings of the TAPS-3.

COMMENTARY. The TAPS-3 is a test of auditory processing appropriate for use for a wide age range of youth. Unfortunately, implying that it is only a modification of previous tests and keeping the acronym does a disservice to the instrument. It could lead professionals to assume that the TAPS-3 is simply one more revision rather than a quite different device.

A CD is provided with the TAPS-3 manual and test booklets. It contains the optional Figure-Ground subtest and additional tracks that aid the examiner in pacing and pronunciation. No rationale was given for why the Figure-Ground subtest is optional. Even if its purpose is one of screening, why should not all examinees receive it?

Given that there could be problems in administering the TAPS-3, the reliability of administration would be increased substantially if the entire test had been recorded on the CD rather than relying on live voice. For example, it would not be necessary for a participant to keep his or her eyes closed during Subtest 1 if the items were presented via the CD.

There are both redundancies and deficiencies in the information provided. Administration and scoring are provided both in the TAPS-3 manual and on the record form. However, little information is presented on the interpretation of scores and what the examiner might actually say to the examinee or his or her parent regarding performance. Determining meaningful information to pass on may be difficult for an examiner who is not statistically knowledgeable.

Unfortunately, the test manual needs careful editing. It contains misstatements and errors, and some tables are difficult to interpret and have misleading legends. Several examples: (a) Table 8.4 contains the correlations of index scores for a sample of 38 individuals who had also been given the WISC-3 (Weschler Intelligence Scale for Children—3). In the following table (Table 8.5) the sample size of presumably the same group of children is substantially different (N = 40 to 53). There is no text that comments on why sample size is different. (b) The legend for Table 8.2 omits reference to the TAPS-UL, yet it is listed immediately below the legend. (c) Table legends are not consistent in stating when statistics were performed on raw scores and when on scaled scores for subtests (e.g., Table 7.4).

The attempt to provide validity information beyond the level of content validity leaves much to be desired. Criterion validity was determined through the adventitious use of IQ data; there was no prospective criterion validity study. Arguments based on the relationship between the previous editions of the TAPS and the TAPS-3 attempt to demonstrate both how different they are and also how similar they are. If both of these are the case, careful delineation of their similarities and their differences should be provided and prospective validity studies conducted.

SUMMARY. The TAPS-3 is an instrument designed to assess various components of auditory processing in individuals 4 years to 18 years, 11 months of age. Because of the need for such an evaluation instrument, the TAPS-3 has potential. Presenting the entire TAPS-3 via CD would increase the reliability of administration. A thorough editing of the test manual is needed to clarify the information that is presented and to reduce the potential for error. Additional information is needed on the meaning of scores (i.e., interpretation) for those examiners who are not statistically sophisticated. Prospective criterion validity studies should be undertaken.

[138]

Test of Childhood Stuttering.

Purpose: Assesses "speech fluency skills and stuttering-related behaviors."

Population: Ages 4-0 to 12-11.

Publication Date: 2009.

Acronym: TOCS.

Scores: 5 Speech Fluency Scores (Rapid Picture Naming, Modeled Sentences, Structured Conversation, Narration, Speech Fluency Index), 4 Observation Rating Scale Scores (Speech Fluency Rating Scale Score, Speech Fluency Rating Scale Index, Disfluency-Related Consequences Rating Scale Score, Disfluency-Related Consequences Rating Scale Index).

Administration: Individual.
Price Data, 2009: $173 per complete kit including examiner's manual (134 pages), picture book, 25 examiner record booklets, and 25 Observational Rating scales; $41 per 25 examiner record booklets; $63 per examiner's manual; $27 per 25 Observational Rating scales; $43 per picture book.
Time: (35-40) minutes for the Speech Fluency Measure; (5) minutes for the Observational Rating Scales.
Authors: Ronald B. Gillam, Kenneth J. Logan, and Nils A. Pearson.
Publisher: PRO-ED.

Review of the Test of Childhood Stuttering by KATHY SHAPLEY, Assistant Professor, Audiology and Speech Pathology Department, and THOMAS GUYETTE, Professor, Audiology and Speech Pathology Department, University of Arkansas at Little Rock, Little Rock, AR:

DESCRIPTION. The Test of Childhood Stuttering (TOCS) is an individually administered measure of fluency for children ages 4–12 years of age. The test authors claim that the test is an efficient alternative to speech sample transcription, which can be time-consuming to complete. The TOCS is composed of three components: the standardized Speech Fluency Measure, Observational Rating Scales, and Supplemental Clinical Assessment Activities. The Speech Fluency Measure is composed of four tasks: Task 1: Rapid Picture Naming in which the child names a series of 40 pictures as quickly as possible. Task 2: Modeled Sentences in which the child is shown two pictures, the examiner models a sentence based on the first picture, and the child should produce a sentence based on the second picture with the same syntactic structure as the one the examiner produced. Task 3: Structured Conversation in which the child is asked to answer three questions about a series of eight pictures. This task is designed to assess stuttering in a dialogue context. Task 4: Narration in which the child is asked to tell a story that corresponds to the pictures that were used in Task 3. The Observational Rating Scales allow flexibility in that they can be administered by the examiner, classroom teacher, or caregivers. The Supplemental Clinical Assessment Activities contain eight activities: clinical interviews, comprehensive analysis of disfluency frequency and types, speech rate analysis, disfluency duration analysis, repetition unit analysis, associated behaviors analysis, stuttering frequency analysis, and speech naturalness analysis.

The directions for the tasks are clear and appear easy to administer. The test authors state that the Speech Fluency Measure has no time limits but typically takes about 20–25 minutes to administer. The Observational Rating Scales takes approximately 5 minutes to complete. The manual does not mention how long it takes to administer the Supplemental Clinical Assessment Activities. The manual provides multiple examples for scoring each task of the Speech Fluency Measure. Examiners are encouraged to audiotape or videotape the entire administration of the test to ensure accuracy in scoring. The Speech Fluency Measure likely requires 15 minutes for an experienced examiner to score.

The TOCS provides three types of scores: raw scores, index scores, and percentile ranks. Each raw score can be interpreted into a descriptive term. To convert the scores the examiner compares the child's performance to the standardization sample of typically developing children (n = 173); to determine a severity rating the examiner compares the child's scores to the standardization sample of children who stutter (n = 123).

DEVELOPMENT. The test authors claim the TOCS was designed to: identify children who stutter, determine the severity of a child's stuttering, document changes in a child's fluency functioning over time, and facilitate research on childhood stuttering. The TOCS uses speech elicitation tasks to identify if a child stutters via rapid picture naming, modeled sentences, structured sentences, and narration. Once the identification has been made then data from the Speech Fluency Measure and the Observational Rating Scales can be used to determine severity. However, the test authors state that additional assessments may be necessary to make "definitive conclusions" regarding the severity of the child's stuttering. The test authors claim the TOCS can be used to evaluate the effects of therapy by comparing pretest and posttest scores. In addition, the test authors claim that the quick administration lends itself to use of the TOCS for research purposes.

TECHNICAL. The standardization sample for the TOCS consisted of 173 typically developing children and 123 children who were identified as stutterers prior to data collection. The test authors do not provide a description of how these children were identified other than to say that the children met "local criteria" for stuttering. The children ranged in age from 4–12 years.

There is an overrepresentation of male students in the standardization sample; however, this is consistent with current literature on childhood stuttering (Guitar & McCauley, 2010). The standardization sample appears to be representative of the U.S. population with regard to ethnicity, Hispanic status, parent education, and family income. However, the entire standardization sample (n = 296) represents only 16 states. Although the raw score conversion tables are collapsed across all ages, the small sample size, low sample sizes per age group, and limited geographic representation raises concerns about the representativeness of the standardization sample.

Measures of reliability were conducted using the children who were identified as stutterers. Coefficient alpha and Standard Errors of Measurement were calculated for each of the four age groups. The alpha coefficient for the Speech Fluency Measure and the Observational Rating Scales ranged from .77–.98 and .83–.94, respectively. However, because no sample sizes were provided for these calculations, the meaningfulness of these values could not be determined. Test-retest reliability coefficients for the Speech Fluency Measure Index and the Observational Rating Index were .91 and .86–.88, respectively. The testing interval was 3 to 10 days. However, these values were calculated on a sample of only nine stutterers from the standardization sample and should be interpreted with caution.

The TOCS examiner's manual reports the following types of validity: content, criterion, concurrent, and construct validity. The TOCS appears to demonstrate adequate evidence of content validity. Reasonable justification is provided for the inclusion of each section in the test and each section appears to examine a representative sample of stuttering behavior. Criterion-related validity examines how well test scores can predict the examinee's behavior in the behavior domain tested. The test authors used the normative sample data to demonstrate how well the test's cutoff scores correctly distinguished stutterers and typically developing children. The strength of this type of validity would have been enhanced if a second data set was used and the criterion data sample were not the same as the normative sample. Concurrent validity examines how well test scores measure the behavior of interest when compared to another, more established, measure of the same behavior. The test authors evaluated the relationship between the Speech Fluency Measure and speech sample analyses of the frequency of disfluencies in the first 100 words of the narration task. Correlations ranged between .53 and .73 for the disfluent children and between .06 and .25 for the typically developing children. These data show moderate support for concurrent validity.

Construct-identification validity is addressed by evaluating a series of hypotheses in which the test authors predicted the outcome based on what is known about stuttering. The test authors tested three constructs: correlation with age, correlation with stuttering, and correlation between the Speech Fluency Measure and the Observational Rating Scales. With regard to the correlation with age, the data do not support a consistent relationship (i.e., coefficients ranged from -.32 to .24). In addressing the second construct (differences among groups), the test authors evaluated the means and standard deviations between the groups using a t-test. Although the means on each measure for children who stutter are larger than the means of those who do not stutter and were found to be statistically significant, the standard deviations for each measure are relatively large and at risk for considerable overlap across the groups. The correlations between the Speech Fluency Measure and the Observational Rating Scale were in the predicted directions and magnitudes supporting the validity of the third construct of the instrument. The empirical support for the validity of test scores would have been more clear if sample sizes had been provided for all analyses.

COMMENTARY AND SUMMARY. The TOCS was designed to be an objective and standardized, individually administered assessment of childhood stuttering in a variety of contexts. The test offers an alternative to speech sample transcription and analysis, a commonly used technique to assess fluency. The test meets its goals of assessing fluency through a variety of tasks and with input from a variety of people (i.e., examiner, teacher, and/or caregiver). Unfortunately, the small standardization sample and limited sample sizes for reliability and validity analyses means the index scores and percentile ranks should be used and interpreted with caution. However, the TOCS appears to be a useful measure for clinicians who wish to use it as a standardized criterion-referenced measure of stuttering.

REVIEWERS' REFERENCE

Guitar, B., & McCauley, R. (2010). *Treatment of stuttering: Established and emerging interventions.* Baltimore: Lippincott Williams & Wilkins.

[139]

Test of Early Language Development-Third Edition: Spanish Version.

Purpose: Designed to identify children in need of intervention in the area of language development and gather information on their strengths and weaknesses in different skill areas involved in language development; the test may also be used "as a measure in research studying language development in young children and to accompany other assessment techniques."
Population: Ages 2-0 to 7-11.
Publication Date: 2007.
Acronym: TELD-3:S.
Scores, 3: Receptive Language, Expressive Language, Spoken Language Ability.
Administration: Individual.
Price Data, 2009: $158 per complete kit including 25 student response forms, 25 profile examiner record books, picture book, manipulatives, and examiner's manual (79 pages); $33 per 25 examiner's record booklets; $33 per examiner's manual; $61 per picture book.
Foreign Language Edition: The test is also available in English (14:388).
Time:(15-40) minutes.
Comments: The test must be administered and interpreted by "fluent Spanish speakers with knowledge of and speaking ability in the appropriate Spanish dialect"; authors also advise that although "results may contribute to the selection of long-term educational goals, they should not be used as the basis for planning day-to-day instructional programs for individual children."
Authors: Margarita Ramos and Jorge Ramos with Wayne P. Hresko, D. Kim Reid, and Donald D. Hammill.
Publisher: PRO-ED.

Review of the Test of Early Language Development–Third Edition: Spanish Version by SANDRA T. ACOSTA, Assistant Professor of Bilingual Education, Educational Psychology, Texas A&M University, College Station, TX:

DESCRIPTION. "The *Test of Early Language Development–Third Edition: Spanish Version (TELD-3:S)* is based on a translation and adaptation of the *Test of Early Language Development–Third Edition (TELD-3*; Hresko, Reid, & Hammill, 1999)" (examiner's manual, p. 1). The TELD-3:S has only one form, and is individually administered and scored manually. The TELD-3:S evaluates the early language development of Spanish-speaking young children (i.e., monolingual or Spanish-dominant) between the ages of 2 years and 7 years 11 months. The purpose of the test is to: (a) identify young children with language delays, (b) identify language strengths and needs in individual children, (c) measure young children's language development in research studies, and (d) accompany other assessments. Particular emphasis is placed on the test as a measure of language delays.

The TELD-3:S consists of two subtests, the 37-item Receptive Language subtest and the 39-item Expressive Language subtest. Each subtest measures a child's word knowledge and acquired grammatical structures. Subtest raw scores are converted to standard scores using the scoring guides in the examiner's manual appendices. Both subtest standard scores are added to yield a composite Spoken Language Ability standard score. Standard scores have a mean of 100 and a standard deviation of 15. Testing kit materials include 7 types of manipulatives, picture book, examiner's manual, and examiner's test record. Red age markers on the test booklet indicate testing entry points. Basal and ceiling levels are established with three consecutive correct answers and three consecutive incorrect answers, respectively.

DEVELOPMENT. The TELD-3:S samples young children's Spanish oral language by measuring two language skill sets: Expressive Language skills (language production) and Receptive Language skills (language comprehension). Three aspects of language are assessed: semantics (verbal knowledge), syntax (word order structures), and morphology (within word structures). Syntax and morphology are combined as grammatical structures.

The initial phase, creating a test item pool, consisted of translating TELD-3 items, written in Standard American English, into Spanish. The pool of translated items was analyzed using qualitative procedures to align the TELD-3:S items to the characteristics of young Spanish-speakers' language development and dialects. These steps included a review of: (a) language development test and developmental checklist formats, (b) curricular materials and maps (i.e., scope and sequence guidelines), (c) expert panelist commentaries on test items and dialectical variations of vocabulary (e.g., Puerto Rican), (d) Spanish language development tests, and (e) compliance with the Standards for Educational and Psychological Testing (American Educational Research Association [AERA], American Psychological Association [APA], & National Council on Measurement in Education [NCME],

1999) relating to test translation and assessment of diverse linguistic groups.

Quantitative item analysis that included the entire normative sample data was conducted to determine item inclusion in the final test instrument. Analytical techniques consisted of item discrimination and item difficulty analyses. Differential item functioning analysis was conducted to detect item bias, occurring when item performance evidences subgroup membership rather than ability. No pilot studies of the TELD-3:S item development process were reported in the manual.

TELD:3-S test directions included common phrases and questions gleaned from Spanish-language assessments. Test data were collected using three item formats: (a) parent or caregiver reports, (b) examiner's observations, and (c) direct observation of tasks during the testing sessions. Finally, scoring key construction was based on a correct-incorrect response format. An assumption of this assessment process common to standardized tests is that nominal-level data from correct-incorrect test items presume all-or-nothing word knowledge (Owens, 1995). Thus, there is no recognition of developing skill knowledge or partially correct responses.

TECHNICAL.

Standardization. The normative sample of Spanish-speaking children (*N* = 1,441), collected between 2002 and 2005, consisted of two groups, U.S. and international. The U.S. group (*N* = 971; 67.4%) was drawn from children residing in: 12 states, including eight states with the highest U.S. Hispanic populations; Washington, DC; and Puerto Rico. Sample demographic subgroups were: geographic area, gender, origin (e.g., Mexican, Cuban), family income, parent educational attainment, and disability status. Sample subgroup percentages were matched with the Hispanic subgroup percentages from the 2000 U.S. Census, and the 2003 Census update. The international group (*N* = 470; 32.6%) was drawn from Mexico (48%), Costa Rica (9%), Chile (31%), and Spain (12%). Of the international group, in addition to gender and national origin subgroups, the Mexican sample added family income based on income groupings provided by the National Institute of Statistics, Geography, and Informatics of Mexico.

Reliability. Three reliability estimates were reported for the TELD-3:S: internal consistency, test-retest, and interscorer. No reliability index was below .82, indicative of high reliability. Internal consistency coefficient alphas and standard errors of measurement (*SEM*) were reported by chronological age intervals (2–7 years) and subgroups (gender and Spanish dialect) using the normative sample as the data source. Coefficient alphas for all age intervals were ≥ .85; subgroup coefficient alphas were slightly higher (≥ .89). Test-retest reliability was analyzed using data from a 30-student sample from Mexico who were administered the TELD-3:S twice at a 2-week interval. The sample consisted of 18 males and 15 females ranging in age from 5-4 years to 7-9 years. Subtest and composite correlation coefficients ranged from .82 to .88.

The interscorer reliability coefficient was calculated using 40 protocols randomly drawn from the normative sample and scored by two bilingual graduate students. Interscorer reliability correlations were .99 for subtests and composite score.

Validity. Evidence of validity was provided by examining test content; oral language as a variable in other language development tests; and the oral language theoretical model (OLTM). Content validity was addressed using qualitative and quantitative analyses for test item analysis and retention in the final test. Average correlation coefficients for item difficulty and discrimination ranged from .54 to .59.

Oral language scores for the TELD-3:S and two language assessments, Clinical Evaluation of Language Fundamentals–Third Edition Spanish (CELF-3S) and Prueba de Lenguaje Inicial (PLI), were compared using data from a U.S. sample of 35 students. Students were ages 6 and 7 years. Scores produced validity coefficients ranging from .72 to .78 (PLI) and .52 to .67 (CELF-3S).

Evidence for validity based on the OLTM was calculated using data from the entire normative sample and consisted of: (a) age differentiation correlations, (b) group differentiation correlations, (c) intercorrelation of TELD-3:S subtests by age, (d) relationship to academic performance (e.g., reading, writing), and (e) relationship to intelligence. First, age discrimination correlation coefficients were positive and high (≥ .80), providing evidence of language maturation. Second, in the group differentiation analysis, all subgroups (gender, age, and dialect) had mean standard scores between 99 and 100. Only developmental delay and language impairment subgroups' mean standard scores were below average (65 and 80, respectively). Finally, receptive and expressive subtest correlation coefficients across age groups ranged from .84 to .55, evidencing a correlational relationship between subtests measuring common skills (verbal and grammatical knowledge).

Validity evidence for the fourth OLTM presumption, the correlational relationship to academic performance and intelligence, was problematic with generally low to moderate coefficients ranging from .24 to .69. Sample characteristics were unreported, and correlational coefficients were corrected for attenuation (i.e., unreliability or insufficient reliability; Mendoza & Mumford, 1987).

COMMENTARY. Overall strengths of the TELD-3:S include population validity, a well-defined and adequate standardized sample, and reliability and validity evidence. Weaknesses relate to printing errors, confusing language in the manual, and analytical issues.

Examiner's manual and examiner record booklet issues. Various errors, inconsistencies between the manual and test booklet, and omissions were noted. The following examples are not exhaustive: (a) normative sample on the test booklet and manual do not agree; (b) Table 7.2 test label is incorrect; (c) the manual is sometimes confusing, not distinguishing clearly between TELD:3 and TELD-3:S item development and selection phases; and (d) test authors noted the inappropriateness of TELD-3:S for bilingual Spanish-speakers, yet the test booklet omits questions about home languages or bilingualism.

Analytical issues. Major issues are double basal scoring procedures and scoring ceilings. First, scoring procedures allow for a double basal, meaning a new basal is established when a student scores three correct responses before reaching a ceiling (i.e., three consecutive incorrect answers). All incorrect items between the first and second basal are calculated as correct. Score inflation may occur as a result. Second, scoring ceiling effects occur at 6 years in both TELD-3:S subtests, possibly depressing language strength identification in some children. Finally, validity evidence generally supports the OLTM; however, ceiling limitations, score inflation due to floating basals, and lack of home language information may increase testing error.

SUMMARY. The TELD-3:S is a language development assessment for monolingual Spanish or Spanish dominant young children. According to the test authors, the normative sample does not support its use with bilingual students whose language development patterns may differ from monolingual students. Analytic issues related to the double basal scoring system and scoring ceiling effects limit its appropriateness for research examining language development/growth and identification of individual strengths and needs, especially in children older than 6 years. The TELD-3:S, a Spanish language development assessment with strong population validity, should be used as a broad measure of Spanish language development for identifying language delays in Spanish-speaking children under 6 years.

REVIEWER'S REFERENCES

American Educational Research Association, American Psychological Association, & National Council on Measurement in Education. (1999). *Standards for educational and psychological testing*. Washington, DC: American Educational Research Association.

Hresko, W. P., Reid, D. K., & Hammill, D. D. (1999). Test of Early Language Development: Third Edition. Austin, TX: PRO-ED.

Mendoza, J. L., & Mumford, M. (1987). Corrections for attenuation and range restriction on the predictor. *Journal of Educational Statistics, 12*, 282-293.

Owens, R. E. (1995). *Language disorders: A functional approach to assessment and intervention* (2nd ed.). Needham Heights, MA: Allyn & Bacon.

Review of the Test of Early Language Development–Third Edition: Spanish Version by ARTURO OLIVÁREZ, JR., Professor and Chair of the Teacher Education Department at the University of Texas at El Paso, El Paso, TX:

DESCRIPTION. The Test of Early Language Development–Third Edition: Spanish Version (TELD-3:S) is an early language test for Spanish-speaking children, that serves as an assessment of spoken language for children from age 2 years 0 months to 7 years and 11 months. The TELD-3:S is an offspring of the Standard American English version of the TELD-3 emphasizing mainly semantic, grammar abilities, and receptive and expressive language systems. The test items were developed to reflect two of the four most common language abilities (Semantics and Grammar) and two widely accepted language systems (Receptive and Expressive language). The TELD-3:S is composed of a Receptive Language subtest (RLS) and an Expressive Language subtest (ELS). Due to the many forms covered by the test items, the test provides a broad picture of a child's overall language ability. The TELD-3:S yields standard scores for each subtest and an overall composite score of general language ability. The TELD-3:S consists of an examiner's manual, a set of manipulatives, examiner record booklet, and a picture book. The RLS is composed of 37 items total, where 24 are semantics items and 13 are grammar items. This collection of items measures the ability of a child to understand spoken language (Spanish). The ELS is composed of 39 items total, 21 of which are semantic items and 18 are grammar items. The intent of these items is to measure children's ability to express themselves verbally in Spanish.

The purpose of the TELD-3:S is to help establish the presence of a language difficulty, if it exists, and to help identify those children who may need further clinical evaluation of their language development abilities. The overall test score is used to determine a child's general spoken language ability. However, as a cautionary note, the developers of the TELD-3:S warn users that the testing results do not determine solely a child's ability to use a language or the diagnosis of a language problem in a short span of time. The test was primarily "designed to complement rather than replace" (examiner's manual, p. 5) any kind of ongoing diagnostic evaluation.

The TELD-3:S was designed to be administered by fluent Spanish speakers. However, because the assessment is conducted entirely in Spanish, test administrators need to be both fluent in Spanish and knowledgeable about the Spanish language in order to guide examinees effectively and properly interpret the test results. The TELD-3:S is untimed. However, the test generally can be completed in one 15–40-minute session. In order to achieve optimal testing, it is recommended the examiner follows test administration guidelines as recommended in the test manual. The developers provide an extensive chart of words used within the test and their corresponding word substitutions from several Latin American countries and Spain.

Both RLS and ELS prompts participants to begin their assessment according to their age level, by establishing entry points preprogrammed chronologically, thus reducing test administration time. Once the appropriate entry point has been established, the participant begins the assessment; a ceiling point is established after three consecutive answers have been missed. Only those items below the established ceiling contribute to the overall raw score. On the other hand, a basal point is established in a variety of ways. For instance, if a participant has struggled to answer correctly three items in a row when trying to determine a ceiling, then the test administrator needs to return to the entry point and administer items in reverse order unitl three correct answers in a row are achieved. At this point, a basal has been reached.

The examiner record booklet, picture book, and manipulatives are the testing objects the test administrator uses to assess the examinee. The booklet consists of a questionnaire type of test, to which the participants either demonstrate their answers or give an oral response. Directions for correct response determination appear directly on each item to assist the examiner and avoid scoring errors (correct = 1 point or wrong = 0 points). Once the test is completed, the examiner can determine raw scores for the two subscales and records them for conversion into a variety of standard score units (i.e., standard scores, percentile ranks, and age equivalents) The TELD-3:S examiner's manual provides all the needed conversion tables in its appendixes.

DEVELOPMENT. According to the test manual, the test norms for each of the subtests and the composite (Spoken Language Ability) are presented in terms of standard scores (Mean = 100 and *SD* = 15). The use of standard scores permits the examiner to make comparisons across subtests, thereby allowing for the computation of a total score or composite. The developers provide a descriptive rating for seven discrete distributional levels and a general description as to what the test's scores measure, thus revealing some of the theoretical underpinnings of the instrument. The RLS goal is to measure overall levels of comprehension or understanding of language, whereas the ELS measures a child's ability to communicate orally.

TECHNICAL. Requests for participation were made through the use of Bilingual educators, bilingual speech-pathologists, and other professional's Internet list servers. The TELD-3:S's final normative sample was composed of 1,441 children residing in the United States, Latin America, and Spain; said sample was collected between January 2002 and May 2005. The selection of examinees from participating countries outside of the United States focused on more systematic sampling procedures correcting for various demographic variables. All of the students in these countries came from private or public preschools, elementary schools, university schools, or denominational schools. All data collection personnel for the U.S. and other participating countries were fluent speakers in the appropriate dialect of the Spanish language. Demographic characteristics of the normative sample derived from the United States yielded proportional stratified samples by geographical areas in the country. Mexican children represented equal proportions reflected by Hispanics in the U.S. followed by children sampled from Central and South America.

A variety of test score reliability procedures were employed by the developers to evaluate item content sampling, internal consistency, and stability of item functioning for both subtests. Internal consistency reliability of TELD-3:S subtests was examined using coefficient alpha. For the Spoken Language Ability standard score, coefficient alphas were computed using Guilford's method (1954, p. 393). The average coefficient for the subtests and the composite yielded moderate to high internal consistency levels among items. For the most part, the standard errors of measurement for these age groups and subtests produced small values. Similar moderate to high internal consistency alphas were observed across gender and geographic location groups.

A very small sample (n = 30) from Mexico was used to establish test-retest reliability. The observed time-sampling reliability values for the subscales and composite scores revealed moderate to high coefficients, mostly in the 80s. The intervening time period was 2 weeks.

A third type of reliability analysis was conducted to determine the amount of test error associated with examiner variability in scoring. A set of 40 completed protocols were independently scored by two graduate students fluent in several Spanish dialects. There was a .99 agreement on the scoring of the two subtests.

The TELD-3:S developers provide compelling evidence of their efforts to examine validity issues surrounding the merits of their instrument in terms of its cumulative evidence, content-related, criterion-related, and construct-related validity. In relation to their efforts to provide evidence of content-description validity, the test authors offer five demonstrations where this type of validity evidence is ascertained. To determine item functioning across two key demographic variables (gender and language), the developers applied logistic regression procedures to all 76 items (Swaminathan & Rogers, 1990). These analyses provided evidence that the TELD-3:S items were functioning similarly across groups of examinees. Of the 304 group comparison analyses conducted, only 9 were deemed significant at the .001 level. These results provide initial evidence of unbiased item functioning for the test's subscales across gender and language groups.

Another type of the evidence provided by the test developers included criterion-related validity and was accomplished by correlating the TELD-3:S raw scores with those of the Clinical Evaluation of Language Fundamentals–Third Edition (CELF-3S; Semel, Wiig, & Secord, 1997) and the Prueba de Lenguaje Inicial (PLI; Ramos & Ramos, 2000). The 12 intracorrelations across these subtests and tests yielded moderate to high coefficients.

Finally, the test authors provided six distinct forms for the demonstration of evidence on construct-identification validity. First, given the developmental nature of the test, children's performances should be strongly correlated with age. The results for this form of evidence yielded a clear ascending pattern in the way mean score performance for different age groups of children improved across time, whereas the relationship across the test's subscales performance and age were found to be very large. Second, because the TELD-3:S purports to measure language ability, its subtests should be able to differentiate between those children with typical developing language skills and those children who are exceptional in the area of language. The test authors demonstrated this type of validity by providing evidence across different demographic grouping variables, by using the mean standard scores for selected subgroups in the normative sample. Those children who were known to have demonstrated language ability performed well whereas those children with known disabilities performed poorly. Third, because oral language and school abilities are highly related, the TELD-3:S should be positively correlated with other measures of academic abilities. The test authors selected four different and well-established measures of academic ability and examined the intercorrelations on more than 18 subtests and the TELD-3:S subtests. The large majority of the intercorrelations (adjusted for attenuation) conducted yielded moderate to high coefficients. Fourth, because the "TELD-3:S measures an important cognitive ability, its scores should correlate significantly with intelligence tests" (examiner's manual p. 43). To confirm this expectation, the test authors used the Test of Nonverbal Intelligence–Third Edition (TONI-3; Brown, Sherbenou, & Johnsen, 1997). Although the coefficients obtained are considered moderate across the TELD-3:S subscales and the composite, the test authors state that these correlations "may be accepted as evidence of the test's construct-identification validity" (examiner's manual, p. 46). Finally, the test authors provided an additional form of construct validity evidence by correlating seemingly related traits between the test's subscales. The results supported this form of evidence given that the large number of subtest intercorrelations produced moderately high to high coefficients across age levels, demonstrating that the TELD-3:S measures the same construct described as spoken language ability by the test authors. The test authors encouraged researchers to cross-validate their findings on this important aspect of the developed test.

COMMENTARY. Learning to speak is one of the most important and visible achievements for a child. The opportunities for sharing needs and wants represents the child's way to start understanding their environment. The importance of learning how to read, how to share experiences, and how to interact with social environments are ever present for the child at this stage of development. The development of an instrument to aid in the early identification then becomes a must for speech therapists and educators to use in order to make appropriate decisions and offer effective interventions. The development and use of psychometrically sound measures becomes paramount in addressing these central issues affecting all children. The TELD-3:S fills this need for the ever growing Spanish-speaking population in the United States by providing an option that may meet some of the needs observed in many educational settings. The most favorable points about the TELD-3:S are evident and include: (a) the simplicity of the entire process of assessment for both subscales, (b) the flexibility it affords for the examiner to assess such important aspects (Receptive and Expressive) of language development, including no restrictions on performance due to time limits, (c) the use of everyday situations, objects, and activities that allow children to understand and act, (d) efficiency in reporting and interpreting examinees' performance at the subscale and composite score levels, (e) the age range for children in the normative sample provides for a wider representation of children currently served by the U.S. educational system, (f) the great efforts made by the test developers in substantiating the test's psychometric soundness, (g) the practical aspects of administering a test of this type within reasonable administration time, and (h) the care taken by the test developers to justify their methods for preventing or minimizing test and item biases, evidenced by their efforts in securing sample representation, not a small task.

There are some minor factors that may affect the overall usefulness of the TELD-3:S. These include: (a) Item response theories could be applied in an effort to improve the final selection of "best" items for each of the subscales. Such procedures may make it possible to achieve the same results with a shorter version of the test; (b) the actual utility of the test's manipulatives is questioned, primarily due to the fact that only three questions (4, 7, and 15) in the RLS appear to have a need for them. Elimination of these may help in the administration of the test and the overall outcome may be not affected at all; and (c) the oversimplification of the overall Language Ability score based on just two subscales. There is a need for the test authors to provide a more in-depth justification for the theoretical perspectives underlying this complex and important phenomenon. These weaknesses do not detract the overall usefulness of the measure and the important impact that it may have in the identification of children's speech problems, but should be considered carefully by those who plan to use the TELD-3:S.

SUMMARY. The careful development of the TELD-3:S signifies an important step in the proper identification of Spanish-speaking children with language problems. These problems will be exacerbated later in the child's daily interaction with others within social and academic settings. The pool of tests that focus on this area of need is very small and scales such as the TELD-3:S fill an important gap, making it a unique assessment tool that addresses critical issues in the understanding of language problems.

Because of the many and varied favorable factors and the potential benefits that appropriate use of this test may have in improving the lives of many Hispanic children, this reviewer endorses the use of the Test of Early Language Development–Third Edition: Spanish Version.

REVIEWER'S REFERENCES

Brown, L., Sherbenou, R. J., & Johnsen, S. K. (1997). Test of Nonverbal Intelligence–Third Edition. Austin, TX: PRO-ED.

Guilford, J. P. (1954). *Fundamental statistics in psychology and education* (2nd ed.). New York: McGraw-Hill.

Ramos, M., & Ramos, J. (2000). Prueba de Lenguaje Inicial. Austin, TX: PRO-ED.

Semel, E., Wiig, E. H., & Secord, W. A. (1997). Clinical Evaluation of Language Fundamentals–Third Edition, Spanish Edition. Columbus, OH: Merrill.

Swaminathan, H., & Rogers, H. J. (1990). Detecting differential item functioning using logistic regression procedures. *Journal of Educational Measurement, 27,* 361-370.

[140]

The Test of Everyday Reasoning.

Purpose: Designed to supplement information on applications for employment, educational assessments, and program evaluations by assessing basic reasoning skills.

Population: Middle school students, high school students, and adults.

Publication Dates: 2000-2007.
Acronym: TER.
Scores, 6: Analysis, Evaluation, Inference, Deductive Reasoning, Inductive Reasoning, Total.
Administration: Group.
Price Data, 2008: $45 per manual (2007, 29 pages); $450 per 100 test forms.
Time: (50) minutes.
Authors: Peter A. Facione and Stephen W. Blohm.
Publisher: Insight Assessment—The California Academic Press LLC.

Review of The Test of Everyday Reasoning by TIMOTHY J. MAKATURA, Adjunct Professor of Psychology, Capella University, Minneapolis, MN:

The Test of Everyday Reasoning (TER) is a recently developed test that is designed to assess the component skills that are necessary for effective critical thinking. This measure was derived from the California Critical Thinking Skills Test (CCTST; 18:21) and continues the test authors' involvement in the development of instruments that may be used to measure the various dimensions of critical thinking. The CCTST was designed to be used with college students or professionals, whereas the TER is intended to be used with younger individuals with a middle school or higher level of education. The TER is theoretically based on the American Philosophical Association's Delphi consensus statement (APA, 1990), which defines critical thinking as "the process of purposeful, self-regulatory judgment. This process gives reasoned consideration to evidence, context, conceptualizations, methods and criteria" (as quoted in TER test manual, p. 6). Working from this foundation, the test authors posit that critical thinking comprises cognitive skills including interpretation, analysis, inference, evaluation, and explanation. The test authors further suggest that certain dispositions are necessary for effective critical thinking and these include open-mindedness, inquisitiveness, cognitive maturity, truth-seeking, analyticity, systematicity, and self-confidence. Although the APA Delphi consensus statement supports the standard definition of critical thinking, support for the additional qualities that reportedly predispose a person to be an effective critical thinker is uncertain.

DESCRIPTION. The TER is a 35-item multiple-choice test that may be administered in an online or paper-and-pencil format. The test authors suggest a 45-minute time limit to complete the test, but this may be altered at the test administrator's discretion. In addition to basic identification information, the test taker may be asked to provide information regarding gender, class level, and/or race, although the use of this information is uncertain because normative information is provided only for the general population. It is interesting to note that the test manual provides frequent reminders to the test taker and test administrator of the need to maintain confidentiality and security of test items.

According to the test manual, each test item is worth one point and there is no penalty for incorrect responses. Scoring is completed by sending the answer sheet to the test publisher and there is no mechanism for scoring to be completed by the test administrator. In fact, the test manual does not indicate which test items comprise each of the summary scales. The test publisher returns total and subscale TER scores for each test taker and descriptive statistics for the group of test takers. Individual results also may be interpreted by comparing individual scores to percentiles listed in the test manual. These percentiles are provided for four samples that are not stratified by age, grade level, or any other characteristic.

DEVELOPMENT. The TER was derived from the California Critical Thinking Skills Test (CCTST) and both tests were developed by Dr. Peter A. Facione and colleagues. The test authors report that the CCTST, which was designed to assess critical thinking in college students, was administered to large samples of high school, technical school, and community college students. Analysis of these results identified 8 items that did not discriminate well between high and low total scores in this population and these items were eliminated. The remaining 26 items were altered to better accommodate lowered age and educational background of this younger group as well as focus the items on everyday situations. Nine additional items were developed and added to the test.

TECHNICAL. Measures of internal consistency reliability were derived using the Kuder Richardson-20 (KR-20). Reliabilities were obtained for four separate groups and ranged from .72 to .89. The four groups included: (a) 145 participants from an Associate Nursing Program at a community college, (b) 201 students from a technical college, (c) 582 students from an all-girls high school with equal numbers of participants from each grade, and (d) 113 participants from the general population aged 18 to 90. Age, race, and gender information are not provided for all groups in this sample.

The test authors provide logical arguments regarding the association between the TER and the factors from the APA Delphi consensus statement regarding critical thinking as evidence of content and construct validity. The strongest evidence for construct validity is the correlation (.77) between the TER and the CCTST, which is based on a sample of 29 participants. The test authors submit that a correlation of .45 between the TER and grade-point average for 575 participants offers evidence of criterion validity. Correlations are also reported between the TER and PSAT scores that range from .50 to .60 for a sample of 408 individuals. Correlations between the TER and scores on the Iowa Educational Development Test ranged from .44 to .55 for a sample of 153 individuals. Correlations between the TER and scores on the ACT ranged from .35 to .52 for a sample of 135 individuals. Although the reported correlations are significant, they tend generally to fall in the moderate range.

COMMENTARY AND SUMMARY. The test authors have made a good attempt to develop a test that measures the multidimensional construct of critical thinking. However, this test is found to be lacking in statistical evidence that supports this contention. The normative sample is certainly large but characteristics of this sample (age, gender, level of education, etc.) are not reported. This omission raises questions regarding the representativeness of the sample, sampling bias, and the potential influence of some demographic factors on performance. There is also some concern regarding the specific relationship between the TER and the APA Delphi consensus statement as the TER subscales do not correspond precisely to the five necessary cognitive skills identified in the consensus statement. The test authors fail to identify items that comprise each of the TER subscales or provide statistical evidence that specific items in a subscale are related. This lack of information regarding subscales limits interpretation of the results. There are also some concerns regarding the lack of test-retest reliability and limited information regarding how test items were developed. This test seems to be appropriate for the general assessment of critical thinking but the results should be interpreted with a great deal of caution due to previously noted limitations.

REVIEWER'S REFERENCE

American Philosophical Association. (1990). *Critical thinking: A statement of expert consensus for the purposes of educational assessment and instruction* ("The Delphi Report"). (ERIC Doc. No. ED 315-423)

Review of The Test of Everyday Reasoning by RENÉE M. TOBIN, Associate Professor of Psychology, and CORINNE ZIMMERMAN, Associate Professor of Psychology, Illinois State University, Normal, IL:

DESCRIPTION. The Test of Everyday Reasoning (TER) is designed to measure critical thinking skills in everyday contexts. The 35-item test consists of three subscales (i.e., analysis/interpretation, inference, and evaluation/explanation) that target five core cognitive abilities selected for inclusion based on a conceptualization of critical thinking established by a consensus study (American Philosophical Association [APA], 1990). Scores are reported for each of the three subscales mentioned above as well as for inductive and deductive reasoning.

Critical thinking is conceived of as having a skills dimension and a dispositional dimension. The TER does not address the dispositional side of critical thinking (i.e., the willingness to think critically). Rather, the TER targets the skills dimension, or the actual cognitive abilities that define critical thinking. To assess dispositions, the test manual suggests the California Measure of Mental Motivation (CM3) for general use, or the California Critical Thinking Disposition Inventory (CCTDI) for use with college populations.

The TER is ideally suited for use with high school and general adult populations because it is assumed that an elementary school education is sufficient for familiarity with the everyday contexts that are presented in the TER. The test does not use technical vocabulary and is written at a sixth-grade reading level. The test can be used with community college or college-aged samples, and has been validated for use in late childhood (i.e., Grades 7–9, beginning at age 12). Because of the wide range of ages, the test is appropriate for use in cross-sectional research.

The TER can be administered online or in paper-and-pencil format. The test manual includes administration instructions for both. The paper-and-pencil format requires a clean test booklet and a CapScore™ answer form for each test taker. Verbatim instructions are provided along with precautions that guard against invalidating the test results. The recommended time limit is 45 minutes. CapScore™ response sheets are returned to Insight Assessment for scanning and scoring. A file will be created that includes the total and subscale scores for each test taker. This file can be sent via email. Alternatively, a PC formatted disk and original response sheets can be returned via surface mail upon request.

The online administration of the TER involves working with a team from Insight Assessments to set up an e-testing system and becoming familiar with the system as a site administrator. Technical support is available to ensure that computers at the e-testing site are compatible with the software with free downloads provided as needed. The site login can be set up in advance with a unique login and password for each user. Alternatively, a unique random login and password can be generated, with test takers instructed to personalize them.

For both versions, sample test items are presented first. For online test takers, sample items provide an opportunity to become familiar with the testing interface. The system allows users to answer questions in any order, and one can return to any question to change an answer. A numbered grid is displayed under the current question, with different colored fonts to indicate which questions have and have not been answered. Questions involving graphs, charts, or figures include the same graphics in the online and paper versions. The computer interface is simple to use and navigate. Online test takers can immediately know their total and subscale scores. Each subscale is described, including the participant's score and the maximum possible score. Percentile rank is provided along with information about how to interpret percentile ranks.

DEVELOPMENT. The TER was developed following a consensus report on the conceptualization of critical thinking (APA, 1990). The panel consisted of 46 experts from various disciplines. The construct of critical thinking was defined as consisting of five core cognitive abilities (analysis, interpretation, inference, evaluation, and explanation) along with metacognitive self-regulation. This conceptualization was later supported by a survey of 600 educators, policy makers, and employers (Jones et al., 1995). The TER was developed from The California Critical Thinking Skills Test (CCTST), which is appropriate for use with college students and professionals. Items were altered or added to be appropriate for the age and educational background of younger and noncollege populations.

Critical thinking, in brief, is characterized as "the process of purposeful, self-regulatory judgment" (test manual, p. 5). The concise conceptualization is that the core cognitive abilities are used in the "process of making a reasoned judgment about what to believe or do" (test manual, p. 6). Lengthier descriptions of core constructs are available in the test manual.

In defining critical thinking this way, the development of test items was focused specifically on response choices about what to do or what to believe, following the evaluation of evidence, charts, or figures. Items are discipline neutral and do not require content area knowledge. Distractor items were chosen to represent well-documented misleading heuristics and fallacies (e.g., hindsight bias, availability heuristic) or dispositional tendencies (e.g., personal bias, hasty generalizations). The items on the TER also can be classified along the dimensions of inductive and deductive reasoning as defined by logicians.

TECHNICAL. Reliability data are reported for four samples: (a) community college students enrolled in a nursing program (N = 145; gender not reported), KR-20 = .78; (b) technical college students (N = 201; 36% female), KR-20 = .76; (c) high school students (Grades 9–12) from a private, all-girls high school (N = 582), KR-20 = .72; and (d) general population sample of individuals (ages ranged from 18–90) in non-health-care-related groups and clubs (N = 113, 82% female), KR-20 = .89. KR-20 coefficients in the range of .65–.75 are considered sufficient for tests that are not intended to target a single factor. Percentile rank norms are presented for an aggregated sample and for each of the four samples.

Content validity. The TER was developed to parallel the consensus study on critical thinking (APA, 1990), targeting the conceptualization of critical thinking as comprising five cognitive skills. The TER combines these into three subscales: analysis/interpretation, inference, and explanation/evaluation. For example, a particular item might involve the evaluation of an argument as either weak or strong, along with the explanation for that evaluation. Therefore, individual items were designed to assess concurrently the ability to evaluate and then to explain or to analyze and interpret. The ability to use the five skills reflexively is acknowledged in the consensus definitions (APA, 1990).

Construct validity. The majority of the assessment specialists who participated in the APA (1990) consensus project agreed that a multiple-choice test could be used as a valid measure of critical thinking skills. The TER includes items designed to engage the test taker's reasoning abilities, and the response choices include well-known reasoning errors or misleading heuristics to differentiate between more and less skilled reasoners. According to the test manual, a .77 correlation was found between performance on the TER and the CCTST with a modest sample of 29 participants.

Criterion validity. Information about the potential for the TER to predict school achievement is reported only in the form of its correlations with other academic predictors, such as GPA (e.g., r = .45 in a sample of 575 girls at a private school, Grades 9–12), PSAT scores, ACT scores, and Iowa Educational Development scores.

COMMENTARY. The major strength of this assessment is its connection to a consensus study of experts from different academic disciplines. The creation of items for this measure is rooted in this interdisciplinary conceptualization of critical thinking. The TER was developed from the CCTST with the goal of assessing the core cognitive abilities that define critical thinking, but without technical vocabulary or domain-specific knowledge. All items are presented in familiar, everyday contexts, making it appropriate for middle school (children as young as 12 years of age), high school, technical school, community college, and general adult populations, as well as college or professional samples. The test length of 45 to 50 minutes lends itself well to administration during the school day for all educational levels.

It is important to note that the TER manual does not provide an answer key; therefore, scores may only be obtained from the test authors, either through their online system or via surface mail. The reported reliability data are biased towards female participants (approximately 85% across three samples). Until additional studies of this measure have been added to the literature, some caution is in order in terms of interpreting the results. As with other first edition manuals, this one is not as polished as future editions are likely to be in terms of proofreading, clarity, and documentation of citations. Generally, the text is comprehensible, but it would benefit from additional editing and the provision of full citations and references throughout the manual. At present, some of the sources cited as supporting the TER's reliability and validity cannot be located.

SUMMARY. The TER a is group-administered test of five core cognitive abilities involved in critical thinking: Analysis, Inference, Evaluation, and Deductive and Inductive Reasoning. Based on the test manual, evidence of the validity and reliability of the TER is limited; however, empirical investigation of this measure by other researchers appears to be growing. Additional research and use will dictate conclusions about its overall utility. In its present form, this measure is recommended for research purposes, but not for clinical use at this time.

REVIEWERS' REFERENCES

American Philosophical Association. (1990). *Critical thinking: A statement of expert consensus for purposes of educational assessment and instruction* ("The Delphi Report"). Newark, DE: American Philosophical Association. (ERIC Document Reproduction Service No. ED315423)

Jones, E., Hoffman, S., Moore, L. M., Ratcliff, G., Tibbetts, S., & Click, B. L., III. (1995). *National assessment of college student learning: Identifying college graduates' essential skills in writing, speech and listening, and critical thinking. Final project report.* Washington, DC: National Center for Educational Statistics. (U.S. Department of Education, Office of Educational Research and Improvement; OERI Publiction NCES 93-001)

[141]

Test of Handwriting Skills—Revised.

Purpose: Designed to assess "neurosensory integration ability as evidenced by manuscript or cursive writing."
Population: Ages 6 to 18.
Publication Date: 2007.
Acronym: THS-R.
Scores: Total score only.
Administration: Group.
Forms, 2: Manuscript, Cursive.
Price Data, 2007: $120 per test kit including 15 manuscript test booklets, 15 cursive test booklets, 30 record forms, manual (190 pages), and training video; $35 per 15 test booklets and record forms (specify manuscript or cursive); $35 per manual; $15 per training video.
Time: (15–20) minutes.
Comments: Examiner's manual contains scoring directions for both manuscript and cursive formats.
Author: Michael Milone.
Publisher: Academic Therapy Publications.

Review of the Test of Handwriting Skills–Revised by PHILLIP L. ACKERMAN, Professor of Psychology, Georgia Institute of Technology, Atlanta, GA:

DESCRIPTION. The Test of Handwriting Skills–Revised (THS-R) is a measure of manuscript (print) and cursive handwriting. The manual indicates that the test can be administered to students between the ages of 6 years, 0 months and 18 years, 11 months. The test is recommended for two uses: to "identify handwriting problems and monitor progress in handwriting, particularly for students with disabilities" and "to determine if neurosensory integration difficulties are contributing to learning problems" (manual, p. 6), although users interested in the second use are advised that the THS-R should be used in conjunction with other "assessments of classroom learning and observations made by trained professionals" (manual, p. 6). The manual states that the test "may be used by a variety of professionals, including occupational therapists, psychologists, learning specialists, diagnosticians, and rehabilitation specialists." The test can be used in "regular or special education settings, as well as guide rehabilitation practices" (manual, p. 10).

The THS-R involves one of two record forms (one for manuscript format and the other for cursive format) that each consist of 10 subtests of increasing complexity. The subtests require the student to write the letters of the alphabet from memory, write letters and numbers from dictation, and copy from example text. The overall test is untimed, though speed measures are made by having the student record progress at timed points in two parts of the test. The test takes roughly 10 minutes to administer. The manual indicates that the test can be administered individually or to small groups of students. For "progress monitoring" the manual recommends that only the first two subtests be administered in a test-retest format, with scores plotted over time. Test administrators are advised also to observe the behaviors of the examinee during the test and record observations on the test form.

Scaled scores for each subtest are computed and summed to provide an overall scaled score, standard score, and percentile rank score. In addition, four ancillary scores are recorded, though these are scaled into one of three categories (*No Concerns, Watch,* or *Test Further*), depending on whether the scores are at or above the 50th percentile, between the 16th and 50th percentile, or below the 16th percentile.

The administration instructions are exceptionally clear and detailed. Users are provided with information about establishing rapport with the examinee and testing in a standardized fashion. The tests must be scored by hand, according to a highly complex set of rules. Instructions for scoring the test are also highly detailed. The manual provides a wealth of information about scoring, and the manual is supplemented by a DVD/CD that reviews the details of the scoring protocol. The DVD is somewhat informal in tone but does provide valuable information about the scoring protocol. (The DVD also mentions that the test "is not intended for regular classroom use. It is a diagnostic assessment that is intended for use in special education and rehabilitation for the diagnosis of certain disabilities that affect handwriting production.") Because of the complexity of the scoring protocol, scoring should only be performed by a highly trained individual.

DEVELOPMENT. The basis for this test is mainly rational, in the sense that the quality of handwriting is viewed as an "indicator of learning disabilities and other neurological issues that affect an individual's performance on academic tasks" (p. 10). Some literature is mentioned in the manual pertaining to the association of handwriting problems with other impairments, but this reviewer considers this analysis as not very extensive. In addition, the manual briefly describes a series of potential interventions associated with improving handwriting skills. The manual does not describe how the subtests and the overall test fit into extant theories or applications of handwriting skills or abilities.

TECHNICAL.

Standardization. The test was normed on a sample of 1,608 students in the U.S.A. between the ages of 6 years, 0 months and 18 years, 11 months. Although no explicit stratification of demographic groups is reported, there appears to be a good representation of different groups in the sample. Scaled score tables are provided for each of the subtests by age. (Although the DVD mentions common gender differences in handwriting performance, there are no reported separate norms for boys and girls in the manual.) The only data reported for identifiable clinical samples were from an ADD/ADHD (Attention Deficit Disorder/ Attention Deficit Hyperactive Disorder) group (N = 28), and a Learning Disability Group (N = 24), though these groups were heterogeneous on age, and only summary statistics are reported for these groups for each subtest, along with scaled score means for matched normal examinees.

Reliability. Internal consistency reliability information is presented for the individual subtests and overall scores by age group. Reliabilities ranged from .61 to .92, depending on the individual subtest. Internal consistency reliabilities for the overall scores are uniformly high (.95 to .98), indicating a high degree of homogeneity across the 10 subtests. Test-retest reliability information was limited to two very small studies (N = 17 for the Manuscript Format, and N = 29 for the Cursive Format) over an average duration of 2 weeks. Given the large standard errors for correlations with these small sample sizes, it was not surprising to note that both individual subtest and overall score test-retest reliabilities were quite modest. The total test-retest reliability coefficient was reported to be r = .82. Test-retest reliabilities for scores from the first and second subtest (which are recommended for progress monitoring) ranged from .71 to .78. These may be a concern for progress monitoring applications, given that these estimates were obtained in the absence of explicit handwriting interventions.

Interrater reliabilities were reported for five raters who had completed training and who had at least 10 hours of prior experience scoring this test. Total score agreement was fair, ranging from .84 to .90. Agreements for subtest scores were lower, ranging from .70 to .93.

Validity. The manual reports that content validity was established from the format of an earlier test (the Test of Handwriting Skills; Gardner, 1998), though few details are provided regarding how the format was selected. No criterion-related validity data are provided. Construct validity was evaluated with respect to developmental changes, that is, median scores on the test by age group. Scores increase from age 6 to age 10, but then decline for the older ages. The manual reports that scores should "increase during the ages at which the children are receiving direct instruction, and then should remain fairly stable, or decrease slightly after the direct instruction stops" (p. 67), though no external evidence was presented to support this assertion. The two small samples of ADD/ADHD and Learning Disability groups were also used to support construct validity. In both cases, mean total standard scores were substantially below matched norm samples, though the overall scores for the two groups were essentially identical to one another. Principal components analyses and factor analyses are reported for the subtest scores, ancillary scores, and total scores. The sample for these analyses is not described, and it was particularly disconcerting to see that the total score measures were included in the analyses, given the part-whole relationship between the total scores and the subtest scores. Also, the speed measure should have been reflected before the analysis, given that substantial negative correlation between the speed measure and the other measures complicates interpretation of the factor solution. Nonetheless, it appeared that two factors or components provided a good representation of the measures, which suggests that 10 subtest scores and 4 ancillary scores should not be interpreted individually. No validity data were reported for correlations with other tests, to allow for an evaluation of convergent and/or discriminant validity. Finally, no data were provided about the results of interventions, or longitudinal tracking of normal development, so it was impossible to ascertain the validity of these measures for "progress monitoring."

COMMENTARY. The manual is generally well written, and in many places the author advises the user to be cautious in the use and interpretation of the test and the various scores. Information about standard errors and the magnitude of differences in subtest scores needed to be considered "significant" were provided, which was an indicator of an appropriate level of rigor in test use. However, the theoretical foundation provided in the manual was quite limited and insufficient for the user to understand the basis for the test content and for its application. Test-retest reliability data were inadequate, and there were no data on the effectiveness of the test in assessing changes in performance under interventions. These shortcomings were especially notable in the context of the recommended uses for the test in terms of progress monitoring. Overall, the validity data were weak, with no attempt made to place the test in the larger context of perceptual-motor skills or differential diagnoses for clinical or educational uses. The scoring regimen also may be so complex as to discourage use by most individuals except those who would use the test on a frequent basis. The manual and DVD provide extensive scoring information, but the DVD is quite long and perhaps overly informal at times.

SUMMARY. The THS-R is a straightforward assessment of handwriting skills in terms of administration, but it is highly complex in terms of scoring. The potential strength of the measure is the rigor of the scoring protocol, but given the paucity of validity information, it is not clear what the utility of the assessments would be. he absence of any demonstrable validity of the test for progress monitoring yields a conclusion that the test should not be recommended for this purpose. The limited data for ADD/ADHD and Learning Disabled groups suggest that the test might be used in conjunction with other indicators for diagnostic purposes, but only to discriminate between normal and nonnormal classifications, because of the absence of differential diagnostic validity data. Other uses of the measure, such as evaluation of normal development patterns, have not been validated. It remains unclear how this assessment would fit into a larger comprehensive assessment protocol because it has unknown relations with other cognitive and perceptual/motor assessments.

REVIEWER'S REFERENCE

Gardner, M. F. (1998). Test of Handwriting Skills. Hydesville, CA: Psychological and Educational Publications, Inc.

Review of the Test Of Handwriting Skills—Revised by GENE SCHWARTING, Associate Professor, Education Department, Fontbonne University, St. Louis, MO:

DESCRIPTION. The author presents the primary purpose of the Test of Handwriting Skills–Revised (THS-R) as the assessment of neurosensory integration skills as manifested in manuscript or cursive writing, with other purposes being to determine if deficits in such abilities are factors in learning difficulties or for progress monitoring as in the Response to Intervention (RTI) model. It is emphasized that this is not a penmanship assessment, but rather to be used to identify handwriting problems. The THS-R may be used by those with an understanding of standardized assessment, with the most likely assessors being occupational therapists, psychologists, or special education teachers. Individuals being tested should have been taught, and be capable of using, all letters of the alphabet with test age ranges from 6 years, 0 months to 18 years, 11 months for manuscript writing assessment and 8 years, 0 months to 18 years, 11 months for cursive writing assessment.

The THS-R consists of a test manual/norms book, examiner's record forms, the examinee's response booklets, and a DVD that provides information on how to score the THS-R. A complete administration involves 10 subtests with four ancillary scores, and is expected to take about 10 minutes to administer and 15 minutes to score. An abbreviated administration using 2 of the subtests would involve significantly less time. Administration can be either individual or in small groups, and the individual being tested may select either manuscript or cursive as the preferred method of writing. Because there are different student response books, switching styles during the test is to be counted as an error. Once the preferred handwriting style is established, the examinee is provided a test booklet, pencil, and verbal directions.

The first two subtests, consisting of writing the alphabet in upper- and lower-case letters, are timed. The remaining eight subtests, which are not timed, involve writing letters, numbers, and simple words to either visual or auditory prompts. Each letter produced by the examinee is scored on a scale from 0 to 3 points following a set of rules as well as a number of examples. Age-based norms tables at 6-month intervals are provided through age 10, with ages 11-12 and 13-18 grouped together. Each subtest converts raw scores to standard scores with a mean of 10 and a standard deviation of 3; subtest scores are summed and converted to a total standard score with a mean of 100 and a standard deviation of 15. Conversion to percentiles, normal curve equivalences, *T*-scores, and stanines is also provided. Ancillary scores measuring the rate of writing, reversals, letters touching when they should not, and errors in upper/lower case are converted to percentile categories.

DEVELOPMENT. The THS-R is a revision of the Test of Handwriting Skills developed by Morrison F. Gardner in 1998, with the purpose, format, and administration procedures being unchanged. The present author reports that the scoring, norms, and development of a composite score are modifications from the original.

TECHNICAL. The THS-R was standardized in 2005-2006 on 1,476 children (the total sample is reported as 1,608 children) between the ages of 6 years, 0 months and 18 years, 11 months. Examinees were to be selected from regular education classrooms, although some individuals with diagnosed disabilities were involved. This norm group was from 80 sites in 34 states, and was selected based upon gender, ethnicity, region of the country, urban or rural settings, and parent education level. When compared to the demographic characteristics of the 2000 U.S. Census, differences were noted with some subgroups; males, Asian Americans, urban residents, and parents with less than a high school education were underrepresented. The size of age groups varied from 99 for 9-year-olds to 154 for 8-year-olds for the manuscript format and from 112 for 10-year-olds to 174 for 11- to 12-year-olds. Ages 13 through 18 were grouped together for both formats, whereas ages 6 through 10 were grouped by each year of age.

Internal consistency reliability, using coefficient alpha for the entire norm group, was computed for each age group noted above. Subtest coefficients varied from .60 to .86 (median = .81) for the manuscript format and from .57 to .98 (median = .86) for the cursive format. Overall internal consistency reliability coefficients by age varied for manuscript format from .95 to .97 and for cursive format from .97 to .98. Standard errors of measurement for the subtests (computed using coefficient alpha) ranged from 1.06 to 1.97 for the manuscript format and 0.58 to 1.96 for the cursive format. Standard errors of estimate by age ranged from 2.44 to 3.10 for the entire manuscript version, and 1.92 to 2.63 for the complete cursive assessment.

Test-retest reliability (average of 14 days between tests) for the subtests with small groups showed significantly greater variability, ranging from .15 to .83 (median = .64) for the manuscript format (n = 17) and from .22 to .82 (median = .68) for the cursive format (n = 29). Overall test-retest reliability was .80 for the manuscript format and .85 for the cursive format. Interrater reliability (five raters) for a sample of 12 manuscript and 41 cursive samples was .89.

Claims to validity are based on several general approaches. Content validity appears to be assumed, as the use of Differential Item Functioning found no item bias. Construct validity involves an increase in raw scores with chronological age through age 10, although they drop past that point due to decrease in formal handwriting instruction and the increased usage of computers. Also, individuals diagnosed as ADD/ADHD (n = 28) or learning disabled (n = 24) obtained significantly lower scores than the general population. Finally, factor analysis found that the THS-R loads into only two factors—Subtests 1 through 10 loaded onto one (Basic Handwriting Skills), whereas the ancillary scores loaded onto another (Ancillary Tasks). Concurrent validity studies are not provided to indicate the relationship of the THS-R with other handwriting or fine motor assessment instruments.

COMMENTARY. The THS-R has a rather narrow focus, concentrating on the mechanics only of the handwriting process with no concern as to the content or purposes of written communication. The authors acknowledge that handwriting no longer receives the emphasis it once did in school, and that the extensive use of computers has made it less important than it was previously. Although the instrument appears to be an improvement over the original THS, the scoring is still subjective, despite the abundance of examples provided. (A valuable training video is provided in the test kit, however.) Questions exist as to both test-retest and interrater reliability, and the minimal discussion of validity also raises concerns.

SUMMARY. If one finds it necessary to use an assessment to measure handwriting only, the THS-R would be useful. However, for individuals having difficulty with their handwriting, providing a word processor appears to be a logical solution.

[142]

Test of Irregular Word Reading Efficiency.

Purpose: Designed to use "the pronunciation of phonetically irregular words to measure reading comprehension."
Population: Ages 3–94.
Publication Date: 2007.
Acronym: TIWRE.
Score: Reading Efficiency Index.
Administration: Individual.
Forms, 3: Form 1, Form 2, Form 3.
Price Data, 2009: $159 per manual (93 pages), 25 record forms, 25 profile forms, and 3 laminated stimulus cards.
Time: (2) minutes.
Comments: Three equivalent forms are to be used to monitor progress over time; a profile form is included with a score log and a table for comparing scores.
Authors: Cecil R. Reynolds and Randy W. Kamphaus.
Publisher: Psychological Assessment Resources, Inc.

Review of the Test of Irregular Word Reading Efficiency by MILDRED MURRAY-WARD, Professor of Education, California State University, Stanislaus, Turlock, CA:

DESCRIPTION. The Test of Irregular Word Reading Efficiency (TIWRE) was published in 2007 by Cecil R. Reynolds and Randy W. Kamphaus. The purpose of the test is to provide "an efficient, effective, and repeatable assessment of reading skill through the use of phonetically irregular words" (professional manual, p. 1). The authors suggest four uses for the TIWRE: (a) A measure of current reading level with age norms that can be compared with intelligence scores; (b) a tool for use in Response to Intervention (RTI) models; (c) a quick estimate of reading skills for use in determining whether self-reports and questionnaires are appropriate for individuals reluctant to reveal a reading difficulty; and (d) an individual reading assessment that is more likely to be valid than a group assessment. The test may be used with persons from 3 to 94 years of age who are without visual or visual perception problems.

The three forms, containing 50 items, can be administered in any order. The first 10–11 items are letters, followed by irregular or sight words. The authors state that the use of such words, rather than regular words or nonsense words, is more reliable because the irregular words are already part of an individual's spoken vocabulary and are less likely to be forgotten even in the face of brain injury. The use of these types of words removes the possibility of a practice effect or other test-taking effects.

Administration is clear; however, the authors do recommend that examiners have training in standardized achievement testing. Examiners may include professional psychologists, school and professional counselors, educational diagnosticians, and special education and classroom teachers, who should have some opportunities for practice assessment and scoring.

The directions for administration include where to begin based on the age of the examinee and what to do if examinees cannot identify letters or words. Examiners enter one point for each correctly pronounced letter or word on the scoring form, along with the test date and examinee's age. Raw scores are converted to the TIWRE Reading Efficiency Index (REI = mean of 100 and a standard deviation of 15), percentiles, *z* scores, NCEs, and qualitative descriptors of reading performance. Score changes are evaluated with the degree of significance of change at the $p \leq .15$ or $p \leq .05$. The profile or record form is used to note scores and score changes and graphically display changes over time.

DEVELOPMENT. The authors began development of the TIWRE by selecting a pool of 200 words of varying difficulty chosen from lists of word frequency and curriculum guides. Review of the resulting word list was a four-step process. First, the authors and publishers' staff (including psychologists) examined the words. Next, doctoral-level reading specialists reviewed the words for type of irregularity and placement in the word list. Third, a panel of ethnically diverse psychologists reviewed the list for words that might be offensive or objectionable to ethnic groups. Finally, a panel of psychologists with various specialties and a measurement expert reviewed the items for appropriateness. The final 164-item word list was used in the standardization form. To establish form equivalency, three forms were derived from the original 164-item standardization version. The resulting forms possessed equivalent item difficulty ranges (.06–.08 to .92–.95), medians (.72 to .73), and standard deviations (.23 to .24).

TECHNICAL.

Standardization. The standardization of the TIWRE was conducted along with the Reynolds Intellectual Assessment Scales (RIAS; 16:213) from 1999 to 2002. The standardization sample consisted of 2,438 individuals, aged 3 to 94, from 41 states, that reflected U.S. population characteristics of age, gender, ethnicity, educational attainment (or parent educational level), and geographic region (U.S. Census, 2001). The TIWRE was normed to create age-corrected normalized standard scores with a mean of 100 and a standard deviation of 15. The norm group was created through Psychological Assessment Resources customers asked to recruit examinees who matched the local community profile. Those recruited matched the sampling matrix plan and were asked to respond to a survey about possible visual difficulties, drug and alcohol use, medications, brain disorders, and other diseases. The inclusion of persons with these conditions did not exceed population proportions. The final sample closely matched the U.S. Census figures in the areas of gender, age, and educational attainment, but contained a higher proportion of participants from the southern United States than in the U.S. Census.

The scores for the TIWRE were created by weighting the raw scores on the basis of age, gender, ethnicity, educational attainment, and geographic regions found in the U.S. Census (2001). Normalized standard scores, including REIs, *z*-scores, NCEs, and percentiles were calculated from raw scores for each of 15 age groups.

Reliability. The reliability of the TIWRE was examined using a standard of reliability coefficients of .80 or higher (with .90 preferred) for individual diagnostic applications. Reliability estimates were calculated for internal consistency, stability, and alternative forms. Internal consistency (coefficient alpha) of the items in each form resulted in median reliability coefficients of .94. Test-retest reliability with an interval of 9 to 39 days resulted in coefficients of .90 to .97. The median of the alternative forms reliability coefficients for pairs of the three forms was .97. In addition, standard errors of measurement (*SEMs*) were calculated for the three forms, resulting in a median value of 3.7.

Validity. Validity of the TIWRE was examined through evidence of internal structure, developmental trends, correlations with other measures, and performance of clinical groups. Evidence of internal structure includes item-scale correlations, content review, and internal consistency coefficients. Evidence of relations was based on correlations with other measures of achievement and intelligence and included comparisons with the Wide Range Achievement Test 4 (WRAT4), the RIAS, and the Kaufman Test of Educational Achievement (KTEA-II). Correlations with all the subscales were statistically significant at $p < .01$. The WRAT4 Word Reading, Sentence Comprehension, Spelling and Reading Composite, and the KTEA-II Word Recognition and Reading Standard Score correlations with the TIWRE were all at or near .70 or higher. The correlations of WRAT4 Math Computation, KTEA-II Reading Comprehension, and all subscales of the RIAS with the TIWRE were lower, ranging from .31 to .54.

In the area of developmental trends, the authors examined the patterns of scores. The patterns matched generally held observations that reading skills grow rapidly in the early years, plateau in the teens, and continue to grow slowly until very late in life.

The evidence for use with clinical groups involved comparisons of scores of small numbers of individuals with 15 different clinical conditions. The demographic characteristics of this group were compared and contained mostly white, some African American, and few Hispanic individuals. Most were identified with polysubstance abuse, traumatic brain injury, child ADHD, or depression conditions. However, the child LD and ADHD conditions were not validated for consistency in diagnoses. The adult and child LD groups, those with mental retardation, traumatic brain injury, stroke or cerebrovascular accident, seizure disorder, and deaf or hearing impaired scored significantly lower than the population mean; whereas the child and adult ADHD groups, those with dementia, anxiety, depression, schizophrenia, bipolar disorder, and polysubstance abuse showed preservation of their reading skills. This conforms to known patterns of reading ability.

COMMENTARY. The TIWRE is a well-developed quick assessment of a major component of overall reading achievement. The authors carefully chose test items and assured the equivalence of the three forms. Reliability indices for internal consistency, test-retest with an interval, and alternative forms were all well above the recommended standards for individual diagnosis of .80. Content validity was well established. The authors provided validity evidence for use of the TIWRE as a measure of current reading level with a score that allows age norms that can be compared with intelligence scores, as was sensitivity to developmental trends and use with clinical groups.

However, the authors did not provide evidence for the remaining uses proposed in the test manual. No evidence of use in Response to Intervention (RTI) models for curriculum-based assessment was presented. In fact, the learning disabled and ADHD individuals who would most likely be involved in RTI were not checked for common diagnostic criteria. The small numbers of persons in the clinical groups suggest that scores for these groups should be cautiously interpreted. Although the TIWRE is a quick assessment for reading, it is not clear that it is an effective tool to determine whether self-reports and questionnaires are appropriate for individuals not wishing to reveal a reading difficulty. No evidence was provided that the TIWRE is more valid than a group reading assessment. In fact, other models of reading that more closely emulate the act of reading extended passages were not used in the validation. Finally, although a reliability study with a short interval was completed, no studies of the TIWRE as a predictor of reading comprehension and future reading performance have been completed.

SUMMARY. The TIWRE is a well-developed tool for assessing a component of reading achievement. The model of use of irregular words to assess reading achievement was well documented with literature. The TIWRE's use in performing quick reading assessments and checking short term reading changes is supported by the test's development. However, this reviewer recommends caution in using the TIWRE for determining reading skills in reluctant examinees or those with clinical diagnoses, predicting long-term future reading performance, or as a tool in RTI unless other measures of reading achievement are used.

Review of the Test of Irregular Word Reading Efficiency by MICHAEL S. TREVISAN, Professor of Educational Psychology, Washington State University, Pullman, WA:

DESCRIPTION. The Test of Irregular Word Reading Efficiency (TIWRE) is an individually administered test designed to provide a measure of reading skill. The test can be applied in both educational and clinical settings. The TIWRE is unique among reading tests, composed entirely of letters and irregular words. Because irregular words cannot be pronounced with knowledge of phonics, the authors argue that the TIWRE is a closer proxy to reading comprehension than other tests that use a combination of regular and irregular words.

The test is composed of 50 items and takes approximately 2 minutes to administer. Each item is composed of a letter or an irregular word that the examinee is asked to read aloud. There are three forms of the test. Test materials include a professional manual, three laminated cards (one for each form) that contain the items, a response form to record whether the examinee responded correctly, and a profile form to record derived scores. Easy-to-follow administration guidelines include a short list of rules to follow. Although no special training is required to administer the test the authors recommend a working knowledge of standardized tests.

A variety of derived scores can be obtained by referring to the conversion (raw to derived score) tables in the appendices of the professional manual. An age-corrected normalized standardized score is offered as the central derived score. Referred to as the reading efficiency index or REI, it has a mean of 100 and a standard deviation of 15, similar to scores often available with many intelligence tests. In addition, the authors offer change score tables to determine whether a reliable change in reading proficiency has occurred after intervention. By comparing two REI scores obtained from different administrations of the TIWRE, one can determine whether the difference between scores is statistically significant (.05 or .15). The authors suggest that for clinical purposes, .15 is a sufficient level for determining significant score differences. Percentile, normal curve equivalent, grade equivalent, and *z* scores are also available. Qualitative descriptors based on REI scores and ranging from significantly below average (REI < 70) to significantly above average (REI ≥ 130) are available to aid clinical interpretation.

DEVELOPMENT. Development of the TIWRE started with identification of the construct to be measured and goals for the assessment. An initial pool of 200 irregular words and letters was subsequently developed. Doctoral-level reading specialists also reviewed the items. Disagreements among review members were ferreted out by referring to the 10th edition of *Merriam-Webster's Collegiate Dictionary* (1997). Additionally, an expert panel of psychologists and other specialists from a variety of underrepresented groups was assembled to screen items that had the appearance of cultural bias. After each review, some items were eliminated although specific criteria for elimination were not mentioned.

TECHNICAL. The standardization sample consisted of 2,438 participants from 41 states. These individuals ranged in age from 3 to 94. The TIWRE was administered at the same time with another test marketed by the publisher, the Reynolds Intellectual Assessment Scales (16:213). Data were obtained from 1999 to 2002. Norming sites were selected to represent all regions of the country. Examiners were obtained through contacts and databases of individuals who had purchased other measures sold by the publisher. Examinees were screened from participation if they had certain physical impairments such as color blindness or uncorrected hearing loss. Gender, ethnicity, age, and educational attainment are demographic variables included in the standardization sampling plan. All examiners for the standardization data collection were specialists or graduate students with knowledge of standardized testing procedures and training in the use of the TIWRE.

All three versions of the test were administered to the same participants. Item difficulty (the proportion of participants answering an item correctly) was computed for each item. The median difficulty value for the items across test forms ranged from .72 to .73, indicating comparability across items and forms. Raw scores were plotted for each age range showing nearly identical curves across forms.

Three types of reliability data were obtained. First, internal consistency reliability coefficients were computed for each form of the test disaggregated by age, gender, and ethnicity. Nearly all coefficients were above .90. Second, correlations between scores from the same test with the same sample at different points in time were obtained. This strategy provides a measure of stability. Most estimates were above .80. The time interval between testings ranged from 9–39 days, with a median value of 21 days. The test-retest sample included 67 individuals across a wide age range. Third, alternative-forms reliability coefficients were computed by correlating scores between forms for each age group. All estimates were above .90.

Consonant with recommendations from the *Standards for Educational and Psychological Testing* (APA, AERA, & NCME, 1999) the authors employed a validity framework to organize validity evidence. The evidence was presented as a validity argument (Shepard, 1993) with explication of the theoretical, logical, and empirical bases for use of the TIWRE.

Included in the validity argument were correlations between the TIWRE and a small number of achievement and cognitive tests and subtests. The magnitude of the correlations between the TIWRE and measures of reading were high, ranging from the upper .60s to mid-.70s. In comparison, correlations with mathematics subtests and intelligence measures were lower. These data further substantiate the TIWRE as a reading test and not just a broad achievement or cognitive measure. In addition, important clinical subgroups (e.g., dementia, children with learning disabilities) were included in the standardization sample. As predicted, almost all average REI scores were significantly lower for these groups as compared to the standardization group as a whole.

COMMENTARY. As the authors note there are many reading measures available for instructional and clinical purposes. The TIWRE is unique in that it is composed entirely of irregular letters and words. The development of the TIWRE, standardization sample and process, and reliability and validity evidence, indicate a professionally constructed test. As a periodic measurement instructor, I would consider using this test to illustrate a test built with high industry standards. As a measurement specialist, I recommend its use for the intended purposes.

The provision for change score tables and decision making could be improved. First, the authors suggest .15 is often used for clinical purposes but do not substantiate this claim. More justification for this decision rule is needed. Second, the standard error used to determine how large the difference has to be between scores in order to claim statistical significance should be the standard error of score differences (Anastasi & Urbina, 1997). This standard error accounts for error in both administrations of the test, and is more appropriate for the score difference use advocated in the manual (rather than the standard error of prediction). For children, the use of the appropriate standard error term could change the difference in scores needed to obtain statistical significance and, therefore, the kinds of clinical decisions that could be made. Third, the *Standards* (AERA, APA, & NCME, 1999) are clear that the results of no single test should be used to make important decisions about individuals. This kind of statement should accompany the TIWRE in general, and use of the statistical significance tables in particular.

One of the components of a validity framework that the *Standards* (AERA, APA, & NCME, 1999) recommends is evidence based on response processes. This component seeks evidence that the observed performance fits the underlying construct. The authors of the TIWRE argue that experimental procedures that could be used to provide this kind of evidence are not feasible. This reviewer agrees. However, there are other procedures that could be used in lieu of a rigorous experiment. As an example, task analysis could be used to understand observed performance on the TIWRE and the underlying construct better. This procedure has been applied to several areas in cognitive psychology (Sternberg, 1981) and could prove useful for this validation purpose.

SUMMARY. The TIWRE is a unique reading measure composed of irregular letters and words. Examinees are asked to pronounce the letters and words. Because they cannot be pronounced by applying phonics rules, the authors argue that the TIWRE is a stronger and clearer proxy for reading comprehension. This reviewer recommends its use. The measure could benefit from enhancements to the statistical significance tables as previously mentioned. Further validity work will help to bolster the evidentiary basis for TIWRE test score use.

REVIEWER'S REFERENCES

American Educational Research Association, American Psychological Association, & National Council on Measurement in Education. (1999). *Standards for educational and psychological testing*. Washington, DC: American Educational Research Association.

Anastasi, A., & Urbina, S. (1997). *Psychological testing* (7th ed.). Upper Saddle River, NJ: Prentice Hall.

Merriam-Webster's collegiate dictionary (10th ed.). (1997). Springfield, MA: Merriam-Webster.

Shephard, L. A. (1993). Evaluating test validity. In L. Darling-Hammond (Ed.), *Review of research in education* (vol. 19, pp. 405-450). Washington, DC: American Educational Research Association.

Sternberg, R. J. (1981). Testing and cognitive psychology. *American Psychologist, 36*, 1181-1189.

[143]

Test of Memory and Learning, Second Edition.

Purpose: Designed to assess the "key features of memory" and to "evaluate learning as reflected in changes in recall and recognition over multiple trials of various stimuli."

Population: Ages 5-0 to 59-11.

Publication Dates: 1994-2007.

Acronym: TOMAL-2.

Scores, 25: 10 Verbal subtest scores (Memory for Stories, Word Selective Reminding, Object Recall, Paired Recall, Digits Forward, Letters Forward, Digits Backward, Letters Backward, Memory for Stories Delayed, Word Selective Reminding Delayed); 6 Nonverbal subtest scores (Facial Memory, Abstract Visual Memory, Visual Sequence Memory, Memory for Location, Visual Selective Reminding, Manual Imitation); 3 core composite

scores (Verbal Memory Index, Nonverbal Memory Index, Composite Memory Index); 6 supplemental composite scores (Verbal Delayed Recall Index, Attention/Concentration Index, Sequential Recall Index, Free Recall Index, Associative Recall Index, Learning Index).
Administration: Individual.
Price Data, 2007: $363 per complete kit including Picture Book A, Picture Book B, 25 profile forms, 25 examiner record booklets, Delayed Recall Cue Cards, Visual Selective Reminding Test Board, 15 vinyl chips, and examiner's manual (2007, 165 pages); $70 per Picture Book A; $80 per Picture Book B; $41 per 25 profile forms; $60 per 25 examiner record booklets; $30 per set of Delayed Recall Cue Cards; $15 per Visual Selective Reminding Test Board; $8 per 15 vinyl chips; $71 per manual (2007, 159 pages).
Time: Core battery (30-35) minutes; Supplemental subtests (25-35) minutes.
Authors: Cecil R. Reynolds and Judith K. Voress.
Publisher: PRO-ED.
Cross References: For reviews by Karen Geller and Susan J. Maller of an earlier edition, see 13:330 (1 reference).

Review of the Test of Memory and Learning, Second Edition by R. ANTHONY DOGGETT, Associate Professor of School Psychology, Mississippi State University, Starkville, MS:

DESCRIPTION. The Test of Memory and Learning, Second Edition (TOMAL-2) is an individually administered instrument designed for evaluating memory function for individuals 5 through 59 years of age. The core battery comprises four verbal subtests (Memory for Stories, Word Selective Reminding, Object Recall, Paired Recall) and four nonverbal subtests (Facial Memory, Abstract Visual Memory, Visual Sequential Memory, Memory for Location), which yield three core indexes (Verbal Memory, Nonverbal Memory, Composite Memory Index). In addition, six supplementary subtests (four verbal, two nonverbal) may be used "when a broader, even more comprehensive assessment of memory is needed" (examiner's manual, p. 11). The four verbal supplementary tests include Digits Forward, Digits Backward, Letters Forward, and Letters Backward, and the two nonverbal subtests include Visual Selective Reminding and Manual Imitation. The supplementary subtests may be used in the derivation of several additional indexes (Attention/Concentration, Sequential Recall, Free Recall, Associative Recall, Learning). The test authors noted that one of the supplementary subtests may be substituted for a core subtest when the core subtest is spoiled or cannot be administered to an examinee. Finally, a delayed recall procedure is available for two of the verbal subtests from the standard battery (Memory for Stories Delayed, Word Selective Reminding Delayed), which yields a Verbal Delayed Recall Index.

The TOMAL-2 should be administered by individuals who have had some formal training in assessment and who hold the appropriate credential in their state of practice. The core and supplemental batteries each require approximately 30 to 35 minutes to complete. The TOMAL-2 yields five types of scores including raw scores, scaled or standard scores, percentile ranks, age equivalents for subtests, and composite indexes. Subtests have been scaled to a mean of 10 and a standard deviation of 3, whereas composite indexes have a mean of 100 and a standard deviation of 15. In addition, other scores (normal curve equivalents, *T*-scores, *z*-scores, stanines) are available in an appendix in the manual. Basal rules are established by age and ceilings are employed to reduce the administration time of all subtests except for two of the subtests (Facial Memory and Word Selective Reminding Delayed). Specific instructions of how to employ ceiling rules are provided in narrative form and further illustrated in figures in the manual. Directions for administering and scoring each subtest are provided in the manual and a shortened version of the directions is provided in the examiner record booklet. Thorough directions are provided for completing the profile summary form, interpreting the TOMAL-2 scores, and prorating when data are missing. A case study is included to further demonstrate these points.

The TOMAL-2 is accompanied by a 159-page manual complete with five chapters discussing the historical perspectives, neurobiology of memory, and need for assessing memory across different age groups as well as the administration, scoring, interpretation, reliability, validity, and standardization of the instrument. Two picture books are included for the TOMAL-2. Picture Book A includes the Facial Memory and Memory for Location subtests and Picture Book B, which is in an easel format, includes the Abstract Visual Memory, Object Recall, and Visual Sequential Memory subtests.

DEVELOPMENT. The test authors initially provided information related to the development of the original TOMAL (Reynolds & Bigler, 1994) in the manual. They further noted that a discussion of the development of the TOMAL was particularly relevant as changes to the item content on the

TOMAL-2 were reported to be "quite minimal" (examiner's manual, p. 89). The rationale provided for the initial development of the TOMAL was to "develop a comprehensive assessment of children's and adolescents' memory skills that was also practical and efficacious" (examiner's manual, p. 90) with the development of the TOMAL-2, extending the assessment of memory and learning into the adult years. Furthermore, the test authors determined on an a priori basis that the TOMAL would include verbal and nonverbal scales as well as an evaluation of delayed recall processes that is continued in the TOMAL-2. The test authors reported that the final development of the TOMAL-2 involved review of the initial development process for the TOMAL as well as consideration of published test reviews, personal experiences, and comments from practitioners who used the instrument.

TECHNICAL.

Standardization. The TOMAL-2 was standardized on a sample of 1,961 individuals residing in 28 states. The normative sample for the TOMAL-2 includes the normative sample from the first edition of the TOMAL as well as new individuals to ensure appropriate matching of current demographic and population characteristics (e.g., geographic region of residence, gender, race, socioeconomic status, educational attainment of parents, exceptionality status, age). The test authors reported that comparison of percentages from the sample for each of these demographic characteristics revealed that the TOMAL-2 closely approximated percentages obtained from the 2002 U.S. Census.

Reliability. The test authors reported internal consistency, test-retest, and interscorer agreement. Internal consistency reliability was reported for the standardization sample across 19 age levels and was represented by alpha coefficients. Median alpha coefficients ranged from .67 to .97 for the Core and Supplementary subtests and from .89 to .91 across the two Verbal Delayed Recall subtests. Median reliability scores ranged from .93 to .96 on the three Core Indexes and from .90 to .98 on the six Supplementary Indexes. The test authors further reported that evaluation of the reliability coefficients for the TOMAL-2 subtest scores and indexes separated by gender and ethnicity revealed no significant differences in reliability estimates when compared to the sample as a whole. Mean test-retest reliability coefficients ranged from .61 to .93 on the Core and Supplementary subtests. The interval between testing sessions was approximately 2 weeks. Mean reliability scores on the two Verbal Delayed Recall subtests ranged from .47 to .88. Mean test-retest reliability coefficients ranged from .81 to .93 on the Core Indexes and from .68 to .94 on the Supplementary Indexes. Pearson correlations between the scaled scores generated by the two independent scorers was .94 or higher for each of the standard scores obtained for all subscales and composite indexes.

Validity. The test authors thoroughly discussed issues related to validity in the manual on pages 87–107 and used standards published by several professional groups (American Educational Research Association, American Psychological Association, & National Council on Measurement in Education, 1999) to guide their evaluation of the validity of the instrument. Evidence for the validity of the TOMAL-2 was evaluated based on test content, response processes, internal structure, relationship with other variables, and consequences of testing. Content validity was evaluated by conducting reviews of other instruments designed to evaluate memory functions and examining the internal reliability coefficients specifically obtained on the TOMAL-2. Additional evidence of validity was initially addressed by evaluating the response processes involved in the assessment and conducting task analyses for various subtests. In addition, correlations between the subtests were evaluated and two sets of factor analysis methods (primary and exploratory models) were conducted. The correlational results revealed statistically significant positive correlations between the TOMAL-2 subtests at $p < .01$. In addition, support for a two-factor and four-factor solution was discussed. Criterion-related validity was established by comparing results from the TOMAL and the TOMAL-2 to other measures of intelligence, achievement, and memory. Overall, correlations between the TOMAL-2 and measures of intelligence and achievement are lower than correlations between IQ tests and achievement, suggesting that the instrument "has a unique contribution to make in the assessment process" (examiner's manual, p. 101). In addition, correlations between the TOMAL-2 and another measure of memory, the WRAML-2 (Sheslow & Adams, 2003), conducted on a sample of 35 adults ranged from .60–.79 indicating a strong relationship between the two instruments. Finally, the test authors addressed the consequences of testing or "consequential" validity of the instrument by conducting evaluations of potential item basis. The test authors found no initial evidence of cultural, gender, or ethnic bias on the TOMAL-2. However, the test authors cautioned examiners to restrict usage of the Verbal Memory subtests to proficient speakers of English.

COMMENTARY. The TOMAL-2 has several noted improvements over the initial version of the instrument. These include: (a) extending the age range from 5 to 59; (b) increasing the overall size of the standardization sample and updating the sample to reflect the current U.S. population; (c) placing the administration instructions and basal, ceiling, and discontinue rules in both the examiner record booklet and the examiner's manual; (d) revising the format of the picture books; (e) reordering the normative tables to follow the order of the subtest presentation; (f) reducing test administration to approximately 30 minutes for core subtests and 30 minutes for supplementary subtests; (g) adding another story to the Memory for Stories subtest to accommodate adult examinees; and (h) addressing additional validity issues by comparing the instrument to another memory instrument. Despite these improvements, the test authors noted that the instrument (a) is not an exhaustive measure of memory and learning, (b) does not assess long-term memory or incidental memory, and (c) can be a difficult test for younger examinees (examiner's manual, pp. 17-18).

SUMMARY. The TOMAL-2 is a standardized, individually administered instrument for evaluating memory function for individuals 5 through 59 years of age. Although efficient for use as an assessment of memory skills, the instrument will be best utilized as a component of a comprehensive assessment battery. Finally, further investigation with populations and instruments other than those used by the test authors will continue to provide valuable information about the psychometric properties and clinical utility of the instrument.

REVIEWER'S REFERENCES

American Educational Research Association, American Psychological Association, & National Council on Measurement in Education. (1999). *Standards for educational and psychological testing*. Washington, DC: American Educational Research Association.

Reynolds, C. R., & Bigler, E. E. (1994). Test of Memory and Learning. Austin, TX: PRO-ED.

Sheslow, D., & Adams, W. (2003). Wide Range Assessment of Memory and Learning—Second Edition. Wilmington, DE: Wide Range.

Review of the Test of Memory and Learning, Second Edition by STEVEN R. SHAW, Assistant Professor of Counselling and Educational Psychology, McGill University, Montreal, Quebec, Canada:

DESCRIPTION. The Test of Memory and Learning, Second Edition (TOMAL-2) is an individually administered measure of different memory functions for persons aged 5 through 59 years. The purpose of the TOMAL-2 is: (a) to emphasize key features of memory that are of inherent clinical interest, the most notable being a distinction between verbal and nonverbal memory; (b) to assess narrow-band aspects of memory such as associative learning and spatial memory; and (c) to evaluate learning as operationalized by changes in recall and recognition over multiple trials. The test authors do not claim that the TOMAL-2 represents a measure of all types of memory, yet it offers a wide-ranging and practical approach to assessing memory.

Administration of the TOMAL-2 requires that the examiner have significant formal training in assessment. Directions for administration are available in the manual and in the examiner record booklet, where all responses are recorded. Information is presented to examinees orally, in the case of some verbal subtests; and with symbols via two picture books. Administration directions are clear. Beginning item points are clearly identified. However, ceiling rules vary across subtests and some vigilance is required to follow the ceiling rules accurately. Scoring rules are clear with multiple examples of correct and incorrect responses provided in the manual. Any clinician with assessment training and experience will have no difficulty learning to administer the TOMAL-2. Time to administer the core battery of the TOMAL-2 is reported to be about 30 minutes for an experienced examiner and an additional 25 to 35 minutes for the supplementary subtests. Four sample administrations averaged 35 minutes for the core battery and 40 minutes for the supplemental subtests.

The TOMAL-2 is made up of a core battery of eight subtests, the scores of which comprise the Verbal Memory Index and Nonverbal Memory Index. There are also six supplemental subtests that are to be used when a more comprehensive assessment of memory is needed. Each subtest has a nominal mean of 10 and standard deviation of 3. The core composites of Verbal Memory Index, Nonverbal Memory Index, and Composite Memory Index are standard scores with a mean of 100 and standard deviation of 15. When supplementary subtests are administered, there are supplementary composite scores of Verbal Delayed Memory, Attention/Concentration, Sequential Recall Index,

Free Recall Index, Associative Recall Index, and Learning Index. All composite scores have a mean of 100 and a standard deviation of 15. Standard scores and percentile ranks are provided in the major tables. Conversion tables for normal curve equivalents, *t*-scores, *z*-score, age equivalents, and stanines are provided.

Extensive information to assist in interpretation is provided in the manual. There are comprehensive descriptions of the clinical significance of composite indices and individual subtests. Moreover, information is provided concerning how to interpret differences among indices and subtests on the basis of statistical significances, relative frequency of occurrence, relevance to the referral question, and consistency with the individual's clinical and background history. There is even a framework from which to analyze items. Although interpretation will be based upon the theoretical orientation of the examiner and the presenting problems of the client, there is much information upon which to develop clinical interpretations.

DEVELOPMENT. The TOMAL-2 has undergone several changes from the original TOMAL. The primary change is that the age range has been extended from ages 5 to 19 on the TOMAL to ages 5 to 59 on the TOMAL-2. The normative sample was updated. Administrative instructions, including basal and ceiling, are now printed on the examiner record booklet and in the manual. The format of the picture book has been clarified. And the subtests Visual Selective Reminding and Digits Forward, which were extraordinarily difficult to administer and score, are now supplementary subtests rather than core subtests.

A potentially useful feature is the use of learning curve analyses. Four subtests—Word Selective Reminding, Object Recall, Paired Recall, and Visual Selective Reminding—have raw scores that can be plotted for each trial of the task. Raw scores can be plotted and compared to raw scores from the normative sample. In this fashion, improvement over time, presumably due to learning, can be analyzed.

TECHNICAL. The TOMAL-2 manual provides detailed evidence on standardization, reliability, and validity.

Standardization. The TOMAL-2 was standardized on a sample of 1,961 persons from 28 states. Of these, 1,477 were between the ages of 5 and 19. For ages 20 to 59, there were 484 members in the standardization sample. Data are reported in 6-month intervals for ages 5 years, 0 months through 8 years, 11 months; 1-year intervals for ages 9 years, 0 months through 19 years, 11 months; and at 10-year intervals for ages 20 years, 0 months through 59 years, 11 months. Because the items have not changed from the TOMAL, the normative data from the TOMAL-2 include the normative data from the original TOMAL. Only 579 people from the total standardization are considered to be new. Only 95 of the persons from ages 5 to 19 represent new assessments. The recycling of standardization data is not necessarily bad because the sample still matches the demographics of the 2000 U.S. Census figures and the items are the same. However, given the well-documented Flynn effect for intelligence tests, older assessment data may not effectively sample the abilities of a more modern cohort (Strauss, Sherman, & Spreen, 2006). Although the construct of memory is moderately correlated with intelligence, the recycling of standardization data is only a potential problem. As yet, there has been no effective description of the Flynn effect for memory tests (Resing & Tunteler, 2007).

Reliability. Internal consistency reliability was calculated for all subtests and indices for all age groups. For the Composite Memory Index, alpha coefficients range from .93 to .97. Subtests and indices demonstrated quite high reliability (generally in the mid .80s to low .90s), making interpretation at the subtest level a possibility. An exception is the Facial Memory subtest, for which alpha coefficients ranged from .46 to .79. Standard errors of measurement are also provided.

Stability was measured in two studies totaling 82 participants. The interval was 2 weeks between the first and second testing. As expected, scores were more stable for adult participants than for children and adolescents. However, stability was within reasonable limits for both samples.

Validity. Evidence for validity is described consistent with the format of the 1999 *Standards for Educational and Psychological Testing* (American Educational Research Association, American Psychological Association, & National Council on Measurement in Education, 1999). Specifically, evidence for validity is provided based on test content, response process, relationship to other variables, internal structure, and evidence based on consequences of testing. There are detailed descriptions of the process for meeting the standards of validity for all five areas.

Evidence based on test content and response process involved review of items, analysis of tryout items, representativeness of items, and expert evaluation of the process involved in responding to each item. Evidence based on internal structure involved a factor analysis that yielded a large general factor. A four-factor solution best explained the data when core and supplemental subtests were used. Yet, there is also evidence that supports the verbal/nonverbal dichotomy. Evidence based on relationships to other variables consists of correlations with achievement tests (i.e., Test of Silent Word Reading Fluency, Test of Silent Contextual Reading Fluency, and Comprehensive Receptive and Expressive Vocabulary Test: Second Edition), tests of intelligence (i.e., Test of Nonverbal Intelligence—Third Edition, Wechsler Intelligence Scale for Children—Revised, Kaufman Assessment Battery for Children), tests of memory (i.e., Wide Range Assessment of Memory and Learning: Second Edition), and analysis of clinical samples (i.e., children with reading disabilities, and children and adolescents with brain injury). No adult clinical populations were evaluated. Evidence strongly supports this facet of validity. However, some evidence was recycled from the original TOMAL and cannot be considered new evidence for the TOMAL-2. Evidence based on the consequences of testing is discussed. Although there is an extensive discussion of bias, no new evidence is presented. There is a general statement that "item functioning is clearly constant across groups for males, females, Whites and non-Whites" (examiner's manual, p. 107). A table is provided showing correlation coefficients for gender (male/female), race (White/Non-White), and ethnicity (Anglo/Non-Anglo) samples for each subtest. Not surprisingly, these coefficients are very high. Although the results would not directly address the technical issue of bias, many examiners would like to know the mean differences among genders and ethnic groups to aid in interpretation of findings.

COMMENTARY. The original TOMAL has long been a part of my clinical practice. Information gained from the TOMAL provides clinical value in addressing the questions of learning disabilities, closed head injuries, long-term effects of chemotherapy and central nervous system radiation, attention deficit hyperactivity disorder, and other clinical questions in pediatric populations. The TOMAL-2 has not changed much in content or organization from the original TOMAL. Whether the age extension from age 19 up to age 59 makes the TOMAL-2 competitive with other adult measures of memory is an open question. The TOMAL-2 is not valid for the assessment of memory in geriatric populations (i.e., older than 59 years of age). Moreover, there may be a lack of sensitivity in the normative sample for adults. There is little reason to drop the Wechsler Memory Scale: Third Edition (Wechsler, 1997), Rey Complex Figure Test and Recognition Trial (Meyers & Meyers, 1996), or Memory Assessment Scales (Williams, 1991) in favor of the TOMAL-2 for adults. Yet, the TOMAL-2 remains one of the psychometrically, theoretically, and clinically strongest measures available of memory for children and adolescents.

SUMMARY. The TOMAL-2 is an individually administered measure of memory for persons from ages 5 to 59. This is a strong measure with excellent psychometric characteristics, ease of use, clinical value, and a strong examiner's manual with a great deal of information to aid in interpretation. The TOMAL-2 continues excellence in the assessment of memory and learning for children and adolescence.

REVIEWER'S REFERENCES

American Educational Research Association, American Psychological Association, & National Council on Measurement in Education. (1999). *Standards for educational and psychological testing.* Washington, DC: American Educational Research Association.

Meyers, J. E., & Meyers, K. R. (1996). Rey Complex Figure Test and Recognition Trial. Lutz, FL: Psychological Assessment Resources.

Resing, W. C. M., & Tunteler, E. (2007). Children becoming more intelligent: Can the Flynn effect be generalized to other child intelligence tests? *International Journal of Testing, 7*, 191-208.

Strauss, E., Sherman, E. M. S., & Spreen, O. (2006). *A compendium of neuropsychological tests: Administration, norms, and commentary* (3rd ed.). New York: Oxford.

Wechsler, D. (1997). Wechsler Memory Scales: Third Edition. San Antonio, TX: The Psychological Corporation.

Williams, J. M. (1991). Memory Assessment Scales. Lutz, FL: Psychological Assessment Resources.

[144]

Test of Preschool Early Literacy.

Purpose: Designed to "identify children at risk of having or developing problems in literacy."

Population: Ages 3-0 to 5-11.

Publication Date: 2007.

Acronym: TOPEL.

Scores, 4: Print Knowledge, Definitional Vocabulary, Phonological Awareness, Early Literacy Index.

Administration: Individual.

Price Data, 2007: $207 per complete kit including examiner's manual (72 pages), picture book, and 25 record booklets; $85 per picture book; $50 per 25 record booklets; $81 per examiner's manual.

Time: (30) minutes.

Authors: Christopher J. Lonigan, Richard K. Wagner, Joseph K. Torgesen, and Carol A. Rashotte.

Publisher: PRO-ED.

Review of the Test of Preschool Early Literacy by RONALD A. MADLE, Licensed Psychologist, Mifflinburg, PA, and Adjunct Associate Professor of School Psychology, The Pennsylvania State University, University Park, PA:

DESCRIPTION. The Test of Preschool Early Literacy (TOPEL) measures abilities associated with early literacy for children ages 3 to 5 years. Its listed uses are to identify children at risk for literacy problems, to assist with documenting progress in literacy intervention programs, and to provide a research measure of early literacy skills.

The TOPEL comes in a colorful storage box that contains a full-color stimulus book, manual, and 25 test forms. Administration takes about 30 minutes; suitably trained professionals, such as early childhood educators, special educators, psychologists, or diagnosticians, can administer the test after studying the manual and giving a recommended five trial administrations.

The three subtests are combined to form a measure of emergent literacy skills—the Early Literacy Index (ELI). The Print Knowledge subtest (36 items) uses pointing to aspects of print, identifying letters, letter-sound correspondences and written words, and saying letters, to assess awareness of the alphabet and early understanding of written language forms and conventions. Single-word and definitional vocabulary is measured on the 35-item Definitional Vocabulary subtest, where the child first names a picture before being asked to describe one of its essential attributes. Finally, the 27-item Phonological Awareness subtest involves deleting specific sounds in words on request (elision) and forming a word (blending) from a series of phonemes.

Administration directions and scoring criteria are clearly stated in the manual. Responses involve either pointing or short answers with binary scoring. Querying is permitted on Definitional Vocabulary for incomplete or vague answers. Subtest administration starts with the first item and continues until a ceiling of three consecutive errors, although two subtests use multiple item sets where each set is administered independent of the others.

Identification and summary information, as well as notes, are provided for on the front and back pages of the record form, with administration directions and items covering the remaining 10 pages. The obtained raw scores are converted to standard scores (mean = 100, *SD* = 15), percentiles, and range descriptors using the typical 10-point bands. The descriptors are Very Poor, Poor, Below Average, Average, Above Average, Superior, and Very Superior. Unfortunately, there is no place to note confidence intervals, which would need to be calculated from the *SEM* tables in the manual, a rather cumbersome procedure for the commonly used 90% confidence interval.

DEVELOPMENT. The TOPEL was developed to provide a downward extension for measuring early literacy or reading readiness skills in preschool children, as most existing measures start at kindergarten or first grade. The test authors note that this permits earlier identification and monitoring of literacy skills, well before the introduction of formal reading instruction. Although several reports are mentioned, the test structure appears to derive largely from *Preventing Reading Difficulties in Young Children* (Snow, Burns, & Griffin, 1998), which identified various problems causing poor reading. Specifically, the reports point to improving vocabulary, phonological awareness, and print knowledge skills before school entrance as preventing many early reading failures. Item development within these areas was guided by examining prior measures of these skills.

TECHNICAL.

Standardization. The standardization sample of 842 children was recruited from 12 states in the four major U.S. geographic regions. Trained personnel collected all data during 2004 to approximate U.S. Census data (U.S. Bureau of the Census, 2001). The sample was stratified on age and then examined by geographic area, gender, race/ethnicity, Hispanic ethnicity, family income, educational attainment of parents, and exceptionality status. An adequate match was obtained for all variables although families with incomes over $75,000 were slightly underrepresented (22% versus 28%). Not surprisingly for a preschool sample, there also were fewer children with disabilities (7%) than the 12% in the Census.

Normative tables use 3-month intervals from ages 3 years, 0 months to age 5 years, 11 months, although the number of children in each group is unspecified. The criteria originally proposed by Bracken (1987) are important to examine for preschool tests. The TOPEL norm divisions are consistent with these criteria. Other criteria relate to floors, ceilings, and item gradients. Floors and ceilings should allow scores of at least two standard deviations from the mean. The ELI meets the floor provisions at all ages but ceiling is lacking for all 5-year-olds. At the subtest level, the floors are inadequate for Print Knowledge until age 5 years, 3 months and for the lowest age group on Phonological Awareness. Definitional Vocabulary, however, has excellent floors at all ages. Print Knowledge and Phonological Awareness ceilings are insufficient from 4 years, 6 months through 5 years, 11 months, whereas Definitional Vocabulary loses acceptable ceilings by 4 years, 0 months. Inspection of the norm tables shows acceptable item gradients except for Phonological Awareness, which has less than the desired 3 raw score points per standard deviation at all ages.

Reliability. The ELI internal consistency coefficient of .96 across ages (.95 to .96) is quite good, as are the Print Knowledge (.95) and Definitional Vocabulary (.94) coefficients. The Phonological Awareness coefficient (.87) is lower but still within acceptable levels. Similar results were obtained for gender and ethnic subgroups. Test-retest stability for the ELI over 2 weeks was .91, with a mean increase of 3 standard score points. The subtests showed 0- to 8-point increases on retesting with coefficients from .81 to .89. Finally, interscorer agreement ranged from .96 for Print Knowledge to .98 for the ELI.

Validity. Content description validity was examined using item selection content rationale, conventional item analysis, and differential item functioning analysis to examine test item bias. Whole sample item analysis confirmed median item difficulties ranging from .20 to .84, whereas all item discrimination indices were .38 or greater.

Differential item functioning analysis, using logistic regression, showed 27 significant comparisons ($p < .001$), although 20 had negligible effect sizes. Six of the remaining seven involved Definitional Vocabulary and four of these effect sizes (three moderate and one large) were with the Hispanic versus non-Hispanic American contrasts. Although the test authors conclude the test is "nonbiased in regard to gender, race, or ethnicity" (examiner's manual, p. 43), the concentration of significant moderate to large effect sizes brings the lack of bias for Hispanics into question.

Construct identification validity was supported by the usual increases in raw score with age, high total score-item correlations, and group differentiation ability. On the latter, ELI mean scores and subtest scores were lower for the African American and bilingual Hispanic American groups. A sample of 154 children from Tallahassee, Florida was studied to investigate construct prediction validity. Six criterion measures were obtained from four early reading, expressive vocabulary, and phonological processing measures. The obtained correlations, when corrected for restriction of age range, varied from .59 to .77 for the subtests. ELI correlations with two criterion measures were .67 and .70.

COMMENTARY AND SUMMARY. Overall, the TOPEL appears to be a useful new test for assessing young children who are at risk for reading or other literacy problems. It can be quickly and easily administered and scored. The standardization sample has been well constructed and the test shows high internal consistency and test-retest reliabilities. The primary weakness, which is not unusual at this age range, is the lack of adequate floors and ceilings across the ages covered. The ELI is acceptable on the lower end for all ranges but cannot produce suitably high scores for 5-year-olds. This will not be a problem if the test is used with average to below average children. The subtests, however, cannot obtain suitably low or high scores at a number of ages. The most pronounced weakness is with Print Knowledge items for 3- and 4-year-olds, which makes the test heavily loaded on oral language below age 5. In spite of these problems, the test should effectively provide early identification of literacy problems as well as a good research measure for early literacy intervention studies.

The ceiling, floor, and item gradient characteristics, however, may limit the utility of the TOPEL to evaluate progress, especially for phonological awareness at the individual child level. The TOPEL should be satisfactory for summative evaluation at the group level, supplemented by curriculum-based approaches for more frequent monitoring of individual child progress.

Finally, the TOPEL may produce lower scores for children of African American and Hispanic American ethnicity. Although this result might be viewed as acceptable for identifying children for interventions, care should be taken to consider bias if the TOPEL is used for the early identification of reading disabilities.

REVIEWER'S REFERENCES

Bracken, B. A. (1987). Limitations of preschool instruments and standards for minimal levels of technical adequacy. *Journal of Psychoeducational Assessment, 5,* 313-326.

Snow, C. E., Burns, M. S., & Griffin, P. (Eds.). (1998). *Preventing reading difficulties in young children.* Washington, DC: National Academy Press.

U. S. Bureau of the Census. (2001). *The statistical abstract of the United States: The national data book.* Washington, DC: U.S. Department of Commerce.

Review of the Test of Preschool Early Literacy by GRETCHEN OWENS, Professor of Child Study, and CLAIRE LENZ, Associate Professor of Child Study, St. Joseph's College, Patchogue, NY:

DESCRIPTION. The Test of Preschool Early Literacy (TOPEL) is a norm-referenced, individually administered test that assesses abilities related to early literacy in children aged 3 years, 0 months to 5 years, 11 months. The test authors list three uses for the TOPEL: (a) to identify children who are likely to have problems learning to read and write, (b) to document progress as a result of intervention, and (c) to measure early literacy-related skills for research purposes.

The TOPEL kit includes an examiner's manual, picture book, and 25 record booklets. Three subtests comprise the TOPEL. The first, Print Knowledge, contains 36 items broken into three item sets: print concepts (such as telling which of four choices is a letter or a word), letter recognition (hearing a letter name or sound and pointing to the correct one from a set of four options), and letter/sound production (saying the name or sound of the letter on the page). For the 35 two-part items in the second subtest, Definitional Vocabulary, the child says the name of a pictured object, then answers a follow-up question about the object (such as what it is used for). The final subtest, Phonological Awareness, contains four sets of items (27 items total) having to do with either elision (the child is asked to say a word without a particular sound) or blending (child combines word parts to make a word). For Set A, the child either points to the picture (out of four) that shows what is left if you take away a given part of a compound word (e.g., "Say toothbrush without brush") or must remove the final sound from a word ("Say cart without the /t/"). Set B is the same task but without pictures. For Set C, the child must combine two words he or she hears into a compound word ("bird – house") or must combine two word parts into a single word (b – ook) and then point to the picture that depicts it (out of four choices). Set D is the same as Set C but without the pictures.

For the Print Knowledge and Phonological Awareness subtests, testing begins with the first item in each of the three or four item sets and continues until the ceiling of three consecutive incorrect responses is reached in each set. (This use of multiple item sets enables the examiner to collect information on the child's responses to different aspects of the same skill.) The Definitional Vocabulary subtest contains only one item set. All children begin with Item 1 and continue until the ceiling of three incorrect responses in a row is reached or the final item is administered. TOPEL results are reported as raw scores, standard scores, and percentile ranks for each subtest. An Early Literacy Index is calculated by combining the scores from the three subtests.

The suggested time requirement is 30 minutes or less. The test authors state that ideally the entire test should be administered in a single session, though testing can be discontinued and resumed later if a child shows signs of fatigue. It is likely that this later session will be needed, especially for older or more skilled children, because each subtest is fairly lengthy and all children, no matter how old, start with the first item in each item set.

Although formal training in administering the TOPEL is not necessary, the test authors recommend that the examiner have knowledge and experience in administering, scoring, and interpreting norm-referenced tests. In addition to familiarity with the examiner manual and the examiner record booklet, and proficiency with the correct application of ceilings in the three subtests, the examiner should also complete five trial administrations before attempting to administer the test.

DEVELOPMENT. The TOPEL is a result of the test authors' longstanding program of research into early literacy development, which has entailed multiple empirical studies involving parents, teachers, and preschool directors as well as young children. The Phonological Awareness and Print Knowledge subtests were developed over time as part of this ongoing research. An iterative process of item analysis and modification led to the final item set for the Print Knowledge subtest, and a new item set based on earlier research was constructed for the Phonological Awareness subtest. The Definitional Vocabulary subtest was added to provide a measure of oral language skills, both single-word expressive vocabulary and, at a deeper level of knowledge, the ability to define words. The specific items on this subtest were chosen based on the frequency with which they appear in children's books and basal reading series. All three subtests were field-tested with samples of 100 or more children.

The normative data were gathered in 2004 and involved 842 children from 12 states. Using the PRO-ED customer files, the test authors asked current users of other early childhood tests to participate in the standardization process. Those who agreed were sent materials for testing 20 children. In addition, the test authors established testing sites in Los Angeles, California; Buffalo, New York; Mandan, North Dakota; and Weatherford, Oklahoma. Standard scores were established using Roid's (1989) continuous norming procedure, as described in the manual.

TECHNICAL. The standardization sample generally approximates 2001 U.S. Census data in terms of geographic area, ethnicity, and parental educational attainment. Children with a variety of exceptionalities are included (7% of the sample, which is lower than the 12% incidence rate for school-age children, but because many preschoolers with learning and behavioral difficulties have not yet received a diagnosis, the seeming underrepresentation appears legitimate). Fewer 3-year-olds (n = 212) are included than 4- and 5-year-olds (n = 313 and 317, respectively).

Evidence of reliability is presented for content sampling, time sampling (test-retest), and scorer reliability. Coefficient alpha estimates indicate very high internal consistency for the Print Knowledge and Definitional Vocabulary subtests (coefficients over .90 at all three ages) and even higher for the composite score (over .95 at all ages). Internal consistency for the Phonological Awareness subtest of .86–.88, although somewhat lower, is still acceptable. Test-retest reliability coefficients for a predominantly female sample (N = 45) were over .80 for subtests and .90 for the composite with 2 weeks between test administrations. Interscorer agreement coefficients were very high (.96 to .98) for two staff members who independently scored 30 protocols.

In the validity chapter of the manual, the test authors provide a review of the professional literature on emergent literacy, which demonstrates a consensus that skills in three areas—oral language, phonological awareness, and print knowledge—serve as the cornerstones for learning to read and write. They then go on to show how the TOPEL incorporates all three. To demonstrate content validity, the test authors describe the rationale that guided their selection of subtests, formats, and item content, citing both theory and empirical research. In addition, conventional item analyses were conducted using the entire normative sample to assure adequate discriminating power, and regression analyses were used to test for item bias related to gender, race, or ethnicity. Only seven items had moderate or large effect sizes that might indicate potential bias. To address criterion-prediction validity, the TOPEL and six other standardized tests of early reading skills and/or vocabulary subtests were given to 154 children. All the TOPEL subtests and the composite had large to very large (.59–.77) relationships with the other measures, particularly among those pairings that tested similar skills. Finally, construct validity was demonstrated by correlating subtest scores with age, and by comparing the performance of children from bilingual homes to Hispanic children from homes where only English is spoken. All results were in the predicted direction, indicating that the TOPEL possesses adequate construct validity.

COMMENTARY. Generally, the TOPEL accomplishes its stated purposes, especially if used with other assessments. Some of its strengths lie in its attractive, colorful, and sturdy packaging; clearly written examiner's manual; and ease of administration and use of tables. The test authors provide an unusually clear and concise discussion of the implications of the test scores for children who score at the above average, average, and below average ranges.

The section of the manual on validity is especially informative, with detailed explanations of all analyses and justifications for their use; it could well serve as a tutorial on test validation. Another refreshing aspect of the manual is the collaborative invitation to professionals who use the TOPEL to send copies of their work to the test authors for inclusion in subsequent editions and a request that they pass along any suggestions for improvements that can help guide further revisions.

In future editions, one useful analysis would be an expansion of the group-differentiation section of the validity chapter to include performance differences between children with exceptionalities and those who are developing normally. Along with this, if the TOPEL is to be used as part of a comprehensive assessment to diagnose learning difficulties (which the test authors caution should not be done with children under age 5 because of an insufficient floor on the TOPEL), we need to see analyses of its ability, using various cut points, to accurately identify those who have literacy problems. Along with the concurrent criterion-related validity studies that are presented, predictive validity studies would also be interesting to show to what extent TOPEL results predict later academic achievement.

A couple of suggestions regarding testing procedure and format: We believe that breaking the administration of the TOPEL into two sessions is advisable and will provide more accurate results. If this is done, administering the Phonological Awareness subtest in a separate session will create a better testing situation because this subtest is difficult, with the directions changing throughout the test. It also might be less confusing for children if the Definitional Vocabulary subtest were broken into two item sets by separating the items that show only a single object to be named from those where the child must come up with a general term for four pictures on the same page.

Finally, there is a strong emphasis in current assessment practices on linking assessment directly to instruction. With the extensive experience they have had working with at-risk children and their teachers and parents, the test authors are well placed to develop and publish a set of proven, evidence-based instructional ideas and activities, either as a chapter in the TOPEL manual or as a set of ancillary materials. With these, educators can more systematically use a child's test results to improve learning. This is particularly important for children whose results indicate that they lack requisite language arts skills, because appropriate remediation provided before the initiation of formal reading instruction can help prevent later academic problems.

SUMMARY. The test authors are to be commended for creating a test based on sound theory and best practices from early childhood literacy research. The consensus among literacy experts is that there are three important indicators of later success in learning to read: print knowledge, vocabulary, and phonological awareness. Though other existing tests look at one or two of these, the TOPEL is unique in including all three. When used as part of a comprehensive evaluation that includes observation, reflection, and informal assessments, the TOPEL can provide direction for educators working with preschool children in the acquisition of literacy skills. It also offers promise as a tool for researchers in the field of early literacy.

REVIEWERS' REFERENCE

Roid, G. H. (1989). *Programs to fit skewed distributions and generate percentile norms for skewed or kurtotic distributions: Continuous norming with the first four moments* (Tech. Rep. No. 89-02). Salem, OR: Assessment Research.

[145]

Test of Understanding in College Economics—Fourth Edition.

Purpose: Intended "to provide norming data for a large national sample of students in [economics] principles classes, allowing instructors to compare performance in their classes on both pretests and posttests to the performance of the national sample of students and instructors."
Population: Introductory economics students.
Publication Dates: 1967-2007.
Acronym: TUCE-4.
Scores: 2 tests: Microeconomics, Macroeconomics.
Administration: Group.
Price Data, 2008: $24.95 per 25 booklets (2007, 44 pages).
Time: (45) minutes.
Authors: William B. Walstad, Michael Watts, and Ken Rebeck.
Publisher: Council for Economic Education.
Cross References: For reviews by Joseph C. Ciechalski and Jennifer J. Fager of the third edition, see 13:335; see also T2:1970 (10 references); for a review by Christine H. McGuire of an earlier edition, see 7:902.

Review of the Test of Understanding in College Economics—Fourth Edition by GEORGE ENGELHARD, JR., Professor of Educational Measurement and Policy, Emory University, Atlanta, GA:

DESCRIPTION. The Test of Understanding in College Economics—Fourth Edition (TUCE-4) can be completed by an individual student in a group setting. It was developed to measure classroom or individual student proficiency in the principles of economics in college classrooms. It consists of two tests designed to represent topics related to Microeconomics and Macroeconomics. There are 30 multiple-choice items in each test. The Microeconomics exam consists of six content categories (percent of items in parentheses): The Basic Economic Problem (6.6), Markets and Price Determination (21.6), Theories of the Firm (28.3), Factor Markets (10.0), Role of Government in a Market Economy (23.3), and International Economics (10.0). The Macroeconomics exam also consists of six content categories (percent of items in parentheses): Measuring Aggregate Economic Performance (13.3), Aggregate Supply and Aggregate Demand (25.0), Money and Financial Markets (13.3), Monetary and Fiscal Policies (28.3), Policy Debates (10.0), and International Economics (10.0). Copies of the test and sample scoring guides are included in the examiner's manual. The authors estimate that the TUCE-4 can be administered in a single class period.

According to the authors, the TUCE-4 has two main objectives: (a) "to offer a reliable and valid assessment instrument for students in principles of economics courses" (examiner's manual, p. 1) and (b) to provide normative data from a national sample so that instructors can compare achievement in their classes with this national sample.

DEVELOPMENT. This revision of the TUCE was a joint effort of the Committee on Economic Education of the American Economic Association and the National Council on Economic Education. Many top economic educators in the country participated in this revision. The high level of involvement by numerous instructors at a variety of colleges and universities is particularly noteworthy. The items included in the Microeconomics and Macroeconomics tests were categorized into the six content areas mentioned above, as well as into cognitive categories of recognition, explicit application, and implicit application. The content of tests did not change much from the earlier versions of the tests. There were 7 entirely new items added for the Microeconomics test, and 10 new items for the Macroeconomics test. The similarity at this version to its predecessor should make it easier for college instructors who have used earlier versions of these tests to maintain some level of interpretability from year to year. Because the content taught may vary across instructors and institutions, potential users should review the items and determine whether or not the TUCE-4 matches the objectives and content of their microeconomics and macroeconomics courses.

TECHNICAL. The authors of the TUCE-4 provide an examiner's manual that includes a description of the psychometric characteristics of the TUCE-4. Throughout the development process, the authors of the TUCE-4 were guided by the *Standards for Educational and Psychological Testing* (AERA, APA, & NCME, 1999), and extensive involvement of key experts in economics.

Normative information is provided for the TUCE-4. The authors recognize that this is not a random sample of all students enrolled in economics classes, but they provide a persuasive argument for use of the matched samples for normative interpretations of the scores. The matched normative data (pretest and posttest scores available for each student) are based on 3,255 students for the Microeconomics test and 2,789 students for the Macroeconomics test. The authors have been very careful to describe the demographic characteristics of these samples. Given the challenges of collecting normative data for college groups, the authors have done a good job. Because the results are very similar for the matched and unmatched data, it seems that only the matched data for students with both pretest and posttest should be used by instructors. The listing of colleges and universities, along with the names of the instructors in the manual, is useful information for the potential user of the TUCE-4.

The TUCE-4 reports the following scores based on this normative sample: raw scores, percentile ranks, and *T*-scores. The authors provide adequate descriptions and cautions for the user on how to interpret these scores.

In the examiner's manual, the authors provide a description of test reliability and standard error of measurement. Internal consistency reliability coefficients (alpha coefficient) are .46 for the pretest and .70 for the posttest for Microeconomics (matched sample), and .51 for the pretest and .77 for the posttest in Macroeconomics (matched sample). No information on test-retest reliabilities is provided. Overall, the posttest reliability coefficients for the TUCE-4 are acceptable, but the pretest scores have very low reliability coefficients and should be interpreted with caution. In particular, the use of the TUCE-4 scores to measure changes in individual student learning is not adequately warranted.

Evidence regarding the validity of the TUCE-4 scores is presented related to item content, conventional item analyses, and group differences. As with other aspects of the development of the TUCE-4, the authors have been very thoughtful and careful in describing and presenting validity evidence for the TUCE-4. Sufficient information is provided for potential users to determine whether or not the TUCE-4 will be useful in making decisions and recommendations about their students.

COMMENTARY. The TUCE-4 is a well-developed instrument that should be considered for use by college instructors who require an assessment of the economics proficiency of their students. The examiner's manual provides information regarding the appropriate uses of the test, cautions about the limitations, and sufficient detail regarding the psychometric quality of the TUCE-4. The examiner's manual does not assume that the reader is an expert in psychometrics, and provides enough detail to teach the potential user about a variety of measurement issues. It should be stressed that the potential user should carefully review the actual items included on the TUCE-4, and verify that the TUCE-4 does indeed reflect the curriculum in their school.

SUMMARY. In summary, the TUCE-4 is a sound assessment that can be used by college instructors to explore the economics proficiency of their students. The supporting material is easy to use, and the psychometric characteristics of the TUCE-4 are acceptable for this type of instrument. Users are provided with an examiner's manual that discusses proper uses of the TUCE-4. Potential users should carefully consider the alignment between the economics curriculum in their schools and the content of the TUCE-4. The TUCE-4 provides a structure for helping economics lecturers around the country to consider student proficiency in economics on a carefully chosen set of topics recommended by a professional organization (National Council on Economic Education). It is quite unusual for a postgraduate organization to create and disseminate tests in this way. Given the importance of economic issues, the authors should be commended for creating a useful tool for college-level instructors of economics.

REVIEWER'S REFERENCE

American Educational Research Association, American Psychological Association, & National Council on Measurement in Education. (1999). *Standards for educational and psychological testing.* Washington, DC: American Educational Research Association.

Review of the Test of Understanding in College Economics—Fourth Edition by JEAN P. KIRNAN, Professor of Psychology, The College of New Jersey, Ewing, NJ:

[The reviewer gratefully acknowledges the contributions of Lauren Wujciski to this critique. Her hard work and insights are greatly appreciated.]

DESCRIPTION. The Test of Understanding in College Economics (TUCE-4) is designed to assess knowledge of basic principles in introductory college economics courses. Sponsored by the National Council on Economic Education (NCEE) and the American Economic Association, the TUCE-4 is the fourth rendition of the instrument, which was first introduced in the 1960s. "The TUCE-4 has two main objectives: (1) to offer a reliable and valid assessment instrument for students in principles of economics courses, and (2) to provide norming data for a large, national sample of students in principles classes, allowing instructors to compare performance in their classes ... to the performance of the national sample" (examiner's manual, p. 1).

Two separate tests are provided, each yielding a single score of the student's mastery of Microeconomics and Macroeconomics, respectively. According to the authors, the Microeconomics test questions represent six subsections that measure The Basic Economic Problem, Markets and Price Determination, Theories of the Firm, Factor Markets, The (Microeconomic) Role of Government in a Market Economy, and International Economics. Similarly, the Macroeconomics test focuses on Measuring Aggregate Economic Performance, Aggregate Supply and Aggregate Demand, Money and Financial Markets, Monetary and Fiscal Policies, Policy Debates, and International Economics. Each test consists of 30 multiple-choice questions that could be administered during a single class period. This recommendation may introduce error variance across school settings as class periods vary in meeting length. There is further confusion regarding the administration time as no specific time limit is cited in the test manual, but a 45-minute limit appears in supplemental materials. Overall, there are no set instructions as to how the test should be administered, including whether the use of calculators is permitted. Additional error variance would be introduced if some professors allowed their use and others did not as four questions on the Macroeconomics test could benefit from the use of a calculator. Scripted verbal instructions for the test administrator, along with specific guidelines on the testing environment and calculator use should be added to ensure standardization.

The items themselves cover a wide content area and also reflect various levels of learning, most of which are beyond recognition and recall, requiring higher levels of thinking and application of economic principles to real world problems or situations. A useful item grid is presented for each test identifying both the content area and learning level for each item. With this information, instructors can assess which areas were covered in their course and properly gauge student performance on those items.

The TUCE-4 is available in paper-and-pencil format with only one version. A scoring key is provided in the back of the examiner's manual; therefore, one can assume that the tests are to be scored by hand or self-programmed Scantron. Local scoring and the single test form contribute to the necessity for test security, especially when used in a pretest/posttest manner to gauge change. The TUCE-4 is relatively inexpensive costing $24.95 for 25 booklets.

DEVELOPMENT. This revision of the TUCE spanned a year and a half and consisted of a combination of content analysis, expert opinion, and statistical evaluation. The sponsoring organizations formed a test Revision Committee, which developed content specifications and then, using the Third Edition of the TUCE (in place since 1991), revised items, deleted items, and added new items as deemed appropriate. Additional modifications were made following a large pilot study. The revisions in the Fourth Edition reflect changes in the content and teaching of macroeconomics with 10 new items, and substantial revisions on most of the 20 other items taken from the TUCE-3. The Microeconomics test has 7 new items with the other 23 items taken from the Third Edition following minor revisions, reflecting more stability in the content of microeconomics.

TECHNICAL. The normative sample was used both to establish comparative data and also for reliability and validity analyses. A total of 3,255 students sat for both the pretest and posttest in Microeconomics with a corollary 2,789 sitting for the Macro exam. These students came from over 40 distinct institutions with adequate representation from schools offering a variety of degree programs. A complete list of participating schools is included and is impressive for the geographical breadth that is represented.

The average pretest score is 31% for Microeconomics and 33% for Macroeconomics with posttest scores of 43% and 47%, respectively. The authors support the low posttest scores by pointing to the fact that item selection for the TUCE-4 was based on a desired 50% correct statistic. The pass rate seems rather low for a measure of course achievement and suggests that the TUCE-4 assesses a broader range of information than would be covered in a single economics course. Individual instructors are wise to follow the authors' caveat that the data "should not be considered as an absolute standard of achievement in economics but a relative measure" (examiner's manual, p. 10) largely due to its normative basis. The importance of comparing course content with test content is critical in interpreting test scores.

Other steps could be taken to provide additional assurances as to the representativeness of the low posttest pass rates. Although the composition of the Review Committee appears to be respected subject matter experts, it is unclear if these individuals are in fact teaching introductory courses in economics. Alternative content validation strategies include examination of content in popular economics textbooks, although this approach does not guarantee that a topic is, in fact, taught. One might utilize a technique whereby the instructors of these courses were to rate each item on the test for inclusion similar to the content validity technique suggested by Lawshe (as cited in Cohen & Swerdlik, 2002).

Tables are provided that present raw scores, percentile ranks, and *T*-scores separately for the pretests and posttests of Micro- and Macroeconomics. Thus, an instructor can reference their class's pretest performance and posttest performance separately to gauge initial knowledge, post-class knowledge, and change relative to these measures in the normative sample.

Reliability was demonstrated through coefficient alpha, a measure of internal consistency, yielding coefficients of .70 and .77 for the Micro and Macro tests, respectively, when administered as posttests. The authors noted that the reliability estimate for the Macro test is unchanged from the earlier version, TUCE-3; for the Micro test, however, the reliability was much lower than the .80 reported for the previous edition. One would expect internal measures of consistency for a cognitive ability test to be .80 or higher and thus the .70 for the Micro test is a concern. Because the TUCE is designed to be taken twice, it might prove useful to demonstrate test-retest reliability as well.

The authors assert that the TUCE-4 has both content and construct validity. Efforts to ensure content validity are clear in the development of the instrument through the work of the Review Committee in establishing content areas, reviewing items from the TUCE-3, revising items on the basis of pilot tests, and review of the instrument by subject matter experts. Although no single statistical technique exists to establish content validity, it would be helpful to delineate the exact process for content review. For example, decision rules for item exclusion/inclusion would be helpful; did an item need to achieve endorsement from a specified percent of the reviewing team?

The main evidence for construct validity is the increase from pretest to posttest scores where a mean difference of 3.4 points (36% improvement) and 4.4 points (45% improvement) are evidenced for the Micro- and Macroeconomics tests, respectively. Additional data on item level improvement are provided for both tests, with all but one item showing an increase in the percent correct from the pretest to the posttest. Other data would be useful to further reinforce the claim of validity. It would be interesting to compare posttest scores with final course grades. Mention was made of administering the instrument to intermediary students. Showing differences in pretest scores between students who never took an economics course and those who were advanced would also provide support.

Further support of construct validity is offered in a comparison of test scores by 15 different factors including demographic information and coursework. Although there is an increase in score from pretest to posttest for all categories, no inferential statistics are provided to determine if the mean differences are statistically significant, although such a claim is made in the manual. Additional analysis of within-category differences would be useful. For example, one would expect that the more economics courses one had taken, the higher the pretest means and the lower the difference between pretest and posttest. This appears to hold true for the Microeconomics test but not for the Macroeconomics test. In the end, construct validity is based upon an accumulation of evidence. The authors do appear to show evidence of adequate construct validity, but the data they currently have could be mined for additional insights.

COMMENTARY. The authors correctly point out that using the TUCE-4 for group or individual evaluation is most effective with a careful comparison of the content of the TUCE-4 with the content and learning objectives of a specific course. As a teaching aid, the instrument can be administered to determine areas of current mastery and areas of deficiency to inform the content and direction of the course. It may be administered posttest to check for understanding. It is useful in research as it provides a standard measure of achievement across instructors and institutions if one is interested in comparing student achievement.

SUMMARY. The TUCE-4 is a carefully constructed instrument with a long history of review and analysis. A lingering concern lies in the interpretation of scores. This single caution reflects the issue of test content relative to course content, which the authors recognize and provide useful item content and item level pass rate information for users.

REVIEWER'S REFERENCE

Cohen, R. J., & Swerdlik, M. E. (2002). *Psychological testing and assessment.* Boston: McGraw-Hill.

[146]

Test of Visual Perceptual Skills, 3rd Edition.

Purpose: Constructed to "determine a child's visual-perceptual strengths and weaknesses."
Population: Ages 4-0 through 18-11.
Publication Dates: 1982-2006.
Acronym: TVPS-3.
Scores: 7 subtests: Visual Discrimination, Visual Memory, Spatial Relationships, Form Constancy, Sequential Memory, Visual Figure-Ground, Visual Closure, Total Score.
Administration: Individual.
Price Data, 2006: $150 per test kit including manual (2006, 88 pages), test plates, and 25 record forms; $40 per manual; $80 per test plates; $30 per 25 record forms.
Time: (30) minutes (untimed).
Authors: Nancy Martin (TVPS-3); earlier editions by Morrison F. Gardner.
Publisher: Academic Therapy Publications.
Cross References: See T5:2724 (13 references); for reviews by Nancy A. Busch-Rossnagel and Joseph W. Denison of an earlier edition entitled Test of Visual-Perceptual Skills (Non-Motor), see 9:1276.

Review of the Test of Visual Perceptual Skills, 3rd Edition by PHILLIP L. ACKERMAN, Professor of Psychology, Georgia Institute of Technology, Atlanta, GA:

DESCRIPTION. The Test of Visual Perceptual Skills, 3rd Edition (TVPS-3) consists of "112 black and white designs chosen from both levels of the previous edition" (manual, p. 9) of the test. The test is described by the publisher as an assessment of "the visual perceptual strengths and weaknesses of students aged 4-0 through 18-11" (manual, p. 5). The items are figural (nonverbal) in content, and range from simple polygons to more complex forms. Two practice items and 16 test items are administered for each of seven different subtests that include Visual Discrimination, Visual Memory, Spatial Relationships, Form Constancy, Sequential Memory, Visual Figure-ground, and Visual Closure. The test is administered individually, and the items have a multiple-choice format. The respondent needs only point to or otherwise indicate the item choice in order for the item to be scored. The test manual indicates that "this format is ideal for use with students who may have impairments in motor, speech, hearing, neurological, or cognitive functions" (manual, p. 5). The test is unspeeded, but the manual reports that administration takes about 30 minutes. In addition to individual subtest scaled scores and a total scaled score, the test provides for derivation of optional index scores for three processes: Basic Processes, Sequential Processing, and Complex Processes. A profile form is provided on the record form for recording individual subtest scaled scores, index scores, and overall score. The manual indicates that "The TVPS-3 may be used by a number of different types of professionals: occupational therapists, school psychologists, learning specialists, optometrists, and rehabilitation specialists" (p. 6). In addition, the manual indicates that "the TVPS-3 may also be used to track progress within a therapeutic and/or educational program" (p. 11).

DEVELOPMENT. The manual provides a description of theories of visual perception and prior research that serve as the basis for including assessments of the seven subtests of the TVPS-3. The manual provides a reasonable level of background about the nature of visual perception abilities, though it provides no information that puts the construct of visual perception abilities into a wider nomological network that includes other nonverbal and spatial abilities, or even the relationship between these abilities and general reasoning or intelligence. As a result, there is an adequate treatment of convergent relationships, but no treatment of discriminant relationships with other major ability traits.

TECHNICAL.

Standardization. The standardization sample for the TVPS-3 consisted of 2,008 students from 38 states in the U.S.A., ranging in age from 4 years, 0 months to 18 years, 11 months. Although it was not clear whether there were any efforts for stratification of the sample, the demographic information presented suggests that the sample was diverse in terms of gender, age, and ethnicity. However, clinical samples were not represented in this standardization sample. Instead, the clinical groups were much smaller and not very diverse. The ADD (attention deficit disorder) sample consisted of 41 individuals, the LD (learning disabled) sample consisted of 35 individuals, and the autistic sample consisted of 13 individuals. Scaled score tables are provided for examinees from age 4 years, 0 months to age 18 years, 11 months. There are no detailed norms for the clinical samples, although means are reported for each of the three groups (which were both heterogeneous by age and differed in average age, so these summary data are meaningless). Another notable shortcoming was that there are no separate norms by gender–something that is especially a concern, given the demonstrated large gender differences on test of visual/spatial abilities like those that make up this test (see Voyer, Voyer, & Bryden, 1995).

Reliability. Internal consistency data are reported for the seven subtest scores and for the total score composite, but no reliability data are reported for the index scores. Although the internal consistency reliability indices appear reasonable on the surface, ranging from .75 to .88 for the subtests and .96 for the total score composite, these results were based on the total standardization sample of 2,008 examinees that ranged in age from 4-18 years. Given that mean subtest scores increased substantially from age 4 years, 0 months to age 18 years, 11 months (by a factor of 2.7 to 4), the internal consistency reliability assessments are probably inflated by the confound of test scores with age differences. In addition, it is highly likely, based on the literature of ability assessment, that reliability of tests given to 4-year-olds will be much lower than the reliability of ability tests given to 18-year-olds (e.g., see Anastasi & Urbina, 1997). Reliabilities for each age group would be needed before one could properly assess the reliability of the subtests and overall scores. Test-retest reliability was assessed in a small sample (N = 42), though again the sample was heterogeneous on age (ranging from age 6 to age 14). The test-retest correlations for the subtests ranged from an unacceptable r = .34 to a more reasonable r = .82. Again, however, given the age heterogeneity of the sample, these correlations most likely overestimate the test-retest reliability of the subtests in a more age-homogeneous sample.

Validity. The manual reports that content validity was determined by the theoretical foundation for the test, and item evaluation was performed with a pilot study of 128 children (ranging in age from 10 to 15). The manual reports that an analysis of item bias was conducted, but no results of the analysis are reported. As evidence for criterion-related validity, the manual reports a correlation between the TVPS-3 overall score and the "Visual Supplement of the Developmental Test of Visual-Motor Integration" (p. 55). For the validation sample of N = 33, the correlation with this other test was r = .67.

As for construct validity, the manual reports that the test shows a positive relationship to chronological age. The manual reports smoothed subtest raw score medians for each age group, and these results appear to show good age differentiation. However, these results also suggest considerable ceiling effects for the older sample, given that *median* performance on some of the subtests is very close to the maximum score (e.g., for all of the scales, the medians for 18-year-olds are above 13.0, and for one scale, the median score is 15.36, but the maximum score on each subtest is 16). Also reported are mean performance levels for the three identified clinical groups (ADD, LD, and Autistic), and an additional "unspecified" diagnosis. All three clinical groups are shown to have normative standard score means significantly below the mean for the standardization sample. However, none of these groups had significantly different scores from the other identified clinical groups. In addition, no data are presented on samples that have impairments in motor, speech, hearing, or other neurological functions mentioned in the test manual.

Results of factor analyses are reported in support of the construct validity of the test. No information is provided about the source of these data or the sample size. The information provided (in terms of eigenvalues from a principal components analysis) suggests that extraction of more than one factor may be ill-advised, given that the first component accounted for 87% of the variance. No information is provided that addresses the fit (or overfit) of these factor solutions. In light of the eigenvalue information provided, it seems doubtful that any other score but a single total index is supported by these data. No validity information is provided concerning the use of the TVPS-3 in the context of "therapeutic" or "educational" (manual, p. 11) programs.

COMMENTARY. A *Mental Measurements Yearbook* review of an earlier edition of the TVPS stated that "the use of the TVPS at this time is not warranted because of the lack of both a rationale and validity evidence" (Busch-Rossnagel, 1985, p. 1596). Although the current edition of the TVPS includes more material in terms of a theoretical rationale, it is seriously lacking in terms of an applied rationale–that is, in terms of what one can do with the information from the test. Although one might infer from the information presented in the manual that the test has a high degree of homogeneity across the seven subtests, and provides an overall test score that increases with age, there is no criterion-related validity information that would suggest the use of the test for any applied purpose. The lack of meaningful construct validity information makes it impossible to determine whether this test provides any value above other tests of nonverbal or spatial abilities, or indeed any markedly different information from an omnibus test of intellectual abilities. The fact that no gender difference information was presented is a substantial concern, given the likelihood that scores differ on this test by gender, and thus, conclusions based on test scores might result in differential impact by gender. The recommendations for use in therapeutic or education programs, or by individuals who are not trained psychometricians (e.g., optometrists), is also a concern, given that these individuals may not have the expertise to evaluate the paucity of data that support any applied use of the TVPS-3.

SUMMARY. The TVPS-3 is an instrument for assessing nonverbal abilities in children that may have some promise for research purposes, in terms of providing a single composite score of ability, based on a format that does not involve the use of language-based materials. Use of the test for much older children (older adolescents) in a normal population is not recommended, because of apparent ceiling effects. Interpretation of individual subtest scores or index scores also cannot be recommended, as these scores have not been demonstrated to be psychometrically differentiable. Finally, the use of this instrument beyond research purposes cannot be recommended, because of the absence of useful reliability and validity information that would be needed to support the use of the test in educational or clinical applications.

REVIEWER'S REFERENCES

Anastasi, A., & Urbina, S. (1997). *Psychological testing* (7th ed.) Upper Saddle River, NJ: Prentice Hall.

Busch-Rossnagel, N. A. (1985). [Review of the Test of Visual-Perceptual Skills (Non-Motor).] In J. V. Mitchell, Jr. (Ed.), *The ninth mental measurements yearbook* (pp. 1595-1596). Lincoln, NE: Buros Institute of Mental Measurements.

Voyer, D., Voyer, S., & Bryden, M. P. (1995). Magnitude of sex differences in spatial abilities: A meta-analysis and consideration of critical variables. *Psychological Bulletin, 117*, 250-270.

Review of the Test of Visual Perceptual Skills, 3rd Edition by BRIAN F. FRENCH, Associate Professor of Educational Psychology (Research, Evaluation, & Measurement), Washington State University, Pullman, WA:

DESCRIPTION. The Test of Visual Perceptual Skills, 3rd Edition (TVPS-3) is an individually administered, multiple-choice test designed to assess the visual perceptual strengths and weaknesses of examinees from 4-0 up to 18-11 years of age. The TVPS-3, with new normative data, replaces all previous age-related versions (i.e., TVPS-R, TVPS-UL-R). The TVPS-3 was designed to be used for "diagnostic and research purposes" (manual, p. 9) by professionals (e.g., school psychologists, educational specialists, optometrists). The test is composed of 112 items measuring seven subdomains (i.e., Visual Discrimination, Visual Memory, Spatial Relationships, Form Constancy, Sequential Memory, Visual Figure-Ground, and Visual Closure). Each item has three or four distractors. The items (black-and-white line drawings) are presented one at a time by the examiner. The examinee selects the correct figure from the choices presented. Examinees can respond via an agreed upon response format (e.g., point to/say the correct answer). A ceiling is reached when either 3 items in a row are incorrect or when all items are administered for a given subtest.

Test administration is straightforward with detailed instructions and scripts in the manual. General training in assessment and familiarity with educational and psychological tests are required to use the TVPS-3. The test authors recommend 30 minutes for test administration, which is untimed with the exception of two subtests, Visual Memory and Sequential Memory. Scoring is completed by the examiner and is straightforward with adequate examples and instructions. Scaled and standard scores as well as percentile ranks and age-equivalent scores are available. Scores are obtained for the seven subtests, the Overall score, and three indices composed of the subtest scores including Basic Processes (Visual Discrimination, Visual Memory, Spatial Relationships, and Form Constancy), Sequencing (Sequential Memory), and Complex Processes (Figure-Ground and Visual Closure).

DEVELOPMENT. The TVPS-3 was based on the definition that visual perception "is how people perceive real objects in real world settings" (manual, pp. 11–12). The assessment is structured around five processes (visual discrimination, spatial relationships, visual memory, figure-ground, and visual closure) identified in the literature (Chalfant & Scheffelin, 1969) as components of visual perceptual abilities. The manual lacks an explanation for the other two constructs measured by the two additional subtests. Several theories are offered for visual perception yet no empirical support is given for selecting the categorization of the construct by Chalfant and Scheffelin. The manual does connect visual perceptual abilities to disabilities (e.g., dyslexia, head injuries) and provides a literature-grounded rationale for why assessing the construct is important.

The development of the TVPS-3 was based, in part, on user feedback obtained by the test publisher, which resulted in retention of existing items to produce one instrument for the entire age range. Specifically, items were selected from the original set of items at the lower and upper end of difficulty (112 items), a pilot study (n = 128) was conducted, and an analysis at the mean and item level was completed. All age ranges were not included in the pilot study. Normative data were collected on 140 items (18 + 2 sample items per subtest), 112 of which were retained from the pilot study. Item analyses, based on Classical Test Theory and the 1-parameter logistic item response theory (IRT) model, and differential item functioning (DIF) analyses were conducted on the retained items, resulting in the final set of items for the seven subtests, each of which contains 16 items plus 2 sample items. Information regarding the item calibration and fit from the IRT analyses or exclusion criteria of items from the DIF analyses was not presented. A DIF method (e.g., logistic regression) suitable for detecting more than uniform DIF would have been preferred.

TECHNICAL. The TVPS-3 was administered to a standardization sample (n = 2,008) in 80 cities from 38 states across the United States. Recruitment focused on users of the previous versions. Comparisons of major categories (e.g., region, gender, race/ethnicity) to U.S. Census data from 2000 demonstrated the sample was relatively representative, with minor exceptions (e.g., urban and rural residence representation). No information was given on disability category representation, which would be helpful to evaluate how well the normative information represents examinees classified in such categories, especially given the diagnostic purpose of the instrument. The raw scores were normalized, transformed into scaled and standard scores, and distributions smoothed to correct for irregularities. No information was given concerning the degree of nonnormality of raw scores. Subtest scaled scores (M = 10, SD = 3) are presented for ages 4-0 through 9-11 in 6-month intervals and for 10-0 through 18-11 in 12-month intervals. Standard scores (M = 100, SD = 15) are provided for the three indices and Overall score. Note that one index is composed of only one subtest. These scores are sums of the scaled scores where age has been factored and scores are not age-separated. Percentile ranks, NCEs, T-scores, and stanine scores based on the standard scores are provided, as are age equivalents based on raw scores.

Internal consistency reliability (alpha coefficients) for the Overall score and the seven subscale scores was .96 and ranged from .75 to .88, respectively. It appears that 18 items (16 + 2 sample items) were used in assessing reliability (manual, p. 49) yet it is clear that sample items are not to be scored. Test-retest reliability values over an unspecified interval for the Overall score was .97 and ranged from .34 to .81 for subtest scores. Information about test-retest sample obtainment was not presented and sample size is reported inconsistently ($N = 63$, $N = 42$). The majority of the sample was 10 and 11 years of age. A lack of information on stability for the lower and upper age ranges is concerning. Standard error of measurement (*SEM*) and confidence intervals for the subtest and Overall scores are presented. The test author is commended for employing correct calculation of the *SEM* and confidence intervals. However, the formula presented for standard error of estimate is incorrect and does not appear to be the one used in the manual. The reviewer's calculations show the correct formula was used in determining the score bands but incorrectly documented in the manual.

Three types of score validity evidence are presented. Content validity was established through the use of items from the previous TVPS versions and through the item analysis process. Stronger evidence presenting information about the test blueprint, how items mapped to specific skills, and item reviews by experts in the area of visual perceptual skills is preferred (e.g., Standard 1.6; AERA, APA, & NCME, 1999). Limited concurrent-related validity evidence was provided by presenting correlations between the TVPS-3 Overall score and the Visual ($r = .67$), Motor ($r = .35$), and Total ($r = .50$) scores from the Developmental Test of Visual-Motor Integration (Beery & Beery, 2004) based on a limited sample ($n = 33$).

Three types of evidence are presented to support construct validity. First, an increase in raw score medians at each age interval was presented, which does not provide strong evidence. Second, contrasting groups evidence among four groups diagnosed with different disabilities (i.e., Learning Disabled, Attention Deficit Disorder, Autistic, and Unspecified) and the standardization sample was presented. Note that little or no justification for the differences between normal functioning examinees and the identified groups was provided. Additionally, the means presented in Table 8.4 and 8.3 in the manual do not match, and the degrees of freedom appear to be incorrect for a two group-independent *t*-test given the stated sample sizes. The reporting of effect sizes is encouraged, as is accurate reporting of *p*-values ($p = 0$ is insufficient). Third, a principal components analysis with varimax rotation and a maximum likelihood factor analysis were conducted on the same data set. A 3- versus 2-factor model was advocated, based on results. Proposed models had limited theoretical support. The manual states "visual perceptual skills have been described as highly interrelated, it is hypothesized that the factor structure would reflect that" (manual, p. 57). However, PCA with varimax rotation assumes no error of measurement and maintains an orthogonal structure (i.e., factor correlations = 0.0). Thus, there is a mismatch between the analysis and proposed structure. Additionally, analytic disconnect between the goal of the analysis and analytic method selected exists. PCA is a data reduction technique and factor analysis is a "search for an underlying structure" technique (e.g., Fabrigar, Leandre, Wegener, MacCallum, & Strahan, 1999). Components of this evidence, especially construct validity, appear to be inaccurate or conducted inappropriately.

COMMENTARY. The TVPS-3 holds promise as a tool that researchers may use in conjunction with other assessments for diagnostic or research purposes. The test author is commended for following many recommendations for test development (AERA et al., 1999), explicitly stating the appropriate cautions about score use and interpretation, and conducting DIF analysis across major groups in the development phase. The measure appears to have some theory to support its development but certainly would benefit from further elaboration. The test author has stated that the test's primary purpose is to provide reliable information on the assessed skills for use by various professionals (e.g., educational specialists). Based on internal consistency estimates of the Overall score, this primary purpose has been met. However, this reviewer would not recommend at this time the TVPS-3 for the additional stated purposes in the absence of the necessary validity information.

The analytic disconnect issues previously mentioned continued with the use of CTT, IRT, and DIF analyses. Specifically, item difficulty and discrimination appeared to be a component of the CTT analysis and item selection, yet models only examining item difficulty were employed for the

IRT and DIF work. Additionally, reporting more details concerning the DIF analysis (e.g., use of purification, subtest vs. total test analysis, effect size use) would allow a more thorough evaluation.

The manual does advocate for scores to be used at the individual level, in combination with other information of sources for diagnostic purposes and encourages use of the subtest scores, the total score, and the three indices. Comparisons are made between learning disabled groups, yet there is no basis for determining which subtest(s) or index differences would be expected between examinees identified and not identified with a disability. Additionally, there is a lack of psychometric information, in general, for the three indices.

It appears more validity evidence was gathered for the TVPS-3 compared to previous versions. However, validity evidence remains too weak to warrant full endorsement of the test score use as advocated by the test maker. For instance, principal components analysis (PCA) was conducted (not well) to provide construct validity evidence. PCA, as well as exploratory factor analysis, does not provide strong validity evidence. Little work is purely exploratory (Crocker & Algina, 1986), especially when the instrument is not new and factor models are proposed. Additionally, conducting more than one EFA (or CFA) on the same data for cross-validation is not recommended as it capitalizes on chance. Such problems, as well as ones outlined above, require attention. Careful and systematic collection of validity evidence that is well documented in the technical manual, for example, is a must-do task for testing programs (Downing, 2006). The TVPS-3 is moving in that direction.

SUMMARY. The TVPS-3 is designed to be an individually administered assessment of visual perceptual skills for use with a population of examinees aged 4 through 18 years. The TVPS-3 offers improvements such as (a) updated norms, (b) the ability to assess a wider age range, (c) more than one response mode, (d) an updated literature review, and (e) an easy-to-use manual and test booklet. With the appropriate psychometric information, this measure could be used in a variety of ways (research, diagnostic evaluations). Unfortunately, score reliability, particularly stability, and score validity, especially at the subtest and index level do not support the inferences from the TVPS-3 scores as advocated by the test maker. This reviewer encourages the continued gathering of the necessary evidence to support the scale's use. Additionally, a refinement of the analytic strategies given the available data would assist in gathering such evidence. In the absence of the said evidence, the TVPS-3 is not recommended for use for decision making about individuals at this time.

REVIEWER'S REFERENCES

American Educational Research Association, American Psychological Association, & National Council on Measurement in Education. (1999). *Standards for educational and psychological testing*. Washington, DC: American Educational Research Association.

Beery, K., & Beery, N. A. (2004). *Developmental Test of Visual Motor Integration, 5th Edition: Administration, scoring, and teaching manual.* Minneapolis: NCS Pearson.

Chalfant, J. C., & Scheffelin, M. A. (1969). *Central processing disorders in children: A review of the research.* Bethesda, MD: Dept. of Health, Education, and Welfare.

Crocker, L., & Algina, J. (1986). *Introduction to classical & modern test theory.* New York: Harcourt Brace.

Downing, S. M. (2006). Twelve steps for effective test development. In S. M. Downing & T. M. Haladyna (Eds.), *Handbook of test development* pp. 3-25. Mahwah, NJ: Erlbaum.

Fabrigar, L. R., Leandre, R., Wegener, D. T., MacCallum, R. C., & Strahan, E. J. (1999). Evaluating the use of exploratory factor analysis in psychological research. *Psychological Methods, 4*, 272-299.

[147]

Texas Functional Living Scale.

Purpose: Intended to be a "performance-based measure of instrumental activities of daily living."

Population: "Individuals ages 16-90 diagnosed with a variety of clinical disorders or requiring an assessment of functional abilities."

Publication Dates: 2006-2009.

Acronym: TFLS.

Scores, 5: Time, Money and Calculation, Communication, Memory, Total.

Administration: Individual.

Price Data, 2009: $149 per complete kit including 25 record forms, 25 response forms, clear plastic bottle, 2 stimulus cards, 5 simulated phone books, and examiner's manual (2009, 104 pages); $15 per 2 stimulus cards; $15 per 5 simulated phone books; $70 per examiner's manual.

Time: (10-20) minutes.

Comments: Initial version also referred to as the Test of Everyday Functional Abilities (TEFA); paper-and-pencil format; examiner must provide the following materials: stopwatch, timer, calendar for the current year, small edible objects/candies to mimic pills, 2 pencils, zip-top bag(s) for money, telephone, 1 $5 bill, 2 $1 bills, 7 quarters, 5 dimes, 5 nickels, and 5 pennies.

Authors: C. Munro Cullum, Myron F. Weiner, and Kathleen C. Saine.

Publisher: Pearson.

Review of the Texas Functional Living Scale by PAM LINDSEY-GLENN, Professor, College of Education, Tarleton State University, Stephenville, TX:

DESCRIPTION. The Texas Functional Living Scale (TFLS) is an individually administered, performance-based scale developed for use with individuals displaying characteristics of a variety of neurodevelopmental, neurodegenerative, and intellectual disabilities. The instrument evaluates the functional abilities, (e.g., daily or independent living skills) of such persons as part of an overall psychological or medical evaluation. The TFLS assesses functional ability skills in instrumental daily activities (IADLs) for individuals ages 16–90. IADLs are described as more complex behaviors related to living independently, such as managing money and paying bills.

The instrument is composed of 24 items measuring an individual's skills in four areas of functioning. These areas are described in subscale ratings related to Time, Money and Calculation, Communication, and Memory. Results may be used as part of a comprehensive medical or psychological evaluation, focused on planning effective programs or evaluating the impact of medical or other interventions.

The test kit contains stimulus cards for some items such as money and time. The examiner's manual provides a list of other items to be provided by the examiner such as a calendar, stop watch, and various coin and bill denominations. The examinee is required to give either an oral or written response to items containing oral and visual cues, depending on the nature of the particular item. The administration instructions are clear and straightforward. The instrument assesses a variety of tasks related to daily functional living such as writing checks, looking up information in a phone book, and so forth. Raw scores and cumulative percentages are recorded for each of the four subscales and an overall *T*-score is calculated for the entire test. The *T*-score is determined by the sum of the four subscale scores. Interpretation guidelines are given for each subscale and for the overall *T*-score.

DEVELOPMENT. The TFLS was developed in response to an increasing need for reliable instruments that describe an individual's independent functioning ability. The skills measured by the TFLS are critical to the development of appropriate programs and interventions that improve an individual's quality of independent living. The work on the instrument began in the mid-1990s with the market version being published in 2009 (examiner's manual, p. ix). The instrument's original purpose was to assess the functional abilities of persons with neurodevelopmental or neurodegenerative disorders, particularly, Alzheimer's disease. However, the current version expands its efficacy for use with individuals who have intellectual disabilities, schizophrenia, and traumatic brain injuries. It was designed to provide relevant information about the examinee's ability to function independently in home and community settings (examiner's manual, p. 3). It was not developed as a "stand alone" measure, but to be used in conjunction with other evaluation data such as tests of memory or cognitive ability.

TECHNICAL. The standardization sample consisted of 800 individuals ages 16–90 with 100 individuals in each age band (e.g., 16–19, 20–29, 30–39, 40–49, 50–59, 60–69, 70–79, & 80–90 years). The standardization data were collected as part of the Wechsler Memory Scale–Fourth Edition (WMS-IV; Wechsler, 2009) standardization. The normative data represent the population of the United States ages 16–90. The participants were selected based on specific demographic variables (e.g., geographic location, educational level, race/ethnicity) based on the 2005 U.S. Census.

The *T*-score has a single norm for all ages with a mean of 50 and standard deviation of 10. The *T*-score uses the sum of raw scores from each subscale. The cumulative subscale percentages are used in place of scaled scores because the typical participants in the norming sample scored a perfect score on each subscale, thus skewing the functional scores. The subscale scores, therefore, are reported in cumulative percentage bands (≤ 2 to > 75) to attenuate for the skewed normative scores (examiner's manual, p. 45).

The reliability coefficients were calculated using a split-half method with a Fisher's z transformation to calculate the average coefficients. A decision-consistency methodology was used to demonstrate reliability between subscales due to the significant highly skewed nature of the subscale scores. Reliability coefficients were adequate to demonstrate test reliability for each age and disability group with an overall average of .75 for typically developing individuals and .92 for the special groups sample. Interrater reliability coefficients were reported as .97 to .99.

The manual provided an excellent description of validity evidence in all three areas of test validity, namely, construct, content, and concurrent. Content validity was evaluated through literature and expert reviews. Adjustments were made based on suggestions from both sources. Construct validity was evaluated throughout the standardization process and modifications were made.

The test authors describe in detail special group studies conducted with targeted populations using the TFLS and other measures of adaptive and/or cognitive abilities. The special studies included populations of participants with Alzheimer's disease, mild-moderate mental retardation, major depressive disorders, schizophrenia, autistic disorder, and traumatic brain injuries. The manual describes in detail how participants for each study were chosen and the validity correlations and mean scores for each. In addition, an extensive description of each concurrent validity study is provided. Data suggested that the TFLS had adequate concurrent validity with instruments having a similar purpose (e.g., ILS), however, poor or moderate correlations with instruments such as those assessing cognition or adaptive behavior (e.g., ABAS-II or WAIS-IV). This result should be expected, however, because the TFLS is a screening instrument designed for a specific purpose and assessment of a limited range of very specialized skills. Instruments such as the ABAS-II or WAIS-IV are not designed to measure the same types of skills as the TFLS purports to measure and are meant as an overall measure of an individual's function. However, the TFLS is appropriate to use in conjunction with other measures such as the WAIS-IV and the ABAS-II.

COMMENTARY. The TFLS is a brief, easy-to-use screening instrument that evaluates an individual's ability to function in four critical lifeskills areas. It has the potential to be a helpful tool if used in conjunction with other assessment data to help plan interventions or evaluate the effectiveness of interventions with a target group of adults. It has clear, straightforward directions and is easy to score. The manual provides interpretive examples; however, the examples are very limited in scope. Alternative prompts are provided for most items, which is very helpful when assessing individuals with cognitive or developmental challenges. Suggestions are also given for examinees with physical challenges.

The downside of the TFLS is the cue cards used for some items. The black and white line drawings would be difficult for some people with developmental disabilities to "pretend" to use or interpret. For example, one item asks the examinee to "act out" the steps to cook a recipe in the microwave. The cue card of the microwave oven is a poor representation. Using real objects or, at least, models of real objects would likely be more effective. A second example is the cue card provided for writing a check and addressing an envelope. The line drawings and cluttered appearance would be difficult to make inferences about for persons with developmental disabilities. The cue card used to simulate a water bill is visually cluttered and would be difficult for a person with developmental disabilities to analyze.

SUMMARY. Overall, the TFLS appears to be a useful screening tool to support comprehensive medical or psychological evaluations. The skills evaluation items are quite limited (24 items), but they could provide an overall impression of an individual's abilities in the four areas assessed. As with all screening instruments, it should be used with caution and in conjunction with other assessment data. Scores from the TFLS should not be used as the sole criterion for making diagnoses, planning programs, or evaluating the success of interventions.

REVIEWER'S REFERENCE

Wechsler, D. (2009). Wechsler Memory Scale–Fourth Edition. San Antonio, TX: Pearson.

Review of the Texas Functional Living Scale by JENNIFER M. STRANG, Clinical Neuropsychologist, Department of Behavioral Health, DeWitt Healthcare Network, Fort Belvoir, VA:

DESCRIPTION. The Texas Functional Living Scale (TFLS) is a performance-based measure designed to assess instrumental activities of daily living (IADLs). The TFLS consists of 24 items assessing the "ability to use analog clocks and calendars, ability to perform calculations involving time and money, ability to utilize basic communication skills in everyday activities, and memory" (examiner's manual, p. 2). The TFLS item requirements vary, ranging from reading a clock display to writing a check to paying a bill. Each item is individually scored from 0 to 1, 0 to 2, or 0 to 3 points. Some items also have a range of 0 to 5 and 0 to 6. A total raw score for each of the four subscales (Time, Money and Calculation, Communication, Memory) is calculated by adding individual item scores within each subscale. A TFLS total raw score is obtained by adding the subscale raw scores; a maximum of 50 points is possible. The subscale raw scores are converted to cumulative percentages, and the TFLS total raw score is converted to a *T*-Score. The manual provides detailed guidelines for interpreting the summary scores and applying qualitative descriptors.

The test is administered individually to examinees ages 16 to 90. The average time to administer the test is less than 15 minutes. A record form is used to administer and score the TFLS; it contains all of the administration, recording, and scoring directions and provides space for recording behavioral observations during test administration. An accompanying response form is needed for Items 4, 5, 6, 13, and 14. The test kit also includes the following materials: a clear plastic bottle, five simulated phone books, and two stimulus cards (Card 1: water bill/microwave and Card 2: food label). Additional required materials to be provided by the examiner include: stopwatch, timer, 12-page wall calendar for the current year, pencil, zip-top bag for money, telephone, small edible objects/candies to mimic pills, and money (1 $5 bill, 2 $1 bills, 7 quarters, 5 dimes, 5 nickels, and 5 pennies). To minimize distractions, the test authors recommend keeping a chair or shelf within easy reach but out of the examinee's view to arrange the test materials. In general, the administration instructions are clear and easy to follow, and helpful icons appear on the record form to indicate materials required in each subtest. Additionally, verbal instructions are highlighted in purple to improve ease of administration.

DEVELOPMENT. According to the test authors, the TFLS "was originally developed in response to the limitations of current functional ability assessment approaches used in patients with Alzheimer disease" (examiner's manual, p. 1). In the past, many assessments of functional capacity relied on reports from family members or other caregivers. Because caregiver reports may be biased by multiple factors, several performance-based functional measures were developed. However, many of these measures have problems of their own that may reduce their validity, reliability, and practicality. Thus, the TFLS was created to provide a brief, easily administered instrument to assess IADLs that are thought to be most susceptible to cognitive decline. Additionally, the test authors hoped to create an instrument that would provide clinically valuable information to aid in differential diagnosis and treatment planning, particularly in relation to an individual's capacity to function independently.

TECHNICAL. The standardization data were collected in conjunction with the Wechsler Memory Scale—Fourth Edition (WMS-IV; Wechsler, 2009) standardization; data from the 2005 U.S. Census guided the stratified sampling of participants. The examiner's manual provides a complete description of the inclusion and exclusion criteria and the demographic characteristics of the nationally representative sample of 800 examinees. The sample was divided into eight age bands with 100 individuals in each band. An equal number of male and female examinees were included in each age group from ages 16 through 59. The older age groups (≥ 60 years) included more females than males. The normative sample was further stratified according to five educational levels, five racial/ethnic categories, and four geographic regions.

Several special group studies were conducted concurrently with standardization to examine the specificity and clinical utility of the TFLS. The special group sample included 212 examinees diagnosed with one of seven disorders: Probable Alzheimer's disease–Mild Severity, Intellectual Disability–Mild Severity, Intellectual Disability–Moderate Severity, Major Depressive Disorder, Traumatic Brain Injury, Schizophrenia, and Autistic Disorder. A sample of participants residing in assisted living facilities or group homes and those requiring caregiver support at home also was collected.

There is some evidence of internal consistency for the TFLS *T*-score, with split-half reliability coefficients ranging from .65 at age 16–19 to .81 at age 60–69. The average across age groups was .75, which is considered a moderate level of reliability. Split-half reliability for the clinical groups generally was quite high, ranging from .63 for Major Depressive Disorder to .97 for the assisted living facility residents, with an average reliability of .92. Two independent raters scored all test protocols; interrater reliability was high, ranging from 97% to 99% agreement. Finally, the TFLS appears to demonstrate good stability over time. Although one would expect some increase in performance due to practice effects, the increase in the TFLS *T*-score was small, suggesting good test-retest reliability. In all, the reliability estimates appear acceptable and are comparable to similar performance-based functional ability measures, such as the Independent Living Scales (ILS; Loeb, 1996).

The test authors also provide validity information based on test content, response processes, internal structure, relationships with other variables, and relationships to other measures. Test content was examined and modified through the use of literature and expert reviews. Earlier versions of the scale were used to develop item content for standardization. Items were reevaluated after the standardization phase to establish a final set of items. Examinee response processes provided additional evidence of validity through the evaluation of frequently occurring incorrect responses. That is, whenever analysis revealed the existence of incorrect but plausible responses, scoring guidelines were changed as appropriate.

External evidence of validity includes correlations between the TFLS and other measures of adaptive functioning, memory, and cognition. The validity of TFLS scores in the aforementioned clinical groups also was examined. In the adaptive functioning domain, the TFLS was compared to performance on the Independent Living Scales (ILS), a similar measure that directly assesses skills required to live independently, and the Adaptive Behavior Assessment System—Second Edition (ABAS-II; Harrison & Oakland, 2003), a self- or other-report measure of adaptive functioning. In a sample of 27 examinees diagnosed with mild to moderate dementia, the research edition of the TFLS apparently showed strong correlations with the ILS, though these data are not printed in the examiner's manual. Nonetheless, the findings suggest measurement of similar constructs. The final edition of the TFLS and the ILS subsequently were administered to a sample of 77 nonclinical examinees. As predicted, correlations in this sample were low to moderate (.14 to .47), given the restricted score range one would expect in a sample of normally developing and aging adults. Likewise, correlations between the TFLS and the ABAS-II were small (.03 to .26), which the test authors suggest are likely due to the restricted range issues and the different format of the instruments. Correlations between the TFLS and ABAS-II in the clinical group sample were significantly higher, ranging from .41 to .80.

Correlations of the TFLS with measures of memory and other cognitive abilities yielded similar findings. In essence, there were low correlations in the normative sample between measures of episodic memory, verbal comprehension, perceptual reasoning, working memory, processing speed, and general cognitive ability, and the TFLS *T*-score. Correlations were higher in the special group sample, ranging from .67 (WMS-IV Auditory Memory) to .80 (Visual Working Memory) on the memory measures and from .71 (WAIS-IV Perceptual Reasoning Index and Processing Speed Index) to .79 (Full Scale IQ). Performance on the TFLS also was compared to the general neuropsychological functioning on the Repeatable Battery for the Assessment of Neuropsychological Status (RBANS). Correlations in the normative sample ranged from .28 (Attention and Delayed Memory) to .44 (Total Scale), suggesting a moderate relationship between neurocognitive functioning and IADLs. Finally, discriminant validity of the TFLS was demonstrated through the special group studies comparing the performance of different clinical groups. As would be predicted, individuals in the Probable Alzheimer's Disease, Intellectual Disability–Mild and Moderate Severity, Schizophrenia, and Autistic Disorder groups all exhibited significantly greater difficulties with IADLs than their matched control groups. Diagnoses of Major Depressive Disorder and Traumatic Brain Injury did not appear to affect performance on the TFLS.

COMMENTARY. The developers of the TFLS appear to have achieved the goals they intended to reach. The TFLS is, indeed, brief, portable and easy to administer, score, and interpret. Of slight inconvenience are the additional materials the examiner must provide. However, this problem is easily alleviated by a few extra minutes of planning and organization. The TFLS has a large and nationally representative normative base and good psychometric properties. Although not discussed in the examiner's manual, the TFLS also appears to have good ecological validity, which is an important factor to consider when evaluating individuals who may resist measures that seem unrelated to the difficulties they are experiencing. Limitations of the TFLS include the requirement of intact fine motor control for successful performance of many of the items, which could result in scores that underestimate an individual's functioning. In such situations, use of the ILS, for example, may be more appropriate given the large number of items on that instrument that require only a verbal response. Additionally, the Memory subscale includes only three items that do not take into account many important aspects of memory, such as the ability to learn and retain new information. Thus, it is strongly recommended that examiners using the TFLS include additional instruments to assess different aspects of memory functioning. A complete picture of memory functioning is especially important for treatment planning in order to build on an individual's strengths and to devise compensatory strategies for an individual's limitations. Finally, continued research with special clinical groups would bolster the clinical applicability of the TFLS. Compared to the normative sample, the special group sample sizes are small and, in some cases, do not cover the full age range, though certain diagnoses, such as Alzheimer's Disease, would naturally restrict the age range of the participants.

SUMMARY. The TFLS is a brief, portable, and easily administered performance-based measure of instrumental activities of daily living related to the capacity to function independently. It is an informative adjunct to traditional neurocognitive assessment and measures of functional capacity that utilize reports from family members or other caregivers. The test authors present detailed information on the instrument's reliability and validity, and they convey a strong rationale for the use of the TFLS to aid in differential diagnosis and treatment planning. In sum, the TFLS is a welcome addition to the rather limited arsenal of psychometric instruments that directly assess independent living skills.

REVIEWER'S REFERENCES

Harrison, P. L., & Oakland, T. (2003). Adaptive Behavior Assessment System–Second Edition. San Antonio, TX: The Psychological Corporation.

Loeb, P. A. (1996). *Independent Living Scales*. San Antonio, TX: The Psychological Corporation.

Wechsler, D. (2009). Wechsler Memory Scale—Fourth Edition. San Antonio, TX: Pearson.

[148]

The Token Test for Children, Second Edition.

Purpose: Designed to identify "children who are significantly below their peers in early receptive language development."
Population: Children ages 3-0 to 12-11.
Publication Dates: 1978–2007.
Acronym: TTFC-2.
Scores: Total score only.
Administration: Individual.
Parts, 4: I, II, III, IV.
Price Data, 2007: $135 per complete kit including 50 examiner record forms, 20 tokens, and manual (2007, 69 pages); $45 per 50 examiner record forms; $30 per 20 tokens; $65 per manual.
Time: 10(20) minutes.
Authors: Ronnie L. McGhee, David J. Ehrler, and Frank DiSimoni.
Publisher: PRO-ED.
Cross References: See T5:2768 (43 references) and T4:2846 (24 references); for reviews by William M. Reynolds and John Salvia of an earlier edition, see 9:1295 (9 references); see also T3:2509 (1 reference).

Review of the Token Test for Children, Second Edition by CHRISTINE NOVAK, Associate Clinical Professor, and ZARABETH GERLING, Doctoral Student, School Psychology Program, The University of Iowa, Iowa City, IA:

DESCRIPTION. The Token Test for Children, Second Edition (TTFC-2) is a rapid screening measure designed to assess receptive language in children ages 3 years, 0 months to 12 years, 11 months. It is updated from a 1978 version developed by DiSimoni. The TTFC-2 has three purposes: "to identify children who are significantly below their peers in early receptive language development" (examiner's manual, p. 2); to serve as a research tool for studying language development in young children; and to accompany other assessment techniques to provide a comprehensive assessment of language. The TTFC-2 is intended to provide a sensitive measure of listening comprehension that is empirically and theoretically grounded. It is deemed useful for estimating language competence when expressive skills are depressed (as in Broca's aphasia) and as a baseline for determining the effectiveness of interventions.

The TTFC-2 requires the manipulation of tokens differentiated by size (large and small) and color (blue, green, yellow, white, and red) in response to verbal instructions. The TTFC-2 includes three verbally presented practice items; if the child fails practice items, test items are not administered. There are 46 test items of increasing difficulty, all of which are administered in consecutive order. Testing time is generally 10–15 minutes; there are no time limits.

Administration and scoring are relatively straightforward. This reviewer believes that rules surrounding repetition of items and modeling correct responses could be stated more clearly. For example, the manual states, "Do not repeat any stimulus item" (p. 6), which is reinforced for situations when the child appears to not be listening; however, later on the same page, the examiner is instructed to repeat the command from the beginning if the child has initiated a response before the entire instruction has been given. Similarly, on the same page, the manual emphasizes "Under no circumstances should you model the correct response" (p. 6); but the examiner is instructed to demonstrate touching the tokens briefly or sequentially if the child holds his or her fingers on the tokens or attempts to touch them both at the same time. The record form is convenient in that it lists the standardized instructions for each item and provides a depiction for the arrangement of tokens. Each item is scored either correct or incorrect and the manual indicates specific requirements for giving credit.

The TTFC-2 yields raw scores, standard scores, percentile ranks, and age equivalents. The authors provide clear explanations of the types of scores and appropriate cautions for relying on a single instrument for decision making. Although limitations of age equivalent scores are referenced, more explicit direction for interpretation might reduce misuse. Additionally, responsible use of test results might be enhanced through more direct prompts for reporting score ranges and the use of confidence intervals in examples.

DEVELOPMENT. The TTFC-2 is an updated version of the Token Test for Children (DiSimoni, 1978), which was designed to meet the need for a quick and easily administered listening comprehension screening test specifically for young children. Despite improvements in administration procedures and increased sample size over adult versions used with children, many technical flaws remained. The current revision represents efforts to ameliorate technical flaws as outlined by Reynolds (1985) in the *Ninth Mental Measurements Yearbook*. Specifically, the authors of the TTFC-2 collected all new normative data and stratified the sample according to geographic region, age, gender, race and ethnicity, and exceptionality status; provided a total score that has a mean of 100 and a standard deviation of 15; revised items to increase difficulty level; expanded instructions for administration, scoring, and interpretation; and conducted studies to demonstrate the reliability of the test and to provide preliminary support for its intended uses.

TECHNICAL.

Standardization. The TTFC-2 normative sample consists of over 100 children at each year level between 3 and 12, with the greatest number at age 9 (n = 153) and smallest number at age 4 (n = 103). According to the manual, these children were drawn from 136 communities representing inner-city, urban, and rural areas. Overall, the sample conforms to the 2001 U.S. Census in terms of region, gender, race, and ethnicity. No information was provided regarding socioeconomic status of the sample, or the specific breakdown by community size. The inclusion of Gifted and Talented students, as well as those identified with select disabilities (i.e., including Specific Language Impairment, Learning Disability, and Mental Retardation), is difficult to evaluate completely because population estimates are not provided for comparison in 3/9 categories; where numbers are provided, there appears to be a fair match.

Data for the whole sample are compared to estimates for the school-aged population, whereas individual age group data are compared to estimates for the U.S. population at large. For the most part, these two referents yield similar percentages; however, the population estimate for the "Other" ethnicity category does not correspond well to race or ethnicity categories reported for the school-age population, which is confusing. With that aside, there is generally good conformity except for substantially more 4-year-olds from the Northeast and fewer of this same group from the South than expected. Although less discrepant, there were also fewer Black 5-year-olds and fewer Hispanic 6-year-olds than might be expected given the Census.

Reliability. The authors present three types of reliability data: internal consistency, test-retest, and interscorer. Scores from the entire standardization sample were used to establish internal consistency for each of the 10 age groups. The coefficient alphas ranged from .80 (3-year-old group) to .95 (9-year-old group) and averaged .90. Considering that the purpose of the test is to provide screening, these alphas appear quite acceptable. Additionally, the alphas for nine subgroups (Male, Female, White, African American, Hispanic, Attention Deficit Hyperactivity Disorder, Learning Disability, Mental Retardation, Specific Language Impairment) ranged from .90 to .98, indicating that the TTFC-2 is equally reliable across the identified subgroups.

Test-retest reliability was determined using a sample of 169 from three southern states; these children ranged in age from 3 to 12 years. Students identified as African American or exceptional were well-represented within this sample, whereas Hispanic students were only represented well in the 3–5-year-old group. Testing occurred 2 weeks apart, resulting in respectable correlations from .93 to .97.

Six professionals independently scored videotaped performances of three different children to establish interscorer reliability. Whether these professionals had any specific training in scoring the TTFC-2 was not indicated; however, all were from professions in which basic training in assessment would be anticipated. The resulting reliability coefficients of .99 point to clarity of scoring criteria.

Validity. Validity was explored via item analysis, including item discrimination, item difficulty, and differential item functioning. Using the standardization sample data, these procedures yielded results that met generally accepted criteria.

The basis for content sampling was described; an independent panel was not utilized to judge the adequacy of sampling from the domain.

Scores from the TTFC-2 were correlated with scores from the Test of Early Language Development—Third Edition, Receptive One-Word Picture Vocabulary Test—2000 Edition, and the Expressive One-Word Picture Vocabulary Test—2000 Edition as preliminary investigations of concurrent validity. The samples used in these studies ranged in age from 3 to 12 years. Again, African American children were well-represented, whereas Hispanic children were minimally included or excluded. Correlations were large as would be expected among language tests, and a higher degree of relation was demonstrated for receptive than for expressive measures consistent with the nature of the TTFC-2.

Several studies were also undertaken to examine the construct validity of the TTFC-2. Mean scores from the standardization sample evidenced steady increases across individual age groups, and raw scores were highly correlated with age consistent with the developmental nature of language skills. Mean scores for demographic subgroups also followed expectation in that there was little variability across gender, race, and ethnicity. However, the mean for Gifted students was above average, whereas means for students with Specific Language Impairment and Learning Disability were below average, but above the means for students with Mental Retardation or Autism.

The TTFC-2 also correlated highly with various measures of academic and cognitive skills, indicating a pattern of higher correlations with subtests purporting to measure listening comprehension, oral language, and verbal ability than subtests focusing on nonverbal skills, writing, or math. Not surprisingly, correlations with measures of processing speed and memory were also in the large to very large range, suggesting potential contribution to performance as indicated by the authors when discussing interpretation guidelines.

COMMENTARY. The strengths of the TTFC-2 include quick administration, easy-to-follow directions, and generally strong psychometric properties. Preliminary evidence to support unbiased results for various demographic groups is presented. Intended applications for which support is lacking include (a) identification of children who may be prone to later academic failure, especially reading; (b) evaluation of specialized interventions to improve language functioning; (c) investigation of effects of language on social emotional functioning; and (d) unique contribution to comprehensive language evaluation.

SUMMARY. The TTFC-2 represents a commendable improvement over the previous Token Test for Children. Its popularity as a useful clinical tool is likely to continue given the test's briefness and tight focus. As such, users are reminded to heed the authors' caution that the TTFC-2 is a screening measure and more comprehensive assessment may be necessary.

REVIEWER'S REFERENCES

DiSimoni, F. G. (1978). The Token Test for Children. Austin, TX: PRO-ED.

Reynolds, W. M. (1985). [Review of The Token Test for Children]. In J. V. Mitchell, Jr. (Ed.), *The ninth mental measurements yearbook* (pp. 1629–1630). Lincoln, NE: Buros Institute of Mental Measurements.

Review of the Token Test for Children, Second Edition by GENE SCHWARTING, Associate Professor, Fontbonne University, St. Louis, MO:

DESCRIPTION. The general purpose of the Token Test for Children, Second Edition (TTFC-2) is to serve as a rapid screening measure of receptive language for children between 3 years, 0 months and 12 years, 11 months of age. In addition, the authors note it might be used for research or as a part of a comprehensive language assessment battery. The TTFC-2 is designed for use by speech-language pathologists, school psychologists, special education teachers, educational specialists, and other personnel trained in standardized test administration. The instrument is not timed, but administration time is estimated as 10 to 15 minutes; if responses are delayed more than 15 seconds, the examiner is encouraged to request a response and issue a score of 0 if none is forthcoming. When used with very young children, a break during the assessment might be considered.

The test kit consists of an administration/scoring manual, record booklets, and a set of 20 "tokens"—small plastic circles and squares in five colors and two sizes. The examiner is to be seated to the side and behind the child rather than the more familiar assessment seating arrangement. Verbal responses are not required of the child for any of the items.

Administration begins with familiarizing the child to the shapes, sizes, and colors of the tokens, which are placed on the table in a specific arrangement. Next, it is emphasized to the child that directions can be given only once for each task of touching the appropriate tokens, and administering three sample items to verify understanding. Then, the entire test, consisting of 46 items divided into four parts, is administered. Part 1 involves 10 tasks using tokens based on three attributes—"Touch the large yellow square." Part 2 involves 10 items of identifying two of the large tokens with two attributes each—involving the touching of items by color and shape; Part 3 also contains 10 tasks using all tokens with three attributes each—color, size, and shape. Part 4 again involves all tokens, but requires more complex directions including basic concepts (e.g., "After touching the red square, pick up the white square"). Thus, the parts are of increasing difficulty, whereas items within each part are of approximately equal difficulty.

Scoring is (1) for a response that is correct in its entirety (no partial credit given), and (0) for incorrect or partially correct responses. Raw scores are converted into standard scores (mean of 100 and standard deviation of 15) and percentiles using the norms tables, with age intervals of the tables ranging from 1 month at 3 years of age to nearly 2 years at ages 11 to 12 years, 11 months. The raw scores can also be converted through a separate table into age equivalents.

DEVELOPMENT. The original Token Test was designed in 1962 by DeRenzi and Vignolo as a tool to assess receptive language deficits in adults with aphasia. A number of versions of this original instrument were produced over the years, with the Token Test for Children being developed by DiSimoni in 1978. This instrument for children ages 3 years, 0 months to 12 years, 6 months utilized the same tokens as the present version. It also involved standardized directions and was normed on over 1,300 children. In the review of this instrument in *The Ninth Mental Measurements Yearbook,* numerous concerns were raised as to the validity, reliability, norms, and type of standard scores obtained. The authors of the TTFC-2 noted those concerns, and attempted to address them in the current instrument. In addition, the authors indicate a number of items from the previous version were deleted and new ones added; however, information as to this process is not provided in the manual.

TECHNICAL. The TTFC-2 was normed in 2004–2005 on a sample of 1,310 children in 22 states. Selection was based on geographic area, gender, race, and exceptionality status, and the 2000 U.S. Census was approximated for each of these characteristics. For each year of age 10–11% of the norm group was included, except for age 4, which was only 8%.

Test reliability was measured a number of different ways. Internal consistency for the entire norm group, using coefficient alpha, varied from .80 at age 3 to .95 at age 9, with an overall average of .90. The resulting standard error of measurement varied from 7 to 3 for the same ages, respectively, with an overall average of 5. When coefficient alpha was used for the disability norm subgroups, the results varied from .90 for children with learning disabilities to .98 for those with mental retardation. Variation based on gender or ethnicity ranged from .96 to .97. Test-retest reliability on 169 children, with a 14-day time interval, ranged from .93–.97 across samples. A limited measure of interrater reliability, conducted with six educational professionals independently scoring three videotaped assessments, was .99.

As with reliability, validity is assessed from several perspectives. Item analysis on the entire norm group indicated that item difficulty varied from .19 at age 3 to .88 at age 12, with an average of .65. Mean scores progressively increase with chronological age, with a correlation of .74 between these scores and chronological age (CA). Mean scores obtained by subgroups of the norm group varied less than 6 points by gender or ethnicity; larger variations were noted for subgroups based on giftedness or verified disabilities.

Concurrent validity was measured through comparing the TTFC-2, the Test of Early Language Development—Third Edition, the Receptive One-Word Picture Vocabulary Test—2000 Edition, and the Expressive One-Word Picture Vocabulary Test—2000. Correlations with receptive language measures were .89 and .84, whereas those with expressive language were .75 and .70. Relationships of the TTFC-2 with academic achievement measures and tests of intelligence were also conducted and reported, with the strongest correlations noted in language-based skills, as anticipated.

In summary, the technical characteristics of the TTFC-2 appear to be solid. The norm group is sufficiently large and representative of the 2000 population. Reliability and validity data are presented in several forms and appear to meet the psychometric standards.

COMMENTARY. This second edition of the Token Test for Children addresses the concerns noted on the initial version through provision of an adequate norm group, change of the standard score format, and adequate documentation of reliability as well as validity. The instrument has been extensively used over the years and is relatively easy to administer and score. The premise of the test, that understanding of 5 colors, 2 shapes, and 2 sizes is adequate to measure receptive vocabulary, is a cause for concern as it would appear instead to be an assessment of auditory memory. In addition, the adequacy of the floor for young children (a raw score of 7 obtains a standard score of 100 at age 3 years) as well as the ceiling for older children (a raw score of 39 of 46 items obtains a standard score of 100 at age 11) also raise questions. However, the authors emphasize that the TTFC-2 is a screening instrument, rather than a diagnostic one, and that it should be used in that manner and provide evidence supportive of construct validity.

SUMMARY. The TTFC-2 is a significant improvement over its predecessor. But it should be considered for screening purposes only.

[149]

Transdisciplinary Play-Based Assessment, 2nd Edition.

Purpose: Designed as a multidimensional approach to identifying service needs, developing intervention plans, and evaluating progress in children.
Population: Birth to age 6.
Publication Dates: 1990-2008.
Acronym: TPBA2.
Scores: 4 domains: Sensorimotor, Emotional and Social, Communication, Cognitive Development.
Administration: Individual.
Price Data, 2009: \$329.95 per 3-volume set with forms CD including Administration Guide for TPBA2 & TPBI2 (2008, 408 pages), Transdisciplinary Play-Based Intervention, 2nd Edition (2008, 672 pages), Transdisciplinary Play-Based Assessment, 2nd Edition (2008, 464 pages), and forms CD; \$149.95 per 3-volume set including Administration Guide for TPBA2 & TPBI2, Transdisciplinary Play-Based Intervention, 2nd Edition, and Transdisciplinary Play-Based Assessment, 2nd Edition; \$54.95 per Transdisciplinary Play-Based Assessment, 2nd Edition; \$59.95 per Transdisciplinary Play-Based Intervention, 2nd Edition; \$54.95 per Administration Guide for TPBA2 & TPBI2; \$39.95 per 5 tablets of forms; \$229.95 per forms CD.
Time: (60-90) minutes.
Comments: Ratings by transdisciplinary team; no domain scores; compares observations to age tables that outline appropriate skills for each age.
Author: Toni Linder.
Publisher: Paul H. Brookes Publishing Co., Inc.
Cross References: For reviews by Terry Overton and Gary J. Stainback of the previous edition, see 13:352.

Review of the Transdisciplinary Play-Based Assessment, 2nd Edition by DAVID R. HOLLIWAY, Assistant Professor, Educational Leadership and Counseling Psychology, Washington State University Tri-Cities, Richland, WA:

DESCRIPTION. The Transdisciplinary Play-Based Assessment, 2nd Edition (TPBA2) and the Transdisciplinary Play-Based Intervention, 2nd Edition (TPBI2) are state of the art, mixed methods, team-based assessment and intervention programs that offer multiple data points on the developmental trends of infants, toddlers, and preschoolers up to age 6. The TPBA has a well-documented history of at least 20 years, but the TPBA2 offers new adaptations consistent with current research on child development and advances in research methodology. The TPBA is a naturalistic, "authentic" play-based assessment that involves a team of caregivers including family, teachers, and other health professionals. This multidimensional team-based approach gathers information over a variety of contexts and over a variety of cognitive, social, and emotional areas. The TPBA2 provides the assessment information for later intervention with the TPBI2. As well, the TPBA2 meets the federal guidelines for IDEA, and the assessment model is supported by the Division of Early Childhood of the Council for Exceptional Children.

The TPBA2 is composed of three separate but interrelated assessment lenses: (a) The Child and Family History Questionnaire (CFHQ), (b) The Family Assessment of Child Functioning (FACF), and (c) the TPBA2 Observation Guidelines and Age Tables. Both professional and parental observations are gathered adding a rich and complete picture of individual children's functioning. The assessment information serves as a basis for creating Individual Education Programs (IEP) and individualized family service plans (IFSP). The transdisciplinary play-based assessment process is clearly outlined in the administration guide for the TPBA2 and TPBI2, using a flow chart that details the coverage and implementation of the assessment process.

The TPBA is an adaptable and integrative assessment model that allows parents and care professionals the ability to plan assessment sessions around a variety of possible settings where parents can be integrated into the play session. The play session creates an assessment context wherein unstructured and structured play is facilitated by a play facilitator. The play session offers a contrast to more standardized question and answer formats because the informal, social nature of the session leads to children who are free to initiate their own play and interactions with others who may be involved in the assessment session.

Play-based assessment is a flexible model of assessment wherein an assessment team and family members, as well as the child being assessed, interact during a play session that typically unfolds over the course of an hour to an hour and a half. The play facilitator moves between unstructured and structured play activities, some initiated by the child and some by the play facilitator. Another team member serves as the family facilitator, dialoguing with family members about their observations of the child.

The session is free flowing and incorporates various types of play, including fine and gross motor activities, social and cognitive play with various props, art and music activities, and so forth. Virtually all aspects of the play session may be shifted or modified as needed to accommodate the child's developmental, emotional, or behavioral needs. During each activity the child is observed in spontaneous play and interactions prior to the play facilitator encouraging higher levels of play activity. Other components included during the play session involve play with parents and, if possible, with a sibling or peer. Family members also leave the room for a few minutes to enable the team to see the child's reaction to separation and reunion. A snack occurs as the final component and provides the team one more opportunity to observe the child's self-help, oral and fine motor, and social skills.

The entire play session is videotaped for later fine tune viewing. It is recommended that when possible and when applicable to individual children, the transdisciplinary team include a speech-language pathologist, a physical therapist, a teacher or psychologist, and, of course, the parent(s). Other care professionals can be included depending on the particular child's needs and the concerns of the parents and the professionals involved in the assessment. The emphasis here is to have multiple perspectives offered in the assessment.

Overall, the multiphase play session allows an assessment team to observe children in spontaneous behaviors, encourages turn-taking through imitation, responds to each child's developmental level, encourages more performance-based scaffolding, provides opportunities for problem solving and creativity, and promotes social interaction. During the assessment session, the team can observe the skills and behaviors of each child, as well as the emotional, social, cognitive, and creative abilities unique to each child.

The TPBA2 serves both assessment and intervention purposes by being flexible and modifiable for each child so that their unique developmental characteristics can be honored. The qualitative nature of the observations makes the information gleaned contextual and specific to each child's learning. The situational aspects observed through the TPBA2 render a more culturally and developmentally sensitive picture of each child's development, allowing that information then to be incorporated into an intervention plan that directly relates to the child's daily routines, life-experiences, and skills.

DEVELOPMENT. Although test development information is not provided in the administration guide for TPBA2 and TPBI2, a thorough discussion is included that focuses on the changing views of childhood assessment, and the changing values and belief about the general nature of assessment. The strengths of authentic assessment versus the limits of standardized testing are compared, suggesting that a more dynamic, natural, holistic, and flexible procedure offers a more detailed account of a child's developmental characteristics. In the TPBI2, an overview of the TPBA offers a child's point of view as if they were going through a "traditional" assessment versus the transdisciplinary approach. For example, traditional standardized tests can offer important screening and diagnostic information that allows for norm-referenced comparisons of children within the same age bracket. With a standardized approach, there is an assumption that the child is of normal developmental accomplishments, understands the language of the assessment, is familiar with the manipulatives that may be used, and assumes there are no developmental disabilities or language constraints. As well, the test authors suggest that a traditional assessment usually involves a lone professional working with the child in a restrictive environment that can inhibit small children from acting natural. One of the biggest limits of standardized assessment is that they can take a deficit view of children by focusing on what the child cannot do, rather than focusing on what could be learned.

On the other hand, in the play-based assessment, the authentic alternative is supported with current professional literature as well. "The TPBA2 derives from the integration of input from hundreds of families, and professionals and the results of current research across many aspects in the field of child development and early childhood special education" (administration guide, p. 3).

TECHNICAL. The TPBA is theoretically sound and has been extensively researched. The original TPBA has a long history since its publication in 1990. Evidence reported in the administration guide for the TPBA2 and the TPBI2 includes interrater reliability, test-retest reliability, and content criterion evidence validity of test scores.

Validity. Construct and content validity were investigated by asking 12 national and international childhood experts (Linder, Goldberg, & Goldberg, 2007) to participate in a survey related to all the content present in the TPBA2. Each expert was asked to respond to how frequently a problem in one subdomain (e.g., Cognitive, Emotional) related to another problem in another subdomain (e.g., Communication) based on a frequency scale of *never, rarely, sometimes, frequently, always.* Across the 28 subdomains that were investigated, 90% of the problems rated by the experts indicated that there was a degree of transdisciplinary influence, suggesting that there is a strong interdependent relationship between subdomains and within domains. This in turn suggested support for the construct definitions utilized in the transdisciplinary assessment and intervention. In addition to the survey, the same 12 experts were asked to comment on each domain, and the definitions of the content for each subdomain within their area of expertise. This evidence also demonstrated that the subdomains are conceptually strong.

Both families and professionals appear to find the transdisciplinary approach useful and a welcome alternative over standardized approaches. The test authors address this finding as social validity. For example, when the TPBA was compared with a standardized assessment, the staff and parental rating for each developmental profile item were compared between each other and compared with the standardized assessment (not named in the guide) the mean agreement was 51.8% for the TPBA and 46.5% for the standardized assessment. Parents also suggested that they were more at ease with the TPBA because they were actual participants in the process and could ask questions during the assessment, a process not available in a more standardized approach.

Reliability. Recent interrater reliability studies indicate that rater scores of the TPBA2 tend to be strong across raters of differing expertise levels and that rater scores can increase with increased training on the assessment. Specifically, four groups of participants (two different 2-day training groups, graduate students studying the TPBA2, and professionals who had used the TPBA2 for the last several years) were asked to observe sections of tape-recorded TPBA play sessions of four different children. The children's developmental level ranged from typical to moderate developmental delay. The raters were given no information on the children. All raters used the TPBA2 Observation Guidelines and Age Tables to determine whether a child was *above average, typically developing, in need of monitoring,* or *a possible candidate for special services.* Across all domains and across all disciplinary groups there was strong agreement. Interrater correlation coefficients ranged from .89 for a 2-day training group to 1.00 for experts who have frequently used the TPBA2.

In the revised administration guide for the TPBA2 and TPBI2 it is suggested that "the level of agreement was greatest for children who were typically developing or had moderate delays. When concerns were mild, observers were more cautious and ratings were spread across Watch and Concern" (p. 23). Also of importance here is to note that when interrater scores were compared between individual assessors and a team of assessors, the teams usually approached 100% agreement, again suggesting that the TPBA2 is very strong when used as a team assessment process.

COMMENTARY. The TPBA and TPBI are well established in early childhood assessment practices. There is not much that could be added to improve what this full package can offer. The play-based process is well supported by research directly focused on the TPBA. In the current research and assessment cultures, "mixed methods" have gained a widely held preference by professional educators and researchers. For example, the American Educational Research Association recently published *The Handbook of Complementary Methods in Education Research* (Green, Camilli, & Elmore, 2006) wherein the major theme through the volume is that no single method is desirable in research but multiple approaches can garner complementary evidence giving a fuller data base to support claims about educational research questions. The TPBA2 is consistent with the AERA's call for integrating methods in research. Other research approaches also emphasize a mixed-methods perspective on gathering data for high-stakes decision making (e.g., deMarrais & Lapan, 2004; Green et al., 2006; Johnson & Onwuegbuzie, 2004; Tashakkori & Teddlie, 2003).

The TPBA is clearly a mixed methods assessment approach offering multiple sources of evidence on the nuanced development of individual children. The TPBA2 and TPBI2 both offer a rich assessment perspective because the assessments are done with collaborative teams including various professionals and parents. The assessments are child-led in that spontaneous play and socialization are encouraged, and the data are collected both formatively and summatively, numerically and qualitatively. One of the strongest components of the TPBA is the video recording of the play session that is made for further study and interrater comparisons. The video allows for multiple viewings of the unique, subtle, and often overlooked interactions that children demonstrate in an open, inviting, play-based environment.

SUMMARY. The research of the past and present support that the TPBA is extensive and impressive. The TPBA2 has strong supporting evidence that it is a comprehensive assessment tool modifiable to any context. The TPBA2 is well suited for identifying children who may have developmental delays and those in need of family and educational services. As well, the TPBA2 is ideal for describing those children who are typically functioning. Few other assessment and intervention programs can offer as extensive and converging perspectives as does the TPBA2 and the TPBI2. The TPBA2 is strongly recommended for early childhood intervention assessments.

REVIEWER'S REFERENCES

deMarrais, K., & Lapan, S. (Eds.). (2004). *Foundations for research: Methods of inquiry in education and the social sciences.* Mahwah, NJ: Lawrence Erlbaum Associates.

Green, J., Camilli, G., & Elmore. P. (2006). *The handbook of complementary methods in education research.* Mahwah, NJ: Lawrence Erlbaum Associates.

Johnson, R., & Onwuegbuzie, A. (2004). Mixed methods research: A paradigm whose time has come. *Educational Researcher, 33,* 14-26.

Linder, T. W., Goldberg, D., & Goldberg, M. (2007). *Validity of "transdisciplinary" as a construct: Implications for assessment and intervention.* Manuscript submitted for publication.

Tashakkori, A., & Teddlie, C. (2003). *Handbook of mixed methods in social and behavioral research.* Thousand Oaks, CA: SAGE Publications.

Review of the Transdisciplinary Play-Based Assessment, 2nd Edition by BECKY L. SPRITZ, Associate Professor of Psychology, Roger Williams University, Bristol, RI:

DESCRIPTION. The Transdisciplinary Play-Based System consists of three volumes designed to guide assessments of and interventions for children's development between the ages of birth through age 6. The package contains the Transdisciplinary Play-Based Assessment, 2nd Edition (TPBA2), the Transdisciplinary Play-Based Intervention, 2nd Edition (TPBI2), and the administration guide for these instruments. This system provides an individualized approach for professionals in Early Intervention and Early Childhood Special Education. A primary goal is the thorough diagnostic assessment of children for mild to moderate developmental delays. Additionally, as noted by the test authors, the consolidation of the TPBA and TPBI is intended to enhance the development and monitoring of effective, functional intervention programs for young children who are identified as having or who may be at-risk for developmental delays.

Four developmental domains are included: Sensorimotor, Emotional/Social, Communication, and Cognitive. These domains are similar to those of other developmental screening and assessment instruments such as the Battelle Developmental Inventory-2 (BDI-2) and the Denver Developmental Screening Test II (DDST-II). Within the TPBA2, guidelines are also provided for screening children's auditory and visual domains.

A child's developmental level is determined via subjective observations and "informed clinical opinion" (administration guide, 2008; p. 10) regarding a child's performance of skills and behaviors relative to peers within each domain. Scoring requires professionals to compare their qualitative evaluations of the child to chronological age descriptions provided in the manuals. The scoring procedure yields subdomain scores indicating either the percentage of delay or the percentage of performance above same-age peers.

No standardized testing materials are provided. Professionals are guided in utilizing familiar toys and materials to assess a child's performance within subcategories of each domain.

DEVELOPMENT. Consistent with the first edition of the TPBA, the assessment and treatment processes espoused within the second edition are grounded in standard practices for early intervention (Sandall, McLean, & Smith, 2000). Such approaches emphasize the ecological validity of the testing situation over other psychometric standards of reliability and validity. Interdisciplinary collaboration and parental involvement in the assessment and treatment processes are also key features of this approach.

New to this edition are tools for gathering relevant child and family information to be used as part of the assessment, including forms for recording child and family history and caregiver reports of daily childcare routines. The manuals have been substantially expanded to provide guidelines for involving caregivers in the assessment process, for orchestrating play to elicit relevant behaviors, and for report writing. Compared to the previous edition, the TPBA2 and TPBI2 are more closely linked to facilitate the assessment to intervention process.

The test authors take steps to acknowledge variation in state eligibility guidelines for assessments and interventions for children with developmental delays. These are noted throughout the manuals and on the respective scoring forms. However, as acknowledged by the test authors, some state guidelines mandate the use of standardized assessment tools for determining eligibility for services. In these cases, the TPBA2 by itself would be an insufficient means by which to evaluate a child's developmental level.

TECHNICAL. Because emphasis is placed upon idiographic assessment, no standardized item set is provided, nor do the test authors provide norms specific to the instrument. The scoring criteria for the instrument are derived from comprehensive reviews of the research literature that vary for each domain. These should not, however, be mistaken for norms. Using this approach is particularly problematic for assessing development in children from economically and culturally diverse groups.

Given the lack of a standardized item set, reliability is reported solely in terms of interrater agreement of videotaped assessments (Linder, 2005). The results indicate strong interrater reliability in classifying normally developing children and children with moderate levels of delay. Professionals were less reliable and accurate in identifying children with mild or questionable delays. Practice effects and familiarity with interdisciplinary team members also influenced agreement.

Issues of validity are also not adequately addressed. Some evidence is provided for the criterion validity of the TPBA2 compared to the Battelle Development Inventory-2 (BDI-2) (DeBruin, 2005), although the test authors note that modifications of the assessment process were required to derive these comparisons. Emphasis is placed on the social validity of the instrument based upon parent perceptions of the TPBA and the BDI-2. This research indicates that parents perceive the TPBA2 to be a more user-friendly means of assessing their child's development.

COMMENTARY. The Transdisciplinary Play-Based Assessment System provides an overarching structure for the assessment and treatment process of young children consistent with standard practices of early intervention. The test authors are extremely well-versed in the field of early childhood interventions and in federal eligibility guidelines for early childhood services. The strength of the system is that it provides a comprehensive strategy for training professionals on how to engage in transdisciplinary assessment and treatment. This individualized approach is likely to provide an ecologically valid picture of a child's developmental strengths and weaknesses that would be extremely useful for guiding interventions and monitoring treatment progress.

Most problematic is the lack of standardization of the TPBA2. Although the test authors themselves acknowledge that the instrument is not a developmental screening tool, the scoring of the instrument in the absence of standardized norms depends heavily on the training and judgment of the professional.

SUMMARY. The second edition of the Transdisciplinary Play-Based Assessment (TPBA2) and its complementary system, the Transdisciplinary Play-Based Intervention (TPBI2), was designed for the diagnostic assessment of children between birth and age 6 who have been identified with or who are at-risk for developmental delays. Although the theoretical foundations of the system are based upon accepted principles for early childhood assessment, its lack of standardization violates the assessment criteria of the *Standards for Educational and Psychological Testing* (AERA, APA, & NCME, 1999). It, therefore, should not be used as a developmental screening or assessment tool on its own. Professionals are strongly cautioned against using the scoring criteria to determine criteria for service eligibility. Some acceptable uses of the tool would be to obtain a qualitative description of a child's developmental strengths and weaknesses and for designing and monitoring early childhood interventions. A recommended list of developmental screening and assessment tools may be obtained from The National Early Childhood Technical Assistance Center (Ringwalt, 2008; http://www.nectac.org/~pdfs/pubs/screening.pdf).

REVIEWER'S REFERENCES

American Educational Research Association, American Psychological Association, & National Council on Measurement in Education. (1999). *Standards for educational and psychological testing.* Washington, DC: American Educational Research Association.

DeBruin, K. A. (2005). *A validation study of TPBA-R with the BDI-2.* Unpublished doctoral dissertation, University of Denver, Colorado.

Linder, T. W. (2005). *Interrater reliability of the revised Transdisciplinary Play-Based Assessment.* Unpublished manuscript, University of Denver, Colorado.

Sandall, S. R., McLeon, M. E., & Smith, B. J. (2000). *DEC recommended best practices in early intervention/early childhood special education.* Longmont, CO: Sopris West.

[150]

Vineland Adaptive Behavior Scales, Second Edition.

Purpose: Designed as an adaptive behavior assessment system that measures self-sufficiency across the life-span.
Population: Birth to age 90-11.
Publication Dates: 1935-2008.
Acronym: Vineland-II.
Scores, 16: 3 Communication scores: Receptive, Expressive, Written; 5 Daily Living Skills scores: Personal, Domestic, Community, Academic (Teacher Rating Form only), School Community (Teacher Rating Form only); 3 Socialization scores: Interpersonal Relationships, Play and Leisure Time, Coping Skills; 2 Motor Skills scores: Gross, Fine; Adaptive Behavior Composite, Maladaptive Behavior Index (optional), Maladaptive Behavior Critical Items (optional).
Administration: Individual.
Foreign Language Edition: Spanish interview and rating forms available for Survey and Expanded Interview forms.
Comments: A revision of the Vineland Social Maturity Scale by Edgar A. Doll.
Authors: Sara S. Sparrow, Domenic V. Cicchetti, and David A. Balla.
Publisher: Pearson.

a) SURVEY INTERVIEW FORM, PARENT/CAREGIVER RATING FORM.
Purpose: Designed to assess adaptive behavior via parent/caregiver report.
Population: Birth to age 90-11.
Price Data, 2009: $154.50 per Survey Forms starter kit including 10 Survey Interview forms, 10 Parent/Caregiver Rating forms, 10 Survey Interview reports to parents, 10 Survey reports to caregivers, and Survey Forms manual (2005, 326 pages); $74 per 25 Survey Interview forms; $74 per 25 Parent/Caregiver Rating forms; $29.75 per 25 Survey Interview forms report to parents; $29.75 per 25 Survey Forms report to caregivers; $103 per Survey Forms manual; $267 per Survey Forms ASSIST™ scoring software for Mac/Windows.
Time: 45(65) minutes.

b) TEACHER RATING FORM.
Purpose: Assessment of adaptive behavior within classroom and school settings.
Population: Ages 3-0 to 18-11.
Price Data: $103 per Teacher Rating Forms starter kit including 10 Teacher Rating Forms, 10 Teacher Rating reports to parents/caregivers, and Teacher Rating Form manual (2006, 238 pages); $68 per 25 Teacher Rating Forms; $29.85 per 25 Teacher Rating Form reports to parents/caregivers; $85.50 per Teacher Rating Form manual; $267 per Teacher Rating Form ASSIST™ scoring software for Mac/Windows.
Time: 20(40) minutes.

c) EXPANDED INTERVIEW FORM.
Purpose: Designed to provide a comprehensive assessment of adaptive behavior via a semistructured interview.
Population: Birth to age 90.
Price Data: $180 per Expanded Interview Form starter kit including 10 Expanded Interview Forms, 10 Expanded Form report to parents, 10 Expanded Form report to caregivers, and Expanded Form manual (2008, 326 pages); $350 per Expanded Form starter kit with ASSIST™ software; $72 per Expanded Interview Forms; $31 per 25 Expanded Form report to parents; $31 per 25 Expanded Form report to caregivers; $85.50 per Expanded Form manual.
Time: 25(90) minutes.

Cross References: See T5:2813 (156 references) and T4:2882 (62 references); for a review by Jerome M. Sattler of an earlier edition, see 10:381 (9 references); for a review by Iris Amos Campbell of an earlier Survey Form and Expanded Form, see 9:1327 (8 references); see also T3:2557 (38 references), 8:703 (23 references), T2:1428 (50 references), P:281 (21 references), 6:194 (20 references), and 5:120 (15 references); for reviews by William M. Cruickshank and Florence M. Teagarden of an earlier edition, see 4:94 (21 references); for reviews by C. M. Louttit and John W. M. Rothney and an excerpted review, see 3:107 (58 references); for reviews by Paul H. Furfey, Elaine F. Kinder, and Anna S. Starr, see 1:1143.

Review of the Vineland Adaptive Behavior Scales, Second Edition by STEPHANIE STEIN, Professor and Chair, Department of Psychology, Central Washington University, Ellensburg, WA:

DESCRIPTION. The Vineland Adaptive Behavior Scales, Second Edition (Vineland-II) represents a significant revision and update of the well-established and popular Vineland Adaptive Behavior Scales (Vineland ABS; Sparrow, Balla, & Cicchetti, 1984), which itself was a revision of Edgar Doll's original Vineland Social Maturity Scale (1935, 1965). The Vineland-II is an individually administered measure of adaptive behavior, which the test authors define as "the performance of daily activities required for personal and social sufficiency" (Survey Forms Manual, p. 6). The age range for the Vineland-II (birth to 90) represents a significant expansion from the Vineland ABS that was intended for individuals from birth to age 18. There continue to be three versions of the Vineland in the latest addition. The two survey forms (Survey Interview Form and Parent/Caregiver Rating Form) differ only with respect to method of administration (interview vs. rating scale). The Expanded Interview Form is intended to provide a more comprehensive measure of adaptive behavior as well as a basis for treatment planning. Finally, the Teacher Rating Form (TRF) is a revision of the Vineland ABS Classroom Edition Form with an expanded age range from ages 3 to 21.

Each of the versions of the Vineland-II measures the same four broad domains of functioning assessed in the Vineland ABS: Communication, Daily Living Skills, Socialization, and Motor Skills. The Communication domain assesses the subdomains of Receptive, Expressive, and Written Communication. The Daily Living Skills domain assesses the subdomains of Personal Skills (eating, dressing, hygiene), Domestic (performance of household tasks), and Community (the use of money, computer, time, telephone, and job skills) on the Survey and Expanded Interview Forms. The subdomains for the TRF have changed to include behaviors that are more relevant to the school environment. The Daily Living Skills subdomains are Personal (same as Survey Form), Academic (understanding of money, math, and time concepts), and School Community (following rules in the classroom and school, attention, and learning approaches). The Socialization domain assesses the person's ability to get along with others and to engage in leisure activities. This domain is further broken down into the subdomains of Interpersonal Relationships, Play and Leisure, and Coping Skills (degree of responsibility and sensitivity demonstrated to others). Finally, the Motor Skills domain (intended for children ages 6 and under) includes the subdomains of Gross and Fine motor skills. This subdomain can be administered to individuals aged 7 and older if a motor deficit is suspected. Finally, there is an optional Maladaptive Behavior domain that can be administered on all but the TRF if problem behaviors are suspected to interfere with the adaptive behavior functioning of individuals aged 3 years and older.

The Survey (Interview Form) and the Expanded Interview Form are both administered to parents and/or caregivers through a semistructured interview format, ranging in administration times from 20 to 60 minutes for the Survey Form and 25 to 90 minutes for the more in-depth Expanded Interview Form. The Survey (Parent/Caregiver Rating Form) and the TRF are both intended to be filled out independently as a rating scale by the respondent (parent, caregiver, or teacher) who is very familiar with the individual. The manuals (a separate one for each version) guide administration by providing suggestions for interview format (where applicable) and determining a starting point for assessment. The detailed scoring guidelines indicate how to score responses obtained through the interview process and how to establish basals and ceilings on each subdomain. The items on the TRF and Survey Forms use a 3-point scale (*Never, Sometimes or Partially, Usually*), whereas the Expanded Form has a 5-point scale (*Almost Always, Often, Sometimes, Rarely, Never*).

A variety of raw and derived scores are provided in the Vineland-II. First, there are clear guidelines for computing subdomain raw scores. Following this step, the tables provide corresponding *v*-scale scores (mean of 15 and standard deviation of 3) for each subdomain and maladaptive behavior raw score. Standard scores (mean of 100 and standard deviation of 15) are available for all of the primary domains and the overall Adaptive Behavior Composite (full scale score). Confidence intervals (based on the standard error of measurement; *SEM*) are provided at the 85%, 90%, and 95% confidence level for both *v*-scores and standard scores. Percentile ranks are also provided for domain scores and the Adaptive Behavior Composite. As with its predecessor, the Vineland-II provides five global adaptive levels as interpretive guides for each subdomain, domain, and Adaptive Behavior Composite: Low, Moderately Low, Adequate, Moderately High, and High. The exception to this pattern occurs in the Maladaptive Behavior subscales and Index that include the descriptive categories of Average, Elevated, and Clinically Significant. Though the manual also provides age equivalent scores for the subdomain raw scores, the test authors are careful to caution against reliance on these scores because of their inherent limitations and likelihood of being misinterpreted. Finally, stanines are provided for the subdomain and domain scores.

The Vineland-II manual provides detailed guidelines for recording scores on the Score Report form and Score Profile and for interpreting each type of score. Interpretive steps include describing the individual's general adaptive functioning (using the Adaptive Behavior Composite score and confidence interval), describing performance in adaptive behavior domains and subdomains, identifying strengths and weaknesses, generating hypotheses about fluctuations in profiles, and describing maladaptive behavior (where applicable).

DEVELOPMENT. The goal of the test authors was to revise the Vineland in response to feedback from clinicians and teachers, to incorporate changing cultural expectations, and to reflect recent research on developmental disabilities. In particular, the revisions in the Vineland-II reflect the greater cultural expectations for adaptive behavior in individuals with developmental disabilities associated with placement in least restrictive living environments. In addition, increased reliance on technology and the need for technological competence is recognized. Furthermore, the need to assess impairments in adaptive functioning in older individuals was addressed.

New items were developed for the Vineland-II to better assess individuals with disabilities who function independently and to improve the diagnostic utility and sensitivity of the measure. An initial pool of over 3,800 items was reviewed by an expert panel, resulting in the elimination of some items and revision of others. The items were then reviewed for relevance and bias by a set of experienced clinicians and the pool was further reduced. Starting with a group of over 5,800 individuals, the remaining items were then tried out on a random sample of 1,843 individuals from the general population and a clinical sample of 392 individuals. The sampling plan controlled for ethnic diversity, sex, SES, geographic region, and community size. The outcome data were analyzed at the item level for developmental sequence, item validity, item placement, clinical sensitivity, bias, and redundancy and at the subdomain level of internal consistency reliability, intercorrelations, and factor structure.

TECHNICAL. A nationally representative sample of individuals, from birth through age 90 (broken down into 20 age groups), comprised the standardization sample for the Survey Interview Form and Parent/Caregiver Rating Form ($n = 3,695$) and the Expanded Interview Form ($n = 2,151$). This sample was pulled from a much larger pool of over 25,000 individuals. Because of rapid developmental changes in the infant years and the need for early identification, a relatively higher proportion of the norm sample was clustered at birth through age 5 (about 30% for the Survey Interview Form; over 40% for the Expanded Interview Form). The TRF was administered to 2,570 teachers and daycare providers (from a larger pool of over 19,000) for 15 age groups of children, ranging from age 3 to 17/18. Even though the TRF is designed for students through age 21, students older than 18 were excluded from the sample because those who remain in secondary school through age 21 are not representative of their age-peers, most of whom are out of school and therefore do not have a teacher to complete the TRF. In all versions of the Vineland-II, the samples were designed to be evenly split between males and females and to match the 2001 U.S. Census data in the areas of race/ethnicity, SES, geographic region, community size, and special education placement. The clinical samples for each instrument included individuals diagnosed with one or more of the following conditions: attention deficit hyperactivity disorder (ADHD), autism (nonverbal or verbal), emotional/behavioral disturbance, hearing impairment, learning disability, mental retardation (mild, moderate, or severe/profound), and visual impairment.

Reliability data for the Vineland-II address internal consistency, test-retest, and interrater/interinterviewer reliability. Coefficient alphas for the TRF and adjusted split-half Pearson correlations for the two other forms are consistently quite strong (mostly mid- to high .90s) for the Adaptive Behavior Composite. The one exception was the Survey Forms (Survey Interview Form and Parent/Caregiver Rating Form) for the ages 32–71, where scores tend to be the highest and therefore are less variable and reliable. The internal consistency reliability for the domain scores is also very good to excellent (mostly high .80s to mid-.90s), with the exception of the slightly lower reliability in the Motor Skills domain. As expected, the internal consistency for the subdomains is lower than for the domains, especially on the Survey Forms. On all forms, the Socialization subdomains appear to be the most reliable, whereas the Receptive subdomain and the Motor subdomains generally have fair reliability. Finally, the internal consistency reliabilities on the optional Maladaptive Behavior subscales and Index are mostly in the range of good to excellent (.70s to low .90s) on the Survey Forms and Expanded Form. Fewer items on this scale probably contribute to the slightly lower reliability coefficients.

The adjusted test-retest reliability coefficients for the TRF (n = 135 students), Survey Forms (n = 414 respondents), and the Expanded Form (n = 220 respondents) are generally good to excellent for the Adaptive Behavior Composite (low .80s. to mid-.90s) Similarly, most of the average domain test-retest reliability coefficients were in the good to excellent range. The two exceptions demonstrated only fair reliability (.70s) on the Expanded Form for ages 0–2, where rapid developmental changes are most likely to occur over short periods of time and on the Survey Form for the teenage group. Average subdomain test-retest reliabilities ranged from fair to excellent. Test-retest reliabilities on the Maladaptive Behavior subscales and Index are mostly in the good to excellent range (.70s to .90s).

Adjusted interrater reliability coefficients for the Adaptive Behavior Composite were mostly moderately strong (.70s to .80s) on the forms that were completed by parents/caregivers (Survey Forms and Expanded Form) and modest (.40s to .60s) for the TRF. Average interrater reliabilities for the domains and subdomains were similar or slightly lower for each form. The relatively low interrater reliability scores on the TRF are explained by the fact that different teachers have varying perceptions and interpretations of students' adaptive behavior. Mostly fair to good interrater reliability scores (.60s to .80s) were obtained on the Maladaptive Behavior subscales and Index except for somewhat lower coefficients on the Survey Forms with the adult population (.39 to .69 for the Parent/Caregiver Rating Form; .59 to .77 for the Survey Interview Form).

Evidence for validity of the Vineland-II focuses on a variety of areas, including test content, test structure, diagnostic accuracy, and concurrent validity with related measures. Content validity evidence demonstrates a link between test content and the theoretical structure of adaptive behavior, as defined by groups such as the American Association on Mental Retardation, the American Psychological Association, and the National Academy of Sciences. In addition, the content of the Vineland-II appears to be representative of the domain of adaptive behavior, demonstrates developmental acquisition of behaviors and skills with age, and has items that are consistent with their assigned subdomains and domains.

In terms of test structure, comparisons between the subdomain, domain, and Adaptive Behavior Composite scores on all forms indicate moderately high correlations, which support the strong influence of overall adaptive behavior on the individual domains and subdomains. Correlations between the subdomains within a domain tend to be slightly stronger than with subdomains across domains. However, overall modest subdomain clustering illustrates the interrelatedness of the adaptive behaviors across domains. Confirmatory factor analysis results on the TRF and Survey Forms indicate that a three- to four-factor model fits the data reasonably well, with a few exceptions.

Diagnostic accuracy was determined by considering whether scores on the Vineland-II systematically corresponded to a variety of clinical groups, including those with diagnoses of mental retardation, autism, ADHD, emotional/behavioral disturbance, learning disability, and visual/hearing impairments. All three of the forms accurately differentiated between clinical and nonclinical populations and, in some cases, reliably distinguished between clinical groups and levels of severity within a diagnosis (i.e., mental retardation). The Vineland-II also identified patterns of behavior typical of individuals with milder diagnoses.

Evidence for the concurrent validity of the Vineland-II was presented by comparing the instrument with related measures. As expected, the adjusted correlations between each of the three Vineland-II forms and the corresponding Vineland Adaptive Behavior Scale form are moderately high, most in the .80s and .90s. Correlations between the different forms of the Vineland-II with each other were also calculated. The relationship between the two forms completed by parents/guardians (Survey Form and Expanded Form) was moderate (.68 to .80 for the Adaptive Behavior Composite). Weaker correlations were found between the TRF and the Survey Form (.32 to .48 for Adaptive Behavior Composite). However, this pattern of relationship between the teacher and parent forms of the Vineland-II is very similar to the early Vineland ABS and likely reflects the fact that the respondents observe the students' behavior in significantly different environments.

Scores from the Vineland-II were also correlated with scores from the Adaptive Behavior Assessment System, Second Edition (ABAS-II; Harrison & Oakland, 2003). The relationship between the two measures varied, depending on the Vineland-II form, the age group, and the type of score (subdomain, domain, or overall composite). The TRF had moderate correlations (.52 to .70) with the ABAS-II when looking at overall composite scores. The strongest areas of similarity were Communication and Socialization. Moderate to moderately strong correlations were also found between the Survey Forms and the ABAS-II composite scores (.69 to .78), though correlations at the subdomain and related skill areas were quite variable ranging from .27 (Health/Safety and Personal for ages 17–74) to .95 (Communication and Expressive Communication for ages 17–74). The most variable correspondence between the Vineland-II and the ABAS-II composite scores was found on the Expanded Form where correlations ranged from a modest .39 for ages 0–5 to a moderately strong .73 for ages 17–82. Subdomain correlations for the youngest age group were generally weak (.19 to .41) but increased with each age group.

Though adaptive behavior and intelligence are different constructs, the Vineland-II was correlated with the WISC-III (all forms), WISC-IV (TRF), and WAIS-III (Survey and Expanded forms). The resulting low correlations between the Adaptive Behavior Composite and the Verbal, Performance, and Full Scale IQ scores from these measures confirm that both types of instruments contribute different kinds of information in the assessment process. Finally, the Vineland-II Survey Forms and TRF were compared with the Behavior Assessment System for Children, Second Edition (BASC-2; Reynolds & Kamphaus, 2004). Even though the BASC-2 is mainly a measure of maladaptive behaviors and the Vineland-II focuses on adaptive behaviors, there are some areas where the scores on the two instruments are closely related. The Maladaptive Behavior Index of the Survey Forms demonstrated a moderately strong correlation with the Behavioral Symptoms Index of the BASC-2 Parent Rating Scales. Furthermore, the TRF Adaptive Behavior Composite demonstrated a moderate to moderately strong negative correlation (-.60 to -.78) with the Behavioral Symptoms Index of the BASC-2 Teacher Rating Scales for individuals ages 6–18. Other patterns of negative correlations between the measures support the construct of adaptive behavior, as conceptualized by the Vineland-II.

COMMENTARY. The Vineland-II is a comprehensive and carefully designed set of rating/interview forms for assessing the adaptive functioning of individuals, ages 0 to 90. The theoretical model represented in the Vineland-II is thoroughly described and well supported by previous and current research. The three manuals include very thorough guidelines for administration, scoring, and interpretation, as well as detailed description of test development, standardization, and technical characteristics. The earlier version of this instrument, the Vineland Adaptive Behavior Scales, was a well-respected instrument and this revision will likely maintain the same strong reputation. The strengths of this instrument include a robust standardization sample, excellent internal consistency and test-retest reliability, and solid evidence for content, concurrent, and construct validity. In addition, the expanded age range for the Vineland-II allows for assessment of age-related adaptive functioning changes in elderly individuals. Furthermore, the increased item density at the youngest ages increases the possibility that developmental delays can be identified early and appropriate interventions can be implemented when they are most likely to lead to improved functioning.

One of the weaknesses of the Vineland-II is relatively weak interrater reliability, especially on the TRF and the Maladaptive Behavior Index of the Survey Forms. However, this is a potential weakness of any rating scale, which requires respondents to quantify their observations of an individual, based on personal experience and varying expectations. Though the interrater reliability of the Vineland-II is lower than preferred, it is still comparable to reported interrater reliabilities of other adaptive behavior measures (Sattler & Hoge, 2006). Another potential weakness of the Vineland-II is inconsistency in the range of scores available by age. The highest scaled scores available vary by age, making it difficult to compare adaptive behavior skills over time for individuals with above average skills (Sattler & Hoge, 2006). Realistically, this is not likely to be a major problem in that the Vineland-II is not typically administered to individuals who are exhibiting higher than average functioning.

SUMMARY. The Vineland-II is an individually administered measure of adaptive behavior with several different rating and interview forms for respondents (parents, caregivers, and teachers) who are very familiar with the individual. The Vineland has a long history of effective use in identifying individuals with adaptive behavior deficits and intervention planning and the recently revised Vineland-II shows promise in continuing this tradition. Even though it is probably one of the better adaptive behavior measures available, users should be cognizant of the inherent limitations of any instrument that relies solely on indirect measures of behavior such as ratings or interviews of third-party respondents.

REVIEWER'S REFERENCES

Doll, E. A. (1935). A genetic scale of social maturity. *The American Journal of Orthopsychiatry, 5*, 180-188.

Doll, E. A. (1965). Vineland Social Maturity Scale. Circle Pines, MN: American Guidance Service, Inc.

Harrison, P. L., & Oakland, T. (2003). Adaptive Behavior Assessment System (2nd ed.). San Antonio, TX: The Psychological Corporation.

Reynolds, C. R., & Kamphaus, R. W. (2004). Behavior Assessment System for Children (2nd ed.). Circle Pines, MN: AGS Publishing.

Sattler, J. M., & Hoge, R. D. (2006). *Assessment of children: Behavioral, social, and clinical foundations* (5th ed.). La Mesa, CA: Jerome Sattler Publisher, Inc.

Sparrow, S. S., Balla, D. A., & Cicchetti, D. V. (1984). Vineland Adaptive Behavior Scales. Circle Pines, MN: American Guidance Service, Inc.

Review of the Vineland Adaptive Behavior Scales, Second Edition by KEITH F. WIDAMAN, Professor and Chair, Department of Psychology, University of California, Davis, CA:

DESCRIPTION. The Vineland Adaptive Behavior Scales, Second Edition (Vineland–II) is an individually administered instrument for assessing adaptive behaviors of persons between the ages of 0 and 90. The adaptive behavior domain is conceptualized as encompassing the four broad dimensions of Communication, Daily Living Skills, Socialization, and Motor Skills, and the Vineland–II also includes an assessment of maladaptive, or problem, behaviors. The Vineland–II is available in several forms. The Survey Interview Form and the Parent/Caregiver Rating Form contain the same set of items. The former is completed by a trained rater based on an interview of an informant (e.g., parent) who knows well the person whose adaptive behaviors are being assessed, whereas the latter is completed by the parent or caregiver of the person being assessed. The Expanded Interview Form contains a more comprehensive set of items and ratings and provides additional information for educational or treatment programming. The Teacher Rating Form yields scores on the same dimensions of adaptive behavior, but focuses on behaviors that occur in classrooms and includes additional items related to basic academic functioning.

Administration instructions are very clearly stated and easy to follow. The Vineland–II takes approximately 20 to 60 minutes to administer, depending on the adaptive levels exhibited by the person assessed. An additional 15 to 30 minutes are needed to hand score the instrument. The instructions for scoring the instrument are nicely formatted and easy to follow, and the manual has several examples of completed protocols with annotations on how discontinue rules were invoked, how to calculate raw scores on each scale, and then how standardized scores are obtained based on scale raw scores. The Vineland–II also has computerized scoring programs that make the computation and interpretation of scores much easier and avoid the many problems that arise in hand scoring of instruments. Standard scores for the four major dimensions are normed to have a mean of 100 and standard deviation of 15, similar to that for intelligence test scores.

DEVELOPMENT. Adaptive behavior is one of two major domains to be assessed when determining whether an individual has mental retardation. That is, professional organizations agree that mental retardation is characterized by subnormal general intellectual functioning accompanied by deficits in adaptive behavior. The original version of the Vineland Adaptive Behavior Scales (Vineland ABS), published in 1984, was the first adaptive behavior instrument standardized on a representative sample of the U.S. population, so that a deviation score cutoff (e.g., a score two standard deviations below the mean or lower) could be employed in parallel to the cutoff that had long been used for intelligence tests. At the time of its initial publication (1984), the VABS was the premier instrument for assessing adaptive behaviors.

The current version of the scale, the Vineland–II, carries a 2005 copyright date. The revision resulting in the Vineland–II was driven by various factors. New versions of tests typically involve the improvement of item content, culling items that are less relevant, and creating new items that are more discriminating, and these were salient goals in the development of this revision. But the test developers also wanted to increase the age range for which the instrument was valid, from 0 to 18 years to 0 to 90 years. They were also interested in increasing the number of items, and therefore the test precision, at very young ages and at the lower levels of each of the scales, to increase the diagnostic accuracy of scores. In pursuing these many goals, the test authors increased the number of adaptive behavior items across the four dimensions on the Survey Interview form by almost 50%, from 261 to 359 items, and increased substantially the numbers of items on the remaining forms as well. In addition to its use in the diagnosis of mental retardation, the Vineland–II is very useful in differential diagnosis and distinguishing among developmental disabilities, such as autism, and providing information relevant for providing programming for individuals with varying levels of adaptive behavior.

TECHNICAL. The Survey Interview and Parent/Caregiver Rating Forms (hereinafter, Survey/Parent forms) of the Vineland–II, for assessing individuals between the ages of 0 and 90 years, were standardized on a nationally representative sample of 3,695 persons. The Teacher Rating Form (hereinafter, Teacher form), used for assessing students between the ages of 3 and 18 years, was standardized on a sample of 2,570 individuals. Both of these norming samples were quite comparable to the U.S. population on key dimensions, such as geographical strata as well as sex, race or ethnicity, and mother's education.

Several different types of reliability coefficients were reported that reflect different psychometric properties of scale scores. Internal consistency reliabilities tended to be in the high .80s for the three primary domains of Communication, Daily Living Skills, and Socialization on the Survey/Parent forms (range: .84–.93); comparable reliabilities were notably higher on the Teacher form (median reliability of .95, range: .93–.97). Resulting standard errors of measurement (*SEMs*) were around 4.5 to 5 points on the Survey/Parent forms and rather narrower (between 2.6 and 4.0 points) on the Teacher form. Test-retest correlations across an approximate 3-week interval averaged in the middle to upper .80s for both the Survey/Parent and Teacher forms. Interinterviewer (or interrater) reliabilities averaged around .75 for the Survey/Parent forms and noticeably lower, around .55, for the Teacher form. Not unexpectedly, given the positive correlations among scores on the three primary domains, all reliability statistics for the Adaptive Behavior Composite–an overall score based on the domain scores–were even more positive, with higher reliabilities and lower *SEMs*.

Information relevant to the validity of the scale scores from the Vineland–II was documented in numerous ways, and only a sampling of validity information can be provided in the context of this short review. One form of validity is the factorial validity of a test. Here, the test developers fit confirmatory factor models to determine whether multiple factors representing each of the postulated domains could be confirmed and whether a single higher order factor successfully explained correlations among the first order factors. Without fail, models with multiple first-order factors and a single higher order factor fit the data well. However, the high correlations among the first-order factors (generally ranging above .80 at the latent variable level) may lead some to question the discriminant validity among the first-order factors. Several group difference comparisons were made, such as comparing scores for persons with mild, moderate, or severe mental retardation with scores obtained for individuals from a nonclinical sample. These comparisons showed that the difference in performance between the nonclinical sample and samples with mental retardation were as expected, with larger differences exhibited by persons with more severe levels of mental retardation. Another type of validity information is the pattern of convergent and discriminant correlations with other measures. The Vineland–II domain scores tended to show moderately strong convergent correlations with comparable scales from the Adaptive Behavior Assessment System, Second Edition, with correlations averaging around .70 for similar scales. With regard to discriminant validity, Vineland–II domain scores tended to correlate at rather low levels with intelligence test scores from the Wechsler tests, correlations generally falling in the range from .10 to .35 for scores from the Survey/Parent forms and in the range from .05 to .50 for the Teacher form.

COMMENTARY. The Vineland–II is a new and improved version of the original Vineland ABS that was the leader among instruments for assessing adaptive behavior upon its publication. Administration procedures are well described, and the methods of obtaining raw scores and scaled scores are clearly described and easy to perform. In addition to hand scoring, the Vineland–II comes with computer programs to ensure accurate computation of all scores. The norming samples for all forms are impressive in size and representativeness of the U.S. population. Moreover, the reliability and validity information provided for the Vineland–II is fairly comprehensive. One issue that is evident in test materials is the difficulty in assessing accurately high levels of adaptive behavior or skill. This implies that the Vineland–II is more accurate at distinguishing among persons scoring at rather low levels than among persons at high levels of adaptive skill. Given the importance of measures of adaptive behavior in the assessment of clinical syndromes such as mental retardation and autism, this is not a problem, but users should expect that scores at high levels of adaptive functioning will have poorer precision (i.e., higher *SEMs*) than those at low levels.

SUMMARY. The Vineland–II was designed to be an easily used, standardized measure of key domains of adaptive behavior–Communication, Daily Living Skills, and Socialization–that play a prominent role in the diagnosis of mental retardation and other developmental disabilities. The instrument clearly meets its goals of ease of use, clear procedures for the calculation of both raw and scaled scores, and clear and comprehensive information regarding its reliability and validity. The Vineland–II deserves to be considered among the best measures of adaptive behavior currently available, and the use of this instrument for making high-stakes decisions regarding individuals is recommended.

[151]

Wechsler Adult Intelligence Scale—Fourth Edition.

Purpose: "Designed to assess the cognitive ability of adolescents and adults"; "provides subtest and composite scores that represent intellectual functioning in specific cognitive domains, as well as a composite score that represents general intellectual ability."
Population: Ages 16-0 to 90-11.
Publication Dates: 1939-2008.
Acronym: WAIS-IV.
Scores, 6: Verbal Comprehension Index, Perceptual Reasoning Index, Processing Speed Index, General Ability Index, Full Scale.
Subtests, 15: Block Design, Similarities, Digit Span, Matrix Reasoning, Vocabulary, Arithmetic, Symbol Search, Visual Puzzles, Information, Coding, Letter-Number Sequencing, Figure Weights, Comprehension, Cancellation, Picture Completion.
Administration: Individual.
Price Data, 2008: $1,079 per complete test kit including Symbol Search scoring key, Coding scoring key, Cancellation scoring templates, 25 record forms, 25 response booklet #1, 25 response booklet #2, administration and scoring manual (2008, 258 pages), technical manual (2008, 218 pages), 2 stimulus books, and Block Design block set.
Time: (59-100) minutes.
Comments: If there are significant differences between Index scores, the General Ability Index can be used to further inform interpretation; Letter-Number Sequencing, Figure Weights, and Cancellation are supplemental subtests for individuals 16-0 to 69-11 only.
Author: David Wechsler.
Publisher: Pearson.
Cross References: For reviews by Allen K. Hess and Bruce G. Rogers of the third edition, see 14:415; see also T5:2860 (1422 references) and T4:2937 (1131 references); for reviews by Alan S. Kaufman and Joseph D. Matarazzo of the revised edition, see 9:1348 (291 references); see also T3:2598 (576 references), 8:230 (351 references), and T2:529 (178 references); for reviews by Alvin G. Burstein and Howard B. Lyman of the original edition, see 7:429 (538 references); see also 6:538 (180 references); for reviews by Nancy Bayley and Wilson H. Guertin, see 5:414 (42 references).

Review of the Wechsler Adult Intelligence Scale–Fourth Edition by GARY L. CANIVEZ, Professor of Psychology, Department of Psychology, Eastern Illinois University, Charleston, IL:

DESCRIPTION. The Wechsler Adult Intelligence Scale-Fourth Edition (WAIS-IV) is the most recent version of the most frequently administered intelligence test for older adolescents and adults, which traces its roots back to the 1939 Wechsler-Bellevue Intelligence Scale (Wechsler, 1939). Consistent with Wechsler's definition of intelligence (i.e., "global capacity"; Wechsler, 1939, p. 229) and all versions of his tests, the WAIS-IV seeks to measure general intelligence through the administration of numerous subtests, each of which is an indicator and estimate of intelligence. The WAIS-IV is a major and important revision of its predecessor and clinicians should appreciate many of the changes.

DEVELOPMENT. In revising the WAIS-IV, several goals were noted in the technical and interpretive manual including updating theoretical foundations, increasing developmental appropriateness, increasing user-friendliness, enhancing clinical utility, and improving psychometric features. Object Assembly and Picture Arrangement subtests were dropped, thus reducing subtests with manipulative objects to one (Block Design), as were Digit Symbol-Incidental Learning and Digit Symbol-Copy. New subtests to the WAIS-IV are Visual Puzzles, Figure Weights, and Cancellation. Verbal IQ (VIQ) and Performance IQ (PIQ) are no longer provided as with the Wechsler Intelligence Scale for Children–Fourth Edition (WISC-IV; 16:262). Administration and scoring rules were modified, easier and more difficult items were added to subtests to improve coverage and range, and discontinue rules were reduced for many subtests. Stimulus materials were enlarged as was writing space for Coding. Item bias investigations were reportedly conducted but data analyses illustrating comparisons or results were not provided. WAIS-IV content and structure are specifically related to current intellectual conceptualizations (Carroll, 1993, 2003; Cattell & Horn, 1978; Horn, 1991) and are explicated with specific reference to the hierarchical nature of intellectual measurement.

TECHNICAL.

Norms and scores. The standardization sample (*N* = 2,200) was obtained using stratified proportional sampling across variables of age, sex, race/ethnicity, education level (or parent education level for ages 16–19), and geographic region. Education level is a likely proxy for SES where accurate information about income is difficult to obtain. Examination of tables in the technical and interpretive manual revealed reasonably close matches to the October 2005 U.S. Census across stratification variables. The technical and interpretive manual notes exclusionary criteria for standardization sample participants related to language, uncorrected sensory impairments and communication limitations, and upper extremity impairments limiting motor performance, as well as current medication use and physical illnesses that might affect cognitive test performance.

Subtest scaled scores (*M* = 10, *SD* = 3) within each of the 13 age groups were obtained using a "method of inferential norming" (technical and interpretive manual, p. 39) where means, standard deviations, and skewness were examined from first through fourth order polynomial regressions with comparison to theoretical distributions and growth curves that produced percentiles for raw scores. Although minor irregularities were reportedly corrected through smoothing, the method of smoothing (statistical vs. hand/visual) was not noted. Due to reported range restriction and norming difficulties, certain process scores remained as raw scores, not standardized scaled scores. The Full Scale IQ (FSIQ), General Ability Index (GAI), and Index scores (*M* = 100, *SD* = 15) were generated by summing subtest scaled scores and normalized with composite score distributions visually smoothed to eliminate irregularities.

Like the WISC-IV, the WAIS-IV uses 10 core subtests to produce the FSIQ. The Verbal Comprehension Index (VCI) and Perceptual Reasoning Index (PRI) are each composed of 3 subtests, whereas the Working Memory Index (WMI) and Processing Speed Index (PSI) are each composed of 2 subtests. Like the WISC-IV, the General Ability Index (GAI) is calculated from the 3 verbal comprehension and 3 perceptual reasoning subtests and may be useful in cases where the FSIQ is unduly influenced by less *g*-oriented subtests (WMI and PSI). The WAIS-IV FSIQ ranges from 40–160 (±4 *SD*) and represents a 2/3 *SD* increase in IQ measurement range over the WAIS-III. This covers a wide enough range of intellectual assessment for most clinical applications.

Reliability. Three types of reliability estimates for WAIS-IV scores are reported in the technical and interpretive manual: internal consistency, test-retest stability, and interscorer agreement; and strong evidence for score reliability is provided. Internal consistency estimates produced by Spearman-Brown corrected split-half or coefficient alpha methods are presented for each of the 13 age groups. Internal consistency estimates across all 13 age groups ranged from .97–.98 for the FSIQ; from .87–.98 for the factor index scores (VCI, PRI, WMI, PSI); and from .71–.96 for the subtests. Standard errors of measurement based on the internal consistency estimates are also included in the technical and interpretive manual. These should be considered best-case estimates because they do not consider other major sources of error such as long-term temporal stability, administration errors, or scoring errors (Hanna, Bradley, & Holen, 1981) known to influence test scores in clinical assessments.

Short-term test-retest stability was investigated for 298 individuals from four age groups with retest intervals ranging from 8–82 days (mean retest interval of 22 days). Stability coefficients were highest for the FSIQ and VCI followed by the PRI, WMI, and PSI scores, and generally lower for the subtests as found in other intelligence tests. Also, mean changes across time were observed with scores at second testing higher and "practice effects" greatest for PRI subtests (Block Design, Visual Puzzles, Figure Weights, and Picture Completion) also observed with the other Wechsler intelligence scales in short-term retest intervals. Research examining long-term stability of WAIS-IV scores is needed to determine which scores and comparisons are consistent across longer time intervals. Such longitudinal investigations are not expected to be included at the time of publication as they would be an undue burden.

Interscorer agreement was examined by comparing two independent scorers of all WAIS-IV standardization record forms. Agreement ranged from .98–.99. Subtests where examiner judgment is involved (Similarities, Vocabulary, Information,

Comprehension) were further examined for interscorer agreement with a sample of 60 randomly selected standardization cases. Three raters (clinical psychology graduate students) independently scored these four subtests, and intraclass correlation coefficients were high, ranging from .91 to .97. These are encouraging results but it remains to be seen if similar results are obtained by clinicians not trained by the publisher in administration and scoring of the WAIS-IV.

Standard errors of measurement are provided based on internal consistency estimates by age group and for the total sample. Estimated true score confidence intervals (90% and 95%) are provided in the administration and scoring manual tables for composite scores. Obtained score confidence intervals are not provided although the formula for calculating them is presented in the technical and interpretive manual. When the assessment question is concerned with estimating the true score of the individual at the time of the evaluation (rather than the long-term estimate), the obtained score confidence interval is appropriate (Glutting, McDermott, & Stanley, 1987; Sattler, 2008). Obtained score and estimated true score confidence intervals will be quite close in cases where the reliability coefficient is high as with the WAIS-IV.

Validity. WAIS-IV score validity estimates were reported based on test content, internal structure (factor structure), relationships with other tests (convergent and divergent/discriminant comparisons), and distinct group differences comparisons. Examination of subtest and index score correlation matrices indicated that subtests within the same domain had higher correlations with each other than with subtests from a different domain. All intersubtest correlations were positive and reflected Spearman's (1904) positive manifold, shared variance, and measurement of the general intelligence factor (*g*). Although Gorsuch (1983) noted the complementary nature of exploratory (EFA) and confirmatory (CFA) factor analytic procedures and general confidence in the latent structure when *both* were in agreement, the WAIS-IV technical and interpretive manual presents *only* CFA analyses. This is a disappointing trend among many of the most recently published intelligence tests, particularly given results of Frazier and Youngstrom (2007) who demonstrated that among tests of cognitive abilities, CFA procedures tend to support the presence of more latent factors than EFA factor extraction criteria such as Horn's parallel analysis (HPA; Horn, 1965), Cattell's scree test (Cattell, 1966), and minimum average partials (MAP; Velicer, 1976).

WAIS-IV correlations with the Wechsler Individual Achievement Test–Second Edition (WIAT-II; Wechsler, 2002) were obtained from 93 16–19-year-old high school students. Typically, high correlations were obtained across academic areas with WAIS-IV FSIQ correlations with WIAT-II composites ranging .65–.88 and ranging .42–.80 for WIAT-II subtests. Relationships between the WAIS-IV and the recently published Wechsler Individual Achievement Test–Third Edition (WIAT-III; Wechsler, 2009) with a small sample (*N* = 59) were similar with WAIS-IV FSIQ correlations with WIAT-III composites ranging .59–.82 and ranging .33–.81 for WIAT-III subtests. Thus, typically strong concurrent relationships with academic achievement measures were observed. Due to the hierarchical nature of the WAIS-IV and the structure of intelligence, it would be more informative to discern the incremental predictive validity of factor index scores above and beyond the FSIQ (cf. Glutting, Watkins, Konold, & McDermott, 2006) in order to discern the relative importance of the factor index scores compared to the FSIQ in predicting academic achievement. If factor index scores are to be of importance in interpretation, they should account for meaningful portions of achievement variance over and above the FSIQ.

A number of small sample special group studies were conducted to examine WAIS-IV differences between the special group and a demographically matched (sex, race/ethnicity, educational level, geographic region) normal control group. As noted in the technical and interpretive manual, these studies and scores on the WAIS-IV should not be used as sole criteria for classification or diagnosis. Special groups examined included individuals identified as intellectually gifted, as well as persons with mild intellectual disability, moderate intellectual disability, borderline intellectual functioning, reading disorder, mathematics disorder, attention deficit-hyperactivity disorder, traumatic brain injury, autism, Asperger's disorder, major depression, mild cognitive impairment, and Alzheimer's dementia. Group differences in expected directions were typically observed but additional research is obviously required to replicate and extend these preliminary studies. It would be of great value to examine the diagnostic utility of WAIS-IV scores in correct classification of individuals with disorders related to intellectual or cognitive difficulties, as distinct group differences are a necessary but not sufficient condition for diagnostic utility.

COMMENTARY AND SUMMARY. The WAIS-IV is a welcome improvement over its predecessor and clinicians will find it a useful and more efficient measure of general intelligence than the WAIS-III for a wide range of individuals and abilities. The large and nationally representative standardization sample for the U.S. is a major strength and internal consistency estimates were uniformly strong across composite scores. The addition of new, creative, and interesting subtests (Visual Puzzles and Figure Weights) provide for better assessment of fluid reasoning–although Figure Weights is a supplemental subtest, so it does not enter into consideration unless replacing one of the core perceptual reasoning subtests. Supplemental subtests are provided (one each for the VCI, WMI, and PSI scales and two for the PRI scale), however; Figure Weights, Letter-Number Sequencing, and Cancellation are not available for 70–90-year-olds. Neither the administration and scoring manual nor the technical and interpretation manual indicate *why* those 70–90 years of age are excluded from these three subtests. Also missing are norms tables for computing factor index scores and the FSIQ when supplemental subtests are used in place of core subtests.

Examination and support of the hierarchical model in CFA was quite informative and use of hierarchical CFA is commendable. Disappointing, however, is the absence of any EFA and use of more accurate procedures to identify how many factors to extract and retain (HPA, MAP). Although CFA procedures support the hierarchical model of intelligence with four first-order factors and higher order *g*, this finding supports the *theoretical* structure. CFA procedures are very useful for testing theory but cannot be directly applied in clinical interpretation (Oh, Glutting, Watkins, Youngstrom, & McDermott, 2004). There are, however, other more practical aspects of test structure that help to determine the viability of the different test scores. Proportions of variance accounted for by the higher order *g*-factor and the four first-order factors are notably absent from the technical and interpretive manual. Subtest specificity estimates are also not provided. Thus, clinicians are unable to judge the relative importance of the factor index scores and subtest scores. If the factor index scores and subtests do not capture sufficient portions of true score variance, their usefulness in assessment will be questionable.

Although the WAIS-IV technical and interpretive manual presents much useful and supportive preliminary reliability and validity information, there is an absence of critical analyses and data to aid the clinician in adequately determining how best to interpret the different available scores. The technical and interpretive manual presents steps in performing profile analysis beyond the FSIQ (i.e., ipsative subtest comparisons, subtest level discrepancies, pairwise subtest comparisons) together with caveats about the common occurrence of strengths and weaknesses in normal subjects, information leading the clinician to a priori suspicion of profile differences, and recommendation for further external corroboration to prevent overinterpretation. However, there is no mention of the extensive research evidence demonstrating that such interpretations have often proven unreliable and invalid (for extensive reviews see Watkins, 2003, and Watkins, Glutting, & Youngstrom, 2005) nor were data presented to demonstrate the utility of such analyses with the WAIS-IV. Standard 1.1 of the *Standards for Educational and Psychological Testing* (AERA, APA, & NCME, 1999) indicates that "a rationale should be presented for each recommended interpretation and use of test scores, together with a comprehensive summary of the evidence and theory bearing on the intended use or interpretation" including scientific evidence that is "inconsistent with the intended interpretation or use" (p. 17). Consequently, clinicians who use the WAIS-IV must become familiar with the totality of evidence and be mindful of Weiner's (1998) advice to "(a) know what their tests can do and (b) act accordingly" (p. 829).

Obviously, there are tremendous amounts of time, effort, and resources devoted to the development and standardization of high quality instruments such as the WAIS-IV and it is impossible for the publisher to provide comprehensive evidence for *all* interpretive methods so reliance on the assistance of additional independent researchers may be of considerable help. Previously, the publisher has sought out and/or granted independent researchers access to the standardization sample data sets for independent research examinations that has helped to further delineate differential reliability and validity of various scores across a number of Wechsler scales (cf., Konold & Canivez, in press). It is hoped that Pearson will continue this practice so that important research may be conducted to help guide clinicians' appropriate WAIS-IV interpretations.

REVIEWER'S REFERENCES

American Educational Research Association, American Psychological Association, & National Council on Measurement in Education. (1999). *Standards for educational and psychological testing.* Washington, DC: American Educational Research Association.

Carroll, J. B. (1993). *Human cognitive abilities: A survey of factor-analytic studies.* England: Cambridge University Press.

Carroll, J. B. (2003). The higher stratum structure of cognitive abilities: Current evidence supports *g* and about ten broad factors. In H. Nyborg (Ed.), *The scientific study of general intelligence: Tribute to Arthur R. Jensen* (pp. 5–21). New York: Pergamon Press.

Cattell, R. B. (1966). The scree test for the number of factors. *Multivariate Behavioral Research, 1,* 245-276.

Cattell, R. B., & Horn, J. L. (1978). A check on the theory of fluid and crystallized intelligence with description of new subtest designs. *Journal of Educational Measurement, 15,* 139-164.

Frazier, T. W., & Youngstrom, E. A. (2007). Historical increase in the number of factors measured by commercial tests of cognitive ability: Are we overfactoring? *Intelligence, 35,* 169–182.

Glutting, J. J., McDermott, P. A., & Stanley, J. C. (1987). Resolving differences among methods of establishing confidence limits for test scores. *Educational and Psychological Measurement, 47,* 607-614.

Glutting, J. J., Watkins, M. W., Konold, T. R., & McDermott, P. A. (2006). Distinctions without a difference: The utility of observed versus latent factors from the WISC–IV in estimating reading and math achievement on the WIAI–II. *Journal of Special Education, 40,* 103-114.

Gorsuch, R. L. (1983). *Factor analysis* (2nd ed.). Hillsdale, NJ: Erlbaum.

Hanna, G. S., Bradley, F. O., & Holen, M. C. (1981). Estimating major sources of measurement error in individual intelligence scales: Taking our heads out of the sand. *Journal of School Psychology, 19,* 370-376.

Horn, J. L. (1965). A rationale and test for the number of factors in factor analysis. *Psychometrika, 30,* 179-185.

Horn, J. L. (1991). Measurement of intellectual capabilities: A review of theory. In K. S. McGrew, J. K. Werder, & R. W. Woodcock (Eds.), *Woodcock-Johnson technical manual* (rev. ed.; pp. 197-232). Itasca, IL: Riverside.

Konold, T. R., & Canivez, G. L. (in press). Differential relationships among WISC-IV and WIAT-II scales: An evaluation of potentially moderating child demographics. *Educational and Psychological Measurement.*

Oh, H. J., Glutting, J. J., Watkins, M. W., Youngstrom, E. A., & McDermott, P. A. (2004). Correct interpretation of latent versus observed abilities: Implications from structural equation modeling applied to the WISC-III and WIAT linking sample. *Journal of Special Education, 38,* 159-173.

Sattler, J. M. (2008). *Assessment of children: Cognitive foundations* (5th ed.). San Diego, CA: Author.

Spearman, C. (1904). "General intelligence": Objectively determined and measured. *American Journal of Psychology, 15,* 201-293.

Velicer, W. F. (1976). Determining the number of components from the matrix of partial correlations. *Psychometrika, 41,* 321-327.

Watkins, M. W. (2003). IQ subtest analysis: Clinical acumen or clinical illusion? *The Scientific Review of Mental Health Practice, 2,* 118-141.

Watkins, M. W., Glutting, J. J., & Youngstrom, E. A. (2005). Issues in subtest profile analysis. In D. P. Flanagan & P. L. Harrison (Eds.), *Contemporary intellectual assessment: Theories, tests, and issues* (pp. 251-268). New York: Guilford.

Wechsler, D. (1939). *The measurement of adult intelligence.* Baltimore, MD: Williams & Wilkins.

Wechsler, D. (2002). Wechsler Individual Achievement Test-Second Edition. San Antonio, TX: The Psychological Corporation.

Wechsler, D. (2009). Wechsler Individual Achievement Test-Third Edition. San Antonio, TX: Pearson.

Weiner, I. B. (1989). On competence and ethicality in psychodiagnostic assessment. *Journal of Personality Assessment, 53,* 827-831.

Review of the Wechsler Adult Intelligence Scale–Fourth Edition by GREGORY SCHRAW, Professor, Department of Educational Psychology, University of Nevada-Las Vegas, Las Vegas, NV:

DESCRIPTION. The Wechsler Adult Intelligence Scale–Fourth Edition (WAIS-IV) provides an individually administered test of intelligence for individuals between 16 and 90 years of age. The WAIS-IV provides a composite of intellectual functioning using 15 separate subtests that are combined into four cognitive skill categories, including Verbal Comprehension (4 subtests), Perceptual Reasoning (5 subtests), Working Memory (3 subtests), and Processing Speed (3 subtests). The total composite scale based on all subtests is interpreted as a measure of general intellectual ability.

The 15 subtests are administered in a prescribed order, which require 2 hours or less to complete for most examinees. Administration guidelines and discontinue rules are stated clearly in the 258-page administration and scoring manual. Detailed scoring rules are provided as well.

DEVELOPMENT. The WAIS-IV is a revision of its immediate predecessors, most notably the WAIS-III. The test has been in continuous use via updated versions since 1939 and retains the same general theoretical and administrative structure. All of the WAIS tests are based on hierarchical models of intelligence such as Spearman's *g* (Spearman, 1923), and the two-factor theory of Cattell (1963), which distinguishes between fluid and crystallized intelligence. Fluid ability is thought to be biologically driven and represents general ability to reason on novel tasks and unfamiliar contexts, whereas crystallized ability represents reasoning and problem solving related to task-specific knowledge and schooling (Ackerman & Lohman, 2006; Carroll, 1993). Fluid and crystallized ability may be combined to create a single composite that measures a general intelligence factor, *g*.

Theoretically, the 15 subtests load on four cognitive factors (i.e., Verbal Comprehension, Perceptual Reasoning, Working Memory, and Processing Speed), which load on fluid and crystallized forms of intelligence, which load on the composite intellectual ability factor known as *g*. Hierarchical models of intelligence are common in cognitive psychology, well researched and supported by 50 years of empirical data. Thus, the theoretical assumptions of the WAIS-IV, as well as the constructs it is purported to measure, are widely recognized as being the most plausible and comprehensive theoretical description of human ability.

TECHNICAL. The WAIS-IV is accompanied by a 218-page technical manual, complete with detailed information about test structure, standardization, reliability and validity, and interpretation of the test. In addition, the interpretation subsection includes an excellent 10-step guide to profile analysis of each examinee based on composites derived from the 15 separate subtests.

The technical manual provides extensive reliability data for individual subtests and composite scores across 13 age bands using coefficient alpha. Coefficients are good to excellent in all cases, ranging from the low .80s to upper .90s. Stability coefficients using test-retest reliabilities are presented for each subtest and composites for four different age bands. Coefficients are good to excellent in all cases, ranging from mid .70s to upper .80s.

Both construct and criterion-related validity are discussed in detail. Regarding construct validity, a variety of confirmatory factor analyses (i.e., statistical tests of a proposed structural relationship among factors) are reported that compared six different structural models, including the four hypothesized factors described above, a one-factor model, and several multifactor combinations. Results typically supported the four-factor model based on Verbal Comprehension, Perceptual Reasoning, Working Memory, and Processing Speed subscores. In addition, structural comparisons between the 16–69 and 70–90 age bands yielded highly similar results.

Regarding criterion-related validity, WAIS-IV subscales and composites were correlated with a variety of other tests, including the WAIS-III, Wechsler Intelligence Scale for Children–Fourth Edition (WISC-IV), and Brown Attention Deficit Disorder Test (Brown ADD). In general, correlations between scores were in the .80 range with tests that measure similar constructs, providing convergent validity evidence. In contrast, WAIS-IV scores were negatively correlated with the Brown ADD scales, providing discriminant validity evidence. A complement of studies also was reported for special and gifted populations.

Detailed information is included about the sampling and standardization plan, including a wide variety of demographic variables at 13 age bands for the nationally representative sample. These percentages closely match national U.S. Census data.

COMMENTARY. The WAIS-IV is an excellent test of intellectual ability and has four important strengths. One is that it provides a strong theoretical framework for the development and interpretation of test scores. The underlying theory is widely accepted and has an abundance of empirical support as well. A second strength is that the 15 subtests provide a comprehensive assessment of basic cognitive skills, especially abilities related to verbal, perceptual, and working memory processing. A third strength is that the test authors provide extensive norming, validation, and standardization data that facilitate inferences drawn about examinees. A fourth strength is that the test includes excellent support documentation such as the technical manual and the administration and scoring manual.

The WAIS-IV possesses two weaknesses. One is that the test is time and labor intensive to administer, score, and interpret; thus, it may be most appropriate when high-stakes decisions are made. A second weakness is that the test assesses what some critics have referred to as "left-brain" or "academic" intelligences, which focus on traditional cognitive abilities an examinee would use in typical school or work settings. In contrast, some experts have argued that social, kinesthetic, interpersonal, and emotional intelligence are not assessed at all by the WAIS (Gardner, 1999).

Although the WAIS-IV focuses only on intellectual ability as it is construed traditionally, it provides an outstanding measure of this construct. Moreover, although some theorists have proposed alternative intelligence factors such as emotional intelligence, there are no readily available measures of these constructs that have comparable reliability, validity, and technical validation equal to the WAIS-IV.

One unresolved yet important issue with the WAIS IV, and many other related measures of intellectual ability, is whether any or all of these skills are fixed or changeable due to instruction or social factors. The manuals do not address this question directly. However, this question is important because it affects how scores are interpreted and used to formulate educational policies, as well as assumptions we make about the relationship between intelligence, creativity, effort and deliberate practice, and worldly success (Ericsson, 2003). Opinions range from those who support the fixed position to social-constructivist orientations that argue that intellectual ability is changeable and context-bound, and perhaps, less important than many people imagine it to be (Winner, 2000).

SUMMARY. The WAIS-IV provides one of the best measures of general intellectual functioning available. It assesses four important dimensions of cognitive ability, including Verbal, Perceptual, Working Memory, and Processing Speed. Research shows that each of these four dimensions is a strong correlate of learning, school achievement, and cognitive development. The test is best suited for high-stakes decision making related to intellectual ability because it is labor-intensive and expensive to administer. Nevertheless, it is extremely comprehensive and provides a reliable and valid measure of intellectual functioning relative to the demands of schooling and academic success.

REVIEWER'S REFERENCES

Ackerman, P. L., & Lohman, D. F. (2006). Individual differences in cognitive functions. In P. A. Alexander & P. H. Winne (Eds.), *Handbook of educational psychology* (pp. 139-161). Mahwah, NJ: Lawrence Erlbaum.

Carroll, J. B. (1993). Human cognitive abilities: A survey of factor-analytic studies. Cambridge, England: Cambridge University Press.

Cattell, R. B. (1963). Theory of fluid and crystallized ability: A critical experiment. *Journal of Educational Psychology, 54*, 1-22.

Ericsson, K. A. (2003). The acquisition of expert performance as problem solving: Construction and modification of mediating mechanisms through deliberate practice. In J. E. Davidson & R. J. Sternberg (Eds.), *The psychology of problem solving* (pp. 31-83). Cambridge, England: Cambridge University Press.

Gardner, H. (1999). Who owns intelligence? *The Atlantic Monthly, 283*, 67-76.

Spearman, C. (1923). *The nature of "intelligence" and the principles of cognition.* Oxford, England: Macmillan.

Winner, E. (2000). The origins and ends of giftedness. *American Psychologist, 55*, 159-169.

[152]

Wechsler Fundamentals: Academic Skills.

Purpose: Designed as "a brief achievement test that measures broad skills in the areas of reading, spelling, and math computation."

Population: Children Kindergarten–Grade 12, adults age 18–50.

Publication Date: 2008.

Scores, 5: Word Reading, Reading Comprehension, Reading Composite, Spelling, Numerical Operations.

Administration: Group and individual.

Forms, 2: A & B.

Price Data, 2009: $182 per examination kit Form A including 25 Summary of Skills Inventory and Word Reading record forms, 25 Spelling and Numerical Operations response booklets, 25 Reading Comprehension response booklets (5 each of Grade K–3, Grade 4–5, Grade 6–8, Grade 9–12, and Adult), word card, and administration and scoring manual (268 pages); $91 per combination set (specify Form A or Form B) including 25 Summary of Skills Inventory and Word Reading record forms, 25 Spelling and Numerical Operations response booklets, and 25 Reading Comprehension response booklets (5 each of Grade K–3, Grade 4–5, Grade 6–8, Grade 9–12, and Adult); $44 per 25 Spelling and Numerical Operations response booklets (specify Form A or B); $10.40 per Word Card (specify Form A or Form B); $44 per 25 Summary of Skills Inventory and Word Reading record forms (specify Form A or B); $93.60 per administration and scoring manual; price information available from publisher for CD for technical and interpretive manual (83 pages).

Time: (45) minutes.

Author: Pearson.

Publisher: Pearson.

Review of the Wechsler Fundamentals: Academic Skills by SUSAN M. BROOKHART, President, Brookhart Enterprises LLC and Duquesne University, Helena, MT:

DESCRIPTION. The Wechsler Fundamentals: Academic Skills test is designed as "a brief achievement test that measures broad skills in the areas of reading, spelling, and math computation" (administration and scoring manual, p. 1). Its technical and interpretive manual (p. 1) further elaborates this purpose: "to create a brief academic inventory with multiple forms that can be administered either in a group or individual format and that corresponds to national grade-level standards." There are four subtests: Word Reading, Reading Comprehension, Spelling, and Numerical Operations. The Word Reading and Reading Comprehension subtest scores are combined for a Reading Composite Score. The Word Reading subtest is administered individually; the other subtests may be administered individually or in groups.

Each of two forms (Form A and Form B) includes a Word Card for the Word Reading test and two test booklets, a Reading Comprehension response booklet (K–3, 4–5, 6–8, 9–12, and Adults), and a Spelling and Numerical Operations response booklet (Kindergarten–Grade 12 and Adults). The materials are clear and well designed. The K–3 Reading Comprehension booklets are printed in color.

For an individual examinee, the examiner selects an item set within the booklet. Start and stop points are indicated for each grade, and may be modified for examinees whose reading or mathematics ability is not typical of his or her grade level. Examinees should take an item set where they get at least two items correct and at least two items incorrect.

All items are scored right/wrong (1/0). For the Word Reading subtest, examinees read from the Word Card as the examiner records their scores for each item. For the Reading Comprehension subtest, examinees read passages and answer multiple-choice questions by marking directly in the booklet. Items assess both literal and inferential comprehension. The Spelling and Numerical Operations booklet has spaces for students to write their answers. For the Spelling test, examinees write spelling words as the examiner dictates them. For the Numerical Operations test, examinees compute the answer to mathematics problems. There is ample space for scratch work.

Each form also includes a record form for the examiner. The record form includes places to record performance, record scores, add confidence intervals, do ability-achievement discrepancy analyses, and note behavioral observations. Examiners determine raw scores for each subtest, then use tables to convert these to weighted raw scores and transform weighted raw scores into grade-based or age-based standard scores. The examiner can then look up the corresponding percentile ranks, NCE scores, stanines, and grade- or age-equivalent scores (respectively).

DEVELOPMENT. The Wechsler Fundamentals: Academic Skills is a revision of the Wechsler Individual Achievement Test-II, Update 2005 (WIAT-II). The Wechsler Fundamentals: Academic Skills technical and interpretive manual describes reviews by content experts and a separate review of several states' standards (which is the only connection to national grade-level standards that this reviewer could see), several state achievement tests (the Stanford Achievement Test, Tenth Edition [SAT10] and the Metropolitan Achievement Test, Eighth Edtition [MAT8], both also Pearson products), published textbooks, (for numerical operations) the NCTM Standards, and (for word reading and spelling) published word lists. Despite its reference to standards, this test is a measure of conventional basic skills. There is no table of specifications to indicate what aspects of various standards were sampled for the test. Except for the inference questions in the Reading Comprehension subtest, the Wechsler Fundamentals: Academic Skills items do not tap higher order thinking.

Pilot studies were conducted during the development phase. Five mini-studies (n = 15 to n = 100) and one national pilot study (n = 950), including students with both verbal and mathematics learning disabilities and with Attention Deficit Hyperactivity Disorder, were conducted.

TECHNICAL.

Standardization. The Wechsler Fundamentals: Academic Skills was normed during 2006–2007, through school and clinical psychologists from around the United States. Thorough descriptions of the various grade- and age-based norm samples are given. The grade-based sample included 2,570 students ages 5 to 19 in Grades K through 12 (so, just under 200 students per grade), half tested in the Fall and half in the Spring. The age-based sample included 2,520 individuals, 720 adults and 1,800 K–12 students. The norming samples seem to be adequate in size, and evidence is presented that they are demographically representative of the U.S. population.

Based on the 2006–2007 data, norms were calculated for Fall, Winter, and Spring. The technical manual describes how weighted raw scores were calculated (using the Rasch model), how standard scores (mean = 100, standard deviation = 15) were derived, and how theoretical distributions were calculated and used to compute percentile ranks. The standardization work for the Wechsler Fundamentals: Academic Skills is clearly and thoroughly described and represents a strength of this test.

Reliability. Several sources of consistency were investigated for the Wechsler Fundamentals: Academic Skills. Internal consistency, test-retest, and interscorer reliability were all addressed.

Internal consistency reliability averaged .84 to .96 across grades for various grade-based subtests. Age-based calculations were similar for school-aged examinees and slightly higher for adults, with subtest average reliabilities across adult age categories of .88 to .96. Internal consistency reliability for the Reading Composite was slightly higher. Standard errors of measurement are reported for each subtest and the Reading Composite, for each grade and age category, and are generally around 3 to 5 standard score points (.2 to .3 standard deviations).

Test-retest reliability was investigated via correlations and also by reporting the standardized differences between the test and the retest. The average test-retest interval ranged from 7 to 8 days across grade and age samples. The average corrected test-retest coefficients for the subtests for the grade-based sample range from the high .70s to the .90s. Test-retest coefficients for the Reading Composite are slightly higher. The average corrected test-retest coefficients for the subtests for the age-based samples, both in school and adult, range from the .80s to .90s, and again the Reading Composite coefficients are slightly higher.

Inspection of the standardized differences, or the effect size that resulted from retesting, indicated mild practice effects. This seems reasonable given the nature of the material. For all except one of the testing purposes listed, the test would only be given once. And, as will be further discussed in the Commentary section, this reviewer would not recommend using the Wechsler Fundamentals: Academic Skills for the purpose of monitoring progress. The existence of a practice effect, although not the main reason for this recommendation, certainly supports it.

Because the Wechsler Fundamentals: Academic Skills has individually administered components and depends on an examiner, interscorer reliability was also investigated. It was found to be excellent (.97–1.00). This is not surprising, given the clarity and specificity of the administration and scoring directions and the straightforward nature of the items.

In summary, the reliability of the Wechsler Fundamentals: Academic Skills has been thoroughly evaluated and reported. At each age and grade level category, all four subtests exhibit adequate to excellent consistency across items (internal consistency), time (test-retest), and scorer.

Validity. The technical manual reports evidence for validity based on response processes, on test content, on internal structure, and on external structure. The resulting body of evidence makes a successful case that the test provides a brief inventory of academic skills in reading, spelling, and mathematics calculation skills, as is claimed.

The response process evidence is all based on expert judgment. There are no think-alouds or other studies of students' actual response processes. Evidence about test content was based on expert judgment and also empirical item analyses. There is ample evidence from conventional item statistics and IRT analyses that the items contribute to their respective subtests.

Internal structure evidence demonstrates that the respective subtests behave as predicted. The Word Reading, Reading Comprehension, and Spelling subtests are more related to one another than they are to the Numerical Operations subtest. Additional internal evidence is found in achievement-ability analyses, where the full-scale, verbal, and performance IQ measures from the Wechsler Abbreviated Scale of Intelligence predict Wechsler Fundamentals: Academic Skills performance as expected. Further, Fall to Spring and grade to grade changes in achievement measure students' progress as expected.

External structure evidence is presented in the form of correlations of Wechsler Fundamentals: Academic Skills scores with WIAT-II scores and with Wide Range Achievement Test: Fourth Edition (WRAT4) scores. Patterns of correlations occur as expected, with reading scales correlating more highly with each other than with mathematics scales, and vice versa. The WRAT4 evidence is more convincing for a validity argument than the WIAT-II evidence. Because the Wechsler Fundamentals: Academic Skills was developed from the WIAT-II it is not surprising that performance on the two is highly correlated.

Validity studies also present evidence that special group performance on the Wechsler Fundamentals: Academic Skills is as expected. Special groups studied included students in gifted and talented programs, students with mild intellectual disabilities, students with learning disabilities in reading and writing, students with learning disabilities in mathematics, and students diagnosed with Attention Deficit Hyperactivity Disorder (ADHD).

Evidence that the test measures basic academic skills in the designated areas seems clear. Less clear is the suitability of the measure for any particular purpose. The administration and scoring manual suggests many possible uses for the test: (a) providing a quick evaluation of school-based skills in schools, colleges, mental health clinics, private practices, rehabilitation clinics, prisons, and residential treatment facilities; (b) providing a second or alternative measure of achievement; (c) monitoring academic progress as a result of intervention; (d) helping vocational counselors outline intervention strategies for academic skills for their clients; and (e) providing a broad measure of academic functioning in adults.

This is a large variety of purposes, and no evidence is given to support a specific purpose. The technical and interpretive manual has a section called "Interpretation," but it is about how to interpret various scores (e.g., percentile ranks), not about interpretation for any specific use. The evidence for construct validity, summarized above, suggests that the Wechsler Fundamentals: Academic Skills does measure the school-based academic skills of word reading, reading comprehension, spelling, and mathematics computation, and thus the purposes that simply require an inventory of basic skills (suggested purposes a, b, and e in the previous paragraph) seem supported.

However, it seems this instrument is too brief to monitor academic progress as a result of intervention (suggested purpose e above). For example, there are only one or two items each for many of the types of mathematics computation sampled. Progress monitoring instruments need to contain detailed samples of the content domain taught (the "intervention") and be deeply curriculum-based.

It also seems that the intervention strategies vocational counselors could suggest based on this instrument (suggested purpose d above) would be similarly un-detailed. For example, for clients with poor reading comprehension scores, the counselor would only have enough information to suggest they work on reading. The broad, brief Wechsler Fundamentals: Academic Skills does not include information that would help identify the nature and type of reading instruction from which a client would benefit. Similarly, in mathematics the test does not yield any diagnostic information that would identify what needed to be learned.

COMMENTARY. The Wechsler Fundamentals: Academic Skills is a carefully crafted test. It is well documented in two very readable manuals. Its administration is straightforward. The psychometric work is based on up-to-date methods and is carefully detailed in the technical manual. The test scores are reliable, allowing confidence in the scores as indicators of word reading, reading comprehension, spelling, and numerical operations.

As a measure of school-based skills in general, the Wechsler Fundamentals: Academic Skills is limited. The claim that the test "corresponds to national grade-level standards" (technical and interpretive manual, p. 1) is misleading. It is true that the four skills are "standards-based" in the sense that they are included in all states' content standards and in professional organization (e.g., NCTM) standards. However, these basic skills comprise a subset of those standards in most cases. Most national grade-level standards include both these basic skills and things like inquiry, analysis, problem-solving, and so on.

The Wechsler Fundamentals: Academic Skills does not seem suitable for use as a tool for progress monitoring or designing interventions. Because it is a brief inventory, there are not enough items on the instrument to evaluate learning progress as a result of specific interventions or prescribe future interventions. No validity studies provide evidence that might contradict this conclusion and support these purposes.

SUMMARY. The most appropriate use of this test, given its validity evidence, is to provide a quick evaluation of school-based skills in settings where trustworthy academic information about an individual is not readily available, or to provide a check on that academic information if its trustworthiness is not known. This is a useful purpose, and it is easy to recommend the test if it is limited to such use.

Review of the Wechsler Fundamentals: Academic Skills by GEORGETTE YETTER, Assistant Professor, School Psychology, Oklahoma State University, Stillwater, OK:

DESCRIPTION. The Wechsler Fundamentals: Academic Skills is a brief norm-referenced test of reading, spelling, and math calculation skills for individuals aged 6–50. It provides four subscale scores (Word Reading, Spelling, Numerical Operations, and Reading Comprehension) and a Reading Composite score. Two parallel test forms (A and B) are available. Three of the four subtests (all except Word Reading) are designed to be administered in either individual or group mode. Testing time averages 55–65 min. The test is administered and scored using paper and pencil.

On the Word Reading subtest, the examinee is provided a list of words and is given approximately 3 seconds to read each word aloud. The Spelling subtest "assesses the ability to spell dictated letters, letter blends, and words" (administration and scoring manual, p. 48). Numerical Operations "assesses the ability to write one-and two-digit numbers; to solve written arithmetic problems involving addition, subtraction, multiplication, and division; to solve written geometric problems; and to solve written algebraic and calculus equations" (administration and scoring manual, p. 53). The Reading Comprehension subtest measures both listening and reading comprehension skills in younger individuals and "the ability to read narrative and informational passages and answer questions based upon those passages" for older individuals (administration and scoring manual, p. 34); questions on this subtest use multiple-choice format.

The Wechsler Fundamentals: Academic Skills produces standard scores with a mean of 100 and standard deviation of 15. Confidence intervals, percentile ranks, normal curve equivalents, and stanines also can be derived. For K–12 students aged 6 through 19, both age-based and grade-based standard scores are available. Age-based scores are reported in 4-month intervals for ages 6 through 13, 1-year intervals for ages 14–16, and in a single 3-year interval for ages 17–19. Grade-based standard scores are reported using Fall, Winter, and Spring norms. For adults not enrolled in secondary school, age-based standard scores are reported for ages 18–19, 20–24, 25–34, and 35–50.

The scoring criteria are straightforward. All items are scored dichotomously (0 or 1). After computing the subtest raw scores, the examiner looks up the corresponding weighted raw scores on tables conveniently printed in the record form.

Age- and grade-based standard scores, confidence intervals, percentile ranks, and other statistics are identified by consulting conversion tables printed in the administration and scoring manual, and they are entered on the cover of the record form.

The record form provides space for graphing the subtest and composite standard scores on a normal curve. It also delineates the seven categories on which the scores are classified: *well below expectations* (below 70), *below expectations* (70–80), *emerging* (80–90), *on-target acquisition* (90–110), *proficient* (110–120), *very proficient* (120–130), and *mastery* (above 130). Additionally, the record form provides space for analyzing the discrepancy between ability and achievement (for individuals aged 6–19 only) by comparison with the Wechsler Abbreviated Scale of Intelligence (WASI; Wechsler, 1999). Both the predicted-difference and simple-difference methods of discrepancy analysis are supported.

DEVELOPMENT. Subtest content was developed by curriculum expert review, comparison with other brief achievement tests, and consultation with textbooks and state standards. The subtests were piloted across the U.S. on over 1,000 individuals, including persons with Specific Learning Disability in Reading/Writing, Specific Learning Disability in Math, and Attention-Deficit/Hyperactivity Disorder (AD/HD). All items were assessed for bias related to gender or ethnicity through informal examination by two language experts and also using statistical analysis.

TECHNICAL. Normative data were gathered in 2006-2007 "by qualified examiners, including school and clinical psychologists, and their access to examinees" (administration and scoring manual, p. 2). Sampling was stratified to reflect the October 2004 U.S. Census data with respect to parent or self-education, race/ethnicity, and geographic region. Examinees who could not speak or understand English were not included in the norm sample. Equal numbers of females and males were represented at each age and grade level.

The grade-based sample consisted of 2,570 individuals, including an unspecified percentage of special education students. Five percent of the norm group had clinical diagnoses and 1% were enrolled in gifted and talented programs. Half of the grade-based data were gathered during the Fall of 2006 and half during the Spring of 2007. Winter norms were derived by interpolating the Fall and Spring scores. The age-based sample consisted of 2,520 individuals aged 6–50 years. Over 90% of the norm group used for developing age-based scores also were part of the grade-based sample.

Internal consistency of the subtests was evaluated using the split-half method. Item response theory was used to rank order the items by difficulty. Items were divided using an odd-even split. The correlation coefficients of the half tests were computed and corrected using the Spearman-Brown formula. The split-half reliabilities computed for all subtests at all ages were good to excellent, within the r = .80 to .90 range (Salvia, Ysseldyke, & Bolt, 2007). Unfortunately, statistics comparing internal consistency by gender and ethnicity were not reported. Moreover, no data were reported to substantiate the equivalence of test Forms A and B. [Editor's Note: The publisher advises that this information is available in an updated technical manual. However, the updated technical manual CD was not provided to Buros or the reviewers after Form B was released. The new form and an updated administration and scoring manual were provided but did not include this updated equivalence information.]

Test-retest stability was computed with samples demographically matched to the U.S. population (U.S. Bureau of the Census, 2004). The corrected Pearson correlation coefficients for all subtests at all ages were in the r = .80 to .90 range, indicating good to excellent stability over a mean period of 7–8 days. Convergent evidence included correlation patterns among the subtests consistent with expectations based on their content. For instance, Word Reading and Reading Comprehension scores were more closely related with each other and with Spelling than they were with Numerical Operations.

Criterion-related evidence was investigated through comparisons with selected subtests from the Wechsler Individual Achievement Test–Second Edition: Update 2005 (WIAT–II; Harcourt Assessment, 2005) and the Wide Range Achievement Test: Fourth Edition (WRAT4; Wilkinson & Robertson, 2006). The measures were administered in counterbalanced order with gender-balanced samples. The corrected correlations with the WIAT-II for Word Reading, Spelling, and Numerical Operations were strong (in the r = .80s); the relationship for Reading Comprehension was lower (r = .69–.73). With school-aged samples, correlations with the WRAT4 Word Reading, Spelling, Math Computation, and Sentence Comprehension subtests were good for Spelling (r = .84–.85), fair for Word Reading and

Numerical Operations (r = .69 and r = .69–.74, respectively), and weaker for Reading Comprehension (r = .60–.63). These relationships were somewhat stronger for adults. As the test authors noted, the weaker correspondence observed at all age levels between the Wechsler Fundamentals: Academic Skills Reading Comprehension scores and those of similar WIAT-II and WRAT4 subtests may be attributable to differences in item formatting. In contrast with the multiple-choice questions of the Wechsler Fundamentals: Academic Skills, the WRAT4 comprehension questions follow a modified cloze format and the WIAT-II questions request free-recall responses.

The technical and interpretive manual does not provide sufficient information to compute coefficients related to discriminant evidence while correcting for attenuation due to measurement error, as recommended by Campbell and Fiske (1959). The correlations it reports using the Kindergarten through Grade 12 sample, however, support the scales' discriminant validity. For example, the weakest relationships with Word Reading and Spelling were found with WRAT4 Math Computation (r = .31 and r = .43, respectively), and the weakest relationship with Numerical Operations was obtained with WRAT4 Word Reading (r = .42). Inexplicably, however, Reading Comprehension was more strongly correlated with WRAT4 Math Computation (r = .50) than with WRAT4 Spelling (r = .44).

To allow for the interpretation of the discrepancy between ability and achievement, the responses of a subset of the normative sample (the linking sample) completed both the Wechsler Fundamentals: Academic Skills and the WASI. Using the predicted-difference method of interpretation, their WASI full-scale IQ scores were used to calculate predicted Wechsler Fundamentals: Academic Skills achievement scores. The predicted achievement was compared with actual achievement and the frequencies were tallied for various levels of divergence. These computations formed the basis for tables that examiners can use to evaluate the significance of an examinee's ability-achievement discrepancy. Two ways of interpreting this discrepancy are available: (a) by reference to the statistical significance of the difference (at the $p < .05$ and .01 levels), and (b) by comparison with the percentage of individuals in the linking sample that exhibited similar degrees of difference (ranging from 1% to 25%). Other tables allow examiners to use the simple difference method for interpreting an examinee's ability-achievement discrepancy. The technical and interpretive manual includes a clear description of the strengths of the predicted-difference method relative to the simple difference method for making educational decisions on the basis of ability-achievement discrepancies, as outlined by McCloskey (2002).

Examiners also can analyze the test-taker's relative strengths and weaknesses by examining differences among his or her subtest scores. As with the ability-achievement discrepancies, tables allow for such interpretation according to (a) the statistical significance of the differences between subtest scores, and (b) the frequency with which various sizes of difference were obtained in the linking sample. The technical and interpretive manual provides a very readable comparison of these interpretation methods, noting that the frequency-of-differences method is likely to be more clinically meaningful.

COMMENTARY. The Wechsler Fundamentals: Academic Skills is easy to administer and to score. It possesses reasonable psychometric characteristics for a screener instrument and it is versatile, in that it can be administered either in individual or group format. Further reliability and validity studies are needed, however, particularly regarding the Reading Comprehension subtest.

SUMMARY. The Wechsler Fundamentals: Academic Skills is a new, potentially useful brief measure of basic academic skills. It may be useful as a norm-referenced school-wide screener for early identification of at-risk students. Educators should take note, however, that the Wechsler Fundamentals: Academic Skills scores in and of themselves are not sufficient for classifying individuals. Any individuals flagged as potentially exceptional by the Wechsler Fundamentals: Academic Skills will require thorough follow-up assessment.

REVIEWER'S REFERENCES

Campbell, D. T., & Fiske, D. W. (1959). Convergent and discriminant validation by the multitrait-multimethod matrix. *Psychological Bulletin, 56*, 81-105.

Harcourt Assessment. (2005). Wechsler Individual Achievement Test–Second Edition: Update 2005. San Antonio, TX: Author.

McCloskey, G. (2002). The WIAT-II, statistical significance of difference scores, and severe discrepancy ability-achievement models: A discussion of important issues. Retrieved March 2010, from http://search-manual-online.com/download/manual/The%20WIAT-II,%20Statistical%20Significance%20of%20Difference%20Scores,%20and/aHR0cDovL21hcmdhcmV0a2F5LmNvbS9QREY1MjBmaWxlcy9-Qc3ljaENvcnAvV0lBVC1JSSUyMGFuZCUyMFNldmVyZSUyMERpc2NyZXBh-bmNpZXMucGRm

Salvia, J., Ysseldyke, J. E., & Bolt, S. (2007). *Assessment: In special and inclusive education* (10th ed.). Boston: Houghton Mifflin.

U.S. Bureau of the Census. (2004). *Current population survey, October 2004: School enrollment supplement file* [CD-ROM]. Washington, DC: Author.

Wechsler, D. (1999). Wechsler Abbreviated Scale of Intelligence. San Antonio, TX: The Psychological Corporation.

Wilkinson, G. S., & Robertson, G. J. (2006). Wide Range Achievement Test: Fourth Edition. Lutz, FL: Psychological Assessment Resources, Inc.

[153]

Wechsler Individual Achievement Test–Third Edition.

Purpose: "Designed to measure the achievement of students" in prekindergarten through Grade 12 in the areas of "listening, speaking, reading, writing and mathematics."

Population: Ages 4-0 to 19-11.

Publication Dates: 1992-2009.

Acronym: WIAT-III.

Scores, 24: 16 subtests (Listening Comprehension, Early Reading Skills, Reading Comprehension, Math Problem Solving, Alphabet Writing Fluency, Sentence Composition, Word Reading, Essay Composition, Pseudoword Decoding, Numerical Operations, Oral Expression, Oral Reading Fluency, Spelling, Math Fluency-Addition, Math Fluency-Subtraction, Math Fluency-Multiplication), 8 composite scores (Oral Language, Total Reading, Basic Reading, Reading Comprehension and Fluency, Written Expression, Mathematics, Math Fluency, Total Achievement).

Administration: Individual.

Price Data, 2010: $625 per complete test kit including Scoring Assistant (Windows only); $117 per 25 record forms and 25 response booklets.

Time: Administration time varies depending on the grade level of the student and the number of subtests administered.

Comments: Examiners may choose to administer one subtest, a subset of subtests, or all 16 subtests; not all subtests contribute to the Total Achievement composite; the Math Fluency subtests do not contribute to the Total Achievement composite; the Early Reading Skills subtest and the Alphabet Writing Fluency subtest are administered to students in prekindergarten through Grade 3 but only contribute to the Total Achievement composite for prekindergarten through Grade 1; the Oral Reading Fluency subtest is administered to students in Grades 1-12 but only contributes to the Total Achievement composite for Grades 2-12; the Spelling subtest is administered to students in kindergarten through Grade 12 but only contributes to the Total Achievement composite for kindergarten through Grade 2; the publisher advises that adult norms for ages 20-50 were published in 2010.

Author: Pearson.

Publisher: Pearson.

Cross References: For reviews by Beth J. Doll and by Gerald Tindal and Michelle Nutter of the Second Edition, see 15:275; see also T5:2861 (4 references); for reviews by Terry Ackerman and Steven Ferrara of a previous edition, see 13:359 (17 references).

Review of the Wechsler Individual Achievement Test–Third Edition by M. DAVID MILLER, Professor, College of Education, University of Florida, Gainesville, FL:

DESCRIPTION. The Wechsler Individual Achievement Test–Third Edition (WIAT-III) is a diagnostic achievement test that is individually administered to students in Grades Prekindergarten (age 4) through 12 (age 19 years and 11 months). [Editor's Note: Adult norms for ages 20–50 were made available to customers in 2010.] The WIAT-III is a revised version of the WIAT-II. The revision was undertaken to develop a more comprehensive test that is responsive to changes in federal mandates and state regulations. Specifically, the WIAT-III is designed to (a) identify academic strengths and weaknesses, (b) inform decisions regarding eligibility for services, placement, or diagnosis of specific learning disabilities, and (c) design instructional objectives and plan interventions. Thus, the primary goal of the WIAT-III is to provide more in-depth academic assessment and intervention recommendations particularly for students who may have specific learning disabilities.

The WIAT-III has added new subtests in Math Fluency and Oral Reading Fluency to provide domain coverage in every achievement area specified by federal law for identifying learning disabilities (*Individuals with Disabilities Education Improvement Act of 2004*). The WIAT-III provides eight composite scores with 16 subtests. The composite scores are Oral Language, Total Reading, Basic Reading, Reading Comprehension and Fluency, Written Expression, Mathematics, Math Fluency, and Total Achievement. The 16 subtests are Listening Comprehension, Oral Expression, Early Reading Skills, Word Reading, Pseudoword Decoding, Reading Comprehension, Oral Reading Fluency, Alphabet Writing Fluency, Spelling, Sentence Composition, Essay Composition, Math Problem Solving, Numerical Operations, Math Fluency–Addition, Math Fluency–Subtraction, and Math Fluency–Multiplication.

Standardized procedures for administration are provided along with the needed testing materials. Testing time for students will vary depending on the age/grade level and the number of subtests being used. Average administration time ranges from 1 minute to 17 minutes.

Standardized scoring procedures are provided. Scoring can be completed by hand or with the Scoring Assistant CD. Several derived scores are available for each subtest: standard scores, percentile ranks, grade and age equivalents, normal curve equivalents, and stanines. Scores are presented as a profile across subtests and/or composites. In addition, confidence intervals and descriptive classifications can be used with the scores for interpretation. Growth Scale Values can be used to track changes over time.

To assist in the identification of specific learning disabilities, the WIAT-III can be used with other cognitive ability standard scores to conduct an ability-achievement discrepancy (AAD) analysis. A second approach for analyzing specific learning disabilities that is available through the Scoring Assistant CD is the Pattern of Strengths and Weaknesses (PSW) discrepancy analysis. Finally, item-level and within-item-level skills analyses can be used to guide the formulation of instructional objectives and interventions.

DEVELOPMENT. The WIAT-III had a conceptual development stage to identify changes from the WIAT-II. This stage included market research with special education practitioners, expert advisory panels, and surveys of experts and examiners. Changes to the WIAT-III were based on stakeholder input, federal and state mandates, and the professional literature. The new test items went through multiple pilot studies and a national tryout before standardization. All practices were consistent with the *Standards for Educational and Psychological Testing* (American Educational Research Association, American Psychological Association, & National Council on Measurement in Education, 1999).

TECHNICAL.

Standardization. Norms were developed with 2,775 students in Grades PK–12. Separate norms are reported for Fall (*N* = 1,400) and Spring (*N* = 1,375). Although the norming sample was not randomly selected, the sample was stratified to reflect the 2005 U.S. Census data. Stratification was done by grade, age, sex, race/ethnicity, education level, and geographic region. The norming samples were constructed so that they were representative of the U.S. population for each grade level, each age level, and total. Students were also added from special groups (e.g., specific learning disabilities, speech or language impairment, intellectual disability, and developmental delay) to be nationally representative.

The norms provide a representative sample of the general U.S. population and are consistent with professional practice. The size of the norming groups does not allow separate norms except by grade or age level.

Reliability. Split-half reliabilities were reported for all subtests and composites by grade and age level with some exceptions. Alphabet Writing Fluency, Sentence Composition, Essay Composition, Oral Expression, and Oral Reading Fluency reported test-retest reliability since there are no item level data. Alphabet Writing Fluency and Math Fluency also used test-retest reliability because they are timed tests.

The average reliability coefficients for all subtests except Alphabet Writing Fluency are .80 and higher for the Fall sample. Reliabilities are slightly lower for the Spring sample. Alphabet Writing Fluency had reliability estimates for each grade level in the Fall sample of .69. The composite reliability estimates exceed .90 with few exceptions. Consequently, the reliability estimates of the subtests and composites are acceptable for most test uses and interpretations. It should be noted that reliability estimates are not reported for the item-level and within-item-level scores that the manual suggests using for planning interventions.

Validity. The recommended interpretations and uses of the WIAT-III are: (a) identifying academic strengths and weaknesses, (b) informing decisions regarding eligibility for services, placement, or diagnosis of specific learning disabilities, and (c) designing instructional objectives and planning interventions. Three primary validity studies are reported: content evidence, convergent evidence, and special group studies.

The content evidence is based on the process used to develop the WIAT-III from the WIAT-II. These studies, consisting of literature and expert reviews (as described in the test development section), are consistent with professional practice and provide validity evidence for interpretations and uses (a) and (b) above.

Convergent evidence is based on correlation studies with the WIAT-III. Studies have been conducted to show the correlation between the WIAT-III and the WIAT-II, as well as the following ability measures: WPPSI-III, WISC-IV, WAIS-IV, WNV, and DAS-II. All correlations were moderate to high (and positive) suggesting strong convergent evidence for interpretation of the subtests and composites.

Studies of special groups provide evidence for informing decisions about eligibility for services, placement, and diagnosis. Matched control groups were compared with the following special groups: academically gifted, mild intellectual disability, reading disorder, disorder of written expression, mathematics disorder, and expressive language disorder. With few exceptions, significant differences were found between the special groups and the matched controls on all subtests and composites. One notable exception was the lack of a difference for most groups on the Alphabet Writing Fluency subtest.

Although the validity evidence collected shows good evidence for some uses of the WIAT-III, no systematic studies have been reported for the third use suggested in the manuals: designing instructional objectives and planning interventions. In addition, no studies are reported on differential evidence for race/ethnicity or gender.

SUMMARY. Overall, the WIAT-III is an achievement battery that is well constructed, has representative norms, and provides solid evidence of reliability and validity. The technical manual provides good evidence for (a) identifying academic strengths and weaknesses, and (b) informing decisions about eligibility for services, placement, and diagnosis of specific learning disabilities. However, the WIAT-III does not provide evidence (reliability or validity) for the suggested use of the test to design instructional objectives and plan interventions. (Note: It may work but the evidence is lacking.) All subtests and composites have strong psychometric properties with the exception of the Alphabet Writing Fluency subtest. Finally, no evidence is provided for differences between race/ethnic or gender groups in test use or interpretation.

REVIEWER'S REFERENCE

American Educational Research Association, American Psychological Association, & National Council on Measurement in Education. (1999). *Standards for educational and psychological testing.* Washington, DC: American Educational Research Association.

Review of the Wechsler Individual Achievement Test–Third Edition by JOHN T. WILLSE, Associate Professor of Educational Research Methodology, University of North Carolina at Greensboro, Greensboro, NC:

DESCRIPTION. The Wechsler Individual Achievement Test-Third Edition (WIAT-III) is designed to assess achievement levels of students from prekindergarten through Grade 12. There are 16 subtests (Listening Comprehension, Early Reading Skills, Reading Comprehension, Math Problem Solving, Alphabet Writing Fluency, Sentence Composition, Word Reading, Essay Composition, Pseudoword Decoding, Numerical Operations, Oral Expression, Oral Reading Fluency, Spelling, Math Fluency–Addition, Math Fluency–Subtraction, Math Fluency–Multiplication), and 8 composite scores (Oral Language, Total Reading, Basic Reading, Reading Comprehension and Fluency, Written Expression, Mathematics, Math Fluency, Total Achievement). All 16 subtests or a subset of those subtests may be administered. Not all subtests contribute to Total Achievement, and which subtests contribute to Total Achievement changes somewhat depending on the grade level of the student.

A comprehensive set of materials are available from the publisher: a complete technical manual, a detailed examiner's manual, a scoring workbook to provide examiners with practice, a scoring assistant CD-ROM, and the testing materials themselves. Although the complete assessment is quite long and involved, the materials should provide an experienced examiner with a solid basis for administering this assessment.

DEVELOPMENT. To guide the revisions from the previous version of the WIAT, several types of advisory panels and focus groups were convened. The revisions from the last edition were made to accomplish several goals. Most, though not all, of these goals were related to improving diagnostic capabilities for both persons with learning disabilities and persons who are academically gifted. Other notable changes/goals include reducing the intended population to students in Grades PK–12 by limiting the age range to 4 years 0 months through 19 years 11 months, strengthening connections to the *Individuals with Disabilities Education Improvement Act of 2004*, making connections to other ability and achievement assessments, and improving usability. [Editor's Note: The publisher advises that in response to customer demand, adult norms for ages 20 to 50 were made available in 2010.] Each change made to the assessment is outlined in the technical manual with appropriate justification given to explain each change. The manual explicitly describes the *Standards for Educational and Psychological Testing* (American Educational Research Association, American Psychological Association, & National Council on Measurement in Education, 1999) as guiding the development of and research on the current edition of the WIAT.

TECHNICAL. A number of research questions related to the revision were addressed in three pilot studies (N = 912, 400, and 180). The next stage included a national tryout of 25 potential scales. This national sample was a stratified sample of 700 typically achieving students. The sample was balanced in terms of key demographics. An additional 30 students were included from each of the following special populations: Mild Intellectual Disability (formerly referred to as mental retardation), Learning Disorder in Reading and/or Writing (LD–RW), Learning Disorder in Math (LD–M), and Academically Gifted (GT). These additional groups were used to provide evidence of diagnostically appropriate floors and ceilings for the scales.

After the three pilot tests and the national tryout, a standardization edition of the WIAT–III was developed. The normative sample was based on a stratified sample of 2,775 students in Grades PK–12 (1,375 in the Spring of 2008 and 1,400 students in the Fall of 2008). The technical manual provides strong evidence that the normative sample was broadly representative of the intended population of test takers.

The test developers appear to have used a reasonable approach for the development of a vertical scale (Rasch; item response theory where appropriate) and standard scores (inferential norming) for reporting. Grade and age equivalents and growth scale values are also available. These grade/age equivalents were developed by taking the median score for each grade or age and extrapolating a smooth curve through the points. This practice is consistent with how others create grade/age equivalents, but, as with all of these types of equivalency scores, the quality of the extrapolation between points is largely unknown.

Reliability. The manual presents reliability estimates from the normative sample. The reliability of each subscale and composite is provided. Separate estimates are provided for the Fall and Spring sample. Reliability is further provided by grade level or age. All reported internal consistency and test-retest estimates for the subscores seem adequate for the purpose (average reliabilities ranging from .83 to .97), with the exception of Alphabet Fluency (where test-retest reliability was less than .70). The eight score composites have average internal consistency reliability estimates ranging from .91 to .98 within the normative sample. Further evidence of stability is presented in the form of the test-retest reliability and again seems adequate, with most stability coefficients greater than .80 and only Alphabet Fluency less than .70. The interval between testing sessions ranged from 2–32 days. The average interval between testing sessions was 13 days for Pre-Kindergarten through fifth grade students and 14 days for sixth through twelfth grade students. The interscorer agreement on the WIAT-III is 98%-99% on the more objective subtests and 91%–99% on more subjective subtests (e.g., Sentence Building agreement was .93). The documentation regarding reliability is quite thorough and includes explanations and additional information that is often omitted from technical manuals (e.g., standard errors of measurement for each scale by grade level).

Validity. The technical manual presents a variety of evidence related to validity. Content validity is addressed in a detailed section providing the theoretical rationale used in test development. Correlations among subscores show a fairly high level of intercorrelation. Most of the correlations among subtests are highest where constructs are closely related (and often contribute to the same score composites). Still, some correlations among composites (e.g., the .91 correlation between Total Reading and Achievement Total) are high enough to allow for some questioning of the uniqueness of information provided by these different composites. Convergent validity evidence is provided by reports of correlations with other commercial achievement and ability assessments. Some initial evidence of construct validity is shown through comparisons of special populations (persons with various disabilities and academically gifted) with matched control groups. The resulting group differences provide support for the validity of the subtests with these populations. However, even the author of the technical manual acknowledges that these studies are more illustrative examples of the assessment's potential than they are definitive studies on the diagnostic quality of the WIAT-III.

COMMENTARY AND SUMMARY. The WIAT-III appears to be a well developed assessment. There is a fair amount of theoretical justification for inclusion of the various subtests. There is a great deal of empirical support for the reliability of the assessment, as well as a strong start to the process of validation with the intended population. The materials that accompany the assessment are extensive and very useful. Further, much of the research from the previous edition will be broadly applicable to this edition as well. Reviews of those previous editions are available and should be consulted.

REVIEWER'S REFERENCE

American Educational Research Association, American Psychological Association, & National Council on Measurement in Education. (1999). *Standards for educational and psychological testing*. Washington, DC: American Educational Research Association.

[154]

Wechsler Memory Scale—Fourth Edition.

Purpose: Developed to "assess various memory and working memory abilities" among "individuals with suspected memory deficits or diagnosed with a range of neurological, psychiatric, and developmental disorders."
Publication Dates: 1945-2009.
Acronym: WMS-IV.
Subtest: Brief Cognitive Status Exam (optional).
Administration: Individual.
Price Data, 2009: $675 per complete test kit including administration and scoring manual (2009, 167 pages), technical and interpretive manual (2009, 258 pages), Stimulus Book #1, Stimulus Book #2, 25 Adult record forms, 25 Older Adult record forms, 25 response booklets, Design and Spatial Addition card set, scoring template, memory grid.
Comments: Roman numerals I and II indicate a subtest's immediate and delayed conditions, respectively; Standard administration guidelines require that 20-30 minutes should elapse between the completion of a subtest's immediate condition and the beginning of the delayed condition.
Author: David Wechsler.
Publisher: Pearson.

a) ADULT BATTERY.
Population: Ages 16-0 to 69-11.
Time: [80-115] minutes.
Scores, 12: 7 subtests; 6 primary (Logical Memory I, Logical Memory II, Verbal Paired Associates I, Verbal Paired Associates II, Designs I, Designs II, Visual Reproduction I, Visual Reproduction II, Spatial Addition, Symbol Span; 1 option (Brief Cognitive Status Exam); 5 indices (Auditory Memory, Visual Memory, Visual Working Memory, Immediate Memory, Delayed Memory).

b) OLDER ADULT BATTERY.
Population: 65-0 to 90-11.
Time: [50-70] minutes.
Scores, 10: 6 subtests; 5 primary (Logical Memory I, Logical Memory II, Verbal Paired Associates I, Verbal Paired Associates II, Visual Reproduction I, Visual Reproduction II, Symbol Span); 1 optional (Brief Cognitive Status Exam); 4 indices (Auditory Memory, Visual Memory, Immediate Memory, Delayed Memory).

Cross References: For reviews by Rik Carl D'Amato and Cecil R. Reynolds of the third edition, see 14:416; see also T5:2863 (431 references) and T4:2940 (117 references); for reviews by E. Scott Huebner and Robert C. Reinehr of an earlier edition, see 11:465 (166 references); see also 9:1355 (49 references), T3:2607 (96 references), 8:250 (36 references), T2:592 (70 references), and 6:561 (9 references); for reviews by Ivan Norma Mensh and Joseph Newman of the original version, see 4:364 (6 references); for a review by Kate Levine Kogan, see 3:302 (3 references).

Review of the Wechsler Memory Scale–Fourth Edition by JERRELL CASSADY, Professor of Educational Psychology, Ball State University, Muncie, IN, and ATHENA DACANAY, Doctoral Student of School Psychology, Ball State University, Muncie, IN:

DESCRIPTION. The Wechsler Memory Scale–Fourth Edition (WMS-IV) is an individually administered measure of various memory and working memory abilities designed for individuals ages 16–90. The test authors claim it is particularly useful to professionals interested in measuring episodic, declarative memory functioning and working memory. "In addition to the assessment of memory functioning, the WMS-IV contains a brief evaluation of cognitive status" (administration and scoring manual, p. 1). There are two batteries included in the WMS-IV: an Adult battery for individuals ages 16–69, and a shorter Older Adult battery for individuals ages 65–90. The Adult battery has seven subtests yielding five index scores and the Older Adult battery has five subtests yielding four index scores.

The administration and scoring manual provides instructions that are clear and easy to follow, addressing administration guidelines, materials needed, manner of recording performance, and scoring for each subtest. A demonstration and/or sample item is administered to all examinees prior to the administration of the start point item on several subtests. The use of illustrations and relevant examples provides effective assistance.

DEVELOPMENT. The test authors report their goals for this revision were to enhance effective assessment by (a) improving clinical sensitivity, (b) decreasing administration time for Older Adults, (c) improving forensic utility, (d) reducing confounding factors, (e) eliminating subtest/construct overlap with WAIS, (f) improving assessment of working memory, and (g) improving ease of administration and scoring.

Several subtests were dropped or modified "due to administration, scoring, or psychometric issues, or to keep the overall battery administration time manageable" (technical and interpretive manual, p. 23). The subtests removed from the

WMS-III to create the WMS-IV were Faces, Family Pictures, Word Lists, Letter-Number Sequencing, Digit Span, Spatial Span, Information and Orientation, and Mental Control. The modified subtests were Logical Memory, Verbal Paired Associates, and Visual Reproduction. New subtests were also added, such as Designs, Spatial Addition, Symbol Span, and Brief Cognitive Status Exam. Developers of the WMS-IV also created a Visual Working Memory Index (VWMI) and improved the content of the Visual Memory Index (VMI) by reducing the confounding impact of construct-related concerns. Finally, scores can be reported and described using contrast scores in addition to three standardized scores (i.e., standard scores, scaled scores, cumulative percentages).

TECHNICAL. The standardization sample for WMS-IV consisted of 1,400 examinees ages 16–90 living in the United States. There were 900 examinees who completed the Adult battery and 500 who completed the Older Adult battery. The sample was divided into 14 age bands, each with 100 participants: 16–17, 18–19, 20–24, 25–29, 30–34, 35–44, 45–54, 55–64, 65–69, 70–74, 75–79, 80–84, and 85–90. Two groups of examinees ages 65–69 were collected; one to complete the Adult battery and the other the Older Adult battery. An equal number of men and women were represented in each age group from ages 16–64. More women than men were included in the older age groups (≥ 65), consistent with the 2005 U.S. Census data proportions. The percentages of the U.S. population according to the 2005 U.S. Census data and the normative sample according to age, sex, education level, race/ethnicity, and geographic region were proportional. A list of exclusion criteria included in the manual (e.g., medical and psychological issues, learning disabilities) was used to disqualify participants from the normative sample.

Normative data are provided separately by age band (Adult and Older Adult) for each index (Auditory Memory Index, Visual Memory Index, Visual Working Memory Index, Immediate Memory Index, and Delayed Memory Index). A method of inferential norming was conducted to determine the means, standard deviations, and skewness of each score "for each of the nine age bands of the Adult and five age bands of the Older Adult normative samples" (technical and interpretive manual, p. 39).

Split-half and coefficient alpha methods were reported for all subtests except the Verbal Paired Associates Word Recall Scaled Score (due to broad variability in number of responses) and recognition memory measures (due to highly skewed score distributions). Stability coefficients were reported for the two exceptions. Overall, subtests demonstrated moderate to high internal consistency (.74–.99).

Internal consistency, using the same methods as the normative sample, was obtained for an independent sample of 555 examinees diagnosed with one of several special needs (e.g., Anxiety Disorder, Attention-Deficit/Hyperactivity Disorder, Asperger's Disorder, Autistic Disorder, Major Depressive Disorder, Mathematics Disorder, Mild Cognitive Impairment, Moderate and Mild Intellectual Disability, Probable Dementia of the Alzheimer's Type–Mild Severity, Reading Disorder, Schizophrenia, Temporal Lobe Epilepsy, and Traumatic Brain Injury). Results of the reliability measures provided additional evidence of validity based on test-criterion relationships, thereby supporting the generalizability of the WMS-IV.

Evidence of other reliability estimates (i.e., test-retest stability, interscorer agreement) to support this instrument were also provided. Reported test-retest reliability (time interval range of 14 to 84 days) of the WMS-IV subtests resulted in mean stability coefficients ranging from .59 to .77 in the Adult battery, and .69 to .81 in the Older Adult battery. Stability coefficients of the WMS-IV indexes ranged from .81 to .83 in the Adult battery and .80 to .87 in the Older Adult battery. Interscorer agreement was very high, ranging from .96 to .99 despite several subtests requiring detailed and interpretive scoring based on established criteria. The high values for internal consistency may in part be explained by the greater ranges of scores for several subtests. The test authors note that "reliability for process scaled scores was lower than primary subtest scaled scores" possibly due to smaller score ranges, "ceiling effects or the use of test-retest reliability" (technical and interpretive manual, p. 45).

Evidence to support the validity of the WMS-IV is substantial. Comprehensive literature and expert reviews were used to develop and refine items. Final subtest and item composition were based on data collected during the pilot and tryout phases. In addition, theoretical and observational sources were used to demonstrate validity based on response processes.

Construct evidence derived from previous versions of the Wechsler Memory Scale based on the internal structure of the scales. The test authors note, however, that moderate correlations between subtests are to be expected because although subtests fall under the same domain, each assesses different abilities. Concurrent evidence is presented, in the form of multiple studies showing modest correlations between WMS-IV and other test measures, including Wechsler Memory Scale–Third Edition (WMS-III), California Verbal Learning Test–Second Edition (CVLT-II), Wechsler Adult Intelligence Scale–Fourth Edition (WAIS-IV), Repeatable Battery for the Assessment of Neuropsychological Status (RBANS), and Delis-Kaplan Executive Function System (D-KEFS).

COMMENTARY. Results from the WMS-III often provided valid and reliable estimates of memory ability for individuals, and thus the test was commonly used in conjunction with information obtained from diagnostic interviews, behavioral observations, and other test scores. The value of the WMS-IV as a measure of memory is increased by the added features and benefits. Improvement of floors across subtests, inclusion of a general cognitive screening tool, enhancement of visual memory assessment, and co-norming with the Wechsler Adult Intelligence Scale-IV, expanded its clinical utility. This version also has enhanced user friendliness by including a brief Older Adult battery, reducing subtest administration time, minimizing visual motor demands, assessing working memory, and modifying story content and administration process. In addition, its improved psychometric properties strengthen its reliability and validity as a measure of memory. They also improved ease of administration and scoring by creating new scoring rules for visual reproduction that are fast, easy, and reliable, eliminating subtests that require rapid changing of stimulus pages, and reducing the amount of rapid visual processing required of the examiner. Although development of the WMS-IV took into account motor limitations, it does not address limitations in a patient's input or output channels (i.e., nonfluent aphasia). For example, in practice, the specified 20–30-minute period between administration of Subtests I and II is not as feasible with persons with aphasia.

SUMMARY. The WMS-IV meets its goals of assessing various memory and working memory abilities for persons aged 16–90. The test modifications were based on user feedback and recent research data reflecting a need for efficiency, in addition to accounting for a changing clinical landscape. Substantial reliability and validity evidence is provided to support the inferences to be made from scores generated by the WMS-IV.

Review of the Wechsler Memory Scale–Fourth Edition by MARY (RINA) M. CHITTOORAN, Associate Professor, Department of Educational Studies, Saint Louis University, St. Louis, MO:

DESCRIPTION. The Wechsler Memory Scale–Fourth Edition (WMS-IV) is an individually administered, norm-referenced, standardized measure of visual, auditory, and working memory in adults (ages 16–69) and older adults (ages 65–90). The memory functions assessed by the WMS-IV are reported in individuals with reported memory deficits or those diagnosed with a variety of neurological and psychiatric disorders. The test is designed to be used by experienced clinicians and assessment personnel and, as such, demands substantial training for administration, scoring, and interpretation. Generally, the test can be administered in 130–190 minutes although immediate and delayed versions of subtests must be administered within 20 to 30 minutes of each other in the same testing session. The Adult Battery includes six primary subtests and the optional Brief Cognitive Status Exam whereas the Older Adult Battery includes four primary subtests and the optional Brief Cognitive Status Exam. Primary WMS-IV subtests include Logical Memory, which assesses narrative memory under free recall, immediate and delayed conditions, Verbal Paired Associates, which assesses verbal memory for associated word pairs, and immediate and delayed conditions; Designs, which assesses spatial memory for novel visual stimuli in both immediate and delayed formats; Visual Reproduction, both immediate and delayed, which assesses memory for nonverbal visual stimuli; Spatial Addition, which assesses visual-spatial working memory; and Symbol Span, which measures visual working memory using unfamiliar visual stimuli.

Test materials include an administration and scoring manual, a technical and interpretive manual, two sets of record forms (one for each age group), Stimulus Books I and II, stimulus cards, an examinee response booklet in which examinees can complete tasks such as copying and reproducing shapes from memory, a scoring grid, and a cardboard grid to be used during administration.

Performance on the WMS-IV is reported as subtest scaled scores with a mean of 10 and a standard deviation of 3, as standard scores with a mean of 100 and a standard deviation of 15, and as percentile ranks. Five index scores may be derived from the primary subtest scaled scores; these include Auditory Memory, Visual Memory, Visual Working Memory, Immediate Memory, and Delayed Memory. Behavioral observations of performance and examinee profiles can lend depth and context to quantitative information.

DEVELOPMENT. The WMS-IV is based on an instrument that was first introduced by David Wechsler in the 1950s as a standardized measure of memory in the clinical setting. The current edition was developed subsequent to extensive literature reviews on memory as well as clinical use of the Wechsler Memory Scale–Third Edition (WMS-III). WMS-IV subtests were shortened or eliminated, and test administration time was considerably reduced. In addition, subtest floors and ceilings and the content of the Visual Memory Index were improved; three new tests (Designs, Spatial Addition, and Symbol Span), a Visual Working Memory Index, and a brief optional mental status exam were added; and contrast score methodology was introduced to assist in interpretation of scores.

The WMS-IV was piloted twice and then underwent a Visual Working Memory Mini-Pilot, and a subsequent tryout with a diverse sample that was similar to the eventual standardization sample. Results of these development efforts were used to modify and refine the WMS-IV.

TECHNICAL. The standardization sample included 1,400 individuals with an equal number of males and females in separate age groups from 16 to 64 years. Racial and ethnic diversity was proportionate to numbers identified in the 2005 U.S. Census, and education level ranged from those who had never attended high school to those with a college degree or higher. Proportional sampling was used to select examinees from the Northeast, South, Midwest, and West. Four hundred and eighty examiners were paid an incentive fee to participate in standardization, and efforts were made to ensure that examiners and scorers were appropriately trained.

Internal consistency reliability coefficients for the normative sample ranged from a low of .66 to a high of .98 with most coefficients higher than .80. Among the index scores, reliability coefficients ranged from a low of .89 to a high of .97 with the majority of coefficients in the mid-.90s. With special group samples (e.g., depression, ADHD), reliability coefficients ranged from a low of .74 to a high of .99. Reliability coefficients for the index scores were, for the most part, in the high .90s. Standard errors of measurement by age group ranged from .42 to 1.72 on the subtest scales and from 2.60 to 4.97 on the index scores. Test-retest reliability was studied by administering the WMS-IV to 244 adults with a mean test-retest interval of 23 days; coefficients ranged from .59 to .87 across all ages. All WMS-IV protocols were scored by two individuals working independently; interscorer reliability ranged from .98 to .99 on subtests that required objective scoring; coefficients were very slightly lower on the two subtests that required subjectivity in scoring.

Regarding validity, content evidence was established by grounding it firmly in the literature on memory and assessment, submitting it to expert reviews, and seeking customer feedback. Evidence of validity based on response processes was gathered by referring to the literature, soliciting expert reviews, and conducting empirical evaluations. Construct evidence was established by referencing earlier versions of the test; moderate correlations between subtests provided evidence of structural integrity and additional studies conducted with both normative and special groups revealed modest correlations. Confirmatory factor analyses were used to test a two-factor model (Visual Memory and Auditory Memory) and a three-factor model (Visual Memory, Visual Working Memory, and Auditory Memory) using the Delayed Memory and Working Memory subtests for the overall sample as well as for three age groups: 16–24, 25–44, and 45–69. Four separate goodness-of-fit statistics revealed higher than expected values for all groups. Both models were adequate to explain the variance for the two older age groups; however, the three-factor model had slightly superior explanatory power than did the two-factor model for those between 16 and 24 years.

Concurrent evidence derived from studies using the WMS-IV and several other tests of memory showed low to moderate correlations with the WMS-III, moderate correlations with the WMS-III Abbreviated, generally low correlations with the California Verbal Learning Test–Second Edition (except for moderate correlations on Verbal Paired Associates and Logical Memory), and low to high correlations with the Children's Memory Scale. Correlations with tests of general cognitive functioning showed coefficients ranging from .40 to .71 on the WAIS-IV index scores and on the

WISC-IV, from .24 to .68 for the index/composite scores and .05 to .55 on the subtest scores. The WMS-IV also showed low to moderate correlations with neuropsychological, academic, and daily living skills measures, both with normative and special samples. Generally, the highest correlations were obtained across similar subtests in the same or related domains.

COMMENTARY. The WMS-IV has a long, distinguished history as one of the few norm-referenced, standardized measures of memory in existence. It is research and theory-based, statistically sound, and has excellent clinical applications. It has impressive internal consistency, excellent interscorer reliability (even on two subtests that require subjective scoring), and good test-retest stability. It demonstrates superior evidence of validity, in the form of content and construct evidence and acceptable concurrent evidence, given the uniqueness of its domains and subtests. The test authors are to be commended for their efforts in developing, piloting, and conducting tryouts of the WMS-IV and for the quality of its standardization sample. Instructions for administration and scoring are extensive and clearly outlined; these are particularly useful for scoring examinee products, a historically difficult task that may be obviated somewhat by the inclusion of sample drawings and clear scoring guidelines. The technical and interpretive manual is thorough and comprehensive. Also included are sample profiles and suggested interventions that enhance the utility of the WMS-IV. This edition of the Wechsler Memory Scale is shorter than its predecessors, thereby decreasing examinee fatigue and improving the quality of obtained results, particularly with older adults. The WMS-IV may be profitably used in conjunction with the WAIS-IV because both tests assess unique but related constructs over the same age span.

Despite its positive features, the WMS-IV has a couple of undesirable features that must be mentioned. For example, the stimulus cards that are designed to be inserted into the cardboard grid are too large for the corresponding spaces and had to be forced into place before they would fit; in fact, two volunteer examinees chose to lay their pieces on top of the grid, instead of fitting them into the appropriate spaces. This might be a significant and frustrating disadvantage to elderly examinees or to those with motor problems. A second concern has to do with the interest level of the subtests from an examinee's perspective, mainly because the same stimuli are used repeatedly (and of necessity) to assess various aspects of memory and working memory. In fact, repetition of tasks on Delayed Recall, Verbal Paired Associates, and Delayed Verbal Production engendered groans of "Oh No!" and "Not again!" from volunteer examinees, who said they had stopped trying because they were so tired of doing the same thing repeatedly. One wonders how this would influence the validity of test results, particularly with older adults. In addition, some of the stimulus items (e.g., stories read out to the examinee) lack appeal; once again, this might influence test results. Another concern has to do with the potential for variation in test administration (e.g., a stimulus page that is to be displayed for 5 or 10 seconds could easily be displayed for a shorter or longer period). Despite the fact that scoring guidelines and samples are available and that interscorer reliability was high when measured with competent, trained volunteer examiners and scorers, the likelihood of subjective and therefore inaccurate scoring could be considerably higher among inexperienced examiners.

SUMMARY. The WMS-IV is an excellent addition to the arsenal of assessment tools available today. This edition of the scale has been vastly improved on the technical front and provides valuable information that was not available with previous editions. There is no comparable standardized measure of memory on the market today and as such, the WMS-IV will be particularly useful to psychologists, neuropsychologists, and educators. The WMS-IV is highly recommended as a comprehensive, technically sound measure of visual and auditory memory in adults and older adults.

[155]

Wechsler Nonverbal Scale of Ability.

Purpose: Designed as a nonverbal measure of general cognitive ability.
Population: Ages 4-0 to 21-11.
Publication Date: 2006.
Acronym: WNV.
Scores, 7: Matrices, Coding, Object Assembly, Recognition, Spatial Span, Picture Arrangement, Full Scale Score.
Administration: Individual.
Levels, 2: Ages 4-0 to 7-11, 8-0 to 21-11.
Price Data, 2007: $675 per complete kit including administration and scoring manual (198 pages), technical and interpretive manual (125 pages), norms booklet (U.S./Canada), stimulus book, 25 record forms, 25 response booklets, spatial span board, object assembly puzzles,

picture arrangement cards, pencil, soft cover carrying case, and Wechsler Nonverbal scoring assistant; $42 per 25 record forms; $31 per 25 response booklets; $210 per object assembly puzzle set; $163 per picture arrangement card set; $130 per administration and scoring manual; $76 per technical and interpretive manual; $26 per norms booklet (U.S./Canada); $130 per stimulus book.
Time: 2-subtest battery: (15-20) minutes; 4-subtest battery: (45) minutes.
Comments: Examinee instructions are delivered via pictorial sequences.
Authors: David Wechsler and Jack A. Naglieri.
Publisher: Pearson.

a) AGES 4-0 to 7-11.
Scores: Matrices (4-subtest battery only), Object Assembly (4-subtest battery only), Recognition, Full Scale Score.

b) AGES 8-0 to 21-11.
Scores: Matrices, Coding (4-subtest battery only), Spatial Span, Picture Arrangement (4-subtest battery only), Full Scale Score.

Review of the Wechsler Nonverbal Scale of Ability by CLEBORNE D. MADDUX, Foundation Professor of Counseling and Educational Psychology, University of Nevada, Reno, Reno, NV:

DESCRIPTION. The Wechsler Nonverbal Scale of Ability (WNV) is an individually administered test of general cognitive ability, with a format "that eliminates or minimizes verbal content" (technical and interpretive manual, p. 1). It is intended for use with examinees between 4 years, 0 months and 21 years, 11 months of age.

The instrument was developed for use "with populations that are diverse in terms of linguistic, educational, cultural, and socioeconomic backgrounds, as well as certain conditions, such as language disabilities and hearing loss" (technical and interpretive manual, p. 1). The manual further states that nonverbal tests such as the WNV are useful for testing minority group children to determine eligibility for gifted programs. It goes on to state that the test is useful across diverse cultural and linguistic groups and across national boundaries for two reasons: (a) because it minimizes the need for receptive language skills and eliminates the effects of varying expressive language skills and mathematical skills on scores of examinees, and (b) because examinee directions are pictorial and make use of little or no verbal instructions, and tasks do not require the examinee to speak.

The WNV includes six subtests, but no examinee will take all six of these. Examinees are divided into two age groups: ages 4 years, 0 months through 7 years, 11 months and ages 8 years, 0 months through 21 years, 11 months. Each age group can be given either a full, four-subtest battery (45 minutes) or a brief, two-subtest battery (20 minutes), all of which will yield a full scale score.

The subtests are Matrices, Coding, Object Assembly, Recognition, Spatial Span, and Picture Arrangement. The full battery consists of the first four of these subtests for individuals in the younger age group, whereas those in the older group take the first two (Matrices and Coding) and the last two (Spatial Span and Picture Arrangement). If the brief, two-subtest battery is elected, those in the younger group take the Matrices and Recognition subtests, whereas those in the older group take the Matrices and Spatial Span subtests.

Four optional scores can also be calculated. The first two are Spatial Span-Forward and Spatial Span-Backward. The manual also includes a method for comparing these two scores. Similarly, scores can be calculated for longest Spatial Span-Forward and longest Spatial Span-Backward. There is also a method provided to compare these two scores.

Test materials come in a large, suitcase-style kit with wheels and a telescoping handle. A spiral-bound administration and scoring manual is well-written and easy to follow with one tabbed section for each of the two age ranges, and appendices containing (a) norms and conversion tables for the scores, (b) critical values and base rate tables for the score analysis, and (c) normative information for the optional analyses of spatial span. There is also a separate technical and interpretive manual.

The administration and scoring manual states that the most innovative aspect of the instrument is the pictorial directions to examinees coupled with gestures and brief verbal prompts in any language (provided in the administration and scoring manual in five languages). According to the manual, these innovations make it possible to administer the test to examinees who are diverse in SES, language, education, or cultural background and those with language disabilities, autism, or those who are deaf or hard of hearing. The manual provides clear and simple directions for administration including start point and discontinue rules for each subtest.

Subtest raw scores are first converted to *T* scores with a mean of 50 and a standard deviation of 10 points. The sum of subtest *T* scores (from either two or four subtests) are then converted to a full scale standard score with a mean of 100 and a standard deviation of 15. Age equivalents are also provided for subtest raw scores and for selected optional scores. Percentile ranks can also be determined for both full scale and subtest *T* scores.

DEVELOPMENT. The subtests of the WNV have been adapted from other Wechsler instruments and from the Naglieri Nonverbal Ability Test–Individual Administration (Naglieri, 2003). The test is different from other Wechsler instruments because the other tests include both verbal and performance items, whereas the WNV seeks to measure general ability exclusively through use of nonverbal items.

Test development included (a) a series of reviews by an international panel, (b) a panel review of the pictorial directions, (c) a series of three pilot studies, and (d) a national tryout. The international panel consisted of researchers and test developers who were asked to review the WNV to ensure that the tests could be used without adaptation in Australia, Canada, France, Germany, the Netherlands, and the United Kingdom. No adaptations were required. A panel of practitioners and researchers reviewed the pictorial directions and commented on the aesthetics of the pictures and the usefulness of the pictorial directions. Some alterations to the directions were made, although no details about these alterations are provided. A list of the panel members is included in the manual, but it is unclear whether this is the same panel referred to earlier as the "international panel" (technical and interpretive manual, p. 7). Three pilot studies were conducted with small numbers of participants (n = 19, 28, and 17) to assess the efficacy of pictorial directions for use in all countries, content of items, adequacy of subtest floors and ceilings, and administration procedures. No further details about these studies are provided.

The national tryout was conducted with an early edition of the test that contained eight subtests. This tryout involved a sample of 229 examinees stratified by age, sex, race/ethnicity, education level, and geographic region of the U.S. The same research questions were used as those used in the pilot studies, and item order was changed based on relative difficulty. In addition, factor-analytic studies were conducted and data were gathered from 78 individuals who were from special groups. No descriptive or inferential statistics or specific methodological details are provided about any of the these activities.

TECHNICAL.

Standardization. The WNV was standardized concurrently in the United States and Canada. In the U.S., normative data were developed with a sample of 1,323 examinees ages 4 years, 0 months through 21 years, 11 months stratified on age, sex, race/ethnicity, education level, and geographic region. The sample was divided into 15 age groups. Full details concerning the stratification procedures are provided, and they appear to be well-conceived and competently carried out. Norms development is also fully described and is also adequate.

Reliability. The manual provides a table of split-half reliability coefficients for subtests, optional scores, and full scale scores by age group, as well as the overall averages across age groups. Indices for the U.S. sample are provided in this review. Internal consistency appears to be adequate. None of the subtest coefficients are below about .70 for any of the 15 age groups, and the subtest coefficients averaged across the age groups range from .74 (Picture Arrangement) to .91 (Matrices). Only the Picture Arrangement subtest has an average coefficient across ages that is below .75. The average coefficient across age groups is .91 for full scale scores derived from both the four-subtest battery and the two-subtest battery. Coefficients for the optional scores are also adequate and average .76 across age groups for Spatial Span-Forward, and .82 across age groups for Spatial Span-Backward. A similar table of coefficients is provided for U.S. special groups (gifted, mild mental retardation, moderate mental retardation, reading and written expression learning disorders, language disorder, English language learners, deaf, and hard of hearing). These are also adequate.

Test-retest reliability was studied with a sample of 61 examinees between the ages of 4 years and 7 years, 11 months and 103 examinees between the ages of 8 years and 21 years, 11 months. The correlation coefficients corrected for variability of the normative sample were calculated separately for younger and older age groups and are low to adequate in magnitude. There is no information given as to how these examinees were selected.

Validity. As evidence of construct validity, the test makers present the results of an intercorrelational study to determine the relationships among subtest and composite scores. For both age groups, the correlation between full scale scores for the two-subtest and four-subtest batteries was found to be .88, and all subtests were found to be significantly correlated with each other. Confirmatory factor-analytic studies using a single-factor model produced specificities for the younger age group that range from .43 to .63 and .32 to .66 for the older age group.

Criterion-related validity was studied by correlating WNV scores with other Wechsler instruments and with two other nonverbal ability tests. These studies make use of relatively small samples and sample selection criteria are not fully disclosed. However, the manual provides complete matrices for each pair of tests including all possible correlations among subtests and more global scores. There is too much information to summarize in this brief review, but results of the study using the WNV and the Wechsler Intelligence Scale for Children–Fourth Edition (WISC-IV; Wechsler, 2003) are interesting, because both instruments are said to be appropriate for ages 6 years to 16 years, 11 months and because the WISC-IV is so widely used. The two-subtest and four-subtest WNV full scale scores produced correlations with the WISC-IV full scale IQ of .58 and .76, respectively. The correlations between the WNV and the WISC-IV Perceptual Reasoning Index were .57 for the two-subtest battery and .66 for the four-subtest battery. Similarly, correlations between the WNV and the Naglieri Nonverbal Ability Test—Individual (NNAT-I; Naglieri, 2003) and the Universal Nonverbal Intelligence Test (UNIT; Bracken & McCallum, 1998) are important because all three are nonverbal ability tests. Full scale score correlations with the NNAT-I were .71 and .73 for the two-subtest and four-subtest batteries, respectively. Full scale score correlations with the UNIT were .62 and .73. This reviewer considers these coefficients to be low, because all three are intended to be nonverbal measures of ability, yet the percent of shared variance ranges from a low of 26% to a high of 53%. Correlations with the Wechsler Individual Achievement Test (WIAT-II; Wechsler, 2001) produced coefficients of .43 and .60 for the two- and four-subtest batteries.

Concurrent validity was investigated by comparing mean scores of a number of special groups with mean scores of a control group matched, in each case, for age, race/ethnicity, and education level. Numbers of examinees in the special groups ranged from 25 to 55. Results of these studies show significant differences between the control group mean and the special group mean in the gifted study, studies of both levels of mental retardation, and the study of language disorders. The significant difference found in the latter group is a cause for concern. The authors make the case that this finding is to be expected because research has shown that children with language disorders tend to have global deficits in cognitive functioning. Nonsignificant differences were found in the study of reading and written expression learning disorders, the study of English language learners, the study of deaf individuals, and the study of hard of hearing individuals. The nonsignificant findings are interesting and seem consistent with the contention that the test is a nonverbal measure of ability. However, the studies used relatively small samples, which compromise statistical power.

COMMENTARY. The WNV is an individually administered nonverbal ability test for use with individuals from age 4 to age 21 years and 11 months. The test is intended for use with culturally and linguistically diverse examinees. Both full (45 minutes) and brief (20 minute) batteries are available. The test is expensive, but is easy to administer and score and the materials are attractive and interesting to examinees. The administration and scoring manual and the technical and interpretive manual are well-written and easy to follow. The pictorial directions make the test unique and particularly appropriate for use with individuals who are not fluent in English.

The theory on which the test is based is somewhat dated, and the manual needs to address this failing in light of the fact that more recent theories have been proposed. Nevertheless, the instrument is unique in its use of pictorial directions, and it can be administered and scored very quickly. Considerable effort has been expended to make the test appropriate for use with culturally and linguistically diverse populations. When a fast screening instrument is needed for use with such examinees, the WNV shows considerable promise.

SUMMARY. The WNV is a well-standardized instrument that has undergone extensive development efforts to ensure that it is appropriate for use with culturally and linguistically diverse populations. Normative procedures were well-done and extensive measures were taken to ensure the sample was representative of the U.S. population. The technical information provided is excellent, although more detail is needed about how samples were obtained for many of the studies that are reported. This is particularly true in the sections devoted to test item development and in the sections that report the results of studies correlating WNV scores with scores from other instruments.

Reliability appears to be adequate, but some questions remain concerning validity. Further research is needed to explain the relatively low correlations between the WNV and scores on the two other nonverbal ability measures. These low correlations might be due to the fact that the WNV makes use of pictorial directions, thus reducing the need for language facility on the part of examinees. More investigations would provide useful information.

REVIEWER'S REFERENCES

Bracken, B. A., & McCallum, R. S. (1998). Universal Nonverbal Intelligence Test. Itasca, IL: Riverside Publishing.

Naglieri, J. A. (2003). Naglieri Nonverbal Ability Test—Individual Administration. San Antonio, TX: Harcourt Assessment.

Wechsler, D. (2001). The Wechsler Individual Achievement Test—Second Edition. San Antonio, TX: The Psychological Corporation.

Wechsler, D. (2003). The Wechsler Intelligence Scale for Children—Fourth Edition. San Antonio, TX: Harcourt Assessment.

Review of the Wechsler Nonverbal Scale of Ability by GERALD TINDAL, Castle–McIntosh–Knight Professor of Education, College of Education, University of Oregon, Eugene, OR:

DESCRIPTION. The Wechsler Nonverbal Scale of Ability (WNV; 2006) is structured with a four-subtest and two-subtest battery and is designed for two different age groups (ages 4 through 7 and 8 through 21). In the younger age group, the four subtests are: Matrices, Coding, Object Assembly, and Recognition; for the older age group, the four subtests are Matrices, Coding, Spatial Span, and Picture Arrangement. When only two subtests are used, Matrices and Recognition are used with the younger age students and Matrices and Spatial Span are used with the older age students. Because the same materials are presented for students of varying ages, a set of rules are used in starting and stopping the test.

Matrices. Geometric figures are presented in a pattern with an element missing and four to five options for completing the pattern are presented below. The student is directed to complete the pattern.

Coding. Five figures or nine numbers are matched to a geometric shape at the top in a series of rows; the figures (or numbers) are presented with a space below each one. The student is directed to insert the correct geometric figure in the space. This subtest is timed.

Object Assembly. A common object is presented in two to eight pieces of a puzzle; the student is directed to assemble the pieces to form a whole. This subtest is timed.

Recognition. A geometric figure is presented to the student for three seconds and then replaced with a set of three to five figures, only one of which is an exact duplicate. The student is directed to identify the matching figure.

Spatial Span. A set of blocks is affixed in a random pattern on a board; the student is directed to touch blocks in the same or reverse order of that demonstrated by the tester.

Picture Arrangement. A set of three to six pictures are presented on cards depicting a series of events reflecting a logical pattern of actions (activities). The student is directed to arrange the cards so they present a logical order. The subtest is timed.

The manipulative materials (Object Assembly puzzles, Spatial Span board, and the Picture Arrangement cards) are each boxed in a very easy-to-access manner with the visual images used in other tasks presented in a well-organized stimulus book. For the Coding subtest, a response booklet and scoring template are presented. All student materials are professionally done by graphic artists, are colorful, and are made of materials that can withstand repeated administrations (heavy cardboard or thick paper). In addition to these student materials, the test kit includes an administration and scoring manual, a record form, and a technical and interpretive manual.

The administration and scoring manual presents clear directions on a number of issues: (a) general administration guidelines, (b) start points, reverse rules, discontinue rules, and timing, (c) scoring rules and record form completion, (d) specific scripted administration in six languages (English, French, Spanish, German, Dutch, and Chinese) separated into the two age-groups, and a series of appendices for presenting norms and conversion tables, critical values for analyzing subtest patterns and base rates, and normative information for analyzing Spatial Span (forward versus backward).

The technical and interpretive manual is organized into six chapters that address (a) an introduction of nonverbal assessment instruments, (b) design and purpose of the scale, (c) research, standardization, and norm development, (d) reliability evidence, (e) validity evidence, and (f) interpretation considerations. Five appendices present intercorrelation tables, tables of correlations with the WIAT II, inclusion criteria for the participation of special group studies, information on examining deaf and hard of hearing students, and a listing of the individuals who have consulted or been involved in the development of the norms.

DEVELOPMENT. Test development is well described and provides a very complete process in which piloting was conducted, followed by national tryouts, item evaluation, and final assembly. Data presented in the technical manual are organized around the central evidentiary analyses proposed in the *Standards for Educational and Psychological Testing* (American Educational Research Association, American Psychological Association, & National Council on Measurement in Education, 1999).

TECHNICAL.

Standardization. The standardization sample is well described with approximately 100 students per grade band sampled from four regions of the U.S. (northeast, northcentral, south, and west). In addition to geographic representation, the sample is well balanced (reflective of the U.S. population) in terms of age, gender, race-ethnicity, and (parent) education level. A separate Canadian normative sample is extensively described. "Mean differences between the Canadian and U.S. samples were observed for all subtest scores: Matrices (.70 points), Coding (1.60 points), Object Assembly (4.00 points), Recognition (2.80 points), Spatial Span (2.30 points), and Picture Arrangement (2.50 points)" (technical and interpretive manual, p. 24).

Reliability. The reliability evidence presents internal consistency values for both subtest levels and the total test for every age (4–21); most of the subtest reliability coefficients are adequate (with somewhat moderate correlations for Picture Arrangement in the U.S. sample). The reliability coefficients are high for the full scale score. For a number of "special groups" the reliability coefficients are high with the exception of Spatial Span-Forward with a few disability groups. Score differences are addressed primarily to guide users in analyzing strengths and weaknesses using critical values (of significance) reported in the administration and scoring manual.

Standard errors of measurement (*SEM*) and confidence intervals are presented for all subtests and age groups; in general, the *SEM* is between 3–5 *T*-score units for most subtests and about 4 *T*-score units for the full scale score. Test-retest stability is reported for all subtests and for both age groups; the correlation between test performances is moderate for subtests and adequate for the full scale score. Interscorer agreement is high (from .88 to .94 for cases in the normative sample).

Validity. Several types of validity evidence are presented. No content-related evidence is presented even though the manual states "evidence of content validity is not based on statistics or empirical testing; rather, it is based on the degree to which the test items adequately represent and relate to the trait or function that is being measured" (technical and interpretive manual, p. 43). The WNV is designed to measure general ability; no such definitions or operationalizations of this construct are presented. Two types of analyses are presented as evidence of the test's internal structure. Using Campbell and Fiske's (1959) convergent and discriminant validity matrix, all subtests are intercorrelated. Most of the coefficients are moderate, indicating a reasonable level of relations that are neither too strong nor too weak. A factor-analytic study is presented using confirmatory factor analysis in different age groups in which communality, specificity, and error variance are estimated; findings show that the unique variance attributable to a particular subtest (specificity) consistently exceeds the error variance; often it is equal to or less than the variance that is common across subtests with *Coding* having the weakest pattern or consistent relation with ability. When a model-fit analysis is used to estimate the population covariance matrix, the findings show a single factor model in the early age group but a significant departure in the older group. Finally, evidence based on relation with other measures presents a series of correlational studies with the *WNV* and a parade of other tests (mostly within the PsychCorp® family). Typically, the findings confirm moderate relations among subtests as well as full-scale scores of both measures. As expected, the coefficients are much lower when using subtests. Another form of criterion-related evidence is the use of special populations: gifted, mild intellectual disabilities, moderate intellectual disabilities, reading and written expression learning disorders, language disorders, English language learners, and deaf and hard of hearing. In all of these studies, the performance of individuals in these groups is as predicted and consistently different than a matched (on age, gender, race-ethnicity, education level, and geographic region) comparison group.

Test interpretation provides the user with a number of options for reporting results that are typical of norm-referenced tests: Standard scores (a *T*-score for subtests with a mean of 50 and standard deviation of 10 and a full scale score with a mean of 100 and standard deviation of 15), percentile ranks, standard errors of measurement and confidence intervals, qualitative descriptive categories, and test age-equivalents. The technical and interpretive manual presents a very clear sequence of steps for summarizing performance, including a subtest analysis and an optional analysis of Spatial Span. Finally, normative information is considered for both the U.S. and Canadian samples.

The subtest analysis provides the tester with information about strengths and weaknesses relative to a normative sample. The technical and interpretive manual also states: "when there is sufficient evidence that an examinee's scores are significantly different from each other or the score is below average, as well as other corroborative evidence, instructional recommendations can be considered" (p. 72). The authors then provide an example using a low Spatial Span score: "One way to help Lucy perform better may be to teach her to use chunking or other mnemonic methods for academic tasks that demand recall of information" (p. 72).

COMMENTARY. The Wechsler Nonverbal Scale of Ability is a very well-designed and developed test that can be used in understanding fairly task-specific performances that may be important in general school functioning. The behaviors that are sampled probably reflect latent traits with relevance for performance on classroom tasks. The test development process is well documented and the test itself is well formatted and packaged for clear and accurate administration. The technical support of the subtests and full test is very complete with well-documented reliability and validity evidence presented in clearly labeled tables.

SUMMARY. The two cautions to note in using this test, however, include the limited information presented about the construct that the test appears to be assessing and the application of results from the test to guide interventions in classrooms. Nonverbal intelligence is a weighty construct that needs more consideration both theoretically and operationally. Yet, little to no information is presented in the test manual to address this construct adequately. Theoretically, it needs to be placed in a nomological net reflecting relations with other constructs, some of which may be more directly observable. Furthermore, application of the results in school tasks needs to be more tenuously considered. Although the test developers provide suggestions for analyzing strengths and weaknesses, this application is likely premature and needs far more empirical (and experimental) research to support the suggestions that are made. Although the results may help guide decisions at the broadest levels of diagnosis and placement into programs, it would be unwise to target specific interventions. Rather, interpretations such as this need to be viewed as hypotheses that warrant vindication using more classroom-relevant measures of achievement related to the specific skill being targeted.

REVIEWER'S REFERENCES

American Educational Research Association, American Psychological Association, & National Council on Measurement in Education. (1999). *Standards for educational and psychological testing.* Washington, DC: American Educational Research Association.

Campbell, D. T., & Fiske, D. W. (1959). Convergent and discriminant validation by the multi-trait, multi-method matrix. In W. A. Mehrens & R. L. Ebel (Eds.), *Principles of educational and psychological measurement: A book of selected readings* (pp. 273-302). Chicago: Rand McNally & Company.

[156]

Western Aphasia Battery—Revised.

Purpose: "Designed to evaluate a patient's language function following stroke, dementia, or other acquired neurological disorder."

Population: Adults with acquired neurological disorders.

Publication Dates: 1980-2007.

Acronym: WAB-R.

Scores, 16: Spontaneous Speech (Information Content, Fluency/Grammatical Competence and Paraphasias, Total), Auditory Verbal Comprehension (Yes/No Questions, Auditory Word Recognition, Sequential Commands, Total), Repetition, Naming and Word Finding (Object Naming, Word Fluency, Sentence Completion, Responsive Speech, Total), Language Quotient, Cortical Quotient, Aphasia Quotient.

Administration: Individual.

Forms, 3: Part 1, Part 2, Bed-Side Administration.

Price Data, 2010: $318 per complete kit including examiner's manual (2007, 153 pages), stimulus book, 25 record forms, 25 bedside record forms, Raven's Colored Progressive Matrices test booklet, and manipulatives; $43 per 20 record forms (Part 1); $32 per 10 record forms (Part 2); $27 per 25 bedside record forms; $124 per stimulus book; $65 per manipulative set; $81 per examiner's manual.

Time: (30-45) minutes for full battery; (15) minutes for bedside administration; (45-60) minutes for the Reading, Writing, Apraxia Contrucional, Visuospatial, Calculation, and Supplemental Writing and Reading section administration.

Comments: Utilizes criterion-referenced scores.

Author: Andrew Kertesz.

Publisher: Pearson.

Cross References: See T5:2873 (74 references) and T4:2949 (33 references); for a review by Francis J. Pirozzolo of an earlier edition, see 9:1362 (1 reference).

Review of the Western Aphasia Battery–Revised by SHAWN K. ACHESON, Senior Research Associate, Duke University Medical Center, Raleigh, NC:

DESCRIPTION. Like the original, the revised version of the Western Aphasia Battery is an individually administered battery of tests intended to assess linguistic competence in a variety of neuropathologies. The test author lays out four primary purposes for the use of this instrument including diagnosis of type and severity of aphasia, establishment of baseline performance against which improvement or decrements can be determined, comprehensive description of linguistic strengths and weaknesses for treatment planning and management, and identification of location and etiology of the source of language impairment. According to the manual, the Western Aphasia Battery–Revised (WAB-R) makes use of a taxonomic table developed with the original WAB to diagnose the specific type of agnosia. This taxonomic procedure is based on four well-established linguistic components: speech fluency, verbal comprehension, repetition, and naming. The target population is described as broad, encompassing both English speaking adolescents and adults.

The WAB-R can be administered by a variety of healthcare professionals with psychometric assessment experience and training. It is used either as a bedside assessment (for which there is a new form) or a more comprehensive assessment using the standard form. The supplemental record form allows for the assessment of additional neurocognitive processes including reading, writing, apraxia, construction, visuospatial ability, and arithmetic calculation. Each form makes use of summed raw scores, some of which are divided by 10 or 20 for reasons that are not described. These modified raw scores are then summed to generate composite scores: Bedside Language Score, Aphasia Quotient, Language Quotient, and Cortical Quotient. Standard scores derived from normative data are not used in this instrument.

DEVELOPMENT. No description is provided concerning the methods and processes used to develop test items, subtests, or composite scores. The new bedside assessment procedure uses selected items from the standard form; however, there is no description of how those items were selected. Convincing rationale is provided for why each domain is used, but there is no description of how each section was developed.

TECHNICAL. The original WAB was standardized on 150 aphasics and 59 controls (ca. 1974). Fifty-six percent of this group were patients at the University of Western Ontario's affiliated teaching hospital, 25% were patients at a veteran's hospital, and 19% were patients at a different hospital. All patients in the aphasia group received an aphasia diagnosis from a physician or speech language pathologist. The majority (76%) had experienced a stroke (cerebral vascular accident). Men outnumbered women 2:1 in this sample. The 59 controls consisted of non-brain-damaged individuals (35.6%), non-dominant-hemisphere injured (29%), and a group of mixed injury individuals (35.6%). The average age was 61.1 years for the aphasic group and 59 for the control group. Both groups had an average of 8 years of education. No standard deviations for age are provided. However, the test instrument is advertised to be normed for individuals age 18–89 on the Pearson Assessment website. Due to the limited demographic information, it is not possible to determine the applicability of this instrument across demographic categories.

The test author provides scant information about a more current standardization sample later in Chapter 5: Standardization of the WAB. This newer sample is reported to contain 215 aphasics. The aphasics consisted of consecutive referrals to the test author's aphasia clinic. The control group was made up of 10 noninjured, age-matched hospital staff and 53 nonaphasic patients with right hemisphere injury. Other than mean age (and *s.d.*), no descriptive or demographic data (e.g., sex, race/ethnicity, or education) are provided for this sample. It is not clear when, and for what purpose, these data were collected beyond the development of the new supplemental tests (Form 2). For example, reliability and validity are discussed prior to the presentation of this additional sample. No mention is made of whether it was included in the analysis of reliability and validity for the standard test.

On the whole, reliability is generally acceptable. Internal consistency reliability for the WAB as a whole was reported to be .91. Intrarater (.92–.99) and interrater (.98–.99) reliability were all very high (except for one subtest, Spontaneous Speech Fluency = .79 in a single rater). Unfortunately, no information is provided concerning the level of training, profession, or WAB familiarity of the raters. This makes it difficult to assess the generalizability of these reliability findings. Test-retest reliability was similarly high. Pearson correlation coefficients between two administrations of the WAB at 1-year intervals was .99, using 22 adults chosen because they had experienced little or no recovery since the onset of aphasia. Subsequent correlations over a 2-year interval for each section score reveals more than adequate correlations. Sixteen of 20 correlations were at or above .85 and only 1 correlation fell below .76. The correlation for Praxis was .45. These test-retest correlations were based on the performance of individuals with chronic aphasic symptoms. The low correlation between the first and second administration of the WAB Praxis section may reveal a differential degree of improvement in Praxis, relative to other WAB sections, or a weakness in the scoring criteria for this particular task.

Despite the otherwise strong reliability, validity of the WAB is not well described. Although correlations between the WAB and the Neurosensory Center Comprehensive Examination for Aphasia (NCCEA) were generally acceptable for individual sections (.82–.92) and the total score (.96), this was the only test of concurrent validity provided. This is all the more problematic given that the NCCEA (Spreen & Benton, 1968) is outdated and only rarely used today. Comparisons between the WAB and the Multilingual Aphasia Exam (Benton, Hamsher, & Sivan, 1994), Reitan's Aphasia Screening Test (Reitan & Wolfson, 1985), or the Boston Diagnostic Aphasia Exam (Goodglass, Kaplan, & Barresi, 2000) would have been far more instructive. The most critical point of validity relates to the numerical taxonomic procedure used to differentiate the various types of aphasia. This section of the manual appears little changed from the original with few references beyond 1977. This does not meet expectations for a test revision published in 2006.

COMMENTARY. The WAB-R provides little benefit beyond the original WAB. Although the test author outlines 12 goals for revision, none provide a valuable addition to the instrument's utility. The manual is poorly organized and appears to be the result of periodic updates based on ancillary data published by the test author. Chapter 5 (Standardization) is written such that it is not clear which data and findings apply to the original WAB and which apply to the WAB-R. The scores generated are not norm-based standard scores and the rationale for the absence of such scores is not well substantiated. There are no explicit procedures described for comparing a patient's level of performance across time, one of the four primary purposes for this instrument. The purpose and validity of the Aphasia Quotient (AQ), Language Quotient (LQ), and Cortical Quotient (CQ) are not well established. For example, the AQ is described as a useful means by which aphasic and nonaphasic patients might be differentiated. However, given the important differences in terms of the nature and location of neural impairment and differences in method of treatment between the various forms of aphasia, a simple distinction between aphasic and nonaphasic offers little utility. Moreover, the taxonomic procedure advocated to differentiate types of aphasia would be sufficient to differentiate impairment of any aphasic typology from nonaphasic impairment. The name (quotient) and character (based on 100 points) of these scores can lead to fundamental misunderstandings of interpretation. These characteristics may lead some less sophisticated clinicians to assume they can be interpreted like intelligence quotients, which are standard scores normally distributed throughout the population with a mean of 100 and a standard deviation of 15. Such assumptions should not be made about the AQ, LQ, or CQ scores on the WAB-R (Sattler, 2008).

SUMMARY. The WAB-R represents a weak revision of a long-established test for aphasia. Although evidence supporting its reliability is acceptable, there is inadequate evidence for validity, no substantive description of item and scale development, and a remarkably limited standardization sample. Any future revision would benefit significantly from a correction of these problems as well as a manual with current references and better organization. The language component of the Neuropsychological Assessment Battery (Stern & White, 2003; 16:163) and the Boston Diagnostic Aphasia Exam (Goodglass, et al., 2000; 17:29) would be more appropriate tools to diagnose aphasia and language impairment.

REVIEWER'S REFERENCES

Benton, A. L., Hamsher, K., & Sivan, A. B. (1994). Multilingual Aphasia Examination (3rd ed.). Iowa City, IA: AJA.

Goodglass, H., Kaplan, E., & Barresi, B. (2000). Boston Diagnostic Aphasia Exam (3rd ed.). Philadelphia: Lippincott.

Reitan, R., & Wolfson, D. (1985). The Halstead-Reitan Neuropsychological Test Battery: Theory and clinical interpretation. Tucson, AZ: Neuropsychology Press.

Sattler, J. M. (2008). *Assessment of children: Cognitive foundations* (5th ed.). San Diego, CA: Sattler Publishing.

Spreen, O., & Benton, A. L. (1968). Neurosensory Center Comprehensive Examination for Aphasia. Victoria, BC: University of Victoria Press.

Stern, R. A., & White, T. (2003). Neuropsychological Assessment Battery. Odessa, FL: Psychological Assessment Resources.

Review of The Western Aphasia Battery–Revised by ANDREW S. DAVIS, Associate Professor, Department of Educational Psychology, Ball State University, and W. HOLMES FINCH, Associate Professor, Department of Educational Psychology, Ball State University, Muncie, IN:

DESCRIPTION. The Western Aphasia Battery–Revised (WAB-R) is a revision of the Western Aphasia Battery that was published in 1982. The WAB-R is a standardized and criterion-referenced test designed to measure a patient's functioning primarily in the area of language. Designed for use with English-speaking adolescent or adult patients with sudden-onset neurological conditions (e.g., stroke) or progressive neurological disorders (e.g., dementia), the WAB-R assesses language and nonlanguage domains. There are a total of eight sections divided into 32 tasks, or subtests. The examiner has several administration options that can shorten the test, including a brief 2-page screening test that can be used as a bedside evaluation. The test author notes that the administration time of the bedside evaluation is 15 minutes, the oral/verbal section administration time is 30–45 minutes, and the remaining tasks take about 45–60 minutes to administer. The test kit comes with most of the objects needed to administer the test, including many common household objects, and the WAB-R Bedside evaluation can use objects typically found in a hospital room or the examiner's possession.

Examiners are able to gather several scores from which to determine a patient's performance. A score can be determined from each of the eight sections, which are Spontaneous Speech, Auditory Verbal Comprehension, Repetition, Naming and Word Finding, Reading, Writing, Apraxia, Constructional, Visuospatial, and Calculation. Three "Quotient" scores can be calculated, which are the Aphasia Quotient, Language Quotient, and the Cortical Quotient. The test author notes that the Aphasia Quotient (AQ) is the "core measure of aphasia" (examiner's manual, p. 6) and is calculated from four section scores: the Spontaneous Speech, Auditory Verbal Comprehension, Repetition, and Naming and Word Finding sections. The Language Quotient (LQ) is composed of tasks that assess spoken and written language. The Cortical Quotient (CQ) is optional, comprising tasks not found on typical assessments of aphasia, including praxis, construction, calculation, and block design and progressive matrices tasks. The WAB-R also provides a classification system that uses an algorithm to sort patients into eight different aphasic diagnoses.

DEVELOPMENT. The WAB-R is a revision of the Western Aphasia Battery (WAB; Kertesz, 1982). The WAB was initially standardized by Kertesz and Poole in 1974 with 150 individuals with aphasia and 59 controls. All members of the aphasic sample had been diagnosed by a physician or speech-language pathologist and were patients at one of three hospitals participating in the study. This sample was used to generate the algorithmic table provided in the WAB-R test manual, which is used to classify individuals by aphasia diagnosis. Some rationale is provided for the cutoff scores for each condition, and the means and standard deviations are reported for patients with different aphasic conditions. The test items were apparently created with increasing levels of difficulty, and a table adapted from the 1974 study shows that difficulty levels were equalized across sections. The criterion used to define difficulty was not explicitly discussed, thus it is unclear whether it was based on classical test theory (i.e., percent of items correctly endorsed), an item response model (e.g., Rasch difficulty values), or some other metric.

The test manual of the WAB-R reports that the WAB underwent two different standardizations, the one listed above and a second with 141 patients with a stroke, 74 patients with different etiologies, and 63 controls. Validity studies were also collected on additional patients with the WAB. The test manual reports that a pilot study for the WAB-R was conducted with 20 participants (14 patients with aphasia and 6 controls). The pilot study participants were evaluated with 10 tasks. The test manual notes that "Examination of the pilot data indicated that modified items were similar in difficulty and frequency of usage ... to the items they were replacing" (examiner's manual, p. 107). However, no tables, data, or figures are provided to show the outcome of the pilot study or what criteria were used to make changes to the WAB-R from the WAB. Indeed, no new information regarding the reliability and validity of the instrument appears to be provided by this pilot sample in the test manual. From the information contained in the test manual, examiners unfamiliar with the WAB will assume that the psychometrics underlying the WAB-R are largely unchanged.

TECHNICAL. The test author reports several studies designed to investigate the validity and reliability of the WAB. They do not, however, appear to have replicated these efforts for the WAB-R. Therefore, the reader must infer that the validity and reliability evidence for the earlier measure is also applicable to this latter version. In terms of criterion-related validity of the WAB, the technical manual reports on a study showing that the mean AQ values for those diagnosed with aphasia was significantly lower than for a control group in the study sample. Results of another study demonstrated that the WAB may have a relatively high false positive rate (approximately .3) for identifying the presence of aphasia, such that they recommend against using only the instrument to diagnose individuals with the disorder, despite its ability to distinguish between patients with aphasia and healthy individuals.

The test author also reported a study of concurrent validity examining the relationship between subscales of the WAB and subscales of the Neurosensory Center Comprehensive Examination for Aphasia (NCCEA; Spreen & Benton, 1968). The correlations reported between subscales of these two measures were uniformly high, ranging from .82 to .96. Thus, to the extent that the NCCEA is itself a valid measure of aphasia, these results demonstrate that the WAB exhibited excellent concurrent validity for the sample of 15 individuals with aphasia who participated in the study. These results should be interpreted in light of the fact that the sample was very small, consisting only of 8 individuals with one type of aphasia (anomic). It is unclear how generalizable these results might be to a more disparate group.

The test author intersperses discussion of reliability and internal consistency with the evidence for validity. Given that an instrument could be reliable but not valid (i.e., an instrument can display a high degree of internal consistency while not being a valid measure of the construct of interest), the organization of this section of the technical manual was somewhat confusing. Nonetheless, if this section is taken at face value, it appears to demonstrate the excellent reliability results taken across a number of different samples. The test author reports an alpha coefficient of .91 for one study, and a Bentler's index value of .97, both of which suggest extremely high internal consistency for the instrument with those samples. Other evidence of the reliability of the WAB for several different samples takes the form of correlations among the subtests (most of which are above .60), test-retest consistency for three different raters (correlations between measurements on the same 10 patients taken at two points in time were nearly all above .90), and test-retest reliability of scores (most correlations were greater than .80). One problem with the reporting of these results, however, is that little or no mention is made regarding the demographic characteristics of the individuals used in the analyses, and the samples were generally small (no more than 35 participants).

A second standardization sample was developed through consecutive referrals to the test author's aphasia clinic. The technical report denotes some of the differences in this sample from the initial group, particularly in terms of the reason for referral. Of particular interest was the use of this group to conduct a taxonomic analysis based on the WAB subscale scores. This statistical technique, which is similar in goal and scope to cluster analysis, identified 10 groups that appeared to be roughly associated with different types of aphasia. Some of these groups presented similar patterns of WAB subscale means, and the test author noted that they may represent only slight variations. It is important to note that several of the groups were very small (<10 participants). The test author argues that this successful clustering of participants based on the WAB subscale suggests that the instrument exhibits a type of criterion-related validity in terms of identifying aphasic subtypes.

In addition to the documentation on the psychometric qualities of the instrument described above, the technical manual for the WAB-R also provides a description of a number of studies in which the WAB was used with individuals diagnosed with dementia. Based on this review of research, the WAB does appear to have the potential for use in identifying aphasia in this specific population.

COMMENTARY. The WAB-R is a revision of the WAB and indeed differs somewhat from the original, including the bedside version, which will be a boon to clinicians working in a hospital setting with patients with limited test-taking skills or who are experiencing fatigue. Other important changes have been made that will also improve the usability and utility of the instrument. The test manual is well-written and the chapter in the test manual, "Rationale and Construction of the WAB," will be especially valuable to newer clinicians or clinicians with limited experience in aphasia. The test assesses a wide range of language functions, including all of the relevant abilities that can present as impaired in patients who present with suspected aphasia. In addition to assessing language, the WAB-R assesses nonlanguage abilities. However, although visual gestalt formation tasks (i.e., block design), dyspraxia, construction problems, and visuo-spatial problems can occur concomitantly with aphasia, some examiners may choose to use more traditional instruments to assess these abilities. Examiners will be particularly interested in the algorithm that is provided in the test manual that can help differentiate aphasia types by test scores.

The psychometric properties of the WAB appear to be adequate. Several types of reliability were assessed with multiple samples, and in nearly all cases the WAB demonstrated a high degree of consistency, across time, across raters, and internally. Of particular interest to clinicians may be the intrarater consistency, which was evaluated using correlations between two measures across time made by the same raters on the same participants. These correlations were above .90, suggesting a very high level of agreement in scores over time for the same participants. The evidence on behalf of the validity of the WAB is not quite as pronounced as that for reliability, though it is by no means deficient. Much of the evidence for validity comes in the form of comparisons with external criteria, such as correlations between the WAB and the NCCEA, and comparisons of WAB subscale means between patients diagnosed with aphasia and a nonclinical sample. In both cases, the WAB performed well. However, there is no information presented regarding the content validity of the measure (review by external experts) nor construct validity (factor analysis or multitrait-multimethod analyses).

Although the available evidence for the WAB paints a positive picture regarding its reliability and validity, there is information lacking that should be included to provide a more complete picture of the utility of the WAB-R. Perhaps first and foremost, there has been very little additional work done with the revised scale. The technical manual reports only one study, based on a sample of 14 patients with aphasia, all of whom were Caucasian and 8 of whom had 16 or more years of education. Thus, the bulk of technical information presented is specific to the older version of the WAB-R, the WAB. This paucity of new work means that potential users must assume that the WAB-R performs similarly to the WAB.

The research that has been conducted on the WAB appears, generally speaking, to have been based upon samples that were predominantly White and male. Although this generalization is not universally true, it does hold for the standardization samples, as well as the sample used with the WAB-R pilot study. Therefore, it is unclear to what extent the instrument is valid for other populations of patients. Finally, although there is positive evidence regarding the validity and reliability of the WAB, as discussed above, there remain certain areas that have not been fully investigated. For example, no factor analysis of the WAB was reported. Such an analysis would be quite useful in establishing the construct validity of the instrument, particularly given the presence of multiple subscales.

SUMMARY. Overall, the WAB-R appears to be a worthy successor to the WAB, including the addition of a bedside evaluation and some revisions of items and materials. The test manual contains quite a bit of information on the original WAB and aphasia. Indeed, the examiner's manual would well serve a training program for clinicians working with patients with aphasia. However, it is important to note that the chapter that discusses the rationale and construction of the WAB, according to the test manual, was previously published elsewhere and was "adapted for this manual" (examiner's manual, p. 24). This issue, although not problematic in isolation, is reflective of the primary concern some users of the WAB-R may express. Although some important changes have been made, many users may wonder how different the WAB-R is from the original, especially because there does not appear to have been new norming or psychometric studies on the WAB-R, at least not reported in the test manual. A small pilot study was conducted with the WAB-R, but it is unclear from the manual how results were used to update the test. Users of the WAB or individuals looking for a test to use with patients with aphasia will likely be satisfied with the current construction of the WAB-R, along with the psychometric qualities of the WAB that would seem to have largely carried over into the WAB-R.

REVIEWERS' REFERENCES

Kertesz, A. (1982). Western Aphasia Battery. New York: Grune & Stratton.

Kertesz, A., & Poole, E. (1974). The aphasic quotient: The taxonomic approach to measurement of aphasic disability. *The Canadian Journal of Neurological Sciences, 1,* 7-16.

Spreen, O., & Benton, A. L. (1968). Neurosensory Center Comprehensive Examination for Aphasia. Victoria, BC: University of Victoria Press.

[157]

Wide Range Achievement Test 4.

Purpose: Designed to "measure the basic academic skills of reading, spelling, and math computation."
Population: Ages 5-94.
Publication Dates: 1940-2006.
Acronym: WRAT4.
Scores, 5: Word Reading, Sentence Comprehension, Spelling, Math Computation, Reading Composite.
Administration: Individual and group.
Levels, 2: Ages 5-7, Ages 8-94.
Forms, 3: Blue, Green, Combined.
Price Data, 2009: $250 per professional manual (2006, 494 pages), 25 blue test/response forms, 25 green test/response forms, 25 blue sentence comprehension response booklets, 25 green sentence comprehension response booklets, set of 2 word reading/spelling cards, set of 3 sentence comprehension cards, and 1 place marker.
Time: (15-45) minutes.
Comments: "The Blue Form and the Green Form can be used interchangeably with comparable results, thus permitting retesting within short periods of time without the potential practice effects that may occur from repeating the same items."
Authors: Gary S. Wilkinson and Gary J. Robertson.
Publisher: Psychological Assessment Resources, Inc.
Cross References: See T5:2879(237 references); for reviews by Linda Mabry and Annie W. Ward of the WRAT3, see 12:414 (111 references); see also T4:2956 (121 references); for reviews by Elaine Clark and Patti L. Harrison, see 10:389 (161 references); for reviews by Paula Matuszek and Philip A. Saigh of an earlier edition, see 9:1364 (103 references); see also T3:2621 (249 references), 8:37 (117 references), and T2:50 (35 references); for reviews by Jack C. Merwin and Robert L. Thorndike of an earlier edition, see 7:36 (49 references); see also 6:27 (15 references); for reviews by Paul Douglas Courtney, Verner M. Sims, and Louis P. Thorpe of the 1946 edition, see 3:21.

Review of the Wide Range Achievement Test 4 by KATHRYN E. HOFF, Associate Professor of Psychology, and MARK E. SWERDLIK, Professor of Psychology, Illinois State University, Normal, IL:

DESCRIPTION. The Wide Range Achievement Test: Fourth Edition (WRAT4) is a norm-referenced achievement test designed to measure the core academic skills of Math Computation, Spelling, Word Reading, and Sentence Comprehension of individuals aged 5–94 years. According to the authors, the WRAT4 was designed to be a simple, time efficient, and technically sound measure. Uses of the WRAT4 include collecting initial evaluation data, screening individuals to identify persons who might need a more in-depth academic assessment, as part of a reevaluation of individuals diagnosed with learning and/or cognitive disorders and evaluating achievement-ability discrepancies to identify specific learning disabilities, determining minimal proficiency levels needed to perform in particular educational or vocational settings, for progress monitoring purposes, or using test results as part of a re-evaluation or a comprehensive evaluation for individuals with learning and/or cognitive disorders. The test kit contains a professional manual, separate blue and green parallel test forms, a response form, a two-sided Word Reading List/Spelling List Card, a Sentence Comprehension Test form, a Sentence Comprehension Card, and a Sentence Comprehension Sample Card.

The WRAT4 includes four subtests: Word Reading, Sentence Comprehension, Spelling, and Math Computation. The WRAT4 is untimed except for the Math Computation subtest, and the authors report administration typically takes between 15 and 25 minutes for children aged 5 to 7 years and 30 to 45 minutes for individuals from 8 to 94 years of age. All parts of the WRAT4 require individual administration by either a trained assessor or a paraprofessional, with the exception of Part 2 of the Spelling and Math Computation subtests which, reportedly, can be administered in a small-group format to participants 8 years or older. The authors state that subtests may be given separately or in combination with one another. There are two forms (Blue form and Green form), containing alternate items, that were designed to be interchangeable with one another. The examiner can choose to administer these forms separately or combine the raw subtest scores from both forms during a single examination period (completion of Combined form summary sheet). It is important to note that the Combined form was not administered to any examinee in the standardization sample. Finally, the user can derive five scores from the WRAT4: one score for each of the four subtests and a Reading Composite score, obtained by combining the Sentence Comprehension and Word Reading standard scores. Scoring is accomplished by summing items within each subtest. Raw scores are converted to norm-referenced scores based on age or grade.

DEVELOPMENT. The WRAT has a long history. The first edition of this measure was published in 1946, and has undergone various revisions. The WRAT4 represents a revision of the WRAT3 that was published in 1993. Although core domains were retained, the WRAT4 includes updated norms, grade-based norms, a Sentence Comprehension measure (added to enhance and expand the reading assessment to include reading comprehension), and an extended age range from 75 (previous edition) to 94 years old. Although the authors made several minor modifications to test items, they strove to retain the "ease of administration and scoring, as well as the significant amount of information gained from a relatively brief investment of testing time" (professional manual, p. 1).

TECHNICAL.

Standardization. The normative sample is based on 3,021 individuals between 5 and 94 years of age. The authors state that the "normative sample was selected according to a stratified national sampling procedure with proportionate allocation controlled for age, gender, ethnicity, geographic region, and educational attainment as an index of socioeconomic status" (professional manual, p. 2). The authors made slight modifications with a weighting procedure to correct for small sampling variations in gender, race/ethnicity, and educational attainment. For example, within the 85–94-year age range, there were a limited number of examinees and what may be a disproportionate number of females (36 females vs. 14 males). Specific demographic information on the grade-based standardization sample (*n* = 1,800) is provided. This sample is composed of data from students enrolled in Grades K-12 from the normative sample. The test authors reported that the grade-based sample included individuals with various types of educational disabilities to the extent that they are represented in the U.S. school population. However, final analyses suggested that all types of disabilities were underrepresented in the WRAT4 sample.

"The WRAT4 norms development process was designed to produce age- and grade-based standard scores" (professional manual, p. 48), including percentile ranks, normal curve equivalents, stanines, grade equivalents, and Rasch ability scaled scores measuring growth across time. However, these Rasch ability scaled scores are not comparable across the four WRAT4 subtests. The manual includes a detailed discussion of the process used to derive the various standard scores.

Reliability. Internal consistency reliability coefficients (coefficient alpha) were presented for single ages 5–12, 2-year age groupings 13–18, 6-year groupings at ages 19–24, and 10-year groups ages 25–94+. The reliability estimates for the four subtests and Reading Composite are excellent for screening purposes and good for individual decision making across most age groups. Median corrected alpha reliability coefficients on the four subtests ranged from .87–.93 by age group and .83–.93 by grade level. Reliability coefficients for the Reading Composite ranged from .95–.96 by age and grade. Reliability coefficients for the Combined form were much higher (.98 for both age and grade), which would be expected considering the Combined form doubles the length of the test. Alternate form reliability was conducted using the parallel Blue and Green forms, and corrected reliability coefficients ranged from .82 (ages 19–34) to .90 (ages 10–11). Alternate form retest reliability data were collected 1 month later on average, and corrected stability coefficients ranged from .68 (Sentence Comprehension for ages 19–94) to .92 (Spelling for ages 19–94) for the age-based sample and ranged from .75 (Math Computation) to .90 (Reading Composite) for the grade level sample. The manual also includes standard errors of measurement (*SEM*) with corresponding confidence intervals for all ages combined but not for individual age levels. No test-retest reliability data, other than one estimate of alternate-forms reliability, are presented.

Person- and item-separation indices are provided for items included on each of the four subtests. For individual subtests, the person-separation reliability coefficients were excellent, ranging from .96–.98 (Blue form) and .95–.98 (Green form), suggesting adequate subtest differentiation. Reliability coefficients for item separation were 1.00 on both the Blue and Green forms. The authors use these person- and item-separation data as an additional estimate of measurement error in test scores.

Validity. There is minimal evidence for what the manual terms internal validity. The authors provide limited information about the development of items, why certain items were included, criteria for item selection, relevancy of items to other indicators, or clear definition of a construct. As evidence of content validity, the authors indicate that 77% of the WRAT4 items were retained from the previous WRAT3 (and earlier test editions), which had reportedly undergone thorough statistical analysis during the WRAT3 standardization and review by outside experts (to ensure freedom from ethnic or gender bias and current relevance). The authors indicate that retaining so many items from the WRAT3 "ensures continuity with the achievement content domains measured by the WRAT3" (professional manual, p. 68) and that items show "universal applicability and relatively little 'aging' or change in their suitability for use over time" (professional manual, p. 69). However, previous reviews of the WRAT3 criticized the content validity of the test (Mabry, 1995; Ward, 1995). The authors use the person-item separation indices as evidence of "the success with which the variables measured by the WRAT4 are adequately defined" (professional manual, p. 65). However, others (Messick, 1989) do not view item separation as a direct measure of item relevance and representativeness.

The authors claim to provide construct validity evidence by demonstrating developmental changes in performance. Specifically, participants' raw scores increase as their age and grade increases, until ages 45–54 when scores gradually begin to decline. These data likely represent that the skills tested are developmental in nature; however, this evidence does not necessarily support that the WRAT4 measures the skills it is designed to assess. The authors also present subtest intercorrelations as evidence for validity internal to the test itself. As expected, there were moderate to strong intercorrelations between subscales, ranging from .79 (Word Reading and Spelling), .63 for Spelling and Math Computation, and .59 for Word Reading and Math Computation, suggesting not all content overlaps (divergent validity).

Differential item functioning, using item difficulty levels, is presented as evidence for the lack of item bias for various groups including Caucasians, African Americans, Hispanics, males, and females. The authors note that "an insignificant number of items were identified as functioning differently" (professionial manual, p. 73), but fail to provide specifics about the criteria they used for eliminating items or deciding how many items were actually eliminated.

Convergent validity was assessed by correlating WRAT4 subtests with similar subtests from an impressive number of well-established achievement tests and cognitive ability measures. The authors also provide data on the relationship between the WRAT4 subtests and the corresponding subtests of the WRAT-Expanded edition. Results indicate moderate to moderately high convergent validity and demonstrate the predicted patterns of relationships. Although evidence of convergent validity is a relative strength, it is important to note that the validity sample was restricted in some cases (e.g., far fewer participants in the upper age range). For example, the validity sample for comparing the WRAT4 to the WAIS-III (n = 58) included only 13 participants over age 35. In other cases, not all age ranges were included (e.g., no students for ages 13 or 15–18).

The authors did conduct analyses of the WRAT4 for special populations; however, the sample sizes were inadequate for a comparison. The sample of individuals with learning disabilities consisted of only 49 individuals, aged 6–18, only one student was included for some ages (6, 15, 17), and older individuals were not included. Interestingly, the sample was more racially/ethnically diverse than the normative sample (43% Caucasian, 18% African American, and 30% Hispanic). Participants in the low (n = 32) and high (n = 45) cognitive ability groups ranged in age from 5 to over 75; however, the sample sizes were also very small. Results indicated that individuals in the matched control condition (matched controls were from the standardization sample) performed significantly better (p < .01) on all four subtests and the Reading Composite than individuals in Learning Disabled (effect sizes .74–.80) and Low Cognitive Ability (effect sizes .74–1.01) groups. For students in the High Cognitive Ability sample, a similar pattern was seen, although the effects were not as strong (effect sizes ranging from .34–.87).

COMMENTARY. The WRAT4 has a long history as a relatively brief measure that is easy to administer by a trained assessment specialist or a paraprofessional. The instructions for administration and scoring are generally straightforward; however, the basal and ceiling rules add some complexity. The WRAT4 includes two parallel forms (Blue and Green). Although the authors indicate the forms are parallel, they present alternate reliability evidence and did not demonstrate that the forms were indeed parallel (i.e., equal means and variances of observed scores.) Further, it appears that the two forms assess slightly different skills. For Mathematics Computation, only the Green form requires participants to evaluate which quantity is greater (two items), calculate a mean score, and complete a compound interest problem; whereas only the Blue form requires participants to write a fraction in simplest form and complete a complex algebra problem.

At times the authors make suggestions in the manual that are not supported by their data. For example, the authors indicate that the examiner can administer some sections in a group format;

however, there were no separate studies of these subtests under the group administration condition (to determine equivalency of the group-administered versus individual-administered subtests). Further, the authors assert that subtests may be administered in any order with a caveat, separately, or all together, despite the test administration in the normative sample being conducted in a specific order. Finally, the authors suggest that test users may conduct an "extended interpretation" to examine differences in subtest standard scores, with such analysis performed using "as many background factors and sources of information about a participant as possible and not rely solely on a single set of numbers derived from a test" (professional manual, p. 28). However, there are limited instructions for how to interpret this analysis and insufficient psychometric rationale to support this recommendation. Thus, it is our opinion that test users should refrain from using this analysis.

The reliability data for the WRAT4 are satisfactory. The most salient limitation of the WRAT4 is validity. Evidence of content and construct validity is minimal, and data supporting the use of the WRAT4 as a diagnostic tool are limited. The authors provided no evidence that the WRAT4 could accurately differentiate between students with various levels of achievement difficulties, although data indicate that a small sample of students with learning disabilities and low cognitive ability students performed lower than the standardization sample. The authors acknowledge that the WRAT4 is less precise when assessing "very able" individuals from late adolescence through middle adult years, especially on the Sentence Comprehension and Word Reading subtests, although such uses are probably not consistent with the primary purposes of the instrument.

Although a test that covers a wide age span could be viewed as a benefit, the associated consequence is limited content validity. Both math and reading tests sample a very limited number of skills. For example, in mathematics computation, the examinee might get only one chance at solving a problem type. The reading assessment covers two areas of reading, but omits areas such as phonemic awareness, knowledge of phonics or alphabetic principle, and vocabulary. Thus, its value for diagnosis, making educational decisions, facilitating interventions, and assessing response to intervention is limited. There are moderate to high correlations between the WRAT4 and other achievement and IQ measures, supporting the use of the WRAT4 for screening purposes; however, it is important to note that only small samples were included in these studies. The authors acknowledge that the WRAT4 results cannot be used in isolation to identify children with learning or cognitive disabilities. However, they also suggest that the test results can be used for reevaluation, determining achievement/ability discrepancies for students with suspected learning disabilities, determining minimal competency levels, measuring growth over time, and for other purposes that involve individual diagnostic decision making for which no validity evidence is presented. Finally, limited data are presented relative to test bias.

SUMMARY. The WRAT4 is a norm-referenced achievement measure designed to measure performance in four areas of academic functioning. The WRAT4 is relatively brief and is easy to administer and score. However, because this test measures academic functioning over such a large age range, there is only a small number of items within each content area and the standardization sample is relatively small for each age group. Further, validity evidence is limited and many purported uses of this test are not fully substantiated. Validity data support the use of the WRAT4 as a quick and relatively easy-to-administer brief screener, and with the results the test user might be able to select individuals for a more in-depth/comprehensive assessment of educational performance. Although this test has a long history, limited validity evidence leads us to conclude that this measure can be recommended for research purposes, but should not be recommended for any type of clinical use except for screening purposes until further validity research has been conducted supporting its use for other purposes.

REVIEWERS' REFERENCES

Mabry, L. (1995). [Review of the Wide Range Achievement Test 3.] In J. C. Conoley & J. C. Impara (Eds.), *The twelfth mental measurements yearbook* (pp. 1108–1110). Lincoln, NE: Buros Institute of Mental Measurements.

Messick, S. J. (1989). Validity. In R. L. Linn (Ed.), *Educational measurement* (3rd ed., pp. 13-103). New York: American Council on Education.

Ward, A. W. (1995). [Review of the Wide Range Achievement Test 3.] In J. C. Conoley & J. C. Impara (Eds.), *The twelfth mental measurements yearbook* (pp. 1110–1111). Lincoln, NE: Buros Institute of Mental Measurements.

Review of the Wide Range Achievement Test 4 by DARRELL L. SABERS, Professor of Educational Psychology, and AMY M. OLSON, Doctoral Student, University of Arizona, Tucson, AZ:

DESCRIPTION. The Wide Range Achievement Test: Fourth Edition (WRAT4) is a revision of the Wide Range Achievement Test: Third

Edition (WRAT3) with editions dating back to 1946. Since the first edition, the WRAT has been designed to assess quickly the "basic academic skills necessary for effective learning, communication, and thinking" (professional manual, p. 1) as well as to provide an initial evaluation of individuals aged 5 to 94 years referred for learning, behavioral, and vocational difficulties. The basic academic skills are measured in four subtests: Word Reading, Spelling, Math Computation, and Sentence Comprehension. The first three are not much different than those offered in the WRAT3, but the Sentence Comprehension subtest is new. Users of the WRAT4 may also choose to combine the Word Reading and Sentence Comprehension standard scores to create a Reading Composite score.

Overall, the subtests are easy to understand and directions for administration are clear. However, a few general administration cautions should be offered: The WRAT4 should not be considered a group test; only the second parts of Spelling and Math Computation can be offered in small groups of no more than five examinees. Additionally, the WRAT4 comes with one large manual that includes administration directions as well as technical data and score conversion appendices. It would perhaps be more convenient for a test administrator to have access only to the information needed to give the test and, hence, require only a smaller manual.

The number correct for each subtest is totaled to obtain a raw score. Standard scores with confidence intervals and percentile ranks are available based on age and grade norms derived from the total sample. The authors are commended for including confidence intervals and asking users to shade them in around standard scores on the score profile sheet as this practice may help reduce overinterpretation of score differences. However, it seems likely that percentile ranks are the most easily interpretable and widely used scores by parents and teachers, and as such, it would also be helpful to include confidence intervals around percentile ranks in future editions. Additionally, the confidence intervals provided have been calculated on the total sample and apply to all ages, but it is difficult to believe that the reliabilities of the WRAT4 subtests do not vary by age.

The authors additionally provide stanines, grade equivalents, and Rasch Ability Scaled Scores (RASS). Stanines are provided with the rationale that the broader score range is appropriate for reporting to students and parents, but percentile ranks and standard scores seem more useful for this purpose. The authors provide grade equivalents for K–12, but caution that the use of grade equivalents is questionable in high school when the curriculum is not taught annually. It seems likely that Word Reading, Spelling, and Sentence Comprehension are included in the elementary curriculum within the context of other academic learning rather than as formal subjects. In fact, the WRAT4 seems to measure more general abilities related to academic achievement rather than achievement directly. With these cautions in mind, perhaps future versions of the WRAT should eliminate grade equivalents entirely. Should the test be considered to measure ability and not content taught in specific grades, person-free item calibration is appropriate and RASS become especially relevant. Additionally, in the opinion of these reviewers, the use of a one-parameter IRT model is well matched to the design of the WRAT4 (the lack of multiple-choice items reduces examinee guessing).

DEVELOPMENT. Primarily, the development of the WRAT4 consisted of editorial review and revision of the WRAT3 Word Reading, Spelling, and Math Computation subtests. Items were dropped and replaced for each subtest, and the lengths of the Word Reading and Spelling subtests were increased. As the newly added subtest, Sentence Comprehension was developed from item specifications to item tryout and expert review. Sentence Comprehension was added to meet criticisms such as those Mabry posed concerning the WRAT3: "No text is read; comprehension is unassessed; no skills other than pronunciation of isolated words are included. On no grounds can this be considered a test of reading" (Mabry, 1995, p. 1108). The authors wished to include a measure of comprehension, and sentences "seemed the next logical step for assessment" in a test that has historically measured knowledge of letters and words (professional manual, p. 34). Although users may find that Sentence Comprehension adds a needed comprehension subtest to the reading skills assessed, reading experts will likely feel that the authors of the WRAT4 have not gone far enough in measuring reading as an academic skill.

TECHNICAL. From a purely technical standpoint, the reliability and validity evidence provided in the manual surpasses that of many small tests. Internal consistency and alternate-form reliability estimates are high, and the inclusion of validity evidence (drawn from correlations between the WRAT4 subtests, with the WRAT-Expanded, with well-known achievement tests, and with well-known ability tests) is an improvement over previous editions. Unfortunately, many of the validity studies have sample sizes too small to demonstrate convergent and discriminant validity sufficiently. Overall, small sample size is the most justified criticism regarding many of the technical issues. Only 3,000 participants were assessed to norm a test designed to cover an 89-year age range and the equating studies include only 300 participants across an 85-year age range; the equating could be enhanced by adding test takers. The authors used stratified quota-based sampling and weighting procedures in order to approximate 2001 U.S. Census data, although Hispanic participants appear to be slightly underrepresented and the authors do not weight by age. There are just too few participants to norm the test adequately across the wide range of ages the WRAT4 is intended to cover.

COMMENTARY. As far back as the first edition in 1946, critics have suggested, "that the test is misnamed, that as a measure of school achievement it has doubtful value" (Sims, 1949, p. 47). We believe it might be better to consider the WRAT a measure of ability rather than academic achievement, and as such, the range of nonschool ages targeted for the test can be better understood. However, should the test be better understood as a measure of ability, the addition of grade-based norms for a test that has traditionally been marketed with age-based norms becomes questionable. Likewise, the interpretation of grade equivalents becomes untenable.

Although the test population is certainly "wide range" in terms of age, the combination of different age levels results in further problems. It is difficult to obtain any meaningful statistical understanding of the total sample. For example, the average score of a sample composed of both kindergarteners and the elderly is difficult to understand in terms of school achievement. Nor would one expect the test to be equally reliable for a fifth grader, parent, and grandparent. Yet, the authors include findings from validity studies that purport to cover the entire age range. More questionable, data important for users to interpret examinee scores, such as confidence intervals and percentile ranks, are drawn from the total standardization sample. The composition of the total sample is far too heavily weighted towards the younger, school-aged groups to be representative of the entire population. In future revisions of the WRAT, the inclusion of subsamples of interest to users may improve interpretation. Inclusion of subsamples of interest may also do much to address another concern: the test seems misdirected as well as misnamed. If the primary use of the test is as an initial screening evaluation for students believed to be at risk for learning difficulties (as is suggested by the inclusion of the validity study demonstrating the WRAT4 scores for students with learning disabilities and low cognitive abilities are lower than their matched counterparts), a wide age range may not be necessary. If the authors intend for the test to be used vocationally or clinically with adults, evidence that the test adequately assesses adults for diagnostic screening purposes needs to be collected.

The WRAT4 authors suggest using both forms of the WRAT4 in order to obtain a longer observation of student performance. Given that problems with the content, particularly with the measurement of reading skills, have been consistently criticized across editions, users desiring a more comprehensive assessment might consider the WRAT-Expanded, reviewed by Engelhard (2005) and Zhang and Walker (2005). The WRAT-Expanded includes reading passages, focuses on a more reasonable age range, and the author was able to attain a larger standardization sample.

The most serious problems for the WRAT4 are not with technical or psychometric issues, but rather in determining what purpose it serves and tailoring it more specifically to that purpose. However, the WRAT has historically been popular despite the enduring nature of many of the criticisms cited here and in reviews of earlier editions. Those who find the WRAT3 useful should be pleased with the improvements in this edition.

REVIEWERS' REFERENCES

Engelhard, G., Jr. (2005). [Review of the Wide Range Achievement Test—Expanded Edition.] In R. A. Spies & B. S. Plake (Eds.), *The sixteenth mental measurements yearbook* (pp. 1136-1138). Lincoln, NE: Buros Institute of Mental Measurements.

Mabry, L. (1995). [Review of the Wide Range Achievement Test 3.] In J. C. Conoley & J. C. Impara (Eds.), *The twelfth mental measurements yearbook* (pp. 1108-1110). Lincoln, NE: Buros Institute of Mental Measurements.

Sims, V. (1949). [Review of the Wide Range Achievement Test.] In O. K. Buros (Ed.), *The third mental measurements yearbook* (pp. 21-22). Highland Park, NJ: The Gryphon Press.

Zhang, B., & Walker, C. (2005). [Review of the Wide Range Achievement Test—Expanded Edition.] In R. A. Spies & B. S. Plake (Eds.), *The sixteenth mental measurements yearbook* (pp. 1139-1141). Lincoln, NE: Buros Institute of Mental Measurements.

[158]

Wide Range Achievement Test Fourth Edition Progress Monitoring Version.

Purpose: Designed "to monitor the progress of students with learning difficulties, students in special education placements, underachieving students in regular educa-

tion, or students who exhibit other conditions that affect school learning."
Population: Ages 5-94.
Publication Dates: 1940-2006.
Acronym: WRAT4-PMV.
Scores, 4: Word Reading, Sentence Comprehension, Spelling, Math Computation.
Administration: Group.
Levels, 6: Level 1 (Grades K-1), Level 2 (Grades 2-3), Level 3 (Grades 4-5), Level 4 (Grades 6-8), Level 5 (Grades 9-12), Level 6 (Grades 13-16).
Forms, 4: Form 1, Form 2, Form 3, Form 4.
Price Data, 2009: $288 per introductory kit including professional manual, 25 level equivalent profile forms, 25 word reading record sheets, 1 word reading list card, 25 sentence comprehension record booklets, set of 3 sentence comprehension cards, 25 spelling response booklets, 1 spelling card, 25 math computation response booklets, and math computation cards.
Time: (15) minutes.
Comments: Adaptation of the Wide Range Achievement Test 4 (18:157).
Authors: Gale H. Roid and Mark F. Ledbetter, with significant contributions by Melissa Messer.
Publisher: Psychological Assessment Resources, Inc.

Review of the Wide Range Achievement Test Fourth Edition Progress Monitoring Version by WILLIAM D. SCHAFER, Affiliated Professor (Emeritus) of Measurement, Statistics, and Evaluation, University of Maryland, College Park, MD:

DESCRIPTION.

Purpose and nature. The Wide Range Achievement Test Fourth Edition Progress Monitoring Version (WRAT4-PMV) is a direct outgrowth of the Wide Range Achievement Test (WRAT4; 18:157) that is intended to allow users to track the progress of academically challenged students over time without expending the resources to give the full WRAT4. It consists of four forms in each of six educational levels in each of four academic areas (96 forms in all). The four content areas tested are: Word Reading, Sentence Comprehension, Spelling, and Math Computation. The six educational (grade) levels are: K–1, 2–3, 4–5, 6–8, 9–12, and 13–16 (college or adult). The professional manual claims that the four forms in each of the 24 grade-level and academic area combinations are "parallel in academic content and psychometrically equivalent" (manual, p. 1). They are intended to allow multiple testing occasions and interpretation of changes between the occasions in each academic area.

Each form consists of 15 items drawn from the WRAT4. Individual administration is necessary for most of the tests. However, administration and scoring are both straightforward and take only about 10 to 15 minutes for each content area. The professional manual claims that raw scores may be compared with each other directly, or may be converted to Level Equivalent (LE) scores that are interpretable across educational levels.

DEVELOPMENT.

Equating. The basis for the WRAT4-PMV is the WRAT4, which has the same grade-level, content area structure. There are two WRAT4 forms, called Blue and Green. Items for each form of the WRAT4-PMV were drawn from the associated pool of WRAT4 items in such a way to create test forms that have similar assessment characteristics in terms of content measured, difficulty, and spread of scores, as estimated using the one-parameter logistic (Rasch) model. Forms 1 and 2 of the WRAT4-PMV were drawn from the WRAT4 Green Form pool and Forms 3 and 4 from the WRAT4 Blue Form pool. In that the professional manual does not describe precisely how that was done, concern may be raised about the actual domain and how it was sampled. For example, in Math Computation at Level 6 (Grades 13–16), just one form includes factoring a binomial and just one (a different one) includes compound interest. One would expect better parallelism of content among so-called equivalent forms.

Norms. The normative sample for the WRAT4-PMV was drawn from the WRAT4 standardization pool. This short-cut approach has appeal in terms of simplicity and the opportunity to include students who represent the intended population for the WRAT4-PMV, which is relatively close to the U.S. population on parent education. Although the gender breakdown is also quite close to the population at Grades K–5 and 6–12, males are underrepresented for Grades 13–16. African Americans are somewhat overrepresented and Hispanics underrepresented. Geographically, the South is overrepresented at all levels.

The short-cut approach also has some drawbacks. Chief among these is that the items were not taken in the same context as they are on the WRAT4-PMV. Item-position effects (e.g., fatigue factors) could affect not only the norms, but also the equivalencies between the forms of the test.

Scales. For each of the four subject-matter areas, two sorts of profile plots over time are available, one for raw scores and the other for LE scores. For raw scores, tables are available that show, for a given score, what change in a subsequent score is statistically significant. These threshold values were developed statistically using regression analyses and are based on the overall standard errors of estimate (prediction) from the equations.

Appendices in the manual can be used to convert raw scores on each form to LE scores. These are intended to be scaled across levels and range from scores below 320 at Level 1 to scores above 550 at Level 6. The manual suggests representing repeated assessments graphically across grade levels, and tables are presented that yield regression-based thresholds for statistically significant differences between LE scores. The optimal time lag for use of these thresholds is not discussed. The manual contains some examples of the use of raw scores and of LE scales.

As with any vertical scale, an LE score on one test may not represent the same achievement level as the same LE score on another test, primarily because of differences in content tested. Perhaps this issue is less important in tests that represent general as opposed to specific curricular achievement constructs such as these. However, it would be helpful for the test materials to include a discussion of the assumptions under which interpretations of growth are reasonable and how to evaluate the importance of these assumptions in representative situations.

TECHNICAL COMMENTARY.

Reliability evidence. KR20 (coefficient alpha) reliability estimates are given for each of the 96 forms. These range from a low of .59 to a high of .91. The higher alpha coefficients seem to be at the lower grades (Level 1) and the lower alphas are generally for Grades 13–16, perhaps because of the increased breadth of content at the higher levels that is still sampled with only 15 items.

In individual administrations, if several items on certain subtests are missed consecutively, the session is terminated and subsequent items are scored as wrong. This creates structural dependencies among the items that can inflate alpha coefficients. The extent to which that may have happened here is impossible to evaluate.

Alternate forms reliabilities are presented within-levels, based on the pools of examinees for the WRAT4 forms. The sample sizes are relatively small, ranging from a high of 264 for within-WRAT4-pool subtests (1 with 2 or 3 with 4), down to 22 for between-WRAT4-pool subtests (however, at Level 1, the between-WRAT4 sample sizes were all less than 20 and were not reported). As with the alpha coefficients, these correlations are higher at the lower levels (from .83 to .92 at Level 1) and lower at the higher levels (from .46 to .77 at Level 6).

Test-retest reliabilities (1-month delay, approximately, on average) were based on data generated by participants in a special study of the WRAT4. Retest intervals ranged from 6 to 89 days, and sample sizes ranged from 26 to 73 participants. The correlations were corrected for sample variability. Average within-form correlations ranged from .77 to .93; average between-form correlations ranged from .63 to .81.

Raw score standard errors of measurement range from a low of .95 to a high of 1.44. These are classical test theory based and apply to all scores on each form. It is generally believed, however, that standard errors of measurement are different for different student scores (i.e., they should be conditional on student scores), and item-response theory (using the Rasch model parameter estimates already available) could have been used to generate the conditional values.

Forms equivalence was evaluated at each level by comparing the average percent correct from form to form (they differ by at most .03) and by a chi-square test of equivalence. The test forms were judged "parallel and equivalent at each level in each of the four subtest areas" (manual, p. 63). However, two factors should be considered in interpreting this finding. First, it should be remembered that the items were selected based on their statistical properties from the WRAT4 norm group and allocated to forms in order to create equivalent measures. Then their equivalence was checked using a sample from the same WRAT4 norm group, which does not provide an independent test. Second, the sample sizes for the various tests of significance are not presented. A communication from the test publisher indicated that these analyses used the sample collected for the WRAT4, which contained about 300 participants at each level. The publisher acknowledged that the samples sizes should have been provided together with the tables that address equivalence.

Validity evidence. The professional manual describes three sorts of evidence for validity: content-related, criterion-related, and construct-related. The content-related evidence rests on the validity of the WRAT4 because the WRAT4-PMV items were sampled from them. The WRAT4-PMV professional manual comments on but does not detail the WRAT4 content-related evidence, so the reader should consult a review of the WRAT4 for a discussion of it.

The criterion-related evidence includes correlations between the WRAT4 subtests and scales of the Woodcock-Johnson III Test of Achievement and the Kaufman Test of Educational Achievement: Second Edition Comprehensive Battery. The correlations are supportive of validity, but the evidence is indirect for the WRAT4-PMV because it is based only on the pools from which the WRAT4-PMV forms were drawn. Direct evidence was reported from four studies, two with well-known tests of achievement, and two with well-known tests of cognitive ability. For the tests of achievement, the sample sizes ranged from 17 to 23 and for the tests of cognitive ability, they ranged from 29 to 68. Not much can be said about correlations based on sample sizes this small, and some of the correlations between math achievement and other achievement traits are very low and even near zero, but the pattern of the other correlations is generally supportive of validity. The correlations between the WRAT4-PMV subtests and those of the tests of cognitive ability are also generally in the predicted directions, except that the WRAT4-PMV Math Computation subtest correlates more strongly with a Verbal Intelligence score than it does with the same battery's Nonverbal Intelligence score.

A positive correlation between age and LE scores is taken as construct-related evidence of validity. The professional manual presents a graph of Word Reading LE scores against age, but does not present the parallel graph for the other three tests. The graph suggests a curvilinear pattern, in which there is a weakening relationship as age increases, with an almost-flat relationship above approximately age 15 years. Several studies involving students with particular characteristics (e.g., learning disabilities, above average intelligence, below average intelligence) generally show the expected relationships on the WRAT4-PMV scales.

Utility. The WRAT4-PMV is easy to administer and score. The materials are attractive and clear. Presenting the scale scores using either of the graphical formats (raw or LE scores) is straightforward, as are the professional manual's descriptions of how to implement its recommendations. The professional manual suggests that the forms be administered in numerical order, and then re-administered in the same order, if necessary, potentially providing multiple opportunities for progress monitoring, although no studies are directly supportive of this intensity of use.

SUMMARY. The WRAT4-PMV is a convenient assessment of achievement in its four tested areas. The reliability and validity evidence is more supportive of the lower levels than the upper levels, perhaps because opportunity to learn the content is more varied as age and educational level increase. This could suggest that a test consisting of only 15 items might never be sufficient to assess achievement for typical older students.

Further work should be undertaken to provide independent evidence of reliability and validity for the WRAT4-PMV as distinct from the WRAT4. Because they are based on very small sample sizes, the independent studies reported in the professional manual are not as helpful as they should be, and the rest of the evidence is taken from WRAT4 data, which was used to develop the WRAT4-PMV in the first place.

The WRAT4-PMV may be recommended as one source of evidence for making educational decisions. However, it is neither long enough nor has it sufficient supporting evidence to use as a sole determiner of important achievement-related decisions for students, especially at the upper age ranges that it is designed to assess.

Review of the Wide Range Achievement Test Fourth Edition Progress Monitoring Version by JOHN J. VENN, Professor, Department of Exceptional Student and Deaf Education, College of Education and Human Services, University of North Florida, Jacksonville, FL:

DESCRIPTION. The Wide Range Achievement Test Fourth Edition Progress Monitoring Version (WRAT4-PMV) is a shorter, adapted version of the Wide Range Achievement Test, Fourth Edition (WRAT4; Wilkinson & Robertson, 2006; 18:157). The test measures the academic progress of students from kindergarten through college with subtests in Word Reading, Sentence Comprehension, Spelling, and Math Computation. The test is divided into six grade levels: K–1, 2–3, 4–5, 6–8, 9–12, and 13–16, and there are four equivalent test forms for each level. Each equivalent form contains 15 items. It takes 10–15 minutes to administer and score the WRAT4-PMV. Portions of the spelling and math subtests may be given in small groups, but the two reading tests must be administered individually. The instrument was designed to be given repeatedly during the school year. When given quarterly, for example, the child would take each of the parallel test forms at the appropriate grade level once, and the results would provide four curriculum-based measurement probes. Use of the instrument in this way produces an independent measure for evaluating progress over time. In addition to giving the instrument quarterly, the WRAT4-PMV manual describes a variety of other progress monitoring procedures. The raw scores from each subtest may be graphically depicted on a profile record sheet. The test materials include separate profile sheets for each subtest, and the profiles are color shaded to indicate the average grade levels. The shading makes it easy to assess student performance quickly as below, on, or above grade level. The profile on the record form also includes tables for identifying significant increases and decreases in performance over repeated administrations. Raw scores may be converted into level equivalent (LE) scores and plotted on a separate LE score profile form. Using the LE scores makes it possible to track student progress across grade levels. An available software scoring program provides automated calculation of raw scores and LE scores. This software includes various graphing and reporting options.

The professional manual describes a variety of procedures for using WRAT4-PMV results with students. These procedures focus on ways to monitor the progress of students with learning problems, especially students receiving special education services. The professional manual also presents ways to assess students who are struggling in the standard general education curriculum as part of the referral process. The instrument was specifically designed to evaluate the quarterly progress of students using the four parallel forms provided for each subtest. The professional manual provides extensive and helpful examples of how to use the test in this way.

DEVELOPMENT. The original Wide Range Achievement Test was published in 1939. The test remained largely unchanged until publication of the WRAT4, which introduced a new subtest for evaluating reading comprehension. Even with this addition, the basic test features including brevity and ease of use remain unchanged as do a majority of the test items. The PMV adaptation responds to the current emphasis on process-based assessment protocols for evaluating progress on an ongoing basis. This objective was accomplished by taking items from the longer WRAT4 and arranging them into brief 15-item WRAT4-PMV equivalent test forms.

TECHNICAL. Rather than conducting a separate norm study, the WRAT4-PMV norms were developed using a sample of 1,929 students selected from a larger sample of WRAT4 normative participants. Because the WRAT4-PMV is essentially a new test, this process for developing norms is problematic. Reliability evidence for the WRAT4-PMV was based on measures of internal consistency, alternate-form consistency, and test-retest reliability using intervals that ranged from 6 to 89 days (mean interval was 31.4 days). Although the reliability coefficients generally fell within an acceptable range, .75 to .91, the sample sizes were quite small. This brings into question the consistency of WRAT4-PMV scores. Much of the validity information in the professional manual references studies conducted to determine the effectiveness of the longer WRAT4. Although WRAT4 validity information is somewhat helpful in establishing the validity of the PMV, it is not sufficient. The professional manual does present some promising validity studies using the WRAT4-PMV including concurrent validity investigations and studies with groups of students including those with learning disabilities. Unfortunately, the sample sizes in these investigations were small. The small sample sizes and the process of norm development represent major weaknesses, and more research needs to be conducted to determine the technical adequacy of the instrument for its intended use as a progress monitoring tool.

COMMENTARY. The WRAT4-PMV is one of several available versions in the WRAT achievement tests series. Unfortunately, this adaptation suffers from many of the same deficiencies as other versions. These include inadequate evidence of technical qualities such as reliability and validity weaknesses and a questionable norm development process. Further, the WRAT4-PMV emphasizes monitoring performance using grade levels even though this type of scoring is fraught with the potential for significant measurement errors. The instrument does provide a way to calculate level equivalent (LE) scores. These scale scores tend to be more reliable than grade equivalent scores. For this reason, evaluators are encouraged to rely on the LE score results rather than grade levels whenever possible. Despite these significant limitations, the design of the WRAT4-PMV is attractive. It provides a quick and easy way to assess students in the major academic learning areas. As a result, practitioners often use this instrument rather than more effective tests that may be less efficient to give, score, and interpret. Given the serious weaknesses of the instrument and to insure accurate measurement of student progress over time, the WRAT4-PMV should be used cautiously and only in conjunction with other progress monitoring measures.

SUMMARY. The WRAT4-PMV consists of a series of 24 brief test forms arranged in six grade levels for assessing student performance over time in the major academic learning areas. The age range of the test is kindergarten through college, and the instrument includes measures of Word Reading, Sentence Comprehension, Spelling, and Math Computation. Although the test is attractively designed, it suffers from a number of deficiencies including serious technical flaws that limit its usefulness as a curriculum-based measure of academic achievement.

REVIEWER'S REFERENCE

Wilkinson, G. S., & Robertson, G. J. (2006). Wide Range Achievement Test, Fourth Edition. Lutz, FL: Psychological Assessment Resources.

APPENDIX

TESTS LACKING SUFFICIENT TECHNICAL DOCUMENTATION FOR REVIEW

Effective with The Fourteenth Mental Measurements Yearbook *(2001), an additional criterion was added for tests reviewed in* The Mental Measurements Yearbook. *Only those tests for which at least minimal technical or test development information is provided are now reviewed. This list includes the names of new and revised tests received since publication of* The Seventeenth Mental Measurements Yearbook *that are lacking this documentation. The publishers have been advised that these tests do not meet our review criteria.*

[159]

Abstract Reasoning Test.
Publisher: Australian Council for Educational Research Ltd. [Australia].

[160]

Attitudes and Values Questionnaire.
Publisher: Australian Council for Educational Research Ltd. [Australia].

[161]

Basic English Literacy Skills Test.
Publisher: Walden Personnel Performance, Inc. [Canada].

[162]

BRIGANCE® Diagnostic Assessment of Basic Skills—Revised Spanish Edition.
Publisher: Curriculum Associates, Inc.

[163]

Career Exploration Inventory: A Guide for Exploring Work, Leisure, and Learning, Third Edition.
Publisher: JIST Publishing, Inc.

[164]

Choosing A College Major.
Publisher: CFKR Career Materials, Inc.

[165]

Compliance with Supervisor's Wishes.
Publisher: Center for Advanced Studies in Management.

[166]

Decision-Making Strategies: A Leadership Inventory.
Publisher: The Center for Management Effectiveness, Inc.

[167]

Diagnostic Test of the New Testament.
Publisher: Association for Biblical Higher Education.

[168]

Dimensional Assessment for Patient Placement Engagement and Recovery.
Publisher: The Change Companies.

[169]

Elementary Student Opinion Inventory.
Publisher: National Study of School Evaluation.

[170]

EQ Index.
Publisher: Center for Advanced Studies in Management.

[171]

Inventory of School Effectiveness.
Publisher: National Study of School Evaluation.

[172]

Job and Vocational Attitudes Assessment Questionnaire and Interview.
Publisher: The Change Companies.

[173]

JOB-O E Career Awareness and Planning, 3rd Edition.
Publisher: CFKR Career Materials, Inc.

[174]

JOB-O 2000+.
Publisher: CFKR Career Materials, Inc.

[175]

Looking at MySELF, Form II.
Publisher: CFKR Career Materials, Inc.

[176]

Major-Minor-Finder [2006 Update].
Publisher: CFKR Career Materials, Inc.

[177]

Manifest Needs Questionnaire.
Publisher: InQ Educational Materials, Inc.

[178]

The Marriage Checkup Questionnaire.
Publisher: Regal Books.

[179]

Music Teacher Self-Assessment.
Publisher: GIA Publications, Inc.

[180]

Organizational Character Index.
Publisher: CPP, Inc.

[181]

Organizational Justice Inventory.
Publisher: Center for Advanced Studies in Management.

[182]

Outcome Assessment and Reporting System.
Publisher: The Change Companies.

[183]

Parker Team Development Survey.
Publisher: CPP, Inc.

[184]

Portland Digit Recognition Test [Revised].
Publisher: Laurence M. Binder, PhD (the author).

[185]

Professional Judgment Rating Form.
Publisher: Insight Assessment—The California Academic Press LLC.

[186]

Psychological Indicator for Assessing Quantities of Love with Regard to Various Types of Love.
Publisher: Dinosaurs, Trees, Religion and Galaxies, Inc.

[187]

Quant Q.
Publisher: Insight Assessment—The California Academic Press LLC.

[188]

Quick Informal Assessment [Third Edition].
Publisher: Ballard & Tighe, Publishers.

[189]

Rahim Leader Power Inventory.
Publisher: Center for Advanced Studies in Management.

[190]

The Retention/Promotion Checklist.
Publisher: Crystal Springs Books.

[191]

School Life Questionnaire.
Publisher: Australian Council for Educational Research Ltd. [Australia].

[192]

Senior South African Individual Scale—Revised.

Publisher: Human Sciences Research Council [South Africa].

[193]

Social-Emotional Wellbeing Survey.

Publisher: Australian Council for Educational Research Ltd. [Australia].

[194]

Support Staff Opinion Inventory.

Publisher: National Study of School Evaluation.

[195]

Survey of Goals for Student Learning.

Publisher: National Study of School Evaluation.

[196]

Survey of Instructional and Organizational Effectiveness.

Publisher: National Study of School Evaluation.

[197]

TEACCH Transition Assessment Profile, Second Edition.

Publisher: PRO-ED.

[198]

Triage Assessment for Psychiatric Disorders.

Publisher: The Change Companies.

TESTS TO BE REVIEWED FOR THE NINETEENTH MENTAL MEASUREMENTS YEARBOOK

By the time each new Mental Measurements Yearbook *reaches publication, the staff at the Buros Institute have already collected many new and revised tests destined to be reviewed in the next* Mental Measurements Yearbook. *Following is a list of tests that meet the review criteria and that will be reviewed, along with additional tests published and received in the next year, in* The Nineteenth Mental Measurements Yearbook.

Auditory Skills Assessment
Autism Spectrum Rating Scale

Behavioral Summary
Brain Injury Rehabilitation Trust Memory and Information Processing Battery
Brigance® Comprehensive Inventory of Basic Skills II
Brigance® Early Child Developmental Inventory
Brigance® Early Childhood Screen II (0-35 months)
Brigance® Early Childhood Screen II (3-5 years)
Brigance® Early Childhood Screen II (K & 1)
Brigance® Head Start Screen
Brigance® Inventory of Early Development II
Brigance® Transition Skills Inventory

The Capute Scales
CASAS Reading Assessments
Childhood Autism Rating Scale, Second Edition
Children's Measure of Obsessive-Compulsive Symptoms
Classroom Assessment Scoring System
Conflict Tactics Scales

Dimensional Assessment of Personality Pathology–Basic Questionnaire

Firestone Assessment of Violent Thoughts-Adolescent

Garos Sexual Behavior Inventory

Harris Infant Neuromotor Test

NICU Network Neurobehavioral Scale

Pediatric Test of Brain Injury

Quick Picture Reading Test

State-Trait Anger Expression Inventory-2: Child and Adolescent

Tasks of Executive Control
Test of Infant Motor Performance
3-Minute Reading Assessments

Winslow Discovery Profile
Winslow Dynamics Profile
Winslow Success Profile

NEW TESTS REQUESTED BUT NOT RECEIVED

The staff of the Buros Institute endeavor to acquire copies of every new or revised commercially available test. Descriptions of all tests are included in Tests in Print *and reviews for all tests that meet our review criteria are included in* The Mental Measurements Yearbook. *A comprehensive search of multiple sources of test information is ongoing, and test materials are regularly requested from publishers. Many publishers routinely provide review copies of all new test publications. However, some publishers refuse to provide materials and others advertise tests long before the tests are actually published. Following is a list of test titles that have been requested but not yet provided.*

The Abel Assessment for Interest in Paraphilias
The Abel Assessment for Sexual Interest
Abilities Forecaster
Ability Profiler
Ability Test
Accuracy Level Test
AccuRater
AccuVision
Achiever
ACT Assessment
The ACT Survey Services [Revised]
Acumen Leadership WorkStyles
Acumen Team Skills
Acumen Team WorkStyles
Adaptiv Resilience Factor Inventory
Admitted Student Questionnaire and Admitted Student Questionnaire Plus
Adolescent Chemical Dependency Inventory
The Adolescent Multiphasic Personality Inventory
Adolescent Self-Report and Projective Inventory
Adult Child Distortion Scale
Adult Health Nursing
Adult Measure of Essential Skills
Adult Memory and Information Processing Battery
Adult Presentence Evaluation
Adult Pretrial Test
Adult Youth Engagement Survey
Advanced Management Tests
Advanced Numerical Reasoning Appraisal
The Advanced Problem Solving Tests
AIMSweb Testing Materials
Algebra
Allied Health Aptitude Test
American Health and Life Styles
The American Tobacco Survey
Apperceptive Personality Test
Applicant Potential Test
Applied Technology Series
Aptitude Assessment
Aptitude Test Battery for Pupils in Standards 6 and 7
Aptitude Test for International Secondary Students
The Arabic Speaking Test
The Area Coordinator Achievement Test
Arithmetic Test, Form A
Arizona Basic Assessment and Curriculum Utilization System for Young Handicapped Children
Armed Services Vocational Aptitude Battery [Revised]
Assertiveness Profile
Assessing Levels of Comprehension
Assessing Semantic Skills Through Everyday Themes
The Assessment of Basic Language and Learning Skills—Revised
Assessment of Collaborative Tendencies [Revised]
Assessment of Competencies and Traits
Assessment of Grandparenting Style
Assessment of Organizational Readiness for Mentoring
Assessment of Sound Awareness and Production
Assessment of Stuttering Behaviors
Attention Battery for Children
Attention Index Survey
Attitude Survey
Auditory Discrimination and Lip Reading Skills Inventory
Australian Law Schools Entrance Test
Australian Technology Network Engineering Selection Test
Autism Diagnostic Interview—Revised
Autism Diagnostic Observation Schedule
Autism Screening Instrument for Educational Planning—Third Edition
Auto Technician
AVIATOR 3
Axis II Personality Checklist

The b Test
Baccalaureate Achievement
Basic Academic Evaluation
Basic Inventory of Natural Language
Basic Nursing Care I and II
The BASICS Behavioral Adjustment Scale
Battelle Developmental Inventory—Spanish, Second Edition
Behavior Assessment Battery for School-Age Children Who Stutter

Behavior Forecaster
Behavior Style Analysis
Behavioral Characteristics Progression (BCP) Assessment Record
Behavioral Intervention Plan
Bell Relationship Inventory for Adolescents
Bilingual Classroom Communication Profile
Bilingual Health and Developmental History Questionnaire
Bilingual Language Proficiency Questionnaire
Bilingual Vocabulary Assessment Measure
The Birkman Method [Revised]
BldgTest
Bracken School Readiness Assessment—Third Edition
Business Personality Indicator

C.I.T.E. Academic Learning Styles
Call Center Survey
The Call Centre Battery
Callier-Azusa Scale: H Edition
CAMDEX: The Cambridge Mental Disorders of the Elderly Examination
Campbell-Hallam Team Leader Profile
"Can-Do" Attitude Test
Canadian Cognitive Abilities Test, Form K
Canadian Tests of Basic Skills, Forms K and L
Candidate and Officer Personnel Survey
Canter Background Interference Procedure for the Bender Gestalt Test
Care of the Adult Client
Care of the Client During Childbearing and Care of the Child
Care of the Client with a Mental Disorder
Career Ability Placement Survey
Career Automotive Retailing Scale
Career Competency Scale for College Students
Career Competency Scale—Sales and Marketing
Career Concerns Checklist: College Edition
Career Finder
Career Guidance Inventory II
Career Interest Profiler
Career Mapper
Career Orientation Placement and Evaluation Survey
Career Personality Questionnaire
Career Portfolio Builder
Career Preference Scale
Career Quest Analysis
Career Selection Questionnaire
Career Values Scale
Careers for Me, Plus
Caregiver-Administered Communication Inventory
CASI Second Edition
Cellular Technician
CERAD Neuropathological Assessment for Alzheimer's Disease
Change Agent Questionnaire
Change Management Effectiveness Profile
Change Style Indicator
Chemical Abuse Scale
Chemical Dependency Assessment Profile
Chemical Reading
Chemistry Test
Child and Adolescent Diagnostic Scales
Child and Adolescent Functional Assessment Scale
Child Health Nursing
Child Health Questionnaire
Child Observation Record (COR) for Infants and Toddlers
Child-focused Toddler and Infant Experiences: Revised Form
Children's Assessment of Participation and Enjoyment/Preferences for Activities of Children
Children's Interaction Matrix
Children's Progress Academic Assessment
Children's Self-Report and Projective Inventory
CLEP Education Assessment Series
Clerical Series Test Modules
Clerical Series Test: Oral Instructions Forms Completion
Clerical Test Battery
Clinical Assessment of Interpersonal Relationships
Clinician-Administered PTSD Scale
Clinician-Administered PTSD Scale for Children and Adolescents
Clock Drawing
Cloze Reading Tests 1-3, Second Edition
CNC Math (Trig. Test)
CNC Operator
Coaching Competencies Questionnaire
Coaching Effectiveness Profile
The Cognitive Assessment of Minnesota
The Cognitive Dissonance Test
Cognitive (Intelligence) Test: Nonverbal
Cognitive, Linguistic and Social-Communicative Scales
Cognitive Process Profile
Cognitive Stability Index
College Board SAT II: Spanish Subject Test
College Board SAT Program
College Board SAT Reasoning Test
College Entrance Test
College Portfolio Builder
College Student Expectations Questionnaire, Second Edition
College Success
Collegiate Assessment of Academic Proficiency [Revised]
Collegiate Learning Assessment
Colorado Malingering Tests
Colorado Neuropsychology Tests
Combustion Control Technician
The Communication Behaviors Inventory II
Communication Competency Assessment Instrument
Communication Effectiveness Profile

Communication Effectiveness Scale
Communication Independence Profile for Adults
Communication Style Inventory
Community Health Nursing
COMPASS Managerial Practices Profile
Competence Assessment to Stand Trial for Defendants with Mental Retardation
Competency-Based Position Analysis
Comprehensive Nursing Achievement–PN
Comprehensive Nursing Achievement–RN
Comprehensive Nursing Achievement Test for Practical Nursing Students
Comprehensive Personality Analysis
Comprehensive Test of Adaptive Behavior—Revised
Comprehensive Test of Nonverbal Intelligence—Second Edition
Computer Optimized Multimedia Intelligence Test
Computer Programmer Ability Battery
Comrey Personality Scales–Short Form
The Concise Learning Styles Assessment
Concussion Resolution Index
Conflict Style Instrument
Copeland Symptom Checklist for Attention Deficit Disorders
COPS Interest Inventory (1995 Revision)
Core Abilities Assessment
Corporate Communication Assessment
Counterproductive Behavior Index
Craft Personality Questionnaire for Sales
Creating a Great Place to Learn
Creativity Questionnaire
Creativity/Innovation Effectiveness Profile
Crichton Vocabulary Scale, 1988 Revision
Criterion-Referenced Articulation Profile
Critical Thinking in Clinical Nursing Practice–PN
Critical Thinking in Clinical Nursing Practice–RN
Critical Thinking Test
Cultural Diversity and Awareness Profile
Customer Care Ability Test
Customer Satisfaction Practices Tool
Customer Service Aptitude Profile
Customer Service Commitment Profile
Customer Service Listening Skills Exercise
Customer Service Simulator
Customer Service Skills Assessment
Customer Service Survey

Data Entry and Data Checking Tests
Data Entry Test
Dealing With Conflict Instrument
DecideX
Decoding-Encoding Screener for Dyslexia
Defendant Questionnaire
Denison Leadership Development Survey
Denison Organizational Culture Survey
Developmental Assets Profile
Developmental Eye Movement Test
Developmental Reading Assessment
Developmental Test of Auditory Perception
The Diagnostic Inventory of Personality and Symptoms
Diagnostic Prescriptive Assessment
Diagnostic Readiness Test–PN
Diagnostic Readiness Test–RN
Differential Aptitude Tests for Schools
Differential Assessment of Autism & Other Developmental Disorders
Differential Screening Test for Processing
Dimensional Assessment of Personality Pathology–Basic Questionnaire
Discovering Diversity Profile
Disruptive Behavior Rating Scale
Diversity & Cultural Awareness Profile
Diversity Survey
Do What You Are Self Discovery Assessment
DOMA—Diagnostic Online Mathematics Assessment
DORA—Diagnostic Online Reading Assessment
The Dot Counting Test
Draw A Person Questionnaire
Drug/Alcohol Attitude Survey
Dynamic Assessment and Intervention: Improving Children's Narrative Abilities
Dynamic Occupational Therapy Cognitive Assessment for Children

Early Literacy Diagnostic Test
Early Motor Control Scales
Easy Assessments
ECHOS Early Childhood Observation System
Edinburgh Reading Tests [2002 Update]
Edinburgh Reasoning Series
Educational Assessment of School Youth for Occupational Therapists
Educational Interest Inventory II
Efron Visual Acuity Test
Elect. & Inst. Technician
Electrical Technician I
Electrical Technician II
Emerging Literacy & Language Assessment
Emo Questionnaire [Revised]
Emotional Competence Inventory—University Edition
Emotional Intelligence Profile
Emotional Intelligence Questionnaire: General and General 360°
Emotional Intelligence Questionnaire: Managerial and Managerial 360°
Emotional Intelligence Style Profile
Emotional Literacy: Assessment and Intervention
Emotional Quotient Scale for Children
Emotional Quotient Scale for Employee
Emotional Smarts!
Employability Skills Inventory
Employee Adjustment Survey
Employee Empowerment Survey

Employee Evaluation of Management Survey
Employee Opinion Survey
Empowerment Development Gauge and Evaluation
Empowerment Management Inventory
Endler Multidimensional Anxiety Scales [including EMAS Social Anxiety Scales]
English and Citizenship Test
Entry Level Police Officer Examination
Essential Skills Assessment
Essential Skills Screener
The Ethical Type Indicator
Evaluating Acquired Skills in Communication—Third Edition
Exam Preparation Inventory
Examining for Aphasia—Fourth Edition
Express Assessments
The Expressive Language Test
Extended DISC
Eysenck Personality Questionnaire [Revised]
Eysenck Personality Scales

FACES IV (Family Adaptability and Cohesion Evaluation Scale)
Facial Recognition
Family Crisis Oriented Personal Evaluation Scales
Family Evaluation Form
Family History Analysis
Fieldwork Performance Evaluation for the Occupational Therapy Student/Fieldwork Performance Evaluation for the Occupational Therapy Assistant Student
15FQ+
Fifteen Factor Questionnaire
Filipino Family Relationship Scale
Filipino Professional/Technical Employee Needs Inventory
Financial Literacy Inventory
Financial Services Suite
Fire Engineer
Fire Inspector and Senior Fire Inspector
Fire Service Administrator (Battalion Chief)
Fire Service Administrator (Captain) 574
Fire Service Administrator (Chief) 578
Fire Service Administrator (Deputy Chief)
Fire Service Supervisor (Sergeant, Lieutenant)
Firefighter Examinations 275.1 and 275.2
Firefighter Test: B-3
Firefighter Test: B-4
FIRO-Business
First Graduate Assessment
Fleishman Job Analysis Survey
Following Instructions Test
Foundations of Nursing
Four Sigma Qualifying Test
French Reading Comprehension Tests
The French Speaking Test
Functional Analysis of Behavior
Functional Communication Profile—Revised
Functional Evaluation of Assistive Technology
Functional Hearing Inventory
Functional Independence Skills Handbook
Functional Vision and Learning Media Assessment
Further Education Reasoning Test

Gardner Social (Maturity) Developmental Scale
Gates-MacGinitie Reading Test, Second Canadian Edition
General Education Performance Index
General Reasoning Test
The German Speaking Test
Goal/Objective Setting Profile
Golden Personality Type Profiler
The Graduate and Management Problem Solving Series
Graduate Appraisal Questionnaire
Graduate Australian Medical School Admission Test
Graduate Program Self-Assessment Service
Graduate Reasoning Test
The Graduation Exam Book
Greens Word Memory Test
Group-Level Team Assessment
Group Literacy Assessment
Group Mathematics Test, Third Edition
Group Perceptions Inventory

Halstead Russell Neuropsychological Evaluation System, Revised
Hare P-Scan Research Version 2
Hare Self-Report Psychopathy Scale III
Harmonic Improvisation Readiness Record and Rhythm Improvisation Readiness Record
Health and Illness: Adult Care
Healthcare Employee Productivity Report
Help for Preschoolers Assessment Strands: Ages 3-6
HELP Strands (Hawaii Early Learning Profile) Ages Birth-3
The HELP Test-Elementary
High Performing Organizations Assessment
High School and College Drop-Out Student Prediction Test
The Highly Effective Meeting Profile
Hill Interaction Matrix [Revised]
Hilson Adolescent Profile-Version D
Hilson Career Stress Inventory
Hilson Caregiver's Questionnaire
Hilson Cognitive Abilities Test
Hilson Job Analysis Questionnaire
Hilson Law Enforcement History Questionnaire
Hilson Life Adjustment Profile
Hilson Life Stress Questionnaire
Hilson Management Inventory
Hilson Management Survey
Hilson Parent/Guardian Inventory
Hilson Personal History Questionnaire
Hilson Relationship Inventory for Public Safety Personnel

Hilson Safety/Security Risk Inventory
Hilson Spouse/Mate Inventory
The Hindi Proficiency Test
Hodder Group Reading Tests 1-3
Hogan Business Reasoning Inventory
Honesty Survey
Honesty Test
Human Job Analysis
Humanics National After-School Assessment Form
Hydraulics

I-7 Impulsiveness Questionnaire
ICT Self-Rating Scale
In-Law Relationship Scale
Individual Directions Inventory
Individualized Mathematics Program
Individualized Systematic Assessment of Visual Efficiency (ISAVE)
Influencing Skills Index
The Influencing Skills Inventory
Influencing Skills Profile
Influencing Strategies and Styles Profile
The Influencing Style Clock
Information and Communications Technology Literacy Assessment
Initial Assessment: An Assessment for Reading, Writing and Maths [New Version]
Insight Pre-School
Insight Primary
Insight Secondary
Integrity Survey
Intercultural Communication Inventory
Interest Check List
Interest Inventory
Interest/Skills Checklist
Internal Customer Service Survey
International Student Admission Test
InterSurvS
Inventory for Assessing a Biblically Based Worldview of Cultural Competence Among Healthcare Professionals
Inventory for Assessing the Process of Cultural Competence Among Healthcare Professionals—Revised
Inventory for Assessing the Process of Cultural Competence Among Healthcare Professionals—Student Version
Inventory of Gambling Situations
Inventory of Leadership Styles
Inventory of Program Stages of Development
Inventory of Religious Activities and Interests
Invest in Your Values
Inwald Personality Inventory—Clinical
Inwald Personality Inventory—Short Version
Inwald Survey 2
Inwald Survey 2-Adolescent Version
Inwald Survey 3
Inwald Survey 4
Inwald Survey 6
Inwald Survey 8
IPI Performance Appraisal Questionnaires
Ironworker

The Janus Competency Identification & Assessment System
The Japanese Speaking Test
Job Observation and Behavior Scale: Opportunity for Self-Determination
Job Requirements Questionnaire
Job Skills Training Needs Assessment
Job Values Inventory
Job-O Enhanced
Jonico Questionnaire
Jordan Dyslexia Assessment/Reading Program
Judgment of Line Orientation
Jung Type Indicator
Junior Scholastic Aptitude Test Battery (Standard 5)
Juvenile Presentence Evaluation
Juvenile Pretrial Test
Juvenile Substance Abuse Profile
Juvenile Treatment Outcome

Kaleidoscope Profile for Educators
The Kaufman Speech Praxis Test for Children
Kendrick Assessment Scales of Cognitive Ageing
Kindergarten Readiness Checklists for Parents
Kohlman Evaluation of Living Skills—Third Edition
Kuder Career Search
Kuder Skills Assessment

Laboratory Technician (Mfg.)
Langdon Adult Intelligence Test
Language Assessment for Grades 3 & 4
Language-Free Programmer/Analyst Aptitude Test
Language Processing Test-Revised
[Law Enforcement] Personal History Questionnaire
Leader Action Profile
Leader Behavior Analysis II for Team Leaders
Leadership & Management Inventory
Leadership Competency Inventory [Revised]
Leadership Development Profile
Leadership Development Series
Leadership Effectiveness Analysis [Revised]
Leadership Effectiveness Profile
Leadership Qualities Scale
Leadership Skills Test
Leatherman Leadership Questionnaire II
Legendary Service Leader Assessment
Life Style Inventory
Lifespace Access Profile
Lifestyle Questionnaire [Selby MillSmith]
Light Industrial Skills Test
Linking Skills Index
Linking Skills Profile
The Listening Comprehension Test 2

Listening & Literacy Index
Listening Effectiveness Profile
Literacy Probe 7–9
The Logical Rorschach
Logramos, Second Edition
Lore Leadership Assessment II
Lowenstein Occupational Therapy Cognitive Assessment Battery [Revised]

The MacArthur Competence Assessment Tool—Criminal Adjudication
Maculaitis Assessment of Competencies II
Magellan 6
Major Field Tests
Making a Terrific Career Happen
Management & Supervisory Skills
Management Behavior Assessment Test
Management Development Questionnaire
Management Effectiveness Profile
Management Practices Inventory II
Management Style Indicator
Management Training Needs Analysis
The Managerial and Professional Profiles
Managing Performance
Manufacturing Suite
Marriage Assessment Inventory
Marshalla Oral Sensorimotor Test
Maternity and Child Health Nursing
Maternity Infant Nursing
Math Grade-Placement Tests
Mathematical Achievement Test
MATRICS (Measurement and Treatment Research to Improve Cognition in Schizophrenia)
Matson Evaluation of Social Skills With Youngsters
Matson Evaluation of Social Skills with Youngsters, Hard of Hearing Version
McGhee-Mangrum Inventory of School Adjustment
The McQuaig System
Me and My World
Measured Success
Measures of Guidance Impact
Mechanical Ability Test
Mechanical Repair Apprentice Battery
Medical College Admission Test
Meeting Effectiveness Questionnaire
Member Satisfaction Survey
Memory and Concentration Test
Memory Complaints Inventory for Windows
Mental Health Concepts
Mentoring Dynamics Survey Online
Metric Assessment of Personality
Michigan Screening Profile of Parenting
Michigan State Suggestibility Profiles
Mill Hill Vocabulary Scales
Millwright Test
Mini-Hilson Life Adjustment Profile
Minnesota Cognitive Acuity Screen
Minnesota Developmental Programming System Behavioral Scales
Minnesota Multiphasic Personality Inventory-2-Restructured Form (MMPI-2-RF)
Mobile Equipment Mechanic
Mobile Equipment Operator
Montgomery Assessment of Language Acquisition
Moray House Tests
Motivation Questionnaire
Motive-A Motivational Analysis
Movement ABC
Movement Assessment Battery for Children—Second Edition
MR/DD Profile
The MSFI College of Law Admission Test
Multi-Digit Memory Test
Multi-Level Management Surveys
Multidimensional Personality Questionnaire
Multiphasic Environmental Assessment Procedure [1998 Revision]
Myself as a Learner Scale Digital

Naglieri Nonverbal Ability Test—Second Edition
The National Corrections Officer Selection Test
The National Firefighter Selection Test & National Firefighter Selection Test—Emergency Medical Services
The National First- and Second-Line Supervisor Tests
The National Police Officer Test [Revised]
NCTE Cooperative Test of Critical Reading and Appreciation
Negotiating Style Instrument
Negotiation Style Instrument
Neitz Test of Color Vision
Nelson Assessment: Mathematics
Networking & Relationship Building Profile
Neuropsychological Aging Inventory
The New Jersey Test of Children's Reasoning
The New Jersey Test of Reasoning [Adult Version]
New Workers Inventory
NOCTI Experienced Worker Assessments
NOCTI Job Ready Assessments
The Nonspeech Test
Normative Adaptive Behavior Checklist—Revised
Norris-Ryan Argument Analysis Test
Numeracy Progress Tests
Numerical Computation Test
Nursing Care During Childbearing and Nursing Care of the Child
Nursing Care in Mental Health and Mental Illness
Nursing Care of Adults, Parts I, II, and III
Nursing Care of Children
Nursing the Childbearing Family
The NYLS Adult Temperament Questionnaire, 2nd Edition

Occupational: Administrative Personnel

Progress in English
Progress in Maths 4-14
Progress in Maths 6-14 Digital
Progressive Achievement Test of Mathematics [2006 Revision]
Progressive Achievement Test of Reading [2008 Revision]
Progressive Achievement Tests in Mathematics–3rd Edition
Project Engineer
Proof Reading Test
ProWrite
Psychiatric Mental Health Nursing
Psycho-Moral and Self-Regulation Scale
PSYGNA personality questionnaire
Pulse Surveys

QO2 Profile [Opportunities/Obstacles Quotient]
QPASS: The Quick Psycho-Affective Symptoms Scan
Qualitative Reading Inventory
Quality Customer Service Assessment
Quality Customer Service Test
Quality Effectiveness Profile
Quality Healthcare Employee Inventory
Quality of Life Questionnaire
Quality of Student Life Questionnaire
Quality of Working Life
Quick Assessments for Neurogenic Communication Disorders

Radio Operator and Senior Radio Operator
Randot Stereotests
Rate Level Test
Rauding Efficiency Level Test
Raven's Progressive Matrices
Reading Efficiency Level Battery
Reading (Electronics & Instrumentation)
Reading (Food Industry)
Reading Grade-Placement Tests
Reading Now
Reading Observation Scale
Reading Power Essentials
Reading Prints & Drawings (Decimal Version)
Reading Progress Scale
Reading Test, Form A
Ready School Assessment
Real Estate Instructor Examination
Reasoning 5-7 Test Series
Recruitment Consultant Questionnaire
Refrigeration Mechanic
Reid Report [29th Edition]
Reinstatement Review Inventory-II
Reiss Profile of Fundamental Motives
Reiss Scales
Reiss Screen
Reiss Screen for Maladaptive Behavior
Relationship Selling Skills Inventory
Reliability Test
Restaurant Manager Assessment Report
Retail Sales Questionnaire
Retail Skills Test
Right-Left Orientation
The Roberts Personality and Motivation Questionnaire
The Roberts Workstyles Profiler
Rorschach's Inkblot Test, Third Edition
Rossetti Infant-Toddler Language Scale

Safety Effectiveness Profile
Sage Vocational Assessment System
Sales Effectiveness Profile
Sales Indicator
Sales Skills
Sales Skills Profile
Salford Sentence Reading Test (Revised)
SALT 2008 Bilingual S/E Version
Salter Environmental Type Assessment
SAT On-Campus Program (Institutional SAT Reasoning Test and SAT Subject Tests)
Scales for Rating the Behavioral Characteristics of Superior Students (Revised Edition)
Scholastic Proficiency Test—Higher Primary Level
Scholastic Reading Inventory
School Child Stress Scale
School Diversity Inventory
The School Leadership Series
School Readiness Tests for Blind Children
Science Research Temperament Scale
Science, Social Studies, and Mathematics Academic Reading Test (SSSMART)
Scoreboard
Secondary Reading Assessment Inventory
Secord Contextual Articulation Tests
Secord-Contextual Articulation Tests & Kit
Self-Assessment Index
Self-Audit
Self-Directed Learning Readiness Scale [Revised]
Self-Directed Team Assessment
Self-Perceptions of College Students
Self-Perceptions of Nurses
Self-Perceptions of Teachers
Self Starter Profile
Seligman Attributional Style Questionnaire
SEPO (Serial Position) Test for the Detection of Guilty/Special Knowledge
Serial Digit Learning
Servant Leadership Inventory Forms A&B
Service Ability Inventory for the Healthcare Industry
Service Skills Indicator
The Sexual Abuse Interview for the Developmentally Disabled
SF-12: Physical and Mental Health Summary Scales
SF-36: Physical and Mental Health Summary Scales
The Shapes Analysis Test

Shore Handwriting Screening for Early Handwriting Development
The Shorr Couples Imagery Test
The Shorr Parent/Child Imagery Test
SigmaRadius 360° Feedback
Simulated Oral Proficiency Interview (SOPI-7 languages)
Single Word Reading Test 6-16
Situational Leadership® [Revised]
Situational Leadership II Leadership Skills Assessment
Six Factor Automated Vocational Assessment System
16+ PersonalStyle Profile
Skil Scale Inventory
SkillCheck Professional Plus
Skills Profiler
Skillscape
Slosson Auditory Perceptual Skill Screener
Slosson–Diagnostic Math Screener
Slosson Intelligence Test—Primary
Slosson Intelligence Test—Revised (SIT-R3)
Slosson Oral Reading Test—Revised 3
Slosson Phonics and Structural Analysis Test
Slosson Visual-Motor Performance Test
Slosson Visual Perceptual Skill Screener
Slosson Written Expression Test
Smell Threshold Test
Social Communication Questionnaire
Social Competency Rating Form
Social Emotional Evaluation
Social Use of Language Programme: Revised Edition
Socially Appropriate and Inappropriate Development
Spanish Articulation Measures
Spanish Language Assessment Procedures [Revised 1995 Edition]
Spanish Language Assessment Procedures, Third Edition
The Spanish Speaking Test
The Spanish Structured Photographic Expressive Language Test—Preschool
The Spanish Structured Photographic Expressive Language Test 3
Spanish Test for Assessing Morphologic Production
Special Abilities Scales
Special Tertiary Admissions Test
Specialty Practice Tests: End-of-Course Exams
Sr. Maint. Tech. Pipefitter
Staff Burnout Scale for Police and Security Personnel
Stages of Concern Questionnaire
Stanford Writing Online Version 1.0
Step One Survey
Stephen's Oral Language Screening Test
Story Recall Test
Strategic Leadership Type Indicator [including 360-Degree Feedback Profile]
Student Aspiration Inventory
Student Engagement Questionnaire
Student Instructional Report II
Stuttering Severity Instrument—Fourth Edition
Substance Abuse Questionnaire
Supervisory Aptitude Test
Supervisory Proficiency Tests
Supervisory Simulator
Supervisory Skills Inventory
Supervisory Skills Test
The Supplementary Shorr Imagery Test
Supplementary Spelling Assessment
SureHire
Survey of Beliefs
Survey of Implementation
The Survey of Quality Values in Practice
Survey of Student Resources & Assets
System for Testing and Evaluation of Potential
System of Interactive Guidance Information, Plus
Systematic Assessment of Voice

Tajma Personality Profile
Tangent Screen
TapDance
Teacher and Student Technology Surveys
Team Assessment System
Team-Building Effectiveness Profile
Team Charter Checkup
Team Climate Inventory
Team Culture Analysis
Team Dimensions Profile
Team Effectiveness Inventory
Team Empowerment Practices Test
Team Leader Competencies
Team Leader Skills Assessment
Team Management Index
Team Management Profile
Team Member Behavior Analysis
Team Performance Assessment
Team Performance Index
Team Performance Profile
Team Performance Questionnaire
Team-Review Survey
Team Skills Indicator
Team Success Profile
Teambuilding Effectiveness
Technology and Internet Assessment
Telemarketing Ability Test
Temperament Comparator [Revised]
Temporal Orientation
TerraNova Online
Tertiary Education Mathematics Test
Tertiary Writing Assessment
Test Alert (Test Preparation)
Test of Adult Literacy Skills
Test of Auditory Reasoning and Processing Skills
Test of General Intellectual Skills
Test of Inductive Reasoning Principles
Test of Language Development—Intermediate—Fourth Edition

Test of Language Development—Primary—Fourth Edition
Test of Oral Reading and Comprehension Skills
Test of Orthographic Competence
Test of Pictures/Forms/Letters/Numbers Spatial Orientation and Sequencing Skills
Test of Pragmatic Language—Second Edition
Test of Problem Solving 2—Adolescent
Test of Reading Comprehension—Fourth Edition
Test of Relational Concepts [Norms for Deaf Children]
Test of Semantic Skills—Intermediate
Test of Semantic Skills—Primary
Test of Silent Reading Skills
Test of Verbal Conceptualization and Fluency
Test of Visual-Motor Skills–Revised
Test of Visual-Motor Skills–Upper Level
Test of Visual-Perceptual Skills (Non-Motor): Revised
Test of Visual-Perceptual Skills (Non-Motor) Upper Level: Revised
Test of Visual-Perceptual Skills, Upper Level
Test of Written Language—Fourth Edition
Tests of General Educational Development [The GED Tests Revision]
Tests of Reading Comprehension, Second Edition
The Texas Oral Proficiency Test
Theological School Inventory
360 By Design
360 Degree Assessment and Development
360° Feedback Assessment
Thurston Cradock Test of Shame
Time Management Effectiveness Profile
Time Management Inventory
Time Mastery Profile
Titmus Stereo Fly Test
Tobacco Use Survey
Tool Knowledge & Use
Total Quality Management Survey
TotalView
TotalView Assessment System
Training Needs Assessment for Modern Leadership Skills
Training Needs Assessment Test
Training Proficiency Scale
Truck Driver Inventory
Trustworthiness Attitude Survey
The Two Cultures Test
Types of Work Index
Types of Work Profile

Undergraduate Assessment Program: Business Test
Undergraduate Medical and Health Sciences Test
Urban District Assessment Consortium's Alternative Accountability Assessments

Valpar Computerized Ability Test
Value Assessment Scale
Value Development Index Form A and Form B
Value Development Index Form C
Values and Motives Questionnaire
Verbal Behavior Milestones Assessment and Placement Program
Victim Index
Visual Form Discrimination
The Vocabulary Gradient Test
Vocational Interest, Experience and Skill Assessment (VIESA), 2nd Canadian Edition

Warehouse & Shipping Reading
Welder, Repair & Maint.
What About You?
The Whitener Group Industrial Assessments
Window on Work Values Profile
Wonderlic Interactive Skills Evaluations, Keyboard and Office Skills
Wonderlic Interactive Skills Evaluations, Software Skills
Woodcock-Johnson III NU: Tests of Achievement, Braille Adaptation
Word Analysis Diagnostic Test
Word Processing Aptitude Battery
The WORD Test 2-Adolescent
Words List
Work Expectations Profile
Work Habits, Attitudes and Productivity Scale [Employee and Student Editions]
Work Personality Profile & Computer Report
Work Preference Questionnaire [1990 Revision]
Work-Readiness Cognitive Screen
Work Skills Series Manual Dexterity
Work Team Simulator
Workplace Aptitude Test
Workplace Ergonomics Profile
Workplace Essentials Profile
Workplace Personality Inventory
Workplace Personality Profile
Workplace Skills Survey–Form E
Writing and Reading Assessment Profile (W.R.A.P.)
Written Language Observation Scale

DISTINGUISHED REVIEWERS

Based on the recommendation of our National Advisory Council, the Buros Institute of Mental Measurements is now making special recognition of the long-term contributions made by individual reviewers to the success of the Mental Measurements Yearbook series. To receive the "Distinguished Reviewer" designation, an individual must have contributed to six or more editions of this series beginning with The Ninth Mental Measurements Yearbook. *The first list below includes those who have now achieved Distinguished Reviewer status by their contribution to six or more editions as of the current* Eighteenth Mental Measurements Yearbook. *The second list includes those reviewers who qualified with their contribution to* The Sixteenth Mental Measurements Yearbook *and/or* Seventeenth Mental Measurements Yearbook *(those who also reviewed in* The Eighteenth Mental Measurements Yearbook *are indicated with an asterisk). By virtue of their long-term service, all these individuals exemplify an outstanding dedication in their professional lives to the principles of improving the science and practice of testing.*

John O. Anderson
Phillip G. Benson
Susan M. Brookhart
Mary "Rina" Mathai Chittooran
Merith Cosden
Gary J. Dean
Thomas W. Guyette
Theodore L. Hayes
Sandra D. Haynes
Anita M. Hubley
Suzanne Lane
Gregory Schraw
Chockalingam Viswesvaran
Sandra B. Ward

DISTINGUISHED REVIEWERS FROM PREVIOUS MENTAL MEASUREMENTS YEARBOOKS

(* Also reviewed for *Eighteenth Mental Measurements Yearbook*)

* Phillip A. Ackerman
* Caroline M. Adkins
* Mark A. Albanese
* Jeffrey A. Atlas
James T. Austin
* Stephen N. Axford
* Patricia A. Bachelor
Laura L. B. Barnes
Ronald A. Berk
Brian F. Bolton
Gregory J. Boyle
Albert M. Bugaj
Michael B. Bunch
Linda K. Bunker
Carolyn M. Callahan
* Karen T. Carey
Janet F. Carlson
JoEllen V. Carlson
* C. Dale Carpenter
* Joseph C. Ciechalski
* Gregory J. Cizek
* Mary M. Clare
Alice J. Corkill
Kevin D. Crehan
* Rik Carl D'Amato
* Ayres G. D'Costa
* Gerald E. DeMauro
* Beth Doll
* George Engelhard, Jr.
Deborah B. Erickson

Doreen Ward Fairbank
Robert Fitzpatrick
John W. Fleenor
* Michael J. Furlong
Ronald J. Ganellen
* Bert A. Goldman
J. Jeffrey Grill
Richard E. Harding
Patti L. Harrison
* Michael R. Harwell
Allen K. Hess
Robert W. Hiltonsmith
* Jeffrey A. Jenkins
Samuel Juni
Randy W. Kamphaus
* Michael G. Kavan
Timothy Z. Keith
Mary Lou Kelley
* Jean Powell Kirnan
Howard M. Knoff
* Matthew E. Lambert
Joseph G. Law, Jr.
* Frederick T. L. Leong
S. Alvin Leung
Rick Lindskog
* Steven H. Long
* Cleborne D. Maddux
* Koressa Kutsick Malcolm
* Rebecca J. McCauley
William B. Michael
* M. David Miller
Patricia L. Mirenda
Judith A. Monsaas
Kevin L. Moreland
Paul M. Muchinsky
Anthony J. Nitko
Janet A. Norris
Salvador Hector Ochoa
Judy Oehler-Stinnett
D. Joe Olmi
* Steven I. Pfeiffer
James W. Pinkney
G. Michael Poteat
Nambury S. Raju
Paul Retzlaff
Cecil R. Reynolds
Bruce G. Rogers
Michael J. Roszkowski
* Darrell L. Sabers
Vincent J. Samar
* Jonathan Sandoval
Eleanor E. Sanford-Moore
William I. Sauser, Jr.
Diane J. Sawyer
* William D. Schafer
* Gene Schwarting
* Steven R. Shaw
* Eugene P. Sheehan
* Jeffrey K. Smith
Jayne E. Stake
* Stephanie Stein
Terry A. Stinnett
* Gabrielle Stutman
Richard B. Stuart
* Hoi K. Suen
* Mark E. Swerdlik
* Gerald Tindal
* Roger L. Towne
* Michael S. Trevisan
Wilfred G. Van Gorp
* T. Steuart Watson
William K. Wilkinson
* Claudia R. Wright
James E. Ysseldyke
Sheldon Zedeck

CONTRIBUTING TEST REVIEWERS

SHAWN K. ACHESON, Senior Research Associate, Duke University Medical Center, Raleigh, NC

PHILLIP L. ACKERMAN, Professor of Psychology, Georgia Institute of Technology, Atlanta, GA

SANDRA T. ACOSTA, Assistant Professor of Bilingual Education, Educational Psychology, Texas A&M University, College Station, TX

EUGENE V. AIDMAN, Senior Research Scientist, Defence Science and Technology Organisation & Senior Lecturer, University of Adelaide, Adelaide, Australia

MARK A. ALBANESE, Professor of Population Health Sciences and Educational Leadership and Policy Analysis, University of Wisconsin School of Medicine and Public Health, Madison, WI

KATHLEEN D. ALLEN, Associate Professor of Education, St. Martin's University, Lacey, WA

CECILIA B. ALVES, Ph.D. Graduate student, Centre for Research in Applied Measurement and Evaluation, Department of Educational Psychology, University of Alberta, Edmonton, Alberta, Canada

JOHN O. ANDERSON, Professor, Department of Educational Psychology, University of Victoria, Victoria, British Columbia, Canada

SHARON ARFFA, Chief of Neuropsychology, The Watson Institute, Sewickley, PA

KATHLEEN B. ASPIRANTI, Doctoral Student in School Psychology, Department of Educational Psychology and Counseling, University of Tennessee, Knoxville, TN

JEFFREY A. ATLAS, Clinical and School Psychologist, SCO Family of Services, Queens, NY

STEPHEN AXFORD Assistant Director of Special Services, Falcon School District 49, Adjunct Faculty Member, University of Colorado at Colorado Springs, Licensed Psychologist, Colorado Springs, CO

PATRICIA A. BACHELOR, Professor of Psychology Emeritus, California State University, Long Beach, Long Beach, CA

SHERRY K. BAIN, Associate Professor Department of Educational Psychology and Counseling, University of Tennessee, Knoxville, TN

SHERI BAUMAN, Associate Professor, Department of Educational Psychology, University of Arizona, Tucson, AZ

ABIGAIL BAXTER, Associate Professor, Department of Leadership and Teacher Education, University of South Alabama, Mobile, AL

PHILIP G. BENSON, Professor of Management, New Mexico State University, Las Cruces, NM

JEFF BERRY, Assistant Professor of Speech Pathology and Audiology, Marquette University, Milwaukee, WI

MICHAEL D. BIDERMAN, Professor of Psychology, University of Tennessee at Chattanooga, Chattanooga, TN

ELIZABETH BIGHAM, Health Psychologist, Lecturer in Human Development, California State University San Marcos, San Marcos, CA

J. M. BLACKBOURN, Associate Professor of Education, University of Mississippi, University, MS

REBECCA BLANCHARD, Doctoral Student in Research, Statistics, and Evaluation, University of Virginia, Charlottesville, VA

PATRICIA BRAZIER-CARTER, Assistant Professor of Speech Language Pathology, Southern University, Baton Rouge, LA

JOHN J. BRINKMAN, Assistant Professor of Psychology and Counseling University of Saint Francis, Fort Wayne, IN

SUSAN M. BROOKHART, President, Brookhart Enterprises LLC and Duquesne University, Helena, MT

RITA BUDRIONIS, Licensed Clinical Psychologist, Licensed Sex Offender Treatment Provider, Director Dominion Sex Offenders Program, Juvenile and Adult, Virginia Beach, VA, and Associate Professor, Department of Psychology, Old Dominion University, Norfolk, VA

ERIC S. BUHS, Associate Professor of Educational Psychology, University of Nebraska-Lincoln, Lincoln, NE

RACHEL D. BURROWS, Doctoral Candidate, University of Maine, Orono, ME

GARY L. CANIVEZ, Professor of Psychology, Department of Psychology, Eastern Illinois University, Charleston, IL

KAREN T. CAREY, Dean, Division of Graduate Studies, Professor of Psychology, California State University, Fresno, Fresno, CA

C. DALE CARPENTER, Associate Dean, College of Education and Allied Professions, and Professor of Special Education, Western Carolina University, Cullowhee, NC

AMBER CARTER, Graduate Assistant, University of Saint Francis, Fort Wayne, IN

JERRELL CASSADY, Professor of Psychology, Department of Educational Psychology, Ball State University, Muncie, IN

TONY CELLUCCI, Professor and Director of the Psychology Training Clinic, Idaho State University, Pocatello, ID

MARY (RINA) M. CHITTOORAN, Associate Professor, Department of Educational Studies, Saint Louis University, St. Louis, MO

DAVID F. CIAMPI, Adjunct Professor, International Homeland Security University Project, Springfield, MA

JOSEPH C. CIECHALSKI, Professor, Department of Counselor & Adult Education, East Carolina University, Greenville, N.C.

GREGORY J. CIZEK, Professor of Educational Measurement and Evaluation, University of North Carolina-Chapel Hill, Chapel Hill, NC

MARY M. CLARE, Professor of Counseling Psychology, Lewis & Clark College, Portland, OR

JEAN N. CLARK, Associate Professor of Educational Psychology, College of Education, University of South Alabama, Mobile, AL

BRANDY L. CLARKE, Pediatric Psychology Intern, Munroe-Meyer Institute, University of Nebraska Medical Center, Omaha, NE

THEODORE COLADARCI, Director of Institutional Research and Professor of Educational Psychology, University of Maine, Orono, ME

MARTA COLEMAN, Instructor, Gunnison Watershed School District, Gunnison, CO

CATHERINE P. COOK-COTTONE, Associate Professor of School Psychology, State University of New York at Buffalo, Buffalo, NY

MERITH COSDEN, Department of Counseling, Clinical, and School Psychology, University of California, Santa Barbara, Santa Barbara, CA

ANDREW A. COX, Professor of Counseling and Psychology, Troy University, Phenix City, AL

MICHAEL K. CRUCE, Nationally Certified School Psychologist, Special Education Department, Lincoln Public Schools, Lincoln, NE

NANCY L. CRUMPTON, Part-time Faculty, Troy University; Part-time Faculty, Walden University; Montgomery, AL

MICHAEL J. CULBERTSON, Illinois Distinguished Fellow, Department of Educational Psychology, University of Illinois-Urbana-Champaign, Urbana, IL

RIK CARL D'AMATO, Professor and Head of the Department of Psychology at the University of Macau, Macau SAR, China

AYRES D'COSTA, Associate Professor, Quantitative Research, Measurement, and Evaluation in Education, The Ohio State University, Columbus, OH

ATHENA DACANAY, Doctoral Student of School Psychology, Ball State University, Muncie, IN

M. MEGHAN DAVIDSON, Assistant Professor of Counseling Psychology, University of Nebraska, Lincoln, NE

ANDREW S. DAVIS, Associate Professor, Department of Educational Psychology, Ball State University, Muncie, IN

GARY J. DEAN, Professor and Department Chairperson, Department of Adult and Community Education, Indiana University of Pennsylvania, Indiana, PA

SHARON deFUR, Professor of Special Education, College of William and Mary, Williamsburg, VA

GERALD E. DeMAURO, Managing Educational Assessment Scientist, American Institutes for Research, Voorheesville, NY

GYPSY M. DENZINE, Associate Dean and Professor of Educational Psychology, Northern Arizona University, Flagstaff, AZ

STEPHAN DILCHERT, Assistant Professor of Management, Baruch College, City College of New York, New York, NY

JOE W. DIXON, Forensic Psychologist and Lawyer, Private Practice, Greenville, NC

R. ANTHONY DOGGETT, Associate Professor of School Psychology, Mississippi State University, Starkville, MS

BETH DOLL, Professor, Department of Educational Psychology, University of Nebraska-Lincoln, Lincoln, NE

STEFAN C. DOMBROWSKI, Professor & Director, School Psychology Program, Rider University, Lawrenceville, NJ

JAMES P. DONNELLY, Clinical Associate Professor, Department of Counseling, School & Educational Psychology, University at Buffalo, Amherst, NY

ANTHONY T. DUGBARTEY, Psychologist, Forensic Psychiatric Services Commission, and Adjunct Associate Professor of Psychology, University of Victoria, Victoria British Columbia, Canada

THOMAS M. DUNN, Associate Professor of Psychological Sciences, University of Northern Colorado, Greeley, CO

CHER EDWARDS, Associate Professor and Chair, Department of Counselor Education, Seattle Pacific University, Seattle, WA

RICK EIGENBROOD, Professor in Education, Seattle Pacific University, Seattle, WA

GEORGE ENGELHARD, JR., Professor of Educational Measurement and Policy, Emory University, Atlanta, GA

CONNIE THERIOT ENGLAND, Professor, Graduate Education, Lincoln Memorial University, Knoxville, TN

RICHARD F. FARMER, Associate Professor of Psychology, East Carolina University, Greenville, NC

JENNIFER G. FILLINGIM, Doctoral Candidate, University of Mississippi, University, MS

W. HOLMES FINCH, Associate Professor, Department of Educational Psychology, Ball State University, Muncie, IN

ROSEMARY FLANAGAN, Associate Professor, Graduate School of Psychology, Touro College, New York, NY

RANDY G. FLOYD, Associate Professor of Psychology, The University of Memphis, Memphis, TN

STEPHEN J. FREEMAN, Professor and Chair, Department of Counseling, Texas A & M University-Commerce, Commerce, TX

BRIAN F. FRENCH, Associate Professor of Educational Psychology (Research, Evaluation, & Measurement), Washington State University, Pullman, WA

MICHAEL J. FURLONG, Professor, Gevirtz Graduate School of Education, University of California, Santa Barbara, Santa Barbara, CA

MARY L. GARNER, Associate Professor of Mathematics, Kennesaw State University, Kennesaw, GA

ZARABETH GERLING, Doctoral Student, School Psychology Program, The University of Iowa, Iowa City, IA

MARK J. GIERL, Professor and Canada Research Chair, Centre for Research in Applied Measurement and Evaluation, Department of Educational Psychology, University of Alberta, Edmonton, Alberta, Canada

BERT A. GOLDMAN, Professor Emeritus, University of North Carolina Greensboro, Greensboro, NC

JORGE E. GONZALEZ, Assistant Professor, Department of Educational Psychology, Texas A&M University, College Station, TX

ERIC GRADY, Psychology Intern, Munroe Meyer Institute, University of Nebraska Medical Center, Omaha, NE

THERESA GRAHAM, Adjunct Faculty, University of Nebraska-Lincoln, Lincoln, NE

ZANDRA S. GRATZ, Professor of Psychology, Kean University, Union, NJ

AMY-JANE GRIFFITHS, Doctoral candidate, Counseling, Clinical, and School Psychology Department, University of California, Santa Barbara, Santa Barbara, CA

THOMAS GUYETTE, Professor, Audiology and Speech Pathology Department, University of Arkansas at Little Rock, Little Rock, AR

LAURA HAMILTON, Senior Behavioral Scientist, RAND Corporation, Pittsburgh, PA

KENNETH M. HANIG, Adjunct Faculty, Department of Psychology, Indiana University South Bend, South Bend, IN

SANDRA M. HARRIS, Assessment Coordinator, College of Social and Behavioral Sciences, Walden University, Minneapolis, MN

MICHAEL HARWELL, Professor, Department of Educational Psychology, University of Minnesota, Minneapolis, MN

THEODORE L. HAYES, Personnel Research Psychologist, U.S. Office of Personnel Management, Washington, DC

SANDRA D. HAYNES, Dean, School of Professional Studies, Metropolitan State College of Denver, Denver, CO

CYNTHIA HAZEL, Assistant Professor, Child, Family and School Psychology, Morgridge College of Education, University of Denver, Denver, CO

CARLEN HENINGTON, Associate Professor of School Psychology, Mississippi State University, Mississippi State, MS

GEORGIA HINMAN, CEO, Hinman Consulting, Madison, WI

KATHRYN E. HOFF, Associate Professor of Psychology, Illinois State University, Normal, IL

THOMAS P. HOGAN, Professor of Psychology, University of Scranton, Scranton, PA

DAVID R. HOLLIWAY, Assistant Professor, Educational Leadership and Counseling Psychology, Washington State University Tri-Cities, Richland, WA

JANET HOUSER, Associate Professor of Health Services Administration, Regis University, Denver, CO

ANITA M. HUBLEY, Professor of Measurement, Evaluation, and Research Methodology, University of British Columbia, Vancouver, British Columbia, Canada

TIFFANY L. HUTCHINS, Lecturer of Communication Sciences, University of Vermont, Burlington, VT

MARC JANOSON, President, Forensic Psychology PC, Manhasset, NY

JEFFREY A. JENKINS, Associate Professor, Roger Williams University, Bristol, RI

KATHLEEN M. JOHNSON, Psychologist, Lincoln Public Schools, Lincoln, NE

KRISTIN JONES, Graduate Student in Educational Psychology, University of Nebraska-Lincoln, Lincoln, NE

H. DENNIS KADE, Naval Medical Center Portsmouth: Substance Abuse Rehabilitation Program, Norfolk, VA and Adjunct Assistant Professor of Psychology, Old Dominion University, Norfolk, VA

ASHRAF KAGEE, Professor of Psychology, Stellenbosch University, South Africa

NEETA KANTAMNENI, Assistant Professor, University of Nebraska-Lincoln, Lincoln, NE

MICHAEL G. KAVAN, Professor of Family Medicine and Professor of Psychiatry, Associate Dean for Student Affairs, Creighton University School of Medicine, Omaha, NE

KARL N. KELLEY, Professor of Psychology, North Central College, Naperville, IL

KEVIN R. KELLY, Head, Department of Educational Studies, Purdue University, West Lafayette, IN
RICHARD T. KINNIER, Professor, Counseling Psychology Program, Arizona State University, Tempe, AZ
JEAN P. KIRNAN, Professor of Psychology, The College of New Jersey, Ewing, NJ
TIMOTHY R. KONOLD, Associate Professor of Research, Statistics, and Evaluation, University of Virginia, Charlottesville, VA
S. KATHLEEN KRACH, Associate Professor, Troy University, Montgomery, AL
JOSEPH C. KUSH, Associate Professor, Duquesne University, Pittsburgh, PA
MATTHEW E. LAMBERT, Clinical Assistant Professor of Neuropsychiatry, Texas Tech University Health Sciences Center, Department of Neuropsychiatry, Lubbock, TX
SUZANNE LANE, Professor of Research Methodology, University of Pittsburgh, Pittsburgh, PA
AIMÉE LANGLOIS, Professor Emerita, Department of Child Development, Humboldt State University, Arcata, CA
CAMILLE LAWRENCE, Doctoral Student in Research, Statistics, and Evaluation, University of Virginia, Charlottesville, VA
THOMAS LAZZARO, Forensic Psychologist in Independent Practice, Syracuse, NY
JEANETTE LEE-FARMER, Associate Professor of Special Education, Marshall University, South Charleston, WV
CLAIRE LENZ, Associate Professor of Child Study, St. Joseph's College, Patchogue, NY
FREDERICK T. L. LEONG, Professor of Psychology, Michigan State University, East Lansing, MI
PAM LINDSEY-GLENN, Professor, College of Education, Tarleton State University, Stephenville, TX
STEVEN LONG, Associate Professor of Speech Pathology and Audiology, Marquette University, Milwaukee, WI
CLEBORNE D. MADDUX, Foundation Professor of Counseling and Educational Psychology, University of Nevada, Reno, Reno, NV
RONALD A. MADLE, Licensed Psychologist, Mifflinburg, PA, and Adjunct Associate Professor of School Psychology, The Pennsylvania State University, University Park, PA
JENNIFER N. MAHDAVI, Associate Professor of Special Education, Sonoma State University, Rohnert Park, CA
TIMOTHY J. MAKATURA, Adjunct Professor of Psychology, Capella University, Minneapolis, MN
KORESSA KUTSICK MALCOLM, School Psychologist, The Virginia School for the Deaf and Blind, Staunton, VA
CAROLINE MANUELE ADKINS, Professor Emeritus, Hunter College, School of Education, City University of New York, New York, NY
WILLIAM E. MARTIN, JR., Professor of Educational Psychology, Northern Arizona University, Flagstaff, AZ
MICHAEL S. MATTHEWS, Assistant Professor of Gifted Education, The University of North Carolina at Charlotte, Charlotte, NC
REBECCA McCAULEY, Professor of Speech & Hearing Science, The Ohio State University, Columbus, OH
MARY J. McLELLAN, Professor, Northern Arizona University, Flagstaff, AZ
TAWNYA J. MEADOWS, Assistant Professor of Pediatrics, Munroe Meyer Institute, University of Nebraska Medical Center, Omaha, NE
FREDERIC J. MEDWAY, Professor of Psychology, University of South Carolina, Columbia, SC
JOYCE MEIKAMP, Professor of Special Education, Marshall University Graduate College, South Charleston, WV
BRAD M. MERKER, Staff Neuropsychologist, Henry Ford Health System, Detroit, MI
M. DAVID MILLER, Professor, College of Education, University of Florida, Gainesville, FL
RAMA K. MISHRA, Neuropsychologist, Department of Psychiatry, Medicine Hat Regional Hospital, Medicine Hat, Alberta, Canada
DEBRA MOORE, Ph.D. Candidate, University of Pittsburgh, Pittsburgh, PA
DAVID MORSE, Professor, Counseling, Educational Psychology and Special Education, Mississippi State University, Mississippi State, MS
MILDRED MURRAY-WARD, Professor of Education, California State University, Stanislaus, Turlock, CA
NYARADZO H. MVUDUDU, Associate Professor, Educational Research, Seattle Pacific University, Seattle, WA
SCOTT A. NAPOLITANO, Psychological and Academic Success Services, P.C., Lincoln, NE
NICOLE L. NIESET, Ph.D. Candidate, Counseling Psychology Program, Arizona State University, Tempe, AZ
AMANDA NOLEN, Assistant Professor, Educational Foundations/Teacher Education, College of Education, University of Arkansas at Little Rock, Little Rock, AR
CHRISTINE NOVAK, Associate Clinical Professor, School Psychology Program, The University of Iowa, Iowa City, IA
LINDSEY O'BRENNAN, University of California, Santa Barbara, Santa Barbara, CA
THOMAS R. O'NEILL, Psychometrician, National Council of State Boards of Nursing, Chicago, IL
ARTURO OLIVÁREZ, JR., Professor and Chair of the Teacher Education Department at the University of Texas at El Paso, El Paso, TX
AMY M. OLSON, Doctoral Student, University of Arizona, Tucson, AZ

DENIZ S. ONES, Hellervik Professor of Industrial Psychology, University of Minnesota, Minneapolis, MN
GRETCHEN OWENS, Professor of Child Study, St. Joseph's College, Patchogue, NY
LINDSAY R. OWINGS, doctoral candidate, University of Maine, Orono, ME
STEVEN I. PFEIFFER, Professor of Educational Psychology and Learning Systems, College of Education, Florida State University, Tallahassee, FL
JULIA Y. PORTER, Associate Professor of Counselor Education, Mississippi State University-Meridian, Meridian, MS
SHAWN POWELL, Instructor of Psychology, Casper College, and private practitioner, Casper, WY
NATALIE RATHVON, Assistant Clinical Professor, The George Washington University, Washington DC; Private Practice Psychologist and School Consultant, Bethesda, MD
JANET REED, Senior Staff Neuropsychologist, Henry Ford Behavioral Health, Division of Neuropsychology, Detroit, MI
BRANDY M. ROANE, Pediatric Psychology Intern, Munroe Meyer Institute, University of Nebraska Medical Center, Omaha, NE
STEVEN V. ROUSE, Professor of Psychology, Pepperdine University, Malibu, CA
KATHERINE RYAN, Associate Professor, Department of Educational Psychology, University of Illinois-Urbana-Champaign, Urbana, IL
DARRELL L. SABERS, Professor of Educational Psychology, University of Arizona, Tucson, AZ
JOHN SAMPLE, Assistant Professor, Adult Education, Florida State University, Tallahassee, FL
JONATHAN SANDOVAL, Professor of Education, University of the Pacific, Stockton, CA
WILLIAM D. SCHAFER, Affiliated Professor (Emeritus) of Measurement, Statistics, and Evaluation, University of Maryland, College Park, MD
MICHAEL J. SCHEEL, Associate Professor, University of Nebraska-Lincoln, Lincoln, NE
STEVEN W. SCHMIDT, Assistant Professor of Adult Education, East Carolina University, Greenville, NC
W. JOEL SCHNEIDER, Assistant Professor of Psychology, Illinois State University, Normal, IL
GREGORY SCHRAW, Professor, Department of Educational Psychology, University of Nevada-Las Vegas, Las Vegas, NV
GENE SCHWARTING, Associate Professor, Education Department, Fontbonne University, St. Louis, MO
NATASHA SEGOOL, Post-Doctoral Fellow, Munroe Meyer Institute, University of Nebraska Medical Center, Omaha, NE
TIMOTHY SHANAHAN, Professor of Urban Education, University of Illinois at Chicago, Chicago, IL
KATHY SHAPLEY, Assistant Professor, Audiology and Speech Pathology Department, University of Arkansas at Little Rock, Little Rock, AR
STEVEN R. SHAW, Assistant Professor of Counselling and Educational Psychology, McGill University, Montreal, Quebec, Canada
EUGENE P. SHEEHAN, Dean, College of Education and Behavioral Sciences, University of Northern Colorado, Greeley, CO
CRAIG S. SHWERY, Assistant Professor, Elementary Education Teaching Programs, University of Alabama, Tuscaloosa, AL
CHRISTOPHER A. SINK, Professor, School Counseling and Psychology, Seattle Pacific University, Seattle, WA
JEFFREY K. SMITH, Professor of Education, University of Otago, Dunedin, New Zealand
RUSSELL W. SMITH, Senior Psychometrician, Alpine Testing Solutions, Henderson, NV
GREGORY SNYDER, Clinical Child and Adolescent Psychologist, Children's Hospital, Omaha, NE
KATHARINE A. SNYDER, Associate Professor of Psychology, Methodist University, Fayetteville, NC
LORAINE J. SPENCINER, Professor of Special Education, University of Maine at Farmington, Farmington, ME
RAYNE A. SPERLING, Associate Professor and Professor-in-Charge of Educational Psychology, The Pennsylvania State University, University Park, PA
BECKY L. SPRITZ, Associate Professor of Psychology, Roger Williams University, Bristol, RI
MARK A. STAAL, Operational Psychologist, U.S. Special Operations Command, Ft. Bragg, NC
MARGOT B. STEIN, Clinical Associate Professor, University of North Carolina at Chapel Hill, Chapel Hill, NC
STEPHANIE STEIN, Professor and Chair, Department of Psychology, Central Washington University, Ellensburg, WA
KAY STEVENS, Associate Dean and Director of Graduate Studies, Texas Christian University, Fort Worth, TX
JAY R. STEWART, Director and Associate Professor, Rehabilitation Counseling Program, Division of Intervention Services, Bowling Green State University, Bowling Green, OH
MARK H. STONE, Adjunct Professor, Aurora University, Aurora, IL
JENNIFER M. STRANG, Clinical Neuropsychologist, Department of Behavioral Health, DeWitt Healthcare Network, Fort Belvoir, VA
GABRIELLE STUTMAN, Private Practice, Westchester and New York City, NY
HOI K. SUEN, Distinguished Professor of Educational Psychology, Pennsylvania State University, University Park, PA
JEREMY R. SULLIVAN, Assistant Professor of Educational Psychology, University of Texas at San Antonio, San Antonio, TX

HAUPING SUN, Doctoral Student, University of Arizona, Tucson, AZ
MARK E. SWERDLIK, Professor of Psychology, Illinois State University, Normal, IL
CONN THOMAS, Professor of Education, West Texas A&M University, Canyon, TX
TRACY THORNDIKE-CHRIST, Assistant Professor of Special Education and Educational Psychology, Western Washington University, Bellingham, WA
GEOFFREY L. THORPE, Professor of Psychology, University of Maine, Orono, ME
GERALD TINDAL, Castle-McIntosh-Knight Professor of Education, College of Education, University of Oregon, Eugene, OR
JONATHAN E. TITLEY, University of Macau, Macau SAR, China
RENÉE M. TOBIN, Associate Professor of Psychology, Illinois State University, Normal, IL
ROGER L. TOWNE, Associate Professor, Department of Communication Sciences and Disorders, Worcester State College, Worcester, MA
MICHAEL S. TREVISAN, Professor of Educational Psychology, Washington State University, Pullman, WA
JOHN J. VACCA, Assistant Professor of Early Childhood Education, St. Josephs University, Philadelphia, PA
RACHEL J. VALLELEY, Associate Professor, Munroe-Meyer Institute and Pediatrics, Munroe-Meyer Institute, University of Nebraska Medical Center, Omaha, NE
JAMES VAN HANEGHAN, Director, Assessment and Evaluation, College of Education, University of South Alabama, Mobile, AL
MATT VASSAR, Curriculum and Outcomes Assessment Coordinator, Oklahoma State University, Tulsa, OK
JOHN J. VENN, Professor, Department of Exceptional Student and Deaf Education, College of Education and Human Services, University of North Florida, Jacksonville, FL
DOLORES KLUPPEL VETTER, Professor Emerita, University of Wisconsin-Madison, Madison, WI
CHOCKALINGAM VISWESVARAN, Professor, Department of Psychology, Florida International University, Miami, FL
CATHERINE WAGNER, Graduate Student in School Psychology, Department of Educational Psychology, Ball State University, Muncie, IN
JOHN F. WAKEFIELD, Professor of Education, University of North Alabama, Florence, AL
DELORES D. WALCOTT, Professor, Western Michigan University, Counseling and Testing Center, Kalamazoo, MI
SANDRA WARD, Professor of Education, The College of William & Mary, Williamsburg, VA
T. STEUART WATSON, Professor of Educational Psychology, Miami University, Oxford, OH
KEITH F. WIDAMAN, Professor and Chair, Department of Psychology, University of California, Davis, CA
JOHN T. WILLSE, Associate Professor of Educational Research Methodology, University of North Carolina at Greensboro, Greensboro, NC
MYRA N. WOMBLE, Associate Professor of Workforce Education, University of Georgia, Athens, GA
MICHAEL F. WOODIN, Assistant Professor of Educational Psychology, Miami University, Oxford, OH
CLAUDIA R. WRIGHT, Professor Emerita, California State University, Long Beach, Long Beach, CA
ROBERT WRIGHT, Professor, Measurement & Statistics, Widener University, Chester, PA
TONY C. WU, Faculty, College of Social and Behavioral Sciences, Walden University, Minneapolis, MN
GEORGETTE YETTER, Assistant Professor, School Psychology, Oklahoma State University, Stillwater, OK
SUZANNE YOUNG, Professor of Educational Research, University of Wyoming, Laramie, WY
CORINNE ZIMMERMAN, Associate Professor of Psychology, Illinois State University, Normal, IL

INDEX OF TITLES

This title index lists all the tests included in The Eighteenth Mental Measurements Yearbook. *Citations are to test entry numbers, not to pages (e.g., 54 refers to test 54 and not page 54). Test numbers along with test titles are indicated in the running heads at the top of each page, whereas page numbers, used only in the Table of Contents but not in the indexes, appear at the bottom of each page. Superseded titles are listed with cross references to current titles, and alternative titles are also cross referenced.*

Some tests in this volume were previously listed in Tests in Print VII *(2006). An* (N) *appearing immediately after a test number indicates that the test is a new, recently published test, and/or that it has not appeared before in any Buros Institute publication other than* Tests in Print VII. *An* (R) *indicates that the test has been revised or supplemented since last included in a Buros publication.*

INDEX OF ACRONYMS

This Index of Acronyms refers the reader to the appropriate test in The Eighteenth Mental Measurements Yearbook. *In some cases tests are better known by their acronyms than by their full titles, and this index can be of substantial help to the person who knows the former but not the latter. Acronyms are listed only if the author or publisher has made substantial use of the acronym in referring to the test, or if the test is widely known by the acronym. A few acronyms are registered trademarks (e.g., SAT); where this is known to us, only the test with the registered trademarks is referenced. There is some danger in the overuse of acronyms. However, this index, like all other indexes in this work, is provided to make the task of identifying a test as easy as possible. All numbers refer to test numbers, not page numbers.*

CLASSIFIED SUBJECT INDEX

The Classified Subject Index classifies all tests included in The Mental Measurements Yearbook *into 18 major categories: Achievement, Behavior Assessment, Developmental, Education, English and Language, Fine Arts, Foreign Languages, Intelligence and General Aptitude, Mathematics, Miscellaneous, Neuropsychological, Personality, Reading, Science, Sensory-Motor, Social Studies, Speech and Hearing, and Vocations. This Classified Subject Index for the tests reviewed in* The Eighteenth Mental Measurements Yearbook *includes tests in 17 of the 18 available categories. (The category of Fine Arts had no representative tests in this volume.) Each category appears in alphabetical order and tests are ordered alphabetically within each category. Each test entry includes test title, population for which the test is intended, and the test entry number in* The Eighteenth Mental Measurements Yearbook. *All numbers refer to test numbers, not to page numbers. Brief suggestions for the use of this index are presented in the introduction and definitions of the categories are provided at the beginning of this index.*

Achievement

Tests that measure acquired knowledge across school subject content areas. Included here are test batteries that measure multiple content areas and individual subject areas not having separate classification categories. (Note: Some batteries include both achievement and aptitude subtests. Such batteries may be classified under the categories of either Achievement or Intelligence and Aptitude depending upon the principal content area.)

See also Fine Arts, Intelligence and General Aptitude, Mathematics, Reading, Science, and Social Studies.

Behavior Assessment

Tests that measure general or specific behavior within educational, vocational, community, or home settings. Included here are checklists, rating scales, and surveys that measure observer's interpretations of behavior in relation to adaptive or social skills, functional skills, and appropriateness or dysfunction within settings/situations.

Developmental

Tests that are designed to assess skills or emerging skills (such as number concepts, conservation, memory, fine motor, gross motor, communication, letter recognition, social competence) of young children (0-7 years) or tests which are designed to assess such skills in severely or profoundly disabled school-aged individuals. Included here are early screeners, developmental surveys/profiles, kindergarten or school readiness tests, early learning profiles, infant development scales, tests of play behavior, social acceptance/social skills; and preschool psychoeducational batteries. Content specific screeners, such as those assessing readiness, are classified by content area (e.g., Reading).

See also Neuropsychological and Sensory-Motor.

Education

General education-related tests, including measures of instructional/school environment, effective schools/teaching, study skills and strategies, learning styles and strategies, school attitudes, educational programs/curriculae, interest inventories, and educational leadership.

Specific content area tests (i.e., science, mathematics, social studies, etc.) are listed by their content area.

English and Language

Tests that measure skills in using or understanding the English language in spoken or written form. Included here are tests of language proficiency, applied literacy, language comprehension/development/proficiency, English skills/proficiency, communication skills, listening comprehension, linguistics, and receptive/expressive vocabulary. (Tests designed to measure the mechanics of speaking or communicating are classified under the category Speech and Hearing.)

Fine Arts

Tests that measure knowledge, skills, abilities, attitudes, and interests within the various areas of fine and performing arts. Included here are tests of aptitude, achievement, creativity/talent/giftedness specific to the Fine Arts area, and tests of aesthetic judgment.

Foreign Languages

Tests that measure competencies and readiness in reading, comprehending, and speaking a language other than English.

Intelligence and General Aptitude

Tests that measure general acquired knowledge, aptitudes, or cognitive ability and those that assess specific aspects of these general categories. Included here are tests of critical thinking skills, nonverbal/verbal reasoning, cognitive abilities/processing, learning potential/aptitude/efficiency, logical reasoning, abstract thinking, creative thinking/creativity; entrance exams and academic admissions tests.

Mathematics

Tests that measure competencies and attitudes in any of the various areas of mathematics (e.g., algebra, geometry, calculus) and those related to general mathematics achievement/proficiency. (Note: Included here are tests that assess personality or affective variables related to mathematics.)

Miscellaneous

Tests that cannot be sorted into any of the current MMY categories as listed and defined above. Included here are tests of handwriting, ethics and morality, religion, driving and safety, health and physical education, environment (e.g., classroom environment, family environment), custody decisions, substance abuse, and addictions. (See also Personality.)

Neuropsychological

Tests that measure neurological functioning or brain-behavior relationships either generally or in relation to specific areas of functioning. Included here are neuropsychological test batteries, questionnaires, and screening tests. Also included are tests that measure memory impairment, various disorders or decline associated with dementia, brain/head injury, visual attention, digit recognition, finger tapping, laterality, aphasia, and behavior (associated with organic brain dysfunction or brain injury).

See also Developmental, Intelligence and General Aptitude, Sensory-Motor, and Speech and Hearing.

Personality

Tests that measure individuals' ways of thinking, behaving, and functioning within family and society. Included here are projective and apperception tests, needs inventories, anxiety/depression scales; tests assessing substance use/abuse (or propensity for abuse), risk taking behavior, general mental health, emotional intelligence, self-image/-concept/-esteem, empathy, suicidal ideation, schizophrenia, depression/hopelessness, abuse, coping skills/stress, eating disorders, grief, decision-making, racial attitudes; general motivation, attributions, perceptions; adjustment, parenting styles, and marital issues/satisfaction.

For content-specific tests, see subject area categories (e.g., math efficacy instruments are located in Mathematics). Some areas, such as substance abuse, are cross-referenced with the Personality category.

Reading

Tests that measure competencies and attitudes within the broadly defined area of reading. Included here are reading inventories, tests of reading achievement and aptitude, reading readiness/early reading ability, reading comprehension, reading decoding, and oral reading. (Note: Included here are tests that assess personality or affective variables related to reading.)

Science

Tests that measure competencies and attitudes within any of the various areas of science (e.g., biology, chemistry, physics), and those related to general science achievement/proficiency. (Note: Included here are tests that assess personality or affective variables related to science.)

Sensory-Motor

Tests that are general or specific measures of any or all of the five senses and those that assess fine or gross motor skills. Included here are tests of manual dexterity, perceptual skills, visual-motor skills, perceptual-motor skills, movement and posture, laterality preference, sensory integration, motor development, color blindness/discrimination, visual perception/organization, and visual acuity.

See also Neuropsychological and Speech and Hearing.

Social Studies

Tests that measure competencies and attitudes within the broadly defined area of social studies. Included here are tests related to economics, sociology, history, geography, and political science, and those related to general social studies achievement/proficiency. (Note: Also included here are tests that assess personality or affective variables related to social studies.)

Speech and Hearing

Tests that measure the mechanics of speaking or hearing the spoken word. Included here are tests of articulation, voice fluency, stuttering, speech sound perception/discrimination, auditory discrimination/ comprehension, audiometry, deafness, and hearing loss/ impairment.

See also Developmental, English and Language, Neuropsychological, and Sensory-Motor.

Vocations

Tests that measure employee skills, behaviors, attitudes, values, and perceptions relative to jobs, employment, and the work place or organizational environment. Included here are tests of management skill/style/competence, leader behavior, careers (development, exploration, attitudes); job- or work-related selection/admission/ entrance tests; tests of work adjustment, team or group processes/communication/effectiveness, employability, vocational/occupational interests, employee aptitudes/ competencies, and organizational climate.

See also Intelligence and General Aptitude, and Personality and also specific content area categories (e.g., Mathematics, Reading).

ACHIEVEMENT

Differential Ability Scales–Second Edition; Ages 2-6 to 17-11; 45
Measures of Academic Progress; Grades 3-10; 73
TerraNova, Third Edition; Grades K–12; 135
Wechsler Fundamentals: Academic Skills; Children Kindergarten-Grade 12, adults age 18-50; 152
Wechsler Individual Achievement Test—Third Edition; Ages 4-0 to 19-11; 153
Wide Range Achievement Test 4; Ages 5-94; 157
Wide Range Achievement Test Fourth Edition Progress Monitoring Version; Ages 5-94; 158

BEHAVIOR ASSESSMENT

Attention Test Linking Assessment and Services; Ages 8-18; 8
BASC-2 Behavioral and Emotional Screening System; Ages 3-18; 10
Behavioral and Psychological Assessment of Dementia; Ages 30-90; 12
Burks Behavior Rating Scales, Second Edition; Ages 4-18; 16
Children's Aggression Scale; Ages 5-18; 25
Children's Organizational Skills Scales; Ages 8-13; 27
Conners 3rd Edition; Ages 6-18; 35
Conners Comprehensive Behavior Rating Scales; Ages 6-18; 33
Devereux Early Childhood Assessment for Infants and Toddlers; Ages 1 month to 36 months; 40
Devereux Student Strengths Assessment; Grades K-8; 41
Differential Scales of Social Maladjustment and Emotional Disturbance; Ages 6-0 to 17-11; 46
Emotional Disturbance Decision Tree; Ages 5-18; 48
Mind Body Wellness Geriatric Rehabilitation and Restorative Assessment System; Ages 55 and up; 76
Pediatric Attention Disorders Diagnostic Screener; Parent- or school-referred children ages 6-12; 89
PsychProfiler; Ages 2-17,ages 18+; 105
Social Skills Improvement System Rating Scales; Ages 3-18 years; 125
Structured Assessment of Violence Risk in Youth; Ages 12-18; 131
Texas Functional Living Scale; "Individuals ages 16-90 diagnosed with a variety of clinical disorders or requiring an assessment of functional abilities"; 147
Vineland Adaptive Behavior Scales, Second Edition; Birth to age 90-11; 150

DEVELOPMENTAL

EDUCATION

ENGLISH AND LANGUAGE

FOREIGN LANGUAGES

INTELLIGENCE AND GENERAL APTITUDE

MATHEMATICS

MISCELLANEOUS

NEUROPSYCHOLOGICAL

PERSONALITY

READING

SCIENCE

SENSORY MOTOR

Bruininks-Oseretsky Test of Motor Proficiency, Second Edition; Ages 4–21; 15
Koppitz Developmental Scoring System for the Bender Gestalt Test, Second Edition; Ages 5-7, 8-85+; 66
Sensory Processing Measure; Ages 5-12; 119
Sensory Profile School Companion; Ages 3-0 to 11-11; 120
Test of Visual Perceptual Skills, 3rd Edition; Ages 4-0 through 18-11; 146

SOCIAL STUDIES

Test of Understanding in College Economics—Fourth Edition; Introductory economics students; 145

SPEECH AND HEARING

Frenchay Dysarthria Assessment–Second Edition; Ages 15-97, 55
The Listening Inventory; Ages 4-17; 70
Overall Assessment of the Speaker's Experience of Stuttering; Individuals 18 and over who stutter; 83
SCAN-3 for Adolescents and Adults: Tests for Auditory Processing Disorders; Ages 13-50; 111
SCAN-3 for Children: Tests for Auditory Processing Disorders; Ages 5-12; 112
Test of Auditory Processing Skills—Third Edition; Ages 4–0 through 18-11; 137
Test of Childhood Stuttering; Ages 4-0 to 12-11; 138

VOCATIONS

A-4 Police Officer Video Test; Candidates for entry-level police officer positions; 1
Administrative Series Modules; Candidates for administrative positions; 2
The Business Critical Thinking Skills Test; Adult business professionals and business students; 17
C-1 and C-2 Correctional Officer Tests; Candidates for entry-level correctional officer positions; 19
C-BDQ Correctional Officer Background Data Questionnaire; Candidates for entry-level correctional officer positions; 18
D-1, D-2, and D-3 Police Officer Tests; Candidates for entry-level police officer positions; 37
ElecTest (Form A, Form A-C, & Form B); Applicants and incumbents for jobs requiring practical electrical knowledge and skills; 47
Employee Wellness Evaluation; Employees seeking counseling; 49
Executive Dimensions; Senior executives; 50
Klein Group Instrument for Effective Leadership and Participation in Teams; Team and group participants of ages 14+; 65
Matrix-Predictive Uniform Law Enforcement Selection Evaluation Inventory; Law enforcement officer candidates; 72
P-BDQ Police Officer Background Data Questionnaire; Candidates for entry-level police officer positions; 84
P-Det 1.0 and 2.0 Police Detective Tests; Candidates for promotion to the police detective position; 85
P-1SV and P-2SV Police Officer Tests; Candidates for entry-level police officer positions; 86
Performance Perspectives Inventory; "[Job] candidates across a broad range of positions"; 91
Picture Interest Career Survey; Ages 10-65; 94
PL-1 and PL-2 Police Administrator Tests (Lieutenant); Candidates for promotion to the police administrator position; 95
The ProfileXT Assessment; Present and potential employees; 100
PST-100SV and PST-80SV Public Safety Telecommunicator Tests; Candidates for entry-level public safety communicator positions; 101

PUBLISHERS DIRECTORY AND INDEX

This directory and index gives the names and test entry numbers of all publishers represented in The Eighteenth Mental Measurements Yearbook. *Current addresses are listed for all publishers for which this is known. This directory and index also provides telephone and FAX numbers and e-mail and Web addresses for those publishers who responded to our request for this information. Please note that all test numbers refer to test entry numbers, not page numbers. Publishers are an important source of information about catalogs, specimen sets, price changes, test revisions, and many other matters.*

A & M Psychometrics, LLC
1611 Utica Ave., #281
Tulsa, OK 74104
Test: 91

Academic Therapy Publications
20 Commercial Boulevard
Novato, CA 94949-6191
Telephone: 800-422-7249
FAX: 415-883-3720
E-mail: atp@aol.com
Web: www.academictherapy.com/
Tests: 69, 70, 137, 141, 146

Acanthus Publishing
343 Commercial St.
Unit 214, Union Wharf
Boston, MA 02109
Telephone: 617-230-2167
FAX: 215-243-7495
E-mail: info@acanthuspublishing.com
Web: www.AcanthusPublishing.com
Test: 23

APR Testing Services
27 Judith Road
Newton, MA 02459-1715
Telephone: 617-244-7405
E-mail: jwiesen@aprtestingservices.com
Web: aprtestingservices.com
Tests: 43, 44

Association for Biblical Higher Education
5575 S. Semoran Blvd., Suite 26
Orlando, FL 32822-1781
Telephone: 407-207-0808
FAX: 407-207-0840
E-mail: exdir@abhe.org
Web: www.abhe.org
Test: 167

Australian Council for Educational Research Ltd.
19 Prospect Hill Road
Camberwell, Melbourne
Victoria 3124
Australia
Telephone: +61 3 9835 7411
FAX: +61 3 9835 7499
E-mail: power@acer.edu.au
Web: www.acer.edu.au
Tests: 9, 81, 105, 159, 160, 191, 193

Ballard & Tighe Publishers
P.O. Box 219
Brea, CA 92822-0219
Telephone: 800-321-4332
FAX: 714-255-9828
E-mail: info@ballard-tighe.com
Web: www.ballard-tighe.com
Test: 188

Castle Consultants
111 Teeter Rock Road
Trumbull, CT 06611
Telephone: 203-375-5353
FAX: 203-375-2999
E-mail: cassie@castleconsultants.us
Web: www.castleconsultants.us
Tests: 6, 114, 115, 116, 117, 118

Center for Advanced Studies in Management
1574 Mallory Court
Bowling Green, KY 42103
Tests: 165, 170, 181, 189

Center for Applications of Psychological Type, Inc.
2815 Northwest 13th Street, Suite 401
Gainesville, FL 32609
Tests: 65, 78

Center for Creative Leadership
One Leadership Place
P.O. Box 26300
Greensboro, NC 27438-6300
Telephone: 336-288-7210
FAX: 336-282-3284
E-mail: info@leaders.ccl.org
Web: www.ccl.org
Test: 50

The Center for Management Effectiveness, Inc.
P.O. Box 1202
Pacific Palisades, CA 90272
Telephone: 310-459-6052
FAX: 310-459-9307
E-mail: info@cmeinc.org
Web: www.cmeinc.org
Test: 166

CFKR Career Materials
P.O. Box 99
Meadow Vista, CA 95722-0099
Tests: 164, 173, 174, 175, 176

The Change Companies
5221 Sigstrom Drive
Carson City, NV 89706
Telephone: 888-889-8866
FAX: 775-885-0643
E-mail: info@changecompanies.net
Web: www.changecompanies.net
Tests: 31, 49, 168, 172, 182, 198

Council for Economic Education
122 East 42nd St.
Suite 2600
New York, NY 10168
Telephone: 800-338-1192
FAX: 212-730-1793
Web: www.CouncilforEconEd.org
Test: 145

CPP, Inc.
1055 Joaquin Road, 2nd Floor
Mountain View, CA 94043
Telephone: 800-624-1765
FAX: 650-969-8608
E-mail: custserve@cpp.com
Web: www.cpp.com
Tests: 36, 123, 128, 129, 180, 183

The Creative Problem Solving Group, Inc.
P.O. Box 648
6 Grand View Trail
Orchard Park, NY 14127
Telephone: 716-667-1324
FAX: 716-667-6070
Web: www.cpsb.com
Test: 122

Crystal Springs Books
10 Sharon Road
P.O. Box 500
Peterborough, NH 03458-0500
Test: 190

CTB/McGraw-Hill
20 Ryan Ranch Road
Monterey, CA 93940-5703
Telephone: 831-393-0700
Web: www.ctb.com
Test: 135

Curriculum Associates, Inc.
153 Rangeway Road
P.O. Box 2001
North Billerica, MA 01862-0901
Telephone: 800-225-0248
FAX: 800-366-1158
E-mail: info@cainc.com
Web: www.curriculumassociates.com
Test: 162

Dinosaurs, Trees, Religion and Galaxies, Inc.
P.O. Box 269052
Chicago, IL 60626
Telephone: 312-316-2055
Web: accelinflation@yahoo.com
Test: 186

GIA Publications, Inc.
7404 South Mason Avenue
Chicago, IL 60638
Telephone: 708-496-3800
FAX: 708-496-3828
E-mail: custserv@giamusic.com
Web: www.giamusic.com
Test: 179

Human Sciences Research Council [South Africa]
Distributed by Mindmuzik Media
P.O. Box 2904 Brooklyn Square
Pretoria
Gauteng 0075
South Africa
Telephone: +27 (0)12-346-6008
FAX: +27 90) 346 4773
E-mail: frikkie@mindmuzik.com
Test: 192

INQ Educational Materials, Inc.
6933 Armour Drive
Oakland, CA 94611-1317
Telephone: 1-888-339-2323
FAX: 1-510-339-6729
E-mail: Paul@YourThinkingProfile.com
Web: www.YourThinkingProfile.com
Tests: 59, 177

Insight Assessment—The California Academic Press LLC
217 La Cruz Avenue
Millbrae, CA 94030
Telephone: 650-697-5628
FAX: 650-692-0141
E-mail: info@insightassessment.com
Web: www.insightassessment.com
Tests: 17, 20, 21, 22, 58, 140, 185, 187

Institute for Personality and Ability Testing, Inc. (IPAT)
P.O. Box 1188
Champaign, IL 61824-1188
Telephone: 217-352-4739
FAX: 217-352-9674
E-mail: custserv@ipat.com
Web: www.ipat.com
Test: 103

International Public Management Association for Human Resources (IPMA-HR)
1617 Duke Street
Alexandria, VA 22314
Telephone: 800-381-8378
FAX: 703-684-0948
E-mail: assessment@ipma-hr.org
Web: testing.ipma-hr.org
Tests: 1, 2, 18, 19, 37, 84, 85, 86, 95, 101, 102, 106

Janelle Publications, Inc.
P.O. Box 811
1189 Twombly Road
DeKalb, IL 60115
Telephone: 800-888-8834
Web: janellepublications.com
Tests: 132, 133

JIST Publishing, Inc.
7321 Shadeland Sta., Ste. 200
Indianapolis, IN 46256-3936
Telephone: 800-648-5478
FAX: 800-547-8329
E-mail: info@jist.com
Web: www.jist.com
Tests: 94, 163

Kaplan DeVries Inc.
1903 G Ashwood Ct.
Greensboro, NC 27455
Test: 67

Kaplan Early Learning Company
1310 Lewisville-Clemmons Road
P.O. Box 67
Lewisville, NC 27023-0609
Tests: 40, 41

Laurence M. Binder, Ph.D.
4900 SW Griffith Dr.
Suite 244
Beaverton, OR 97005
Telephone: 503-626-5246
FAX: 503-626-1686
E-mail: pdxlarry@aol.com
Test: 184

Learning by Design
P.O. Box 5448
Evanston, IL 60201-5448
Test: 126

Multi-Health Systems, Inc.
P.O. Box 950
North Tonawanda, NY 14120-0950
Telephone: 800-456-3003
FAX: 888-540-4484
E-mail: CUSTOMERSERVICE@MHS.COM
Web: www.mhs.com
Tests: 24, 27, 32, 33, 34, 35, 68, 72, 104

National Study of School Evaluation
1866 Southern Ln.
Decatur, GA 30033-4033
Tests: 169, 171, 194, 195, 196

Northwest Evaluation Association
5885 SW Meadows Road, Suite 200
Lake Oswego, OR 97035-3256
Test: 73

Paul H. Brookes Publishing Co., Inc.
P.O. Box 10624
Baltimore, MD 21285-0624
Telephone: 800-638-3775
FAX: 410-337-8539
E-mail: custserv@brookespublishing.com
Web: www.brookespublishing.com
Tests: 4, 5, 149

Pearson
5601 Green Valley Drive
Minneapolis, MN 55437
Telephone: 800-627-7271 or 952-681-3232
FAX: 800-632-9011 or 952-681-3299
E-mail: pearsonassessments@pearson.com
Web: www.pearsonassessments.com
Tests: 7, 10, 11, 13, 14, 15, 26, 30, 45, 51, 57, 63, 74, 75, 80, 82, 83, 87, 88, 97, 98, 107, 111, 112, 120, 125, 127, 147, 150, 151, 152, 153, 154, 155, 156

PRO-ED
8700 Shoal Creek Blvd.
Austin, TX 78757-6897
Telephone: 800-897-3202
FAX: 800-397-7633
E-mail: info@proedinc
Web: WWW.PROEDINC.COM
Tests: 42, 46, 54, 55, 66, 96, 99, 136, 138, 139, 143, 144, 148, 197

Professional Resource Press
P.O. Box 15560
Sarasota, FL 34277-1560
Tests: 53, 60, 71, 77

Profiles International, Inc.
Profiles Office Park
5205 Lake Shore Drive
Waco, TX 76710-1732
Test: 100

PSI Services, LLC
2950 N. Hollywood Way, Ste. 200
Burbank, CA 91595
Test: 91

Psycho-Educational Services
5114 Balcones Woods Drive
Suite 307-163
Austin, TX 78759
Web: www.psycho-educational.com
Test: 56

Psychodiagnostics, Inc.
3155 Patrick Lane, Suite One
Las Vegas, NV 89120
Telephone: 866-530-7742
FAX: 888-214-4393
E-mail: psyinfo@psychodiagnostics.com
Web: www.psychodiagnostics.com
Test: 79

Psychological Assessment Resources, Inc.
16204 N. Florida Avenue
Lutz, FL 33549-8119
Telephone: 800-331-8378
FAX: 800-727-9329
E-mail: custsupp@parinc.com
Web: www.parinc.com
Tests: 3, 12, 25, 28, 39, 48, 52, 61, 62, 76, 90, 92, 93, 109, 131, 134, 142, 157, 158

Psychological Services Press
92 Bowman St.
Hamilton, Ontario L8S 2T6
Canada
Telephone: 1-905-527-0129
FAX: 1-905-527-5726
E-mail: PS-support@sympatico.ca
Web: www3.sympatico.ca/itrofimova/PS-STQ.htm
Test: 130

Ramsay Corporation
Boyce Station Offices
1050 Boyce Road
Pittsburgh, PA 15241-3907
Test: 47

Regal Books
c/o Gospel Light
1957 Eastman Ave.
Ventura, CA 93003
Test: 178

Scholastic Testing Service, Inc.
480 Meyer Road
Bensenville, IL 60106-1617
Telephone: 1-800-642-6787
FAX: 630-766-8054
E-mail: stesting@email.com
Web: www.ststesting.com
Test: 64

SPSI-A, LLC
P.O. Box 147
Oshtemo, MI 49077-1078
Test: 124

Stoelting Co.
620 Wheat Lane
Wood Dale, IL 60191-1164
Telephone: 630-860-9700
FAX: 630-860-9775
E-mail: psychtests@stoeltingco.com
Web: www.stoeltingco.com/tests
Test: 8

Targeted Testing Inc.
1109 Trout St. BHR
Okeechobee, FL 34974
Telephone: 863-824-7542
FAX: 863-763-8216
E-mail: info@targettest.com
Web: www.targettest.com
Test: 89

Walden Personnel Performance, Inc.
1445 Lambert-Closse, Suite 301
Montreal, Quebec H3H 1Z5
Canada
Telephone: 514-989-9555
FAX: 514-989-9934
E-mail: ssilver@waldentesting.com
Web: www.waldentesting.com
Test: 161

Western Psychological Services
12031 Wilshire Blvd.
Los Angeles, CA 90025-1251
Telephone: 310-478-2061
FAX: 310-478-7838
Web: www.wpspublish.com
Tests: 16, 29, 38, 108, 110, 113, 119, 121

INDEX OF NAMES

This index indicates whether a citation refers to authorship of a test, a test review, or a reviewer's reference for a specific test. Numbers refer to test entries, not to pages. The abbreviations and numbers following the names may be interpreted as follows: "test, 73" indicates authorship of test 73; "rev, 86" indicates authorship of a review of test 86; "ref, 45" indicates a reference in one of the "Reviewer's References" sections for test 45. Reviewer names mentioned in cross references are also indexed.

SCORE INDEX

This Score Index lists all the scores, in alphabetical order, for all the tests included in The Eighteenth Mental Measurements Yearbook. *Because test scores can be regarded as operational definitions of the variable measured, sometimes the scores provide better leads to what a test actually measures than the test title or other available information. The Score Index is very detailed, and the reader should keep in mind that a given variable (or concept) of interest may be defined in several different ways. Thus the reader should look up these several possible alternative definitions before drawing final conclusions about whether tests measuring a particular variable of interest can be located in this volume. If the kind of score sought is located in a particular test or tests, the reader should then read the test descriptive information carefully to determine whether the test(s) in which the score is found is (are) consistent with reader purpose. Used wisely, the Score Index can be another useful resource in locating the right score in the right test. As usual, all numbers in the index are test numbers, not page numbers.*

MONITORING ASSESSMENT QUALITY IN THE AGE OF ACCOUNTABILITY

A Conference Celebrating
70 Years of the *Mental Measurements Yearbook* Series
and
30 Years of the Buros Center at the University of Nebraska-Lincoln
April 9-10, 2010
The University of Nebraska-Lincoln

Opening Comments

Kurt F. Geisinger
Director, Buros Center for Testing, University of Nebraska-Lincoln

The papers that follow relate to an interesting history of one of the preeminent research and public service institutions that has impacted psychology, psychological practice, and education for over 70 years. These papers were presented at a symposium held in April 2010 on the campus of the University of Nebraska-Lincoln and they celebrate both the birthday of the Buros Institute of Mental Measurements and the anniversary of its marriage with the University of Nebraska-Lincoln. This institution was founded by a single individual, Oscar Buros, in New Jersey, but in the late 1970s it migrated to the University of Nebraska-Lincoln, where it has remained true to its original mission but continues to transform itself to meet this mission.

Like an elderly individual whose age is only rarely and unwillingly divulged, it is not entirely clear how old the Buros unit actually is. On one hand, we do know that it came to the University of Nebraska approximately 30 years ago, this academic year. We also know that the first *Mental Measurements Yearbook* was published in 1938, so by some definitions, it actually will be about 72 years old. I would like to begin these comments with a statement from a book review of *The 12th Mental Measurements Yearbook*, edited by Jane Close Conoley and James Impara, both of whom have written chapters for this set of papers. This review was written for a journal by Dr. Robert M. Thorndike, who also has written a chapter for this section of *The 18th Mental Measurements Yearbook.* In that review, he pointed out that the Buros Institute was founded in 1935. When we set up the celebration of the 70th birthday of the Buros Institute, we believed it to be approximately the 70th birthday of the publication of the first *Mental Measurements Yearbook* by Oscar Buros. Thorndike's representation related to the beginning of Oscar's work, and we do not know definitively when that work actually began. In either case, this institute has a long history, one we believe is worth celebrating with these papers documenting some aspects of its distinguished history.

Oscar Buros obviously could not be here, given that he passed in 1978. Luella Buros, whose paintings continue to grace our offices, and whose connection to the University of Nebraska led to the founding of the Buros Institute here in Lincoln, left this earth in 1995. We thank both of them for their leadership in the pioneering effort that led to the ultimate establishment of what is the Buros Center for Testing today.

Dr. Cecil Reynolds, who was the interim director of the Buros Institute and who helped bring it to the University of Nebraska, begins this section with a description of its movement to the University of Nebraska. Dr. Reynolds is now Professor Emeritus at Texas A&M University and an active consultant.

Dr. James Mitchell, the second director of the Buros Institute of Mental Measurements, was invited to contribute to our celebration, but his health did not permit him to do so. James wrote me recently and told me of how he came to know Oscar through his frequent communications with Luella. He reports that Oscar and Luella were quite a team. I note that although only one of us currently working at the Buros Center knew either Oscar or Luella personally, James Mitchell referred to them in the following manner, "They were a team, and quite a team they were ... You couldn't help admiring their marriage as well as their work." Another of Dr. Mitchell's recollection related to the work of the Institute. He stated that the work was immense and overwhelming, made doable only by the value of the product that emerged. He closed

ISBN 978-0-910674-61-4, *The Eighteenth Mental Measurements Yearbook.*

by commenting that he believed he got the Buros Institute off to a good start at Nebraska, where it continued to be the "Consumer Reports of the Testing Industry."

Under the third director of the Institute, Dr. Barbara Plake, who also has contributed a chapter for this portion of this *Yearbook*, the Institute had a child, named BIACO, the Buros Institute for Assessment Consultation and Outreach. This institute helped to address the needs of tests that were not commercially available. She also was able to delegate some of the editing of the *Yearbooks* to individuals such as Jack Kramer, Jane Close Conoley, and James Impara. Two of these editors are with us today and have contributed to this description of our history, and they have charted some future directions for us.

Barbara was so taken by Jim Impara's work that she decided that she would resort to any action, including marriage, to keep him here at Buros. I note, too, for those of you who do not know Dr. Plake, she retired from the University but by no stretch of the imagination is she retired. As psychology department chair at Fordham, I used to say that Anne Anastasi retired was still my most well-published faculty member. I would not be surprised if Barbara is still surpassing most of the faculty in publications. At the same time, she is an active consultant and co-chair of the test standards development committee.

Another individual who was involved in the early days of the Institute at Nebraska is Dr. Terry Gutkin, who we also thank for making an important contribution to this section. Dr. Chad Buckendahl, another contributor to this collection of articles, began his work as a graduate assistant in Buros and left as a highly valued Director of BIACO, earning a doctorate along the way. We extend thanks to each of these contributors.

We wanted someone who was, in fact, independent of The Buros Center to make some final comments in this section describing our history. We are extremely pleased to have Dr. Robert M. Thorndike do so. Dr. Thorndike wrote reviews for four different *Mental Measurements Yearbooks* and, as I mentioned previously, wrote a book review of another *Yearbook*. In keeping with the Buros requirement to avoid conflicts of interest, I note he did not write a review of a *Yearbook* in which he submitted a review.

I served at two institutions of higher education as the chief academic officer. Both institutions were about 50 years old. At both institutions I helped to set up university archives because if one does not capture the history of an institution, it will be lost forever. That is one of the justifications for this representation of our history, both live at the April 2010 conference and in writing in this section of the *The Eighteenth Mental Measurements Yearbook*. We wanted to learn about the history of the Buros Institute while all these participants are still active and to keep that history for posterity. Another reason relates to the importance of celebration. Although it would have been nice to have the celebration at the same time that the *The Eighteenth Mental Measurements Yearbook* was published, we decided that to have the celebration prior to the publication and then be able to include the papers in the *Yearbook* would be a bonus, especially for our long-time contributors and those who have purchased so many of the *Yearbooks* as references. As I write this introduction, that Buros has existed something like 70-75 years is worth noting. Why? Well, for those of you about my age or so, please recall Hayes Modem, Pan American Airlines, AMC or American Motors, Montgomery Ward, Levitz Furniture, Osborne, Commodore and Kaypro Computers, Crazy Eddie, and Studebaker. For those of you a bit younger, how about Circuit City, Alltel, Wilson Leather, Linens & Things, CompUSA, Talbots Kids, and Sharper Image? Buros has continued to exist because we have adapted, because there is a need for our product, and because we have been frugal.

The very fact that we are having this celebration and producing these historical papers is in keeping with the goals of Oscar Buros to improve the science and practice of testing. The papers that are included in this section of the *Yearbook* are important and presented by first-rate, internationally recognized scholars. These papers and the conference that spawned them served as something of a first for the Buros Center. This event was our first foray into continuing education. Some individuals in the audience actually received continuing education credits for their observation of the presentations. This activity is one in which we believe Buros will become more active.

I have a few people to thank regarding the conference and the resultant papers. One of the advantages of being a director of an institute is that one can have an idea, yet encourage others to make it happen. Robert Spies and Brett Foley were, with me, the initial planners for the conference and for identifying and contacting the presenters/writers. As plans progressed, all of the contributors agreed to make presentations and subsequently to commit them to writing. The only sadness we had was in relation to potential speakers from industrial-organizational psychologists—some of whom have had a major role with Buros (e.g., Paul Sackett, Milt Hakel, and Neal Schmitt), but whose national meeting coincided with the timing of this meeting. As the planning for the conference continued to progress, Janet Carlson and Theresa Glanz took on many of the tasks that needed doing, and the rest of the staff, Linda Murphy, Gary Anderson, Katherine Chin, and Rasma Strautkalns all found new elements in their job descriptions. Linda Murphy, as she does so effectively, agreed to edit the documents as they came in. Several graduate assistants, especially Carina McCormick, also lent a hand from time to time. Let me take a moment to thank them all not only for their wonderful work in setting up this conference and producing the papers, but also in keeping the Buros Center for Testing the successful organization that it continues to be, some 70 years after its founding. We hope that you find these papers illuminating.

The Road to Huskerville: How Did the Buros Institute Get from New Jersey to Nebraska?

Cecil R. Reynolds
Texas A&M University

First, how did it get to be the Buros Institute (and what did the Russians have to do with it)?

The Road to Huskerville: How did it get here? I'm going to tell you my version. It was originally in New Jersey and it was kind of a tight fit. It was housed in the home of Oscar and Luella Buros. It started in the basement and gradually consumed all three floors of their home except for a small living area on the third floor. One of the reasons it came here was that it needed space. Nebraska has the vast expanse of space. But how did it get to be the Buros Institute and what did the Russians have to do with it?

The Buros staff asked me to cover just a little bit of how it got started, before it got here. It started with the Great Depression and a vibrant young aspiring statistician. Had it not been for the Great Depression, there might not be a Buros Institute. Oscar had a Master's degree in Psychology from Teachers College at Columbia, and most of what I know about him is from my conversations with Luella, which I think is better than what has been written about him, and several papers Oscar wrote about the Institute's early days, including some of its struggles. She said his heart was always in measurement and statistics, and his intent was

Tight quarters at the early Buros Institute in Highland Park, New Jersey.

This is a transcript of this conference presentation.

ISBN 978-0-910674-61-4, *The Eighteenth Mental Measurements Yearbook.*

to get a doctoral degree in statistics. Because of the depression, there was very little funding and he couldn't get money to continue his schooling, so he had to quit to support his family. When he couldn't finish his degree in statistics, he got a job as a teacher and subsequently became a principal at an elementary school. He was never able to finish the doctoral degree in statistics.

But he continued to learn and contribute...

He continued to study statistics, and he learned on his own. He published in statistics, and as far as we know, he is the only nondoctoral fellow ever of the American Statistical Association, an honor based on his contributions to statistics and measurement. He even earned a Fulbright senior lectureship in statistics. Oscar seemed never to let any setbacks hold him in abeyance for long; he moved forward.

He was a professor at Rutgers University and a consultant on assessment to many institutions, including West Point. When they decided to identify leadership skills more objectively, they came to Oscar to assist in identifying the right objective means for doing so. His work there was later cited publicly by John Kennedy.

He was concerned with the quality of books and tests...

He was concerned, all this time, with the quality of both books and tests that related to statistics and measurement. His first concerns actually started out with books being written in the field of statistics. He started out critiquing statistics textbooks. He wrote several books, early on, critiquing textbooks, and he published these. They didn't do very well (there was a limited market). But that is where he started.

In the late 1920s, when he became a teacher, we see a huge increase in the number of psychological and educational tests being published (post-WWI), and people were beginning to write books critiquing these tests. The increase in tests and testing was not just in the U.S., but all over the world. The U.S. really took leadership of those efforts, however. Oscar was very dissatisfied with the quality of the reviews of tests that were coming out. He thought they were very subjective; there were no quantitative criteria and there were no consistent guidelines for reviewing or evaluating tests. They did not exist. Eventually Oscar developed guidelines for reviewers to have some kind of consistency. He derived a consistent set of topics reviewers have to address that persists today in the Buros guidelines for reviewers.

Still a young scholar, Buros pondered ways to improve the world of psychological testing...

While he was still a young scholar, Oscar pondered ways to improve the world of psychological testing. That was his goal. It was about that same time that he was inspired (or prodded) by the founding of the organization that would become Consumer Reports.

It should come as no surprise the Buros Yearbooks came to be considered the "Consumer Reports" of the testing industry...

Consumer's Research, Inc. was founded, and Oscar took great notice of that. Hopefully, it is not a big surprise to hear that the Buros *Yearbooks* began to be referred to as the Consumer Reports of the testing industry. Giles Ruch, inspired by the founding of Consumer's Research, Inc. in the late 1920s, wrote in 1933: "There is a great need for a fact-finding organization which will undertake impartial, experimental, and statistical evaluations of tests...in much the same way that Consumer's Research is attempting to furnish reliable information to the average buyer." This was Oscar's original goal for the institute.

So in 1934, he published a comprehensive bibliography of research on all tests available in the English language. That was the start, but it was a very small part of what Oscar wanted to do.

In 1938, the first *Yearbook* was published, but it wasn't a yearbook then. In fact, they were never yearbooks. There was some initial intent to do this once a year, but Luella said that faded pretty fast. When the first *Yearbook* was published, it set off significant tremors in the testing industry. As Luella and Oscar described it, it generated some correspondence from publishers and authors of tests, none of them being particularly happy. There were threats of lawsuits and angry letters from authors of tests. Oscar recounted a letter he got from a test author that explained all of the things Oscar had done wrong and all of the things he was upset about in the review. The author thought about going further with this, but he didn't consider it worthwhile because he stated the review and the *Yearbook* itself would be of no influence having come from Oscar. Turns out he was wrong. The Buros Institute has probably been one of the most influential entities on the quality of psychological and educational tests of any institution or individual, anywhere, ever. Publishers pay attention. One of the things that publishers do is keep files with the Buros reviews and other published reviews on the test on file. The first thing we do when we have a meeting to start a revision of a test is pull those reviews and say "what do we need to do better in the next version of this test?" Every major publishing company starts the revision process by looking at the Buros reviews. I can't imagine what would be more influential than that. It has had tremendous impact.

His original goal to design research and collect data to test the tests and the claims of their authors and publishers being unrealistic, even to Oscar…

Oscar's original goal was to design research and collect data to test the tests and the claims of authors and publishers. This was unrealistic. He wanted to go out and conduct validity and reliability studies, and do the work to see if the tests could do what the authors and publishers said the tests could do. He realized very early that he couldn't do that.

Goals for the Institute

He adopted a separate set of goals that have guided the Institute. His goals for the Institute, as he phrased them: he wanted to provide comprehensive and up-to-date bibliographies of recent tests published in all English-speaking countries. And he was very obsessive and compulsive about generating those reference lists. It was a monumental task to continue to compile these, particularly in the absence of computers. There was a lot of hand and foot work, because there was a lot of running around. They had to go to libraries all over the Northeast. He also wanted to have comprehensive, accurate bibliographies on construction, validation, uses, and limitations of specific tests. But what the *Yearbooks* are best known for is Oscar's clear desire and guidance in producing frankly critical test reviews, written by persons of "outstanding ability." He wanted to represent more than one viewpoint, and he wanted to assist test users in making more intelligent test selection.

And perhaps even to help husbands defend themselves against the growing threat of "Magazine Tests." If any of you get Redbook or House and Garden, you know it's easy to get into trouble.

Financial Struggles

There were financial struggles early on for the Buros Institute. In order to produce the *1938 Yearbook*, Oscar sought a grant from Rutgers University. He asked them for $65,000 to support the preparation of the *1938 Yearbook*, but he got a $350 grant instead and it was from the American Council on Education (ACE). Rutgers gave him nothing. Luella never forgot and never forgave Rutgers University for that slight and their lack of confidence in Oscar. Everyone assumed that when Oscar passed on, the Institute would go to Rutgers. Luella's response to that, as she told it to me, was not "no," but "hell no." Her version of it was that Rutgers was probably the last place it would go because they had fought for Rutgers support all those years and were constantly denied.

For the second *Yearbook*, published in 1940, they actually received a WPA grant and were able to hire some staff and support work on it for about 6 months. But ultimately, the Institute survived by Oscar and Luella Buros making their home the home of the Buros Institute and the Gryphon Press. The Gryphon Press was their imprint. That was a name they chose, appropriately, from "Alice in Wonderland." This was a whole new dimension in the testing world.

October 4, 1957

In 1957, an interesting thing happened. Russia solved the financial problems of the Buros Institute with its surprise successful launch of Sputnik. Oscar reported that the ensuing infusion of federal funds for the identification of talent in schools was a direct result of Sputnik. The Russians were getting ahead. We couldn't have that, right? So money came to the schools to identify talent, and it led to an enormous surge in orders for the 1959 *Mental Measurements Yearbook* because test users were looking to use tests to identify talent in schools, and they needed to know which tests to use. All of a sudden they turned to the Buros Institute. This was the major financial turning point for the Buros Institute, when these federal funds came to the public schools to identify talented youth. And, of course, psychologists began to develop more tests. You'll see another bump if you look at numbers of tests being developed. That saved the Institute's hide in a lot of ways. Oscar and Luella were spending everything they had to keep the Institute going, not because they thought this was going to happen and it was going to be a huge financial success, but because it was what Oscar was devoting his life to doing. The Russians made them profitable.

Yearbooks of Oscar and Luella Buros

The *1938 Mental Measurements Yearbook*, the *1940*, and then the first one to be called by a number, *The Third Mental Measurements Yearbook* in 1949, the *Fourth* in 1953, the *Fifth* in 1959, the *Sixth* in 1965 (you can see they're really not yearbooks), the *Seventh* in 1972 (which had to be expanded to two volumes), and then the *Eighth Mental Measurements Yearbook*, which would be their last, in 1978, was published just after Oscar's death. The *Yearbooks* since then, the *Ninth* through the *Eighteenth* are from the Buros Institute of Mental Measurements from Nebraska.

Oscar Buros in 1977

Oscar lecturing in 1977. I think this was at Iowa, maybe. He was talking about the issues of statistics underlying tests. He was very interested in that, and there was a very interesting controversy that occurred back in the 1950s with Oscar's interest in statistics. Oscar developed a new mathematical model for deriving reliability coefficients. He circulated that among a group of individuals from whom he sought commentary. Shortly after that, a measurement professional named Lee Cronbach published a seminal paper developing a reliability coefficient known as coefficient alpha, whose formula happened to be the same as the formula Oscar had derived and was circulating for feedback from the statistical community.

This led to some correspondence and some disagreement, some of it rather vitriolic. Lee and Oscar had some bitterness over coefficient alpha. It was never settled. Oscar always believed that Lee had gotten a jump start on alpha from looking at his work, without acknowledging it. Having known Lee well, I don't believe that was the case. I think, as often happens in science, the timing was right, the foundation had been laid, and it was two independent scholars, working along the same trail, who arrived at the same conclusions at about the same time. Lee took his immediately to publication, whereas Oscar circulated his work among colleagues to get feedback. That's what I think happened. It was a quite interesting time to read about, and an interesting thing to discuss with Luella. It was another one of those things that was still on her mind, even in the 1980s.

Oscar died in March of 1978 when the indexing, the final task for *The Eighth Mental Measurements Yearbook*, was being started, after 45 years of dedication to the improvement of psychological tests and measurements. That was his true missionary hope; he really wanted tests and measurements in our field to be the best that they could be, and that's what he had promoted throughout his career.

About 2 weeks later, I met Luella Buros for the first time, this time on the telephone. That happened as a result of being in the right place at the right time. I was sitting in my major professor's office (Alan Kaufman) and we were going over some research that I was trying to work on, and the phone rang. He took the call, and it was someone who had called to tell him that Oscar Buros had died. Not having particularly good social skills, my first question was "What do you think will happen to the Buros Institute?" He said he had no idea. He was sure they would have plans for it, but he didn't know what.

I hadn't graduated yet, and it continued to bug me a little bit. I was interviewing at different places, and about to interview at Nebraska. I began to think about that, and it continued to bug me, so about 2 weeks later I tracked down the phone number and called the Buros Institute. I asked whoever answered the phone what the plans were for the Institute. I had no idea who answered the phone there, but it was Luella. She was very nice and she said, "Well, we're just putting *The Eighth Mental Measurements Yearbook* to bed and I haven't had time to think about it; what did you have in mind?" I talked with her, without really knowing who this was just yet, about how incredibly important I thought the Institute was and what they had done, and how I thought it was so important that it needed to continue. Now knowing that I was talking to Luella, I think that had a lot to do with why it ended up at Nebraska. She said that she would think about that, and she hadn't really had time to do that yet, and would I call her back? I called her a few weeks later, after they had finished the indexing, and she said she'd been thinking about it, and what she had decided to do was put out a very informal request for proposals to see who might be interested in taking over the institute, and that's what she did. She put out an RFP.

Luella Buros

Luella was life partner and wife to Oscar. They married December 21st, 1925. She was truly a partner. She was a nationally renowned artist in the 1930s, whose paintings were exhibited in many museums. She won the National Academy of Women Artists' gold medal for her painting in the 1930s. She became a nationally renowned photographer after that. She quit painting in the early 1940s to support the Institute with her full time efforts. They didn't have money for people to design the books and do the layout and those types of things. Luella, being an artist, picked up those skills very quickly and set aside her career, which was a substantial one, as an artist, which surely would have made her a lot more money than the Buros Institute given the quality of her paintings, the awards that she had been winning, and that her paintings were being put in museums and taken on exhibits throughout the country. She gave all that up to design the *Yearbooks*. She was truly Oscar's life partner and devoted to the task.

She did have time, because they liked to travel between *Yearbooks*, to become a photographer. I don't know what happened to her collection of photographs, but she had a monumental collection of black and white photography, and she had some really amazing pictures. She became very well known as a photographer at that time. She was a world traveler, explorer, adventurer, and she and Oscar, because of Luella, collected primitive art. They traveled throughout Africa, and in many places that they went, they would ship a Land Rover ahead of them and simply take off in it once they arrived. Luella told me that there were still places that they went, they were the first "white-skinned people" that some of the villagers had ever met. They began to collect art from these villages, which they later donated to the University of Nebraska. It is quite a collection. I remember seeing it for the first time and being amazed.

They had hundreds of pieces and were considering giving some of it away. Someone suggested that it was such a wonderful collection and went back so far that they should see if the Smithsonian was interested. In the mid-1970s, the Smithsonian Institution gave them an appraisal of that art that was between three and five million dollars. Luella never did do anything with it. She couldn't bring herself to let go of it—she kept it all stuffed in boxes throughout their home in New Jersey and later in a country home in Delaware. It was like her paintings. When she gave up her art career, she attempted to find every painting she had ever sold and buy them back. She wanted her entire collection. She got most of them back, but there are still a few out there in museums that refused to sell them back. I believe that the remainder are housed at the Institute and her family has some. But she did get most of them back.

Winner of NAWA Award

See the Buros Institute website (www.unl.edu/buros/bimm/html/artpage.html) for a photograph of Luella's painting, "Coastal Landscapes," that won the National Academy of Women Artists' gold medal in the 1930s. This one is housed in the library at the Buros Institute.

Her war protest painting from 1939

Luella was very much a pacifist. She also did some paintings in protest of what was going on with war developing in Europe. See the Buros Institute website (www.unl.edu/buros/bimm/html/artpage.html) for a photograph of Luella's painting, "Street Musicians." Luella told me that she painted this as a war protest and that she had seen these men. These were disabled veterans of WWI that she had seen in Times Square. Her style was realism;

and her paintings were, indeed, very real looking. She painted this from memory to protest the war in Europe in the 1930s. This is also hung in the Oscar K. Buros Library of Mental Measurements at the Buros Institute, and it is very profound and moving to see in person as she captured the emotions of these men so well.

Luella Buros...

Luella designed the Buros Yearbooks, and they actually won awards from the printing industry. They awarded them and designated them books of distinction because of their outstanding design. She was gracious, independent, witty, talented, and generous. I can't say enough good things about her. She's one of my most favorite people that I've ever met in my entire life. She is the benefactor of the Buros Institute of Mental Measurements in many ways. My sense is that she didn't just gift the Institute with all of the worldly things that it has, the money, the books, the library, but she also was a wonderful carrier of Oscar's philosophy. Knowing Luella and hearing her talk about it, you couldn't help but adopt it. She understood it, devoted her life to it, and made so many sacrifices for it; if you understood the importance of it, then you had to adopt it when you heard her talk about it.

The Road to Huskerville...the Last Legs

I had talked to Luella a couple of times before she decided to send out the RFP. In the meantime, I got a job at Nebraska. My first faculty position, fresh out of school, and I was just young and dumb enough to think we could pull off something like this, and brash enough not to be deterred. I really didn't have good enough social skills to hear "no" very well, so I began to talk to people here (at UNL) about this and the fact that Luella was going to put together this RFP.

My next call to Luella Buros...

So during my next call to Luella, she talked about putting together and putting out this RFP and what she would be interested in through doing that. I talked with her in some detail about it and she put out the call.

And then what happened...

Next, I came to Lincoln, and I pitched it to Terry Gutkin. Here I am, brand new faculty, walking in during July of 1978, having had these conversations; nobody knows me, and I talked to Terry about this. Terry knew about the Institute and its importance, but he needed me to teach. He liked the idea; he was a little reticent, but said that we needed to talk to some people. He pitched it to Ken Orton (Educational Psychology Department Chair at that time) and his response was that it might be interesting but he didn't think so. We got him to pitch it to Bob Egbert, the Dean of the Teacher's College at UNL at that time. Bob Egbert took notice. He thought it really was interesting but he didn't know whether they had the budget, but said they really should talk to Ned Hedges.

Bob pitched it to Ned who was in charge of Academic Affairs. Ned kind of liked the idea, but he didn't know anything about it because he's an English professor. Ned started making phone calls to colleagues around the country who knew something about this area. Ned called me and said, "You know, I've been talking to other administrators around the country and there's something to this; this is a big deal. We ought to take a serious look at it." He pitched it to Bob Lovitt because Bob was in a similar position, but for research at the University. Bob Lovitt was the tie to the Nebraska Foundation, and that's where they thought they could get funding. They agreed to give up to a half a million dollars to acquire the Institute and move it here. That was a lot of money to come up with, especially for a rookie faculty member in 1978.

So I wrote the proposal. I had help with that, particularly from Ned. Ned funded me for a quarter time release and a quarter time graduate assistant to help me put that proposal together and write it. I did and it had to go through all the university things that these things have to go through, and somebody finally signed off somewhere and said I could send it to her.

And then there were three...

Luella chose three proposals to look at in detail, and one of them was ours. The other two that she chose were from Teacher's College at Columbia and AERA (American Educational Research Association). She invited each of us for a site visit.

Luella scheduled a site visit with each of us. Ned Hedges, Bob Lovitt, and I went for UNL...

When we rang the doorbell and Luella answered the door, we knew that the Institute belonged to the University of Nebraska. Luella opened the door, ignored Ned and Bob, took me by the arm and led me in. The first thing she said to me was "you remind me of a young, energetic Oscar, when we got married." We came on in, and then she realized there were other people with me, and she turned and talked to them a little bit, and then pretty much ignored them the rest of the time. She kept holding my arm and took me through the whole Institute. I have no idea why, but we immediately connected. We could talk about it, and I knew a lot about the Institute and its work and what it had done, and she, of course, liked that. But we knew. It was really clear.

It was very interesting, when we got back, because shortly after that, she called and said "it's yours." We went back out there to talk over the details, and I'm not sure if she was insulted or not, but I always thought that she looked a little bit like she was because we hadn't talked about money. I only had a half a million dollars in my pocket so when we went back, one of the things I asked her was how much money she wanted for the Institute. That was when I got that little bit of a hurt look from her. She said, "I don't want any money; I'm giving it to the University." She gave us everything, including some cash to operate for the first year. She gave us the whole thing because she wanted to honor the work of the Institute, and she wanted to honor Oscar and his lifetime of work. She mentioned that if we did a good job, there might be other gifts down the road.

A year later, we went down to see her and introduce her to Jim Mitchell, and it was quite interesting. As we were leaving, Luella said, "Do you need any money to help with the Institute?" We said, "We're doing okay; I think we're going to be all right. We've got some funding for this and the University is paying the salaries." She said, "Well, just in case," and she wrote us a check for another $25,000 just to make sure we had a little extra money for the Institute that year.

A little bit more about who she was; she was feisty at times. When she was in her 80s, she still liked to travel, and she went to South America with a senior citizen's group. She was hiking in the mountains while they were touring. I talked to her when she got back, and she said, "It was hike 1,000 feet, sit and rest; hike 1,000 feet, sit and rest. I am never going on another tour with a bunch of old people in my life." She later drove a 30-foot RV from New Jersey to Arizona alone. It was who she was and what she did.

So, that's how it got here…

I'm going to leave it to others to recount the modern history. My fervent hope still remains that Oscar's original goals will persist as the prime directive for the work of the Institute, and when possible, that the Institute will also find ways to give back to the people who promote the enhancement of standards and products in psychological testing and measurements. Find ways to give back to those people who are promoting the goals of the Institute who may not work there. Find ways to recognize and promote those people as well; those people who are true to Oscar's goals. I know that Oscar and Luella would have wanted it that way.

And I also know, they would have loved the library!

Oscar had a great love of libraries. He had always wanted to have the library that he had to be accessible, but he could never make it that way. They were just too cramped. I know that he would have loved the new Buros Library and so would Luella. (For photographs of the Buros Library see www.unl.edu/buros/bimm/html/library.html)

Assessing the Validity of Test Scores

James C. Impara
Consultant
&
Professor Emeritus, University of Nebraska-Lincoln

The concept of the validity of test scores is neither new nor well understood by many of those who review tests for *The Mental Measurements Yearbook* (*MMY*) series. It is, however, well understood by those in advertising. Many of you will remember the TV commercial that had a little old lady who gave the tagline: "Where's the beef?" If you are old enough to remember that commercial (actually, from a test reviewer's perspective, "Where's the validity evidence?"), you may still think validity has three principal elements: content, criterion related (predictive and concurrent), and construct. Well, get with it, folks: Things, especially the way the validity of test scores is characterized, have changed.

The unitary perspective of validity has been widely accepted in the measurement profession and has been incorporated in the *Standards for Educational and Psychological Testing* (American Educational Research Association-AERA, American Psychological Association-APA, & National Council on Measurement in Education-NCME, 1985 and 1999; hereafter *Standards*). Moreover, this unitary conceptualization of validity has been supported by the *Standards* since the 1985 edition. By unitary concept, it is meant that the evidence for validity supports the intended interpretation of the test score and is focused on the construct associated with that interpretation[1]. Note that the assignment of the validity concept is to test scores and how they are interpreted. Validity is considered to be a property of the score interpretation, not a property of the test.

If you don't believe me that many, actually most, *MMY* reviewers still think of validity as being an attribute of tests and as having three distinct elements named above, observe the following commentary and quote from Cizek, Koons, and Rosenburg (2007) in their paper examining the way validity was represented in 283 test reviews in *The Sixteenth Mental Measurements Yearbook* (16th MMY; Spies & Plake, 2005). Cizek et al. (2007) indicated that about 24% of the reviewers in the *16th MMY* correctly ascribed validity to test scores. Of the remaining reviews, about 30% ascribed validity to the test and the remaining reviews were unclear as to whether validity was a property of the test or of the interpretation of the scores. Moreover,

> Regarding unitary view of validity, it appears to be far more widely articulated in theory than embraced in practical test validation. Only 7 of the 283 reviews (2.5%) used language that connoted a unitary view of validity; by far the most common perspective taken was that of differing "kinds" of validity. Given this finding, it is not surprising that only 27 of the reviews (9.5%) cited either the definitive chapter on validity by Messick (1989) or the current *Standards for Educational and Psychological Testing* (AERA/APA/NCME, 1999) both of which unambiguously explicate and endorse the unitary conceptualization. (Cizek et al., 2007, p. 12)

It seems clear that some *MMY* reviewers are not paying attention. Validity has been considered an attribute to score interpretation and as a unitary concept for at least 25 years.

---

[1]An important exception to the unitary position on validity is presented by the Uniform Guidelines on Employee Selection Procedures (1978), which most measurement professionals believe to be very outdated.

ISBN 978-0-910674-61-4, *The Eighteenth Mental Measurements Yearbook.*

A major change in the 1999 *Standards* is associated with Messick's (1989) *Educational Measurement* (3rd Edition) chapter in which he extends the unitary conceptualization of the validity of test scores to include the notion of consequential validity, which was, and continues to be, somewhat controversial. Kane's (2006) more recent representation of validity in the fourth edition of *Educational Measurement* continues the notion of test score validity as a unitary notion and also promotes the notion of consequential validity.

Although there are several theorists who have taken positions on what validity is and how evidence of validity might be characterized (e.g., Messick, 1989; Kane, 2006), the relevant benchmark for *MMY* reviewers in terms of what validity is and how it should be characterized in test reviews is found in the *Standards* (1999). Because the charge to the Joint Committee that is currently revising the *Standards* (1999) did not specify the need for substantive changes in the notions associated with validity, I have assumed that Chapter One (Validity) will not change substantially.

Overview of the 1999 Standards Related to Validity

Chapter One of the *Standards* (1999) comprises the principal discussion of validity. It is appropriate that this first chapter focuses on validity because validity evidence is the sine qua non required for the use of any test. The chapter begins with a definition of validity: "the degree to which evidence and theory support the interpretations of test scores" (*Standards*, 1999, p. 9).

Chapter One of the *Standards* does not provide a history of the development of the validity concept, but it does discuss a variety of perspectives associated with the nature of validity evidence, suggesting that different kinds of tests with varying score interpretations may require different types of evidence to support the intended score interpretations. In terms of the nature of the evidence that is appropriate to support validity, some statistical methods have influenced the nature of the evidence, as have advances in, and greater acceptance of, qualitative evidence associated with the different forms that validity evidence may take.

Different validity propositions may be associated with the different uses of test scores and these differing propositions also suggest differing kinds of evidence. Because appropriateness of the interpretation may change over time, the need for providing validity evidence over the life of the test is also important. That need suggests that prior to any initial use of the test the user should have validity evidence to evaluate the appropriateness of the intended score interpretations. Moreover, as the test continues to be used, additional validity evidence to support the intended interpretation of the scores is also important. This is much like the pharmaceutical model for medicines, although somewhat less rigorous, and also the model used by auto manufacturers to decide if a recall is needed. Unlike drugs and cars, however, there is no government oversight of the testing industry and that's where the *MMY* comes into play.

Once the general discussion of validity is completed (this is really a "must read" section of Chapter One, and this paper does not do it justice), there is another narrative section that describes sources of validity evidence. This section describes in some detail the following evidentiary sources, which are expanded later in this paper:

1. Evidence based on test content
2. Evidence based on response processes
3. Evidence based on internal structure
4. Evidence based on relations to other variables
   a. Convergent and discriminant evidence
   b. Test-criterion relationships
   c. Validity generalization
5. Evidence based on the consequences of testing

The final narrative section of the chapter is a brief discussion about the need to integrate the various sources of validity evidence. This section specifies, "the validity of an intended interpretation of test scores relies on all the available evidence" (*Standards,* 1999, p. 17). This section reminds the test user (and reviewer) that the presentation of validity evidence incorporates all the elements of the testing process, beginning with test construction and including equating, standard setting, and the fairness of the testing process and score interpretation for all examinees.

The narrative discussion is followed by the actual standards. There are 24 specific standards associated with validity in Chapter One[2]. These 24 standards expand and elaborate on the narra-

[2]It may be argued that some standards in later chapters may also have implications for validity, but such standards are not considered in this paper.

tive in important ways, by providing a statement of the standard and comments to aid the user in understanding what is meant by the standard, and how the standard might be interpreted. For example:

> STANDARD 1.2
> The test developer should set forth clearly how test scores are intended to be interpreted and used. The population(s) for which a test is appropriate should be clearly delimited, and the construct that the test is intended to assess should be clearly described.
> *Comment:* Statements about validity should refer to particular interpretations and uses. It is incorrect to use the unqualified phrase "the validity of the test." No test is valid for all purposes or in all situations. Each recommended use or interpretation requires validation and should specify in clear language the population for which the test is intended, the construct it is intended to measure, and the manner and contexts in which test scores are to be employed. (*Standards,* 1999, pp. 17-18)

Selection of this particular standard was not arbitrary. Based on the observations of Cizek et al. (2007), reviewers need to be reminded of this notion and with the notion that validity is a unitary concept.

The remainder of this presentation focuses on the different types of validity evidence. There are examples of what the evidence might look like and for what sorts of tests the evidence may be appropriate. There are far too many types of evidence within each of the various categories to be comprehensive, but an attempt is made to illustrate how evidence may be presented for each type of evidence. Also, although there are suggestions about the types of tests for which the type of evidence may be most appropriate, it can easily be argued that each type of evidence can be applied to virtually all tests, so the types of tests may be considered somewhat arbitrary.

Evidence Based on Test Content

Appropriate types of tests for which evidence of test content may provide evidence of validity include achievement tests, tests used in credentialing (licensure and certification), and employment tests. There may also be circumstances when such evidence may be appropriate for evaluating aptitude tests and psychological tests.

Descriptions of how evidence of test content may be presented include:

- Curriculum analysis (including examining curricular outlines, course syllabi, textbooks, teachers' lesson plans, teachers' assignments, teachers' tests).
- State or local content standards.
- Job/task analysis.
- Detailed domain definitions, descriptions, and delineations.
- Development of a table of specifications that is based on the curriculum analysis, content standards, and/or job/task analysis.
- Review of job-, or content-related materials.
- Description of how the test development process relied on the curriculum analysis, content standards, and/or job/task analysis.
- Results of focus groups or other interactions with stakeholders who have examined test content for relevance and appropriateness.
- Results of expert review of the relationship between the test items and the curriculum analysis, content standards, and/or job/task analysis (this might be called an alignment study or evidence of the adequacy of domain sampling).
- Detailed description of the psychological construct and theoretical framework, including a review of relevant research and literature.
- A detailed discussion of the relationship between the theoretical framework and the content.
- A description of expert panels that are used to conduct alignment studies; including the qualifications of the panelists, the number of panelists, and the procedures used to conduct the study.
- If item production algorithms are used, the evidence might include a description of the nature of the algorithms and how they assure content coverage. Similarly, if item "cloning" strategies are used, how these strategies relate to the curriculum analysis, content standards, and/or job/task analysis.
- The time frame within which the curriculum analysis, content standards, and/or job/task analysis was completed and the item/test development completed, and the test introduced.
- If the test is computer adapted, there may be a description of how the item presentation algorithm assures the comprehensiveness of

content coverage. That is, how does the adaptive test meet the table of specifications?

- There may be a description of the population and sample on which the test was field-tested and the experience/exposure of that population and sample to the content being measured described.
- There may be a discussion or cautions about elements of the test content that may be associated with construct irrelevant variance (e.g., a mathematics computation test that has a high reading load, or using a norming population that is principally English speaking, then administering the test to examinees whose first language is not English).

Clearly not all of these pieces of evidence will be presented for every test. Depending on the test and its purpose, however, some of these elements may be offered in support of validity of the interpretation of test scores for any test for which such evidence is appropriate.

Evidence Based on Response Processes

Appropriate types of tests for which evidence of response processes may be applied might include tests that assess cognitive processes, attitude and other scales that may have some responses that are more "socially correct" than others, measures that require observations (e.g., teacher evaluations), physical assessments, or measures that require raters to rate behaviors or score the responses of others.

Descriptions of how evidence of response processes may be presented include:

- Reports of interviews with examinees about what they were thinking/doing when responding to various prompts (i.e., think-aloud protocols).
- Reflection and analysis of the examinees' responses as they relate to the theoretical construct that is intended to be assessed.
- Analysis of progressive development of responses (e.g., in a writing exercise, looking at progressive drafts up to the final essay to see if the growth that is intended is occurring).
- For physical or developmental assessments, recordings and analyses of examinee reactions (e.g., eye movements, response times, and behavioral strategies such as tying shoelaces or purchasing items).
- For behavioral assessments, relationships between items and such techniques as functional Magnetic Resonance Imaging (fMRI) taken while performing the items.
- For computerized tests, an examination of examinee response times may reveal insights about understanding item content.
- DIF-types of studies to examine possible cultural differences across populations that may impede or enhance understanding performance requirements associated with the test. That is, do different cultures perceive the construct in the same way?
- Interview or other data that reflect on how observers/judges/scorers may differentially react to examinee behaviors/responses. That is, are all observers/judges/scorers responding to the same stimulus in the same way and not being "influenced by factors that are irrelevant to the intended interpretation." (*Standards*, p. 13).

Evidence Based on Internal Structure

This type of evidence is applicable to virtually all tests. There are many ways to look at internal structure including interrelationships among test items, test parts, how different populations relate to test items or parts, and the structure of the test in terms of its dimensionality relative to the theoretical perspective underlying the test scores and their interpretations.

Descriptions of how evidence of internal structure may be presented include:

- Exploratory and confirmatory factor analyses (i.e., does the factor structure match the theoretical modeling of dimensions?).
- Cluster analysis or other forms of profile matching to predict membership in nominal or other disjoint groups.
- Subtest intercorrelations.
- Internal consistency reliability or the interrelationships among items is appropriate for tests that are intended to be homogeneous or unidimensional.
- Item to total score correlations (item discrimination).
- Distractor analyses.
- A description of the item format and whether the format may result in a restriction of range of total scores.
- An analysis reflecting that items are sensitive to instruction.
- DIF studies and other data related to item discrimination. Note that items that show

DIF may be consistent with theoretical expectations, so not all DIF is necessarily "bad."

- Data related to "item fit."
- An analysis of the test assembly algorithm for computerized tests (e.g., Linear on the Fly Testing, LOFT).
- An analysis of the item selection algorithm for computer adaptive tests (to ensure that the table of specifications is covered in the adaptive test).

Evidence Based on Relations to Other Variables

This type of evidence is applicable to virtually all tests. Historically, this element of validity evidence probably is the most well defined and most highly emphasized. It is the broadest of the evidence categories and it includes such familiar terms as convergent and discriminant evidence, test-criterion evidence (perhaps better known as predictive and concurrent evidence), and validity generalization. The latter term and procedure is most often used in education and employment settings.

Descriptions of how evidence of relations to other variables may be presented include:

- A rationale for deciding which variables or investigative strategies were used to collect the validity evidence.
- A description of the nature and psychometric characteristics of the other variables used to provide validity evidence.
- Convergent evidence.
    - Correlations or other measures of association with variables that purportedly measure the same construct using either the same or a different method of measuring the construct (such data would be found in a multi-trait, multi-method matrix–MTMM matrix).
    - Correlations, or other measures of association, with variables that purportedly measure similar, but not the same, constructs.
    - Investigations that examine whether individuals whose scores indicate the presence of the construct belong to groups that have been identified using other means as having the construct (also called the known groups method).
    - Investigations that look at gradations among examinees who have the construct in varying degrees.
- Discriminant evidence.
    - Correlations or other measures of association with variables that purportedly measure different constructs (may be found in a MTMM matrix).
    - Correlations or other measures of association with variables that purportedly measure related but dissimilar constructs (may be found in a MTMM matrix).
    - Investigations that examine whether individuals whose scores indicate the absence of the construct belong to groups that have been identified using other means as not having the construct (also called the known groups method).
- Test-criterion relationships.
    - The time frame within which the test and criterion data are gathered. If in close conjunction, then the evidence will be more concurrent, whereas if the time span is somewhat longer, then the evidence will be more predictive.
    - Correlations, or other measures of association, with one or more criterion variables.
    - Descriptions, statistical and other, of the criterion variable, including the way the criterion was measured and the psychometric characteristics of the criterion variable(s).
    - A rationale describing the basis for selecting the criterion variable(s).
    - A description of the sample(s) used to conduct the validity studies, including a description of the sampling population, the sample sizes, the time frame within which the test was administered and the criterion measures taken.
    - Prediction estimates (e.g., R square values for different subpopulations).
    - Evidence that the scores provide incremental evidence (i.e., the measure provides a statistically significant increase in the R square over and above other measures used to predict the same criterion).
    - Evidence of cross-validation studies.
    - Discriminant, logistic, or other regression analyses or tables that show how well the test assigns examinees into multiple groups or treatments.
    - Data related to selection ratios associated with placement or other decisions (e.g., admit or not, hire or not).

  - Correlations corrected for attenuation or range restrictions.
  - If there is a cut score involved in the decision process, then a description of how the cut score was set may be provided. Such a description may include the methods for setting the cut score, a description of the cut score panel (if a panel was used), including the number of panelists, the qualifications of the panelists, and other relevant data. If there was no panel and the cut score was set empirically, then evidence of the statistical design and other relevant details may also be provided.
  - An estimate of the measurement and/or prediction error and its impact (e.g., estimates of false positives and false negatives).
- Validity generalization
  - Meta-analysis of criterion-related validity studies across a variety of settings or times using the same or similar criterion variables.
  - Data related to corrections for statistical artifacts such as sampling fluctuations, variations in test scores across studies, variations in the reliability estimates of criterion variables.
  - Comparisons between local validation studies and meta-analytic studies.
  - Meta-analyses of generalizability studies using the following facets: "(a) differences in the way the predictor construct is measured, (b) the type of job or curriculum involved, (c) the type of criterion measures used, (d) the type of test takers, and (e) the time period in which the study was conducted." (*Standards,* 1999, p. 15)
  - Meta-analyses of variables other than criterion variables. Such variables might include studies associated with different testing conditions (e.g., accommodations for disabled examinees), populations (e.g., students who have been coached or not).

Evidence Based on Consequences of Testing

This type of evidence is also applicable to virtually all tests. It is the most recent consideration to be added to the *Standards* (1999) and perhaps the most controversial. This type of evidence focuses on both intended and unintended consequences of testing. The *Standards* caution test users to differentiate between "issues of validity and issues of social policy" (*Standards*, 1999, p. 16.) The *Standards* (1999) offer a number of clarifying examples to help the reader distinguish between social policy and the validity issues. A principal distinction focuses on construct relevant variance (e.g., employment tests that incorporate necessary job skills, which results in individuals belonging to different groups being hired at different rates because of their test scores) and construct-irrelevant variance (e.g., employment tests that assess skills that are only peripherally related to job skills, which results in individuals belonging to different groups being hired at different rates because of their test scores) or construct underrepresentation (e.g., a test intended to assess math computation skills that focuses principally on addition and subtraction and ignores other operations).

The test manuals and other sources of evidence that are likely to be provided by publishers will probably focus on positive aspects of the consequences of testing. It will be up to the reviewer to examine the evidence provided and consider what evidence of consequences may be absent and then to raise questions about potential negative consequences.

Much of the evidence listed above for other categories may also represent evidence of the consequences of testing. Descriptions of how evidence of consequences of testing may be presented include:

- Evidence that the use of the test scores for making decisions about examinees results in more accurate decisions than would be made without using the test.
- Evidence that the content of the test is consistent with the table of specifications.
- Evidence that shows the test is at an appropriate level of difficulty for the examinee population to which it is administered.
- Studies showing that examinees have been exposed to the content of the test (for achievement tests).
- Studies showing the job-relatedness of the test (for employment and credentialing tests).
- Studies of bias and DIF and explanations for tests that either discriminate across different examinee groups or show different results associated with group membership, with an explanation of how the DIF should be interpreted. That is, is the DIF consistent with theoretical expectations?

- Studies showing that placements (or other decisions) resulting from the use of the test scores are consistent with the intended use of the scores and that such placements do not produce harmful labels for placed examinees.
- Studies that show that alternative uses of the test scores, other than those for which the test was initially intended, do not result in harmful impacts on examinees.
- Displays of score reports that explicitly discourage inappropriate use or interpretation of scores.
- Results of legal actions where the "company" lost the suit, provided by publishers to discourage inappropriate use of the test.
- Discouragement by the publisher of making an important decision about an examinee based on the results of a single measure.
- Evidence that the treatment intervention predicted by the score was effective (i.e., the treatment produced the intended change in the examinee).
- Discussion by the publisher/author actively discouraging uses of the test scores that are not supported by research.

Clearly there are many more types of data or discussions wherein evidence of the consequences of testing may be found. More difficult to find are examples of negative consequences. Reviewers should be alert to omissions from the data that may suggest potential negative consequences that may be associated with the use of a test.

Integration of Evidence and the Need for Ongoing Studies

The *Standards* (1999) encourage providing a variety of evidence to support validity arguments. Moreover, publishers and test users are encouraged to promote ongoing studies to support the validity arguments associated with a test. Often tests may be used for purposes other than their intended purpose (e.g., an omnibus achievement test intended to show achievement status and growth may be used for grade-to-grade promotion) and studies are needed to validate such uses.

The evidence of the validity of test scores begins with the description of the need for the test and is followed by descriptions of the test development process; the psychometric characteristics of the tests (e.g., item statistics, reliability); appropriate administration and scoring procedures; actionable test security procedures, methods used for scaling, equating, and setting cut scores; and procedures put in place to assure fairness for all examinees (*Standards,* 1999, p. 17).

References

American Educational Research Association, American Psychological Association, & National Council on Measurement in Education. (1999). *Standards for educational and psychological testing.* Washington, DC: American Educational Research Association.

Cizek, G. J., Koons, H. K., & Rosenberg, S. L. (2007, May). *Chronicling and questioning validity: Mental Measurements Yearbook as a context for investigating sources of evidence for high-stakes tests.* Paper presented at the Buros Institute Invitational Conference honoring Barbara S. Plake, Lincoln, NE.

Equal Employment Opportunity Commission, Civil Service Commission, Department of Labor, & Department of Justice. (1978). Adoption by four agencies of Uniform Guidelines on Employee Selection Procedures. *Federal Register, 43,* 38290-38315.

Kane, M. (2006). Validation. In R. L. Brennan (Ed.), *Educational measurement* (4th ed., pp. 17-64). Westport, CO: American Council on Education and Preager.

Messick, S. (1989). Validity. In R. L. Linn (Ed.), *Educational Measurement* (3rd ed., pp. 13-103). New York: American Council on Education and Macmillan.

Spies, R. A., & Plake, B. S. (Eds.). (2005). *The sixteenth mental measurements yearbook.* Lincoln, NE: Buros Institute of Mental Measurements.

Back to the Future: Some Reflections on the Buros Institute of Mental Measurements

Jane Close Conoley
&
Rafael J. C. Hernandez
University of California, Santa Barbara

Marking the Buros Institute of Mental Measurements' 40 years at the University of Nebraska-Lincoln caused us to reflect and inquire about the roots of modern psychological measurement and imagine its future. What follows is a brief report of the results of these reflections about the trajectory of measurement between 19th and early 20th Century experimental psychology and 21st Century advancements in biological measurement related to psychological and educational variables. The question of how the Buros Institute might adapt to a changed scientific landscape associated with the assessment of human functioning is posed.

The prestigious accomplishments of the Buros Institute have been built primarily on reviews of paper-and-pencil tests for the past 72 years. Although innovations such as computer-assisted and adaptive delivery systems have been incorporated into the Buros review process easily, the 21st Century may offer some additional challenges to reaching the goal of comprehensive reviews of commercially available tests. These challenges may come from a number of sources, but for this brief look at possible futures, the potential of measurement based on biological markers associated with important psychological and cognitive functions is suggested.

Ironically, the earliest history of psychological measurement was dominated by physiological approaches (Wundt, 1910). Psychologists have always been interested in measuring human and animal characteristics with the goal of understanding and perhaps controlling cognitive, social, and emotional behaviors. Some of the earliest psychological measurements were called psychophysiological measures. They relied on close observation of biological responses to stimuli. The measures included galvanic skin response, heart rate, blood pressure, length of gaze, retinal dilation, eye movements, reaction times, and many others. Early, pioneering researchers studied the structure of the mind, memory, learning, attention, abnormal behavior, and a variety of values and attitudes (e.g., religious beliefs) using these approaches.

At the dawn of the 20th Century, however, psychophysiological measures remained in the laboratories of experimental psychologists and "paper and pencil" assessments became the norm to describe intelligence, creativity, vocational interests and aptitudes, and personality and behavioral traits or states. The only regularly used approach from early psychophysiological research apparent then and now in many tests is reaction time (RT) either directly measured as response latency (a relatively rare approach) or more commonly in timed tests. Jensen and Munro (1979) argued persuasively for the use of RT and movement time as markers of speed of information processing and showed their high correlation with more standard tests of intelligence, but their influence was minimal on many commercially available tests (except neuropsychological batteries).

Studies of genetic contributions to intelligence, psychopathology, resilience, temperament, and so on characterized early psychology inquiry

ISBN 978-0-910674-61-4, *The Eighteenth Mental Measurements Yearbook.*

and remain common today as a research area (e.g., Rutter, Moffitt, & Caspi, 2005). Twenty-first Century genetic research greatly surpasses early understandings of missing, double, or damaged genetic material by investigating the interplay of genetic expression with environmental contexts. In fact, although the highly publicized focus of genetic research has been on the mapping of the human genome, modern research illustrates the importance of the complex interaction between genes and multiple environments predicting genetic expression in ways that reflect Gutkin's (this volume) call for measurement approaches that capture information about entire ecosystems rather than molecular understandings of individuals.

These advances in genomics and biological measurement along with the exploding knowledge base associated with cognitive neuroscience caused us to wonder if our current understanding of humans as integrated beings–not mind and body, but highly adapted and intelligent bodies–would revolutionize psychological measurement and, thus, the focus of the Buros Institute. That is, will the testing paradigm move from reporting frameworks to direct assessment approaches of genetic and biological markers of psychological constructs? For example, could intelligence be measured not by quantifying people's verbal or written responses to various stimuli, but by a direct measurement of some brain structure, chemical level, or neural activity pattern?

Recent news about the relationship between thalamic dopamine D2 receptor densities, creativity, and schizophrenia might be a harbinger of such an approach (de Manzano, Cervenka, Karabanov, Farde, & Ullen, 2010). These researchers found that both highly creative people and individuals with schizophrenia show low densities of these receptors in the thalamus. Increasing sophistication and accessibility of techniques to measure physiological structures and states make discoveries such as these increasingly likely. For example, the findings about receptor densities used Positron Emission Tomography (PET) as the measurement technique. Other now frequently used approaches to study brain activity or map parts of the brain include functional magnetic resonance imaging (fMRI), electroencephalograms (EEG), tonal activity, magnetoencephalography (MEG), and cortical oscillations (e.g., Ardila, 2007; Desikan et al., 2009; DeYoung, Hirsh, Shane, & Papademetris, 2010; Kujala et al., 2000).

In addition to these neural mapping approaches, levels of various body chemicals have been used to assess psychological constructs. These include glycogen, oxytocin, acetylcholine, androgens, estradiol and follicle-stimulating hormone, cortison, and serotonin (e.g., Rajewska & Rybakowski, 2003).

Research using the above mentioned techniques and substances have illustrated biological associations with cognitive, social, and behavioral variables that most would intuit as having strong biological bases such as emotional expressions of love, anger, fear, anxiety and depression, expressions of masculinity and femininity, emotional regulation (e.g., sensation seeking), and levels of cognitive impairment.

Perhaps more surprising, however, are findings that link various biological markers to memory, math performance and math/spatial/visual skills, perspective taking, object recognition, decision making, social cognition, implicit attitudes, number sense, coping with pain, selective attention, childhood play behavior, reading, resilience, insight, perspective-taking, claustrophobia, and agoraphobia. Given that our current science assumes that every psychological trait or state has a physiological base, this merely suggestive list will likely grow exponentially over the next decade.

How might the Buros Institute adapt to a scientific landscape that may eventually evaluate traditional test scores based on verbal or written responses to be gross measures of variables when compared to highly precise physiological measures of the same variables? How will traditional psychometric constructs such as validity, reliability, norms, and item behavior translate to such approaches? The Institute has focused its work only on commercially available, English-language tests. Will such focus seem quaint and provincial in just a few years?

A transitional step between paper-and-pencil tests and direct physiological measurements may be the development of experimental cognitive tasks. This work may provide a clue to the future role of the Buros Institute. A compelling example of the experimental cognitive task approach is the *Measurement and Treatment Research to Improve Cognition in Schizophrenia Program* (MATRICS, http://www.matrics.ucla.edu/matrics-overview/). This large-scale National Institutes of Health effort developed a battery of very precise cognitive tasks/tests meant to tap the cognitive deficits associated with the disease (e.g., speed of processing, attention, vigilance, verbal and nonverbal working memory, verbal learning, reasoning and problem solving, visual learning, and social cognition). These targeted assessments facilitated the development and monitoring of drugs to relieve these cognitive deficits (Carter, 2005). The work required a strong collaboration between cognitive neuroscientists and psychometricians because of daunting issues related to test-retest reliability and the predictive validity of the scores to the functional status of the participants with schizophrenia.

Although these experimental cognitive tasks are not direct biological measurements, their sensitivity to individual differences is similar to the challenges inherent in psychophysiological assessments. That is, the responses to these tasks, like biological markers, are extremely sensitive to slight changes in context (time of measurement, co-morbid conditions, age, sex, and so on) (e.g., Heath, Bishop, Hogben, & Roach, 2006). It seems that even the most advanced measures of cognitive functioning require psychometric critique to ensure valid and reliable uses of the scores.

Thus, should the Buros Institute evolve to include critiques of biological markers of psychological and educational constructs, reviews investigating the validity of the measure may always be needed. Although the future will certainly deliver unexpected challenges to the professionals at the Buros Institute, the need for careful review of assessment approaches will remain and may require unprecedented cooperation between medical/neuroscience experts with psychometric experts to explore how microscopic amounts of biological material can be used to illuminate human capacities and characteristics.

References

Ardila, A. (2007). What can be localized in the brain: Toward a "factor" theory on brain organization of cognition. *International Journal of Neuroscience, 117*, 935-969.

Carter, C. S. (2005). Applying new approaches from cognitive neuroscience to enhance drug development for the treatment of impaired cognition in schizophrenia. *Schizophrenia Bulletin, 31(4),* 810-815.

de Manzano, Ö., Cervenka, S., Karabanov, A., Farde, L., & Ullén, F. (2010). Thinking outside a less intact box: Thalamic Dopamine D2 receptor densities are negatively related to psychometric creativity in healthy individuals. *PLoS ONE 5(5):* e10670. doi:10.1371/journal.pone.0010670.

Desikan, R. S., Cabral, H. J., Hess, C. P., Dillon, W. P., Glastonbury, C. M., Weiner, M. W., Schmansky, N. J., Greve, D. N., Salat, D. H., Buckner, R. L., & Fischl, B. (2009). Automated MRI measures identify individuals with mild cognitive impairment and Alzheimer's disease. *Brain, 132,* 2048–2057.

DeYoung, C. G., Hirsh, J. B., Shane, M. S., & Papademetris, X. (2010) Testing predictions from personality neuroscience: Brain structure and the big five. Psychological Science. doi:10.1177/0956797610370159, Retrieved April 1 from http://pss.sagepub.com/content/early/2010/04/03/0956797610370159.

Gutkin, T. (2010). Assessment in the science of clinical practice: Where do we go from here? Included in presentations from the Buros Center Conference for Monitoring Assessment Quality in the Age of Accountability, *The eighteenth mental measurements yearbook* (pp. 827-836). Lincoln, NE: Buros Institute of Mental Measurements.

Heath, S. M., Bishop, D. V. M., Hogben, J. H., & Roach, N. W. (2006) Psychophysical indices of perceptual functioning in dyslexia: A psychometric analysis. *Cognitive Neuropsychology, 23(6),* 905–929.

Jensen, A. R., & Munro, E. (1979). Reaction time, movement time, and intelligence. *Intelligence, 3(2),* 121-126.

Kujala, T., Myllyviita, K., Tervaniemi, M., Alho, K., Kallio, J., & Naatanen, R. (2000). Basic auditory dysfunction in dyslexia as demonstrated by brain activity. *Psychophysiology (The International Journal of the Society for Psychophysiological Research), 37,* 262-266.

Rajewska, J., & Rybakowski, J. K. (2003). Depression in premenopausal women: Gonadal hormones and serotonergic system assessed by D-fenfluramine challenge test. *Progress in Neuro-Psychopharmacology & Biological Psychiatry, 27,* 705–709.

Rutter, M., Moffitt, T. E., & Caspi, A. (2005). Gene-environment interplay and psychopathology: Multiple varieties but real effects. *Journal of Child Psychology and Psychiatry, 47(3-4),* 226-261.

Traub, R., & Whittington, M. (2010). *Cortical oscillations in health and disease.* New York: Oxford University Press.

Wundt, W. (1910). *Principles of physiological psychology.* New York: The Macmillan Company.

Assessment in the Service of Clinical Practice: Where Do We Go From Here?

Terry Gutkin
San Francisco State University, California

INTRODUCTION

I am approaching my talk for this Buros measurement conference from the perspective of a clinician who is a user of tests. Despite possessing a reasonable level of psychometric expertise, I am not a psychometrician per se. First and foremost I am a school psychologist. I use tests to assist in my work addressing clinical problems. As a clinician, however, I have a very strong sense that progress in professional practice can only be as good as the measurement technology available for our work. For me, clinical practice is tied directly to data gathering and data gathering is tied to measurement, and that is what brings me here to this measurement conference sponsored by the Buros Center for Testing.

What are the most important practice needs facing our field at this point in time? What would move clinical practice forward? My focus for this talk will be on identifying these directions and then attempting to relate them to measurement advances that are necessary to support this desired progress.

For the purposes of this talk I have identified three crucial future directions for clinical practice. Subsequent to detailing these, I will examine the demands these new clinical directions will create for the measurement community. Because of my personal professional expertise in school psychology I am going to focus this talk primarily on schools and children. However, nothing that I am going to address is in any way limited to those settings or populations. The points I will be making pertain just as much to professional practice in virtually all settings and with virtually all client groups.

CHANGING THE UNIT OF CLINICAL ANALYSIS

The first point I wish to address is the idea of changing the unit of clinical analysis. When I discuss this I will not be focusing on issues pertaining to psychometric units (e.g., standard scores). Instead I will address modifying the unit of analysis for clinical practice. Specifically, on whom or what should we focus our professional services?

The Medical Model vs. The Ecological Model

Traditionally, professional psychologists have relied on what has been termed the medical model. Essentially, our clinical practice has been based on the assumption that human behavior is primarily a function of the internal characteristics of people, with the external environment playing a much lesser role. Quoting from the introduction of the fourth edition of the *Diagnostic and Statistical Manual (DSM-IV-TR)* (American Psychiatric Association, 2000, p. xxxi) as it describes the nature of mental health disorders, "whatever its original cause, it must currently be a manifestation of behavioral, psychological, or biological dysfunction *in the individual* [emphasis added]." Psychology, psychiatry, and virtually all other related mental health professions have created a science that is based almost exclusively on intrapersonal phenomena. Although I am certainly not going to dismiss intrapsychic variables as unimportant, I wish to highlight an alternative

ISBN 978-0-910674-61-4, *The Eighteenth Mental Measurements Yearbook.*

perspective that holds greater potential for effective service delivery to individual clients and our society at large. I am referring to ecological views of human functioning. From an ecological perspective, human behavior is a function of intrapersonal characteristics as they interact with the environments that pervasively surround them. It is this interaction between people and their environments that is the key to understanding, predicting, and changing human behavior (Table 1).

Table 1

Medical Versus Ecological Models of Human Behavior

Traditional Medical Model Behavior = f (PERSON, environment)
Ecological Model Behavior = f (Person X Environment)

There are a number of major theorists who have espoused ecological perspectives. Chief among them is Urie Bronfenbrenner (1979), who has masterfully illuminated the nature of interlocking micro-, meso-, exo-, and macro-environmental systems and their potential impact on human experience. Historically, Kurt Lewin (1951) might be identified as one of the earliest ecological thinkers, with Roger Barker (1965, 1968), Albert Bandura (1978), and Dante Cicchetti (Cicchetti & Toth, 1997) among many others following in his footsteps. There has also been a lot of work in the clinical literature addressing the translation of ecological theory into professional practice. Within school psychology, I've written quite a bit on this topic (e.g., Gutkin & Conoley, 1990; Sheridan & Gutkin, 2000), with a recent chapter (Gutkin, 2009) providing my latest and most thorough discussion. A book in counseling psychology, entitled *Ecological Counseling* (Conyne & Cook, 2004), sheds very important insights into the provision of ecologically based services for counseling psychologists. Finally, Widiger and Trull (2007), two clinical psychologists writing in *The American Psychologist,* capture the essence of ecological thinking as it is applied to the arena of mental health. They wrote, "Most (if not all) mental disorders appear to be the result of a complex interaction of an array of interacting biological vulnerabilities and dispositions with a number of significant environmental, psychosocial events" (p. 80). The underlying commonality in all of this work is the central idea that both intrapersonal and environmental factors are crucial to explaining human behavior, and that neither one is sufficient in and of itself.

Recent work in the area of genetics shows how ecological thinking has emerged even in bodies of research where previously we would have least expected to find it. Rusk and Rusk (2007, pp. 4-5) write,

> there is a growing recognition by biologists that the environment determines which genes are expressed and how they are expressed. Although biological processes are the essential mechanisms mediating all physical and psychological functioning, micro- and macro-environments determine which of these genes are being turned on or off, from conception until death.

Consider the following simple example. Children may have special genetic skills in music; however, if they are not exposed to music and/or music lessons they may never get to utilize this genetic potential and may fail to exhibit any special musical abilities throughout their lifespan. As such, even when it comes to variables that are quintessentially biological in nature, limiting our understanding exclusively to intrapersonal phenomena in isolation to how these variables interact with the environment leads to an inadequate understanding of human functioning.

Students vs. Ecosystems as the Unit of Clinical Analysis

Clearly, the traditional unit of analysis in professional psychology has always been the individual client. For school psychologists, that has meant focusing virtually all of our clinical attention on referred students. Over time we have developed innumerable tests and procedures that allow us to understand what is going on inside students, from their biology and neurology to their personality and learning styles. That is where we have put our energy and expertise. I want to suggest in this talk, however, that by focusing single-mindedly on the inner life of students that we have overlooked a vast array of enormously important information that is at least as vital if we wish to serve our clients effectively. The problems experienced by children are not just the result of what goes on inside the child. They are also a function of what happens in the environments that surround children, such as their home, school, extended family, peers, community, and society, to name just a few of the most relevant variables (Figure 1). These all interact with the student and they all interact with each other. Together they form a living ecosystem, where change anywhere reverberates everywhere.

In my latest writing on ecological school psychology (Gutkin, 2009, p. 479) I tried to capture the essence of how ecosystems can impact the lives of children in a school setting.

> A national economic recession (macro-system) results in a local school board deciding to cut costs by increasing its student-teacher ratio (exo-system). Bobby is a 4th grade student in this school district. Since entering school he has had to struggle somewhat with academics and a variety of mild behavior problems, but he has been able to progress successfully despite these challenges. Bobby's 4th grade teacher, Ms. Smith, who cares deeply about him (micro-system), has a number of additional difficult students transferred into her class from a school in the district that was closed due to budget cuts (meso-system). Ms. Smith's professional life is further complicated by the school district (exo-system) listing her school as one that is not making adequate yearly progress (AYP) according to the guidelines stipulated by No Child Left Behind (macro-system). The principal of the school begins to place considerable pressure on all of the teachers to bring up the school's test scores (meso-system). Ms. Smith is no longer able to devote as much personal time to Bobby and he begins to fall progressively further behind academically (micro-system). Bobby's harried teacher eventually refers him for special education services (micro-system). He is diagnosed as learning disabled and placed part-time in a resource program with a teacher who has little patience for his "needy" behaviors (micro-system). For Bobby, failure experiences in school become increasingly prevalent and by the end of the 4th grade he "turns off" to learning and begins to escalate his acting out in a variety of ways at home (micro-system) and school (micro-system). As the next academic year begins, the district budget crisis worsens (exo-system) resulting in progressively higher student-teacher ratios throughout the school district (meso-system) and at Bobby's school (micro-system). The resource teacher informs Bobby's 5th grade teacher that he is a difficult student who needs stern discipline (meso-system). The 5th grade teacher puts Bobby's parents on notice that she will not tolerate his "disruptive and disrespectful" behaviors (meso-system). This leads to increasing pressure at home from his parents to "straighten up and fly right" (micro-system) and ultimately a change in his relationship patterns at school resulting in a new, less academically oriented circle of friends (micro-system). As the 5th grade ends, Bobby is moving on to middle school with poor basic academic skills, a "bad attitude," and a preference for peers who see little value in education.

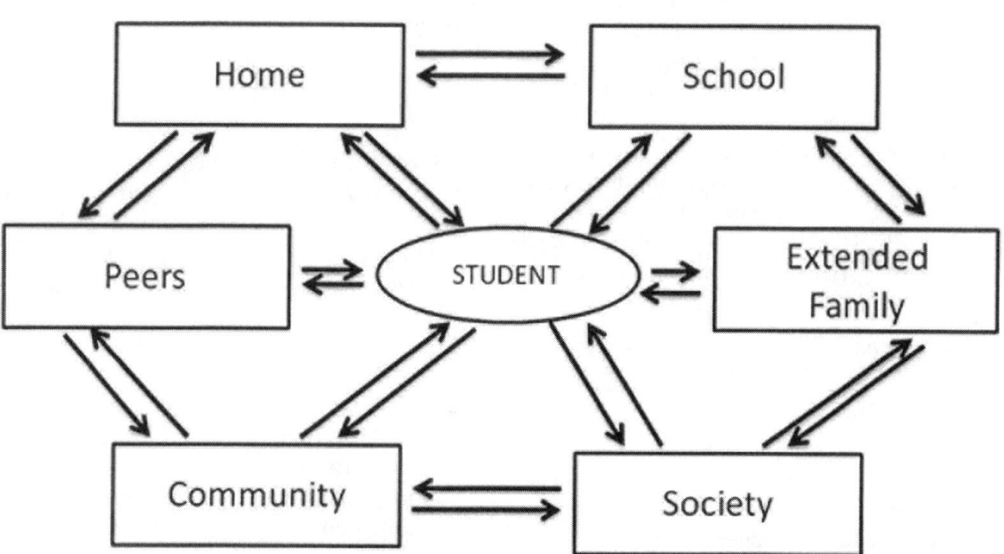

Figure 1. Ecological Model of Student Behavior.

Ecosystems provide a much more sophisticated and accurate picture of student behavior and dysfunction than focusing exclusively on the intrapersonal characteristic of children, and as such the ecological model provides us with much more powerful perspectives than those that have been employed traditionally. It helps us, for example, to understand the high level of recidivism for substance abusers. Regardless of whatever psychological or medical cures you might put "inside" a client while under treatment, the impact of being re-exposed to a culture of substance abuse among family, peers, and/or community members is often enough to negate all prior intervention efforts and gains. An ecological perspective also sheds important light on the rash of eating disorders (e.g., anorexia, bulimia) among young women in our country. "Can it be a coincidence that the dramatic rise of these serious problem behaviors mirrors the shift in our culture toward a standard of female beauty that is based on extreme thinness? Logic, the research literature, and the work of leading therapists suggest otherwise" (Gutkin, 2009, p. 467). Most importantly the ecological model helps explain why, despite decades of effort, the link between traditional diagnostic systems and specific efficacious treatment methods remains tenuous at best (e.g., Widiger & Trull, 2007). Because people who share identical diagnoses will likely vary widely in terms of their ecosystems, it comes as no surprise that the diagnostic category of individuals is not a good predictor of their responsiveness to particular treatments.

Thinking and working ecologically is the challenge that faces clinicians on a day-to-day, case-to-case basis, even though most clinicians do not currently conceptualize their work in this manner. To move practice toward the ecological model, however, will require some major advances from the measurement community.

Implications for Assessment and Testing

A new generation of assessment instruments will have to be developed if clinicians are to begin utilizing the ecological model in their daily professional practice. Currently, almost all measures in both psychology and education focus entirely on the internal workings of clients. Two new thrusts are needed.

First, given the powerful impact of micro-, meso-, exo-, and macro-environmental systems, we need an armamentarium of tools that help us measure salient characteristics of environments (e.g., home, school, work, community). To advance clinical practice we must move away from what Sarason (1981, p. 827) termed a "psychology of the individual" and move toward grasping the nature of functioning ecosystems. We need a range of instruments to measure environments that is as large, sophisticated, and diverse an array as we currently have to measure people. Second, and perhaps even more importantly, there is an urgent need to develop assessment methodologies that allow practitioners to assess and diagnose the interaction *between* persons and their environments. Measurement of the person and environment in isolation from each other will not be sufficient. It is the interaction between the two that must command our attention most of all.

Moving toward ecologically based clinical practice, which will allow clinicians to change their unit of analysis from individuals to living ecosystems, will simply not be possible if the necessary measurement tools are not created. I want to suggest here, at a conference hosted by the Buros Center for Testing, that more time and resources be spent fostering the development and refinement of contextualized measures of human functioning. "More of the same" will simply not provide the tools that practitioners need to move to the next level of clinical practice.

Moving in the Right Direction

Fortunately, progress toward measuring environments and the interactions of people within their environments has begun (Ysseldyke & Burns, 2009). In schools, for example, we have some instruments that have shifted the unit of clinical analysis toward ecosystems rather than individuals. The *Functional Assessment of Academic Behavior* (*FAAB;* Ysseldyke & Christenson, 2002) and the *MainStream Code for Instructional Structure and Student Academic Response* (*MS-CISSAR*; Carta, Greenwood, Schulte, Arreaga-Mayer, & Terry, 2009) are two of the best examples. These instruments simultaneously examine variables pertaining to students, teacher behaviors, the structure and provision of instruction, classroom and home environments, and the interaction among all these different entities. Although only a rudimentary start to developing assessments for ecosystems, it is a start nonetheless.

RESPONDING TO OUR NATION'S MENTAL HEALTH AND EDUCATION PANDEMICS

The second major point I will discuss in my talk is the fact that our nation is experiencing crises in both mental health and education. The problems that we face in 2010 are severe and pervasive enough to warrant the label of "pandemic." To underscore the breadth and depth of these problems I will cite a number of startling and disconcerting statistics, beginning with those for the general population and then shifting to those for children and youth in particular.

Some Relevant Statistics

General Population

- Each year 25% of Americans have a diagnosable mental health disorder (approximately 75 million people), with 60% of this group (approximately 45 million people) experiencing problems that can be characterized as either moderate or severe (Kessler, Chiu, Demler, & Walters, 2005). These statistics come from a nationally representative survey of 10,000 people conducted by the National Institute of Mental Health.
- According to the World Health Organization (WHO), 85% of Americans with diagnosable disorders (approximately 60 million people) will not receive mental health treatment within a year and 70% (approximately 50 million people) will never receive specialized mental health care (WHO World Mental Health Survey Consortium, 2004).
- The annual cost of mental health treatment expenditures and lost economic output is about $220 billion, third only to cancer and coronary disease (DeVol & Bedroussian, 2007).
- According to the Centers for Disease Control and Prevention, antidepressants are now the most frequently prescribed category of medications in the nation (Burt, McCaig, & Rechtsteiner, 2007).

Children and Adolescents: Mental Health

- The U.S. Department of Health (1999) reports that 20% of America's youth experience the signs and symptoms of a *DSM* disorder each year.
- Data indicate that 10% of our nation's children and adolescents suffer from mental illness severe enough to result in significant functional impairment (National Advisory Mental Health Council Workgroup on Child and Adolescent Mental Health Intervention Development and Deployment, 2001).
- Strein, Hoagwood, and Cohn (2003) report that 70% of children in need of mental health treatment do not receive any such services.
- The opening sentence of the summary section of the Surgeon General's report addressing the state of mental health care for young people indicates that the "foremost finding is that most children in need of mental health services do not get them" (U.S. Department of Health and Human Services, 1999).

Children and Adolescents: Education

- A public school student is suspended every second and drops out of school every 11 seconds (The Children's Defense Fund, 2008).
- "About two-thirds of public school 4th graders cannot read at grade level; 6 out of 10 cannot do math at grade level.... Seven out of 10 public school 8th graders cannot read or do math at grade level" (The Children's Defense Fund, 2008, pp. 55-56).

The Way Forward

Given the previous statistics, it should be obvious that "business as usual" is not really a very good option for professional psychologists or the clients they serve. The rate at which new cases are being created (i.e., the incidence rate) seems to be far outstripping the rate at which we "cure" them. The number of troubled, dysfunctional children and adults is rising faster than we can possibly serve them. In my mind the most appropriate metaphor is that of a boat taking on water. What happens when water pours into a boat faster than it can be bailed out? The boat sinks. And that is what we are facing if one looks at contemporary mental health and education statistics. So what are we going to do? What is the way forward and what does this have to do with measurement?

The traditional approach to psychological treatment has been to wait passively for people to become "ill" and then attempt to cure those we encounter once they fall victim to serious psychological and educational dysfunction. Albee (1999) observed, however, that "no mass disorder has ever been eliminated by treating one person at a time" (p. 133) or attempting to cure those who are already casualties.

In light of these realities, we need to be shifting towards population-based services and a public health orientation. At least within the field of school psychology, a lot of scholars have already made this leap conceptually. At the *Future of School Psychology Conference* (D'Amato, Sheridan, Phelps, & Lopez, 2004), for example, a great deal of attention was given to moving toward a public health orientation as a way to address the pandemics we face. Likewise, in *School Psychology: A Blueprint for Training and Practice III* (Ysseldyke et al., 2006), published by the National Association of School Psychologists for the purposes of providing a roadmap for the future development of the field, movement in the direction of greater emphases on population-based services was highlighted as a crucial step needing to be taken. On a more general level and external to the profession of school psychology, Huppert (2009) recently presented a compelling statistical argument founded essentially on the nature of the normal curve. She argues that if we wish to have the greatest possible impact on the largest number of people, we would be better off to focus our energies on achieving small improvements for those falling near the center of the normal distribution (a public health orientation) rather than expending the bulk of our resources on those falling at the extremities (the traditional approach of clinical services in psychology and education).

A population-based service approach would include a heavy emphasis on primary and secondary prevention efforts. Based on a comprehensive review of the literature and a substantial array of empirical research, it is clear that prevention provides a highly efficacious set of tools for working with young people (e.g., Durlak, 2009). Clearly, prevention services need to be integrated more pervasively into the mix of clinical work undertaken by psychologists. To address the mental health and education pandemics, however, authors such as Seligman (2008), Keyes (2007), and numerous others (see Snyder & Lopez, 2002) go an important step further. They argue that psychologists and society must be promoting positive mental and educational health in addition to preventing disturbance, as health is substantially more than the simple absence of illness. All of this and more will be required if we are to successfully address the mental health and educational pandemics documented earlier.

Implications for Assessment and Testing

To achieve this dramatic restructuring of psychological services, it will be necessary to expand clinical assessment far beyond its current boundaries. For example, our current focus on assessing individuals one at a time will have to be extended to facilitate the assessment of broadly based population-based services. To succeed in the development of preventive intervention strategies, new methodologies for assessing environments will be crucial given that so much of the work in prevention is directed toward environmental manipulations. If we wish to promote mental and educational health rather than simply address illness and dysfunction, it will demand the creation of a large array of reliable and valid tests that measure constructs such as wellness, competence, resilience, flourishing, flow, etc.

Currently we have a fully developed science of individual human dysfunction. To create an adequate body of knowledge to support necessary new service delivery paradigms focusing on population-based services, prevention and health promotion will require major advances and changes in testing and assessment instruments. Who better than the Buros Center for Testing to facilitate our movement forward in these endeavors?

Moving in the Right Direction

Despite the daunting tasks in front of us, I'm pleased to report that we are seeing the early stages of progress that will support professional practices intended to address the mental health and education pandemics. Within the field of school psychology, one of the best examples can be found in the ClassMaps methodology developed by Doll, Kurien, LeClair, Spies, Champion, and Osborn (2009). This is important work because it provides clinicians with assessment tools that facilitate prevention as well as remediation services, the proactive promotion of educational success, the creation of healthy and enriched environments for students, and intervention plans that can be targeted toward individuals, classrooms, and/or entire schools. On a much broader scale, extending far beyond children and school-based services, the World Health Organization has published its *International Classification of Functioning, Disability, and Health* (ICF; World Health Organization, 2001). This complex and expansive approach to developing clinical services is explicitly premised on promoting prevention, ecological conceptualizations of human functioning, and the creation of environments that advance human psychological health. A principal stumbling block to realizing all the potential benefits of the ICF, however, is the lack of instrumentation to measure many of the constructs upon which this system is based. As I've been suggesting throughout this talk, however, this important set of new approaches to clinical services will neither thrive nor find its way into standard psychological practice without new and effective measurement tools.

MOVING FROM SNAPSHOTS TO MOVING PICTURES

Traditionally, the use of measurement in clinical practice is largely limited to ascertaining formal and/or informal diagnoses. That is, clients are assessed along relevant dimensions to determine their status on a wide array of continua. As a result of testing, clinicians garner a comprehensive view of their client's current level and manner of functioning. Although the value of data such as these is obvious, they are nonetheless too limited for optimal service provision. The crucial missing element is information regarding responsiveness to treatment over time. In effect, although traditional testing methods give us high resolution "snapshots" of each client's current status, they fail to provide us with "movies" showing how clients improve (or fail to improve) in response to intervention. Addressing this need is the third, and final, major point of my presentation.

Particularly in this era of accountability, it is not enough to know a client's current status at the point of diagnosis. Clinicians need data pertaining to progress monitoring, performance tracking, and formative evaluation to determine whether interventions currently in force should be continued, revised, or replaced. Without data to inform their decision making in this regard, clinicians are left to draw upon a range of subjective sources of information (e.g., clinical intuition, past experience) that are subject to well-documented errors emerging from a variety of cognitive heuristics (Macmann & Barnett, 1999; Watkins, 2009). What is needed are measurement devices that are compatible with data-based decision making over time as clients are provided with treatment.

Progress monitoring is already a vital and accepted element of virtually all medical practice, allowing physicians to maximize the benefits they provide to their patients. Following a diagnosis of cancer, for example, physicians continuously monitor progress via a wide array of tests (e.g., blood draws, CAT scans, body temperature). These data allow medical practitioners to determine whether sufficient progress is being made and whether modifications to the current treatment regimen have to be instituted. Analogous measurement approaches for psychologists would be equally powerful in optimizing clinical services.

Implications for Assessment and Testing

To effectively impart progress monitoring, performance tracking, and formative evaluation types of data for clinicians, psychological tests must possess a number of characteristics. Among these would be the ability to provide repeated test administrations without producing client reactivity. For most contemporary paper-and-pencil tests in psychology, this is a significant problem. There are only a limited number of times that clients can be administered most of the frequently used assessment devices in our field without engaging a variety of reactive responses (e.g., boredom, memory of prior responses, fatigue). Additionally, in light of contemporary resource constraints, tests would have to be amenable to efficient administration, scoring, and interpretation. This could also be challenging for some of the more complex constructs that are routinely measured in psychological evaluations (e.g., intelligence). Finally, to be useful in progress monitoring, psychological tests would have to produce change scores or other measures of progress that are sensitive and reliable enough to be employed effectively in normal practice. Because most current psychometric devices were not designed for repeated applications with the same clients, this could also prove to be a difficult set of obstacles to overcome with many extant instruments.

Ideally, test instruments would not only meet the prior criteria, but would also possess some of the following desirable characteristics that would allow them to be particularly useful within a context of performance monitoring. Tests might not only provide information on client improvements (or the lack thereof) but could also inform clinicians about variables related to treatment integrity (i.e., whether an intervention is being implemented correctly). Lack of client progress means entirely different things in the presence of high versus low treatment integrity. The former would direct a clinician to modify the intervention being employed, whereas the latter would be more suggestive of a need to implement the treatment more accurately/appropriately before making any decision about retaining or revising the therapeutic plan. Another helpful function for test instruments employed within a progress monitoring paradigm would be to provide clinicians with recommendations for empirically validated treatments based on the performance of clients on the test. That is, client scores and/or patterns of results would be explicitly linked to treatment recommendations derived through empirical research. Information such as this would help direct psychologists to alternative intervention plans in those cases when formative evaluation indicated that clients were not making sufficient progress.

Moving in the Right Direction

At least within the field of school psychology, meaningful forward movement can be reported, although much progress remains to be made. A number of different assessment methodologies have been employed to facilitate progress monitoring during the provision of clinical services in the areas of mental health, behavior change, and educational growth. One of the most interesting approaches to emerge recently is the response to intervention (RTI; Jimerson, Burns, & VanDerHeyden, 2007) methodology. RTI was designed initially to assess whether students were responsive to empirically validated interventions, as a means for determining if they had a learning disability and thus were in need of special education. This approach is being generalized in some schools to tracking progress across time for students experiencing academic problems, regardless of disability status, with demonstrated empirical success (Greenwood & Kim, in press). Curriculum-based assessment (CBA; e.g., Hintze, 2009) is another successful tool in wide use in schools that is intended to monitor student academic progress over time. Although there are a number of different CBA models, they all focus on repeated measurement of student skills in the curriculum being taught. The end product is graphs of learning trajectories that clearly show whether students are making satisfactory progress over the weeks and months of each particular school year. And last, but certainly not least, is functional behavioral assessment (FBA), which has a vast empirical record of effectively tracking progress of student behavior change over time (e.g., Steege & Watson, 2009). Based primarily on behavioral psychology, FBA employs single-subject research designs to monitor client behavior change as clinical interventions are implemented in school, home, and community settings.

SUMMARY AND CONCLUSIONS

Three of the most pressing needs facing contemporary professional psychologists are to: (a) develop interventions based on ecosystems rather than being limited to intrapersonal variables, (b) move towards prevention and population-based services as a means for addressing extant mental health and education pandemics, and (c) shift clinical evaluations away from static diagnostic "still pictures" towards data-based decision making that is founded on progress monitoring, performance tracking, and formative evaluation. In this talk I have attempted to explore each of these areas, pointing out how none of these can be accomplished by clinicians without the necessary measurement technology being developed to make it possible. As a world leader facilitating improvements in tests and measurement, it is hoped that the Buros Center for Testing can play an active role in helping to bring forth and then critically evaluate progress in each of these potentially vital emerging areas of development.

REFERENCES

Albee, G. W. (1999). Prevention, not treatment, is the only hope. *Counselling Psychology Quarterly, 12*, 133-146.

American Psychiatric Association. (2000). *Diagnostic and statistical manual of mental disorders IV-TR*. Washington, DC: Author.

Bandura, A. (1978). The self-system in reciprocal determinism. *American Psychologist, 33*, 344-358.

Barker, R. G. (1965). Explorations in ecological psychology. *American Psychologist, 20*, 1-14.

Barker, R. G. (1968). *Ecological psychology*. Stanford, CA: Stanford University Press.

Bronfenbrenner, U. (1979). *The ecology of human development*. Cambridge, MA: Harvard University Press.

Burt, C. W., McCaig, L. F., & Rechtsteiner, E. A. (2007). Ambulatory medical care utilization estimates for 2005.

Advance data from vital and health statistics; no. 388. Hyattsville, MD: National Center for Health Statistics.

Carta, J. J., Greenwood, C. R., Schulte, D., Arreaga-Mayer, C., & Terry, B. (2009). Code for instructional structure and student academic response: Mainstream version (MS-CISSAR). In C. Utley, C. R. Greenwood, S. H. Reynolds, K. Douglas, H. Bannister, & J. M. Kim (Eds.), *EBASS-Mobile: Ecobehavioral Assessment System Software.* Kansas City, KS: Juniper Gardens Children's Project, Institute for Life Span Studies, University of Kansas.

Cicchetti, D., & Toth, S. L. (1997). Transactional ecological systems in developmental psychopathology. In S. S. Luthar, J. A. Burack, D. Cicchetti, & J. R. Weisz (Eds.), *Developmental psychopathology: Perspectives on adjustment, risk, and disorder.* New York: Cambridge University Press.

Children's Defense Fund. (2008). The State of America's Children 2008. http://www.childrensdefense.org/child-research-data-publications/data/state-of-americas-children-2008-report.pdf.

Conyne, R. K., & Cook, E. P. (Eds.). (2004). *Ecological counseling: An innovative approach to conceptualizing person-environment interaction.* American Counseling Association: Alexandria, VA.

D'Amato, R. C., Sheridan, S. M., Phelps, L., & Lopez, E. C. (Eds.). (2004). Psychology in the Schools, School Psychology Review, School Psychology Quarterly, and Journal of Educational and Psychological Consultation Editors Collaborate to Chart School Psychology's Past, Present, and "Futures." *School Psychology Review* [Special issue], *33*(1).

DeVol, R., & Bedroussian, A. (2007). *An unhealthy America: The economic burden of chronic disease.* Santa Monica, CA: Milken Institute.

Doll, B., Kurien, S., LeClair, C., Spies, R., Champion, A., & Osborn, A. (2009). The ClassMaps Survey: A framework for promoting positive classroom environments. In R. Gilman, E. S. Huebner, & M. J., Furlong (Eds.), *Handbook of positive psychology in schools* (pp. 213-227). New York: Routledge/Taylor & Francis Group.

Durlak, J. A. (2009). Prevention programs. In T. B. Gutkin & C. R. Reynolds (Eds.), *The handbook of school psychology (4th ed.,* pp. 905-920). New York: Wiley.

Greenwood, C. R., & Kim, J. M. (in press). Response to Intervention (RTI) Services: An ecobehavioral perspective. *Journal of Educational and Psychological Consultation.*

Gutkin, T. B. (2009). Ecological school psychology: A personal opinion and a plea for change. In T. B. Gutkin & C. R. Reynolds (Eds.), *The handbook of school psychology* (4th ed., pp. 463-496). New York: Wiley.

Gutkin, T. B., & Conoley, J. C. (1990). Reconceptualizing school psychology from a service delivery perspective: Implications for practice, training, and research. *Journal of School Psychology, 28*, 203-223.

Hintze, J. M. (2009). Curriculum-based assessment. In T. B. Gutkin & C. R. Reynolds (Eds.), *The handbook of school psychology* (4th ed., pp. 397-409). New York: Wiley.

Huppert, F. (2009). A new approach to reducing disorder and improving well-being. *Perspectives on Psychological Science, 4*, 108-111.

Jimerson, S. R., Burns, M. K., & VanDerHeyden, A. M. (Eds.). (2007). *Handbook of response to intervention: The science and practice of assessment and intervention.* New York: Springer.

Kessler, R. C., Chiu, W. T., Demler, O., & Walters, E. E. (2005). Prevalence, severity, and comorbidity of 12-month DSM-IV disorders in the National Comorbidity Survey Replication. *Archives of General Psychiatry, 62,* 617-627.

Keyes, C. L. M. (2007). Promoting and protecting mental health as flourishing: A complementary strategy for improving national mental health. *American Psychologist, 62*, 95-108.

Lewin, K. (1951). *Field theory in the social sciences.* Harper & Row: New York.

Macmann, G. M., & Barnett, D. W. (1999). Diagnostic decision making in school psychology: Understanding and coping with uncertainty. In C. R. Reynolds & T. B. Gutkin (Eds.), *The handbook of school psychology (3rd ed.,* pp. 519-548). New York: Wiley.

National Advisory Mental Health Council Workgroup on Child and Adolescent Mental Health Intervention Development and Deployment. (2001). *Blueprint for change: Research on child and adolescent mental health: Executive summary and recommendations (publication01-4986).* National Institutes of Health: Bethesda, MD. http://www.colorado.gov/cs/Satellite?blobcol=urldata&blobheader=application%2Fpdf&blobheadername1=Content-Disposition &blobheadername2=MDT-Type&blobheadervalue1=inline%3B+filename%3D671%2F781%2FBlueprintformentalhealth%2C0.pdf&blobheadervalue2=abinary%3B+charset%3DUTF-8&blobkey=id&blobtable=MungoBlobs&blobwhere=1227308931294&ssbinary=true

Rusk, T. N., & Rusk, N. (2007). Not by genes alone: New hope for prevention. *Bulletin of the Menninger Clinic, 71*, 1-21.

Sarason, S. B. (1981). An asocial psychology and a misdirected clinical psychology. *American Psychologist, 36*, 827-836.

Seligman, M. E. P. (2008). Positive health. *Applied Psychology: An International Review, 57*, 3-18.

Sheridan, S. M., & Gutkin, T. B. (2000). The ecology of school psychology: Examining and changing our paradigm for the 21st century. *School Psychology Review, 29*, 485-502.

Snyder, C. R., & Lopez, S. J. (Eds.). (2002). *Handbook of positive psychology.* New York: Oxford University Press.

Steege, M. W., & Watson, T. S. (2009). *Conducting school-based functional assessments: A practitioner's guide.* New York: Guilford.

Strein, W., Hoagwood, K., & Cohn, A. (2003). School psychology: A public health perspective I. Prevention, populations, and systems change. *Journal of School Psychology, 41*, 23-28.

U.S. Department of Health and Human Services. (1999). *Mental health: A report of the surgeon general.* Rockville, MD: U.S. Department of Health and Human Services.

Watkins, M. W. (2009). Errors in diagnostic decision making and clinical judgment. In T. B. Gutkin & C. R. Reynolds (Eds.), *The handbook of school psychology* (4th ed., pp. 210-229). New York: Wiley.

Weisz, J. R., Sandler, I. N., Durlak, J. A., & Anton, B. S. (2005). Promoting and protecting youth mental health through evidence-based prevention and treatment. *American Psychologist,* 60, 628-648.

WHO World Mental Health Survey Consortium. (2004). Prevalence, severity, and unmet need for treatment of mental disorders in the World Health Organization world mental health surveys. *Journal of the American Medical Association, 291*, 2581-2590.

Widiger, T. A., & Trull, T. J. (2007). Plate tectonics in the classification of personality disorder: Shifting to a dimensional model. *American Psychologist, 62,* 71-83.

World Health Organization. (2001). *International Classification of Functioning, Disability and Health (ICF).* Geneva, Switzerland: Author.

Ysseldyke, J., & Burns, M. (2009). Functional Assessment of Instructional Environments for the Purpose of Making

Data-Driven Instructional Decisions. In T. B. Gutkin & C. R. Reynolds (Eds.), *The handbook of school psychology* (4th ed., pp. 410-433). New York: Wiley.

Ysseldyke, J. E., & Christenson, S. L. (2002). The Functional Assessment of Academic Behavior. Longmont, CO: Sopris West.

Ysseldyke, J., Morrison, D., Burns, M., Ortiz, S., Dawson, P., Rosenfield, S., Brenna, K., & Telzrow, C. (2006). School psychology: A blueprint for training and practice III. Bethesda, MD: National Association of School Psychologists.

Strategies for Evaluating Educational Assessments

Chad W. Buckendahl
Alpine Testing Solutions

At the outset, I want to thank the volume editors, Robert Spies, Janet Carlson, Kurt Geisinger; the managing editor, Linda Murphy; and all of the staff at the Buros Center for Testing for their continuing efforts to continue the path that Oscar and Luella Buros envisioned. I further appreciate the opportunity to contribute a paper to help celebrate the Buros Institute of Mental Measurements' more than 70 years of serving as an external monitor of quality for commercially available tests.

Like most of the contributors to this set of papers, I have a personal connection with the Buros Center for Testing that began as a graduate student in the Buros Institute of Mental Measurements and evolved within the Buros Institute for Assessment Consultation and Outreach. This second institute was an extension of Oscar's vision that Luella graciously supported. And though there are additional individuals who likely deserve credit for fostering that support, the leadership of Barbara Plake and Jim Impara in developing this additional area of Buros's mission of teaching, research, and service was invaluable. As an early career practitioner and researcher, working in Buros provided me with a range of experiences that could be matched by very few organizations and for those opportunities, I will be forever grateful.

The substantive goals of this paper are threefold. First, I will describe strengths and weaknesses of common approaches for evaluating educational tests and testing programs. Second, I will discuss the different reasons why organizations may or may not participate in an external evaluation. Third, I will touch on where I see opportunities for Buros and the measurement community to play an increasing role in education policy deliberations.

As a precursor to discussing these goals, it is important to note the different sources of evaluative criteria that researchers and practitioners can use as a guide. A primary source for the measurement community is the jointly produced *Standards for Educational and Psychological Testing* (American Educational Research Association, American Psychological Association, & National Council on Measurement in Education, 1999). These expectations continue to evolve to respond to changes in the field and are discussed in more detail by Plake (2010, this volume). Because the *Standards* are voluntary and not comprehensive, additional resources have been developed to guide practice. Some of these include the *Guidelines for Computer-Based Testing* (Association of Test Publishers, 2000), the *International Guidelines for Computer-Based and Internet Delivered Testing* (International Test Commission, 2005), and the *International Test Commission Guidelines for Translating and Adapting Tests* (International Test Commission, 2010). Though broad in their expectations, they serve as useful information for testing programs to develop comprehensive validation frameworks based on the context of intended uses and interpretations of test scores.

Existing Evaluation Models

Researchers have long called for external evaluation of educational (and other) tests and testing programs (e.g., Buckendahl & Plake, 2006; Buros, 1938; Downing & Haladyna, 1996; Madaus, 1992; Ruch, 1925) and described a number of models for such reviews. Each of these strategies has strengths and weaknesses that make them more or less desirable for different reasons. In this section, I discuss some of these models, their strengths, and weaknesses.

ISBN 978-0-910674-61-4, *The Eighteenth Mental Measurements Yearbook.*

ANSI

Although not currently active with evaluating tests within the educational arena, the American National Standards Institute (ANSI) has the potential to become involved at some point given shifting education policy at the U.S. federal level. This organization and its evaluation and accreditation model is noted, but not discussed in great detail because it plays primarily in the credentialing testing space. However, given its pseudo-government positioning, it could be viewed as a potential "external" body by federal policymakers if a single organization is ever tapped to have legislated or regulatory authority. ANSI's model for test and testing program evaluation at the time of this writing involved the use of reviewers similar to many peer review processes. Its primary challenge is to remain independent of the potential conflicts of interest that occur when using individuals from the same industry it is evaluating. There are the dual directional effects of leniency and stringency related to potential secondary gain that often make it difficult to interpret the outcomes of such reviews.

Buros Center for Testing

The Oscar and Luella Buros Center for Testing, through its Buros Institute of Mental Measurements (BIMM) and the Buros Institute for Assessment Consultation and Outreach (BIACO), has a longstanding history of serving as an independent organization for test reviews that is detailed in Reynolds (2010, this volume). As described in this collection of papers, BIMM has more than 70 years of experience coordinating the evaluation of commercially available tests and then publishing these reviews in the *Mental Measurements Yearbook* (MMY) series. BIACO fulfills a complementary market niche by reviewing tests and testing programs that are not commercially available. These types of reviews are custom audits or evaluations that are also discussed as a separate model below.

The external review model employed by BIMM has a number of strengths, specifically, the consistent efforts of Oscar and Luella Buros and the staff of the Buros Center for Testing at the University of Nebraska-Lincoln, who have spent decades developing and refining the review processes to continue to publish the MMY sustaining the Institute's reputation. This tenure in evaluating commercially available tests is unmatched. Second, the MMY series is publicly disseminated to add a layer of transparency in the review process that allows consumers to have access to the information contained in the reviews rather than it being an internal or proprietary process.

Among the models discussed in this paper, it is the closest model of independence given the selection process for reviewers, fact checking, and editorial processes. However, it is important to vigorously maintain that independence. For example, at the time of this writing, the homepage of Buros's web site promoted a lecture series that it jointly sponsors with a well-known test publisher. This situation is potentially problematic because it raises concerns about potential conflicts of interest regarding the relationship between this publisher and Buros. Although I am not discouraging assessment literacy development among scholars, practitioners, and users, Buros's unique position within the testing community places a greater burden on their efforts to avoid real or perceived conflicts of interest.

Although Buros's history as a resource for external evaluation information for commercially available tests is strong, its ability to be consistently seen as the primary resource for noncommercial tests is uneven. This observation is driven, in part, by some of the market forces that influence testing organizations' willingness to participate in an external review process. For both the commercial and noncommercial space, there is a reliance on cooperation from publishers in the testing industry and related agencies that requires a necessary balance of the healthy tension of external review. Another challenge to Buros's model within the commercial space is a lack of enforcement ability for poor science or practice. Changes in these situations may then be driven by public or peer pressure to modify practice in response to a reaction to published reviews.

U. S. Department of Education Peer Review

Because the focus of this paper is specifically on educational assessments, I have chosen to include the federal peer review process that state student assessment and accountability programs have been required to undergo under the regulations that emerged from the *No Child Left Behind Act of 2001* (NCLB, 2002). Similar to other peer review processes, external reviewers, intended to have expertise with test development, psychometrics, and education policy evaluate evidence provided by state departments of education about their assessment and accountability programs. Summaries of these reviews are provided to the U.S. Department of Education as recommendations or suggestions based on the interpretation of the reviewers. Final decisions about whether evidence meets the intended policy expectations are determined by federal decision makers. Although this particular model for reviewing tests does not have the extensive history of other evaluation or accreditation programs, it has had a direct impact on testing practice.

There are some notable strengths of this review approach. The federal Peer Review Guidance defines and provides an intended common set of expectations across states. Although these expectations may be viewed as somewhat redundant to the *Standards for Educational and Psychological Testing* (AERA, APA, & NCME, 1999), the *Standards* are voluntary, whereas the Peer Review expectations inform funding decisions that are backed by regulatory authority. An additional strength of the process is that the feedback from peer reviewers and the federal policymakers has had a direct influence on assessment science and practice. An evaluation of whether that influence has been a positive or negative consequence is debatable.

Based on what I have just discussed as strengths of the federal peer review process, the next few comments may be viewed as backhanded compliments. Although Peer Review Guidance defines a common set of expectations, the interpretation of these expectations and the feedback provided to state departments of education has been uneven. Davis and Buckendahl (2007) describe this concern in more detail through a review of publicly disseminated letters sent to state departments of education. This paper described concerns about peer reviewer selection, training, recommendations from peer reviewers for changes to testing programs, and the clarity of information provided by the U.S. Department of Education in their dissemination materials.

A larger concern about the federal peer review process is the potentially chilling effect it has had on the advancement of measurement science in educational assessment. In some instances, rather than evaluating the appropriateness of a particular methodology for a validation study (e.g., alignment, standard setting), peers and/or federal decision makers have recommended specific methodologies and rejected equivalent alternative approaches. Although this is likely a result of limited knowledge of the measurement literature by the peer reviewers or decision makers, scientific advancement of the field can be stifled.

Custom Evaluation

The final model I will discuss is the catch-all category of custom evaluation. Many educational testing programs do not fit neatly within the commercially available or state assessment program space. In these instances, a customized approach is often used to respond to the specific evaluation questions for a testing program sponsor. The seeming flexibility of these types of test evaluation experiences has its own strengths and weaknesses.

A primary advantage of such a custom approach is to be able to directly target a program's unique validation framework (i.e., a development and validation agenda that is aligned with the program's intended uses and interpretations of test scores) with the evaluation questions and evidence collection. For example, an educational testing program may have specific questions about evaluating security (e.g., potential item exposure, cheating behavior) or developing score reports for multiple stakeholder audiences. Such an evaluation also has the potential to provide more comprehensive and formative feedback on targeted aspects of the testing program. Depending on the impetus for the evaluation and the dissemination policies, it may also be possible for evaluators to get more candid responses from the program's stakeholders who may be concerned about negative consequences if the stakes of the outcome are higher. In these customized instances, the ability for a program sponsor to potentially keep any conclusions or feedback confidential may be viewed as another benefit.

Although the flexibility of a customized evaluation model may be a benefit for a particular testing program, there are limitations for both the program and for the broader community of potential users. For a program that is looking for some comparability with similar products or programs within their market space, there is likely a lack of comparability in the evaluation plan and implementation. Further, in these instances, the motivation for conducting a custom evaluation may be for market-based reasons that do not align with a goal of public disclosure of the outcomes or recommendations. As such, the lack of dissemination would make it difficult for both the program and potential users to be able to compare their program's outcomes with others. However, custom evaluations may also be required by legislative or other policy requirements that necessitate a measure of public dissemination. Next, I briefly describe one of these situations as an example.

An Illustration

The Evaluation of the *National Assessment of Educational Progress* (NAEP): Final Report (Buckendahl et al., 2009) serves as an example of a custom evaluation of a testing program that was necessitated by the federal legislation that authorized the program. NAEP is the United States' educational assessment program designed to monitor the achievement and progress of the nation's students. The scope of this program combined with limited time and resources made a comprehensive evaluation infeasible. Therefore, a negotiated evaluation design was constructed based on an interpretation of the authorizing legislation, the policy context of the evaluation questions from the legislation, and through collaboration with key program stakeholders. To inform the evaluation and to respond to the policy needs, the final design revolved around a series of studies that reviewed extant materials, conducted interviews with key stakeholders, and conducted independent data collection and analyses.

The specific studies were divided into two categories: evaluation of the breadth of the development and validation methods and outcomes for the program; and special studies that explored targeted areas of the program in greater depth through independent research. The breadth of the program was evaluated through a lifecycle audit that reviewed the design, development, administration, and psychometric characteristics that are typically found in test review models. The special studies evaluated a new methodology for recommending achievement levels, compared how NAEP's achievement levels aligned with international measures (i.e., Trends in International Mathematics and Science Study [TIMSS], Programme for International Student Assessment [PISA], and Progress in International Reading Literacy Study [PIRLS]), evaluated score reporting practices for the program, conducted a score equity assessment to evaluate stability of scale scores across states, and reviewed methods for evaluating alignment of domain representation on assessments.

Although interested readers are encouraged to go to the full report, I will briefly describe the primary finding from the evaluation because I expect that it applies to many testing programs whether they are in the educational sector or not. Our evaluation team's major finding from the report was that the NAEP program did not have a clearly defined and transparent validity agenda driven by the intended uses and interpretations of test scores. Not surprisingly, a primary recommendation that emerged from this finding was for NAEP to develop such a plan. Because of the range of stakeholders for the NAEP program, the external advisory committee that provided periodic feedback during the evaluation discouraged a specific model to avoid a potential misinterpretation that it was prescriptive. However, such a validation framework might include systematic collection of validity evidence that focuses on three levels: core elements (e.g., operational needs, defensibility of primary interpretations), policy reactions (e.g., flexibility to respond to unexpected questions or research studies that are raised by changing policy), and innovation (e.g., a macro picture of where the program is and where it is going in its evolution). An outcome of a custom audit like the one described above would likely be actionable suggestions and recommendations that are consistent with the testing program's intended uses and interpretations of their scores.

Motivation for External Review

As noted in the introductory section, there are different reasons why publishers or agencies may participate in or seek out external evaluation of their testing programs. Three of these factors are discussed in this section.

A primary motivation for state K-12 student assessment programs to participate in an external review is an accountability requirement within the NCLB legislation that requires such a review. Mandated, independent audits or evaluations are not uncommon among programs that are funded by public or private resources. However, the consequences associated with poor performance in these reviews are a new wrinkle for these types of testing programs.

A second factor that often motivates educational assessment programs to seek external review is the risk of potential legal challenge. This is particularly important for programs that are using assessment information to inform higher stakes decisions about individual students (e.g., graduation, promotion, retention), but may also apply to how accountability systems for schools and teachers may be developed. Because legal challenges for assessment programs generally revolve around issues of domain specification, fairness, reliability, and decision making, these areas would likely be highlighted in a targeted evaluation of these sources of validity evidence in the program.

Although probably not considered as the initial motivation in the minds of some organizations, another factor that motivates many testing programs is the professional responsibility for ensuring that our development and validation practices and outcomes are adhering to the *Standards for Educational and Psychological Testing* (AERA, APA, & NCME, 1999). An accountability system for the measurement profession and testing industry should not be interpreted as an onerous concept. Professions are generally defined, in part, by a code of ethics and some type of accountability or enforcement mechanism; yet, within the testing community, we are hesitant to move beyond the voluntary nature of our professional *Standards*.

The business realities of the educational testing industry lend themselves to an additional factor that motivates organizations in their decision to seek out or participate in external review. From a more positive perspective, these market-based factors may involve seeking accreditation as recognition from a third party that can be leveraged as part of co-branding the reputation of the accrediting body with the reputation of the participating organization. Even without the additional benefits of accreditation, there is greater potential credibility when an external evaluator or organization can provide both formative and summative feedback about a testing program's strengths and weaknesses relative to a set of professional expectations.

On the more sinister dark side, though, is the reverse scenario of a testing organization being unwilling to participate in external review as a hedge against the potential for receiving a bad review or revealing potentially poor practice. In a competitive market environment, organizations may perceive greater risk to submit tests for review through either the *MMY* series or through customized evaluations, particularly if they have already been successful in their business model. Because assessment literacy among consumers varies widely, the incentive to ensure that tests and testing programs meet professional expectations likely correlates positively with the level of assessment literacy within the targeted population of consumers. *Caveat emptor* indeed.

A Related Anecdote

As readers are likely aware, the invited papers in this collection were an extension of a conference held in celebration of the more than 70 years of service for the Buros Institute of Mental Measurements. One of the most enjoyable components of this conference as an attendee was to hear some of the anecdotes from individuals who had interacted with Oscar and Luella Buros before and after the Institute came to the University of Nebraska-Lincoln. My own contribution to the parade of inside stories was not as interesting as the personal anecdotes, but was related to the concept of market-based motivational factors that was discussed above as something that publishers or organizations consider when submitting a test for review.

A few years ago, the Chancellor of the University of Nebraska-Lincoln advanced an initiative to bring all departments, programs, and research centers under a common logo that would extend to letterhead and other University publications. This was a laudable effort to establish the University's "brand" and communicate a shared vision of that brand. However, this goal had two potential unintended consequences for Buros. Specifically, because Buros was recognized in the market as an independent source for critically candid test reviews, this reputation could be damaged if it were subsumed under a heading of another department or center at the University of Nebraska that produced a test that could be reviewed by Buros. A favorable review of such a test may not be perceived as credible if both entities are part of the same organization.

A second and more concerning factor was that the Buros Institute had a 40+ year history prior to its arrival at the University of Nebraska-Lincoln in the 1970s. Thus, changing the branding of the Institute in the early 2000s after then a 60+ year history had the potential to create consumer confusion in the marketplace regarding the organization. Because the Buros Center for Testing essentially functions as a self-supported entity within the University, such a change could also have been damaging to the "business" model of the Institute. In collaboration with the Center's director, Dr. Barbara Plake, we prepared a reasoned argument and scheduled a meeting with the Chancellor to make our case. Fortunately for us, Chancellor Harvey Perlman had previously been Dean of UNL's College of Law where he had taught torts as a substantive area of law and had research expertise specifically in trademark infringement, consumer confusion, and related intellectual property law.

After presenting our case and using some of the Chancellor's own research to support our request to maintain the Buros branding to protect its independence, he agreed with our position with little discussion and granted Buros a waiver of the University's policy to maintain the long-established brand. Thus, at the time of that decision, only two divisions of the University of Nebraska-Lincoln–the Buros Center for Testing and the Athletic Department–were authorized to use logos that were different from the official University policy. Chancellor Perlman also deserves special thanks for his understanding of the potential impact that weakening the Buros brand may have had for both the Institute and the University.

Opportunities for Buros

The entertaining thought experiment involved in discussing potential future directions in reviewing educational assessments is that readers would need to revisit this paper after a few years to either marvel at the foresight or ridicule the ignorance. My sense is that there will likely be a little of each for future readers to glean from this section. There are three areas where I think Buros has potential for growth or renewal opportunities.

With more education policy being driven at the federal level, we will likely see more common assessments delivered across consortia of states. In these situations, a review of the technical characteristics of assessments would likely occur at the consortia level and likely not be considered a commercially available assessment. However, the unusual paradox of greater involvement by a large, centralized entity is contrasted by an emphasis on classroom-based information that has utility for formative or benchmarking purposes. Many of these will be commercial products characterized as formative, benchmark, and interim assessments and will be purported to be aligned with national and international standards. This potential resurgence in commercially available educational assessments may swing the pendulum back to a market where Buros has its most stable history and experience.

Another area where Buros could expand its testing program evaluation services is in the area of custom audits and evaluation. Although it would be an expansion of the model that is currently applied to commercially available testing programs, the increasing number of educational assessments and programs that are not considered commercially available would benefit from the critically candid reviews for which Buros is well known. Effectively operating in that space may necessitate actively seeking partnerships or outsourcing opportunities with regulatory or government agencies.

In either instance, Buros will be challenged to assert itself as the primary source of information on the technical quality of tests and testing programs. As discussed earlier in this paper, there have been additional evaluation models that have entered the space in addition to the varying factors that motivate organizations to participate or not in an external review process. This challenge, particularly in the educational assessment market, will persist in the continuation of federal legislation and related policy initiatives that have the potential to further reduce the flexibility that consumers have in identifying assessments or developing customized programs that are designed to meet their needs.

Conclusions

A primary assumption when providing information about any substantive topic such as investing as part of retirement planning is a level of domain specific literacy. We have a similar assumption when providing information about tests and testing programs. Specifically, when providing evaluative information about the validity evidence that a particular testing program does or does not have to support the intended uses and interpretations of their scores, we assume that readers understand the criticality of whether the current evidence supports their intended use(s) or whether additional validity evidence would be necessary. A challenge, then, for members of the testing community that often discuss the importance of assessment literacy, myself included, is to define what we mean by the term and what we really expect different audiences to understand about test development, validation, and psychometric characteristics of tests relative to their intended uses. Laying this groundwork could better communicate the expectations we have for potential users.

As implied above, another area where I think the broader educational testing community could benefit itself is in the area of how we characterize testing professionals. For example, psychometricians do not currently have a license or certification requirement. This means that anyone can (and many do) represent themselves as a psychometrician. Although I am not suggesting that we will have a stampede of people rushing to enter the field, the expectations for characterizing oneself as a psychometrician should be more than simply being able to spell the title correctly on a business card. Such a credential, particularly if it is administered by one or more of the organizations that sponsor the *Standards*, would add credibility to the profession and ultimately respond to a potential threat that a regulatory agency without subject matter expertise could potentially assume that role. Further, as the expectations promulgated by the professional community, the *Standards* could serve as guidance for developing the program.

In closing, it is difficult to capture accurately the history of the Buros Institute and more specifically the legacy of Oscar and Luella Buros within the testing community in few words, but I have some thoughts that capture the spirit. During free blocks of time during my visits to Washington, DC, I usually gravitate to one or more of the Smithsonian museums. At the American History museum there was an exhibit that documented Thomas Edison's persistent efforts to develop a sustainable lighting option as an alternative to gas that could be scaled to consumers. A quote attributed to Edison as part of this exhibit, "If you want to be successful, first make some enemies," referenced his direct challenge to the gas company, but resonated with me. Specifically, I generalized this perspective to Oscar's passionate concern for consumers and users who may be unintentionally misusing tests that were poorly constructed or had little or no validity evidence to support the intended uses and interpretations purported by the publisher. To continually improve the science and practice of testing, we should be courageous enough to actively share this concern.

References

American Educational Research Association, American Psychological Association, & National Council on Measurement in Education. (1999). *Standards for educational and psychological testing*. Washington, DC: American Educational Research Association.

Association of Test Publishers. (2000). *Guidelines for computer-based testing*. Washington, DC: Author.

Buckendahl, C. W., Davis, S. L., Plake, B. S., Sireci, S. G., Hambleton, R. K., Zenisky, A., & Wells, C. S. (2009). *Evaluation of the National Assessment of Educational Progress: Final report*. Washington, DC: U. S. Department of Education.

Buckendahl, C. W., & Plake, B. S. (2006). Evaluating tests. In S. Downing & T. Haladyna (Eds.), *Handbook of test development* (pp. 725-738). Mahwah, NJ: Lawrence Erlbaum Associates.

Buros, O. K. (Ed.) (1938). *The nineteen thirty-eight mental measurements yearbook*. Highland Park, NJ: Gryphon Press.

Davis, S. L., & Buckendahl, C. W. (2007, April). *Evaluating NCLB's peer review process: A comparison of state compliance decisions*. Paper presented at the annual meeting of the National Council on Measurement in Education, Chicago, IL.

Downing, S. M., & Haladyna, T. M. (1996). A model for evaluating high-stakes testing programs: Why the fox should not guard the chicken coop. *Educational Measurement: Issues and Practice, 15*(1), 5-12.

International Test Commission. (2010). *International test commission guidelines for translating and adapting tests*. [http://www.intestcom.org]

International Test Commission. (2005). *International guidelines on computer-based and internet delivered testing*. Granada, Spain: Author.

Madaus, G. F. (1992). An independent auditing mechanism for testing. *Educational Measurement: Issues and Practices, 11*(1), 26-31.

No Child Left Behind Act of 2001 (2002). Pub. L. No. 107-110, 115 Stat. 1425.

Plake, B. S. (2010). Impact of the Testing Standards. Included in presentations from the Buros Center Conference for Monitoring Assessment Quality in the Age of Accountability, *The eighteenth mental measurements yearbook* (pp. 844-853). Lincoln, NE: Buros Institute of Mental Measurements.

Reynolds, C. R. (2010). The road to Huskerville: How did the Buros Institute get from New Jersey to Nebraska? Included in presentations from the Buros Center Confrence for Monitoring Assessment Quality in the Age of Accountability, *The eighteenth mental measurements yearbook* (pp. 810-816). Lincoln, NE: Buros Institute of Mental Measurements.

Ruch, G. M. (1925). Minimum essentials in reporting data on standard tests. *Journal of Educational Research, 12*, 349-358.

Impact of the Testing Standards

Barbara S. Plake
Director Emeritus
Buros Center for Testing
University of Nebraska-Lincoln

The *Standards for Educational and Psychological Testing* ("Testing Standards") is a joint publication by the American Educational Research Association (AERA), American Psychological Association (APA), and the National Council on Measurement in Education (NCME). First published in 1954, there have been several editions of the Testing Standards over the ensuing years (1966, 1974, 1985, 1999). The first edition, entitled *Technical Recommendations for Psychological Tests and Diagnostic Techniques*, was issued by APA alone. In 1955, AERA and NCME published their own document on achievement tests. Both of these documents primarily focused on test development and the type of information test publishers should provide to test users in publications such as test manuals. The next edition, called *Standards for Educational and Psychological Tests and Manuals*, was published in 1966 jointly by APA, AERA, and NCME and was the product of a committee with membership across the associations. The 1974 edition included standards for employment and college admission testing and addressed test development, test use, and reporting instead of just focusing on test development and technical documentation. The 1985 edition made a dramatic shift toward a unitary concept of validity theory as represented in the change in title to *Standards for Educational and Psychological Testing*. In 1999, *Standards for Educational and Psychological Testing* was again revised, and in this revision the definition of "test" was broadened to encompass a wider range of instruments and assessments as well as emphasizing their use in the decision-making process, highlighting that validity and reliability were a function of the interpretation and use of test results, not of the test itself. A revision to the 1999 Testing Standards is currently in process; more about this revision will be presented later in this document.

The intent of the Testing Standards is to promote the sound and ethical use of tests and provide a basis for evaluating the quality of testing practice (AERA, APA, & NCME, 1999, p. 8). The purpose of these Standards, as specified in the 1999 edition, is to provide criteria for the evaluation of tests, testing practices, and the effects of test use (p. 9). Therefore, it is clear that the Testing Standards aims to provide information for test developers and users about the key elements in a testing program that would inform the development, selection, and use of test products. Tests are broadly defined:

> A test is an evaluative device or procedure in which a sample of an examinee's behavior in a specified domain is obtained and subsequently evaluated and scored using a standardized process. While the label *test* is ordinarily reserved for instruments on which responses are evaluated for their correctness or quality and the terms *scale* or *inventory* are used for measures of attitudes, interest, and dispositions, the *Standards* uses the single term *test* to refer to all such evaluative devices. (AERA, APA, & NCME, 1999, p. 2, italics in original)

Several important philosophical changes have occurred regarding validity theory since 1954. The most notable change in validity theory has been in the shift from proposing four distinct types of validity to representing all types of validity as a unitary concept. Before 1954, test validity was a singular concept in that it was thought to exist if a test score correlated highly with the test's criterion (Bingham, 1937; Cureton, 1950; Gulliksen, 1950). In 1954,

ISBN 978-0-910674-61-4, *The Eighteenth Mental Measurements Yearbook.*

the idea of test validation was multifaceted but fragmented. The 1954 Test Standards considered four types of validity: predictive, concurrent, content, and construct. The type of validity that should be used for test validation was that strategy that was more appropriate for the planned use of the test. The 1966 Test Standards took a small step toward unification by suggesting only three types of validity (predictive and concurrent validity were merged into criterion validity). And, although these standards still proposed that the most appropriate type of validity was that strategy that matched the planned test use, it also suggested that one might want to use more than one approach. In the 1974 Testing Standards, the three distinct types of validity remained intact; however, the concern of test validation began to shift from choosing a strategy based on test use to choosing a strategy based on the inferences made regarding the test scores. The 1985 Testing Standards made a dramatic shift toward a unitary concept by stating that validity is "the appropriateness, meaningfulness, and usefulness of specific inferences made from the test scores" (p. 9). These Testing Standards regarded content, criterion, and construct validity as types of evidence about validity rather than three distinct types of validity. The conception of validity also evolved in the 1999 Testing Standards. The 1999 Testing Standards states "validity refers to the degree to which evidence and theory support the interpretations of test scores entailed by proposed uses of tests" (p. 9). For more about the evolution of validity theory, see Shepard (1993) and Geisinger (1992).

Another change over the years is what is being evaluated with regard to tests. In the earlier edition, tests were "validated"; or statements were made that validity for a test had been "established." Over the years, the focus has shifted from the test as the focal point of validation to the use or interpretation of the test scores that need to be validated. Further, evidence was gathered to support the intended use or interpretation, but this was viewed as an ongoing process. Because validity evidence was based on uses of test scores, a first step was to identify the intended uses and interpretations, through what is today called the "validity framework" or "validity argument" (Kane, 2001). There is controversy in the field about where the limits and responsibility for making a validity argument falls, whether on the test developer or on the test user. Some argue that it is unreasonable to hold test developers responsible for validity evidence for uses that were not intended by the developer. Others maintain that when uses not intended by the developer are reasonable to anticipate, the developer has a responsibility for gathering evidence to support or disclaim such uses. On the other hand, when unanticipated and unintended consequences arise, there is still debate on how such evidence should be obtained and by whom.

Other areas of changes are obvious over the publications of the Testing Standards. As noted previously, both the sponsoring organizations have changed (starting with only APA in 1954 and adding AERA and NCME in subsequent years) as well as the titles of the editions. Further, the number of standards has continued to grow, from 180 in 1985 to 264 in 1999. Other changes are in the amount and purpose of the introductory text for each chapter (signaling perhaps a change in intended audience). Up through the 1974 Testing Standards, introductory material was brief and mostly technical in nature. The 1999 Testing Standards expanded the introductory text for each chapter, aiming to serve an educational goal because it was noted that a large number of graduate classes were using the 1985 Testing Standards as required texts. Finally, another major change in the 1999 Standards was the discontinuance of identifying standards using priority language such as "primary," "secondary," and "conditional." The 1999 Standards discontinued this practice because it was felt by the authors that different standards take on more or less importance and relevance based on the type of test and its use. Further, there was concern that when a standard was designated as "desirable" it was more or less ignored. Such a system of prioritization of the standards set up a mentality that only those designated as "primary" needed serious consideration. Some argue, however, that the elimination of "primary standards," which were perceived as required for all tests and test uses, has changed the standards to a more aspirational level (Camara & Lane, 2006). This change has been both lauded and criticized in the following years and is a matter of discussion by the current revision team.

As discussed later in this paper, the charge to the Joint Committee for the Revision of the 1999 Standards includes considering ways to communicate critical/overarching standards or requirements for sound testing practices. How this will play out in the revision is still a matter of discussion and debate among the committee members.

Use of the Testing Standards

According to the Introduction to the 1999 Testing Standards, the intended uses are to (a) promote sound and ethical use of tests, (b) provide a basis for evaluating the quality of testing practices, and (c) provide a frame of reference to assure all relevant issues in test design, development, and use are addressed. However, the Testing Standards also caution about literal application of the standards without thoughtful considerations and professional judgment. Thus professional judgment should consider (a) knowledge of behavioral science, psychometrics, and the standards in the professional field; (b) the degree to which the intent of the standard has been satisfied by the test developer and user; (c) alternatives that are readily available; and (d) research and experiential evidence regarding feasibility of meeting the standard.

The Testing Standards have been used in court cases challenging the technical quality or use of specific assessments for particular uses. Some examples where the Testing Standards have contributed substantively to court decisions include the *Debra P. v. Turlington (1979)* and the *GI Forum v. Texas Education Agency (1999)* cases. Sireci and Parker (2006) argue that the courts have systematically used a lower standard for technical quality than is detailed in the Testing Standards. This same line of evidence regarding the courts and requirements in the Testing Standards can be found in Buckendahl and Hunt (2005). Further, it is now common practice for Requests for Proposals issued by states, for example, to include a statement regarding compliance with the *Standards for Educational and Psychological Testing* by the bidding vendors. In addition, some technical manuals (for example, California Test Bureau/McGraw Hill's manual for the Missouri assessment program: http://dese.mo.gov/divimprove/assess/tech/documents/2009-MAP-Technical-Report.pdf) directly relate how the components of the testing program are in congruence with these Testing Standards.

Closer to home, both the Buros Institute of Mental Measurements (BIMM) and the Buros Institute for Assessment Consultation and Outreach (BIACO) rely heavily on the Testing Standards for their work. BIMM provides reviews of the technical quality of commercially available tests through its *Mental Measurements Yearbook* series. Reviewers are recruited from professionals in the relevant field to the test and are provided guidelines for their reviews that are based on the Testing Standards. BIACO developed a program for review of the technical quality and possible accreditation of proprietary assessment programs. This program has criteria for test quality that were developed to be in compliance with the Testing Standards.

Further, NCME developed a set of standards for the ethical use of tests and testing practices (Schmeiser, 1992) that used the Testing Standards as a foundation. More recently, a document tentatively titled "Operational Best Practices," is being developed by several testing advocates that is intended to be complementary to the Testing Standards but provides operational examples of testing practices that would be in compliance with the Testing Standards. Those involved in the development of this document include people from state departments of education, testing vendors, and others who have a vested interest in testing practices.

Empirical Evidence of the Impact of the Standards

In the late 1990s, Jessica Jonson and I (Jonson & Plake, 1998) conducted a study designed to evaluate the use of the Testing Standards in the reviews of commercially available tests in the *Mental Measurements Yearbook* (*MMY*). The focus of this study was to examine whether *MMY* reviews have shown sensitivity to the change in the conceptualization of validity over the last 50 years. As indicated previously, over the last 50 years, validity has changed from a set of types (content, concurrent, criterion, construct) to a unified construct with evidence provided to support the intended score interpretations and use. The Jonson and Plake study examined how these changes in the conceptualization of validity have impacted validity practices, as evidenced by the criteria used by *MMY* reviewers in their evaluation of the validity information.

Therefore, the purpose of the Jonson and Plake study was to compare the criteria for validity that were articulated in the current Testing Standards at the time of the review published in the relevant *MMY* with the concept of validity as characterized in the relevant edition of the Testing Standards. In order to achieve this goal, several steps needed to be completed. First, it was necessary to operationalize validity requirements over the history of validity theory. Next, a set of tests needed to be identified that spanned this historical period so that the same test would be the basis for the *MMY* review over the time span covered by the reconceptualization of validity. Then, an examination of the *MMY* reviews of these tests was used to evaluate types of validity evidence provided by reviewers of these tests in appropriate time-period *MMY*s. Finally, a comparison was made of the relevant validity theory to *MMY* reviewers' comments.

To accomplish Step 1, five distinct periods on the evolution of validity theory were identified: Period 1: pre-1954; Period 2: 1955-1966; Period 3: 1967-1974; Period 4: 1975-1985; Period 5: 1986-1998. For the pre-1954 period, the criteria for evaluating validity came from the *Essentials of Psychological Testing* (Cronbach, 1949), which considered a singular concept in that validity was thought to exist if a test score correlated highly with a test's criterion. Also, in 1954 the idea of test validation consisted of four types of validity: content, predictive, concurrent, and construct. The 1974 Testing Standards took two small steps toward unification of the types of validity by (a) merging predictive and concurrent validity into criterion validity and (b) indicating the use of more than one validity approach for a test. The three distinct types of validity still remained in the 1974 Testing Standards, but test validation began to shift from choosing a strategy based on test to choosing a strategy based on the inferences made regarding test scores. The 1985 Testing Standards present validity as a unified concept.

In the next step, a decision needed to be made regarding which type of commercially available assessments would be considered in the study. For a variety of reasons, it was decided that achievement tests would be the focus of the study. This was decided in part because achievement tests were more likely to include information about the original "types" of validity, more so than some intelligence or psychological assessments. Through an examination of commercially available achievement tests that had been reviewed over the 50-year period for this study, two tests were selected: The Metropolitan Achievement Test (MAT) and the Wide Range Achievement Test (WRAT). These tests had reviews in each of the *MMY* volumes published in 1938, 1941, 1953, 1965, 1978, 1985, 1989, and 1995.

Next, using the same validity criteria that emerged from an examination of the Testing Standards, the reviews in the editions of the *MMY* for the MAT and WRAT were coded by how the validity evidence was reported in the reviews. This allowed for a cross-walk between the validity requirements identified in the Testing Standards and the evidence that was identified by the reviewers in the *MMY* over the volumes of the *MMY* and across editions of the Testing Standards.

The results indicated that across the years of the *MMY* reviews, the most prevalent validity evidence identified in the reviews centered on aspects of content. Face validity, per se, was only mentioned in the pre-1954 era, but it was talked about in every review of the MAT and WRAT across volumes of the *MMY*. This came in terminology such as "appearance of relevant content"; perhaps this was a foreshadowing of what we would today refer to as "content alignment."

Discussions in the *MMY* reviews of construct validity also appeared across the years and *MMY* volumes. Requirement for construct validity evidence has increased in the Testing Standards following the 1974 edition, but especially so following the unified conceptualization of validity articulated in the 1985 edition of the Testing Standards. This suggests that the *MMY* reviews were in congruence with the evolving conceptualization of validity as articulated in the Testing Standards.

The Jonson and Plake study was completed prior to the release of the 1999 Testing Standards. The discussion of validity requirements in the 1999 Testing Standards was heavily influenced by the reconceptualization of validity by Messick (1989), which organized the concept of validity into two facets. One facet was the source of justification for testing, which was further divided into two components: evidential and consequential. The second facet, outcome of testing, was divided into two components: test interpretation and test use. The purpose of Messick's conceptualization of validity was to extend the concept of validity beyond test score meaning to test score use, value implications, and social consequences.

As discussed earlier, the definition of validity in the 1999 Testing Standards, consistent with Messick's conceptualization, presents validity as the degree to which evidence and theory support the interpretations of test scores entailed by the intended uses of the tests. This definition brings together the component of justification for testing (intended inferences) and outcomes of testing (intended uses). Text of the standards for validity in the 1999 Testing Standards identifies requirements for providing a rationale for each intended interpretation that would provide theoretical and empirical evidence to support these intended uses or interpretations. Further, there are standards in the 1999 Testing Standards that address the notion of both intended and unintended consequences of test use.

It would be interesting to repeat the Jonson and Plake study using the current Testing Standards to see how the Messick validity theory, as characterized by the 1999 Testing Standards, has affected the reviews of these same achievement tests in the reviews of these instruments in recent *MMY*s. It would be particularly interesting to see how the evidence for consequential validity has been presented in the *MMY* reviews, not only of these two tests, but across tests for educational and psychological assessments. Research along these lines has been conducted by Cizek, Koons, and Rosenberg (in press). As mentioned earlier, the notion of consequential validity has been controversial since the publication of the 1999 Testing Standards. One way to examine the impact of the standards for consequential validity would be to examine the reviews prepared since the 1999 Testing Standards to reveal whether this topic is discussed by the *MMY* reviewers. Cizek et al. (in press) did exactly that, looking at the nearly 300 reviews in the *Sixteenth MMY* (Spies & Plake, 2005). Their results were somewhat discouraging from the perspective of the impact of the validity conceptualization promoted in the 1999 Testing Standards. Hardly any of the reviews mentioned consequential validity at all, and when they did, the information was not directly congruent with the intended notion of consequential validity. Another topic for consideration in such a study would be how the unified concept of validity is still being discussed by the reviewers or whether there is a tendency to still think of validity in terms of specific types. This might be differentially presented in the area of psychology or business, for example. Again, this was a topic addressed in the Cizek et al. (in press) study. Disappointing results were also found because only 7 of the reviews in *The Sixteenth MMY* mentioned the notion of a unified concept of validity and that was introduced as early as 1985! Expanding the Cizek et al. (in press) study to more *MMY*s or by general content category, such as educational, psychological, or occupational might provide insights into where the more progressive concepts of validity may be taking hold.

Most of the research to date on the impact of the Testing Standards had focused on the reconceptualization of validity in the Testing Standards and how that has affected assessment practice. In fact, most of this paper has focused on changes in validity theory as documented in the Testing Standards. There have been other changes over the years in both the topics covered in the Testing Standards and in their theoretical conceptualization. Changes in reliability theory, especially with the introduction of generalizability theory as an integrated approach to reliability, were introduced into the Testing Standards in 1999. More emphasis has also been introduced in the Testing Standards to topics such as policy analysis, program evaluation, and testing of examinees with disabilities. Very little research has been done to look into the impact of these other changes to the Testing Standards. These are some ideas for research that might serve as thesis or dissertation fodder.

Current Revision Process for the Testing Standards

The Management Committee for the Revision of the 1999 Testing Standards is composed of representatives from APA (Wayne Camara, Chair), AERA (Suzanne Lane), and NCME (David Frisbie). The Management Committee is responsible for operational details, such as soliciting comments, monitoring the budget, and negotiating publication options. One of the first actions of the Management Committee was to solicit comments from the field about areas that needed revision. They did this through a web-based process that asked agencies, groups, and individuals to prepare comments using a structured electronic format. Invitations to make comments were communicated mostly through the sponsoring organizations' newsletters, websites, and other communication vehicles. Agencies and organizations were also contacted and asked to submit comments through the website. Once the comments were received, the Management Committee did a content analysis to examine both the extent of needed revisions and the areas where revisions were needed. This resulted in a charge that identified areas where revisions should be focused (see Appendix A for the text of the Charge to the Committee).

Once the charge was developed, the next task for the Management Committee was to appoint the co-chairs for the Joint Committee for the revision of the 1999 Testing Standards. Lauress Wise and

I were asked to serve as co-chairs. Then, together with the co-chairs, the Management Committee identified the members of the Joint Committee. The members of the Joint Committee are identified in Table 1.

Table 1.

Members of the Joint Committee for the Revision of the 1999 Standards for Educational and Psychological Testing.

Barbara Plake, co-chair, University of Nebraska-Lincoln
Lauress Wise, co-chair, HumRRO
Linda Cook, Educational Testing Service
Fritz Drasgow, University of Illinois
Brian Gong, National Center for Assessment
Jo-Ida Hansen, University of Minnesota
Laura Hamilton, Rand Corporation
Joan Herman, CRESST/UCLA
Michael Kane, Educational Testing Service
Michael Kolen, University of Iowa
Antonio Puente, University of North Carolina-Wilmington
Nancy Tippins, Valtera Corporation
Paul Sackett, University of Minnesota
W. Denny Way, Pearson
Frank Worrell, University of California-Berkeley

Two members of the 1999 Joint Committee are also members of the current Joint Committee: Paul Sackett (co-chair of the 1999 Joint Committee) and Jo-Ida Hansen. It was decided to seek overlap in membership with the 1999 Joint Committee to foster continuity. This was also the case with the Joint Committee for the 1999 Standards where there was carryover in some members from the 1985 Joint Committee. In the past, no Joint Committee members were employed by testing companies, as it was thought that such members might have a conflict of interest. For the current Joint Committee, that restriction was relaxed. Initially two members of the Joint Committee were from testing companies (Linda Cook, Educational Testing Service and W. Denny Way, Pearson). Subsequent to being appointed to the Joint Committee, Michael Kane changed his affiliation from the National Conference of Bar Examiners to Educational Testing Service. However, with the appointment of each Joint Committee member, it was made clear that they were to exercise their own professional judgment in their thoughts and deliberations and not to represent organization or other affiliations. In addition to having members from testing companies, the current Joint Committee also has members from business and non-profit organizations: Laura Hamilton (RAND), Brian Gong (National Center for Assessment), Nancy Tippins (Valtera Corporation), and Lauress Wise (HumRRO).

As mentioned earlier, based on the invitation to comment, the Management Committee identified major areas for consideration in the revision of the 1999 Standards. These five areas focused on (a) accessibility and fairness for all examinees, (b) accountability and educational testing, (c) technology advances in testing, (d) workplace testing including employment and certification, and (e) format of the Standards including ways of prioritizing the Standards. To tackle these issues in the revision, the Joint Committee created four major "theme teams." The first team, focusing on access and fairness, is led by Linda Cook and has as its members Joan Herman, Barbara Plake, Antonio Puente, and Frank Worrell. The second team, led by Brian Gong and with Laura Hamilton, Michael Kane, and Michael Kolen is addressing accountability and educational testing. Technology is the main focus of the third team, which is led by Denny Way and has Fritz Drasgow and Lauress Wise as members. Workplace is the topic for the fourth team, which is lead by Nancy Tippins and has Jo-Ida Hansen and Paul Sackett as members. The goal of this approach was to have groups of Joint Committee members work collaboratively on issues related to the charge. In addition to this organization, each member of the Joint Committee serves as lead authors for revisions to each of the 15 original chapters in the 1999 Testing Standards. These lead authors have a support group that consists of members from each of the theme teams, called cross-team collaborators. Once the lead author has made revisions to the chapter, his or her cross-team collaborators serve as initial sounding-boards and reviewers prior to sharing the chapter's revision with the full committee. This structure is being used to get the revised chapters ready for full committee review and discussion.

The charge to the committee, as mentioned earlier, has five major components. The first component, access and fairness for all examinees, has three subsections. The first deals with the use of accommodations and modifications for testing. Within accommodations and modifications, the charge addresses (a) differentiating when a test change is to be considered an accommodation or a modification, (b) the appropriateness of different test changes for students with disabilities and English language learners, (c) broadening the consideration of other groups such as young children and older adults, (d) when and whether it is appropriate to flag scores when the test has been changed or administered under nonstandard conditions, and (e) how to conduct comparability studies for valid score interpretations, especially in instances with small sample sizes. The second component of the charge for accessibility and fairness deals with the adequacy of score translations and ways to conduct comparability studies to ensure valid score interpretations from translated tests. The final component for consideration from the charge for accessibility and fairness is the notion of designing assessments with accessibility in mind, sometimes called Universal Design.

The charge also addressed the area of accountability in educational settings. Four major components were identified in that charge to the Joint Committee from the Management Committee: (a) validity and reliability requirements for accountability systems; (b) issues of scoring, scaling, and equating; (c) matters of policy and practice for accountability systems; and (d) use of formative and interim assessments in educational settings and for accountability uses.

Technology was another area addressed in the charge. Within the charge, the following components were identified for consideration in the revision of the 1999 Testing Standards: (a) innovative item formats, (b) validity of the use of automated scoring and score reports, (c) security issues with internet delivered tests, and (d) issues with web-accessible data, including data warehousing.

For workplace testing, the charge considered five major areas: (a) validity and reliability requirements for certification, licensure, and promotion tests; (b) issues when tests are administered only to small populations of job incumbents; (c) requirements for tests for new, innovative job positions that do not have incumbents or job history to provide validity evidence; (d) assuring access to licensure, certification, and promotion tests for examinees with disabilities; and (e) differential requirements for certification and licensure and employment tests.

Formatting concerns were also part of the charge from the Management Committee. No surprise, one of the considerations for the Joint Committee is whether, and if so, how to indicate any prioritization of the standards. As discussed previously, the 1999 Testing Standards discontinued the practice of identifying some standards as primary, conditional, or desirable. The charge to the Joint Committee emphasized that without such prioritization, less direction is provided to the user about how to interpret and use the standards. In addition the Joint Committee was charged to reconsider the organization of the chapters and to work to create an integrated document that is consistent in tone, complexity, and technical language.

With the charge and committee membership in place, the Joint Committee's initial meeting was in January 2009. Since then, the committee has met approximately every 3 months with the goal of having a draft ready for public review following their December 2010 meeting. At that time, there will be an open review period of 3–4 months; again, that review will be completed using a web-based system. Following the review, it will be the task of the Joint Committee to make revisions to respond to the comments and reactions from the open review. The second version will then be submitted to the sponsoring organizations for approval. The targeted release date for the revised Testing Standards is 2012.

Conclusions

The Testing Standards have a long and important history in educational and psychological testing. Starting in the mid-1950s the testing community has relied on these standards to guide both theory and practice. There is strong evidence that the Testing Standards both respond to and change test design, development, administration, and use. Over the years there have been calls for putting more teeth into the Testing Standards by imposing sanctions for test practices that are out of compliance with these standards. Although bad testing practices have important negative consequences, it is likely that imposing sanctions for these practices through a control agency would in the long run hinder progress in test practices because there would be so much focus on avoiding malpractice suits that innovations would be limited if not discouraged. Therefore, voluntary compliance with the Testing Standards should be encouraged, but not legislated.

The Oscar and Luella Buros Center for Testing (BCT) plays an important role in the promotion of the Testing Standards. Through the reviews published in the *Mental Measurements Yearbook* series focus on the Testing Standards is maintained. Reviewers are instructed to use the current Testing Standards when completing their reviews. Further, through the test accreditation program under the auspices of BIACO, the Testing Standards are again front and center in the work of the Buros Center for Testing. Long live the Testing Standards and the BCT!

References

American Educational Research Association, American Psychological Association, & National Council on Measurement in Education. (1999). *Standards for educational and psychological testing.* Washington, DC: American Educational Research Association.

American Psychological Association. (1954). Technical recommendations for psychological tests and diagnostic techniques. *Psychological Bulletin, 51*, 201-238.

American Psychological Association, American Educational Research Association, & National Council on Measurement in Education. (1966). *Standards for educational and psychological tests and manuals.* Washington, DC: Author.

American Psychological Association, American Educational Research Association, & National Council on Measurement in Education. (1974). *Standards for educational and psychological tests.* Washington, DC: American Psychological Association.

American Psychological Association, American Educational Research Association, & National Council on Measurement in Education. (1985). *Standards for educational and psychological testing.* Washington, DC: American Psychological Association.

Bingham, W. V. (1937). *Aptitudes and aptitude testing.* New York: Harper.

Buckendahl, C. W., & Hunt, R. (2005). Whose rules? The relation between "rules" and "law" in testing. In R. Phelps (Ed.), *Defending standardized testing* (pp. 147-158). Mahwah, NJ: Erlbaum.

California Test Bureau/McGraw Hill. (2009). *Technical Manual, State of Missouri, Grades 3–8, Reading and Communication Arts.* (http://dese.mo.gov/divimprove/assess/tech/documents/2009-MAP-Technical-Report.pdf)

Camara, W., & Lane, S. (2006). A historical perspective and current views on the Standards. *Educational Measurement: Issues and Practice, 25*, 35-41.

Cizek, G. J., Koons, H. K., & Rosenberg, S. L. (in press). Chronicling and questioning validity: *Mental Measurements Yearbook* as a context for investigating the sources of evidence for high-stakes tests. To appear in J. A. Bovaird, K. F. Geisinger, & C. W. Buckendahl (Eds.), *High stakes testing in education: Science and practice in K-12 settings.* Washington, DC: APA Books.

Cureton, E. E. (1950). Validity. In E. F. Lindquist (Ed.), *Educational measurement* (pp. 621-694). Washington, DC: American Council on Education.

Cronbach, L. J. (1949). *Essentials of psychological testing.* New York: Harper & Brothers.

Debra P. v. Turlington, 474 F. Supp. 244 (M.D. Fla. 1979) *aff'd in part, rev'd in part*, 644 F.2nd 397 (5th Cir. 1981); *on remand*, 564 F. Supp. 177 (M.D. Fla. 1983), *aff'd*, 730 F.2d 1405 (11th Cir 1984).

Geisinger, K. F. (1992). The metamorphosis of test validation. *Educational Psychologist, 27*, 197-222.

GI Forum et al. v. Texas Education Agency, et al., NO.SA 97-CA-128, U.S. District Court, W.D. of Texas, San Antonio, TX.

Gulliksen, H. (1950). *Theory of mental tests.* New York: John Wiley.

Jonson, J. L., & Plake, B. S. (1998). A historical comparison of validity standards and validity practices. *Educational and Psychological Measurement, 58*, 736-753.

Kane, M. T. (2001). Validation. In R. L. Brennan (Ed.) *Educational measurement* (4th ed., pp. 17-65). Washington, DC: American Council on Education Praeger.

Messick, S. (1989). Validity. In R. L. Linn (Ed.), *Educational measurement* (3rd ed., pp. 13-103). Washington, DC: American Council on Education.

Schmeiser, C. B. (1997). Ethical codes in the professions. *Educational Measurement: Issues and Practice, 11*, 5-11.

Shepard, L. A. (1993). Evaluating test validity. *Review of Educational Research, 19*, 405-450.

Sireci, S. G., & Parker, P. (2006). Validity on trial: Psychometric and legal conceptualizations of validity. *Educational Measurement: Issues and Practice, 25*, 27-34.

Spies, R. A., & Plake, B. S. (Eds.). (2005). *The sixteenth mental measurements yearbook.* Lincoln, NE: Buros Institute of Mental Measurements.

Appendix A

Charge to the Joint Committee for the Revision of the 1999 Standards for Educational and Psychological Testing by the Management Committee

Charge to the Committee

Charge and Scope of Work

The committee will review and consider each of the comments received by the three organizations in their call for comments on the current Standards. Based on a review of the comments received, the Management Committee expects five main areas of focus for the committee. The five areas are:

1. Changes due to technological advances in testing.
2. Changes associated with the increased use of tests for accountability and educational policy-setting.
3. Access for all examinee populations.
4. Issues associated with work-place testing.
5. Scope and formatting of the Standards.

(a.) Technological Advances

Technological advances have changed the way tests are delivered, scored, and interpreted and, in some cases, the nature of the tests themselves. Issues for consideration include:

1. Reliability and validity considerations for new item formats, such as interactive computer tasks and simulations.
2. Security issues for tests delivered over the internet.
3. Validity issues associated with use of:
   - automated scoring algorithms,
   - automated score reports and interpretations.
4. Issues related to computer-generated score reports and reports (test results) delivered electronically or over the internet.
5. Issues related to security and confidentiality of web-accessible storage of test data, including data warehouses.

(b.) Accountability and Educational Policy-Setting

Under No Child Left Behind, there has been a dramatic increase in the use of tests for accountability. In such cases, test results have important consequences for third parties such as school administrators and teachers, although not always for the examinees themselves. Federal peer review procedures have required assurances of reliability and validity that often go beyond requirements of the current Test Standards. Attention to the overall technical quality of tests and score interpretation is required. High school tests are used as a graduation requirement and there have been questions about how the current Standards should be interpreted in these cases. In general, the validity and reliability of individual and aggregated scores used for accountability purposes need to be addressed. Some examples of issues to be considered are:

1. Use of a single test (whether or not scores resulting from retesting or repeat testing are sufficient for using more than one score for high stakes decisions) as the sole source of high stakes decisions (e.g., graduation, promotion).
2. Growth modeling, gain scores, and other methods of estimating aggregated performance or growth based on individual or school/district performance and characteristics.
3. Distinguishing among commercial formative and benchmark assessments (as well as item banks), their appropriate uses, and validation evidence required in interpreting scores from them.
4. Validity and reliability requirements for reporting individual or aggregate performance on subscales (skills or diagnostics) and for instructing users in appropriate interpretations of such scores or data (e.g., as they impact between or within student and school comparisons, validity considerations in subscore interpretation).
5. How test alignment studies should be documented and used to demonstrate the validity of score interpretations regarding mastery of required content standards.
6. Issues or requirements when linking assessments (e.g., concordances, linkages, and equating).
7. How to balance privacy concerns for individual examinees, teachers, and administrators while meeting information needs for policy-makers.
8. Incorporating error estimates and interpretive guidance in score reports, including subscores and diagnostic reporting for individuals and groups.
9. Issues related to the appropriate role of practice and test prep, especially in contrast to admissions testing or credentialing.
10. Provide additional guidance on score accuracy, especially when used to classify individuals or groups into performance regions or other bands on a score scale.

(c.) Access for all Examinee Populations

In making tests accessible to all examinees, there has been much debate about the appropriateness of accommodations provided to some or all examinees that may need them in demonstrating what they know and can do. Some examples of issues raised in this debate are:

1. Appropriate ways to determine or establish the impact of different types of accommodations and modifications on intended interpretations and uses of the resulting scores, including differentiation of accommodations and modifications.
2. Appropriate testing accommodations for English language learners as well as for examinees with disabilities.
3. Appropriate testing accommodations for a variety of groups (e.g., older populations, pre-K).
4. Reporting or flagging results for examinees receiving different test accommodations, including when aggregating scores.

5. Comparability of scores with and without accommodations and limits on validity.
6. Translations, in terms of language-to-language or language-to-symbol (Braille) and the kinds of evidence needed to demonstrate adequacy of translation and comparability of scores from the two (or more) versions.
7. Issues in designing assessments that are appropriate for all individuals (e.g., universal design).

(d.) Workplace Testing

Tests are being used in the workplace for certification and promotion decisions as well as for initial selection. Some issues to consider in this area include:

1. Issues relating to the validity and reliability of test scores and how such information is communicated and determined in certification, licensure, and promotion decisions about individuals.
2. Validity and reliability requirements when tests are administered only to small populations of job incumbents so as to preclude the use of common statistical evidence.
3. What standards are needed, or what stipulations to current standards need to be considered, for new, innovative job positions that do not have incumbents or job history to provide evidence for validity?
4. What standards are needed to assure access to licensure, certification, and promotion tests for examinees with disabilities, which may limit participation in regular testing sessions?
5. Considering ways to clarify standards relating to certification and licensure testing from employment testing.

(e.) Scope and Format Considerations

Some standards are generally applicable-across test uses, settings, and modes of administration and scoring, whereas other standards are applicable to only particular test uses, settings, or modes of administration and scoring. The next revision of the Test Standards should identify those standards that must be addressed, either across all test uses or in particular settings, as opposed to those standards that are conditional based on the context or other limiting factors. A method for differentiating the importance of standards should be used.

The Standards are relevant to any standardized or commercial, and large-scale or clinical assessments, including formative or benchmark assessment systems. Although the Standards are not intended to be applied to teacher-made tests, the general principles for good testing practices apply to all contexts, including classroom assessments.

Consideration in the revision to:

1. Correcting confusing or erroneous statements.
2. Ensuring the product has a more even level of technical language across chapters, and that terms are used in a consistent fashion (same meaning) throughout.
3. Presenting the chapters with a more consistent "voice."
4. Including more cross-referencing and indexing, or otherwise identifying standards that are primary or essential in most if not all applications and situations.
5. Revisiting the initial statements regarding purpose of the Standards.
6. Expanding the introduction to describe the types of test users who should be familiar with the Standards and why (e.g., test users, policy makers setting assessment policies, managers of testing programs).

Some Ruminations on the Past, Present, and Future of Psychological Measurement

Robert M. Thorndike
Professor Emeritus
Western Washington University

When Dr. Geisinger asked me to speak at this conference honoring the work of Oscar Buros and the Buros Center he said he wanted someone who could provide a long-term perspective. Well, I suppose that in one sense that makes me uniquely qualified because my family has been at this business of psychological measurement, man, boy, and now daughter, for over 110 years, almost the entire span of its existence. My grandfather, Edward L. Thorndike (call him EL for short) earned his doctorate under James McKeen Cattell, one of the earliest pioneers in a discipline that he had christened mental testing, in 1898, and we have been at it ever since. In fact, EL produced the first American textbook on psychological measurement in 1904, having previously developed a number of instruments to measure various characteristics ranging from learning in cats and fish to intelligence in people. Much of the rest of his career was spent inventing ways to measure human traits as diverse as skill in handwriting and the social structure of cities, but his primary interest was in measuring human intelligence and using those measurements to improve education. EL believed so strongly in the utility of the scientific method as a means to improve education and in the inherent quantifiability of the world that he wrote in 1914, "If a thing exists, it exists in some amount; and if it exists in some amount, it can be measured." And again in 1918, "Whatever exists at all exists in some amount. To know it thoroughly involves knowing its quantity as well as its quality." On the other side of the coin, a student once sent me some lines from an E. E. Cummings poem after I had been critical of a paper she had written, "While you and I have lips and voices which are for kissing and to sing with who cares if some one-eyed son of a bitch invents an instrument to measure Spring with." I guess it all depends on your perspective.

Near the end of EL's career, all but one year of which was spent at Teachers College, Columbia University, he was joined on the TC faculty by his son, Robert L. Thorndike (RL for short), who had recently completed his doctorate under Percival Symons at the Columbia main campus. RL also spent almost his entire career at Teachers College, except for a 4-year sabbatical with the Army Air Force Aviation Psychology Program during World War II where he worked with J.P. Guilford, Lyle Jones, and other measurement types on developing selection batteries for pilots and bombardiers. He also focused on measuring intelligence and its influence on human performance, particularly academic performance. First with Irving Lorge and later with Elizabeth Hagen, he authored widely used ability measures and books on measurement theory and application. Both EL and RL strongly believed that education could be improved by knowing a child's strengths and weaknesses and tailoring their educational experiences to fit the child's abilities. Neither, however, believed that the same expectations should be held for all children. They would have opposed most vigorously the idea that the curriculum should be set so all students would succeed. They valued individual differences and the use of measurement to identify those differences and maximize each child's achievement.

In 1964, I (call me RM for short; notice that we change one letter per generation) was trying to decide where to go to graduate school, having changed my major from chemistry to, of all things, the psychology of cats. Although I had followed

ISBN 978-0-910674-61-4, *The Eighteenth Mental Measurements Yearbook.*

EL and RL to Wesleyan University, I knew for certain that I did not want to go to Columbia. One shadow is bad enough; with two I knew I would never see the sun. I didn't get quite as far away from New York City as possible, but I did get half way there, the University of Minnesota, where I was dragged by my developing interests into quantitative psychology. You know the old saying that a PhD's education becomes narrower and narrower until she knows everything about nothing. Well, I became an expert on an obscure statistical technique known as canonical correlation. Then, just to demonstrate my independence still further, I took a position literally as far away from Columbia as possible, the wilds of northwest Washington, teaching educational measurement. I spent my entire career at Western Washington University, where my daughter, who did her doctoral work here at the University of Nebraska as a Buros Fellow in the early 1990s, is now on the faculty of education. It remains to be seen whether her son will make it five generations in psychological measurement.

So now you have my credentials to serve as senior curmudgeon of this conference. I actually do have a family connection with the Buros Center. But it goes deeper than that. I am proud to say that I knew Oscar K. Buros personally. I first met him when I was a newly minted PhD at Minnesota in the spring of 1970 and later at various APA and Psychometric Society meetings. Oscar and Harold Gulliksen, two of the aging giants of measurement at the time, were visiting the Minnesota campus and I was asked to join them for lunch. Oscar complained about the unequal revenue stream from the *Yearbooks* from year to year and the havoc it raised with his income taxes.

The Students for a Democratic Society was having its national meeting that week at the U of M and as we exited the faculty club on the fifth floor of the Student Union we looked out over a sea of radical students filling the quad. We looked for all the world like the Polit Bureau reviewing a May Day parade in Moscow, fur hats and all. I sometimes wonder whether there is a picture of us somewhere in the FBI's files.

A few years later Oscar asked me to review two tests for the *Eighth MMY*. At the time no one knew it would be his last effort. He died before publication was complete, but the work that he began in the depression of the 1930s and that has been ably carried on by the staff of the Buros Center for Testing here at the University of Nebraska for the last 30 years will be an ongoing monument to his career. His emphasis on advancing the quality of measurement in Psychology made him a kindred spirit to my family.

As one of his very last projects, Oscar gave a talk up the road a ways at the University of Iowa, one of the strongholds of educational measurement and the home of his old friend, E. F. Lindquist, who was the father of electronic test scoring. The paper was published in *Educational Researcher* in 1977 and reprinted near the end of Volume 2 of the *8th MMY*. It makes interesting reading even today, and I think it appropriate that I should take it as my point of departure.

In his talk, Oscar was asked to look back on the last 50 years of changes in educational and psychological measurement. The picture he painted was not very complimentary. He argued that, except for progress in electronic scoring and analysis of tests, few if any advances had been made. By the mid 1920s psychologists had developed measuring methods and instruments for essentially all of the traits that the tests of the 1970s covered. No new item types had been developed and, in fact, reliance on electronic scoring had reduced the variety, and also possibly the validity of item formats. He noted that attempts to assess some traits, such as character, had been abandoned. With the exception of a few advances that depend on improved computer technology and a greater sensitivity to the shortcomings of psychological assessments, I'm afraid much the same can be said today. Almost all of the most widely used tests of 2010 are relatively minor revisions of instruments that were available in 1960, and the best-known tests, such as the Stanford-Binet, the Wechsler scales, the Strong Vocational Interest Blank and the MMPI, were around when Buros published the first *MMY* over 70 years ago. There are a few exceptions, such as the Woodcock-Johnson, the Das-Naglieri Cognitive Assessment System, and the Universal Nonverbal Intelligence Test, which explore some new ground, but on the whole it is a picture of stasis, of reupholstering the old furniture.

I believe that one of the great mistakes that the measurement community has made over the last 70 years is its almost universal reliance on norm-referencing of test scores. When Alfred Binet introduced his instrument for measuring what he called judgment in 1905, he insisted that what should be reported was the "mental level" reached by the examinee as an index of the kind and complexity of tasks the person could perform. All three editions of his instrument reported test results in terms of the number of mental puzzles the child could solve. Because, in the second and third editions of the test, the items were grouped by the age at which the average child could solve them, performance was sometimes referred to as mental age, although Binet did not use this term and objected to it because of its inherent normative meaning.

When Henry Goddard and Lewis Terman brought Binet-type scales to the United States around 1910, they introduced the norm-referenced expression of performance suggested by Stearn, the intelligence quotient or IQ, which at that time was calculated as mental age divided by chronological age. The average IQ was, by definition, 1.00. In the 1920s it became common practice to multiply the ratio by 100 to remove the decimal point. Thus, an average IQ of 100 was born. Although the metric has changed to that of deviation scores standardized to have a mean of 100 and a standard deviation of 15, the basic idea of reporting performance as relative position in an appropriate reference group remains almost universal. There are times when this is an appropriate metric, but as Oscar noted over 30 years ago, there are many situations where it is not.

As most of you are probably aware, one problem with norm-referenced scores is that they do not show change very well. In fact, a highly reliable test of a stable trait like mental ability will show essentially no change in an individual's norm-referenced score from year to year because the person's relative position in the group will not change. But this is hardly what is happening in a good educational program or in normal human development. A rising tide lifts all boats, so the fact of growth is hidden by the deeper water. In 1997, at a conference at the University of Kansas (why do all these things happen in the Midwest?) I suggested that we abandon norm-referencing for a scale that would show the actual growth in mental ability from year to year, just as Binet had done. This call was not original with me. Dick Woodcock had been making the argument for years, but few were listening. It seems obvious to me that in the current climate of educational accountability a norm-free scale of achievement would be highly desirable.

I am happy to report that a few test developers have made movement in this direction. The fifth edition of one of the oldest tests still in use, the Stanford-Binet, has introduced what the publishers call Change Sensitive Scores or CSSs based on the technology of item response theory. The metric yields a mean score of 500 for 10-year-olds and is the same scale that is used for similar scores on the third edition of the Woodcock-Johnson. This I see as one of the few changes in the last 30 years that represents a real advance, but the advance is one of technology and practice, not of theory or test design. The basic theory on which IRT is based was developed by L. L. Thurstone in the 1920s in his work on scaling attitudes. Parenthetically, the publishers of the Binet also took a step backward by reintroducing IQ as the label for the norm-referenced scores produced by the test. In the SB-4 these had been called standard age scores to get away from the cultural baggage that surrounds the term IQ.

A simplified version of Thurstone's theory was applied to ability measurement by E. L. Thorndike in an instrument he called the CAVD (for the cognitive dimensions of Comprehension, Arithmetic, Vocabulary, and Direction-following) in 1926. Each of the four CAVD tests was made up of 17 testlets of 10 items each, and all items of a testlet were of equal difficulty. The testlets were equally spaced over the range of human ability from average 2-year-old to very superior adult. Thirteen additional levels were available for measuring subhuman intellect, producing what EL believed to be a ratio scale of intelligence. For a year between high school and college EL's son, RL, worked as a lab assistant in developing this test, which is why you will see echoes of the CAVD in the 4th edition of the Binet, of which RL was the senior author. The only substantive difference between the methods Thurstone developed and those of unidimensional IRT is the probability distribution used to generate the underlying scale, the cumulative normal for Thurstone versus the logistic in IRT, and the justification for the latter is algebraic and computational tractability, not theoretical superiority.

There has been a second form of technical progress which, together with IRT, has changed, and perhaps sometimes improved the landscape of mental measurement, the use of computers to assist in test administration, although we have not gone as far as we might in this regard, or perhaps we have gone too far. At the time I was finishing my graduate work at Minnesota, Dave Weiss was working on developing Computer Adaptive Testing or CAT. CAT works hand in hand with IRT to produce the most efficient use of testing time. As Thurstone demonstrated in the 1920s, we only get useful information from a test item when we are unsure how the examinee will respond. I use the term "unsure" to make the point that this applies to typical performance items as well as maximum performance items.

An item that an examinee will always get correct or always answer in the same way gives us no information about the person's status on the trait. For example, I would get no information about the vocabulary ability members of this audience if you can successfully define a word like "sleepy" because you can all correctly define virtually any word that is this common in the language. Your position on the trait is far enough above words of this difficulty that we can be certain you will get them correct, but we do not know how far above that point any one of you is, and we cannot differentiate between any two of you. Likewise, we would get no information about your vocabulary ability if you failed to define correctly words such as "oscitant" or "fracidinous" because I suspect these words are obscure enough that few, if any of you know them.

We get maximum information from those items where our uncertainty about your response is greatest. The IRT or Latent Trait model makes this clear by scaling both the items and the examinees on the latent trait. In the simplest version, IRT items are placed on the scale at the point where their ability requirement is at 50%, the inflection point of the curve that describes the probability function for the item. This is the point that yields the greatest discrimination between examinees. Persons are scaled by the item difficulty where their probability of a correct response is 50%, the point of greatest uncertainty as to their response. What CAT does is allow us to select for presentation those items that the examinee's past performance indicates will yield the greatest amount of information, the items closest to his estimated scale value. As a result, two examinees who start the test at the same place may receive quite different selections of subsequent items, depending on their pattern of responses. Because each item is selected to yield maximum information, given what we already know, we get more information for a test of a given length. Performance is then reported in some suitable metric, but in a well-developed test the scale is independent of the characteristics of the reference group. The scores are therefore free of the shortcomings of a norm-referenced scale and can easily show changes in level of performance over time or with instruction.

This brings us to another area where the history of testing has been one of progress followed by retreat, now followed by progress. The year 1904 was a banner year for measurement theory. Not only did EL provide the first systematic treatment of measurement theory, Charles Spearman published two related papers that have had a profound effect on psychological and educational measurement. The first, proposing a theory about the dependability of measurement, has led to the development of reliability theory. Spearman argued that any measurement is a composite of two elements, the true position of the person on the trait in question and a random error in this particular observation.

To illustrate the point, I would like each of you to make an estimate of my height in feet and inches. This is a rudimentary form of measurement, but similar to ones often used in clinical practice. Now, how many of you think I am less than 6 feet tall? Don't cheat ...6'...6'1"... Notice that because my true height is the same for all of you, your measurements form a distribution of errors. Also, consider the errors that are likely to occur when we try to measure characteristics that are not as directly observable and well defined as height.

In the form of an equation, each of your observations can be expressed as

Observed score (X) = True score (T = 6'3") + error of measurement ($\pm$ E, the amount by which your estimate deviated from 6'3")

Obtaining measurements on a group of people, reliability, then, can be viewed as the ratio of the variation in True Scores to the variation in Observed Scores and reflects the stability of each person's relative position in the group. The standard deviation of the errors of measurement, known as the standard error of measurement, provides an index of the absolute stability of performance or the uncertainty of our estimate. (Parenthetically, EL expressed frustration in 1905 that communication was so slow; he believed Spearman's theoretical development would have added greatly to his measurement book.)

In practice, it is difficult and expensive, sometimes impossible, to obtain multiple independent measurements of individuals to calculate the needed variances. Much of reliability theory as it developed over the next 70 years involved inventing or conceptualizing different ways to estimate these true and error components. RL published an elaborate classification of sources of test variance in his 1948 book, *Personnel Selection*. He showed that different ways to estimate reliability characterize different sources of variance as true score or error. As Oscar pointed out in his 1977 talk, the single administration methods for estimating reliability that had become almost universal by the 1970s, KR-20 and coefficient alpha, did not give appropriate values for test reliability, but frequently these are still the only reliability estimates offered in test manuals.

The good news here is that in the last 30 years IRT has provided a better way to estimate what we are really interested in, the accuracy with which a given test score estimates a person's status on the trait in question. You will be relieved to know that I will not be going into the mathematical details. They are available, at least in summary form, in most contemporary measurement texts, including mine. However, we can get a feel for what the test gives us without equations.

First, we assume that the test in question measures a person's status on some unitary underlying continuous trait of ability, personality, vocational interest, or whatnot. Each item provides an independent measure of the person's position on the trait. For ability measures, this is usually a pass-fail dichotomy, but does not need to be. Other item formats, such as Likert attitude scales, may give graduated assessments. Whatever the format, the item has a correlation with total score, and total score is used as a proxy for the underlying trait. The higher this correlation, the better the item differentiates between people at different levels of the trait. This is called the item discrimination index. This discrimination index can be converted into a measure of the amount of information each item provides, known as the item information function. Items with high discrimination differentiate sharply, but over a narrow range. The limiting case is a Guttman scale item where the probability of a correct response goes instantly from zero to one, but such items rarely exist in practice. Items with moderate discrimination differentiate less sharply, but yield useful information over a broader range. By taking the information provided by each item that the examinee has attempted, we can calculate the total test information. The square root of the inverse of the test information is an estimate of the standard error of measurement resulting from the unique test that this person has taken at this point in time. This may not seem like a big deal, but trust me, it is a significant advance over what we were doing 30 years ago. Test developers should be encouraged to provide ways to estimate test information indexes. My optimistic crystal ball tells me that testing will trend in this direction.

Spearman's second 1904 paper proposed that the intellectual performance required by any test consisted of combination demands for general mental ability and an ability specific to that particular test. The theory became known as the Two-Factor Theory. On this issue Spearman and EL differed dramatically and they carried on a debate in the journals and the popular press for another 30 years, Spearman advocating a single general ability and Thorndike, because of his connectionist psychology, expressing belief in a quasi-infinite number of specific factors or neural bonds. Literally thousands of papers have been written on this topic, some even by me, but most of the psychometric community has come to be convinced by the massive study John Carroll conducted in the 1980s and published in 1993 that they both were right in their own way. Today most cognitive ability tests at least pay lip service to the Cattell-Horn-Carroll or CHC theory. Using an Apple IIe computer that might take up to 8 hours for a single analysis, Carroll, who would turn on the computer and go to bed, expecting to get his results in the morning, found evidence for about 70 fairly narrow and specific factors that could be grouped into about nine correlated broad factors. These in turn give rise to a general cognitive ability similar to the one Spearman proposed. The Woodcock-Johnson Psycho-Educational Battery is the currently available test adhering most closely to CHC theory, whereas the Wechsler scales, the Stanford-Binet-Fifth Edition, and numerous other tests claim to measure subsets of the nine broad CHC factors.

Spearman's Two-Factor theory spawned one of the most popular and widely misused statistical techniques in mental testing, factor analysis. In the years BC (that's before computers), factor analysis was a computationally demanding procedure, not lightly undertaken. For example, in the largest study conducted up to that time (1938) Thurstone extracted what he termed the 11 Primary Mental Abilities from a set of over 50 tests given to about 250 examinees. The analysis took 10 staff years using all of the latest equipment and every available shortcut. When I replicated the analysis in 1969 it took 6 computer seconds using a machine that filled a modest-sized building and a program I had written myself. Today, you can do the same analysis on a laptop using SPSS in not much more than the blink of an eye. That's progress, but maybe not.

Beginning in the late 1960s computers and program packages made factor analysis available to everyone, so everyone did one. Because computers do exactly what they are told to do, regardless of what the data may be, and because many journal reviewers possessed only a rudimentary knowledge of factor analytic theory, vast numbers of senseless factor analyses made their way into the professional literature. The same goes on today, but with more sophistication, and this has implications for the *Mental Measurements Yearbooks* and the Buros Center now and in the future.

Let me give you a fairly sophisticated example of what I am talking about. Many of you are probably familiar with what is commonly misnamed confirmatory factor analysis. You may also know it by a variety of brand names such as LISREL, EQS, AMOS, et cetera. These programs are all descendants of statistical work begun in the late 1960s by Karl Jöreskog under the name "Restricted Maximum Likelihood Factor Analysis" and subsequently released by him and Dag Sörbom in the program called LISREL, short for linear structural relations. Notice that Jöreskog called this restricted factor analysis, not confirmatory factor analysis, and his term is more accurate because the factor solution is restricted by fixing various of the parameters of a model. This usually takes the form of fixing some factor loadings to zero. The rest of the loadings, and perhaps the factor correlations, are freely estimated by the program to fit the data as closely as possible. Actually, these models are much more general than just factor analysis, but measurement applications more commonly use only the factor analytic capabilities of the programs.

We must now return to Spearman's measurement model. Recall that observed scores are viewed as composed of true and error components. The error component of a score is generally assumed to be a random event and therefore uncorrelated with anything in the universe. Factor analysis decomposes the true score portion of a set of observations into a set of contributing sources, called common factors, that may or may not be correlated. They are assumed to be correlated in the CHC model. Traditional factor analysis as practiced by Thurstone, and pretty much everyone else until about 1980, determined the positions of the factors according to one or another statistical principle, most often what is called principal axes, but none of the factor loadings were specified beforehand. The factors would then be rotated to a position of greatest psychological meaningfulness, often called simple structure.

With restricted factor analysis some or all of the loadings are specified before the analysis begins, and the program attempts to produce a solution that is as close as possible to the one specified. This is called fitting a model to the data. Measures of the goodness of this fit are generally based on a chi-squared statistic that measures a lack of fit. Large values of fit statistics such as the normed-fit index indicate small differences between the model specified by the user and the best approximation obtainable from the data. With other measures, such as the root-mean-squared-residual or RMSR, small values indicate close fit. Most programs produce both types of fit indices. Sometimes the proposed model does not fit the data very well, and this is where the mischief can begin.

My case in point is the fifth edition of the Stanford-Binet. The test was designed to measure five factors from the CHC model. Each factor was represented by 1 verbal test and 1 nonverbal test. The 5 verbal tests also can be combined to yield a Verbal IQ score and the 5 nonverbal tests likewise produce a Non-Verbal IQ. The combination of all 10 tests produces an estimate of general cognitive ability or IQ. For various technical reasons the publisher's statistical staff split each of the 10 tests in half to provide four measures of each of the five CHC factors when conducting the restricted factor analysis. They reported in the test manual that the model fit the data reasonably well. In addition, they fit a two-factor verbal-non-verbal model for which they also reported satisfactory results.

In my younger days I was somewhat of a data analysis nut; I would analyze data just for the fun of it. Now, I play golf. When the new Binet came out in 2003 I requested the correlation matrices from the publisher, and Riverside generously provided them. I attempted to replicate the results published in the manual to use as a training example for my graduate students. To my surprise, although I could get the verbal-non-verbal factor results to come out within the two-digit accuracy of the correlations I had been given, I could not get the five-factor solution to give anything close to what was published in the manual. The fit statistics were not good at all. When I analyzed the correlation matrices using old-fashioned unrestricted factoring procedures and required the program to keep five factors, the result was one general factor and nonsense. Rotation did not help.

Puzzled by this, I sent my input file to the publisher together with the output I had obtained. They informed me that they had used commonly applied model-modification procedures to improve model fit. These procedures tell you how much the fit will improve if certain parameters that were fixed (usually to zero) are allowed to be freely estimated from the data. Freeing parameters always improves fit, but sometimes not very much. The modifications suggested by the computer for the five-factor model with the SB5 involved allowing several of the error terms for the observed variables to be correlated. This makes neither psychometric nor substantive sense. Unless there is a compelling reason, such as data that form a time-series model, allowing what are assumed to be random events to take on non-zero correlations violates a basic measurement assumption. The bottom line for the Binet is that this aspect of the publisher's evidence for construct validity of the five factors claimed for the SB5 is substantially flawed. At most, the verbal-nonverbal scores and the general cognitive ability score can be trusted. The bottom line more generally is that powerful statistical procedures can often be made to torture data until they will tell you anything you want to hear, regardless of the consequences for the psychometrics or for science.

I bring this issue up because this is the kind of checking *MMY* reviewers should be performing on the tests they review if we are to see the kind of progress in mental measurement that Oscar Buros spent his life promoting. Independent replication of analyses is fundamental in science (remember cold fusion) and test publishers should be expected to make the data on which they base their validity claims available for independent verification. If a reviewer is not capable of performing this kind of analysis, it should be done by Buros Center staff. Test publishers have a product to sell, and the people on their statistical staffs are not necessarily competent in psychometrics. I assume that the people who did the analysis of the Binet were simply following orders to get the best fit possible and did not appreciate the logical error and psychometric heresy they were committing. I have encountered similar sophisticated mathematics but naive psychometrics in dealings with the people at SPSS. As an aside, when I reviewed the revision of the K-ABC (Kaufman Assessment Battery for Children) for the *MMY* a few years ago, I was able to replicate the published results without resorting to torture and said so in my review. So my second crystal ball prediction, which is more of a hope than a forecast, is that test reviewers and test users will demand more and better evidence of the validity of the inferences test publishers claim for the scores their tests produce.

Earlier I mentioned that one of the advances of the last 30 years has been the development of Computer Adaptive Testing, but that it may not all be positive. The increased efficiency of adaptive tests is definitely a positive change, yielding more information or more accurate scores for a given amount of testing time. Computers have also essentially eliminated clerical errors from test scoring and reporting. The computer is not going to incorrectly score a response or use the wrong table to look up a standardized score. However, this comes at a potential cost. Computerized testing, adaptive or otherwise, may not adapt to changes in the examinee during testing. Once you have given an answer to an item and moved on to the next question there is often no way for you to go back and change your answer, even if you realize later that your answer was wrong. Suppose, for example, we have an analogies item of the following form:

God is to Dog as Was is to
A) Now B) Won C) Jesus D) Saw

When you first read this item it may not seem to make any sense, particularly if previous items have been semantic analogies such as "hot is to cold as light is to dark," so you either guess or leave the item blank. Later in the test you encounter another spatially based analogy and realize that the relationship is one of spelling reversal. Clearly, the correct answer to the earlier analogy is D) Saw because the first two items are related by reversal. Suppose there were six items that used this format and you only discovered the clue on the last item. In the old-fashioned paper-and-pencil test you would have been able to go back and correct your answers to the other five items, thereby substantially increasing your score. With some computerized testing, whether it is adaptive or not, this option is unavailable. With adaptive tests in particular, changing your response after having answered some later items would play havoc with the item-selection algorithm. I am particularly sensitive to this issue because it happened to me on the Miller Analogies Test 45 years ago with two types of relationships. I estimate that my score would have been about 10 points lower if I had not been able to go back and change some of my answers, and that might have been the difference between getting into grad school or not. My grandson has complained of being unable to correct errors he later discovered on computerized tests he has taken. This is an area that I believe needs more consideration than it has received and I hope that the future of measurement will address the issue.

I would now like to shift gears and speculate a little on where we may go from here. I do this with great trepidation. Most of you are old enough to remember the catastrophic world-wide famine that reduced the planet's population by 25% in the 1980s. If you don't remember it, that is probably because it didn't happen, although we were told by Paul Ehrlich that it was an absolute and unavoidable certainty in his 1968 book, *The Population Bomb,* if we did not change our ways. Similar fantastic predictions about the end of the world as we know it have been made for centuries and continue to be made today, in particular by the climate change doomsayers. On the bright side, Ehrlich has lived long enough to experience some of the ridicule that has attended the failure of his forecasts. My predictions will be somewhat more modest.

My first prediction, which hardly involves much risk, is that the role of computers in testing will expand. New and better programs will be written for test administration and for test score interpretation and report writing. It may even come to pass that the work of Arthur Jensen and his colleagues on the relationship between reaction time and cognitive ability, requiring very precise timing of both stimulus and response, will be found to have practical application as a culture-free measure of intelligence. However, the place where I see the most immediate expansion of computers is in what I call computer-assisted test administration. Most computerized tests today are substitutes for group testing in that the items are often in a multiple-choice select-response format. The examinees may be either alone or in groups, but the item format is usually that of a traditional paper-and-pencil test, only presented on a computer screen. It could also be a fill-in-the-blank format where the response is typed in.

A few years ago I suggested to Riverside Publishing, the publisher of the Binet, that computer programs be developed to assist the clinician or counselor with individually administered cognitive tests. The fourth and fifth editions of the Binet are complicated to administer, requiring almost instantaneous scoring of free-response answers to the test questions by the test administrator and quick decisions about what items to administer next. Other tests, such as some of the Wechsler subtests and the subtests of the Das-Naglieri Cognitive Assessment System, require precise timing of multiple parts of the test as well as rapid scoring. All of these factors place a heavy load on the examiner. Numerous studies have found frequent administration errors in these tests, even with experienced examiners. When, for recreation, RL re-scored all 5,000 of the Binet-4 standardization protocols he was appalled at the number of mistakes in addition, item selection, norms table used, and so forth, and these were experienced clinicians and counselors working under closer-than-usual supervision. In the real world of test use the problem is likely to be much worse and to go undetected.

If responses to verbally administered items are submitted to a computer, either typed in or using voice-recognition software, scoring of the responses becomes faster and more accurate. Responses can be compared to a larger catalog of answer alternatives, and the information is stored digitally for easy subsequent analysis. The computer can then select or suggest the next item to be administered, essentially eliminating errors in item selection. We also have the possibility of an individually administered adaptive test, and perhaps better yet from the clinician's point of view, the chance to explore more deeply some areas that initial testing has highlighted by having the computer present additional items specific to that concern. Using item information from the items already administered to estimate the standard error of measurement, testing can be continued until any desired degree of precision is reached. I have couched this discussion in terms of ability testing, but the generalization to testing in other clinical situations is straightforward.

Computers also may make new item formats possible. I don't know what these will be, but I can imagine having examinees rearrange stimuli on a computer screen rather than manipulating objects on a table. The computer could also ask the examinee to try again if the first answer was incorrect, or give hints, thereby providing a measure of the degree to which the examinee could profit from corrective feedback, which is often more relevant than a static test score to educational intervention. Extended response items such as essays could be administered and scored, perhaps including presentations of probes when answers are unclear. Susan Embretson has been working on software that generates new items from item generation rules. There may come a time when ability tests can be tailored to the interests of examinees based on their responses to questions about their favorite activities. Or, test items can be embedded in video games to maximize the engagement of children for whom tests are an alien or hostile concept.

I am not going to speculate about where social attitudes about testing will be in 20 years, but I am sure they will be different than now. Psychological and educational testing has always taken place in a complex social and cultural environment, which it has also helped to shape. Advances in testing between 1900 and 1920 led to a euphoric period when it seemed the measurement millennium was just around the corner. By the 1930s attitudes had changed and become much more critical. Enter Oscar Buros and efforts by the measurement community to police itself. These efforts have continued, with greater or lesser success, in the form of the *MMY*s and the various sets of guidelines for test development and practice initiated in the 1950s by the APA, AERA, and NCME. The professional associations that use tests have tried to be responsive to the changing culture, but I fear that sometimes we have sacrificed good science for social ends. This is a choice and a set of trade-offs that will continue to impact test development and testing practice.

The last 30 years have been quite a ride. Perhaps in another 20 years my daughter, Tracy, will be able to address a 50th anniversary conference at the Buros Center and comment on the failures of my predictions.

Closing Thoughts: A Look to the Future

Kurt F. Geisinger
Director, Buros Center for Testing
University of Nebraska-Lincoln

These closing thoughts are focused on where Buros is going in the next 70 years. One of the reasons for this set of papers and the conference on which they were based in the first place was to reconsider the history of an institution founded by a single individual, one supported by a faithful wife and loyal employees to be certain, but generally a single individual. It was a team of individuals who brought this New Jersey institution westward to Nebraska, and a good number of those people have participated in the conference that led to these papers and, indeed, have contributed papers for this appendix to the *Mental Measurements Yearbook.* I would like to extend thanks to members of two groups: those individuals who helped to bring the Buros Institute, now the Buros Center to this University in Nebraska; and those who have written papers for this history of the Buros Center for Testing.

I am also pleased to state that this paper and those preceding it are being published in *The Eighteenth Mental Measurements Yearbook.* We believe that these papers represent an important component of the history and practice of the profession of testing.

My masters advisor, William A. Owens (see Mumford, Stokes, & Owens, 1990; Owens, 1976), was a long-term leader in psychological measurement. His specialty within industrial psychology was what has been called "biodata." These data are generated by the completion of questionnaires on which the respondent answered questions about his or her background and previous experiences. Such measures have been found to be highly predictive in industry and in education, right up there with general developed mental ability. During his many professional years at Purdue University and the University of Georgia, every incoming freshman completed these biographical questionnaires at freshmen orientation and their records over their years in college were followed and compared to their self-portrayals of their background as freshmen. Although one could make many conclusions about such findings, a simple summarization would be the oft-quoted line that the best predictor of future behavior is past behavior. In fact, a single item relating to the number of books in one's home as one grew up correlated with eventual college GPA about as well as the major standardized tests. That simple statement is my primary justification for hosting this conference. The future of the Buros Center for Testing will in large measure be determined by the values, the actions, and the decisions made in the past. I felt, and I continue to believe, that we needed to document the history of our center. As people leave the profession and even this earth, the history of organizations disappears, never to be formulated and examined. That was one reason why we invited both Oscar Kris Buros, James Mitchell, Cecil Reynolds, and Ned Hedges to this celebration and we were very pleased that Kris, Cecil, and Ned were able to come and James was able to send us a letter with some of his reflections. This summer the Buros Center for Testing will begin a full-fledged strategic planning process. Some of the comments I make in the remaining sections of this talk predict outcomes that will emerge from that planning process.

Just as our test reviewers describe how a particular test is developed, how the Buros Center for Testing has been developed impacts what it is today and what it will be in its future. In brief, I

ISBN 978-0-910674-61-4, *The Eighteenth Mental Measurements Yearbook.*

believe the Buros Center for Testing has a bright future, one entirely consistent with its past values and orientation. Let me describe where I think it will be going. I am going to begin with a description of where the oldest unit in the Buros Center for Testing is likely to go and then move in turn to the newer units. I will close with some general comments about the overall Buros Center for Testing, our umbrella organization.

The Buros Institute of Mental Measurements

The Buros Institute of Mental Measurements is, with the culmination, publishing *The Eighteenth Mental Measurements Yearbook*. Near future predictions are always easier to make than longer term ones. I will make a prediction, this one a long-term prediction. As long as the Buros Center for Testing continues to exist, we will always review tests for users and encourage the improvement in testing practice. We will take on the review of new kinds of measures as called for in the papers by Jane Close Conoley and Terry Gutkin in this section. That prediction was another easy one, I think. So let's move on to some more difficult predictions.

Those using our test reviews have in the past 15-20 years been increasingly accessing them electronically rather than in the *Yearbooks*. Reviews are available via the Buros website for a small fee, and the vast majority of university libraries in the United States provide access to these documents through the Ebsco or Ovid databases. More than one person I have known for a long time, upon hearing that I had accepted a position at Buros some 4 years ago asked me if Buros was still publishing the Mental Measurements reviews as books, or whether all of our dissemination was via electronic media. We still do publish the *Yearbooks* and I hope we always will. As the son of a librarian, I love books. I love reading books, I love holding books, I love looking at their bindings, I love smelling them. But whether we continue to publish *The Mental Measurements Yearbooks* as a print medium or not, a decision that will ultimately be a business rather than a moralistic decision, we will continue to review tests.

I note that there is a new procedure going into effect soon. We have made the decision to purchase some tests for review; we cannot be held hostage by publishers who do not send them to us. We need to review our budget model in this regard, but one of the foundations with whom we talked this past year felt that this was the only way for us to operate. To continue our mission successfully, we must evaluate all tests, especially those of consequential use.

We also have been encouraged in some ways to change the way we review tests. Among the strategies that have been floated by me are the following: that we should review all the tests ourselves and that we should use a 1-to-5 scale, perhaps frowning faces to smiling faces, to characterize tests, or at least certain qualities of tests. Let me address each of these, perhaps just in a sentence. In addition to the near impossibility of reviewing all tests ourselves, I believe that there are advantages in having the profession as a whole engage in the process. Such actions demonstrate that we as a profession police ourselves. Moreover, I know that there are advantages in getting more than one perspective on a test; such diversity of opinions is what leads to knowledge and proper decision making and urges users to be informed themselves.

I find the frowning to smiling scale to be overly simplistic. For example, validity coefficients and reliability coefficients must be interpreted in context. Dr. James Impara's paper could even be expanded to our need to focus validation on score interpretation for a particular purpose. What leads to a smile in one context might generate tears in another. Although our reviews are brief, complexity of the review consideration is often the rule of thumb.

Changes in the testing industry and in our related professions have been impacting our work evaluating tests. The consolidation of test publishing companies in the industry has probably reduced the number of new tests being published: fewer companies mean fewer tests. Fewer tests mean fewer reviews. Thus, the pacing between the publication dates of our *Mental Measurement Yearbooks* is being extended, although this does not impact our regular updating of reviews available electronically.

Perhaps in response to the consolidations of large testing companies, there appear to be more tests that are published by some very small test publishers, publishers that may only publish a single test or two, and by companies whose primary work is not testing. Many of these companies neither have the resources to perform the research that we would need to see to be able to review the test nor the desire to publish technical test manuals. To the extent that they can publish and sell tests without engaging in significant validation work, one can understand their position, although Buros cannot accept such a position and we will always take stands against such actions. At Buros we may need to take a tougher stance on publishers who market instruments without performing the requisite research.

Many more educational tests are not commercially available per se. Twenty or 30 years ago, most educational tests were developed, marketed, and sold nationally. Tests such as the Iowa Test of Educational Development, the Metropolitan Achievement Tests, the California Achievement Tests, and a few others, which were widely used then, continue to be available, but virtually all states have test developers build tests just for them. In fact, one of the markets for these published tests today is for students who are home schooled. As previously noted, the tests used by most states currently are not commercially available and hence fail to meet our present review criteria. One major foundation this past year actually contacted the Buros Center for Testing and discussed with us the possibility that we could evaluate such tests for the public. To be sure, such an effort would be well within our mission, but it is beyond our capacity at this time and it is not yet clear how such efforts would be funded, especially given the number of states, the number of different test levels or grades within each test, the number of different forms within states, the changing of tests from year to year, and so on. I am not saying that we would not or should not engage in this activity, but that at present it is hard to imagine how any organization could perform this work. You may know that our second unit, the Buros Institute for Assessment Consultation and Outreach does work with such tests. Nevertheless, we see the need for reviews of tests that are not commercially available but are quite impactful on society, education, and healthcare.

In so many contexts today, we know that the world is shrinking. Increasingly, testing companies are cross-national, if not world-wide. We have discussed the possibility of reviewing tests in other languages, for other cultures. We cannot make this move yet. The difficulty of dealing with different languages and cultures is not yet surmountable for us, but I expect in the future we will need to address such tests. If we do not, someone else will. My work with the International Test Commission and with some of the international test review agencies has made it clear to me that we have systems in place for test reviewing that are far beyond everything else in the world. We will be taking a first baby step within the next year by developing a *Tests in Print* in Spanish for tests available around the world in that language.

Let me also mention some of the current day threats to our experience in test evaluation. One of the worst threats to our continuation as we have existed relates to the well-documented drop in testing expertise among psychologists (Aiken, West, & Millsap, 2008). Frankly, the loss of testing courses in the graduate psychology curriculum has been well-documented, and it is concerning. Our reviewers must know a certain amount of psychometrics and psychological testing to be able to write reviews effectively. Presently, we have reason to worry about this change. Moreover, we also know that the average age of our current reviewers is increasing, many of our long-term reviewers are retiring and choosing not to review tests into their retirement, and new reviewers have, in general, different backgrounds than their predecessors. On the other hand, psychometrics as a discipline seems increasingly to be moving into education or educational psychology departments. The training of such individuals is often quite strong psychometrically, but I share my own fear that too many of such individuals have learned little about psychology content other than what they have seen on certain educational achievement tests. For example, I read a draft review of an individually administered clinical instrument in the past couple of years where the reviewer, someone from a large-scale educational testing background, faulted the test for not having a norm sample comparable for a large-scale, machine-scored instrument. Similarly, a former hat that I wore as a chair of a psychology department that housed a doctoral program in psychometrics brought me into contact with a great number of graduates of educational testing programs seeking employment. In many cases, these individuals told me that they could not teach even a single undergraduate course in psychology other than those related to statistics. Evaluating tests requires of the reviewer that he or she know something about psychometrics, but also something about content of the test. It is increasingly difficult to find such individuals in some cases. Finally, I also believe that there are fewer individuals with what I will call a broader scope.

Professionalism in the 21st Century in psychology and educational psychology generally leads to a very focused specialization. Presently, many of the larger professional associations are noticing a loss of memberships and of attendees at their annual conferences as members increasingly affiliate with more specialized associations. This specialization has come with certain associated costs, however. Some reviews that I have read in recent years were written by people in one field, let's say educational testing or vocational counseling, and they were evaluating tests in another related field, such as personnel selection, and some of their comments indicated a surprising narrowness of their foci and a reduced ability to evaluate a test the use of which is even somewhat different from those that they personally use more frequently. In the history of psychology, a common course was called Applied Psychology or Fields of Applied Psychology. In such courses, students learned about the variety of different venues where psychologists work and come to appreciate these differences. Such courses, and experience working with psychologists and researchers in other areas, I believe, helps one understand the breadth of our discipline and to consider approaches that those in related fields use. James Mitchell's recent letter to me mentioned the absolute criticality of identifying and using well-qualified reviewers in our process. We need to seek broadly educated individuals with both psychometric expertise and content expertise.

Buros Institute for Assessment Consultation and Outreach

The Buros Institute for Assessment Consultation and Outreach, BIACO, has been in existence for some 16 years as I write this paper in 2010. During that time it has worked primarily for states in the realm of educational testing, but also for cities, the nation, and licensing and certification boards. Our client base will probably continue although it is always changing. Since I have been at Buros, a very limited sampling to be certain, we have primarily performed independent alignment studies, standard settings, applied research, equating, and test credentialing. I'll say a few words about each. Alignment studies have become a critical component of the states-located, standard-based education testing and assessment. In general, states develop the standards to guide and control their curricula and subsequent testing programs. Typically, they hire a testing firm to develop tests to assess these standards grade by grade. In some cases, the same testing firms perform these alignment studies to determine the extent to which an independent group, most typically teachers, consider the items to be measuring the standards that the item writers intended for them. We believe that when the firm that develops the items also controls the study to assess what they are measuring, there is a potential for a conflict of interest. This situation is ideal for Buros where we pride ourselves on our independence. That there sometimes have been penalties for states whose tests do not align with the state standards is a condition that has raised the stakes of these decisions. We can also expect that the need for alignment studies may well be greatly reduced given that many states have come together for what has been called common core standards in reading and mathematics, a process that is also under way as I write this paper. Although such an action might have detrimental impact on the business model for BIACO, I can only be supportive of this important and, perhaps, overdue action. This movement should lead to fewer tests, I believe, and these examinations should be of higher quality. Remembering that we embody Oscar Buros' vision of being the *Consumer Reports* of the testing industry, I believe that this action should lead to fewer, higher quality tests that are more thoroughly studied and researched in ways that will make it easier to make validation judgments. It will make states more collaborative with each other, which I also think is potentially advantageous. Dr. Chad Buckendahl made a similar comment in his paper. Moreover, I have had concerns whereby certain decisions are based on non-psychometric criteria such as the raw numbers of items rather than scale reliability, validity, domain coverage, and the like.

Standard setting has been of great interest to Drs. Plake, Impara, Buckendahl, and me, all members and former members of BIACO. In my mind, when we perform standard setting, we are focusing on the practice of testing in a way that makes tests most useful and defensible. Professional judgment is always critical in any aspect of this process. Standard setting has been overly stressed, in my opinion, by No Child Left Behind, where the scores on many statewide tests are broken into as many as 5-8 proficiency levels. We need other ways to show that growth is occurring rather than a student progressing from one performance level to the next. Newer growth models may help reduce the number of categories that are needed and permit us to identify instructional growth in ways that I believe are more psychometrically defensible.

To the best of my knowledge, our recent work in equating is a relatively new activity for the Center. Many states wish to identify changes over years, but, of course, they cannot use the same test forms or items in consecutive years due to their exposure. In my opinion, testing companies are generally remarkably talented in equating test forms year to year. Nevertheless, errors can occur on one hand, and these same companies may also have pressure placed on them to equate tests where the data simply do not fit in the manner in which one would like. Our role has been to come into such situations independently and to check the work of experts. Given that there are a number of different psychometric approaches to equating and different software packages, many of which lead to differences that may sometimes be of consequence, there is also basic research that is needed in this arena and I think Buros should be a part of this effort.

In terms of applied research, in recent years, we have engaged in a number of applied studies from interrater reliability on high stakes tests, to the reliability of mixed format tests, the evaluation of reading tests for a state, the psychometrics of so-called alternate assessments for states, and the analysis of survey data. BIACO is small and small size can be a benefit when one is both flexible and willing to change what we do within the limits of our expertise. We are nothing if not adaptable.

Our work in test accreditation is perhaps most like our work in BIMM. There are organizations that produce and use tests, often high-stakes tests such as tests that permit individuals to join professions. These tests are not commercially available and are, therefore, outside the realm of BIMM. As Dr. Barbara Plake mentioned in her paper, we do have our own test standards that are based upon the *Standards for Educational and Psychological Testing* (1999) and we apply those standards to such testing programs. One testing program that we accredited in the past year, that of the Federation of State Boards of Physical Therapy, found that the process was a very positive one, one that encouraged professionalism and adherence to professional standards. Accreditation reviews are one more way in which we fulfill our mission of improving the science and practice of testing.

Buros Institute for Assessment Literacy

During the early 1990s, Dr. Barbara Plake as Director of the Buros Institute of Mental Measurements envisioned the Buros Center for Testing composed of three institutes, including the current Buros Institute of Mental Measurements and the Buros Institute of Assessment Consultation and Outreach as well as one additional institute. We now are committed to the foundation of a third institute to deal with assessment literacy, although we are also committed to a name that does not sound phonetically like "bile." I have already explained how many recently trained psychologists and educational testing experts have what I will call "assessment holes in their background." Older professionals, too, need updating, including learning how to administer new tests, how to interpret scores, what validation means, how validation has changed, and so on.

One of the other big needs in the opinion of many is the need to upgrade the knowledge base of many politicians on the state and national levels who are making educational policy and educational testing decisions. We believe that this audience, too, is in need of information that would help them make decisions about testing more related to the quality of data produced by tests.

There is a continuing need to educate teachers about testing, too; but we believe that others are already meeting this need and it is not our first priority. Nevertheless, we ask for advice from others as we set up this new institute. We think that members of testing companies, state departments of education, professionals such as psychologists and speech therapists, and politicians are all in need of greater assessment literacy.

Conclusion

In conclusion, the Buros mission is to improve the science and practice of testing. It is clear that the Buros Institute of Mental Measurements has enabled our profession to move forward and to permit professionals to choose which test is most likely to meet their needs. We have heard from some publishers who tell us the reviews even help them improve tests. Dr. Cecil Reynolds made this point in his paper. Similarly, the Buros Institute for Assessment Consultation and Outreach has helped states to use tests more appropriately and effectively. Finally, given the uses of testing and assessments in our society, we believe that there are a number of audiences where education and training on test-related matters could improve testing practices as well.

There has been one change in the role of Buros since coming to Nebraska. Although it is not part of our mission, per se, one important component of our work at Nebraska is the training of graduate students as part of the BIMM, BIACO, and our newly envisioned Assessment Literacy Institute. We believe that a major piece of our work is the education of our graduate students, without whom our work would probably be impossible.

My last comment relates to the nature of work within the Buros Center. We not only produce great products, but we have some fun in so doing and the staff is remarkably caring and conciliatory. One member of our team continually refers to us as a family, wording that I believe is totally appropriate. I searched for words that I could use to characterize the employees at Buros; the best I could do is that they are all very different, but they are all good souls. Today, let me thank you for reading this selection of papers that detail the history, the work, and perhaps even the future of our fine organization.

References

Aiken, L. S., West, S. G., & Millsap, R. E.. (2008). Doctoral training in Statistics, Measurement, and Methodology in Psychology: Replication and extension of the Aiken, West, Sechrest, and Reno (1990) survey of Ph.D. programs in North America. *American Psychologist, 63,* 32-50.

Mumford, M., Stokes, G. S., & Owens, W. A. (1990). *Patterns of life history: The ecology of human individuality.* Hillsdale, NJ: Erlbaum.

Owens, W. A. (1976). Background data. In M. D. Dunnette (Ed.), *Handbook of industrial and organizational psychology* (pp. 609-644). Chicago: Rand-McNally.